PRAISE FOR
RUNNING ON PLENTY AT WORK

"This is a beautiful and wise book full of tips that will motivate and inspire you to work in a more balanced way."
MAGGIE BEDROSIAN, CO-AUTHOR,
LOVE IT OR LOSE IT: LIVING CLUTTER-FREE FOREVER

"Schmidt and Kurth provide us with a practical guide to creating renewal in our everyday lives. This is a welcome addition to a growing field of interest."
FREDERIC HUDSON, PH. D. AUTHOR,
THE ADULT YEARS: MASTERING THE ART OF SELF-RENEWAL
AND PAMELA MCLEAN, PH. D., CEO,
THE HUDSON INSTITUTE OF SANTA BARBARA

"This book provides important reflections on the timely topic of renewal at work. The tips are based on real life examples of people dealing with critical issues of renewal at work."
ANN MCGEE-COOPER, ED. D., AUTHOR, *YOU DON'T HAVE TO GO FROM WORK EXHAUSTED!* AND *TIME MANAGEMENT FOR UNMANAGEABLE PEOPLE*

"An enthusiastic reference for re-thinking our attitudes to workplace behavior and performance. The Renewal at Work Self-Assessment tool offers insights that can be put to use immediately."
PAUL WILSON, AUTHOR, *CALM AT WORK*

RUNNING ON PLENTY AT WORK

RENEWAL STRATEGIES FOR INDIVIDUALS

KRISTA KURTH, Ph.D.

AND

SUZANNE ADELE SCHMIDT, Ph.D.

RENEWAL RESOURCES PRESS, POTOMAC, MD

Running on Plenty at Work
Renewal Strategies for Individuals
by Krista Kurth, Ph.D. and Suzanne Adele Schmidt, Ph.D.

Published by Renewal Resources Press
A Division of Renewal Resources LLC
9428 Garden Court
Potomac, MD 20854 USA
www.renewalatwork.com

Copyright © 2003
First printing 2003

Printed in the United States of America

Cover and interior design by Kim Leonard, Bookcovers.com.
Interior illustrations by Barbara Quinn.
Printed and bound by Boyd Printing.

Publisher's Cataloging-in-Publication Data
(Provided by Quality Books, Inc.)

Kurth, Krista.
    Running on plenty at work : renewal strategies for
individuals / by Krista Kurth, Suzanne Adele Schmidt. --
1st ed.
    p. cm.
    Includes bibliographical references and index.
    LCCN 2002094210
    ISBN 0-9716994-0-2

    1. Self-actualization (Psychology) 2. Success in
business. 3. Conduct of life. 4. Rejuvenation.
I. Schmidt, Suzanne Adele. II. Title.

BF637.S4R86 2003   158.1

DEDICATION

CONTENTS

Part One: Embarking on the Road to Renewal

Part Two: Traveling through the Seasons of Renewal

Acknowledgments

Over the course of the last year, we learned that no book comes into this world alone—rather a book comes in on the wings of angels. Our cadre of angels is glorious and selfless. Their names and contributions follow.

With gratitude to:

Our proofreaders and editors for all of their constant encouragement, careful editing, solid advice, and useful feedback. They include: Daniel Davis, MD, Reverend Doug Wysockey-Johnson, Nancy Joie Watkins, Rae Thompson, Rosi Lovdal, and Maggie Bedrosian.

Our superb administrative team, Diana Bivona and Amy Pavlock, for their unending support and enthusiasm for this project, preparing drafts "just one last time," and performing tasks that rival the best of detectives. Their caring assistance made this book possible.

Our illustrator, Barbara Quinn for playfully and creatively capturing in pictures our ideas of the road to renewal and the seasons of renewal.

Our cover and book designer, Kim Leonard for her solid and calm response to our many changes and requests in the "eye of the book preparation storm."

Our marketing coach, Allen D'Angelo for unswerving belief in us and gently pushing us to grow and stretch how we think about and approach marketing.

Our clients and associates for encouraging us and supporting us both emotionally and financially, and providing a workplace laboratory where we could further develop our ideas about the practice of renewal at work. Special thanks to: Rod MacAlister of Conoco, Claiborn M. Carr III of The Gardens Ice House and Tri-City Eagles, and Reid M. Knight of Howard Hughes Medical Institute.

PERMISSIONS

PREFACE

The Origin of the Idea of Running on Plenty at Work

Our interest in renewal at work grew out of our personal experiences in the workplace and our work with clients over the past 10 years. The actual concept of "running on plenty at work" came to us as a result of our research on individual revitalization in start-up organizations. We surveyed a number of women entrepreneurs about how they renewed themselves during the workday and had asked if they were willing to talk with us about their experience of renewal at work. One woman responded by saying, "The thought of talking to you about renewal is very, very scary to me because I feel as if I have been running on empty for years. Please call. It's time to talk." Touched deeply by this woman's words, we became inspired to write about how people can work in a way that was the opposite of running on empty. This is how the idea of *"running on plenty at work"* was born.

Why We Wrote This Book

Like the woman in our survey, many white-collar professionals are experiencing a lack of energy, well-being and balance at work. The statistics on work habits in America paint a vivid picture of hectic and fast-paced workplaces. People report feeling overwhelmed at work. They say they are putting in longer hours, working faster and harder, and enjoying less free time at home due to the blurring of work and personal boundaries caused by the advances in computer and networking technology. Many professionals are expected to be available via phone, email, or beeper 24 hours a day, seven days a week. Given this situation, it is no surprise that studies also indicate that illnesses related to work stress and burnout are on the rise.

Fortunately, there is another way! From our own experience with burnout and renewal, and from our research and work with clients, we know that working nonstop is detrimental to performance and well-being. We also know that there is a more effective way to work—that taking time for renewal at work can enhance people's accuracy, efficiency, and productivity, along with their personal well-being.

Relying on our knowledge and experience with renewal, we started by writing tips to support professionals in renewing four aspects of themselves at work—physical, mental, emotional, and spiritual. We intentionally generated ideas that required few precious resources (time and money) and yet resulted in people feeling revitalized. As we began to share our thoughts with our clients, we felt encouraged by their positive and enthusiastic responses and began to further develop our approach to renewal at work. We created a series of renewal sessions for a few of our main clients, including Conoco and Howard Hughes Medical Institute, where we tested and honed our renewal strategies. At the same time, we added renewal tips to our Web site. Based on the feedback we received, it was clear that there was a large need for information about renewal in the workplace. So we decided to write about our approach by expanding upon the tips on the Web site, to make this information available to a wider audience. The result of our efforts is this book.

Who Should Read This Book

We wrote *Running on Plenty at Work* primarily for white-collar workers who are facing non-stop change, working long hours, and looking for more balance in their work lives. The book is relevant to the wide range of readers—from ambitious young professionals to successful, middle-aged executives—who are experiencing job burnout in the current environment of rapid change.

We also wrote this book with practitioners in mind—human resource managers, organizational consultants, and coaches who help employees identify and implement strategies for working in more balanced and productive ways. And, although the primary focus of this book is renewal **at work**, it is also meant for readers interested in balancing their personal as well as their work lives. Many of the strategies in this book can be applied to other contexts.

Our Individual Stories

This book is living proof of the axiom that "we teach what we most need to learn." Our exploration into how to work in a more renewing way came about after we each experienced the painful results of living unbalanced lives. Our stories are different, and yet there are similar threads running through them. What follows is how we each were called to the mission of "renewal at work."

Krista's Story:

When Krista began to have an inkling that she might need to learn to live and work in a different way, she was working full-time, going to graduate school at night, volunteering in her faith community, and was a single mother of a very active young boy. Krista had always been smart and very competent, so she thought that even though people were saying to her, "How do you do it all?" she could handle it. In fact, she did not think twice about it. Until one day, she began to realize that her schedule **was** taking a toll on her and her son. Something had to give. Turning to her family for support, she quit her consulting job, which was draining her physically as well as spiritually, to finish her Ph.D.

However, the years of burning the candle at both ends had already done their damage. Shortly after finishing her course work in the fall of 1990, Krista came down with a flu from which she could not seem to recover. One month went by and then two. Barely being able to get out of bed, with little energy, achy muscles, and excruciating headaches, she went to see a doctor. After many tests and visiting numerous doctors, she was diagnosed with chronic fatigue syndrome. The prescription was "aggressive rest therapy," which basically meant doing nothing but resting—no work at all. She took a leave of absence from school and hired someone to help care for her son and herself.

It was not an easy time, physically, mentally, emotionally or spiritually. In addition to doing nothing so that her body could heal, Krista had to deal with the mental and emotional pain of giving up all of her concepts and feelings about herself in relation to work. She had totally identified with being competent, reliable, intelligent, and capable of doing anything and everything—so much so, that

that is how she proved her worth to herself and the world. Now that she could do very little, she went through an identity crisis along with the physical one, which brought with it a sense of depression. Krista had to find a new way of being in, and relating to, the world, and a new way of anchoring her self worth. She spent many hours in doctors', therapists', and acupuncturists' offices and many hours praying and reading spiritual literature.

Gradually, over the course of two years, with much help and support (particularly from her husband whom she met during this time), Krista healed physically, transformed her self identity, overcame her depression, and grew spiritually, all of which eventually influenced her doctoral research and her future work. She came out of the illness knowing that living according to spiritual teachings and living in a balanced way at work and home was the only way in which she could remain healthy and live a joyful loving life. She also realized that making a meaningful contribution to the world was more important than being perfectly competent.

Krista decided to do her doctoral dissertation on individuals in business who live according to a spiritual perspective of service at work. Her research project was exhilarating for her and spiritually inspiring. Upon graduating, she decided to start a consulting practice that would focus on helping people in businesses and other organizations integrate their deeply held values with their work and take care of their own and others' well-being. She also made a commitment to work in a way that honored her own spiritual values and well-being.

Suzanne's Story:

Suzanne was always active and busy in all arenas of her life. She liked to push the envelope—just to see how much she could accomplish. When she was taking classes for her Master's degree, she worked full-time at an outdoor school that required her to be on 24-hour call two days a week. The other two days of the workweek found Suzanne teaching all day and then driving an hour and a half to graduate school. One night a week—after being in class for three hours—she participated in a staff meeting. Every weekend she studied. There was little time for recharging her batteries.

When she left education and began to work in the field of corporate Human Resource Management, Suzanne also taught courses at the local college. She was working full time and taking courses toward her Ph.D. At the same time, Suzanne was actively involved in her professional society, the American Society for Training and Development, at both the local and national levels, and participated in her church on many levels. She also kept up with her family of origin and often drove many hours to attend family celebrations. She thrived on being able to do it all.

Suzanne was managing Human Resources in an organization that encouraged innovation, something that was very important to her, when the leadership of the company changed. She was asked to be less forward-looking and to manage the Human Resources department according to an antiquated personnel model. Suzanne's spirit was greatly impacted and she began to feel as if she was no longer being nourished in her workplace.

It is not surprising that eventually the negative workplace environment and the toll of living in a harried way caught up with Suzanne. Her spirit and body both suffered and she developed a very serious case of bronchial asthma from which she took a long time to recover. The medication that she needed to take reeked havoc with her body and emotions. During this time she wondered what direction she should take. In 1994, she attended a retreat at the Kirkridge Retreat Center facilitated by Parker Palmer, entitled "Gifted and Called: Where Do I Go from Here?" During her time at Kirkridge, she began to wonder if she was being called to a different kind of work and a different way of working. At the same time, she began meeting with a wonderful spiritual director, Reverend Jane Quinn, who helped Suzanne explore the questions of God's call in her life and how she could live and work in a more life giving way.

In 1995, Suzanne decided to leave her corporate employer and start her own organizational development consulting practice. Her focus was to help organizations create workplaces where the human spirit would be honored and nurtured.

Our Collective Story

We were introduced to each other by Peter Vaill, Ph.D., well-known consultant, author of several books on management, and one of

Krista's professors and doctoral advisors. Peter knew of Krista's interest in spirituality in the workplace. At the time Suzanne was facilitating a Spirit at Work dialogue group that he attended. He thought we would have a lot to talk about. Little did he know that he was planting the seeds of our future partnership! We hit it off immediately upon meeting and agreed to do some work together. We spoke at a number of conferences on spiritual renewal at work and also taught graduate level leadership courses together at the University of Maryland's University College.

Then one day, at the end of one of our work meetings, Suzanne told Krista that she had been contemplating and talking with her spiritual director about the direction she wanted to go in her work. She wanted to share her ideas with Krista. Since we only had 15 minutes left before we had to leave, Suzanne quickly shared that she was thinking about becoming a renewal coach. The next morning Krista sat for her regular morning meditation and was surprised to find Suzanne's vision for her work bubbling up in her meditation. Ideas just kept flowing and Krista realized that she was supposed to do renewal work too. The possibility crossed her mind that maybe she and Suzanne were supposed to do it together and form a business.

So, we met to talk about a potential partnership, and the more we talked, the more excited—and scared— we became. The idea of working together was very appealing. At the same time, we were two very independent women who did not want to lose our individual autonomy and individual ways of working. We spent the next three months exploring the mission and vision for the possible company, the values we wanted to work by, the beliefs we both held, the types of clients we wanted, the kinds of services we would offer, and how we would organize and handle finances. We talked about how we would work together, manage and deliver projects, and how we would resolve disagreements. Basically, we talked about all the possible opportunities and pitfalls we could think of and, in the end, decided we would form a partnership. In January 1998, Renewal Resources was born!

As we began doing more renewal work together, we came to realize that not everyone who has experienced extreme burnout has the option of leaving his or her workplace. It was these people who were feeling the brunt of stress in the workplace that we felt called to serve and support in renewing themselves right where they are. Our vision has led us to develop processes to assist individuals and organizations in creating workplaces where renewal is welcomed and practiced.

Since 1998, we have been consulting with, speaking to, and coaching many individuals and organizations who want to lead more renewing and productive lives at work. We are grateful that the clients we envisioned attracting have asked for our services. Although not an exhaustive list, some of our clients include: Alstom Power, Chautauqua Institution, Central Atlantic Conference of the United Church of Christ, Conoco, the Environmental Protection Agency, the Food and Drug Administration, Howard Hughes Medical Institute, IBM, Silicon Graphics International, Social and Scientific Systems, The Gardens Ice House, The Tri-City Eagles, and University United Methodist Church. While, in most cases, we have not identified individuals from our client's organizations by using their full names, their stories are woven into the fabric of this book.

How We Practice What We Preach

When you are hard-wired to achieve, like we are, it takes vigilance to make work and life style changes. Writing this book has caused each of us to commit even more fully to practicing what we preach. Some days we are more successful with our own renewal practices than others. For the most part, we create an oasis in our workday by scheduling time for lunch and stretch breaks. Many days, we follow individual practices that renew us spiritually. We take real vacations and refrain from checking email and voice mail while we are away.

We each have a corner of the world where we get away from it all. Suzanne spends a portion of every summer at Chautauqua Institution in Chautauqua, New York—a beautiful spot in western New York on a large lake—where things are slower and the spirit and mind are renewed. One summer Suzanne wrote in her journal that Chautauqua must have been the kind of place that Christ had in mind when He said to his disciples, "Come away with me, my beloved, and rest awhile."

Krista spends time throughout the year at Shree Muktananda Ashram, a Siddha Yoga spiritual retreat site in the Catskill Mountains in New York state. There, she relieves herself of stress (the definition of the Indian word ashram is "a place where worldly fatigue is removed") by participating in meditation retreats and courses on spiritual topics and practices. Krista also renews herself by spending peaceful moments at a lake near the ashram where she and her husband own a cabin. She spent numerous days there writing material for this book, pausing frequently to look out the big picture window to the lake beyond.

We hope that our book inspires and motivates you to join us in the rewarding practice of renewal at work.

KRISTA AND SUZANNE
POTOMAC AND GERMANTOWN, MARYLAND
NOVEMBER 2002

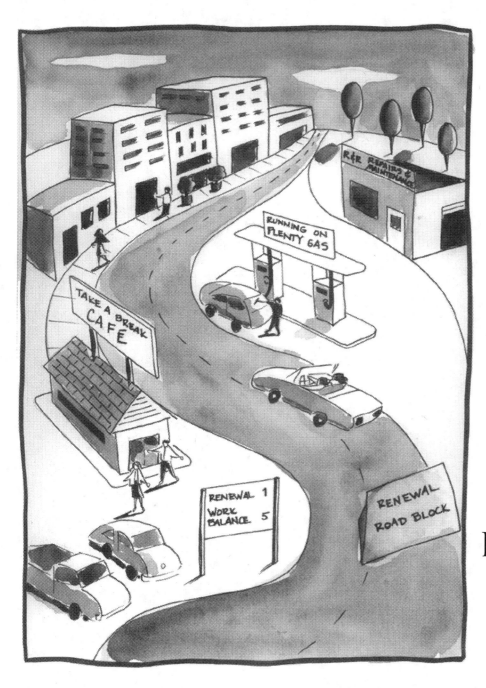

Part one

EMBARKING
ON THE
ROAD TO
RENEWAL

How to Prepare Yourself for Running on Plenty at Work

"We should not hurry, we should not be impatient, but we should confidently obey the eternal rhythm. That's the road to take; find the absolute rhythm and follow it with absolute trust."

Nikos Kazantzakis, *Zorba the Greek*

Deciding to Take the Trip

Do you have a sense of calm, balanced well-being on the job? Do you feel like you are running close to plenty at work? If you answered "no" to these questions, you are reading the right book at the right time. If you answered "yes," reading this book will help sustain your ability to work in a way that renews you. In reading this book you have an opportunity to follow the "eternal rhythm" at work and travel the Road to Renewal on a regular basis. The ideas you find along the way will keep you running on plenty at work.

Navigating the Road to Renewal

The Road to Renewal may be an unfamiliar, or infrequently traveled, highway to you. Here is a road map containing the trip highlights to help you know what to expect along the way as you read.

In Part One (Chapters 1–7), you will learn:

- Why it is important to run on plenty
- What running on plenty means
- How you can actually learn to run on plenty at work
- How you can work with and overcome the roadblocks and "gas guzzling" activities in your work life
- Car metaphors that provide an interesting and light way to understand renewal

In Part Two (Chapters 8–19), you'll find:

- Guidance for navigating through the seasons of renewal at work
- Monthly renewal themes
- Related weekly themes for the four weeks of each month
- Tips and exercises for each week
- Resources for each month (located at the end of the book)

Understanding the Road Signs

Throughout the book you will find the following elements to assist you as you travel on the Road to Renewal at work.

Reflection Questions

Reflection Questions — To help you deepen your thinking and understanding of renewal

Inspirational Quote

Quotes — To inspire you

Key Point

Key Points — To remind you of important items

Renewal Tips — To help you renew yourself

Renewal Exercises — To do at work

Identifying Your Trip Options

There are a number of ways to travel the Road to Renewal. Here are a few of the trip possibilities. You can:

- Read the book all the way through and use the material to create your own practice of renewal.
- Work first with the material in Part One and then work with the monthly theme, tips, and exercises. The monthly chapters are independent of each other so you can start with the month in which you are reading the book. You do not have to wait until January to start renewing yourself!
- Choose a theme that captures your interest and work with the tips in that chapter.
- Renew a specific aspect of your being—body, mind, emotions, and spirit—by using the Quick Reference Guides located in the back of the book.

Whatever option you choose, you will want to keep a journal for noting your answers to the various exercises and questions in this book. You have several options with the exercises and reflection questions. You can practice the exercises as you read them or save them for a later time. You can choose to answer all of the reflection questions at once, answer them over a period of time or respond only to those that resonate with you.

The sooner you begin your trip, the better for you. Your work will profit for having traveled the Road to Renewal! In fact, today is a perfect day to begin your journey to revitalization at work! Buckle up and start your engine...

WHY RUNNING ON PLENTY AT WORK IS IMPORTANT

Self-renewal consists of the conscious, regular steps you take to rejuvenate and revitalize yourself. It's the primary way to prevent burnout and rekindle your spark of excitement about your work—keeping it flourishing, even in tough, trying work settings.
— ROBERT K. COOPER, PH. D., *THE PERFORMANCE EDGE*

Contemplating the Importance of Running on Plenty

Until now, you may have thought little about why renewal is important. Your decision to read this book is an important first leg on your journey toward running on plenty at work. This book will increase your understanding of renewal at work and why you want to run on plenty instead of empty. Before reading further, you may want to reflect on why you are interested in this topic.

Reflection Questions

Take two to three minutes to reflect and/or write about each of the following questions:

1. What does running on plenty at work mean to me?
2. Why am I interested in renewal at work?
3. Why is renewal at work important to me?
4. What do I hope to gain from renewing myself?

Many people never even consider the possibility of running on plenty at work. Often, when they consider revitalizing themselves, they typically think they have to find time after work to do it, or they believe they will renew themselves after all their obligations are met, something which usually never happens! While it is true that some methods of renewal require you to take time off work and put aside all your seemingly endless tasks, you do not have to always find time outside of work to refuel.

Certainly, the whole idea of renewal in the workplace runs counter to the cultural norms surrounding work in the United States and a business mentality that is based on the Protestant work ethic. Many people in organizations believe that the amount of time they work is directly related to their productivity—a belief that is supported by many workplace policies and behaviors. This attitude results in people taking few or minimal breaks, skipping lunch, and working longer and longer hours.

Statistics paint a hectic picture of Americans and their work habits. Consider the following:

- Nearly 50 percent of all U.S. workers feel overwhelmed by a growing number of job tasks and longer working hours (Families and Work Institute, 2001).
- Sixty eight percent of employees say that they have to work very fast and eighty percent say that they have to work very hard (Families Work Institute, 1998).
- Fifty percent of workers in a survey conducted by Integra reported that they often spend 12-hour days on work-related duties and an equal number of people frequently skip lunch (Integra Survey, 2001).
- Fifty-five percent of workers take 15 minutes or less for lunch (1997 survey cited in *Life is not Work, Work is not Life*, Robert K. Johnston, Ph.D. and J. Walker Smith, Ph.D.).

These work practices come with a high personal price. The results are high levels of stress, a lack of work/life balance, burnout, and family distress. Essentially, the outcome leads to running on empty! This book encourages you to work in a different way—to claim responsibility for creating a renewing work rhythm for yourself.

Reflecting on a Renewal Tale

So, how do you learn to work with ease? There is a story, adapted from a Zen tale that offers some insight.

> *A young, ambitious manager went to her wise CEO and said earnestly, "I am devoted to studying how you work with such effectiveness and ease. How long will it take me to master it?" The wise CEO's reply was casual, "One year." Impatiently, the ambitious manager*

answered, "But I want to master it faster than that. I will work very hard. I will work everyday, ten or more hours a day if I have to. How long will it take then?" The wise CEO thought for a moment and replied, "Five years."

Learning from the Renewal Tale

Reflection Questions

 Take two to three minutes to reflect and/or write about each of the following questions:
1. What are the main points of the story?
2. How does this story relate to my own approach to work?
3. What can I learn for myself from this story?

Lesson 1: Renewal is best learned using an easy approach

As you may have already concluded, renewal is best studied in a replenishing and easy manner. As the young woman in the story discovered, you cannot master renewal by working longer and harder. You are actually less productive and effective when you toil too intensively or extensively. If you want to have a productive and renewing work life, you will learn more quickly if you pace yourself and approach the education process in a low key way. Like Einstein said, "you cannot solve a problem with the same kind of thinking that got you into the situation in the first place."

Key Point

 "You are actually less productive and effective when you toil too intensively or extensively."

The good news is that the approach to work that you seek is already at your disposal. In the story the young ambitious manager could have worked in the same manner as the wise CEO by simply choosing to work at a slower pace than she had been. In other words, working with effectiveness and ease are readily available for you to claim, making it easy for you to attain renewal at work.

In her book *Come With Me,* Naomi Shihab Nye writes:

> *"To the quiet minute between two noisy minutes*
> *It is always waiting, ready to welcome us—*
> *Tucked under the wing of the day."*

Renewal is waiting for you at work. You'll find it "tucked under the wing" of your workday.

Lesson 2: Renewal contributes to performance effectiveness

In the Renewal Tale, the ambitious manager believed that the key to working with effectiveness and ease was work longer and harder. She learned from the wise CEO that her perception was inaccurate. The truth is that working harder and longer does not necessarily contribute to one's effectiveness. In fact, as suggested in the story, it can negatively effect overall performance and take longer to achieve goals. As you may know from experience, when you do not take breaks, when you keep "pushing" yourself, you tend to make mistakes and it takes longer and longer to complete your tasks.

In fact, it can take up to five times more energy to complete a task when you are fatigued than it would if you were to renew yourself first. This is because your mind is "wired" for taking periodic rests or breaks and it "shuts down" spontaneously if you do not take a break. You have probably experienced this if you have tried to read while being tired. You end up reading the same paragraph over and over again because nothing seems to register in your mind. Or you make simple, easily avoidable mistakes that you would never make when you are feeling rested. Taking the time to nourish your body by simply scheduling lunch gives you energy to perform effectively the remainder of the day.

Inspirational Quote

"One of the simplest and most effective ways to counteract fatigue is through scheduling and design of work breaks. American, European, and Japanese research substantiate the need for short daily work breaks to revitalize the body and mind, measurably increasing job satisfaction, productivity, and quality control."

ROBERT K. COOPER, PH.D., *THE PERFORMANCE EDGE*

Lesson 3: Renewal contributes to sustained work performance

In the story, the wise CEO works at an easy and steady pace, which allows him to renew himself and remain effective over the long run. Recent research on the way executives work, reinforces the lesson of the story. In her book *Thriving in 24/7*, Sally Helgesen states that senior executives never seem to hurry, while the people around them are more frantic in their approach to their work. The way in which senior executives carry themselves reflects their conviction that they have value and absolutely nothing to prove. If you make a habit of working with ease by practicing renewal everyday, particularly when the pressure is off and you have reserve energy, it will allow you to develop the skills you will need to be readily available when "the pressure is on." It is sort of like having a "renewal savings account" from which you can draw in times of chaos, stress or demand.

The fable, the Wild Boar and the Fox, emphasizes the same point. *Once upon a time, a Wild Boar stood under a tree and rubbed his tusks against the trunk. A Fox passing by asked him why he thus sharpened his teeth when there was no danger threatening from either huntsman or hound. He replied, "I do it advisedly; for it would never do to have to sharpen my weapons just at the time I ought to be using them."*

Inspirational Quote

"It is what you do now when you do not have to do anything that makes you what you want to be when it is too late to do anything about it."

ROBERT J. GARY, RETIRED EXECUTIVE VICE PRESIDENT,
GENERATION TXU, DALLAS TEXAS

Reviewing the Benefits of Renewal

In conclusion, running on plenty at work is important because when you replenish yourself, you can:

- produce quality work
- maintain a strong sense of purpose
- be creative
- make effective decisions
- handle challenging situations when they arise
- enjoy what you do

- live a balanced life
- take care of yourself
- interact with others in valuable ways
- benefit from clearer intuition
- sustain energy and enthusiasm for your work

Assessing Your Need for Renewal

About now you may be wondering, "Do **I** need to renew myself at work?" To help you gain some clarity about your need for rejuvenation, take a few minutes to complete the Renewal at Work Self-Assessment that follows.

This instrument is based on Frederic M. Hudson, Ph.D.'s characteristics of self-renewing adults and our evolving thinking in the area of proactive renewal at work. In his book, *The Adult Years: Mastering the Art of Self Renewal,* Hudson writes that self-renewing adults: 1) are value driven, 2) are connected to the world around them, 3) require solitude and quiet, 4) pace themselves, 5) have contact with nature, 6) are creative and playful, 7) adapt to change, 8) learn from their disappointments and losses, 9) never stop learning, and 10) are future oriented.

The assessment takes into account our ideas about taking responsibility for your own renewal at work, as well as incorporates our thoughts on integrated well-being at work. Our integrated model of renewal at work includes the four key aspects of human beings: 1) body, 2) mind, 3) emotions, and 4) spirit. The instrument also integrates our ideas about living a balanced life outside of work, which is essential to peoples' well-being at work. You will find it helpful to take this assessment now and again six months from now, after you begin to incorporate renewal into your daily work life.

Renewal At Work Self-Assessment (Abbreviated Version)

Instructions: For each of the items listed that follow, circle the number that best indicates how you currently think or feel about yourself at work.

Key: Not true of me – 1; Slightly True of Me – 2; Mostly True of Me – 3; or Very True of Me – 4

	Not True	Slightly True	Mostly True	Very True
Section 1				
1. I act on my need for a break, food, or physical exercise during the workday.	1	2	3	4
2. I pace myself at work balancing high-energy tasks with time to replenish myself.	1	2	3	4
3. I work a reasonable number of hours.	1	2	3	4

Total Score for Section 1 = _____

Section 2				
4. I look for opportunities to learn and use new skills at work.	1	2	3	4
5. I spend some small portion of each workday in quiet.	1	2	3	4
6. I seek openings to be creative and playful at work.	1	2	3	4

Total Score for Section 2 = _____

Section 3				
7. I sustain work relationships through listening and empathizing with others, and doing small acts of kindness for others.				
8. I forgive others and myself for errors and learn from disappointments at work.	1	2	3	4
9. I have developed and work according to my life mission/purpose statement.	1	2	3	4

Total Score for Section 3 = _____   1   2   3   4

Section 4

		Not True	Slightly True	Mostly True	Very True
10.	I take time during my workday to rejuvenate myself by connecting with nature in some way.	1	2	3	4
11.	I see my work as an opportunity to serve others.	1	2	3	4
12.	I ask for inner guidance or call upon a higher power for help during my workday.	1	2	3	4

Total Score for Section 4 = _____

Section 5

		Not True	Slightly True	Mostly True	Very True
13.	I take all of my vacation days.	1	2	3	4
14.	I follow a regular fitness program by exercising 3 times a week for 20 minutes.	1	2	3	4
15.	I spend time with friends and family on a regular basis.	1	2	3	4

Total Score for Section 5 = _____

Scoring and Interpreting the Renewal at Work Self-Assessment (Abbreviated Version)

Step One: Assessment

Tally your scores for each section. Transfer the scores for each section to the "Your Score" column. Notice the aspects with which each section corresponds.

Section:	Your Score	Renewal Quadrant	Need for attention	Change Strategy
Section 1		Body		
Section 2		Mind		
Section 3		Emotions		
Section 4		Spirit		
Section 5		Work-Life balance		

Step Two: Interpretation

Compare your scores for each section with the table that follows to discover the corresponding level of need for attention and change strategy associated with your scores. Insert the corresponding need for attention and change strategy comments into the scoring chart above.

Score for each section	Need for attention	Change Strategy
11 +	None	None
8-10	Somewhat	Observe
0-7	Probably	Take Action

If you scored 11–12 on any portion of the assessment, you are doing very well in renewing that aspect of yourself. Consequently, you do not need to take any further actions in that area. You can focus your attention on other areas in which you scored lower

If you scored between 8–10 on any portion of the assessment, you are doing fairly well in renewing that aspect of yourself. Take some time to observe yourself to determine if there are any minor shifts that you could make to enhance this area.

If you scored between 3–7 on any portion, you probably need to pay close attention to this aspect of your life. Review the questions on the assessment for sections in which you scored below 8 and identify at least one specific behavior you could improve in that area.

Step Three: Application

Using the information from the assessment scoring table, reflect on how well you are renewing yourself at work. You can use the questions that follow to guide your thinking. Then, identify at least one specific action you can take to enhance your well-being in any areas where you scored below 8. Utilize the matrix in the back of the book to find specific tips and exercises for renewing that particular aspect—body, mind, emotions, and spirit.

1. What aspects of my renewal at work require attention?
2. What would be realistic renewal goals for me to set? What resources (time, people, and money) will help me attain these goals?

THE EXPERIENCE OF RUNNING ON PLENTY AT WORK

> *"It is essential that everyone find new ways to break away from work at work, and savor even a minute's reprieve from the rush and roar of the daily grind. This is one way to begin bringing a revitalized sense of being home for a few minutes wherever you happen to be, even at work."*
>
> ROBERT K. COOPER, PH.D., AND AYMAN SAWAF, *EXECUTIVE EQ*

Defining Renewal

The most basic definition of renewal (or as we like to call it, "running on plenty") is to make new again, to rejuvenate, or to refresh. In the context of renewal at work, renewal means regularly taking the time to revitalize yourself during your workday so that you always have enough energy on which to run. The goal of renewal is to be able to perform well at work, be available to those you care for at work and at home, sustain your own well-being, and experience the joy of being alive. Renewal involves balancing your personal needs with the demands of work and caring for others, so that you have fresh energy for yourself and your activities.

When you renew yourself you reestablish your connection with the core of your being. You reconnect with the steady center within you, and with what is most important to you. In order to rejuvenate yourself, you have to give yourself permission to stop and pause momentarily from focusing on work or helping others. To refuel, you need to temporarily step back from your daily activities and all the things you have to do and take time to simply be in the present moment. This will allow you to reconnect with the sources of energy, creativity, wisdom, balance, and inspiration within yourself.

Key Point

"Renewal involves balancing your personal needs with the demands of work and caring for others so that you have fresh energy for yourself and your activities."

In practical terms, renewal is an on-going process that involves taking time on a daily basis to replenish and nurture yourself. Because you naturally expend energy on all the activities you engage in during the course of the day, you need to counterbalance the outflow of energy and take conscious action to replenish yourself. This is not something that happens automatically.

Everyone needs to be aware about renewing themselves because it is not typically taught in formal schooling or in the workplace. Society does not lift up role models that demonstrate how to live and work in renewing ways. However, even though you may not have learned so far how to integrate renewal into your life so far, you **can** learn how to replenish your energy on an on-going daily basis. All you need to do is make it a priority and pay attention to your own needs!

Inspirational Quote

"Daily renewal is a statement about how you wish your day and, ultimately your life, to unfold. It is your soul speaking to your heart, and your heart translating to your mind, and your mind giving your body directions. It is ultimately an expression of self-love."
OPRAH WINFREY AND BOB GREENE, *MAKE THE CONNECTION*

There are many different areas in which you may choose to renew yourself throughout the day. How you replenish yourself depends on your needs and your focus. Different aspects of your being get depleted and need refueling at different times. Because your work demands that you use your mind, body, emotions, and spirit each day, you may need to replenish yourself physically, mentally, emotionally, and/or spiritually in different ways. Likewise, you may need to revitalize one of your specific skills or attitudes, your creativity, your enthusiasm, or your ability to listen to others. The key is to constantly be aware of what parts of you are depleted and adjust the replenishment appropriately.

Describing the Feeling of Renewal

Regardless of what aspect of yourself you are renewing, there are some common qualities that are present when you feel like you are running on plenty. You are probably already familiar with them.

Reflection Questions

 Take two to three minutes to reflect and/or write about each of the following questions:
1. How do I know when I am renewed?
2. What does it feel like to run on plenty?

Typically, when you feel renewed you feel more whole, more integrated, more steady and more in touch with your work and life than when you are experiencing burnout. Other words that participants in our Running on Plenty at Work Workshops have used to describe their experiences of renewal include feeling:

less judgmental	lighter
more creative	flexible
more connected	centered
invigorated	at ease
less caught up in crises	more accepting
at peace with themselves and work	alive
more meaning and direction at work	free
more aware of their own needs	open
more intuitive	

Are these qualities you want to have at work? Would you like to feel this way more often during your workday? You can, by starting with a simple renewal activity like *conscious breathing*.

Renewing Yourself Simply

Conscious breathing is something you can do anywhere, even in the midst of your work. This powerful tool can renew all four aspects of your being — mind, body, emotions, and spirit. When you breathe in a deep and conscious way your mind becomes quiet, your body relaxes, you release stressful emotions, and you connect with your spirit.

Key Point

 "Conscious breathing, if practiced regularly, will take you a long way down the road to renewal and will enhance your performance at work."

Essentially, the breath is the thread that runs through and connects these four aspects of your being. If you pay attention to your breathing and its effects on you, the connection becomes obvious. Take for instance the connection between your body and mind or your body and emotions. When you are upset, your breathing is shallow, restricted, and fast. And when you are calm your breathing is deeper and more relaxed. Knowing this fact about breathing is very useful when you are feeling tense or upset. When you practice deep, steady breathing, you use your body to relax, release emotional tension, and trigger a calming effect on your mind. Wellness expert, Herbert Benson, M.D., calls this the Relaxation Response and claims that this "natural restorative phenomenon is common to all of us."

Inspirational Quote

"It is suggested strongly [by research] that you could use your mind to change your physiology in a beneficial way, [to] improve [your] health..."

HERBERT BENSON, M.D., *THE WELLNESS BOOK*

Learn to breathe consciously and rehearse it several times each day. Practice when you are on hold on the phone, in the middle of a meeting, when things are getting tense, or when you are sitting in your car at a red light on the way to work.

Conscious breathing, if practiced regularly, will take you a long way down the road to renewal and will enhance your performance at work. There are numerous other ways to replenish yourself described in this book, many of which you can do right in the midst of your work. So travel on...

Exercise: Practicing Conscious Breathing

Note: Throughout this book, you will find exercises such as this one and guided imagery scripts that are difficult to do and read at the same time. To facilitate doing these exercises with ease, you may want to tape record the instructions and then play them back to guide you through the exercise.

1. Sit up straight with your back erect, yet relaxed.
2. Keeping your eyes open, focus your attention on your breathing. Become aware of the flow of air moving in and out of your body as you inhale and exhale through your nose.
3. As you feel yourself relaxing a bit, begin to allow your breathing to become deeper and longer. Allow the air to move all the way down into your abdomen, pushing your tummy outward, and then feel it filling up your chest cavity, expanding your ribs all around, front, sides, and back. And then exhale, fully and slowly, allowing the air to move all the way out from the top of the chest all the way into your abdomen.
4. Breathe this way for a few minutes until you feel relaxed.

You can do this exercise anywhere, anytime, for as long as you like. Experiment with it and create your own variations. You might try what Brian Luke Seaward suggests in *Stand Like a Mountain, Flow Like Water*. While focusing consciously on your breathing, visualize the air coming into your lungs as a cloud of clean, pure energized air. Imagine that the clean, fresh air you are breathing in has the power to clear your mind of distracting thoughts and replenish your body. Imagine the fresh air circulating throughout your body. And then, as you exhale, visualize the air leaving your body as a dark dirty cloud, representing all your tension and frustrations. With each breath, allow the clean fresh air to enter and circulate and rejuvenate your body, and with each exhalation of dark, stale air, your body releases its stress and tension.

How to Keep Yourself
Running on Plenty at Work

> "You have to learn the appropriate ... methods to [relax].... Once you have mastered these techniques, they can be put to work anywhere. Simply to be able to close one's eyes, detach, and relax can be very refreshing and allows one to return to work in a more creative and less combative frame of mind."
>
> ROBERT S. ELIOT, M.D., *FROM STRESS TO STRENGTH*

Keeping Yourself Running on Plenty

It is common place to pick up a popular magazine these days and read about some product or workshop bound to relieve your stress. Indeed, these are enticements for us to get away from it all. There are a variety of other restorative approaches that require less time and effort to implement. Approaches to renewal generally fall into one of the following three categories:

Going on Retreats

This method of reducing stress involves suspending regular life for a period of time, going away from work and home with a goal of returning renewed. Sometimes vacations can be viewed as renewal retreats. However, many people come back from vacations exhausted from doing too much. It is important for everyone to periodically suspend all the busy activity in their lives and create time to focus exclusively on their renewal. Retreats can vary in length and scope, depending upon your need and income. They can be as short as an afternoon or as long as a month. Some people choose a spiritual retreat center, while others head for a remote log cabin in the mountains. Some prefer a quiet day at the spa as a way of "going on retreat."

Setting Aside Daily Personal Time

This approach involves scheduling time in your day for renewing activities such as exercise, meditation, prayer, and play. Typically, these activities are done before or after work, or during breaks scheduled into the workday. The time allotted for these activities is shorter than retreat activities and easier to arrange.

Engaging in Renewal Activities in "Real Time"

This option entails doing renewal activities in the midst of your work, such as the breathing exercise described earlier. Other examples include repeating positive affirmations, praying, expressing enthusiasm and gratitude, looking for the larger meaning and purpose in work activities, performing small acts of kindness, being playful at work, or appreciating the moment.

Choosing the Right Mixture of Fuel for Running on Plenty

If you want to make renewal a way of life, you will want to include all three techniques in your renewal "fuel mixture." For instance, you could begin your day with an invigorating walk, schedule breaks into your workday, and go on retreat twice a year. Experiment until you find a combination that works for you. Remember, your goal is to identify a formula that renews your body, mind, emotions and spirit.

The activities you choose should reflect your lifestyle and preferences. There is no "one fuel fits all" when it comes to renewal. Thankfully, there are numerous renewal techniques from which you can pick and choose to help revitalize yourself. The lists on the following pages should get you thinking about the right renewal mix for you!

Key Point

"Remember, your goal is to identify a formula that renews your body, mind, emotions, and spirit."

Some Ways To Renew Your Body

Engage in Physical Exercise
- Aerobics
- Dance
- Garden
- Learn a new sport
- Play golf
- Play tennis
- Practice yoga
- Run
- Swim
- Walk

Eat Healthy Meals and Snacks
- Be aware of the effects of food on your body
- Cook and eat nutritious, delicious food
- Drink adequate water
- Pay attention to your diet

Relax
- Do aromatherapy
- Get a massage
- Get enough sleep
- Meditate
- Practice deep, steady breathing
- Rest
- Soak in a bath
- Take naps
- Do nothing

Some Ways to Renew Your Mind

Rest Your Mind
- Daydream
- Listen to moving water
- Listen to music
- Look at a meaningful object: picture, quote, or symbolic object
- Meditate
- Practice visualization

Focus Your Mind
- Bring your attention to the present
- Give tasks your full attention
- Repeat centering phrases

Develop Your Mind
- Contemplate thought-provoking questions
- Develop your intuition
- Interpret your dreams
- Learn a new hobby, activity, or skill
- Practice positive imaging
- Read inspiring literature
- Reflect on your life purpose
- Repeat positive affirmations

Some Ways to Renew Your Emotions

Express Emotions
- Cry
- Express passion and joy
- Hug others (with their permission)
- Sing a song!
- Speak to friends about feelings
- Vent anger in healthy ways
- Write in a journal

Cultivate Positive Attitudes
- Develop an attitude of gratitude
- Observe the beauty around you
- Replace negative thoughts with positive ones
- Seek and appreciate the moment
- Think about what brings you joy

Engage in Uplifting Activities
- Celebrate
- Create a personal mission statement
- Engage in creative activities; crafts, art, music, poetry
- Have fun—tell jokes, laugh, and express humor
- Play spontaneously
- "Perform random kindness and senseless acts of beauty"
- Sing or listen to music
- Spend time with high energy, uplifting people
- Volunteer your time and talents to help others in need

Some Ways to Renew Your Spirit

Engage in Spiritual Practices
- Meditate
- Perform sacred rituals
- Practice gratitude
- Pray
- Read spiritual literature
- Repeat names of God or do rosaries
- Serve others
- Sing spiritual songs, chant

Open Yourself to the Divine
- Ask for inner guidance
- Be aware of God's presence everywhere
- Be in silence
- Direct your thoughts to God
- Forgive yourself and others
- Look for larger meanings and purposes
- Spend time in nature
- Visualize being blessed

Recognizing What Is Renewing

Inspirational Quote

"New research suggests the uppermost priority for self renewal may be healthful pleasures—finding ways to do more of what you love to do and taking greater advantage of life's unvarnished golden moments to lift your spirits and put a little more fun back into your life."

ROBERT COOPER, PH.D., *PERFORMANCE EDGE*

As you can see, renewal activities come in a variety of forms. In her book, *You Do Not Have to Go Home from Work Exhausted!* Ann McGee-Cooper, Ed.D., states that many things that divert you from the work at hand are revitalizing. Although renewal techniques vary, they all have common characteristics that make them renewing. The following list should help you determine whether or not you have an effective renewal method. It is renewing if it:

- Takes your mind away from work and redirects your attention in a calming way
- Allows you to be reflective and turn your attention toward yourself
- Is fun to do and brings you pleasure
- Reenergizes you
- Changes, positively, your state of mind and your level of awareness

Reflection Questions

Take two to three minutes to reflect and/or write about each of the following questions:

1. In what ways do I like to renew myself?
2. What renewal activities work best for me at home?
3. What renewal activities work best for me at work?

Finding Creative Ways to Refuel at Work

It is no surprise that some renewing activities that you like to do at work are easier and more appropriate to do than others. Some renewal methods may require more time than you typically have available at work or may be only suitable to do outside the workplace. However, if you are creative you can find ways to do renewal practices right at work that you would typically do at home or on vacation.

For instance, Lillie, who participated in one of our workshops, shared that her preferred way to renew herself physically was to take a hot bath with nice smelling oils. Taking a bath at work is not an option. We suggested that she think about how to modify this activity so that she could use it at work. She came up with a great idea. Lillie decided to take a wash cloth with aromatic oil on it to work and use the microwave to create a hot, wet cloth, like the towels you get at some restaurants or on some long airplane flights. She could refresh herself at work by wiping her face and neck with the towel, breathe in the soothing aroma, and allow the warmth to relax her neck.

Another person, Parker, who loves to play chess at home, puts a magnetic chessboard on his office door with a sign inviting people to make a move using the white pieces. He checks the board periodically throughout the day, sees what move his coworkers have made, and then makes a move himself. This activity does not take much of Parker's time during the day and gives him a fun way to interact with people at work. Parker takes a short break and uses his mind in a way that is renewing for him.

Key Point

"If you are creative you can find ways to do renewal practices right at work that you may not find time for at home."

Donna, who works in advertising, reports that what renews her emotionally is cooking and entertaining. She brings her latest culinary creations to work and invites her colleagues to join her for lunch in the conference room. Her pleasure is twofold because she cooks and connects with her colleagues. Donna is renewed and so are her coworkers because she provides a venue in which they can relax and enjoy one another's company as well as healthy, low fat food.

Finally, Helena, who works as a librarian at a private school, finds that complete silence renews her spirit. During the weekend she likes to read and spend time by herself. Throughout the school day many of the teachers who come in the library for their breaks want to talk with Helena, making it difficult for her to find quiet in her own library. During her break, she goes to the public library, which is next door. She enjoys the silence there and returns to the school library with her spirits renewed.

Reflection Questions

 Take two to three minutes to reflect and/or write about each of the following questions:

1. What renewal activities can I do at work that require a short break?
2. Which of my preferred renewal activities require a longer break?
3. What renewal activities can I do in the midst of my work?
4. How can I creatively refuel myself at work?
5. How can I integrate renewal activities into my workday that I would not ordinarily do at work?

How to Practice Preventive Maintenance

> *"(Idling) is the most relaxed, energy–efficient way for a car engine to operate. Humans can work that way too."*
>
> PAUL WILSON, *CALM AT WORK*

Taking a Tip from Your Car

It is no secret that preventive maintenance enhances the performance and often extends the life of an automobile. In his book, *Calm at Work*, Paul Wilson explains that idling is the most relaxed, energy efficient way for a car engine to operate. Human beings work that way too. Research into work habits has shown that the human body can only work a certain amount of time without a rest before performance begins to deteriorate. This time is known as the Rest-Activity Cycle. The average person's cycle is 90 to 120 minutes.

Knowing what smart car maintenance entails and following the guidelines in your owner's manual are not always synonymous. Your approach to personal renewal might be like your approach to car maintenance. You may know what you need to do to renew yourself and even how you might integrate your preferred renewal activities into your work settings. Yet, doing it may be another matter.

Prior to reading this book, you were probably already aware of how you like to revitalize yourself, but have found it difficult to practice renewal on a regular basis. Do not worry! You are not alone. Many people have good intentions and tell themselves that they will renew themselves later—at home on the weekend—or they will take a vacation but they never get around to it because of all the things they have to do in their lives. This is akin to eventually getting around to taking your car in for a much needed oil change.

It may be challenging for you to renew yourself regularly—to habitually do it—to see it as a crucial activity worthy of scheduling into your day. It is important to explore how to more effectively integrate renewal into your busy days.

Understanding Your Maintenance Options

Taking responsibility for your own renewal requires awareness of your options, a commitment to implement the option best suited for your particular situation, and the discipline to manage your own maintenance. There are two complementary approaches to renewal—one reactive and the other proactive. You can choose to repair yourself after a break down and refuel your gas tank after it is completely empty (reactive renewal)—or you can follow a regular maintenance schedule and refill your tank before it becomes depleted (proactive renewal).

Paying Attention to Repair Needs

Reactive renewal starts with an awareness that you are depleted in some way. You respond to that need in a way that brings replenishment. This is how most people approach renewal and it is often done ineffectively. There are two aspects that are necessary for reactive renewal to be effective: **awareness** and **action.** You first are aware of the need for renewal and then you act in a specific way—engage in some activity—that addresses your need. These two aspects of reactive renewal may seem quite obvious and elementary. Yet, how often do you actually pay attention to the signals that your body, mind, emotions, and spirit send you every day? And how often, once you are aware of these signals, do you choose to do something to respond to them?

You can delay your response to the need for renewal until your body "ups the ante" and you get sick. Or perhaps you do pay attention to signals that indicate you need to refuel, but you end up responding in a way that does not actually refresh you. For instance, how many times have you plunked down in front of the television at the end of a long day because you felt you had no energy? And what was the end result? You often ended up feeling more drained than revitalized at the end of the evening. The secret to renewal is to choose activities that will give you energy and make you feel better, not depleted.

Again, the car analogy is helpful. Have you ever run out of gas in your car? Many believe that this is a female affliction. But Suzanne's husband, Dan, ran out of gas two times during the first six months they dated. As she went to rescue him for a second time, she asked him, "Didn't you look at your gas gauge?" To which Dan replied, "Of course! But I thought I could make it."

How many people run their bodies on empty believing that they "can make it?" By the way, Dan instituted a new policy after the second episode. He now fills the tank when it is half-empty. How does he know to fill the car? By looking at the gauge! Although you do not have a fuel gauge like a car, you do have signals that let you know when you are running on empty.

Key Point

"How often do you actually pay attention to the signals that your body, mind, emotions, and spirit send you every day?"

You can learn and become more conscious of the indicators that point to a need for renewal, both the signals you get from your mind, body, emotions, and spirit throughout the day and the messages you get from the people and situations around you. Paying attention to the signals and responding accordingly is the key to practicing reactive renewal.

Reflection Questions

Take two to three minutes to reflect and/or write about each of the following questions:
1. How do I know when I need to renew myself?
2. What are the typical signals I get when I need to revitalize myself?
3. How do I typically respond or react to the signals I receive?

If you stop and think about it, you probably already know many indicators of the need for renewal. However, knowing about them does not necessarily translate into recognizing them when they are happening. The more familiar you are with these signs, the more you will be likely to respond to them in "real time." Review the following list of signs that you need renewal.

Signals That You Need Renewal

You most likely need to refuel in some way when—

You feel a lack of:	Or when you experience yourself as:	Or if you find yourself:
• Commitment to work • Connection with colleagues • Creativity • Enthusiasm and energy • Interest in your work • Joy • Motivation for the work you are doing • Purpose and meaning • Satisfaction • Sense of humor	• Angry • Cranky • Depleted • Frustrated • Having to reread or redo your work • Impatient • Making careless errors • Mentally blocked or confused in your thinking • Moody • Procrastinating • Restless • Tense • Tired	• Working obsessively • Bored • Easily upset • Forgetting important information • Nervous • Not able to keep focused on your work • Powerless • Unable to make clear decisions • Worrying excessively

Because you may not be used to paying attention to these indicators, it is helpful to check in periodically with yourself during the day to see if any of the signs that you need to renew yourself are present.

Exercise: Checking In with Yourself

To check in with yourself:
1. Take a pause in your activity and bring your attention to your own experience in the present moment. You may want to close your eyes and take a few deep breaths.
2. Ask yourself "How do I feel at this moment?" or "What do I need right now?"
3. Listen for your own answer and trust the information you get.
4. Follow up and act on the information.

Key Point

"Awareness is one of the first steps in making a change."

It is also helpful to discover and pay attention to those activities that regularly consume you. Once you know what drains you, you can begin to choose renewal rather than depletion. You may be able to eliminate these exhausting activities from your schedule. Of course, there will be some you cannot avoid. For those activities, you can make sure to plan renewing and counterbalancing exercises before, during, and after the fatiguing situations. You might also think about how you could modify depleting activities. For instance, if you are a perfectionist, maybe you can experiment with performing at the 100 percent level rather than at 120 percent. Better still, pick out some things you can do at 80 percent level to conserve your energy for those tasks and goals truly worthy of 100 percent.

You can pay more attention to and work with those things, both externally and internally, that stop you from revitalizing yourself, even when you are aware of the need for renewal. Awareness is one of the first steps in making a change. If you know what blocks your renewal process, then you have a better chance of overcoming those obstacles. Use your will power to take appropriate action when the need arises.

Practicing Preventive Maintenance

You know that you need to do more than just "go in for repairs" when your vehicle is run down. Over the long run, if you want your vehicle to perform at peak levels you must practice preventative maintenance. You need to follow the suggested guidelines in the owner's manual. Similarly, to run on plenty and work at optimum energy levels, you need to engage in regular renewal practices to avoid getting depleted in the first place. Proactive renewal is the human form of preventive care.

Proactive renewal involves building renewal activities into the day on an ongoing basis so that you do not wait until you are beyond exhaustion to take care of yourself. This is the scheduled regular, preventive maintenance or the "apple a day" approach. This is what keeps you (and your car) from needing major repairs. In the case of your car, a major repair might mean a new transmission or a new engine. In the case of yourself, a major repair might involve a serious health problem or work performance issue.

Key Point

"Proactive renewal involves building renewal activities into the day on an ongoing basis so that you do not wait until you are beyond exhaustion to take care of yourself."

There are many ways you can create renewal moments during the day. For instance, Krista meditates almost every morning before going to work and reads inspirational and devotional books during different times of the day. Suzanne writes in her personal journal and sets aside time for praying each day. It has taken years for us to find the right activities and timing that works best for each of us. And from time to time, as life circumstances have changed, we have taken time to adjust our timing to fit our new situation. For instance, when Krista's oldest son went away to college last year she modified when she meditated and added a new creative activity to her schedule. We know that it is a challenge to set aside time every day to proactively renew yourself. Certainly there are some days when we do not. But, we also know that the days when we think we do not have the time for renewal are probably the days when we need it the most. We have learned from experience that our work goes better and we serve our clients in more effective ways when we build some renewal into our daily routines.

Inspirational Quote

"Work, work, from early to late. In fact, I have so much to do I that I shall spend the first three hours in prayer."
VELT DIETRICH, MARTIN LUTHER'S SCRIBE AND COMPANION

An important key to proactive renewal is to give yourself permission to incorporate renewal activities into your day and to see them as essential to success. A helpful framework is to think of renewal as a necessary piece of your work and as important activities that will help you achieve whatever goals you have set for yourself that day. When you at first begin to integrate renewal into your daily life in a proactive way, start with small and simple activities. Here are some helpful guidelines for creating moments of proactive renewal in your day.

1. To renew yourself, use times during the day when you do not have to do focused thinking. For instance:
   - Listen to inspirational tapes in your car on the way to work.
   - When getting ready for work, play inspiring music, or meditate.
   - During lunchtime, stretch or exercise.
   - While standing in lines, do breathing exercises.
   - While waiting on hold on a phone call, practice positive imaging.
   - While in the bathroom, repeat centering phrases to yourself.
2. Schedule renewal moments in your daily calendar. Consider this to be "catch your breath time," when you can nourish yourself, literally and figuratively. For example:
   - When doing complex work, schedule brief renewal breaks every hour or so. Lydia, an environmental engineer, sets her timer on her computer to go off every 60 minutes and then each hour she takes a one-minute break.

- On regular days, schedule two short activities, one in the morning and one in the afternoon.
- Make sure you take time to hydrate yourself and nourish your body. Rather than relying on the "junk food" from the vending machine, keep a bottle of water, dried fruit, or nuts at your desk.
- On very busy days, incorporate renewal activities into the midst of your work activities—like focusing on the positive, and doing deep, steady breathing.
- When you have a work activity you know is draining, schedule a renewing activity before and/or after the depleting activity. Rachel, who is a trainer and an off the chart extrovert, schedules calls with upbeat clients and colleagues in the middle of a particularly difficult course development project.

3. Pay attention to what renews you and schedule these activities into your day and week. Place your needs on par with all your other work and family priorities.

4. Experiment with finding new ways to renew yourself. Learn which activities work best in which settings and how best to address your different physical, mental, emotional, and spiritual needs.

5. Get support from friends, family, and coworkers for renewing yourself. Choose a renewal partner, someone at work with whom to share your renewal plans. You can check in with each other, ask how things are going, and remind each other to renew yourselves. In high activity work crunches, ask yourself, "How am I going to renew myself today?" Wait until you hear a satisfactory answer!

6. Discover and create places at work that are conducive for your renewal experience. For instance, you may find that taking a breather in the bathroom works for you. Maybe there is a quiet nook in your office where you can go on your breaks. Your office may be located in a setting that enables you to take walks outside near your building. Perhaps your company can create a special renewal room at the workplace. If there is nowhere in your work environment that is naturally suitable for renewal,

you can create a mini renewal environment by decorating your office with plants, a small water garden, posters or pictures that support your renewal. In her office, Suzanne has a monthly calendar of the Chautauqua Institution in New York, her road to renewal every summer. Just by glancing at that calendar, Suzanne is transported to her beloved Chautauqua.

7. Invite others to join you in group renewal activities, such as discussing work issues while taking a walk together. You might even encourage your organization to schedule activities such as:
   - Company picnics and/or parties
   - Creating a company renewal room where people can do renewal activities
   - Volunteering together
   - Celebrating successes and milestones

6

Overcoming Roadblocks to Running on Plenty at Work

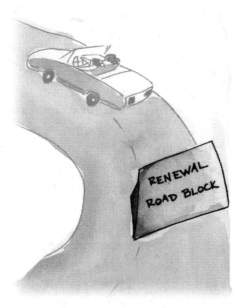

"Stand up to your obstacles and do something about them. You will find they have not the strength you think they have."

NORMAN VINCENT PEALE,
WORDS OF WISDOM 4U QUOTES

Managing Your Response to Roadblocks

As you travel on the Road to Renewal, hazards, and roadblocks can often get in the way. Typically, when you stop to think about what impedes your renewal, the first thing that comes to mind are all the situations and people around you that cause problems. Some of the roadblocks that you might recognize are:

- "My boss is too demanding and would think I was slacking off if I took time for renewal."
- "I have too much to do to take the time for renewal."
- "The company where I work expects me to put in long hours."
- "On my team, I have difficult or incompetent coworkers who cause me to spend more time and energy."

Sound familiar? Each and every day you face very real and numerous challenges in your work environment. Often you cannot control or change your external environment. Ultimately, all you have control over is how you respond to the challenges life presents. Taking responsibility for your own state of well-being and understanding what depletes you are key to renewal at work.

Reflection Questions

Take two to three minutes to reflect and/or write about each of the following questions:

1. How do I deplete myself at work?
2. What stops me from renewing myself at work?
   a. Which of these are organizational challenges?
   b. Which of these are my personal challenges?
   c. Over which of these do I have control?
   d. How can I respond to these challenges?

Preventing a Leaky Tank

Over time, gas tanks in cars can develop leaks. When this happens, one remedy is to patch the tank. Like cars, people can also unconsciously leak their energy source. The good news is you can repair the leaks in your personal fuel tank!

Regardless of the kind of environment you work in and the kinds of external challenges to renewal that you may face, there are many ways in which you cause leaks in your own "personal tank." In the course of the day, you may use more "gas" than necessary and often unintentionally create more mental and physical exhaustion than is required. You drain valuable energy whenever you:

1. Have stress-producing expectations about work
2. Are not aware of what is important to you
3. Do activities that are depleting, redundant, or not necessary
4. Engage in negative thinking, or *stinkin' thinkin'*

Fuel Leak One: Stress-Producing Work Expectations

When you expect a task to be stressful or tiring, you create a self-fulfilling prophecy. The mental picture alone can lower productivity and the expectations can even dictate when your energy will run out. The way to patch this leak in the tank and overcome this way of depleting yourself is to complete a reality check, like the one in the following exercise.

Exercise: Conducting Your Own Reality Check

1. Spend some time uncovering the expectations you have about your work. Contemplate and note what you think and say to yourself about what you think will happen at work.
2. Assess how accurate your expectations are. Do they really reflect reality?
3. If they do reflect reality, schedule more renewal breaks into your day.
4. If they do not reflect reality, revise your expectations about what you think and say to yourself about work. Create statements that you can say to yourself about your work that would be more accurate and renewing.

Key Point

 "When you expect a task to be stressful or tiring, you create a self-fulfilling prophecy."

It is important to remember that when depleted, you tend to see things in a more negative light and this makes it more difficult to assess your situation accurately. It is much easier to assess what is really going on when you are not exhausted. It is recommended that you take a brief renewal break before you check out your expectations. In his book, *The Performance Edge*, Robert Cooper, Ph.D. writes about research conducted by Harvard psychology professor Ellen J. Langer. Langer's findings indicate that alternating different kinds of work, shifting mental focus throughout the day and taking short breaks all help prevent fatigue and boost energy by shaking you free of mental exhaustion.

Reflection Questions

 Take two to three minutes to reflect and/or write about each of the following questions:

1. What expectations about work do I have that cause me to deplete myself unnecessarily?
2. How can I revise these expectations so that I am renewed rather than depleted?

Fuel Leak Two: Lack of Clarity and Purpose

When you are not certain about what you want or what is important in your life, you may find yourself expending lots of energy and going nowhere. On the other hand, when you know what you want and what is important to you, you are able to make choices more easily and act in ways that take you farther down the road to renewal. To patch the leak in your tank, the solution is obvious. You need to get clear about what is important to you and use this information to prioritize what you do on a daily basis.

Here is a fun story that illustrates the importance of identifying what is most important to you.

There once was a young boy who loved candy. Imagine his delight when he came upon a huge candy jar containing one hundred different kinds of candy. He eagerly reached in trying to get one of every kind of candy. As he tried to remove his hand from the jar, he realized that he was stuck. Dropping a few pieces of candy from his hand, he tried again with no luck. He made two more attempts dropping only a few pieces of candy each time. In frustration he looked down at the huge amount of goodies in his hand and realized that many of the candies he had greedily grabbed he would never eat! In that moment he understood that what he really wanted was chocolate. Armed with this realization, he dropped all the candies and started all over again. This time he picked up only one piece of each type of chocolate. He now held the ten pieces of candy that were most important to him and was able to remove his hand easily from the jar.

Reflection Questions

Take two to three minutes to reflect and/or write about each of the following questions:

1. Do I focus on the chocolates in my "candy jar at work" (what is important to me) or do I spend more time trying to get all the goodies?
2. What are the "chocolates" or most important things for me to focus on at work?
3. What can I do to ensure that I stay focused on what is most important to me at work (instead of getting my hand stuck in a candy jar with a handful of candy that I do not need)?

Fuel Leak Three: Unnecessary and Depleting Activities

In addition to ignoring what is important to you, you might spend a lot of time working on activities that do not further your goals. Perhaps you take on more than is necessary because you feel compelled to respond to all of the demands made by others. Maybe you may feel obligated to respond to all of the emails and phone calls you get the moment you receive them.

Ah...but, you have another option...simply say "no." The most obvious way to stem the fuel leak in many situations is to learn to say "no." Learn to set some boundaries on what you are willing to do and when you can do it. For some reason, many people in our culture find it difficult to say "no." Some people believe they must be accessible and responsive all the time. But if you prioritize and create some boundaries, you can actually be more productive and responsive in the long run. When you say "no" to less important things, it gives you the opportunity to say "yes" to other more important things.

Inspirational Quote

"It is easy to say no when there is a deeper yes burning inside."
ANONYMOUS

There are many ways to say no. Here are a few of them:
- The "Outright No, Never No"—"I cannot/will not do what you are asking at all."
- The "Not Now No" or the "Postponed Yes"—"I cannot help you right now. Can I get back to you later (in a few minutes, hours or days)?"
- The "Supportive No"—"I cannot do what you are asking me to do. Can I help you find someone who can?"
- The "Creative Solution No"—"I cannot do what you are asking. Can we find another way of resolving the situation?"

In her book *Time Management for Unmanageable People*, Ann McGee-Cooper, Ed.D., suggests rehearsing how you will say no. McGee-Cooper recommends delivering your no "graciously, thoughtfully, and firmly." Even with rehearsal, saying "no" is not always easy, especially for women. Suzanne was reminded of this through a memento she found in her mother, Alice's things. Alice, some one who was always available to help everyone, left behind a note from a class she had taken years ago. The note contained the phrase "A Type B Woman is one who is everything to everybody" and listed three solutions to the Type B Woman's dilemma: "learn to say no," "negotiate," and "say, I can't do that, I need help." What a great reminder Alice left for her two daughters that it is okay to say no!

Inspirational Quote

"The purpose of learning to say no is to give yourself control over your own time."

ANN McGEE-COOPER, ED.D.,
TIME MANAGEMENT FOR UNMANAGEABLE PEOPLE

Reflection Questions

Take two to three minutes to reflect and/or write about each of the following questions:
1. To what do I have a difficult time saying "no?"
2. What gets in my way of saying "no?"
3. How can I say "no" more often at work?
4. What can I say "no" to at work?

Fuel Leak Four: Negative Thinking

Finally, your energy can be depleted if you get caught up in narrow, "no way out," or hopeless thinking. What you focus on influences your behavior. You probably have had a moment in your life of *stinkin' thinkin'* that influenced how you responded to a situation and subsequently drained your energy. Constantly thinking "I'm late, I'm late, for a most important date," becomes how you behave in the world. This increases your stress level. If you have ever been late for a meeting because you were stuck in traffic and spent time worrying about getting there on time, then you know how this way of thinking can make you tense. However, if you relax and realize that the time at which you arrive is out of your control, then you will feel much better when you do finally arrive. The situation is the same regardless of how you respond. The only thing that is different is what you think about the event and how you respond.

Reflection Questions

Take two to three minutes to reflect and/or write about each of the following questions:
1. Do I have any examples of *stinkin' thinkin'* that I frequently repeat to myself at work? If so, what are they?
2. What positive thoughts or words could I use to replace the negative thoughts or words?

Bypassing Your Own Roadblocks to Renewal

Sometimes you can set up your own roadblocks on the Road to Renewal. You sabotage or hinder your own renewal. Although your obstacles may seem familiar, they can make your trip hazardous. Here is a list of the most common and dangerous self-imposed obstacles:

Roadblock One: You think you do not have enough time to renew yourself.

Roadblock Two: You think you need to take care of others first.

Roadblock Three: You allow others' perceptions to drive you.

Roadblock Four: You hold certain beliefs that are not in keeping with renewal.

Roadblock Five: You do not want to change your behavior or daily patterns.

Reflection Questions

Take two to three minutes to reflect and/or write about each of the following questions:
1. What roadblocks do I create when it comes to renewal at work?
2. Which of my roadblocks can I remove from the Road to Renewal?

Roadblock One: Thinking There is Not Enough Time

"Eliminating unproductive or depleting activities from the workday will free up time to renew yourself — even if for a brief time during your workday."

Perhaps you do not take time to renew yourself because you **think** there is not enough time to get every thing done and still fit renewal activities into the day. You may think that if you take time to renew yourself everything will not get done. Take heart! You can remove this roadblock! Begin by examining whether there are unproductive tasks and actions you are doing that can be eliminated from your daily activities. Ask yourself if you are spending time worrying about meeting deadlines instead of putting energy into the task at hand. Determine whether you fritter or give away time to unproductive or nonessential, depleting activities. Make certain that you are prioritizing your activities and focusing on the most important ones. Eliminating unproductive or depleting activities from the workday will free up time to renew yourself—even if for a brief time during your workday. Remember, also, that when you are stressed, pausing to renew yourself enables you to be more productive and to use your time better.

Reflection Questions

Take two to three minutes to reflect and/or write about each of the following questions:

1. What unproductive tasks and actions can I eliminate from my daily activities?
2. How do I fritter or give away my time to unproductive or nonessential depleting activities?
3. How can I better prioritize my activities so that I can get more done and make time for renewal?
4. How can I better manage my daily schedule so I can incorporate renewal activities into it?

Roadblock Two: Taking Care of Others First

Maybe you do not renew yourself because you think you need to take care of others first. You may make time for everyone else in your life and everything else on your list but yourself. Sometimes this is because you have been conditioned to think of others first with little regard for yourself. As a result you do not pay attention to your own needs. This phenomenon is especially true for women.

In general, American culture encourages people to work, work, work, and feel guilty if they schedule renewal time or activities into their day. You might think that if you take time for yourself you are being selfish. You may think that you do not deserve renewal time. You may feel that you have to prove your worthiness by being available to others or by working all the time.

One way to remove this obstacle is to realize that to be truly available to others and be productive, you need to care for yourself first. You serve as a role model for others when you take the time to replenish yourself. You set the example that it is all right to renew oneself.

Most major religions or faith traditions encourage service to others, as well as personal contemplation. At the heart of these teachings, however, is balance. You focus on the "inward journey" in order to have the necessary energy to sustain yourself for the "outward journey." Taking time for yourself replenishes you for your work in the world.

Reflection Questions

Take two to three minutes to reflect and/or write about each of the following questions:

1. On a scale of 1 to 10 (1 = Never, 5 = Sometimes, and 10 = Always), how often do I put others' needs in front of my own at work?
2. If my score is 5 or above, in what instances do I put others' needs in front of my own and for what reasons?
3. What specific actions could I take to balance my needs at work with the needs of others?

Roadblock Three: Allowing Others' Perceptions to Influence You

In addition to your own perceptions, you may also allow the perceptions of others to drive what you do. This is not uncommon in a society driven by what those around us think. Some people buy houses, cars, and clothes, and choose partners, careers, and friends, all based on making an impression on others. This attitude is pervasive in a workplace where individuals overextend themselves so the individual in the next office does not think they are slacking off.

Pushing yourself too hard can be depleting. You are so busy trying to please others or being perfect that you lose sight of your authentic self and what you need. Worrying about what others might think makes it difficult to enjoy the present moment and renew yourself. For instance, you might be reluctant to sit briefly with your eyes closed because of the fear that the boss will think you are not doing your work or that your office mates will think you are weird when doing yoga stretches.

The way to overcome this roadblock is to cultivate a sense of self-confidence and detachment from others' opinions about your life. When you are certain that you are doing what is best for you—that your activities benefit both your well-being and work - it is easier to make decisions based on what you choose, rather than what coworkers may think. Initially, you may find it challenging to put aside concerns about others' impressions. However, if you do something to renew yourself at work, in spite of your fear, eventually it will become more natural to be self-directed. To help you alter your decision making criteria, whenever you find yourself heeding what you think other people may be saying about your actions, pause and reflect on what you know is most beneficial for you and your work. Then act on that idea.

Roadblock Four: Holding Beliefs that are Counter Productive to Renewal

Many of the roadblocks people create for themselves have to do with the attitudes they hold about renewal and work. There are a number of assumptions in the work world that hinder you from renewing yourself (refer to the examples in the exercise that follows).

Obviously, the way to overcome this roadblock is to replace these ineffective beliefs with more productive and life enhancing beliefs. Examining your beliefs about renewal is critical to dealing with the roadblocks to renewal.

Reflection Questions

Take two to three minutes to reflect and/or write about each of the following questions:
1. What beliefs or ideas do I have that stop me from renewing myself at work?
2. What beliefs would be more supportive of my personal renewal at work?

Exercise: Clarifying Beliefs That Support Renewal

1. Take a few minutes to review the following table to identify beliefs in Column 1 that are counter-productive to renewal.
2. Reflect on the beliefs you hold that are in opposition to renewal at work. Make a note in your journal of your counter-productive thoughts, both those from the table and those that emerged during the contemplation.
3. Study Column 2 for beliefs that are in alignment with renewal that can be used instead of those listed in Column 1.
4. Examine the beliefs that you jotted down in step two. Consider how to replace those statements with ones that are supportive of renewal. Use your journal to note all of the new statements.
5. Refer to your journal whenever you discover yourself thinking a counter-productive thought. Find a statement to use instead and repeat it to yourself several times.

Column 1: Beliefs Counterproductive to Renewal	Column 2: Beliefs Supportive of Renewal
People are like machines. If they work harder and longer, they will produce more.	People are live, dynamic organisms. They need to renew their bodies, minds, emotions, spirit and energy daily. The longer they work at one time without doing this, the less productive they get. People need to take regular, periodic breaks to sustain high levels of productivity and quality work.
Faster is better. The faster people work, the more quickly the work will get done. The more quickly they get things done, the better the work will be.	Slowing down is advantageous. Some problems and decisions are best resolved using slow-paced, intuitive thinking. People make fewer mistakes this way.
Breaks take away from work. Because there is so much to do, people do not have time to take breaks and renew themselves.	Breaks are essential for work. People think better and have more energy when they take regular breaks. Taking renewal breaks actually shortens the amount of time needed to complete work.

Roadblock Five: Being unwilling to change behavior

Key Point

"Changing your life and making a commitment to renewal at work requires discipline and conscious effort."

Regular renewal requires that you take responsibility for your own well-being. This means that you must choose to change some of your behaviors or daily patterns. You may even have to let go of long-held attitudes and behaviors that impede your self renewal. The thought of changing your ways can be frightening. You might be like many others who find it is much easier to talk about renewal and changing their life than to actually do it. Look at the number of New Year's resolutions that go unfulfilled!

Changing your life and making a commitment to renewal at work requires discipline and conscious effort. To gain strength for the journey, select a renewal partner with whom you can share your renewal goals and plans. You can choose to be accountable to each other for your goals. Develop one or two very specific renewal goals or activities that you would like to incorporate into your work life. Share them with your renewal partner and act on them together. Once you have been successful at integrating them at work you can add one or two new activities.

Reflection Questions

Take two to three minutes to reflect and/or write about each of the following questions:

1. How can I take more responsibility for my own well-being at work?
2. What behaviors and patterns that hinder my renewal do I need to change?
3. What will help me remain committed to taking action and renewing myself?
4. Who might be an appropriate "renewal partner?" When will I contact him/her?

7

MAKING A COMMITMENT TO RUNNING ON PLENTY AT WORK

"...If we want to change our life toward balance, we must be very clear in our desire to change and very committed to our desire to follow through with it."

JOAN KOFODIMOS, *BALANCING ACT*

Making a Case for Renewal

You have made good progress on understanding what is required to travel on the Road to Renewal. You have looked at what renewal is, how to incorporate in into your day, and what gets in the way of your renewal at work. Now comes the most important leg of the journey—making a commitment to running on plenty at work. Near the end of a long road trip, you may find yourself asking questions like "Why did I take this trip in the first place?" or "Is this trip worth it?" You might be asking yourself similar kinds of questions about renewal at work right now, like "Is it worth all the effort?"

Hopefully, we have convinced you in Part One of this book to make a commitment to running on plenty at work. Doing so benefits both you and your work. Here is a summary of the reasons why you want to do this:

Reason One: Practicing renewal at work allows you to be productive and effective.

Research shows if you work too long at mental tasks, the time you need to solve problems increases five fold. If you do not take a planned pause, the brain unplugs. Renewing yourself by taking planned breaks enhances your accuracy, efficiency, and performance!

Reason Two: Taking time for renewal may directly impact your: 1) outlook toward your work, 2) creativity, and 3) decision-making ability.

Studies support the link between job satisfaction and self renewal. You are less likely to experience burnout at work if you regularly renew yourself. You will be more positive towards your work, more creative, more likely to make decisions, and more energetic.

Practicing renewal at work is a safeguard against chronic fatigue, low energy, irritability, and a negative attitude towards yourself and your job. All of these have a direct impact on the quantity and quality of your work. Renewing yourself on a regular basis throughout the day prevents burnout and contributes to the rekindling of your enthusiasm at work.

Reason Three: Renewing yourself at work can contribute to healthier personal and social relationships, protect against illness, and promote longevity.

Renewing yourself at work, will positively impact your personal life as well your professional life. When you go home at the end of the workday energetic and calm, you are in a better position to lead a balanced life. You will have energy for your family, your spiritual life, and your hobbies. Mary Oliver's poem *The Journey,* contains the powerful line "to save the only life you can." Making a commitment to renewal at work is taking action "to save the only life you can save"...your own. When you practice renewal you are in a sense "saving" yourself by being a good steward of your resources.

Key Point

"When you go home at the end of the workday energetic and calm, you are in a better position to lead a balanced life."

Reflecting on Your Need for Renewal

You now know why making a commitment to renewal is important. You might find the following reflection questions helpful when thinking about moving forward.

Reflection Questions

Take two to three minutes to reflect and/or write about each of the following questions:

1. In what specific ways am I already renewing myself at work?
2. Which activities that I am already doing would I like to do more regularly?
3. Which aspects of my being (body, mind, emotions, spirit) would I like to renew more frequently?
4. What **new activities** can I do to help me renew these aspects of myself?
5. How can I better integrate or schedule renewal activities into my workday?
6. What times of the day are easiest for me to engage in renewal activities?
7. When are the times when I most need renewal during the day?
8. How can I remind myself to "check-in" during the day to see if I need to take a renewal break?
9. How can I get support for renewing myself on a regular basis? Who can I turn to for support?
10. What are the best ways for me to overcome the roadblocks to renewal in my life?
11. To what am I willing to commit on a regular basis to renew myself and ensure that I run on plenty instead of empty?

Making a Positive Change in Your Life

Sometimes the idea of making a change in your life can be overwhelming, let alone actually making it happen. Change experts recommend approaching change one step at a time. Choose one simple goal or behavioral change and then work on that one item until it becomes a part of your life. Research shows that if you practice a new behavior every day for 28 days, you are more likely to master it.

Begin your commitment to staying on the Road to Renewal right now by taking a moment to choose one renewal activity you would like to incorporate into your daily schedule.

Exercise: Making a Personal Commitment to Running on Plenty

1. If you have spent time thinking about your responses to the reflection questions in the book, then you are ready to run on plenty at work. If you have not done this, take some time to answer the reflection questions on the previous page.

2. Next, take a few minutes to review your answers. As you read over your responses, pay attention to which activities you are most attracted. Then choose one activity to which you are willing to commit for the next 28 days.

3. Once you have selected the activity, spend some time thinking about exactly how you are going to practice it for the next 28 days. Write down what you are going to do and where and when you are going to do it.

4. Post your commitment someplace where you can refer to it often during the month.

5. Choose someone with whom you can talk on a daily or weekly basis to share your progress. Many people find it helpful to share their plan with a friend, family member, or co-worker, who can be their "renewal partner" and support them in their commitment.

Staying on the Road to Renewal

Key Point

"Sustained renewal takes continual effort, ongoing awareness and commitment, and often requires learning new behaviors."

Once you have begun to develop a regular renewal practice at work, you are off to a good start. Here are some helpful guidelines for staying on the Road to Renewal:

1. **Pay attention to the signals along the way.**
   Your body, mind, emotions, and spirit are giving you signals about your energy level and your needs throughout the day. Respond to these signals by engaging in a renewal activity. Observation and personal awareness are major keys to self renewal.

2. **Engage in a range of renewal activities at work over time.**
   Choose activities that nurture all four parts of your being (body, mind, emotions, and spirit). Pay special attention to those areas you typically neglect. And remember, the busier you are, the more you need to replenish yourself!

3. **Incorporate both reactive and proactive renewal into your workday.**
   Be responsive to your needs for refreshment. Be regular in refueling whether you are on running on empty or not. Renewal requires practice and foresight!

4. **Research different ways to renew yourself at work.**
   Check the list of resources at the end of this book for other ideas. Visit our web site at www.renewalatwork.com. Email us about what is working for you!

5. **Take time to renew yourself outside of work.**
   Think about your renewal at home. Go on occasional personal renewal retreats. You will feel more renewed. Your capacity to renew yourself in the midst of all the activity at work will be strengthened. The more you renew yourself the better you get at it.

6. Elicit support from others.

Get support from others at work and home for engaging in renewal. Find ways to support each other. If you find walking replenishes you, invite a colleague to discuss business while you take a walk. Consider hiring a coach who can help you set and meet renewal goals. We have found in our work with coaching clients that examining how to enhance their renewal at work positively impacts them both professionally and personally.

7. Experiment with renewing yourself and discover which methods work best for you.

Periodically try different renewal activities. One way to do this is to turn to Part Two of this book. There are monthly themes and weekly renewal tips related to the seasons. Each week contains at least three different activities that you can try.

Sustained renewal takes continual effort, ongoing awareness and commitment, and often requires learning new behaviors. All your hard work will pay off with a life that is happier, healthier, and more productive. We wish you all the best in your efforts to keep running on plenty at work. May your travels on the Road to Renewal be fulfilling!

"Our destiny is to journey on the river of change, and this calls for a capacity to adventure well—at all times, in all seasons. Self-renewing adults are trained for the journey they are on. Adventure is what they seek and want... We can prepare to live fully in the world that we have—no matter what. We can learn to sustain passion, joy, and purpose throughout our years."

FREDERIC M. HUDSON, PH.D.
MASTERING THE ART OF SELF RENEWAL

P
a
r
t

T
w
o

TRAVELING
THROUGH
THE
SEASONS
OF
RENEWAL

INTRODUCTION TO PART TWO

In reading Part One, you set out on the Road to Renewal and acquired an understanding of what renewal is and how to begin to integrate it into your work life. And if you completed all the exercises in the first half of the book, you are well on your way to running on plenty at work! Part Two provides more fuel and directions for traveling farther down the road, through the seasons of renewal. Specifically, you will find:

- Twelve chapters, one for each month of the year
- Twelve renewal themes, each one associated with the season and month in which it appears
- Four weekly areas of focus in each month that are related to that month's theme
- Specific tips, exercises, and fables to enhance your ability to understand and travel the Road to Renewal

Identifying Your Trip Options

As was mentioned at the beginning of Part One, there are a number of ways to travel the Road to Renewal. Here are a few of the trip possibilities for Part Two. You can:

- Read all of Part Two at one time and then choose the tips that speak to you the most to practice at work. If you read the whole section at once, you may find that some of the tips in one month seem similar to tips in another month. While the themes are different in each month, a few of them are related to and reinforce each other. Also, certain tips and ideas are repeated in a different context to help you strengthen your ability to renew yourself in that area.

- Read a chapter a month and experiment with the tips in that chapter. Although Part Two begins with a chapter representing January, you do not have to wait until January to start renewing yourself! The monthly themes are independent of each other so you can start with the month in which you pick up the book.
- Try all of the tips listed under each of the four weeks in a month, or select the tips to which you are most drawn. To expand your capacity for renewal, experiment with a few tips that feel less comfortable to you. It is good to work with a particular theme for four weeks. Remember, research shows that if you practice something new for 28 days, you are more likely to master it.
- Choose a monthly theme that captures your interest and work with the tips in that chapter.
- Renew a specific aspect of your being—body, mind, emotions, or spirit—by using the Quick Reference Guides located in the back of the book.

Whatever option you select, use a journal for noting your answers to the various exercises and questions in this part of the book. Again, you have several options with the exercises and reflection questions. You can practice the exercises as you read them or save them for a later time. You can choose to answer all of the reflection questions at once, answer them over a period of time, or respond only to those that resonate with you.

The sooner you begin to travel through the seasons of renewal, the more likely you will be running on plenty all year long! So, select your route and begin the second part of your journey!

8

JANUARY

TRANSFORM YOUR RELATIONSHIP WITH TIME AT WORK

> *"Clock time is a part of us—and it is something to be valued, something to be used. But we must learn to keep a different kind of time as well, if we are to savor life most fully."*
>
> STEPHEN RECHTSCHAFFEN, M.D., *TIME SHIFTING*

Introduction

The first month of the year is a great occasion to appreciate the wonderful gift of time. As another year begins you have an opportunity to ponder the question of how you "used" your time the previous year and how to make the best use of your days during the coming year. It is a great time to pause and consider your goals and make resolutions that enable you to live in a renewing way during the New Year.

You are probably familiar with the old adages "time marches on" and "time waits for no one." It seems that for ages people have experienced a love-hate relationship with time. When it comes to renewal, be sure of this—your relationship to time is directly related to your approach to personal renewal. When altering your relationship with time, you automatically enhance your ability to run on plenty. Instead of working to the tune of "Beat the Clock," you can sing that old favorite by the Rolling Stones "Time is on my Side."

You know that time and how you use it is important both at work and at home. Many people, however, think of time as a limited resource (which it is) that needs to be controlled (which it cannot be). They see it as something to be spent and something of which they never have enough. In order to get everything done, they try to speed up time, save it, and do more with less of it. Essentially, they treat time as if it were simply and solely a concrete, linear, quantitative, and finite commodity.

This approach to time is deeply rooted in our western society. In fact, so much so, that many individuals are unaware of the impact this way of living has on their lives. Arlie Hochschilds in *The Time Bind* suggests that the patterns of people's workdays—with deadlines and schedules and interruptions—shape their lives and relationships with others more than they know. You may be one of many American workers who live by the clock, day planner book, or electronic planner. If this is so, you are living by "Chronos" time, a word developed by the Greeks to describe clock time. Although this modern approach to time enables you to be busy and productive, it also drains you and adds a great deal of stress to life.

Inspirational Quote

"You have a choice about how you live your life, about how you spend your time. You can either continue with the way things are and hope it gets better, or you can do something about it."
CHERYL RICHARDSON, *TAKE TIME FOR YOUR LIFE*

You do not have to live with this limited and stress-producing view of time at work (or at home for that matter). You can choose to spend time in a way that is nourishing. A more rejuvenating approach is that of "Kairos" time. Kairos, a second word created by the Greeks, points to unique moments in time where meaningful activity occurs. The Judeo-Christian faith traditions often refer to Kairos time as "God's time." which suggests that this type of time is sacred. In Kairos time, there is space for being, rather than just doing, and for paying attention to your purpose at work. This spacious kind of time is rhythmic, cyclical, and qualitative in nature and full of significance. Dorothy C. Bass writes about this sense of time in *Receiving the Day*. She says "time resonates with meaning...As we seek to live well within it, we are caught again and again in issues that are profoundly spiritual." Time when seen from a qualitative and spiritual point of view—instead of being a limited resource—is ultimately a gift full of rich possibilities.

If you choose to adopt a more spiritual view and step into the gift of the present moment, you will be able to expand your sense of time into an experience of "timelessness" and ease. Although you may spend most days entrenched in linear Chronos or "clock-time," you **can** transform your relationship with time at work. And when you do, relationships are more rewarding, time spent alone is more peaceful, and work is more renewing and productive.

Reflection Questions

Take two to three minutes to reflect and/or write about each of the following questions:

1. What do I believe about time?
2. What is my current relationship with time and how do I feel about it?
3. What effect does my relationship with time have on my mind, body, emotions, and spirit?
4. How can I change my relationship with time so that I work in a more renewing way?

Week One: Decide What is Really Important in Your Life

It is easy to let time "slip away." Before you know it, what is really important has fallen off the radar screen. A great first step in getting your arms around this "time thing" is to reflect on what is really important to you. Here are some ways to get started.

Take inventory of exactly how you invest your time

Evaluate what you actually do each day. What you do points to what you value enough to invest your time. Once your present time allocations are identified, think about whether or not these issues are where you really want to focus your attention and energy. If not, make adjustments. Also make changes that will help you live in a balanced way. The following exercise will help you assess your time utilization.

Key Point

"Time, when seen from a spiritual point of view, is ultimately a gift full of rich possibilities."

Exercise: Evaluating How I Invest My Time at Work and Home

1. Evaluate how you invest your time in a given week. You can create a table in your journal, like the one that follows, to jot down your thoughts.
2. Make a guess about how much time you spend each week in each category of your life and write them down in the second column of the table in your journal.
3. Review your time estimates and reflect on what the information is saying about what the present priorities are, and how much balance you have, in your life. Remember you tend to devote time to what is important to you.
4. Given what you see, are there any adjustments to make in how to invest your time? Make note of any adjustments in the third column of the table in your journal. Also record what you will do to make the desired adjustments real.
5. Then act on your new ideas!

Example of An Inventory for Evaluating How I Invest my Time		
Area	Estimated Hours Spent/Week	Adjustments to Time Spent
Work matters		
Commuting/Work Related Travel		
Work Related Tasks (other than email and returning phone calls, meetings)		
Emails and Returning Calls		
Meetings		
Interacting with Others (one on one)		
Professional Development		
Breaks		
Personal Matters		
Personal maintenance like eating, dressing		
Physical Exercise		
Family		
Home/Life Maintenance		
Social Life/Friendships		
Spiritual Life		
Creative Activities		
Free/Personal Time		
Sleep		
Self Improvement		

Clarify your priorities

Assess what is most important at this point in your life and on what you choose to concentrate during the coming year. This kind of assessment requires self-inquiry. Set aside an afternoon or morning to reflect on what is most important to you right now in your personal life outside work and also at work. After deciding what your top priorities are for this year, determine how much time you want to devote to them.

Every January each of us, Krista and Suzanne, sets aside a day to think and write about our personal and professional priorities for the year. Once we are clear on our individual goals, we meet to share and discuss them with each other. Then we create our business goals for the year with our personal preferences in mind. This process allows us to make both individual and professional plans in alignment with what is most important to each of us. It enables us to support each other in staying true to our stated priorities throughout the year.

Example of a Table for Noting My Top Priorities in Life		
Top Five Life Priorities	Actual Amount of Time Invested/Week	Desired Amount of Time Invested/Week

Example of a Table for Noting My Top Priorities at Work		
Top Five Work Priorities	Actual Amount of Time Invested/Week	Desired Amount of Time Invested/Week

Exercise: Devoting Time to My Top Priorities

1. Think about what you choose to give time and energy to this year. Get philosophical. Consider what your priorities would be if this year were all you had left to live!

2. Then, if you are a linear thinker create a table like the ones on the previous page to list the top five priorities in both your personal and work life. If you are a visual thinker, use colored markers on a blank sheet of paper to capture your ideas.

3. Now, go back to your lists or drawings and think about how much time you invest in each of the ten items each week. Write down your best guess of actual time spent beside each of your priorities.

4. Next, reflect on the amount of time currently given to your top priorities. Are you investing enough time on each priority? Do you provide the top priorities the time and attention they deserve? How much time and attention would you ideally like to devote to each top priority? Write down the desired amount in the third column of both tables in your journal or create a new drawing of how you would like to devote your time.

5. Then think about what adjustments you need to make to align your daily activities with your desired time allocations. For instance, if family is your number one priority in life and you are spending 90 percent of your time working, you know an opportunity for an adjustment awaits you! What do you need to stop doing in order to align your time investment with your top priorities? What do you need to start doing? And what do you need to continue doing? Be realistic about the adjustments you make. New habits need time to take hold. The more realistic you are about your revisions the more likely you are to be successful with the desired changes.

Nancy, the only obstetrician gynecologist in her small town in the northwest, reports that after she found herself knee deep in the middle of a serious bout with burnout she examined her priorities. She knew that she could not be good to her patients if she was not good to herself. So she made her own health and well-being a priority by scheduling time each day for exercise and meditation and going on retreat four times a year.

Key Point

"Devote your time to your top priorities."

Use your priorities to make decisions about how you invest your time
Post your priorities in a place where you can see them. Refer to them when making decisions about how to dedicate your time at work and at home. For instance, before agreeing to serve on a professional association committee related to your work, think about that activity in light of your priorities and where your current attention is focused. Is this pursuit in alignment with your current priorities? Will this opportunity further what you most value? If you agree to serve on the committee, will you have to decrease time devoted to other priorities to create space for this new activity? Once you have answered these questions and are certain that adding the new endeavor is in keeping with your priorities, your homework is done and you can feel comfortable about the decision.

Inspirational Quote

"Experience takes place in time, so time is the ultimate scarce resource we have. Over the years, the content of experience will determine the quality of life. Therefore one of the most essential decisions any of us can make is about how one's time is allocated or invested."
MIHALY CSIKSZENTIMIHALYI, *FINDING FLOW*

Week Two: Realize the Preciousness of Time

Willie Jolley, author of *It Only Takes a Minute to Change Your Life*, shares with his audiences the following words often attributed to Benjamin Mays, Ph.D.:

I have only just a minute, only 60 seconds in it.
Forced upon me, cannot refuse it. Did not seek it, did not choose it.
But it is up to me to use it.
I must suffer if I lose it, give account if I abuse it.
Just a tiny little minute, but an eternity in it.
So ladies and gentlemen, use your minutes wisely.

This poem is a prompt to remember the importance of enjoying and using time wisely. It is possible to interpret this verse as a directive to actively use all of your time. However, from the perspective of running on plenty, it means making the most of your valuable time here on Earth and taking time to "smell the roses." When you recognize that life is precious and that the amount of time you have is unknown and limited, you can choose to devote part of the day to experiencing the gift you have been given. Here are some ways to recognize the preciousness of the gift of time this week.

Inspirational Quote

"To wish for time is to wish for life, for the opportunity to live with fullness and vitality. Therefore, time calls for artful attention on our part."
THOMAS MOORE, QUOTED IN *TIME SHIFTING*

Plan your day with the preciousness of time in mind

Begin the workday by thinking about the preciousness of the time before you and how to appreciate this gift by living fully. Ask yourself questions like, "Given my priorities, what would best enable me to live this day well and make full use of the time in it? What would be the best investment of my time? How can I fully experience the gift of time today?" Once you have an idea of what activities would be most beneficial, incorporate them into your schedule.

Appreciate the gifts you receive from time

Create an occasion during which you appreciate the gifts that time allows you to enjoy. Since time is life, when you recognize all of the many wonderful opportunities that life affords you, you are automatically acknowledging the preciousness of time. One way to appreciate your time is to pause during or at the end of the day before going home to reflect on the non-material gifts you received. Or stop during the day to experience the gift of a particular moment while it is happening. Whenever we, Suzanne and Krista, have a day-long meeting, we pause for lunch. Before eating we share a moment of silence and then say what we are grateful for that day. It renews us and reminds us of all the opportunities we have in life.

During a tough work week when it is difficult to see the gifts in your workplace, make it a point to go outside during a sunset to just focus on the beauty of that instant and the gift of being able to enjoy it. It can also be helpful to think about and list what you are able to do with your valuable life. To jump-start your thinking, here is an example of Suzanne's list:

What Time Allows Me To Do

Give and receive love	Connect with my family
Be married to a loving partner	Do work I love
Laugh	Build a business
Speak and write	Extend the gift of hospitality
Make new friends and keep the old	Sing
Worship God	Pray
Make people laugh	Make a living and make a life
Journal	Read
Have a great business partner	Belong to a professional
Walk, swim, travel	society
Visit museums	Eat at quaint inns
Live by my values	Interact with great clients
	Serve others

Find ways to remind yourself of how precious time is

It is easy to get caught up in daily activities and tasks and to forget about how short life can sometimes be. It is human nature to be complacent and think you have all the time in the world. Do not wait for a personal tragedy or world crises to occur to remind you. Look for prompts that you can place in your workspace and gaze at everyday. For instance, pin up a poem or listen to a song about time, bring a memento to work of something you love to do when the gift of time is at your disposal, or put a reminder on a screen saver. You might even set aside time to contemplate how temporary life really is. Some faith traditions advocate thinking about death as a way of remembering to live each day fully.

Krista has the following saying, taken from a talk given by her spiritual teacher, Gurumayi Chidvilasananda, after September 11, 2001, posted in her office that reminds her that human life is precious.

"Thank you for expanding your understanding and realizing that you are responsible for spreading the importance of human life by giving love and respect.... Look into the eyes of your brothers and sisters and give and receive love. Continually access your own deeper power, so that you can literally send your blessings to everyone everywhere who needs to experience them."

Key Point

"Life is precious. Live it well."

Take a vacation ASAP

Plan your next vacation today and then take it! Many people put off taking a vacation and one day realize that they have not had a holiday in years. You probably know someone who boasts about not taking vacations or has saved up all their vacation time for "down the road." Since time is precious and you never know how much time is left, enjoy time with your loved ones now. Do something you love to do each year. Taking time off work will renew you and possibly even extend your life. Health experts say that people can decrease their risk of a heart attack by one third if they take one week of vacation a year. This is particularly true if the vacation is work-free.

If you are used to being available 24 hours a day, seven days a week, you may find it challenging to take a work-free vacation. Gil Gordon, author of *Turn It Off*, describes how difficult it was for him the first time he went on vacation to not check his messages every day. Instead of relaxing, he worried about missing "the crucial call." However, after a few trips, he became accustomed to it and realized that business and life would go on if he were not always available. The key for taking a work-free vacation is to make arrangements prior to going away with customers, coworkers, and others who expect to hear from you. If they know ahead of time that you will not be available and who they can contact instead, they and your business will be fine. You will come back feeling refreshed with more clarity and energy to tackle the work on your desk. Give yourself the gift of time off work!

Week Three: Step into the Present Moment

The pace of life is so fast today that many people do not experience their life as it is happening. Stop to think about it—how much of your day is spent worrying about what to do next or thinking about what happened earlier? Instead of paying attention to what is occurring in the present moment, most people focus their attention either in the past or the future. And yet, it is in the present moment that life is truly lived and time takes on a different quality.

By concentrating in the present, you begin to experience the freedom and serenity of the moment, which is ultimately renewing. As Peter Russell, author of *Waking Up in Time*, says, "a mind in the present is free to experience what is." You may have felt this freedom for yourself at some point in life—a moment where you were fully absorbed in what you were doing, or when you stepped outside of time. Maybe you felt a heightened sense of awareness and a connection with your self and the world. In that moment, there were no concerns nor stress, just a sense of ease and vitality. Mihaly Csikszentmihalyi, Ph.D., the author of *Finding Flow*, calls this the *flow state*. In the *flow state*, you are so present to what is occurring in the moment that you are unaware of the passing of time and action is effortless. You automatically know what to do and how to adjust to changes as they occur. There is a short story called "Going with the Flow" that beautifully illustrates the experience of giving yourself to the present moment.

There once was an old man who accidentally fell into the river rapids leading to a high and dangerous waterfall. Onlookers feared for his life. Miraculously, he came out alive and unharmed downstream at the bottom of the falls. People asked him how he managed to survive. "I accommodated myself to the water, not the water to me. Without thinking, I allowed myself to be shaped by it. Plunging into the swirl, I came out with the swirl. This is how I survived."

Here are some ways to bring the gift of that experience—the gift of the present moment—fully and more often into your daily life.

Take time each day to pay attention to yourself in the present moment

Pause for a few minutes and focus on what you are experiencing at that time. Jon Kabat-Zinn, Ph.D., in *Wherever You Go There You Are* suggests "stopping, sitting down, and becoming aware of your breathing once in a while throughout the day." You can pause for five minutes, or even a few seconds. Let yourself fully accept whatever you are experiencing in the present moment. Pay attention to how your body feels, what you are thinking, how you are feeling, and the state of your spirit. Do not try to change anything at all. Simply breathe and let whatever is occurring in your body, mind, emotions, and spirit be as it is. Stay in the moment and just observe yourself. Make a habit of paying attention to all four aspects of your being.

Focus fully on the task before you

Bring all of your attention to what you are doing in the present moment. Often when you are working you create stress by thinking about how much work there is to do, when you have to have it finished, and/or the results you need to create. Instead of using energy to do the work at hand, you spend time focused on the future that is out of your control. You will be pleasantly surprised at how effective it is to give all of your attention to what you are doing and to doing it well. You will get more done and feel less stressed in the process. As Dorothy Bass in *Receiving the Day* says, "freedom from bondage to the past and from fear for the future releases energies for bold and creative living."

Krista experienced the benefits of focusing on the task at hand when she was completing her doctoral dissertation. The thought of writing such a large document that was to be critiqued by six professors at times made the task daunting for her. Whenever she focused on the upcoming doctoral defense, she would begin to worry about whether her research paper was good enough and her writing became more of a struggle. She discovered that the only way to deal with her anxiety and keep working was to suspend any thoughts about the future and give all her attention to the material she was working on at the time. She learned that the more she did this, the easier and better the writing became and her anxiety dissipated.

Inspirational Quote

 "It is the full involvement of flow that makes for excellence in life...Only after the task is completed do we have the leisure to look back on what has happened, and then we are flooded with gratitude for the excellence of that experience."

MIHALY CSIKSZENTMIHALYI, PH.D., *FINDING FLOW*

 Concentrate on your current emotions in difficult situations Become aware of what you are feeling whenever you have a strong reaction to a situation. Instead of ignoring your emotions and allowing them to direct your behavior, take a moment to observe what you are feeling. Recognize that you are probably feeling intensely because the event has triggered an unconscious memory of a past experience that was upsetting. Allow yourself to experience the energy of the emotion as it is in that moment. Let yourself tolerate not acting on any impulses to do something in response to your feelings. If you can stay still and observe your emotions, instead of identifying with and acting on them, then the energy your emotions carry will dissipate and you will no longer be identified with the past in that instant.

Inspirational Quote

 "Intense presence is needed when certain situations trigger a reaction with a strong emotional charge... Once you can feel what it means to be present, it becomes easier to simply choose to step out of the time dimension whenever time is not needed for practical purposes and move more deeply into the Now."

ECKHART TOLLE, *PRACTICING THE POWER OF NOW*

Experience the present through your senses

Step into the present moment by using the physical senses to bring your awareness into the here and now. Take a few minutes to look around and pay attention to what you see. Become aware of the light, colors, textures, and objects in the room. Listen to the sounds in the world around you. Hear all of the various and different kinds of noises of which you are typically unaware. Sniff the air and smell the odors floating there. Feel the clothes draped on your body and your chest moving as the air flows in and out of your lungs. Once you have experienced each of the senses, expand your awareness and step more deeply into the present moment. Become conscious of the silent space around and within you. See if you can experience the silent presence of the objects around you or the silence in between the sounds. Feel the energy subtly vibrating in the cells of your body. When you feel complete in the experience, pay attention to how alive you feel.

Inspirational Quote

"If all the blood surging through your body were suddenly to sing...if all the oxygen in your cells were to play music...if your bones were to paint pictures and your organs were to dance, what would this moment be?"
MAGGIE BEDROSIAN, *LIFE IS MORE THAN YOUR TO-DO LIST*

Week Four: Live Each Day Fully

When you contemplate the passing of time and realize that time on this Earth is limited, you become motivated to live life fully and invest your time in meaningful activities. You become inspired to "live the breadth as well as the depth of your life," as author Diane Ackerman writes. Awareness of the preciousness of life typically becomes heightened after a crisis and your motivation increases to take full advantage of your time. This is what happened to Sharon, a Public Relations consultant, after September 11, 2001.

On that day, Sharon was putting on a press conference on Capitol Hill when news came of the World Trade Center and Pentagon incidents and a possible plane headed towards the Capitol. In the chaos that ensued as the building she was in was evacuated, she had a moment where she clearly saw how beautiful life is and felt very grateful to be alive. Since that day, Sharon says that the ordinary concerns that used to occupy her day, such as focusing on money and looking for recognition from others, have become less important. She is no longer willing to put off things until later. Instead, she gives herself to what is happening now and is only interested in doing meaningful work that matters to her. She pays more attention to people around her than she used to and looks for ways to help them. She spends more time with her family and ends every conversation with "I love you."

This week, use the following tips to assist you in living each day as completely as possible, as Sharon is inspired to do.

Say what is in your heart on and off the job

Take time each day to let people in your life know just how important they are to you. This sage advice applies to those with whom you work and live. Somehow American workers have come to believe that they should "park" who they are at the door when they go to work. This month you can counteract that behavioral norm by recognizing someone important in your worklife. Ask yourself questions like, "if today was the last day I was to see my favorite coworker, what would I say to that coworker?" Then say it to them! Choose another colleague the next day to whom to express your affection.

Inspirational Quote

"Without dreams, without risks, only a trivial semblance of living can be achieved."

MIHALY CSIKSZENTMIHALYI, PH.D., *FINDING FLOW*

Follow your as yet unfulfilled dreams

Take some time to recall all those things you have dreamed of doing, learning, contributing, or experiencing at work and in your personal life and have not yet done. Choose one and do it today. One of the best ways to be serious about living life fully is to get focused on what still could be and then use your time to work on those actions. When you make an intention to follow your dreams and put your energy behind them, the dreams will come true. And chances are you will lead a rich life and make a contribution to the surrounding world.

Each January Suzanne and a group of other professional women gather to create collages. Each woman's poster contains pictures and phrases that capture her personal and professional dreams for the coming year. The "Poster Girls"—as they affectionately refer to themselves—review the past year's poster and their hopes for the new year. For two years Suzanne's collage has featured our book as a dream and now that wish is a reality!

Exercise: Recollecting and Acting on My Dreams

This exercise is a right-brain activity. Even if you are a linear thinker, give it a try. If you like, after you have experimented with this more holistic method, create a list of activities you have dreamed of doing and have not yet done, along with a list of actions to realize your dreams. Note: This exercise requires a fairly large chunk of uninterrupted time. You may want to consider completing it at home.

1. Set aside some time when you will not be disturbed. Have several pieces of paper and some colored markers or pencils handy.

2. Put aside any thoughts of work or tasks that need to be done. Take a few deep breaths and allow yourself to relax.

3. When you are relaxed, begin to reminisce about all the dreams you have had over the course of your life and have not yet acted upon. Allow yourself to recall things that you have always wanted to do, learn, contribute, and experience—both at work and in your personal life.

4. As an idea comes to mind, choose a color and, anywhere on the paper, write down the activity or draw an image representing your interest. As new ideas arise, choose another color and write or draw them. You can use similar colors for activities that seem related and/or place them near each other on the paper.

5. Once you have portrayed all the dreams you can recall for now, look at what you have depicted. Are there any similarities and/or connections between the activities or images? If so, draw any relationships you see. If you do not observe any

associations, reflect on whether or not the activities fall into any categories and indicate them on the page.

6. Next, look at the page of dreams and pay attention to which activities or categories stand out the most for you right now. Identify which dreams you would most like to follow at this point in your life. **It works best to focus on one to three ideas.**

7. Take a second piece of paper and using colored pencils write down on different areas on the page each activity that you identified as a dream to follow. Place a circle around each idea.

8. Then begin to brainstorm all the steps and ways in which you can realize the dream. As you think of an idea, write it down near the activity to which it is related and draw a line connecting it and the circled activity. (Note: This is a form of *mind mapping*, a technique described by Tony Buzan in *The Mind Map Book*. You can find an example of a mind map in Chapter 10 of this book.)

9. When you can no longer think of any ideas to write down, look at your Dream Map and choose the activity and related steps that appeal to you the most.

10. Next, think about when and how you are going to put them into action! And then, do it!

Key Point

"When you make an intention to follow your dreams and put your energy behind them, the dreams will come true."

Identify a maxim for your life and live it!

Choose a saying that has a lot of meaning for you and can provide you guidance for living a full life. Find ways to remind yourself of this maxim so that you can put it into action regularly. Write it down in your date book or palm pilot, create a screen saver, and/or talk with people about your guiding principles. Suzanne's mother, Alice, had a motto that she dependably lived by throughout her life—

"Family, Friends, and Faith." The strength of her commitment became very apparent at the end of her life. As she bravely lived with cancer for three and a half years, she continued to focus on family, friends, and faith. In fact, one of her final acts was to dictate notes to send to friends and family on their birthdays in the coming year. In the weeks following Alice's death, her maxim was heard over and over again. It was clear that Alice's slogan guided how she spent her time and made life decisions. Take some time to think about a saying that has special meaning for you and can last a lifetime.

"To every thing there is a season,
And a time to every purpose under heaven."
THE WESTMINSTER STUDY EDITION HOLY BIBLE,
ECCLESIASTES 3:1, KING JAMES VERSION

9

FEBRUARY

BE LOVE'S TOUCH AT WORK

> *Be love's touch...Choose to do what you must...Let Love be your reason."*
>
> MARSHA SINETAR, *HOLY WORK*

Introduction

Since February 14th is Valentine's Day in the United States every year, the month of February is often associated with love. Seems like the perfect time to explore how you can bring more love into everyday life, even at work! Love is one of the most powerful and revitalizing forces in the world. It renews as it fills people with joy and a sense of connection and belonging. Imagine how much richer and healthier your life and work place will be if you widen the circle of those with whom you share your love. Why not make February the month to renew yourself and those around you by applying love's touch at work?

Obviously if you are going to express love at work, you have to broaden your definition of it beyond the romantic love typically connected with Valentine's Day. What description of love makes sense in the workplace? Although love is difficult to define concretely because it is limitless, it does have many visible forms of expression. You are expressing love whenever you give to others, are generous in your interactions, show care, concern, respect and kindness for others, or do something to uplift, nurture, or protect someone.

Love is something that is not typically talked about in the workplace. Many people might say, "what's love got to do with it (work)?" Yet, if you stop and think about it, you know that love is what unites people most strongly and gives real meaning to their lives. Sigmund Freud, the famous father of 20th-century psychology, claimed that love and work are the two most important aspects of life. Given their crucial role, it makes sense to bring the two together. This can easily happen since, as Kymn Harvin Rutigliano suggests in the following quote from *The New Bottom Line*, love has a natural place at work:

> *"If people truly are the heart of business (how could it be otherwise, since without people there is NO business), and love is the heart of people, then does not it stand to reason that love does have a place— a central place—in business?"*

Key Point

> *"Love has many visible forms of expression at work: generosity, care, concern, respect and kindness."*

Given that love is central to everyone, taking the time to share your love with those at work will be renewing and become a source of inspiration for others. All it takes is one simple act of genuine love for love to spread. In *Words to Love By*, Mother Teresa shares how one loving touch can multiply into many:

> *I never look at the masses as my responsibility.*
> *I look at the individual.*
> *I can only love one person at a time.*
> *I can only feed one person at a time*
> *Just one, one, one...*
> *So you begin... I begin.*
> *I picked up one person —*
> *Maybe if I did not pick up that one person,*
> *I wouldn't have picked up 42,000.*
> *The whole work is only a drop in the ocean.*
> *But if I did not put the drop in,*
> *The ocean would be one drop less.*
> *Same thing for you,*
> *Same thing in your family,*
> *Same thing in your business.*
> *Wherever you go*
> *Just begin... one, one, one.*

Begin as Mother Teresa did and take one small step each day towards being love's touch this month. The tips that follow offer some suggested ways to express love at work.

Reflection Questions

Take two to three minutes to reflect and/or write about each of the following questions:
1. In what ways do I experience love at work and how does it effect customers, coworkers, and me?
2. In what ways do I already share and/or express love at work?
3. How can I express love more often at work?
4. What stops me from expressing love at work?
5. What do I love about my work?

Week One: Find Simple Ways to Let People at Work Know You Care

One of the ways of being love's touch is to perform simple acts of kindness that let people know you care. James Autry, poet, author of *Love and Profit* and former President of Meridith Corporation's magazine group, advocates treating the people with whom you work with love and creating a caring environment in the workplace. In fact, he believes that "good management is largely a matter of love." Here are some simple ways to express your love at work this week.

Show people you care in fun and creative ways

Be inventive in honoring your coworkers and/or customers. For instance, take pictures of your colleagues making a contribution to the workplace and post them in a place where they can be seen by all coworkers. Or invite clients to send pictures of them doing activities they love, using your product or services. Create a collage with the pictures and display it in a welcoming and popular location.

Cheryl, an administrative assistant who works in the life sciences industry, is fond of taking pictures at employee events. Over the years, she has amassed boxes full of employee photos. When her company announced a downsizing she created collages for people leaving the organization. She creatively crafted a story about each person from carefully cut photos, using interesting scissors, and added a thought about the person in the center of the collage. She then framed her work and presented it to her fellow employee. Cheryl's gifts provided her colleagues with memorable mementos and made them feel special.

Get to know your coworkers, consumers, or your boss better
Invite a team member, your boss, or someone you do not know that well to have lunch or a healthy snack with you. Over lunch or a snack, share something about your life with them. Ask about their activities, family, background, and what they love to do. Invite them to talk about the high point and low point of their week and share yours with them. Or inquire about the most important lessons they have learned in their career.

We, Suzanne and Krista, typically have lunch with each of our regular clients at least once a year. Instead of focusing on our work with them, we spend time thanking them for their support, talking with them about what is new in their lives, and generally having a good time. Often we invite their spouses or significant others to join us. As a result of our time together, our clients have become our friends.

Inspirational Quote

"You can only love one person at a time...So just begin, one, one, one."
MOTHER TERESA, *WORDS TO LOVE BY*

Offer your support and encouragement to someone at work
Maybe your boss is feeling stressed and maybe a coworker has a lot on his or her plate. Let them know you see how hard they are working and ask them if there is anything you can do to help. If a colleague is having a particularly difficult time, you might want to see if everyone in your office is willing to donate one hour of their vacation time to this person so he or she could take a day off. Do what you can to make their day easier.

Judy, a management consultant, values highly the consultants with whom she works. She makes a point of offering her support to them when they are in challenging situations. Once when she was in a meeting with Krista, a colleague who was out of town on a stressful project called. Judy interrupted the meeting to speak with the person. She listened to, empathized, and then brainstormed with the consultant ways to work with the situation to make the most of it. Before hanging up she told the person that they would not agree to future projects that were as stressful as this one. Then she ended the conversation by saying, "I love you." It was clear that Judy's priority was to assist and care for those who work with her.

Jack, a financial executive, makes himself available to discuss career plans with people on his staff, even if it means they will leave the company. He said, "When people progress to the point where there are not any opportunities for growth in our company, we encourage them to go out and seek something elsewhere."

Perform acts of kindness for your colleagues and customers

Do small favors for people at work. For instance, offer to pick up a coworker's lunch while you are getting yours. On your way to the copy machine ask an officemate if he needs to have anything copied. Or give your boss words of encouragement and appreciation. Think about how to show you care in a personal way. Everyone has his or her own way of feeling appreciated. Ask yourself questions like, "What would each of my coworkers think was caring?" "How can I show my care and concern for each person individually?" "What small act can I do to make their workday easier, to brighten up their day, to make them feel loved and cared for?" Write the ideas down as a reminder of what you are going to do. Then do something for at least one person each day this week.

Inspirational Quote

"Sometimes you just connect,
Like that,
No big thing maybe
But something beyond the usual business stuff....
Listen.
In every office you hear the threads
of love and joy and fear and guilt
the cries for celebration and reassurance,
and somehow you know that connecting those threads
is what you are supposed to do..."

JAMES AUTRY, EXCERPT FROM THE POEM "THREADS"
IN *LOVE AND PROFIT*

Week Two: Take Care of the Work Environment

Marsha Sinetar, in *Holy Work,* suggests paying attention to how we bring "beauty, order, or 'Love's touch'" to our lives. One way of doing this is to take care of the physical space in which you and your coworkers work. People feel uplifted when they spend time in beautiful and inviting environments. Take time each day to think about how to bring beauty to your workplace. Then at the end of the day, make a note of the ways in which you took care of the workplace environment. Here are some ideas to get you started.

Create a beautiful environment in your own individual workspace

Set up a space you love to be in. If you work in an office, clear the desk of any unnecessary clutter. Put pleasing pictures on the wall. Place attractive plants on your desk or shelves, if light allows. Get one of those desk fountains. Do whatever feels right to you. And then take time each week to keep it looking and feeling beautiful.

The great thing is that each person's idea of a beautiful workspace is different. For instance, Gail, an educational administrator, loves Teddy Bears. Her office has pictures of Teddy Bears on the wall and small stuffed bears on the desk and shelves. Sometimes she even wears her Teddy Bear vest to work! Another person, Rae, who is a writer, has an elegant desk on which to work and bookshelves filled with her favorite books. When she is writing she turns the small fountain in the corner on to create soothing sounds in her office. Krista has several shelves next to her desk that hold all her family pictures. (She has a very large family!) She has placed her desk so that she can look outside at the woods and a serene statue of Buddha meditating placed in a strategic location to remind her to remain calm during the workday.

Inspirational Quote

"Make lovely some small space of your cosmos."
MARSHA SINETAR, *HOLY WORK*

Make your workspace feel welcoming to others

Stand in the door of your workspace and look at it as if you were coming in to meet with the person who works in the space. As you look around ask questions like, "Do I feel welcomed by the physical space here?" "Is there a comfortable place for me to sit or be?" "Is there a place for me to put down a beverage or papers?" "Is the furniture arranged in a welcoming way?" Then, based on your experience, think about specific ways to make the workspace more welcoming.

Bill, a manager in a federal agency, keeps a jar of licorice in his office for his coworkers. When his colleagues stop by his office for their afternoon snack, Bill makes it a point to catch-up on their lives. His fellow employees are now in on the act and help restock Bill's licorice supply.

Look for opportunities to bring love's touch to other's workspaces

Give a small gift to someone who has done something you appreciate that will brighten up his or her workspace and day. For instance, leave a single flower on their desk as a surprise. Place a plant in the conference room or reception area for all to see. Pay attention to which of your teammates' workspaces or other common areas are in need of some care and love. Then come up with your own way of bringing beauty to these places. Rod, a manager in a company that advocates for certain international issues, brings items from his travels abroad for staff members to put in their offices. He also posts inspiring and thought-provoking quotes in the office lunchroom each week.

Take the lead in raising awareness about renewing workspaces
Invite others in the office, including top management, to think about how, collectively, everyone can make the work environment more appealing, comfortable, uplifting, and welcoming. Collect information to share with management on the impact of color, light, and office layout on well-being and productivity.

In the past decade the amount of research done on the role of light and color in human health has increased. Studies show that light and color can affect mood, memory, sleep, learning, and productivity. How you design and decorate your office does make a difference. For instance, blue is supposed to have a calming effect and pink seems to be the color of love. Suzanne capitalizes on this information by decorating her office in blue and mauve as a way of creating a space where people feel calm and cared for. Some helpful resources to explore include *The Power of Color: Creating Healthy Interior Spaces* by Sara O. Marberry and Laurie Zagon, *Color Voodoo for the Office* available as an e-book on www.colorcom.com, and *Color in Public Spaces* by Kenneth Foote.

Week Three: Love Your Work

Recently there has been much written on finding the work that you love and finding your true calling in life. There is also something to be said for loving what you do, whether or not it is the type of job you have always wanted. Some people do not have the opportunity to search for, or have not yet found, their "true vocation." And even if you are already doing the work you love, every job has aspects that are difficult and less enjoyable. It is in these circumstances that knowing how to love what you do makes all the difference. The following fable, called "More Is Not Enough," borrowed from the Zen Stories web site (www.zenstory.html), illustrates the power of appreciating what you are currently doing.

Once upon a time, there was a stone cutter who was dissatisfied with himself and with his position in life. One day he passed a wealthy merchant's house. Through the open gateway, he saw many fine possessions and important visitors. "How powerful that merchant must be!" thought the stone cutter. He became very envious and wished that he could be like the merchant. To his great surprise, he suddenly became the merchant, enjoying more luxuries and power than he had ever imagined, but envied and detested by those less wealthy than himself.

Soon a high official passed by, carried in a sedan chair, accompanied by attendants and escorted by soldiers beating gongs. Everyone, no matter how wealthy, had to bow low before the procession. "How powerful that official is!" he thought. "I wish that I could be a high official!"

Then he became the high official, carried everywhere in his embroidered sedan chair, feared and hated by the people all around. It was a hot summer day, so the official felt very uncomfortable in the sticky sedan chair. He looked up at the sun. It shone proudly in the sky, unaffected by his presence. "How powerful the sun is!" he thought. "I wish that I could be the sun!" Then he became the sun, shining fiercely down on everyone, scorching the fields, cursed by the farmers and laborers. But a huge black cloud moved between him and the earth, so that his light could no longer shine on everything below. "How powerful that storm cloud is!" he thought. "I wish that I could be a cloud!"

Then he became the cloud, flooding the fields and villages, shouted at by everyone. But soon he found that he was being pushed away by some great force, and realized that it was the wind. "How powerful it is!" he thought. "I wish that I could be the wind!" Then he became the wind, blowing tiles off the roofs of houses, uprooting trees, feared and hated by all below him. But after a while, he ran up against something that would not move, no matter how forcefully he blew against it—a huge, towering rock. "How powerful that rock is!" he thought. "I wish that I could be a rock!"

Then he became the rock, more powerful than anything else on earth. But as he stood there, he heard the sound of a hammer pounding a chisel into the hard surface, and felt himself being changed. "What could be more powerful than I, the rock?" he thought. He looked down and saw far below him the figure of a stone cutter.

This week heed the lesson that the stone cutter discovered and look for contentment where you are. Use the tips that follow to help you love what you do right now.

Share what you love about your work

Let people in the office know what you love about your work and how much you like working where you are. Whenever you feel excited about a project, or something new you are learning, share those feelings with others. Your interest and love will uplift everyone. We, Krista and Suzanne, let each other know almost weekly how much we love what we do and how much we appreciate working with each other. Claire, a factory worker, spends five to ten minutes talking and joking with her coworkers about what they like about their job before they begin work each morning. She says that everything is done with a good feeling all day.

Key Point

"Knowing how to love what you do makes all the difference."

Do your daily tasks with an inner attitude of love

Pause as you begin your day and think about what you love about the office and work. Focus on why you decided to do this particular kind of job or what you receive from the workplace each day. Then throughout the day, periodically pause and recall your morning reflection. Allow the feelings and energy that naturally arise during your reflection to be present during your daily work activities. Or while doing your work tasks, consciously do them with the utmost care and in a loving way. Explore your own way of doing work with love. Arnie, the owner of a retail business, consciously strives to do his work with love. In the morning before he begins his daily work activities, he pauses as a way of remembering why he is working and then evokes feelings of love and offers his work to God. Then, throughout the day, he brings his mind back to the experience of love that he evoked in the morning and returns to the task at hand with an attitude of love.

Key Point

"On your most difficult days, "act as if" you love what you are doing. You will be pleasantly surprised how it changes your inner attitude towards your work."

Love the difficult tasks and moments at work
Momentarily step back from a task when you find yourself struggling or disliking what you are doing. Take a few moments to reflect on and reconnect with why you love your career or the original motivation for choosing your job. Or consider how your work in general makes a contribution to the world. Then, keeping this bigger perspective in mind, reflect on how the current task contributes to the success of your work. Another approach to reconnecting with your work is to pay attention to what you can learn from the moment. Identify what you can bring to the moment that is uplifting or will make a difference in how you feel. And on the most difficult days, if none of these methods work, "act as if" you love what you are doing. You will be pleasantly surprised how it changes your inner attitude.

This practice got us through the detailed editing of the book. Paying attention to minute details, such as making sure that there is only one space after a period instead of two, is one of our least preferred activities. During the process, we playfully recognized our weakness in editing, talked about how important having a clean and consistently organized manuscript was for our graphic person and our readers, and relied heavily on friends and our administrative assistant to help us catch items we missed. This allowed us to like the task as much as we could.

Inspirational Quote

"You can not love the journey if you hate the steps."
Maggie Bedrosian and Barbara Hemphill, *Love it or Lose it*

Week Four: Become a Source of Love at Work

Probably the most powerful way of being love's touch is to expand your own capacity for being a source of love for others. As Richard Carlson, Ph.D. suggests in *Do not Sweat the Small Stuff,* if we want a life filled with love, "the effort must start within us. Rather than waiting for other people to provide the love we desire, *we* must be a vision and source of love." Here are some ways to be a source of love at work.

Inspirational Quote

"Love at work is beyond softness and niceness. It includes whether people really respect and care about one another, whether they reach out and help, whether they protect one another's dignity, and whether they give without (too many) strings attached."
Jack Hawley, Ph.D., *Reawakening The Spirit In Work*

Give your full attention to your colleagues when they are speaking

Make a goal this week to really listen to at least one person in your workplace each day. Take the time to listen to them, even when you might want to do otherwise. Instead of thinking about what you are going to say next, pay attention to their words and the feelings underneath the words. See if you can understand what they are saying from their perspective. It is amazing how little it takes to listen and what a big impact it has. The benefits listening can elicit, in terms of building relationships and demonstrating care, are limitless. When people are listened to, they feel cared for and are often in a better place to focus on their work.

David, a lawyer, makes a conscious effort to listen to others and understand their perspectives. He says, "When I listen, I go outside myself to be with the other person without having my ego involved. And I find that listening intently, listening with my heart and mind, listening with everything I am is a great gift I can bring to the encounter. I can be there for the person."

Key Point

> *"Treat others as you would treat yourself if you loved yourself unconditionally."*

Treat your coworkers and clients with love and respect

Take time each day this week to be aware of your colleagues and customers and to extend care and love towards them. It is easy to get caught up in what you are doing and lose sight of those with whom you work. So make time to think about how you most like to be treated and then interact with others in this way. One caveat to this method: people are often harder on themselves and treat themselves with less respect than they do others. Why not treat others as you would treat yourself if you really loved yourself unconditionally? And then treat yourself this way as well!

Think loving thoughts of others

Silently wish your coworkers well and send caring thoughts to them throughout the day. You can think good things about them, send them blessings, or pray for them without their knowing you are doing it. This activity is particularly transformative for relationships with people with whom you are having difficulty at work! You will be amazed how sending loving thoughts to a "difficult person" can change the way you interact with and respond to that person.

Recently, Betty, a supervisor in a Human Resources Department, told Krista how thinking positive thoughts about two coworkers with whom she was having difficulty was helping her relate differently with them. Instead of thinking about how incompetent she thought one of them was, Betty began to silently send her colleague well-wishes in her work and to look for ways in which the person did great work. With the second individual, instead of avoiding the coworker because she found her difficult to work with, Betty began to consider what gifts this teammate brought to the department and what lessons Betty could learn from her. The result of Betty's efforts was that she began to get along better with each person and feel okay about working with them. She even found herself offering support and encouragement to them in ways that surprised them all!

Inspirational Quote

"We must give love the same close attention we give other things these days; we must move nearer to love and become better at it."
Jack Hawley Ph.D., *Reawakening The Spirit In Work*

Practice Loving Kindness

Evoke feelings of love and kindness within yourself this week and then direct those feelings to people with whom you work. The Eastern faith traditions have a method for cultivating and sharing love and compassion called the Loving-Kindness Meditation. While there are many variations that are used, the practice involves sitting quietly with your eyes closed and focusing on allowing feelings of love to arise within. Once you have evoked love and compassion, first direct these feelings to yourself and then extend them out to others in an expanding circle. The natural outcome of sending blessings to yourself and others is that you often become moved to respond to others and situations in your daily life in benevolent ways. You naturally respond more often with love. You can experiment with finding your own way to practice loving kindness. Or you can use some of the methods suggested by long time practitioners like Sharon Salzburg in *Loving Kindness* or Jon Kabat-Zinn, Ph.D., in *Wherever You Go There You Are*, both of whom inspired the meditation in the exercise that follows.

Exercise: Evoking Loving Kindness

This exercise is best done, initially, in a quiet place where you can remain undisturbed for ten to fifteen minutes. Once you are familiar with the process you can do it anywhere, even with your eyes open.

Read the following instructions completely once or twice before doing the exercise. You can also record yourself reading them. Then play them back and guide yourself through the meditation exercise. If you choose to record the exercise, leave pauses between the sentences so you have time to experience what the instructions are guiding you to do.

1. Assume a comfortable upright posture, with your spine elongated and feet flat on the floor. Close your eyes. Take a few deep breaths and then become aware of any sensations in your body. Notice any tension in your body, any tightening of muscles, any feelings that may be coming from your work situation at this time.

2. As you become aware of a particular sensation, notice that feeling for a moment and then allow your breath to flow into the area of your body where you notice the sensation, relaxing the body in that spot. Then, scan your body and breathe into any remaining areas of sensation, tension, or tightness.

3. Now focus attention on your breath. Allow your breathing to become steady and even and pay attention as your breath moves in and out of the center of the chest—as it moves in and out of the center of the heart region—the place from where love and kindness arise.

4. Allow feelings or images of love, kindness, or compassion to arise within you. Imagine the loving kindness moving from the heart region down into your legs and feet. Feel it moving upward into the arms, neck, and face until it radiates through out your whole being.

5. Allow yourself to bathe in the warmth and acceptance of your own loving kindness as if you were a small child held in your mother's or father's arms. Bask in the energy of loving kindness, breathing it in and breathing it out, as if it were a lifeline, passing along nourishment. From this place of love, wish yourself well. Imagine that loving kindness is radiating throughout your whole being, nourishing your spirit.

6. Now that you have established yourself as a center of loving kindness, begin to let your feelings radiate outward towards others. You can direct your feelings to those whom you think are suffering at work—to people at work you have a hard time with—to people you do not know—or even to whole groups and organizations.

7. Whomever you choose, visualize their essential selves. Then from the center of love within you, wish them well—that they not suffer, that they come to know their true way in the world, that they may experience love, kindness, and acceptance in life.

8. As you extend your compassion towards others, notice if you feel called to act differently at work. If an action arises in your awareness, ask if you wish to commit to making such an effort. If your response is affirmative, imagine yourself carrying it out in a loving and compassionate manner. If you are not yet ready to make that particular commitment, simply hold the idea in your awareness for a few moments, and give yourself permission to offer love and compassion at another time or in another way.

9. Come gently out of meditation whenever you feel complete in the exercise. It is best to take some time in opening your eyes. You may want to take a few deep breaths and slowly move your body first. Take a few minutes to write down the experience and any thoughts or feelings that were evoked during the meditation.

10. Then, enact any ideas that you feel committed to performing.

"Meanwhile, these three remain: faith. hope, and love; and the greatest of these is love."
GOOD NEWS BIBLE, 1 CORINTHIANS 13:13
(TODAY'S ENGLISH VERSION)

10

MARCH

NOURISH YOUR CREATIVITY AT WORK

"The creative process is as natural as breathing. We all use it, but most of us are not even aware of it. It is subtle, mysterious, and happens on a subconscious level."

SALLI RASBERRY AND PADI SELWYN, *LIVING YOUR LIFE OUTLOUD*

Introduction

In the Northern Hemisphere, nature begins its annual process of renewal during the month of March. New life emerges from the dormancy of winter. The Earth starts to warm up under the shifting sun. Sleepy bulbs pop their heads out of the dark soil. Birds fly north to mate and nest. The natural world is making itself anew. With all the creative energy occurring in the world around you, this month is the perfect time to explore how you too can foster your creativeness.

What comes to mind when you think about the word "creative?" You might think this word only applies to professional artists, performers, and inventors. Think again! The creative process is inherently a part of all human life. Your workday is filled with numerous opportunities to express your creativity. Every time you act there is a chance to produce something that has never before existed. You are virtually unlimited in the ways to be creative in your daily work life. You do not have to invent something that wins a Nobel Prize to be creative, suggests Dr. Teresa Amabile, a psychologist at Brandeis University who researches creativity. As long as what you do is original and works, you are being creative. Because the workplace is one of the largest ground-breaking arenas (although one of the least recognized), opportunities for innovation and resourceful problem solving abound there, such as:

- taking a new approach to a familiar problem
- handling a conflict between coworkers in a different way
- improving work processes and procedures
- creating innovations in management methods

- solving a problem collaboratively
- providing innovative services to customers
- developing a groundbreaking idea or original product
- coming up with an inspired way to take care of less fortunate members of your community
- finding better ways to express your values at work
- discovering new approaches to your daily work
- uncovering methods for doing more with less

Creativity is particularly important in today's fast paced environment. The speed of change demands that you be able to think quickly on your feet and respond resourcefully.

As customer and organizational requirements vary, new solutions and products are necessary for success. All of this requires creativity on your part, as well as resiliency. Keeping up with all these day-to-day demands necessitates finding ways to renew yourself. Fortunately, utilizing creative processes to meet work challenges can also be a means of renewing yourself. When you are creative you renew your mind and enhance your sense of vitality.

Inspirational Quote

"When creativity is in full fire, people can experience what athletes and performers call the 'white moment.' Everything clicks. Your skills are so perfectly suited to the challenge that you seem to blend with it. Everything feels harmonious, unified, and effortless."
DANIEL GOLEMAN, PAUL KAUFMAN, AND MICHAEL RAY,
THE CREATIVE SPIRIT

Reflection Questions

 Take two to three minutes to reflect and/or write about each of the following questions:

1. What is the most creative thing I have ever done in my life? What creative talents did I demonstrate?
2. Who best represents my image of a creative person? What creative characteristics does this person possess? Which of these creative characteristics do I possess?
3. What actions do I regularly take to nourish my creative side at work?
4. What actions can I add to my daily routine to encourage my own creativity?

Week One: Be Curious About Everything

According to Mihaly Csikszentmihalyi, Ph.D., author of *Creativity: Flow and the Psychology of Discovery and Invention*, one of the first steps toward a more creative life is the cultivation of curiosity and interest, or doing things for their own sake. Begin this week by being curious about work-related and non-work related things.

Key Point

"Your workday is filled with numerous opportunities to express your creativity."

 Be inquisitive every day at work

Allow yourself to be as curious as a child and ask "why?" throughout the day. Be pleasantly surprised by unexpected occurrences. Pose questions during meetings to create better understanding and idea sharing. Talk with people who are not in your field or department. Inquire about what work problems they are trying to solve. Find out what is piquing their curiosity. Read trade journals and other magazines and listen to National Public Radio for new ideas. Then, see if you can apply any of the information you are discovering to your work setting.

Hank, a former superintendent of schools in a large metropolitan area, learned from his three-year-old daughter how to be curious.

When he went on walks with her, he noticed that she stopped and examined everything. If she saw an ant, she would sit down on the ground for a few minutes and watch it moving along. She also asked many questions of him, like "Why is the ant carrying that?" "Where is he taking it?" "Is he going to eat it?" and so on. After spending time in this way with her, he found that his own ability to stop and examine what was going on at work was enhanced. This heightened sense of curiosity led to him exploring new possibilities and to going outside of his normal sources of information for ideas when developing a new curriculum.

Inspirational Quote

"Creativity is a vital force without which we can exist, but not truly live."
ANN CUSHMAN, *"ARE YOU CREATIVE?"*

Explore your interests at work

When something at work sparks your interest, make time to explore the idea or activity that got your attention. Like a child, follow what catches your eye. Explore why it appeals to you. Discover as much as possible about the subject and look at how it can be integrated into what you do at work. Csikszentmihalyi writes that "life is nothing more than a stream of experiences—the more widely and deeply you swim in it, the richer your life will be." Make this exploratory approach a new way of thinking, feeling, and acting at work.

Krista reads books and articles from many different disciplines that she likes to draw upon when working with clients. She has both an Idea Book, given to her by a colleague, in which she writes ideas that she wishes to explore and a file where she keeps articles that have interesting ideas and examples. Many of the ideas have been incorporated into the information she shares with consulting clients and the creative experiments that she encourages her coaching clients to do.

Look at work questions in a new and creative way

Bring a fresh perspective to your work by using new approaches for exploring work issues. Be creative! Study the issue similar to how children investigate nature. Look at the situation from all sides.

Imagine that you can physically see the issue. Then, metaphorically, look at it up close. Pick it up and see how it feels and how it moves. Put yourself into the experience. You could also spend some actual time in nature, studying the trees, insects, birds, and butterflies. Pay attention to what you can learn from nature and then apply those lessons to your work-related problem.

The inventors of Pringles® potato chips took a lesson from nature in coming up with their product idea. They realized that people did not like broken or crushed potato chips and decided to do something about this issue. They thought about leaves and how these delicate miracles of nature are easily crushed. They thought about how leaves can be preserved by layering them and putting them in a protective cover. This led them to thinking about how to preserve potato chips. The rest is history. Nature's lessons guided the birth of Pringles® in a can!

Exercise: Looking at Challenges with New Eyes

Here is one way to look at work challenges creatively and from a different perspective.

1. Identify a work-related challenge to which you would like to bring a new perspective.
2. Select and list three to five different types of animals.
3. Ask yourself how each animal would look at and/or respond to the situation. For instance, ask yourself "How would a polar bear (moose, snake, turkey, tortoise, fly, shark, ant, elephant, mouse, or bird) solve this work dilemma?"
4. Write down all of your ideas, no matter how "silly" you may think they are.
5. Review the notes and consider how they help you think about the work situation in a new way. Decide which concepts can be applied to your challenge and come up with an action plan.

Learn something new at work every month

Make a list or create a mind map of all the skills, information, techniques, and activities you would like to learn at work. Then, choose one every month to investigate and study. Read a trade journal in your field or a book on leadership. Ask a coworker to cross-train you on some aspect of their job. Sign up for an online course. Keep up with the latest software and e-mail changes. Take an adult learning course on advanced Microsoft PowerPoint®, and dazzle your coworkers by adding pizzazz to your next PowerPoint® presentation. The ideal goal is to learn something new every day, at work and at play!

Suzanne has an interest in the brain and ways of expanding the brain's potential. She makes it a point to spend time with LaDonna Bates, her friend and fellow Chautauqua faculty member, discussing the brain. LaDonna has always read the latest on brain research and recommends books to Suzanne. Suzanne then weaves the new ideas that she learns about the brain and mental renewal into her presentations. It is not unusual to find Suzanne demonstrating brain exercises and encouraging her audiences to incorporate them into their daily routine.

Week Two: Be Playful at Work

You may be wondering "is there a connection between playfulness and creativity?" Good question. Here is how the authors of *The Creative Spirit* see the link:

> *"There is a paradox: Although creativity takes hard work, the work goes more smoothly if you take it lightly. Humor greases the wheels of creativity. One reason is that when you are joking around, you're freer to consider any possibility—after all, you're only kidding. Having fun helps you disarm the inner censor that all too quickly condemns your ideas as ludicrous."*

The key to being playful is to break out of your normal habits of action, thought, and perception for a short period of time. Brenda Ueland, the author of *If You Want to Write*, advocates cultivating the playful idleness that children have as a way of enhancing creativity. She writes, "At such times, you are being slowly filled and recharged with warm imagination, with wonderful, living thoughts." This week allow yourself to get out from under old, familiar ways and reinvent your approach to creativity at work. If after you have experimented with the tips here, you are interested in learning more about play at work, Chapter 13 (Play at Work) offers many more ideas on the subject!

Give yourself permission to do playful things at work

Have fun at work. Allow yourself to be personal and playful during meetings and working sessions. Everyone at work might think of you as the "serious, hard-driving, professional type." As such, you might believe you are supposed to behave in certain ways. Breaking out of such a restrictive role or mindset gives you and those around you permission to lighten up. Maybe this newfound fun behavior will spark an idea for a new product or a different approach to work.

Here is an example of someone who broke away from others' perception of him. Allen, a corporate Vice President of Finance with whom Suzanne has worked, is a pretty serious and "all business" kind of guy. At the beginning of a three-day outdoor team building program, the VP asked if he could borrow a jester's hat that Suzanne was going to use later in the day. Then, he wore it when introducing Suzanne and kicking off the whole program. His willingness to loosen up served as inspiration to the participants who were about to be challenged in their own personal and professional growth.

Use toys to spark creativity at work

Think about the toys you loved to play with as a child. Buy some and bring them to work. Look at your kids' (or a friend's kids') toys for ideas. Nerf® Balls, stuffed animals, musical instruments, or action toys are great choices for work. Ron, a Vice President of Human Resources, keeps a karate action figure on his desk. A client bought it for him as a symbol of the VP's ability to negotiate benefits and compensation packages with the skill of a martial arts master.

In the middle of a particularly difficult brain storming session, break out the toys! You never know how they will inspire people. One proven training approach to exploring how to improve manufacturing lines is to ask workers to build a model of the current line with tinker toys. They then rebuild the model with an eye toward making improvement upgrades. Tinkertoys come in handy in numerous settings. A group of doctoral students in Management Science at George Washington University used Tinkertoys to build a mobile that illustrated the common factors among three key theorists on organizational change and behavior. They called the mobile

"Tinkering with Theories" and presented it by holding an "Art Gallery Opening" at the graduate school.

Read something funny everyday at work

Keep funny books or cartoons in your desk at work and read them daily. Then ask yourself, "How would the cartoon character or comedian solve this problem?" "What would Dave Barry do if he were in my shoes?" "How would Charlie Brown, Lucy, or Snoopy® respond to the situation?" Your responses to these types of questions will add to your fun, boost creativity, and just might lead to the solutions for which you are searching. If you do not have any funny books or do not know where to go to find cartoons or jokes, go to the humor section of a bookstore, get the Sunday comics, or check out some of the joke sites online. When you find something funny online share it with your coworkers and friends. Dan, the medical officer mentioned before in our book, regularly sends jokes and stories via e-mail to his colleagues. Everyone has a good laugh and Dan has fun finding funny stories to share, which is easy for him to do because so many people send him items in return!

Draw pictures of key points rather than taking notes at a meeting

Draw images that represent the ideas being discussed instead of taking linear notes. Or create a *mind map* of the ideas generated during the conversation. Look at your drawings after the meeting and see how they might inform the issue you were discussing. Perhaps you will draw images that will be helpful in designing a new logo for a product. Or perhaps somewhere buried in your drawing might be the answer to a tricky product distribution issue.

Some organizations bring in facilitators to "draw" the proceedings of their meeting. For instance, author and consultant Meg Wheatley has artist Nusa Maal of Sense Smart, Inc., capture ideas as people speak during her workshops on dialogue. Using this approach is a great way to signal to people that this meeting is not "business as usual and creativity is welcome here."

Mind mapping is a technique that was created by Tony Buzan. You start with a concept in a circle in the middle of a page. You then write down associated ideas around the circle and draw connections between them, like the example that follows. For more information on *mind mapping*, see the creativity section in the resource list at the end of the book.

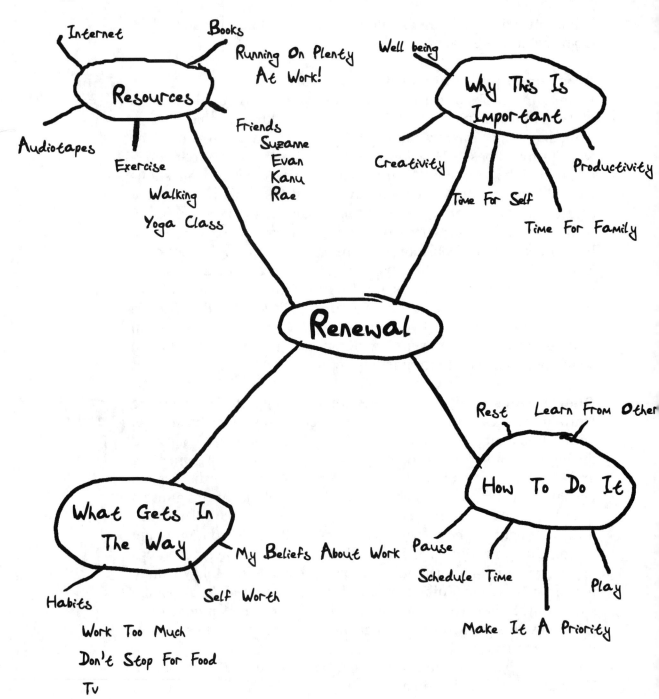

"Using innovative and fun processes during discussions is a great way to signal to people that this meeting is not 'business as usual and creativity is welcome here.'"

Week Three: Take Time to Reflect and Relax

Taking time out is one of the most powerful ways to honor your creativity. Salli Rasberry and Padi Selwyn claim that "highly creative achievers make time for themselves a priority, because they know, consciously or intuitively, that recharging the creative batteries happens during downtime. Getting in touch with your creative rhythm is critical to creative health." In other words, taking time for reflection and relaxation is crucial! Constant busyness is not a good prescription for creativity. The Greeks believed that leisure provided the opportunity to dream, imagine, and create. They considered repose essential primarily because they thought that creativity was important. Without rest, there is no creativity. This week slow down and nourish your creativity by taking some time to rest and relax.

Inspirational Quote

"The imagination needs noodling—long, inefficient, happy, idling, dawdling, and puttering."

BRENDA UELAND, *IF YOU WANT TO WRITE*

Schedule reflection into your daily schedule at work

Set aside time in your calendar at the beginning of the week for intentional reflection during the day. You may choose to contemplate at the beginning or end of the day. You may find it works best to sit down and think after a big customer meeting before running off to your next meeting. Taking a few minutes to stop your regular activity, collect yourself, and think about work events will better enable you to be present and creative in your next meeting. It also helps you have more clarity about the situation at hand.

Rod, the manager who deals with international issues mentioned in an earlier chapter, has found that it is crucial for him to spend time each morning thinking about his priorities for the day. He intentionally arrives at the office a half an hour early whenever he is able so that he can sit quietly and reflect on his day. He also likes to take a moment to read a passage from the Bible when there is a challenging issue that he must face later in the day. It helps to guide his decisions and actions and enables him to be prepared for the day.

Key Point

 "Taking time for rest and relaxation is crucial for creativity. Slow down and nourish your creativity."

Pay attention to your unique work rhythms

 Keep track of your energy levels and the time of day when you do your most creative work. If mornings are the most productive time, schedule your more difficult tasks at this time. If late in the afternoon is your creative time, use this period of the day for activities that require more inventiveness. Save less productive times for routine tasks that require less mental and physical energy.

Nancy, the physician in the Northwest whom you may recall reading about previously in the book, pays particular attention to how patients are scheduled. She alternates patients who might need a great deal of attention with those who are post-operative and may need less attention. In this way, she can work in a way that honors her needs and allows her to be refreshed throughout the day and fully available for her patients.

Build pauses into your workday

 Enhance your creativity by taking breathers throughout the day. Pausing or momentarily changing the activity in which you are engaged is particularly helpful when you find yourself stumped or feeling less productive. As Charles Thompson says in *What a Great Idea*, "If at first you do not succeed, take a break." This is a great reminder for lengthy, unproductive staff meetings, long stretches at the computer, or intense problem solving sessions. Taking a brief rest will revive you. You will return to work with a fresh perspective. Your solutions will reflect your renewed state. Many of Einstein's ideas came to him when he was taking a pause from his work. If Einstein's experiences are any indicator, a creative idea may come to you in the midst of your interlude. Often the best ideas arise when you are not consciously thinking about an issue. The idea for Krista's doctoral research occurred to her when she was sitting in a garden soaking up the sun. Suzanne swears by "the water cure." Either taking a shower or sitting by a body of water provides a venue for working out her most complex professional and personal challenges.

Set aside some uninterrupted time each week

Create time when you can work without any interruptions. It can be difficult to concentrate and come up with creative solutions when your work is frequently being disrupted. Some people create times when they have their calls held so they can focus completely on the task at hand. Some organizations even block off time each week as "interruption free time" during which no internal meetings are scheduled or visits to coworkers' offices are made. Use your uninterrupted time to finish important tasks, reflect on work issues, brainstorm solutions, engage in creative activity, or simply to rest. Suzanne sets aside 15 minutes each day to read a current magazine. She often reads *Cooking Light,* which emphasizes both cooking light recipes and "living and working light." The reading is rejuvenating and she usually can weave some of the newly acquired information or ideas into her work.

Week Four: Work with Your Creative Roadblocks

Everyone experiences creative roadblocks. They are a natural part of the innovative process. The trick to moving beyond them or detouring around them is to accept and work with them. Surrendering to your own timing and process will nourish your creativity in the long run. Here are some ways to honor the ebb and flow of your creative routine.

Acknowledge the voice of judgment within you

Realize that everyone has a critical voice that sometimes hinders or limits his or her creativity. Your voice of judgment is that part within that disapproves of what you are doing, makes you afraid to do it and makes you feel depressed after not doing it. Whenever you are feeling blocked at work, take some time to listen to and write down what your voice of judgment is saying. Pay attention to the kinds of messages your voice of judgment is sending and find ways to restate or change those thoughts to ones that are more supportive of your creative efforts. If sharing with others is comfortable, talk with someone about what is delaying your creative process. Acknowledging your block to someone else is a good first step in getting unstuck.

Inspirational Quote

 "The biggest block to living a creative life is the voice of blame and criticism within each of us: the voice of judgment. A good way to deal with it is to acknowledge you have it!"

DANIEL GOLEMAN, PAUL KAUFMAN, AND MICHAEL RAY, *THE CREATIVE SPIRIT*

 Identify what is holding you back from being creative at work Take some time to look at how and why you stop yourself from expressing your creativity at work. Although everybody has the potential to be inventive, many people hold back because of the belief that they are not capable, they are afraid of what others might think, or that their way of being creative is not appropriate in the workplace. It takes courage to look at how and why you hold yourself back. It can also be quite freeing when you pinpoint the obstacles, because then you can move beyond them. Use the following exercise to help identify and discard the key barriers to living out your dreams imaginatively.

Inspirational Quote

 "The creative is the place where no one else has been. You have to leave the city of your comfort and go into the wilderness of your intuition. You can not get there by bus, only hard work and risk and by not quite knowing what you're doing. What you'll discover will be wonderful. What you'll discover will be yourself."

ALAN ALDA, *THE QUOTATIONS PAGE*

Exercise: Identifying and Discarding Your Main Barriers

1. Take a piece of paper and write down your dreams for your work and career.
2. Beside each item, write several reasons for not moving toward that dream. Include fears, resources, family, intimate relationships, and lack of specific skills. Make note of any reasons that you think hinder your creativity and lack of action. Be negative, really negative!
3. Then, say goodbye to your list and burn it!
4. Start a new list. Write down your dreams again and this time note all the reasons why you can achieve these dreams at work! Include the skills and characteristics that will help you achieve the dreams. List creative ways to achieve your dreams! Keep this list handy and refer to it often.

Key Point

"Your voice of judgment is that part of you that disapproves of what you are doing… Pay attention to the messages your voice of judgment is sending and substitute them with thoughts that are more supportive of your creative efforts."

Let go of how you think the creative process should function
Yield to your unique course of inventive action. Discard any expectations you have about how "things should happen" and allow your creative process to take its own direction. Although the workplace has many ideas about how problems get solved, the most innovative solutions and most successful products often come from those times when people abandon the rules. It is when you let go of controlling what should be taking place that you leave room for real creativity to emerge.

Exercise: Letting Go of Your Creative Blocks

Here are two approaches to help release the inner obstacles to your creativity.

Letting go physically

1. Sit in a chair with your hands resting comfortably on your legs.
2. Bring to mind the cause of your creative block. For instance, a critical thought, a fear of not being good enough, or a lack of energy may produce your block.
3. Keeping the source of your roadblock in mind, begin to tense your legs and keep them tense as you successively and steadily tense your abdomen, chest, shoulders, arms, neck, and jaw. Imagine that the tension in your body represents what is hindering your action. Hold all your muscles tense for a moment.
4. Now relax and imagine that in releasing the tension your creative blocks have been freed as well. You have just let go. How did it feel?

Letting go mentally

1. Sit quietly for a few minutes and reflect on what thoughts, beliefs, or expectations are interfering with your creative process. Choose one that you think is the largest obstacle.
2. Now imagine that your chosen idea is actually represented by something you are wearing. It can be a shoe, watch, ring, scarf, bracelet, or tie. Imagine without a doubt that this mental block is contained entirely within the article you are wearing. The thought and the article have now fused into one.
3. Then, take it off! Observe what you are experiencing as you let go of this mental obstacle.
4. If after doing this exercise you still feel that your beliefs are limiting your creativity, think of a supportive phrase or thought that you can use to replace the creative obstacle whenever it crosses your mind.

April

Spread Seeds of Enthusiasm at Work

"Even one enthusiastic [person] with a deep sense of mission and purpose can inspire those around to achieve their very best, so let enthusiasm begin with YOU!"

BARBARA GLANZ, *CARE PACKAGES FOR THE WORKPLACE*

Introduction

I t is April, the season of renewal! The new life that springs from winter's cold ground, now warmed by the sun, can bring lightness to your steps. Like the spring flowers, you too can come alive, warmed by the light and liveliness of spring and buoyed by the passing of winter, as the following verse from the Song of Solomon (2:11-13, *The Holy Bible,* New King James Version) indicates.

> *For lo, the winter is past.*
> *The rains are over and gone.*
> *The flowers appear on the earth.*
> *The time of the singing of birds is come*
> *And the voice of the turtledove is heard in our land.*

At this time of year, it is easy to feel enthusiastic as spring brings with it a renewing burst of joy. Drawing on the season's natural light and on your own physical, emotional, and spiritual energy, you can become rejuvenated and filled with vitality at home and at work.

Key Point

 "Enthusiasm spreads as easily as seeds blown by the wind. It can spill over into all areas of your life."

The word enthusiasm derives from the Greek word *entheos,* which means, "filled with God" or "from the spirit within." Even though you may feel energized by the natural world's coming alive, your enthusiasm actually originates from your inner being and then radiates outward to the world. According to the Webster dictionary, enthusiasm is also defined as "intense or eager interest; zeal, fervor." And since enthusiasm originates inside, your zeal can be directed towards almost anything you are interested in—your faith, a specific cause, family, and especially work.

The great thing about enthusiasm is that it spreads as easily as seeds blown by the wind. Enthusiasm for one aspect of life can spill over into other areas of life. This means that you can take steps to cultivate and spread enthusiasm in your daily work. Keep in mind that each person has his or her own way of expressing enthusiasm. You can be as animated as a cheerleader or share your passion in a quiet and wholehearted manner. Find the style that best suits you.

There is an old saying that one who plants a garden lives by faith. Similarly, cultivating enthusiasm at work also requires trust. As the verse from E.B. White suggests, it is the grace within you that allows the seeds of enthusiasm to grow.

> *Before the seed there comes the thought of bloom,*
> *The seedbed is the restless mind itself.*
> *Not sun, soil alone can bring to border*
> *This rush of beauty and this sense of order.*
> *Flowers respond to something in the gardener's face—*
> *Some secret in the heart, some special grace.*

This month tap into the renewing energy within you so that you can cultivate and spread the seeds of enthusiasm in the "garden" that is the workplace. If you bring enthusiasm to work, you will experience a greater sense of fulfillment and will renew your connections with others. Enthusiasm is contagious. Like flowers moving toward the sun, people naturally gravitate toward and enjoy working with those who are genuinely enthusiastic.

The key is to begin to look at work as full of possibilities for spreading the seeds of your enthusiasm. One place to start is to uncover how you experience enthusiasm at work, cultivate it, and share it with others.

Reflection Questions

 Take two to three minutes to reflect and/or write about each of the following questions:

1. In what ways do I experience enthusiasm while at work?
2. In what ways do I already share or spread the seeds of enthusiasm at work?
3. How can I express enthusiasm more often at work?
4. What stops me from experiencing and sharing enthusiasm at work?
5. How can I overcome my barriers to experiencing and sharing enthusiasm at work?

Week One: Cultivate Enthusiasm for Your Work

Enthusiasm, like a garden, often requires cultivating and nurturing to grow. Like most people, you may not always feel enthusiastic about your work. And yet, it is your attitude towards work that makes the biggest difference in how renewing you find your job and the workplace.

Richard Carlson, Ph.D., relates a story in *Don't Sweat the Small Stuff* that demonstrates the difference that a person's attitude can make. There were two construction workers who were asked by a reporter, "What are you doing?" The first complained that he was "virtually a slave, an underpaid bricklayer" who wasted his day's away, placing bricks on top of each other. The second worker replied, "I'm the luckiest person in the world... I get to be a part of creating important and beautiful pieces of architecture. I help turn simple pieces of brick into exquisite masterpieces." The moral of the story, according to Carlson, is that "we see in life what we want to see. If you search for ugliness you'll find plenty of it... But the opposite is also true. If you look for the extraordinary in the ordinary, you can train yourself to see it." Here are some ways in which you can teach yourself to feel enthusiasm at work this week.

Key Point

 "Enthusiasm, like a garden, often requires cultivating and nurturing to grow."

Explore your own enthusiasm for your job

Make a list of things that you thoroughly enjoy about work. You can do the exercise that follows to help make note of what you are enthusiastic about at work. Refer to it once a day this week, particularly during moments where you feel frustrated or dissatisfied with your work. Notice how you feel after recalling what you are excited about at work. Then bring renewed enthusiasm to what you are doing in that moment.

Joie, a friend of ours, recently changed jobs after a company buyout. She took a pay-cut, has less responsibility, is not utilizing her college degree, and has added 40 minutes to her commute. In spite of all of the drawbacks, Joie has found things about which to be enthusiastic at work. She recognizes that she has a wonderful working space with a breath taking view of the sunset from her seventeenth floor office and her coworkers appreciate her contributions.

Exercise: Identifying My Enthusiasm at Work

You can do this exercise using a table like the one that follows, or you can draw a mind map of your ideas.
1. Identify and note as many characteristics of work about which you are enthusiastic. Think about aspects related to the nature of the work, the location, the people with whom you work, and the working environment.
2. Then reflect on and make note of why you are excited about each item.

A Table for Identifying Aspects of Work About Which You are Enthusiastic		
Category	What am I enthusiastic about at work?	Why am I enthusiastic about this aspect of work?
My work itself—the type of work, amount of work, working hours, *etc.*		
The people with whom I work—coworkers, supervisor, customers, suppliers, *etc.*		
The organization in which I work—the size, structure, culture, *etc.*		
The working environment—the atmosphere, physical space, location, commute time, *etc.*		
The society in which I work—the benefit work brings to others, the economy, the culture, *etc.*		
Other		

Act enthusiastic, even when you are not feeling it

"Act as if" you are feeling enthusiastic. Like the second brick layer in the previous story, you can choose to see work in an inspiring light. If past attempts at generating enthusiasm for an aspect of your work did not produce positive feelings, make another attempt. If it is still difficult to shift the way you see work, seek out the help of someone else in the workplace to help you cultivate your passion. Let them know you are working on generating enthusiasm for a specific aspect of your work. See if they have any "gardening" tips.

Let go of what gets in the way of your enthusiasm at work

Take some time this week to become aware of what you need to let go or change. Sometimes, for a garden to grow best, you have to dig up the earth to loosen or aerate the soil, prune the plants, or do some weeding. Explore what needs to be pruned, weeded, or dug up. What stops you from feeling enthusiastic about your work? It may be your thoughts or beliefs about work or other people in the workplace, or it may be that your enthusiasm is dampened by fatigue. Whatever it is that gets in the way, see if you can let it go so more space can be created for your enthusiasm and inspiration to emerge. Remember that spring is a welcomed season because it follows the colder, darker winter. As the following brief Zen story suggests, you cannot feel your natural enthusiasm unless you make room for it!

One day, a university professor went to visit a famous Zen master. While the master quietly served tea, the professor talked about Zen. The master poured the visitor's cup to the brim, and then kept pouring. The professor watched the overflowing cup until he could no longer restrain himself. "It is overfull! No more will go in!" the professor blurted. "You are like this cup," the master replied, "How can I show you Zen unless you first empty your cup."

Inspirational Quote

 "New seed is faithful. It roots deepest in places that are most empty."
CLARISSA PINKOLA ESTES, PH.D., *FAITHFUL GARDNER*

Exercise: Creating Space for Enthusiasm to Grow

Here are two exercises to help you "empty your cup" and let go of what gets in the way of expressing and enjoying your enthusiasm. They may seem familiar, since they are adapted from the letting go exercises in the previous chapter.

Objectifying and Letting Go of Beliefs

1. Sit quietly for a few minutes and reflect on what thoughts or beliefs are roadblocks to your enthusiasm at work. Make a note in your journal of each thing that is a potential pothole on your journey to renewal at work.
2. Choose one item from the list that you think is the largest obstacle.
3. Now imagine that the obstacle is actually represented by something you are wearing. It can be a shoe, watch, ring, scarf, bracelet, or tie. Imagine without any reservation that the hurdle is contained entirely within the article you are wearing. The obstacle and the article have now fused into one.
4. Then, take it off! Observe what you are experiencing as you let go of this mental obstacle.

Getting Rid of Obstacles to Enthusiasm

1. Take a piece of paper and write down all the things that get in the way of your enthusiasm at work. Include fears, resources, thoughts, beliefs, salary, type of work, amount of work, the commute, coworkers, your boss, the work environment—any thing that blocks or drains your enthusiasm. Give yourself permission to be negative. Really negative!
2. Now take the list, say goodbye to it, and do something with it that symbolizes getting rid of those obstacles. You can cut it into pieces with scissors—holding an image of pruning your garden. Shred it in the shredder. Turn it into a paper airplane and fly it out the window. Burn it! Do whatever feels best to you.

> *"Let go of beliefs that block you from creating more space for your enthusiasm and inspiration to emerge."*

Welcome whatever happens at work with enthusiasm

Adopt the attitude that everything in life happens for the best. Although at first you may not feel enthusiasm for a situation that is challenging, look for the ways in which the situation helps you to grow or the ways in which it could be positive. Look for ways in which the situation may make your work or working relationships better. Search for those little magical seeds that when nurtured can blossom into magnificent perennial flowers.

About ten years ago, Bob, a manager at a large hardware computer company, learned that situations usually do turn out for the best, even though when you are going through them it does not seem that way. When Bob's daughter was one year old she was diagnosed with Leukemia. Bob and his wife, Anne, who worked for the same company, spent many months going back and forth to the local Children's Hospital. Their colleagues were very supportive and set up a schedule for providing them with frozen meals each week, as well as gave them some of their vacation days to use. Their daughter began to respond to treatment and one day they were told that she might be able to go home soon. They enthusiastically drove home only to find that there had been a fire in their house that morning.

Luckily their neighbors had called the fire department and only their kitchen was damaged. There was too much smoke and fire retardant in the house for them to sleep there that night so after calling their insurance agent they went to a hotel. The next morning when they arrived at the house to meet the agent, they discovered that vandals had broken in overnight, had spray painted sayings all over the walls, had stopped up the sinks, and flooded the house. The agent assured them that they were fully covered and that the kitchen would be repaired, the walls repainted, and the carpets replaced.

Feeling overwhelmed they left to meet with the doctor at the hospital about their daughter's homecoming. Imagine their amazement when the doctor told them that they would have to create a clean and germ free environment for their daughter—by repainting the walls and replacing the carpet—because her white blood cell count was so low! They looked at each other and burst out laughing and crying at the same time. When they calmed down they were able to explain to the doctor what had just happened at home and that the insurance company was going to take care of everything!

As if this experience was not enough to convince them that everything happens for the best, they had another experience a short while later. While in the midst of getting the house repaired Anne discovered she was pregnant, something they had not been trying to do. At first they despaired a bit. How were they going to handle having an infant when they had to spend so much time taking care of their very ill, first child? A few months after their daughter came home from the cancer ward, she came out of remission and began to get very ill again. The doctors told them there was not much they could do with traditional methods, but there was a new "cord blood" procedure that had only been done four times before. It entailed using compatible blood cells from an umbilical cord for a transfusion. By this time, Anne was due to give birth in a few months. They agreed to do the procedure and scheduled it and a Cesarean operation on her expected due date. Anne gave birth to another daughter and the transfusion went well. Both girls are alive and healthy today. The eldest was declared completely cancer-free five years after the birth of her sister!

This unbelievably true story does not have much to do with the workplace, but it does show that we never really know how things will turn out. They can turn out for the best even when it seems like you are living your worst nightmare.

Key Point

"Adopt the attitude that everything happens for the best and discover how challenging situations could be positive in the long run."

Week Two: Share the Seeds of Enthusiasm with Others at Work

Once you have cultivated enthusiasm for your own work it becomes easy to share this positive attitude with others. An interesting thing happens when you do share your zeal with others, the enthusiasm spreads throughout the "garden" of the workplace like seeds carried by the wind. Most likely your enthusiasm will inspire others to spread their own seeds of enthusiasm. This week's tips offer suggestions for ways to disperse enthusiasm at work.

Share your zeal with others at work each day this week

Express your enthusiasm at work. Since you have already spent some time last week cultivating your enthusiasm, there is a lot to share. Let folks at work know when you are excited about a particular aspect of work. Make a point of letting people know what you enjoy about working with them and watch your enthusiasm spread to your colleagues at work!

Ann, a college professor who teaches English and serves on a not-for-profit board of directors with Suzanne, has a real gift for showing quiet enthusiasm. When things look financially or spiritually challenging for the organization, Ann has a way of quoting just the right poem that provides hope and inspiration for the group. Hearing Ann's poems helps the board think of new possibilities for their work in the world.

Look for signs of enthusiasm around you at work

Pay attention to expressions of enthusiasm by others this week. Chances are there are other people in your workplace who are naturally enthusiastic or who are actively cultivating enthusiasm, just like you are doing. Watch them and allow their enthusiasm to bolster your own. If you feel comfortable you may choose to acknowledge their enthusiasm and let them know how much it positively impacts you.

Seek out others at work that are enthusiastic

Be courageous and approach enthusiastic coworkers. Make a point to spend time with them. Positive feelings are contagious. When you get in a room with other enthusiastic people, the total amount of enthusiasm grows. Take the time to talk with your spirited colleagues about what their enthusiasm is about, as well as how they cultivate their enthusiasm. You will learn and keep the enthusiasm flowing.

Seeking out someone enthusiastic is an easy task for Krista. Suzanne is one of the most cheerful and uplifting persons in the world. And that is not an exaggeration! Whenever we go to a conference, Krista, who is more of an introvert, rides on Suzanne's wake of enthusiasm and meets all the people who quickly become Suzanne's friends. Krista has also learned from Suzanne how to be more enthusiastic herself. As a result she is more playful and energetic when giving speeches and conducting workshops.

Help others at work find their own enthusiasm

Spend some time this week identifying people at work that may require support and then share your enthusiasm with them. Just like there are certain plants that need more care in order to bloom, some people need assistance to feel or express enthusiasm for their work. If someone approaches you to complain about their work, encourage them to look at their work in a more positive way that evokes enthusiasm. You may want to ask them some of the questions you have been exploring like, "What do you enjoy about work?" Or "What can you learn from this situation that will help you in the future?"

Week Three: Serve Others Enthusiastically

Often when people are busy at work they do not always offer their time and attention enthusiastically to others. This week adopt an attitude of enthusiastic service. Your manner will make a difference to the people with whom you interact. Chances are your enthusiasm will spread to others and you will receive some of it back in return.

Smile at everyone with whom you interact this week

Connect with the people whom you pass and/or interact with by smiling at them. Smiling takes little effort and reaps big rewards for both you and the persons with whom you are interacting. It is good to practice smiling even when you do not necessarily feel like it. Focus on shifting your inner attitude and "act-as-if" you really mean it. It will benefit both you and the person at whom you are smiling. If you find smiling difficult to do when you do not feel it, read a poem like the one in the inspirational quote that follows to bring a smile to your face. Or motivate yourself by recollecting the benefits that smiling brings. Research studies show that a genuine smile increases the production of serotonin, the brain chemical that makes you feel happy. Smiling connects you with other people and gives your face a workout. You use more than 16 muscles every time you smile.

Remember to smile even when talking with someone on the phone and particularly if you are dealing with a problem. Although they may not be able to see your face, people will sense your smile coming through in the tone of your voice and in the positive energy you evoke. You may want to place a mirror on the desk so you can see yourself and remember to smile while talking on the phone.

Add friendly notes or inspirational quotes to your correspondence

Let others know how much you appreciate your working relationship with them. Whether it is putting a genuine thank you note on the bottom of a customer invoice or adding an inspirational quote on service to your regular business correspondence or email, the note will let people know you are enthusiastic about working with and serving them. Rod, the manager whom you might have already encountered in our book, is a master at writing notes of appreciation. He regularly writes notes to coworkers, clients, suppliers, and others whom he meets during the course of his work. He always lets the individual know how much he appreciates them as a person, working with them, and what they do for him. Those who receive cards from Rod always feel deeply acknowledged and are uplifted by his enthusiasm. We have been the recipients of numerous cards from Rod. His enthusiasm is so present that we have dubbed him the head of our fan club!

Inspirational Quote

Try Smiling

"When the weather suits you not,
Try smiling.
When the coffee isn't hot,
Try smiling.
When your neighbors don't do right,
Or your relatives all fight,
Sure 'tis hard, but then you might
Try smiling.
Doesn't change the things, of course—
Just smiling.
But it cannot make them worse—
Just smiling.
And it seems to help your case,
Brightens up a gloomy place,
Then, it sort o' rests your face—
Just smiling."

AUTHOR UNKNOWN

Enthusiastically support your coworkers

Respond enthusiastically this week whenever a coworker makes a request of you. Thank them for turning to you and do what you can to support them in their request. Even if it is a busy time and there is a lot of work to do, you can still enthusiastically acknowledge their trust in you. Let them know you are happy to help them and then negotiate a way (place, time, method) in which to support them and still meet your own work needs. They will appreciate your positive attitude and feel supported in their work.

Go the extra mile in serving your customers

Go out of your way this week to do more than usual in responding to your customers' requests, problems, and questions. Instead of focusing on everything that needs to be done, or on seeing customer calls as interruptions, give everything you have to the issue at hand. Allow yourself to be totally present to the person with whom you are speaking. Bring your enthusiasm for work into the interaction with them. To help you remember whom benefits from your service, create a mural or collage using thank-you notes from and photos of your direct customers or indirect end-users.

One of our clients, The Gardens Ice House, offers children's birthday parties complete with cake, ice cream, prizes, and of course, ice skating. When the children arrive at the rink on their special day, they are greeted by huge digital sign bearing their name in lights and wishing them a Happy Birthday. Susan, the staff member who arranges the parties, goes the extra mile by putting the birthday child's name in lights. Each year, following their party, children receive a birthday card from the rink.

Week Four: Tap into the Wellspring of Enthusiasm Within

Since by definition enthusiasm has to do with being filled with God or the Spirit of life, it is in essence a spiritual experience. Although some people do not typically think about spirituality in relation to their work, you can experience the divine and joyful nature of life itself by tapping into the wellspring of enthusiasm inside you while at work. This reservoir is not dependent on external circumstances and is consequently always available. By choosing to pay more attention to the source of natural joy within you during the workday, you will be renewed spiritually and will work with a happy, enthusiastic heart. And, as the following statement from Proverbs suggests, you will always be nourished: "He that is of merry heart hath a continual feast." (*The Westminster Study Edition Holy Bible*, Proverbs 15:15, King James Version)

> ## Exercise: Enjoying Enthusiasm
>
> This is a subtle exercise that may take some practice to experience fully. Whenever you feel deeply satisfied or experience pleasure at work, you can tap into the natural source of your enthusiasm by completing the following steps:
>
> 1. Become aware of your feelings of pleasure or satisfaction. Maybe you just finished a long-term project or signed a contract on which you have been working long and hard to bring to closure. Or maybe you are enjoying a moment of pleasure at work.
> 2. Allow yourself to revel in and savor the situation and your positive feelings.
> 3. Then mentally focus on the experience of pleasure itself. Let go of the specific circumstances that evoked your feelings and become aware of the basic energy inherent in your emotions. Try to trace the energy of your feelings to their internal source in your consciousness.
> 4. Rest for a few minutes in this interior space.

Spend time each day immersed in the inner fountain of joy and enthusiasm

Schedule time during the workday to turn your attention to the fountain of joy that is deep inside. At work there are many ways to tap into your inherent source of joy—meditating, praying, listening to music, laughing, thinking of loved ones, walking in nature, looking at the clouds moving in a bright clear sky, or even eating chocolate! Experiment with what evokes joy in you and allow yourself to spend some time reveling in it for a few minutes each day. Pay attention to the time of day that works best for you to do this—first thing in the morning before your day starts, just after lunch when your energy is waning, or after a disappointing meeting. Joe, an insurance agent, meets with other agents at lunch to study and discuss the Bible. He says that it gives them an opportunity to recharge their batteries and focus on something they enjoy without leaving work.

Use natural moments of enthusiasm to lead to the source of your joy.

Expand your experience of enthusiasm by using moments at work where you feel enthusiastic to take you to the source of internal joy. There are many exercises in the eastern spiritual traditions where people use the energy of a naturally occurring moment to carry them to the source of that experience inside. For instance, instead of quickly eating a piece of chocolate (or something else that gives great pleasure when eaten), eat it slowly and savor the flavor and pleasure it provides.

 Experience enthusiasm by remembering the divine and joyful nature of life itself

Practice evoking feelings of enthusiasm at work by remembering or focusing on the joyful nature of life. In their purest and most expansive forms, enthusiasm and joy are independent of external activities and circumstances. Therefore, you can experience enthusiasm even when there is little going on at work externally to evoke the feeling in you. By focusing attention on the essential positive qualities of life, you can generate feelings of enthusiasm from within.

> *"He that is of merry heart hath a continual feast."*
> THE WESTMINSTER STUDY EDITION HOLY BIBLE,
> PROVERBS 15:15, KING JAMES VERSION

MAY

HONOR THE SACRED AT WORK

> *"The whole of the universe declares the glory of God at work. Just as it is the nature of the Infinite to create, to be at work, it is the nature of every person to be creative, to be working."*
>
> EUGENE CALLENDER, D.MIN., *DARSHAN* MAGAZINE, VOL. 32

Introduction

May is a wonderfully alive month! Spring comes into full bloom and Mother Nature dresses herself in a glorious variety of brilliant colors in flowers, trees, birds, and insects. During this time of year, as the weather gets warmer and you spend more time outdoors, it is easy to appreciate the wonders of life and become drawn to the natural splendor around you. When there is a vibrant relationship with the natural energy of life, you automatically feel alive, renewed, and connected with the world. Native American writer N. Scott Momaday captures this experience in his poem "The Delight Song of Tsoai-Talee" from *The Gourd Dancer*.

> *You see, I am alive, I am alive*
> *I stand in good relation to the earth*
> *I stand in good relation to the gods*
> *I stand in good relation to all that is beautiful...*
> *You see, I am alive, I am alive!*

Although you may experience a sense of aliveness when you are in nature, you may not always feel in touch with the sacredness of life in that moment. What, exactly, is "the sacredness of life?" W.L. Reese describes it in the *Dictionary of Philosophy and Religion* as "an outward and visible sign of an inward and spiritual grace." Sacredness is the experience of feeling blessed and connected to life in a way that makes you wish to treat everything in that moment with great reverence. Chances are you have had some of these moments of deep recognition. Yet, because the signs of grace are often subtle, you may not always be aware of them in the midst of daily life.

Key Point

> *"When you are in relationship with the natural energy of life, you automatically feel alive, renewed, and connected with the world."*

There is a great analogy that illustrates how you can better see the inner sacredness amongst your regular activities. Have you ever tried to see through a wooden fence to the other side? If you have, you know that if you focus only on the fence when walking by, you are not able to see the garden or yard beyond. You just see the wooden fence. However, if you shift your attention to look through or beyond the fence, then something amazing happens—your eyes adjust to each fleeting glimpse through the cracks between the boards in the fence and you get a remarkably good view of what is on the other side. The narrow slits between the wood blur together as you walk by, giving you insight into what lies beyond the fence.

The physical world is like the fence. The surface appearance masks the sacred beauty within—not because the world is impenetrable, but because of the way you look at it. It is so easy to focus on the fences in life—the thoughts, feelings, activities, people, and events—that make up the world. Yet, in doing so, you miss the sacredness that shows through the spaces and pervades everything. This holiness is always present. You just shift your focus to perceive it. How you see the world and what you focus on affects what is actually seen.

At this point, you might be wondering what sensing and honoring the sacredness of life has to do with work. This may be the first time you have thought about the sacredness of your work. However, it is not a new concept. The world's faith traditions have always encouraged people to connect with the sacred in the midst of ordinary life. For example, the Christian faith advocates glorifying God through your household duties and work; Judaism encourages sanctifying ordinary daily experiences; and Islam asks people to look for indications of God's activity in everything going on around them. However, you do not have to follow a particular religion or adhere to any specific theological traditions to experience the blessedness of life. By taking the time to look a little more closely at your daily experiences, you will come into contact with sacredness in moments of beauty, love, creativity, joy, and service, as well as in nature. Everyone has access to this experience. Consequently, you can make daily life more holy simply by recognizing the sacredness that already exists in everything around you.

Essentially, if you look at work from a spiritual point of view, all the people, objects, and places with which you come in contact can be reminders and reflections of the sacredness of life. In fact, work itself can be experienced as sacred. If you take the time to pay attention to and honor the blessedness of life at work, then you will discover that it is possible to access in your daily life the same sense of aliveness you experience in nature. Honoring the sacred at work leads to a renewed sense of personal energy and a deep sense of connection and meaning. It also beneficially impacts your work and working relationships.

Key Point

"You can make your work life more holy simply by recognizing the sacredness that already exists in everything around you."

Imagine how those you work with might feel if you were to honor the inner grace within them. Imagine what impact recognizing their holiness would have on how you work together. At a minimum, if you were to open yourself to sensing and respecting the divine in others, you would be more compassionate and open-minded towards them. This would help build the trust and connection that are needed for high-performing work to happen. It would give you an opportunity to be connected to the wellspring of life itself, right there in the midst of your work. This month, honor the sacred while at work and see for yourself what happens!

Reflection Questions

Take two to three minutes to reflect and/or write about each of the following questions:

1. What does honoring the sacredness of work mean to me?
2. In what ways do I experience the sacred at work?
3. What stops me from seeing my work as sacred?
4. What steps can I take to experience my work as sacred more often?

Week One: Pay Attention to the Sacredness of Everyday Items at Work

Sacredness is already present in everything. Like the fence analogy in the introduction suggests, you need to shift the focal point. Remind yourself that even at work you are "standing on holy ground." This week, turn up the volume on your senses and see what is revealed to you at work. When you begin to look for the holiness in life, to look beyond "the fences" of the visible world around you, sights and experiences that were previously hidden from you become apparent. Here are some ways to pay attention to the sacredness of everyday things at work.

Inspirational Quote

"If you cultivate a vibrant curiosity and welcome the reports of your senses, you will see that the world is alive and moving toward [you] with rare epiphanies and wonderful surprises."
FREDERIC AND MARY ANN BRUSSAT, *SPIRITUAL LITERACY*

Give thanks for the everyday things you use in your work life
Express your appreciation for the items that you use everyday at work and the blessings they provide. The familiar phrase "God is in the details" implies that even the most mundane activities and tools at work can be seen as holy. The list of objects that contribute to your work is substantial. How often do you give thanks for the technology and engineering behind the electric lighting in the office? Your computer, printer, scanner, and other tools of productivity are powered by this same source of energy. What about the chair and desk where you work everyday? Or the implements and paper used to take notes during meetings? Apply the exercise that follows to honor the everyday items that make your work easier.

Road to Renewal

Exercise: Honoring the Simple Tools of Your Work Life

1. Identify the many everyday things in your office for which you are grateful. Use a table, like the one that follows, to list your ideas or, if you prefer, create a mind map.

2. Think about the blessings each item brings into your life and what your work life would be like without each one.

3. Then make a note of why you are thankful for each object. You might even want to think about all the energy and creativity that has gone into making these objects, including the attention of the people who made it possible for you to use these items. Here are a couple of examples.

   a. One item that Krista is very thankful for is small, colorful Post-It® Notes. She uses them for planning and scheduling her work. They allow her to avoid rewriting to-do lists and brighten up her office at the same time. She is aware of the creative energy that went into coming up with the idea, as well as the office supply deliveryman who delivers them to her office door with a smile each month. She also is grateful for the large windows in her office that allow light to come in where she sits at the computer, and for the fact that light exists so she can see all the colors in front of her.

   b. Suzanne is thankful for all the mauve office accessories that adorn her antique oak desk and file cabinet. They make a warm and cozy place for her to write and work. She also appreciates the soft watercolor of Cape May, New Jersey, which provides her with beauty each time she looks up from her desk; and the two chairs that provide a perfect place for a chat with Krista or a client. She loves the books that fill her office and cannot imagine working without her library. And then there are the computer, printers, scanner, and fax, all of which make her work life easier.

An Example of a Table to Use for Giving Thanks for Everyday Work Items	
Everyday Work Item	The Reasons Why I Give Thanks for This Item

Reflect at the end of the day on how sacredness was apparent to you
Take time at the end of the day to look back and notice the moments
of truth, insight, connection, and inspiration that happened during
your workday. Although grace-filled moments occur every day, it is
important to acknowledge them consciously or be explicitly aware
of them when they actually take place. Look for the most simple of
instances, like the person who held a door open as you struggled to
find a free hand, or the colleague who took time to support you on a
project. To help identify sacred moments at work, ask yourself
questions such as:

- "What blessings were inherent in the day?"
- "When did I experience being connected with the wholeness of life?"
- "How was divinity reflected in the people I met today?"
- "Where did I meet God today?"

Once when Krista was driving home from meeting with a client,
she experienced a prolonged sense of oneness. It was as if she could
almost see what the quantum physicists call the unified field of
energy. She understood that she was an element woven into this
continuum and she felt completely a part of the fabric of life. From
this place of connection, she realized how events happen at the right
moment and she had a deeper understanding of the role that she
and her client played in each other's lives.

Key Point

"Even at work you are standing on holy ground."

Recite poems or prayers that celebrate the sacredness of work
Commemorate your awareness of the sacredness of your everyday activities by reading or reciting poems or prayers that celebrate work and its many blessings. Take some time to discover poets like James Autry or David Whyte, both who write poems that are relevant to work life. Write your own poems and prayers to recite whenever you want to celebrate work. You might also turn to spiritually inspired authors like Kahlil Gibran or Marianne Williamson, who wrote the following lines in one of her prayers in *Illuminata*: "I dedicate this work to you. Use it to shower Your love into the world."

Several years ago, Krista wrote a simple poem while attending a leadership conference that reminds her of why she really works. It reads, "As I watch my destiny unfold, My heart melts like gold. My focus will not swerve, For I am here to serve." In addition to having this poem above her desk she also has the following quote from Gurumayi Chidvilasananda on the wall:

> *"While performing your duty, expect neither approval or disapproval.*
> *Do your work with the utmost love. This love alone will attract grace,*
> *and all that you do will become the worship of God. You will see your*
> *own Self in this worship."*

Suzanne regularly recites a line from a Twelve Step Program prayer, "God, I offer myself to Thee—to build with me and do with me as Thou wilt."

Talk with others about sacredness at work
Invite a small group of colleagues to have lunch and discuss what you think is sacred about your work, why it is blessed, and what you do to pay attention to it during the day. Then ask your colleagues what they find sacred about their work. It will give a lift to everyone's day and everyone may discover some new ways to see work as holy. There is power in naming what you see as sacred. Such power multiplies as other people name what is hallowed for them. However,

when talking about sacredness at work, it is important to be sensitive to and accepting of the differences in beliefs held by others and to refrain from imposing your beliefs on them. It is best to create a safe conversational environment in which everyone present is open, honest, and caring in their interactions and genuinely shares their personal experiences.

More people these days are eager to engage in this type of conversation. A poll done in 1999 on spirituality in the workplace found that about half of the people questioned had talked about their faith in the workplace sometime during the past 24 hours. Many of those who are doing so are creating regular groups where they can talk about spiritual issues with each other during lunchtime or after work. One estimate suggests that there are about 10,000 such groups in U.S. workplaces. One group that has received some publicity is the Spiritual Unfoldment Society at the World Bank. Employees get together once a week during lunch to listen to guest speakers and/or discuss a variety of spiritual topics and issues.

Week Two: Consecrate Your Work

Many people only focus on the sacredness of life one day a week. They reserve Saturdays or Sundays as their holy time, when they go to their place of worship or enjoy time with family and friends, celebrating all of life's blessings. Yet, you can treat each and every day this way. You can claim workdays as holy, too. Here are some ideas to consecrate (make holy) your work.

Acknowledge the blessings inherent in your work

Take time this week to think about the many gifts you receive from your specific job and what the job enables you to do for others. Invest time reflecting on the reasons why you think these particular blessings are present in your life. Remember to include the tough parts of your job. Although difficulties at work can be very challenging, they also provide you with gifts. Be aware, as the following Taoist story illustrates, that blessings often come in surprising ways.

> *There was an old farmer who had worked his crops for many years.*
> *One day his horse ran away. Upon hearing the news, his neighbors*

*came to visit. "Such bad luck," they said sympathetically. "May be,"
the farmer replied. The next morning the horse returned, bringing with
it three other wild horses. "How wonderful," the neighbors exclaimed.
"May be," replied the old man. The following day, his son tried to
ride one of the untamed horses, was thrown, and broke his leg. The
neighbors again came to offer their sympathy on his misfortune. "May
be," answered the farmer. The day after, military officials came to the
village to draft young men into the army. Seeing that the son's leg was
broken, they passed him by. The neighbors congratulated the farmer
on how well things had turned out. "Maybe," said the farmer.*

Exercise: Embracing the Good Things at Work

1. Create a form in your journal, like the one that follows, to begin a list of your work-related blessings. For example, Suzanne's blessings include both 1) being able to talk easily and 2) being a speaker/trainer.

2. After noting the good fortune your work provides, reflect and write down the reasons why this particular item is a blessing. For instance, Suzanne feels that her ability to talk easily allows her to be a better speaker/trainer and that this directly enables her to make a difference in people's lives while doing something she loves.

3. When thinking about all the ways in which work is a blessing, also go back in time and consider the patterns in your life that have led to your current work. For instance, when Suzanne was in first grade she went to the nurse's office. Although she was not feeling well, she was able to carry on a "healthy" conversation. When Suzanne's dad came to pick her up, he was told by the school nurse "Mr. Schmidt, you have a lovely daughter there. And can she ever talk! Maybe she was vaccinated with a phonograph needle?" Even in the first grade, Suzanne was doing her work in the world: "talking."

4. Keep the list where you can see it on a regular basis and update it monthly. Each time you see it, be aware of how fortunate you are to be doing the work you do.

An Example of A Table for Reflecting on Work-Related Blessings	
Blessing in my Work	Why This is a Blessing

Meditate on or pray for your work

Consecrate your work by reflecting on it in a spiritual way. Take some time to think about how your work is holy work. During your meditation or prayer, give thanks for your work or ask that your work be a blessing to others as well. As an alternative, you may choose to perform a specific ritual in which you bless your work. Krista often pauses before beginning a project and says a prayer, asking for blessings for the work and the people involved, as well as wishing the project to be an instrument of greater good. If you engage in this practice of praying for work often, you may discover that tasks take on new meaning and you begin to sense the invisible moments of grace more often.

Many people pray for or meditate on their work. Charito, an executive of an international consulting company, prepares for the day by praying for everyone in the company, asking that she and her employees "have the wisdom, the support, and the strength to do the very best to serve others in our work." Another CEO of a financial group, Wayne, uses meditation to look at his work, to see the patterns and connections. He remarked, "Instead of working hard, meditating is like standing back and letting the gift appear—what the answer is in terms of relationships, strategies, and designs."

Doug Wysockey-Johnson, the Executive Director of a faith based, not-for profit organization which is located in Washington, DC, goes to the Washington National Cathedral once a month to use the Cathedral Center for Prayer and Pilgrimage. During his day at the center, Doug prays for his work, his organization, and discernment about decisions facing him at his work. This once a month ritual plays a significant role in Doug's recognition of the sacredness of his work.

Key Point

> *"Work is made holy when you accept it as a sacred gift."*

Recognize that your work is a privilege and serves a greater purpose

Take a moment each day this week, or whenever you are feeling down about your work or challenged by it, to become aware of how work is a privilege. Step back and look at the bigger picture. Realize how many people in the world would be thankful for the kind of opportunity you have. Consider that you might be here on this Earth to fulfill a greater purpose other than being happy in this moment. Think about how your work might be part of a bigger sacrifice (in the sense of being a part of making something great happen). Explore how and why what you accomplish in the workplace is linked to a greater purpose.

For many people, their greater purpose at work involves serving and enhancing the well-being of others and life on the planet. Arnie, the retailer mentioned earlier, says that seeing his work as service is the thing that gives real meaning to his life. Robert, a VP in a large commercial real estate company, sees his work as his "calling" or vocation. He believes that the corporation is "a vehicle that God has created to enable us to develop different skills and parts of ourselves so that we can serve." And Paul, the former CEO of an international education organization, feels that the true purpose of his work is to give of himself in service. When he does that, he is satisfied. He often asks himself, "Of how much service have I been today?"

Embrace your current work

Accept your job as the work meant for you right now. Instead of focusing on the next job or the job you wish you had, explore the ways in which your work is just right for you at this point in time, at this point in your personal and professional development. Staying engaged in the present situation will allow you to do the work you are being asked to do in the moment. There is something to be said for working by faith and doing the very best possible for as long as you are in the current position at work. That is not to say that all work is perfect or that all work assignments are perfect matches. It is just a reminder that work is made holy when you accept it as a sacred gift, as your mission to do in the here and now. When you embrace your current work, you may be surprised at what happens.

This is what happened to Linda, a woman who Krista met at a leadership conference a few years ago. Linda was deeply dissatisfied with her job and came to the seminar hoping to get clarity on what she wanted to do. She had been searching for a new job for months and nothing had come of her efforts. Although she left the conference still unclear about her "true" work in the world, she felt less desperate than when she had arrived. She said that she could stick out her current job a little longer while she continued her search. A year later, Krista ran into Linda at another conference and inquired about Linda's job situation. With a big smile on her face, Linda said that she was still at the same organization and was loving it! When Krista asked what had happened to change things, Linda replied, "When I got back from the conference last year, I decided that while I was looking for a new job I would give myself to what I was currently doing, instead of focusing on what I didn't like. The interesting thing is, the more I focused on giving myself to my work, the more I began to like it. And my relationships with the people with whom I was working began to change. Things got so good, that I decided to stop looking for another job and stay where I was! It has been the best year! Who would have thought this would happen?"

Rhonda Neel would have! She conducts workshops on "Taking Your Job From Ordinary to Extraordinary." She says that the difference between a happy and an unhappy employee has less to do with the actual job itself and more to do with how people approach it, how they think about it, and the personal responsibility they take for it.

Week Three: Consider Your Work as Sacred

When seen from a spiritual point of view, all work can be thought of as an expression of creative divine energy. It can be considered to be both the invisible and visible activity of God. All work carries with it a meaning and connection with your purpose in life that goes beyond the mundane activities you perform each day. Expand your view of your work as sacred by practicing the tips provided here.

Inspirational Quote

 "All work is spiritual work. All work has meaning beyond the surface realities of a job, a production schedule, a product, or a paycheck. All work concerns spirit and soul and involves our ability to connect them with surface realities."

DICK RICHARDS, *ARTFUL WORK*

Become aware of the contribution you make to the world through your work

Reflect on how your work helps make the world a better place. The sacredness of your vocation becomes clearer when you see how your work makes a difference to society and the planet. Make a mental note of the positive impact your work has on humanity and the environment. Whose lives does your work touch? How does your work make other people's lives easier or better? If you find yourself not sure how to answer, know that you do not have to be involved in an altruistic occupation to make a contribution. Think of the ways in which your work enhances the well-being of others. For instance, Dan, the medical officer and physician at the Food and Drug Administration mentioned earlier, could simply see his work as reviewing new drugs for approval. Instead, he speaks about his work as helping the development and marketing of new drugs that will stop the spread of STI's (Sexually Transmitted Infections) in the world. He talks about the fact that his work touches millions of lives. When viewed in this way, his work becomes a sacred trust.

You might be thinking, "Of course, what Dan does contributes to others' well-being! Can someone in a more mundane job see the contribution they make?" The answer is, "Yes." Patricia Bovarie writes about Linda Kouch, a customer service representative in a call center who loves her work, in an ASTD article "Lessons from the Call Center." Linda makes and responds to calls all day long. You might think that it would be tiring to deal with people all day long, but Linda feels like she is making a difference in people's lives. She says in the article, "Everybody is different. And everybody has a different story. You just listen to people and let them talk about their lives...but at the end of the call when I know I've made their day better that's really rewarding."

"There is a creative energy in work that is somehow tied to God's creative energy. If we can understand that connection, perhaps we can use it to transform the workplace into something remarkable."
GREGORY F. A. PIERCE, QUOTED IN "GOD AND BUSINESS"

Discover the joy inherent in your work

Elevate your awareness of the holiness of life by focusing on the joy that your work brings. Sacredness and joy are closely linked. While you may not always feel joyful at work, you can experience joy by evoking and being open to it. Explore how your work brings you joy overall. Then identify more specifically the different situations and people that bring you joy each day. For instance, Krista generally gets great joy from working as a coach and consultant. She feels energized and alive when doing this work. More specifically, she enjoys having conversations with long-term clients with whom she has established close relationships. Krista takes pleasure in these conversations, since they are usually thought provoking and uplifting. She also delights in synthesizing new material and creating innovative programs for clients. She likes being able to read the latest books and apply new ideas to her work with clients.

"We have a right to and a need for joy in our work...Much of our living is about our work. There is no creation without some joy."
MATTHEW FOX, *THE REINVENTION OF WORK: A NEW VISION OF LIVELIHOOD FOR OUR TIME*

Discern the deeper meaning of your work

Contemplate the meaning that work provides for you. Sacredness and meaning are also closely related. By exploring the deeper meaning of your work, you can uncover its sacredness. Go beyond the typical answer such as, "My work allow me to provide for my family." Consider how your work is an expression of creative divine energy, how it is essential to the work of the greater whole. Look for the ways in which work enables you to participate in the divine process of creation. Discover how the divine manifests itself through you at work. Think about how work is related to your most profound purpose in life. For instance, Krista believes that her ultimate reason for living is to use her gifts and talents to serve humanity and become fully and continually aware of the divine energy pervading all life. As a result she periodically takes time to appreciate how work enables her to uplift others and further both her own spiritual growth and that of her clients. She frequently prays, meditates, and opens herself to inner guidance while at work so that she can make room for the divine to work through her.

Key Point

"Sacredness and meaning are also closely related. By exploring the deeper meaning of your work, you can uncover its sacredness."

Week Four: Be Still and Experience the Sacred at Work

By slowing down, holding still, and being silent, you can become aware of the sacredness within and around you. As writer Sue Patton Thoele, quoted in *The Wonders of Solitude*, puts it, "Only in the oasis of silence can we drink deeply from our inner cup of wisdom," That sacred place where words and activity come to a halt is a necessary part of a full life. Yet holding still is counter culture to the way many Americans do things. The great American society is FAST. Fast is not necessarily good or healthy and it is certainly not a way to experience the divine. Make an effort this week to create your own slower pace and develop a daily ritual of taking sacred time to be still and silent. Here are some ways to get started.

Schedule short intervals each morning and afternoon to be still Put on the brakes and sit quietly with yourself for ten minutes each morning and afternoon. During this time, allow yourself to do nothing, to just "be" and notice what feelings, thoughts, and experiences arise. At first you may feel uncomfortable stopping your activity and being still. If you can remain quiet for some time, eventually you will begin to experience a sense of peace and calm. Treat these periods as sacred by scheduling them just as you would any other meeting. Be firm about this because it is easy to say, "Ah, it is only ten minutes." Quiet time can make all the difference in your work and for you. For this week, allow yourself to "be still and know," twice a day, everyday. Then make it a permanent, sacred way of working. For example, Robert Shapiro, former CEO of Monsanto, incorporated meditation twice a day into his daily schedule at work.

Connect with the sacredness of the world around you

Spend a few minutes each day absorbing the wonder of nature. Gaze out a window at the clouds, go outside and feel the gentle breezes, take time to smell the roses (both literally and figuratively), or focus on the amazing variety of trees, flowers, insects, and birds in your local environment. Nature abounds with the sacred and is a key source of renewal. Spending time in the natural world allows the mind to rest and is a reminder that you are a part of something larger than you—something truly holy.

Inspirational Quote

"Come away with me, my beloved, and rest awhile."
JESUS, *HOLY BIBLE*, MARK 6:31 (ADAPTED)
SOURCE, MICHAEL NOYES' WEB SITE

Take a mini-spiritual retreat each day

Create a twenty-minute retreat, either at work or home, each day. Rachel Harris, Ph.D., in her book *20-Minute Retreats*, advises that you should replenish your soul daily by taking refuge from worldly activities. You might take a walk every morning before the rest of the world wakes up so that you can take in all of nature without interruptions from other people. Or you might find a quiet park to visit at lunch. You may choose to do yoga in a quiet room somewhere in the office or at night before going to bed. Or you might write in a journal or read a passage from an inspirational book every morning or during a break. As we mentioned earlier, Krista meditates and Suzanne journals and prays. We both find that these practices reconnect us with the sacredness of our lives and help us run on plenty for the entire day.

"A retreat can be anything that allows us to intentionally enter another world where time slows to nonexistence, silence prevails, and a certain tranquility permeates the atmosphere."

RACHEL HARRIS, PH.D., *20-MINUTE RETREATS*

Rest at least once a week

Refrain from doing work and personal chores at least one day a week and allow your mind, body, emotions, and spirit to relax and renew. Many professionals work 60-hour weeks and then go home to a multitude of household tasks. And for many people working on the weekends is the norm. When you spend most of your time working, you deplete yourself and leave little room for the experience of sacredness. To function effectively and to come into contact with the divine, humans require both rest and quietude. The concept of Sabbath, introduced in the Hebrew Scriptures, honors the fact that even God rested on the seventh day. Why should humans be any different? Do yourself a favor and allow yourself to be at leisure at least one day this week. Your family and friends will be glad to be with you. You will be glad to feel more relaxed and at peace when you return to work.

"No workplace can be truly alive... until we insist that our work will not be the humdrum product of a sleeping spirit but a glorious monument to who we really are."

JOHN COWAN, *THE COMMON TABLE*

JUNE

PLAY AT WORK

"Sometimes we simply need to unlearn our polarized belief that only work is important and realize that without refreshing, renewing play, we lower our capacity for high-quality work and our ability to enjoy life fully."

ANN McGEE-COOPER, ED.D.,
TIME MANAGEMENT FOR UNMANAGEABLE PEOPLE

Introduction

Summer is here and it is time to play! For many people, June brings to mind pleasant memories of the end of school and the beginning of "lazy, hazy, crazy days of summer." Do you remember the exhilaration you felt when the final bell rang on that last day of school and everyone ran out into the day, finally free to play? For some people, summer meant family reunions with favorite aunts, uncles, and cousins, with games, picnics, and ice cream for all. For others, the days were spent at summer camp playing "Capture the Flag," and the biggest worry of the day was how to pull a really good prank on the counselor. Maybe you spent hours swimming and hanging out with your friends at the pool, lake, or "old watering hole."

Would you love to reclaim some of the joy and freedom you felt back then? One way to do this is to play at work. Playing at work may at first glance seem like an impractical idea. It is certainly not the norm in most organizations. After all, who has the time in the midst of all the demands to stop working and to play? Besides, play is kids' stuff! While these statements might reflect typical beliefs held by many in the work world, pleasure and fun do not have to be relegated to kids or life outside work. Play is essential to renewal at work and can be easily incorporated into your daily life. As Pat Kane, an advocate of creating a play ethic in our society and author of the article "Play for Today" says, "meaningful work and serious play can become the same thing."

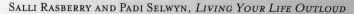

"The best times occur in our lives when we are playful, wild, and spontaneous. Some of our most playful moments become our most cherished memories."

SALLI RASBERRY AND PADI SELWYN, *LIVING YOUR LIFE OUTLOUD*

Essentially, play increases enjoyment and brings many other benefits to both you and your work. For instance, playing at work can have a positive impact on the following attributes of work:

- Productivity—because play invigorates you
- Creativity—because play allows you to experiment with new ideas in non-threatening ways
- Mental clarity—because play enables you to see the world in new ways, improves memory, and leads to sharper reasoning
- Relationships with coworkers—because you have fun together and build trust
- Morale and job satisfaction—because you have more fun while doing work, attending meetings, and serving on committees
- Ability to learn—because play provides you with multiple ways to take in information
- Well-being—because play makes you laugh, increases optimism, and relieves stress

The bottom line is you feel better, perform better, and are more renewed when you play at work! It makes you and life more interesting. As the old saying goes, "all work and no play makes Jack a dull boy (or Jill a dull girl)!"

So how do you actually play at work? Contrary to popular belief, play is not the opposite of work. Nor is play idle time. You do not have to stop working to play. You can play anywhere, anytime because in reality, play has more to do with your attitude than with any particular activity. Whenever you do something, bring a spontaneous, creative, curious, humorous, experimental mindset to what you are doing! Do something unexpected! Be willing to look silly or goofy! By acting in these fun ways, you are creating openings to play at work. In addition to supporting you in cultivating a playful attitude, this month's tips also offer a variety of ways to incorporate play into your work

Reflection Questions

Take two to three minutes to reflect and/or write about each of the following questions:
1. Do I consider myself playful? Do I value play and make time for it in my daily life?
2. In what ways do I currently play while at work?
3. What stops me from being playful at work?
4. How can I play more often or be more playful at work?

Week One: Give Yourself Permission to Play at Work

If you are thinking, "I am not a very playful person," you are not alone. Many people gradually lose the natural playfulness they had as children and by adulthood they have forgotten how to play. There are also many messages and beliefs that people absorb over time that stop them from being playful as adults. You may have been conditioned, both by parents and the culture in which you work, to value work more than play. Do you remember ever being told "You cannot go out to play until all your homework and chores are done?" Maybe at some point you were told that you were not funny or creative. Perhaps your first boss told you that work is a serious matter and not an appropriate place to play. To fit in, you suppressed all natural playfulness. You might be a task- or results-oriented person who believes that play is unproductive and a waste of time because it does not always produce a concrete end product.

Key Point

"The bottom line is you feel better, perform better, and are more renewed when you play at work!"

While your beliefs and attitudes on work and play have served you well in many instances, always valuing work over play means that you wind up not playing. The solution to this problem is to give yourself permission to play—both at work and outside work. While you do not want to throw all your work to the wind, you can always work with a playful attitude. Here are some ways to begin to give yourself permission to play at work.

Study the benefits of play

Do some research on the benefits of play at work, particularly if you are someone who has to be convinced about the advantages. Sometimes it helps to have data on the benefits of a new activity to assist in changing your beliefs. Check out the resources on play listed at the end of the book or go online to get information on the benefits of play and related topics like humor, laughter, and creativity at work. (Check out www.deepfun.com) Once you know how much play can positively impact your well-being and work, you will have more concrete and rational reasons for giving yourself permission to play at work. You can also look for data to support playing at work in the experiences of people around you. Identify the most playful persons in your organization and watch to see how productive they are. You might also turn to your own experience for information. Recall work moments when you had fun doing something and what the results were. Or recollect your most fun class in high school or college and how easy it was to learn in that class and how much the experience is still with you today.

Key Point

> *"Once you know how much play can positively impact your well-being and work, you will have more concrete and rational reasons for giving yourself permission to play at work."*

Explore your beliefs about work and play

Set aside some time to think about the attitudes and beliefs about work and play that you have inherited. Pay attention to which beliefs support you and which ones stop you from playing. The following exercise offers one way of exploring what you think about play at work.

> ## Exercise: Exploring Beliefs about Work and Play
>
> 1. Make a list (or create a mind map) of all the messages you have received from parents, teachers, coaches, bosses, and coworkers about work and play. For instance, you may have heard a message like "You have to finish all your work before you can play."
> 2. Once you have completed the list, review it to see how many of the messages support being playful and how many stop you from playing. Think about how each of these messages impacts your playfulness at work.
> 3. Next create a new list with only supportive and positive statements about work and play. In creating this second list, rephrase some of the negative messages on your first list to be more encouraging. For instance, "You have to get all your work done before you can play" can be rewritten to read, "If I take some time to play in the middle of work, it will help me work better."
> 4. Post the second list somewhere where you can see it and read it several times a day, every day this week. If you catch yourself thinking a thought that blocks you from being playful at work, look at the list and choose a positive statement to repeat to yourself.
> 5. Notice how your attitude towards play changes over the course of the week.

Krista became more aware of her opinions on play when her son, Andrew, was getting his art portfolio ready to apply to art colleges. She became very anxious when Andrew would go off to "hang out" (play) with friends instead of working on his portfolio. After reflecting on her anxiety, she realized that her feelings were being triggered by her belief that "you havExpectationsr work done before you play or it won't happen." She understood that this deeply held thought was making her think Andrew would not finish his portfolio or that because he did it at the last minute he would not get into art school. She began working on letting this thought go by replacing it with the idea that he would successfully complete his portfolio. It helped her even more to let go of her old belief when Andrew was accepted at every school to which he applied, including one of the top art schools in the country! It became very obvious to Krista that you do not always have to get your work done to play. You can play and still be successful in your work.

Get "unstuck"

Experiment with playing at work, even if you feel you cannot do it. You may believe it is difficult to do and that you have no choice in the matter. It is not that you do not want to be playful, you just do not see how it can be done. You may not know how to play at work or you may not see yourself as a playful person. You may fear experiencing serious consequences (like losing your job) if you play at work. You believe you must keep working in the same old way. In other words, you feel stuck! Trapped with no way out! Ann McGee-Cooper, Ed.D., in *Time Management for Unmanageable People*, describes what getting "stuck" at work can be like:

> *"Usually when we have a big work load, the first thing to go is fun time and we go into a negative and unproductive spiral—the more we work, the more tired we get, the less creative or open minded we are, and the less we accomplish, so we get further behind and then we think we have no time for play."*

The way to get unstuck is to realize that when it comes to play at work you have more choice and more time than you think. Step back and look at your situation objectively. Talk it over with a friend to see if you may be over-exaggerating the potential negative consequences of playing at work and/or ignoring the costs of not playing. Explore how you are contributing to being stuck and brainstorm a list of choices you can make. Choose an alternative that makes you stretch outside your comfort zone and act on it!

Key Point

> *"The way to get unstuck is to realize that when it comes to play at work you have more choice and more time than you think."*

Go ahead and just play

Take a risk and play at work. Do not worry about being awkward, making a fool out of yourself, having other people judge you, or being afraid that playing will affect your job performance. Stop focusing on any fears you may have, take a deep breath and, simply play! In other words, just do it!

The key to taking action is to recognize your fears and act anyway. Start with small steps, like getting a few toys for the office, wearing a funny tie or earrings to work, or writing a staff memo in a bright color. After you have taken action, notice whether the outcome you feared took place. Most likely you will find that what you were worried about did not happen. Continue to take play risks and notice what happens. Eventually your fears will fade away. You may discover that it is not worth worrying about what other people think because most people do not care that much about you playing at work. Before you know it, you will be giving yourself permission to play freely and thinking thoughts like, "Why waste all that time and energy worrying when I could be playing and working instead?"

Suzanne chairs the Personnel Committee for Faith at Work, a not-for-profit organization located in Washington, DC. One October the committee had a particularly challenging agenda, including items that concerned serious discussions about the future direction of the organization. Since it was Halloween, Suzanne brought animal noses for each committee member. The meeting began with members wearing their animal noses and having a really good laugh as they took a picture to share with the Board of Directors. This moment of levity allowed the group to approach their very important work with a modicum of lightness and good humor.

Week Two: Learn How to Play at Work from Kids

Even though as an adult you may have forgotten how to play, you can recapture the energy playing brings by relearning it. One of the best ways to learn about play is to turn to the experts—kids! As Matt Weinstein, the author of *Managing to Have Fun*, says "playfulness is a forgotten language that adults can easily relearn. Once we recall that feeling of jubilation that we once knew as children, we can even make work fun." This week allow yourself to become the student of a master of play. Then take what you learn to work. Even if you are already fairly good at playing at work, take some time to relearn some lessons from the kids in your life. Play is a process that benefits from practice and regular renewal. Here are some ways to stay young by learning about play from children.

> *"We do not stop playing because we become old, we grow old because we stop playing."*
>
> OLIVER WENDELL HOLMES, *BRAINY QUOTES*

Spend time playing with a child

Make a date to play with a young child in your life. When you get together, allow the child to be the leader. Permit him or her to direct what you do and follow the lead. Join in his or her world. Get down on the floor and play a part in making up the rules as you go along, engaging in "make believe" conversations, and following your whims. It may take you a few times to let go of being in control and to follow along. It takes time to unlearn our adult, competitive, goal-oriented behavior and relax into the spontaneous process of play. After the play date, take a few moments to notice how you feel. It is likely that you will feel both relaxed and energized. Also, take some notes on what you learned and how to apply these lessons to playing at work. For instance, you may notice that the child you were with asked a lot of silly questions, said whatever came to his or her mind, and liked to try new things. You might then experiment with asking some fun questions, saying silly things or what you are really thinking, and trying new ways of doing things at work. Play with magical thinking or bring your own toys to work!

This is what Peter, the owner of a recruiting firm, did. He had been too busy to spend as much time with his 10 year-old son as he wished. So, since he was working with his coach to develop more playfulness at work, he invited his son to go with him to a toy store and help him pick out some toys for the office. As payment for his son's "consulting services" Peter bought his son a football he wanted and they played with it in the hallway when they got back to the office.

Taking time to learn from and speak with children is important regardless of your station in life. There is a wonderful story written by Tony Payton that appeared in *The Washingtonian Magazine* about Former President, Jimmy Carter and Jack Walsh, a political consultant from Boston. When Jimmy was President of the United

States, he called Jack to ask him to serve in a major role in Carter's reelection campaign. Jack was not home, but his young son answered the phone. President Carter talked to the young boy for quite a while and told him a story about bunny rabbits. When Jack came home, his son told him that "the mayor" had called from the White House and that "the mayor" had told him a story. Jack could barely believe his ears. When he called The White House, Jack heard the President say "Thanks for calling back." Could it be that President Carter learned some of his peace making skills from children?

Observe children at play

Put aside some time this week to go to a playground to watch children at play. It can be renewing and you can learn a lot simply from observing children at play because they naturally have a playful attitude. Kids always have time to play. They perfect play. Life for them is full of opportunities to play. Make note of what you observe about their positive play behavior and think about how, while at work, you can do what they do. For example, children play simply for the pleasure of it—because it feels good. They are also very active, always on the move, stretching the limits of their bodies and minds. They are very curious and will follow whatever catches their attention. They use their imaginations and honor the signals they get from their bodies. They insist that others pay attention to and nurture them.

How might you be different at work if you did what kids do? Take your observations and apply them to your next meeting. Ask others to pay attention to what each person says at the meeting. Figure out ways to nurture your colleague's ideas in the meeting. Suzanne was working with a group of women who participated in a physical challenge course. After they had successfully completed their activities, she asked about their experience. The women reported that watching their children do similar exercises on school field trips gave them courage for successfully completing the course. They said "After all. Why should the kids get to take all the risks?" The women were pleased that they had learned from their children to playfully face the obstacles before them on the course.

"It can be renewing and you can learn a lot simply from observing children at play because they naturally have a playful attitude."

Recall your own childhood

Recollect your own experience as a child to recapture some of your own youthful playfulness. Because everyone is a kid at heart, you do not have to rely solely on other children to learn about playfulness. There are many ways to recall your own childhood and bring it into the present moment. Think back to what you loved to do as a child during the summer. Then find a way to do that activity now. Remember some of the zany things you said and did as a kid. Then, say or do something silly at work this week. You might also recall something that you were curious about as a child and have yet to explore. Explore it now. Rediscover a childhood pleasure. Dan, the medical researcher at the Food and Drug Administration you may have read about previously in the book, and his work colleague, Norm, both loved Laffy Taffy® candy as kids. They take turns buying Laffy Taffy® for one another at work. Dan reports that when they eat their Laffy Taffy® and read the riddle on the wrapper during the workday they are reminded to "lighten up."

Exercise: Incorporating Childhood Activities into Your Work

Salli Rasberry and Padi Selwyn, in *Living Your Life Outloud*, recommend the following exercise for learning to play:

1. Make a list (or mind map) of all the activities you loved to do as a child.
2. Review the list, and imagine yourself doing each activity. Recall how you felt while doing your favorite types of play.
3. After going over the entire list, look at it again. Are there any activities you would enjoy doing now? How can you use the information to create play opportunities at work now?
4. Make a second list of all the things you wished to do or learn as a child and have yet to do. Think about what you would enjoy now and how you could incorporate those activities into work.

Week Three: Plan for Play at Work

Even if you give yourself permission to play and learn from kids, failing to consciously incorporate play into daily life will result in very little play. It is important for your work and well-being to refresh yourself through play and explicitly plan play into the day. Play is a renewing resource that is as important to your emotional, mental, physical and spiritual health as are other activities like exercise, rest, quiet time, and productive work.

Inspirational Quote

 "Each day, and the living of it, has to be a conscious creation in which discipline and order are relieved with some play and pure foolishness."
MAY SARTON, QUOTED IN
TIME MANAGEMENT FOR UNMANAGEABLE PEOPLE

 ### Add play to your "to-do" list

Include at least one play activity to your list of work activities each day. If you have a hard time thinking of play activities to add to the "to-do" list, make a separate list of all the things you enjoy doing and wish you had time for. Your list might include talking with a friend, playing golf, drawing, writing letters, listening to music, reading a good book, or learning a craft. Be creative in how to do these activities at work. For example, while you may not be able to leave work to play golf, you could read a golf magazine or practice your putting in the office at lunch. When you first begin to add play to your to-do list, you may feel it is taking time away from work. However, pay attention to the impact that playing has on you and your work. You will soon notice that play actually reenergizes you, allowing you to get more done in less time. You may even have energy left at the end of the day or a long meeting!

We know five partners of a start-up business who experienced the importance of including play on their action list. They were having a long orientation meeting for nine new employees. There was a lot of material to cover in the amount of time they had so they were tempted to focus all their time on sharing information. In the end, they decided to spend half an hour at the beginning of the meeting doing a fun activity with the new employees. Everyone was divided up into four groups (including the partners) and given props such as grass skirts and balloons. Each group was given 15 minutes to come up with a skit that depicted one of the services the business offers. To make things more interesting, the skits were set to music and no speaking was allowed. They had a hilarious time presenting and figuring out what the skits represented. The activity helped the new employees bond with each other and the partners, and the energy that was created by it helped them all get through the long meeting that followed.

Schedule play at work

Make play dates with yourself at work. Consciously set time aside for play by putting it into your daily schedule. Write your play dates in your calendar—in pen! Think about the times during the day when you could most benefit from some play. For instance, you might schedule a play period directly after a long and serious meeting, or in the early afternoon when your energy wanes a bit. Scheduling a brief play date about an hour after lunch will probably improve your energy and help you think better the rest of the afternoon. Sarah, an office administrator in an association, finds great delight in making hooked rugs. She hangs an unfinished rug on her office wall and each day at lunch she makes a "play date" with herself to spend some time doing what she loves.

Inspirational Quote

"Make a point to add playtime all through your calendar and then notice the significant improvement in energy, enthusiasm, flexibility, teamwork, and productivity you experience. Creative, balancing play can be worth a lot!"

ANN MCGEE-COOPER, ED.D.,
TIME MANAGEMENT FOR UNMANAGEABLE PEOPLE

Remind yourself to play

Create ways to prompt yourself to play. You may have reached the point where you are now able to give yourself permission to play and are beginning to schedule it into the calendar. However, you may discover that the busyness of life takes over and, despite all good intentions, you forget to make or take time to play. It can be challenging to learn a new habit, particularly if you are in an environment that does not directly support that behavior. Develop as many ways to remind yourself as possible.

Experiment with writing a note in your calendar and highlighting the play dates using a bright color. You might create an eye-catching or fun screen saver. You might leave sticky notes with reminders on them in many strategic places around you. In the beginning it is a good idea to surround yourself with reminders. Make them as personal as possible—things to which you can relate—and then place them in multiple locations. Put them in spots where you will be surprised by them or move them around so they do not fade into the background of your awareness.

Write yourself a play prescription today

Have fun in small doses whenever you are feeling depleted in any way—physically, mentally, emotionally, or spiritually. Write yourself a prescription for play. Take some mini-renewal breaks (two to five minutes in length) several times a day. There are many ways to have moments of fun at work. For example, you might keep cartoon books (like Dilbert™ or Calvin and Hobbes™) in your office to read during a break. Or work on a puzzle or word game for a few minutes. You might even play around with drawing, doodling, or writing silly poems. There are many games and toys you can keep in the office with which to play, such as Koosh® basketball, yo-yos, Slinkys®, Hula Hoops®, wind up toys, squishy stress toys, and Cosmo Cranium®, to name just a few.

After playing football in the hall with his son, Peter, the recruiter mentioned earlier, decided that it would be fun to play Frisbee® or football at work. Every so often now, he invites the employees to join him outside to play at lunchtime. He also occasionally sends memos to people in the office by turning it into a paper airplane and flying it over the top of the cubicle dividers.

Week Four: Infuse Play into Your Work Activities

Because play also involves a particular a way of thinking as much as it does specific kinds of activity, you do not always have to stop work to play. You can be playful right in the midst of your work! Remember, the best work, the most satisfying work, the most productive work is also the most fun. This week while doing your work, think playfully and infuse fun into your work activities. The goal is to become so playful at work that the boundary between work and play disappears.

Look at situations with a humorous eye

Take your work more lightly this week and laugh at some of the work situations and yourself. Instead of getting upset or stressed when things at work do not go your way, look at what is going on with a humorous eye. Humor is a kind of play. Remind yourself that life can be funny and unpredictable and that the situation is not as serious as it might seem at first glance. Look for something to laugh about in the situation. This is not always easy to do, particularly in the moment. Because it is easier to laugh at yourself and the situation after-the-fact, it is effective to use tools, such as cartoons about worklife, to help. If you are having trouble seeing the humor in the situation, look at some relevant cartoons.

For instance, if you are prone to working on your vacation imagine this cartoon that one of Suzanne's friends gave her as a reminder to relax on vacation. The cartoon depicts a woman on the beach sitting at a desk complete with phone and in-basket, all of which she has built from sand. She is sitting at the desk looking extremely stressed—probably waiting for the phone to ring—and her husband says " For heaven's sake, Blanche, relax!" Next time you are tempted to take your work on vacation with you, think about how silly Blanche looked at the beach.

Key Point

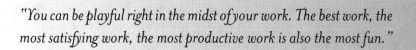

"You can be playful right in the midst of your work. The best work, the most satisfying work, the most productive work is also the most fun."

Find playful ways to express yourself at work

Communicate in playful ways at work. Dan, Suzanne's husband, enjoys wearing fun socks and ties to work. On golf day, he wears a tie and socks adorned with golf balls. On Valentine's Day, he wears a heart tie with matching socks that play "Let Me Call You Sweetheart." Although his job is serious, wearing his fun ties and socks brings lightness to his and his colleagues' work. (We will not tell you about the matching underwear that Suzanne says he wears!)

Here are some ways that you can express yourself playfully at work:

- include positive, humorous messages in your e-mails
- write your memos in crayon or colored markers or pens
- give yourself a playful title—Suzanne refers to herself at the "The Queen of Fun"—or call yourself a player not a worker
- incorporate cartoons in your presentations or reports that speak to the topic in a fun way—or include a cartoon with a client note or invoice
- bring to work a fun picture that makes people laugh and leave it on a coworker's desk with a note to pass the picture along to someone else, with a note to pass it on again.
- write prescriptions for play for your colleagues and team members
- bring pretzels or licorice to pass around the office on an obscure holiday, like Ground Hog's Day.

Will your colleagues think you are a little crazy? Perhaps! Will they enjoy themselves? Yes!

Play with representations of ideas

Create representations of your ideas whenever you are working on a new idea or project. For instance you can draw your ideas on paper, create models out of LEGOS®*, Tinkertoys, or blocks, or create 3-D pictures on the computer so you can look at your idea from all angles. The point is to make your ideas more concrete and play with a variety of possible scenarios. Explore ways in which other people play with concepts at work. There are many ideas included in *Jump Start Your Brain*, written by Doug Hall.

* The Lego company now has a product available called Lego Serious Play®. It is an innovative process that uses play and LEGO® bricks as a means to enhance business performance.

"[Play at work] is about improvising with the unanticipated in ways that create new value. Any tools, technologies, techniques, or toys that let people improve how they play seriously with uncertainty is guaranteed to improve the quality of innovation.... You cannot be a serious innovator unless you are willing and able to play."

MICHAEL SCHRAGE, *SERIOUS PLAY*

Find ways to mix business with pleasure

At work this week, be inventive about mixing business with pleasure. There are many ways to blend the two. Awhile ago, Suzanne planned a meeting with a group of fellow colleagues. The meeting was scheduled for June 14, Flag Day, and one of Suzanne's favorite annual holidays. Suzanne's colleagues decorated her office in red, white, and blue and arranged for Uncle Sam to visit during the meeting! What great fun everyone had! The activity took about 15 minutes and it kept people energized all day!

Here are some other examples of ways to mix pleasure with business:

- Energize meetings by doing some fun exercise together or by playing music in the background. *The Mozart Effect* by Don Campbell describes how some classical music has a beneficial affect on productivity, creativity, and well-being.
- Celebrate with others at work every month. Celebrate work milestones, coworkers birthdays, the arrival of a season, or a holiday. If you are in a very playful mood, you could even invite everyone to dress in a costume that is in keeping with the occasion.
- Do something unexpected for the people with whom you work. Matt Weinstein in *Managing to Have Fun* describes a situation in which a man placed a walky-talky inside a puppet and left it in a busy office location that he could see without being noticed. Whenever someone walked by the puppet, he would use his part of the walky-talky to make the puppet talk. Some people actually stopped and had conversations with the puppet! Find your own way to surprise people in your office.

- Write a poem or limerick about a recent work event, project, or team that can be shared with your coworkers. For example, Norm who works as a medical officer for the Food and Drug Administration writes poems about his colleagues and the products that they review. An all time group favorite is Norms' limerick about Viagra.
- Learn a fun skill and show it off at work. For instance, become skilled at a magic trick or practice performing a silly activity from books like *Totally Useless Skills* by Rick Davis.
- Choose a familiar tune, cheer, or song and create your own lyrics to go with it. Teach it to your coworkers and sing it at appropriate moments. Michael Aronin, a much-admired member of the National Speakers Association (NSA) who lives with and makes fun of his Cerebral Palsy, spoke at NSA's 2002 national convention. The NSA Washington, DC chapter was so proud of him that they sang a song (that Suzanne wrote for him) with great enthusiasm at dinner one night. The song was to the tune of Michael Row the Boat Ashore and poked fun at the fact that Michael did not fall when he was talking—something about which Michael himself was happy! He likes the song so much he is going to feature it in a book about his life.
- Keep a collection of 'wild and crazy" hats and other costume props in your office. Wear one of them when you are feeling inspired and invite colleagues who visit your office to put one on as well. Suzanne is known for her crazy hats and props. They are one of the first things you notice when you walk into her office.
- Most of all—have fun!

14

JULY

RELAX AT WORK

"If you can learn to be calm when you need to ... and no matter what circumstances or workmates do to test your patience... you'll still feel good about your work. You'll cope better, you'll enjoy a zest for life that stressed people only fantasize about, and you'll look forward to going to work each day with a childlike enthusiasm."

PAUL WILSON, *CALM AT WORK*

Introduction

July brings to mind that time of year when life tends to slow down a bit. You may find yourself taking time to relax and enjoy the longer, warmer days of summer. Decks become a place to unwind and hammocks beckon! July is often when people take time off from work, either by leaving early or going on vacations. Incorporating relaxation into your daily routine does not need to rely solely on "getting away from it all." You can learn from the natural pull that comes with summer how to rest and revitalize yourself in the midst of work.

About now, you may be thinking that relaxation is out of place at work. You are there to perform tasks, rather than take it easy. So, what is the point of relaxing at work? Learning to relax is at the heart of working and living well. It is also important for your creativity, resiliency, and productivity. Approaching your work in a tranquil manner also allows you to respond to stressful situations with flexibility and objectivity. As Naomi Levy says in her article "Change Your Life...Take a Day of Rest," "True rest gives us a completely different perspective on all of life's difficulty. It allows us to heal, to reflect, to give thanks, and to face whatever lies ahead with a renewed sense of calm."

Key Point

"Learning to relax is at the heart of working and living well."

Essentially, calmness and relaxation are good for you and your work, and they are good for your organization as well. Paul Wilson in *Calm at Work* suggests that calm, enthusiastic employees generate higher output, and that means fewer industrial problems, more work completed each hour, and reduced staff turnover. And as the following brief fable suggests, relaxation is good for the whole organization.

Once upon a time, the members of the Body held a meeting and decided to rebel against the Belly. The leader of the rebellion fueled the members' conviction to act by saying "Why should we be perpetually engaged in administering to the Belly's wants, while the Belly does nothing but take its rest, and enjoy itself in luxury and self-indulgence?" The Members carried out their resolve and with great flourish refused their assistance to the Belly. The whole Body quickly became debilitated. For the first time understanding the importance of rest and nourishment for the whole organism, the hands, feet, mouth, and eyes repented of their folly and asked the Belly to teach them about relaxation.

Key Point

"Calm and relaxation are good for you and your work, and they are good for your organization as well."

The challenge associated with relaxing at work is that in addition to thinking it is unproductive, many people find it difficult to unwind on the job. They do not know how to relax effectively. They hurry to attain a state of relaxation, thus defeating the goal of working in a calm way. They think they can only rest when they are away from work. It is common to hear people say, "I cannot wait until my vacation because I can FINALLY relax." This message suggests that vacation is the only way to get a time off from work. Why not do something different this month? Instead of waiting until your vacation to get some relaxation, take some time each day at work to unwind right where you are.

Reflection Questions

 Take two to three minutes to reflect and/or write about each of the following questions:

1. What is my attitude towards relaxation at work?
2. When was the last time I relaxed at work? What were the positive benefits that came from that moment of relaxation at work?
3. What stops me from relaxing at work?
4. What can I do to relax more at work?

Week One: Practice Simple Acts of Relaxation at Work

When you are not used to relaxing, the thought of finding time to do so might be intimidating. The best advice for chartering unknown territory is to take it slowly. Start with simple ways of relaxing at work. Here are a few high-leverage, low-time commitment relaxation exercises for the workplace.

Inspirational Quote

 "...Relaxation cannot be hurried. We must have faith that our slow, circuitous journey will take us in the end to the land of calm perspectives..."

MIKE GEORGE, *LEARN TO RELAX*

Relax your body

Pay attention to your body's signals when it comes to relaxing. Your body will let you know when you need to rest. One simple way to loosen up at work is to rub your forehead gently. Place your elbows on a table and rest your head in your hands with your thumbs on the sides of your cheeks and your fingers pointing upward on your forehead. Pressing lightly, slowly move your fingers back and forth across your forehead or in circles. Rub your temples and then holding your head with your fingers, massage your jaw with your thumbs. Use your thumbs to press behind your ears and along the back of your head where it connects with the neck. These actions will relax your facial muscles. Rachel Harris, Ph.D., writes in *20 Minute Retreats* that as the muscles of the face loosen, the rest of the body unwinds. Keep it simple and relax your whole body by rubbing your forehead.

Pause and breathe when the phone rings

Instead of jumping when the phone rings at work, why not pause and take a moment to breathe? Thich Nhat Han, a Vietnamese monk, is attributed with the idea of using the ring of the phone as a signal to take a long breath. As was mentioned in Part One, *conscious breathing* is a simple and very effective method for renewing yourself. Now you have an easy way to practice it—breathe when the phone rings! Imagine the person calling hearing a calm, relaxed voice on the other end. One of our editor friends tried this technique after reading about it. She found it so helpful that she now pauses and lets the phone ring three times before answering.

Inspirational Quote

"...Something as mundane and distracting as the phone can become a tool for incorporating small but persistent acts of renewal into our everyday lives."

SALLY HELGESEN, *THRIVING IN 24/7:*
SIX STRATEGIES FOR TAMING THE NEW WORLD OF WORK

Slow down at work

Demonstrate an air of calmness by slowing down this week at work. This can be a challenge for most people. When it comes to work, most Americans like to do everything fast, from thinking quickly to responding rapidly. Hurrying and multi-tasking seem to be the standard operating procedures in the workplace. Although working in this harried way may have made it possible for you to cram 29.8 hours of activity into a 24-hour day, it contributes to a false sense of being able to do it all, even if it is all at the same time and nothing gets done right. The downside of working at a feverish pace is that you are never fully present for anything or anyone at work. You are too busy thinking about what is next, to listen clearly and completely to others and observe thoroughly what is going on around you. Do yourself a favor by slowing down, multi-tasking less, and participating in work more fully. In doing so, you will be able to pay closer attention in the moment, work in a more relaxed and productive way, and bring a welcome sense of calm to yourself and your colleagues.

This may be a completely new way of working for you. Start out taking "baby steps" (literally); walk slowly. Then move into speaking at a slower pace than you normally do. Eventually try thinking more slowly and reflectively. Watch and see what happens. You may actually find yourself exhibiting a calm and relaxed demeanor!

Inspirational Quote

"In the name of God, stop a moment, cease your work, look around you."
LEO TOLSTOY, THE QUOTATIONS PAGE

Do nothing at work

Take two minutes, once in the morning and once in the afternoon, when you do nothing. Forget multi-tasking! Turn off your cell phone! Give yourself the gift of relaxation by allowing yourself to stop completely. Stopping is not easy in the typical workplace where people are expected to work faster and faster. The act of doing nothing will require courage on your part. The rewards can be great. Make an attempt this week to start doing nothing at work! Keep track of how your day goes after these episodes of non-doing.

Krista allows the animals she sees from the window to remind her to stop and do nothing. The deer that live in the woods behind the office often pause and stand very still. Occasionally there is a hawk that rests for awhile on a branch nearby. Krista takes advantage of their presence to stop working and become as quiet as they are. Sometimes she even has a staring contest with a deer that has come close enough to the window for them to see each other clearly. Krista always returns to her work refreshed from these moments of doing nothing.

Inspirational Quote

"...Non-doing doesn't have to be threatening to people who feel they always have to get things done. They might find they get even more "done," and done better, by practicing non-doing. Non-doing simply means letting things be and allowing them to unfold in their own way."
JON KABAT-ZINN, PH.D., WHEREVER YOU GO, THERE YOU ARE

Week Two: Come to Work Rested

Although relaxation during the day is crucial to productivity and performance at work, daily (or rather nightly) rest also has a significant impact on your workday. Robert Cooper, Ph.D., the author of *The Performance Edge*, explains that oftentimes your success, or even your survival at work, is dependent upon consistent focus, alertness, and top performance, every single day. You perform best when you are well rested.

Sleep deprivation is rampant in North America. In fact, research indicates that over 50 percent of Americans are sleep deprived. This may be attributed to longer work days, increased responsibilities, and the emergence of an American dream that includes getting, buying, and doing more and more. Here are some things you can do to acquire a good night's rest.

Inspirational Quote

"True rest spills over into our weeks, our years, our very lives."
NAOMI LEVY, *"CHANGE YOUR LIFE...TAKE A DAY OF REST"*

Reclaim your right to sleep

Take back your right to a good night's sleep, every night, even if it runs counter to the messages you get at work. One manager in a large Fortune 500 Company was overheard saying to her employees, "You can sleep when you retire." If you follow this manager's advice and continue to get inadequate sleep you will hurt your performance and reduce your longevity. Research indicates that sleep deprivation negatively impacts both your work and your health. Make an effort to stop working late. Turn off the TV early. Put down your book! Make certain that you sleep a reasonable number of hours each night this month. Even the biblical story of creation includes a good rest for God. The authors of Genesis write that God created the world in six days and rested on day seven. If God rested after working so can you.

The employee whose manager said, "You can sleep after you retire," got so stressed that she decided to take care of herself. She cut back on her hours at work so she was only working 10 hours a day, took time every day to walk outside and made sure she got a good night's rest. At first she was concerned that she was not working hard enough. But, after discovering that she was able to successfully complete all of her projects and also reclaim her sleep and personal time, she was able to let go of her guilt. She is now enthusiastic about living and working in a different way.

Inspirational Quote

"...Research confirms that consistent sleep deprivation results in loss of motivation and decreased productivity; a reduced ability to learn and remember; feelings of irritability, anger and unhappiness; increased job errors; slower healing; and lowered resistance to disease. Sleep loss or poor rest can also obstruct creative innovation."

ROBERT COOPER, PH.D., *THE PERFORMANCE EDGE*

Maintain a peaceful sleeping environment

Refrain from working in bed. Does your picture of yourself in bed include a laptop and a stack of folders? If so, change that picture now by moving the laptop and folders back to your desk. Struggling with a work challenge before you try to fall asleep almost guarantees a night of fitful sleep. In fact, the tradition of Feng Shui (the Chinese art of the placement of objects) recommends no books in the bedroom as they may interfere with your sleep. Others, however, may find books to be comforting. What do you need to maintain your peaceful sleeping environment? Think about it and act on your ideas.

Establish a regular sleep pattern

Go to bed and get up at the same time each day. It is also wise to establish a bed time ritual that prepares you for a good night sleep. For instance, some people keep a gratitude journal in which they list things and events for which they are grateful for that day. Suzanne's parents, Richard and Alice, always ended their day by saying the Lord's Prayer before going to sleep. In the winter, Krista likes to lie on a heating pad for a few minutes. The warmth relaxes her and makes her sleepy.

If you already have a regular sleep ritual and pattern that enables you to get seven to eight hours of sleep a night, good for you! If not, keep track of your sleep pattern for one week. Evaluate it to see how you might obtain consistent, adequate rest. See the exercise that follows for an idea of how to keep track of your sleep pattern.

Exercise: Tracking My Sleep Pattern

1. Choose a typical workweek during which to track your sleep pattern.
2. At the beginning of the week, write down what you know about your typical sleep pattern and how rested you feel.
3. Each night before going to bed make a note of how you feel, what activities you did the hour before going to bed and what you did to prepare for sleep.
4. In the morning upon rising, make a note of how you slept and how rested you feel. Note on a chart similar to the one that follows what time you went to bed, what time you rose, and how many hours you slept.
5. At the end of the week, look at the notes and discover what your sleep pattern has been for the week. Reflect on how rested you feel and whether or not your sleep pattern is serving you well. Write down any insights about the impact of your sleep habits on your energy and work.
6. Think about any changes you would like to make in your sleeping pattern or habits.
7. If you decide to alter the pattern, note the modifications you choose to make and put them into place in the next week.
8. During the second week, repeat the process that you completed the first week, making note of how you feel and how your altered sleep pattern is impacting your energy and work.

(See next page for sleep pattern tracking chart)

My Sleep Pattern During the Week of _____

Day	How I Felt at Bedtime	What I Did the Hour Before Bed	How I Prepared for Sleep	Bed Time	Rise and Shine	Hours Slept
Monday						
Tuesday						
Wednesday						
Thursday						
Friday						
Saturday						
Sunday						

Greet the day calmly and gently

Plan a gentle start to your day. Awaken to classical or quiet music. If the news disturbs you, hold off listening to it until later. Many people begin their day by reading something inspirational. Consider ways that you might begin the day in a calm and relaxed way. Derrick gets up early each morning before his wife and children. In the quiet of the morning, he shaves and then plays his flute. Later he wakes his children by playing their favorite songs on the flute allowing them to start their day off calmly and gently, too.

Week Three: Practice the Fine Art of Napping at Work

Even if you come to work rested, a nap is still a good idea. Does taking a nap at work seem preposterous to you? Consider this: a 25-year study on the effects of napping at work reveals that for over 90 percent of workers an afternoon nap increases productivity and their creative and problem solving skill. Napping at work is not as far-fetched an idea as it might seem. A few companies actually sanction naps and provide napping rooms. For instance, Yarde Metals in Connecticut encourages napping at work to give employees a break and help them stay alert. They provide a napping area where people can unwind. Other companies like Sprint and Deloitte Consulting in Pittsburgh also have specially designed areas, called "napnasiums," where employees can rest.

Inspirational Quote

"Workplace napping is a natural, no cost way to increase worker productivity."
WILLIAM A. ANTHONY, PH.D., & CAMILLE W. ANTHONY, PH.D.,
THE ART OF NAPPING AT WORK

If you are fortunate enough to work for a forward-thinking company with napping privileges, you are set to implement this week's tips. If not, you will want to practice the fine art of napping in a low-key manner by starting out with small actions and working your way up to a full-blown nap at your break or lunchtime.

Read *The Art of Napping at Work*

Become knowledgeable about research on, and strategies for, napping at work. The easiest and most entertaining way to do this is to read *The Art of Napping at Work* by William A. Anthony, Ph.D., and Camille W. Anthony, Ph.D. The Anthonys' book provides ideas about how to overcome attitudinal and environmental barriers to napping. It also describes favorite workplace napping places. You might even take a nap in between chapters if you are so moved!

 ### Rest your eyes

Not yet ready for a full-blown nap at work? Begin by resting your eyes. James Joseph, author of *Working Wonders*, recommends simply closing your eyes and cupping your hands over them. Do not put pressure on the eyes, but make sure that your eyes are in total darkness. Then use deep breathing to relax, clearing your mind of all thoughts. You might even try little beanbag eye pillows (usually a flaxseed-filled silk pillow with a soothing herbal scent). Suzanne uses one that has a lavender scent—used in aromatherapy to instill calmness—and it smells and feels great!

 ### Nap during your break

Find a place to nap during your break. According to Camille Anthony, a useful nap can be as short as ten minutes. A nap seems like a perfect way to spend a short break. Chances are that after your ten-minute nap you will be alert again. Bill, a financial advisor, found an old chair that was going to be discarded in the hallway at his office. He put the chair in a closet and goes there for his naps. The Anthonys suggest letting your coworkers know you are napping so you are not disturbed. They also recommend using an alarm clock to wake you after 20 minutes and briefly doing something physical to shake off any grogginess before returning to your desk.

 ### Sleep for twenty minutes during a portion of your lunch

Eat lunch and then put your head down on your desk. If you nap in your office, turn off the ringer on the phone and close the blinds if possible. If napping in the office is not an option, try your car. Twenty minutes, which is the typical amount of time for a workplace nap, should be just right. You'll awake rested, but not groggy. Alan, a benefits specialist in a large bank quoted in Sue Shellenbarger's article "From Office Catnaps to Lunchtime Jogs," regularly takes a nap at work during lunch. He says that he wakes up "refreshed and ready to calculate another retiree's benefits. I am vastly more productive when my mind is fresh."

Week Four: Develop an Easy Attitude towards Your Work

American companies are hiring humor consultants to help their organizations become more relaxed and joyful. One such consultant, Charles Metcalf, talks about the concept of *terminal professionalism*. This means that people are just too darn serious about themselves at work! Such an outlook works against creating a relaxed atmosphere for workers or their companies.

Key Point

"When you laugh, you are renewing all aspects of your being. And it is easier to feel relaxed when you are laughing."

Work is a great gift and a wonderful blessing. Why not work in a way that demonstrates that belief and is more relaxed? Think about your own approach to work. Do you laugh? Do you spread joy? Do you experience ease while working? Or do people run the other way when you start with "gloom and doom" rhetoric? Is the glass at work "half empty" or "half full" for you? Think about ways you could take yourself less seriously at work and contribute to a sense of relaxation in the workplace. Here are some ways to get started.

Laugh often at work

Find things to laugh about every day this week. Doing so keeps things in perspective for you and your colleagues. Laughter heals the body, mind, emotions, and spirit. When you laugh, it renews all aspects of your being. It is much easier to feel relaxed when you are laughing. A wonderful article appeared in the *Washington Post* about an executive who signs all of his correspondence with bright crayon. What a fun way to keep yourself and the recipients of your correspondence laughing!

Exercise: Reflecting on My Levity at Work

1. Recall a situation at work to which you responded with some levity and humor.
2. Reflect on your behavior and write answers to the following questions on a piece of paper.
   a. What was my behavior like? How lightly did I behave? Why did I behave the way I did?
   b. What did I find humorous about the situation?
   c. What allowed me to take the situation lightly?
   d. What can I learn from this situation that I can apply to other situations in the future?
3. Reread your notes and write down any additional insights you have about bringing levity to work situations in the future.
4. Date and sign the paper in crayon or colored ink. Draw a smiley face on the paper and keep it in your desk drawer for future reference.

Stay relaxed in the face of urgent requests

Learn to distinguish between real and imagined crises at work. Remain calm, examine the situation, and rush only on those items that truly demand immediate action. These days, many people approach their work as if everything is urgent. As a result, their perception becomes skewed and they are no longer able to distinguish a true crisis from a less critical matter. Remember the lesson of Chicken Little? He went around saying, "the sky is falling, the sky is falling," when it wasn't. Then, when it mattered, no one listened to him because of his past allegations.

Instead of acting like Chicken Little whenever you are faced with a potentially urgent item, allow yourself to think, "Everything is alright. Stay calm." Then, ask the questions that will help you focus on what requires your immediate attention. Be courageous in

Key Point

"Hurrying in and of itself adds stress to an already overflowing plate. Hurrying impacts your effectiveness as well as your zest for your work and your life for that matter."

pointing out that not everything at work is a crisis. When everything is treated as an emergency, you end up rushing and completing your work in a hurry. This approach contributes to the workplace epidemic of *hurry sickness*. What do you profit by hurrying? Not much. Hurrying in and of itself adds stress to an already overflowing plate. Hurrying impacts your effectiveness as well as zest for your work and life for that matter.

Suzanne's former minister, Reverend Fred Shaw, preached one of the most memorable sermons of his career the Sunday morning that he learned his father had died. Fred must have had a thousand things to do, including driving many miles to be with his mother and assisting with the funeral arrangements. It would have been easy for Fred to hurry through the sermon and dismiss "his flock" early. He instead preached calmly and steadfastly and no one in the congregation suspected that he was facing an emergency. At the end of the sermon he told the group assembled what had happened and that he had preached that Sunday because he was doing the work that "God has called him to do." Reverend Shaw was an exquisite example of grace under pressure at work that Sunday morning.

Inspirational Quote

"By constantly hurrying, we not only poison the quality of our individual lives, we also undermine our own ultimate value by adopting a demeanor that suggests that we are at someone else's beck and call, rather than moving through life comfortably, at our own pace, in accord with our own inner rhythm and light."
SALLY HELGESEN, *THRIVING IN 24/7: SIX STRATEGIES FOR TAMING THE NEW WORLD OF WORK*

Adopt a long-term, bigger perspective of work

Think about what matters in the long run, both at work and in your life in general, whenever you find yourself working in crisis mode. Remember that life is precious and that one day you will leave this Earth. Will any of what you are worrying or hurrying about matter when you depart? Humorist and stress specialist, Loretta LaRoche's book title says it all—*Relax: You May Only Have a Few Minutes Left.*

Elisabeth Kubler-Ross, noted researcher on death and dying, is attributed with saying that no one on his or her deathbed ever utters the words "I wish I had worked more." Most people wish they had stopped long enough to enjoy the simple pleasures of life.

Key Point

"Remember that God did not put you in charge of the Universe. You are not responsible for making sure everything works out all right."

Allow yourself to slow down, gain perspective, and suspend your sense of responsibility for a few minutes each day. Remember that God did not put you in charge of the Universe. You do not have to make sure that everything works out all right! Recently, Krista gave Suzanne a refrigerator magnet with the following saying on it to help them both remember that they do not have to do it all: "Good morning. This is God. I will be handling all your problems today. I will not need your help. So have a good time. I love you."

"Teach me the art of taking minute vacations of slowing down. Remind me each day that the race is not always to the swift—that there is more to life than increasing its speed."

WILFERD A. PETERSON,
EXCERPT FROM "SLOW ME DOWN, LORD!"
IN *ADVENTURES IN THE ART OF LIVING*

15

AUGUST

CREATE BALANCE AT WORK

"Our long-term effectiveness as employees or entrepreneurs is at risk if we spend week after week working at a fast pace and with little time to disengage and turn off our computers, cell phones, and brains."

GIL GORDON, *TURN IT OFF*

Introduction

Toward the end of the summer, when August rolls around, the pace of work slows down as large numbers of people go on vacation. For those of you who remain at work while others are away, this is a time for catching up and creating a sense of balance at work. Of course, for those of you who take time off during this period, it is an opportunity to rejuvenate. Yet the sense of balance and relaxation you bring back with you from holiday may not last very long once you step back into your fast-paced work routine. To sustain your equilibrium, it is necessary to find ways to create balance in your life at work.

Living a balanced life at work is important year round, both for personal reasons and for responding to the rapid, non-stop change at work. Balance at work contributes to resiliency, a skill that is critical for dealing with the high-speed changes in the workplace and world.

Inspirational Quote

"As more and more people bring balance into their work and life-style, a creative resilience forms a solid foundation that is necessary to support the rapid change taking place across the globe."

Ann McGee-Cooper, Ed.D., *You Do Not Have to Go Home from Work Exhausted*

What comes to mind when you think about creating balance at work? For some people, it means balancing the time spent at work with personal life and activities outside of work. In this instance, you might view balance as being similar to a scale. The goal is to counter balance the weight of work by paying proportionate attention to your personal life outside of work. Another way of looking at balance is to see your life as a harmonious, integrated whole. The goal is to be engaged in a fluid process of arranging how to use your time based on what you value most. It requires slowing down, stepping back, looking at the bigger picture, and making small adjustments to bring your actions into alignment with what is important to you.

No matter how you view balance, it is something that calls for continuous attention. Because of the ever-changing demands of life, it is unlikely that you can put your life into balance once and for all. As new circumstances arise, you will be called to make new choices about what is important to you and to adjust how to invest your time. Because people tend to slip into routines, you may find it necessary to rebalance your life periodically. You may have drifted into spending time on activities that are no longer important to you. Creating balance also requires flexibility and creativity. A solution to balancing your life may be effective at one point in time and not at another. Stay flexible, find new solutions, and give yourself time to pay attention to the balance in your life. An inspirational resource to get you thinking about this topic is *Life is Not Work, Work is Not Life* by Robert K. Johnston and J. Walker Smith.

Since you spend most of the day at work, it makes sense to focus on what adjustments you can make at work to bring more balance to your life. By achieving a sense of balance there, you will have energy left over for yourself, friends, and family. But what does balance at work look and feel like? Although you may experience balance in your own unique way, some of the characteristic traits include:

- Feeling that there is time to do everything you choose to do
- Completing priority tasks including important items that are less urgent
- Having time to renew yourself at work on a regular basis
- Having energy at the end of the workday

This month's tips provide multiple ways to help you experience these traits and create balance at work!

Reflection Questions

Take two to three minutes to reflect and/or write about each of the following questions:

1. How balanced do I feel at work and in my life?
2. Do I value balance at work and make time for it? How do I currently create balance at work?
3. What gets in the way of my achieving balance at work? How can I overcome the barriers (both internal and external) to experiencing balance at work?
4. How can I create more balance at work? What would an ideal balanced day at work be like for me?

Week One: Take an Interlude at Work

One way to live in balance is to pay attention to your physical and personal needs while at work. Although the human body and mind are designed to frequently rest, many people ignore the signals their bodies send them about needing to pause. Research shows that about 50 percent of Americans do not take a lunch break or even eat lunch at all. Contrary to popular belief, we are more effective and productive, as well as happier and healthier, when we take frequent short breaks throughout the day to take care of ourselves. Here are some ways to create more balance in your daily work life.

Eat lunch everyday

Take advantage of your lunchtime everyday this week to get away from work and to nourish yourself. You can also use your lunch hour to do errands, spend time with friends, or relax. To maintain the mental or emotional steadiness associated with balance, your body requires fuel. Make sure to take time to eat a healthy meal with food you really enjoy. It is also helpful to focus on only one activity at a time during lunch. According to Pragito Dove, the author of *Lunchtime Enlightenment,* if you eat and read or work on the computer at the same time, your attention is divided and that creates stress. Setting aside time for eating allows you to savor your food and experience the nourishment and pleasure that comes with dining.

Take water breaks

Instead of taking coffee breaks, leave your work tasks to get water. Recent research shows that most Americans do not drink enough water. Being dehydrated affects your physical health and productivity. Set a goal to drink at least six to eight glasses of water a day. Drink this much even if you are not thirsty. Experts say that waiting until you are thirsty is too long. You are already dehydrated. If taking a break that often is unpractical, keep a bottle of water with you. The great thing about this strategy is that it has a natural renewal mechanism built right into it. The more water you drink, the more often you will need to take a break to visit the rest room!

Key Point

"Contrary to popular belief, we are more effective and productive, as well as happier and healthier, when we take frequent short breaks throughout the day to take care of ourselves."

Attend to your personal business

Many people put in so many hours at work that they have little time left for taking care of personal business after work. If you tend to put in long hours at work, set aside a few times during the day to take care of some of your personal affairs. Take a few minutes to make a personal phone call, plan a vacation, go to the dry cleaners, go on a brief shopping trip, buy a gift for a family member, or write a letter or thank you note to a friend. Take some time upon arriving in the morning to plan something reasonable to do for yourself and add it to your schedule. Then use your work breaks to follow through on the plan.

Although you may be concerned about taking time for your personal business during the work day, more people are using some of their time at work for individual activities. This phenomenon has been coined "undertime." According to Sue Shellenbarger, columnist with the *Wall Street Journal* and author of "What You Need to Know About 'Undertime' Rules," more and more employees are taking "undertime." She says that it is essential both for work life balance and for peak performance and creativity.

Stretch during your workday

Pay attention to the signals your body sends and you will become aware of the need for physical self-renewal. One of the easiest ways to reinvigorate yourself is to incorporate stretches into the daily work regime. If you have been sitting at the computer for a long time, chances are your neck and shoulders will be stiff and tense. The following exercises are great for relieving stress in the upper body and neck, and are easy to do at a desk. Belinda, an investment advisor, regularly makes an effort to remember to do stretches to loosen up her hips and lower back when she has been sitting for a long time. Sitting in her office chair, she does a simple twist to each side several times and then takes turns crossing one ankle over the other knee, leaning forward to stretch her hip muscles.

Exercise: Stretching at Work

There are many brief stretching and yoga exercises that you can do right in the office. They are easy to do. They require little room or time, so you can do them right in your workspace, in your work attire. They feel good and provide great release from stress! If you are interested in learning more, there are several books, including *Office Yoga: Simple Stretches for Busy People* by Darrin Zeer, that outline numerous exercises you can do easily at work.

Neck and Shoulder Roll

Many people carry tension in their neck and shoulders, particularly if they sit at desks and computers all day long. To release tension from your neck and shoulders:

1. Sit or stand up straight. Shrug one shoulder at a time towards your ear. Do this three times on each side.
2. Next, roll both shoulders up, forward, and back three times. Then reverse the direction for three rolls. Take a deep breath.
3. Now, while exhaling, allow your chin to slowly drop towards your chest. Let your head rest in this position for a moment, feeling the stretch in the back of your neck. On an inhale, bring your head up and let the back of your head move towards your back. Then, gently move your head up and down, chin to chest and back, several times, remembering to breath as you move.

4. Bringing your head back into a neutral position, slowly turn your head to the right side, as if you are trying to look over the right shoulder. Then move your head to the other side, as if trying to look over the left shoulder. Alternate looking to each side three times.

5. Finally, drop your right ear towards the right shoulder and gently roll your head down and forward, moving your chin across the chest and up, ending with the left ear dropped towards your left shoulder. Do not roll your head backwards. Instead, reverse the direction, rolling your head down, moving the chin from left to right. Roll your head forward three times in each direction.

6. End by bringing your head into an upright position. Pause, take a breath and feel the difference in the neck and shoulders. Do this exercise any time you feel tension in your neck and shoulders.

Torso Stretch

People also carry tension in their chests, which makes it difficult to breathe fully. To release tightness and create more room in your torso:

1. Sit or stand upright. Raise both arms over your head until they are next to your ears. Stretch your arms and hands as straight as you can and take a deep breath, exhaling fully.

2. Next, take a hold of the right wrist with your left hand. Exhaling, slowly bend at the waist and move to the left. Feel the stretch along the right side of your torso. Take a few deep breaths and then return to an upright position.

3. Switch hands, taking a hold of the left wrist with your right hand. Again, exhaling, slowly bend at the waist and move to the right. Feel the stretch along the left side of your torso. Take a few deep breaths and return to an upright position.

4. Repeat this exercise two more times for each side. Then, lower your arms to your sides and take a deep breath. Feel the difference in the torso. Do you feel as if there is more room in the chest area? Are you breathing more freely and fully?

Week Two: Pace Yourself Throughout the Day and Week

In order to have a sense of balance at work it is essential to pace yourself. If you are always rushing from one activity to the next, you will most likely find yourself off balance and exhausted at the end of the day or week. To be most effective and run on plenty it is important to create a work schedule that enables you to get work done at a tempo that leaves you feeling well, rather than worn out. Do you remember the childhood tale of the tortoise and the hare? To refresh your memory, here is a modified version.

One day the cocky hare challenged the wise tortoise to a race. Much to everyone's surprise, the tortoise agreed. They agreed on the course and arranged to meet by a certain tree in the morning. That night the tortoise went home to rest while the hare partied with his friends, confident that he would win.

The next morning all the animals in the wood were there to watch the race. The hare, anxious to start, bounced up and down at the starting line while the tortoise slowly made his way over to him. As the tortoise reached the tree, he began to say "good luck" to the hare. But the hare did not even hear him because just then the starting bell rang and the hare took off down the road at top speed. By the time the hare got half way to the finish line, he was exhausted. Breathing heavily, he collapsed by the side of the road. Checking to see where the tortoise was, the hare decided that since he could barely see the tortoise, he had plenty of time to sleep and still win the race.

Meanwhile, the tortoise slowly and steadily made his way down the road, eventually passing the exhausted and sleeping hare. A long while later, the hare awoke to the crowd's shouts and realized that the tortoise was very close to the finish line. He got up quickly, feeling groggy and still a bit worn out, and started off down the road after the tortoise. He rounded the final curve, thinking he still had a chance to outrun the tortoise when he saw the tortoise cross the finish line. He couldn't believe it. The slow tortoise had outrun him!

One key lesson of this fable is that a slower, steady pace over the long run is what gets you to the finish line. If you push yourself too much you will wear yourself out and not successfully meet your deadlines. There are many ways to establish an even, balanced rate of activity at work. Here are a few suggestions.

Balance your most demanding tasks with less demanding ones

Instead of packing the day or week with one demanding activity after another, schedule your work so that you have some less challenging tasks mixed in with more challenging ones. Allow time to prepare for the demanding activities and time to rejuvenate yourself after them. For instance, when you schedule meetings, build in times to prepare for the meeting and to do some follow up planning after the meeting. Only schedule a few meetings in a single day. If you arrange too many meetings in a row, little time will be available to take care of yourself and other necessary tasks, such as planning, returning phone calls, and responding to e-mails.

Rod, the manager who has been described several times before, learned this lesson himself when he filled his calendar with one meeting after another for several weeks in a row. He found that he was too busy to prepare properly for all of the meetings. Because he had not planned any time for following up on the action items that resulted from the meetings, some important actions did not get done. After discussing different time management issues with his business coach, whenever it was in his control he scheduled fewer meetings in a day and made sure he included time on his calendar to prepare for and implement ideas from all his meetings.

Follow your body's natural rhythms

Get to know your body's energy cycles and then schedule work to take advantage of those natural rhythms. When do you think best? When do you have the most physical energy? Schedule your more challenging tasks during those periods of the day when you can be most productive and leave the less difficult activities for times when you are moving more slowly. It is important to honor your need to slow down. Recognize that you are a human organism that needs to move at different paces at different times. Krista, for instance, always schedules a day of paper work following a major training event. This kind of planning allows her to honor the fact that she usually thinks less clearly when she is tired, and she takes care of necessary tasks that require less mental energy at the same time.

Work only as long as is required to achieve results

Over the course of this week, examine how many hours you are working and how well you are using the time. Develop a chart to track your work hours. Evaluate your daily work patterns. (You can use the exercise that follows to help you). Are you working 14-hour days and taking work home on the weekends? Sometimes working this hard is necessary. Perhaps you are spending more time at work than is required because you are doing unnecessary tasks or spending a lot of energy engaged in unproductive activities, such as worrying about events over which you have no control. Or you may have very high standards and be trying to attain a level of perfection that is not necessary for the task at hand. Is there a way in which you can use time more wisely so that you can work only 40 hours a week and still obtain the outcome you desire?

Many individuals operate as if the number of hours they spend at work equates with productivity and leads to great results. Instead of focusing on the amount of time spent at work, this month pay attention to accomplishing your goals. As the following fable suggests, the value is in the worth, not in the number.

> Once upon a time, a controversy prevailed among the beasts of the field as to which of the animals deserved the most credit for producing the greatest number of whelps at a birth. They rushed clamorously into the presence of the Lioness and demanded of her the settlement of the dispute. "And you," they said, "how many sons have you at a birth?" The Lioness laughed at them, and said: "Why! I have only one; but that one is altogether a thoroughbred Lion."

Begin this week by asking if there is a way to focus on the quality of your work rather than the number of hours. Is there a way to reduce the number of hours you work and still achieve the results you are seeking? Make a commitment this week to work a maximum of eight to ten hours each week day, with no work on weekends, and to leave your work behind when you go home. While it is possible to create a sense of balance at work, chances are you will have a difficult time maintaining your balance if you spend all the time working. It is essential to have time in the evenings and weekends for relaxation, play, and other activities outside of your job.

Exercise: Evaluating my Work Patterns and Hours

1. Choose a typical work week during which you track your work hours.
2. Create a chart, like the one that follows, to keep track of the number of hours you work each day that week, including the weekend.
3. At the end of the week, evaluate how productive you were during the hours worked and how effectively and wisely you used the time. Ask yourself questions like:
   a. Did I need to spend so much time working this week?
   b. How productive was I and did I work effectively and efficiently?
   c. Did I have enough time and energy for personal and family activities this week?
4. Finally, determine whether or not your answers reveal an opportunity for making adjustments in your working patterns.
   a. If you discovered that you invested the right amount of time at work, were productive and effective, and had time for personal activities, then congratulate yourself for maintaining some balance and continue to monitor the number of hours you work and how productive, efficient, and effective you are.
   b. If, on the other hand, you had no time or energy for your personal life or that you were not as productive as you would have liked, then give some thought to how to spend fewer hours and be more effective and efficient while at work. Make a note of a few specific adjustments you can make and then implement them.

(Please see next page for Work Hour Log)

My Work Hour Log for the Week of _____

Day	Hours Worked	Evaluation of Productivity	Evaluation of Effectiveness	Evaluation of Efficiency
Monday				
Tuesday				
Wednesday				
Thursday				
Friday				
Saturday				
Sunday				
Total Hours Worked				

*"While it is possible to create a sense of balance at work, chances are you will have a difficult time maintaining your balance if you spend **all** the time working."*

Form boundaries around your work

Instead of accepting all of the work requests that come your way this week, create some balance and pace yourself by forming boundaries around what you are willing to accept. Find ways to say no, compromise, delegate, or share work! Do what you can within limits. Many people in the workplace agree to do more work than they can realistically complete at any given time. As a result they push themselves and feel overwhelmed because they have too much to do. Sound familiar? Though you may believe that you should be available to everyone at all times, it is more productive for you and for your work to say "no" some of the time.

Review Chapter Six to refresh your memory on the different ways to say no. Explore some of the resources at the end of this chapter. Scan *Time Management for Unmanageable People* by Ann McGee-Cooper, Ed.D., for ideas. Read *Turn It Off* by Gil Gordon who offers excellent suggestions about how to have constructive conversations with your manager, coworkers, and customers on the subject of boundaries. Alternatively, complete the following exercise.

Inspirational Quote

"It is better to say no. Otherwise in the long run you'll suffer burnout, become frustrated, make mistakes and you will let people down. Trying to do everything depletes your physical, emotional, financial and time reserves."

MILLARD MACADAM, QUOTED IN
"GUARDING YOUR TIME: HOW TO SAY NO"

Exercise: Practicing Saying No

If you are new to, or completely uncomfortable with, saying "no" at work, you may find it helpful to practice ahead of time, before you actually need to say it. Remember, it *is* possible to say no without damaging your relationship with the person making the request.

Practice One:

1. Think of a person who typically makes requests that add to your workload. Make a guess as to a specific request he or she might make in the near future.
2. Think of and write down the different ways you could respond to this person's request graciously. (See Chapter Six)
3. Practice saying each response out loud. Pay attention to how you feel while verbalizing each possible response. Which response feels most gracious, comfortable, and realistic to you?
4. The next time the person makes a request of you, remember this practice session and decline in a gracious way.

Practice Two:

1. Invite a coworker or friend to do a role-play exercise with you.
2. Ask your partner to make a work-related request.
3. Respond by declining the request.
4. Share with the colleague or friend how you felt about your response. How comfortable did you feel saying no to their request? Do you think you were effective? What might you do differently next time?
5. Then, ask your partner to give feedback on your response. How did he or she feel when you said no? How does he or she think you did? Does he or she have any suggestions?
6. Do the exercise again, using the information you obtained from doing the first role-play to refine your response.
7. Invite your partner to switch roles so he or she can take a turn at practicing saying no.

Week Three: Balance Your Energy Replacement

To create balance at work it is important to replenish your energy in a balanced way. Since you expend physical, mental, emotional, and spiritual energy at work, it is best to pay attention to revitalizing each of these dimensions of your being. This does not mean that you have to do something every day to replenish your energy in each of these areas. You can pay attention over time to balancing your energy replacement.

Inspirational Quote

> *"It inspires me to look at the whole picture of my life and the way it is balanced over periods of time rather than by day or week. I am moving from a checklist mentality (...did I get my walk in today...how is my social life this week?) to assessing where I am putting most of my energy, how balanced I feel, and whether I feel like anything is missing."*
> SHEILA ADAMS, *"LIFE AND WORK: BALANCING OR JUGGLING?"*

Renew yourself physically

Pay attention to your physical energy throughout the day. If possible, get moving early in the morning by taking the stairs to your office. Consider forming a morning yoga class and holding it in a conference room with a video player and monitor. This way you can simply use a yoga tape to guide the group. Later in the day, whenever you are feeling tired, do something to rejuvenate yourself physically. Energize yourself by simply getting up from the desk and strolling around your work area. Do a few deep knee bends or swing your arms around your head. Skip or run in place for one minute.

Schedule physical exercise into your workday. Take a walk outside as part of your lunchtime in order to keep your energy high after the noon meal. Ed, a marketing manager, even holds a few meetings during his walks. He talks on the cell phone with his coworkers who are out of town while taking a walk outside. If it is cold outside, bundle up or walk inside the building. Suzanne reports that her best workday lunch walks were when she worked in Buffalo and had to wear two coats in the winter to keep warm. Talk about invigorating!

Key Point

"Become aware of the signals that indicate that you are ready for a mental refresher, like making mistakes, having to read a sentence over and over again, and forgetting what you were going to say in the middle of a sentence."

Refresh your mind at least five times a day

Because you use your mind continually at work, it is important to refresh your mental energy frequently throughout the day. You may have noticed that after an hour or so of concentrated effort you begin to think less clearly. This is because the mind is naturally wired to take a rest every 60-90 minutes. (Remember the rest-activity cycle that was mentioned in Part One?) Make an effort this week to pause and revitalize yourself mentally *before* you begin to get tired. You may even choose to set an alarm to go off every hour as a reminder to revitalize yourself. Become aware of the signals that indicate that you are ready for a mental refresher, like making mistakes, having to read a sentence over and over again, and forgetting what you were going to say in the middle of a sentence. Review the activities for renewing your mind in Part One and select one to do.

Practice the art of "constructive rest" for your mind. Suzanne first learned about this approach when she led a retreat in which one of the participants, Shirley, taught the group an exercise that is often associated with yoga. At the retreat, everyone lay down on the floor on their backs, placed the lower half of their legs on a chair, closed their eyes, and rested quietly for 10 minutes. The retreat participants all reported feeling surprisingly "clear headed" and well rested after only ten minutes. Try this in your office with the door closed or commandeer the conference room at lunchtime and ask your colleagues to join you.

Pay attention to your emotional state

Take time to stop and consider how you are doing emotionally in relation to work. Most people attend to their physical and mental renewal and often ignore their emotional condition. This week, pay attention to how you are feeling. Are you overwhelmed or are you feeling content? Are you dissatisfied or happy while at work? Do you dislike working in a team or enjoy collaborating with coworkers?

Once you are clear about your feelings, do something to enhance them or bring them into balance. For instance, if you feel happy at work, share your feelings with colleagues. Let them know why you like working where you do. If you have negative feelings, take some time to take care of your emotional state. What would help you feel more positive about the situation? Do you simply need to "vent" some of your feelings or is there something that you can do to make the situation work better? How can you create some peace of mind for yourself?

Bob Younglove, author of *SPONSOR SUCCESS: A Workbook for Turning Good Intentions Into Positive Results*, often speaks about keeping your "hot buttons" from being pushed by making an "emotional adjustment." Bob describes his own method for making an emotional adjustment as follows: "First, I take a slow deep breath. As I breathe out I relax all my muscles—my shoulders, my stomach, and my forehead. Second, I take another slow deep breath and as I breathe out I say to myself, 'this too shall pass.' Next, I practice the *art of taking a minute vacation*. To help me do this, I look at a photograph of my favorite vacation spot at the beach. I close my eyes and mentally jump into the picture. I imagine the warmth of the sun on my back as I stroll the beach, listen to the sound of the waves, smell the salt air, and look out at the crystal blue water. Almost immediately I begin to feel better. To finish up my emotional readjustment, I remember how lucky I am to be alive, to have job, a future, and a sense of humor. I take responsibility for the fact that no one is going to ruin my day, unless I let them…and I not going to let anyone or anything keep me from being happy."

Uplift your spirit at work

Figure out what gives your spirit a lift and do it at work. Sometimes people get so caught up in the external "goings-on" of the job that they do not notice the impact work is having on their spirit. It is important to raise your spirit. When you feel uplifted you work better and bring an open heart and mind to what you are doing. Some people find it energizing to connect with others at work by placing a call to ask, "How is it going?" Others find their spirits lifted by spending some time in silence at work. This week get in touch with what renews you spiritually at work and find a way to incorporate that activity into the workday.

Robert, the VP of the commercial real estate company mentioned earlier in the book, uplifts himself spiritually by thinking of God as his partner at work and quietly acting in accordance with his spiritual values. He claims that working in this way gives him a clearer sense of what he is doing. He says, "The positive thing about being on a faith journey is that you avail yourself of spiritual resources that enable you to see connections and build bridges that I think only with the grace of God you are able to build. It adds a whole other resource that enables you to be more effective as a manager and as an advisor." Another person, Bill, a Chief Financial Officer of a non-profit organization, makes time during the day to be quiet and to pray. He says that this helps him feel as if he is "going through the day in a prayer of love and praise" and his work days appear easier.

Week Four: Reprioritize and Simplify Your Work

In today's fast-paced, high-demand work environment, everything seems to be urgent. In this situation, you may have difficulty prioritizing activities because all the tasks on your to-do list seem important. As a result, you try to do it all and inevitably end up overwhelmed and frustrated because the list keeps getting longer. One of the best ways to overcome the constant external pressure is to step back, reprioritize, and simplify your work.

Step back and reprioritize

When faced with an urgent request, ask for a few minutes to think about it before responding. Take time to step back and consider how important the request is in light of all your other activities and priorities. Reflect on what is most important to your work before making a decision. Think about how much time it will take to complete the task and exactly when you will do it. If you decide to accept the request, think about how you can reprioritize and reschedule the other items on your to-do list for that day (or for as long as necessary).

When we were in the thick of writing this book, we came to the realization that we had too much on our work plates. In addition to writing our book, we were busy starting a second business with some other colleagues. After much serious dialogue and careful contemplation about our priorities, we decided to remove ourselves from the second business. At the same time, Suzanne was asked to serve as an officer in her local chapter of the National Speakers Association (NSA). Although it was a great honor to be asked, Suzanne reflected on the time commitment necessary to perform responsibly for her NSA chapter and declined the offer. Many times during the writing and marketing of our book, we have given thanks that we were able to step back and say no.

Key Point

> *"One of the best ways to overcome the constant external pressure is to step back, reprioritize, and simplify your work."*

Simplify your to-do list

If you are like most people, your daily or weekly to-do list is too ambitious. Do you regularly feel frustrated because there are always more items on your list than you can ever get done? The best way to deal with this frustration is to simplify your expectations about how much can realistically be accomplished in any given day or week and then carefully select what you schedule. You can define your list by doing one or more of the following:

1. Combine tasks or overlapping activities to shorten your list. For instance, set aside time during the day to return all non-urgent calls or create a to-file pile and put the papers away at the same time.
2. Limit the amount of time spent on each task. Allow yourself to lower your standards of excellence for some tasks. You do not have to do everything perfectly! If you can do an adequate job on a low priority or non-urgent item in a short amount of time, give yourself permission to devote more time to other important tasks.
3. Delegate items on your list.
4. Delete items from the list, particularly if it is a non-essential item that has been on the list for a few weeks.

Straighten up your work area

Clear away the clutter on your desk or in your computer files. You will be amazed how rejuvenating it can be to straighten up the work area. Getting rid of disorder can bring surprising balance and freedom to work. As Suzanne was moving her home office to a new house, she took the opportunity to sort everything and discard a good many items. She also labeled or indexed the material she kept. Suzanne now spends less time searching for items and has more time to take a renewal recess in the afternoon. If you are looking for ideas on how to straighten up your work area, read Barbara Hemphill's book, *Taming the Paper Tiger at Work*. You will find simple guidelines for getting the tiger in your work area under control.

Key Point

"Straightening up the work area can be rejuvenating and can bring balance and freedom to work."

Visualize balance at work

Set aside ten minutes each day this week to step back from your normal routine and visualize yourself experiencing balance at work. Visualizing is a technique that many successful, professional athletes use to improve their performance. It enables you to subtly align your intention with your actions and create a shift in the way you operate. Give it a try! You can use the exercise on Visualizing Balance at Work to help you imagine that you are living and working in a sustained and renewing way.

Exercise: Visualizing Balance at Work

Read the exercise instructions several times until you become familiar with them. Then put them aside and complete the exercise on your own. As an alternative, record the instructions on an audiotape and play them back.

1. Sit upright in a chair and take a few deep breaths. Close your eyes and allow yourself to relax.

---

2. Begin to imagine yourself at work. See yourself entering the workplace, feeling calm and energized. Imagine yourself moving through the day—performing tasks, responding to requests, making decisions—at a pace that feels comfortable and easy. Be very specific in your visualization. Notice the light and colors in the room around you. Pay attention to the physical surroundings. Visualize specific tasks. What exactly are you doing and how are you doing it in a balanced way? Notice what you hear...see...smell...feel...and touch.

3. Hear yourself talking with your coworkers in a calm and even tone of voice. Feel the space and ease in your conversations. See yourself handling important situations with equanimity. Picture yourself reprioritizing tasks and events as the day proceeds—saying "no" to some requests and responding affirmatively to others. Imagine yourself knowing which activities are truly important and remaining relaxed in the face of other people's sense of urgency.

4. Imagine yourself engaging in various renewal activities during the day. Notice how you are aware of your physical, mental, emotional, and spiritual energy and how you revitalize yourself in each of these areas at different times during the day. Maybe you pause to stretch mid-morning and get a fresh glass of water; eat lunch and run a personal errand; write a note of appreciation to a friend and change activities to give your mind a rest in the afternoon; notice how much you enjoy your work and coworkers; and take a few moments at the end of the day to silently express your gratitude.

5. Imagine leaving work at the end of the day, knowing you have accomplished the most important goals for the day, feeling satisfied with your work and having enough energy to enjoy an evening at home. Picture yourself doing an activity after work that refreshes you and imagine getting a good night's rest.

6. Take a few deep breaths and slowly open your eyes.

"I have seen first-hand that life is not work and work is not life, and from that I have learned that only a life in balance is truly a life in full."

ROBERT K. JOHNSTON, PH.D.
AND J. WALKER SMITH, PH.D.,
LIFE IS NOT WORK, WORK IS NOT LIFE

16

September

Make a New Commitment to Your Work

"Commitment is a personal investment or consignment in the face of
uncertain outcome. If the outcome were a sure thing, no commitment
would be required."

PETER BLOCK, *STEWARDSHIP*

Introduction

When September arrives, it is back to school and work after vacation. The lazy days of summer are over and it is time to get back on track. During the summer, people are more relaxed and less intensely focused on work, often letting things slide. So, September is a good time to reflect on and make a new commitment to your work and life's mission. Doing so will reinvigorate you and allow you to contribute fully to work with a renewed passion and vigor.

One of the best ways to make a fresh pledge to your work is to re-examine what motivates and inspires you. When you have determined why you are doing the type of work you have chosen, it is easy to refocus attention on what is important at this point in time. Clarifying your motivation is also a great preparation for identifying or refining your life's mission. Remembering the original inspiration for your career choice can help you recognize the deeper meaning of your work or assist in redefining your life's purpose.

Inspirational Quote

"If, as employees, our commitment is low, then our connection to the organization is weak and we offer less of our energy and skills in service of it. High commitment leads to the opposite result: We want to give our energy and skills."

DENNIS T. JAFFE, CYNTHIA D. SCOTT, GLENN R. TOBE,
REKINDLING COMMITMENT

Recommitting to your life mission or even a large project at work can be challenging, especially if you do not know what the outcome will be. Pledging yourself to something when you know the end result is easy. The most arduous form of commitment requires stepping out in faith—without knowing what will happen—saying "I am in," and staying motivated and dedicated to the purpose, regardless of what happens.

This is what Moses did. You might be familiar with the Biblical story of Moses leading his people through the desert to the Promised Land.

During his 40 years in the desert, Moses faced both unending hardships, as well as blessings. At one point, Pharaoh, having second thoughts about letting the people go with Moses, sent soldiers and six hundred chariots to capture them and bring them back. Moses prayed to God, asking that he be shown the way to escape the soldiers. God directed Moses to follow a route that led right to the edge of the Red Sea. As Moses and his frightened people stood there with a huge body of water ahead and the six hundred chariots in hot pursuit, he was told to part the waters with a rod that he had carried with him through the desert. Moses had made a commitment to God that he would lead the Israelites and place his trust in God. So, he did what he was instructed to do, without knowing what the outcome would be. God caused a great wind to blow over the waters, opening up a passageway through which Moses and his people could cross. They walked across—not knowing how the waters had parted or whether the soldiers would catch up with them. Many say that it was their great faith that gave them favor in God's eyes. And in fact, the Red Sea (which closed again after the Israelites had safely crossed) drowned all of Pharaoh's men as they tried to follow Moses and his people.

Inspirational Quote

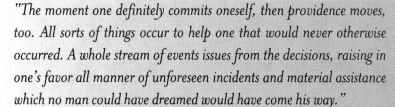

"The moment one definitely commits oneself, then providence moves, too. All sorts of things occur to help one that would never otherwise occurred. A whole stream of events issues from the decisions, raising in one's favor all manner of unforeseen incidents and material assistance which no man could have dreamed would have come his way."
JOHANN WOLFGANG VON GOETHE, *PAST FORWARD*

Moses stayed committed—even in the face of unbelievable circumstances—and then acted on his faith. Commitment without action is meaningless. Action is the visible sign that you are serious about carrying out your commitments. Reflecting on promises to yourself and others at work is the first important step. Making a commitment and taking action is the second. And getting support for sustaining that action is the third.

Key Point

"Commitment without action is meaningless. Action is the visible sign that you are serious about carrying out your commitments."

Sustaining momentum for carrying out your mission at work requires a variety of types of support. It helps to have people who can both inspire and hold you accountable to your commitment to work. While recommitting to your work, how about renewing the promises you made earlier in the year to refresh yourself during the workday? Remember, renewal activities provide the sustained energy you need to accomplish your mission and achieve your goals.

If you have read this book in chronological order, there are many renewal ideas that you can implement. You may find it helpful to go back and review the tips for Chapter 8, Week One: Decide What's Really Important in Your Life, and Chapter 12, Week Two: Consecrate Your Work and Week Three: Consider Your Work as Sacred. These sections provide support for thinking about priorities and purpose at work. This month's tips help you take action to renew yourself and your commitment to your most important goals.

Reflection Questions

Take two to three minutes to reflect and/or write about each of the following questions:

1. How do I feel when I am committed to my work?
2. Do I need to recommit to my work right now? If so, what are the signals that lead me to this conclusion?
3. What are the advantages to committing to my work?
4. What one action could I take that would rekindle my commitment to work?

Week One: Understand Your Motivation and Inspiration to Work

Understanding what motivates and inspires you to work is key to remaining committed. Just as life circumstances change over time, so can what motivates and inspires you to work. As a young person, your motivation and inspiration may differ from someone who has worked for a number of years. Early on in your career, motivation for working may be grounded in a desire for advancement and recognition. As you mature, motivation for working often centers on leaving a legacy, such as mentoring younger workers or making a meaningful contribution to society or the workplace.

If you find your commitment to work is waning, or you feel that it is time to recommit to your job, begin by looking at what motivates and inspires you to work. Doing so can often provide the impetus for reconnecting to your career.

Inspirational Quote

"The key to motivation is motive... It's what gives us the energy to stay strong in hard moments. It gives us the strength to say "no" because we connect with a deeper "yes!" burning inside. If a goal isn't connected to a deep "why," it may be good, but it usually isn't best. We need to question the goal."

STEPHEN R. COVEY, *FIRST THINGS FIRST*

This week take time to clarify the inspiration for your life's work and the goals associated with your mission. Examine your objectives and change those that no longer hold meaning for you or are unrealistic. Once you make any necessary adjustments, you will be better able to make a fresh start toward linking your purpose in life with your work.

Key Point

"When you have determined why you are doing the type of work you have chosen, it is easy to refocus attention on what is important."

Explore your inspiration at work

Remember why you are doing your work. In the midst of your hectic workday, it is easy to loose sight of what is inspiring about your work. Ask yourself "what inspires me to work?" Make a list of your reasons using a table like the one shown in the exercise that follows. Your answers may provide just the energy you need to be more inspired and committed to your work. Or your answers might just spark you to see the deeper reasons for working or to see your work as a gift.

Exercise: Reviewing What Is Inspiring About My Work

1. List or draw a mind map of everything that you find inspiring about work. Or use a table like the sample one that follows. If you are having difficulty thinking of items to include, recall the original reason why you chose your line of work. Think about the people with whom you work or, as the tips in Chapter 12, Week Three suggest, consider the contribution that your work makes to the greater community outside the workplace.
2. Reflect on and note the reasons why these items are inspiring to you.
3. Review your list or mind map every day this week and notice if and how your motivation and commitment to work increases. If your commitment is still low, implement more of the tips in this chapter.

Example of Table for Listing What Is Inspiring About My Work	
What Inspires Me At Work?	What About It Is Inspirational?

Identify the most inspiring event of your work life in which you played a part

Think back on your entire work life and identify the most inspirational moment in it. Examine the answer and your memory to see if elements that were a part of that situation are a part of your work today. If not, explore how you can make them part of your work now.

Many years ago, Suzanne worked as a music director in a program for differently-abled children. Tracy, a boy who was autistic, went through almost a whole summer without singing one song. As the children rehearsed for the yearly talent show and used the microphone for the first time, Tracy made his way quietly to the mike. To everyone's surprise, Tracy began singing the songs he had silently learned that summer! All he needed was a little extra stimulation to motivate him. To this day, Suzanne uses music in her training programs because of the power that music has to heal and to reach places that other learning methodologies cannot.

Inspirational Quote

"Thank You for Your faith in me that such a glorious mission has been placed in my hands."

MARIANNE WILLIAMSON, *ILLUMINATA*

Ask others what they find inspiring about their work

Be courageous and invite your colleagues and clients to share what is important and heartening to them at work. From them, you may find new inspiration for your own work or clarify your mission in life further. One Labor Day, a colleague of ours asked a group of preachers, a retired army captain, and a physician, all in the 50- to 60-year old range, who work in not-for-profit organizations and government agencies, what they found inspirational about their work. Our colleague thought that because these individuals all worked in very different settings and had varied backgrounds that their answers would differ. Instead, there was a thread of similarity running through their responses. For the most part, they were inspired by "the moments in which they served as catalysts for others' growth and the opportunity to discover new things about themselves and life." Our colleague reports it was enlightening as well as uplifting to hear the group's answers.

Read about people who follow their life's work or mission

Become inspired by others' life purposes. Reading about the lives of those who see their work as a means of making a difference in the world can be motivating and uplifting. It can also help to identify what matters to you at work. Often *Parade* (the Sunday magazine included in many US national newspapers), *Reader's Digest*, and *Guideposts* feature stories of people living out their life's mission— often in spite of obstacles and difficult challenges. You can also explore courageous stories of those who are living our their Christian mission by logging onto www.FaithAtWork.com and clicking onto the *Faith At Work Magazine*. Typically the stories we have mentioned are short and can easily be read during a work break. Consider having a "helping" of *Chicken Soup for the Soul at Work* stories with your lunch.

One story we read in the September 1, 2002, edition of *Parade* described Mattie J. T. Stepanek, a 12-year old poet with three best-selling books, who suffers from a neuromuscular disease that claimed the lives of three of his siblings. What inspires Mattie is his zeal for world peace. He and his mother, who both use wheelchairs, travel across the United States in a specially-designed van donated by Oprah Winfrey. They spread Mattie's message of hope and ideas for peace in the world.

When you read the stories of people who follow their life's purpose, you are reminded that acting to fulfill your mission requires persistence in the face of challenges. There is a story told of Mother Teresa about this very matter. Someone once suggested to Mother Teresa that service might be easier for her than for some others. After all, she had no house, no car, no possessions, and no husband. She replied that was not true and held up her ring, which symbolized her marriage to Christ. She went on the say that "He can be very difficult sometimes."

Week Two: Develop or Revisit the Mission Statement for Your Life's Work

Written mission statements can be very powerful. They identify what is most important and help you keep focused on your purpose in life and work. They also serve as a guide in making decisions and prioritizing all the many items on your "to do" list. Revisiting your mission statement can help refocus and re-inspire you to get "back on track." Having a mission statement can help ground you when work or life presents a surprise blind curve in the road ahead.

"Mission statements identify what is most important and help you keep focused on your purpose in life and work."

If you already have a written mission statement for your life's work, this is an opportunity to revisit and refine it. If you have yet to write a statement, begin to gather ideas for your statement this week. Whether you are composing or revising your statement, it is important to know that mission statements are alive and organic. A good mission statement stands the test of time and, at the same time, can expand and change to include new ideas and experiences.

Writing a statement is just the first step. In order to give life to your mission over time, it is helpful to revisit it periodically and revise the goals that support it. Think of this process as a tune-up for yourself. Avoid delaying your personal tune-up. The sooner you get started, the sooner you will be able to focus on what is most important.

Inspirational Quote

"A year from now you will wish you had started today."
Karen Lamb, *Time Management Guide*

Consult resources for developing or revising your mission statement

Discover how to create an effective personal mission statement. In his book *First Things First*, Stephen R. Covey provides excellent tools for devising a meaningful mission statement that describes your life's work. Consult Covey's book for assistance in fine-tuning your current statement, if you have one, or for guidance in writing your first statement, if you do not already have one.

Over the years many individuals have relied on Covey's formula for developing their statements. Ask around and see if other people are willing to share their reactions to writing their vision using Covey's process. There are several other resources available if Covey's suggestions do not resonate with you. These resources include: *Zen and the Art of Making a Living* by Laurence C. Boldt, *Living with Vision* by Linda Marks, *The Power of Purpose* by Richard J Leider, and *The Path* by Laurie Beth Jones.

Create or review your life's work mission statement

Write or revise a mission statement once you have decided on an approach that works for you. After it is complete, ask significant others in your life to read the statement to see if it sounds like you and makes sense based on what they know about you. Then post it in a prominent place where you can read and evaluate it. Examine the words to see if they inspire you to take action. Ask if this statement will work for you over the long haul. See if your mission statement has threads of what have been sources of inspiration throughout your life. If necessary, make any appropriate changes to make your statement reflect your purpose and inspiration.

Ed, a consultant we know, has a mission statement that reflects his desire to use his abilities to help change how business is done so that people can develop themselves personally, as well as professionally. The first part of his purpose statement reads as follows: "My purpose is to use my creativity, courage, speaking/ teaching abilities, and my understanding of scientific and human transformative principles to help transform ...how business is practiced today, so that people in business can develop themselves materially and spiritually, and apply this...for the greatest benefit of themselves, their companies, our society, and the natural world. The business entity I lead is a positive force for this change."

Other people have shorter mission statements that reflect their key goals in life or work. For instance, Juliet, the president of a real estate company, has a briefer mission statement. She says, "The most important goal for me is to do my part as a woman and business leader for the future of our city." Laurie, the president of a food processing company, states, "I want to continue being involved in meaningful social-political and business economic issues that affect positive attitudes towards women, Mexicans, and other Latinos." Janis' statement is more general. She claims, "the most important thing for me now is to live each day as fully as possible. I want to stay interested in life, to laugh often, and to give love."

"You want a mission statement that will work for you over the long haul, one that has threads of what have been sources of motivation throughout your life."

Develop goals to support your mission statement

Think about how best to implement your purpose or life's work at this point in time. Develop specific goals that support the mission that inspires you. Begin with short-term goals and then work on your long-term goals attaching attainable target dates to each set of goals. As you develop these objectives, consider the various areas of life that require renewal in order to sustain the energy to live out your life's work. In his book, *The 7 Habits of Highly Effective People*, Stephen R. Covey describes four critical areas to include—1) physical (exercise, nutrition, stress management), 2) mental (reading, visualizing, planning, writing), 3) spiritual (value clarification and commitment, study, and meditation), and 4) social/emotional (service, empathy, synergy, intrinsic security).

Review your mission statement daily and your goals weekly

Place your mission statement in your appointment book or on the computer screen to keep it in front of you on a regular basis. Some individuals post their statement on a bathroom mirror at home as a means of seeing their mission first thing in the morning and last thing at night.

Returning to your mission statement and goals can bring about powerful results. One young college woman we know wrote a goal for herself when she was twelve years old. Her goal simply read "Attend Harvard and swim on the Harvard team." Each and everyday she read her goal. Six years later she was studying and swimming at Harvard.

Week Three: Get Support for Implementing Your Goals

The various "Twelve Step" programs that have worked miracles in so many people's lives are based on the principle of accountability. The programs encourage participants to seek out sponsors and to call other members weekly to offer and get support. The success of these programs is often attributed to the fact that individuals are accountable to someone every day for their actions.

Inspirational Quote

"Many hands make light work."

LEROY W. JONES, *SPARKLE PEOPLE*

If you find sticking to your goals difficult or challenging, learn from the experience of "Twelve Step" programs and get support. You can improve the success of achieving your goals by turning to other caring individuals for assistance. Allow others the privilege of helping you stay true to your mission and goals. Your support system can range from one person to an entire group. Here are some ideas to help you get started in gathering support.

Ask for help on an informal basis in accomplishing goals

Seek out a coworker or professional colleague as a sounding board whenever you would like assistance in working towards a particular work goal. Check in with this person from time to time to provide an update. An easy way to manage this process is to e-mail this person your progress report on a frequent basis and ask for feedback.

Key Point

"You can improve the success of achieving your goals by turning to other caring individuals for assistance. Allow others the privilege of helping you stay true to your mission and goals."

Seek out an accountability partner

Select a colleague whom you trust and share your mission and goals with that person. Ask him or her to help you keep on track with your plan by meeting regularly to review your progress. Offer to return the favor to them by being their accountability partner. This strategy requires an ongoing commitment on your part and the part of your colleague.

Right from the beginning, set-up a formal schedule for reporting to one another. Set aside at least one hour a month to communicate with one another in person or by phone. Share, in writing, progress on your goals and plans for the next steps. Keep a record of your meeting by writing down those actions to which each of you has agreed. Begin your next meeting by reporting how well you did since you last met.

You may opt to find a paid coach to serve as your accountability partner. This is a role that we often play with our coaching clients. The old adage that "one values that for which one pays" applies here. If you hire a coach, you may find yourself more focused and willing to follow through on your action plans than you would working with a colleague for free.

We have hired a fitness consultant, Cindi Olson of Fitness Works Wonders located in Germantown, Maryland, to help remind us to exercise, something we both resist doing. We drew up a "fitness contract" with Cindi and she calls us on a regular basis to see if we are sticking to our agreement. Many times we are not, but we improve when we know it is time to report to or meet with Cindi. In turn, we are helping her be accountable about writing her book.

Inspirational Quote

"No one of us is as smart as all of us."

ANONYMOUS

Form a Mastermind Group

Invite a number of colleagues or professional friends to join you in creating a group in which you support each other in achieving your goals. One of the most successful forms of group assistance is the Mastermind Group. The premise behind Mastermind Groups is accountability through community. Mastermind Groups are usually comprised of 6 to 10 individuals who may have similar backgrounds (many professional speakers belong to a Mastermind Group) or different backgrounds. Members may be located in the same city or in different parts of the country. Groups may meet in person or over the phone. This type of gathering works best for those who desire help with problem-solving, are looking for inspiration from others, and are willing to trust a small group of individuals with personal information.

Each group works differently and establishes its own operating guidelines as to frequency of meetings and ground rules. For the most part, all Mastermind Groups provide a place where members can gain support and be accountable for a "stretch goal" in their lives. Most Mastermind Groups allot focused time for members to speak at each meeting. During this period, members present a challenge for which they are seeking support and advice. Follow-up meetings include a "report out time." For more information about forming a group of your own, refer to Christine W. Zurst's online article, "Leaders Gain Valuable Insights Through Mastermind Groups."

Ruth, who is a trainer and speaker, uses her Mastermind Group to challenge her to become a more effective presenter. When she has a major new presentation, she practices the new material with the group. Members give feedback and once she has presented to her client, she reports back at the next group meeting, sharing what went well and how she could improve next time.

Inspirational Quote

 "Two heads are always better than one, but how about 6, 8, or 10 heads?"
CHRISTINE W. ZURST, "LEADERS GAIN VALUABLE INSIGHTS THROUGH MASTERMIND GROUPS"

Create a "Personal Board of Advisors"

 Hold yourself accountable by forming a volunteer board of advisors. Many small business owners use this approach. Anyone can use an advisory board, regardless of their career endeavors. The concept of using a board of advisors is simple. You invite a variety of people, with different careers, whom you respect to be on your board. Then you meet with the board as a group once or twice a year to report on your progress. They, in turn, respond to the report by challenging you to stretch and providing you with encouragement. The meeting can be as formal or informal as you make it. At different times during the year, you can also call on an individual member of your board to advise you on an area of their expertise. Krista serves on the personal advisory board of a friend and client. They go to lunch when he has an issue to discuss regarding his personal mission in life. You can find guidance for forming a personal board of advisors in an online article by Vance Caesar, Ph.D., entitled "Use a Personal Board of Advisors to Be Successful."

Inspirational Quote

"It's easy to see the benefits of having your own life-board of advisors: focus, accountability, and resources that accelerate results and reduce effort."

VANCE CAESAR, PH.D.,
"USE A PERSONAL BOARD OF ADVISORS TO BE SUCCESSFUL"

Week Four: Include Renewal at Work in Your Commitment Plan

It is common to think about your goals in terms of only job-related tasks. However, renewal activities enable you to be most productive in the short term. They also provide energy over the long run to make your mission a reality. Remember, as was discussed in Part One, that renewal activities are a necessary piece of your work and one of the key factors that will help you achieve your goals. In order to work with renewed vigor, establish a few renewal goals for yourself, both for this month and the upcoming year. Here are some tips that will jump-start your thinking about creating goals to keep yourself running on plenty at work.

Commit to one friendship at work

Think about your colleagues at work and set a goal to make a new friend or deepen an existing relationship with one of them. Many people believe that they do not have time for friendships at work. Taking the time to foster friendships at work can lighten your load, provide a place to connect, and give you a place to be heard—all of which is renewing to your spirit. We have made a point of being friends as well as business partners. Our friendship has sustained us both in times of personal and business hardships. It has also helped us choose to deal with issues between us in respectful and caring ways because we personally value and love each other.

Learn more about Emotional Intelligence

Develop your understanding of the importance of maintaining good relationships at work and dealing effectively with your own and others' emotions. Recent research shows that emotional intelligence is a much more accurate predictor of professional success than intellectual intelligence. Those individuals who are emotionally intelligent are aware of both theirs and others emotions, understand the impact that emotions have on behavior, are able to care for themselves emotionally, and use emotions constructively in interactions with others. You can learn more about emotional intelligence and how it can enhance your work performance by reading the work of Daniel Goleman, Ph.D. He has written several books on the subject, including *Emotional Intelligence, Emotional Intelligence at Work,* and *Primal Leadership: Realizing the Power of Emotional Intelligence.*

Move your body every hour or two at work

Think of ways you can move your body at work throughout the workday and set a goal to implement these ideas. Ask children you know about "Brain Gym®" exercises they may do in school. These specific activities are designed to integrate left brain/right brain functions. According to www.braingym.org, Brain Gym® "consists of twenty-six easy and targeted activities that bring about rapid and often dramatic improvements in concentration, memory, and physical coordination." In other words, these exercises renew you both physically and mentally. You can learn more about Brain Gym®

at work by reading *Brain Gym for Business* by Gail Dennison, Paul Dennison, Ph.D., and Jerry Teplitz, J.D., Ph.D. Incorporate Brain Gym® concepts into your work day by trying the exercise which follows.

Exercise: Renewing Your Body and Mind

1. Standing, take turns swinging your arms, one at a time, in front of you, making figure eight's several times with each arm. Reverse your pattern. Repeat three times.
2. Raising your left knee upward, touch your left knee with your right hand. Then, switch sides and touch your right knee with your left hand. Repeat three times.
3. Bending your left leg behind you, touch your left heel behind your back with your right hand. Then, change sides and touch your right heel with your left hand behind your back. Repeat three times.
4. Placing one hand on the top of your head, and one hand on your belly, repeatedly pat the top of your head gently, while also rubbing your belly. Switch hands, placing the opposite hands on top of your head and belly. Repeat the patting and rubbing.
5. When you have completed all four exercises, take a moment to explore how you feel before returning to your work activities.

Relax your brain during the workday

Commit to a daily goal of relaxing your mind at work. In his book, *Mozart's Brain and the Fighter Pilot*, Richard Restak, M.D. makes the case for "relaxing your brain." Restak claims that relaxing the brain is a perfect antidote to stress and over-stimulation. He suggests a simple exercise for resting the mind: focus on the scene before you and then close your eyes. With your eyes closed, try to recall every detail of the scene. Then open your eyes to check for anything that you may have missed to complete the mental picture. Close your eyes again and hold that completed picture in your mental awareness. Restak states, "Contrary to what you might expect, this imaging exercise provides relief from mental fatigue rather than worsens it."

"We must understand the urgency and importance of our mission if we are to fulfill it."

LAURIE BETH JONES, *THE PATH*

17

OCTOBER

APPRECIATE ABUNDANCE AT WORK

Introduction

Traditionally, the fall is a time of harvest, a time for the farmers to gather in the fruits of their labors and for all of us to celebrate the abundance of life. Although much of western society has left agricultural rhythms behind in the move to the technological age, the modern workplace is still an appropriate place to acknowledge the bounty that flows from your efforts. If you think about it, work is itself the very foundation of wealth. As the Bible and other faith traditions state, it is "by the sweat of your brow you shall eat." Simply being able to work for a living is a form of wealth, for work allows you to expand and share your personal resources (skills and knowledge). Work can bring a sense of happiness and satisfaction, which are important forms of abundance.

What comes to mind when you think of abundance? Most people associate the word abundance with having and acquiring a bounty of possessions and money. However, if you look at abundance only in material terms, you restrict both your understanding of, and access to, the many forms of wealth. If you wish to fully appreciate prosperity, then it is essential to expand your vision of abundance beyond a desire for objects alone. You can experience affluence mentally, emotionally, and spiritually, as well as financially and physically.

Inspirational Quote

"Profit may take the form of increased energy, improved satisfaction, a new friendship, monetary income, or any other net expansion of joy or happiness."

JAMES CRAIG GREEN, "SMALL PROFITABLE STEPS"

You may have a wealth of knowledge and wisdom, a plethora of skills and abilities, lots of love, a bounty of moral virtues, a multitude of friends and family, profuse happiness, complete satisfaction, a feeling of total freedom, and a sense of overflowing fullness. In fact, the word "abundance" is derived from the Latin word "abundare," which means to overflow. Its original meaning refers to the ability to recognize, appreciate, and celebrate **all** that you have and experience in life.

Key Point

"You can experience affluence mentally, emotionally, and spiritually, as well as financially and physically."

When you have such an expanded definition of abundance, you come to realize that prosperity is not solely about acquiring more possessions and money. Abundance is about increasing inner wealth, those attributes that are intrinsically unlimited—love, care, harmony, respect, peace of mind, and a willingness to work for the good of humanity.

Once you recognize the prosperity that already exists in your life, you have some choices to make about what to do with it. First, you can either allow your prosperity to blossom or diminish. You might unconsciously choose to diminish the value of your wealth by saying something like, "I could have done better." Or you could choose to celebrate your abundance by acknowledging all that you have accomplished and the results you received from your work. Second, you can either claim all of the credit for your prosperity, saying, "Look what I did," or recognize those who had a hand in your success.

Key Point

"Abundance is about increasing our inner wealth, those attributes that are intrinsically unlimited—love, care, harmony, respect, peace of mind, and a willingness to work for the good of humanity."

Finally, you can choose to gather in all of the bounty and keep it for yourself, or you can recognize that ultimately nothing truly belongs to you. You are a steward of everything that you have. True abundance comes from sharing what you have. This month's tips will help you make these choices by giving ways to cultivate an attitude of abundance, be a steward of your resources, and recognize and share abundance at work.

Reflection Questions

Take two to three minutes to reflect and/or write about each of the following questions:

1. How do I feel about abundance in my life? What are my beliefs and attitudes about it?
2. How aware am I of abundance at work?
3. What gets in the way of my recognizing and welcoming abundance at work?
4. How can I cultivate an attitude of abundance at work?
5. In what ways can I share my abundance more often at work?

Week One: Recognize Your Abundance at Work

Sometimes, in the midst of your hectic work schedule, you may overlook the prosperity that is all around you. You may forget to celebrate what you have and what you are working towards. Recognizing abundance at work entails slowing down enough to realize the assets you have, both material and intangible. Here are some ways to be more aware of the abundance that already exists in your life.

Become aware of the plentitude of life around you

Expand your overall sense of prosperity by paying attention to the profusion of life in general. Instead of neglecting the many resources life provides, or focusing on your lack of resources (time, money, or other means) at work, notice how life itself is plentiful. Perceive the magic of everyday life and connect to the beauty of the world. Observe the nice variety of people around you at work. Look out the window and see the multitude of ways in which nature expresses its riches at this time of year. Glance around your workspace and survey the number of items that are available to help you perform your work. Listen to the variety of sounds in your environment. Feel the collection of objects in your workspace. Then, with a renewed awareness of abundance, return to the work at hand. Note if there is any difference in your energy and attention to work.

Key Point

> *"Recognizing abundance at work entails slowing down enough to realize the assets you have, both material and intangible."*

Assess your abundance at work

Set aside some time to consider the abundance that exists in your life at work. Explore the variety of ways in which your work life is rich and plentiful. Observe the many obvious, and subtle, ways in which your workdays are full of prosperity. Do you have a meaningful job? Are you successful in your career? Do you have motivation, skills, and resources to get things done at work? Are you able to draw on your knowledge, experience, and inner strength to deal with challenges and change at work? Do you have numerous opportunities to learn? Use the exercise below to help you become even more abundantly aware of all the true wealth you possess.

Inspirational Quote

> *"All prosperity begins in the mind and is dependent only upon the full use of our creative imagination."*
>
> RUTH ROSS, *THE QUOTATIONS PAGE*

Exercise: Assessing Abundance at Work

1. Use the categories in the following example to reflect on the many ways in which your work life is prosperous.
2. Make a note, draw a picture, make a collage, or create a mind map of all the ideas that surface.
3. Keep your list, picture, or mind map in a place where you can see it frequently, such as in your day planner or desk drawer.
4. Refresh your memory and awareness of the abundance at work by reviewing your ideas each day or week.

An Example of an Assessment of Abundance

Category	Ways in which my work life is abundant:
Mentally	1. I have a lot of knowledge about my field of work 2. I have many opportunities to be creative at work and develop myself personally and professionally 3. I get to use my skills and talents at work
Physically	1. I have plenty of energy for my job 2. My working conditions are good 3. I am able to exercise in the gym at work
Financially	1. I am paid what I am worth 2. I have health insurance and other benefits at work 3. I have promotional opportunities 4. I work in an industry that provides room for professional growth
Emotionally	1. I have lots of motivation 2. I laugh often at work and am in a good mood 3. I love my work
Spiritually	1. I do meaningful work 2. I make a positive contribution to the world 3. I love what I do and the people with whom I work
Relationally	1. I have good relationships with my coworkers 2. My work hours allow me to spend enough time with my family
Materially	1. I have enough resources to get things done 2. I work in a pleasant environment with many nice objects around me

Key Point

"Success is striving for something you believe in and living a life that enables you to accomplish both meaningful professional results and a satisfying personal life."

Acknowledge your success

Recognize your professional achievements and the abundance associated with them. Acknowledge what you have accomplished at work, the money you have earned, and the accolades you have received in your field. Recognize the more subtle and important aspects of success, such as personal fulfillment, the attainment of inner contentment, and strength in the face of adversity. Success is more than just money and achievements. It is also striving for something you believe in and persisting in putting forth effort towards your goal, no matter what happens in the long run. It is living a life that enables you to accomplish both meaningful professional results and a satisfying personal life.

Inspirational Quote

"Not what we have, but what we enjoy, constitutes our abundance."
JOHN PETIT-SENN, *CYBER NATION*

Enjoy your abundance

Take pleasure in all the forms of success and richness in your life. Allow yourself to feel good about what you have done at work. Acknowledge that you deserve what you have achieved. Then, instead of always pushing on to accomplish more, avail yourself of the benefits of your abundance. Take time to relish the fruits of your labor. Acquiring possessions and money and accomplishing great things in life have much more meaning when you are able to experience the inner aspects of success, and enjoy what you have helped to create. Like the fisherman in the following story, make the most of what you have today.

A Story about Enjoying Abundance

**(Adapted first by Charles MacInerney and then by us
from a popular story circulating on the Internet)**

There once was an American CEO who, while vacationing in Mexico, became fascinated with a local fisherman. Each day, he watched the fisherman set out in the morning and return in the afternoon with fish. One day the fisherman returned early. The CEO, interested in why the fisherman was not working all day, approached him and inquired why he was back so early. Smiling, the fisherman pointed to the fish in the boat and said, "The fish were biting today and I caught what I needed in an hour!"

The CEO, stunned by the fisherman's lack of work ethic, asked, "What will you do with the rest of the day?" The fisherman grinned and replied, "After lunch I will take a rest. Then, in the afternoon, I will play with my children. In the evening I will spend time with my friends."

The CEO, thinking he could help the fisherman with his business, began to offer his advice. "You know, since the fish are biting so well today, you could go back out and catch even more fish that you could sell in the market. If you continue to fish all day when the fish are biting, you will soon be able to buy another boat. I bet that within a few years, you could even have a small fishing fleet. In time, you might even be able to open your own fish market and one day you could own an entire fishing empire!"

When the CEO paused to take a breath, the fisherman, who was perplexed by the CEO's monologue, quickly jumped in and said, "Why would I want to do all that?" The CEO smiled and replied, "Why, after you have built your empire, you could sell it and then really enjoy life!" The fisherman responded, saying, "That is what I am already doing!" And he walked away to go take a rest, see his children, and have dinner with his friends.

Week Two: Cultivate an Attitude of Abundance

If you look to the world to supply you with a steady stream of wealth and prosperity, you will end up being disappointed. People's desires are seldom completely fulfilled by the circumstances of life. If you wish to expand your abundance at work, another approach is necessary. To be content and live abundantly at work, it is essential to look within yourself and cultivate a mindset of prosperity.

Inspirational Quote

"What we are really seeking in life is an inner affluence."
MARSHA SINETAR, *TRUE WEALTH*

Abundance is as much a way of thinking as it is the acquisition of the material items one desires. Each person has a choice about what he or she thinks and how he or she perceives the world. You can choose to view the world as a place of scarcity or you can perceive the rich beauty and plentiful blessings that surround you. Whatever you choose to believe will influence how you behave and what is actually experienced. For instance, if you are worried about having enough, you might hoard resources and be seen by others as stingy and selfish. On the other hand, if you think, "there is enough to go around," you might share what you have and in return receive much from others. Given the power of beliefs, it makes sense to nurture an outlook of plenty if you wish to increase the abundance in your life. Here are some ways to get started.

Enhance your positive beliefs and attitudes about prosperity

Reflect on the beliefs and attitudes you hold towards abundance and wealth. Are you always wanting more from the job or are you satisfied with what you have? Do you work to acquire more power or do you see ways you can already serve and make a contribution? Do you focus on what is wrong with the situation or cultivate solution-oriented thinking? Do you believe that success is primarily about climbing the career ladder or do you feel that true wealth comes from living a meaningful life?

Contemplate questions like the ones just listed and invest some time thinking about what is enough for you. Also, pay attention to whether or not your thoughts increase or decrease your sense of prosperity. Do you feel that the cup is half empty or half full most of the time? Do you believe you have to fight and compete for recognition and success or do you think there is plenty of everything to go around? Do you think you do not deserve to live well or do you feel worthy of having an abundant life? Do you envy others who have material wealth or do you celebrate their success and yours?

Explore these types of questions by writing down your positive and negative beliefs on two different pieces of paper. Then, create positive statements to replace the negative ones whenever they come to mind.

Be content with your present level of assets

Be satisfied with what you have at work. Instead of wanting more— more time, more resources, more support, more skills, more money, etc.—allow yourself to accept and be pleased with what is on hand. Think thoughts like, " I do my very best with what I have" or "What I have is enough." Then explore how you can achieve your goals with the resources currently available. As the Lao Tsu quote suggests, true contentment and prosperity comes when you adopt a point of view that welcomes what you already have.

Inspirational Quote

"Be content with what you have;
    rejoice in the way things are.
When you realize there is nothing lacking,
    the whole world belongs to you."
        LAO-TSU, *TAO TE CHING: THE BOOK OF THE WAY*

Nancy, the only obstetrician gynecologist in her small town in the northwest, worked long hours and built up a successful practice. Over the years, she worked more and earned more, but she enjoyed her patients less. Her discontentment led to serious burnout and Nancy began to look at why she went into medicine in the first place. She realized her initial motivation was more about healing people and less about increasing her earning power. After some considerable soul searching, she decided to cut back on her hours and sought the assistance of local family physicians to handle routine births and gynecological exams. Nancy reports that she is much happier now and feels better about herself and her patients.

Act as if your work life is abundant

Whenever you find yourself thinking thoughts of scarcity or having a difficult time perceiving the richness around you, think positively. Imagine that you already have all the prosperity and wealth you desire. Then act as if what you are thinking is true. If it helps, you can repeat statements or affirmations like the one Ernest Holmes makes in *The Science of Mind*: "Life lies open to me rich, full, abundant. My thought, which is my key to life, opens all doors for me." Sometimes it is the most challenging circumstances that help us to see the abundance in our lives. So, use a perceived adversity to your advantage. Allow it to guide you to welcome the plenty in your life.

Inspirational Quote

"If we had no winter, the spring would not be so pleasant; if we did not sometimes taste of adversity, prosperity would not be so welcome."
ANNE BRADSTREET, *THE QUOTATIONS PAGE*

Exercise: Reaffirming Abundance at Work

1. Take five minutes to brainstorm as many positive phrases (affirmations) as you can about your abundance at work.
2. Review your list and select the one with which you resonate the most.
3. If necessary, rephrase the statement so that it is written in the present tense. Here is an example: "I have all the resources necessary to do excellent work."
5. Then, every day for 28 days, write or repeat the phrase at least 10 times. This process will help you develop an abundant and content mindset.

Explore the dynamics of creating prosperity

Reflect on what you know about how growth and creativity work in the world. What kinds of lessons do you notice about generating abundance? What messages and adages have you learned pertaining to how prosperity is generated? Two that come to mind are "You reap what you sow," and "Give and you shall receive." Are there others you can think of? To get some additional ideas about the dynamics of abundance, go online or to a local library or bookstore. Numerous books and articles exist that offer information on how to generate more prosperity in your life. A few of them include *Simple Abundance, The 40 Day Prosperity Plan, The Abundance Book, Open Your Mind to Prosperity,* and *The Dynamic Laws of Prosperity.*

Many people have memorized the passage "The Lord is my shepherd. I shall not want" from the 23rd Psalm found in the Hebrew scriptures. Reverend Canon Eugene Sutton, the Director of the Cathedral Center for Prayer and Pilgrimage asked a group of individuals who were about to walk the labyrinth at Washington National Cathedral to look at this familiar line in a new way. He encouraged them to repeat "The Lord is my shepherd. I have all that I need" as they made their way around the labyrinth.

Week Three: Be a Good Steward of Abundance

Those who understand abundance in spiritual terms, know that nothing truly belongs to them. Since they cannot take anything physical with them when they leave this earth, they realize they are essentially caretakers of all the resources available to them while they are alive. Like Buddha taught, they know that "one must count nothing as one's own in the midst of abundance."

Inspirational Quote

"Surplus wealth is a sacred trust which its possessor is bound to administer in his lifetime for the good of the community."
ANDREW CARNEGIE, *PPR QUOTES*

Once you accept that you are a steward of abundance, you naturally begin to think about how best to take care of any accessible wealth and how to use it well. You also begin to shift, as Jae Malone says in an article on abundance, from focusing on your own prosperity to thinking about how to create wealth for everyone. Here are some suggestions for being a good caretaker of abundance at work.

Use your resources wisely

Make conscious decisions about how you utilize resources to make the most of what you have. Discover ways to employ your assets, both professionally and personally, to the fullest extent. Judiciously use the means you have available, having faith that there will be enough to go around. Protect and nurture your wealth, without hoarding it. Operate from a spirit of cooperation and put your wealth to use in ways that bring about positive outcomes for you, coworkers, and the organization.

At work, make reasonable charges to your expense account, without going overboard. Treat others with whom you work with respect, for they are your most important resources. Encourage your company to spend surplus funds on community projects that benefit many people. At home, allocate your budget to items that will make the biggest contribution to the local or global community. Become a volunteer and offer your time and skills to a local charity.

Conserve some of your wealth

Whenever you have an abundant supply of a resource, set some aside, if possible, for non-urgent tasks or for the future. Start small. Put away whatever you can afford. Reserve ten minutes for a piece of work that you have been continuing to put aside or for something you enjoy doing. Then add another five minutes to that reserved time each subsequent day, so that you eventually build up to having 30 minutes set aside for your chosen activity on the fifth day. (On day one, you have 10 minutes for your activity; on day two, 15 minutes; day three, 20 minutes, and so on.) Or refrain from spending any surplus work budget dollars on frivolous or unnecessary items. Instead, allocate a part of your surplus to a future project. Although this act may be bucking the norm—after all, if you do not spend all of your budget this year, you may not get an increase or your allocation may even be decreased—you will be making resources available for others to spend on needed projects.

Inspirational Quote

"When prosperity comes, do not use all of it."

CONFUCIUS, *CYBER QUOTATIONS*

Live simply at work

Use the minimum amount of resources necessary to complete your work. Look for ways to recycle materials, avoid over-utilization of raw materials, and leverage tasks to serve multiple purposes. When you live simply at work, you reduce the stress on the environment and leave ample supplies for others. Start conserving now and avert disaster. A young "dot com" company in the Washington, DC area was in financial trouble and, rather than laying off its employees, the company's executives asked their staff to identify creative ways to save money. Motivated to save their jobs, this company's employees began a variety of cost-saving measures, such as coordinating overnight mailings. Instead of sending three packages to the same customer, the mailings were combined into one. They pulled together as a team and demonstrated their abilities to be good stewards of their company's resources. Unfortunately, the lesson of stewardship was learned too late and the company folded.

Focus on the unlimited inner resources you have available to you, like the ability to create joy for others and do something well for its own sake. As Jae Malone suggests in the article "From Abundance," living modestly entails shifting your focus from wanting more power and material goods to making connections and appreciating life. When you take time to concentrate on the intrinsic beauty and function of the resources at and outside work, then you discover your needs are less than expected.

Key Point

"When you live simply at work, you reduce the stress on the environment and leave ample supplies for others."

Remember that you are a steward

Find ways to keep in mind that everything you have comes from the Creator of all life. Remind yourself often that work provides you wealth that in turn affords the opportunity to practice stewardship. Post a reminder somewhere in the office or in your daily planner about your role as a steward. Locate a poem or prayer that you repeat every day. Or create a statement that affirms your role as caretaker. Take for example such as the following lines from a prayer in *Illuminata* written by Marianne Williamson: "[May money] flow freely into me and through me, that it might bless my life and the life of others... Whatever money comes to me, may it be used to serve [humanity]."

Week Four: Share Your Abundance with Others

When you have a prosperity mindset, you recognize that the planet is abundant with life and resources. You understand that wealth is like water, it either flows freely or it gets stagnant and disappears. You are motivated to give what you have. You share ideas and actions freely because you know that abundance flourishes when kept running and channeled in productive ways. Instead of competing for resources and striving to have more than others, you look for ways to collaborate and to share your riches.

Key Point

"True abundance comes from sharing what you have."

Donate a portion of your abundance to others

Allocate some of your time to helping coworkers. When you receive positive feedback for a project, make sure to acknowledge those who assisted you, directly and indirectly, in being successful. Offer an hour of your vacation time to someone who seems stressed. Support your coworkers' projects during budget meetings by offering them a small portion of your budget. Buy a small gift for your boss or assistant using some of your year-end bonus money. Or you might offer financial support from your business like Jackie does. After contemplating the abundance in her life and the amount of resources available to most people in the developing world, Jackie decided to offer a large share of her business profits to a non-profit organization that gives micro-loans to women in developing countries. She feels that she has so much and wants to support economic opportunities for other women in the world. When you give with a generous attitude you open the floodgates of abundance and eventually end up receiving more than you ever imagined in return.

The story of the Loaves and Fishes in the Christian scriptures demonstrates the principle of sharing abundance.

> *The story goes that Christ was talking to a multitude of 5,000 people and they were hungry. Jesus had compassion on them and tells the disciples to feed the people. The disciples question the wisdom of this because it would take six months of wages to feed the 5,000 gathered. So Jesus asks the disciples what they have and they reply "five loaves and two fish." In the story, Jesus blesses the five loaves and two fish and they multiply so that the entire crowd is fed.*

One interpretation of the story suggests that the people, upon seeing that the disciples were willing to share all they had, offered up what they had brought and shared with others as well. Parker Palmer, in *The Active Life: Wisdom for Work, Creativity, and Caring*, says, "Jesus wanted to help people … act out of the reality of abundance." Palmer suggests that a crucial transition occurs in your ability to understand "the potential of abundance" when you look at what you already have, at "the gifts and resources" that are available for you to share with others.

Inspirational Quote

"*This is the time of loaves and fishes.*
People are hungry and one good word is bread for a thousand."
DAVID WHYTE, *HOUSE OF BELONGING*

Share your inner wealth and talents with others

Develop a list of ways in which you can share some of your prosperity both at work and outside of work. Make a commitment to offer something to someone at least once a day. You may wish to refer back to the "Assess your abundance at work" tip in Week One to help recall what you have to give to others, as well to boost your motivation for sharing. As Cheryl Richardson, in *Take Time for Your Life*, suggests:

> *"When your cup is full, you naturally want to share with others. Being of service and offering your support to those in need brings you closer to others in a way that adds richness to your life."*

How you share your wealth with coworkers and others depends upon what you have to contribute. If you have been blessed with great baking abilities, perhaps you could bake something and bring it into work or give it away in the name of your organization. One of our computer industry clients baked goodies for the fire station personnel located near their office and delivered them on the one-year anniversary of the September 11, 2001 tragedy. If you have the gift of an easy smile, then you might dress up like a clown once a week and make children in the terminal care ward of a local hospital laugh. Maybe you have a talent for making people feel good about themselves and are in great physical shape. You might consider running with your local high school's cross country team a few days a month and becoming a mentor for some young adults. Whatever the decision, you will soon discover that sharing your abundance is as natural as flowing water.

A Story about Sharing Abundance

(adapted from a story on the Web site, Zen Stories to Tell your Neighbors)

> *One day a small pond, thinking it knew best, demanded from the river flowing by it, "Why do you give all your water to the ocean? It doesn't care about you. You are wasting your wealth." Silently, the river flowed on. "Let me give you some advice," continued the pond. "Even*

with all your water you can't make the ocean any less salty. I recommend that you reserve your riches for yourself." At this, the river replied, "I can't help it, my friend. It is my nature to give."

The pond, feeling rebuffed, turned away saying, "You'll regret not taking my advice." And the river just continued to flow, offering itself to the ocean, while the pond held on to all its water. As time passed, the miserly pond began to stagnate. All life in it eventually died and finally it completely dried up. The river, however, flowed on to the ocean where, invisibly, the surface waters evaporated. Gentle winds gathered moisture in the clouds and carried it back to the mountains, where it fell again as rain, feeding the river and keeping its waters fresh and pure forever.

> "Dear God, I wish to have whatever abundance You see fit for me. Amen"
> MARIANNE WILLIAMSON, *ILLUMINATA*

November

Cultivate Gratitude at Work

> *"Gratitude is the inward feeling of kindness received. Thankfulness is the natural impulse to express that feeling. Thanksgiving is the following of that impulse."*
>
> Henry Van Dyke, *Angel Fire Gratitude Quotes*

Introduction

November is a natural time for focusing on gratitude. It is the month when Americans traditionally celebrate Thanksgiving. It is also the time in the agricultural cycle where gratitude is most appropriate. After you have reaped the fruits of your labor and experienced abundance, it is fitting to give thanks for all that you have received. Some spiritual traditions advise setting aside time during the year for giving thanks. Ancient Hebrew law, for example, directs people to offer gratituStresser the harvest is reaped.

Life does offer a bounty of gifts. Yet, in spite of the fact that many American people have what they need, quite a few struggle with expressing gratitude for all that they have. U.S. society can breed greed and an entitlement mentality that can make it difficult for people to remember to give thanks for what they have. Some people only give their full attention to being grateful during the times set aside for giving thanks—times such as Thanksgiving. It seems that often inStressidst of all the busyness they forget to pause and be thankful. They forget to appreciate their blessings and to be grateful for the gifts received from work, others, nature, and life itself.

Key Point

"Life does offer a bounty of gifts. Yet, in spite of the fact that most people have what they need, many struggle with expressing gratitude for all they have."

Key Point

"With attention and practice, gratitude can become a way of life at work."

How often do you pause and give thanks for what you have? And when you do, do you express gratitude for your work? Charles Kingsley said, "Thank God every morning when you get up that you have something to do which must be done." Suzanne's father, RichStressho faces many physical challenges and is now limited in what he can do, says "I get up every morning with things to accomplish and I am grateful for something—regardless of how small—to work toward every day."

With attention and practice, gratitude can become a way of life at work. There are a multitude of ways you can express it—through praise, thanks, affirmation, offering, humor, prayer, wonder, awe, and service. This month's tips provide ideas and motivation for increasing your expression of gratitude at work.

Reflection Questions

Take two to three minutes to reflect and/or write about each of the following questions:

1. Do I think gratitude has a place in the workplace? If so, why is it good to give thanks at work?
2. In what ways do I experience gratitude at work?
3. In what ways do I express thanks at work?
4. What hinders me from expressing gratitude in the workplace?
5. In what ways can I increase my expression of gratitude at work?

Week One: Expand Your Understanding of Gratitude

Gratitude has the power to transform. Think about how a genuine and sincere "thank you" can alter your day. Yet, some people believe that expressing heart-felt thanks at work is inappropriate because people are being paid to do their work, which is thanks enough. There are many ways that gratitude can make a difference to people at work. For instance, in times of upheaval, people often feel anxious and disconnected. Saying thank you during times like this is a way to connect with your coworkers. This week learn more about the transforming power of gratitude in the workplace.

Inspirational Quote

"Gratitude
Opens our hearts
Connects us with others
Shows us life's blessings
Helps us get more out of life
Brings out the best in us and others
Reminds us of how abundant our lives are
Helps us remember the source of all that we have"

KRISTA KURTH

Read about gratitude

Become familiar with others' stories and views about gratitude and giving thanks. Many people have given considerable thought to the topic of gratitude and have written words of encouragement that can serve as a road map for finding ways of expressing thanks. This week explore the ideas found in *Simple Abundance: A Daybook of Comfort and Joy* by Sarah Ban Breathnach or the stories compiled by Louise L. Hay in *Gratitude: A Way of Life*. These resources will lift your spirits and provide inspiration for practicing how to express gratitude.

Surf the Internet for gratitude related Web sites

Go online to explore sources of information on giving thanks. The Internet has a wealth of inspirational quotes, stories, and practical ideas to help you deepen your understanding of gratitude. There are a variety of sites that feature stories about gratitude. Two sites in particular focus solely on gratitude and thankfulness: www.gratefulness.org, and www.bethankful.com. Take some time during lunch to go online to discover how others say thanks. Some sites have a place for readers to add their ideas, so you can submit thankful thoughts about your blessings at work.

Inspirational Quote

"No duty is more important than that of returning thanks and expressing gratitude."

ANONYMOUS

Learn from others how to express gratitude

Take time to listen to and watch how others express gratitude. Grateful and gracious people are all around and willing to provide you with models. Perhaps you know managers who know how to say "thanks" to their team members in meaningful ways. If so, listen to what they say and how it is said. In *Workforce Magazine,* Ann Perl tells about the chairman and CEO of Global Management Systems Inc., Hilton Augustine, and his approach to expressing gratefulness to his fellow employees. Augustine writes personal thank you notes, mentions specific contributions, and sends them to employees' homes. He believes that employees get extra accolades when they open the notes in front of their family members and significant others.

Inspirational Quote

"Let your heart be awakened to the transforming power of gratefulness."

SARAH BAN BREATHNACH,
THE SIMPLE ABUNDANCE JOURNAL OF GRATITUDE

Explore the power of gratitude

Experience the great restorative powers of gratitude. It has the power to change you and the workplace. As Sarah Ban Breathnach writes in her *Simple Abundance Journal of Gratitude,* "When we offer thanks to God or to another human being, gratitude gifts us with renewal, reflection, reconnection." Contemplate and write about your experiences of the power of gratitude. How have you been touched by others' expressions of thanks? How have you transformed situations or made a difference in other people's lives by sharing your gratitude?

Almost everyone has experienced the power of unexpected expressions of gratitude. Suzanne recalls a time, over a decade ago, when she was counseling clients at an outplacement center. Although she enjoyed this work, she found that some clients were often angry, extremely resistant to change, and not easily motivated. However, there was one client, Judy, who responded differently. After Judy found a new job she wrote a heartfelt thank you note in which she thanked Suzanne for her role in assisting "God to make a way where there was no way." To this day, Suzanne cherishes Judy's expression of thanks. It still holds great meaning and inspires Suzanne as she coaches other clients in difficult situations.

Key Point

"Gratitude has the power to change you and the workplace."

Week Two: Cultivate an Attitude of Gratitude at Work

Once you are more familiar with the general concept of gratitude, how others express their thanks, and the transforming power of gratefulness, you become ready to deepen the practice of giving and demonstrating thanks at work. It will have a profound effect upon your work. As Ann Perle suggests in her article featured on the MTM Recognition Web site, "Gratitude is an emotion that opens us up to seeing life in a more positive light and having feelings of goodness, joy, and love. It makes the workplace more meaningful."

Inspirational Quote

"Apply gratitude at work and remember that at the end of each business process—and at steps along the way—there are human hearts."
AUTHOR UNKNOWN, *BE THANKFUL QUOTE ARCHIVE*

Become aware of all the things for which you are thankful

Take time each day to notice the things at work for which you are grateful. If you have already completed last month's exercises, Reaffirming Abundance at Work and Assessing Abundance at Work, begin by reviewing your answers. Then develop a list of "Top Ten Things to Be Thankful For at Work." Place the list where you can see and refer to it at the beginning and end of each workday. Regularly review your list and revise it as appropriate.

Everyday, Krista makes sure to make note of what she is thankful for at work. She is grateful for doing work that she loves, for having great colleagues and clients, for having adequate financial resources, and for being able to work at home many days. At difficult times, she is particularly thankful for all the support she receives from others—the computer guys who keep her computer working, her assistant who takes care of so many details, and all the reliable suppliers who provide services to her and the business.

Exercise: Meditating on Your Blessings

This exercise is best done, initially, in a quiet place where you can remain undisturbed for ten to fifteen minutes. Once you are familiar with the process, it can be done anywhere, even with your eyes open.

Read the following instructions completely one or two times before doing the exercise. Alternatively, record yourself reading them, then play them back to guide yourself through the meditation exercise. If you choose to record the exercise, leave pauses between the sentences to allow time to experience what the instructions are guiding you to do.

1. Assume a comfortable upright posture, with your spine elongated and feet flat on the floor. Close your eyes. Take a few deep breaths and then become aware of any sensations in your body. Notice any tension in your body, any tightening of muscles, any feelings that may be coming from your work situation at this time.

2. As you become aware of a particular sensation, notice that feeling for a moment and then allow your breath to flow into the area of your body where the sensation is felt, relaxing the

body in that spot. Then, scan your body and breathe into any remaining areas of sensation, tension, or tightness.

3. Now focus your attention on your breath. Allow your breathing to be steady and even. Become aware of the rhythmic pattern of your breathing.

4. InStresseelings or images of gratitude and thanksgiving to arise from within. Imagine your thankfulness moving from the heart region down into your legs and feet. Feel it moving outward and upward into your arms, neck, and face, until it radiates throughout your whole body.

5. Begin to meditate on all that has been given to you. Start with the workplace and focus on the people at work, the work itself, and the positive impact of your work. Next move to your personal life, again focusing on the people, material, and non-material gifts.

6. After you have gathered in all your blessings, one-by-one, offer a word of thanks to God or the universe for each of the specific items before you.

7. Come gently out of meditation whenever you feel complete in the exercise. It is best to take some time in opening your eyes. You may want to take several deep breaths and slowly move your body first. Take a few minutes to write about your experience and any thoughts or feelings that you had during the meditation. Use this as an opportunity to expand your list of "Top Ten Things to Be Thankful For at Work."

8. Then work the rest of the day with a grateful heart and peaceful mind.

Keep a daily gratitude journal

Each day write down three to five things for which you are grateful. This daily ritual helps to develop your "attitude of gratitude." By noting all the things for which you are grateful, you are making an inventory of all that you have, instead of all that you want. As Dr. Richard Carlson suggests in *Don't Sweat the Small Stuff*, if you do this, "your life will start appearing much better than before. For perhaps the first time in your life, you'll know what it means to feel satisfied."

The practice of keeping a gratitude journal has received a great deal of exposure in the last few years due to Oprah Winfrey. After Oprah became familiar with Sarah Ban Breathnach's book *Simple Abundance*, she strongly encouraged her viewers to take up the daily ritual of keeping a gratitude journal because of the positive impact it could have on their lives. In an article that appeared in *Online Noetic Network*, Ban Breathnach is quoted as saying, "I swear to you that if you start giving thanks for five things everyday and do it for sixty days you will say that it absolutely turned your life around!" The Research Project on Gratitude and Thanksgiving, funded by the John Templeton Foundation, concurs with this statement. The study (the summary of which is highlighted at www.bethankful.com) found that those who kept gratitude journals felt better about their lives as a whole, and were more optimistic about the upcoming week, compared to those who wrote about hassles or neutral life events.

For those of you reading this who might be thinking that this activity appeals more to females or "right-brained types," think again. When Suzanne, who had been keeping a gratitude journal for years, suggested to her newlywed, "left-brained" husband that they keep the journal together, he agreed. Every night before going to bed, they each began to list three things for which they were grateful that day. Today Dan is so much into this practice that he now takes the lead for the bedtime ritual.

Key Point

"By noting all the things for which you are grateful, you are making an inventory of all that you have, instead of what you want."

A Story about Being Grateful for What You Have
(Adapted from "Teaching Tales: The Way You Like It")

There once was a man who lived with his wife and six children in a tiny, cramped house. His family's living quarters were crowded and everyone was always getting in each other's way. The man was at his wit's end and went to the Rabbi to ask for advice. When the man told the Rabbi of his plight, the Rabbi responded, "Will you promise to do exactly what I tell you?" When the man responded with a "Yes," he heard the Rabbi say, "Then things will get better." The Rabbi went on to ask if the man owned any animals. Indeed the man owned one goat, one cow, and several chickens. The Rabbi instructed the man to bring all the animals into the house.

The man went home and did as he was instructed. Soon his small house was filled with his family, the animals, and much confusion. The next day, the man ran back to the Rabbi in desperation. When the Rabbi greeted him, the man shouted, "What have you done to me? Things are just awful!" The Rabbi instructed the man to remove the chickens from the house. The man ran home and did as he was instructed. But the next day he was right back at the Rabbi's door pleading for more help as the goat was eating the furniture. The Rabbi told him to remove the goat from house. Again, the man did as he was instructed. And the next day he was back to see the Rabbi about the cow. The Rabbi directed the man to remove the cow, which the man did. The next day the man showed up at the Rabbi's house smiling. He said gratefully, "With the animals gone, things are quiet and we have room to spare! Things did get better!"

Exercise: Keeping a Daily Gratitude Journal

1. Find a time convenient for listing your items. Some people choose to write in their journal at bedtime. Others find the evening meal a good time to involve family members in this daily remembrance of gratitude. You will have greater success in developing the practice of keeping a gratitude journal if you do it at the same time each day.

2. Focus on your day by reflecting on those things at work for which you are grateful. Then focus on those things away from work for which you are grateful.

3. List your five items in a gratitude journal or in a table like the one that follows.

Day	Five Things for Which I am Grateful Today
Monday	1. 2. 3. 4. 5.
Tuesday	1. 2. 3. 4. 5.
Wednesday	1. 2. 3. 4. 5.
Thursday	1. 2. 3. 4. 5.
Friday	1. 2. 3. 4. 5.
Saturday	1. 2. 3. 4. 5.
Sunday	1. 2. 3. 4. 5.

Inspirational Quote

"Blessed are those who delight in the way things are and keep their hearts open, day and night."
HOLY BIBLE, PSALMS 1:1-2 (ADAPTED FROM *THE ENLIGHTENED HEART*)

Be specific when you give thanks

State your thanks in precise terms. When you are expressing your gratitude to someone at work, mention everything for which you are grateful. Hearing the details of how someone made a difference to you and your work is music to many people's ears. You may also reap an additional reward. Remember the old adage, "What gets noticed, gets repeated." Your words may serve to motivate coworkers to stretch themselves toward greater accomplishments.

Inspirational Quote

"The authentic expression of gratitude reduces fear and anxiety while creating a sense of belonging. This makes us feel safer to apply our creativity, new ideas, and innovation to our work."
MICHAEL STONE, AMERICAN SOCIETY FOR TRAINING AND
DEVELOPMENT CONFERENCE, 2002

Say thanks with your body

Use your body to demonstrate gratefulness. This tip follows the guidelines of many faith traditions that suggest kneeling while giving praise. By getting your body into the act of showing gratitude you renew yourself both physically and spiritually.

At this point, you might be wondering just how to incorporate kneeling into the workday when you give thanks. Although this approach might not fit your workplace culture, there may be other ways to demonstrate your gratefulness physically. For instance, you might choose to bow to someone using the age-old Namasté pose—bowing your head towards your hands folded in a prayer position in front of your chest. As you do this, think, "the divine in me thanks the divine in you." We know many professional speakers who end their programs in this way. If people in your workplace accept physical contact, a slight touch on the arm or a gentle arm around the shoulder as a means of showing thanks might be appropriate. You will want to consider how the person with whom you are interacting will respond to a physical gesture of thanks. In some cases, you may even be able to give a hug to the person whom you are thanking. Many of our long-term clients give us hugs, both in greeting and in gratitude.

Week Three: Give Thanks In All Things—Even Your Difficulties

The Christian scriptures tell us to give thanks in all circumstances. You might be thinking that practicing gratitude is one thing, while giving thanks for your adversities is another matter. Yet, as you face difficulties you become stronger and better able to withstand the rigors of change. Suzanne recalls a time that she was facilitating a job search course for a group of laid-off employees. She asked the group, "What was the worst thing that could happen to you?" One woman raised her hand and said, "The worst thing that could ever happen to me has already happened—my divorce. And I'm grateful that it has prepared me to face any change—including finding a new job." This week's tips provide ideas about how to find the gift in your trials and tribulations at work.

Inspirational Quote

"Give thanks in all circumstances."

HOLY BIBLE, 1 THESSALONIANS 5:18A
(NEW REVISED STANDARD VERSION)

Be grateful for your mistakes

Give thanks for your errors at work. Think about your mistakes as "miss-takes"—opportunities to do things again and expand your horizons and your skills. Your errors could prove to be a gateway to your greatest achievements. It is well known that Edison failed miserably many times before inventing the light bulb. The creation of Post-It Notes were really a result of an experiment gone wrong.

> *"Your mistakes could prove to be a gateway to your greatest achievements."*

Accept your difficult colleagues

Learn from all of your coworkers—especially the ones who challenge you the most. Those colleagues who seem the most difficult are often the exact people who can teach you the lessons for which you will be most grateful. Several years ago, Suzanne worked with a colleague named Phil. They were polar opposites with some overlapping job responsibilities. None of this made for an easy working relationship. One time Phil sent out a corporate-wide memo without informing Suzanne first. The memo announced a change that directly impacted the services Suzanne provided her clients. In spite of the fact that Suzanne is usually fairly easy going, she was so mad that she gave Phil a "piece of her mind." In retrospect, she wished she had sought to understand Phil first before speaking her mind. After Phil heard her heated delivery, he said, "I made a mistake. I'm sorry. Haven't you ever made a mistake?" Suzanne learned one of the most important workplace lessons of her life that day. Since then, she thinks about the mistakes she makes and seeks to hear the other person's perspective before providing constructive criticism.

Express your thanks in writing to difficult customers

Write a note of thanks to those who have caused you some grief at work. The act of documenting your thanks in writing to difficult customers and clients provides you with powerful learning opportunities. An article featured on the Work At Home Index Web site suggests a Thanksgiving ritual that allows you to thank those who may have hurt you or your business. The article suggests listing the names of five people who have brought benefits to your business in the past year. (That is the easy part!) And then, it recommends listing the names of five people who have brought grief to you or your business this past year. Then address an envelope to all ten people. Write a thank-you note to one of the persons on your list every week over the next ten weeks. It will be a cinch to write the notes to those individuals who have brought you benefits. Start there and be specific about everything for which you are thankful. Next write notes to those who have brought you grief and again be specific about your thanks. The author of the article offers some encouragement for composing notes to those difficult clients: "How are you supposed to find something to be thankful for when a relationship has been troubled, perhaps even damaging to your bottom line? I propose that you cannot afford to have a loss that you do not learn from. You clearly have something for which to be grateful."

Week Four: Complete the Cycle of Gratitude

Gratitude has the potential to be the gift that keeps on giving. For all gifts there are recipients and the possibility for them to pass on the kindness shown to them. When you do kind acts for others because of something for which you are grateful, this is completing the cycle of gratitude—of giving and receiving. Often you are able to thank and return a kindness to the person who has done something nice. Other times, instead of repaying the person who has done something for you, you do something for someone else as a way of expressing gratitude for what you have received. Think about the positive impact you can have on the workplace if you take this cycle to heart and give something for everything you receive. This week's tips encourage you to find ways to complete the cycle of gratitude at work. Who knows? You might be part of a chain reaction of never-ending acts of kindness and gratitude.

Inspirational Quote

"Blessed are those that can give without remembering and those who can receive without forgetting."

ANONYMOUS

Practice unconditional gratitude at work

Express your gratitude even if you believe that someone does not deserve it. Michael Stone, in his presentation at the 2002 conference of the American Society of Training and Development, told his audiences:

"giving unconditional gratitude means that we are one hundred percent responsible for this expression, regardless of the circumstances. The expression of gratitude frees us and others from pain and stress. It replaces our frustration with a sense of peace, joy, and happiness."

A little forgiveness on your part can mean a great deal to coworkers. Once when Krista was facilitating a workshop with another consultant, the person did not pay attention to the design they had created together. Without warning Krista or discussing it, she changed the order of activities in the middle of the workshop, leaving Krista to come up with something different on the spot when it was her turn to facilitate the next activity. When Krista raised the issue with the consultant at the break, the person apologized, but said that she had been inspired to make the change. Krista explained that it was important for them to work together and although the person agreed, she did the same thing in the afternoon. By the end of the day, Krista was quite upset and her irritation came through in her voice when talking with her co-facilitator. The other consultant was surprised and offended by Krista's tone and they parted without thanking each other.

Later that evening, Krista received a call from the consultant who was still upset about the way in which Krista had spoken to her. Krista apologized and thanked her for calling to resolve the issue and for doing the workshop with her. Krista's willingness to express regret and gratitude, even though she was unhappy with what the facilitator had done, opened up the conversation and they were able to talk about how they could work better together in the future.

Keep passing on your gratitude

Find ways to keep thankfulness flowing around the workplace. Although the following strategy has been applied in the home setting, it could be adapted to your work setting. Tom, who serves on Faith at Work's Board of Directors with Suzanne, told her about giving "SHMILY's." SHMILY stands for "See How Much I Love You." The way one gives a SHMILY is to write it in unique and surprising ways and leave it around for another person to find. Tom wrote the word SHMILY in white twinkle lights for his wife, Laurel, to see when she looked out their kitchen window at night. Laurel returned the SHMILY by calling ahead to a conference Tom was attending and asking the registrar to add a sticky note to Tom's badge bearing the word "SHMILY." Then it was Tom's turn. He used Hershey Kisses® to write SHMILY on the wooden floor he was refinishing in their Victorian home. Tom reports that the SHMILY exchange has been going on for over a year. Why not think of a way to begin a gratitude activity that could make the rounds at your workplace? Perhaps SHMILWWY (See how much I love working with you) is a good possibility? Or come up with another fun acronym to use.

Demonstrate your gratitude in extraordinary ways to those with whom you work.

Go the extra mile to show your gratitude at work. Rosemarie, a bookstore employee, is grateful for her work and shows it in a variety of ways. She hand writes a note with each of her customer service mailings. Rosemarie knows that this is not necessary, but reports that it makes her feel good because she knows it makes the recipient feel good. In addition, she takes such a personal interest in the customers—by smiling, looking into their eyes, and speaking to them when they approach her. Consequently, she sells the highest number of discount cards for the store each month. Rosemarie does not realize any commission for the card sales—just the satisfaction that she has shown gratefulness for her work through extraordinary attention to the customers.

" *There is a calmness to a life lived in Gratitude, a quiet joy.* "
RALPH BLUM, *ANGEL FIRE GRATITUDE QUOTES*

19

DECEMBER

CELEBRATE AT WORK

> *"Celebrations infuse life with passion and purpose. They summon the human spirit. They reattach us to our human roots and help us soar toward new visions. They touch our hearts and fire our imaginations. They bond people together and connect us to shared values and myths. Ceremonies and rituals create community, fusing individual souls with the corporate spirit."*
>
> TERRENCE E. DEAL AND M. K. KEY, *CORPORATE CELEBRATION*

Introduction

December is a natural time to celebrate. It is a time when good feelings abound, song is in the air, and people gather to honor each other warmly. For many people, this month is an occasion to pay tribute to the light of their faith tradition. During Chanukah, candles are lit and songs are sung in honor of the original miracle of light that happened centuries ago. Tapers are also lit during Kwanzaa, the African festival that pays homage to seven key principles of life. On Christmas, the birth of Christ, who is considered the light of the world by Christians, is celebrated in 150 countries. All around the globe, people observe the passing of the old and the promise of the new on New Year's Eve, often by lighting a candle at midnight. The actual coming of the light is commemorated on the Winter Solstice as the days begin to get longer.

All of these traditional events make it easy to focus on rejoicing at work this month and creating a celebratory energy that will carry you into the New Year. When you mark events that occur in your life with a festive ceremony, this renews the inner connection to your true self. You honor the deeper meaning of life and express that which you value. In addition to being fun, celebrations also provide a forum both for reveling in your successes and for gathering support and creating hope in times of difficulty. Celebrating allows you to step out of the daily routine and reconnect with your heart—with joy, laughter, and vitality—which leads to a renewed commitment to your work.

Ceremonies also help to strengthen relationships at work because they create a sense of collective spirit. They are a way of coming together to share stories during both good and bad times. Essentially, celebrations at work are part of the culture that provides the symbolic glue that unites people in mutually working toward a common vision. They help an organization's members adjust to changing situations and supply what Terrence Deal and M. K. Key in *Corporate Celebrations* call "high-octane fuel" or "spiritual juice."

Key Point

> *"Celebrating at work allows you to step out of the daily routine and reconnect with your heart—with joy, laughter, and vitality—which leads to a renewed commitment to your work."*

So how do you celebrate at work? It helps to understand what celebration really is. In its most basic form, celebration is the commemoration of a noteworthy situation in a way that is both meaningful and memorable to those involved. Often, ceremony and ritual are included in celebrations because they enhance the meaning of the special event. Everyone regularly participates in rituals. For instance, singing the happy birthday song is one ritual with which everyone is familiar. Rituals are occasions that are designed and have specific elements that are repeated each time that the ritual is performed. Because of this repetition, people have shared expectations of what to do and can therefore easily participate.

Ceremonies are typically larger than, and often include, rituals, and they tend to be different each time they occur. Wedding ceremonies, for example, vary depending upon those planning them. Yet, all ceremonies have exclusive preparations made and time set aside for a particular purpose. Often a special atmosphere is created for the event and drama, incantations (speeches), food, and music are included. Examples of familiar work ceremonies include retirement parties, company or division anniversaries, and company product "kick-off" meetings.

Inspirational Quote

> *"Ritual and ceremony undergird, interpenetrate, and intertwine with all aspects of corporate life: recognition, rewards, quality, teamwork, and leadership. Celebration is an integral element of culture, and provides the symbolic adhesive that welds a community together."*
> TERRENCE E. DEAL AND M.K. KEY, *CORPORATE CELEBRATION*

While the ceremonies, rituals, and celebrations with which everyone is most acquainted tend to be large and complex affairs, they do not always have to be this way. You can celebrate something by yourself or with a few people just as well as you can with a whole group or organization. You can also make celebrations as simple or as elaborate as you wish. The most important thing on which to focus is the purpose of the commemoration and what will make it significant for those involved. This month's tips help you create expressive rituals, pay tribute to your cowLovers, celebrate through song, and learn how to celebrate at work.

Reflection Questions

Take two to three minutes to thinkLove/or write about each of the following questions:

1. How often do I celebrate at work and how do those celebrations affect my work, coworkers, and me?
2. What rituals are meaningful to me and how can I perform them at work?
3. How can I celebrate my own achievements and the successes of others more often?
4. To what extent do I incorporate music and song into my celebrations?
5. How can I further enhance ceremonies at work with music and other art forms?

Week One: Learn to Celebrate

In today's fast paced work culture, people do not plan and conduct celebrations at work very often. Many feel as if they do not have the time, the resources, and skills, or the knowledge to pull off a good party or ceremony. This week give yourself and your coworkers a gift and learn how to plan and hold celLovetions at work.

Key Point

"In its most basic form, celebration is the commemoration of a noteworthy situation in a way that is both meaningful and memorable to those involved."

Research different ways to celebrate at work

Explore the components of a good celebration. According to Terrence Deal and M.K. Key, the authors of *Corporate Celebrations,* each celebration is unique, and also contains many universal attributes that are included in most ceremonies. They are:

- A focal point, like a theme or person to honor, that is the reason for the event
- A design or order of elements that serves as the framework for the ceremony
- A specific space that is set aside where people can gather as a community
- Aesthetics, like decorations, flowers, and lighting that create a special setting
- Music or sounds that have meaning for the participants
- Stylized behavior, such as parades, dances, processions, or rituals to honor someone or something
- Stories or speeches that convey values and important messages
- Costumes or symbols, like flags or specific colors, that connote affiliation

Go online to find out more information about ways to celebrate. Talk with an event planner about what they do. Read books on celebrations such as *Fan Fare for a Feather: 77 Ways to Celebrate Practically Anything* by Vivienne Margolis, Kerry Townsend Smith, and Adele Weiss. Write down in your journal all of the ideas that are of interest or that you can apply in the work environment. For instance, you might choose to learn about Kwanzaa, a holiday that honors seven key principles, as well as ancestors who forged paths from which people today benefit. You might then create a ceremony to acknowledge the founders of your company or organization. Or you could set aside seven days during which to focus on how the seven principles of Kwanzaa (unity, self-determination, collective work and responsibility, cooperative economics, purpose, creativity, and faith) are present in and support your work.

Key Point

"*You can make your celebrations as simple or as elaborate as you wish.*"

Recall meaningful celebrations in your life

Think about ceremonies and events in your life that you have enjoyed or found momentous. What was special about each of these favorite celebrations? What moved you? What was joyful about them? What did you like about the event? What did others receive from participating in the festivity? What can you learn from those situations that can be applied to celebrations at work? Write down your experiences and ideas in your journal or create a celebration notebook that you can turn to when designing a ceremony at work.

Celebrate your successes

Honor yourself and all that you have achieved this year. You do not have to wait for others to acknowledge you. Do it for yourself! Schedule a special time to review the year and make note of all your accomplishments at work, both large and small. If you completed the exercises and experimented with the tips in Chapter 17 on Abundance, then you are already aware of your many successes. If not, spend some time now to write down or draw in your journal all the achievements you wish to celebrate. Think about the goals attained, the learning acquired, and the service you provided to others. Consider the small wins, the near misses, the lessons discovered from mistakes and failures, and the improvements made throughout the year. If you have difficulty thinking of things to commemorate, think about what others have said about you during the year. Reread any letters of recognition, thank you notes, and positive performance appraisals you have received to remind you of your successes.

Key Point

"*Sit quietly for a moment and absorb all that you have accomplished.*
Then, do something to honor and celebrate you."

Once you have depicted all the items you can recall, sit quietly for a moment and absorb all that you have accomplished. Then, do something to honor and celebrate you. While at work, give yourself a pat on the back. Write yourself a congratulatory letter. Invite a colleague or significant other to lunch and share your achievements with each other. After work, have a glass of wine and give yourself a toast. Create a montage using pictures from old magazines that portray your achievements. Put on some music and do a jig or a little dance. Buy a special gift. Whatever you decide to do, select something that is meaningful to you and makes you feel rewarded.

Inspirational Quote

"Celebrations are quite literally life-giving forces... Celebrations—whether to recognize the accomplishment of one person or to cheer the achievements of many—are opportunities to promote individual health, but also opportunities for leaders to build healthier groups."

JAMES M. KOUZES AND BARRY Z. POSNER,
ENCOURAGING THE HEART

Organize a celebration at work

Think about what you would most like to celebrate at work. Then invite some of your coworkers to join you in creating a communal expression of recognition. Use the information obtained from your exploration of celebrations to design and plan the ceremony. Make a commitment to produce an event that is both unique and meaningful. There are as many ways to rejoice as there are people to celebrate. And you do not have to have a large budget to be successful. Be creative and have fun.

If you have little time to plan, be spontaneous about celebrations at work. In fact, in their Employment Recruitment and Retention Newsletter, Ragan Communications recommends following an approach they call "guerilla celebrations," which are spur-of-the-moment events. This strategy adds an element of surprise and innovation to workplace celebrations. If you are looking for an occasion to celebrate, consult Chase's Calendar of Events published annually by NTC Contemporary Publishers. You will find all kinds of reasons to "make merry" in this reference. OPP!, a specialty gift store in Providence, Rhode Island, uses this publication to encourage their employees to celebrate on a regular basis. On Willie Nelson's birthday, the staff wore bandanas to work. If you pay a visit to Party Universe® in Germantown, MD (our favorite place to buy celebration supplies) at Halloween or most other holidays, you will find the staff dressed in festive garb. The customers like to come to the store just to see what the staff will come up with next.

When we first began our partnership and incorporated our business we had a gathering of friends, colleagues, and clients. In preparation for the event, we covered one wall in the room with large sheets of white paper and placed many colored markers nearby. Then during the celebration we asked people to write or draw what renews them at work on our "renewal wall." It was both fun and educational for everyone. Later in the gathering, Rae, a colleague of ours, facilitated a ritual where people offered their well wishes for our business. Everyone gathered around a pot of soil and a bowl of seeds that were placed on a table in the middle of the room. Rae invited everyone to think of a one or two word blessing they would like to give our business and us. Then, one by one when they were ready, people picked up some seeds and said their blessing out loud as they planted their seeds in the pot of soil. People wished many wonderful things for us such as success, learning, great clients, and good associates. After the celebration, the pot became a living metaphor for our business. We watered it and fed it, just as we nourished our business, and slowly tender shoots began to appear. Since we did not know what seeds had been planted, it was fun to see the shoots sprout, turn into plants, begin to grow buds and blossom along with our business.

Key Point

"There are as many ways to rejoice as there are people to celebrate."

Week Two: Pay Tribute To Your Coworkers And Customers

Recognizing the people with whom you interact everyday is one of the best ways to celebrate at work. Research shows that employees want to be appreciated more than they want to receive additional money from their employers. According to an article on her Web site (www.corpstory.com), Evelyn Clark, the President of a marketing communication firm and corporate storyteller, states that the benefits of appreciating others include the following:

- People feel seen and acknowledged for who they are and what they do
- People are inspired to enhance their performance
- People are proud to be associated with the organization

However, if you chose to pay tribute to specific colleagues and clients, it is important to do it in a way that is meaningful and enjoyable for the persons whom you are celebrating. Being genuine and specific when honoring someone requires you to be thoughtful. Make an effort to understand what is appropriate culturally (both within the organization and the person's background) and know what the person likes.

Several years ago, Scott, one of our colleagues, turned 40. Scott, a died-in-the-wool introvert and no fuss kind-of-guy, told his wife that he definitely did not want a party. His wife, who loved parties, e-mailed all of his family and friends asking them to write a letter in Scott's honor. She also asked everyone to pretend that there was going to be a party. When he walked into a friend's huge family room on his birthday, he expected to find family and colleagues. Instead he found a new guitar and a memory book (with all the letters people had written) in the middle of the room. He was deeply touched that his wife paid such careful attention to how he most wanted to be celebrated. Suzanne, who also loves parties, learned a great lesson from Scott's wife and abstained from planning a huge party for her husband's sixtieth birthday. Instead, knowing that Dan is fond of ties and quilts, Suzanne asked all of his friends and family to send ties and scarves to make a quilt for his birthday, which she quietly gave to him on his birthday.

This week experiment with paying tribute to your colleagues and customers by telling positive stories about them, praising them, and giving them tokens of your appreciation.

Key Point

> *"When you tell stories about colleagues' achievements, you offer encouragement and make people feel valued."*

Tell stories of accomplishment and appreciation

Notice how your coworkers and customers support you. Then share your observations with others at work. Tell stories about the successes that you see occurring in your workplace. When you tell stories about colleagues' achievements, you offer encouragement and make people feel valued. Stories are one of the most effective ways to recognize people, touch their hearts, and communicate what is important.

Evelyn Clark, author of the article "Fire Up Employees and Please Your 'Customers'—Tell Your Stories!" writes how Jim Sinegal, cofounder and CEO of Costco Wholesale, uses stories to convey corporate values and to illustrate how those values are being played out. One of his favorite stories is about fish. The story is about a meat department buyer who, over a five-year period, markedly improved the quality of the fresh salmon Costco sold while also lowering the price. The high quality salmon fillet now costs 20% less than it did five years ago. Jim retells this story again and again because it illustrates the company's goal of delivering value to customers through high quality products at low prices.

There are numerous ways to tell stories at work:

- write what you see happening and send e-mails to customers and coworkers
- send a story to the company newsletter
- during a meeting tell teammates what you have observed
- encourage a colleague who is disappointed about a particular work outcome by telling them a story about how they have helped you
- be creative and develop a skit to share at a company event
- create a collage or tell stories with pictures and post them in the office on a bulletin board

In *Encouraging the Heart*, James Kouzes and Barry Posner tell a story about a furniture company that has a bragging board near to the entrance where all the employees hang their coats. In the beginning, the manager pinned notes of appreciation there. However, soon employees also began to attach notes to the board that were written to coworkers recognizing them for their accomplishments. Then they began to put up pictures and notices of items of which they were proud, like new grandchildren and college degrees earned.

Inspirational Quote

"By making achievements public, you encourage the person being recognized and the hearts of those who witness the award."
JAMES M. KOUZES AND BARRY Z. POSNER, *ENCOURAGING THE HEART*

Exercise: Finding Stories to Tell

There are numerous stories being acted out every day in the workplace. All it takes is an interest in observing and listening. Here is a process for recognizing the stories in your organization so you can share them with others.

1. At least once a week, walk around your workplace several times in one day and observe what is going on. What are your coworkers doing? And how are they doing it? What stands out or is impressive as you walk around your organization? What items do they have displayed in their offices?

2. Initiate conversations with colleagues and clients everyday. Listen to what they are talking about. What projects are they completing? What challenges are they having and how are they successfully overcoming them? What goals do they have and how are they achieving them? What excites them? What are they celebrating? Pay attention to the language they are using to describe their experiences as well as the jokes they are telling about themselves and the occupation. Many occupations have their own language, tools, and customs.

3. Each time you return after walking around, take a few minutes to jot down in your journal the positive and noteworthy situations that caught your attention. You may also choose to get a special notebook or folder in which to collect the stories.

4. Then, during the week, share the stories and what impressed you about them with the people from whom you acquired the stories as well as others in the organization, especially customers.

Praise people at work

Become a "yay-sayer," someone who affirms and praises others regularly. The word "praise" comes from the Latin root "preci-are" which means to prize. Similarly, the Oxford English Dictionary defines praise as proclaiming the worth, excellence, or merits of something, or speaking highly of someone. The idea behind these definitions is that people laud what they value. This week find praise-worthy qualities and behaviors exhibited by others around you, including your boss, colleagues, and customers. Then extol their virtues. Meaningful appraisal requires knowledge. Make an effort to get to know those with whom you work so that you can offer genuine admiration. Pay attention to what your colleagues are good at accomplishing. Notice how generous your customers are. Compliment people on their uplifting personal characteristics. Praise others even when you do not necessarily feel like doing it. You will find that your own state of mind becomes transformed. When you voice praise it opens your heart as well as those whom you are honoring.

A Federal employee we know completed a complicated and controversial project before it was due. He worked outside his usual discipline to help his colleagues who were swamped with other projects. Upon completion of the project, his manager wrote an e-mail to the entire division praising his work in very specific terms. The manager also gave a bag of goodies with a ski hat for the employee (who loves to ski) and hot chocolate for his wife (who love to sit in front of fireplace drinking hot chocolate while her husband skis). The employee was touched by the way his manager paid attention to what was important to him.

Inspirational Quote

"Make a habit of catching people doing something right."
KEN BLANCHARD, *THE ONE MINUTE MANAGER*

Give Tokens of Appreciation

Let others know how much you value their presence and contribution by giving them a small gift. Giving to others is one of the most meaningful ways to celebrate and December is a natural time to grace others in this manner. You do not have to be a manager to offer your coworkers or customers awards, gifts, certificates, or notes of appreciation. There are many ways to recognize others simply and inexpensively. For instance you can create an award on your computer to give to a special customer. Krista's husband, Evan, created a special diploma recognizing her integrity, determination, and spiritual courage during her dissertation research. He asked all the members of her doctoral committee to sign it and then gave it to her at the dissertation defense meeting.

Inspirational Quote

"Storytelling is an important and magical vehicle for bringing people together and for passing along what's important in a culture. Stories are avenues to the spirit."
SALLI RASBERRY AND PADI SELWYN, *LIVING YOUR LIFE OUTLOUD*

There are also commercial cards you can purchase that have meaningful sayings on them that are appropriate for the workplace. Barbara Glanz, speaker and author of *Care Packages for the Workplace*, hands out Pass It On™ cards at her seminars and asks participants to give them to someone who has done something to make a difference in their lives. The cards, which are published by Argus Communications in Allen, Texas, have sayings such as, "Some people make the world more special just by being in it" or "The difference between ordinary and extraordinary is that little 'extra'!" On the back of the cards the words "pass it on" are written. JoAnna Brandi, a customer care consultant also has Dare to Care postcards that have inspiring pictures and sayings on them. You can find out more about the Dare to Care postcards at www.customerretention.com. Of course, you can create your own card and gifts, or even write a poem, to express your appreciation. In *Care Packages for the Workplace*, Barbara Glanz writes about Jim, an operations coordinator of a public power company, who composes and sends poems to coworkers to celebrate their work and their birthdays.

Another classical way of celebrating is to offer food to others. December is a great time of year to give the gift of food. Bake something fun, like holiday cookies, and give them to colleagues and customers. Amy, our former administrative assistant, bakes unusual cookies every year and presents them to various people in decorative containers. Try giving a gift to someone whenever you are feeling a bit down. It will make them feel great and will create a climate of generosity—both at work and within you.

In 2002, the Washington, DC metropolitan area was plagued by a series of sniper attacks. At the end of the siege, the girls field hockey team from Quince Orchard High School, part of the Montgomery County Public Schools in Maryland, decided to present Charles Moose, Chief of Police for Montgomery County, a balloon bouquet for all he had done to lead to the capture of the suspects. At the end of a grueling news conference late one evening, the girls visited Chief Moose. When asked what the chief had said upon receiving the balloons, the girls said "Nothing. He just had tears in his eyes."

Inspirational Quote

"Rewards and recognition, to be truly meaningful, should be given to the individual in a way that says, 'YOU are special'."
BARBARA GLANZ, *CARE PACKAGES FOR THE WORKPLACE*

Week Three: Rejoice At Work Through Music

Music is one of the most universal modes of celebrating. People from most national and religious traditions all over the world include song in their festivities. This is because music touches people like no other medium can do. It connects individuals—energizing and renewing them, inspiring them, and opening up their hearts. It is a potent healing and creative force that evokes and expresses deep emotion. Basically, music unlocks the best part of people!

Suzanne believes strongly in the renewing power of music. She remembers traveling in Europe alone as a young woman many years ago. She felt homesick, was tired of wearing the same clothes over and over, and longed for a hamburger. (This was before the days of McDonalds in Europe.) She was waiting in an extremely long line to tour the salt mines in Salzburg, when suddenly a group of students started singing a nonsense song that she had sung in the outdoor school where she taught. In that moment, she felt one with the world and forgot her homesickness.

"Make joyful noise!"

HOLY BIBLE, PSALMS 66:1A (NEW REVISED STANDARD VERSION)

Opportunities to rejoice through music at work abound. Yet many people are hesitant to incorporate it into their workday because it is not the norm. What they are forgetting is that music can be of great benefit in the workplace. Don Campbell, author of *The Mozart Effect*, writes that research shows music can boost productivity, foster endurance, and generate a sense of safety and well-being. It can also strengthen memory and learning as the following Yiddish folktale, "The Rabbi's Melody," illustrates:

> Once upon a time, there was a great Rabbi who explained the Torah to his students every evening. One day, he noticed an old man among the students who seemed to be trying to understand what he was saying. It was clear from the look on the old man's face that he was struggling.
>
> When the Rabbi concluded his talk, he invited the old man to join him in his study and asked the man if he had understood the teachings. The old man lowered his head and admitted that he had been unable to comprehend what the great teacher was saying. He explained that he had been a simple workingman with little education who had spent his life supporting his family. "All I can do is to recite the Psalms," he said, "and I don't understand them very well either. But now that my children are grown I am drawn to study the Torah. So I have come to study with you because I hear you befriend everyone. Tell me what I must do to understand the scriptures."
>
> The Rabbi replied with great compassion, "What you have heard me explaining today was a teaching of the Baal Shem Tov. If you haven't understood what I said in words, I will help you by singing a song. Listen, for all of the Baal Shem's thought is hidden in it."
>
> Then the Rabbi began to sing a sweet melody, one phrase after the other. The old man listened in rapt attention as if he had been turned into a pillar of attention. The more the Rabbi sang, the brighter the

man's face became and a warm flush of happiness surged through him.
When the Rabbi finished singing, the man cried out, "I understand, I
understand! Dear Rabbi." From then on, the Rabbi sang that same
melody at the end of his talks as a way of clarifying them, just in case
there was someone there who did not fully understand his discourse.

Like the Rabbi in the story, wise people throughout the ages have taught and celebrated through music and song. We encourage you to use music in the workplace this week to celebrate and invigorate yourself and others.

Inspirational Quote

"The Ancients sang their way all over the world. They sang the rivers and the ranges, the saltpans and sand dunes.... They wrapped the whole world in a web of song."

EXCERPT FROM AN ABORIGINAL STORY BY BRUCE CHATWIN,
THE SONGLINES

Sing your own song at work

"Toot your horn" and celebrate at work by identifying a song that represents success for you. If you are musically inclined, write a song for yourself. Select music that resonates with, inspires, or moves you. Sarah Ban Breathnach, author of *Simple Abundance*, claims that "finding the personal music that calls to us authentically can be empowering...." Play or sing that song whenever you accomplish a key goal, deal gracefully with a difficult situation, or just want to celebrate. Dance playfully when you sing the song or listen to it. If you feel comfortable, share the song with teammates so they know when you are celebrating a triumph. Play your music every day to inspire your ongoing success.

David plays inspiring music on his flute everyday to celebrate and prepare for work. He told us "As a result of playing my flute, I am more stable and able to be a rudder in times of change in my workplace." David plays his instrument at home. However, if you are a musician, you might consider bringing your instrument to work. What a treat it would be for your coworkers if you played music during lunch.

> *"Music is a powerful healer, if we open to it, and no music is more powerful in this regard than the sound of our own voice in song... No matter [what kind of song]—for every particular feeling state and life situation, there is a perfect song that can help us contact and express ourselves better than any other method I know."*
>
> ELLIOT SOBEL, *WILD HEART DANCING*

Use music to generate hope during challenging times

Select some songs or music that inspires you. Then play or sing them when you are in the midst of difficult situations at work. Like Julie Andrews in the movie *The Sound of Music,* you can uplift yourself by singing about your favorite things. If you feel brave enough, invite your coworkers to sit quietly and listen to inspiring music during a troublesome meeting. Sing a meaningful song together when facing organizational challenges or world crises. The song "America the Beautiful" took on great meaning for many people after 9/11. They found great hope and healing in singing it together. As Pete Seeger writes in his introduction to *Rise Up Singing,* "there's hope for the world" when we sing. Everyone benefits from what Mitchell L. Gaynor, M.D. calls, in *Sounds of Healing,* the restorative properties of music.

> *"Music touches people like no other medium can do. It connects individuals, energizes and renews, inspires and opens the heart. It is a potent healing and creative force that evokes and expresses deep emotion."*

Allow music to speak for you

Consider including music in a formal presentation you are giving. Find a song that captures people's attention or one that celebrates the group's success. A few years ago, when Krista gave a presentation on love in business, she used two song titles to engage her listeners:

"What's Love Got to do With It?" by Tina Turner and "Love is the Key" by Tuck and Patti. Incorporating music into a speech makes it more interesting. It also increases the likelihood that your listeners will remember what you said, particularly if you actually sing the songs yourself!

You can also ask others to think of songs that encapsulate their feelings or ideas. There is power in allowing music to speak for you. The results are pretty amazing. We often facilitate sessions with groups in the midst of transition. We like to begin these sessions by asking, "What song comes to mind when you think about the current situation and why?" We were working with a group from the EPA and asked each person to describe his or her vision for the workplace. One woman responded by using song titles. Her sharing motivated other people to think about songs for themselves.

Using the name of a song to speak for you is a non-threatening way to open up a discussion. It helps, if you are the person asking the group to name a song, to lead the way in giving an example of your own. People feel safer sharing their feelings and ideas if you speak first.

Inspirational Quote

"Where speech fails, then music begins. It is the natural medium for the expression of our emotions—the art that expresses in tones our feelings which are too strong and deep to be expressed in words."
CHARLES W. LANDON, *QUOTATIONS ABOUT*

Create a celebration with music

Invite your coworkers to create a celebration of song. December is a good time to do this since so many holiday traditions have songs associated with them. Ask people to submit the words and music of meaningful tunes from their faith and spirited songs from family rituals. Once you have collected them, make copies and have a sing-a-long that includes a variety of songs. Invite different people to lead the singing. You might ask people to dress up or decorate the area in the office where everyone will gather.

A group of employees at Carnegie Mellon University in Pittsburgh takes this idea to new heights. Each December, they create a light show in their hall. As you enter their work area, you are greeted by colorful, twinkling light displays that rival the best New York City holiday windows. All the while, seasonal music plays in the background. Employees from all over the university wait each year to attend this group's "Light-Up Night." The staff dedicates their own time (lunch breaks, hours before and after work, and even their vacation days in some cases) to put this together. What a great way to celebrate and lift everyone's spirits!

Week Four: Perform Rituals at Work

All over the world, people have cultural, religious, familial, and secular traditions that they regularly observe in their daily lives. Rituals are performed to mark important transitions, to recognize special occurrences and passages, and to answer a deep need for healing. Familiar ceremonies include birthday and graduation parties, marriage ceremonies, retirement banquets, New Year's Eve celebrations, religious festivals, community fairs, office gatherings, company picnics, and team-building events.

Rituals differ from celebrations in that they are more symbolic, are done intentionally to evoke meaning, and enable you to connect with yourself and others in deep and rewarding ways. They are right-brain activities that engage all four aspects of your being. They generate a specific mindset, emotional state, and heightened awareness, that brings about a change in your physiological status. Your body becomes more aligned and responsive to the intent expressed in the ceremony. Rituals energize you, generate renewed motivation, and make you aware of past and potential future successes. This week learn how to perform rituals so that you can celebrate both the organization's and your personal precious moments and transitions, and use them to help let go of emotional pain in difficult times.

Inspirational Quote

"Ritual is an activity or action done with the intention that inducts you into deeper parts of yourself and life. They engage our hearts, our minds (through focus), and our bodies (through physical gesture or posture). The power of ritual lies in its ability to nourish on a very deep level."
NANCY MONSON, "RITUAL IN THE LIVES OF CHILDREN"

Learn how to create rituals

Explore what goes into designing a meaningful ritual. There is no right or wrong way to create or perform a ritual. Most rituals have an order, a focus, and create a certain mental and emotional state. They express your purpose in a symbolic way, and they have a beginning and an end. Many ceremonies end with the sharing of food and drink. Find out what holds meaning for you and is appropriate for the purpose at hand. Plan the event carefully and set aside an appropriate time and place for the ritual to occur. Most people also like to prepare for the ritual so they can make a transition from regular activities and be fully present during the ritual.

Inspirational Quote

"When we pay attention to the details and invest parts of ourselves in a ritual, it comes alive for us."

SALLI RASBERRY AND PADI SELWYN,
LIVING YOUR LIFE OUTLOUD

To learn more about ritual, explore your cultural and familial traditions. Research articles online or read books on the subject. A few publications to explore include *Lights of Passage: Rituals and Rites of Passage for the Problems and Pleasures of Modern Life* by Kathleen Wall, Ph.D., and Gary Ferguson, *Ritual: Power, Healing and Community* by Malidome Somé, and *Feeding the Spirit: Creating Your Own Festivals, Ceremonies and Celebrations* by Nancy Brady Cunningham.

Discover the rituals in your organization

Look for the rituals that are already a part of your organization's tradition. Inquire about their origin. Make note of the meaning and feelings that are evoked by participating in the events. Explore the different ways in which transitions are marked and significant moments are recognized where you work. Different departments may have different rituals. There may be some that are held organization-wide. One large hospital system in New York City has an annual employee recognition ceremony that all employees are invited to attend. Each year one person is selected to be specially honored. Kathryn, an internal organization consultant and skilled story teller, interviews coworkers about that person. She then writes a story or poem about the person and his or her contribution to the company that is presented at the ceremony.

Inspirational Quote

> *"Human beings have used ritual for centuries as an important way of consciously recognizing and supporting a life event. When a new transition is celebrated it is imbued with meaning and importance."*
> AMBER BOTTELSEN, *"THE POWER OF RITUAL"*

Start a new ritual in your department or company

Select a significant occurrence at work that is currently not being recognized and design a meaningful way to commemorate it. It can be something small and simple around which you would perform an individual ritual. It can be an event or person that you would like to honor in a public ceremony. In addition to more routine transitions that take place in organizations (like retirements and company anniversaries), consider holding a ritual to honor the less obvious milestones. Think about commemorating the team meeting production goals or honoring someone's contribution to the transformation of a work process that made things easier for everyone. Alternately, add a ritual to a current company celebration.

Whatever you choose to commemorate, design a ritual that is appropriate to the subject and preference of those participating. Invite a few of your colleagues to join in planning it so that everyone can respect differences and build on common bonds. Remember, your goal is to create a sense of occasion and a feeling of significance, which you can do very simply. As an example, every New Year's Eve, Krista invites her family to join her in front of the fire to describe the top five non-material gifts they received during the year and the five non-material events or lessons to which they are looking forward in the New Year. This ritual can easily be adapted for the workplace. At an appropriate time, ask your teammates to share what have been the best parts of the year or month and to what they wish to aspire in the New Year or next month.

You can also create other small rituals that can be performed all year long. For example, we have several practices that are meaningful and allow us to make transitions between activities in our daily work life. As mentioned earlier in the book, we consciously take a moment of silence before beginning all our business meetings. It allows us to clear our minds, offer a silent prayer, and bring our attention fully to the present. We also pause for a moment of silence before eating lunch to help us make the transition between work and nourishing our bodies. During lunch we talk about non-work related items. We feel it is important for general well-being and the integrity of our work to "walk our talk" and renew ourselves through these little rituals.

If you want to create your own ritual, use the following exercise created and presented by Tiffany Montavon and Kathryn Wysockey-Johnson at a workshop entitled "Marking the Passages as Sacred" during the 2002 Sacred Circles event at the Washington National Cathedral. Tiffany and Kathryn of Arlington, Virginia have assisted others in developing rituals to celebrate important individual and organizational passages. They believe that good ritual connects participants to both their immediate community and to that which is sacred, or larger than themselves.

Exercise: Creating Your Own Ritual At Work

1. Identify a transition or event at work you wish to mark with a ritual.
2. Contemplate and note in your journal why it is important to mark the event. (For example: because it is imminent, it needs to be honored, I want to celebrate or mourn it, etc.)
3. Consider how you will connect personally with the ritual by answering the following questions in your journal:
   a. What do I expect to happen at the event?
   b. What five adjectives best describe the event or person for whom the ritual is intended? How can I make the ritual reflect the event or person for whom it is intended?
   c. Is there a natural element (water, fire, earth, air) that feels appropriate to incorporate into the ritual?
   d. Is there a specific color—one to which I am drawn—that feels pertinent to use?
   e. How do I want others and myself to feel at this ritual? (for example: connected, joyful, peaceful, resolved, honored, humbled, etc.)

f.   How do I want others and myself to feel after this ritual? (for example: acknowledged, strengthened, empty, full, blessed, content, complete, opened, etc.)

    g. What do I want to name the event?

    h. Do I want this ritual to be serious, humorous, or a combination of the two?

4. Reflect on how you will include sacred elements in the ritual by answering the following questions:

    a. Does my organization or my faith or cultural tradition have a ritual or ceremony that I want to adapt for this event?

    b. What components of this tradition are helpful to me now, as I create this ritual?

    c. Do those individuals participating need to shed anything from their faith tradition to be present to this ritual?

    d. What are some symbols (organizational, cultural, or sacred) associated with this event that I can incorporate into the ritual?

    e. What kind of space do I want to create for this event?

    f.   Is silence important to include?

5. Think about the amount of community involvement the ritual requires by responding about the following questions:

    a. Do I need other people to help me plan or facilitate this ritual, or do I need to do it by myself?

    b. Am I providing/implementing this occasion for others, or do I want to be the recipient?

    c. Who needs to be present at the event?

    d. Do I want to invite others to offer something during the ritual (e.g. a prayer, song, dance, work of art, poem, action, special food, light/extinguish a candle)?

6. Plan the logistics of the event by thinking about the following considerations:

    a. How will the ritual begin and end?

    b. Who will lead it?

    c. What is the ideal location for it?

    d. What is the ideal time to hold it—day or night, time of month or year?

    e. Are there instructions/preparations of which others need to be aware (such as songs to be practiced)?

> f. What readings, if any, will be used? Do I or the honoree have favorite or appropriate authors, poets, or readings? Do I want to write something to be read at the ritual myself, or ask others to do so?
> g. What other important details do I need to think about and plan?
> 7. Finally, once you have reflected on all of the questions, draw or doodle an image that comes to mind as you picture this ritual. How does your drawing inform how you feel about the ritual?

Inspirational Quote

"Ritual provides us with rich opportunities to coalesce as a community and to rejoice in life's rhythms. It compounds our joy as we mark significant passages, and it diminishes our sorrow during times of pain."

SALLI RASBERRY AND PADI SELWYN,
LIVING YOUR LIFE OUTLOUD

Use ritual to provide comfort during tough times

Pay attention to and recognize the losses and difficult situations at work by creating a symbolic event. Most people do not typically think about creating a celebration when things do not go as planned, when goals are not met, or when calamities occur—when people are laid-off or businesses collapse. However, when the downs as well as the ups in work life are acknowledged, you are able to both learn from those times and move on to new things. Rituals can provide comfort and hope. They help you mourn losses and obtain the motivation required to keep working in difficult situations. They free emotional energy so that you can say "Yes" to the challenging times in life.

> *"Especially in a world of rapid change, we need to pay as much attention to loss as to gain, to demise as to growth, to disaster as to triumph. Otherwise, people are deprived of the ceremonial support of letting go, reaching closure, maintaining hope, and moving on."*
>
> TERRENCE E. DEAL AND M. K. KEY, *CORPORATE CELEBRATION*

This month, experiment with creating rituals that help you let go of things you cannot change, that provide closure, that assist you in dealing with disappointments, and that create a sense of healing in the midst of tough times at work. Rod, the manager we have mentioned in several chapters of this book, consciously planned a number of rituals and events for his staff to deal with the impact of change and loss during a company-wide merger. During the early stages of the merger process, he had frequent meetings to discuss their feelings about the uncertainty created by the transition, giving them an opportunity to acknowledge their loss. He hired Renewal Resources to conduct a workshop on the impact of change on personal well-being and work performance. During a regular office planning retreat, he asked everyone to share, on index cards, what they appreciated about each of their teammates. Then, when it was clear that the office would be closing and people would be reassigned to different departments, he also asked us to facilitate a meeting in which staff members were invited to discuss the impending change. They talked about the great things they had created together as a team and shared what they would miss about working together. They also spoke about the opportunities that the merger provided them, planned ways to stay in touch with each other, and organized a number of good-bye parties. While all of these events did not eliminate their sense of loss, the rituals did help them acknowledge and deal with it better. They also helped the staff appreciate each other and prepare for the changes ahead. Follow their example and use rituals to help you move through the difficult times in your work life.

"Celebration is vital to the human psyche. All of us have an emotional craving, a deep-seated need to participate in ritual and ceremony. When we do... our chests swell with palpable feeling connecting us to our inner selves, to others, and to the enduring human spirit."

TERRENCE E. DEAL AND M. K. KEY,
CORPORATE CELEBRATION

RESOURCES

Part One

Balancing Act: How Managers Can Integrate Successful Careers and Fulfilling Personal Lives (Jossey-Bass Management Series), Joan Kofodimos. (New York: Jossey-Bass, 1993).

Calm at Work, Paul Wilson. (New York: Plume, 1999).

Come With Me, Naomi Shihab Nye. (New York: HarperCollins, 2000).

Dream Work, Mary Oliver. (New York: Grove/Atlantic,).

Executive EQ: Emotional Intelligence in Leadership & Organizations, Robert K. Cooper, Ph.D. and Ayman Sawaf. (New York: Grosset/Putnam, 1996).

From Stress to Strength: How to Lighten Your Load and Save Your Life, Robert S. Eliot, M.D. (New York: Bantam Doubleday Dell Pub, 1995).

Life is Not Work, Work is Not Life: Simple Reminders for Finding Balance in a 24/7 World, Robert K. Johnston, Ph.D. and J. Walker Smith, Ph.D. (California: Wildcat Canyon Press, 2001).

Make the Connection: Ten Steps to a Better Body and a Better Life, Bob Greene and Oprah Winfrey (contributor). (New York: Hyperion, 1996).

Stand Like Mountain, Flow Like Water: Reflections on Stress and Human Spirituality, Brian Luke Seaward. (Florida: Health Communications, 1997).

The Adult Years: Mastering the Art of Self-Renewal, Frederic M. HudCommitmentYork: John Wiley & Sons, 1999).

The Performance Edge, Robert K. Cooper, Ph.D. (Boston: Houghton Mifflin Company, 1991).

Thriving in 24/7: Six Strategies for Taming the New World of Work, Sally Helgesen. (New York, Free Press [div. of Macmillian, Inc., 2001).

Time Management For Unmanageable People, Ann McGee Cooper with Duane Trammell. (New York: Bantam Books, 1994).

Wellness Book: The Comprehensive Guide To Maintaining Health And Treating Stress Related Illness, Herbert Benson, M.D. and Eileen Stuart, R.N., M.S. (New York: Simon & Schuster, 1993).

Words of Wisdom 4 U Web site, www.wow4u.com

You Don't Have To Come Home from Work Exhausted!: A Program to Bring Joy, Energy and Balance to your Life, Ann McGee Cooper with Duane Trammell and Barbara Lau. (New York: Bantam Books, 1992).

Zorba the Greek, Nikos Kazantzakis. (New York: Scribner Paperback Fiction, 1996).

Part Two

Chapter 8: January (Transform Your Relationship with Time at Work)

Finding Flow: The Psychology of Engagement With Everyday Life, Mihaly Csikszentmihalyi, Ph.D. (New York: Basic Books, 1998).

It Only Takes a Minute to Change Your Life, Willie Jolley. (New York: St. Martin's Press, 1997).

Life is More than Your To-Do List: Blending Business Success with Personal Satisfaction, Maggie McAuliffe Bedrosian. (Vermont: B.C.I. Press, 1995).

Mind Map Book: How to Use Radiant Thinking to Maximize Your Brains Untapped Potential, Tony Buzan. (New York: Dutton, 1996).

Practicing The Power of Now: Essential Teachings, Meditations, and Exercises from the Power of Now, Eckhart Tolle. (California: New World Library, 2001).

Receiving the Day: Christian Practices for Opening the Gift of Time (The Practices of Faith Series), Dorothy C. Bass. (California: Jossey-Bass, 2001).

Take Time for Your Life: A Personal Coach's Seven Step Program for Creating the Life You Want, Cheryl Richardson. (New York: Broadway Books, 1999).

The Time Bind: When Work Becomes Home and Home Becomes Work, Arlie Russell Hochschild. (New York: Metropolitan Books, 1997).

The Westminster Study Edition Holy Bible, King James Version. (Philadelphia: Westminster Press, 1948).

Time Shifting: Creating More Time to Enjoy Your Life, Stephen Rechtschaffen, M.D. (New York: Doubleday, 1996).

Turn It Off: How to Unplug from the Anytime-Anywhere Office Without Disconnecting Your Career, Gil E. Gordon. (New York: Three Rivers Press, 2001).

Waking Up In Time: Finding Inner Peace in Times of Accelerating Change, Peter Russell (California: Origin Press, 1992, 1998).

Wherever You Go, There You Are: Mindfulness Meditation in Everyday Life, Jon Kabat-Zinn, Ph.D. (New York: Hyperion, 1994).

Chapter 9: February (Be Love's Touch at Work)

Color Voodoo #6, Color Voodoo for the Office, Jill Morton. (Hawaii: Color Voodoo Publications). www.colorvoodoo.com.

Don't Sweat the Small Stuff... And It's All Small Stuff, Richard Carlson, Ph.D. (New York: Hyperion, 1997).

Good News Bible (Today's English Version). (Tennessee: Thomas Nelson, 1993).

Holy Work: Be love. Be blessed. Be a blessing. Marsha Sinetar. (New York: Crossroad Publishing Co., 1998).

Love and Profit: The Art of Caring Leadership, James A. Autry. (New York: William Morrow & Co., 1991).

Love It or Lose It: Living Clutter-Free Forever, Maggie Bedrosian and Barbara Hemphill. (Rockville, MD: BCI Press, 2003).

Loving-Kindness: The Revolutionary Art of Happiness, Sharon Salzberg. (Boston: Shambhala Publications, 1995).

Reawakening the Spirit in Work: The Power of Dharmic Management, Jack Hawley, Ph.D. (California: Berrett-Koehler Publishers, 1993).

Research Papers Series Color in Public Spaces: Toward a Communication-Based Theory of the Urban Built Environment, Kenneth Foote. (Illinois: University of Chicago, 1983).

The New Bottom Line: Bringing Heart and Soul to Business, Ed. John Renesch and Bill DeFoore. (California: Sterling & Stone, 1996).

The Power of Color: Creating Healthy Interior Spaces, Sara O. Marberry and Laurie Zagon. (New York: John Wiley & Sons, 1995).

Wherever You Go, There You Are: Mindfulness Meditation in Everyday Life, Jon Kabat-Zinn, Ph.D. (New York: Hyperion, 1994).

Words to Love By, Mother Theresa. (Indiana: Ava Maria Press, 1989).

Zen stories Web site, www.zenstory.html

Chapter 10: March (Nourish Your Creativity at Work)

"Are You Creative?" Ann Cushman. (Minneapolis, MN: Utne Reader) www.utne.com (1992).

Cooking Light Magazine, (Tampa, FL: Time, Inc.). www.cookinglight.com

Creativity: Flow and the Psychology of Discovery and Invention, Mihaly Csikszentmihaly, Ph.D. (New York: HarperCollins, 1996).

If You Want to Write, Brenda Ueland, (Minnesota: Graywolf Press, 1997).

Living Your Life Out Loud: How to Unlock Your Creativity and Unleash Your Joy, Salli Rasberry and Padi Selwyn. (New York, Pocket Books, 1995).

Mind Map Book: How to Use Radiant Thinking to Maximize Your Brains Untapped Potential, Tony Buzan. (New York: Dutton, 1996).

The Creative Spirit, Daniel P. Goleman, Paul Kaufman and Michael Ray. (New York: Dutton, 1992).

The Quotations Page, www.quotationspage.com

What a Great Idea!: The Key Steps Creative People Take, Charles N. Thompson. (New York: HarperCollins, 1992).

Chapter 11: April (Spread Seeds of Enthusiasm at Work)

C.A.R.E. Packages For The Workplace: Dozens of Little Things You Can Do To Regenerate Spirit At Work, Barbara Glanz. (New York: McGraw-Hill, 1996).

Don't Sweat the Small Stuff... And It's All Small Stuff, Richard Carlson, Ph.D. (New York: Hyperion, 1997).

Poems and Sketches of E.B. White, E.B. White. (New York: Harper and Row, 1981).

The Faithful Gardener: A Wise Tale About That Which Can Never Die, Clarissa Pinkola Estes, Ph.D. (San Francisco: Harper, 1995).

The Holy Bible, New King James Version. (Tennessee: Thomas Nelson, Inc., 1989).

The Westminster Study Edition Holy Bible, King James Version. (Philadelphia: Westminster Press, 1948).

Chapter 12: May (Honor the Sacred at Work)

20-Minute Retreats. Rachel Harris, Ph.D. (New York: Henry Holt, 2000).

Artful Work, Dick Richards. (California: Berrett-Koehler Publishers, Inc. 1995).

Darshan Magazine, vol. 32, (South Fallsburg, New York: SYDA Foundation, November 1989).

DeepFUN, www.deepfun.com

Dictionary of Philosophy and Religion: Eastern and Western Thought, William L. Reese. (New Jersey: Humanities Press, Atlantic Highlands, 1996).

"God and Business," Marc Gunther. Fortune.com, July 9, 2001.

Illuminata: A Return to Prayer, Marianne Williamson. (New York: Riverhead Books, 1995).

"Lessons from the Call Center," Patricia, Boverie. www.astd.org, 5/15/02.

Life After Mississippi, James A. Autry. (Mississippi: Yoknapatawpha Press, 1989).

Nights Under a Tin Roof, James A. Autry (Mississippi, Yoknapatawpha Press, 1983).

Spiritual Literacy: Reading the Sacred in Everyday Life, Frederic and Mary Ann Brussat. (New York, Scribner, 1996).

The Common Table, John Cowan. (New York: HarperBusiness, 1993).

The Gourd Dancer, N. Scott Momaday. (New York: Harper & Row, 1976).

The Heart Aroused: Poetry and the Preservation of the Soul in Corporate America, David Whyte. (New York: Doubleday, 1996).

The Holy Bible, Mark 6:31, adapted by Micheal Noyes. www.michaelnoyes.com

The Prophet, Kahlil Gibran. (New York: Random House, 1976).

The Reinvention of Work: A New Vision of Livelihood For Our Time, Matthew Fox. (California: HarperCollins Publishers, 1994).

The Wonders of Solitude, Ed. Dale Salwak. (California: New World Library, 1998).

Chapter 13: June (Play at Work)

Brainy Quotes, www.brainyquotes.com/quotes

Jump Start Your Brain, Doug Hall with David Wecker. (Indiana: Warner Books, 1996).

Living Your Life Out Loud: How to Unlock Your Creativity and Unleash Your Joy, Salli Rasberry and Padi Selwyn. (New York, Pocket Books, 1995).

Managing to Have Fun, Matt Weinstein. (New York: Simon & Schuster, 1996).

"Al Gore, That Snake," Tony Payton. *Washingtonian Magazine* 38.2. (November, 2002).

"Play for Today," Pat Kane, (2000, October 22). *The Observer.* (West Hudson Publishing Company) www.theobserver.com.

Serious Play: How the World's Best Companies Simulate to Innovate, Michael Schrage. (Massachusetts: Harvard Business School Press, 1999).

The Mozart Effect, Don Campbell. (New York: Avon Books, 1997).

Time Management For Unmanageable People, Ann McGee Cooper with Duane Trammell. (New York: Bantam Books, 1994).

Totally Useless Skills: 75 Great Ways to Play at Work, Rick Davis. (New Hampshire: Hobblebush Books, 1996).

Chapter 14: July (Relax at Work)

20-Minute Retreats. Rachel Harris, Ph.D. (New York: Henry Holt, 2000).

Adventures in the Art of Living, Wilferd A. Peterson. (New York: Simon & Schuster, 1968).

Calm at Work, Paul Wilson. (New York: Plume, 1999).

"From Office Catnaps to Lunchtime Jogs," S. Shallenbarger (2002). *www.careerjournal.com*.

Learn to Relax: A Practical Guide to Easing Tension and Conquering Stress, Mike George. (Nevada: Chronicle Books, 1998).

"Change Your Life...Take a Day of Rest," Naomi Levy, (1998, October 11). *Parade Magazine*, pp.12-13.

Relax – You May Only Have a Few Minutes Left, Loretta LaRoche. (New York: Villard, 1998).

"Tales of Grabbing Undertime at Work," S. Shallenbarger (2002). www.careerjournal.com/columnists/workfamily/20020517-workfamily.html.

The Art of Napping at Work: The No-Cost Natural Way to Increase Productivity and Satisfaction, William A. Anthony, Ph.D. and Camille W. Anthony, Ph.D. (California: Larson Publishing, 1999).

The Performance Edge, Robert K. Cooper, Ph.D. (Boston: Houghton Mifflin Company, 1991).

Thriving in 24/7: Six Strategies for Taming the New World of Work, Sally Helgesen. (New York, Free Press [div. of Macmillian, Inc.], 2001).

To Begin Again: The Journey Toward Comfort, Strength and Faith in Difficult Times, Naomi Levy. (New York: Ballatine Publishing Group, 1999).

"What You Need to Know About Office Undertime Rules," S. Shallenbarger. www.careerjournal.com/columnists/workfamily/20020419-workfamily.html, 9/27/02.

Wherever You Go, There You Are: Mindfulness Meditation in Everyday Life, Jon Kabat-Zinn, Ph.D. (New York: Hyperion, 1994).

Working Wonders: 60 Quick Break Techniques to Beat Burnout, Boast Productivity and Revive Your Workday, James Joseph. (California: Berkley Publishing Group, 1998).

Chapter 15: August (Create Balance at Work)

"Guarding Your Time: How To Say No," Jan McDaniel. www.bluesuitmom.com/career/balance/say

Life is Not Work, Work is Not Life: Simple Reminders for Finding Balance in a 24/7 World, Robert K. Johnston, Ph.D. and J. Walker Smith, Ph.D. (California: Wildcat Canyon Press, 2001).

"Life and Work: Balancing or Juggling?" Sheila Adams. www.selfgrowth.com/articles/adams5.htm

Lunchtime Enlightenment, Pragito Dove. (New York: Penguin Putnam, 2002).

Office Yoga: Simple Stretches for Busy People, Darrin Zeer. (Nevada: Chronicle Books, 2000).

"What You Need to Know About Office Undertime Rules," S. Shallenbarger. www.careerjournal.com, 9/27/02.

SPONSOR SUCCESS: A Workbook for Turning Good Intentions Into Positive Results, Bob Younglove. (Maryland: American Literary Press, 2002).

Taming the Paper Tiger at Work, Barbara Hemphill. (Florida: Kiplinger Books, 1998).

Time Management For Unmanageable People, Ann McGee Cooper with Duane Trammell. (New York: Bantam Books, 1994).

Turn It Off: How to Unplug from the Anytime-Anywhere Office Without Disconnecting Your Career, Gil E. Gordon. (New York: Three Rivers Press, 2001).

You Don't Have To Come Home from Work Exhausted!: A Program to Bring Joy, Energy and Balance to your Life, Ann McGee Cooper with Duane Trammell and Barbara Lau. (New York: Bantam Books, 1992).

Chapter 16: September (Make a New Commitment to Your Work)

Brain Gym for Business: Instant Brain Boosters for On-the-Job Success, Gail Dennison, Paul Dennison, Ph.D., and Jerry Teplitz, J.D., Ph.D. (Ventura: Edu-Kinesthetics, Incorporated, 1994).

"Use a Personal Board of Advisors to Be Successful," Vance Caesar, Ph.D. www.smallbusinessresources.com.

Emotional Intelligence: Why It Can Matter More than IQ, Daniel Goleman. (New York: Bantam Books, 1997).

Faith at Work™ Magazine. (Falls Church, VA: Faith At Work, Inc.) www.FaithAtWork.com.

First Things First, Steven R. Covey. (New York: Simon & Schuster, 1996).

Guideposts Magazine, 16 E 34 St, New York NY 10016. www.guideposts.com

Illuminata: A Return to Prayer, Marianne Williamson. (New York: Riverhead Books, 1995).

Living with Vision: Reclaiming the Power of the Heart, Linda Marks. (Santa Monica: Sigo Press, 1991).

Mozart's Brain and the Fighter Pilot: Unleashing Your Brain's Potential, Richard Restak, M.D. (Kentucky: Harmony Books, 2002).

PARADE Magazine. (New York) www.parade.com

Past Forward: Past Life Healing, Higher Self-Counseling,
www.healpastlives.com

Primal Leadership: Realizing the Power of Emotional Intelligence, Daniel
Goleman, Richard E. Boyatzis, and Annie McKee. (Massachusetts:
Harvard Business School Press, 2002).

Reader's Digest Magazine. (Pleasantville, New York: Reader's Digest).
www.rd.com.

*Rekindling Commitment: How to Revitalize Yourself, Your Work, and Your
Organization* (The Jossey-Bass Management Series), Dennis T. Jaffe,
Cynthia D. Scott, and Glenn R. Tobe. (New York: Jossey-Bass, 1994).

Spark People, www.sparkpeople.com.

Stewardship: Choosing Service Over Self-Interest, Peter Block. (San Francisco:
Berrett-Koehler Publishers, 1996).

The 7 Habits of Highly Effective People: Powerful Lessons in Personal Change,
Steven R. Covey. (Pennsylvania: Running Press Book Publishers, 2000).

The Path: Creating Your Mission Statement for Work and for Life, Laurie Beth
Jones. (New York: Hyperion Press, 1998).

The Power of Purpose, Richard J. Leider. (New York: Fine Communications,
2000).

Working With Emotional Intelligence, Daniel Goleman. (New York: Bantam
Books, 1999).

"Time Management Guide," Karen Lamb. www.time-management-
guide.com

*Zen and the Art of Making a Living: A Practical Guide to Creative Career
Design* Laurence G. Boldt. (New York: Penguin Putnam, 1999).

"Leaders Gain Valuable Insights Through Mastermind Groups," Christine
W. Zurst. www.emergingleader.com

Chapter 17: October   (Appreciate Abundance at Work)

Cyber Nation, www.cyber-nation.com/victory/quotations/subjects/quote_abundance.html

Cyber Quotations, www.cyberquotations.com/sorted/qProsperity.htm

"From Abundance?" Jae Malone. www.lightmatrix.org/prosperity/abundance.html

Good News Bible: English Version. (New York: American Bible Society, 2001).

House of Belonging, David Whyte. (Washington: Many Rivers Press, 1997).

Illuminata: A Return to Prayer, Marianne Williamson. (New York: Riverhead Books, 1995).

Open Your Mind to Prosperity, Catherine Ponder. (California: DeVorss & Company, 1984).

PPR Quotes, www.pprsites.tripod.com/pprquotes/PPR-Quote-Wealth.htm

"Small Profitable Steps", James Craig Green. www.pw1.netcom.com/~zeno7/smalstep.html

Take Time for Your Life: A Personal Coach's Seven Step Program for Creating the Life You Want, Cheryl Richardson. (New York: Broadway Books, 1999).

Tao Te Ching—"The Book of the Way," Lao Tsu, translated by Stephen Mitchell (New York: Harper and Row, 1988).

The 40 Day Prosperity Plan, John Randolph Price. (California: Hay House, 1996).

The Abundance Book, John Randolph Price. (California: Hay House, Inc., 1996).

The Active Life: Wisdom for Work, Creativity, and Caring, Parker Palmer. (HarperSanFrancisco; San Francisco, 1991).

The Dynamic Laws of Prosperity, Catherine Ponder. (New York: Buccaneer Books, 1993).

The Quotations Page, www.quotationspage.com

The Science of Mind, Ernest Holmes. (New York: Penguin Putnam Books for Young Readers, 1988).

True Wealth, Marsha Sinetar. (Colorado: Sounds True, 1994).

Zen Stories to Tell Your Neighbor, www.rider.edu/users/suler/zenstory/ zenstory.html

Chapter 18: November (Cultivate Gratitude at Work)

Angel Fire Web site, www.angelfire.com

"A Story about Being Grateful for What You Have," Adapted from "Teaching Tales: The Way You Like It," retold by Aaron Zerah, www.beliefnet.com

Be Thankful Web site, www.bethankful.com

Charles Kingsley, www.colleenscorner.com

Don't Sweat the Small Stuff… And It's All Small Stuff, Richard Carlson, Ph.D. (New York: Hyperion, 1997).

Gratefulness Web site, www.gratefulness.com

Gratitude: A Way of Life, Louise L. Hay. (California: Hay House, 1998).

"Gratitude and Forgiveness in the Workplace," Michael Stone. www.astd.org,

"Have an Attitude of Gratitude," Ann Perle. www.mtmrecognition.com

"Highlights from Research Project on Gratitude and Thanksgiving," Robert A. Emmon and Michael E. McCullough, study Co-Investigators for John Templeton Foundation. www.bethankful.com

Holy Bible, Psalms 1:1-2 (adapted from *The Enlightened Heart: An Anthology of Sacred Poetry,* edited by Stephen Mitchell. (New York: Harper & Row Publishers, 1989).

Holy Bible (New Revised Standard Version). (Tennessee: Thomas Nelson Inc., 1989).

"Open for Business: The Gratitude Survey," www.work-at-home-index.net

Simple Abundance Journal of Gratitude, Sarah Ban Breathnach. (Indiana: Warner Books, 1997).

Simple Abundance: A Daybook of Comfort and Joy, Ban Breachnach. (New Jersey: Universe Publishing, 1998).

"The Power of Gratitude," Jill Lawrence, 4/16/98. www.nhne.com/storiesquotes/gratitude.html

Chapter 19: December (Celebrate at Work)

C.A.R.E. Packages For The Workplace: Dozens of Little Things You Can Do To Regenerate Spirit At Work, Barbara Glanz. (New York: McGraw-Hill, 1996).

Corporate Celebration: Play, Purpose, & Profit at Work, Terrence E. Deal and M. K. Key. (California: Berrett-Koehler Publishers, 1998).

Dare to Care postcards, JoAnna Brandi, www.customerretention.com

Fanfare for A Feather: 77 Ways to Celebrate Practically Anything, Vivienne Margolis, Kerry Townsend Smith, and Adele Weiss. (California: Resource Publications, 1991).

Feeding the Spirit: Creating Your Own Festivals, Ceremonies and Celebrations, Nancy Brady Cunningham. (California: Resource Publications, 1988).

"Fire Up Employees and Please Your "Customers"—Tell Your Stories!" Evelyn Clark. www.corpstory.com/articles

Holy Bible (New Revised Standard Version). (Tennessee: Thomas Nelson Inc., 1989).

"Guerilla Celebrations". Employment Recruitment and Retention Newsletter. (Chicago, Illinois: Ragan Communications, Inc.)

Encouraging the Heart: A Leader's Guide to Rewarding and Recognizing Others, James M. Kouzes and Barry Z. Posner. (New York: John Wiley & Sons, 1998).

Lights of Passage: Rituals and Rites of Passage for the Problems and Pleasures of Modern Life, Kathleen Wall. (New York: Holt, Henry & Company, 1995).

Living Your Life Out Loud: How to Unlock Your Creativity and Unleash Your Joy, Salli Rasberry and Padi Selwyn. (New York, Pocket Books, 1995).

Modern Life, Kathleen Wall, Ph.D. and Gary Ferguson. (California: DeVorss & Company, 1994).

Pass It On™ cards. (Allen, TX: Argus Communications).

Rise Up Singing: The Group Singing Songbook, edited by Peter Blood-Patterson. (Pennsylvania: Sing Out Publications, 1991).

"Ritual in the Lives of Children," Nancy Monson. www.runningriver.sprout.org/articles/ritual.shtml

Ritual: Power, Healing and Community, Malidome Somé. (New York: Penguin Putnam, 1997).

Simple Abundance: A Daybook of Comfort and Joy, Ban Breachnach. (New Jersey: Universe Publishing, 1998).

The Drop that Became the Sea trans. by Kabir Helminski and Relik Argar (Putney: Threshold Books, 1989).

The Mozart Effect, Don Campbell. (New York: Avon Books, 1997).

The One Minute Manager, Ken Blanchard. (New York: HarperCollins, 1981).

"The Power of Ritual," Amber Bottelsen. www.everevolving.com/rituals/rituals_articles.html

The Songlines (London: Pan Books Ltd, 1988).

The Sounds of Healing: A Physician Reveals the Therapeutic Power of Sound, Voice & Music, Mitchell L. Gaynor, M.D. (Pennsylvania: Diane Publishing Company, 2002).

"The Study of Music in Public Schools," Charles W. Landon. www.quotations.about.com.

Wild Hearts Dancing: A Personal One-Day Quest to Liberate the Artist & Lover Within, Elliot Sobel. (New York: Simon & Schuster, 1994).

Yiddish Folktales, edit. by Beatrice Silverman Weinrieich, trans. by Leonard Wolf. (New York: Pantheon Books, 1988).

Quick Reference Guides

QUICK REFERENCE GUIDE TO TIPS

This guide has been created to help you easily identify tips that will address specific renewal needs. The four different aspects of your being (B = Body, M = Mind, E = Emotions, and S = Spirit) are listed on the right hand side of the page and the general themes and names of the tips are indicated on the left. You can use this guide in the following two ways: 1) Read the names of the tips, select one that resonates with you, and then look in the right hand columns to determine which aspects of your being the tip will renew. Note that some tips help you renew several different areas while others result in the renewal of only one area. 2) Decide which aspect(s) of your being you want to renew, then use the right hand columns to help you determine which tips will address that particular area. Select the tip that you feel is most relevant to and supportive of your current situation.

Name of Month/Theme/Tip	Page #	B	M	E	S
Chapter 8: January — Transform Your Relationship with Time					
Decide what is really important in your life					
Take inventory of exactly how you invest your time	70	B	M	E	
Clarify your priorities	72	B	M	E	
Use your priorities to make decisions about how you invest your time.	74		M		
Realize the preciousness of time					
Plan your day with the preciousness of time in mind.	75		M	E	S
Appreciate the gifts you receive from time.	75			E	S
Remind yourself of the preciousness of time.	76		M		S
Take a vacation ASAP!	77	B	M	E	S
Step into the present moment					
Take time each day to pay attention to yourself in the present moment.	79	B	M	E	S
Focus fully on the task before you.	79		M		
Concentrate on your current emotions in difficult situations	80			E	
Experience the present through your senses	81	B	M		
Live each day fully					
Say what's in your heart on and off the job	82			E	
Follow your as-yet, unfulfilled dreams	83			E	S
Identify a maxim for your life and live it!	84		M		S

Name of Month/Theme/Tip	Page #	B	M	E	S
Pace yourself throughout the day and week					
Balance your most demanding tasks with less demanding ones	197	B	M		
Follow your body's natural rhythms	197	B			
Work only as long as is required to achieve results	198	B	M	E	S
Form boundaries around your work	201	B		E	
Balance your energy replacement					
Renew yourself physically	203	B			
Refresh your mind at least five times a day	204		M		
Pay attention to your emotional state	204			E	
Uplift your spirit at work	205				S
Reprioritize and simplify your work					
Step back and reprioritize	206		M	E	
Simplify your to-do list	207		M		
Straighten up your work area	208	B		E	
Visualize balance at work	208	B	M	E	S
Chapter 16: September - Make a New Commitment to Your Work					
Understand your motivation and inspiration to work					
Explore your inspiration at work	216		M	E	
Identify the most inspiring event of your work life in which you played a part	216			E	
Ask others about what they find inspiring about their work	217			E	
Read about people who follow their life's work or mission	217		M	E	S
Develop or revist the mission statement for work					
Consult resources on developing or revising your mission statement	219		M		
Create or review your life's work mission statement	220		M	E	S
Develop goals to support your mission statement	221		M	E	
Review your mission statement daily and your goals weekly	221		M	E	S
Get support for implementing your goals					
Ask for help on an informal basis in accomplishing goals	222			E	
Seek out an accountability partner	223			E	
Form a Mastermind Group	223		M	E	
Form a "Personal Board of Advisors"	224		M	E	
Include renewal at work in your goals					
Commit to one friendship at work	226			E	S
Learn more about Emotional Intelligence at Work	226		M	E	

QUICK REFERENCE GUIDE TO EXERCISES

This guide has been created to help you easily identify exercises that will address specific renewal needs. The four different aspects of your being (B = Body, M = Mind, E = Emotions, and S = Spirit) are listed on the right hand side of the page and the general themes and names of the exercises are indicated on the left. You can use this guide in the following two ways: 1) Read the names of the exercises, select one that resonates with you, and then look in the right hand columns to determine which aspects of your being the exercise will renew. Note that some exercises help you renew several different areas while others result in the renewal of only one area. 2) Decide which aspect(s) of your being you want to renew, then use the right hand columns to help you determine which exercises will address that particular area. Select the exercise that you feel is most relevant to and supportive of your current situation.

Chapter/Month/Exercise	Page #	B	M	E	S
Chapter 3: The Experience of Running on Plenty at Work					
Practicing Conscious Breathing	22	B	M	E	S
Chapter 5: How to Practice Preventative Maintenance					
Checking In With Yourself	36	B	M	E	
Chapter 6: Overcoming Roadblocks to Running on Plenty					
Conducting Your Own Reality Check	43		M	E	
Clarifying Beliefs with Support Renewal		B	M	E	
Chapter 7: Making a Commitment to Running on Plenty at Work					
Making a Personal Commitment to Running on Plenty	52	B	M	E	S
Chapter 8: January - Transform Your Relationship with Time					
Evaluating How I Invest My Time at Work and Home	71	B	M		
Devoting Time to My Top Priorities	73	B	M		
Recollecting and Acting on My Dreams	83			E	S
Chapter 9: February - Be Love's Touch at Work					
Evoking Loving-Kindness	102	B	M	E	S

INDEX

INDEX

ABOUT THE AUTHORS

Krista Kurth, Ph.D. and Suzanne Adele Schmidt, Ph.D. have spent the last decade of their work focused on helping others to lead more renewing and productive lives at work. This book, *Running on Plenty at Work: Renewal Strategies for Individuals,* is the culmination of what they have learned in their work with clients. It is the first in a series on renewal in the workplace.

They are cofounders of Renewal Resources, a consulting and publishing firm dedicated to the renewal and revitalization of individuals and organizations. Together, they have designed and delivered a wide variety of training programs and seminars, including their unique "Mastering Personal Renewal at Work" program. Their specialties include personal and organizational renewal, leadership development, team building, and enhanced interpersonal communication. In addition to their writing, coaching and consulting work, they also deliver presentations at local, national and international events.

Both Krista and Suzanne live in the Washington, DC metropolitan area where they frequently meander on the Road to Renewal in the midst of the cosmopolitan chaos there. Suzanne's favorite renewal activity is driving in her convertible—top down—with her athletic husband, Dan. Krista loves to find quiet back roads and moments to meditate, away from her active and sports-oriented teenage sons and husband.

Over the years, they have assisted organizations in a variety of ways—both contributing their unique gifts to those with whom they work. Krista brings her love of service and her extensive background in business, organization development, psychology, and spiritual and renewal practices to her work. Her own personal experience and her abiding interest in helping people be more true to themselves at work inspired original research on the topic of spiritual renewal at work. Suzanne's life long passion is to enhance interpersonal and team dynamics in the workplace. She is masterful in employing games, initiatives, celebrations, and outdoor activities to spark her clients' enthusiasm for learning to work and live in more productive ways.

Both Dr. Schmidt and Dr. Kurth have practical and academic backgrounds in business and organization development work. Dr. Schmidt completed her doctorate at the University of Pittsburgh in Education and received a Masters in Counseling from Slippery Rock University in Pennsylvania. Dr. Kurth received her doctorate in Organization Development from George Washington University and her MBA from the University of Washington in Seattle, WA. Prior to founding Renewal Resources, Suzanne worked as a consultant in her own firm, as well as managed human resources for Life Technologies and Westinghouse Electric Corporation. Krista also operated her own consulting practice, prior to teaming up with Suzanne, as well as held a range of other managerial and consulting positions, including one with KPMG Peat Marwick.

To contact the authors:

Krista Kurth, Ph.D.
9428 Garden Court
Potomac, MD 20854
301-765-9551
krista@renewalatwork.com

Suzanne Adele Schmidt, Ph.D.
18920 Falling Star Road
Germantown, MD 20874
301-601-1990
suzanne@renewalatwork.com

Disclaimer

This book is designed to provide information on renewal strategies for individuals at work. It is sold with the understanding that the publisher, Renewal Resources Press, a division of Renewal Resources LLC, and the authors are not engaged in rendering psychological or other professional services. If psychological or other expert assistance is required, the services of a competent professional should be sought.

Every effort has been made to provide a guide to renewal that is as complete and accurate as possible. However, there *may be mistakes*, both typographical and in content. Therefore, this text should be used as a general guide for renewal. Furthermore, this manual contains information that is current only up to the printing date.

The purpose of this book is to educate and entertain. The authors and publisher shall have neither liability nor responsibility to any person or entity with respect to any loss or damage caused, or alleged to have been caused, directly or indirectly, by the information in this book.

Why We Chose to Contribute to Enterprise Development™ International

 Since 1998, Renewal Resources has been blessed with a profitable business and wonderful clients who have helped us to grow our business. When it came time to apply for a small loan to fund our publishing company, Renewal Resources Press, our bank approved our application almost overnight. The Washington, DC area, where we are based, provides rich training and networking opportunities for women entrepreneurs. We have been fortunate to participate in many activities aimed at enhancing our business.

We know that women entrepreneurs in other parts of the world face huge obstacles as they try to start up their businesses. In many corners of the earth, women's poverty is such that they are blocked from traditional forms of credit. As a way of passing on our gratitude for those who have helped us, we are making a donation to Enterprise Development™ International from the proceeds from this book.

Founded in 1985, Enterprise Development™ International is a nonprofit organization serving the poor to free themselves from poverty. In the past seventeen years, Enterprise Development™ International has worked in more than fifty countries to provide business training and small loans to the hard-working poor so they can start or expand their businesses.

To learn more about Enterprise Development™ International, contact them at 10395 Democracy Lane, Fairfax, Virginia 22030; Phone: 703-277-3360; Web site: www.endpoverty.com.

Renewal Resources Press

9428 Garden Court
Potomac, MD 20854
www.renewalatwork.com

BOOK ORDER FORM

Phone Orders: Call (800) 877-2693 and select option 2
 In keeping with the idea of running on plenty, phone orders are taken
 Monday through Friday from 8 AM until 4 PM ET

Fax orders: Copy, complete, and send this form to (518) 436-7433

Online orders: Go to our Web site: www.renewalatwork.com and click on
 the book cover on our home page. Follow the instructions for ordering.

Mail orders: Copy, complete and mail this form to Renewal Resources,
 18920 Falling Star Road, Germantown, MD 20974

Please send ____ copies of *Running on Plenty at Work: Renewal Strategies for Individuals.*

(Large order discounts: 10 –24 copies: 10% discount, 25–30: 15% discount).
I understand that I may return any of them for a full refund—for any reason, no
questions asked.

Please send more FREE information on:

☐ Other Books   ☐ Speaking/Seminars   ☐ Programs   ☐ Consulting

Name:_____ Company Name:_____
Shipping Address:_____
City: _____ State: _____ Zip: _____
Day Time Telephone: _____
Email address: _____

Sales tax: Please add 8.5% sales tax for books shipped to New York addresses and 5% sales tax for
books shipped to Maryland addresses.

Shipping:

Within the U.S.A: Add $5.00 for first book and $2.00 for each additional book.
International: Add $10.45 for first book; $5.00 for each additional book (estimate).

Payment: ☐ Check   ☐ Credit card:
                          ☐ Visa   ☐ MasterCard   ☐ AMEX

Card number: _____

Name on card: _____ Exp. Date: _____

Signature: _____

Renewal Resources Press

9428 Garden Court
Potomac, MD 20854
www.renewalatwork.com

BOOK ORDER FORM

Phone Orders: Call (800) 877-2693 and select option 2
   In keeping with the idea of running on plenty, phone orders are taken
   Monday through Friday from 8 AM until 4 PM ET

Fax orders: Copy, complete, and send this form to (518) 436-7433

Online orders: Go to our Web site: www.renewalatwork.com and click on
   the book cover on our home page. Follow the instructions for ordering.

Mail orders: Copy, complete and mail this form to Renewal Resources,
   18920 Falling Star Road, Germantown, MD 20974

Please send ____ copies of *Running on Plenty at Work:*
Renewal Strategies for Individuals.

(Large order discounts: 10 –24 copies: 10% discount, 25–30: 15% discount).
I understand that I may return any of them for a full refund—for any reason, no
questions asked.

Please send more FREE information on:
☐ Other Books   ☐ Speaking/Seminars   ☐ Programs   ☐ Consulting

Name:_____ Company Name:_____
Shipping Address:_____
City: _____ State: _____ Zip: _____
Day Time Telephone: _____
Email address: _____

Sales tax: Please add 8.5% sales tax for books shipped to New York addresses and 5% sales tax for
books shipped to Maryland addresses.

Shipping:
Within the U.S.A: Add $5.00 for first book and $2.00 for each additional book.
International: Add $10.45 for first book; $5.00 for each additional book (estimate).

Payment: ☐ Check   ☐ Credit card:
                ☐ Visa   ☐ MasterCard   ☐ AMEX

Card number: _____

Name on card: _____ Exp. Date: _____

Signature: _____

EVIDENCE-BASED PRACTICE

in Nursing & Healthcare

A GUIDE TO BEST PRACTICE

- **Bernadette Mazurek Melnyk, PhD, RN, CPNP/PMHNP, FNAP, FAAN**
  Associate Vice President for Health Promotion
  University Chief Wellness Officer
  Dean, College of Nursing
  The Ohio State University
  Columbus, Ohio

  Associate Editor, Worldviews on Evidence-Based Nursing

  Partner, ARCC llc; President, COPE for HOPE, Inc.

  Founder and Chair, National Association of Pediatric Nurse Practitioners' (NAPNAP)
  KySS (Keep your children/yourself Safe and Secure) Campaign
  Promoting the Mental Health of Children, Teens & Families

  Member, The United States Preventive Services Task Force

- **Ellen Fineout-Overholt, PhD, RN, FNAP, FAAN**
  Clinical Professor and Director
  Center for Advancement of Evidence-Based Practice
  Arizona State University College of Nursing & Health Innovation
  Phoenix, Arizona

  Partner, ARCC llc

second edition

Wolters Kluwer | Lippincott Williams & Wilkins
Health
Philadelphia · Baltimore · New York · London
Buenos Aires · Hong Kong · Sydney · Tokyo

Acquisitions Editor: Hilarie Surrena
Product Manager: Helen Kogut
Vendor Manager: Cynthia Rudy
Design Coordinator: Joan Wendt
Illustration Coordinator: Brett MacNaughton
Manufacturing Coordinator: Karin Duffield
Prepress Vendor: SPi Technologies

2nd edition

Library of Congress Cataloging-in-Publication Data
Melnyk, Bernadette Mazurek.
    Evidence-based practice in nursing & healthcare : a guide to best practice / Bernadette Mazurek Melnyk, Ellen Fineout-Overholt.—2nd ed.
        p. ; cm.
    Other title: Evidence-based practice in nursing and healthcare
    Includes bibliographical references and index.
    ISBN 978-1-60547-778-7
  1. Evidence-based nursing. 2. Evidence-based medicine. I. Fineout-Overholt, Ellen. II. Title. III. Title: Evidence-based practice in nursing and healthcare.
    [DNLM: 1. Evidence-Based Nursing—methods—Practice Guideline. 2. Nurse Clinicians—Practice Guideline. WY 100.7 M527e 2011]

    RT42.M44 2011
    610.73—dc22

2010007467

Care has been taken to confirm the accuracy of the information presented and to describe generally accepted practices. However, the author(s), editors, and publisher are not responsible for errors or omissions or for any consequences from application of the information in this book and make no warranty, expressed or implied, with respect to the currency, completeness, or accuracy of the contents of the publication. Application of this information in a particular situation remains the professional responsibility of the practitioner; the clinical treatments described and recommended may not be considered absolute and universal recommendations.

The author(s), editors, and publisher have exerted every effort to ensure that drug selection and dosage set forth in this text are in accordance with the current recommendations and practice at the time of publication. However, in view of ongoing research, changes in government regulations, and the constant flow of information relating to drug therapy and drug reactions, the reader is urged to check the package insert for each drug for any change in indications and dosage and for added warnings and precautions. This is particularly important when the recommended agent is a new or infrequently employed drug.

Some drugs and medical devices presented in this publication have Food and Drug Administration (FDA) clearance for limited use in restricted research settings. It is the responsibility of the health care provider to ascertain the FDA status of each drug or device planned for use in his or her clinical practice.

CCS0213

I dedicate this book to my loving, understanding, and supportive family:
my husband, John, and my three daughters, Angela, Megan, and Kaylin,
as well as to my father, who always taught me that anything can be
accomplished with a spirit of enthusiasm and determination.

Bernadette Mazurek Melnyk

The second edition of this book is dedicated to my precious family, Wayne and
Rachael, who are my inspiration; to my Mom, Virginia Fineout, who believes
in me and what we are trying to accomplish; and in loving memory of
my Dad, Arthur J. Fineout, who taught me to think critically,
apply what I learned, and never give up.

Ellen Fineout-Overholt

Anne Wojner Alexandrov, PhD, APRN, CCRN, FAAN
Professor
University of Alabama at Birmingham
Birmingham, Alabama

Chapter 10

Karen Balakas, PhD, RN, CNE
Professor and Director of Clinical Research/EBP
  Partnerships
Goldfarb School of Nursing
Barnes-Jewish College
St. Louis, Missouri

Chapter 14

Patricia E. Benner, PhD, RN, FRCN, FAAN
Professor Emerita (former Thelma Shobe Endowed
  Chair in Ethical and Spirituality)
Department of Social and Behavioral Sciences
University of California San Francisco
San Francisco, California

Chapter 7

Donna R. Berryman, MLS
Assistant Director of Education and Information
  Services
School of Medicine and Dentistry
University of Rochester
Rochester, New York

Chapter 3

Cecily L. Betz, PhD, RN, FAAN
Associate Professor of Clinical Pediatrics
Department of Pediatrics
Keck School of Medicine
Director of Nursing Training
Director of Research
USC Center for Excellence in Developmental
  Disabilities
Children's Hospital
Los Angeles, California
Editor-in-Chief
*Journal of Pediatric Nursing: Nursing Care of
  Children and Families*

Chapter 16

Barbara B. Brewer, PhD, RN, MALS, MBA
Director of Professional Practice
John C. Lincoln North Mountain Hospital
Phoenix, Arizona

Chapter 10

Terri L. Brown, MSN, RN, CPN
Research Specialist
Texas Children's Hospital
Houston, Texas

Chapter 9

Donna Ciliska, PhD, RN
Scientific Co-Director of the National Collaborating
  Centre for Methods and Tools and Professor
School of Nursing
McMaster University
Hamilton, Ontario, Canada

Chapter 11

Robert Cole, PhD
Associate Professor of Clinical Nursing
University of Rochester
Rochester, New York

Chapter 17

John F. Cox III, MD
Assistant Professor of Clinical Medicine
School of Medicine and Dentistry
University of Rochester
Rochester, New York

Chapter 13

Laura Cullen, MA, RN, FAAN
Evidence-Based Practice Coordinator
University of Iowa Hospitals and Clinics
Iowa City, Iowa

Chapter 11

Deborah Dang, PhD, RN, NEA-BC
Director of Nursing
Practice, Education, Research
Johns Hopkins Hospital
Baltimore, Maryland

Chapter 11

Alba DiCenso, PhD, RN
Professor
School of Nursing
McMaster University
Hamilton, Ontario, Canada

Chapter 11

Doris Grinspun, PhD, RN
Executive Director
Registered Nurses' Association of Ontario
Toronto, Ontario, Canada

Chapter 8

Marilyn J. Hockenberry, PhD, RN, PNP-BC, FAAN
Professor of Pediatrics, Hematology/Oncology
Baylor College of Medicine
Houston, Texas

Chapter 9

Sheila Hofstetter, MLS, AHIP
Health Sciences Librarian
Arizona State University
Noble Science and Engineering Library
Tempe, Arizona

Chapter 3

Linda Johnston, PhD, RN
Professor and Chair of Neonatal Nursing
  Research
The Royal Children's Hospital
Parkville
Deputy Head of School and Associate Head
  (Research)
School of Nursing
The University of Melbourne
Murdoch Children's Research Institute
Melbourne, Australia

Chapter 5

June H. Larrabee, PhD, RN
Professor and Clinical Investigator
West Virginia University and West Virginia
  University Hospitals
Charleston, West Virginia

Chapter 11

Victoria Wynn Leonard, RN, FNP, PhD
Assistant Professor
University of San Francisco School of Nursing
San Francisco, California

Chapter 7

Robin P. Newhouse, PhD, RN, CNAA, BC
Assistant Dean
Doctor of Nursing Practice Studies
Associate Professor
School of Nursing
University of Maryland
Annapolis, Maryland

Chapter 11

Dónal P. O'Mathúna, PhD
Senior Lecturer in Ethics, Decision-Making
  and Evidence
School of Nursing
Dublin City University
Glasnevin, Dublin, Ireland

Chapters 5 and 20

Bethel Ann Powers, RN, PhD
Professor and Director
Evaluation Office
University of Rochester School of Nursing
Rochester, New York

Chapters 6, 18, and Appendix C

Tom Rickey, BA
Manager of National Media Relations and Senior
  Science Editor
University of Rochester Medical Center
Rochester, New York

Chapter 16

Brett W. Robbins, MD
Associate Professor of Medicine and Pediatrics
University of Rochester
Rochester, New York

Chapter 13

Jo Rycroft-Malone, PhD, MSc, BSc (Hon), RN
Professor of Health Services and Implementation
  Research
School of Healthcare Sciences
Bangor University
Frowheulog, Bangor, United Kingdom

Chapter 11

Alyce A. Schultz, PhD, RN, FAAN
Consultant
EBP Concepts, Alyce A. Schultz & Associates,
  LLC
Chandler, Arizona

Chapter 11

Kathryn A. Smith, RN, MN
Associate Director for Administration
USC University Center for Excellence in Developmental Disabilities
Children's Hospital
Associate Professor of Clinical Pediatrics
Keck School of Medicine
University of Southern California
Los Angeles, California

Chapter 16

Julia Sollenberger, MLS
Director
Health Science Libraries and Technologies
University of Rochester Medical Center
Rochester, New York

Chapter 3

Cheryl B. Stetler, PhD, RN, FAAN
Consultant
EBP and Evaluation
Amherst, Massachusetts

Chapter 11

Kathleen R. Stevens, RN, EdD, FAAN
Professor and Director
Academic Center for Evidence-Based Nursing
The University of Texas Health Science Center
  at San Antonio
San Antonio, Texas

Chapter 4

Susan B. Stillwell, DNP, RN, CNE
Clinical Associate Professor and Expert EBP
  Mentor
College of Nursing and Health Innovation
Arizona State University
Phoenix, Arizona

Chapters 2 and 13

Nancy Watson, PhD, RN
Associate Professor and Director
John A. Hartford Foundation Community
  Initiative & Center for Clinical Research
  on Aging
University of Rochester School of Nursing
Rochester, New York

Appendix I

Kathleen M. Williamson, PhD, RN
Clinical Associate Professor and Associate
  Director
Center for the Advancement of Evidence-Based
  Practice
College of Nursing and Health Innovation
Arizona State University
Phoenix, Arizona

Chapter 13

As the first decade of the new millennium comes to a close, our nation is struggling to deal with a mounting disease and economic burden that is unsustainable and largely preventable. Embedded within the greatest science and technology the world has ever seen is an antiquated anachronistic inefficient "sick" care system in desperate need of evidence-based transformation. From practitioners who are rewarded to care for your illnesses episodically but not to keep you healthy to citizens who either by choice or by circumstance engage in behaviors deleterious to their health that ultimately adds to the national preventable disease and economic burden, we have no choice at this juncture but to embrace the best evidence-based practices in order to create a true healthcare system focused on the citizen/patient with the value proposition being providing the best prevention strategies and care to all citizens at the least cost.

My colleagues in nursing are leaders and equal partners in this evidenced-based journey that should put us on a path to optimal health and wellness as well as cost-effective quality care for all. Like many of you, I have appreciated health care through a range of experiences and perspectives. As someone who has delivered care as a Special Forces combat medic, paramedic, registered nurse, trauma surgeon, and also as a Health System CEO and as Surgeon General of the United States, I know and embrace the power of evidence-based practices.

Dean Melnyk and Professor Fineout-Overholt have once again assembled a world class group of academic and clinical nurse leaders who have authored a state-of-the-art delineation of the pathway needed to scientifically dissect and decipher best practices as well as translate them into practice.

This book transcends nursing and will benefit all health practitioners whose aim is to pursue excellence in their practices.

The future is upon us and nursing continues to lead and shape our health future both clinically and academically.

Richard H. Carmona, MD, MPH, FACS
17th Surgeon General of the United States
Distinguished Professor, Zuckerman College of Public Health
University of Arizona

As clinicians, we all aspire to providing the best healthcare possible for our patients, and evidence-based practice (EBP) is an essential tool in pursuing this aspiration. Healthcare practitioners who provide evidence-based care can be confident that the health and longevity of their patients will benefit. For nurses, EBP must be implemented with fidelity to the culture of compassion and caring that is fundamental to clinical practice. I believe this book provides guidance for practice that optimizes both critical elements of health care.

One of the goals of EBP is to reduce practice pattern variation. Some skeptics have faulted this aspect of EBP as being oriented toward saving costs by not providing care. However, fully implementing EBP more often translates to providing more care to more individuals and achieves cost savings through the appropriate use of the care we know works, while discouraging care that does not work, that has minimal impact on health status, or for which we have insufficient evidence of efficacy.

Healthcare technology continues to move faster than the research needed to evaluate its value. Our current healthcare system often supports the use of new technologies well before the evidence is in, and often we are later proven wrong. But EBP should not be viewed as "just stand there—don't do something"; it is assuring that first and foremost, we do the right thing.

There is ample evidence that the healthcare system does not always do the right thing, even when well supported by evidence. For example, of the 2.5 million annual deaths in the United States, at least half of them could be addressed directly by evidence-based preventive services. The potential of delaying more than a million deaths a year by implementing just what we know now, without any new technologies, provides an imperative that we as healthcare providers must not continue to ignore.

This second edition of *Evidence-Based Practice in Nursing & Healthcare: A Guide to Best Practice* by Melnyk and Fineout-Overholt continues to provide a landmark reference to EBP for health care students, practitioners, researchers, and faculty. I applaud the work of each of the contributors and support the translation of the principles outlined in this book into nursing practice.

Ultimately our education, training, and life-long learning are rooted in science, so a commitment to EBP is the only logical course of action. I hope that all users of this book go on to become active EBP providers, as well as EBP zealots. Our patients will clearly benefit.

Ned Calonge, MD, MPH
Chief Medical Officer, Colorado Department of Public Health and Environment
Chair, US Preventive Services Task Force

There are many published interventions/treatments that have resulted in positive outcomes for patients and healthcare systems that are not being implemented in clinical practice as well as many qualitative findings that are not incorporated into care. It is our continued desire to accelerate the rate at which research findings are translated into practice that stimulated our decision to revise *Evidence-Based Practice in Nursing & Healthcare*. There has been some progress in the adoption of evidence-based practice (EBP) as the standard of care over the past few years; however, there is still much work to be done for this paradigm to be used daily in practice by point-of-care providers. The daunting statistic that it takes an average of 17 years to move research findings into practice is still a reality in many healthcare institutions across the globe. Therefore, increased efforts are needed to provide the tools that point-of-care clinicians need in order to use the best evidence from research and their practices to improve their system, practitioner, and patient outcomes.

We still, and will always, believe that anything is possible when you have a big dream and believe in your ability to accomplish that dream. It was the vision of transforming healthcare with EBP, in any setting, with one patient-clinician encounter at a time and the belief that this can be the daily experience of both clients and practitioners, along with our sheer persistence through many "character-building experiences" during the writing and editing of the book, that culminated in this user-friendly guide that assists all healthcare professionals in the delivery of the highest quality, evidence-based care in order to produce the best outcomes for their patients.

This second edition of *Evidence-Based Practice in Nursing & Healthcare* was revised to assist healthcare providers with implementing and sustaining EBP in their daily practices and to foster a deeper understanding of the principles of the EBP paradigm and process. In working with healthcare systems and clinicians throughout the nation and globe, we have learned more about successful strategies to advance and sustain EBP. Therefore, you will find new material throughout the book, including new chapters and tools to advance EBP.

This second edition also cultivates a foundational understanding of the steps of EBP, clarifies misperceptions about the implementation of EBP, and provides readers with practical action strategies for the implementation of evidence-based care so that widespread acceleration of EBP at the point of care will continue across the country and globe until the lived experience of practicing from the EBP paradigm becomes a reality.

This second edition of *Evidence-Based Practice in Nursing & Healthcare* contains key, usable, and relatable content for all levels of practitioners and learners, with many exemplars that bring to life the concepts within the chapters. For those who want to build their knowledge and skills, this book contains the foundational steps of EBP. For those clinicians who desire to stimulate or lead a change to EBP in their practice sites, this book has information and practical strategies/models on how to introduce change, how to overcome barriers in implementing change, and how to conduct an outcomes assessment of that change. For those in advanced roles or educational programs, the chapters on generating quantitative and qualitative evidence as well as how to write a successful grant proposal will be of particular interest. For educators in the clinical and academic settings, we have included specific chapters on teaching EBP in those settings. The most important issue for teaching others about EBP is to make the paradigm and process understandable for the learner. With that goal in mind, we believe that this book will continue to facilitate a change in how research concepts and critical appraisal are being taught in clinical and academic professional programs throughout the country.

Features

We are huge proponents of cognitive-behavior theory, which contends that how people think directly influences how they feel and behave. We believe that how an individual thinks is the first step toward or away from success. Therefore, new **inspirational quotes** are intertwined throughout our book to encourage readers to build their beliefs and abilities to actively engage in EBP and accomplish their desired goals.

With the rapid delivery of information available to us, **web alerts** direct readers to helpful Internet resources and sites that can be used to further develop EBP knowledge and skills.

New to This Edition

New chapters include

- *Chapter 10*   Focuses on the role of evaluating practice outcomes.
- *Chapter 12*   Details how to create a vision to motivate a change to best practice.
- *Chapters 17 and 18*   Provide step-by-step principles for generating both qualitative and quantitative evidence when little evidence exists to guide clinical practice.
- *Chapter 20*   Addresses the ethics of evidence use and generation.

New content includes

- **"real-life" examples** to assist the reader in actualizing important concepts and overcoming barriers in the implementation of evidence-based care
- **unique evidence hierarchies for different clinical questions** because one hierarchy does not fit all questions
- **successful strategies for finding evidence**, including new resources such as evidence summaries and synopses
- **rapid critical appraisal checklists, evaluation tables, and synthesis tables** that provide efficient critical appraisal methods for both quantitative and qualitative evidence
- information about how to **factor in a clinician's expertise and patient preferences/values when making decisions** about patient care
- **the role of the EBP mentor**, a key factor in the sustainability of an EBP culture, including evaluation of the role with the valid and reliable **EBP beliefs, implementation, and organizational culture and readiness scales**
- discussion of **EBP models by their original creators** to assist learners as they build a culture of EBP
- information on how to **write a successful grant proposal** to fund an EBP implementation project or research study
- information on how to **disseminate evidence to other professionals, the media, and policy makers**
- Multiple appendices with many tools that will help healthcare providers implement EBP

Resources for Students and Instructors

A variety of ancillary materials are available to support students and instructors.

Resource CD-ROM. A variety of tools are available on the accompanying CD-ROM to assist students, clinicians, and educators in their quest for delivering evidence-based care to achieve best outcomes.

Additional resources for students can be found online at thePoint.LWW.com/Melnyk2e.

Instructor's Resource CD-ROM. This comprehensive resource includes the following:

- A Test Generator, containing 300 multiple choice questions
- PowerPoint presentations
- An Image Bank, containing images from the text in formats suitable for printing, projecting, and incorporating into Web sites
- And more!

Resources for Instructors are also available online at thepoint.LWW.com/Melnyk2e

A Final Word from the Authors

Finally, we want to thank each of you who have shared valuable feedback to us on the benefits and challenges you have had in learning about and applying knowledge of EBP. We continue to believe in constructive feedback and would welcome any readers of our book to convey to us what was most helpful for them and what can be done to improve a future edition.

It is important to remember that a spirit of inquiry and lifelong learning are foundational to practicing based on the EBP paradigm. These principles underpin the EBP process so that this problem-solving approach to practice can cultivate an excitement for implementing the highest quality of care. As you travel on your EBP journey, remember that it takes time and becomes easier when the principles of this book are placed into action with enthusiasm on a consistent, daily basis.

Whether you are first learning the steps of the EBP process, leading a successful EBP change effort, or generating evidence to make a difference at the point of care, we want to encourage you to keep the dream alive and, in the words of Les Brown, "Shoot for the moon. Even if you miss, you land among the stars." We hope you are inspired by and enjoy the following EBP RAPP.

Evidence-based practice is a wonderful thing,
Done with consistency, it makes you sing.
PICOT questions and learning search skills;
Appraising evidence can give you thrills.
Medline, CINAHL, PsychInfo are fine,
But for Level I evidence, Cochrane's divine!
Though you may want to practice the same old way
"Oh no, that's not how I will do it" you say.
When you launch EBP in your practice site,
Remember to eat the elephant, bite by bite.
So dream big and persist in order to achieve and
Know that EBP can be done when you believe!

© *2004 Bernadette Melnyk*

Bernadette Mazurek Melnyk and Ellen Fineout-Overholt
Note: You can contact the authors at
500 North 3rd Street
Phoenix, Arizona 85004
Bernadette.Melnyk@asu.edu
Ellen.Fineout-Overholt@asu.edu

acknowledgments

This book could not have been accomplished without the support, understanding, and assistance of many wonderful colleagues, staff, family, and friends. I would first like to acknowledge the outstanding work of my coeditor and cherished friend, Ellen—thank you for all of your efforts, wonderful friendship, attention to detail, and ongoing support throughout this process. I could not have accomplished this revised edition without you. Since the first edition of this book, I have grown personally and professionally through the many opportunities that I have had to teach and mentor others in EBP across the globe—the lessons I have learned from all of you have been incorporated into this book. I thank all of my mentees for their valuable feedback and all of the authors who contributed their time and valuable expertise to this book. Along with my wonderful husband and daughters, I am appreciative for the ongoing love and support that I receive from my mother, Anna May Mazurek, my brother and sister-in-law, Fred and Sue Mazurek, and my sister, Christine Warmuth, whose famous words to me "Just get out there and do it" have been a key to many of my successful endeavors. I also would like to thank my wonderful colleagues and staff at the Arizona State University College of Nursing and Health Innovation for their support, understanding, and ongoing commitment to our projects and their roles throughout this process. Finally, I would like to acknowledge Helen Kogut for her assistance with and dedication to keeping this project "on track."

Bernadette Mazurek Melnyk

My goal for this second edition of the book is for more students, clinicians, clinical educators, faculty, and researchers to adopt the EBP paradigm as their own. Ownership of practice is imperative for healthcare to be transformed. I want to thank each of you who have shared with me personally the value of the first edition of this book to your learning and to the difference you have made in patients' lives and experiences with their health and healthcare. It has been my privilege to hear your enthusiasm for changing for the better how "it has always been done." You have inspired me to continue to keep our dream alive for healthcare transformation, one client–clinician relationship at a time.

I could not have written and edited this second edition of the book without the support of my family. The love and laughter of my dear husband, Wayne, and my precious 9-year-old daughter, Rachael, have kept me focused. They are and always will be my inspiration for what I do. Through her support in the writing of this and the first edition, my mother, Virginia (Grandginny), has become more of an evidence-based consumer, which is what I wish for all of us. My brother, John, and his family, Angela, Ashton, and Aubrey, have provided me with many inspirational moments, particularly in their music. To have had the privilege of working with Bern for these past 20 years has been a pleasure. Together we have helped each other grow and achieve goals that neither of us could have accomplished individually—that is a partnership that is worth preserving. All of these and many others have prayed for me throughout this journey, for which I am truly grateful.

In addition, I would like to thank the folks at Lippincott Williams & Wilkins for helping us to live our dream. I so appreciate the many wonderful contributors to this work and the common goal that binds us together—improving healthcare. I am very grateful for their investment throughout the writing of this second edition.

Finally, as I walk this path, working with sole focus to assist others in improving healthcare outcomes through sustainable evidence-based practice, I realize even more that I am sustained through my relationship with my Savior and Friend, who always has my best in mind, for which I am eternally grateful.

Ellen Fineout-Overholt

xix

contents

Contents

Steps Zero, One, Two: Getting Started

> *To accomplish great things, we must not only act but also dream; not only plan, but also believe.*
>
> *Anatole France*

Making the Case for Evidence-Based Practice and Cultivating a Spirit of Inquiry

Bernadette Mazurek Melnyk and Ellen Fineout-Overholt

It is now widely recognized throughout the globe that **evidence-based practice** (EBP) is key to delivering the highest quality of healthcare and ensuring the best patient outcomes. Findings from numerous studies have indicated that an evidence-based approach to practice versus the implementation of clinical care that is steeped in tradition or based upon outdated policies results in a multitude of improved health, safety, and cost outcomes, including a decrease in patient morbidity and mortality (McGinty & Anderson, 2008; Williams, 2004). When clinicians know how to find, critically appraise, and use the best evidence in clinical practice, and when patients are confident that their healthcare providers are using evidence-based care, optimal outcomes are achieved for all.

Although there is an explosion of scientific evidence available to guide clinical practice, the implementation of evidence-based care by health professionals is typically not the norm in many healthcare systems across the United States and globe. However, when healthcare providers are asked whether they would personally like to receive evidence-based care if they found themselves in a patient role, the answer is resoundingly "yes!" For example:

- If your child was in a motor vehicle accident and sustained a severe head injury, would you want his neurologist to know and use the most effective, empirically supported treatment established from randomized controlled trials (RCTs) to decrease his intracranial pressure and prevent death?

- If your mother was diagnosed with Alzheimer's disease, would you want her nurse practitioner to give you information about how other family caregivers of patients with this disease have coped with the illness, based on evidence from well-designed qualitative and/or descriptive studies?

- If you were diagnosed with colon cancer today and were faced with the decision about what combination of chemotherapy agents to choose, would you want your oncologist to share with you the best and latest evidence regarding the risks and benefits of each therapeutic agent as generated from prior clinical trials with other similar cancer patients?

Definition and Evolution of Evidence-Based Practice

In 2000, Sackett, Straus, Richardson et al. defined EBP as the conscientious use of current best evidence in making decisions about patient care. Since then, the definition of EBP has been broadened in scope and referred to as a lifelong problem-solving approach to clinical practice that integrates

- A systematic search for as well as critical appraisal and synthesis of the most relevant and best research (i.e., **external evidence**) to answer a burning clinical question
- One's own clinical expertise, which includes **internal evidence** generated from outcomes management or quality improvement projects, a thorough patient assessment, and evaluation and use of available resources necessary to achieve desired patient outcomes
- Patient preferences and values (Figure 1.1)

Unlike **research utilization,** which has been frequently operationalized as the use of knowledge typically based on a single study, EBP takes into consideration a synthesis of evidence from multiple studies and combines it with the expertise of the practitioner as well as patient preferences and values (Melnyk & Fineout-Overholt, 2005).

What is Evidence?

Evidence is a collection of facts that are believed to be true. **External evidence** is generated through rigorous research (e.g., **RCTs** or **cohort studies**) and is intended to be generalized to and used in other settings. An important question when implementing external evidence from research is whether clinicians can achieve results in their own clinical practices that are similar to those derived from a body of evidence (i.e., can the findings from research be translated to the real-world clinical setting?). This question of transferability is why measurement of key outcomes is still necessary when implementing practice changes based on evidence. In contrast, **internal evidence** is typically generated through practice initiatives, such as **outcomes management** or **quality improvement projects** undertaken for the purpose of improving clinical care in the setting in

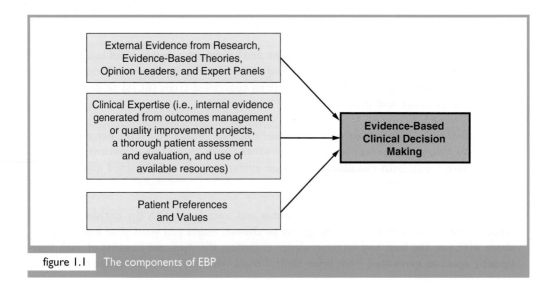

unit one

4

figure 1.1   The components of EBP

which it is produced. Researchers generate new knowledge through rigorous research (i.e., external evidence), and EBP provides clinicians the tools to translate the evidence into clinical practice and integrate it with internal evidence to improve the quality of healthcare and patient outcomes.

Unfortunately, there are many interventions (i.e., treatments) that have substantial empirical evidence to support their use in clinical practice to improve patient outcomes that are not routinely used. For example, findings from a series of RCTs testing the efficacy of the COPE (Creating Opportunities for Parent Empowerment) Program for parents of critically ill/hospitalized and low-birth-weight premature infants have supported that when parents receive COPE (i.e., an educational–behavioral skills building intervention that is delivered by clinicians to parents at the point of care through a series of brief DVDs, written information, and activity workbooks) versus an attention control program, COPE parents: (a) report less stress, anxiety, and depressive symptoms during hospitalization; (b) participate more in their children's care; (c) interact in more developmentally sensitive ways; and (d) report less depression and posttraumatic stress disorder symptoms up to a year following their children's discharge from the hospital (Melnyk, 1994; Melnyk, Alpert-Gillis, Feinstein, et al., 2004; Melnyk, Feinstein, Alpert-Gillis, et al., 2006; Melnyk & Feinstein, 2009). In addition, the premature infants and children of parents who receive COPE versus those whose parents who receive an attention control program have better behavioral and developmental outcomes as well as shorter hospital stays, which could result in billions of dollars of healthcare savings for the U.S. healthcare system if the program is routinely implemented by hospitals (Melnyk et al., 2006; Melnyk & Feinstein, 2009). Despite this strong body of evidence, COPE is not a standard of practice in many hospitals throughout the nation.

In contrast, there are many practices that are being implemented in healthcare that have no or little evidence to support their use (e.g., double-checking pediatric medications, routine assessment of vital signs every 2 or 4 hours in hospitalized patients). Unless we know what interventions are most effective for a variety of populations through the generation of evidence from research and practice data (e.g., outcomes management, quality improvement projects) and how to rapidly translate this evidence into clinical practice through EBP, substantial sustainable improvement in the quality of care received by U.S. residents is not likely (Shortell, Rundall, & Hsu, 2007).

Components of Evidence-Based Practice

Although evidence from systematic reviews of RCTs has been regarded as the strongest level of evidence (i.e., Level 1 evidence) on which to base practice decisions about treatments to achieve a desired outcome, evidence from descriptive and qualitative studies as well as from opinion leaders should be factored into clinical decisions when RCTs are not available. Evidence-based theories (i.e., theories that are empirically supported through well-designed studies) also should be included as evidence. In addition, patient preferences, values, and concerns should be incorporated into the evidence-based approach to decision making along with a clinician's expertise, which includes (a) clinical judgment (i.e., the ability to think about, understand, and use research evidence; the ability to assess a patient's condition through subjective history taking, thorough physical examination findings, and laboratory reports), (b) internal evidence generated from quality improvement or outcomes management projects, (c) clinical reasoning (i.e., the ability to apply the above information to a clinical issue), and (d) evaluation and use of available healthcare resources needed to implement the chosen treatment(s) and achieve the expected outcome. See Figure 1.2.

Clinicians often ask how much and what type of evidence is needed to change practice. A good rule of thumb to answer this question is that there needs to be strong enough evidence to make a practice change. Specifically, the level of evidence plus the quality of evidence equals the strength of the evidence, which provides clinicians the confidence that is needed to change clinical practice. (See Box 1.1.)

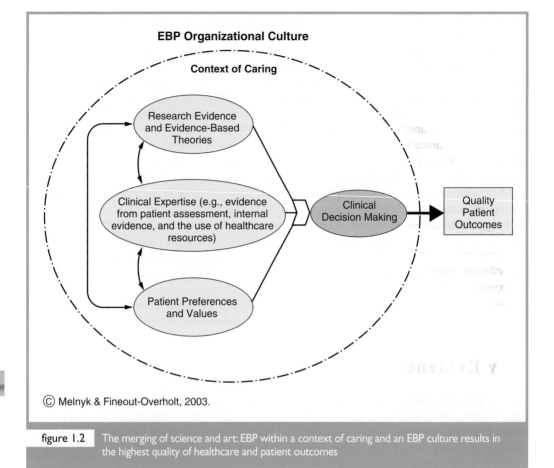

© Melnyk & Fineout-Overholt, 2003.

| figure 1.2 | The merging of science and art: EBP within a context of caring and an EBP culture results in the highest quality of healthcare and patient outcomes |

Origins of the Evidence-Based Practice Movement

The evidence-based practice movement was founded by Dr. Archie Cochrane, a British epidemiologist, who struggled with the efficacy of healthcare and challenged the public to pay only for care that had been empirically supported as effective (Enkin, 1992). In 1972, Cochrane published a landmark book that criticized the medical profession for not providing rigorous reviews of evidence so that policy makers and organizations could make the best decisions about healthcare. Cochrane was a strong proponent of using evidence from RCTs because he believed that this was the strongest evidence on which to base clinical practice treatment decisions. He asserted that reviews of research evidence across all specialty areas need to be prepared systematically

box 1.1

The Level of the evidence + Quality of the evidence = Strength of the Evidence →
Confidence to act upon the evidence and change practice!

through a rigorous process and that they should be maintained to consider the generation of new evidence (The Cochrane Collaboration, 2001).

In an exemplar case, Cochrane noted that thousands of low-birth-weight premature infants died needlessly. He emphasized that the results of several RCTs supporting the effectiveness of corticosteroid therapy to halt premature labor in high-risk women had never been analyzed and compiled in the form of a systematic review. The data from that systematic review showed that corticosteroid therapy reduced the odds of premature infant death from 50%–30% (The Cochrane Collaboration, 2001).

Dr. Cochrane died in 1988. However, as a result of his influence and call for updates of systematic reviews of RCTs, the Cochrane Center was launched in Oxford, England in 1992, and The Cochrane Collaboration was founded a year later. The major purpose of the Center and international Collaboration is to assist individuals in making well-informed decisions about healthcare by developing, maintaining, and updating systematic reviews of healthcare interventions and ensuring that these reviews are accessible to the public (The Cochrane Collaboration, 2001).

Further information about the Cochrane Center and Collaboration can be accessed at **http://www.cochrane.org/cochrane/cc-broch.htm#cc**

Why Evidence-Based Practice?

The most important reasons for consistently implementing EBP are that it leads to the highest quality of care and the best patient outcomes (Reigle, Stevens, Belcher, et al., 2008; Talsma, Grady, Feetham, et al., 2008). In addition, EBP reduces healthcare costs and geographic variation in the delivery of care (McGinty & Anderson, 2008; Williams, 2004). Findings from studies also indicate that clinicians report feeling more empowered and satisfied in their roles when they engage in EBP (Maljanian, Caramanica, Taylor, et al., 2002; Strout, 2005). With recent reports of pervasive "burnout" among healthcare professionals and the pressure that many influential healthcare organizations exert on clinicians to deliver high-quality, safe care under increasingly heavy patient loads, the use and teaching of EBP may be key not only to providing outstanding care to patients and saving healthcare dollars (Titler, Cullen, & Ardery, 2002), but also to reducing the escalating turnover rate in certain healthcare professions.

Despite the multitude of positive outcomes associated with EBP and the strong desire of clinicians to be the recipient of evidence-based care, an alarming number of healthcare providers do not consistently implement EBP or follow evidence-based clinical practice guidelines (Fonarow, 2004; Melnyk, Fineout-Overholt, Feinstein et al., 2004). Findings from a survey to assess nurses' readiness to engage in EBP conducted by the Nursing Informatics Expert Panel of the American Academy of Nursing with a nationwide sample of 1,097 randomly selected registered nurses indicated that (a) almost half were not familiar with the term *evidence-based practice*, (b) more than half reported that they did not believe their colleagues use research findings in practice, (c) only 27% of the respondents had been taught how to use electronic databases, (d) most did not search information databases (e.g., Medline and CINAHL) to gather practice information, and (e) those who did search these resources did not believe they had adequate searching skills (Pravikoff, Pierce, Tanner, et al., 2005).

On a daily basis, nurse practitioners, nurses, physicians, pharmacists, and other healthcare professionals seek answers to numerous clinical questions (e.g., In postoperative surgical patients, how does relaxation breathing compared to cognitive-behavioral skills building affect anxiety? In adults with dementia, how does a warm bath compared to music therapy improve sleep? In depressed adolescents, how does cognitive-behavioral therapy combined with Prozac compared to Prozac alone reduce depressive symptoms?). An evidence-based approach to care allows healthcare providers to access the best evidence to answer these pressing clinical questions in a timely fashion and to translate that evidence into clinical practice to improve patient care and outcomes.

Without current best evidence, practice is rapidly outdated, often to the detriment of patients. As a classic example, for years, pediatric primary care providers advised parents to place their infants in a prone position while sleeping, with the underlying reasoning that this is the best position to prevent aspiration in the event of vomiting. With evidence indicating that prone positioning increases the risk of sudden infant death syndrome (SIDS), the American Academy of Pediatrics (AAP) released a clinical practice guideline recommending a supine position for infant sleep that has resulted in a decline in infant mortality caused by SIDS (AAP, 2000). As another example, despite strong evidence that the use of beta-blockers following an acute myocardial infarction reduces morbidity and mortality, these medications are considerably underused in older adults in lieu of administering calcium channel blockers (Slutsky, 2003). Therefore, the critical question that all healthcare providers need to ask themselves is Can we continue to implement practices that are not based on sound evidence and, if so, at what cost (e.g., physical, emotional, and financial) to our patients and their family members?

Even if healthcare professionals answer this question negatively and remain resistant to implementing EBP, the time has come when third-party payers are beginning to provide reimbursement only for healthcare practices whose effectiveness is supported by scientific evidence (i.e., pay for performance). Furthermore, hospitals are beginning to be denied payment for patient complications that develop when evidence-based guidelines are not being followed. In addition to pressure from third-party payers, a growing number of patients and family members are seeking the latest evidence posted on websites about the most effective treatments for their health conditions. This is likely to exert even greater pressure on healthcare providers to provide the most up-to-date practices and health-related information. Therefore, despite continued resistance from some clinicians who are skeptical or who refuse to learn EBP, the EBP movement continues to forge ahead.

Another important reason that clinicians must include the latest evidence in their daily decision making is that evidence evolves continually. As a classic example, because of the release of findings from the Prempro arm of the Women's Health Initiative Study that was sponsored by the National Institutes of Health, the clinical trial on hormone replacement therapy (HRT) with Prempro was ceased early—after only 2.5 years—because the overall health risks (e.g., myocardial infarction, venous thromboembolism, and invasive breast cancer) of taking this combined estrogen/progestin HRT were found to be far greater than the benefits (e.g., prevention of osteoporosis and endometrial cancer). Compared with women taking a placebo, women who received Prempro had a 29% greater risk of coronary heart disease, a 41% higher rate of stroke, and a 26% increase in invasive breast cancer (Hendrix, 2002a). For years, practitioners prescribed long-term hormone therapy in the belief that it protected menopausal women from cardiovascular disease because many earlier studies supported this practice. However, there were studies that left some degree of uncertainty and prompted further investigation (i.e., the Prempro study) of what was the best practice for these women. As a result of the Women's Health Initiative Study, practice recommendations changed. The evolution of evidence in this case is a good example of the importance of basing practice on the latest, best evidence available and of engaging in a lifelong learning approach (i.e., EBP) about how to gather, generate, and apply evidence.

Another recent example is an RCT that was funded by the National Institutes of Health, which compared the use of the medication Metformin, standard care, and lifestyles changes to activity, diet, and weight loss to prevent type 2 diabetes in high-risk individuals. The trial was stopped early because the evidence was so strong for the benefits of the lifestyle intervention. The intervention from this trial was translated into practice within a year by the Federally Qualified Health Centers participating in the Health Disparities Collaborative, a national effort to improve health outcomes for all medically underserved individuals (Talsma et al., 2008). This rapid transition of research findings into practice is what needs to become the norm instead of the rarity.

Key Initiatives Underway to Advance Evidence-Based Practice

The gap between the publishing of research evidence and its translation into practice to improve patient care often takes 17 years (Balas & Boren, 2000) and continues to be a major concern for healthcare organizations as well as federal agencies. In order to address this research–practice time gap, major initiatives such as the federal funding of EBP centers and the creation of formal task forces that critically appraise evidence in order to develop screening and management clinical practice guidelines have been established.

The Institute of Medicine's Roundtable on Evidence-Based Medicine is helping to transform the manner in which evidence on clinical effectiveness is generated and used to improve healthcare and the health of Americans. Its goal is that, by the year 2020, 90% of clinical decisions will be supported by accurate, timely, and up-to-date information that is based on the best available evidence (McClellan, McGinnis, Nabel, et al., 2007). The Roundtable convenes senior leadership from multiple sectors (e.g., patients, healthcare professionals, third-party payers, policy makers, and researchers) to determine how evidence can be better generated and applied to improve the effectiveness and efficiency of healthcare in the United States (Institute of Medicine of the National Academies, n.d.). It stresses the need for better and timelier evidence concerning which interventions work best, for whom, and under what types of circumstances so that sound clinical decisions can be made. The Roundtable places its emphasis on three areas:

- Accelerating the progress toward a learning healthcare system, in which evidence is applied and developed as a product of patient care;
- Generating evidence to support which healthcare strategies are most effective and produce the greatest value; and
- Improving public awareness and understanding about the nature of evidence, and its importance for their healthcare (Institute of Medicine of the National Academies, n.d.).

A second key initiative to advance EBP is the United States Preventive Services Task Force (USPSTF), which is an independent panel of experts in primary care and prevention who systematically review the evidence of effectiveness and develop recommendations for clinical preventive services, including screening, counseling, and preventive medications. Emphasis is placed upon which preventive services should be incorporated by healthcare providers in primary care and for which populations. The USPSTF is sponsored by the Agency for Healthcare Research and Quality (AHRQ), and its recommendations are considered the gold standard for clinical preventive services (AHRQ, 2008). EBP centers, funded by AHRQ, conduct systematic reviews for the USPSTF and are the basis upon which it makes its recommendations. The USPSTF reviews the evidence presented by the EBP centers and estimates the magnitude of benefits and harms for each preventive service. Consensus about the net benefit for each preventive service is garnered, and the USPSTF then issues a recommendation for clinical practice. If there is insufficient evidence on a particular topic, the USPSTF recommends a research agenda for primary care for the generation of evidence needed to guide practice. The USPSTF produces a *Guide to Clinical Preventive Services* (2008) that includes its recommendations on screening (e.g., breast cancer screening, visual screening, colon screening), counseling, and preventive medication topics along with clinical considerations for each topic. This guide provides general practitioners, internists, pediatricians, nurse practitioners, nurses, and family practitioners with an authoritative source for evidence to make decisions about the delivery of preventive services in primary care.

> The current Guide to Clinical Preventive Services can be downloaded free of charge from **http://www.ahrq.gov/clinic/pocketgd.htm**

Another initiative to advance EBP is the National Consortium for the Advancement of Pediatric and Adolescent Evidence-based Practice (NCPAEP), which was launched in 2007 at the first U.S. EBP Leadership Summit focused on children and adolescents, with funding by the AHRQ (Melnyk, Fineout-Overholt, Hockenberry, et al., 2007). The NCPAEP was formed because of the urgent need to accelerate EBP and to generate evidence rapidly to support best practices to improve health outcomes for children, teens, and families. Several nationally recognized EBP experts and healthcare leaders from a number of children's hospitals and universities across the United States participated in the summit. The consortium's vision is to be a leading organization for pediatric and adolescent EBP, with a mission to promote interdisciplinary EBP and collaborative research for improving child and adolescent health outcomes across the care continuum. Activities of the consortium include creating evidence-based guidelines where none exist, advancing EBP through education and skills building, conducting multisite research and EBP projects to generate external and internal evidence to guide clinical practice, and sharing best practices.

The Magnet Recognition Program by the American Nurses Credentialing Center is also facilitating the advancement of EBP in hospitals throughout the United States. The program was started in order to recognize healthcare institutions that promote excellence in nursing practice. Magnet-designated hospitals reflect a high quality of care. The program evaluates quality indicators and standards of nursing practice as defined in the American Nurses Association's (2004) *Scope and Standards for Nurse Administrators*. Conducting research and using EBP are critical for attaining Magnet status (Reigle et al., 2008). Hospitals are appraised on evidence-based quality indicators, which are referred to as Forces of Magnetism. The Magnet program is based on a model with five key components: (a) transformational leadership; (b) structural empowerment; (c) exemplary professional practice; (d) new knowledge, innovation, and improvements, which emphasize new models of care, application of existing evidence, new evidence, and visible contributions to the science of nursing; and (e) empirical quality results, which focus on measuring outcomes to demonstrate the benefits of high-quality care (American Nurses Credentialing Center, 2008).

The Steps of Evidence-Based Practice

The seven critical steps of EBP (summarized in Box 1.2) include

0. Cultivate a spirit of inquiry
1. Ask the burning clinical question in the format that will yield the most relevant and best evidence (i.e., PICOT format, which is discussed later in this chapter)
2. Search for and collect the most relevant and best evidence to answer the clinical question (e.g., searching for systematic reviews, including meta-analyses)
3. Critically appraise the evidence that has been collected for its **validity**, **reliability**, and **applicability**, then synthesize that evidence
4. Integrate the evidence with one's clinical expertise and the patient's preferences and values to implement a clinical decision
5. Evaluate outcomes of the practice decision or change based on evidence
6. Disseminate the outcomes of the EBP decision or change

---

box 1.2

The Steps of the EBP Process

0. Cultivate a spirit of inquiry.

1. Ask the burning clinical question in PICOT format.

2. Search for and collect the most relevant best evidence.

3. Critically appraise the evidence (i.e., rapid critical appraisal, evaluation, and synthesis).

4. Integrate the best evidence with one's clinical expertise and patient preferences and values in making a practice decision or change.

5. Evaluate outcomes of the practice decision or change based on evidence.

6. Disseminate the outcomes of the EBP decision or change.

Step 0: Cultivate a Spirit of Inquiry

Before embarking on the well-known steps of EBP, it is critical to cultivate a **spirit of inquiry** (i.e., a consistently questioning attitude toward practice) so that clinicians are comfortable with and excited about asking questions regarding their patients' care as well as challenging current institutional or unit-based practices. Without a culture that is supportive of a spirit of inquiry and EBP, individual and organizational EBP change efforts are not likely to succeed and sustain (Fineout-Overholt, Melnyk, & Schultz, 2005; Rycroft-Malone, 2008). A culture that fosters EBP promotes this spirit of inquiry and makes it visible to clinicians by embedding it in its philosophy and mission of the institution.

Key elements of an EBP culture include

- A spirit of inquiry where all health professionals are encouraged to question their current practices
- A philosophy, mission, and clinical promotion system that incorporate EBP
- A cadre of EBP mentors who have in-depth knowledge and skills in EBP, mentor others, and overcome barriers to individual and organizational change
- An infrastructure that provides tools to enhance EBP (e.g., computers for searching at the point of care, access to key databases, ongoing EBP educational and skills building sessions, EBP rounds and journal clubs)
- Administrative support and leadership that values and models EBP as well as provides the needed resources to sustain it
- Regular recognition of individuals and groups who consistently implement EBP

Step 1: Formulate the Burning Clinical PICOT Question

In step 1 of EBP, clinical questions are asked in **PICOT format** (i.e., *P*atient population, *I*ntervention or *Issue* of interest, *C*omparison intervention or group, *O*utcome, and *T*ime frame) to yield the most relevant and best evidence. For example, a well-designed PICOT question would be: In teenagers (the patient population), how does cognitive-behavioral skills building (the experimental intervention) compared to yoga (the comparison intervention) affect anxiety (the outcome) after 6 weeks of treatment (the time frame)? When questions are asked in a PICOT format, it results in an effective search that yields the best, relevant information and saves an inordinate amount of time (Fineout-Overholt & Johnston, 2005; Melnyk & Fineout-Overholt, 2002a). In contrast, an inappropriately formed question (e.g., What is the best type of intervention to use with teenagers who are anxious?) would lead to a search outcome that would likely include hundreds of nonusable abstracts and irrelevant information.

For other clinical questions that are not intervention focused, the meaning of the letter *I* can be "issue of interest" instead of "intervention." An example of a nonintervention PICOT question would be: How do new mothers who have breast-related complications perceive their ability to breast-feed past the first 3 months after their infants' birth? In this question, the population is new breast-feeding mothers, the issue of interest is breast-feeding complications, there is no appropriate comparison group, the outcome is their perception of their ability to continue breast-feeding, and the time is the 3 months after their infants' birth.

When a clinical problem generates multiple clinical questions, priority should be given to those questions with the most important consequences or those that occur most frequently (i.e., those clinical problems that occur in high volume and/or those that carry high risk for negative outcomes to the patient). For example, nurses and physicians on a surgical unit routinely encounter the question: In postoperative adult patients, how does morphine compared to hydromorphone affect pain relief? Another question might be: In postoperative patients, how does daily walking compared to no daily walking prevent pressure sores? The clinical priority would be answering the question of pain relief first, as pain is a daily occurrence in this population, versus putting a priority on seeking an answer to the second question because pressure ulcers rarely occur in postoperative adult patients. Chapter 2 provides more in-depth information about formulating PICOT questions.

Step 2: Search for the Best Evidence

The search for best evidence should first begin by considering the elements of the PICOT question. Each of the key words from the PICOT question should be used to begin the search. The type of study that would provide the best answer to an intervention or treatment question would be systematic reviews or meta-analyses, which are regarded as the strongest level of evidence on which to base treatment decisions (Guyatt & Rennie, 2002). There are different levels of evidence for each kind of PICOT question (see Chapter 2 for more in-depth discussion). Although there are many hierarchies of evidence available in the literature to answer intervention PICOT questions (e.g., Guyatt & Rennie; Harris, Hefland, Woolf, et al., 2001), we have chosen to present a hierarchy of evidence to address these questions that encompasses a broad range of evidence, including systematic reviews of qualitative evidence, also referred to as meta-syntheses (see Box 1.3). A **systematic review** is a summary of evidence on a particular topic, typically conducted by an expert or expert panel that uses a rigorous process for identifying, appraising, and synthesizing studies to answer a specific clinical question. Conclusions are then drawn about the data gathered through this process (e.g., In adult women with arthritis, how does massage

---

box 1.3

Rating System for the Hierarchy of Evidence for Intervention/Treatment Questions

Level I: Evidence from a systematic review or meta-analysis of all relevant RCTs

Level II: Evidence obtained from well-designed RCTs

Level III: Evidence obtained from well-designed controlled trials without randomization

Level IV: Evidence from well-designed case-control and cohort studies

Level V: Evidence from systematic reviews of descriptive and qualitative studies

Level VI: Evidence from single descriptive or qualitative studies

Level VII: Evidence from the opinion of authorities and/or reports of expert committees

Modified from Guyatt, G., & Rennie, D. (2002). Users' guides to the medical literature. Chicago, IL: American Medical Association; Harris, R. P., Hefland, M., Woolf, S. H., Lohr, K. N., Mulrow, C. D., Teutsch, S. M., et al. (2001). Current methods of the U.S. Preventive Services Task Force: A review of the process. American Journal of Preventive Medicine, 20, 21–35.

compared to pharmacologic agents reduce pain after 2 weeks of treatment? In women, what factors predict heart disease in older adulthood?). Using a rigorous process of well-defined, preset criteria to select studies for inclusion in the review as well as stringent criteria to assess quality, bias is overcome and results are more credible. Population health stands a better chance for improvement when there is effective integration of scientific evidence through systematic reviews that are made available to influence policy makers' decisions (Sweet & Moynihan, 2007).

Many systematic reviews incorporate quantitative methods to summarize the results from multiple studies. These reviews are called **meta-analyses**. A meta-analysis generates an overall summary statistic that represents the effect of the intervention across multiple studies. Because a meta-analysis can combine the samples of each study included in the review to create one larger study, the summary statistic is more precise than the individual findings from any one of the contributing studies alone (Ciliska, Cullum, & Marks, 2001). Thus, systematic reviews and meta-analyses yield the strongest level of evidence on which to base practice decisions. Caution must be used when searching for systematic reviews as some evidence reviews or narrative reviews may be labeled systematic reviews; however, they lack the rigorous process that is required of true systematic reviews (Fineout-Overholt, O'Mathúna, & Kent, 2008; Newhouse, 2008). Although studies are compared and contrasted in narrative and integrative reviews, a rigorous methodology with explicit criteria for reviewing the studies is often not used, and a summary statistic is not generated. Therefore, conclusions and recommendations by authors of narrative and integrative reviews may be biased.

In addition to the Cochrane Database of Systematic Reviews, the journals *Worldviews on Evidence-Based Nursing* and *Nursing Research* frequently provide systematic reviews to guide nursing practice across many topic areas. More information on *Worldviews* and *Nursing Research* can be found at **http://www.wiley.com/bw/journal.asp?ref = 1545–102X** and **http://www.nursingresearchonline.com/**

Evidence-based clinical practice guidelines are specific practice recommendations grouped together that have been derived from a methodologically rigorous review of the best evidence on a specific topic. Guidelines usually do not answer a single specific question, but rather a group of questions about care. As such, they have tremendous potential as tools for clinicians to improve the quality of care, the process of care, and patient outcomes as well as reduce variation in care and unnecessary healthcare expenditures (Fein & Corrato, 2008). The National Guideline Clearinghouse (visit http://www.guideline.gov) provides a mechanism to access detailed information on clinical practice guidelines for healthcare professionals, healthcare systems, and the public. The purpose of the National Guideline Clearinghouse is to further the dissemination and use of the guidelines. Examples of two guidelines housed at the National Guideline Clearinghouse include

- *Screening for Illicit Drug Use* by the USPSTF (2008)
- *Practice Guideline for the Treatment of Patients With Alzheimer's Disease and Other Dementias* by the American Psychiatric Association (2007)

It is important to note the latest publication date of clinical practice guidelines, as many guidelines need updating so that the latest evidence is included in making practice recommendations. Although clinical practice guidelines have tremendous potential to improve the quality of care and outcomes for patients as well as reduce healthcare variation and costs, their success depends on a highly rigorous guideline development process and the incorporation of the latest best evidence. In addition, guideline success depends on implementation by healthcare providers (Fein & Corrato, 2008; Graham, Harrison, Brouwers, et al., 2002). More information about guideline development and implementation can be found in Chapter 10.

A toolkit to enhance the use of clinical practice guidelines is available from the Registered Nurses' Association of Ontario and can be downloaded from its website at **http://ltctoolkit.rnao.ca**

If syntheses (e.g., systematic reviews, meta-analyses) are not available to answer a clinical practice treatment question, the next step should be a search for original RCTs that are found in databases such as MEDLINE or CINAHL (Cumulative Index of Nursing and Allied Health Literature). If RCTs are not available, the search process should then include other types of studies that generate evidence to guide clinical decision making (e.g., nonrandomized, descriptive, or qualitative studies). Chapter 3 contains more detailed information on searching for evidence.

Step 3: Critical Appraisal of Evidence

Step 3 in the EBP process is vital, in that it involves critical appraisal of the evidence obtained from the search process. Although healthcare professionals may view critical appraisal as an exhaustive, time-consuming process, the first steps of critical appraisal can be efficiently accomplished by answering three key questions as part of a rapid critical appraisal process in which studies are evaluated for their validity, reliability, and applicability to answer the posed clinical question (summarized in Box 1.4):

1. **Are the results of the study valid? (Validity)** That is, are the results as close to the truth as possible? Did the researchers conduct the study using the best research methods possible? For example, in intervention trials, it would be important to determine whether the subjects were **randomly assigned** to treatment or control groups and whether they were equal on key characteristics prior to the treatment.
2. **What are the results? (Reliability)** For example, in an intervention trial, this includes (a) whether the intervention worked, (b) how large a treatment effect was obtained, and (c) whether clinicians could expect similar results if they implemented the intervention in their own clinical practice setting (i.e., the preciseness of the intervention effect). In qualitative studies, this includes evaluating whether the research approach fits the purpose of the study, along with evaluating other aspects of the study.
3. **Will the results help me in caring for my patients? (Applicability)** This third critical appraisal question includes asking whether (a) the subjects in the study are similar to the patients for whom care is being delivered, (b) the benefits are greater than the risks of treatment (i.e., potential for harm), (c) the treatment is feasible to implement in the practice setting, and (d) the patient desires the treatment.

The answers to these questions ensure relevance and transferability of the evidence to the specific population for whom the clinician provides care. For example, if a systematic review provided evidence to support the positive effects of using distraction to alleviate pain in postsurgical patients

box 1.4

Key General Critical Appraisal Questions

1. Are the results of the study valid? (Validity)
2. What are the results? (Reliability)
3. Will the results help me in caring for my patients? (Applicability)

between the ages of 20 and 40 years, those same results may not be relevant for postsurgical patients who are 65 years or older. In addition, even if an RCT supported the effectiveness of a specific intervention with a patient population, careful consideration of the risks and benefits of that intervention must be done before its implementation. When critically appraising a body of evidence to guide practice decisions, it is important to not only conduct rapid critical appraisal of the studies found in the search but also to evaluate all of the studies in the form of an evidence synthesis so that it can be determined if the findings from the studies are in agreement or disagreement. A synthesis of the studies' findings is important in order to draw a conclusion about the body of evidence on a particular clinical issue. Unit 2 in this book contains in-depth information on critical appraisal of all types of evidence, from expert opinion and qualitative studies to RCTs and systematic reviews.

Step 4: Integrate the Evidence With Clinical Expertise and Patient Preferences to Make the Best Clinical Decision

The next key step in EBP is integrating the best evidence found from the literature with the healthcare provider's expertise and patient preferences and values to implement a decision. Consumers of healthcare services want to participate in the clinical decision-making process, and it is the ethical responsibility of the healthcare provider to involve patients in treatment decisions (Melnyk & Fineout-Overholt, 2006). Even if the evidence from a rigorous search and critical appraisal strongly supports that a certain treatment is beneficial (e.g., HRT to prevent osteoporosis in a very high-risk woman), a discussion with the patient may reveal her intense fear of developing breast cancer while taking HRT or other reasons that the treatment is not accept- able. Moreover, as part of the history-taking process or physical examination, a comorbidity or contraindication may be found that increases the risks of HRT (e.g., prior history of stroke). Therefore, despite compelling evidence to support the benefits of HRT in preventing osteoporosis in high-risk women, a decision against its use may be made after a thorough assessment of the individual patient and a discussion of the risks and benefits of treatment.

Similarly, a clinician's assessment of healthcare resources that are available to imple- ment a treatment decision is a critical part of the EBP decision-making process. For example, on follow-up evaluation, a clinician notes that the first-line treatment of acute otitis media in a 3-year-old patient was not effective. The latest evidence indicates that antibiotic A has greater efficacy than antibiotic B as the second-line treatment of acute otitis media in young children. However, because antibiotic A is far more expensive than antibiotic B and the family of the child does not have prescription insurance coverage, the practitioner and parents together may decide to use the less expensive antibiotic to treat the child's unresolved ear infection.

Step 5: Evaluate the Outcomes of the Practice Change Based on Evidence

Step 5 in EBP is evaluating the evidence-based initiative in terms of how the change affected patient outcomes or how effective the clinical decision was with a particular patient or practice setting. This type of evaluation is essential in determining whether the change based on evi- dence resulted in the expected outcomes when implemented in the real-world clinical practice setting. Measurement of outcomes is important to determine and document the impact of the EBP change on healthcare quality and/or patient outcomes. If a change in practice based on evi- dence did not produce the same findings as demonstrated in rigorous research, clinicians should ask themselves a variety of questions (e.g., Was the treatment administered in exactly the same way that it was delivered in the study? Were the patients in the clinical setting similar to those in the studies?). Chapter 10 contains information on how to evaluate outcomes of practice changes based on evidence. See Figure 1.3 for the key steps of EBP to improve quality healthcare.

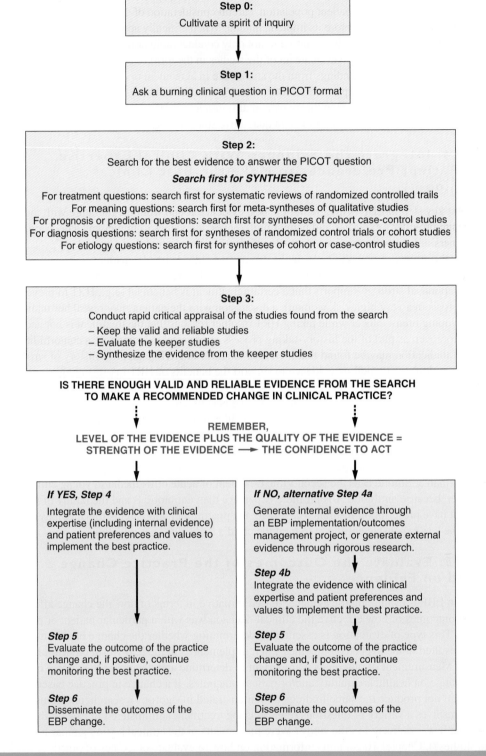

figure 1.3   Steps of the EBP process leading to high quality healthcare and best patient outcomes
© Melnyk & Fineout-Overholt, 2009

Step 6: Disseminate the Outcomes of the Evidence-Based Practice Change

The last step in EBP is disseminating the outcomes of the EBP change. All too often, clinicians achieve many positive outcomes through making changes in their care based upon evidence, but those outcomes are not shared with others, even colleagues within their same institution. As a result, others do not learn about the outcomes and clinicians as well as patients in other settings do not benefit from them. It is so important for clinicians to disseminate outcomes of their practice changes based on evidence through such venues as oral and poster presentations at local, regional, and national conferences; EBP rounds within their own institutions; journal and newsletter publications; and lay publications. Specific strategies for disseminating evidence are covered in Chapter 16.

Some online tutorials that teach the steps of EBP include
- Teaching/Learning Resources for Evidence Based Practice at Middlesex University in London at **http://www.mdx.ac.uk/www/rctsh/ebp/ main.htm**
- The University of Rochester Medical Center Library at **http://www.urmc. rochester.edu/HSLT/Miner/resources/evidence_based/index.cfm**

Obstacles and Opportunities

Healthcare providers are struggling to deliver evidence-based care while managing demanding patient loads and attempting to keep pace with the volume of journal articles related to their clinical practices.

Barriers to Evidence-Based Practice

Nurses, physicians, and other health professionals cite a number of barriers to EBP that include

- Lack of EBP knowledge and skills
- Misperceptions or negative attitudes about research and evidence-based care
- Lack of belief that EBP will result in more positive outcomes than traditional care
- Voluminous amounts of information in professional journals
- Lack of time and resources to search for and appraise evidence
- Overwhelming patient loads
- Organizational constraints, such as lack of administrative support or incentives
- Lack of EBP mentors
- Demands from patients for a certain type of treatment (e.g., patients who demand antibiotics for their viral upper respiratory infections when they are not indicated)
- Peer pressure to continue with practices that are steeped in tradition
- Resistance to change
- Lack of consequences for not implementing EBP
- Lack of autonomy over practice and incentives
- Inadequate EBP content and behavioral skills building in educational programs along with the continued teaching of how to conduct rigorous research in baccalaureate and master's programs instead of teaching an evidence-based approach to care (Fineout-Overholt, et al., 2005; Hannes, Vandersmissen, De Blaeser, et al., 2007; McGinty & Anderson, 2008; Melnyk, Fineout-Overholt, et al., 2004; Melnyk, Fineout-Overholt, Feinstein, et al., 2008; Melnyk, Fineout-Overholt, Stetler, et al., 2005).

Facilitators of Evidence-Based Practice

To overcome the barriers in implementing EBP, there must be champions at all levels of practice (i.e., clinicians who believe so strongly in the EBP paradigm that they will do what it takes to facilitate it in their daily practice and their organizational culture) and an EBP culture with mechanisms to support the cause (Fein & Corratto, 2008; Fineout-Overholt et al., 2005). For healthcare professionals to advance the use of EBP, misconceptions about how to implement practice based on the best available evidence need to be corrected, and knowledge and skills in this area must be enhanced (Fineout-Overholt et al.). It also must be realized that changing behavior is complex and influenced by multiple factors, including beliefs, attitudes, resources, and the availability of evidence to change practice (McGinty & Anderson, 2008).

Facilitating conditions that have been found to enhance EBP include

- Support and encouragement from leadership/administration that foster a culture for EBP
- Time to critically appraise studies and implement their findings
- Research reports that are clearly written
- Evidence-based practice mentors who have excellent EBP skills as well as knowledge and proficiency in individual and organizational change strategies (Melnyk, 2007; Melnyk & Fineout-Overholt, 2002b; Melnyk, Fineout-Overholt et al., 2004; Newhouse, Dearholt, Poe, et al., 2007)
- Proper tools to assist with EBP at the point of care (e.g., computers dedicated to EBP; computer-based educational programs; Hart, Eaten, Buckner, et al., 2008)
- Clinical promotion systems that incorporate EBP competencies for advancement (Newhouse et al., 2007)
- Evidence-based clinical practice policies and procedures (Oman, Duran, & Fink, 2008)
- Journal clubs and EBP rounds

Overcoming Barriers to Evidence-Based Practice

For evidence-based care to become the "gold standard" of practice, EBP barriers must be overcome. Federal agencies, healthcare organizations and systems, health insurers, policy makers, and regulatory bodies must advocate for and require its use. Funding agencies must continue to establish translational research (i.e., how findings from research can best be transported into clinical practice to improve care and patient outcomes) as a high priority. Interdisciplinary professionals must work together in a collaborative team spirit to advance EBP. In addition, healthcare organizations must build a culture for EBP and devise clinical promotion ladders that incorporate its use.

As an initial step, barriers and facilitators to EBP along with organizational culture and readiness for system-wide implementation of EBP must be assessed within an organization. Surveys or focus groups should first be conducted with healthcare providers to assess their baseline knowledge, beliefs, and behaviors regarding EBP (Melnyk, Fineout-Overholt, & Mays, 2008). Objective documentation of the status of EBP is essential to demonstrate a change in outcomes, even when there is a subjective consensus of the leaders regarding the state of EBP in their agency. An additional benefit of conducting surveys or focus groups at the outset of any new EBP initiative is that research shows that these strategies also are effective in raising awareness and stimulating a change to evidence-based care (Jolley, 2002).

As part of the survey or focus group, clinicians should be asked about their baseline knowledge of EBP as well as to what extent they believe that implementing EBP will result in improved care and better patient outcomes. This is a critical question because knowledge alone usually does not change behavior (Melnyk, 2002). Although healthcare providers must possess basic knowledge and skills about EBP, it is critical for them to believe that EBP will produce better outcomes in order for changes in their practices to occur (Melnyk, Fineout-Overholt, & Mays, 2008).

> *Belief at the beginning of any successful undertaking is the*
> *one ingredient that will ensure success.*
> **William James**

Healthcare providers who do not believe that EBP results in improved care and patient outcomes need to be exposed to real case scenarios in which evidence-based care resulted in better outcomes than care that was steeped in traditional practices. For example, many primary care providers continue to prescribe antidepressants as the sole treatment for depressed adolescents when RCTs have indicated that medication in combination with cognitive-behavioral therapy is better than medication alone in reducing depressive symptoms (Brent, Emslie, Clarke, et al., 2008; Melnyk & Moldenhauer, 2006). In addition, although rigorous systematic reviews of the effectiveness of metered-dose inhalers (MDIs) versus nebulizers in administering bronchodilators to children with asthma have indicated that MDIs are just as effective with fewer side effects, less emergency room time, and less hospital admission, nebulizers continue to be the preferred route of administration in many emergency rooms (Mason, Roberts, Yard, et al., 2008).

Correcting Misperceptions

Because misperceptions about EBP constitute another barrier to its implementation, clarifying these perceptions and teaching the basics of EBP are critical to advancing evidence-based care. For example, many practitioners believe that searching for and critically appraising research articles is an overwhelming, time-consuming process. However, practitioners who have this belief frequently have not had exposure to databases such as the Cochrane Library and the National Guideline Clearinghouse, which can provide them with quick, easily retrievable systematic reviews and evidence-based guidelines to inform their practices. In addition, because many educational curricula continue to teach the in-depth critique of a single study versus time-efficient approaches to the gathering and critical appraisal of a body of empirical studies, clinicians may have the misperception that the EBP process is not feasible in the context of their current practice environments. Therefore, the basics of EBP (e.g., how to formulate a searchable question that will yield the best evidence, how to search for and rapidly critically appraise studies, how to synthesize the evidence) must be taught first in order to create baseline knowledge and skills.

The teaching of EBP can and should be accomplished with multiple strategies, including continuing education conferences; interactive workshops; and dissemination of educational materials, such as journal articles, textbooks, and informational handouts (Davies, 2002). The best learning method incorporates the teaching of didactic information with interactive behavioral skills. Therefore, creating opportunities for clinicians to practice the skills that they are learning about in didactic sessions is superior to didactic sessions alone.

More detailed information about teaching EBP can be found in Chapters 14 and 15. Moreover, three active EBP centers housed in nursing schools in the United States can serve as resources for the teaching and implementation of EBP.

1. The Academic Center for Evidence-Based Nursing (ACE) at the University of Texas Health Science Center at San Antonio
http://www.acestar.uthscsa.edu/
2. The Center for the Advancement of Evidence-Based Practice (CAEP) at Arizona State University College of Nursing & Health Innovation
http://nursing.asu.edu/caep
3. The Sara Cole Hirsch Institute for Best Nursing Practice Based on Evidence at Case Western Reserve School of Nursing
http://fpb.case.edu/Centers/Hirsh/

Both ACE and CAEP offer annual national EBP continuing education conferences for nurses and other interdisciplinary healthcare professionals, some of which have been funded by AHRQ. Preconference interactive workshops also are held in conjunction with ACE's and CAEP's annual conferences. The CAEP workshops focus on such topics as the foundations of EBP, implementing and sustaining EBP in healthcare systems, and teaching EBP. The Academic Center for Evidence-Based Nursing preconference workshops have varied in their focus from teaching EBP to systematic reviews. The CAEP offers an online 17-credit graduate/post-master's certificate in EBP and EBP mentorship immersion programs for clinicians and faculty. The Sara Hirsch Institute also offers a certificate through a continuing education program in implementing best nursing practices. The Academic Center for Evidence-Based Nursing has a summer institute that offers academic and continuing education opportunities for those interested in learning more about EBP.

Centers for EBP also have been established internationally in countries such as Australia, New Zealand, Hong Kong, Germany, the United Kingdom, and Canada. The mission of most of these centers is to educate clinicians through workshops or formal courses on EBP or to conduct systematic reviews.

Other reputable sources of information about EBP are from abstraction journals, such as *Evidence-Based Medicine, Evidence-Based Nursing, Evidence-Based Mental Health,* and *Evidence-Based Health Policy & Management*. These are other mechanisms through which professionals can find evidence to guide their practice. These journals summarize high-quality studies that have important clinical implications and provide a commentary by an expert in the field. The commentary addresses strengths and limitations of the research reviewed. In addition, EBP columns to guide practice regularly appear in professional journals such as *Pediatric Nursing* and *Maternal-Child Nursing*.

Questioning Clinical Practices, Changing Practice With Evidence, and Evaluating Impact

Never stop questioning!
S u s a n   L.   H e n d r i x

After basic EBP knowledge and skills are attained, it is important for healthcare professionals to ask questions about their current clinical practices (e.g., In neonates, how does the use of pacifiers compared to no pacifiers reduce pain during intrusive procedures? In adult surgical patients, how does heparin compared to antiembolic stockings prevent deep vein thrombosis within the first 2 months after surgery?). Efforts also should be made to prioritize practice problems within an organization or practice setting. One strategy for prioritizing practice problems is described by Rosenfeld, Duthie, Bier, et al. (2000), who conducted a survey and focus groups with nurses in a large academic health center to develop specific action plans around particular patient problems. Once high-priority areas were recognized, it was helpful to identify colleagues who had an interest in the same clinical question so that a collaboration could be formed to search for and critically appraise the evidence found. The results of this search and appraisal could be shared with colleagues through a variety of mechanisms (e.g., journal clubs, EBP practice rounds, or informational handouts). If a current practice guideline does not exist, one can be developed and implemented. However, guideline development is a rigorous endeavor, and adequate time must be allotted for the individuals who will complete the work (Davies, 2002). Useful processes for developing and implementing clinical practice guidelines are described in Chapter 8. To complete the EBP process, evaluation of the key outcomes of evidence implementation is essential to determine its effects on the process and outcomes of care.

Change to EBP within an organization or practice requires a clear vision, a written strategic plan, a culture in which EBP is valued and expected, and persistence to make it happen. In addition, the chance to succeed in making a change to EBP and sustaining it will be greater where there is administrative support, encouragement and recognition, EBP mentors, expectations for EBP as contained in clinical promotion criteria, interdisciplinary collaboration, and allocated resources. It is often best to start with a small evidence-based change with high impact, especially when there is skepticism about EBP and elevated levels of stress or complacency within a system, rather than to expect a complete change to EBP to happen within a short period of time. For example, finding a mechanism for routinely discussing evidence-based literature, such as journal clubs or EBP rounds that can spark interest and enhance "buy-in" from colleagues and administration, may be a wonderful start to facilitating a change to EBP.

> *I don't think there is any other quality so essential to success of any kind as the quality of perseverance. It overcomes almost everything, even nature.*
> **John D. Rockefeller**

Further information about how to infuse EBP into clinical settings is provided in Chapters 9 and 11, which review a variety of specific EBP strategies and implementation models. In addition, Chapter 12 outlines assessment strategies for determining an organization's stage of change. It also provides multiple suggestions for motivating a vision for change to best practice, based primarily on evidence-based organizational change principles. For two case examples on how evidence-based care can positively impact patient outcomes, see Appendix A: EBP in Action. These two case examples are success stories of how EBP can improve both the process and outcomes of patient care. Countless examples similar to these can be found in the literature. Evidence-based success stories stem from first asking compelling clinical questions, which emphasizes the need to cultivate a never-ending spirit of inquiry within our colleagues, our students, and ourselves. These two case examples, along with the Women's Health Study, teach a valuable lesson: Never stop questioning because providers need to take evidence-based responsibility for clinical decisions and stay up to date with data that can further support or dramatically change their practice standards (Hendrix, 2002b). Once that spirit of inquiry is cultivated within us and our clinical settings, the journey toward a change to EBP will begin.

We have come to a time when the credibility of the health professions will be judged by which of its practices are based on the best and latest evidence from sound scientific studies in combination with clinical expertise, astute assessment, and respect for patient values and preferences. The chance to influence health policy also rests on the ability to provide policy makers with the best evidence on which to make important decisions. However, it is important to remember that high-quality healthcare also depends on the ability to deliver EBP within a context of caring, which is the merging of science and art.

For EBP to evolve more quickly, commitments to advancing evidence-based care must be made by both individuals and organizations. Basic and graduate professional programs must teach the value and processes of EBP, leveled appropriately (see Chapter 13). Doctoral programs must prepare researchers and leaders who advance EBP through the generation of new knowledge from research to support the most effective practices, as well as the testing of established and new models of EBP implementation so that it can be determined which models are most effective on both staff and patient outcomes. Researchers and practitioners across disciplines also must unite to produce evidence on the effectiveness of numerous practices and to answer high-priority, compelling clinical questions, as well as to determine how best those initiatives or interventions can be best translated into practice.

The time has come for practitioners from all healthcare professions to embrace EBP and quickly move from practices that are steeped in tradition or based on outdated policies to those that are supported by sound evidence from well-designed studies. In doing so, patients, healthcare professionals, and healthcare systems will be able to place more confidence in the care that is being delivered and know that the best outcomes for patients and their families are being achieved.

Knowing is not enough; We must apply. Willing is not enough; We must do.

Goethe

references

Agency for Healthcare Research and Quality. (2008). U.S. Preventive Services Task Force. Retrieved on July 15, 2008, from http://www.ahrq.gov/clinic/USpstfix.htm

American Academy of Pediatrics. (2000). *Changing concepts of sudden infant death syndrome: Implications for infant sleeping environment and sleep position*. Elk Grove Village, IL: American Academy of Pediatrics.

American Nurses Association. (2004). *Scope and standards for nurse administrators*. Silver Spring, MD: Author.

American Nurses Credentialing Center. (2008). *Magnet model components and sources of evidence*. Silver Spring, MD: American Nurses Credentialing Center.

Balas, E. A., & Boren, S. A. (2000). *Managing clinical knowledge for healthcare improvements*. Germany: Schattauer Publishing Company.

Brent, D., Emslie, G., Clarke, G., Wagner, K. D., Asarnow, J. R., Keller, M., et al. (2008). Switching to another SSRI or to venlafaxine with or without cognitive behavioral therapy for adolescents with SSRI-resistant depression: The TORDIA randomized controlled trial. *JAMA, 299*(8), 901–913.

Ciliska, D., Cullum, N., & Marks, S. (2001). Evaluation of systematic reviews of treatment or prevention interventions. *Evidence-Based Nursing, 4,* 100–104.

Cochrane, A. L. (1972). *Effectiveness and efficiency: Random reflections on health services*. London: Nuffield Provincial Hospitals Trust.

The Cochrane Collaboration. (2001). *The Cochrane Collaboration—Informational leaflets*. Retrieved January 22, 2002, from http://www.cochrane.org/cochrane/cc-broch.htm#cc

Davies, B. L. (2002). Sources and models for moving research evidence into clinical practice. *Journal of Obstetric, Gynecologic, and Neonatal Nursing, 31,* 558–562.

Enkin, M. (1992). Current overviews of research evidence from controlled trials in midwifery obstetrics. *Journal of the Society of Obstetricians and Gynecologists of Canada, 9,* 23–33.

Fein, I. A., & Corrato, R. R. (2008). Clinical practice guidelines: Culture eats strategy for breakfast, lunch, and dinner. *Critical Care Medicine, 36*(4), 1360–1361.

Fineout-Overholt, E., & Johnston, L. (2005). Teaching EBP: Asking searchable, answerable clinical questions. *Worldviews on Evidence-Based Nursing, 2*(3), 157–160.

Fineout-Overholt, E., Melnyk, B. M., & Schultz, A. (2005). Transforming health care from the inside out: Advancing evidence-based practice in the 21st century. *Journal of Professional Nursing, 21*(6), 335–344.

Fineout-Overholt, E., O'Mathúna, D. P., & Kent, B. (2008). How systematic reviews can foster evidence-based clinical decisions. *Worldviews on Evidence-Based Nursing, 5*(1), 45–48.

Fonarow, G. C. (2004). Role of in-hospital initiation of carvedilol to improve treatment rates and clinical outcomes. *American Journal of Cardiology, 93*(9A), 77B–81B.

Graham, I. D., Harrison, M. B., Brouwers, M., Davies, B. L., & Dunn, S. (2002). Facilitating the use of evidence in practice: Evaluating and adapting clinical practice guidelines for local use by health care organizations. *Journal of Obstetric, Gynecologic, and Neonatal Nursing, 37,* 599–611.

Guyatt, G., & Rennie, D. (2002). *Users' guides to the medical literature.* Chicago, IL: American Medical Association.

Hannes, K., Vandersmissen, J., De Blaeser, L., Peeters, G., Goedhuys, J., & Aertgeerts, B. (2007). Barriers to evidence-based nursing: A focus group study. *Journal of Advanced Nursing, 60*(2), 162–171.

Harris, R. P., Hefland, M., Woolf, S. H., Lohr, K. N., Mulrow, C. D., Teutsch, S. M., et al. (2001). Current methods of the U.S. Preventive Services Task Force: A review of the process. *American Journal of Preventive Medicine, 20,* 21–35.

Hart, P., Eaten, L., Buckner, M., Morrow, B. N., Barrett, D. T., Fraser, D. D., et al. (2008). Effectiveness of a computer-based educational program on nurses' knowledge, attitude, and skill level related to evidence-based practice. *Worldviews on Evidence-Based Nursing, 5*(2), 78–84.

Hendrix, S. L. (2002a). Implications of the women's health initiative. *A Supplement to the Female Patient,* November, 3–8.

Hendrix, S. L. (2002b). Summarizing the evidence. *A Supplement to the Female Patient,* November, 32–34.

Institute of Medicine of the National Academies. (n.d.). *Roundtable on evidence-based medicine.* Retrieved July 15, 2008, from http://www.iom.edu/CMS/28312/RT-EBM.aspx

Jolley, S. (2002). Raising research awareness: A strategy for nurses. *Nursing Standard, 16*(33), 33–39.

Maljanian, R., Caramanica, L., Taylor, S. K., MacRae, J. B., & Beland, D. K. (2002). Evidence-based nursing practice, Part 2: Building skills through research roundtables. *Journal of Nursing Administration, 32*(2), 85–90.

Mason, N., Roberts, N., Yard, N., & Partridge, M. R. (2008). Nebulisers or spacers for the administration of bronchodilators to those with asthma attending emergency departments? *Respiratory Medicine, 102*(7), 993–998.

McClellan, M. B., McGinnis, M., Nabel, E. G., & Olsen, L. M. (2007). *Evidence-based medicine and the changing nature of health care.* Washington, DC: The National Academies Press.

McGinty, J., & Anderson, G. (2008). Predictors of physician compliance with American Heart Association Guidelines for acute myocardial infarction. *Critical Care Nursing Quarterly, 31*(2), 161–172.

Melnyk, B. M. (1994). Coping with unplanned childhood hospitalization: Effects of informational interventions on mothers and children. *Nursing Research, 43,* 50–55.

Melnyk, B. M. (2002). Strategies for overcoming barriers in implementing evidence-based practice. *Pediatric Nursing, 28,* 159–161.

Melnyk, B. M. (2007). The evidence-based practice mentor: A promising strategy for implementing and sustaining EBP in healthcare systems. *Worldviews on Evidence-Based Nursing, 4*(3), 123–125.

Melnyk, B. M., Alpert-Gillis, L., Feinstein, N. F., Crean, H., Johnson, J., Fairbanks, E., et al. (2004). Creating opportunities for parent empowerment (COPE): Program effects on the mental health/coping outcomes of critically ill young children and their mothers. *Pediatrics, 113*(6), 597–607 (electronic pages).

Melnyk, B. M., & Feinstein, N. (2009). Reducing hospital expenditures with the COPE (Creating Opportunities for Parent Empowerment) program for parents and premature infants: An analysis of direct healthcare neonatal intensive care unit costs and savings. *Nursing Administrative Quarterly, 33*(1), 32–37.

Melnyk, B. M., Feinstein, N. F., Alpert-Gillis, L., Fairbanks, E., Crean, H. F., Sinkin, R., et al. (2006). Reducing premature infants' length of stay and improving parents' mental health outcomes with the COPE NICU program: A randomized clinical trial. *Pediatrics, 118*(5), 1414–1427.

Melnyk, B. M., & Fineout-Overholt, E. (2002a). Key steps in evidence-based practice: Asking compelling clinical questions and searching for the best evidence. *Pediatric Nursing, 28,* 262–263, 266.

Melnyk, B. M., & Fineout-Overholt, E. (2002b). Putting research into practice: Rochester ARCC. *Reflections on Nursing Leadership, 28*(2), 22–25.

Melnyk, B. M., & Fineout-Overholt, E. (2005). *Evidence-based practice in nursing & healthcare. A guide to best practice* (1st ed.). Philadelphia, PA: Lippincott, Williams & Wilkins.

Melnyk, B. M., & Fineout-Overholt, E. (2006). Consumer preferences and values as an integral key to evidence-based practice. *Nursing Administration Quarterly, 30*(1), 123–127.

Melnyk, B. M., Fineout-Overholt, E., Feinstein, N. F., Li, H., Small, L., Wilcox, L., et al. (2004). Nurses' perceived knowledge, beliefs, skills, and needs regarding evidence-based practice: Implications for accelerating the paradigm shift. *Worldviews on Evidence-Based Nursing, 1*(3), 185–193.

Melnyk, B. M., Fineout-Overholt, E., Feinstein, N. F., Sadler, L. S., & Green-Hernandez, C. (2008). Nurse practitioner educators' perceived knowledge, beliefs, and teaching strategies. *Journal of Professional Nursing, 24*(1), 7–13.

Melnyk, B. M., Fineout-Overholt, E., Hockenberry, M., Huth, M., Jamerson, P., Latta, L., et al. (2007). Improving healthcare and outcomes for high-risk children and teens: Formation of the national consortium for pediatric and adolescent evidence-based practice. *Pediatric Nursing, 33*(6), 525–529.

chapter 1

23

Melnyk, B. M., Fineout-Overholt, E., & Mays, M. (2008). The evidence-based practice beliefs and implementation scales: Psychometric properties of two new instruments. *Worldviews on Evidence-Based Nursing, 5*(4), 208–216.

Melnyk, B. M., Fineout-Overholt, E., Stetler, C., & Allan, J. (2005). Outcomes and implementation strategies from the first U.S. EBP leadership summit. *Worldviews on Evidence-Based Nursing, 2*(3), 113–121.

Melnyk, B. M., & Moldenhauer, Z. (2006). *The KySS guide to child and adolescent mental health screening, early intervention and health promotion.* Cherry Hill, NJ: NAPNAP.

Newhouse, R. P. (2008). Evidence synthesis: The good, the bad, and the ugly. *Journal of Nursing Administration, 38*(3), 107–111.

Newhouse, R. P., Dearholt, S., Poe, S., Pugh, L., & White, K. M. (2007). Organizational change strategies for evidence-based practice. *Journal of Nursing Administration, 37*(12), 552–557.

Oman, K. S., Duran, C., & Fink, R. (2008). Evidence-based policy and procedures: An algorithm for success. *Journal of Nursing Administration, 38*(1), 47–51.

Pravikoff, D. S., Pierce, S. T., Tanner, A., Bakken, S., Feetham, S. L., Foster, R. L., et al. (2005). Evidence-based practice readiness study supported by academy nursing informatics expert panel. *Nursing Outlook, 53*, 49–50.

Reigle, B. S., Stevens, K. R., Belcher, J. V., Huth, M. M., McGuire, E., Mals, D., et al. (2008). Evidence-based practice and the road to Magnet status. *Journal of Nursing Administration, 38*(2), 97–102.

Rosenfeld, P., Duthie, E., Bier, J., Bowar-Ferres, S., Fulmer, T., Iervolino, L., et al. (2000). Engaging staff nurses in evidence-based research to identify nursing practice problems and solutions. *Applied Nursing Research, 13*, 197–203.

Rycroft-Malone, J. (2008). Evidence-informed practice: From individual to context. *Journal of Nursing Management, 16*(4), 404–408.

Sackett, D. L., Straus, S. E., Richardson, W. S., Rosenberg, W., & Haynes, R. B. (2000). *Evidence-based medicine: How to practice and teach EBM.* London: Churchill Livingstone.

Shortell, S. M., Rundall, T. G., & Hsu, J. (2007). Improving patient care by linking evidence-based medicine and evidence-based management. *JAMA, 298*(6), 673–676.

Slutsky, J. (2003). *Clinical guidelines: Building blocks for effective chronic illness care. Slide presentation at web-assisted audio conference, "Causes of and Potential Solutions to the High Cost of Healthcare."* Rockville, MD: AHRQ.

Strout, T. D. (2005). Curiosity and reflective thinking: Renewal of the spirit. In Clinical scholars at the bedside: An EBP mentorship model for today [Electronic version]. *Excellence in Nursing Knowledge.* Indianapolis, IN: Sigma Theta Tau International.

Sweet, M., & Moynihan, R. (2007). *Improving population health: The uses of systematic reviews.* New York, NY: Milbank Memorial Fund.

Talsma, A., Grady, P. A., Feetham, S., Heinrich, J., & Steinwachs, D. M. (2008). The perfect storm: Patient safety and nursing shortages within the context of health policy and evidence-based practice. *Nursing Research, 57*(1 Suppl), S15–S21.

Titler, M. G., Cullen, L., & Ardery, G. (2002). Evidence-based practice: An administrative perspective. *Reflections on Nursing Leadership, 28*(2), 26–29, 46.

U.S. Preventive Services Task Force. (2008). *Guide to clinical preventive services, 2008.* Rockville, MD: Agency for Healthcare Research and Quality. Available at http://www.ahrq.gov/clinic/pocketgd.htm

Williams, D. O. (2004). Treatment delayed is treatment denied. *Circulation, 109,* 1806–1808.

Asking Compelling, Clinical Questions

Ellen Fineout-Overholt and Susan B. Stillwell

A prudent question is one-half of wisdom

Francis Bacon

How healthcare professionals seek and use information has changed over the past several decades (e.g., the Internet; electronic health records with evidence-based clinical decision support systems; Leggat, 2003). Over the past few years, significant strides have been made to make information even more readily available online (e.g., full text articles, books on personal assistant devices). In addition, growing complexity of patient illness has required practitioners to become increasingly more proficient at obtaining information they need *when* they need it. Access to reliable information is necessary to this endeavor (Biermann & Aboulafia, 2007) as well as clinicians definitively identifying what they want to know and what they need to access (Fineout-Overholt & Johnston, 2005). Additionally, resources (e.g., computers, databases, and libraries) have to be in place to ensure that practitioners can retrieve needed information so that they can perform the best patient care possible. Not all practice environments have or allow these resources. Estabrooks, O'Leary, Ricker, and Humphrey (2003) found that although nurses were increasing their use of the Internet and e-mail at home, their work use was not comparable. There are many variables that influence whether a practitioner has the capacity to gather information quickly (e.g., financial ability to purchase a computer, availability of Internet service providers); however, every clinician must be able to articulate the clinical issue in such a way that it maximizes the information obtained with the least amount of time investment. Hence, the first step in getting to the right information is to determine the "real" clinical issue and describe it in an answerable fashion, that is, a searchable, answerable question. However, skill level in formulating an answerable question can be a barrier to getting the best evidence to apply to practice (Fleigel, Frohna, & Mangrulkar, 2002; Green & Ruff, 2005). This chapter provides the practitioner with strategies to hone their skills in formulating a clinical question to minimize the time spent in searching for relevant, valid evidence to answer it.

A Needle in a Haystack: Finding the Right Information at the Right Time

The key to successful patient care for any healthcare professional is to stay informed and as up to date as possible on the latest best practices. *External* pressure to be up to date on clinical issues increasingly comes from patients, employers, certifying organizations, and insurers (Centers for Medicare & Medicaid Services [CMS], 2006; Greiner & Knebel, 2003). The clinician's personal desire to provide the best, most up-to-date care possible along with expectations from healthcare consumers that practice will be based on the latest and best evidence fosters evidence-based practice (EBP). However, the desire to gather the right information in the right way at the right time is not sufficient. Practical, lifelong learning skills (e.g., asking focused questions, learning to search efficiently) are required to negotiate the information-rich environment that every clinician encounters. With the amount of information that clinicians have at their disposal today, finding the right information at the right time is much like weeding through the haystack to find the proverbial needle. If one has any hope of finding the needle, there must be some sense of the needle's characteristics. Formulating the clinical question is much like identifying the characteristics of the needle. Question components guide the searching strategies undertaken to find answers. Knowing how to sift through the haystack is also important (see Chapter 3 for searching strategies).

Huang, Lin, and Demnar-Fushman (2006) found in a study examining the utility of asking clinical questions in **PICOT format** (i.e., P: population of interest; I: intervention or issue of interest; C: comparison of interest; O: outcome expected; T: time for the intervention to achieve the outcome) that when clinicians asked clinical questions for their patient's clinical issues, their format almost always fell short of addressing all the aspects needed to clearly identify the clinical issue. Two out of 59 questions contained an intervention (I) and outcome (O), but no other components (P, C, or T), although these aspects were appropriate. Currie et al. (2003) indicated that approximately two thirds of clinicians' questions are either not pursued or answers are not found even though pursued. However, if properly formulated, the question could lead to a more effective search. In addition, in a randomized controlled trial (RCT) examining the effect of a consulting service that provides up-to-date information to clinicians, Mulvaney et al. (2008) found that such a knowledge broker improves the use of evidence and subsequent care and outcomes. However, without having a well-built question to communicate what clinicians genuinely want to know, efforts to search for or provide appraised evidence likely will be less than profitable.

The Haystack: Too Much Information

Although there is a plethora of information available and increasingly new modalities to access it, news of clinical advances can diffuse rather slowly through the literature. Additionally, only a small percentage of clinicians access and use the information in a timely fashion (Cobban, Edgington, & Clovis, 2008; Estabrooks et al., 2003; MacIntosh-Murray & Choo, 2005; McCloskey, 2008; Pravikoff, Tanner, & Pierce, 2005). Clinicians are challenged with the task of effectively, proactively, and rapidly sifting through the haystack of scientific information to find the right needle full of the best applicable information for a patient or practice. In a study about information-seeking behavior in nurse practitioners (NPs), Cogdill (2003) found that NPs most frequently used colleagues, drug reference manuals, textbooks, and protocol manuals as information sources. In addition, Cogdill found that NPs were more likely to find answers to questions about drug therapy from a print resource and to discuss needs about diagnosis with a colleague. Scott, Estabrooks, Allen, et al. (2008) found that uncertainty in clinicians' work environment promoted a disregard for research as relevant to practice. To reduce this uncertainty and facilitate getting the right information at the right time, EBP emphasizes first asking a well-built question, then searching the literature for an answer to the question. This will better prepare all clinicians to actively discuss the best available evidence with colleagues.

The EBP process focuses on incorporating good information-seeking habits into a daily routine. Pravikoff et al. (2005) indicated that not all nurses were engaged in daily information seeking, supporting the notion that, in a busy clinical setting, there is seldom time to seek out information. The purchase of a good medical text and regular perusal of the top journals in a specialty were once considered adequate for keeping up with new information, but scientific information is expanding faster than anyone could have foreseen. The result is that significant clinical advances occur so rapidly that they can easily be overlooked. Reading every issue of the top three or four journals in a particular field from cover to cover does not guarantee that clinicians' professional and clinical knowledge is current. With the increase in biomedical knowledge (especially information about clinical advances), it is clear that the traditional notion of "keeping up with the literature" is no longer practical. Before the knowledge explosion as we know it today, Haynes (1993) indicated that a clinician would have to read 17–19 journal articles a day, 365 days a year to remain current. This compels every clinician to move toward an emphasis on more proactive information-seeking skills, starting with formulating an answerable, patient-specific question.

Digitization and the Internet have improved accessibility to information, regardless of space and time; however, these innovations have not resolved the issue of finding the right information at the right time. It is important to become friendly with and proficient at utilizing information technology, including the Internet and other electronic information resources, which means that clinicians must be skilled in using a computer. Access to computers at the point of care is also essential. The information needed cannot be obtained if the clinician has to leave the unit or seek an office to locate a computer to retrieve evidence. Proficient use and access to computers are essential to EBP and best practice. In addition, other barriers described by nurses and other healthcare professionals to getting the right information at the right time include (a) a low comfort level with library and search techniques and (b) a lack of time to search for the best evidence (Melnyk & Fineout-Overholt, 2002; Pravikoff et al., 2005; Sackett, Straus, Richardson, et al., 2000). However, recent evidence indicates that successful searches may be much more dependent on the question formulation than search process (Schardt, Adams, Owens, et al., 2007). In a study conducted to determine the obstacles to answering questions, Ely, Osheroff, Ebell et al. (2002) found that difficulty in formulating an answerable question included the complexity of a patient's specific question, not having enough patient data, uncertainty of the scope of the question, uncertainty regarding the wording of the question, and difficulty in modifying questions to match the PICOT format. These barriers to finding the necessary evidence to improve patient outcomes can be adequately addressed through clinicians first learning to ask a searchable, answerable question.

The important thing is not to stop questioning

Albert Einstein

Asking Searchable, Answerable Questions

Finding the right information amidst an overwhelming amount of information in a timely way is imperative. The first step to accomplish this goal is to formulate the clinical issue into a searchable, answerable question. It is important to distinguish between the two types of questions that clinicians might ask—background questions and foreground questions. **Background questions** are those that need to be answered as a foundation for asking the searchable, answerable **foreground question** (Fineout-Overholt & Johnston, 2005; Straus, Richardson, Glasziou, et al., 2005). Background questions are described as those that ask for general information about a clinical issue. This type of question usually has two components: the starting place of the question (e.g., what, where, when, why, and how) and the outcome of interest (e.g., the clinical diagnosis). An example of a background question is: How does the drug acetaminophen work to affect fever? The answer to this question can be found in a drug pharmacokinetics text. Another example of a background question is: How does hemodynamics differ with positioning? This answer can be found in textbooks, as well. Often, background questions are far broader in scope than foreground questions. Clinicians often want to know the best method to prevent a clinically undesirable outcome. For example, What is the best method to prevent pressure ulcers during hospitalization? This question will lead to a foreground question, but background knowledge is necessary before the foreground question can be asked. In this example, the clinician must know what methods of pressure ulcer prevention are being used. Generally, this information comes from knowledge of what is being used in clinicians' practices and what viable alternatives are available to improve patient outcomes or it may come from descriptive research, such as survey research. Once the methods most supported are identified, clinicians can formulate the foreground question and ask, between the two most effective methods of pressure ulcer prevention, which one will work best in my population? If a clinician does not realize that the question at hand is a background question, time may be lost in searching for an answer in the wrong haystack (e.g., electronic evidence databases versus a textbook).

Foreground questions are those that can be answered from scientific evidence about diagnosing, treating, or assisting patients in understanding their prognosis. These questions focus on specific knowledge. In the first two background question examples, the subsequent foreground questions could be: In children, how does acetaminophen compared to ibuprofen affect fever? and In patients with acute respiratory distress syndrome, how does the prone position compared to the supine position affect hemodynamic readings? The first question builds on the background knowledge of how acetaminophen works but can be answered only by a study that compares the two listed medications. The second question requires the knowledge of how positioning changes hemodynamics (i.e., the background question), but the two types of positioning must be compared in a specific population of patients to answer it. The foreground question generated from the third background question example could be: In patients at risk for pressure ulcers, how do pressure mattresses compared to pressure overlays affect the incidence of pressure ulcers? The answer provided by the evidence would indicate whether pressure mattresses or overlays are more effective in preventing pressure ulcers. The most effective method will become the standard of care. Recognizing the difference between the two types of questions is the challenge. Sackett et al. (2000) state that a novice may need to ask primarily background questions. As one gains experience, the background knowledge grows, and the focus changes to foreground questions. Although background questions are essential and must be asked, it is the foreground questions that are the searchable, answerable questions and the focus of this chapter.

Clinical Inquiry and Uncertainty in Generating Clinical Questions

Where clinical questions come from (i.e., their origin) is an important consideration. On a daily basis, most clinicians encounter situations for which they do not have all the information they need (i.e., uncertainty) to care for their patients as they would like (Ely et al., 2002; Scott et al., 2008). The role of uncertainty is to spawn **clinical inquiry**. Clinical inquiry can be defined as a process in which clinicians gather data together using narrowly defined clinical parameters to appraise the available choices of treatment for the purpose of finding the most appropriate choice of action (Horowitz, Singer, Makuch, et al., 1996).

Clinical inquiry must be cultivated in the work environment. To foster clinical inquiry, a level of comfort must be had with uncertainty. Scott et al. (2008) define uncertainty as the inability to predict what an experience will mean or what outcome will occur. Lindstrom and Rosyik (2003) state that uncertainty is a sequela of ambiguity. Clinicians live in a rather ambiguous world. What works for one patient may not work for another patient. The latest product on the market claims that it is the solution to wound healing, but is it? Collaborating partners in caring for complex patients have "their" way of providing care. Formulating clinical questions in a structured, specific way, such as with PICOT formatting (discussed later in this chapter), assists the clinician in finding the right evidence to answer those questions and to decrease uncertainty. This approach to asking clinical questions facilitates a well-constructed search. Schardt et al. (2007) found that that using PICOT templates improved clinicians' skills to search PubMed for answers to burning clinical questions. These successes then foster further clinical inquiry.

Clinical circumstances, such as interpretation of patient assessment data (e.g., clinical findings from a physical examination or laboratory data), a desire to determine the most likely cause of the patient's problem among the many it could be (i.e., differential diagnosis), or simply wanting to improve one's clinical skills in a specific area, can prompt five types of questions. These five types of foreground questions are (a) intervention questions that ask what intervention most effectively leads to an outcome; (b) prognosis/prediction questions that ask what indicators are most predictive of or carry the most associated risk for an outcome; (c) diagnosis questions that ask what mechanism or test most accurately diagnoses an outcome; (d) etiology questions that ask to what extent a factor, process, or condition is highly associated with an outcome, usually an undesirable outcome; or (e) meaning questions that ask how an experience influences an outcome, the scope of a phenomenon, or perhaps the influence of culture on healthcare. Whatever the reason for the question, the components of the question need to be considered and formulated carefully to efficiently find relevant evidence to answer the question.

Posing the Question Using PICOT

Focused foreground questions are essential to judiciously find the right evidence to answer them (Schardt et al., 2007). Foreground questions should be posed using PICOT format. Thoughtful consideration of each component can provide a clearly articulated question. Table 2.1 provides a quick overview of the PICOT question components. Well-built, focused clinical questions drive the subsequent steps of the EBP process (The Cochrane Collaboration, 2006).

The patient population (P) may seem easy to identify. However, without explicit description of who the population is, the clinician can get off on the wrong foot in searching. The *Cochrane Handbook for Systematic Reviews of Interventions* (The Cochrane Collaboration, 2006) suggests careful consideration of the patient and the setting of interest. Limiting the population to those in a certain age group or other special subgroup (e.g., young adult females with lung cancer) is a good idea if there is a valid reason for doing so. Arbitrary designations for the patient population will not assist the clinician in retrieving the most relevant evidence.

The intervention or issue of interest (I) may include but is not limited to any exposure, treatment, diagnostic test, or predictor/prognostic factor, or it may be an issue that the clinician is interested in, such as fibromyalgia or a new diagnosis of cancer. The more specifically the intervention or issue of interest is defined, the more focused the search will be.

The comparison (C) needs special consideration as it is sometimes appropriate to include in a question and at other times does not need to be included. If the "I" is an intervention, the comparison can be a true control, such as a placebo, or another treatment, which is sometimes the usual standard of care. For example, a clinician wants to ask the question, in disabled, elderly patients (P), how does the use of level-access showers (I) compared to bed bathing (C) affect

table 2.1   PICOT: Components of an answerable, searchable question

PICOT	
Patient population/disease	The patient population or disease of interest, for example: • Age • Gender • Ethnicity • With certain disorder (e.g., hepatitis)
Intervention or issue of interest	The intervention or range of interventions of interest, for example: • Therapy • Exposure to disease • Prognostic factor A • Risk behavior (e.g., smoking)
Comparison intervention or issue of interest	What you want to compare the intervention or issue against, for example: • Alternative therapy, placebo, or no intervention/therapy • No disease • Prognostic factor B • Absence of risk factor (e.g., nonsmoking)
Outcome	Outcome of interest, for example: • Outcome expected from therapy (e.g., pressure ulcers) • Risk of disease • Accuracy of diagnosis • Rate of occurrence of adverse outcome (e.g., death)
Time	The time involved to demonstrate an outcome, for example: • The time it takes for the intervention to achieve the outcome • The time over which populations are observed for the outcome (e.g., quality of life) to occur, given a certain condition (e.g., prostate cancer)

patient hygiene (O)? The intervention of interest is level-access showers, and the comparison is the usual care of bed bathing. In a meaning question, the "I" is an issue of interest. For example, a meaning question may be, How do parents (P) with children who have been newly diagnosed with cancer (I) perceive their parent role (O) within the first month after diagnosis (T)? In this question, there is no appropriate comparison to the issue of interest, and "C" is not found in the question.

The outcome (O) in the intervention example above is patient hygiene and the outcome of the meaning question above is the parental role. Specifically identifying the outcome (O) in a question enables the searcher to find evidence that examined the same outcome variable, although the variable may be measured in various ways.

In some questions, there may be more than one outcome of interest found in a study, but all of these outcomes fall under one umbrella. For example, the question may be, In preschool-age children, how does a flavored electrolyte drink compared to water alone affect symptoms of dry mouth, tachycardia, fever, and irritability? Instead of formulating the question this way, it would be better to use the umbrella term dehydration for all these symptoms that are listed. The question would then be, In preschool-age children, how does a flavored electrolyte drink compared to water alone affect dehydration (e.g., dry mouth, tachycardia, fever, irritability)? Specifying the outcome will assist the clinician in focusing the search for relevant evidence.

A time frame (T) associated with the outcome also may be part of asking a PICOT question. For example, In family members who have a relative undergoing cardiopulmonary resuscitation (P), how does presence during the resuscitation (I) compared to no presence (C) affect family anxiety (O) during the resuscitation period (T)? In the intervention example given earlier, there is no specific time associated with bathing or showering to achieve patient hygiene. However, for the meaning question example, it would be important to consider that the 1st month after diagnosis may be a critical time for parental role to be actualized for this population; therefore, a time frame is included in the question. To answer this question, studies would be sought that would have collected data to evaluate parental role for a period of a month after diagnosis. Time (T) and comparison (C) are not always appropriate for every question; however, population (P), intervention or issue of interest (I), and outcome (O) must always be present.

Three Ps of Proficient Questioning: Practice, Practice, Practice

The best way to become proficient in formulating searchable, answerable questions is to practice. This section includes five clinical scenarios that offer you the opportunity to practice formulating a searchable, answerable question. Read each scenario and try to formulate the question using the appropriate template for the type of question required (see Box 2.1 for a list of all question types and templates). Templates are guides and are designed to assist you in formulating each question

chapter 2

31

---

box 2.1

Question Templates for Asking PICOT Questions

Intervention

In _____ (P), how does _____ (I) compared to _____ (C)
affect _____ (O) within _____ (T)?

Prognosis/Prediction

In _____ (P), how does _____ (I) compared to _____ (C)
influence/predict _____ (O) over _____ (T)?

Diagnosis Or Diagnostic Test

In _____ (P) are/is _____ (I) compared with _____ (C)
more accurate in diagnosing _____ (O)?

Etiology

Are _____ (P), who have _____ (I) compared with those without _____ (C) at _____ risk for/of _____ (O) over
_____ (T)?

Meaning

How do _____ (P) with _____ (I) perceive _____ (O)
during _____ (T)?

clinical scenario 2.1

Intervention Example

Glenda, a 45-year-old Caucasian woman, 5'6" weighing 250 pounds, presented to her primary care provider (PCP) with complaints of malaise and "pressure in her head." The physical examination revealed that she was hypertensive (blood pressure 160/98). Her PCP discussed putting her on an ACE inhibitor for 6 months; however, Glenda wanted to try exercise and dietary alterations to promote weight loss as she had heard on the evening news that for every 10 pounds of weight loss, blood pressure was reduced by 5 mm Hg. You want to make sure that Glenda is safe, so you inform her that you are going to do a little homework to find out the latest evidence.

and ensure that components of the question (i.e., PICOT) are not missed. Once you craft your questions, read the paragraphs that follow for help in determining the success of your question formulation.

Clinical Scenario 2.1 is about an intervention. Given the suggested format below for an intervention question, fill in the blanks with information from the clinical scenario.

In _____ (P), how does _____ (I) compared to _____ (C) affect _____ (O) within _____ (T)?

Remember that a well-formulated question is the key to a successful search. The question could be, In middle-aged Caucasian obese females (BMI > 30 m²) (P), how does weight loss (I) compared to daily administration of ACE inhibitors (C) affect blood pressure (O) over 6 months (T)? A more general background question might read, In overweight women, what is the best method for reducing high blood pressure? Background knowledge would be necessary to know what effective methods were available for reducing blood pressure in this population. Intervention questions are about what clinicians do; therefore, it is important to be able to determine *the* best intervention to achieve an outcome. Once the question has been answered with confidence (i.e., well-done studies agree on *the* intervention to achieve the outcome), the next step would be establishing that intervention as the standard of care.

In this example, the patient's concern has to do with her motivation to lose weight and her prior experience with a family member who did not have successful results with ACE inhibitors. She is asking the clinician to provide her with information about how successful she can be with what she prefers to engage versus what may be the accepted practice. Therefore, the "I" is the intervention that is most desired (e.g., weight loss) and the "C" is often what is the current standard of care or usual practice (e.g., ACE inhibitors).

The evidence to answer this type of question requires substantiated cause and effect relationships. The research design that best provides this information is an RCT. An RCT is defined as having three key elements: (a) an intervention or treatment group that receives the intervention, (b) a comparison group that has a comparison intervention, and (c) random assignment to either group (i.e., assignment of patients to either the experimental or comparison group by using chance, such as a flip of a coin). The groups are evaluated on whether or not an expected outcome is achieved. In the example, we would look for studies that had a defined sample (e.g., overweight women) with common characteristics (e.g., BMI > 30 m²) that were randomly assigned to the intervention (i.e., weight loss program) and the comparison (i.e., daily ACE inhibitors) and evaluate if the desired outcome was achieved (i.e., reduction in blood pressure values). Ideally, we would search for a synthesis or compilation of studies that would have compared how daily administration of ACE inhibitors and exercise and weight loss affected blood pressure. A synthesis of these RCTs is considered level one evidence to answer this type of question.

Keep in mind that syntheses are always level one evidence, no matter what kind of question you may be asking. Table 2.2 provides an example of a clinical question and the leveling of evidence that would answer that question. The level one evidence is listed first. If well done (i.e., bias is minimized through rigorous research methods), this is the type of research that would give us the valid information that would enable us to have confidence in the findings. With each drop in the level of evidence, the confidence in the findings drops. Hence, it is always the best idea to search for level one evidence first, keeping in mind the type of question that will indicate the study design, which would be synthesized as level one evidence for that question (e.g., intervention questions would require a synthesis of RCTs as level one evidence).

In the desired RCTs found in our example, the blood pressure values for both groups would be evaluated after they received either what is called the experimental intervention (i.e., weight loss) or the comparison intervention (i.e., ACE inhibitor). It is important that the

table 2.2 Examples of different types of clinical questions using PICOT format and the hierarchy indicating the best type of evidence to answer the given question

Questions	Levels of Evidence to Answer This Type of Question
Intervention: In patients living in a long-term care facility who are at risk for pressure ulcers (P), how does a pressure ulcer prevention program (I) compared to the standard of care (e.g., turning every 2 hours) (C) affect signs of emerging pressure ulcers (O)? **OR** **Diagnosis or diagnostic test:** In patients with suspected deep vein thrombosis (P) is d-dimer assay (I) compared with ultrasound (C) more accurate in diagnosing deep vein thrombosis (O)?	1. Systematic review/meta-analysis (i.e., synthesis) of RCTs 2. RCTs 3. Nonrandomized controlled trials 4. Cohort study or case–control studies 5. Meta-synthesis of qualitative or descriptive studies 6. Qualitative or descriptive single studies 7. Expert opinion
Prognosis/Prediction: In patients who have a family history of obesity (BMI > 30) (P), how does dietary carbohydrate intake (I) predict healthy weight maintenance (BMI < 25) (O) over six months (T)? **OR** **Etiology:** Are fair-skinned women (P) who have prolonged unprotected UV ray exposure (>1 hour) (I) compared to darker-skinned women without prolonged unprotected UV ray exposure (C) at increased risk of melanoma (O)?	1. Synthesis of cohort study or case–control studies 2. Single cohort study or case–control studies 3. Meta-synthesis of qualitative or descriptive studies 4. Single qualitative or descriptive studies 5. Expert opinion
Meaning: How do middle-aged women (P) with fibromyalgia (I) perceive loss of motor function (O)?	1. Meta-synthesis of qualitative Studies 2. Single qualitative Studies 3. Synthesis of descriptive studies 4. Single descriptive studies 5. Expert opinion

Prognosis Example

Shawn is a 63-year-old gentleman who has been diagnosed with prostate cancer. He has been married to his wife, Laura, for 40 years and is greatly concerned about his ability to be physically intimate with her should he pursue surgery as a treatment method. He mentions that he is most interested in living his life fully with as much normality as he can for as long as he can. He comes to you requesting information about whether or not having surgery will be the best plan for him.

evaluation of the outcome occurs after the individuals receive the intervention; otherwise, causality is in question. Also, it is important that all other factors (e.g., age, comorbidities, genetic predisposition to high blood pressure) that may influence the outcome (e.g., blood pressure) be considered and key factors be accounted for (i.e., controlled for—one of the reasons it is called a RCT). When these factors are controlled for, and if it is shown that weight loss does just as good or a better job than ACE inhibitors in reducing blood pressure, clinicians can confidently prescribe weight loss as an alternative intervention to manage high blood pressure for those who prefer it.

Clinical Scenario 2.2 contains a scenario about prognosis. The following is the format for prognosis questions. Fill in the blanks with information from the clinical scenario.

In _____ (P), how does _____ (I) compared to _____ (C) influence or predict _____ (O)?

The prognosis/prediction question for this example could read, in elderly patients with prostate cancer (P), how does choosing to undergo surgery (I) compared to choosing not to undergo surgery (C) influence lifespan and quality of life (O)? Prognosis/prediction questions assist the clinician in estimating a patient's clinical course across time. This type of question allows inference about the likelihood that certain outcomes will occur. Clinical issues that may lend themselves to be addressed with a prognosis/predictive question could involve patients' choices and future outcomes. The difference in prognosis or prediction questions and intervention questions is that the conditions (I & C) cannot be randomized due to the potential for harm (i.e., this would be unethical). In these questions, the "I" is the issue of interest (e.g., choice to have surgery) and the "C" is the counter to the issue of interest (i.e., the negative case) (e.g., choice not to have surgery). This is an important distinction for prognosis/predictive questions. Therefore, an answer to a prognosis/prediction question would require a study that examined a group of people with an identified condition (e.g., prostate cancer) that self-selected the issue of interest and counter issue (e.g., choosing surgery or not) and were observed over time to evaluate the likelihood of an outcome occurring or not. In the example, we would look for studies that followed a group of elderly people with prostate cancer (a cohort) who chose to have surgery (I) or not (C) and then evaluated how the elderly people reported their quality of life and how long they lived. This is called a cohort study. A single cohort study (i.e., not a synthesis) would be considered level two evidence for prognosis/prediction questions (see Table 2.2). If there were a synthesis of cohort studies examining elderly people with prostate cancer who had surgery or not and their relationship between their choice and their quality of life and how long they lived, then that would be level one evidence. Case–control studies are another study design that can be used to answer this kind of question and, they are further discussed in Chapter 5.

Clinical Scenario 2.3 is about diagnosis. Given the format for diagnosis questions, fill in the blanks with information from the clinical scenario.

> ### clinical scenario 2.3
>
> ## Diagnosis Example
>
> Brenda, a 33-year-old woman who is gravida 2 para 1 and in her sixth month of pregnancy, tells you that her right side is extremely tender and she feels rather nauseous, which is new for her. Her pregnancy is high-risk and she has been on bed rest for 3 weeks to prevent preterm labor. You are suspicious of appendicitis, but upon ultrasound you are not sure. You consider getting a CT scan to confirm your diagnosis; however, you are not sure of the benefits of its accuracy in comparison to its risks.

In _____ (P) are/is _____ (I) compared with _____ (C) more accurate in diagnosing _____ (O)?

Questions about diagnosis are focused on determining how reliable a test is for clinical practice. Risks of the test, likelihood of misdiagnosis of a high-risk outcome, and cost of the test are some of the considerations for how such questions would be answered. Benefit of the test to patients is the overall goal of these kinds of questions. In the clinical example, the question could read, in pregnant women with suspected appendicitis (P), is ultrasound followed by computed tomography (CT) (I) compared with ultrasound alone (C) more accurate in diagnosing appendicitis (O)?

The evidence to answer this type of question requires substantiated certainty that the diagnostic test will reliably provide a true positive (i.e., the outcome does exist and is diagnosed accurately by the test) or true negative (i.e., the outcome does not exist and is diagnosed as such accurately by the test). The research design that best provides this information (level one) is a synthesis of RCTs; this design involves groups that randomly (i.e., by chance) received a diagnostic test and a comparison diagnostic test and are then evaluated based on the presence or absence of the expected outcome (i.e., diagnosis). Sometimes, however, it would be unethical to randomly assign a diagnostic test to some patients and not others because the risks for the diagnostic test or misdiagnosing the outcome are too high. In this situation, the best research design to answer the question would be a cohort study (see Table 2.2). This is the case in the example, as a CT scan would expose the fetus to considerable radiation. Therefore, we would look for studies that had a defined sample of pregnant women with suspected appendicitis who had the intervention (e.g., ultrasound with follow-up CT) and the comparison (e.g., ultrasound alone) as a matter of course. Most commonly, the comparison is the test considered to be the "gold standard" for the industry. The outcome would be determined by actual documentation of appendicitis in these women.

Clinical Scenario 2.4 contains an etiology scenario. Given the format for etiology questions, fill in the blanks with information from the clinical scenario.

> ### clinical scenario 2.4
>
> ## Etiology Example
>
> A 40-year-old woman with asthma comes to the clinic for her regularly scheduled physical examination. She has been listening to the radio and an expert indicated that beta-adrenergic agonists may help her manage her asthma. However, she is apprehensive since she had a friend who died after using this type of medication. She would like to know if this is likely to happen to her if she includes this medication in her asthma management plan.

Are _____ (P), who have _____ (I) compared with those without _____ (C) at _____ risk for/of _____ (O) over _____ (T)?

In the example, the question could read, Are adult patients with asthma (P), who have beta-adrenergic agonists prescribed (I) compared with those without prescribed beta-adrenergic agonists (C), at increased risk for death (O)? In this case, the "T" would not be necessary.

Etiology questions help clinicians to address potential causality and harm. These questions can be answered by cohort or case–control studies that indicate what outcomes may occur in groups over time; however, it requires an abundance of longitudinal studies that consistently demonstrate these relationships for there to be confidence in the causality. For example, it is commonly believed that smoking "causes" lung cancer; however, there are people who defy this conviction by smoking all of their adult lives and have not been diagnosed with lung cancer. Potential causality from case–control or cohort studies must be carefully interpreted. RCTs are the only design that establishes with confidence a cause and effect relationship between an intervention and an outcome. However, the difference in an etiology/harm question and an intervention question is that the conditions (I & C) cannot be randomized due to the potential for harm—often that is the reason for the question.

In the clinical scenario, potential for harm is the focus of the question. It is important to know the harm associated with an intervention. As always, it is preferable to search for syntheses first. To answer this type of question, the desired research design would be cohort or case–control studies in which groups of people with a given condition (e.g., asthma) were prescribed either the interventions of interest (i.e., I [e.g., beta-adrenergic agonists] or the comparison of interest [e.g., no beta-adrenergic agonists]) by their healthcare providers and were observed over time to evaluate the likelihood of a suspected outcome (e.g., death) (see Table 2.2). In the example, we would look for studies that followed a group of adults with asthma that took beta-adrenergic agonists and adults with asthma that did not take beta-adrenergic agonists and determine the number of deaths in each group.

Clinical Scenario 2.5 contains a scenario about meaning. The following is the format for meaning questions. Fill in the blanks with the information from the clinical scenario.

How do _____ (P) with _____ (I) perceive _____ (O) during _____ (T)?

---

clinical scenario 2.5

Meaning Example

You are caring for Jim, a 68-year-old gentleman, who has been in the intensive care unit (ICU) for 3 weeks. He is now extremely tenuous and could go into cardiac arrest at any moment. Your patient is ventilated; he is on several intravenously infused medications to maximize his cardiac function; and has continuous monitoring of heart rhythm, blood pressure, and oxygenation. Jim's daughter is very involved in her dad's care. She asks many questions about how his care is progressing and wants to be informed of any nuances. She raises a question about whether or not she would be welcome to be present should her dad go into cardiac arrest and have to be resuscitated. The healthcare team is adamantly opposed to her presence. She tells you it would be important to her dad and to her to be together during such a difficult situation, and she cannot understand the perspective of the healthcare team. To facilitate the best outcomes for your patient and his daughter, you determine to find evidence to inform decision making.

In this example, the question could read, How do family members (P) with a critically ill relative who is being resuscitated (I) perceive healthcare providers' responses to their presence (O) during the resuscitation (T)?

This question is remarkably different from the others that we have discussed. You may notice that a "C" is not present in this question. It is not required as there is no comparison to their family members' resuscitation (I) in regard to the healthcare providers' perceptions (O). The emphasis is on how the family members experience the resuscitation of their family member, particularly in regard to the healthcare providers' responses to their presence during the resuscitation. The best evidence to answer this type of question would be qualitative in method. A synthesis of qualitative studies would be considered level one evidence (see Table 2.2). Research designs such as an RCT, cohort, or case–control would not be able to provide the data required to answer this question. Therefore, we would look for qualitative studies, such as a phenomenological study (see Chapter 6), to answer this question.

All of these examples and templates are for practicing. There may be various ways in which to ask a certain type of question; however, all the appropriate components must be present in the question. Clinicians, whether novice or expert, who use the PICOT format to construct a clinical question ensure that no component is missed and increase the likelihood that the question is answered (Huang et al., 2006). Consider your clinical scenario and try to identify the PICOT components specifically. Then formulate the question in a complete sentence. Carefully consider which template may work for the clinical situation driving your question, as it is not wise to try to form cookie-cutter questions (e.g., applying the intervention template to every situation), because some important component(s) most assuredly will be missed.

When evaluating the appropriateness of each question that arises from clinical issues you are most concerned about, consider the cost, feasibility, and availability of the intervention, diagnostic test, or condition, as these can preclude the ability to apply the evidence to clinical practice. These issues also influence ethical considerations for implementing the best evidence (see Chapter 20).

Why Work Hard at Formulating the Question?

Without a well-formulated question, the clinician is apt to search for wrong, too much, or irrelevant information. Honing one's skills in formulating a well-built question can provide confidence that the search will be more successful and timely. From their vast experience, Sackett et al. (2000) identified that formulating a searchable, answerable question is the most difficult step in the EBP process. However, they also suggested several other benefits from constructing good questions, including clearly communicating patient information with colleagues, helping learners more clearly understand content taught, and furthering the initiative to become better clinicians through the positive experience of asking a good question, finding the best evidence, and making a difference. Various web-based resources can assist you in understanding how to formulate a searchable, answerable question.

Find web-based information on formulating searchable, answerable questions at the following websites:
- Centre for Evidence-Based Medicine University of Toronto:
  http://www.cebm.utoronto.ca/practise/formulate/
- Arizona State University Center for the Advancement of EBP
  http://nursing.asu.edu/caep/pico.htm
- Studentbmj.com: International Medical Student's Journal:
  http://www.studentbmj.com/back_issues/0902/education/313.html

Formulating a well-built question is worth the time and effort it takes. A well-formulated question facilitates a focused search (Schardt et al., 2007; Stone, 2002), decreasing searching time and improving search results. Formulating a well-built question is step 1—and as some have said, the most challenging—toward providing evidence-based care to patients (Schlosser, Koul, & Costello, 2007; Straus et al., 2005).

> *Reason and free inquiry are the only effectual agents against error*
>
> *Thomas Jefferson*

references

Biermann, J. S., & Aboulafia, A. J. (2007). Web-based resources for orthopaedic oncology information. *Clinical Orthopaedics & Related Research, 459*, 192–194.

Centers for Medicare & Medicaid Services. (2006). *Post-acute care reform plan*. Retrieved July 8, 2008, from http://www.cms.hhs.gov/SNFPPS/Downloads/pac_reform_plan_2006.pdf

Cobban, S. J., Edgington, E. M., & Clovis, J. B. (2008). Moving research knowledge into dental hygiene practice. *Journal of Dental Hygiene, 82*, 21.

Cogdill, K. W. (2003). Information needs and information seeking in primary care: Study of nurse practitioners. *Journal of the Medical Library Association, 91*(2), 203–215.

Currie, L. M., Graham, M., Allen, M., Bakken, S., Patel, V., & Cimino, J. J. (2003). Clinical information needs in context: An observational study of clinicians while using a clinical information system. *American Medical Informatics Association Annual Symposium Proceedings/AMIA Symposium*, 190–194.

Ely, J. W., Osheroff, J. A., Ebell, M. H., Chambliss, M. L., Vinson, D. C., Stevermer, J. J., et al. (2002). Obstacles to answering doctors' questions about patient care with evidence: Qualitative study. *British Medical Journal, 32*(1), 1–7.

Estabrooks, C., O'Leary, K., Ricker, K., & Humphrey, C. (2003). The internet and access to evidence: How are nurses positioned? *Journal of Advanced Nursing, 42*, 73–81.

Fineout-Overholt, E., & Johnston, L. (2005). Teaching EBP: Asking searchable, answerable clinical questions. *Worldviews on Evidence-based Nursing, 2*(3), 157–160.

Fleigel, J., Frohna, J. G., & Mangrulkar, R. S. (2002). A computer-based OSCE station to measure competence in evidence-based medicine skills in medical students. *Academic Medicine, 77*, 1157–1158.

Green, M. L., & Ruff, T. R. (2005). Why do residents fail to answer their clinical questions? A qualitative study of barriers to practicing evidence-based medicine. *Academic Medicine, 80*, 176–182.

Greiner, A., & Knebel, E. (2003). *Health professions education: A bridge to quality*. Washington, DC: Institute of Medicine & National Academy Press.

Haynes, R. (1993). Where's the meat in clinical journals? *ACP Journal Club, 119*, A23–A24.

Horowitz, R., Singer, B., Makuch, R., & Viscoli, C. (1996). Can treatment that is helpful on average be harmful to some patients? A study of the conflicting information needs of clinical inquiry and drug regulation. *Journal of Clinical Epidemiology, 49*, 395–400.

Huang, X., Lin, J., & Demnar-Fushman, D. (2006). Evaluation of PICO as a knowledge representation for clinical questions. *American Medical Informatics Association Proceedings*, 359–363.

Leggat, S. (2003). Turning evidence into wisdom. *Healthcare Papers, 3*(3), 44–48.

Lindstrom, T., & Rosyik, A. (2003). Ambiguity leads to uncertainty: Ambiguous demands to blood donors. *Scandinavian Journal of Caring Sciences, 17*, 74–71.

MacIntosh-Murray, A., & Choo, C. W. (2005). Information behavior in the context of improving patient safety. *Journal of the American Society of Information Science & Technology, 56*, 1332–1345.

McCloskey, D. J. (2008). Nurses' perceptions of research utilization in a corporate health care system. *Journal of Nursing Scholarship, 40*, 39–45.

Melnyk, B. M., & Fineout-Overholt, E. (2002). Putting research into practice. *Reflections on Nursing Leadership, 28*(2), 22–25, 45.

Mulvaney, S., Bickman, L., Giuse, N., Lambert, E., Sathe N., & Jerome, R. (2008). A randomized effectiveness trial of a clinical informatics consult service: Impact on evidence-based decision-making and knowledge implementation. *Journal of the American Medical Informatics Association, 15*, 203–211.

Pravikoff, D., Tanner, A., & Pierce, S. (2005). Readiness of U.S. nurses for evidence-based practice. *American Journal of Nursing, 105*, 40–50.

Sackett, D. L., Straus, S. E., Richardson, W. S., Rosenberg, W., & Haynes, R. B. (2000). *Evidence-based medicine: How to practice and teach EBM*. Edinburgh: Churchill Livingston.

Schardt, C., Adams, M. B., Owens, T., Keitz, S., & Fontelo, P. (2007). Utilization of the PICO framework to improve searching PubMed for clinical questions. *BMC Medical Informatics and Decision Making, 7*(16), 1–6.

Schlosser, R., Koul, R., & Costello, J. (2007). Asking well-built questions for evidence-based practice in augmentative and alternative communication. *Journal of Communication Disorders, 40*, 225–238.

Scott, S., Estabrooks, C., Allen, M., & Pollock, C. (2008). A context of uncertainty: How context shapes nurses' research utilization behaviors. *Qualitative Health Research, 18*, 347–357.

Stone, P. (2002). Popping the (PICO) question in research and evidence-based practice. *Applied Nursing Research, 16*, 197–198.

Straus, S. E., Richardson, W. S., Glasziou, P., & Haynes, R. B. (2005). *Evidence-based medicine: How to teach and practice EBM* (3rd ed.). Edinburgh: Churchill Livingston.

The Cochrane Collaboration. (2006). *Handbook for systematic reviews of interventions: Section 4: Formulating the problem.* Retrieved July, 10, 2008, from http://www.cochrane.org/resources/handbook/Handbook4.2.6Sep2006.pdf

chapter 2

39

Finding Relevant Evidence to Answer Clinical Questions

Ellen Fineout-Overholt, Donna R. Berryman, Sheila Hofstetter, and Julia Sollenberger

> *Searching is half the fun: life is much more manageable when thought of as a scavenger hunt as opposed to a surprise party.*
>
> *Jimmy Buffett*

In any clinical setting, there are numerous information resources (e.g., journal literature, practice-based data, patient information, text books) to answer a variety of questions about how to improve patient care or clinical procedures and protocols. For example, a patient in the medical intensive care unit (ICU) is being treated for refractory atrial fibrillation without much success. After exhausting a range of treatment options, a collaborating clinician remembers hearing that clonidine, a well-known antihypertensive medication, has been used successfully elsewhere and wonders whether it would work on this patient. With the delays in treatment success, the patient has become more and more concerned as treatment after treatment fails. The patient requests some help in understanding how she can reduce her anxiety. While other members of the healthcare team seek out what the evidence says about the use of clonidine, you formulate the following PICOT question about how to address the patient's anxiety: In adult ICU patients undergoing difficult treatment plans, how does music therapy compared to planned quiet affect anxiety during their hospitalization? Using the PICOT question as a guide, you conduct an efficient, thorough search for evidence to address the clinical question (Fineout-Overholt, Hofstetter, Shell, et al., 2005). Upon finding several recent randomized controlled trials (RCTs) that corroborate positive benefits of music therapy, you share this with the healthcare team and initiate music therapy for your patient.

Finding the right information to answer a given question often depends on the source of the information (Table 3.1). When clinicians explore only one source of information, they

table 3.1 **Sources of external evidence**

Resources	Free or Subscription Required*	Document Types	Search Method	Mobile Device Access
ACP Journal Club	• Subscription • Individual (ACP members receive web access as benefit of membership)	• Synopses of single studies and reviews • Expert clinical commentary • FT	• KW • KP	Yes
BMJ Clinical Evidence	• Subscription • Individual	• Summaries of evidence with recommendations • Clinical commentary • FT	• KW • Disease condition (e.g., diabetes) • Category (e.g., gastrointestinal)	Yes
CINAHL	• Subscription • Individual	• Journal article citation and abstract of primary studies, reviews, and synopses • FT (with FT subscription)	• KW • CV	No
Cochrane Databases	• Subscription • Individual • Free website access with restricted content • Pay-per-view options	• CDSR—FT systematic review • DARE—citation and abstract summary of systematic review not completed by Cochrane • CENTRAL—citation and abstract of clinical trials Note: Three of the five Cochrane databases are described here	• KW • CV (i.e., MeSH if you know the heading)	No
Dynamed	• Subscription • Individual	• Summaries of evidence • FT	• KW • Topic	Yes
Essential Evidence Plus	• Subscription • Individual	• POEMs (Patient Oriented Evidence that Matters) synopses of evidence • Clinical practice guidelines and guideline summaries • FT	• KW • Topic	Yes
Evidence-Based Nursing	• Subscription (individuals or institutions)	• Synopses of single studies and reviews • Expert clinical commentary • FT	• KW • KP	No
MEDLINE	• Free via PubMed • Available as subscription from other vendors	• Journal article citation and abstract of primary studies, reviews, and synopses • FT (with FT subscription)	• KW • CV • Clinical queries	Yes
NGC	• Free	• Clinical practice guidelines • Syntheses of selected guidelines • FT	• KW • Category	Yes

(table continues on page 42)

chapter 3

41

table 3.1 **Sources of external evidence** (continued)

Resources	Free or Subscription Required*	Document Types	Search Method	Mobile Device Access
PIER (Physician's Information & Education Resource)	• Subscription • Individual	• Summaries of evidence for point-of-care issues in internal medicine • FT	• KW • Topic • Organ system	Yes
PsycINFO	• Subscription • Individual	• Journal article citation and abstract of primary studies, reviews, and synopses • FT (with FT subscription)	• KW • CV	No

* Institutional subscription is implied; separate listing if individual subscription available

CV, controlled vocabulary; FT, full text; KW, keyword; KP, key phrase.

may conclude that there is no evidence to answer their question. For example, if clinicians are searching for RCTs to answer the sample clinical question and only search a web-based search engine (e.g., Yahoo or Google), they may not find any recent trials. Instead, they find a case study that is presented in a journal. The temptation may be to ignore the case study and conclude that there is no evidence to answer the question; however, to discard a case study would be inadvisable. While it may not be able to answer the clinical question fully and confidently indicate a practice change, a case study can inform clinical care. When searching for answers to clinical questions, all evidence should be considered; however, caution must be used when deciding about practice changes that are based solely on evidence that may contain substantial bias (e.g., case studies). Table 3.2 contains categories of clinical questions and the corresponding type of evidence that would best answer the question.

Since time is of the essence in finding answers to clinical questions, searching for evidence that has already been appraised for the quality of the study methodology and the reliability of its findings is desirable. This is called preappraised literature and can range from **meta-analytic systematic reviews** to synopses of single studies. Since these golden nuggets have already been critically appraised for clinicians, the work they need to do to determine whether or not they have reliable information can be minimized. Therefore, the time from finding the evidence to application can be reduced with this type of resource. Systematic reviews are the type of preappraised synthesis of studies that is the heart of evidence-based practice (EBP; Stevens, 2001). However, there is often not enough quality research to address all clinical issues with a synthesis; there may be only a few primary studies that exist—the question is where to find them. Clinicians looking for answers to their questions can access many sources of evidence reviews, synopses, summaries, and primary studies to efficiently and effectively locate the nuggets; however, it is often like finding the proverbial needle in a haystack.

Tools for Finding the Needle in the Haystack

Given the consistent need for current information in healthcare, frequently updated bibliographic and/or full-text databases that hold the latest studies reported in journals are the best, most current choices for finding relevant evidence to answer compelling clinical questions (see Clinical Scenario 3.1).

table 3.2 **Types of studies to answer clinical questions**

Examples of Clinical Questions	Best Evidence Design to Answer the Question
In patients with acute respiratory distress syndrome, how effective is prone positioning on weaning parameters compared with supine positioning?	Systematic reviews and meta-analyses Single RCTs
In pregnant women, how does prenatal care compared to no prenatal care affect a healthy delivery and a healthy baby?	Well-controlled, nonrandomized experimental studies
How do spouses with a loved one who has Alzheimer's disease perceive their ability to provide care?	Qualitative
What are the coping mechanisms of parents who have lost a child to AIDS?	Descriptive studies
What are the national standards for the prevention and management of wandering in patients with Alzheimer's disease who live in long-term care facilities?	Evidence-based clinical practice guidelines Opinion reports of experts and professional organizations

clinical scenario 3.1

A 45-year-old mother of three has been newly diagnosed with asthma. She tells you that her friend who has asthma takes a medication that is long acting. She wonders why the one she has been prescribed is short acting. She asks you about whether there is support for the medication she has been prescribed (Salbutamol). You search the literature to help her with the answer. The PICOT question for the search is as follows: In adults with asthma (P), how does salbutamol (I) compared with salmeterol xinafoate (C) affect asthma symptoms (O)?

Upon searching the Cochrane Database of Systematic Reviews, you find two systematic reviews that recommend the longer-acting medication (Tee, Koh, Gibson, et al., 2007; Walters, Walters, & Gibson, 2002). In an effort to gain more information, you look for an evidence-based guideline in the NGC database, searching with the keywords *short-acting beta agonist*, *long-acting beta agonist*, and *asthma*. The search reveals five guidelines. One is helpful to you as a healthcare provider (Singapore Ministry of Health, 2008). On the basis of these two pieces of evidence and your patient's concerns, you discuss the plan of care and the patient's concerns with the healthcare team.

The use of a standardized format, such as PICOT (see Chapter 2), to guide and clarify the important elements of the questions is an essential first step toward finding the right information to answer them. Generally, PICOT questions are expressed in everyday clinical terminology. Often, in searching for the best evidence to answer a PICOT question, clinicians encounter databases that have their own database-specific language that can help the searcher navigate a myriad of available studies and articles. This language is designed to eliminate or minimize errors that occur because of linguistic usage or spelling. Learning how to navigate through different databases is imperative for successfully retrieving relevant evidence. Novices to this type of searching are wise to consult a medical librarian who can assist them in this process.

After formulating a well-built PICOT question, the next step is to determine the source from which the best evidence is most likely available. Clinicians need **peer-reviewed research** to answer their questions, and most often the source of that evidence will be a database of published studies. These databases contain references to the healthcare literature, including books or journal publications, that are usually discipline specific (i.e., allied health, nursing, medicine, psychology). Choosing the right databases and being familiar with their language are essential to a successful, expedient search for answers to a clinical question.

In addition, there are resources that are available to assist busy clinicians with the best available evidence. While these resources save time, clinicians need to know how the appraisal process was conducted to ensure that the preappraised evidence is trustworthy. For example, one resource may be critically appraised topics (CATs; http://www.ebmny.org/cats.html). While some CATs are well done and reliable, others may not be. Knowledge of the PICOT question, the best type of evidence to answer it, and critical appraisal are essential for clinicians to know which of these resources (i.e., the haystack) is the best to search for the desired information.

Tool I: Sources of External Evidence—Description of the Haystack

Answers to clinical questions may be found in a variety of resources, ranging from practice data found in the healthcare record (i.e., **internal evidence**) to research articles in journals (i.e., **external evidence**), all of which have been moving increasingly from print to digital formats. The transition of evidence to electronic format has been fundamental to the emergence of new external evidence resources for supporting clinical decision making at the point of care. These resources contain timely clinical topic summaries and are designed to provide both background information and the best available external evidence to improve patient care.

Types of Evidence Resources

Textbooks and Journals. Healthcare professionals can consult a good textbook to refresh their knowledge of a specific condition or physiologic mechanism (i.e., background information; see Chapter 2), particularly if it is unusual (e.g., noncompaction cardiomyopathy or the clotting cascade), whether the text is in print or electronic format. To answer a specific question over and above general knowledge, however, textbooks are insufficient, as the discussion may be either incomplete or out of date. A journal article is the typical source from which to find an answer to this kind of question (i.e., foreground question; see Chapter 2), if there is one to be found. The journal literature is generally where all new ideas first enter the healthcare knowledge base. Journals contain a number of publication types, including systematic reviews, article synopses, research articles, narrative reviews, discussion articles, news items, editorials, and letters to the editor (listed from most useful to least in answering foreground questions).

Consolidated Resources and Beyond. Over the past decade, we have seen that the number and range of information databases that contain clinical evidence of varying levels have grown and flourished. Far beyond bibliographic databases that contain citations and abstracts to individual research articles (e.g., MEDLINE®, CINAHL®), there has evolved this new genre of information resource that holds within it "nuggets" of evidence to help the clinician make patient care decisions without searching the primary research literature every time.

Haynes (2007) characterized and organized the growing universe of evidence-based resources using a pyramid framework. A simplified version of this pyramid is presented in Figure 3.1. In the pyramid's base are contained original research articles. Bibliographic databases in which the original research articles are indexed (e.g., MEDLINE, CINAHL, or PsycINFO®) form the foundation of the healthcare literature. These databases contain the largest number and widest variation of articles describing clinical research. This is the original source of current research and holds the most reliable information; however, finding the evidence within these

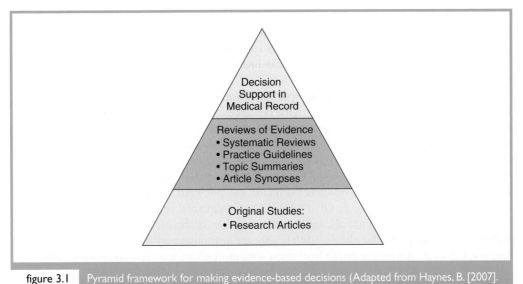

databases and appraising the worth of the articles to practice require specific knowledge and skill.

The next level of the pyramid entitled *Reviews of Evidence* contains preappraised literature, which, when done well, can be considered a "gold mine" of evidence. New consolidated resources (e.g., Clinical Evidence, Dynamed, Essential Evidence Plus, First Consult) have been designed to answer both background and foreground questions. They include comprehensive disease summaries, some as extensive as the equivalent of 40 print pages, that are formatted with sections and subcategories that are easily selected or expanded. These summaries include many hyperlinks to electronic journal articles or practice guidelines. They combine a textbook-like resource with easy access to the evidence contained in the journal literature—a format easily usable by busy clinicians. These resources can contain many types of evidence, ranging from **systematic reviews**, **clinical practice guidelines**, **health topic summaries** to **article synopses**. Reviews within these resources are written by individuals or panels of experts who have evaluated the available evidence, determined its worth to practice, and made recommendations about how to apply it to a particular clinical issue. While these sources of evidence are preappraised, it is important that the clinician understand the appraisal process used by each source of evidence to determine if the information contained within them is reliable for clinical decision making.

The pyramid's top layer, entitled *Decision Support in Medical Record,* describes the ideal situation, a **clinical decision support system** integrated into the **electronic health record** (EHR). Here, data on a specific patient are automatically linked to the current best evidence available in the system that matches that patient's specific circumstances. Upon matching the evidence with patient data, the clinical support system assists clinicians with evidence-based interventions for that patient. There are currently few of these decision support systems in use, and those that do exist are not always completely evidence based or current (Haynes, 2007). Effective use of these resources requires that practitioners value the use of evidence in daily practice and have the knowledge and skills to utilize the given information.

The shape of the pyramid is significant in terms of the number of resources available. Although there are millions of original research articles on the bottom layer, the number of highly functioning computerized decision support systems is very few. The number of conditions covered by evidence reviews is somewhere in between. One reason for this disparity in resources is the time and money it takes to develop highly sophisticated EHR systems with integrated current evidence, systematic reviews, practice guidelines, summaries, and synopses—all requiring updating on a regular basis.

Table 3.1 includes the names of specific information resources that fall into the bottom two sections of the pyramid. Only three of the resources (i.e., National Guideline Clearinghouse [NGC], MEDLINE, and Cochrane Databases) are available to all healthcare providers no matter where they practice because they are government-sponsored databases. All of the others are available to individuals and/or institutions on a subscription basis. It is important to note that MEDLINE is produced by the National Library of Medicine (NLM) and is available free of charge through PubMed® (http://www.ncbi.nlm.nih.gov/pubmed) but can also be obtained for a cost via commercial vendors (e.g., Ovid®, EBSCO). Commercial vendors offer their own search interfaces, full-text articles/journals, and a variety of other databases, which can provide unique features that attract particular clients. Each healthcare institution may have a different array of database offerings, depending on the institution size, professions it serves, and library budget.

Tool 2: Gathering the Right Evidence From the Right Source

Healthcare professionals, faculty, librarians, and students are all very busy in their roles and desire a reliable, efficient source of evidence. The key is to know how to match the sources of evidence with the question to be answered.

Which Resource or Database Is a Good Match?

Evidence that is reliable, accurate, and consistent is needed to reduce the risk, uncertainty, and time involved in clinical decision making that is focused on promoting desired patient outcomes. With all of the resources potentially available to clinicians, the first step in finding the answer to their clinical questions is to search for evidence in synthesized, preappraised resources (e.g., **Cochrane Database of Systematic Reviews** [CDSR], Database of Reviews of Effectiveness [DARE], American College of Physicians [ACP] Journal Club, and the journal, *Evidence-Based Nursing* [EBN] see Table 3.1 for more information on these resources). Finding the evidence in full text (i.e., electronic copies of articles available online) can promote timely decision making. While there are open source full-text articles available (i.e., no fee), a subscription is required to access most full-text journals (see Table 3.1). For example, in the CDSR, only an abstract of the systematic reviews can be obtained without a subscription. To obtain the full systematic review, either an individual or an institutional subscription is required.

For point-of-care decisions, clinicians may choose to consult one of the preappraised summaries or synopsized resources listed earlier. However, when making practice changes, it is important to either find a synthesis that has conducted an exhaustive search (i.e., found all that we know on the topic) or get as close to that as possible by searching multiple databases to ensure that studies are not missed. Searching authoritative, subject-specific, bibliographic databases that index scientific communities' scholarly, peer-reviewed research provides the next resource for the best available evidence to clinicians. For example, searching MEDLINE, with its range of core journals cutting across disciplines and numbering in the thousands, enables clinicians to obtain a large chunk of the evidence that exists on a topic. However, solely searching MEDLINE would be a limitation, in that other databases index other journals not covered in MEDLINE and studies in those journals would not be known to clinicians; therefore, key knowledge that may impact outcomes could be missed. Other healthcare databases to consider include the Cumulative Index of Nursing & Allied Health Literature (CINAHL) and PsycINFO, the database of psychological literature. Healthcare covers a wide range of topics. If a question focuses on issues that are not indexed within the mainstream healthcare databases, a healthcare librarian can recommend other databases that can provide evidence to answer a PICOT question (e.g., Educational Resources Information Center [ERIC], Business Abstracts [ABI], Computing Reviews, Social Sciences Citation Index [SSCI]).

When searches in indexed bibliographic databases do not lead to sufficient quality evidence and clinicians wish to explore what other evidence (e.g., **grey literature**) is available, they may choose to turn to web-based free resources, such as Google. Searching any web-based, non-indexed search engines, such as Google and Google Scholar, can provide value; however, caution should be used and careful evaluation of the evidence retrieved from these sources is required. MacColl (2006) indicates that Google's best contribution to healthcare evidence base may be its identification of grey literature (i.e., reports, conference proceedings, and other research studies that may not have been published or indexed). Additionally, MacColl indicated that Google has a unique citation mechanism called "known item searching" in which searchers who have only bits and pieces (e.g., author's name, a few words from an article title) can retrieve a full citation. Clinicians should keep in mind that Google is known for citing older resources, and older resources may not be relevant for answering clinical questions that may lead to practice change. Web-based search engines, such as Google and Google Scholar, are insufficient as sole sources of evidence. Shultz (2007) indicated that searching Google can involve time wasters in searching, and the evidence-based practitioner risks missing reliable evidence when searching them solely, as these resources are not indexed and have no limits that can be set to refine the search. With these resources, having the correct keywords is essential, as without them, evidence can be elusive.

For more about evaluating information on the Internet, visit:
http://www.lib.berkeley.edu/TeachingLib/Guides/Internet/
EvalForm_General_Barker.pdf
http://nccam.nih.gov/health/webresources/webresources.pdf
http://www.lib.unc.edu/instruct/evaluate/web/checklist.html

chapter 3

47

Final Key Resource for Finding Evidence: Collaboration With Healthcare Librarians

An essential step in achieving success is knowing the extent of one's resources. Collaboration with healthcare librarians who are savvy about EBP is essential to get efficient answers to clinical questions. While all clinicians may not be expert searchers, each one should have the skills to be able to search and find their own answers as they have time and resources to do so. However, there are occasions when time is short and system infrastructures must be in place to facilitate finding evidence to answer the clinical question. To bring in the librarian at this late date, however, will not serve the process or outcome well. Healthcare librarians are involved in the culture shift toward EBP. They are the knowledge brokers and knowledge miners of healthcare. Without their involvement in establishing an EBP culture, important pieces will be missed. Librarians can be helpful at any point in the search; however, librarians shine when clinicians have attempted to search multiple databases and other resources but do not find the evidence they seek. Often librarians work their remarkable magic and can find evidence to answer a clinical question. As you plan your approach to establishing EBP, consider some advice and "take your librarian to lunch."

Get to know what is available in your organization to help you hone your searching skills. Get to know your healthcare librarian and share what your interests are in improving healthcare outcomes. Key concepts to the clinician–librarian collaboration are dialogue, role delineation, and purpose. Talk about how PICOT questions are the drivers of searches.

Discuss how keywords are a wonderful start to searching, but not sufficient to close the search. Explore the most effective way for clinicians to get the data now.

Currently, some healthcare professionals are finding evidence at the bedside. However, in 2030, it is hopeful that all healthcare professionals will be evidence-based clinicians, conducting rapid, efficient searches *at the bedside,* often in sources of evidence that will not be primary electronic databases. For this to occur, collaboration between librarians and clinicians will be instrumental in exploring how to access information rapidly and efficiently. As information experts, librarians are partners with clinicians in achieving the mission of transforming healthcare from the inside out. The desired effect of the clinician–librarian collaboration is synergy that leads to consistent best practices by clinicians to achieve optimal outcomes for healthcare consumers.

Tool 3: Understanding Database Structure and Searching the Databases

When searching databases for evidence, clinicians need to be aware of features common to most databases. Understanding the structure and content of a particular information resource before attempting to search it is critical. Without this background, the search terms and strategies used may not yield the desired information, or the chosen database may not contain the information sought.

Types of Databases

Prior to the mid-1990s, knowledge-based databases were of two types: bibliographic and full-text databases. Now, however, point-of-care resources combine these two elements in a single resource that houses evidence summaries on clinical topics along with references to supporting primary articles. Examples of both types of databases as well as hybrid databases that contain both bibliographic and full-text information will be discussed. Bibliographic databases contain article citations that point to the location of the article in the journal literature. They include information about the publication that makes it easy to find, such as author, article title, journal name and volume, publisher, and/or an abstract. Citations rarely include the **full text** of the published item. Box 3.1 is an example of a bibliographic record from MEDLINE, a bibliographic database, obtained through PubMed.

A bibliographic record (i.e., citation) can include many details about the item, including the terms that were used to describe the content, but it does not contain the full text of the article as part of the record. Other examples of bibliographic healthcare databases are CINAHL, which indexes citations dealing with healthcare issues across multiple healthcare disciplines, and PsycINFO, which indexes articles dealing with psychological topics.

Full-text information resources contain whole articles or books, including the text, charts, graphs, and other illustrations. These electronic versions may be enhanced by supplemental data (i.e., in spreadsheets), by multimedia content, and/or by hypertext links to other articles and supporting references. Full-text resources most often take the form of online journals or books (e.g., *Evidence-Based Nursing* journal or Harrison's Online) but can also include the full text of practice guidelines (NGC) or systematic reviews (Cochrane Library). The hybrid database is designed for the point-of-care provider, with patient care recommendations supported by links to general patient care information, evidence-based articles, reviews, synopses, and guidelines. Some examples of hybrid databases are First Consult and Clinical Evidence.

Content of Databases

A clinician must be familiar with what databases and other information resources are available and what they contain before determining the value of searching it for answers to particular clinical questions. Databases can contain references to articles, the full text of the articles, entire

box 3.1

Example of a Bibliographic Record from the MEDLINE Database

Testing an Intervention to Promote Children's Adherence to Asthma Self-Management
Burkhart PV, Ravens MK, Oakley MG, Abshire DA, and Zhang M

College of Nursing, University of Kentucky, Lexington, KY 40536–0232, USA
pvburk2@uky.edu

Purpose: To test the hypothesis that compared with the control group, 7- through 11-year-old children with persistent asthma who received asthma education plus a contingency management behavioral protocol would show higher adherence to peak expiratory flow (PEF) monitoring for asthma self-management and would report fewer asthma episodes. *Design and methods:* A randomized, controlled trial was conducted with 77 children with persistent asthma in a southeastern U.S. state. Both the intervention and the control groups received instruction on PEF monitoring. Only the intervention group received asthma education plus contingency management, based on cognitive social learning theory, including self-monitoring, a contingency contract, tailoring, cueing, and reinforcement. At-home adherence to daily PEF monitoring during the 16-week study was assessed with the AccuTrax Personal Diary Spirometer, a computerized handheld meter. Adherence was measured as a percentage of prescribed daily PED uses at Weeks 4 (baseline), 8 (postintervention), and 16 (maintenance). *Results:* At the end of the baseline period, the groups did not differ in adherence to daily PEF monitoring nor at Week 8. At Week 16, the intervention group's adherence for daily electronically monitored PEF was higher than that of the control group. Children in either group who were ≥80% adherent to at least once-daily PEF monitoring during the last week of the maintenance period (Weeks 8–16) were less likely to have an asthma episode during this period compared with those who were less adherent. *Conclusions:* The intervention to teach children to adhere to the recommended regimen for managing their asthma at home was effective.

Publication Types:

- Randomized Controlled Trial
- Research Support, N.I.H., Extramural

MeSH Terms:

- Asthma/epidemiology
- Asthma/prevention and control*
- Asthma/psychology
- Chi-square distribution
- Child
- Computers, handheld
- Female
- Health promotion
- Humans
- Male
- Nursing assessment
- Nursing education research

(box 3.1 continues on page 50)

chapter 3

49

box 3.1 (continued)

- Nursing evaluation research
- Patient compliance/psychology*
- Patient education as topic/organization and administration*
- Peak expiratory flow rate*
- Prevalence
- Program evaluation
- Reinforcement (psychology)
- Self care*/methods
- Self care*/psychology
- Single-blind method
- Southeastern United States/epidemiology
- Spirometry
- Statistics, nonparametric

Grant Support

- R15 NR08106–01/NR/United States NINR
- PMID: 17535313 [PubMed - indexed for MEDLINE]

Source: Pubmed@http://www.ncbi.nlm.nih.gov/pubmed/

books, dissertations, drug and pharmaceutical information, and other resources (e.g., news items, clinical calculators). To determine which databases to search, clinicians must consider the clinical question and which databases will contain relevant evidence. Evidence can come from multiple databases that primarily serve certain disciplines (e.g., nursing and allied health, medicine, biomedicine, psychology, social sciences). Searching only one database will limit clinicians in retrieving the best evidence to answer their questions.

Searching Databases

To effectively find an answer to questions, clinicians need to understand a few details about the databases they are searching, such as (a) is the evidence current? (b) will controlled vocabulary or keywords be more effective in getting to the best evidence quickly?

Often clinicians wonder how many years back they should search. Some have indicated that searching back 5 years is sufficient; however, this may not be adequate to discover evidence that can address the clinical issue. While there is no rule for how far back to search for evidence, clinicians may need to search until they can confidently indicate that there is little or no evidence to answer their clinical question or that they feel confident that what evidence they have found represents the body of evidence that exists. For example, Dr. Priscilla Worral of SUNY Upstate Healthcare System, in a situation in which clinicians in the ED were using salt pork to prevent rebleeding from epistaxis, indicated that she had to search for articles back to the late 1800s to find relevant evidence to her clinical question (P.S. Worral, personal communication, 2001). To accomplish the goal of finding "all that we know" about a topic, databases must have a span of years of evidence available for clinicians to search for the databases to contain the best answers to questions. Knowing that evidence is current is another consideration. Clinicians must be aware of the years covered in a bibliographic database. The Cochrane Library's systematic reviews, for instance, always state the most recent update date. Other resources also require investigating how current they are. For example, some online textbooks and point-of-care resources are updated daily and some only every year. If there is no known date for evidence (e.g., Internet sources of evidence), it may be outdated and not readily applicable.

Keyword and Controlled Vocabulary Searching

Keyword searching is searching using simple, everyday language. The inherent challenge is that all synonyms (e.g., research, evidence, studies, study, investigation) must be included in the search or items will be missed. Some search engines, databases, and other sources of evidence are searched completely by keywords (e.g., Google). If web based, these search engines retrieve information by looking strictly for the occurrence of the term(s) somewhere in the items to be searched. In databases, the keyword search yields evidence if there is a match between the word entered and what is found in the title and/or abstract. If a different term is entered, evidence may be missed. For example, in keyword searching, you get (and only get) articles that match the terms that you put into the search. This may sound like a good thing, but it is very difficult to know every synonym of a word and every spelling variation. For example, the keyword entered is *behavior*, which would yield any title or abstract (i.e., a record) that contained the word *behavior* in it. All records with the alternative spelling *behaviour* in the title or abstract would be missed. In addition, different spellings of singulars and plurals (e.g., *mouse* and *mice*) must be included or evidence will be missed.

Using keywords can be ambiguous and jargon-laden. Consider the following question: Are people diagnosed with AIDS more likely to acquire pneumonia in the community than the elderly? An example of a keyword search for this question might start with the word *AIDS*. This search would include articles on other types of aids, such as visual aids, aid to dependent children, and hearing aids. In addition, this search would retrieve only articles containing the word *AIDS*. Those articles that used *acquired immune deficiency syndrome* or *acquired immunodeficiency syndrome* would be potentially missed. A well-known example of a controlled vocabulary is Medical Subject Headings (**MeSH**), which are the set of terms used by the NLM to describe the content of articles indexed in MEDLINE. If the MeSH term *acquired immunodeficiency syndrome* was searched, all of these articles would contain information about acquired immunodeficiency syndrome. Searching with keywords can be helpful, especially when no controlled vocabulary term exists to adequately describe the topic searched. When a topic is so recent that there is likely to be very little available in the journal literature, using keywords may be the best way to find relevant evidence because controlled vocabulary for the topic is unlikely. For this reason, the importance of carefully formulating the PICOT question cannot be overemphasized. Using unambiguous, nonjargon terms to describe the PICOT components of the clinical question will assist in obtaining the best search in the shortest time.

Scholarly databases, which use keyword searching, also have enhanced search retrieval by assigning subject terms from a controlled vocabulary to each item. Controlled vocabulary can also be referred to as subject headings, thesaurus, or taxonomies in healthcare databases. The content of an article will determine which controlled vocabulary (i.e., category or subject heading) it falls under (e.g., fibromyalgia or fatigue). These controlled vocabulary terms are used to help the searcher find information on a particular topic, no matter what words the author may use to refer to a concept in the text. For example, cancer can be described using keywords such as tumor, neoplasm, mass, or with words with prefixes such as onco- or carcino- or suffixes such as -oma. If a database incorporates controlled vocabulary with keyword searching, regardless of what words the author used in the article, when searchers type their words into the search box of the database, the database does what is called "mapping" and finds the controlled vocabulary terms that best match the keyword. Using controlled vocabulary, searchers can broaden their searches without having to consider every synonym for the chosen keyword. For example, articles about cardiac carcinomas or heart tumors will be retrieved using the controlled vocabulary subject heading *heart neoplasms*.

Many controlled vocabulary systems also have a hierarchical structure that helps the searcher retrieve the more specific terms that fall under a general term. In searching a general MeSH term such as *heart diseases,* the PubMed search engine automatically maps keywords to controlled vocabulary and retrieves every specific term that is listed under it in the hierarchical structure (called a "tree structure"). This search retrieves articles ranging from myocardial infarction to familial hypertrophic cardiomyopathy and everything in between—all at one time. Some search engines, rather than doing it automatically, offer the user the option of including, or not including, all of the specifics under a general term (e.g., Ovid presents the option to "explode" the subject heading, which means to include all the specific terms indented under a more general heading).

Including the narrower terms in the controlled vocabulary (i.e., explode) can be advantageous for searches when broad terms are needed; however, it can be disadvantageous because the searcher may find papers that are not necessarily helpful in answering the clinical question. However, when clinicians use the explode feature and perhaps retrieve irrelevant articles, they can eliminate most of them by setting appropriate limits and combining controlled vocabulary term searches using the PICOT question as the guide. Therefore, exploding the search term when using controlled vocabulary is recommended. Some search systems enable the searcher to click on the controlled vocabulary heading and see the other narrower headings in the hierarchical thesaurus. This option helps the searcher create the most relevant search by making a decision about whether to explode terms in the search.

An example of the usefulness of the explode function is a search to find information on food poisoning. In MEDLINE, the MeSH term *food poisoning* is the broad subject heading that describes various types of food poisoning, including botulism, ciguatera poisoning, favism, mushroom poisoning, salmonella poisoning, and staphylococcal poisoning. Using this heading to initiate the search and then exploding it means that the name of each of those types of food poisoning is a part of the search without entering each one into the search strategy, saving clinicians' time. In PubMed's MeSH search, the term you enter is automatically exploded. In the search, you have to instruct PubMed to NOT explode the term.

Most large bibliographic databases, such as MEDLINE, CINAHL, and PsycINFO, use a controlled vocabulary to describe the content of the items it references. Most search engines will attempt to map the keyword entered in the search box to a controlled vocabulary subject heading. This assists the searcher in finding relevant evidence without the need to know the subject heading up front. For example, in most search engines, the term *Tylenol* is mapped to the generic term *acetaminophen*, as is the European term *paracetamol*, or any of the following that are acetaminophen types of pain relievers: *tempra, panadol, datril, valgesic, valadol, tussapap, tralgon, tapar, tabalgin,* and *pyrinazine*. As a system searches the controlled vocabulary heading *acetaminophen*, any article using the term *Tylenol* or any of the other words above will be retrieved because an indexer cataloged it under that heading, regardless of the term used in the article. There is a caveat to controlled vocabulary searching: This mapping process may not be efficient with very current topics that have only recently entered the literature. In these cases, a controlled vocabulary term likely is not available; therefore, keyword searching, using synonyms or variant forms of the word, may yield more relevant results. In some cases, truncation should be considered, which is using special symbols in combination with words or word parts to enhance the likelihood of finding relevant studies. Truncation is usually indicated by a word or part of a word followed by an asterisk (*). In PubMed, the asterisk is used to replace any number of letters at the end of the word. For example, in PubMed, to truncate *adolescent*, one would use *adolescen** to retrieve *adolescent, adolescents,* or *adolescence.*

Some evidence-based resources do not have controlled vocabulary, or there must be knowledge of controlled vocabulary terms that may not be commonplace to use them. For example, the Cochrane Library can be searched using MeSH or keywords. To search using the MeSH option, you have to know the MeSH term you want to search. If you use MeSH often, you may know the term you want to search and easily can make use of this feature. However, given that this information resource is relatively small, searching with keywords, including synonyms, can retrieve a reasonable number of relevant articles. Nevertheless, keyword searching requires some creativity; the searcher must think of all the different ways that an author could have referred to a particular concept. To maximize your search, keep in mind the caveats about keyword searching that were described earlier in this chapter.

Combining and Limiting Searches

In a focused search for a clinical topic using the PICOT question as the framework for the search, clinicians may choose to enter multiple concepts simultaneously into the search system. The disadvantage to this method is that there is no way to determine which concept has the most evidence available. To assist with knowing what evidence exists to address the terms entered into the search box, clinicians can enter the terms from the PICOT question into the search box one at a time. By entering them one at a time, especially in very large databases (e.g., MEDLINE, CINAHL, PsycINFO), the number of hits (i.e., articles or studies that contain the searched word) for each individual term searched can be known. For example, searching MEDLINE for the keywords *Tylenol* and *pain* separately yielded 67 and 180,694 hits, respectively; however, when searching them together, *Tylenol AND pain*, the yield was 32. There is clearly more evidence about pain than Tylenol. It is important to consider that out of a possible 67 studies, only 32 were found that addressed both terms. To enter each PICOT term individually may not be possible with every search due to competing clinical priorities; however, it is the best method to fully understand what evidence exists to answer the clinical question.

When combining controlled vocabulary or keywords, the Booleans AND and OR are usually used. Using AND is appropriate when clinicians wish both of the combined terms to appear in the final record. Since AND is a restrictive word (i.e., both words must appear), it will reduce the size of the final yield (i.e., number of studies retrieved). If the goal of the search is to explore what is available, using OR can be helpful, as either one or the other or both of the terms are desired in the final record. When keyword searching using synonyms, OR is often used. Each search system has its own unique way of combining terms. For example, one system may require typing in the word AND or OR, while another may offer the ease of clicking on a "combine" option and specifying the correct connector.

Consider an example that illustrates the principle of combining search terms. A clinician began searching for articles to answer the following question: In patients with suspected schizophrenia, how does magnetic resonance imaging (MRI) compared to computed tomography (CT scan) assist in accurate diagnosis of the disorder? The search would begin with entering the keywords *MRI*, *CT scan*, *schizophrenia*, and *diagnosis* into the search engine. If there is an option of controlled vocabulary, it would be used. The yields from the searches of the terms *MRI* and *CT scan* could first be combined with the outcome of the searches for the terms *schizophrenia* and *diagnosis* using AND (i.e., [MRI AND CT scan] AND schizophrenia AND diagnosis) because this search would theoretically yield the best answer to the question. However, if few results were found, more exploration can be accomplished by combining the yields of the searches for MRI and CT scan using the Boolean connector OR and then combining with the outcome using AND (i.e., [MRI OR CT scan] AND schizophrenia AND diagnosis). This search can provide some insight into the answer to the question; although, it won't answer it completely.

Clinicians should consider that different search engines process terms in the search box in different ways; therefore, use caution when searching various databases in multiple search engines. They may not all be searched using the same search strategy. For example, PubMed automatically puts an AND between the words, as does Google. Other search engines may look for the words first as a phrase, while other search systems automatically put OR between the terms. Before combining terms in a large bibliographic database, know how the search engine treats the terms it is given.

Since bibliographic databases are very large, often there are more citations retrieved than are reasonable to address to determine relevance, even after the searcher has combined all of the main concepts of the search. The "limit" function is designed to help the searcher pare down the large results list. This is a great tool when considering how to increase the relevance of the final search cohort. Choosing the limit function leads one to a set of options for limiting the results by various parameters (e.g., language, human studies, publication year, age, gender, publication type, full text). An important limiting option in a bibliographic database with a controlled vocabulary is to designate the search terms as the main point of the article. When indexers assign subject terms for MEDLINE, CINAHL, and PsycINFO, they will index both the major and the minor concepts within the articles. In Box 3.1, the asterisk (*) beside some MeSH terms denotes the main points of the article. Many search systems permit the searcher to limit the search to articles where a particular concept is the main point, or focus, of the article. For example, Ovid provides the "focus" option to the left of its controlled vocabulary subject heading. Using this limit is aimed at increasing the relevancy of the retrieved articles.

Another option, full text, limits the search to only those articles that are available electronically. The ease of full-text retrieval can be tempting; however, clinicians can miss evidence by limiting their search to only those articles where full text is readily available. While an increasing number of journals do provide their articles in full text, all journals do not. Although limiting to full text can be a useful tool to get a rapid return on a search, clinicians must keep in mind that there may be relevant studies that are not captured in such a limited search. The quality of the full-text evidence will assist in determining whether the missing evidence is essential to safe and effective clinical decision making (see Chapters 4–8 on critical appraisal).

It is important to note that full-text articles are not part of the bibliographic record and are not in the database itself. Rather, links have been created that connect the search to the free full-text article available somewhere on the web or to the article in an electronic journal for which the library in your institution has paid a subscription fee for institutional access. If neither of these conditions exists, then the link may lead you to the journal's website and you will be asked to pay a fee to access the full text of the article. Box 3.1 is a bibliographic record from the bibliographic database MEDLINE that contains an example of buttons at the top of the citation that link the searcher from the bibliographic database to the full text of the article.

If it is preferable not to pay the publisher for this article, know that the library that you are affiliated with can get the item for you through interlibrary loan. Some libraries offer this service at no charge and others charge a fee per article. Contact your librarian to request the article. If there is no librarian to partner with regarding the evidence you need, you can register to use a document delivery service through the NLM called Loansome Doc®, using the instructions at the following link: http://www.nlm.nih.gov/pubs/factsheets/loansome_doc.html. This service requires you to establish a relationship with a nearby library and there may be a fee for each document, depending on that library's policies.

The final limit setting is not done in the search, but in the strategy for retrieving studies to review as evidence. Once a search yields a number of potential matches, or hits, the clinician is wise to have established specific conditions beforehand that will assist in determining which hits, or articles, are "keepers" and which will be discarded. These conditions are called **inclusion** and **exclusion criteria**. Often, many of the criteria have been applied in the search strategy as limits. However, there are occasional articles/studies that are not relevant to answering the question but still slip through the best search strategy. Stating inclusion and exclusion criteria upon which to judge a study will focus the return of the search to provide the most relevant evidence.

An inclusion criterion may be that a clinician will accept only studies with samples that are equally balanced in regard to gender. An exclusion criterion may be that the clinician will not accept studies that compare three different medications. These stipulations for acceptable studies cannot be met through the search strategy. Often, the abstract is not adequate to address all of the inclusion and exclusion criteria. The entire study may need to be obtained to determine whether it is a keeper.

Keepers: Managing Citations of Interest

Once a search is completed, each database will provide options for dealing with citations of interest. Most databases provide methods for printing, saving, or e-mailing citations. Each database may also provide other specialized features for dealing with selected citations: PubMed has the Clipboard, while EBSCO uses folders. Databases may also allow users to set up individual accounts that allow customization of certain features or the ability to save desired settings. Familiarizing yourself with these options can spare you frustration and may save you a great deal of time. Collaborate with a librarian to determine the easiest way to learn about these time-saving options provided by any given database. In addition, many databases provide "Help" documentation that can assist users in learning to use these helpful features of a database.

Saving Searches: Why and How

Saving the method of searching (i.e., how you went about the search) is imperative if you want to repeat the search or communicate the search to someone else. The only way to have the search details so that they can be replicated is to save it when you conduct the initial search. Each search engine offers different mechanisms for saving a search. Let's take the example of updating a healthcare policy and procedure. An in-depth search is completed that yielded relevant studies upon which to base the recommendations in the now updated policy. The next review cycle comes along; however, without a saved search, the review group will have to start from scratch. With a saved search, they simply run it to determine what is new since the last revision of the policy.

Organizing Searches

Often there is a need to organize the evidence found, as it can become overwhelming just by the sheer volume (Fineout-Overholt et al., 2005). Practitioners need to be able to organize evidence in a variety of ways to best serve clinicians as they journey through the various steps of the EBP process and search various databases. The entire team working on a clinical change project can have quick access to necessary resources through web-based password-protected folders (i.e., bibliographic management software [BMS]), thereby supporting team communications, work distribution, turnaround of critical appraisal sessions, defense of practice changes, and other knowledge transfer initiatives.

Bibliographic management software is designed to offer options that save, search, sort, share, and continuously add, delete, and organize promising citations. Some web-based examples include RefWorks and EndNote®. Many libraries provide access to these types of software programs for their users; therefore, readers should check with their library before purchasing any BMS software. If clinicians must select a BMS product, they need to compare purchase/subscription fees, features, ease of use, and speed. Approximate annual fees for individuals can range from $100 to $300 per year, depending upon vendor/desired features.

Practitioners can work with teams in multiple sites or their own institution using a web-based BMS that is designed to import/export citations from all of the commonly searched bibliographic databases as well as sort the citations by author, journal title, and keywords. Organizing the evidence in folders such as clinical meaningfulness, specific PICOT concepts, or strength of evidence allows the teams to add to and keep track of the relevant information they have about their common clinical issue. Through sharing citations with the team or organizing them for their own initiatives, clinicians can reduce the time invested in evidence retrieval and improve access to current information for the entire team.

Tool 4: Choosing the Right Database

Of the many databases that index healthcare literature, some are available through several vendors at a cost, some are free of charge, and some are available both free of charge and through a vendor for a fee. For example, as noted previously, depending on the search options desired, MEDLINE can be accessed free of charge through the NLM's PubMed or obtained for a cost through other providers (e.g., Ovid). Table 3.1 contains information about access to some of the available databases.

This chapter focuses primarily on the following databases:

- Cochrane Databases
- NGC
- MEDLINE
- CINAHL
- Excerpta Medica Online (EMBASE)
- PsycINFO

MEDLINE and CINAHL are among the best-known comprehensive databases and can arguably be described as representing the scientific knowledge base of healthcare. However, the amount of information in healthcare exceeds the capacity of either of these databases. In addition to MEDLINE and CINAHL, there are other databases available, some of which are highly specialized, and their numbers are growing in response to the desire for more readily available information (e.g., Up-to-Date, Clinical Evidence).

> *Curiosity is the wick in the candle of learning.*
>
> **William Arthur Ward**

Cochrane Databases

Classified as an international not-for-profit organization, The Cochrane Collaboration represents the efforts of a global network of dedicated volunteer researchers, healthcare professionals, and consumers who prepare, maintain, and promote access to The Cochrane Library's six databases: Cochrane Database of Systematic Reviews (CDSR), Database of Reviews of Effectiveness (DARE), **Cochrane Central Register of Controlled Trials** (CENTRAL), **Cochrane Methodology Register**, Health Technology Assessment Database, and NHS Economic Evaluation Database.

The Cochrane Library's "gold standard" database is the CDSR. It contains Cochrane full-text systematic reviews and should be searched first to answer intervention questions. Although the CDSR is a fairly small database, in part because systematic reviews are still relatively new in the history of healthcare, the CDSR contains a large number of valuable, synthesized (i.e., critically appraised, compiled, and integrated) RCTs. Unlike MEDLINE (e.g., 16 million citations) and CINAHL (e.g., 3 million citations), the CDSR contains a few thousand citations and is limited to a single publication type—systematic reviews—including meta-analyses. A single word search in the MEDLINE or CINAHL databases can easily result in thousands of hits. Because the CDSR is a small database, the broadest search is likely to retrieve only a small, manageable number of hits. This makes the database easy to search and the results easy to review. When reading the search results, the label "Review" refers to a completed Cochrane review and the label "Protocol" applies to Cochrane reviews that are in the initial stages of gathering and appraising evidence. It is helpful to know that protocols are in the pipeline; however, it can be disappointing not to find a full review. Protocols can provide background information, the objectives and methods for developing the review in progress, and an expected completion date for the review.

If a full Cochrane review is retrieved during a search, clinicians can save time because they do not need to conduct the critical appraisal and synthesis of primary studies, as that has already been done. However, clinicians need to critically appraise the systematic review itself. Chapter 5 contains more information on critically appraising systematic reviews. A Cochrane review can be quite lengthy, which is particularly important when printing.

Clinicians without a paid subscription to The Cochrane Library can still access almost all of its collection of six databases for free at: http://www.cochrane.org/. The Cochrane Library provides free access to the abstracts of the systematic reviews. However, without a subscription, access to the full-text Cochrane review is restricted. First check to see if your library has a subscription to the Cochrane Library. In addition, full-text reviews can be available if institutions and organizational libraries have licensing agreements with vendors who bundle the CDSR with other databases. If these options are not available, another option is to access the full-text version of a review by paying for it separately, called pay-per-view. This option is offered on each abstract summary page.

The Cochrane DARE database is produced by the Centre for Reviews and Dissemination at the University of York, UK. The DARE database complements the CDSR by quality assessment and summarizing of reviews that are not produced by The Cochrane Collaboration.

The Cochrane CENTRAL database serves as the most comprehensive source of reports of controlled trials. It includes 310,000 trial reports from MEDLINE, 50,000 additional trial reports from EMBASE, and the remaining 170,000 reports from other sources such as other databases and hand searching. It also includes citations of reports of controlled trials that are not indexed in MEDLINE, EMBASE, or other bibliographic databases; citations published in many languages; and citations that are available only in conference proceedings or other sources that are difficult to access (Dickersin et al., 2002).

> The databases produced by The Cochrane Collaboration can be accessed via **http://www.cochrane.org.**

National Guideline Clearinghouse

The NGC is a comprehensive database of evidence-based clinical practice guidelines and related documents that provide physicians, nurses, and other healthcare professionals and stakeholders with detailed information on the latest management and maintenance of particular health issues, along with how the guideline was developed, tested, and should be used (e.g., an algorithm). Guidelines are systematically developed statements about a plan of care for a specific set of clinical circumstances involving a particular population. In other words, clinical practice guidelines address several PICOT questions, compiling the evidence into a set of evidence-based recommendations that can be easily applied by clinicians. The best intervention guidelines are based on rigorous scientific evidence obtained from systematic reviews or RCTs. Some guidelines that are consensus of expert opinion, while not the strongest evidence, still can assist in decision making.

The NGC is a government-supported database that was initiated by the Agency for Healthcare Research and Quality (AHRQ) within the U.S. Department of Health and Human Services. The agency has a mission to improve the quality, safety, efficiency, effectiveness, and cost effectiveness of health. The NGC provides the following benefits: (a) structured summary abstracts with links to the full-text guidelines, when available, or links to ordering information for print copies; (b) syntheses of selected guidelines that cover similar topics; (c) expert commentary on issues of interest to the guideline community; (d) a guideline comparison feature that allows users to generate side-by-side evaluation of two or more guidelines; and (e) downloads to a mobile device.

> The NGC can be found at **http://www.guideline.gov.**

MEDLINE

MEDLINE is one of the world's largest searchable bibliographic databases covering medicine, health, and the biomedical sciences, and it is available 24 hours a day on any computer in the world with Internet access. The NLM also leases the MEDLINE data to vendors. These types of companies load the database into their own user interfaces with unique features and sell subscriptions to libraries and others. It is important to acknowledge that the original file of indexed citations is the same MEDLINE product in PubMed as in any of these other vendors' versions of the file. It contains citations from more than 5,200 biomedical journals in medicine, nursing, pharmacy, dentistry, and allied health. The database is updated daily and has abstracts for over 52% of its articles, with 80% of its citations in English.

MEDLINE has worldwide coverage, including many non-English languages, though it tends to focus on North American journal articles. MEDLINE uses a controlled vocabulary, MeSH, to facilitate searches.

> The MEDLINE database is available free of charge through PubMed at **http://www.ncbi.nlm.nih.gov/pubmed.**

unit one

CINAHL

The Cumulative Index of Nursing & Allied Health Literature (CINAHL) database is produced by Cinahl Information Systems and contains article citations with abstracts, when available, from 13 nursing and allied health disciplines. Articles are retrieved from journals, books, drug monographs, dissertations, and images that are sometimes difficult to locate in other databases. The CINAHL database is usually accessed through libraries but can be accessed through a personal CINAHL direct subscription via the Cinahl Information Systems website (http://www.ebscohost. com/cinahl/). The CINAHL database includes more than 3 million journal articles from 1982 to present. About 70% of the citations in CINAHL also appear in the MEDLINE database. The CINAHL database also has a controlled vocabulary. It is an English language database and available through various vendors.

> The CINAHL database is available at **http://www.ebscohost.com/cinahl/.**

EMBASE

Excerpta Medica Online (EMBASE) is the major European biomedical and pharmaceutical database indexing in the fields of drug research, pharmacology, pharmaceutics, toxicology, clinical and experimental human medicine, health policy and management, public health, occupational health, environmental health, drug dependence and abuse, psychiatry, forensic medicine, and biomedical engineering/instrumentation. The EMBASE database is indexed using the controlled vocabulary EMTREE as well as MeSH. The EMBASE database currently has more than 19 million indexed records from more than 7,000 peer-reviewed journals. Yearly, EMBASE adds more than 600,000 articles to the database, 80% of which have full abstracts. EMBASE requires a subscription to access its indexed articles.

The EMBASE database is available at **http://www.embase.com/**.

PsycINFO

PyscINFO is a bibliographic database that indexes publications from the late 1800s to present. This database of scholarly literature in psychology, behavioral sciences, and mental health contains more than 2 million citations, 7% of which are books and 11% dissertations. Professionals in psychology and related fields such as psychiatry, education, neuroscience, nursing, and other health-care disciplines can find relevant evidence in this database to answer specific clinical questions.

PsycINFO is available at **http://www.apa.org/psycinfo/**.

Searching the literature can be both rewarding and challenging, primarily because the volume of healthcare literature is huge. The MEDLINE database alone provides reference to more than 17 million citations; however, it cannot cover *all* worldwide healthcare journals. Searching multiple databases can increase the number of relevant articles in any search. The databases discussed here and others impose organization on the chaos of the journal literature. Each database offers coverage that is broad and sometimes overlapping. Knowing which databases to search first and for what information is imperative for a successful, efficient search.

> *Never give up, for that is just the place and time that the tide will turn.*
>
> **Harriet Beecher Stowe**

Example: How to Search PubMed

PubMed is a broad database produced and maintained by the National Center for Biotechnology Information (NCBI) at the NLM. In 2009, this bibliographic database contained more than 19 million citations to articles from more than 5,200 journals published worldwide (NLM, 2009). At its web debut in 1997, the oldest citations in PubMed were from 1966, but that has changed dramatically since 2003 when the first group of older citations (1.5 million citations to journal articles dated 1953–1965) was added to the database. As of 2009, the oldest citations date back to 1945. Since NLM has been indexing the medical literature since 1879, it is highly probable that the date of the oldest citations in PubMed will continue to slowly creep backward in time while current citations continue to be added.

PubMed is freely accessible on the Internet at http://www.pubmed.gov. However, NCBI has made it possible for libraries to link their electronic and print serial holdings to citations in the database, making it easy for their clientele to access full-text articles through the

PubMed database. Such access is via a specialized URL that facilitates this linking. Therefore, it is important for anyone affiliated with a library to check with that library to learn the most efficacious way to access PubMed.

PubMed covers several subject areas, including

- Biomedical sciences
- Nursing
- Dentistry
- Veterinary medicine
- Pharmacy
- Allied health
- Preclinical sciences
- Health policy
- Bioinformatics
- Health administration
- Standards and practice guidelines
- Health-related technology

PubMed also contains access to the information that makes up the foundation and midsection of the Haynes Evidence Pyramid: original research studies and reviews of evidence. PubMed provides free online access to the MEDLINE database, which resides within the PubMed database; however, not everything in PubMed is in the MEDLINE database.

Citations in PubMed that are in MEDLINE are indexed with MeSH terms. Citations that are in PubMed but not in MEDLINE are *not* indexed with MeSH terms. Every citation in PubMed contains a status tag at the end of the citation. The majority of citations start out as electronically submitted by publishers to the database and have a status tag that says "[PubMed—as supplied by publisher]." In general, these are the newest citations in PubMed. During the indexing process, the status tag will change to "[PubMed—in process]." When indexing is complete, the citation's status tag changes to "[PubMed—indexed for MEDLINE]." It is then that the citation becomes part of MEDLINE.

Approximately 8% of the PubMed database is not indexed with MeSH terms. This has implications for searchers. Since only the citations marked "[PubMed—indexed for MED-LINE]" are indexed with MeSH terms, *only* MEDLINE citations can be retrieved by using MeSH terms to search the database. Constructing a search in PubMed using only MeSH terms will exclude all the nonindexed citations in PubMed. In reality, this means that the newest citations in the database may not be retrieved. In healthcare, it is crucial to retrieve the most current information. Nonindexed citations in the PubMed database can only be retrieved by using keyword searching. Effective searching in PubMed requires the use of *both* MeSH terms and keywords. In PubMed, the NLM developed automatic term mapping, which takes the terms typed into the search box, maps them to any appropriate MeSH terms, and uses keywords in the search. It effectively searches *both* indexed and nonindexed citations (i.e., PubMed and MEDLINE).

For example, consider the following question: In children with otitis media (P), how does waiting (I) compared to immediate antibiotic treatment (C) affect time for infection resolution (O)? To answer this question, you could begin by entering *otitis* into the search box in PubMed as one search term and run the search. On the right-hand side of the search results page is a box that says "Search Details" and there you will see how PubMed used automatic term mapping to process the search, shown in Box 3.2.

In another example, consider the following PICOT question: How do women (P) diagnosed with breast cancer (I) perceive their own mortality (O)? As an initial step to answer this question, you could type *breast cancer* as one of the search terms in the search box in PubMed

Details of PubMed Automatic Term Mapping for *Otitis*

"otitis"[MeSH Terms] OR "otitis"[All Fields]

- ■ The "otitis"[MeSH Terms] portion of the search will retrieve relevant information from the MEDLINE database.
- ■ The "otitis"[All Fields] portion of the search will retrieve information from the nonindexed portion of the database.

and run the search. Click on "Details" to see how PubMed used automatic term mapping to process the search, as shown in Box 3.3.

Automatic term mapping makes sure that both the indexed and the nonindexed portions of the database are searched. In addition, a particular logic has been built into automatic term mapping to make it even more effective. There are three steps to this process:

1. **MeSH term:** Automatic term mapping first looks for a match between what is typed into the search box and a table of MeSH terms. If there is a match with a MeSH term, the MeSH term plus the keyword will be used to run the search.
2. **Journal title:** If there is no match with a MeSH term, what has been typed in the search box is next compared to a table of journal titles. If there is a match, the journal title is used to run the search.
3. **Author name:** If there is no match with either a MeSH term or a journal title, the words in the search box are then compared to a table of author names. If there is a match, that author name is used to run the search.

Automatic term mapping begins with the words entered into the search box as a single unit. If it cannot find a match in any of the three tables, it will drop the word that is furthest to the right in the search string, look at the remaining words, and run through the three steps of automatic term

Details of PubMed Automatic Term Mapping for *Breast Cancer*

"breast neoplasms"[MeSH Terms] OR ("breast"[All Fields] AND "neoplasms"[All Fields]) OR "breast neoplasms"[All Fields] OR ("breast"[All Fields] AND "cancer"[All Fields]) OR "breast cancer"[All Fields]

- ■ The "breast neoplasms"[MeSH Terms] portion of the search will retrieve relevant information from the indexed portion of the MEDLINE database, since breast cancer is not a MeSH term.
- ■ The ("breast"[All Fields] AND "neoplasms"[All Fields]) OR "breast neoplasms" [All Fields] OR ("breast"[All Fields] AND "cancer"[All Fields]) OR "breast cancer"[All Fields] portion of the search will retrieve information from the nonindexed portion of the database

mapping, looking for a match. If a match is found, then automatic term mapping will use the match (MeSH term, journal title, or author name) plus the keyword as part of the search and return to process the term that was previously dropped. An example of this process can be found in Box 3.4.

Once a search has been run, PubMed provides the option to further refine retrieval by using limits. Simply click on the Advanced Search link located just above the search box in PubMed. Limiting to certain dates of publication, certain languages, human or animal studies, and types of publications (e.g., clinical trial, meta-analysis) is also one of the options. Figure 3.2 shows some examples of the many limits that can be applied.

When reviewing search results in PubMed, it may appear that the citations are listed in chronological order with the most recent citation appearing first, but that is not the case. Search results appear in the order in which they were added to the database. This means that the citation that sits in the no. 1 spot is the citation that meets the search criteria and was most recently added

---

box 3.4

An Example of PubMed Automatic Term Mapping

PICOT question: In children with head lice (P), how does shampoo (I) compared to mayonnaise (C) affect lice demise (O)? As a *beginning* step, you type *head lice shampoo* into the search box in PubMed and run the search. This is what will appear in the "Details":

("pediculus"[MeSH Terms] OR "pediculus"[All Fields] OR ("head"[All Fields] AND "lice"[All Fields]) OR "head lice"[All Fields]) AND shampoo[All Fields]

And here is how Automatic Term Mapping did the processing:
Automatic Term Mapping will

1. Look at *head lice shampoo* as a single unit and it will find
   - No match to a MeSH term
   - No match to a journal title
   - No match to an author name
2. Drop *shampoo*, the word on the far right of the search string.
3. Process the remaining words *head lice* to find
   - Head lice maps to the MeSH term *pediculus*
   - Use "pediculus"[MeSH Terms] as the first part of the search
   - **OR** in "pediculus"[All Fields] OR ("head"[All Fields] AND "lice"[All Fields]) OR "head lice"[All Fields] to capture information from the non-indexed part of the database
4. Go back and look at the term that was previously dropped, *shampoo,* and find
   - No match to a MeSH term
   - No match to a journal title
   - No match to an author name
5. Look for the term *shampoo* in [All Fields]; **AND** it into the search

Final result:

("pediculus"[MeSH Terms] OR "pediculus"[All Fields] OR ("head"[All Fields] **AND** "lice"[All Fields]) OR "head lice"[All Fields]) **AND** shampoo[All Fields]

This method can facilitate busy clinicians finding relevant evidence quickly since PubMed automatically maps keywords to controlled vocabulary behind the scenes. Terms can be typed into the search box in PubMed and automatic term mapping can do its work to retrieve relevant studies.

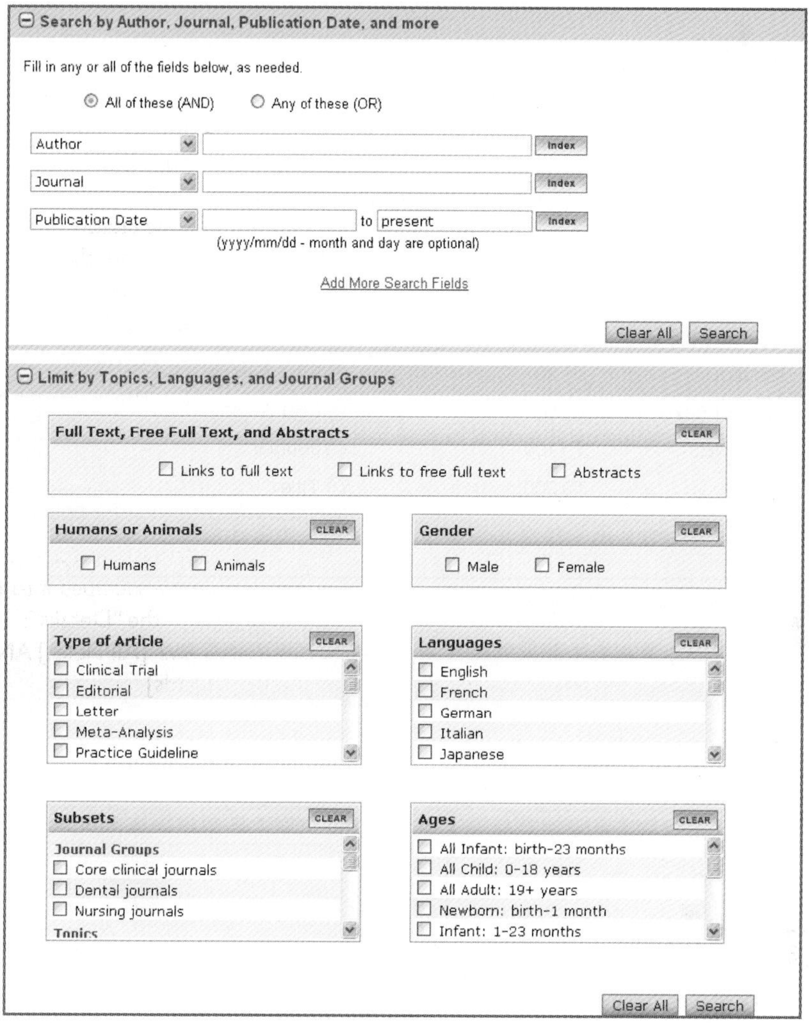

Source: *http://www.ncbi.nlm.nih.gov/pubmed/*

figure 3.2   Limits in PubMed

to the database. To find the most recently published article, use the "Sort by Pub Date" option that can be found in the Display Settings dropdown menu (Figure 3.3).

The search strategy carefully designed using PICOT as a guide is entered into the search box in PubMed and run. The appropriate limits have been applied. The results have been sorted as desired. The most useful of these are found in Figure 3.3. To further separate the citations of interest from others, PubMed provides the "Send To" options (e.g., e-mail, clipboard; Figure 3.4).

This has been a brief introduction to PubMed. Additional information on searching PubMed can be found from

- Tutorials provided by NLM and available via the "Tutorials" link on the blue sidebar of the PubMed homepage or directly from http://www.nlm.nih.gov/bsd/disted/pubmed.html

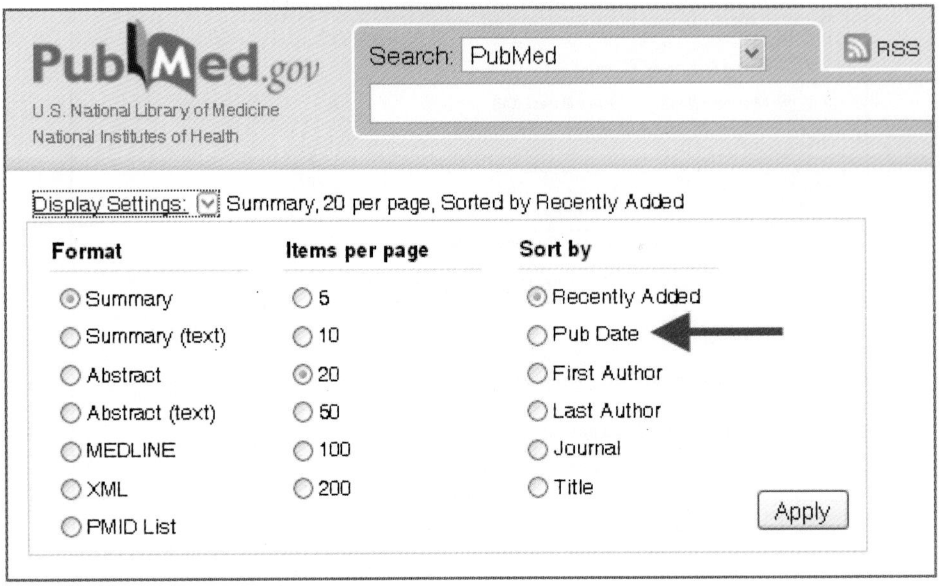

Source: *http://www.ncbi.nlm.nih.gov/pubmed/*

figure 3.3   Tip on sorting citations in PubMed

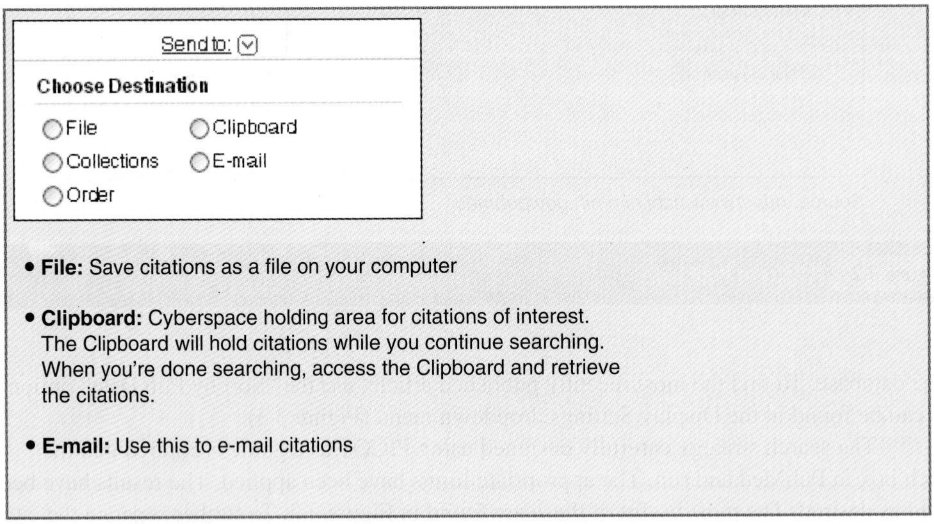

- **File:** Save citations as a file on your computer

- **Clipboard:** Cyberspace holding area for citations of interest.
  The Clipboard will hold citations while you continue searching.
  When you're done searching, access the Clipboard and retrieve
  the citations.

- **E-mail:** Use this to e-mail citations

Source: *http://www.ncbi.nlm.nih.gov/pubmed/*

figure 3.4   The most useful "Send To" options in PubMed: a mechanism to manage citations of interest

- The PubMed Help document, which is available online at http://www.ncbi.nlm.nih.gov/books/bv.fcgi?rid = helppubmed.chapter.pubmedhelp
- PubMed training manuals and resources, which are available online at http://www.nlm.nih.gov/pubs/web_based.html
- Healthcare librarians in your facility or in a partnering agency

Tool 4: Help Finding the Needle: Specialized Search Functions

Many database providers have designed specialized search functions to help busy healthcare practitioners find evidence as quickly as possible. This section discusses the specific search functions available in PubMed, Ovid, and EBSCO that can assist in finding relevant evidence quickly.

PubMed Clinical Queries and Health Services Research Queries

PubMed provides several options for busy clinicians: Clinical Queries and Health Services Research Queries. Both are freely available to all users and are easily accessed via the "Special Queries" link on the blue sidebar of the PubMed home page.

The Clinical Queries section provides two very useful search options: Clinical Study Category and Systematic Reviews. **Search by Clinical Study Category** provides a quick way to pull evidence from the PubMed database. When using this feature, search terms must be entered in the query box, the type of clinical question being asked must be indicated (etiology, diagnosis, therapy, prognosis, or clinical prediction guide), and the scope of the search must be indicated (broad or narrow), as shown in Figure 3.5.

When a search is run, PubMed applies specific search filters to limit retrieval to the desired evidence. This means that PubMed automatically adds terms to the search in order to hone in on just the evidence needed. A quick look at the "Details" box after running a search will show what terms were added. PubMed also provides a link to the filter table that shows the different search filters and the terms associated with them.

Find Systematic Reviews is located on the Search by Clinical Study Category page (Figure 3.6) and works somewhat like the Search by Clinical Study Category, in that PubMed automatically enhances the search by restricting retrieval to Systematic Reviews. Run a search using this feature and then check the "Details" box to see that PubMed automatically adds "AND

chapter 3

65

Search by Clinical Study Category

This search finds citations that correspond to a specific clinical study category. The search may be either broad and sensitive or narrow and specific. The search filters are based on the work of Haynes RB et al. See the filter table for details.

Search [   ] [Go]

Category	Scope
○ etiology	⦿ narrow, specific search
○ diagnosis	○ broad, sensitive search
⦿ therapy	
○ prognosis	
○ clinical prediction guides	

Source: *http://www.ncbi.nlm.nih.gov/pubmed/*

figure 3.5 Special search tips: Search by Clinical Study Category

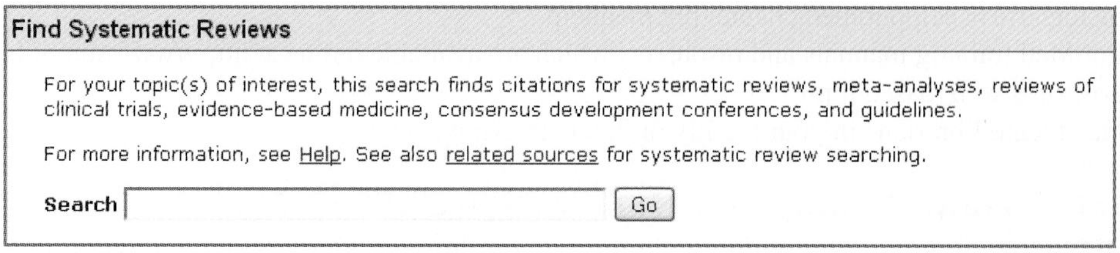

Find Systematic Reviews

For your topic(s) of interest, this search finds citations for systematic reviews, meta-analyses, reviews of clinical trials, evidence-based medicine, consensus development conferences, and guidelines.

For more information, see Help. See also related sources for systematic review searching.

Search [   ] Go

Source: *http://www.ncbi.nlm.nih.gov/pubmed/*

figure 3.6   Special search tips: Search by Find Systematic Reviews

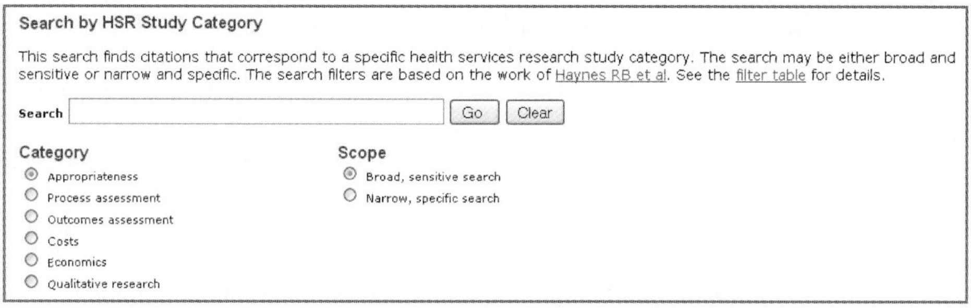

Search by HSR Study Category

This search finds citations that correspond to a specific health services research study category. The search may be either broad and sensitive or narrow and specific. The search filters are based on the work of Haynes RB et al. See the filter table for details.

Search [   ] Go   Clear

Category
○ Appropriateness
○ Process assessment
○ Outcomes assessment
○ Costs
○ Economics
○ Qualitative research

Scope
◉ Broad, sensitive search
○ Narrow, specific search

Source: *http://www.ncbi.nlm.nih.gov/pubmed/*

figure 3.7   Special search tips: Search by HSR Study Category

systematic[sb]" to the search. Systematic Reviews in the PubMed database are coded as such so that little addition to the search easily locates those citations.

Health Services Research (HSR) Queries have been developed by the National Information Center on Health Services Research and Health Care Technology (NICHSR). As noted before, this function is available via the "Topic Specific" link on the Advanced Search page or on the bottom of the PubMed home page, as displayed in Figure 3.7. These HSR Queries may be of special interest to nurses who are often looking for evidence that is cross disciplinary or qualitative in nature. These function very much like the Search by Clinical Study Category in that a search is enhanced using special search filters. However, the HSR Queries address different types and areas of research, including

- Appropriateness
- Process assessment
- Outcomes assessment
- Costs
- Economics
- Qualitative research

Once search terms have been entered, a category chosen, and the scope of the search selected, simply click "Go" and the search will be run with appropriate filters applied. Check the "Details" box to see what terms were added to the search. Links are provided to both the filters and the definitions of the categories.

More information about PubMed Queries can be found at
http://www.ncbi.nlm.nih.gov/entrez/query/static/clinical.shtml.

Clinical Queries in Ovid

Ovid Clinical Queries (OCQ) is an innovation designed to be used in the EBP searching process to limit retrieval to best evidence and what Ovid refers to as "clinically sound studies." To access OCQ, a searcher enters search statements in the main search box. A number of retrieved journal citations display as "Results" on Ovid's main search page within "Search History." To limit retrieved results, select "Additional Limits" to view Ovid's menu of limits. Find the Clinical Queries' dropdown menu and select the clinical query that best serves the purposes of your PICOT question.

The OCQ dropdown menu offers limits that retrieve clinically sound studies. Searchers select a query based on what the PICOT question is targeting (e.g., therapy, diagnosis, prognosis, reviews, clinical prediction guides, qualitative studies, etiology, costs, economics). Additionally, within each query, there are options to further refine the search. This refinement is described as restricting retrieval to clinically sound studies. The refinement options include "Sensitive" (i.e., most relevant articles but probably some less relevant ones), "Specific" (i.e., mostly relevant articles but probably omitting a few), and "Optimized" (i.e., the combination of terms that optimizes the trade-off between sensitivity and specificity). The use of these queries requires a level of searching expertise that can be perfected through practice.

Evidence-Based Practice "Limiter" in EBSCO

Journal databases typically offer options for limiting search results to allow quick retrieval of the most relevant and focused citations. "Limiters" that are commonly offered allow you to narrow your citation search by options such as publication type, age groups, gender, clinical queries, language, peer reviewed, and full text. EBSCO CINAHL provides an additional option within its "Special Interest" category of limits called "Evidence-Based Practice." Selecting the EBP limiter allows you to narrow your results to articles from EBP journals, about EBP, research articles (including systematic reviews, clinical trials, meta-analyses, and so forth), and commentaries on research studies.

A Final Tool: Time and Money

Producing, maintaining, and making databases available is financially costly and time-consuming. Although computer technology has revolutionized the print industry and made it easier to transfer documents and information any time around the world in seconds, the task of producing databases still relies on people to make decisions about what to include and how to index it. Databases produced by government agencies, such as MEDLINE, are produced with public money and are either very inexpensive or without cost to the searcher. The MEDLINE database is available to anyone in the world who has access to the Internet through PubMed. The data in MEDLINE can be leased at no cost by vendors and then placed on a variety of search engines to be accessed by healthcare providers, librarians, and others. Private organizations that produce biomedical databases, such as CINAHL or the CDSR, license their product, usually to libraries but also by subscription to individuals. If there is no in-house library, it is worth the time and effort to locate libraries in the area and find out their access policies for these databases.

For clinicians to practice based on evidence, access to databases is necessary. Cost for access to databases includes subscriptions, licensing fees for users of the database, hardware, software, Internet access, and library staff to facilitate its use (if available). Institutions must make decisions about what databases to subscribe to, and these decisions may be based on the resources available. Not all healthcare providers have libraries in their facilities. In these situations, clinicians or departments can consult with partnering librarians about securing access to databases that they consider critical to evidence-based care.

Although there is a cost associated with searching databases for relevant evidence, regular searching for answers to clinical questions has been shown to save money. Researchers conducted an outcome-based, prospective study to measure the economic impact of MEDLINE searches on the cost both to the patient and to the participating hospitals (Klein, Ross, Adams, et al., 1994). They found that searches conducted early (i.e., in the first half) in patients' hospital stays resulted in significantly lower cost to the patients and to the hospitals, as well as shorter lengths of stay.

Computerized retrieval of medical information is a fairly complex activity. It begins by considering the kind of information needed, creating an answerable question, planning and executing the search in an appropriate database, and analyzing the retrieved results. Clinicians must remember the costs of both searching and obtaining relevant evidence, as well as the costs of not searching for and applying relevant evidence.

> *Do not go where the path may lead, go instead where there is no path and leave a trail.*
> **Ralph Waldo Emerson**

How to Know You Have Found the Needle

Successfully searching for relevant evidence is as important as asking a well-built PICOT question. For clinicians to get the answers they need to provide the best care to their patients, they must determine the appropriate database, use controlled vocabulary, use limits, and meet specified criteria to navigate the database maze. In addition, clinicians must consider the cost of *not* searching for the best evidence. Commitment to finding valid, reliable evidence is the foundation for developing the skills that foster a sound strategy, which, in turn, helps in reducing frustration and time. Box 3.5 contains the steps of an efficient search.

The key to knowing whether the needle has been found is in further evaluation of the selected studies from a successfully executed search. This evaluation method is called *critical appraisal*, the next step in the EBP process. Some journals are dedicated to the preappraisal of existing literature. Most of these articles are not syntheses (e.g., systematic reviews), but rather critical appraisals of current single studies. For example, the journal *Evidence-Based Nursing* reviews 140 general medical, specialist, and nursing journals to identify research that would be clinically meaningful to nurses. Appraisals of 24 studies (both quantitative and qualitative) are published quarterly. The *ACP Journal Club* is another publication dedicated to preappraised literature. More than 100 journals are scanned for evidence relevant to clinicians. Specific criteria are applied to the appraised articles, and the appraisals are published bimonthly in the journal. These types of journals assist the clinician in reducing the time it takes from asking the question to applying valid evidence in decision making.

> *Do what you can, with what you have, where you are.*
> **Theodore Roosevelt**

> **box 3.5**
>
> ## Steps to an Efficient Search to Answer a Clinical Question
>
> ■ Begin with PICOT question–generated keywords.
> ■ Establish inclusion/exclusion criteria *before* searching so that the studies that answer the question are easily identifiable.
> ■ Use controlled vocabulary headings, when available.
> ■ Expand the search using the explode option, if not automatic.
> ■ Use available mechanisms to focus the search so that the topic of interest is the main point of the article.
> ■ Combine the searches generated from the PICOT keywords that mapped onto controlled vocabulary, if the database does not automatically do this for you.
> ■ Limit the *final* cohort of studies with meaningful limits, such as year, type of study, age, gender, and language.
> ■ Organize studies in a meaningful way using BMS.

Next Steps

There needs to be some discussion about when a thorough search to answer a compelling clinical question yields either too little valid evidence to support confident practice change (i.e., inconclusive evidence) or no evidence. In most cases, clinicians are not in positions to do full-scale, multisite clinical trials to determine the answer to a clinical question, and the science may not be at the point to support such an investigation. However, determining what is effective in the clinician's own practice by implementing the best evidence available can generate internal evidence. In addition, generating external evidence by conducting smaller scale studies, either individually or with a team of researchers, is an option. Chapters 4–8 address how to generate evidence to answer clinical questions. However, the starting place for addressing any clinical issue is to gather and evaluate the existing evidence using strategies and methods described in this chapter.

references

Dickersin, K., Manheimer, E., Wieland, S., Robinson, K. A., Lefebvre, C., Mcdonald, S., et al. (2002). Development of the Cochrane Collaboration's Central Register of Controlled Clinical Trials. *Evaluation & the Health Professions, 25*(1), 38–64.

Fineout-Overholt, E., Hofstetter, S., Shell, L., & Johnston, L. (2005). Teaching EBP: Getting to the gold: How to search for the best evidence. *Worldviews on Evidence-Based Nursing, 2*(4), 207–211.

Haynes, B. (2007). Of studies, syntheses, synopses, summaries, and systems: The "5S" evolution of information services for evidence-based healthcare decisions. *Evidence-Based Nursing, 10*(1), 6–7.

Klein, M. S., Ross, F. V., Adams, D. L., & Gilbert, C. M. (1994). Effect of online literature searching on

lengthy of stay and patient care costs. *Academic Medicine, 69*, 489–495.

MacColl, J. (2006). Google challenges for academic libraries. *Ariadne, 46.* Retrieved August 10, 2008, from http://www.ariadne.ac.uk/issue46/maccoll/intro.html

National Library of Medicine (2009). *Fact sheet: PubMed®: MEDLINE® retrieval on the world wide web.* Retrieved November 19, 2009, from http://www.nlm.nih.gov/pubs/factsheets/pubmed.html

Shultz, M. (2007). Comparing test searches in PubMed and Google Scholar. *Journal of the Medical Library Association, 95*, 442–445.

Singapore Ministry of Health (2008). *Management of asthma.* Singapore: Author. Retrieved June 30, 2009, from http://www.guidelines.gov

Stevens, K. R. (2001). Systematic reviews: The heart of evidence-based practice. *AACN Clinical Issues: Advanced Practice in Acute and Critical Care, 12*(4), 529–538.

Tee A., Koh, M. S., Gibson, P. G., Lasserson, T. J., Wilson, A., & Irving, L. B. (2007). Long-acting beta2-agonists versus theophylline for maintenance treatment of asthma. *Cochrane Database*

of Systematic Reviews, 3. Art. No.: CD001281. DOI:10.1002/14651858.CD001281.pub2.

Walters, E. H., Walters, J. A. E., & Gibson, P. G. (2002). Regular treatment with long acting beta agonists versus daily regular treatment with short acting beta agonists in adults and children with stable asthma. *Cochrane Database of Systematic Reviews, 3.* Art. No.: CD003901. DOI: 10.1002/14651858.CD003901.

Step Three: Critically Appraising Evidence

Critically Appraising Knowledge for Clinical Decision Making

Kathleen R. Stevens

> *Knowledge, the object of Knowledge, and the Knower are*
> *the three factors which motivate action*
> *Friedrich von Schiller*

Practitioners who want to know which actions to take in a given clinical situation are asking clinical questions. For example, in adult surgical patients, how do videotaped preparation sessions compared to one-to-one counseling affect preoperative anxiety? In home-bound older adults, how does a fall prevention program compared to no fall prevention program affect the number of fall-related injuries? In an attempt to select the most effective action, each clinical decision made or action taken is based on knowledge. This knowledge derives from a variety of sources, such as research, theories, experience, tradition, trial and error, authority, or logical reasoning.

In addition to the knowledge gained from their clinical experiences, many healthcare providers are compelled to create and use evidence from research to determine effective strategies for implementing system-based change to improve care processes and patient outcomes. Often, this array of knowledge and evidence is so diverse that clinicians are challenged to determine which action(s) will be the most effective in improving patient outcomes.

The critical appraisal of such knowledge for decision making is one of the most valuable skills that the clinician can possess in today's healthcare environment. Distinguishing the best evidence from unreliable evidence and unbiased evidence from biased evidence lies at the root of the impact that clinicians' actions will have in producing their intended outcomes.

Knowledge Sources

The healthcare professions have made major inroads in identifying, understanding, and developing an array of knowledge sources that inform clinical decisions and actions. We now know that

73

systematic inquiry in the form of research produces the most dependable knowledge upon which to base practice. In addition, practitioners' expertise and patients' choices and concerns must be taken into account in providing effective and efficient healthcare. Research, expertise, and client choices are all necessary evidence but each alone is insufficient for best practice.

In the past, most clinical actions were based solely on logic, tradition, or conclusions drawn from keen observation (i.e., expertise). Although effective practices sometimes have evolved from these knowledge sources, the resulting practice has been successful less often than hoped for in producing intended patient outcomes. Additionally, conclusions that are drawn solely from practitioner observations can be biased because such observations usually are not systematic. Similarly, non–evidence-based practices vary widely across caregivers and settings. The result is that, for a given health problem, a wide variety of clinical actions are taken without reliably producing the desired patient outcomes. That being said, the process for generating practice-based evidence (e.g., **quality improvement data**) has become increasingly rigorous and must be included in sources of knowledge for clinical decision making.

It is well recognized that systematic investigation (i.e., research) holds the promise of deepening our understanding of health phenomena, patients' responses to such phenomena, and the probable impact of clinical actions on resolving health problems. Following this realization, research evidence has become highly valued as the basis for clinical decisions.

The research utilization (RU) and evidenced-based practice (EBP) movements have escalated attention to the knowledge base of clinical care decisions and actions. In the mid-1970s, RU represented a rudimentary approach to using research as the prime knowledge source upon which to base practice. In the early stages of developing research-based practice, RU approaches promoted using results from a single study as the basis for practice.

Several problems arise with this approach, particularly when more than one study on the same topic has been reported. Multiple studies can be difficult to summarize and may produce conflicting findings, and large and small studies may hold different conclusions. To improve the process of moving research knowledge into practice, mechanisms to enhance the evidence produced through research have improved as well as more sophisticated and rigorous approaches for evaluating research have been developed. These approaches are largely embodied in the EBP paradigm.

What is important is to keep learning, to enjoy challenge, and to tolerate ambiguity. In the end there are no certain answers

Martina Horner

Weighing the Evidence

The EBP movement catapults the use of knowledge in clinical care to new heights of sophistication, rigor, and manageability. A key difference between the mandate to "apply research results in practice" and today's EBP paradigm is the acknowledgement of the relative weight and role of various knowledge sources as the bases for clinical decisions.

"Evidence" is now viewed and scrutinized from a clinical epidemiological perspective. This means that the practitioner takes into account the validity and reliability of the specific evidence when clinical recommendations are made (Stevens, Abrams, Brazier, et al., 2001). The EBP approach addresses variation in ways of managing similar health problems and the deficit between scientific evidence and clinical practice. In other words, it makes clear the evidence underlying effective practice (i.e., best practice) and specifies actions for addressing insufficient scientific evidence. In addition, EBP methods such as systematic reviews increase our ability to manage the ever-increasing volume of information produced in order to develop best practices.

Best practice is not new to healthcare providers. For example, mandatory continuing education for licensure in many states is regulatory testimony to the value of staying abreast of new developments. However, emphasis on best practice has shifted from keeping current through traditional continuing education to keeping current with the latest and best available evidence that has been critically appraised for quality and impact. Reliance on inexplicit or inferior knowledge sources (e.g., tradition or trial and error) is rapidly becoming unacceptable practice in today's quality-focused climate of healthcare. Rather, the focus is changing to replacing such practices with those based on a quality of knowledge that is said to include certainty and, therefore, predictability of outcome.

> *We don't receive wisdom; we must discover it for ourselves*
>
> *after a journey that no one can take for us or spare us.*
>
> *Marcel Proust*

Certainty and Knowledge Sources

The goal of EBP is to use the highest quality of knowledge in providing care to produce the greatest positive impact on patients' health status and healthcare outcomes. This entails using the following knowledge sources for care:

- Valid research evidence as the primary basis of clinical decisions
- Clinical expertise to best use research by filling in gaps and combining it with practice-based evidence to tailoring clinical actions for individual patients' contexts
- Patient choices and concerns for determining the acceptability of evidence-based care to the individual patient

In clinical decisions, the key criterion for quality of underlying knowledge is certainty. Certainty is the level of sureness that the clinical action will produce the intended or desired outcome. Because clinical actions are intended to assist patients in achieving a health goal, we can say with high certainty that what we do with patients is likely to move them toward that intended goal. To appraise certainty, the practitioner must first uncover the source of knowledge underlying the contemplated clinical action and then appraise the quality of that knowledge.

> *The intuitive mind is a sacred gift and the rational mind is*
>
> *a faithful servant*
>
> *Albert Einstein*

Rating Strength of the Scientific Evidence

Evidence-based practice experts have developed a number of taxonomies to rate varying levels of evidence as well as "strength of evidence" (i.e., the level of evidence plus the quality of evidence). These assessments of the strength of scientific evidence provide a mechanism to guide practitioners in evaluating research for its applicability to healthcare decision making. Most of these taxonomies or hierarchies of evidence are organized around various research designs. Many refer to the syntheses of randomized controlled trials (RCTs) as a research design of highest order, and most taxonomies include a full range of evidence, from systematic reviews of RCTs to expert opinions. However, simply leveling evidence is not sufficient for assessing quality or impact of evidence.

According to the Agency for Healthcare Research and Quality (AHRQ, 2002), grading the strength of a body of evidence should incorporate three domains: quality, quantity, and consistency. These are defined as follows:

- Quality: the extent to which a study's design, conduct, and analysis have minimized selection, measurement, and confounding biases (internal validity) (p. 19)
- Quantity: the number of studies that have evaluated the question, overall sample size across all studies, magnitude of the treatment effect, and strength from causality assessment, such as relative risk or odds ratio (p. 25)
- Consistency: whether investigations with both similar and different study designs report similar findings (requires numerous studies) (p. 25)

In an AHRQ study (2002) in which 109 resources for evaluating evidence were reviewed to determine if they met the above criteria, 7 of 19 systems for reviewing evidence were judged to include all three domains. Four of the seven indicated that systematic reviews of a body of literature represented the highest level of evidence, and five of the seven included expert opinion as evidence. Box 1.3 in Chapter 1 presents a sample system to determine the level of evidence for intervention questions. The level combined with the quality of the evidence that is assessed through critical appraisal reflects the strength of evidence, which determines the impact.

Appraising Knowledge Sources

Critical appraisal of evidence is a hallmark of EBP. Although critical appraisal is not new, it has become a core skill for those who plan to use evidence to support healthcare decisions (Stevens et al., 2001). The evolution of EBP from evidence-based medicine (EBM) has heavily influenced the current emphasis on critical appraisal of evidence. At times, EBP has been criticized as having a sole focus on appraisal of RCTs. However, EBM leaders did not intend for appraisal of RCTs to be the final point of critical appraisal. The *Cochrane Handbook for Systematic Reviews of Interventions* (Higgins & Green, 2008), the most highly developed methodological source for conducting systematic reviews, states that RCTs are the first focus of current systematic reviews; however, other evidence is reviewed when relevant, making explicit that the focus on RCTs is an interim situation (Box 4.1).

EBP methodologists are actively developing and using methods for systematically summarizing the evidence generated from a broad range of research approaches, including qualitative research. Evidence from all health science disciplines and a broad array of healthcare topics, including nursing services, behavioral research, and preventive health, are available to answer clinical questions (Stevens, 2002).

The meaning of *evidence* is fully appreciated within the context of best practice, which includes the following (Stevens, 2002):

- Research evidence
- Clinical knowledge gained via the individual practitioner's experience
- Patients' and practitioners' preferences
- Basic principles from logic and theory

> **box 4.1**
>
> ## Randomized Controlled Trials and Systematic Reviews
>
> Early on, the Cochrane Collaboration expressed through its colloquia and the *Cochrane Reviewers' Handbook*, an explanation of their focusing initial efforts on systematic reviews of RCTs: Such study designs are more likely to provide reliable information about 'what works best' in comparing alternative forms of healthcare (Kunz, Vist & Oxman, 2003). At the same time, the Collaboration highlighted the value of systematically reviewing other types of evidence, such as that generated by cohort studies, using the same principles that guide reviews of RCTs. "Although we focus mainly on systematic reviews of RCTs, we address issues specific to reviewing other types of evidence when this is relevant. Fuller guidance on such reviews is being developed." (Clarke & Oxman, 2003, no pagination)

An important task in EBP is to identify which knowledge is to be considered as evidence for clinical decisions. The knowledge generated from quantitative and qualitative research, clinical judgment, and patient preferences forms the crucial foundation for practice. Depending on The particular source of knowledge, varying appraisal approaches can be used. The chapters in Unit 2 describe appraisal approaches for the main types of evidence and knowledge to guide clinical practice:

- Evidence from quantitative research
- Evidence from qualitative research
- Clinical judgment
- Knowledge about patient concerns, choices, and values

The authors of the following chapters apply generic principles of evidence appraisal to the broad set of knowledge sources used in healthcare. The purpose of critically appraising these sources is to determine the certainty and applicability of knowledge, regardless of the source.

Understanding Internal Evidence and Tracking Outcomes of Evidence-Based Practice

Evidence is a collection of facts that grounds one's belief that something is true. While external evidence is generated from rigorous research and is typically conducted to be used across clinical settings, internal evidence is that generated by outcomes management, quality improvement, or EBP implementation projects. Unlike external evidence, the generation of internal evidence is intended to improve clinical practice and patient outcomes within the local setting where it is conducted (see Chapter 1).

A number of scientifically sound systems of quality indicators provide the foundational evidence for tracking quality of care over time. The value of such evidence is that impact of improvement in innovations can be traced, overall performance can be documented at regular intervals, and areas for improvement can be targeted for intervention. Several of these quality indicator systems offer opportunities for individual healthcare agencies to survey their own agencies and compare their results to national benchmarks. Three of these quality indicator systems that generate internal (i.e., practice-based) evidence are described in the following sections.

Agency for Healthcare Research and Quality
National Healthcare Quality Report

A notable addition to national quality indicators in the United States is the AHRQ *National Healthcare Quality Report*. The purpose of the report is to track the state of healthcare quality for the nation on an annual basis. In terms of the number of measures and number of dimensions of quality, it is the most extensive ongoing examination of quality of care ever undertaken in the United States or in any major industrialized country worldwide (AHRQ, 2007).

This evidence is used as a gauge of improvement across the nation. These reports measure trends in effectiveness of care, patient safety, timeliness of care, patient centeredness, and efficiency of care. Through these surveys, clinicians can locate indices on quality measures, such as the percentage of heart attack patients who received recommended care when they reached the hospital or the percentage of children who received recommended vaccinations.

The first report, in 2004, found that high-quality healthcare is not yet a universal reality and that opportunities for preventive care are often missed, particularly opportunities in the management of chronic diseases in the United States. Subsequent surveys have found both that healthcare quality is improving in small increments (about 1.5%–2.3% improvement) and that more gains than losses are being made. Core measures of patient safety improvements reflect gains of only 1% (AHRQ, 2007). This national data as well as others described in the following sections can be helpful to organizations making clinical decisions. Best practice would be when these data are combined with external evidence supporting action to improve outcomes.

National Quality Forum

Other internal evidence useful in quality improvement may be gleaned from a set of quality indicators that were developed by the National Quality Forum (NQF). The NQF is a not-for-profit membership organization created to develop and implement a national strategy for healthcare quality measurement and reporting. The NQF is regarded as a mechanism to bring about national change in the impact of healthcare quality on patient outcomes, workforce productivity, and healthcare costs. It seeks to promote a common approach to measuring healthcare quality and fostering system-wide capacity for quality improvement (NQF, 2008).

Recently, the NQF endorsed a set of 15 consensus-based nursing standards for inpatient care. Known as the "NQF-15," these measures represent processes and outcomes that are affected, provided, and/or influenced by nursing personnel. These factors and their structural proxies (e.g., skill mix and nurse staffing hours) are called *nursing-sensitive measures*. The NQF's endorsement of these measures marked a pivotal step in the efforts to increase the understanding of nurses' influence on inpatient hospital care and promote uniform metrics for use in internal quality improvement and public reporting activities. The NQF-15 includes measures that examine nursing contributions to hospital care from three perspectives: patient-centered outcome measures (e.g., prevalence of pressure ulcers and inpatient falls), nursing-centered intervention measures (e.g., smoking cessation counseling), and system-centered measures (e.g., voluntary turnover and nursing care hours per patient day; NQF, 2008).

National Database of Nursing Quality Indicators

In 1998, the National Database of Nursing Quality Indicators® (NDNQI®) was established by the American Nurses Association to facilitate continued indicator development and further our understanding of factors influencing the quality of nursing care. The NDNQI provides quarterly and annual reports on structure, process, and outcome indicators to evaluate nursing care at the unit level. The structure of nursing care is reflected by the supply, skill level, and education/ certification of nursing staff. Process indicators reflect nursing care aspects such as assessment, intervention, and registered nurse job satisfaction. Outcome indicators reflect patient outcomes that are nursing-sensitive and improve if there is greater quantity or quality of nursing care, such as pressure ulcers, falls, and IV infiltrations. There is some overlap between NQF-15 and NDNQI as a result of the adoption of some of the NDNQI indicators into the NQF set. The NDNQI repository of nursing-sensitive indicators is used in further quality improvement research.

Combining Internal and External Evidence

At the core of local quality improvement and generation of internal evidence is the planned effort to test a given change to determine its impact on the desired outcome. **The Plan-Do-Study-Act (PDSA) cycle** has become a widely adopted and effective approach to testing and learning about change on a small scale. In PDSA, a particular change is planned and implemented, results are observed (studied), and action is taken on what is learned. The PDSA cycle is considered a scientific method used in action-oriented learning (Speroff & O'Connor, 2004). The original approach is attributed to Deming and is based on repeated small trials, consideration of what has been learned, improvement, and retrial of the improvement. The PDSA cycle tests an idea by putting a planned change into effect on a temporary and small-trial basis and then learning from its impact. The approach suggests a conscious and rigorous testing of the new idea. Small-scale testing incrementally builds the knowledge about a change in a structured way. By learning from multiple small trials, the new idea can be advanced and implemented with a greater chance of success on a broad scale (Institute for Healthcare Improvement, 2010). Combining PDSA with external evidence that corroborates the practice change increases the effectiveness of the carefully evaluated outcome for sustained change.

Four stages of PDSA cycle include

PLAN: Plan the change and observation
DO: Try out the change on a small scale
STUDY: Analyze the data and determine what was learned
ACT: Refine the change, based on what was learned, and repeat the testing.

Finally, the action is based on the probability that the change will improve the outcome; however, without external evidence to support this improvement, the degree of certainty for any PDSA cannot be 100%.

Overviews of Following Three Chapters

About Quantitative Evidence

The nature of evidence produced through quantitative research varies according to the particular design utilized. Chapter 5, "Critically Appraising Quantitative Evidence for Clinical Decision Making," details the various types of quantitative research designs, including case studies, case–control studies, and cohort studies, as well as RCTs, and concludes with a discussion of systematic reviews. Distinctions among **narrative reviews**, **systematic reviews**, and **meta-analyses** are drawn. Helpful explanations about systematic reviews describe how data are combined across multiple research studies. Throughout, critical appraisal questions and hints are outlined.

About Qualitative Evidence

Given the original emphasis on RCTs (experimental research design) in EBP, some have inaccurately concluded that there is no role for qualitative evidence in EBP. Chapter 6, "Critically Appraising Qualitative Evidence for Clinical Decision Making," provides a compelling discussion on the ways in which qualitative research results answer clinical questions. The rich understanding of individual patients that emerges from qualitative research connects this evidence strongly to the elements of patient preferences and values—both important elements in implementation of EBP.

About Clinical Judgment and Patients' Contributions

Chapter 7, "Patient Concerns, Choices, and Clinical Judgment in Evidence-Based Practice," outlines the roles of two important aspects of clinical care decision making: patient choices and concerns and clinical judgment. The discussion emphasizes patient preferences not only as perceptions of self and what is best but also as what gives meaning to a person's life. The role of clinical judgment emerges as the practitioner weaves together a narrative understanding of the patient's condition, which includes social and emotional aspects and historical facts. Clinical judgment is presented as a historical clinical understanding of an individual patient—as well as of psychosocial and biological sciences—that is to be combined with the evidence from scientific inquiry. Three components of clinical judgment are discussed: experiential learning, clinical forethought, and clinical grasp. This discussion represents a significant contribution to EBP; it is one of only a few discussions elucidating the role of clinical expertise and patient values, choices, and concerns in clinical care.

Critical appraisal of evidence and knowledge used in clinical care is a requirement in professional practice. These chapters will provide a basis for understanding and applying the principles of evidence appraisal to improve healthcare.

> *Knowledge speaks, but wisdom listens*
>
> *Jimi Hendrix*

references

Agency for Healthcare Research and Quality. (2002). *Systems to rate the strength of scientific evidence*. (AHRQ Pub No. 02-E016). Rockville, MD: Author. Retrieved October 21, 2008, from http://www.ahrq.gov/clinic/tp/strengthtp.htm

Agency for Healthcare Research and Quality. (2007). *National healthcare quality report*. Retrieved November 21, 2008, from http://www.ahrq.gov/qual/qrdr07.htm

Higgins, J. P. T., & Green, S. (Eds.) (2008). *Cochrane handbook for systematic reviews of interventions* Version 5.0.1 [updated September 2008]. The Cochrane Collaboration. Available from www.cochrane-handbook.org

Institute for Healthcare Improvement (IHI). (2010). *Plan-Do-Study-Act (PDSA)*. http://www.ihi.org/IHI/Topics/ChronicConditions/AllConditions/HowToImprove/ChronicTestingChanges.htm. Accessed January 31, 2010.

Kunz, R., Vist, G., & Oxman, A. D. (2003). Randomisation to protect against selection bias in healthcare trials (Cochrane Methodology Review). In *Cochrane Library, 1*. Oxford: Update Software.

National Quality Forum. (2008). *About us*. Retrieved October 20, 2008, from http://www.qualityforum.org/about/

Speroff, T., & O'Connor, G. T. (2004). Study designs for PDSA quality improvement research. *Quality Management in Health Care, 13*(1), 17–32.

Stevens, K. R. (2002). The truth, the whole truth…about EBP and RCTs. *Journal of Nursing Administration, 32*(5), 232–233.

Stevens, A., Abrams, K., Brazier, J., Fitzpatrick, R., & Lilford, R. (Eds.) (2001). *The advanced handbook of methods in evidence based healthcare*. London: Sage Publications.

Critically Appraising Quantitative Evidence for Clinical Decision Making

Dónal P. O'Mathúna, Ellen Fineout-Overholt, and Linda Johnston

> *The reason most people never reach their goals is that*
> *they don't define them, or ever seriously consider them as*
> *believable or achievable. Winners can tell you where they*
> *are going, what they plan to do along the way, and who will*
> *be sharing the adventure with them.*
>
> *D e n i s   W a t l e y*

Clinicians read healthcare literature for various reasons. Some do it solely in an attempt to keep up to date with the rapid changes in care delivery. Others may have a specific clinical interest and want to be aware of the current research results in their field. With the advent of the evidence-based practice (EBP) healthcare movement, clinicians are increasingly reading literature to help them make informed decisions about how best to care for and communicate with patients to achieve the highest quality outcomes (Fineout-Overholt, Melnyk, & Schultz, 2005; Guyatt, Rennie, Meade, et al., 2008; Melnyk, Fineout-Overholt, Stone, et al., 2000).

However, few practitioners, if any, can keep up with all the research being published (Haynes, 1993). With current competing priorities in healthcare settings, it is challenging to determine which studies are best for a busy practitioner to use for clinical decision making. In addition, researchers may propose various, sometimes contradictory, conclusions when studying the same or similar issues, making it quite challenging to determine which studies can be relied on. Even the usefulness of preappraised studies such as systematic reviews are sometimes difficult to discern. As an evidence-based practitioner attempts to answer clinical questions, the quandary becomes how to critically appraise the studies found to answer the question and then determine the strength of the evidence (i.e., the confidence to act) from the gestalt of all the studies (i.e., more than a summary of the studies). In **critical appraisal**, the research is evaluated for its strengths, limitations, and value/worth to practice (i.e., how well it informs clinician decision making to impact outcomes). Clinicians cannot focus only on the flaws of the research, but must weigh the limitations with the strengths to determine a study's worth to practice. Appraising research is similar to how a jeweler appraises gemstones, weighing the characteristics of a diamond (e.g., clarity, color, carat, and cut) before declaring its worth (Fineout-Overholt, 2008).

First, it is important to determine the best match between the kind of question asked and the research methodology available to answer the question (see Chapter 2, Table 2.2). The notion of levels of evidence is described in Chapter 2, and those levels will be referred to here as critical appraisal of different quantitative research methodologies.

Hierarchy of Evidence

A **hierarchy of evidence** provides guidance about the types of studies, if well done, that are more likely to provide reliable answers to the clinical question. There are various hierarchies, or levels, of evidence; which hierarchy is appropriate depends upon the type of clinical question being asked. For intervention questions, the hierarchy of evidence ranks quantitative research designs (e.g., systematic review of **randomized controlled trials** [RCTs]) as providing higher levels of confidence that the studies will have reliable answers to these questions than designs with lower levels of confidence (e.g., descriptive studies).

An RCT is the best research design for providing information about cause-and-effect relationships. A systematic review of RCTs provides a compilation of what we know about a topic from multiple studies addressing the same research question, which ranks it higher in the hierarchy than a single RCT. Thus, the higher a methodology ranks in the hierarchy, the more likely the results of such methods are to represent objective findings and the more confidence clinicians can have that the intervention will produce the same health outcomes in similar patients for whom they care.

The hierarchy of evidence for intervention questions assists clinicians to know that a systematic review (i.e., a synthesis of these studies) of a large number of high-quality RCTs documenting that research studies' findings agree (i.e., have **homogeneity**) is the strongest and least-biased method to demonstrate confidence that the intervention will consistently bring about an outcome (Fineout-Overholt, O'Mathuna, & Kent, 2008; Guirguis-Blake, Calonge, Miller, et al., 2007; Guyatt et al., 2008; Phillips, Ball, Sackett, et al., 2001). Such systematic reviews have been called the "heart of EBP" (Stevens, 2001).

Critical Appraisal Principles for Quantitative Studies

It can be exasperating if a search of the literature to answer a clinical question reveals multiple studies with findings that do not agree. Also disappointing can be finding a study in which researchers found that a promising intervention is no more effective than a placebo; particularly when an earlier study reported that the same intervention was beneficial. Given the resulting confusion and uncertainty, it is reasonable for clinicians to wonder if external evidence (i.e., research) reveals consistent results.

Ideally, all studies would be designed, conducted, and reported perfectly, but that is not likely. Research inherently has flaws in how it is designed, conducted, or reported; however, study results should not be dismissed or ignored on this basis alone. Given that all research is not perfect, users of research must learn to carefully evaluate research reports to determine their worth to practice. This evaluation is called critical appraisal and hinges on three overarching questions to consider when appraising any study (O'Rourke & Booth, 2000):

1. Are the results of the study valid? (Validity)
2. What are the results? (Reliability)
3. Will the results help me in caring for my patients? (Applicability)

The critical appraisal process provides clinicians with the means to interpret the quality of studies and determine the applicability of the synthesis of multiple studies' results to their particular patients (Crombie, 1996; O'Rourke & Booth, 2000).

When appraising quantitative studies, it is important to recognize the factors of validity and reliability that could influence the study findings. Study validity and reliability are determined by the quality of the study methodology. In addition, clinicians must discern how far from the true result the reported result may be (i.e., compare the study result to the outcome that can be replicated in practice). Since all studies have some flaws, the process of critical appraisal should assist the clinician in deciding whether a study is flawed to the point that it should be discounted as a source of evidence (i.e., the results cannot be used in practice). Interpretation of results requires consideration of the **clinical significance** of the study findings (i.e., the impact of the findings clinically), as well as the **statistical significance** of the results (i.e., the results were not found by chance).

Are the Study Results Valid? (Validity)

The validity of a study refers to whether the results of the study were obtained via sound scientific methods. Bias and/or confounding variables may compromise the validity of the findings (Goodacre, 2008a). The less influence these factors have on a study, the more likely the results will be valid. Therefore, it is important to determine whether the study was conducted properly before being swayed by the results. Validity must be ascertained before the clinician can make an informed assessment of the size and precision of the effect(s) reported.

Bias

Bias is anything that distorts study findings in a systematic way and arises from the study methodology (Polit & Beck, 2007). Bias can be introduced at any point in a study. When critically appraising research, the clinician needs to be aware of possible sources of bias, which may vary with the study design. Every study requires careful examination regarding the different factors that influence the extent of potential bias in a study.

An example of bias could be how participants are selected for inclusion into the different groups in an intervention study. This selection may occur in a way that inappropriately influences who ends up in the experimental group or comparison group. This is called selection bias and is reduced when researchers **randomly assign** participants to experimental and comparison groups. This is the "randomized" portion of the RCT, the classic experimental study. In an RCT, all other variables should be the same in each group (i.e., the groups should be homogenous). These studies are prospective and the participants are monitored over time. Differences in the outcomes should be attributable to the different interventions given to each group. A controlled trial in which researchers do not properly randomly assign participants to study groups will have a different appraisal, and likely a different outcome, when compared with one using the best randomization methods, as there is inherently more bias in poorly randomized studies. Other study designs (e.g., quasi experimental, cohort, case studies) do not randomly allocate participants and risk introduction of selection bias into the research.

Figure 5.1 shows how participants could be selected for an experimental study. For example, researchers want to study the effect of 30 minutes of daily exercise in the elderly who

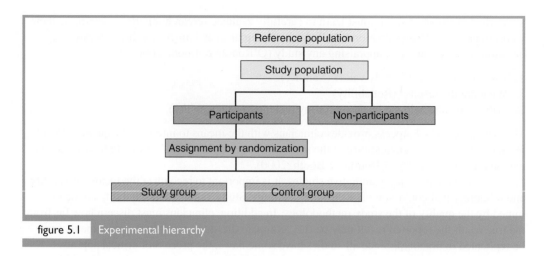

figure 5.1   Experimental hierarchy

are over 80 years of age. The ideal, but usually infeasible, sample to include in a study is the reference population; that is, those people in the past, present, and future to whom the study results can be generalized. In this case, the reference population would be all elders over 80 years of age. Given the difficulty in obtaining the reference population, researchers typically use a study population that they assume will be representative of the reference population (e.g., a random sample of elders over 80 years of age who live in or within a 25 mile radius of a metropolitan city in a rural state).

However, clinicians need to keep in mind that bias could be introduced at each point where a subgroup is selected. For example, the study population will include some people willing to participate and others who refuse to participate in the study. If potential participants volunteer to be involved in the study (i.e., a convenience sample), the volunteers may have some characteristic that could influence the final results in some way. For example, in a study of the impact of exercise on the health of elders over 80 years of age, those elders who play games at a local senior center and volunteer for the study may have a more positive attitude toward exercise, which may impact the study outcomes. This type of effect is particularly relevant in studies where people's attitudes or beliefs are being explored because these may be the very characteristics that influence their decision to participate or not (Polit & Beck, 2007). Evidence users must be aware that despite the best efforts of the investigators to select a sample that is representative of the reference population, there may be significant differences between the study sample and the general population.

Another type of bias in RCTs is introduced by participants or researchers knowing who is receiving which intervention. To minimize this bias, participants and those evaluating outcomes of the study are kept blind or "in the dark" about who receives each intervention (i.e., the experimental and the comparison). These studies are called double-blind studies.

Another element known to introduce bias is a well-intentioned person acting as a gatekeeper, particularly in studies involving vulnerable populations. For example, researchers conducting a study with patients receiving palliative care may have difficulty recruiting sufficient number of people into the study because the patients' caregivers may consider it too burdensome to ask the patients to participate in research at a difficult time in their lives. This introduces bias into the study and may ultimately exclude the very people who could benefit from the research.

Another concern that may influence study results is measurement bias (i.e., how the data are measured). For example, *systematic error* can occur through using an incorrectly calibrated device that consistently gives higher or lower measurements than the actual measurement.

Another example of measurement bias is that data collectors may deviate from established objective data collection protocols or their individual personality traits may affect the eliciting of information from patients in studies involving interviews or surveys. Longitudinal studies, in general, have challenges with measurement bias.

One type of longitudinal, retrospective study that compares two groups is a **case–control** study, in which researchers select a group of people with an outcome of interest, the cases (e.g., cases of infection), and another group of people without that outcome, the control cases (e.g., no infection). Both groups are surveyed in an attempt to find the key differences between the groups that may suggest why one group had the outcome (i.e., infection) and the other did not. Participants respond to surveys about what they did in the past. This is referred to as recall. Studies that rely on patients remembering data are subject to "recall bias" (Callas & Delwiche, 2008). Recall may be affected by a number of factors. For example, asking patients with brain tumors about their past use of cellular phones might generate highly accurate or falsely inflated responses because those patients seek an explanation for their disease, compared with people who do not have tumors and whose recall of phone use may be less accurate in the absence of disease (Muscat, Malkin, Thompson, et al., 2000). Bias can be a challenge with case–control studies in that people may not remember things correctly. In addition, "information bias" can lead researchers to record different information from interviews or patient records if they know which participants are cases and which are controls (Callas & Delwiche).

Another longitudinal study that has to battle information bias is a **cohort study**. This type of study focuses prospectively on one group of people who have been exposed to a condition and another group that has not. For example, people living in one town might be put into one cohort and those in another town into a second cohort—the town they lived in would be the selection criterion. All of the participants would be followed over a number of years to identify differences between the two cohorts that might be associated with differences between the towns and specific outcomes (e.g., environmental factors and breast cancer).

Cohort studies also can be conducted by selecting one group of people and monitoring them over years. The comparison cohorts are selected based on the data gathered during the study. For example, the largest cohort study of women's health is the Nurses' Health Study. More than 121,000 nurses were enrolled in the study in 1976 and were mailed questionnaires every 2 years. Several correlations have been identified through this study. For example, women who sleep 7 hours per night have the lowest risk of death, with those sleeping more or fewer hours having higher risk of mortality (Patel, Ayas, Malhotra, et al., 2004). The cohorts were selected from within the Nurses' Health Study based on answers to a question about sleep duration (e.g., 7 hours a night, more than 7 hours a night, and less than 7 hours per night) and followed over 14 years.

In longitudinal studies, loss of participants to follow-up also may contribute to measurement bias. Not reporting losses to follow-up may mask the real reason for observed differences between the experimental intervention and control groups of patients. Possible reasons for loss of participants (i.e., study attrition) could include unforeseen side effects of the intervention or burdensome data collection procedures. Such losses can lead to noncomparable groups and misleading results. Chapter 17 contains more information on these quantitative designs and reducing bias.

Contamination is another form of measurement bias. This occurs when participants originally allocated to a particular group or arm of a study are exposed to the alternative group's intervention (i.e., the comparison intervention). For example, in a study of asthmatic school children that compares retention of asthma management information given to the children in written form and by video, results may be compromised if those in the video group lend their videos to those in the written information group. Another example would be if patients in a placebo-controlled trial somehow become aware that they have been assigned to the placebo group and, believing they should be in the intervention arm of the study, find some way to access the intervention.

In critical appraisal of a research study, specific questions should be asked about the report to identify whether the study was well designed and conducted or whether risks of bias were introduced at different points. Appendix D contains rapid critical appraisal checklists for quantitative study designs as well as qualitative studies that provide standardized criteria to be applied to each study methodology to determine if it is a valid study.

Confounded Study Results

When interpreting results presented in quantitative research papers, clinicians should always consider that there may be multiple explanations for an intervention effect reported in a study. A study's results may be confounded when a relationship between two variables is actually due to a third, either known or unknown variable (i.e., a confounding variable). The confounding variable relates to both the intervention (i.e., the exposure) and the outcome, but is not directly a part of the causal pathway (i.e., the relationship) between the two. Confounding variables are often encountered in studies about lifestyle and health. For example, clinicians should consider the possibility of confounding variables when researchers reported a link between the incidence of headaches among hospital workers who fasted for Ramadan and their caffeine intake (Awada & al Jumah, 1999). Headache sufferers consumed significantly more caffeine in beverages such as tea and coffee compared to those who did not get headaches. The reduction in caffeine consumption during fasting for Ramadan led to caffeine withdrawal, which the researchers stated was the most likely cause of the headaches. Intuitively, this may sound likely; however, if the study population includes people engaged in shift work, which is very likely since the participants were hospital staff, the irregular working hours or a combination of variables may have facilitated the headaches, not solely caffeine withdrawal. Figure 5.2 demonstrates how confounding variables can lead to confusing results. The shift work is related to both the exposure (i.e., reduced high caffeine intake and subsequent withdrawal) and the outcomes (i.e., headaches). However, it is not directly causal (i.e., irregular working hours do not cause headaches).

When critically appraising a study, clinicians must evaluate whether investigators considered the possibility of confounding variables in the original study design, as well as in

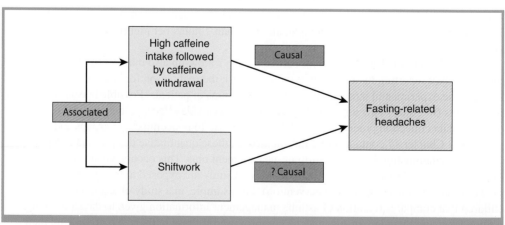

figure 5.2   Model of possible confounding variables in a study examining the association between caffeine intake and symptoms

the analysis and interpretation of their results. Minimizing the possible impact of confounding variables on a study's results is best addressed by a research design that utilizes a randomization process to assign participants to each study group. In this way, confounding variables, either known or unknown, are expected to equally influence the outcomes of the different groups in the study.

Confounding variables may still influence a study's results despite investigators' best efforts. Unplanned events occurring at the same time as the study may have an impact on the observed outcomes. This is often referred to as history. For example, a study is launched to determine the effects of an educational program regarding infant nutrition (i.e., the experimental intervention group). The control group receives the usual information on infant growth and development provided at maternal and child health visits. Unknown to the researchers, the regional health department simultaneously begins a widespread media campaign to promote child health. This confounding historical event could impact the results and thereby, make it difficult to directly attribute any observed outcomes solely to the experimental intervention (i.e., information on infant nutrition). Finally, inclusion and exclusion criteria should be used to select participants and should be prespecified (i.e., a priori). Often these criteria can be controls for possible confounding variables (see Appendix D).

What Are the Results? (Reliability)

Quantitative studies use statistics to report their findings. Having evaluated the validity of a study's findings, the numerical study results need to be examined. Clinicians planning to use the results of quantitative studies need a general understanding of how to interpret the numerical results. The main concerns are how large the reported intervention effect was and how precisely that effect was estimated. Together, these determine the reliability of study findings. The concern here is not simply to understand the study results, but to evaluate how likely it is that the intervention will have the same result when clinicians use it in their practices. In critical appraisal, this is where the numerical data reported in the results section of a study are examined.

> *Nothing in the world can take the place of Persistence...*
> *Persistence and determination alone are omnipotent. The*
> *slogan 'Press On' has solved and always will solve the*
> *problems of the human race.*
> *Calvin Coolidge*

Reporting the Study Results: Do the Numbers Add Up?

In all studies, the total number of participants approached and the number consenting to participate in the study should be reported. In addition, in RCTs, the *total number* in each group or arm of a study (e.g., intervention or comparison group) should be reported, as these values will usually form the denominator in subsequent critical analyses of study findings (see Table 5.1).

In the results section and subsequent analyses, the numbers of participants with various outcomes of interest are reported as n. The clinician should evaluate whether the sum of all n values equals the original N (i.e., total sample) reported (see Table 5.1). This is particularly important, as a discrepancy represents loss of subjects to follow-up (i.e., attrition). Participants may withdraw from a study for various reasons, some of which are very relevant to the validity of the study results. Regardless of the reasons, researchers should account for any difference in the

table 5.1 **Measures of effect**

Exposure to Intervention	Expected Outcome Occurred		
	Yes	No	Total
Yes	a	b	a + b
No	c	d	c + d
Total	a + c	b + d	a + b + c + d

Note: *a + b is the total number of study participants in the intervention arm of the study.*

a is the number of participants exposed to the intervention who had the expected outcome.

b is the number of participants exposed to the intervention who did not have the expected outcome.

c + d is the total number of study participants in the unexposed or comparison arm of the study.

c is the number of participants not exposed to the intervention who nevertheless had the expected outcome.

d is the number of participants not exposed to the intervention and who had the expected outcome.

a + c is the total number of study participants, both exposed and not exposed to the intervention, who had the expected outcome occur.

b + d is the total number of study participants in the control and intervention groups who did not have the expected outcome occur.

a + b + c + d is the total number of study participants, N.

final number of participants in each group compared to the number of people who commenced the study. For example, a study reporting the effectiveness of depression management that uses frequent individual appointments with a professional may report fewer participants at the end of the study than were originally enrolled. The high attrition rate may have occurred because participants found it difficult to attend the frequent appointments. A well-conducted study would attempt to discover participants' reasons for withdrawing. These factors are important to consider because sometimes even if interventions were found to be effective in the study, they may be impractical to implement in a clinical setting.

Magnitude of the Effect

Quantitative studies are frequently conducted to find out if there is an important and identifiable difference between two groups. Some examples could be: (a) why one group is diagnosed with breast cancer and not the other group, (b) the quality of life for older people living at home compared to those living in nursing homes, or (c) outcomes of taking drug A compared to taking drug B. A study will pick one or more outcomes to determine whether there are important differences between the groups. The magnitude of effect refers to the degree of the difference or lack of difference between the various groups (i.e., experimental and control) in the study. The effect is the rate of occurrence in each of the groups for the outcome of interest. It is helpful when trying to determine the magnitude of effect to use what is called a two-by-two table, such as Table 5.2, in which are listed in one column those who had the outcome and in the other column are listed those without the outcome. The exposure to the intervention/condition and the comparison for those with the outcome and those without the outcome are featured across the rows.

Statistical tests, conducted by researchers to determine if the effects differ significantly between groups, often are included in such tables. While it is important for clinicians to understand what these statistics mean, they do not need to carry statistical formulae around in their heads to critically appraise the literature. Some knowledge of how to interpret commonly used statistical tests and when they should be used is adequate for the appraisal process. However, keeping a health sciences statistics book nearby or using the Internet to refresh one's memory can be helpful when evaluating a study.

table 5.2 Two by two table of smokers and nonsmokers incidence of ukillmeousus*

Condition	Outcome: Incidence of Ukillmeousus		
	Yes	No	Total
Smokers	3	97	100
Nonsmokers	2	98	100

*Ukillmeousus is a hypothetical disease

Table 5.2 presents data to assist in understanding how to use this kind of table. The outcome chosen here is dichotomous, meaning that the outcome is either present or absent (e.g., Do you smoke? Either a "yes" or "no" answer is required). Data also can be continuous across a range of values (e.g., 1 to 10). Examples of continuous data include age, blood pressure, or pain levels. Dichotomous and continuous data are analyzed using different statistical tests. The effect measured in the hypothetical study was whether smokers or nonsmokers developed ukillmeousus or not (i.e., dichotomous data, with an outcome of either "yes" or "no").

Another approach to evaluating the response of a population to a particular disease is reporting the risk of developing a disease (e.g., how likely it is that a smoker will develop the disease at some point). Other terms used to describe outcomes are *incidence* (i.e., how often the outcome occurs or the number of newly diagnosed cases during a specific time period) or *prevalence* (i.e., the total number of people at risk for the outcome or total number of cases of a disease in a given population in a given time frame). For the purposes of this discussion about understanding the magnitude of a treatment effect, the focus will be on risk. People are often concerned about reducing the risk of a perceived bad outcome (e.g., developing colon cancer), usually through choosing the treatment, screening, or lifestyle change that best minimizes the risk of the outcome occurrence.

Strength of Association

In the context of the example in Table 5.2, the risk is the probability that a smoker who is currently free from ukillmeousus will develop the disease at some point. This risk can be expressed in a few different ways. The absolute risk of smokers developing ukillmeousus, often referred to as the probability (i.e., risk) of the outcome in the exposed group (Re), is 3 out of 100, (i.e., 0.03, 1 in 33, or 3%). This is derived by dividing the number of those who had the outcome by the total number of those who could have had the outcome (i.e., 3/100). The risk for nonsmokers developing ukillmeousus (i.e., the probability of the outcome occurring in the unexposed group [Ru]) is 2 out of 100. This risk also can be expressed as a proportion, 1 in 50 (0.02), or percentage, 2%. Table 5.3 contains the general formulas for these and other statistics. Using Table 5.1 with Table 5.3 will help in applying the formulas to studies' results or clinical situations.

When comparing groups, whether testing an intervention or examining the impact of a lifestyle factor or policy, people are often concerned about risk. Some examples of common concerns about risk include (a) colon screening to reduce the risk of colon cancer deaths; (b) high-fiber, low-fat diets to reduce the risk of cardiovascular disease; (c) high school coping intervention programs to reduce the risk of suicide in adolescents; and (d) lipid medications reducing the risk of a cardiovascular disease. Often, we are interested in the difference in risks of an outcome between a group that has a particular intervention and one that does not. When groups differ in their risks for an outcome, this can be expressed in a number of different ways. One way to report this is the absolute difference in risks between the groups. The **absolute risk reduction** (ARR) for an undesirable outcome is when the risk is less for the experimental/condition group

table 5.3 **Statistics to assist in interpreting findings in healthcare research**

Statistic	Formula	Ukillmeousus Example
Absolute risk (AR)	Risk in exposed (Re) = a/(a + b) Risk in *unexposed* (Ru) = c/(c + d)	3/(3 + 97) = 3/100 = 0.03 2/(2 + 98) = 2/100 = 0.02
Absolute risk reduction (ARR)	Ru – Re = ARR	Not appropriate
Absolute risk increase (ARI)	Re – Ru = ARI	0.03 – 0.02 = 0.01 0.01 × 100 = 1%
Relative risk (RR)	RR = Re/Ru	0.03/0.02 = 1.5
Relative risk reduction (RRR)*	RRR = {|Re – Ru|/Ru} × 100%	{|0.03–0.02|/0.02} = 0.01/0.02 = 0.5 × 100 = 50%
Odds ratio (OR)	Odds of exposed = a/b	Odds of smokers 3/97 = 0.03
	Odds of unexposed = c/d	Odds of nonsmokers 2/98 = 0.02
	OR = (a/b)/(c/d)	OR 0.03/0.02 = 1.5

Note: |Re – Ru| means only positive values are used, which gives RRR the same value whether ARR or ARI is used.

than the control/comparison group. The **absolute risk increase** (ARI) for an undesirable outcome is when the risk is more for the experimental/condition group than the control/comparison group. These values can also be referred to as the risk difference (RD).

In the previous example, the risk for the undesirable outcome of ukillmeousus is higher in the smoker (i.e., condition) group than in the comparison group (i.e., nonsmokers). Therefore, the ARI is calculated as 3% (risk [or probability] of ukillmeousus for smokers) −2% (risk for ukillmeousus for nonsmokers) = 1% (or, in proportions, 0.03 − 0.02 = 0.01). To put it in a sentence, the absolute risk for developing ukillmeousus for smokers is 1% higher than the risk for nonsmokers.

Risks between two groups also can be compared using what is called **relative risk** or risk ratio (RR). This indicates the likelihood (i.e., risk) that the outcome would occur in one group compared to the other. The group with the particular condition or intervention of interest is usually the focus of the study. In the example, the condition is smoking. Relative risk is calculated by dividing the two absolute risk values (condition of interest/intervention group divided by control group). In the example, the RR is AR for smokers/AR for nonsmokers: 0.03/0.02 = 1.5. To use it in a sentence, smokers are 1.5 times more likely to develop ukillmeousus compared to nonsmokers. Relative risk is frequently used in prospective studies, such as RCTs and cohort studies. If the outcome is something we want, an RR greater than 1 means the treatment (or condition) is better than control. If the outcome is something we do not want (ukillmeousus), an RR greater than 1 means the treatment (or condition) is worse than control. In the example, the outcome of ukillmeousus is not desirable and the RR is greater than 1, therefore the condition of a smoker is worse than the control condition of a nonsmoker.

A related way to express this term is the **relative risk reduction** (RRR). This expresses the proportion of the risk in the intervention/condition group compared to the proportion of risk in the control group. It can be calculated as a percentage by taking the risk of the condition (3%) minus the risk of the control (2%), dividing the result by the risk for the control, and then multiplying by 100; ([0.03 − 0.02]/0.02) × 100 = 50%. To state this in a sentence, being a nonsmoker decreases the likelihood (i.e., RRR) of developing ukillmeousus by 50% relative to being a smoker.

Notice here the importance of understanding what these terms mean. An RRR of 50% sounds more impressive than a 1% RD (i.e., ARR). Yet both of these terms have been derived from the same data. Other factors must be taken into account. For example, a 1% ARR may not be very significant if the disease is relatively mild and short-lived. However, it may be very significant if the disease is frequently fatal. If the differences between the groups are due to treatment options, the nature and incidence of adverse effects will also need to be taken into account (see Example One later in this chapter).

When trying to predict outcomes, "odds" terminology arises frequently. In quantitative studies, calculating the odds of an outcome provides another way of estimating the strength of association between an intervention and an outcome. The odds of the outcome occurring in a particular group is calculated by dividing the number of those exposed to the condition or treatment who had the outcome by the number of people without the outcome, not the total number of people in the study (see Table 5.3). In the example comparing smokers and nonsmokers, the odds of a smoker getting the disease are 3/97 = 0.031. The odds of a nonsmoker getting ukillmeousus are 2/98 = 0.020. The **odds ratio** (OR) is the odds of the smokers (0.031) divided by the odds of the nonsmokers (0.020) = 1.5. To use it in a sentence, smokers have 1.5 times greater odds of developing ukillmeousus than nonsmokers. As seen in this example, the OR and RR can be very similar in value. This happens when the number of events of interest (i.e., how many developed the observed outcome) is low; as the event rate increases, the values can diverge.

Interpreting results that are presented as an ARR, ARI, RR, or OR sometimes can be difficult, not only for the clinician but also for the consumer—an essential contributor to the healthcare decision-making process. A more meaningful way to present the study results is through the calculation of the **number needed to treat** (NNT). Number needed to treat (NNT) is a value that can permit all stakeholders in the clinical decision to better understand the likelihood of developing the outcome if a patient has a given intervention or condition. The NNT represents the number of people who would need to receive the therapy or intervention to prevent one bad outcome or cause one additional good outcome. If the NNT for a therapy was 15, this would mean 15 patients would need to receive this therapy before you could expect one additional person to benefit. Another way of putting this is that a person's chance of benefiting from the therapy is 1 in 15. The NNT is calculated by taking the inverse of the ARR (i.e., 1/ARR). For example, if smoking cessation counseling is the treatment, the outcome is smoking cessation, and the ARR for smoking cessation is 0.1, the NNT to see one additional person quit smoking using this treatment is 1/0.1 or 10. Ten people would need to receive the counseling to help one more person stop smoking.

A related parameter to NNT is the **number needed to harm** (NNH). This is the number of people who would need to receive an intervention before one additional person would be harmed (i.e., have a bad outcome). It is calculated as the inverse of the ARI (i.e., 1/ARI). In the ukillmeousus example, the ARI for the condition of smoking versus nonsmoking was 0.01; the NNH is 1/0.01 = 100. For every 100 persons who continue to smoke, there will be one case of ukillmeousus. While one case of ukillmeousus in 100 smokers may seem small, if we assume that this disease is fatal, clinicians may choose to put more effort and resources toward helping people stop smoking. The interpretation of a statistic must be made in the context of the severity of the outcome (e.g., ukillmeousus) and the cost and feasibility of the removal of the condition (e.g., smoking) or the delivery of the intervention (e.g., smoking cessation counseling).

Interpreting the Results of a Study: Example One. You are a clinician who is working with patients who want to quit smoking. They have friends who have managed to quit by using nicotine chewing gum and wonder whether this also might work for them. You find a clinical trial that measured the effectiveness of nicotine chewing gum versus a placebo (Table 5.4). Among

table 5.4 The effectiveness of nicotine chewing gum

	Outcome		
Exposure	Quit, *n* (%)	Did Not Quit, *n* (%)	Total
Nicotine gum	1,149 (18.2)	5,179 (81.8)	6,328
Placebo	893 (10.7)	7,487 (89.3)	8,380
Total	2,042	12,666	

those using nicotine chewing gum, 18.2% quit smoking (i.e., risk of the outcome in the exposed group [Re]). At the same time, some participants in the control group also gave up smoking (10.7%; i.e., risk of the outcome in the unexposed group [Ru]). The RD for the outcome between these groups (i.e., these two percentages subtracted from one another) is 7.5% (i.e., the ARR is 0.075). The NNT is the inverse of the ARR, or 13.3. In other words, 13 smokers need to use the gum for one additional person to give up smoking. Nicotine gum is a relatively inexpensive and easy-to-use treatment, with few side effects. Given the costs of smoking, treating 13 smokers to help 1 stop smoking is reasonable.

The size of the NNT influences decision making about whether or not the treatment should be used; however, it is not the sole decision-making factor. Other factors will influence the decision-making process and should be taken into account, including patient preferences. For example, some smokers who are determined to quit may not view a treatment with a 1 in 13 chance of success as good enough. They may want an intervention with a lower NNT, even if it is more expensive. In other situations, a treatment with a low NNT also may have a high risk of adverse effects (i.e., a low NNH). Clinicians may use NNT and NNH in their evaluation of the risks and benefits of an intervention; however, simply determining that an NNT is low is insufficient to justify a particular intervention (Barratt, Wyer, Hatala, et al., 2004). Evidence-based clinical decision making requires not only ongoing consideration, but an active blending of the numerical study findings, clinicians' expertise, and patients' preferences.

> *Energy and persistence conquer all things.*
>
> **B e n j a m i n   F r a n k l i n**

Measures of Clinical Significance

It is very important that the clinician involved in the critical appraisal process consider the results of a study within the context of practice by asking the question, Are the reported results of actual clinical significance? When appraising a study, clinicians trying to interpret the significance of study findings need to be aware that the way in which the results are reported may be misleading. For example, the ARR reported in study results is calculated in a way that considers the underlying susceptibility of a patient to an outcome and thereby, can distinguish between very large and very small treatment effects. In contrast, RRR does not take into account existing baseline risk and therefore, fails to discriminate between large and small treatment effects.

Interpreting the Results of a Study: Example Two. In a hypothetical example, assume that researchers conducted several RCTs evaluating the same antihypertensive drug and found that it had an RRR of 33% over 3 years (Barratt et al., 2004). A clinician is caring for two 70-year-old women: (a) Pat, who has stable, normal blood pressure and her risk of stroke is estimated at 1% per year; and (b) Dorothy, who has had one stroke and although her blood pressure is normal, her risk of another stroke is 10% per year. With an RRR of stroke of 33%, the antihypertensive medication seems like a good option. However, the underlying risk is not incorporated into RRR, so in making clinically relevant decisions, the ARR must be examined. In the first study conducted on a sample of people with low risk for stroke, the ARR for this medication was 0.01 or 1%. In the second study, conducted on a sample of individuals at high risk for stroke, the ARR was 0.20 or 20%.

Without treatment, Pat has a 1% risk per year of stroke, or 3% risk over 3 years. An ARR of 1% means that treatment with this drug will reduce her risk to 2% over 3 years. From the low-risk study (i.e., the participants looked most like Pat), 100 patients would need to be treated before one stroke would be avoided (i.e., NNT). Without treatment, Dorothy has a 10% risk of stroke each year, or 30% over 3 years. From the second study (i.e., the participants looked most like Dorothy), with an ARR of 20%, the drug would reduce her risk to 10% over 3 years, and five patients would need to be treated to reduce the incidence of stroke by one (i.e., NNT). In this case, it appears that this medication can be beneficial for both women; however, Dorothy will receive more benefit than Pat. The clinical significance of this treatment is much higher when used in people with a higher baseline risk. The ARR and NNT reveal this, but the RRR does not.

For both of these patients, the risk of adverse effects must be taken into account. In these hypothetical RCTs, researchers found that the drug increased the RR of severe gastric bleeding by 3%. Epidemiological studies have established that women in this age group inherently have a 0.1% per year risk of severe gastric bleeding. Over 3 years, the risk of bleeding would be 0.3% without treatment (i.e., Ru) and 0.9% with the medication (i.e., Re), giving an ARI of 0.6%. If Pat takes this drug for 3 years, she will have a relatively small benefit (ARR of 1%) and an increased risk of gastric bleeding (ARI of 0.6%). If Dorothy takes the drug for 3 years, she will have a larger benefit (ARR of 20%) and the same increased risk of gastric bleeding (ARI of 0.6%). The conclusion holds then that Dorothy is more likely to benefit from treatment than Pat; however, the final decision will depend on their preferences (i.e., how they weigh these benefits and harms).

Precision in the Measurement of Effect

Random Error. Critical appraisal evaluates systematic error when checking for bias and confounding variables. This addresses validity and accuracy in the results. However, error also can be introduced by chance (i.e., random error). Variations due to chance occur in almost all situations. For example, a study might enroll more women than men for no particular reason other than pure chance. If a study was to draw some conclusion about the outcome in relationship to it occurring in men or women, the interpretation would have to consider that the variations in the outcome could have occurred due to the random error of the unplanned disproportionate number of men to women in the sample. If participants were not randomly assigned to groups, very sick people could enroll in one group purely by chance and that could impact the results. A hospital could be particularly busy during the time a research study is being conducted there, and that could distort the results. Random error can lead to reported effects that are smaller or greater than the true effect (i.e., the actual impact of an intervention which researchers do their best to determine, though they can never be 100% certain they have found it). Random error impacts the precision of a study finding. The chances of random error impacting the results can be reduced up to a point by study design factors such as increasing the sample size or increasing the number of times measurements are made (i.e., avoiding measurements that are a snapshot in time). When repeated measures of the same outcome are similar in a study, it is presumed that there is low random error. The extent to which random error may influence a measurement can be reported using statistical significance (or *p* values) or by confidence intervals (CIs).

Statistical Significance. The aim of statistical analysis is to determine whether an observed effect arises from the study intervention or has occurred by chance. In comparing two groups, the research question can be phrased as a hypothesis (i.e., what we think will happen) and data collected to determine if the hypothesis is confirmed. For example, the hypothesis might be that an experimental drug relieves pain better than a placebo (i.e., the drug has effects beyond those of suggestion or the personal interactions between those involved in the study). Usually for a study, researchers describe what they expect to happen as their study hypothesis. The null hypothesis (i.e., that there is *no difference* in effect between the drug and placebo) is the counter position to the primary hypothesis. When an intervention study is conducted and statistical analysis is performed on study data (i.e., hypothesis testing), a *p* value is calculated that indicates the probability that the null hypothesis is true. The smaller the *p* value, the less likely that the null hypothesis is true (i.e., the decreased likelihood that the study findings occurred by chance); therefore, the more likely that the observed effect is due to the intervention. By convention, a *p* value of 0.05 or less is considered a statistically significant result in healthcare research. This means that generators and consumers of healthcare research agree that it is acceptable for the study findings to occur by chance 1 in 20 times.

While *p* values have been commonly reported in healthcare literature, they have been debated for many years (Rothman, 1978). Very small *p* values can arise when small differences are found in studies with large samples. These findings can be interpreted as statistically significant, but may have little clinical meaningfulness. Conversely, studies with small sample sizes can have strongly associated outcomes with large *p* values, which may be dismissed as statistically not significant, but could be clinically meaningful. Part of the problem is that *p* values lead to an "either-or" conclusion (i.e., statistically significant or not significant) and do not assist in evaluating the strength of an association (Carley & Lecky, 2003). In addition, the "cutoff" of $p \leq 0.05$ is set arbitrarily, and it contributes to dichotomous decision making. Hence, studies reporting only *p* values tend to be classified as statistically significant (i.e., a positive finding) or statistically not significant (i.e., a negative study finding). The impression given is that the intervention is either useful or useless, respectively. In clinical settings, the study finding is more or less likely to be useful depending on several other factors that clinicians have to take into account when hoping to obtain similar results with their patients. Consider the example highlighted by Table 5.5 (Brower, Lanken, MacIntyre, et al., 2004).

table 5.5 **Two by two table of the incidence of death in comparing high PEEP to low PEEP**

Exposure	Outcome (Death)		
	Yes	No	Total
High PEEP	76	200	276
Low PEEP	68	205	273
Absolute risk (AR)	Re = a/(a + b) Ru = c/(c + d)	Re = 76/(76 + 200) = 0.28 Ru = 68/(68 + 205) = 0.25	
Absolute risk increase (ARI)	Re − Ru = ARI	0.28 − 0.25 = 0.03 × 100 = 0.03 ± 1.96 √{0.28 (100 − 0.28)/276} + {0.25(100 − 0.25)/273}	3% increase in risk of death with high PEEP
CI for ARI	ARI ± 1.96 √{Re (100-Re)/a + b} + {Ru(100-Ru/c + d}	0.03 ± 1.96√{0.10 + 0.09} 0.03 ± √0.19 0.03 ± /− 0.44	95% CI: −0.41 to 0.47

Patients can require mechanical ventilation because of different injuries and diseases. However, mechanical ventilation itself can cause further lung damage, especially if high tidal volumes are used. Table 5.5 gives the results of an RCT in which patients were assigned to low or high positive end-expiratory pressure (PEEP). The ARI for death in the high-PEEP group was 13%. When researchers investigated whether or not there was a difference in the groups, they found that the probability of the null hypothesis (i.e., no differences in the groups) being true was $p = 0.48$. Therefore, the researchers concluded that there were no significant differences in mortality between the two levels of PEEP. However, if the study is simply classified as "statistically not significant," other important information can be missed.

Interpreting the Results of a Study: Example Three. Another potential problem with p values occurs if researchers collect a lot of data without clear objectives (i.e., hypotheses) and then analyze it all looking for significant correlations. In these situations, it is more likely that chance alone led to significant results. When the level of statistical significance for the p value is set at 0.05, the probability of saying that the intervention worked when it did not (i.e., getting a false positive result) can be calculated as $(1 - 0.95)$ or 0.05 (i.e., 1 in 20 positive results will be found by chance). Multiple hypothesis testing is a commonly found example of poor research design (Goodacre, 2008b). When two hypotheses are tested, the probability of a chance finding is increased to $[1 - (0.95 \times 0.95)]$ or 0.0975 (i.e., about 1 in 10 positive results will be found by chance). With five tests, the probability moves to 0.23 (i.e., almost a one in four chances that a positive result will be found by random chance).

There are circumstances in which testing several hypotheses may be legitimate (e.g., when several factors are known to impact an outcome). In such cases, there are statistical analyses that can avoid the problems of multiple hypothesis testing (e.g., the Bonferonni Correction; Bono & Tornetta, 2006). Researchers generally select one primary outcome; however, secondary outcomes also may be appropriate when they arise from the study's conceptual background and objectives. In contrast, "fishing expeditions" or "data dredging" occurs when the sole purpose of data collection is to find statistically significant results. Often a clue to data dredging is when subgroups are created without any conceptual basis and these groups differ significantly on an outcome. Subgroups should be planned prior to starting the study (i.e., a priori) and should be formed based on the conceptual framework that underpins the study. For example, a large RCT of high-dose steroids to treat spinal cord injuries has been criticized for its multiple statistical tests (Bracken, Shepard, Holford, et al., 1997). More than 100 p values were presented in the report without specifying which one was planned as the primary analysis (Bono & Tornetta). For example, the main results table gave 24 p values for various outcomes at different time intervals, of which one was statistically significant. With the convention for probability set at $p < 0.05$, 1 positive test in every 20 tests is likely to be found by chance; therefore, 1 positive test out of the 24 tests in the study example would very likely be due to chance. One positive finding was that patients had statistically significant better neurological outcome scores when treated with intravenous steroids within 8 hours of a spinal cord injury. However, no significant differences in neurological outcomes were found for the entire study population. One problem was that the 8-hour cutoff was not identified prior to the study being conducted, nor was there evidence from basic research as to why treatment prior to 8 hours would make a significant difference (Coleman, Benzel, Cahill, et al., 2000). Researchers, including one involved in the original study, have expressed concerns that multiple statistical tests were run until a statistically significant difference was discovered, resulting in an artificially created subgroup (Lenzer, 2006). This has important clinical implications as this study continues to determine the standard of care even though many clinicians and researchers have questioned the reliability of its conclusion (Lenzer & Brownlee, 2008). Statistical significance cannot be the sole marker for whether or not a study finding is valuable to practice. Clinical meaningfulness (i.e., the clinician can achieve similar outcomes to the study) is another mechanism that can assist the practitioner in evaluating the value of a study's results to patient care.

Confidence Intervals. A CI describes the range in which the true effect lies with a given degree of certainty. In other words, the CI provides clinicians a range of values in which they can be reasonably confident (e.g., 95%) that they will find a result when implementing the study findings. The two most important values for clinicians are the study point estimate and the CI. The point estimate, given the study sample and potentially confounding variables, is the best estimate of the magnitude and direction of the experimental intervention's effect compared with the control (Higgins & Green, 2008). Clinicians need to know to what degree the study intervention brought about the outcome, and they need to know how confident they can be that they can achieve similar outcomes to the study. In general, researchers present a 95% CI, which means that clinicians can have 95% confidence that the value they can achieve (i.e., the true value) falls within this range of values.

Although a CI can be calculated easily, it is not the calculation that clinicians need to remember; rather, they need to understand what information the CI provides. A confidence interval is appropriate to provide clinical meaningfulness for the measured effect of (a) an intervention in one group, (b) the difference the intervention made between two groups, or (c) the intervention's effect with multiple samples pooled together in a **meta-analysis**. A confidence interval's range can be expressed numerically and graphically (see Figure 5.3).

The width of the CI is the key to its interpretation. In general, narrower CIs are more favorable than wider CIs. The narrower the CI around the study point estimate, the less the margin of error for the clinician who is choosing to implement the study findings. In Figure 5.3, the CI is wider; therefore, clinicians would not have much confidence in the study findings. When the CI contains the line of no difference (also called the line of no effect), the difference between the groups (i.e., the study point estimate) is not statistically significant. The CI in Figure 5.3 crosses the center line that indicates no effect (i.e., contains the numerical value); therefore, the results are not statistically significant. The actual numerical value for this line can vary depending on the statistic used (e.g., for OR or RR, no effect = 1; for effect size, no effect = 0).

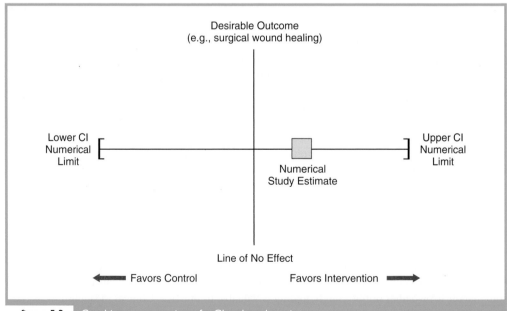

figure 5.3   Graphic representation of a CI and study estimate

Confidence interval width can be influenced by sample size. Larger samples tend to give more precise estimates of effects (i.e., narrower CI) and tend to more likely yield statistically significant effects. In Figure 5.4, outcome estimates for the intervention and control groups and the accompanying CIs are shown for two studies. In the second study, the sample size is doubled and the same values are found. Though the mean values remain the same, the 95% CI is more narrowly defined. Clinicians can have more confidence in the findings of the second study. For continuous outcomes (e.g., blood pressure), in addition to sample size, the CI width also depends on the natural variability in the outcome measurements. Because of the limitations of *p* values, healthcare journals, more commonly, ask for the statistical analyses to report CIs (Goodacre, 2008b).

The information provided by a CI accommodates the uncertainty that is inherent in real-world clinical practice. This uncertainty is not reflected when interventions are described solely as either statistically significant or not. While we can never be absolutely certain whether or not an intervention will help our patients, we can be reasonably confident in the outcome when we have a narrow CI and an effective intervention.

Interpreting the Results of a Study: Example Four. Look over the data found in Table 5.5, from the study comparing the incidence of death with high PEEP and low PEEP in mechanical ventilation (Brower et al., 2004). The study point estimate indicates that those participants with low PEEP had lower mortality rates. While the difference in death rate between the two groups was not statistically significant (CI crosses the line of no effect with ARI = 0; *p* = 0.48), the 95% CI provides additional information that is clinically meaningful for patient care. The 95% CI for ARI is narrow (−0.41 to 0.47), indicating that clinicians can have confidence that they too can get a very small increase in mortality rates by using high PEEP with mechanically ventilated patients (see Figure 5.5). However, even a small increase in death is not desirable. This information is clinically meaningful, despite not being statistically significant. However, though the study findings are clinically meaningful, it would be unwise to conclude whether or not to use high PEEP based solely on the better or worse mortality rates found in this single study. To arrive at a more definitive conclusion, trials with more subjects would be needed to establish that these findings were not by chance (e.g., the study CI would not cross the line of no effect).

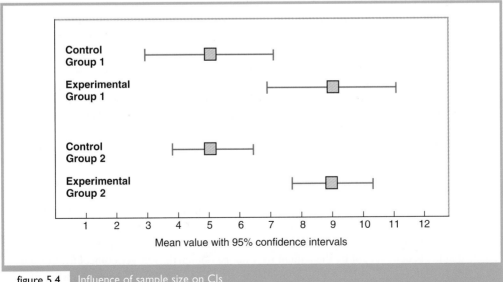

figure 5.4   Influence of sample size on CIs

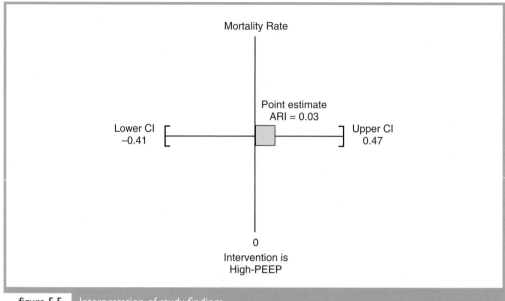

figure 5.5 Interpretation of study findings

In addition, since the outcome is death, it would be advisable to decrease the acceptable error to 1 in 100 or a 99% CI.

Interpreting the Results of a Study: Example Five. Confidence intervals also can be useful in examining the clinical significance of trials with statistically significant results. A blinded, multi-center trial enrolled almost 20,000 patients with vascular disease and randomized them to either aspirin or clopidogrel (CAPRIE Steering Committee, 1996). Both drugs have been recommended to reduce the risk of serious adverse events, especially ischemic stroke, myocardial infarction, or vascular death. Researchers found an annual risk of these outcomes of 5.32% with clopi-dogrel (i.e., Re) and 5.83% with aspirin (i.e., Ru), giving an RRR of 8.7% in favor of clopidogrel ($p = 0.043$; 95% CI, 0.3%–16.5%).

As discussed earlier, for clinical decision making, the NNT expresses study results more meaningfully. This is calculated as the inverse of the ARR. In this case, the ARR = 0.51% (95% CI, 0.02%–0.9%) and the NNT = 1/(0.51%) = 100/0.51 = 196. Put into a sentence, 196 patients would need to be treated with clopidogrel instead of aspirin for one serious adverse event to be avoided each year. Sometimes, clinicians consider comparing NNT per 1,000 patients; for this example, for every 1,000 patients treated with clopidogrel instead of aspirin, about five serious adverse events would be avoided each year (i.e., adverse events avoided per 1,000 patients = 1,000/196 = 5.1).

While the differences between the two groups are statistically significant, the CI can help evaluate clinical significance. Clinicians could discuss with patients what value of RD, which is the same as the ARR, would be viewed as meaningful to them. The value would depend on many factors. Let us assume that a patient with a similar profile to those in this RCT decided to change from aspirin only if he or she could be 95% confident of a 1% RD. Even though the trial is statistically significant, the RD that is viewed as clinically significant by the patient has not been met. Though the CI may include the value chosen by the patient, there is still some chance that the benefit sought by the patient may not be obtained. A larger clinical trial would be needed to reduce the width of the CI and allow greater precision in determining the point estimate.

Will the Results Help Me in Caring for My Patients? (Applicability)

The last couple of examples have moved into the area of applying results to an individual patient or local situation. Clinicians who are appraising evidence should always keep application to patients in mind as the ultimate goal. Each study design has specific questions that, when answered, assist clinicians in critically appraising those studies to determine their worth to practice (i.e., validity, reliability, and usefulness for clinical decision making). Several study designs will be discussed later in the chapter regarding their distinctive appraisals and how to interpret the results for application to patient care.

Preliminary Questions to Ask In A Critical Appraisal

Quantitative research papers generally follow a convention when presenting results. This approach can assist with critical appraisal. The process through which a study is critically appraised applies standardized criteria to each study. The previous section has examined three questions that should be asked of all studies, although the literature on critical appraisal may phrase these questions differently. Each study design will have additional specific questions that fall under each of the three major questions. In addition, overview questions will be asked of each quantitative study (see Box 5.1).

Why Was the Study Done?

A clear explanation of why the study was carried out (i.e., the purpose of the study) is crucial and should be stated succinctly in the report being critically appraised. This can be elaborated on in the aims of the study. The brief background literature presented in a study should identify the gap that this research was designed to fill. This provides the reader with an understanding of how the current research fits within the context of reported knowledge on the topic. Clear descriptions of how researchers conducted their statistical analyses assist the reader in evaluating the reliability and applicability of the study results and protect against data dredging.

---

box 5.1

Overview Questions for Critical Appraisal of Quantitative Studies

- Why was the study done?
- What is the sample size?
- Are the measurements of major variables valid and reliable?
- How were the data analyzed?
- Were there any untoward events during the conduct of the study?
- How do the results fit with previous research in the area?
- What does this research mean for clinical practice?

What is the Sample Size?

The study sample size should be sufficient to ensure reasonable confidence that the role of chance is minimized as a contributor to the results and that the true effect of the intervention will be demonstrated. Researchers should conduct an a priori (i.e., done before starting the study) calculation called a power analysis, that assists them in determining what the sample size needs to be to minimize findings that are based on chance (i.e., reduces Type I error). This should be reported in the methods section of the research report. If a power analysis is not reported, no assumptions can be made about the adequacy or inadequacy of the sample size for minimizing chance findings. Sometimes ethical, economic, and other practical considerations impact the sample size of a study. Careful consideration of how the sample size affects the validity of findings should be considered when appraising a study.

Are the Measurements of Major Variables Valid and Reliable?

The concepts of validity and reliability discussed regarding a study's results differ from the concepts of validity and reliability discussed in the measurement of outcomes. In this section of the chapter, the focus is on how well an instrument measures a concept (i.e., the accuracy and consistency of the measures). A valid instrument is one that measures what it is purported to measure. For example, an instrument that is expected to measure fear should indeed measure fear and not anxiety. A reliable instrument is one that is stable over time (i.e., it performs the same way each time responders answer the questions) and is composed of individual items or questions that consistently measure the same construct. Several statistical techniques can be applied to instrument results to determine their reliability (e.g., Cronbach's alpha).

Published research reports should discuss the validity and reliability of the outcome measures used in the study in the methods section. Investigators should address issues or concerns they have with the validity or reliability of the measurement of study outcomes in the discussion section of the research report. It is important for the critical appraiser to keep in mind that without valid and reliable measurement of outcomes, the study results are not clinically meaningful.

How Were the Data Analyzed?

Clinicians do not need to be familiar with a large number of complex approaches to statistical analysis. Even experts in statistics have challenges keeping up with current statistical techniques. Researchers reviewed articles published in the journal *Pediatrics* and found that readers who were very familiar with the 10 most common statistical concepts would still encounter unfamiliar statistical procedures in the journal's articles (Hellems, Gurka, & Hayden, 2007). The authors reported that an anonymous reviewer of their article commented, "I have never heard of some of these, and I teach this stuff!" Although challenging, clinicians need a general understanding of how to interpret some common statistical tests and the types of data that are appropriate for their use. For those new to critical appraisal, spotting common mistakes in statistics can be a great opportunity to learn the methods (Bono & Tornetta, 2006; Lang, 2004). Some common statistical errors include

- *Focusing only on the **p value***. Choosing a statistical test because it gives the answer for which the investigator had hoped (e.g., statistical significance) is ill-advised. A statistical test should be chosen on the basis of its appropriateness for the type of data collected. Authors should give clear justifications for using anything other than the most commonly used statistical tests.
- *Data dredging, or conducting a large number of analyses on the same data*. This can be problematic because the more analyses conducted, the more likely that a significant result will be found due only to chance.

● *Confusing statistical significance with clinical importance.* A small difference between large groups may be statistically significant, but be such a rare event that few will benefit from it. For example, if an intervention reduces blood pressure by 2 mm Hg, the finding might be statistically significant in a study with a large sample, but it would not be clinically meaningful. On the other hand, a large difference between small groups may not be statistically significant, but may make an important clinical difference.

● *Missing data.* Incomplete data is surprisingly common, and, when noted, should raise questions during critical appraisal. Researchers should indicate in their report how they addressed any incomplete data. If this issue is not addressed, the problem may be an oversight in the report, a restrictive word count from the publisher, or a poorly conducted study—all of which should be considered carefully. If the issue is an oversight in reporting or word count restriction, contacting the researcher is in order to discuss how missing data were addressed.

● *Selective reporting.* Inappropriately publishing only outcomes with statistically significant findings can lead to missing data (Dwan, Altman, Arnaiz, et al., 2008). A flow chart is an efficient mechanism to account for all patients in a study and show how the various groups progressed through the study. Figure 5.6 gives an example of how a flow chart visually summarizes the study design and how the numbers of subjects were used in the statistical analyses.

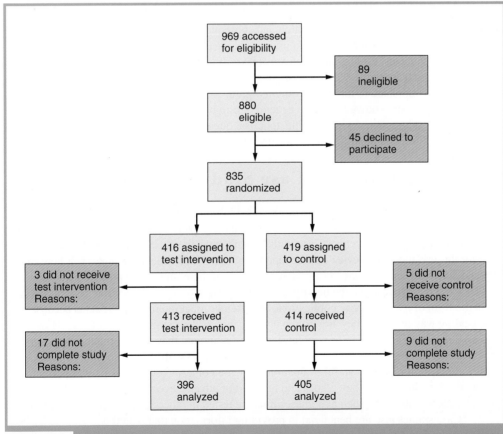

figure 5.6   Study participants flowchart

Were There Any Untoward Events During the Conduct of the Study?

During critical appraisal, it is important to understand how problems that arose during a study influenced the final results. These issues may be unpredictable and occur randomly or they may arise because of a flaw or flaws in the original study design. One such problem is loss to follow-up (i.e., study attrition), which results in missing data and introduction of bias. Research reports should provide explanations for all adverse events and withdrawals from the study and how those events affected the final results.

How Do the Results Fit With Previous Research in the Area?

Except on rare occasions when researchers investigate completely new areas of interest, studies fit into a growing body of research evidence. A study report should begin with the **systematic review** of previous literature that substantiates why the research was conducted. In a study report, the evidence review is the context in which the current research is meaningful. This review should provide confidence that the researchers took advantage of previous researchers' experiences in conducting studies on this topic. In addition, the discussion section of the report should discuss the study findings in the light of what is already known and how those findings complement or contradict previous work. In writing the report, the evidence review and discussion should be framed in such a way that the clinician will understand the purpose and context of the research.

What Does this Research Mean for Clinical Practice?

The point of critical appraisal of all research and subsequent evidence-based decision making in healthcare is to apply research findings to improve clinical practice outcomes. Therefore, asking what the research means for clinical practice is one of the most important questions to keep in mind during critical appraisal. Clinicians should look at the study population and ask whether the results can be extrapolated to the patients in *their* care.

While it is imperative that these general questions are asked of every study, it is also important to ask additional, design-specific appraisal questions to determine the worth of each study to clinical decision making. The following sections provide those design-specific questions.

Critical Appraisal of Case Studies

Case studies, also called case reports, are historically ranked lower in the hierarchy of evidence for intervention questions because of their lack of objectivity (Chapter 1, Box 1.2). In addition, publication bias could be a factor, since most case studies found in the literature have positive outcomes. Evidence for this was found in a review of case reports published in Brazilian dental journals between 1994 and 2003 (Oliveira & Leles, 2006). More than 99% of these studies had positive outcomes.

Case reports describe the history of a single patient (or a small group of patients), usually in the form of a story. These publications are often of great interest to clinicians because of the appealing way in which they are written and because of their strong clinical focus. However, since case reports describe one (or very few) person's situation, they are not reliable for clinicians to use as the sole source of evidence. They must be used with caution to inform practice, and any application requires careful evaluation of the outcomes. Case studies play important roles in alerting clinicians to new issues and rare and/or adverse events in practice and to assist in hypothesis generation. Any such hypotheses must be tested in other, less bias-prone research.

Case studies also are beneficial in providing information that would not necessarily be reported in the results of clinical trials or survey research. Publications reporting a clinician's experience and a discussion of early indicators and possible preventive measures can be an

---

clinical scenario 5.1

You are caring for an infant 4 days after cardiac surgery in the pediatric intensive care unit. Platelets and albumin were administered the night before because of the infant's abnormal clotting profile. In consultation with the healthcare team, you remove the pulmonary artery catheter. You notice continuous ooze from the site and a marked deterioration in the patient's condition. Cardiac tamponade is diagnosed, and the patient requires a reopening of the sternotomy and removal of 200 mL of blood from the pericardial sac. At the end of your shift, you wonder how rare such a complication is in this patient population and decide to look at the literature.

---

extremely useful addition to the clinician's knowledge base. Given that a case series would present a small number of patients with similar experiences or complications and their outcomes, statistical analyses are rarely, if ever, appropriate. A major caution that impacts critical appraisal of case studies is that the purpose of such studies is to provide a patient's story about little-known health issues and not to provide generalizations applicable to the general population.

What the Literature Says: Answering a Clinical Question

In Clinical Scenario 5.1, the clinical question you may want to ask is, In infants who have had cardiac surgery (P), how often does removing pulmonary artery catheters (I) influence cardiac tamponade (O) within the first week after surgery (T)? In your search, you find a recent case study that describes a similar complication to one you have just experienced: Johnston, L. J., & McKinley, D. F. (2000). Cardiac tamponade after removal of atrial intracardiac monitoring catheters in a pediatric patient: Case report. *Heart & Lung, 29*(4), 256–261.

The article is a case report of one patient who experienced cardiac tamponade after removal of a pulmonary artery catheter. The article focuses on describing the pathophysiology of tamponade. The report states that this complication occurs with a frequency rate of 0.22%. The authors give details of their experience with a single patient and provide some recommendations for limiting the potential for bleeding complications in this patient population. You take a copy of the paper to your unit for discussion. You realize that this one case study is not enough to make practice change, so you search for stronger studies (e.g., controlled trials) to assist in developing an addition to your unit protocol manual to create awareness of possible complications arising from removal of monitoring catheters and how to prevent such complications.

Critical Appraisal of Case–Control Studies

A **case–control** study investigates why certain people develop a specific illness, have an adverse event with a particular treatment, or behave in a particular way. An example of a clinical question for which a case–control study could be the appropriate design to provide an answer would be, In patients who have a family history of obesity (BMI > 30) (P), how does dietary carbohydrate intake (I) influence healthy weight maintenance (BMI < 25) (O) over 6 months (T)? Another clinical question that could be answered by a case–control study could be, In patients who have cystic fibrosis (P), how does socioeconomic status (I) influence their engagement with and adherence to their healthcare regimen (O)?

Investigators conducting a case–control study try to identify factors that explain the proposed relationship between a condition and a disease or behavior. The case–control method selects individuals who have an outcome (disease, adverse event, behavior) and retrospectively looks back to identify possible conditions that may be associated with the outcome. The characteristics of these individuals (the cases) are compared with those of other individuals who do not have the outcome (the controls). The assumption underpinning this methodological approach is that differences found between the groups may be likely indicators of why the "cases" became "cases."

For example, case–control methodology was used to address a clinical issue in identifying the connection between a rare cancer in women and diethylstilbestrol (DES) use by their mothers when they were pregnant (Herbst, Ulfelder, & Poskanzer, 1971). A prospective design would have been challenging because the adverse event took 20 years to develop and an RCT could not be used for ethical reasons (i.e., it would be unethical to ask pregnant women to take a drug to determine whether or not it increased the risk of birth defects). Eight women with the cancer (vaginal adenocarcinoma) were enrolled in the study as cases, and 32 women without cancer were enrolled as controls in the study. Various risk factors were proposed, but found to be present in cases and controls. In contrast, mothers of seven of the women with cancer (i.e., cases) received DES when pregnant, while none of the controls' mothers did. The association between having the cancer and having a mother who took DES was highly significant ($p < 0.00001$) and was subsequently demonstrated in cohort studies (Hatch, Palmer, Titus-Ernstoff, et al., 1998; Troisi, Hatch, Titus-Ernstoff, et al., 2007). The combination of (a) the huge impact vaginal adenocarcinoma had on women's lives, (b) the final outcome of death, and (c) the strong association established between the occurrence of the cancer and mothers taking DES while pregnant led to a common acceptance that DES causes this cancer. However, causation cannot be established by a case–control study. Instead, a strong association was found between taking DES while pregnant and vaginal adenocarcinoma in the adult child. In addition, this case–control study played an important role is alerting people to the potential adverse effects of using any medications during pregnancy.

Rapid Appraisal Questions for Case–Control Studies

There are three rapid appraisal questions for all studies: Are the results of the study valid? What are the results? Do the results apply to my patients? Each of these questions has design-specific issues that must be answered before case–control studies can assist the clinician in decision making. Rapid critical appraisal is intended to quickly determine if a study is worthy of consideration (see Box 5.2).

---

box 5.2

Rapid Critical Appraisal Questions for Case–Control Studies

1. Are the Results of the Study Valid? (Validity)
   a. How were the cases obtained?
   b. Were appropriate controls selected?
   c. Were data collection methods the same for the cases and controls?
2. What Are the Results?
   a. Is an estimate of effect given (do the numbers add up)?
   b. Are there multiple comparisons of data?
   c. Is there any possibility of bias or confounding?
3. Will the Results Help Me in Caring for My Patients?
   a. Were the study patients similar to my own?
   b. How do the results compare with previous studies?
   c. What are my patients/family's values and expectations for the outcome?

Are the Results of the Study Valid? (Validity)

How Were the Cases Obtained? When appraising a case–control study, the clinician first determines how the cases were identified. The investigators should provide an adequate description or definition of what constitutes a case, including the diagnostic criteria, any exclusion criteria, and an explanation of how the cases were obtained (e.g., from a specialist center, such as an oncology unit, or from the general population). In the DES study, all the cases were identified in the same hospital in Boston over a period of a few years (Herbst et al., 1971). Cases coming from one geographical area could represent another explanation for the findings. Controls also would need to be from the same geographical area to control for that possible confounding variable.

      The source of the cases has important implications for the appraisal of the study. For example, recruitment of patients from an outpatient chemotherapy unit could include patients with well-established and managed disease and exclude those who are newly diagnosed. Bias could be introduced when cases are recruited from a general population because the potential participants could be at various stages in their disease or have a degree of the behavior of interest. Similarly, bias may arise if some of those cases sought are not included in the study for whatever reason. Patients who choose to become involved in research studies can have characteristics that distinguish them from those who avoid research studies. Care must be taken to ensure that these characteristics are not confounding variables that may influence the relationship between the condition being investigated and the outcome.

Were Appropriate Controls Selected? Selection of controls should be done so that the controls are as similar as possible to the cases in all respects except that they do not have the disease or observed behavior under investigation. In the DES study, the control women were born within 5 days of a case in the same hospital and with the same type of delivery and were from the same geographical area (Herbst et al., 1971). In general, controls may be selected from a specialist source or from the general population. The controls in case–control studies may be recruited into the study at the same time as the cases (concurrent controls). Alternatively, they may be what are referred to as historical controls (i.e., the person's past history is examined, often through medical records). Case–control studies with historical controls are generally viewed as lower on the hierarchy of evidence than those studies with concurrent controls, because there is more likelihood of bias.

Were Data Collection Methods the Same for the Cases and Controls? Data collection is another potential source of bias in a case–control study. Recall bias, which is inaccurately remembering what occurred, needs to be considered because of the retrospective approach to determining the possible predictive factors. For example, people who have developed a fatal disease may have already spent a considerable amount of time thinking about why they might have developed the disease and therefore be able to recall in great detail their past behaviors. They may have preconceived ideas about what they think caused their illness and report these rather than other factors they have not considered.

      In contrast, the disease-free controls may not have considered their past activities in great detail and may have difficulty recalling events accurately. The data should ideally be collected in the same way for both the case and control groups. Blinding of the data collector to either the case or the control status or to the risk factors of interest assists in reducing the inherent bias in a case–control approach and thus provides more accurate information.

Additional Considerations. The possibility of confounding variables needs to be considered when interpreting a case–control study. Confounding variables are other extrinsic factors that unexpectedly (or unknowingly) influence the variables expected to be associated with the outcome. A case–control study reported a strong association ($p = 0.001$) between

> ### clinical scenario 5.2
>
> A concerned relative follows you into the hall from the room of a family member who has just been diagnosed with a rare brain tumor. He tells you he recently saw a program on television that described research linking cellular phone use to the development of some forms of cancer. His relative has used a cellular phone for many years, and he wonders whether that may have caused his relative's tumor. You would like to know what the research literature has to say about this issue.

coffee consumption and pancreatic cancer (MacMahon, Yen, Trichopoulos, et al., 1981). The researchers stated that if the association was borne out by other research, it would account for a substantial proportion of the cases of pancreatic cancer in the United States. However, other research failed to replicate these findings, which are now regarded as false positive results (Type II error—accepting that there was an effect when in fact there was none). Individuals with a history of diseases related to cigarette smoking or alcohol consumption were excluded from the control group, but not the cases (Boffetta, McLaughlin, La Vecchia, et al., 2008). These activities are highly correlated with coffee consumption, suggesting that coffee consumption may have been lower among the controls than among the cases because of how the cases were selected. This methodological error generated an uncontrolled confounding variable that may have been the reason for the apparent association between coffee and pancreatic cancer and gives an alert appraiser reason to question the validity of the study findings. All findings must be carefully evaluated to determine the validity of the findings and how valuable they are to practice.

What the Literature Says: Answering a Clinical Question

The clinical question for Clinical Scenario 5.2 could be, In patients admitted with brain tumors (P), how does cell phone usage (I) influence brain tumor incidence (O)? When conducting a quick search of the literature, you find the following study and believe it may help answer the question from the family member in your practice: Inskip, P., Tarone, R., Hatch, E., Wilcosky, T., Shapiro, W., Selker, R., et al. (2001). Cellular-telephone use and brain tumors. *New England Journal of Medicine, 344*(2), 79–86.

Enrolled in the study were 782 case participants with histologically confirmed glioma, meningioma, or acoustic neuroma. Participants came from a number of hospitals. The control participants were 799 patients admitted to the same hospitals as the cases but with nonmalignant conditions. The predictor measured was cellular phone usage, which was quantified using a personal interview to collect information on duration and frequency of use. Once the details of the study are evaluated, the general critical appraisal questions should be answered. The rapid critical appraisal questions for case–control studies found in Box 5.2 can assist in critically appraising this study to determine its value to the care of this particular patient and family.

Are the Results of the Study Valid? (Validity)

This case–control study describes in detail how cases were selected from eligible patients who had been diagnosed with the various types of tumors. Tumor diagnosis was confirmed by objective tests. Validity can be compromised in case–control studies if cases are misdiagnosed. Control patients were concurrently recruited from the same healthcare centers and were matched for age, sex, and ethnicity. A research nurse administered a computer-assisted personal interview with the patient or a proxy if the patient could not participate.

Participants were asked about the frequency of cellular phone usage. Reliance on recall rather than a more objective way to measure cell phone usage is a weakness in this study. Other studies have used computer databases of actual cell phone usage to overcome this limitation (Guyatt et al., 2008). While case patients were matched on certain demographic variables, other variables that influenced the outcome may not have been considered. In addition, recall bias would be a serious threat to the validity of this study. Although the data analysis did not support the hypothesis that cellular phone usage causes brain tumors, possible inaccuracies in patient recall or use of different types of cellular phones raise questions about the validity of the results. Overall, the study suggested that cellular phone usage does not increase or decrease the risk of brain tumors. This conclusion is supported by basic research showing that the radio frequencies used in cellular phones are not carcinogenic and the absence of a theoretical basis for such effects (Trichopoulos & Adami, 2001). However, because of the study's limitations and risk of bias, further research is needed on this issue. Clinicians can have some confidence in the validity of this study's findings; however, complete confidence is not possible.

What Are the Results? (Reliability)

Comparisons were made between those who never or very rarely used a cellular phone and those who used one for more than 100 hours. The RR for cellular phone usage were RR = 0.9 for glioma (95% CI, 0.5–1.6); RR = 0.7 for meningioma (95% CI, 0.3–1.7); RR = 1.4 for acoustic neuroma (95% CI, 0.6–3.5); and the overall RR = 1.0 (95% CI, 0.6–1.5) for all tumor types combined. While some studies indicated that the RR of certain types of brain tumors increased with cell phone use, the overall result from this group of studies indicated an RR of 1. This indicates that a person who has used a cell phone for more than 100 hours is just as likely (RR 1.0) to have a tumor as someone who has not used a cell phone. The CIs reportedly give us an estimate of the precision of the measurement of effect of cell phone use in this study. Note that all the CIs in this example include the value of 1. Remember that when the CI contains what is called the line of no effect, which for RR is 1, the results are not statistically significant.

For example, from this study's findings, the RR for meningioma was 0.7 with a CI of 0.3–1.7, which includes 1 and therefore is not statistically significant. Since in this study the sample size is moderate to large, we would expect the CIs to be narrow. The narrower the CI, the more precise the finding is for the clinician (i.e., the more likely clinicians can get close to the study finding). A 95% CI enables clinicians to be 95% confident that their findings, if they do the same thing (e.g., use the cell phone for so many hours), will be within the range of the CI. In studies with a high-risk outcome (e.g., death), having 95% confidence in knowing the outcome they will achieve may not be sufficient. In studies of these types, clinicians will want to know more specifically what they can expect and would be likely to choose a 99% CI.

Will the Results Help Me in Caring for My Patients? (Applicability)

When evaluating the results of this study and the associated limitations, it is difficult to find helpful information for clinical decision making. When critically appraising all studies, a basic aspect of applicability is to evaluate the study patients in comparison with the patients to whom the evidence would be applied (i.e., the clinician's own patients). Since this study has known limitations, it is more challenging to determine if the results would lead directly to selecting or to avoiding cell phone use. However, the results of the study assist researchers in understanding the need for more research about cell phone usage and the possible sequelae of brain tumors. For the patient's family members, the information from this one study would not be definitive. To provide appropriate counsel to healthcare consumers, it would be important to find other studies that could help answer the clinical question.

chapter 5

107

Critical Appraisal of Cohort Studies

The **cohort study** design is especially suitable for investigating the course of a disease or the unintended consequences of a treatment (Fineout-Overholt & Melnyk, 2007; Guyatt et al., 2008). A *cohort* refers to a study population sharing a characteristic or group of characteristics. There are two ways to conduct a cohort study, with and without a control group. Without a control group, researchers identify one cohort exposed to the characteristic and follow that cohort over time to determine the existence of an outcome. For example, a cohort could be adolescents experiencing their first episode of psychosis or school-aged children who have had audible wheezing in the last 6 weeks. If a condition that is being observed requires a comparison group, then the study must be designed as such. For example, assessing the impact of congenital heart disease on an infant's cognitive and motor development could be best undertaken in a study that matched a cohort of infants with congenital heart disease with a similar control cohort without disease or with an unrelated condition. As with case–control studies, exposed and unexposed cohorts should otherwise have a similar risk of the target outcome.

Since cohort studies generally follow people over a period of time to determine their outcomes, they are longitudinal. In prospective studies, a cohort exposed to a drug, surgery, or particular diagnosis may be followed for years while collecting data on outcomes. For example, in studying DES and cancer, cohort studies have been running since the initial case studies reported in the 1970s and now involve three generations of people who have been impacted by this association (Troisi et al., 2007). Since such prospective studies can take many years to complete, cohort studies often are retrospective. In retrospective studies, the outcome under investigation (e.g., occurrence of a disease or condition) has already occurred and researchers go even further into the past to select those characteristics they believe might be associated with the given outcome. The cohort is followed from that point forward to determine what influenced the development of the outcome and when those influences occurred. Since participants are not randomly assigned to a cohort, cohort studies do not have an experimental research design. These studies therefore have the limitations of all observational studies.

An example of the limitations that may accompany a cohort study can be seen in the data supporting or refuting the benefits of hormone replacement therapy for heart health. A meta-analysis of 16 cohort studies of women taking postmenopausal estrogen therapy concluded that the medication gave women a lower risk of coronary heart disease (CHD) with an RR of 0.5 and 95% CI of 0.44–0.57 (Stampfer & Colditz, 1991). Practice was based on these studies for quite a long time; however, standards of care were challenged when the highly publicized Women's Health Initiative RCT showed that hormone replacement therapy actually increased the risk of CHD in postmenopausal women (Rossouw, Anderson, Prentice, et al., 2002). The quandary for clinicians is which studies provide the most valid and reliable evidence for making decisions with their patients. Randomized controlled trials are the strongest evidence for making decisions about interventions; however, without the existence of this type of evidence, cohort studies may be the only evidence to guide practice.

Rapid Appraisal Questions for a Cohort Study

The design-specific rapid critical appraisal questions for cohort studies that can assist the clinician in quickly determining the value of a cohort study can be found in Box 5.3.

Are the Results of the Study Valid? (Validity)

Was There a Representative and Well-defined Sample of Patients at a Similar Point in the Course of the Disease? When appraising a cohort study, establishing the characteristics of the patients or clients under study is important. These characteristics, such as the severity of

> ### box 5.3
>
> ## Rapid Critical Appraisal Questions for Cohort Studies
>
> 1. Are the Results of the Study Valid?
>   a. Was there a representative and well-defined sample of patients at a similar point in the course of the disease?
>   b. Was follow-up sufficiently long and complete?
>   c. Were objective and unbiased outcome criteria used?
>   d. Did the analysis adjust for important prognostic risk factors and confounding variables?
> 2. What Are the Results?
>   a. What is the magnitude of the relationship between predictors (i.e., prognostic indicators) and targeted outcome?
>   b. How likely is the outcome event(s) in a specified period of time?
>   c. How precise are the study estimates?
> 3. Will the Results Help Me in Caring for My Patients?
>   a. Were the study patients similar to my own?
>   b. Will the results lead directly to selecting or avoiding therapy?
>   c. Would the results be used to counsel patients?

symptoms or stage in the illness trajectory, will strongly influence the impact an intervention may have on the patient's condition or the resulting outcomes. A suitably detailed description of the population and how the cohorts were defined (i.e., how the exposure [and nonexposure, if appropriate] cohorts were established) is necessary for the clinician to draw any conclusions about the validity of the results and whether they are generalizable to other populations.

Was Follow-up Sufficiently Long and Complete? The length of follow-up for a cohort study will depend on the outcomes of interest. For example, wound breakdown as a consequence of an early discharge program after surgery would require a shorter follow-up period than a study examining hospital admissions for management of acute asthma subsequent to an in-school education strategy. Insufficient time for outcomes to be demonstrated will bias the study findings.

Clinicians appraising a cohort study would need to evaluate if people withdrew from the study, and if so, why (i.e., to determine if there something unique about those participants). Patients enrolled in a cohort study, particularly over a long time, may be lost to follow-up. Furthermore, the condition of interest in a cohort study may predispose patients to incomplete or noncompliant participation in a study. Cohort studies involving patients with a terminal or end-stage illness commonly must deal with patients dying during the study before follow-up data are completely collected. While unavoidable, the extent of loss to follow-up may bias the study results.

Were Objective and Unbiased Outcome Criteria Used? When evaluating outcomes in the cohort, researchers can use both subjective and objective measurements. Subjective measures introduce bias (e.g., recall) into the study; whereas, ideally, objective measures have less bias and provide more reliable data. Patient self-reporting and clinician diagnosis are outcome measures that are subject to some bias. Objective measures will be based on a reference standard, such as a biochemical test or clinical interview conducted by a psychologist. Research reports should contain the validity and reliability of the measures that were used. The clinician also should integrate clinical expertise with appraisal skills when thinking about the measurement of the outcomes of interest.

Did the Analysis Adjust for Important Prognostic Risk Factors and Confounding Variables?

Clinicians need to consider what, if any, other prognostic (i.e., predictive) factors could have been included in the study, but were not. If there are other factors identified, clinicians must determine how those would affect the validity of the current findings. In addition, other factors must be considered that could muddy the relationships among the existing identified factors and the outcomes. For example, a cohort study may be designed to study the risk of gastric bleeding in nonsteroidal anti-inflammatory drug (NSAID) users compared to nonusers. Incidence of gastric bleeding (i.e., the event rate) is so low that an enormous number of participants would be needed for an RCT, making a cohort study more feasible. However, a cohort of NSAID users may inherently be older than a cohort of NSAID nonusers and bring with them increased risk for gastric bleeding. In this case, age could be a confounding variable if it is not controlled for when selecting the cohorts.

What are the Results? (Reliability)

What is the Magnitude of the Relationship Between Predictors (i.e., Prognostic Indicators) and Targeted Outcome?

For cohort studies, clinicians must determine the final results. Often studies may report an incident rate or a proportion for the outcome occurring within the exposed and unexposed cohorts as well as the differences in those rates or proportions. Evaluating the strength of association between exposure and outcome is imperative (e.g., RR, ARR, or NNT).

How Likely is the Outcome Event(s) in a Specified Period of Time?

Often the strength of association is provided for a given time period. For example, researchers may state that the NNT is 15 with an antihypertensive medication to prevent one more stroke within 3 years.

How Precise are the Study Estimates?

Confidence intervals must be provided, along with *p* values, to determine precision of the findings (i.e., whether a clinician can replicate the results).

Will the Results Help Me in Caring for My Patients?

Were the Study Patients Similar to My Own?

As with all studies, it is important to note how similar or dissimilar the sample is to the clinicians' patients.

Will the Results Lead Directly to Selecting or Avoiding Therapy? And Would the Results Be Used to Counsel Patients?

After clinicians evaluate the findings to see if they are reliable and applicable to their patients, they must determine how they can be used to assist those patients

---

clinical scenario 5.3

You have been working in a community mental health program for a number of years. Young people who have experienced their first episode of schizophrenia make up a large proportion of your client base. Your colleagues have suggested that differences in the disease and social course of schizophrenia may arise depending on clients' age at onset. You volunteer to find a paper for the next journal club that investigates the influence of age at onset on the symptom-related course of the disease.

in their healthcare management. Caution must be used here, as cohort studies are not RCTs and inherently have bias in their design; therefore, there is less confidence in the replication of their findings. Nevertheless, providing information to patients regarding the study findings is important to having evidence-based consumers who use the best evidence to make their healthcare decisions.

What the Literature Says: Answering a Clinical Question

The clinical question for Clinical Scenario 5.3 could be, In adolescent patients who have schizophrenia (P), how does age of onset (I) influence the social course of the disease (O)? The following study may help answer the question about adolescents and schizophrenia: Häfner, H., Hambrecht, M., Löffler, W., Munk-Jørgensen, P., & Riecher-Rössler, A. (1998). Is schizophrenia a disorder of all ages? A comparison of first episodes and early course across the life-cycle. *Psychological Medicine, 28*(2), 351–365. Using the rapid critical appraisal questions, this study will be evaluated to determine whether it provides valid, relevant evidence to address this clinical question.

The participants in the study were 1,109 patients first admitted to a mental health institution with a broad diagnosis of schizophrenia at age 12–20, 21–35, or 36–59 years. Symptoms were assessed at 6 months and at 1, 2, 3, and 5 years after first admission. The outcome measured was symptom severity as determined by scores on the symptom-based Present State Examination (PSE), using a computer program to arrive at diagnostic classifications (PSE-CATEGO). The higher the score on the PSE-CATEGO, the more severe the illness.

Are the Results of the Study Valid? (Validity)

There are several questions that help determine if a cohort study is valid. The first is, Was there a representative and well-defined sample of patients at a similar point in the course of the disease? Since the participants in this study were admitted into the study at their first admission and their onset and course before the first admission were assessed retrospectively with a standardized instrument, the study sample seems representative for patients at similar points for schizophrenia. The second question is, Was follow-up sufficiently long and complete? In this study, ensuing symptoms and social consequences were prospectively followed over 5 years. Although there was no explanation for why a 5-year follow-up period was chosen, nor was any information given on losses to follow-up, 5 years is probably sufficiently long enough for follow-up. The third question is, Were objective and unbiased outcome criteria used? Symptomatology, functional impairment, and social disability were assessed by clinically experienced, trained psychiatrists and psychologists using previously validated instruments. The fourth and final question to assess study validity is, Did the analysis adjust for important prognostic risk factors? In the study, symptoms of schizophrenia as well as onset of formal treatment were considered for their impact on functional impairment and social disability. Given these methods, the study findings are valid and can help in determining practice.

What Are the Results? (Reliability)

In this study, participants with early-onset schizophrenia, especially men, presented with higher PSE-CATEGO scores than did study participants with late-onset disease. In men, symptom severity decreased with increasing age of onset. In women, symptom severity remained stable, although there was an increase in negative symptoms with late onset. Disorganization decreased with age, but delusions increased markedly across the whole age of onset range. The main determinant of social course was level of social development at onset. Inferential statistics were used to determine any differences between groups, and *p* values were reported; however, there were no CIs provided, and precision of the effect is difficult to determine.

Some of the study participants are similar in age and social development to those in your clinic population. Although much of the data show trends rather than statistically significant differences, the authors of the study developed some suggestions about why any differences exist that are clinically meaningful. You and your colleagues could use this information, along with other studies, to plan early intervention programs with the goal of limiting the negative consequences of schizophrenia in young people. This study is applicable to your practice and should assist in making decisions. Always keep in mind, however, that any time you use evidence to make clinical decisions, subsequent evaluation of the difference the evidence makes in your own practice is essential.

> *Persistence is the twin sister of excellence. One is a matter*
> *of quality; the other, a matter of time.*
> *Marabel Morgan*

Critical Appraisal of Randomized Controlled Trials

Randomized controlled trials are the most appropriate research design to answer questions of efficacy and effectiveness of interventions because their methodology provides confidence in establishing cause and effect (i.e., increased confidence that a given intervention leads to a particular outcome). As individual studies, RCTs rank as Level II evidence in the hierarchy of evidence because a well-conducted study should have a low risk of bias. A synthesis of RCTs is considered Level I evidence for answering questions about interventions for the same reason (see Chapter 1, Box 1.2). An RCT compares the effectiveness of different interventions. This can involve one treatment group getting the intervention under investigation and a comparison treatment group receiving another intervention (e.g., current standard of care for the same outcome) to determine which is better at producing the outcome. The interventions studied could be the experimental treatment compared to a comparison group, with the comparison group receiving no intervention (i.e., true control group), a placebo, or the usual standard of care. Randomized controlled trials are experimental studies in which participants are *randomly* assigned to each intervention in what are often referred to as the "arms" of a study. An RCT often has two arms, but may have more than two, such as when an intervention is being compared with no intervention and with a placebo. Randomized controlled trials also are prospective and longitudinal in that participants are studied over a period of time to assess the effects of an intervention or treatment on selected outcomes.

In crossover trials, participants are given the experimental intervention and then the comparison or placebo-controlled intervention in consecutive periods and thus serve as their own controls. For example, a crossover design was used to study the effectiveness of two combinations of dental hygiene products on bad mouth odor (Farrell, Barker, Walanski, et al., 2008). The study used four periods in which participants were randomly assigned to either combination A (antibacterial toothpaste, antibacterial mouth rinse, and an oscillating-rotating toothbrush) or combination B (regular toothpaste and manual toothbrush). The participants were allowed 2 days between each intervention to permit the effects of the previous intervention to subside or washout, hence the name "washout period." Combination A led to a 35% reduction in bad breath as determined by an instrument widely used to measure breath volatiles ($p < 0.001$). Crossover trials allow comparisons of the same participants' responses to the two interventions, thus minimizing variability caused by having different people in each intervention group. The crossover design works well for short-lasting interventions, such as the dental hygiene products used in this study. The major concern with crossover trials is carryover, in which the effects of the first intervention linger into the period of testing of the second intervention (Higgins & Green, 2008). It is important to consider this introduction of bias when critically appraising a crossover trial.

Randomized controlled trials, in general, are sometimes considered to be overly artificial because of the control investigators exert over most aspects of the study. Predetermined inclusion and exclusion criteria are used to select participants and provide a homogeneous study population (i.e., all the participants in the sample are alike). The investigators must carefully consider how to recruit participants for the intervention, the control, and the comparison groups before starting the study. The outcomes of interest also are predetermined. Since some suggest that the results of an RCT are really only generalizable to the particular population studied in the trial because of this artificiality, two approaches to conducting RCTs have been developed.

The two approaches to conducting RCTs are called the efficacy study and the effectiveness study. The efficacy has to be established first (i.e., how well does the intervention actually work) before an effectiveness trial is done (i.e., how well does the intervention work in the real world). The distinction rests with the sort of research question that each study attempts to answer (Goodacre, 2008b). In an efficacy study (sometimes also called an explanatory study), everything is controlled as tightly as possible to ensure the two groups differ only in regard to how they respond to the intervention. Such studies give the best information on whether and how well the intervention works, but may not be as readily applicable to clinical practice (Lang, 2004). Effectiveness studies are about the pragmatic value of an intervention in clinical practice. In an effectiveness study, controls are kept to a minimum to ensure the research setting is as similar to routine practice as possible. In contrast, efficacy studies are designed to explain how or why an intervention works, usually in ideal circumstances. While the degree to which RCT findings are generalizable must be kept in mind when applying the results to individual patients, RCTs remain the most valid and rigorous study design for assessing the benefits or harms of an intervention and supporting cause and effect relationships.

Rapid Appraisal Questions for Randomized Controlled Trials

Are the Results of the Study Valid? (Validity)

Although all the issues and standard appraisal questions discussed earlier in this chapter apply to RCTs, there are additional questions that are specific to this methodology. Rapid appraisal questions for RCTs can assist the clinician in quickly determining a particular study's value for practice (see Box 5.4).

Were the Subjects Randomly Assigned to the Experimental and Control Groups? Because the purpose of an RCT is to determine the efficacy or effectiveness of an intervention in producing an outcome, without it being by chance, the groups assigned to either the experimental treatment or the comparison need to be equivalent in all relevant characteristics (e.g. age, disease severity, socioeconomic status, gender) at the beginning of the study, before the intervention is delivered. The best method to ensure baseline equivalency between study groups is to randomly assign participants to the experimental treatment or intervention and to the comparison or placebo-controlled group. This became more obvious when awareness of bias in observational studies arose in the 1980s. Several studies were published that showed how observational studies tended to have more favorable outcomes than an RCT on the same research question (Kunz & Oxman, 1998). In one early review, the researchers found significant differences between the outcomes of 145 trials investigating different treatments for acute myocardial infarction (Chalmers, Celano, Sacks, et al., 1983). Within this body of evidence, the frequency of significant outcomes

box 5.4

Rapid Critical Appraisal Questions for Randomized Controlled Trials

1. Are the Results of the Study Valid?
   a. Were the subjects randomly assigned to the experimental and control groups?
   b. Was random assignment concealed from the individuals who were first enrolling subjects into the study?
   c. Were the subjects and providers kept blind to study group?
   d. Were reasons given to explain why subjects did not complete the study?
   e. Were the follow-up assessments conducted long enough to fully study the effects of the intervention?
   f. Were the subjects analyzed in the group to which they were randomly assigned?
   g. Was the control group appropriate?
   h. Were the instruments used to measure the outcomes valid and reliable?
   i. Were the subjects in each of the groups similar on demographic and baseline clinical variables?
2. What Are the Results?
   a. How large is the intervention or treatment effect (NNT, NNH, effect size, level of significance)?
   b. How precise is the intervention or treatment (CI)?
3. Will the Results Help Me in Caring for My Patients?
   a. Were all clinically important outcomes measured?
   b. What are the risks and benefits of the treatment?
   c. Is the treatment feasible in my clinical setting?
   d. What are my patients/family's values and expectations for the outcome that is trying to be prevented and the treatment itself?

for observational trials for a given treatment was 25%, for nonconcealed RCTs was 11%, and for concealed RCTs was 5%. The average RRR for a myocardial infarction per study type was 34%, 7%, and 3%, respectively. More recent comparisons of study designs have found that observational studies can produce similar results to RCTs with certain types of interventions, which suggests that the general quality of observational studies has improved (Benson & Hartz, 2000; Concato, Shah, & Horwitz, 2000).

In a large review of treatments for 45 conditions, researchers found that while randomized and nonrandomized trials of the same treatment tend to agree on whether the treatment works, they often disagree on the size of the effect (Ioannidis, Haidich, Pappa, et al., 2001). Observational studies may often be preferred in evaluating the harms of medical treatments; however, RCTs of the same treatments usually found larger risks of harm than observational trials, though not always (Papanikolaou, Christidi, & Ioannidis, 2006). In general, it appears that if the clinician chooses which patients receive which treatment or if patients self-select the treatment they will receive, important demographic and clinical variables are introduced that impact the outcomes. Where possible, random assignment should be used to minimize such bias.

The method of randomization should be reported in the methods section of the published research report. To avoid selection bias, the random sequence for assigning patients should be unpredictable (e.g., a random number table, a computer random number generator, or tossing a coin). Researchers sometimes assign participants to groups on an alternate basis or by such criteria as the participant's date of birth or the day of the week, but these methods are not adequate because the sequence can introduce bias. For example, something may be systematically different about the participants who present on a particular day of the week. This kind of assignment is called *pseudo-* or *quasi-randomization* and has been shown to allow assignment bias (Schulz & Grimes, 2002b). Often such approaches are used because they are more convenient; however, the higher risk of bias makes them less desirable.

Variations on the simple randomization method described previously do exist. *Cluster randomization* is a method whereby groups of participants are randomized to the same treatment together (Torgerson, 2001). The unit of measurement (e.g., individual clinician, patient unit, hospital, clinic, or school) in such a study is the experimental unit rather than individual participants. When critically appraising a cluster randomized trial, attention must be paid to whether the results were analyzed properly. A review of such trials in primary care found that 41% did not take account of the clustering in their analyses (Eldridge, Ashby, Feder, et al., 2004). *Block randomization* is where participants from groups with characteristics that cannot be manipulated (e.g., age, gender) are randomly assigned to the intervention and control groups in equal numbers (i.e., 40 men out of a group of 100 men and 40 women out of a group of 100 women). *Stratified randomization* ensures an equal distribution of certain patient characteristics (e.g., gestational age or severity of illness) across the groups.

Was Random Assignment Concealed from the Individuals Who Were First Enrolling Subjects Into the Study? Bias can be introduced when recruiting participants into a study. If those recruiting know to which group the participants will be assigned, they may recruit those going into the intervention group differently than those going into the comparison or control group. Therefore, random assignment should be concealed until after the participants are recruited into the study. This can be accomplished with a method as simple as having designated recruiters who are not investigators or by placing the assignment in an envelope and revealing the assignment once recruitment is complete, to something as elaborate as using an assignment service independent of the study investigators. Using a sealed, opaque envelope to conceal the randomly generated treatment allocation can be susceptible to bias if recruiters are determined to ensure a specific allocation for a particular participant (Schulz & Grimes, 2002a). This susceptibility was illustrated in a study in which researchers anonymously admitted they had held semiopaque envelopes up to a bright light to reveal the allocation sequence or searched a principal investigator's files to discover the allocation list (Schulz, 1995). While such investigators may have rationalized that their actions were well intended, they probably introduced bias into their studies, which could have undermined the conclusions. To avoid such issues, a central research facility could be used where someone other than the study researchers phone or fax the enrollment of a new participant. The central facility determines the treatment allocation and informs the researcher. Such *distance randomization* removes the possibility of researchers introducing bias by attempting to ensure that a patient receives the treatment they believe would be most beneficial; however, there is increased cost to this option, which may prohibit using it.

Were the Subjects and Providers Kept Blind to Study Group? Blinding, sometimes referred to as "masking," is undertaken to reduce the bias that could arise when those observing the outcome know what intervention was received by the study participants. Clinicians may be familiar with the term *double blind*, in which neither the person delivering the intervention nor the participant receiving it knows whether it is the treatment or comparison intervention; however, they may not be as familiar with other degrees of blinding, such as *single blind* and *triple blind* (Devereaux, Manns, Ghali, et al., 2001). All research reports need to describe precisely how groups were blinded to treatment allocation. Double-blinding is very important because it mitigates the placebo effect (i.e., participants respond to an intervention simply because they received something rather than the intervention itself being effective). Studies have demonstrated that the size of a treatment effect can be inflated when patients, clinicians, data collectors, data analyzers, or report authors know which patients received which interventions (Devereaux et al.). When everyone involved is blinded, the expectations of those involved in the study are less likely to influence the results observed.

The degree of blinding utilized in a study partly depends on the intervention being studied and the outcome of interest. For example, death as an outcome is objective and unlikely to be influenced by knowledge of the intervention. However, quality of life or pain scores are relatively subjective measures and may be influenced by the participant's knowledge, if outcomes are self-reporting, or by the health professionals' knowledge, if they are collecting the data.

The **placebo** intervention is another method used for blinding. When investigators report on using a placebo, it should appear like the treatment in all aspects. For example, a placebo medication should look, smell, and taste just like the experimental drug and should be given via the same mode of delivery. A placebo can be developed for many types of interventions. Surgical procedures have been tested in patient-blinded trials using "sham surgery" in which patients receive only an incision. Although ethically controversial, they are viewed by some as necessary to adequately evaluate surgical procedures (Heckerling, 2006).

When the intervention cannot be blinded, usually due to ethical considerations, researchers can ensure that outcome assessment is blinded to reduce bias. For example, patients with burns could be allocated to either the currently used dressing type or an experimental bio-engineered dressing. The patients and their caregivers would be aware of the dressing that they were receiving; however, through taking photographs of the wounds and having assessors score the degree of healing without knowing which patients received which dressing, healing could be measured in a blinded fashion.

Were Reasons Given to Explain Why Subjects Did not Complete the Study? Researchers conducting RCTs prospectively follow people over a period of time, sometimes for years. When critically appraising such studies, the research consumer should examine the number of participants originally enrolled in the study and compare that number with the final numbers in the analyzed outcome data. Ideally, the status of every patient enrolled in the study will be known at the study's completion and reported. When large numbers of participants leave a study and therefore have unknown outcomes, the validity of the study is potentially compromised. Participants may leave a study for many reasons. They may have withdrawn because they had an adverse outcome, died, felt the protocol was too burdensome, or because their symptoms resolved and they saw no need to return for assessment. When critically appraising a study, it is important to consider whether those who were lost to follow-up differed from those who finished the trial. Although a commonly accepted dropout rate is 20% or less (i.e., 80% retention), this arbitrary rate is inadvisable as a sole marker of study validity. Consider that researchers conducting a well-done study with participants who are severely ill plan to enroll more participants than what they know they will need according to a **power analysis**, which was done to reduce making a Type II error (i.e., accepting that the intervention really did not work, when it did). They enroll more participants because they know that there is a high likelihood they will have a high dropout rate. For example, if they know they need 100 participants to ensure that they do not make a Type II error by power calculation, and they anticipate a 50% dropout rate, they then enroll 200 participants to ensure that they have at least 100 participants at the end of the study. This is why it is important to note not only the number of participants who completed the study, but also other factors that influence such studies (e.g., conducted over very long periods or involving severely ill participants) that may lead to higher dropout rates that are unavoidable. Often researchers will compare the demographic variables of those who dropped out of the study to those who remained in the study. They also may assess the impact of loss to follow-up by assuming the worst outcome for those who withdrew and by repeating the analysis. If researchers find that this worst case scenario has the same treatment effect, clinicians can consider that the validity of the study has not been compromised.

Were the Follow-up Assessments Conducted Long Enough to Fully Study the Effects of the Intervention? In critically appraising an intervention study, clinicians consider how long it takes for the intervention to produce the outcome. For example, if a study of the effect of two prophylactic methods on incidence of deep vein thrombosis in hip replacement patients were to evaluate the outcome at discharge, insufficient time would have passed to adequately evaluate the outcome. The follow-up assessment would need to be at least 2 months out for the intervention (i.e., prophylaxis) to achieve the outcome (i.e., incidence of deep vein thrombosis). In critically appraising a study, one timeframe will not apply to all studies. Clinicians should use their experience with patient populations to guide them in determining the appropriate timeframe for a study.

Were the Subjects Analyzed in the Group To Which They Were Randomly Assigned? Another way to ask this question is, Was an intention to treat analysis conducted? Despite the best efforts of investigators, some patients assigned to a particular group may not receive the allocated treatment throughout the entire study period. For example, some people allocated an experimental drug might not take it. Then clinicians must decide whether those participants' outcomes should be included with the control group who received a placebo or with the treatment group to which they were assigned. Imagine an RCT of a new patient information DVD. If some of those assigned to the control intervention hear about the DVD and borrow a copy, should their outcomes be included with the experimental group? In the Chocolate Happiness Undergoing More Pleasantness (CHUMP) study (Chan, 2007), participants in one treatment group traded treatments with another treatment arm of the study, muddying the treatment analysis for both these arms of the study.

One approach to addressing these cross-contamination issues could be to exclude from the analysis the data of everyone who did not adhere to their assigned intervention. However, this approach could potentially introduce bias as patients who change treatment or drop out of a study may be systematically different from those who do not. The intention to treat principle states that data should be analyzed according to the group to which the patient was originally allocated. Researchers follow this principle to preserve the value of random assignment (Busse & Heetveld, 2006). If the comparability of groups is to be maintained through the study, patients should not be excluded from the analysis or switched.

The intention to treat principle tends to minimize Type I error, in which investigators conclude that a difference does exist between intervention and comparison groups when it really does not. It is desirable to minimize Type I error as clinicians need to be confident that when they use an intervention based on a body of evidence (i.e., studies' findings) that the findings from the study are true, and the intervention is effective (i.e., true positive). However, the approach has been criticized as being too conservative and more susceptible to Type II error, in which results indicate that no difference exists when, in fact, there is one (see Table 5.6). One alternative for researchers is to analyze patients according to the intervention they actually obtained in the study (i.e., per protocol analysis), but this method is extremely vulnerable to bias. Clinicians must keep in mind that any study that has substantial deviation from the protocol has methodological problems in its design and should be evaluated extremely carefully as far as worth to practice (Ruiz-Canela, Martínez-González, & de Irala-Estévez, 2000).

Another alternative for researchers would be to exclude patients from final data analysis. It is commonly accepted that patients who were actually ineligible to be enrolled in the trial and who were mistakenly randomized may be excluded, as well as patients who were prematurely enrolled in a trial but who never received the intervention. Excluding large number of these patients from analysis may not introduce bias; however, clinicians should consider the implications these reductions would have on sample size and how that would influence the ability to detect important differences (Fergusson, Horwood, & Ridder, 2005).

Was the Control Group Appropriate? The only difference between the experimental and control groups should be the study intervention. What the researchers choose for the comparison

table 5.6 Implications of study results found by chance

		Study Result	
		Researchers Found that the Intervention Worked (i.e., alternative hypothesis is true)	Researchers Found that the Intervention Did Not Work Better than the Comparison Intervention (i.e., null hypothesis is true)
Reality options	True positive (statistically significant, $p < 0.05$)	On target finding	Oops—made a **Type II error** (false negative— said it really did not work, when it did)
	True negative (statistically not significant, $p > 0.05$)	Oops—made a **Type I error** (false positive—said it really did work when it did not)	On target finding

or control intervention can assist in understanding whether or not the study results are valid. If an intervention involves personal attention, time spent with participants, or other activities, the participants in the treatment group must be provided the same attention, time, or activities as the comparison group. This is because the attention, time, or other activity could impact the outcomes. For example, an RCT was conducted to evaluate the effect of a complementary therapy, Therapeutic Touch (TT), on women's mood (Lafreniere, Mutus, Cameron, S., et al., 1999). Participants in the experimental group removed their shoes, laid on a hospital bed, and listened to soft music while receiving TT. They rested for 5–10 minutes and were taken to a testing room where they completed study questionnaires. Those in the control group went directly to the testing room to complete the questionnaires, without any of the attention or time that the experimental group received. The indicators of mood differed significantly between the groups, but the choice of control made it inappropriate to attribute the differences to TT alone. The soft music, relaxing environment, 10 minutes of rest, or any combination of those confounding variables could have contributed to the observed outcomes, making the study findings unreliable for clinicians to use in practice.

If treatments used in a research study are to be used in clinical practice, a clear description of the intervention and control is essential. If the detail is unclear, clinicians' delivery of the interventions may differ, thereby resulting in a different outcome. For example, drug dosages, details of written information given to participants, or number of clinic visits, if relevant, should be described adequately. The description of the interventions in the methods section also should report any other interventions that differed between the two groups, such as additional visits from practitioners or telephone calls, because these may affect the reported outcomes.

Were the Instruments Used to Measure the Outcomes Valid and Reliable? The instruments researchers use to measure study outcomes are important in determining how useful the results are to clinicians. If the measures are valid (i.e., they measure what they are intended to) and they are reliable (i.e., the items within the instrument are consistent in their measurement, time after time), then clinicians can have more confidence in the study findings. Chapter 17 has more information on validity and reliability of outcome measurement.

Were the Subjects in Each of the Groups Similar on Demographic and Baseline Clinical Variables? Sufficient information about how the participants were selected should be provided in the research paper, usually in the methods section. The study population should be appropriate for the question the study is addressing. Clinicians can decide whether the results reported are relevant to the patients in their care. The choice of participants may affect the size of the observed treatment effect. For example, an intervention delivered to people with advanced disease and cared for in a specialist center may not be as effective for or relevant to those with early-stage disease managed in the community.

The characteristics of all intervention groups should be similar at baseline if randomization did what it is expected to do. These data often are the first data reported in the results section of a research paper. This can include demographic variables of the groups, such as age and gender, stage of disease, or illness severity scores. Investigators generally indicate if the groups differed significantly on any variables. If the groups are different at baseline, clinicians must decide whether these reported differences invalidate the findings, rendering them clinically unusable.

As an example, let's say that researchers attempted to determine the effectiveness of oral sucrose in alleviating procedural pain in infants. The participating infants were randomized to treatment (sucrose) or control (water) groups. Statistical tests found that the two groups did not differ significantly in gestational age, birth weight, and the like. However, by chance and despite the appropriate randomization, a statistically significant difference in the severity of illness scores existed between the two groups and in the number of infants in each group who used a pacifier as a comfort measure. As clinicians evaluate these results, they must decide about the usefulness of the study findings. If the outcome of interest was incidence of infection, these differences may be irrelevant. However, in the hypothetical study described here, the outcome (i.e., pain scores associated with a procedure) could very well be influenced by the infants' use of a pacifier for comfort. In this case, the baseline differences should be taken into account when reporting the observed effects. If the groups are reported as being significantly different on certain baseline variables, clinicians should look for how investigators controlled for those baseline differences in their statistical analyses (e.g., analysis of covariance tests).

What Are the Results? (Reliability)

How Large is the Intervention or Treatment Effect and How Precise is the Intervention or Treatment? How the size and precision of the effect are reported is extremely important.

As discussed earlier in this chapter, trials should report the total number of study participants assigned to the groups, the numbers available for measurement of outcomes, and the occurrence or event rates in the groups. If these data are not reported, the measures of effect, such as RR and OR, cannot be calculated. Confidence interval and/or *p* values (or the information required to calculate these) should also be included in the results presented to identify the precision of the effect estimates.

Clinicians have to decide on the usefulness or clinical significance of any statistical differences observed. As discussed earlier, statistically significant differences and clinically meaningful differences are not always equivalent. If the CI is wide and includes the point estimate of no effect, such as an RR of 1 or a reported *p* value of greater than 0.05, the precision of the measurement is likely to be inadequate and the results unreliable. Clinicians cannot have confidence that they can implement the treatment and get similar results. Clinicians must also ask, since the results are not significant and the CI is wide, if it is possible that the sample size was not large enough. A larger sample would likely produce a narrower CI. In addition, trials are increasingly conducted across a large number of healthcare sites. If the findings are consistent across different settings, clinicians could be more confident that the findings were reliable.

Will the Results Assist Me in Caring for My Patients? (Applicability)

Are the Outcomes Measured Clinically Relevant? Evidence-based practice requires integration of clinical expertise with the best available research evidence and patient values, concerns, and choices. Clinicians need to utilize their own expertise at this point in the critical appraisal process to decide whether the outcomes measured in a study were clinically important. They

> ### clinical scenario 5.4
>
> At a recent meeting of the surgical division managers of your hospital, the budget was discussed. An idea was proposed that a legitimate cost-cutting measure may be found by discharging women earlier after surgery for breast cancer. Debate about the advantages and disadvantages of such a change to health service provision continued until it was decided to investigate the available evidence.

also need to assess whether the timing of outcome measurement in relation to the delivery of the intervention was appropriate (Roland & Torgerson, 1998). For example, it may be important to measure the effectiveness of an intervention, such as corticosteroid administration in the management of traumatic brain injury, by measuring survival to discharge from the intensive care unit. However, in determining the effectiveness of a cancer therapy, survival to 5 years may be more relevant. Outcome measures such as mortality would appear appropriate in these examples but would not likely be relevant in trials with patients with dementia or chronic back pain. Quality of life scores or days lost from work would be more useful measures in the studies of these types of conditions.

Investigators may be interested in more than one outcome when designing a study, such as less pain and an improved quality of life. Researchers should designate the primary outcome of interest in their research report, and should clarify what outcome formed the basis of their a priori power calculation (assuming one was carried out). This should minimize problems with multiple measures or data dredging in attempts to ensure that a significant result is found.

What the Literature Says: Answering a Clinical Question

The following study may begin to help answer the question that arises from Clinical Scenario 5.4, In women who have had surgery for breast cancer (P), how does early discharge (I) compared with current length of stay (C) affect coping with the challenges of recovery (O) (physical and psychosocial)?: Bundred, N., Maguire, P., Reynolds, J., Grimshaw, J., Morris, J., Thomson, L., et al. (1998). Randomised controlled trial of effects of early discharge after surgery for breast cancer. *British Medical Journal, 317,* 1275–1279. Using the general critical appraisal questions, clinicians can critically appraise this study to determine whether it provides valid, reliable, and relevant evidence.

The participants in the study were 100 women who had early breast cancer and who were undergoing (a) mastectomy with axillary node clearance ($n = 20$) or (b) breast conservation surgery ($n = 80$). The intervention and comparison were early discharge program versus routine length of stay. The outcomes measured were physical illness (i.e., infection, seroma formation, shoulder movement) and psychological illness (i.e., depression and anxiety scores). The timing of follow-up was first preoperatively, then 1 and 3 months postoperatively.

Are the Results of the Study Valid? (Validity)

After patients were recruited into the study, they were randomized in clusters for each week of admissions by a research nurse who opened a sealed envelope containing the randomization code. A flowchart was provided in the report to identify the recruitment, participation, and follow-up of participants. Before the study began (i.e., a priori), a power calculation was undertaken to determine how large the sample needed to be to lessen the chance of accepting that there was no effect when there was one (i.e., Type II error). Participants were analyzed using the intention to treat analysis. Participants were not blinded to the intervention and no mention was made of whether the investigators assessing the outcomes were blinded. A detailed description of the intervention and the control management was given. The groups were reported as similar at baseline. Based on these methods, the study results should be considered valid.

What Are the Results? (Reliability)

Results are expressed as OR with 95% CI, and *p* values are provided where there was statistical significance. Women discharged early had greater shoulder movement (OR 0.28; 95% CI, 0.08–0.95) and less wound pain (OR 0.28; 95% CI, 0.10–0.79) at 3 months compared with the standard length of stay group. Symptom questionnaire scores were significantly lower in the early discharge group at 1 month. It is difficult to determine whether there were clinically meaningful differences in the psychological measures because a total of six tools were used to measure psychological illness. Multiple measurements in themselves are more likely to lead to significant results.

Will the Results Help Me in Caring for My Patients? (Applicability)

The results presented in this research report are those of a planned interim analysis (i.e., the analysis was done to confirm that there were no adverse consequences of early discharge). This approach is reasonable to protect the participants. The results of the full study, when and if completed, would be important to evaluate. From this interim analysis, it would appear that early discharge might be appropriate if women are given sufficient support and resources. However, an outcome that may affect the usefulness of the findings is cost. A cost analysis was not undertaken, so further research that addresses this point may need to be found and appraised before making any final decisions about changing an entire health service model. Based on these issues, this evidence will assist clinicians to consider early discharge but will not answer the clinical question of whether it is the best option for most women who have had surgery for breast cancer.

chapter 5

121

Critical Appraisal of Systematic Reviews

A systematic review is a compilation of similar studies that address a specific clinical question (see Table 5.7). To conduct a systematic review, a detailed search strategy is employed to find the relevant evidence to answer a clinical question. The researchers determine beforehand what

table 5.7 Definitions of different types of research evidence reviews

Review	Definition
Systematic review	A compilation of like studies to address a specific clinical question using a detailed, comprehensive search strategy and rigorous appraisal methods for the purpose of summarizing, appraising, and communicating the results and implications of all the research available on a clinical question. A systematic review is the most rigorous approach to minimization of bias in summarizing research.
Meta-analysis	A statistical approach to synthesizing the results of a number of studies that produces a larger sample size and thus greater power to determine the true magnitude of an effect. Used to obtain a single-effect measure (i.e., a summary statistic) of the results of all studies included in a systematic review.
Integrative review	A systematic review that does not have a summary statistic because of limitations in the studies found (usually due to heterogeneous studies or samples).
Narrative review	A research review that includes published papers that support an author's particular point of view and usually serves as a general background discussion of a particular issue. An explicit and systematic approach to searching for and evaluating papers is usually not used.

inclusion and exclusion criteria will be used to select identified studies. Systematic reviews of RCTs, considered Level I evidence, are found at the top of the hierarchy of evidence for intervention studies (see Chapter 1, Box 1.2). Systematic review methodology is the most rigorous approach to minimization of bias in reviewing studies.

A systematic review is not the same as a literature review or narrative review. The methods used in a systematic review are specific and rigorous, whereas a narrative review usually compiles published papers that support an author's particular point of view or serve as a general background discussion for a particular issue. A systematic review is a scientific approach to summarize, appraise, and communicate the results and implications of several studies that may have contradictory results.

Research trials rarely, if ever, have flawless methodology and a large enough sample size to provide a conclusive answer to questions about clinical effectiveness. Archie Cochrane, an epidemiologist after whom the Cochrane Collaboration is named, recognized that the increasingly large number of RCTs of variable quality and differing results were seldom made available to clinicians in useful formats to improve practice. "It is surely a great criticism of our profession that we have not organised a critical summary, by specialty or subspecialty, adapted periodically, of all relevant randomised controlled trials" (Cochrane, 1979, p. 9). For this reason, the systematic review methodology has been gradually adopted and adapted to assist healthcare professionals take advantage of the overwhelming amount of information available in an effort to improve patient care and outcomes. According to the Cochrane Collaboration, which facilitates the production of healthcare systematic reviews and provides much helpful information on the Internet, the key characteristics of a systematic review are (Higgins & Green, 2008).

- A clearly stated set of objectives with predefined eligibility criteria for studies
- An explicit, reproducible methodology
- A systematic search that attempts to identify all studies that would meet the eligibility criteria
- A standardized assessment of the validity of the findings of the included studies, for example, through the assessment of risk of bias
- A systematic presentation of the synthesis of studies, including the characteristics and findings of the studies included in the review

A systematic review is a form of *secondary research* because it uses previously conducted studies. The study types discussed previously in this chapter would be *primary research* studies. Because it is such an obviously different research approach, it requires unique critical appraisal questions to address the quality of a review.

> *Life is either a daring adventure or nothing.*
>
> *H e l e n   K e l l e r*

Specific Critical Appraisal Questions for Systematic Reviews

Systematic reviews have multiple phases of development, with each one designed to reduce bias. This entire process requires attention to detail that can make it time consuming and costly (O'Mathúna, Fineout-Overholt, & Kent, 2008). Clinicians have specific questions that they must ask in appraising a systematic review (see Box 5.5), just as they should do with other study designs to determine their value for practice. (Please note that the discussion below of critical appraisal of systematic reviews follows a slightly different format than prior research design sections.)

---

box 5.5

Rapid Critical Appraisal Questions for Systematic Reviews

1. Are the Results of the Review Valid?
   a. Are the studies contained in the review RCTs?
   b. Does the review include a detailed description of the search strategy to find all relevant studies?
   c. Does the review describe how validity of the individual studies was assessed (e.g., methodological quality, including the use of random assignment to study groups and complete follow-up of the subjects)?
   d. Were the results consistent across studies?
   e. Were individual patient data or aggregate data used in the analysis?
2. What Were the Results?
   a. How large is the intervention or treatment effect (OR, RR, effect size, level of significance)?
   b. How precise is the intervention or treatment (CI)?
3. Will the Results Assist Me in Caring for My Patients?
   a. Are my patients similar to the ones included in the review?
   b. Is it feasible to implement the findings in my practice setting?
   c. Were all clinically important outcomes considered, including risks and benefits of the treatment?
   d. What is my clinical assessment of the patient and are there any contraindications or circumstances that would inhibit me from implementing the treatment?
   e. What are my patient's and his or her family's preferences and values about the treatment under consideration?

Are the Results of the Study Valid? (Validity)

Phase 1 of a systematic review identifies the clinical practice question to be addressed and the most suitable type of research design to answer it. The next step, Phase 2, develops inclusion criteria for the studies to be kept and exclusion criteria for those studies that will not be included in the analysis. These steps are completed prior to gathering any evidence.

Once Phase 2 of planning is completed, Phase 3 begins the process of searching for and retrieving published and unpublished literature related to the study question. Rigorous search strategies are developed to ensure that research findings from all relevant disciplines and in all languages are found. Multiple computer databases (e.g., MEDLINE, CINAHL, EMBASE) are searched, as well as conference proceedings, dissertations, and other "grey literature." Grey literature is unpublished studies or studies published by governmental agencies or other organizations that are not peer-reviewed (Hopewell, McDonald, Clarke, et al., 2007). The section of the research report that discusses Phase 3 includes answers to the critical appraisal questions, Are the studies contained in the review RCTs? Does the review include a detailed description of the search strategy to find all relevant studies?

Systematic reviews minimize bias by the way in which the literature pertaining to the research question is identified and obtained. The research literature comprises the raw data for a review. When appraising a systematic review, the clinician looks for a detailed description of the databases accessed, the search strategies used, and the search terms. The databases should be specified, as should the years searched. The authors should indicate whether the retrieved information was limited to English language studies only. MEDLINE and CINAHL are probably the best known healthcare publication databases for such studies. Although these databases index thousands of journals, not all journals are indexed by any one database. If reviewers limit their search to English language sources, they risk biasing the research they may find that addresses that particular research question. EMBASE is a European database of healthcare research, and many other databases exist in non-English languages. However, the cost of accessing these databases and translating non-English language papers may create challenges.

Search terms used should be clearly described so the reader can make an informed decision about whether all relevant publications were found. For example, a review of antibiotic therapy for otitis media might use the search terms *otitis media* and *glue ear*. However, *red ear* also is used commonly for this disorder, and omission of the term from the search strategy may lead to the review missing some studies. Most electronic databases provide an index or thesaurus of the best terms to use in searching, such as MeSH terms in MEDLINE (O'Mathúna et al., 2008).

Both published and unpublished research should be identified and retrieved where possible because of the issue of publication bias, which occurs when publication of a study's results is based on the direction (positive or negative) or significance of the findings (Phillips, 2004). Publication bias arises for several reasons and means that the results of systematic reviews or meta-analyses that include only published results could be misleading. Including grey literature in the search strategy is one way to overcome publication bias. Reviewers will commonly search relevant journals by hand, called hand searching, and examine the reference lists of previously retrieved papers for possible studies. In addition, a review will usually specify whether researchers in the field of interest were contacted to identify other studies. Additionally, authors of retrieved studies may be contacted if information in the publication is missing or insufficient to make a decision regarding inclusion. This process of literature retrieval can be costly, and clinicians need to consider whether the absence of such an exhaustive search affects the conclusions drawn in the review.

In addition, clinicians should be able to clearly see from the systematic review which studies were included and which were excluded. The studies are usually presented in a table format and provide clinicians with information about the study populations, settings, and outcomes measured. Ideally, included studies should be relatively homogenous (i.e., the same) with respect to these aspects. Reasons for exclusion, such as study design or quality issues, also should be included in a table. The information presented in these tables assists clinicians to decide whether it was appropriate to combine the results of the studies.

Publication bias is used to describe the findings that studies reporting a positive result have a greater chance of being published (Decullier, Lhéritier, & Chapuis, 2005). Thus, inclusion of only published studies in a systematic review may result in biased reporting of the effect of an intervention. Clinicians need to be reassured that all reasonable attempts were made to retrieve both published and unpublished studies. When unpublished studies are not included, the size of any effect is likely to be exaggerated. One way researchers may indicate that they evaluated the presence of publication bias is through the use of a statistical test called the "funnel plot." This method is a scatterplot in which each study's sample size is plotted on the horizontal axis and each study's effect size is plotted on the vertical axis of the graph. When the risk of publication bias is low, a symmetrical inverted funnel is expected. An asymmetrical plot may indicate selection bias through the absence of some studies.

The next critical appraisal question, Does the review describe how validity of the individual studies was assessed (e.g., methodological quality, including the use of random assignment to study groups and complete follow-up of the subjects)? can be answered in the section of the report about Phases 4 and 5 of a systematic review. These phases involve assessing the quality and validity of the included studies. The systematic review should report precisely how this was conducted and against what criteria evaluations were made. A clear report of how the review was conducted can assist the clinician in determining the worth of the gathered studies for practice.

The critical appraisal process itself shows that primary research is of varying quality. A rigorous, high-quality systematic review should base its primary conclusions only on high-quality studies. A clear description of the basis for quality assessment should be included in the review. Although a review with a rigorous methodology that includes only RCTs is considered the highest level of evidence for intervention questions, other clinical questions (e.g., questions of prognosis) that are not appropriate for an RCT design also should include the types of study designs that are most appropriate to answer those questions (e.g., cohort studies).

The systematic review report should inform clinicians about how data were extracted from the individual studies (Phase 6) and provide an overview of the evaluation of the included studies (Phase 7). Data are extracted and assessment of the quality of studies in the review is conducted independently by at least two members of the review team. The independent assessment further reduces the possibility of bias regarding evaluation of the studies. This process should be discussed in a systematic review as well as how the researchers resolved any disagreement they may have had regarding study findings.

The studies included in a systematic review often have varying designs and inconsistent results, which may allow for only a descriptive evaluation of the studies. When studies are similar enough to be combined in a quantitative synthesis (e.g., comparing effect size, ORs), this can be very helpful to clinicians. The statistical approach to synthesizing the results of two or more studies is called a meta-analysis. A meta-analysis is a systematic review, but not all systematic reviews are meta-analyses (Fineout-Overholt et al., 2008). When critically appraising these studies, clinicians must keep in mind that overviews or integrative reviews do not apply statistical analyses to the results across studies, generally because the studies in review are not amenable to that kind of analysis. Instead, these reviews or evidence syntheses often culminate in recommendations based on descriptive evaluations of the findings, or they indicate to clinicians that the included studies on a given topic cannot be synthesized, for a myriad of reasons. This section of the study report is helpful in answering the following critical appraisal questions: Were the results consistent across studies? Were individual patient data or aggregate data used in the analysis? The latter question reflects whether pooling the data was suitable or not from across the included studies. If it is possible (i.e., the researchers studied the same variables, defined them the same way, measured them the same way), given what you know about the sample size from your prior reading, consider how researchers could have more reliable findings with a larger pooled sample (e.g., 1,000), than 10 smaller samples (e.g., 100).

Chance alone would suggest that some variation will arise in the results of individual studies examining the same question. The differences in studies and the reported findings (i.e., heterogeneity) can be due to study design. Formal statistical methods can be used to test whether there is significant heterogeneity among the studies that precludes them being combined. Generally, reviewers will report using such a test. However, as with all statistical tests, statistical significance is not the same as clinical meaningfulness.

What are the Results? (Reliability)

The results section of the systematic review can address the following critical appraisal questions: How large is the intervention or treatment effect (e.g., NNT, NNH, effect size, level of significance)? How precise is the intervention or treatment? Common statistics seen in systematic reviews are ORs and effect sizes. If the study is a meta-analysis, these values will assist the clinician in determining the magnitude of effect. The CI is the indicator of the preciseness of the study findings (i.e., can clinicians get what the researcher got, if they repeat the intervention?).

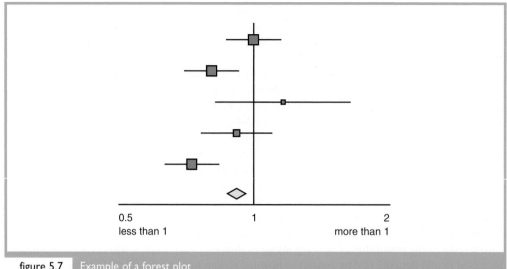

0.5
less than 1

1

2
more than 1

| figure 5.7 | Example of a forest plot |

A major advantage of a systematic review is the combining of results from many studies. In meta-analyses, combining the results of several studies produces a larger sample size and thus greater power to accurately determine the magnitude of the effect. Because of the strength of this type of evidence, this relatively new methodology has become a hallmark of EBP (Stevens, 2001).

Meta-analysis is the statistical method used to obtain a single-effect measure of the summarized results of all studies included in a review. While the technique may sound complicated, clinicians do not require even moderate understanding of the mathematics involved in such methods. A solid understanding of how to interpret the results is what is needed. The meta-analysis of a number of trials recognizes how sample size of the studies may influence findings and, thereby, provides a more precise estimate of treatment effect than individual studies. A "forest plot" (see Figure 5.7) is a diagrammatic representation of the results of trials included in a meta-analysis, along with their CIs. You can now apply what you learned from the explanation of OR and CI given earlier in this chapter. In the forest plot, each square is the measure of effect of an individual study, and the horizontal line shows its CI. The larger the square, the more important the contribution of that particular study is to the meta-analysis (Lewis & Clarke, 2001). The diamond at the bottom of the forest plot is the summary treatment effect of all studies, with the vertical points of the diamond being the result and the horizontal points of the diamond being the CI for that overall result.

To interpret these data, clinicians must consider the outcome first. If there is no difference in outcomes between the treatment and control groups, the resulting OR is 1.0. If the CI crosses the line of no treatment effect (OR = 1.0), the study is not statistically significant. If the outcome is something you do not want (e.g., death, pain, or infection), a square to the right of the line means that the treatment was worse than the control in the trial (i.e., there were more deaths in the treated group compared to the comparison or control group). Usually, this is not the desired result. For a negative outcome, the desired result is to see the treatment decrease the outcome, and this would be reflected in a square to the left of the line of no effect. A square to the left of the line means that the treatment was better, which is what would be desired for outcomes you want (e.g., stopping smoking or continuation of breastfeeding).

The forest plot gives a way to make an informed estimate of study homogeneity. A forest plot with study estimates that are scattered all over and have wide CIs suggests excessive heterogeneity in the measurement and precision of effect. Bringing together all of the studies to answer a particular clinical question provides important information; however, studies often are too dissimilar to combine their results. If possible, reviewers can quantify the effectiveness of the intervention in a summary statistic that can be compared across these studies. Alternatively, the studies may not be of sufficient quality to combine or compare, which provides information to researchers regarding the need for additional high-quality research.

Another caveat about appraising a systematic review is that clinicians must watch for reports in which reviewers have analyzed by subgroups when no overall effect was found. Study subsets may be analyzed on the basis of particular patient demographics or methodological quality of the included studies. However, in such an analysis, the purpose of the initial randomization to treatment and control groups in the underlying studies is essentially lost because the balance afforded by randomization does not extend to subgroupings after the fact. However, some subgroup analyses may be legitimate. For example, if an overall effect is found, but individual studies varied widely in quality, subgroup analysis based on study quality may be warranted and important. For example, researchers conducting a meta-analysis of chromium supplements for diabetes found some beneficial outcomes, but when subgroup analyses were conducted based on study quality, those studies with the lowest quality had significantly more favorable outcomes than the high-quality studies (Balk, Tatsioni, Lichtenstein, et al., 2007). This suggests that the overall beneficial results of the meta-analysis were unduly influenced by low-quality studies and therefore the overall results of the meta-analysis should be applied with caution in clinical practice.

Another caveat for clinicians to look for is a sensitivity analysis, which is done to help determine how the main findings may change as a result of pooling the data. It involves first combining the results of all the included studies. The studies considered of lowest quality or unpublished studies are then excluded, and the data is reanalyzed. This process is repeated sequentially, excluding studies until only the studies of highest quality are included in the analysis. An alteration in the overall results at any point in study exclusion indicates how sensitive the conclusions are to the quality of the studies included.

The final issue for clinicians in critically appraising this portion of a systematic review is to determine if the reviewers justified their conclusions. Evidence-based practice requires integrating the best evidence with clinical expertise and patient values, choices, and concerns. Poor-quality systematic reviews exist, just as there are poor-quality primary studies. Clinicians need to ask whether the interpretations of the reviewers are justified and valid based on the strength of the evidence presented in the review.

Will the Results Help Me in Caring for My Patients? (Applicability)

The final questions in critically appraising systematic reviews are (a) Are my patients similar to the ones included in the review? (b) Is it feasible to implement the findings in my practice setting? (c) Were all clinically important outcomes considered, including risks and benefits of the treatment? (d) What is my clinical assessment of the patient and are there any contraindications or circumstances that would inhibit me from implementing the treatment? and (e) What are my patient's and his or her family's preferences and values about the treatment under consideration? Common sense may appear to answer some of the questions, but without careful attention to them, important application issues can be missed.

Interpreting the Results of a Study: Example Six. You are thinking of establishing an early discharge program for first-time mothers, but are concerned that such a program may be associated with unplanned readmissions for breast-feeding related problems. You find three RCTs with different sample sizes. The smallest study ($n = 50$) reports that there is no difference in readmissions between the early discharge and routine length of stay groups. A study with a larger sample size ($n = 100$) reports an increase in readmissions in the experimental group. The study with the largest sample size ($n = 1,000$) reports an increase in readmissions in the control group. All three

---

clinical scenario 5.5

Nursing staff on your unit in a residential elder care facility have just completed an audit of falls in the previous 12 months. A total of 45 falls were documented during the period, but the actual number could have been higher. Interested and concerned clinicians meet to discuss the results and consider options for reducing this incidence. A few people bring copies of trials with them that discuss the efficacy of fall prevention programs that incorporated various interventions. All the trials look like high-quality studies but they all show different results. Which one to believe? It would be nice to have one study that summarizes all the available evidence for you and presents the implications for clinical practice.

---

studies are rigorously conducted trials with very similar patient demographics. How can these three studies be synthesized for clinical decision making?

While the study with the larger sample size is more likely to capture the variation in the reference population and thus represent a more accurate estimation of the effect of such a program, the other studies need to be considered as well, as they may have small samples, but clinically meaningful results. Ideally, you would like to have a meta-analysis that combines the results of all three studies and pools the study samples. This would provide a sample size of 1,150 and important evidence to guide decision making.

What the Literature Says: Answering a Clinical Question

The following study may help answer the clinical question for Clinical Scenario 5.5, In elders (P), how do fall prevention programs (I) compared to no fall prevention (C) affect fall rates (O)?: Gillespie, L., Gillespie, W. J., Robertson, M., Lamb, S., Cumming, R., & Rowe, B. (2003). Interventions for preventing falls in elderly people. *Cochrane Database of Systematic Reviews, 4.** In this systematic review, the objective was to assess the effects of interventions designed to reduce the incidence of falls in elderly people. It included people living in the community, in institutional care, or in hospital care. The search strategy was designed and conducted by the Cochrane Musculoskeletal Group. MEDLINE (1966–2001), EMBASE (1988–2001), CINAHL (1982–2001), National Research Register, and Current Controlled Trials were searched. A hand search of reference lists of articles was conducted, and field researchers were contacted. The selection criterion was that studies had to be randomized trials of interventions designed to minimize the effect of or exposure to risk factors for falling in elderly people. Main outcomes of interest were the number of fallers or falls. Trials reporting only intermediate outcomes were excluded. The data collection and analysis methods involved two reviewers independently assessing the trial quality and extracting data. Data were pooled using the fixed effect model where appropriate. In the fixed effect model, the

> traditional assumption is that the event rates are fixed in each of the control... and treatment groups. Any variation in the observed event rates is then attributed to random chance. If the trials being combined are truly clinically homogeneous and have been designed properly (for example, with balanced arms), which is the situation that will commonly pertain, then in this (and only in this) case it is appropriate to pool raw data. (Moore, Gavaghan, Edwards, et al., 2002, p. 3)

The main findings were that beneficial interventions included muscle strengthening; group exercise; home hazard assessment and modification; withdrawal of psychotropic medication; and

---

*In 2010 this review was withdrawn and replaced by two reviews: one focused on the community and one on institutions (Gillespie, et al., 2009; Cameron, et al., 2010).

multidisciplinary, multifactorial risk factor screening. Interventions of unknown effectiveness included nutritional supplementation, pharmacologic therapies, hormone replacement therapy, fall prevention programs in institutional settings, and interventions using a cognitive/behavioral approach alone.

The reviewers' conclusions were that interventions to prevent falls that are likely to be effective are now available. Costs per fall prevented have been established for four of the interventions. Some potential interventions are of unknown effectiveness, and further research is indicated.

Are the Results of the Study Valid? (Validity)

Only RCTs that met quality inclusion criteria were included in the review. A large number of databases were searched, and both English and non-English language sources were searched. Two reviewers independently assessed the quality of trials and extracted the data. Tables of included and excluded studies were provided. These methods produced valid results.

What Are the Results? (Reliability)

Relative risk or risk ratio and 95% CI were given for interventions likely to be of benefit, such as a program of muscle strengthening (RR 0.80; 95% CI, 0.66–0.98) and home hazard assessment and modification (RR 0.64; 95% CI, 0.49–0.84). Pooled study results were tested for heterogeneity, and the authors acknowledged that cluster randomized study results could not be pooled with individually randomized study results, because a falsely narrow CI would be calculated.

Will the Results Help Me in Caring for My Patients? (Applicability)

Although there was variation in the study settings, types of patients, and interventions included in this review, the authors provided a description of the circumstances in which a particular intervention may be beneficial. Economic outcomes were not reported, and there were no trials of reducing the serious consequences of falls. Given the clinical question of reducing falls in an elder care facility, the evidence is applicable.

> *When a resolute young fellow steps up to the great bully,*
> *the world, and takes him boldly by the beard, he is often*
> *surprised to find it comes off in his hand, and that it was*
> *only tied on to scare away the timid adventurers.*
> *Ralph Waldo Emerson*

Evaluation & Synthesis: Final Steps In Critical Appraisal

Critical appraisal includes rapid critical appraisal, as described throughout the chapter, as well as digging deeper. Once studies have been defined as keepers, they should be melded together into a synthesis upon which to base practice and standards of care. Clinical decisions at the point of care may use already synthesized or synopsized resources, as described in Chapter 3; however, when sustainable practice changes are required, careful evaluation and synthesis of evidence are necessary. To provide best care, we must act on what we currently know and understand from what we synthesize as the best available evidence (Fineout-Overholt, 2008).

table 5.8 Example of headings for an evaluation table

Citation of a Single Study	Theoretical or Conceptual Framework	Study Design and Method	Sample Characteristics and Setting	Names and Definitions of Major Variables	Outcomes Measures	Data Analysis	Findings	Level and Quality of Evidence
Jones and Smith (2009)	ARCC	RCT	EBPM ACC EBPM M/S	IV = MS DV = NrsS	WSI	*t*-Test	NSD	Level II
Smith and Jones (2007)	ARCC	RCT	EBPM Peds NM	MS NrsS	WSI JS	*t*-Test	EBPM SD NM, $p < 0.001$	Level II

ACC, acute and critical care; ARCC, Advancing Research & Clinical practice through close collaboration; DV, dependent variable; EBPM, EBP mentors; IV, independent variable; JS, job satisfaction; M/S, Medical/Surgical; MS, managerial style; NM, nurse managers; NrsS, nurse satisfaction; NSD, no significant difference; Peds, Pediatrics; RCT, randomized controlled trial; SD, significantly different; WSI, Work Satisfaction Index.

Each individual study should be evaluated using an evaluation table like the one found in Table 5.8. The essential elements are listed as headings for the table. There may be other headings that clinicians feel are important to their studies, which can be added. The PICOT question is the driver for the evaluation table and synthesis tables. For example, with data analysis, while many statistics may be reported in a study, only those statistics that assist you in answering your clinical question should be placed in the table. As well, only the findings that are relevant to the clinical question should be placed in the table. Keeping the order of information placed in the table clear and simple is imperative for comparisons across studies for synthesis. Some suggestions to make the table user-friendly are to: (a) use abbreviations (e.g., RCT) with a legend for interpretation, (b) keep the order of the information the same in each study (e.g., MS would appear at the top of the variables section for each study), and (c) place similar statistics in the same order in each study for easy comparison (Fineout-Overholt, 2008). Appendix E contains templates for evaluation and synthesis tables for conducting an evidence review.

Synthesis occurs as clinicians enter the study data into the evaluation table (Fineout-Overholt, 2008). Each study is compared to the others for how it agrees or disagrees with the others in the table. Some examples of the columns that would be included in the table are study design, sample characteristics, and major variables studied. Using the last column to document the level of evidence as well as the quality assists the clinician to quickly peruse the strength of the evidence that leads to the confidence to act on that evidence to impact outcomes (Fineout-Overholt).

Fineout-Overholt (2008) outlines some principles of synthesis that can assist clinicians in making determinations about how to use the data extracted from across the studies. These principles of synthesis include making decisions about which study details and findings need to be synthesized. The clinical question drives this decision making. Often, clinicians can cluster studies around different aspects of methods or findings (e.g., study design, interventions, outcome measurement, or findings). Synthesis requires a thoughtful consideration of inconsistencies as well as consistencies across studies. These can give great insights into what is not known, what is known, and what researchers need to focus on to improve the body of evidence to address a particular clinical question. Pulling together the conclusions or major findings from a study can be of great help in clinical decision making. In addition, carefully discussing how studies' strengths,

table 5.9 **Example of headings for a synthesis table***

Sample Clinical Question: In adolescents at risk for depression (P), how does relaxation and visual imagery (I₁) and/or music (I₂) compared to yoga (C) affect depression (O) over 5 months (T)?

Study Author	Year	Number of Participants	Mean Age (or other sample characteristic that is pertinent to your question)	Study Design	Intervention	Major Finding that Addresses Your Question
Carrigan	2001	15	15	R	Yoga	↓ D
Johnson	2005	280	17	Q	Relaxation/ visual imagery	— D
Meade	1999	51	19	Q	Music	↓ D
Smith	2008	1,400	14	R	Relaxation/ visual imagery + music	↑ D

*Example is hypothetical.

D, depression; Q, quasi-experimental study; R, randomized controlled trial (all studies measured depression using the Beck Depression Scale); ↓, decreased; ↑, increased; —, no effect.

limitations, and level of evidence match or do not match can assist in the final conclusion of what should be done in practice. Synthesis tables are the best way to formulate and communicate the information that is essential for comparison across studies (see Table 5.9). A caveat about synthesis is in order here: Synthesis is not reporting the findings of consecutive studies; rather, it is combining, contrasting, and interpreting a body of evidence to reach a conclusion about what is known and what should be done with that knowledge to improve healthcare outcomes.

Evaluation and synthesis tables differ in that evaluation tables contain information about each individual study, while synthesis tables contain only those aspects of the individual studies that are common or unique across studies (e.g., study design, outcomes, findings). Such tables should have the advantages of clarity and simplicity. Synthesis tables enable clinicians to confidently make clinical decisions about the care that is provided to their patients by making evidence from studies readily useable for clinical decision making (Fineout-Overholt, 2008). Chapter 9 speaks to implementation of evidence, which is the next step after critical appraisal (i.e., rapid critical appraisal, evaluation, and synthesis).

Conclusion

Evidence-based healthcare decision making requires the integration of clinical expertise with the best available research evidence and the patients' values, concerns, and choices. To do this, clinicians must develop skills in critically appraising available research studies and applying the findings. The validity of study findings depends upon how well researchers use study design principles and how different designs best match the clinical question under investigation. Clinicians must understand these aspects of studies to utilize research appropriately to improve practice. Accessing and regularly using one of the many critical appraisal skills guides available will help the clinician learn more about the scientific basis for health management and lead to more informed decision making and better patient outcomes (see Appendix D). Completing the critical appraisal process with evaluation and synthesis of studies will boost clinicians' confidence to act on strong evidence to change outcomes.

references

Awada, A., & al Jumah, M. (1999). The first-of-Ramadan headache. *Headache, 39*(7), 490–493.

Balk, E. M., Tatsioni, A., Lichtenstein, A. H., Lau, J., & Pittas, A. G. (2007). Effect of chromium supplementation on glucose metabolism and lipids: A systematic review of randomized controlled trials. *Diabetes Care, 30*(8), 2154–2163.

Barratt, A., Wyer, P. C., Hatala, R., McGinn, T., Dans, A. L., Keitz, S., et al. (2004). Tips for learners of evidence-based medicine: 1. Relative risk reduction, absolute risk reduction and number needed to treat. *Canadian Medical Association Journal, 171*(4), 353–358.

Benson, K., & Hartz, A. J. (2000). A comparison of observational studies and randomized, controlled trials. *New England Journal of Medicine, 342*(25), 1878–1886.

Boffetta, P., McLaughlin, J. K., La Vecchia, C., Tarone, R. E., Lipworth, L., & Blot, W. J. (2008). False-positive results in cancer epidemiology: A plea for epistemological modesty. *Journal of the National Cancer Institute, 100*(14), 988–995.

Bono, C. M., & Tornetta III, P. (2006). Common errors in the design of orthopaedic studies. *Injury, 37*(4), 355–360.

Bracken, M. B., Shepard, M. J., Holford, T. R., Leo-Summers, L., Aldrich, E. F., Fazl, M., et al. (1997). Administration of methylprednisolone for 24 or 48 h or tirilazad mesylate for 48 h in the treatment of acute spinal cord injury: Results of the Third National Acute Spinal Cord Injury Randomized Controlled Trial. National Acute Spinal Cord Injury Study. *Journal of the American Medical Association, 277*(20), 1597–1604.

Brower, R. G., Lanken, P. N., MacIntyre, N., Matthay, M. A., Morris, A., Ancukiewicz, M., et al. (2004). Higher versus lower positive end-expiratory pressures in patients with the acute respiratory distress syndrome. *New England Journal of Medicine, 351*(4), 327–336.

Bundred, N., Maguire, P., Reynolds, J., Grimshaw, J., Morris, J., Thomson, L., et al. (1998). Randomised controlled trial of effects of early discharge after surgery for breast cancer. *British Medical Journal, 317*(7168), 1275–1279.

Busse, J. W., & Heetveld, M. J. (2006). Critical appraisal of the orthopaedic literature: Therapeutic and economic analysis. *Injury, 37*(4), 312–320.

Callas, P. W., & Delwiche, F. A. (2008). Searching the biomedical literature: Research study designs and critical appraisal. *Clinical Laboratory Science, 21*(1), 42–48.

Cameron, I. D., Murray, G. R., Gillespie, L. D., Robertson, M. C., Hill, K. D., Cumming, R. G., & Kerse, N. (2010). Interventions for preventing falls in older people in nursing care facilities and hospitals. *Cochrane Database of Systematic Review*, 1.

CAPRIE Steering Committee. (1996). A randomised, blinded, trial of clopidogrel versus aspirin in patients at risk of ischaemic events (CAPRIE). *Lancet, 348*(9038), 1329–1339.

Carley, S., & Lecky, F. (2003). Statistical consideration for research. *Emergency Medicine Journal, 20*(3), 258–262.

Chalmers, T. C., Celano, P., Sacks, H. S., & Smith Jr, H. (1983). Bias in treatment assignment in controlled clinical trials. *New England Journal of Medicine, 309*(22), 1358–1361.

Chan, K. (2007). A clinical trial gone awry: The Chocolate Happiness Undergoing More Pleasantness (CHUMP) study. *Canadian Medical Association Journal, 177*(12), 1539–1541.

Cochrane, A. L. (1979). 1931–1971: A critical review, with particular reference to the medical profession. In *Medicines for the Year 2000* (pp. 1–11). London: Office of Health Economics.

Coleman, W. P., Benzel, E., Cahill, D., Ducker, T., Geisler, F., Green, B., et al. (2000). A critical appraisal of the reporting of the National Acute Spinal Cord Injury Studies (II and III) of methylprednisolone in acute spinal cord injury. *Journal of Spinal Disorders, 13*(3), 185–199.

Concato, J., Shah, N., & Horwitz, R. I. (2000). Randomized, controlled trials, observational studies, and the hierarchy of research designs. *New England Journal of Medicine, 342*(25), 1887–1892.

Crombie, I. (1996). *The pocket guide to critical appraisal*. London: BMJ Publishing Group.

Decullier, E., Lhéritier, V., & Chapuis, F. (2005). Fate of biomedical research protocols and publication bias in France: Retrospective cohort study. *British Medical Journal, 331*(7507), 19.

Devereaux, P. J., Manns, B. J. H., Ghali, W. A., Quan, H., Lacchetti, C., Montori, V. M., et al. (2001). Physician interpretations and textbook definitions of blinding terminology in randomized controlled trials. *Journal of the American Medical Association, 285*(15), 2000–2003.

Dwan, K., Altman, D. G., Arnaiz, J. A., Bloom, J., Chan, A. W., Cronin, E., et al. (2008). Systematic review of the empirical evidence of study publication bias and outcome reporting bias. *PLoS ONE, 3*(8), e3081.

Eldridge, S. M., Ashby, D., Feder, G. S., Rudnicka, A. R., & Ukoumunne, O. C. (2004). Lessons for cluster randomized trials in the twenty-first century: A systematic review of trials in primary care. *Clinical Trials, 1*(1), 80–90.

Farrell, S., Barker, M. L., Walanski, A., & Gerlach, R. W. (2008). Short-term effects of a combination product night-time therapeutic regimen on breath malodor. *Journal of Contemporary Dental Practice, 9*(6), 1–8.

Fergusson, D. M., Horwood, L. J., & Ridder, E. M. (2005). Tests of causal linkages between cannabis use and psychotic symptoms. *Addiction, 100*(3), 354–366.

Fineout-Overholt, E. (2008). Synthesizing the evidence: How far can your confidence meter take you? *AACN Advanced Critical Care, 19*(3), 335–339.

Fineout-Overholt, E., & Melnyk, B. (2007). Evaluating studies on prognosis. In N. Cullum, D. Ciliska, & B. Hayne (Eds.), *Evidence-based nursing: An introduction*. London: Blackwell.

Fineout-Overholt, E., Melnyk, B., & Schultz, A. (2005). Transforming health care from the inside out: Advancing evidence-based practice in the 21st century. *Journal of Professional Nursing, 21*(6), 335–344.

Fineout-Overholt, E., O'Mathúna, D. P., & Kent, B. (2008). Teaching EBP: How systematic reviews can foster evidence-based clinical decisions: Part I. *Worldviews on Evidence-Based Nursing, 5*(1), 45–48.

Gillespie, L., Gillespie, W., J., Robertson, M., Lamb, S., Cumming, R., & Rowe, B. (2003). Interventions for preventing falls in elderly people. *Cochrane Database of Systematic Reviews, 4.*

Gillespie, L. D., Robertson, M. C., Gillespie, W. J., Lamb, S. E., Gates, S., Cumming, R. G., & Rowe, B. H. (2009). Interventions for preventing falls in older people living in the community. *Cochrane Database of Systematic Review, 2.*

Goodacre, S. (2008a). Critical appraisal for emergency medicine: 1. Concepts and definitions. *Emergency Medicine Journal, 25*(4), 219–221.

Goodacre, S. (2008b). Critical appraisal for emergency medicine 2: Statistics. *Emergency Medicine Journal, 25*(6), 362–364.

Guirguis-Blake, J., Calonge, N., Miller, T., Siu, A., Teutsch, S., Whitlock., E., et al. (2007). Current processes of the U.S. Preventive Services Task Force: Refining evidence-based recommendation development. *Annals of Internal Medicine, 147*(2), 117–122.

Guyatt, G., Rennie, D., Meade, M. O., & Cook, D. J. (2008). *Users' guide to the medical literature: A manual for evidence-based clinical practice* (2nd ed.). New York: McGraw Hill.

Häfner, H., Hambrecht, M., Löffler, W., Munk-Jørgensen, P., & Riecher-Rössler, A. (1998). Is schizophrenia a disorder of all ages? A comparison of first episodes and early course across the life-cycle. *Psychological Medicine, 28*(2), 351–365.

Hatch, E. E., Palmer, J. R., Titus-Ernstoff, L., Noller, K. L., Kaufman, R. H., Mittendorf, R., et al. (1998). Cancer risk in women exposed to diethylstilbestrol in utero. *Journal of the American Medical Association, 280*(7), 630–634.

Haynes, R. B. (1993). Some problems in applying evidence in clinical practice. *Annals of the New York Academy of Sciences, 703*, 210–224.

Heckerling, P. S. (2006). Placebo surgery research: A blinding imperative. *Journal of Clinical Epidemiology, 59*(9), 876–880.

Hellems, M. A., Gurka, M. J., & Hayden, G. F. (2007). Statistical literacy for readers of *Pediatrics*: A moving target. *Pediatrics, 119*(6), 1083–1088.

Herbst, A. L., Ulfelder, H., & Poskanzer, D. C. (1971). Adenocarcinoma of the vagina: Association of maternal stilbestrol therapy with tumor appearance in young women. *New England Journal of Medicine, 284*(15), 878–881.

Higgins, J. P. T ., & Green, S. (Eds.) (2008). *Cochrane handbook for systematic reviews of interventions, Version 5.0.1.* Retrieved January 8, 2009, from http://www.cochrane-handbook.org

Hopewell, S., McDonald, S., Clarke, M., & Egger, M. (2007). Grey literature in meta-analyses of randomized trials of health care interventions. *Cochrane Database of Systematic Reviews, 2.*

Inskip, P., Tarone, R., Hatch, E., Wilcosky, T., Shapiro, W., Selker, R., et al. (2001). Cellular-telephone use and brain tumors. *New England Journal of Medicine, 344*(2), 79–86.

Ioannidis, J. P. A., Haidich, A. B., Pappa, M., Pantazis, N., Kokori, S. I., Tektonidou, M. G., et al. (2001). Comparison of evidence of treatment effects in randomized and nonrandomized studies. *Journal of the American Medical Association, 286*(7), 821–830.

Johnston, L. J., & McKinley, D. F. (2000). Cardiac tamponade after removal of atrial intracardiac monitoring catheters in a pediatric patient: Case report. *Heart and Lung, 29*(4), 256–261.

Kunz, R., & Oxman, A. D. (1998). The unpredictability paradox: Review of empirical comparisons of randomised and nonrandomised clinical trials. *British Medical Journal, 317*(7167), 1185–1190.

Lafreniere, K. D., Mutus, B., Cameron, S., Tannous, M., Giannotti, M., Abu-Zahra, H., et al. (1999). Effects of therapeutic touch on biochemical and mood indicators in women. *Journal of Alternative and Complementary Medicine, 5*(4), 367–370.

Lang, T. (2004). Twenty statistical errors even *YOU* can find in biomedical research articles. *Croatian Medical Journal, 45*(4), 361–370.

Lenzer, J. (2006). NIH secrets government funded data concealment. *New Republic.* Retrieved January 8, 2009, from http://www.ahrp.org/cms/index2.php?option=com_content&do_pdf = 1&id = 398

Lenzer, J., & Brownlee, S. (2008). An untold story? *British Medical Journal, 336*(7643), 532–534.

Lewis, S., & Clarke, M. (2001). Forest plots: Trying to see the wood and the trees. *British Medical Journal, 322*(7300), 1479–1480.

MacMahon, B., Yen, S., Trichopoulos, D., Warren, K., & Nardi, G. (1981).Coffee and cancer of the pancreas. *New England Journal of Medicine, 304*(11), 630–633.

Melnyk, B., Fineout-Overholt, E., Stone, P., & Ackerman, M. (2000). Evidence-based practice: The past, the present, and recommendations for the millennium. *Pediatric Nursing, 26*(1), 77–80.

Moore, R., Gavaghan, D., Edwards, J., Wiffen, P., & McQuay, H. (2002). Pooling data for number needed to treat: No problems for apples. *BMC Medical Research Methodology, 2*, 2.

Muscat, J., Malkin, M., Thompson, S., Shore, R., Stellman, S., McRee, D., et al. (2000). Handheld cellular telephone use and risk of brain cancer. *Journal of the American Medical Association, 284*(23), 3001–3007.

Oliveira, G. J., & Leles, C. R. (2006). Critical appraisal and positive outcome bias in case reports published in Brazilian dental journals. *Journal of Dental Education, 70*(8), 869–874.

O'Mathúna, D. P., Fineout-Overholt, E., & Kent, B. (2008). Teaching EBP: How systematic reviews can foster evidence-based clinical decisions: Part II. *Worldviews on Evidence-Based Nursing, 5*(2), 102–107.

O'Rourke, A., & Booth, A. (2000). *Critical appraisal and using the literature.* ScHARR Guides. School of Health and Related Research, University of Sheffield. Retrieved January 8, 2009, from http://www.shef.ac.uk/~scharr/ir/units/

Papanikolaou, P. N., Christidi, G. D., & Ioannidis, J. P. A. (2006). Comparison of evidence on harms of medical interventions in randomized and nonrandomized studies. *Canadian Medical Association Journal, 174*(5), 635–641.

Patel, S. R., Ayas, N. T., Malhotra, M. R., White, D. P., Schernhammer, E. S., Speizer, F. E., et al. (2004). A prospective study of sleep duration and mortality risk in women. *Sleep, 27*(3), 440–444.

Phillips, B., Ball, C., Sackett, D., Badenoch, D., Straus, S., Haynes, B., et al. (2001). *Oxford Centre for Evidence-Based Medicine levels of evidence.* Retrieved January 8, 2009, from http://www.cebm.net/index. aspx?o = 1047

Phillips, C. V. (2004). Publication bias *in situ. BMC Medical Research Methodology, 4*, 20.

Polit, D., & Beck, C. (2007). *Nursing research: Generating and assessing evidence for nursing practice* (8th ed.). Philadelphia: Lippincott Williams & Wilkins.

Roland, M., & Torgerson, D. (1998). Understanding controlled trials. What outcomes should be measured? *British Medical Journal, 317*(7165), 1075.

Rossouw, J. E., Anderson, G. L., Prentice, R. L., LaCroix, A. Z., Kooperberg, C., Stefanick, M. L., et al. (2002). Risks and benefits of estrogen plus progestin in healthy postmenopausal women: Principal results from the women's health initiative randomized controlled trial. *Journal of the American Medical Association, 288*(3), 321–333.

Rothman, K. J. (1978). A show of confidence. *New England Journal of Medicine, 299*(24), 1362–1363.

Ruiz-Canela, M., Martínez-González, M. A., & de Irala-Estévez, J. (2000). Intention to treat analysis is related to methodological quality [letter]. *British Medical Journal, 320*(7240), 1007–1008.

Schulz, K. F. (1995). Subverting randomization in controlled trials. *Journal of the American Medical Association, 274*(18), 1456–1458.

Schulz, K. F., & Grimes, D. A. (2002a). Allocation concealment in randomised trials: Defending against deciphering. *Lancet, 359*(9306), 614–618.

Schulz, K. F., & Grimes, D. A. (2002b). Generation of allocation sequences in randomised trials: Chance, not choice. *Lancet, 359*(9305), 515–519.

Stampfer, M. J., & Colditz, G. A. (1991). Estrogen replacement therapy and coronary heart disease: A quantitative assessment of the epidemiologic evidence. *Preventive Medicine, 20*(1), 47–63.

Stevens, K. R. (2001). Systematic reviews: The heart of evidence-based practice. *AACN Clinical Issues, 12*(4), 529–538.

Torgerson, D. J. (2001). Contamination in trials: Is cluster randomisation the answer? *British Medical Journal, 322*(7282), 355–357.

Trichopoulos, D., & Adami, H-O. (2001). Cellular telephones and brain tumors. *New England Journal of Medicine, 344*(2), 133–134.

Troisi, R., Hatch, E. E., Titus-Ernstoff, L., Hyer, M., Palmer, J. R., Robboy, S. J., et al. (2007). Cancer risk in women prenatally exposed to diethylstilbestrol. *International Journal of Cancer, 121*(2), 356–360.

Critically Appraising Qualitative Evidence for Clinical Decision Making

Bethel Ann Powers

> *What is important is to keep learning, to enjoy challenge,*
> *and to tolerate ambiguity. In the end there are no certain*
> *answers*
> *Martina Horner*

All scientific evidence is important to clinical decision making, and all evidence must be critically appraised to determine its contribution to that decision making. Part of critical appraisal is applying the clinician's understanding of a field of science to the content of a research report. Qualitative research may not be as familiar to practitioners as quantitative research, especially in terms of how it can be useful in guiding practice. Therefore, this chapter provides information to help clinicians with

● **Appraisal of qualitative evidence for clinical decision making**

● **Language and concepts that will be encountered in the qualitative literature**

● **Aspects of qualitative research that are known to have raised concerns for readers less familiar with different qualitative methods**

● **Issues surrounding the use of evaluative criteria that, if not understood, could lead to their misuse in the appraisal of studies and subsequent erroneous conclusions**

With adequate knowledge, practitioners can extract what is good and useful to clinical decision making by applying appropriate method-specific and general appraisal criteria to qualitative research reports. Glossary boxes are provided throughout the chapter to assist the reader in understanding common terms and concepts that support and structure the chapter discussion.

It is important for clinicians to gain the knowledge and ability required to appreciate qualitative studies as sources of evidence for clinical decision making. As with all knowledge, application is the best way to gain proficiency. Readers are invited to review a demonstration of how to use the appraisal guide at the end of the chapter (see Box 6.18) with a variety of sample articles found in Appendix C. Reading these articles is the best way to fully appreciate how to apply the guide. First-hand appraisal of qualitative studies requires active engagement with the evidence. This chapter prepares clinicians to engage with and move beyond the material presented to apply it when appraising the research in their particular fields of practice.

> *Learning is not attained by chance; it must be sought for*
>
> *with ardor and attended to with diligence*
>
> *Abigail Adams*

The Contribution of Qualitative Research to Decision Making

Multiple types of qualitative research are present in cross-disciplinary literature. However, those clinical practice questions that focus on interventions, risk, and etiology require different hierarchies of evidence that do not designate qualitative evidence as "best evidence." When addressing the meaning question, qualitative research is considered level one evidence. Herein lie both a challenge and an opportunity for clinicians to utilize qualitative evidence to answer their questions about quality patient care.

Expanding the Concept of Evidence

Clinical trials and other types of intervention research have been a primary focus of evidence-based practice (EBP) from its inception as a clinical learning strategy used at McMaster Medical School in the 1980s. As well, the international availability of systematic reviews provided by the Cochrane Collaboration and the incorporation of intervention studies as evidence in clinical decision support systems has made this type of evidence readily available to point-of-care clinicians. Selection of studies evaluated in EBP reviews to answer intervention questions is guided by evidence hierarchies that focus on quantitative research. In turn, reviews to answer meaning questions are guided by evidence hierarchies that must focus on qualitative research. In years past, when compared with quasi-experimental and nonexperimental (i.e., comparative, correlational, descriptive) designs, randomized controlled trials (RCTs) easily emerged as the designated gold standard for determining the effectiveness of a treatment. With new hierarchies of evidence that assist in identifying the best evidence for different kinds of questions, the extent of influence of the one-size-fits-all "rules of evidence" (i.e., determination of weakest to strongest evidence with a focus on support of the effectiveness of interventions), that in the past has tended to dominate discussions within the EBP movement, has been minimized; however, the use of qualitative studies still remains less clear than is desirable for clinical decision making (Milton, 2007; Powers & Knapp, 2006b). In strength-of-evidence pyramids (i.e., a rating system for the hierarchy of evidence) that are proposed as universal for all type of clinical questions, qualitative studies are ranked at or near the base, along with descriptive, evaluative, and case studies, signifying weaker forms of evidence. These, then, are compared with other research designs that examine interventions, with the strongest being

RCTs at or near the apex. This is a misrepresentation of the qualitative research genre because applying the linear approach used to evaluate intervention studies hardly fits the divergent purposes and nonlinear nature of these research traditions and designs. It is now understood that systematic reviews of RCTs serve as best evidence for intervention questions. Best evidence for diagnosis and prognosis questions are systematic reviews of descriptive prospective cohort studies. Grace and Powers (2009) have proposed recognition of two additional question domains: human response and meaning. They argue that the strongest evidence for these question types, which are of particular importance for nursing practice, arise from qualitative research traditions. This supports the use of different evidence hierarchies for different types of questions (see Chapter 2 for more information on levels of evidence that are appropriate for different types of questions).

Furthermore, a need to balance scientific knowledge gained through empirical research with practice-generated evidence and theories in clinical decision making has been noted to be part of the work of expanding the concept of evidence (Fineout-Overholt, Melnyk, & Schultz, 2005; Powers & Knapp, 2006a). That is,

> For a more comprehensive description of evidence-based… practice [,]… evidence must extend beyond the current emphasis on empirical research and randomized clinical trials, to the kinds of evidence also generated from ethical theories [e.g., based on standards, codes, and philosophies], personal theories [e.g., derived from autobiographical experience and insights], and aesthetic theories [e.g., represented by examples of aesthetic criticism and the creative arts]. (Fawcett, Watson, Neuman, et al., 2001, p. 118)

Efforts to expand the concept of evidence are consistent with fundamental tenets of the EBP movement. A clear example is the conceptual framework put forward in this chapter in which the goal of EBP is the successful integration of the following elements of clinical care (see Figure 1.2):

- Best research (e.g., valid, reliable and clinically relevant) evidence
- Clinical expertise (e.g., clinical skills, past experience, interpretation of practice-based evidence)
- Patient values (e.g., unique preferences, concerns, and expectations)
- Patient circumstances (e.g., individual clinical state, practice setting, and organizational culture)

In the past, research evidence seems to have been the portion of the EBP paradigm that has received the most attention, with literature focusing on helping practitioners develop their skills in retrieving, critically appraising, and synthesizing largely quantitative studies. There is growing awareness, however, that "qualitative research may provide us with some guidance in deciding whether we can apply the findings from quantitative studies to our patients [and] can help us to understand clinical phenomena with emphasis on understanding the experiences and values of our patients" (Straus, Richardson, Glasziou, et al., 2005, p. 143). Knowledge derived from syntheses of qualitative and quantitative research evidence pertaining to a clinical issue enables the integration of all elements of EBP in a manner that optimizes clinical outcomes.

Recognizing Research Relevant to Practice

Science and art come together in the design and execution of qualitative studies. Before clinicians can critically appraise qualitative research, they must have an appreciation for and basic knowledge of its many methodologies and practices, which are rooted in the social and human sciences. Questions asked by qualitative researchers are influenced by focus of these traditions on in-depth understanding of human experiences and the contexts in which the experiences occur.

In the health sciences, knowledge generated by qualitative studies may contain the theoretical bases for explicit interventions. However, studies that promote better understanding of what health and illness situations are like for people, how they manage, what they wish for and expect, and how they are affected by what goes on around them also may influence practice in other ways. For example, heightened sensitivity or awareness of life from others' vantage points may lead to changes in how persons feel about and behave toward one another, as well as prompt reflection on and discussions about what practical actions might be taken on an individual basis or a larger scale.

Significant growth in qualitative health science literature over recent decades has occurred at least in part because these approaches were capable of addressing many kinds of questions that could not be answered by quantitative, including quantitative descriptive, research methods. Because of the expansion and evolution of qualitative methods, clinicians across disciplines will encounter a more varied mix of articles on different clinical topics. Therefore, to keep up to date on the latest developments in their fields, practitioners need to be able to recognize and judge the validity of relevant qualitative as well as quantitative research studies.

> *The heights by great men reached and kept were not obtained by sudden flight. But they, while their companions slept, were toiling upward in the night.*
> *Thomas S. Monson*

Separating Wheat from Chaff

When we critically appraise a study, we act as the wind that blows away the chaff (i.e., imperfections) so that which is good and useful remains. There are no perfect studies. Therefore, the task becomes one of sifting through and deciding whether good and useful elements outweigh a study's shortcomings. To critically appraise qualitative research reports, the reader needs a sense of the diversity that exists within this field (i.e., a flavor of the language and mindset of qualitative research) to appreciate what is involved in using any set of criteria to evaluate a study's validity (or trustworthiness) and usefulness. This decreases the possibility of misconstruing such criteria because of preconceived notions about what they signify and how they should be used. The following sections provide brief overviews of how qualitative approaches differ and a synthesis of basic principles for evaluating qualitative studies.

Managing Diversity

Qualitative research designs and reporting styles are very diverse. In addition, there are many ways to classify qualitative approaches. Therefore, it is necessary to be able to manage this diversity through an awareness of different scientific traditions and associated research methods and techniques used in qualitative studies.

External Diversity Across Qualitative Research Traditions

Qualitative research traditions have origins within academic disciplines (e.g., the social sciences, arts, and humanities) that influence the theoretical assumptions, methods, and styles of reporting used to obtain and convey understanding about human experiences. Therefore, despite similarities in techniques for data gathering and management, experiences are viewed through different lenses, studied for different purposes, and reported in language and writing styles consistent with the research tradition's origins. Among qualitative traditions commonly used in health sciences research are ethnography, grounded theory, phenomenology, and hermeneutics.

box 6.1

Ethnography Research Terms

Culture: Shared knowledge and behavior of people who interact within distinct social settings and subsystems.

Participant observation: The active engagement (i.e., observation and participation) of the researcher in settings and activities of people being studied (i.e., everyday activities in study informants' natural settings).

Fieldwork: All research activities carried out in and in relation to the field (informants' natural settings).

Key informant: A select informant/assistant with extensive or specialized knowledge of his/her own culture.

Emic and etic: Contrasting "insider" views of informants (emic) and the researcher's "outsider" (etic) views.

Ethnography. Ethnography involves the study of a social group's **culture** through time spent combining **participant observation** (see Box 6.1), in-depth interviews, and the collection of artifacts (i.e., material evidence of culture) in the informants' natural setting. This appreciation of culture—drawing on anthropologic theory and practice—provides the context for a better understanding of answers to specific research questions. For example, cultural understanding may help answer questions about:

- People's experiences of health/illness in their everyday lives (e.g., methods-focused article on use of ethnography in breastfeeding disparities [Cricco-Lizza, 2007]; study about everyday life of children living with juvenile arthritis [Guell, 2007]).
- Issues of concern to caregivers (e.g., study of the role of pediatric critical care nursing unit culture in shaping research utilization behaviors [Scott & Pollock, 2008]; study of nursing assessment of pain on two postoperative units [Clabo, 2007]).
- Individuals' experiences in certain types of settings (e.g., study of experiences of adult patients and staff in the ward culture of a trauma unit [Tutton, Seers, & Langstaff, 2007]; study of dying in a nursing home [Kayser-Jones, 2002; Kayser-Jones, Schell, Lyons, et al., 2003]).

Fieldwork is the term that describes all research activities taking place in or in connection with work in the study setting (i.e., field). These activities include the many social and personal skills required when gaining entry to the field, maintaining field relationships, collecting and analyzing data, resolving political and ethical issues, and leaving the field. Researchers may have **key informants** (in addition to other informants) who assist them in establishing rapport and learning about cultural norms. Research reports are descriptions and interpretations that attempt to capture study informants' **emic** points of view balanced against the researcher's **etic** analytic perspectives. These efforts to make sense of the data also may provide a basis for generating a theory (Wolf, 2007).

Grounded Theory. The purpose of grounded theory, developed by sociologists Glaser and Strauss (1967), is to generate a theory about how people deal with life situations that is "grounded" in empirical data and that describes the processes by which they move through experiences over time. Movement often is expressed in terms of stages or phases (e.g., stages/phases of living with a chronic illness, adjusting to a new situation, or coping with challenging circumstances). For example, Beck (2007) described an emerging theory of postpartum

---

box 6.2

Grounded Theory Research Terms

Symbolic interaction: Theoretical perspective on how social reality is created by human interaction through ongoing, taken-for-granted processes of symbolic communication.

Pragmatism: Theoretical perspective that problems of truth and meaning need to be arrived at inductively; understood in terms of their utility and consequences; and modified to fit the circumstances of time, place, and the advent of new knowledge.

Constant comparison: A systematic approach to analysis that is a search for patterns in data as they are coded, sorted into categories, and examined in different contexts.

Theoretical sampling: Decision making, while concurrently collecting and analyzing data, about the data and data sources that are needed further to develop the emerging theory.

Saturation: The point at which categories of data are full and data collection ceases to provide new information.

Core variable: A theoretical summarization of a process or pattern that people go through in specified life experiences.

---

depression using grounded theory. In an additional example, Copeland and Heilemann (2008) used grounded theory to describe the experience of mothers striving to obtain assistance for their adult children who are violent and mentally ill. Philosophical underpinnings of this tradition are **symbolic interaction** and **pragmatism** (Wuest, 2007; see Box 6.2). Data collection and analysis procedures are similar to those of ethnographic research, but the focus is on symbolic meanings conveyed by people's actions in certain circumstances, resultant patterns of interaction, and their consequences.

The goal is to discover a core variable through procedures of **constant comparison** (i.e., coding, categorizing, and analyzing incoming data while continually seeking linkages by constantly comparing informational categories with one another and with new data) and **theoretical sampling** that directs data gathering toward **saturation** of categories (i.e., completeness). The *core variable*, or **basic social process** (BSP), is the basis for theory generation. It recurs frequently, links all the data together, and describes the pattern followed, regardless of the various conditions under which the experience occurs and different ways in which persons go through it. In the literature, the reader may encounter terms that are used to further describe the types of BSP (e.g., a basic social psychological process [BSPP]; a basic social structural process [BSSP]). Researchers typically will describe the meaning of these terms within the context of the study. Mordoch and Hall (2008) described two interrelated BSPPs in their study of children's perceptions of living with a parent with a mental illness. One process—"finding the rhythm"— helped children manage day-to-day living and staying connected to parents through stages of "monitoring" and "adjusting." The other process—"maintaining the frame"—was used to create a safe distance in relationships with parents through stages identified as "preserving myself" and "gauging."

Phenomenology. Phenomenology is the study of **essences** (i.e., meaning structures; see Box 6.3) intuited or grasped through descriptions of **lived experience**. Husserl's philosophy described lived experience (i.e., the lifeworld) as understandings about life's meanings that lie outside of a person's conscious awareness. Thus, in studying the meaning, or essence, of an experience

box 6.3

Phenomenology/Hermeneutics Research Terms

Essences: Internal meaning structures of a phenomenon grasped through the study of human lived experience.

Lived experience: Everyday experience, not as it is conceptualized, but as it is lived (i.e., how it feels or what it is like).

Introspection: A process of recognizing and examining one's own inner state or feelings.

Bracketing: Identifying and suspending previously acquired knowledge, beliefs, and opinions about a phenomenon.

Phenomenological reduction: An intellectual process involving reflection, imagination, and intuition.

Hermeneutics: Philosophy, theories, and practices of interpretation.

(phenomenon), researchers need to recognize their own personal feelings (**introspection**) and suspend their beliefs about what the experience is like (**bracketing**), particularly if they are using the Husserlian approach to phenomenology. Interpretive insights are derived by collecting experiential descriptions from interviews and other sources and engaging in intellectual analytic processes of reflection, imagination, and intuition (**phenomenological reduction**). Use of certain philosophers' perspectives to direct the analysis (e.g., Husserl, Heidegger, Merleau-Ponty) can affect methodological processes.

Phenomenology, represented as a school of thought within philosophy, offers perspectives shaped through ongoing intellectual dialogues rather than explicit procedures. Descriptions of research processes have come from outside of the parent discipline of philosophy. Processes often cited are

- The philosophically, language-oriented, descriptive–interpretive phenomenology of educator Max van Manen (the German Dilthey-Nohl and the Dutch Utrecht schools of phenomenological pedagogy). An example of this type of phenomenology would be a study of the experience of parents who have a child with autism (Woodgate, Ateah, & Secco, 2008).
- The empirical descriptive approaches of the Duquesne school of phenomenological psychology (i.e., Giorgi, Colaizzi, Fischer, and van Kaam). An example of this type of phenomenology would be a study of the impact of birth trauma on breast-feeding (Beck & Watson, 2008).

Examples of phenomena of interest to clinical researchers include what various illness experiences are like for persons or how a sense of hope, trust, or being understood is realized in their lives. Insights offered through research reports range in style from lists of themes and straightforward descriptions (i.e., empiric descriptions) to philosophical theorizing and poetizing (i.e., interpretations). In writing about the usefulness of phenomenology in pediatric cancer nursing research, Fochtman (2008) asserts the perspective that, "only when we truly understand the meaning [e.g. what it means to have cancer as a child or adolescent] can we design interventions to ease suffering and increase quality of life" (p. 191).

Hermeneutics. Hermeneutics has a distinct philosophical history as a theory and method of interpretation (originally associated with the interpretation of Biblical texts). However, various philosophers (e.g., Dilthey, Heidegger, Gadamer, Hirsch, and Ricoeur) have contributed to its development beyond a focus on literal texts to viewing human "lived experience" as a text that is to be understood through the interpreter's dialogical engagement (i.e., thinking that is like a thoughtful dialog or conversation) with life.

There is not a single way to practice hermeneutics. A variety of theories and debates exist within the field. However, although separated by tradition, it also may be associated with phenomenology and certain schools of phenomenological thought. Thus, "hermeneutic phenomenology" sometimes is the terminology used to denote orientations that are interpretive, in contrast to, or in addition to, being descriptive (van Manen, 1990/1997). For instance, Evans and Hallett (2007) draw on the hermeneutic traditions of Heidegger and Gadamer in their study of the meaning of comfort care for hospice nurses. The complex realities of nurses' work in comfort care settings are presented under the thematic headings of: comfort and relief, peace and ease, and spirituality and meaning. A fuller appreciation of how the process contributes to understandings that have implications for clinical practice is best acquired through firsthand reading of these types of reports, engaging reflectively with the actual words of the written text, and experiencing the total effect of the narrative.

Internal Diversity Within Qualitative Research Traditions

Qualitative research traditions vary internally as well as externally. For example, there are several reasons why ethnographic, grounded theory, or phenomenologic accounts may assume a variety of forms, including:

● When a tradition acts as a vehicle for different representational styles and theoretical or ideological conceptualizations
● When historical evolution of a tradition results in differing procedural approaches
● When studies differ individually in terms of their focus on description, interpretation, or theory generation

Representation and Conceptualization. **Representation** of research findings (i.e., writing style, including authorial voice and use of literary forms and rhetorical devices) should not be a matter of dictate or personal whim. Rather, it is part of the analytic process that, in qualitative research, gives rise to a great variety of representational styles. Articles and entire texts have been devoted to the topic of representation (Atkinson, 1992; Denzin, 1997; Mantzoukas, 2004; Morse, 2007; Richardson, 1990; Sandelowski, 1998b, 2004, 2007; van Manen, 1990/1997, 2002; Van Maanen, 1988; Wolcott, 2001, 2002). Qualitative research reports may be conversational dialogs. They may contain researchers' personal reflections and accounts of their experiences; poetry, artistic, and literary references; hypothetical cases; or fictional narratives and stories that are based on actual data, using study informants' own words in efforts to increase sensitivity and enhance understanding of a phenomenon.

Thus, although researchers should not abuse artistic license, readers also should not see a research report as unconventional if that report is enriched by using an alternative literary form as a faithful representation that best serves a legitimate analytic purpose. If the representation is meaningful to the reader, it meets a criterion of analytic significance in keeping with these traditions' scholarly norms. For example, qualitative researchers have used health theater (i.e., dramatic performance scripts) to make research findings more accessible and relevant to select audiences (Kontos & Naglie, 2006, 2007; Sandelowski, Trimble, Woodard, et al., 2006; Smith & Gallo, 2007). Further examples of different representational strategies in qualitative health research are the uses of poetic forms (Furman, 2006) and autoethnography (i.e., personal/autobiographical experience; Foster, McAllister, & O'Brien, 2005).

Some standard forms of representation also are used with ethnographic, phenomenological, and grounded theory designs to bring out important dimensions of the data. For example, Creswell (2007) discussed how case studies and biography can serve as adjuncts to these types of studies as well as traditions in their own right.

> **box 6.4**
>
> ## General Qualitative Research Terms
>
> **Representation:** Part of the analytic process that raises the issue of providing a truthful portrayal of what the data represent (e.g., essence of an experience; cultural portrait) that will be meaningful to its intended audience.
>
> **Case study:** An intensive investigation of a case involving a person or small group of people, an issue, or an event.
>
> **Biography:** An approach that produces an in-depth report of a person's life. Life histories and oral histories also involve gathering of biographical information and recording of personal recollections of one or more individuals.
>
> **Critical inquiry:** Cultural critique guided by theories/approaches to the study of power interests between individuals and social groups, often involving hegemony (domination or control over others) associated with ideologies that operate to create oppression and constrain multiple competing interests in order to maintain the status quo.
>
> **Feminist epistemologies:** A variety of views and practices inviting critical dialog about issues arising in areas of social life that involve such concerns as inequality, neglect of diversity, exploitation, insensitivity, and ethical behavior.

Major qualitative traditions also may be vehicles for distinctive theoretical or ideological concepts. For example, a critical ethnography combines ethnographic methods with methods of **critical inquiry** or cultural critique. The result has been described as "conventional ethnography with a political purpose" (Thomas, 1993, p. 4). The reader should expect to find an integration of empirical analysis and theory related to a goal of emancipation from oppressive circumstances or false ideas. For example, Varcoe (2001) conducted a critical ethnography of how the social context of the emergency room influenced the nursing care of women who had been abused.

Similarly, feminist research, traditionally, has focused critique on "issues of gender, gender relations, inequality, and neglect of diversity" (Flick, 2006, p. 77). However, a feminist perspective may be brought to bear on research interest in any area of social life that would benefit from the establishment of collaborative and nonexploitative relationships and sensitive, ethical approaches. Examples include how researchers deal with boundary issues that arise in qualitative health research on sensitive topics (Dickson-Swift, James, Kippen, et al., 2006) and how the quality of written reports may be enriched by inclusion of researchers' embodied experiences (Ellingson, 2006). "In short, rather than a focus on [feminist] methods, [current] discussions have now turned to how to use the methods [informed by a variety of different **feminist epistemologies**, i.e., ways of knowing and reasoning] in a self-disclosing and respectful way" (Creswell, 2007, p. 27) (see Box 6.4).

Historical Evolution. Use over time may refine, extend, or alter and produce variations in the practice of a research tradition. One example of this within anthropology is the developing interest in **interpretive ethnography** (see Box 6.5). This occurred as researchers crossed disciplinary boundaries to combine theoretical perspectives from practices outside of the discipline to inform their work (e.g., the humanistic approaches of phenomenology and hermeneutics; **discourse analysis**, evolving from **semiotics** and **sociolinguistics**; and **critical theory**). Of course, said influencing practices may also be qualitative approaches in their own right. Examples include

box 6.5

General Qualitative Research Terms

Interpretive ethnography: Loosely characterized as a movement within anthropology that generates many hybrid forms of ethnographic work as a result of crossing a variety of theoretical boundaries within social science.

Axial coding: A process used to relate categories of information by using a coding paradigm with predetermined subcategories in one approach to grounded theory (Corbin & Strauss, 2008; Strauss & Corbin, 1990).

Emergence: Glaser's (1992) term for conceptually driven ("discovery") vs. procedurally driven ("forcing") theory development in his critique of Strauss & Corbin (1990).

Theoretical sensitivity: A conceptual process to accompany techniques for generating grounded theory (Glaser, 1978).

Discourse analysis: Study of how meaning is created through the use of language (derived from linguistic studies, literary criticism, and semiotics).

Semiotics: The theory and study of signs and symbols applied to the analysis of systems of patterned communication.

Sociolinguistics: The study of the use of speech in social life.

Critical theory: A blend of ideology (based on a critical theory of society) and a form of social analysis and critique that aims to liberate people from unrecognized myths and oppression in order to bring about enlightenment and radical social change.

Starks and Trinidad's (2007) inclusion of discourse analysis in a comparison of three qualitative approaches that can be used in health research and Stewart and Usher's (2007) discussion of the use of critical theory in exploring nursing leadership issues.

Another example of historical evolution within a tradition began with controversy between Glaser and Strauss, the originators of grounded theory over Strauss' interpretation of the method (Corbin & Strauss, 2008; Strauss & Corbin, 1990, 1998), which included *axial coding,* a procedure not featured in earlier texts (Chenitz & Swanson, 1986; Glaser, 1978; Glaser & Strauss, 1967). Axial coding involves the use of a prescribed coding paradigm with predetermined subcategories (e.g., causal conditions, strategies, context, intervening conditions, and consequences) intended to help researchers pose questions about how categories of their data relate to one another. Glaser (1992) objected to forcing data into a fixed model. He argued that his examples of 18 different coding families that may be used to systematically link categories of data (Glaser, 1978) illustrate but do not limit possibilities for analysis, where coding should be driven by conceptualizations about data. These and other concerns (e.g., inattention to earlier developed ideas about BSPs and saturation of categories) led Glaser to assert that Strauss and Corbin's model is a new method no longer oriented to the discovery, or **emergence**, of theory (i.e., grounded theory method as originally conceived by himself and Strauss; Melia, 1996).

These and subsequent developments in grounded theory not only offer clear choices between Straussian and Glaserian methods of analysis but also between both Glaser's and Strauss and Corbin's versions and other approaches that expand its interpretive possibilities, as a growing number of scholars apply grounded theory's basic guidelines to research agendas that involve a wider variety of philosophical perspectives and theoretical assumptions (Bryant & Charmaz, 2007; Charmaz, 2006).

---

box 6.6

General Qualitative Research Terms

Thick description: Description that does more than describe human experiences by beginning to interpret what they mean.

Description, Interpretation, and Theory Generation. Qualitative researchers amass many forms of data: recorded observations (fieldnotes), interview tapes and transcripts, documents, photographs, and collected or received artifacts from the field. There are numerous ways to approach these materials.

All researchers write descriptively about their data (i.e., the empirical evidence). The act of describing necessarily involves interpretation of the facts of an experience through choices made about what to report and how to represent it. Researchers also refer to Geertz's (1973) notion of **thick description** (as opposed to thin description; see Box 6.6) as what is needed for interpretations. Thick description not only details reports of what people say and do but also incorporates the textures and feelings of the physical and social worlds in which people move and—always with reference to that context—an interpretation of what their words and actions mean. "Thick description" is a phrase that "ought not to appear in write-ups of qualitative research at all" (Sandelowski, 2004, p. 215). Rather, it is a quality that needs to be demonstrated in the written presentation.

Describing meaning in context is important because it is a way to try to understand what informants already know about their world. Informants do not talk about that which they take for granted (i.e., tacit, personal knowledge) because their attention is not focused on it. And sometimes what they do is different from what they say because everyday actions in familiar settings also draw on tacit understandings of what is usual and expected. Thick descriptions attempt to take this into account. They are the researchers' interpretations of what it means to experience life from certain vantage points through written expression that is "artful and evocative" as well as "factual and truthful" (Van Maanen, 1988, p. 34).

It is the researcher's choice to report research findings in more factual, descriptive terms (allowing the empirical data to speak for themselves) or more interpretive terms (drawing out the evidence that illuminates circumstances, meanings, emotions, intentions, strategies, motivations). But this mostly is a matter of degree for researchers whose work in a designated tradition tends to push them toward more in-depth interpretation. Additionally, the venue and intended audiences influence decisions about how to represent research findings.

Theory generation also is a proper goal in ethnography and an essential outcome in grounded theory. In these traditions, theories are empirical evidence-based explanations of how cultural, social, and personal circumstances account for individuals' actions and interactions with others. Analyzed data supply the evidence in which the theories are "grounded." Theory generation is not expected in phenomenologic or hermeneutic approaches. The purpose of these studies is to understand and interpret human experience (i.e., to provide a mental picture or image of its meaning and significance), not to explain it (e.g., to describe or theorize about its structure and operation in terms of causes, circumstances, or consequences).

Qualitative Descriptive Studies. Descriptive studies may be used in quantitative research as a prelude to experiments and other types of inquiry. However, qualitative descriptive studies (see Box 6.7) serve to summarize factual information about human experiences with more attention

> ### box 6.7
>
> ## General Qualitative Research Terms
>
> **Qualitative description:** Description that "entails a kind of interpretation that is low-inference [close to the "facts"] or likely to result in easier consensus [about the "facts"] among researchers" (Sandelowski, 2000b, p. 335).
> **Naturalistic research:** Commitment to the study of phenomena in their naturally occurring settings (contexts).
> **Field studies:** Studies involving direct, firsthand observation and interviews in informants' natural settings.

to the feel of the data's subjective content than that tends to be found in quantitative description. Sandelowski (2000b) suggests that researchers "name their method as qualitative description [and] if... designed with overtones from other methods, they can describe what these overtones were, instead of inappropriately naming or implementing these other methods" (p. 339).

Generic Qualitative Studies. Researchers may identify their work in accordance with the technique that was used (e.g., observation study or interview study). Other generic terms are **naturalistic research** (Lincoln & Guba, 1985), largely signifying the intellectual commitment to studying phenomena in the natural settings or contexts in which they occur, or **field study**, implying research activities that involve direct, firsthand observations and interviews in the informants' natural settings.

Qualitative Evaluation and Action Research Studies. Some studies that use qualitative research techniques need to retain their unique identities. For example, evaluation of educational and organizational programs, projects, and policies may use qualitative research techniques of interviewing, observation, and document review to generate and analyze data. Also, various forms of **action research**, including **participatory action research** (PAR; see Box 6.8), may use field techniques of observation and interviewing as approaches to data collection and analysis. Examples are the use of PAR to explore the chronic pain experienced in older adults

> ### box 6.8
>
> ## General Qualitative Research Terms
>
> **Qualitative evaluation:** A general term covering a variety of approaches to evaluating programs, projects, policies, and so forth using qualitative research techniques.
> **Action research:** A general term for a variety of approaches that aim to resolve social problems by improving existing conditions for oppressed groups or communities.
> **Participatory action research (PAR):** A form of action research that is participatory in nature (i.e., researchers and participants collaborate in problem definition, choice of methods, data analysis, and use of findings); democratic in principle; and reformatory in impulse (i.e., has as its objective the empowerment of persons through the process of constructing and using their own knowledge as a form of consciousness raising with the potential for promoting social action).

---

box 6.9

General Qualitative Research Terms

Observation continuum: A range of social roles encompassed by participant observation and ranging from complete observer to complete participant at the extremes.

Fieldnotes: Self-designed observational protocols for recording notes about field observations.

Analytic notes (memos): Notes that researchers write to themselves to record their thoughts, questions, and ideas as a process of simultaneous data collection and data analysis unfolds.

(Baker & Wang, 2006) and as an approach for improving Black women's health in rural and remote communities (Etowa, Bernard, Oyinsan, et al., 2007).

Favored Research Techniques

Favored techniques used in qualitative research reflect the needs of particular study designs. It is appropriate for them to appear last in a discussion of methods because techniques do not drive research questions and designs. They are the servants, not the masters, and they are not what makes a study qualitative. Nevertheless, a secure knowledge of techniques and their uses has important consequences for successful execution and evaluation of studies.

Observation and Fieldnotes. In fieldwork, observation, combined with other activities, takes on different dimensions, sometimes described as complete observer, observer as participant, participant as observer, and complete participant (Flick, 2006). **Participant observation** (i.e., active engagement of the researcher in settings and activities of people being studied; Box 6.9) encompasses all of these social roles with less time spent at the extremes. Most time is spent in the middle where distinctions between observer as participant and participant as observer are blurred. This is similar to everyday life in which the emphasis shifts back and forth as people take more or less active roles in interactions (e.g., speaking and listening, acting and watching, taking the initiative and standing by), depending on the situation.

     Fieldnotes are self-designed observational protocols for recording notes about field observation. Most are not actually recorded in the field, where researchers may only be able to do "jottings" (e.g., phrases and key words as memory aids) until it is possible to compose an expanded account. Fieldnotes are highly detailed records of all that can be remembered of observations, as well as researcher actions and interactions. They may include maps and drawings of the environment, as well as conversations and records of events. **Analytic notes** (also called *reflective notes* or *memos*) are notes researchers write to themselves about ideas for analysis, issues to pursue, people to contact, questions, personal emotions, understandings, and confusions brought into focus by writing and thinking about the field experience. This process illustrates how data collection and analysis occur simultaneously throughout the study.

Interviews and Focus Groups. Although a variety of interview forms and question formats are used in qualitative research, their common purpose is to provide ways for informants to express and expand on their own thoughts and remembrances, reflections, and ideas. Informal conversational interviews that occur in the natural course of participant observation are of the **unstructured, open-ended** type (Box 6.10). Formal interviews, however, often involve the use of interview guides that list or outline in advance the topics and questions to be covered. Inter-

---

box 6.10

General Qualitative Research Terms

Unstructured, open-ended interviews: Informal conversations that allow informants the fullest range of possibilities to describe their experiences, thoughts, and feelings.

Semistructured interviews: Formal interviews that provide more interviewer control and question format structure but retain a conversational tone and allow informants to answer in their own ways.

Structured, open-ended interviews: Formal interviews with little flexibility in the way the questions are asked but with question formats that allow informants to respond on their own terms (e.g., "What does... mean to you?" "How do you feel/ think about... ?").

Focus groups: This type of group interview generates data on designated topics through discussion and interaction. Focus group research is a distinct type of study when used as the sole research strategy.

---

views remain conversational, and the interviewer has the flexibility in deciding sequence and wording of questions on the basis of how the conversation is flowing, but the **semistructured interview** approach makes data collection more comprehensive and systematic from one informant to another.

Some studies also use **structured, open-ended** question formats, where informants answer the same exactly worded question(s) but are free to describe their experiences in their own words and on their own terms. Although this discussion covers several interview methods, it does not exhaust possible interview approaches.

Group interviews may be used in addition to individual interviews in field research. In recent years, **focus groups** have been used in combination with other forms of data collection in both qualitative and quantitative research studies to generate data on designated topics through discussion and interaction. Group moderators direct interaction in structured or semistructured ways, depending on the purpose of the interview. For example, Perkins, Barclay, and Booth (2007) reported a focus group study of palliative care patients' views on priorities for future research that, as the qualitative component of a mixed method study, was used in the development of a questionnaire for a larger quantitative patient survey.

When used as the sole research strategy, the focus group interview represents a distinct type of study with a history in marketing research. Thus, researchers should limit their naming of the method to "focus group" and refer to primary sources for information on specific focus group strategies when planning to use this as the central data collection technique (e.g., Krueger & Casey, 2000).

Narrative and Content Analysis. Analysis in qualitative research involves extracting themes, patterns, processes, essences, and meanings from "textual data" (i.e., written materials such as fieldnotes, interview transcripts, and various kinds of documents). But there is no single way to go about this. For instance, narrative, discourse, and content analysis are examples of broad areas (paradigms) within which researchers work; each comprises many different approaches.

Narrative analysis is concerned with generating and interpreting stories about life experiences. It is a specific way to understand interview data, representing it in the form of "truthful fictions" (Sandelowski, 1991, p. 165). Kleinman's (1988) *The Illness Narratives* is a well-known example in the medical literature. Other examples include Bingley, Thomas,

Brown, et al.'s (2008) discussion of narrative analysis approaches that may be of use in palliative care and Edwards and Gabbay's (2007) study of patient experiences with long-term sickness. Although qualitative researchers commonly deal with stories of individuals' experiences, narrative analysis is a particular way of dealing with stories. Therefore, the term should not be used casually to refer to any form of analysis that involves narrative data.

Discourse analysis is a term covering widely diverse approaches to the analysis of recorded talk. The general purpose is to draw attention to how language/communication shapes human interactions. "Discourse analysts argue that language and words, as a system of signs, are in themselves meaningless; it is through the shared, mutually agreed-on use of language that meaning is created" (Starks & Trinidad, 2007, p. 1374).

Current examples from clinical literature of discourse analysis are sparse and varied, primarily due to the existence of multiple discourse analysis techniques but no single method.

Discourse analysis uses "conventional" data collection techniques to generate texts… [which] could be interview transcripts, newspaper articles, observations, documents, or visual images…Although the methods of generating texts and the principles of analysis may differ…the premises on which the research being reported has drawn need to be clearly articulated. (Cheek, 2004, pp. 1145–1146)

An example is Graffigna and Bosio's (2006) analysis of how the setting shapes conversational features of face-to-face versus online discussions about HIV/AIDS.

Qualitative **content analysis** is most commonly mentioned in research reports in connection with procedures that involve breaking down data (e.g., coding, comparing, contrasting, and categorizing bits of information), then reconstituting them in some new form, such as description, interpretation, or theory. Ethnographers refer to this as *working data* to tease out themes and patterns. Grounded theorists describe *procedural sequences* involving different levels of coding and conceptualization of data. Phenomenologists also may use **thematic analysis** as one of many analytic strategies. Hsieh and Shannon (2005) discussed three approaches to qualitative content analysis. To avoid confusion, it should be noted that there are forms of quantitative content analysis that use very different principles to deal with narrative data in predetermined, structured ways.

Sampling Strategies. *Sampling* decisions involve choices about study sites or settings and people who will be able to provide information and insights about the study topic. A single setting may be chosen for in-depth study, or multiple sites may be selected to enlarge and diversify samples or for purposes of comparison. Some studies of human experiences are not specific to a particular setting. Within and across sites, researchers must choose activities and events that, through observation and interview, will yield the best information. For example, if in a study of elderly individuals' adjustment to congregate living, data gathering is limited to interviews in individuals' private quarters, there will be a loss of other individuals' perspectives (e.g., family members, service providers) and the ability to observe how participants interact with others in different facets of community life.

Choice of participants (i.e., informants or study subjects in qualitative studies) is based on a combination of criteria, including the nature and quality of information they may contribute (i.e., **theoretic interest**), their willingness to participate, their accessibility, and their availability. A prominent qualitative sampling strategy is purposeful.

Purposeful/purposive sampling (Box 6.11) enables researchers to select informants who will be able to provide particular perspectives that relate to the research question(s). In grounded theory, this is called **theoretical sampling** (i.e., sampling is used in specific ways to build theory). **Nominated** or **snowball sampling** also may be used, in which informants assist in recruiting other people they know to participate. This can be helpful when informants are in a position to recommend people who are well informed on a topic and can provide a good interview. **Volunteer/convenience samples** also are used when researchers do not know potential informants

---

box 6.11

General Qualitative Research Terms

Purposeful/purposive sampling: Intentional selection of people or events in accordance with the needs of the study.

Nominated/snowball sampling: Recruitment of participants with the help of informants already enrolled in the study.

Volunteer/convenience sampling: A sample obtained by solicitation or advertising for participants who meet study criteria.

Theoretical sampling: In grounded theory, purposeful sampling used in specific ways to build theory.

---

and solicit for participants with the desired experience who meet study inclusion criteria. With all types of sampling, researcher judgment and control are essential to be sure that study needs are met.

Researchers' judgments, based on ongoing evaluation of quality and quantity of different types of information in the research database, determine the number and variety of informants needed (Creswell, 2007; Marshall & Rossman, 2006). Minimum numbers of informants needed for a particular kind of study may be estimated, based on historical experience. For example, 30–50 interviews typically meet the needs of ethnographic and grounded theory studies, whereas six may be an average sample size for a phenomenologic study (Morse, 1994). However, if a study involves multiple interviews of the same people, fewer informants may be needed. And if the quality of information that informants supply is not good or sufficient to answer questions or saturate data categories, more informants will be needed. Decisions to stop collecting data depend on the nature and scope of the study design; the amount, richness, and quality of useable data; the speed with which types of data move analysis along; and the completeness or saturation (Morse, 2000).

> An adequate sample size… is one that permits—by virtue of not being too large—the deep, case-oriented analysis that is a hallmark of all qualitative inquiry, and that results in— by virtue of not being too small—a new and richly textured understanding of experience. (Sandelowski, 1995, p. 183)

Random sampling, used in quantitative studies to achieve statistically representative samples, does not logically fit with purposes of qualitative designs (i.e., to seek out people who will be the best sources of information about an experience or phenomenon). In addition, relying on random sampling would delay saturation in qualitative studies (i.e., possibly producing too much of some and not enough of other needed data) and result in oversaturation (i.e., unmanageable volume) that also would not serve well for decision making (Morse, 1998b).

Data Management and Analysis. Qualitative studies generate large amounts of narrative data that need to be managed and manipulated. Personal computers and word processing software facilitate data management (Box 6.12), including:

- Data entry (e.g., typing fieldnotes and analytic memos, transcribing recorded interviews)
- "Cleaning," or editing
- Storage and retrieval (e.g., organizing data into meaningful, easily located units or files)

Data manipulation involves coding, sorting, and arranging words, phrases, or data segments in ways that advance ongoing analysis. Various types of specialized software have been developed

---

box 6.12

General Qualitative Research Terms

Qualitative data management: The act of designing systems to organize, catalog, code, store, and retrieve data. (System design influences, in turn, how the researcher approaches the task of analysis.)

Computer-assisted qualitative data analysis: An area of technological innovation that in qualitative research has resulted in uses of word processing and software packages to support data management.

Qualitative data analysis: A variety of techniques that are used to move back and forth between data and ideas throughout the course of the research.

---

to support management and manipulation of textual data. There is no inherent virtue in using or not using qualitative data analysis software (QDAS). It is wise to consider the advantages and disadvantages (Creswell, 2007). Most important to remember is that QDAS packages, unlike statistical software, may support but do not perform data analyses. And users need to be certain that the analyses they must perform do not suffer as a result of inappropriate fit with the limits and demands of a particular program or the learning curve that may be involved.

Data analysis occurs throughout data collection to ensure that sampling decisions produce an appropriate, accurate, and sufficiently complete and richly detailed data set to meet the needs of the study. Also, to manage the volume of data involved, ongoing analysis is needed to sort and arrange data while developing ideas about how to reassemble and represent them as descriptions, theories, or interpretations.

Sorting may involve making frequency counts, coding, developing categories, formulating working hypotheses, accounting for negative cases (instances that contradict other data or do not fit hypotheses), or identifying concepts that explain patterns and relationships among data. Research design and specific aims determine one of the many analytic techniques that will be used (e.g., phenomenological reduction, constant comparison, narrative analysis, content analysis).

Similarly, the results of data analysis may take many forms. A common example is thematic analysis that systematically describes recurring ideas or topics (i.e., themes) that represent different yet related aspects of a phenomenon. Data may be organized into tables, charts, or graphs or presented as narratives using actual quotes from informants or reconstructed life stories (i.e., data-based hypothetical examples). Data also may be presented as typologies or taxonomies (i.e., classification schemes) that serve explanatory or heuristic (i.e., illustrative and educational) purposes (Porter, Ganong, Drew, et al., 2004; Powers, 2001, 2005). As noted previously in discussing issues of representation, researchers also may use drama, self-stories, and poetry to immerse the reader in the informants' world, decrease the distance between the author and the reader, and more vividly portray the emotional content of an experience.

Mixing Methods. It is unhelpful to view qualitative research as a singular entity that can be divorced from the assumptions of the traditions associated with different methods or reduced to an assemblage of data collection and analysis techniques. Because there are so many choices that necessarily involve multilevel (e.g., paradigm, method, and technique; Box 6.13) commitments (Sandelowski, 2000a), seasoned researchers have cautioned against nonreflective, uncritical mixing of qualitative perspectives, language, and analytic strategies (i.e., hybridized qualitative studies) to produce results that do not meet rigorous scholarly standards. This is coupled with a concern about researchers who rely on textbooks or survey courses for direction in lieu of expert

> ### box 6.13
>
> ## General Qualitative Research Terms
>
> **Paradigm:** A world view or set of beliefs, assumptions, and values that guide all types of research by identifying where the researcher stands on issues related to the nature of reality (ontology), relationship of the researcher to the researched (epistemology), role of values (axiology), use of language (rhetoric), and process (methodology; Creswell, 2007).
>
> **Method:** The theory of how a certain type of research should be carried out (i.e., strategy, approach, process/overall design, and logic of design). Researchers often subsume description of techniques under a discussion of method.
>
> **Techniques:** Tools or procedures used to generate or analyze data (e.g., interviewing, observation, standardized tests and measures, constant comparison, document analysis, content analysis, statistical analysis). Techniques are method-neutral and may be used, as appropriate, in any research design—either qualitative or quantitative.

mentorship. The concern is that their ability to recognize within-method and across-method subtleties and nuances, identify decision points, and anticipate consequences involved in the research choices they make may be compromised as a result of the insufficient depth of understanding afforded by these limited knowledge bases (Morse, 1997a). Novice readers of qualitative research (and beginning researchers) are advised first to learn about pure methods so that they will be able to proceed with greater knowledge and confidence, should they later encounter a hybrid (combined qualitative) or mixed-method (combined qualitative and quantitative) approach.

Appraising Individual Qualitative Studies

A variety of method-specific and general criteria have been proposed for evaluating qualitative studies. In fact, there is a large variety of rules related to quality standards, but there is no agreed-upon terminology or preset format that bridges the diversity of methods enough to be able to dictate how researchers communicate about the rules they followed. And only part of the judgment involves what researchers say they did. The other part is how well they represent research results, the effect of the presentation on readers, and reader's judgments about whether study findings seem credible and useful.

Method-Specific Evaluative Criteria

Some criteria for evaluating scientific rigor specifically relate to central purposes and characteristics of traditional methods. For example, ethnography's historic emphasis on understanding human experience in cultural context is reflected by six variables proposed by Homans (1955) to evaluate the adequacy of field studies: *time*, *place*, *social circumstance*, *language*, *intimacy*, and *consensus*.

Elaboration on these variables relates to values placed on prolonged close engagement of the researcher with study participants, active participation in daily social events, communication, and confirmation of individual informant reports by consulting multiple informants. Appraisals of an ethnographic/field study's accuracy (credibility) may be linked to how well values such as these appear to have been upheld.

---

box 6.14

Glaser and Strauss' Evaluative Criteria for a Grounded Theory Study

■ **Fit:** Categories must be indicated by the data.
■ **Grab:** The theory must be relevant to the social/practical world.
■ **Work:** The theory must be useful in explaining, interpreting, or predicting the study phenomenon.
■ **Modifiability:** The theory must be adaptable over time to changing social conditions.

Similarly, the ultimate goal of grounded theory-influenced evaluative criteria was summarized by Glaser and Strauss (1967) as: *fit*, *grab*, *work*, and *modifiability* (see Box 6.14).

The pedagogic, semiotic/language-oriented approach to phenomenology of van Manen's (1990/1997) is reflected in his four conditions or evaluative criteria of any human science text. The text must be *oriented*, *strong*, *rich*, and *deep* (see Box 6.15).

These are just a few examples of how active researchers working within specific traditions have conceptualized their craft. Because there is such diversity in qualitative inquiry, no single set of criteria can serve all qualitative approaches equally well. But there have been efforts to articulate criteria that may more generally apply to diverse qualitative research approaches (Creswell, 2007; Flick, 2006; Marshall & Rossman, 2006). The method-specific criteria to some extent drive these general criteria. However, the primary driver for the variety of attempts to develop general criteria has been perceived as communication gaps between qualitative and quantitative researchers whose use of language and world views often differ. Despite these attempts, there is no agreement among qualitative researchers about how or whether it is appropriate to use the general appraisal criteria.

General Criteria for Evaluating Qualitative Studies

Examples of general evaluative criteria are those proposed by Lincoln and Guba (1985) that offer qualitative equivalents to quantitative concepts of validity and reliability. These help explain the scientific rigor of qualitative methods to quantitatively oriented persons. But it has been argued that by framing discussion on the basis of the belief structures of quantitative researchers and drawing attention away from other criteria of equal importance, the criteria fail to address paradigmatic differences. The differences reflected by qualitative researchers' world views are in the ways they perceive reality as subjective and multiple (i.e., the ontological issue); the way they

---

box 6.15

van Manen's Evaluative Criteria for a Phenomenological Study

■ **Oriented:** Answers a question of how one stands in relation to life and how one needs to think, observe, listen, and relate
■ **Strong:** Clear and powerful
■ **Rich:** Thick description/valid, convincing interpretations of concrete experiences
■ **Deep:** Reflective/instructive and meaningful

view the relationship between the researcher and the researched as close and collaborative (i.e., the epistemologic issue); the belief that all research is value laden, and biases that are naturally present need to be dealt with openly (i.e., the axiologic issue); the conviction that effective use of personal and literary writing styles are key to meaningful representation of research results (i.e., the rhetorical issue); and the ways in which inductive logic is used to draw out and encourage development of emerging understanding of what the data mean (i.e., the methodologic issue) (Creswell, 2007).

Thus, Guba and Lincoln (1994) acknowledge that although their criteria "have been well received, their parallelism to positivist criteria makes them suspect… [and, therefore,] the issue of quality criteria… is not well resolved" (p. 114).

Trustworthiness Criteria

When appraising qualitative research, applying Lincoln and Guba's (1985) trustworthiness criteria can be helpful. These criteria include *credibility*, *transferability*, *dependability*, and *confirmability* (see Box 6.16).

Credibility. Credibility (paralleling internal validity) is demonstrated by accuracy and validity that are assured through documentation of researcher actions, opinions, and biases; negative case analysis (e.g., accounting for outliers/exceptions); appropriateness of data (e.g., purposeful sampling); adequacy of the database (e.g., saturation); and verification/corroboration by use of multiple data sources (e.g., triangulation), validation of data and findings by informants (e.g., member checks), and consultation with colleagues (e.g., peer debriefing).

Some caveats about the above indicators of credibility merit mentioning. Member checks can be problematic when researchers' findings uncover implicit patterns or meanings of which informants are unaware. Thus, they may not be able to corroborate findings and may need to reexamine the situation and "check out results for themselves" (Morse, 1994, p. 230).

Also, member checks are seldom useful for corroborating reports that are a synthesis of multiple perspectives because individuals are not positioned well to account for perspectives beyond their own. Therefore, member checks should be seen as an ongoing process for assuring that informants' recorded accounts accurately and fairly reflect their perceptions and experiences. But as an ultimate check on the final interpretation of data, they are not required; it is up to the researcher to decide when and how they may be useful (Morse, 1998a; Sandelowski, 1993, 1998a). As a result, when reading a qualitative report, member checks may or may not be present.

Peer debriefing involves seeking input (substantive or methodological) from knowledgeable colleagues as consultants, soliciting their reactions as listeners, and using them as sounding boards for the researcher's ideas. It is up to the researcher to decide when and whether peer debriefing will be useful. It is important to distinguish peer debriefing from quantitative researchers' use of multiple raters and expert panels. In qualitative research, it is not appropriate to use

---

box 6.16

Lincoln and Gubas' Evaluative Criteria: Trustworthiness Criteria

- Credibility
- Dependability
- Transferability
- Confirmability

individuals outside of the research to "validate" the researcher's analyses and interpretations because these are arrived at inductively through closer contact and understanding of the data than an outside expert could possibly have (Morse, 1994, 1997b, 1998a; Sandelowski, 1998a). Because peer debriefing may not always be useful, the reader should not expect to encounter this credibility criterion in every qualitative report.

Transferability. Transferability (paralleling external validity) is demonstrated by information that is sufficient for a research consumer to determine whether the findings are meaningful to other people in similar situations (analytic or theoretical vs. statistical generalizability). The practical usefulness of a qualitative study is judged by its:

- Ability to represent how informants feel about and make sense of their experiences
- Effectiveness in communicating what that information means and the lessons that it teaches

Is has been thought that because qualitative studies did not meet generalizability standards for quantitative studies, the results were not generalizable. However, the extent to which research-based understandings can be applied to experiences of individuals in similar situations (i.e., transferability) defines a study's generalizability. Therefore, it is misleading to say that results of qualitative studies are not generalizable (Sandelowski, 1996). When the reader holds this idea or encounters it in the literature, it usually means that there is a lack of understanding about the differences between statistical generalization and analytic or theoretic generalization. The former pertains to mathematically based probabilities with which implications of study findings can be extended to a larger population, consistent with the purposes of quantitative research designs. The latter pertains to logically and pragmatically based possibilities with which implications of study findings can be extended to a larger population, consistent with the purposes of qualitative research designs.

Dependability. Dependability (paralleling reliability) is demonstrated by a research process that is carefully documented to provide evidence of how conclusions were reached and whether, under similar conditions, a researcher might expect to obtain similar findings (i.e., the concept of the audit trail).

Confirmability. Confirmability (paralleling objectivity) is demonstrated by providing substantiation that findings and interpretations are grounded in the data (i.e., links between researcher assertions and the data are clear and credible).

Other general criteria are linked to concepts of credibility and transferability but relate more to the effects that various portrayals of the research may have. For example, a second set of criteria developed by Guba and Lincoln (1989) have overtones of a critical theory view that when the goal of research is to provide deeper understanding and more informed insights into human experiences, it also may prove to be empowering (Guba & Lincoln, 1994).

Authenticity Criteria

Box 6.17 lists Guba and Lincoln's (1989) evaluative *authenticity criteria. Fairness* is the degree to which informants' different ways of making sense of experiences (i.e., their "constructions") are evenly represented by the researcher. *Ontological authenticity* is the scope to which personal insights are enhanced or enlarged. *Educative authenticity* is the extent to which there is increased understanding of and appreciation for others' constructions. *Catalytic authenticity* is how effectively the research stimulates action. *Tactical authenticity* is the degree to which people are empowered to act.

Ontological and educative authenticity, in particular, is at the heart of concerns about how to represent research results. That is, to transfer a deeper understanding of a phenomenon to the reader, researchers may strive for literary styles of writing that make a situation seem more "real" or "alive." This also is called making use of *verisimilitude*, an important criterion of

---

box 6.17

Guba and Lincoln's Evaluative Criteria: Authenticity Criteria

- ■ Fairness
- ■ Ontological authenticity
- ■ Catalytic authenticity
- ■ Tactical authenticity
- ■ Educative authenticity

---

traditional validity (Creswell, 2007; Denzin, 1997). It refers to any style of writing that *vicariously draws readers into the multiple realities of the world that the research reveals*, seen from both informant and researcher perspectives.

Evaluation Standards

The authenticity criteria (Guba & Lincoln, 1989) are not as well recognized or cited as regularly as Lincoln and Guba's (1985) trustworthiness criteria. The reason that many quantitative researchers and practitioners appreciate the latter is that they are understandable and seek to impose a sense of order and uniformity on a field that is diverse and difficult to understand. Thus, some readers have greater confidence in qualitative reports that use the classic trustworthiness criteria terminology to explain what researchers did to assure *credibility, transferability, dependability*, and/or *confirmability*. However, it does not mean that reports that do not do so are necessarily deficient. Many qualitative researchers and practitioners resist parallelism (i.e., using words that mirror the concepts and values of quantitative research) because they think that it may detract from better method-specific explanations of their research (a matter of training and individual preference). Some also think it could undermine the integrity of qualitative methods themselves (a matter of principle). Furthermore, they know that examples of procedures to ensure quality and rigor are more or less appropriate for different kinds of qualitative studies and, therefore, attempts to talk about the general properties of qualitative designs and findings pose many constraints. As a result, there is a threat to integrity if general criteria come to be viewed as rigid rules that must apply in every instance. Therefore, it is incumbent upon nonqualitative researchers and practitioners to assimilate more details about the differences, similarities, and nuances of this large field of research than they might at first prefer in order to conduct a fair and accurate appraisal of qualitative reports.

Walking the Walk and Talking the Talk: Critical Appraisal of Qualitative Research

This chapter began by comparing critical appraisal of individual research reports with separating wheat from chaff. Separating out the chaff involves applying the reader's understanding of the diversity within the field of qualitative research to the content of the report. Then extracting what is good and useful involves applying the appropriate method-specific and general evaluative criteria to the research report. Using the guide in Box 6.18 to appraise qualitative research studies depends on a degree of familiarity with the preceding introduction to the diversity of characteristics, language, concepts, and issues associated with this field.

The guide adopts the EBP format of basic quick appraisal questions followed by questions of a more specific nature. However, there are caveats. One is that no individual study will contain the most complete information possible about everything in the appraisal guide. Sometimes, as in quantitative reports, the information really is available, built into the

box 6.18

Rapid Critical Appraisal of Qualitative Evidence

Are the Results Valid/Trustworthy and Credible?

1. How were study participants chosen?
2. How were accuracy and completeness of data assured?
3. How plausible/believable are the results?

Are Implications of the Research Stated?

1. May new insights increase sensitivity to others' needs?
2. May understandings enhance situational competence?

What is the Effect on the Reader?

1. Are results plausible and believable?
2. Is the reader imaginatively drawn into the experience?

What were the Results of the Study?

1. Does the research approach fit the purpose of the study?

How does the Researcher Identify the Study Approach?

1. Are language and concepts consistent with the approach?
2. Are data collection and analysis techniques appropriate?

Is the Significance/Importance of the Study Explicit?

1. Does review of the literature support a need for the study?
2. What is the study's potential contribution?

Is the Sampling Strategy Clear and Guided by Study Needs?

1. Does the researcher control selection of the sample?
2. Do sample composition and size reflect study needs?
3. Is the phenomenon (human experience) clearly identified?

Are Data Collection Procedures Clear?

1. Are sources and means of verifying data explicit?
2. Are researcher roles and activities explained?

Are Data Analysis Procedures Described?

1. Does analysis guide direction of sampling and when it ends?
2. Are data management processes described?
3. What are the reported results (description or interpretation)?

(box continues on page 158)

> **box 6.18** *(continued)*
>
> ### How are Specific Findings Presented?
>
> **1.** Is presentation logical, consistent, and easy to follow?
> **2.** Do quotes fit the findings they are intended to illustrate?
>
> ### How are Overall Results Presented?
>
> **1.** Are meanings derived from data described in context?
> **2.** Does the writing effectively promote understanding?
>
> ### Will the Results Help me in Caring for My Patients?
>
> **1.** Are the results relevant to persons in similar situations?
> **2.** Are the results relevant to patient values and/or circumstances?
> **3.** How may the results be applied in clinical practice?

design itself but dependent on reader's knowledge of the method. At other times, because the volume of data and findings may require a series of reports that focus on different aspects of the research, authors sometimes direct readers to introductory articles that are more focused on the methods and broad overviews of the study. Also, space limitations and a journal's priorities determine the amount of detail that an author may provide in any given section of the report.

> *That inner voice has both gentleness and clarity. So to get*
> *to authenticity, you really keep going down to the bone, to*
> *the honesty, and the inevitability of something.*
> *Meredith Monk*

Putting Feet to Knowledge: Walking the Walk

It is time to put feet to the knowledge the reader has gained through this chapter. The reader is encouraged to use Appendix C that demonstrates a rapid critical appraisal application of the appraisal guide for qualitative evidence. The appendix contains 10 exemplars of qualitative research reports. The range of topics appearing in the literature confirms that clinical researchers across professions and specialty areas are "walking the walk and talking the talk" with regard to using a variety of qualitative approaches with attendant methodologies, terms, and concepts as discussed and defined previously.

Choice of exemplars presented here was guided by the following criteria:

- A mix of recent articles (from 2008) representing a variety of concerns across different areas of clinical interest
- A range of qualitative research designs that illustrate the achievement of valid results
- A range of research purposes that illustrate a variety of ways in which results may help readers care for their patients

The source of these studies was *Qualitative Health Research,* an interdisciplinary journal that addresses a variety of healthcare issues and is an excellent resource for individuals seeking good examples of qualitative methods. Factors that may affect reader response to the appraisal of articles using the rapid critical appraisal format are

1. Individual preference: In the real world, people choose the topics that interest them.
2. The ease with which the report submits to appraisal: Appreciation and understanding of qualitative reports depend on individual reading of and engagement with the report in its entirety. Therefore, the articles lose some of their communicative and evocative qualities when parsed apart and retold.

The results of the appraisal process combined with individual preference may affect the studies' initial appeal. Because in every case evaluations of an article's plausibility and generalizability (transferability) require the use of independent reader judgments, firsthand reading is recommended.

> *Changes may not happen right away, but with effort even the difficult may become easy.*
>
> **Bill Blackman**

Keeping it Together: Synthesizing Qualitative Evidence

Synthesizing qualitative evidence is not a new endeavor, given the history of the *meta-study* in the social sciences. A meta-study is not the same as a critical literature review or a secondary analysis of an existing data set. Instead, meta-studies involve distinct approaches to the analysis of previously published research findings in order to produce new knowledge (a synthesis of what is already known). In quantitative research, *meta-analysis* is the research strategy designed to ask a new question on multiple studies that address similar research hypotheses using comparable methodologies, reanalyzing and combining their results to come to a conclusion about what is known about the issue of interest. In qualitative research, various strategies for performing *meta-synthesis* have been proposed. In an article by Thorne, Jensen, Kearney, et al. (2004), these scholars presented their distinct perspectives on meta-synthesis methodology in order to, first, underscore what it is not (i.e., it is not an integrative critical literature review) and, then, to explore the various methodological conventions used and/or recommended by this panel of authors.

The result of various approaches to qualitative meta-synthesis can be a formal theory or a new refined interpretive explanation of the phenomenon. For example, Kearney (2001), using a grounded formal theory approach, analyzed 13 qualitative research reports and synthesized a middle-range theory of women's responses to violent relationships. She found that "within cultural contexts that normalized relationship violence while promoting idealized romance, these women dealt with the incongruity of violence in their relationships as a basic process of enduring love" (p. 270).

Thorne, Paterson, Acorn, et al. (2002) presented insights about a body of qualitative evidence related to the experience of chronic illness gained through use of general meta-method approaches developed within sociology and anthropology. Their findings uncovered a tension between conceptualizations of chronic illness (e.g., loss vs. opportunity for growth) that suggested the need for "a functional model of chronic illness…to account for both possibilities, focusing its attention on, for example, how we might know which conceptualization to engage in any particular clinical encounter" (p. 448). The methodological approach that was used is described in greater detail in *Meta-Study of Qualitative Health Research: A Practical Guide to Meta-Analysis and Meta-Synthesis* (Paterson, Thorne, Canam, et al., 2001).

Sandelowski and Barroso (2003) used meta-summary and meta-synthesis techniques in an ongoing study of research conducted on HIV-positive women. Their findings in this report, in part, revealed that "motherhood itself positioned these women precariously between life as a normal woman and life as a deviant one" (p. 477). Women's response to "mortal and social threats of HIV infection and the contradictions of Western motherhood embodied in being an HIV-positive mother…was to engage in a distinctive maternal practice [described as] *virtual motherhood*" (p. 476). A detailed description of how to perform qualitative research synthesis, including illustrative examples from this research, is provided in their *Handbook for Synthesizing Qualitative Research* (Sandelowski & Barroso, 2007). Further examples of meta-synthesis include Hammell's (2007a, 2007b) meta-synthesis of qualitative findings on the experience of rehabilitation and factors contributing to or detracting from the quality of life after spinal cord injury, and a meta-ethnographic approach to the synthesis of qualitative research on adherence to tuberculosis treatment by Atkins, Lewin, Smith, et al. (2008).

Despite the lack of a single set of agreed-upon techniques for synthesizing qualitative studies, there is an appreciation for the basic definition and underlying purposes of meta-synthesis and the general procedural issues that any approach to it will need to address. Basically, meta-synthesis is a holistic translation, based on comparative analysis of individual qualitative interpretations, which seeks to retain the essence of their unique contributions. Although individual studies can provide useful information and insights, they cannot give the most comprehensive answers to clinical questions. A benefit of meta-synthesis methods is that they provide a way for researchers to build up bodies of qualitative research evidence that are relevant to clinical practice.

Specific approaches to meta-synthesis need to address issues of:

- How to characterize the phenomenon of interest when comparing conceptualizations and interpretations across studies
- How to establish inclusion criteria and sample from among a population of studies
- How to compare studies that have used the same or different qualitative strategies
- How to reach new understandings about a phenomenon by seeking consensus in a body of data where it is acknowledged that there is no single "correct" interpretation (Jensen & Allen, 1996)

Appraisal of meta-synthesis research reports requires an appreciation for the different perspectives that may be guiding the analysis. Mechanisms described by Sandelowski and Barroso (2007) for promoting valid study procedures and outcomes include:

- Using all search channels of communication and maintaining an audit trail (Rodgers & Cowles, 1993) tracking search outcomes as well as procedural and interpretive decisions
- Contacting primary study investigators
- Consulting with reference librarians
- Independent search by at least two reviewers
- Independent appraisal of each report by at least two reviewers
- Ensuring ongoing negotiation of consensual validity (Belgrave & Smith, 1995; Eisner, 1991) facilitated by collaborative efforts by team members to establish areas of consensus and negotiate consensus in the presence of differing points of view
- Securing expert peer review (Sandelowski, 1998a) by consultation with experts in research synthesis and with clinical experts

Written reports will vary in their use or mention of these approaches and in their detailing of research procedures. Readers will have to be alerted about references to a named methodology; explanation of the search strategy that was used; clarity in the manner in which findings (data that comprise the study sample) are presented; and the originality, plausibility, and perceived usefulness of the synthesis of those findings.

> *You will come to know that what appears today to be a sacrifice will prove instead to be the greatest investment that you will ever make.*
>
> *Gorden B. Hinkley*

references

Atkins, S., Lewin, S., Smith, H., Engel, M., Fretheim, A., & Volmink, J. (2008). Conducting a meta-ethnography of qualitative literature: Lessons learnt. *BMC Medical Research Methodology, 8,* 21.

Atkinson, P. (1992). *Understanding ethnographic texts.* Newbury Park, CA: Sage.

Baker, T. A., & Wang, C. C. (2006). Photovoice: Use of a participatory action research method to explore the chronic pain experience in older adults. *Qualitative Health Research, 16,* 1405–1413.

Beck, C. T. (2007). Teetering on the edge: A continually emerging theory of postpartum depression. In P. L. Munhall (Ed.), *Nursing research: A qualitative perspective* (4th ed., pp. 273–292). Sudbury, MA: Jones & Bartlett.

Beck, C. T., & Watson, S. (2008). Impact of birth trauma on breast-feeding. *Nursing Research, 57,* 228–236.

Belgrave, L. L., & Smith, K. J. (1995). Negotiated validity in collaborative ethnography. *Qualitative Inquiry, 1,* 69–86.

Bingley, A. F., Thomas, C., Brown, J., Reeve, J., & Payne, S. (2008). Developing narrative research in supportive and palliative care: The focus on illness narratives. *Palliative Medicine, 22,* 653–658.

Bryant, A., & Charmaz, K. (Eds.) (2007). *The SAGE handbook of grounded theory.* London: Sage.

Charmaz, K. (2006). *Constructing grounded theory: A practical guide through qualitative analysis.* London: Sage.

Cheek, J. (2004). At the margins? Discourse analysis and qualitative research. *Qualitative Health Research, 14,* 1140–1150.

Chenitz, W. C., & Swanson, J. M. (1986). *From practice to grounded theory.* Menlo Park, CA: Addison-Wesley.

Clabo, L. M. L. (2007). An ethnography of pain assessment and the role of social context on two postoperative units. *Journal of Advanced Nursing, 61,* 531–539.

Copeland, D. A., & Heilemann, M. V. (2008). Getting "to the Point": The experience of mothers getting assistance for their adult children who are violent and mentally ill. *Nursing Research, 57,* 136–143.

Corbin, J., & Strauss, A. (2008). *Basics of qualitative research: Techniques and procedures for developing grounded theory* (3rd ed.). Thousand Oaks, CA: Sage.

Creswell, J. W. (2007). *Qualitative inquiry & research design: Choosing among five approaches* (2nd ed.). Thousand Oaks, CA: Sage.

Cricco-Lizza, R. (2007). Ethnography and the generation of trust in breastfeeding disparities research. *Applied Nursing Research, 20,* 200–204.

Denzin, N. K. (1997). *Interpretive ethnography: Ethnographic practices for the 21st century.* Thousand Oaks, CA: Sage.

Dickson-Swift, V., James, E. L., Kippen, S., & Liamputtong, P. (2006). Blurring boundaries in qualitative health research on sensitive topics. *Qualitative Health Research, 16,* 853–871.

Edwards, S., & Gabbay, M. (2007). Living and working with sickness: A qualitative study. *Chronic Illness, 3,* 155–166.

Eisner, E. W. (1991). *The enlightened eye: Qualitative inquiry and the enhancement of educational practice.* New York: Macmillan.

Ellingson, L. L. (2006). Embodied knowledge: Writing researchers' bodies into qualitative health research. *Qualitative Health Research, 16,* 298–310.

Etowa, J. B., Bernard, W. T., Oyinsan, B., & Clow, B. (2007). Participatory action research (PAR): An approach for improving Black women's health in rural and remote communities. *Journal of Transcultural Nursing, 18,* 349–357.

Evans, M. J., & Hallett, C. E. (2007). Living with dying: A hermeneutic phenomenological study of the work of hospice nurses. *Journal of Clinical Nursing, 16,* 742–751.

Fawcett, J., Watson, J., Neuman, B., Hinton-Walker, P., & Fitzpatrick, J. J. (2001). On theories and evidence. *Journal of Nursing Scholarship, 33,* 115–119.

Fineout-Overholt, E., Melnyk, B., & Schultz, A. (2005). Transforming health care from the inside out: Advancing evidence-based practice in the 21st century. *Journal of Professional Nursing, 21*(6), 335–344.

Flick, U. (2006). *An introduction to qualitative research* (3rd ed.). London: Sage.

Fochtman, D. (2008). Phenomenology in pediatric cancer nursing research. *Journal of Pediatric Oncology Nursing, 25,* 185–192.

chapter 6

161

Foster, K., McAllister, M., & O'Brien, L. (2005). Coming to autoethnography: A mental health nurse's experience. *International Journal of Qualitative Methods, 4*, 1–13.

Furman, R. (2006). Poetic forms and structures in qualitative health research. *Qualitative Health Research, 16*, 560–566.

Geertz, C. (1973). *The interpretation of cultures.* New York: Basic Books.

Glaser, B. G. (1978). *Theoretical sensitivity.* Mill Valley, CA: Sociology Press.

Glaser, B. G. (1992). *Emergence vs. forcing: Basics of grounded theory analysis.* Mill Valley, CA: Sociology Press.

Glaser, B. G., & Strauss, A. L. (1967). *The discovery of grounded theory: Strategies for qualitative research.* New York: Aldine.

Grace, J. T., & Powers, B. A. (2009). Claiming our core: Appraising qualitative evidence for nursing questions about human response and meaning. *Nursing Outlook, 57*(1), 27–34.

Graffigna, G., & Bosio, A. C. (2006). The influence of setting on findings produced in qualitative health research: A comparison between face-to-face and online discussion groups about HIV/AIDS. *International Journal of Qualitative Methods, 5*(3), Article 5. Retrieved, September 16, 2008, from http://www.ualberta.ca/~iiqm/backissues/5_3/pdf/graffigna.pdf

Guba, E. G., & Lincoln, Y. S. (1989). *Fourth generation evaluation.* Newbury Park, CA: Sage.

Guba, E. G., & Lincoln, Y. S. (1994). Competing paradigms in qualitative research. In N. K. Denzin & Y. S. Lincoln (Eds.), *Handbook of qualitative research* (pp. 105–117). Thousand Oaks, CA: Sage.

Guell, C. (2007). Painful childhood: Children living with juvenile arthritis. *Qualitative Health Research, 17*, 884–892.

Hammell, K. W. (2007a). Experience of rehabilitation following spinal cord injury: A meta-synthesis of qualitative findings. *Spinal Cord, 45*, 260–274.

Hammell, K. W. (2007b). Quality of life after spinal cord injury: A meta-synthesis of qualitative findings. *Spinal Cord, 45*, 124–139.

Homans, G. C. (1955). *The human group.* New York: Harcourt Brace.

Hsieh, H.F., & Shannon, S. E. (2005). Three approaches to qualitative content analysis. *Qualitative Health Research, 15*, 1277–1288.

Jensen, L. A., & Allen, M. N. (1996). Meta-synthesis of qualitative findings. *Qualitative Health Research, 6*, 553–560.

Kayser-Jones, J. (2002). The experience of dying: An ethnographic nursing home study. *The Gerontologist, 42*, 11–19.

Kayser-Jones, J., Schell, E., Lyons, W., Kris, A. E., Chan, J., & Beard, R. L. (2003). Factors that influence end-of-life care in nursing homes: The physical environment, inadequate staffing, and lack of supervision. *The Gerontologist, 43*, 76–84.

Kearney, M. H. (2001). Enduring love: A grounded formal theory of women's experience of domestic violence. *Research in Nursing & Health, 24*, 270–282.

Kleinman, A. (1988). *The illness narratives: Suffering, healing & the human condition.* New York: Basic Books.

Kontos, P. C., & Naglie, G. (2006). Expressions of personhood in Alzheimer's: Moving from ethnographic text to performing ethnography. *Qualitative Research, 6*, 301–317.

Kontos, P. C., & Naglie, G. (2007). Expressions of personhood in Alzheimer's disease: An evaluation of research-based theatre as a pedagogical tool. *Qualitative Health Research, 17*, 799–811.

Krueger, R., & Casey, M. (2000). *Focus groups: A practical guide for applied research* (3rd ed.). Thousand Oaks, CA: Sage.

Lincoln, Y. S., & Guba, E. G. (1985). *Naturalistic inquiry.* Beverly Hills, CA: Sage.

Mantzoukas, S. (2004). Issues of representation within qualitative inquiry. *Qualitative Health Research, 14*, 994–1007.

Marshall, C., & Rossman, G. B. (2006). *Designing qualitative research* (4th ed.). Thousand Oaks, CA: Sage.

Melia, K. M. (1996). Rediscovering Glaser. *Qualitative Health Research, 6*, 368–378.

Milton, C. L. (2007). Evidence-based practice: Ethical questions for nursing. *Nursing Science Quarterly, 20*, 123–126.

Mordoch, E., & Hall, W. A. (2008). Children's perceptions of living with a parent with a mental illness: Finding the rhythm and maintaining the frame. *Qualitative Health Research, 18*, 1127–1144.

Morse, J. M. (1994). Designing funded qualitative research. In N. K. Denzin & Y. S. Lincoln (Eds.), *Handbook of qualitative research* (pp. 220–235). Thousand Oaks, CA: Sage.

Morse, J. M. (1997a). Learning to drive from a manual? *Qualitative Health Research, 7*, 181–183.

Morse, J. M. (1997b). "Perfectly healthy, but dead": The myth of inter-rater reliability. *Qualitative Health Research, 7*, 445–447.

Morse, J. M. (1998a). Validity by committee. *Qualitative Health Research, 8*, 443–445.

Morse, J. M. (1998b). What's wrong with random selection? *Qualitative Health Research, 8*, 733–735.

Morse, J. M. (2000). Determining sample size. *Qualitative Health Research, 10*, 3–5.

Morse, J. M. (2007). Quantitative influences on the presentation of qualitative articles. *Qualitative Health Research, 17*, 147–148.

Paterson, B. L., Thorne, S. E., Canam, C., & Jillings, C. (2001). *Meta-study of qualitative health research: A practical guide to meta-analysis and meta-synthesis.* Thousand Oaks, CA: Sage.

Perkins, P., Barclay, S., & Booth, S. (2007). What are patients' priorities for palliative care research? Focus group study. *Palliative Medicine, 21*, 219–225.

Porter, E. J., Ganong, L. H., Drew, N., & Lanes, T. I. (2004). A new typology of home-care helpers. *Gerontologist, 44*, 750–759.

Powers, B. A. (2001). Ethnographic analysis of everyday ethics in the care of nursing home residents with dementia: A taxonomy. *Nursing Research, 50*, 332–339.

Powers, B. A. (2005). Everyday ethics in assisted living facilities: A framework for assessing resident-focused issues. *Journal of Gerontological Nursing, 31*, 31–37.

Powers, B. A., & Knapp, T. R. (2006a). Evidence. In B. A. Powers & T. R. Knapp (Eds.), *A dictionary of nursing theory and research* (3rd ed., pp 54–56). Thousand Oaks, CA: Sage.

Powers, B. A., & Knapp, T. R. (2006b). Evidence-based practice (EBP). In B. A. Powers & T. R. Knapp (Eds.), *A dictionary of nursing theory and research* (3rd ed., pp. 56–58). Thousand Oaks, CA: Sage.

Richardson, L. (1990). *Writing strategies: Reaching diverse audiences*. Newbury Park, CA: Sage.

Rodgers, B. L., & Cowles, K. V., (1993). The qualitative research audit trail: A complex collection of documentation. *Research in Nursing & Health, 16*, 219–226.

Sandelowski, M. (1991). Telling stories: Narrative approaches in qualitative research. *Image: Journal of Nursing Scholarship, 23*, 161–166.

Sandelowski, M. (1993). Rigor or rigor mortis: The problem of rigor in qualitative research revisited. *Research in Nursing & Health, 16*, 1–8.

Sandelowski, M. (1995). Sample size in qualitative research. *Research in Nursing & Health, 18*, 179–183.

Sandelowski, M. (1996). One is the liveliest number: The case orientation of qualitative research. *Research in Nursing & Health, 19*, 525–529.

Sandelowski, M. (1998a). The call to experts in qualitative research. *Research in Nursing & Health, 21*, 467–471.

Sandelowski, M. (1998b). Writing a good read: Strategies for re-presenting qualitative data. *Research in Nursing & Health, 21*, 375–382.

Sandelowski, M. (2000a). Combining qualitative and quantitative sampling, data collection, and analysis techniques in mixed-method studies. *Research in Nursing & Health, 23*, 246–255.

Sandelowski, M. (2000b). Whatever happened to qualitative description? *Research in Nursing & Health, 23*, 334–340.

Sandelowski, M. (2004). Counting cats in Zanzibar. *Research in Nursing & Health, 27*, 215–216.

Sandelowski, M. (2007). Words that should be seen but not written. *Research in Nursing & Health, 30*, 129–130.

Sandelowski, M., & Barroso, J. (2003). Motherhood in the context of maternal HIV infection. *Research in Nursing & Health, 26*, 470–482.

Sandelowski, M., & Barroso, J. (2007). *Handbook for synthesizing qualitative research*. New York: Springer.

Sandelowski, M., Trimble, F., Woodard, E. K., & Barroso, J. (2006). From synthesis to script: Transforming qualitative research findings for use in practice. *Qualitative Health Research, 16*, 1350–1370.

Scott, S. D., & Pollock, C. (2008). The role of nursing unit culture in shaping research utilization behaviors. *Research in Nursing & Health, 31*, 298–309.

Smith, C. A. M., & Gallo, A. M. (2007). Applications of performance ethnography in nursing. *Qualitative Health Research, 17*, 521–528.

Starks, H., & Trinidad, S. B. (2007). Choose your method: A comparison of phenomenology, discourse analysis, and grounded theory. *Qualitative Health Research, 17*, 1372–1380.

Stewart, L., & Usher, K. (2007). Carspecken's critical approach as a way to explore nursing leadership issues. *Qualitative Health Research, 17*, 994–999.

Straus, S. E., Richardson, W. S., Glasziou, P., & Haynes, R. B. (2005). *Evidence-based medicine: How to practice and teach EBM* (3rd ed.). Edinburgh: Elsevier.

Strauss, A. L., & Corbin, J. (1990). *Basics of qualitative research: Grounded theory procedures and techniques*. Newbury Park, CA: Sage.

Strauss, A. L., & Corbin, J. (1998). *Basics of qualitative research: Techniques and procedures for developing grounded theory* (2nd ed.). Thousand Oaks, CA: Sage.

Thomas, J. (1993). *Doing critical ethnography*. Newbury Park, CA: Sage.

Thorne, S., Jensen, L., Kearney, M. H., Noblit, G., & Sandelowski, M. (2004). Qualitative metasynthesis: Reflections on methodological orientation and ideological agenda. *Qualitative Health Research, 14*, 1342–1365.

Thorne, S., Paterson, B., Acorn, S., Canam, C., Joachim, G., & Jillings, C. (2002). Chronic illness experience: Insights from a metastudy. *Qualitative Health Research, 12*, 437–452.

Tutton, E., Seers, K., & Langstaff, D. (2007). Professional nursing culture on a trauma unit: Experiences of patients and staff. *Journal of Advanced Nursing, 61*, 145–153.

Van Maanen, J. (1988). *Tales of the field*. Chicago: University of Chicago Press.

van Manen, M. (1990/1997). *Researching lived experience*. London, Ontario: University of Western Ontario & State University of New York Press.

van Manen, M. (2002). *Writing in the dark: Phenomenological studies in interpretive inquiry*. London, Ontario: University of Western Ontario.

Varcoe, C. (2001). Abuse obscured: An ethnographic account of emergency nursing in relation to violence against women. *Canadian Journal of Nursing Research, 32*, 95–115.

Wolcott, H. (2001). *Writing up qualitative research* (2nd ed.). Thousand Oaks, CA: Sage.

Wolcott, H. (2002). Writing up qualitative research… better. *Qualitative Health Research, 12*, 91–103.

Wolf, Z. R. (2007). Ethnography: The method. In P. L. Munhall (Ed.), *Nursing research: A qualitative perspective* (4th ed., pp. 293–330). Sudbury, MA: Jones & Bartlett.

Woodgate, R. L., Ateah, C., & Secco, L. (2008). Living in a world of our own: The experience of parents who have a child with autism. *Qualitative Health Research, 18*, 1075–1083.

Wuest, J. (2007). Grounded theory: The method. In P. L. Munhall (Ed.), *Nursing research: A qualitative perspective* (4th ed., pp. 239–271). Sudbury, MA: Jones & Bartlett.

Acknowledgment

The author wishes to thank Jeanne T. Grace PhD, RN, WHNP and anonymous reviewers for reading and commenting on earlier drafts of this chapter.

Steps Four and Five: Moving from Evidence to Action

Patient Concerns, Choices, and Clinical Judgment in Evidence-Based Practice

Patricia E. Benner and Victoria Wynn Leonard

The right to search for truth implies also a duty: One must not conceal any part of what one has recognized to be true.

A l b e r t   E i n s t e i n

Nursing like medicine involves a rich, socially embedded clinical know-how that encompasses perceptual skills, transitional understandings across time, and understanding of the particular in relation to the general. "Clinical knowledge is a form of engaged reasoning that follows modus operandi thinking, in relation to patients' and clinical populations' particular manifestations of disease, dysfunction, response to treatment, and recovery trajectories. Clinical knowledge is necessarily configurational, historical… (i.e., the immediate and long-term histories of particular patients and clinical populations), contextual, perceptual, and based upon knowledge gained in transitions…. [Through articulation], clinical understanding becomes increasingly articulate and translatable at least by clinical examples, narratives and puzzles encountered in practice" (Benner, 1994, p. 139).

The use of research-based evidence in clinical practice is nearly as old as clinical practice itself. To qualify as a self-improving practice rather than a closed practice, it has always been incumbent on the practitioner to bring the latest and most accurate scientific information into any decision made on a patient's clinical problem. To improve or change tradition, nursing must demonstrate ongoing knowledge development and critical evaluation of science and practice.

In simpler times, there was little controversy about the "best" practice because scientific research was yet to proliferate into the multibillion-dollar enterprise that it has now become. "Evidence" was hard to come by and usually anecdotal. The most effective clinicians were keen observers who knew their patients and communities well, often caring for them over long periods of time.

What is new about the current evidence-based practice (EBP) movement in this time of expanding scientific research and information is the attempt to aggregate data in ever larger meta-analytic studies for application by responsible but hurried practitioners who often are working in impersonal practice settings and caring for large numbers of patients they seldom know well.

This enterprise of aggregating data relieves practitioners of some of the time-consuming reading, evaluating, and weighing of all of the published research relevant to their clinical practices. The body of health literature is expanding exponentially and is expected to double in 19 years. Clinicians' feelings of being overwhelmed by research "evidence" will certainly grow along with the literature, as will the need for a way to "digest" it. But the myth that enough "scientific evidence" exists to drive practice completely creates its own set of problems. That is why a critical evaluation of the strengths and weaknesses of the available evidence for any particular patient situation is so crucial to effective EBP.

Best Evidence: Research and Patient Concerns

Although the concept of applying "best evidence" in a clinical decision seems straightforward, it is actually very complex. Skillful critical thinking is needed to evaluate the evidence for its robustness and scientific rigor. Moreover, it needs to be considered in light of the patient's concerns and preferences. The patient's concerns and preferences are crucial because most clinical situations are underdetermined (i.e., knowledge and information are incomplete), and the particular patient and circumstance are changing across time. The patient's diagnosis may be imprecise and the degree of pathophysiology uncertain, and the patient's responses to particular interventions will vary.

Good clinical judgment requires the most critical and up-to-date appraisal of existing science and application of this evidence where it is most relevant to a particular patient's concerns and disease trajectory.

In thinking critically about EBP, a two-pronged approach is useful. First the validity of the evidence itself needs to be examined carefully. This involves assessing the way the research was conceived and funded as well as how the findings were disseminated (or not). Second, how the evidence is applied to clinical decision making must be examined because expert clinical decision making is a much more nuanced and multidimensional process than the straightforward application of evidence. Clinical decision making and application of evidence requires good clinical judgment that includes the patient's concerns, preferences, and choices.

If clinical judgment could be reduced to a 1:1 application of evidence to particular cases, practice could be completely standardized and applied in a strictly technical manner, accomplishing exact replication and reproduction of findings from the general to the particular case (to be discussed as "techne" later in this chapter).

Clinical trials constitute a high level of "best evidence" in EBP. Other levels of relevance include basic empirical bench and epidemiological science, narrative inquiry on illness experience and disease trajectories, case studies, and other qualitative research (discussed in other chapters). Even if clinical trials alone provided best evidence for a particular patient, the reliability of the trial must be critically evaluated, just as is required in all science (see Box 7.1 for an in-depth discussion of potential flaws in research evidence). To enhance good clinical judgment and to have confidence in clinical practice guidelines generated by "best evidence," we need "better evidence" as urgently as we require the "best" of what evidence is available to us. System reforms need to be directed upstream—where research and evidence generation begin— rather than midstream, where EBP tries to make the best of a situation at a point where critical biases are already anchored. Reconceiving research to eliminate upstream biases and to enhance clinical judgment will require restructuring the way we execute clinical research.

box 7.1

Thinking Critically About Clinical Trials

When evaluating evidence generated by randomized controlled trials (RCTs), practitioners need to consider increasing threats to valid results caused, for example, by dropout rates and by several other factors:

■ Exclusivity—the exclusion of women, children, minorities, elderly people, and individuals with mixed diagnoses and/or comorbid conditions from most clinical trials
■ Conflicts of interest—on the part of the investigators
■ Inappropriate involvement of research sponsors—in the design and management of RCTs
■ Publication bias in disseminating trial results

Exclusivity

The exclusion of women, children, minorities, and those with complex chronic medical problems from most clinical trials raises very basic issues of justice and fairness, in addition to issues of validity of generalization of findings. These excluded populations constitute most of the population being treated with clinical practice guidelines generated by "best evidence." Until clinical trials can become more inclusive, the argument that patients are being treated based on the best evidence *for them* is usually not technically true.

Conflicts of Interest

Currently, between $300 and $600 million is needed to develop a single new drug. This cost is rising as pharmaceutical companies look for new drugs for chronic conditions. Trials to establish efficacy *of drugs* for chronic conditions require large subject pools and lengthy study periods. They must be conducted at multiple centers to ensure statistical validity. Approximately 70% of the money for clinical drug trials in the United States comes from industry rather than from the National Institutes of Health (NIH; Bodenheimer, 2000). In fact, the majority of NIH funding is directed toward basic science research (DeAngelis, 2000). Thus, pharmaceutical companies are conducting the lion's share of clinical research in the United States. The threat of conflict of interest to the development of unbiased clinical practice guidelines is a significant problem that must be addressed squarely by clinicians who use good clinical judgment in evaluating evidence for clinical decisions for particular patients.

Inappropriate Involvement of Research Sponsors

The vested interests of corporate sponsors of research are in the favorable review of their products, leading to approval by the U.S. Food and Drug Administration (FDA) and the ability to profitably market their products to both clinicians and consumers. This vested interest shapes which products are chosen for development (this is the reason for the moniker *orphan* for drugs with limited profitability) and how the evidence for their use is generated.

A significant outcome of sponsor involvement may be exemplified in clinical practice guidelines. These guidelines provide specific clinical recommendations for particular

(box continues on page 170)

box 7.1 *(continued)*

diagnostic entities. In a study designed to quantify the extent and nature of interactions between authors of clinical practice guidelines and the pharmaceutical industry, Choudhry, Stelfox, and Detsky (2002) found that 87% of authors had some form of interaction with the pharmaceutical industry, and 59% had relationships with companies whose drugs were considered in the guidelines they authored. Some 55% indicated that the guideline creation process with which they were involved had no formal process for declaring these relationships. This is why critical appraisal of the relevant evidence is a central part of the practitioner's clinical judgment.

Publication Bias in Disseminating Trial Results

Angell (2000) in a *New England Journal of Medicine* editorial entitled "Is Academic Medicine for Sale?" reports that the *Journal* requires that guest editorial writers have no important financial ties to companies that make products related to the issues they discuss. Because of this relatively stringent attempt to prevent bias in the *Journal,* Angell reports, they routinely encounter difficulty in finding experts to write editorial reviews who do not have financial relationships with corporations producing products related to the reviews. This is especially true, she reports, in disciplines that involve the heavy use of expensive drugs and devices. Brennan (1994), also in a *New England Journal of Medicine* editorial ("Buying Editorials"), recounts being approached by a public relations firm asking whether she would be interested in writing an editorial for a medical journal. More accurately, the firm proposed that its editorial staff write the editorial for her review before submission under her name. The caller told Brennan that the entire project would be funded by a pharmaceutical manufacturer; her firm was merely the intermediary. She would be paid $2,500 for her time.

Traditionally, pharmaceutical companies contracted with academic research scientists to conduct clinical trials. Increasingly, though, corporate funding is now being channeled into contract research organizations (CROs). CROs are for-profit, independent contractors whose sole purpose is to coordinate and expedite clinical trials. During the 1990s, pharmaceutical companies increased the use of CROs from 40% to 80% (Rettig, 2000). At the same time, clinical study grant funding grew by more than 20% annually (CenterWatch, 2002). The result is a major shift in the way clinical research is being funded and conducted.

Academic centers continue to lose research dollars. They currently participate in about 50% of trials, down from 80% 5 years ago (Association of Clinical Research Professionals, 2002). With the movement of clinical research away from academic centers, there is also a shift in the oversight of research. The more public and regulated space of academic research centers, where objectivity has always been the goal of research, is being replaced by the private, profit-driven, largely unexamined culture of CROs. This shift becomes more troublesome when one considers the expansion of CROs into activities such as medical writing for journals, including the ghost writing of "guest editorials" for peer-reviewed journals.

The validity of inferences made from any study sample depends on knowing that the sample is representative of the relevant population. Making valid inferences from meta-analytic synthesis requires that the sample of studies reviewed be representative of all studies that have been carried out.

> **box 7.1** *(continued)*
>
> Evidence-based practice (EBP) requires the practitioner to search for all available evidence, published and unpublished. That is why EBP is made easier by meta-analyses or integrative reviews that have done the work for the practitioner. One criterion to discern an overview article's "worth" is if the authors speak to whether or not they have covered ALL the relevant studies, published and unpublished.
>
> Many welcome the expansion of links between the private and public sectors. Some see it as the inevitable result of the growth of technology and the need for its dissemination and the reality of funding streams for clinical research. Others are understandably cautious. These relationships have the potential to both extend and despoil the growing body of clinical knowledge.

Even if the universe of clinical trials were perfect and meta-analysis could generate a perfect summary of what is known about treatment of a particular problem, practitioners would still have to proceed with caution. The logic of EBP provides a static snapshot of a conclusion based on aggregate evidence about one general condition to produce a yes or no decision. The clinician still must make a clinical judgment about a particular patient, usually with a complex particularized medical history and patterns of responses.

The practitioner must judiciously consider relevant patient particularities and concerns in making clinical decisions, such as gender, age, socioeconomic class, and illness experiences. In the patient's narrative, the particular clinical history, the social concerns, and the lifeworld concerns are revealed in ways that get covered over with just straight clinical information gathering.

Scannell (2002) argues that EBP "strives to be a little too much of everything… by proposing a system of medical knowledge that tries to eliminate subjective bias on one hand (in data collection and analysis) while invoking it on the other (through clinical applications that incorporate the subjective values of patients and the clinical judgments of physicians)" (p. 7). This is wonderfully illustrated in a *New York Times* article entitled "When Doctors Say Don't and the Patient Says Do" (Siegel, October 29, 2002).

Marc Siegel describes a determined 93-year-old woman who is a tap dancer and a former teacher of dance at Julliard. For the past 50 years, she was an avid tap dancer at amateur shows and recitals, until it was discovered that she had a "bulging disc in her neck and tissue so inflamed that it encroached on the space intended for the spinal cord, the crucial super-highway of the nervous system" (p. 7, Section F, Col. 1). All scientific evidence on prognosis for someone of her age undergoing spinal surgery unanimously showed that the risks outweighed the benefits, even though this particular patient's heart was in excellent health and she was also in excellent physical condition. When the risks of surgery were enumerated and weighed against the almost certain continued pain and incapacitation without the surgery, the woman asked, "Can the surgery make me dance again?" The physician replied, "It's possible." "Then," the woman responded, "I'll take my chances." A neurosurgeon who was willing to do the surgery was obtained. When the patient returned to the physician's office after surgery, she appeared to be a vigorous woman whose vitality was returning. Her walking had already progressed beyond her presurgical capacities.

Several weeks later, the physician received an invitation to her first postsurgical tap dancing recital. The woman explained, "You see, we patients are not just statistics. We don't always behave the way studies predict we will."

Clinical Judgment in Evidence-Based Practice

This story reveals the inextricable links between ethical and clinical decision making and the problematic implications of applying population-based research findings to individual patients. Good clinical judgment requires that the clinician discern what is good in a particular situation. The patient never offers an average statistical life to a possible medical intervention. Each patient has only one particular life and is concerned with his or her particular chances.

Every clinical judgment has ethical aspects about the goods and potential harms in a particular situation. The clinician must engage in a fiduciary relationship with the patient—acting in the patient's best interests and doing as little harm and as much good as possible. Scientific medicine separates the social from the medical in ways that nursing and doctoring particular patients never can. This patient presented clinical evidence that she experienced an exceptional health and fitness level, far different from projections based on the "average" 93-year-old person. One can imagine many different age-based scenarios with 30- or 60-year-olds who may be in extremely fragile health and who would require adjusted decisions based on their lower fitness and health levels. Social aspects, however, weighed in heavily in this decision, as in most other clinical decisions. The patient explained that tap dancing was her life. She literally could not imagine a life without tap dancing. She also had a robust confidence in her physical and emotional ability to withstand the surgery successfully. It is her life and her choice, and in the end, her outcomes proved that she was right.

This illustrates EBP at its best, where the science is there and indicates one path for treatment, but the patient's concerns and a realistic estimate of what is possible (for this exceptionally fit and active older woman) guide choices and decision making. Good clinical judgment always includes notions of good practice and a fiduciary relationship with the patient. The clinician used good clinical judgment in evaluating the medical feasibility of the woman's preferred decision and helped her find a surgeon who also found the risks acceptable. In the end, all clinicians learned from this exceptional patient. Including patients' central concerns, their history and information, preferences, and values in clinical decision making is a key to proficient EBP.

Nurses and doctors point out that they weave together a narrative understanding of their patients' condition that includes social and emotional aspects as well as many relevant current and historical clinical facts of the case (Benner, 2001; Benner et al., 1996; Cassel, 1991; Hunter, 1991; Tanenbaum, 1994; Wulff, Pederson, & Rosenberg, 1990).

Elements of Good Clinical Judgment

Clinical judgment requires knowing the patient (Tanner, Benner, Chesla, 1993) and entails reasoning across time about the particular through changes in the patient's condition and/or changes in the clinician's understanding of the patient's situation (Benner, Hooper-Kyriakidis, & Stannard, 1999, p. 10–11). Clinicians use evidence based on psychosocial sciences and basic sciences (e.g., physiology, anatomy, biochemistry, pharmacology, genetics), reasoning across time about the patient's transitions and history, an understanding of the patient's particular concerns, and evidence that draws on a comparative analysis of research, not only on the results of randomized clinical trials (RCTs). It is a dangerous simplification to imagine that evidence from clinical trials could apply directly to a particular patient care decision without evaluating the validity of the clinical trial and its relevance for that particular patient. The evidence must always be interpreted by the clinician in terms of what she or he knows about the way the evidence was obtained and in light of the clinician's interpretations of the patient's concerns, history, family and cultural context, and disease trajectory.

Summary results of comparative evidence from clinical trials must also be critically evaluated. As noted earlier, crucial questions about possible flaws in the research must be considered. Were there biased commercial influences in the design, presentation, or dissemination of the research? What is the credibility of the research and how well can it be directly applied to particular patients? Sometimes the research is robust and convincing; at other times, it is weaker and more conflicted. Still at other times, the relevant clinical trial research for a particular patient has not yet been done. Practice patterns, skills, and clinical insights are never infallible; they need constant clarification (i.e., thoughtful questioning and reflection about particular patient outcomes and a careful review of the basic science and its effectiveness).

Clinical Judgment and Self-Improving Practices

To continuously improve a practice, different clinical interventions and consequent outcomes must be compared. The goal is for a practice to be a self-improving practice through science and experiential clinical learning and correction, rather than a closed or deteriorating tradition that repeats errors. A self-improving practice can be compared with a closed traditional practice that depends only on past patterns rather than correction from experiential learning and science. A self-improving clinical practice depends on experiential learning and clinical inquiry of every practitioner in the everyday course of their practices.

Experiential Learning

Experience, as noted by Gadamer (1976), is never a mere passage of time or exposure to an event. To qualify as experience, it requires a turning around of preconceptions, expectations, sets, and routines or adding some new insights to a particular practical situation. Experiential learning is at the heart of improving clinical judgment.

Experiential Learning: Techne and Phronesis

Dunne (1997) revisits the distinction that Aristotle made between *techne* and *phronesis*. In EBP, techne (i.e., the art or skill involved in deliberately producing "something") involves producing outcomes by a means-ends strategy, whereby the *maker or producer* governs the outcome by mastering the means of its production. When nurses talk about establishing prespecified outcomes, they are talking about outcomes that can be the only predictable outcomes of techne; for example, known blood pressure parameters in the responses of a particular patient to specific drug dosages within a narrow time frame. When influence, persuasion, patient concerns, preferences, fear, or other emotions are involved, outcomes cannot be prespecified because the outcomes depend on mutual agreements and situated possibilities for the patient and clinician, and on too many complex variables.

By contrast, phronesis, which is good judgment applied to human conduct (or to clinical practice), cannot rely strictly on a means-ends rationality determined by preset norms, standards, or separation of means and ends. Phronesis involves reasoning across time about changes in the particular patient's condition and changes in the clinician's understanding. For instance, a clinical guideline that specifies outcomes without identifying means for achieving the outcome for a particular patient is a good example of separating means and ends. Therefore, phronesis involves ethical comportment, clinical judgment, and a respectful fiduciary relationship with the patient and family. Phronesis depends on a patient–clinician relationship that allows discernment of the human concerns at stake and encourages a patient to disclose the concerns with confidence and trust in the safety of the relationship. Good patient–clinician relationships can guide actions and treatments that are in tune with the needs, concerns, and autonomy of the patient.

When means and ends are radically separated, both can be distorted and understanding lost about which good ends are worthy and how to create them. For example, one cannot separate the means of respectful and trustworthy communication with a patient from the ends of respect for the patient's autonomy and concerns. Nursing and medicine are compelled by safety and efficiency to use techne in situations where outcomes are predictable and reliable. However, it is false logic to assume that a clinical problem is amenable to simple standardized technical applications (techne) when reasoning about the *particular* (i.e., the patient's condition and/or changes in the clinician's understanding and/or patient/family notions of good) may alter technical and statistical prescriptions, as they did in the case of the tap dancer who did not fit the statistical profiles.

It is wise to establish solid scientific direction that can alleviate the uncertainty and risk of human judgments when possible. However, it is unwise to mistake a situation that requires clinical judgment about a particular patient and inappropriately apply a standard guideline that does not fit the situation because of clinical, ethical, social, or psychological reasons. Again, the woman who wanted to continue her rewarding life as a tap dancer had good reason to risk surgery, and it would have been less than good ethical and clinical judgment to deny her request.

Risks and Cautions

A risk of practice that depends on outcomes research based on the evaluation of clinical trials is that the practice works best in remedial situations in which current practices achieve below average outcomes for the patient populations. Practice that achieves lower than average success rates in light of evidence from multicenter clinical trials can guide practice improvement. However, in some situations, outcome success exceeds standardized expected success rates because of innovations and advanced practice skills in the local situation. In such cases, practice based on evidence from the multicenter trials must be critically evaluated to avoid degrading above-standard practice to the average success rates.

If an excellent center of practice is developing new lines of therapy and the level of skillfulness achieves what other centers do not, it is counterproductive to bring the outcomes down to the "standard" of practice when they are above the standard. Variation below the standard must be brought up to the standard. This is the remedial work of benchmarking. But practice that achieves above-standard outcomes should not be lowered to the standard; otherwise, the practice would cease to be innovative and self-improving.

Kierkegaard (1962) called this a dangerous form of leveling that results when public averages are used to adjust practice to fit public norms, regardless of the level of a particular practice. A self-improving practice needs to meet minimal standards, be engaged in ongoing improvements and experiential learning, raise standards in everyday practice, and evaluate intermittent external updates from scientific studies and practice guidelines.

Technical cure and restorative care cannot be mutually exclusive for the clinician. Basic natural sciences, evidence from clinical trials and other research, psychosocial sciences, and clinical judgment are partnered with the patient's concerns and changing condition, and all are implicated in discerning the best course of action in particular clinical situations. When nursing, medicine, and other healthcare practices are understood as *practices* that encompass more than the science and technologies they use to effect cures, all types of relevant knowledge can be brought to bear on the relational, particular, and ethical dimensions of the patient/family and healthcare. Notions of good are intrinsic to nursing as a socially organized practice. For example, accuracy, not error; attentiveness, not neglect; recognition practices, not depersonalization are notions of good that are internal to being a good nurse.

In most cases, good and poor nursing care can be recognized by nurses, even though it would be impossible to list formally all the precise behaviors and comportments of excellent nursing care. Kassirer (1992) noted that in medicine, "Controlled studies guide us in the right direction, but only occasionally do patients match the study population precisely. The art of medicine involves interpolating between data points" (p. 60).

Tanenbaum (1994), drawing on Kassirer, notes, "The experienced physician reworks patient, intervention, and outcome variables to set his expectations for the case at hand" (p. 37). It is not possible to list or formalize explicitly all aspects or features of an underdetermined social practice such as nursing, law, or social work. Philosophers call this problem the "limits of formalization" (Dreyfus, 1992). Likewise, the practical knowledge embedded in the traditions of science cannot be made completely formal and explicit (Lave & Wenger, 1991; Polanyi, 1958). Every complex social practice has a combination of formal theoretical knowledge and skilled practical know-how. Practical skilled know-how includes tacit and explicit knowledge.

Clinical Expertise

Everyday practical comportment of nurses includes a foreground of focused attention and a background that guides their perception and action. Science and technology formalize the reasoning and knowledge associated with scientific experiments to the extent possible. But even scientists have social influences that shape their practices and practical skilled know-how that escapes notice and formalization. It sometimes mistakenly appears that thinking within a particular scientific discipline is restricted to what can be made "formalizable," that is, turned into formal models, lists of formal criteria, or operational definitions. However, as Kuhn (1970) demonstrated through historical examples, every scientific community (such as clinical practitioners) has tacit, social, and nonrationalizable aspects to its scientific work. These aspects, for example, may include the use of metaphors, insights about what constitutes an interesting scientific problem, skillful know-how in conducting experiments, and other particularized practices, to name a few.

The practice of a particular discipline such as nursing or a science such as biochemistry contains the ethos or notions of what counts as good nursing or good scientific practice. In practice disciplines such as nursing and medicine, the ethos (i.e., ethics or notions of good) of practice influences what is considered relevant science, just as advances in scientific knowledge influence practice.

Experiential learning in clinical practice is a way of knowing, and it contributes to knowledge production. It also should influence the development of science. Viewing practitioners who actively learn from their practices as contributors to knowledge production further illustrates a nontechnological understanding of what constitutes a practice. That is, even though the practitioners use technology, they do not imagine that simple mechanical or production processes are all that is involved. Practitioners must use skillful attunement, discernment, interaction, and judgment in a facilitating relationship with the patient (Dunne, 1993).

Physicians also describe their clinical work as coming to know a patient (Tanner et al., 1993) and gaining a good clinical grasp, as described by Tanenbaum (1994) in an ethnographic study of everyday doctoring:

> The doctors I studied also did interpretive work. Virtually every senior physician spoke of the volume and complexity of medical information. "The number of complicating factors— parameters per patient—is unbelievable." And I observed attending physicians work and rework what they knew in order to make sense of an individual case. Doctors would find it "bothersome," or would be "confused" when they could not get a patient's pieces to "fit": "I don't put him together very well." They frequently used a visual metaphor in which their work was to discern "an emerging picture." One attending physician likened knowing a patient to viewing a canvas, arguing that computer manipulation of patient data "is like describing a painting," not incorrect exactly, but incomplete. According to this informant, the physician, like the viewer, comprehends a whole that is greater than the sum of its parts, and this grasp of a meaningful medical whole has been documented elsewhere—as perceiving a gestalt, getting a joke (Wartofsky, 1986), or calling up a prototype (Groen & Patel, 1985, p. 32).

Ethical and clinical perceptual acuity and good clinical judgment are central to safely practicing evidence-based nursing. Good clinical judgment depends on knowing the patient, understanding his or her concerns, preferences, history, and understanding of the illness, as well as the best relevant scientific knowledge (Benner & Wrubel, 1982; Blum, 1994; Vetleson, 1994). Theoretical and scientific knowledge alone are not sufficient to ensure that nurses will form helpful relationships with patients or that nurses will notice and correctly identify early signs and symptoms or therapy, anxiety, or suffering. This is true even though the nurse may know theoretically what the formal characteristics of these patient conditions are. The most formal measurements cannot replace the perceptual skills of the nurse in recognizing when a measurement is relevant and what the measurement means, which are at the center of good clinical judgment.

In addition, following the *course* of the patient's development of signs and symptoms (i.e., the trajectory or evolution of signs and symptoms) informs the clinician's understanding of the relevance of the signs and symptoms. The context and temporal unfolding of signs and symptoms is important. This creates the need for reasoning about the patient's transitions, not just considering a static list of signs and symptoms. The practitioner who applies algorithms or makes particular clinical judgments based on aggregate outcomes data alone ignores, at great peril, the clinical know-how, relational skills, and the need for reasoning across time that are essential for effective patient care (Halpern, 2001).

The value of EBP depends on the ongoing development of good clinical discernment and judgment combined with valid scientific evidence in actual practice. The Dreyfus Model of Skill Acquisition (Benner, 2001; Dreyfus, 1979) is based on determining the level of expertise in practice that is evident in particular situations. It elucidates strengths in the practice situation, as well as omissions or problems. Situated practice capacities (i.e., expertise as enacted in a particular situation) are described rather than traits or talents of the practitioners (i.e., these traits and talents exist separate from a particular situation).

At each stage of experiential learning (novice, advanced beginner, competent, proficient, expert), clinicians can perform at their best. For example, one can be the best advanced beginner possible, typically during the first year of practice. However, no practitioner can become more skilled without experience, despite the necessary attempts to make practice as clear and explicit as possible through care guidelines and clear instructions. If the nurse has never encountered a particular clinical situation, support from other clinicians, additional information, and experiential learning are required to accurately assess and manage the clinical situation. For example, referring to critical pathways is not the same as recognizing when and how these pathways are relevant or must be adapted to particular patients. Experiential learning that leads to individualization and clinical discernment is required to render critical pathways sensible and safe. Such individualization requires clinical discernment based on experience with past whole concrete clinical situations. This ability to make clinical comparisons between whole concrete clinical cases without decomposing the whole situation into its analytical components is a hallmark of expert clinical nursing practice. Each patient/clinician encounter requires understanding the particular patient's illness experience. Such an understanding of the particular patient is required for all health care practitioners. Such humanistic values are, as Eric J. Cassel (condensed and cited by Frankford, 1994) argues, essential also to good doctoring.

> Proponents of medical humanism have stressed that good doctoring involves more than attending to disease. Illness is simply greater than a biomedically conceived problem. For example, when pneumonia develops in an elderly, grieving, socially isolated widower, in part because his inflamed arthritic knee has reduced his level of activity and led to malnourishment, it does little good simply to diagnose and treat that pneumonia and then send him back to the life-context from which he came. Diagnosis and treatment of the pneumonia is essential, of course, but alone it is insufficient because the cause of the illness is not only the pneumococcus that invaded his lungs. Rather, the cause derives from a unique and personal and social context: From the standpoint of the process, that is, an illness, it is artificial to

stop at the boundaries of the body. The story of the old man includes the social facts of his solitude, the personal matter of his bereavement, his living conditions, his bad knee, his failure to maintain proper nutrition, the invasion of the pneumococcus, its progress in his lungs, his worsening infection, collapse, being discovered, being brought to the hospital, antibiotics, respirator support, and so on (Cassel, 1991, p. 13).

Accordingly, as Cassell has shown, good doctoring must consist of attending to this entire story of illness, and it must be a process of inserting values and treating the whole person. Instead of reducing patients to a few variables, whether stipulated by biomedical or social scientific positivism, doctors must be encouraged to contextualize their patients' problems because "clinicians treat particular patients in particular circumstances at a particular moment in time, and thus they require information that particularizes the individual and the moment" (Cassel, 1991, as cited by Frankford, 1994, p. 769).

A renewing, coherent, recognizable professional identity requires that practitioners develop notions of good that are constantly being worked out and extended through experiential learning in local and larger practice communities. These notions of good guide the judicious use of a range of sciences, ethics, and humanities used in their practices. Practice is a way of knowing, as well as a way of comporting oneself in practice (Ruddick, 1989; Taylor, 1993, 1994). A self-improving practice directs the development, implementation, and evaluation of science and technology. Clinical judgment requires moral agency (i.e., the ability to affect and influence situations), relationship, perceptual acuity, skilled know-how, and narrative reasoning across time about particular patient transitions. As Joseph Dunne notes (1997):

> A practice is not just a surface on which one can display instant virtuosity. It grounds one in a tradition that has been formed through an elaborate development and that exists at any juncture only in the dispositions (slowly and perhaps painfully acquired) of its recognized practitioners (p. 378).

How Narratives Inform Clinical Understanding

A narrative mode of description best captures clinical judgment and experiential learning because a narrative can capture chronology, the concerns of the actor, and even the ambiguities and puzzles as the story unfolds (Benner, 1984; Benner, Tanner, & Chesla, 1996; Hunter, 1991).

Rubin (1996) points out that the agent/actor's concerns organize how the story is told, what is included or left out, and even where the story begins and ends. Nurses' clinical narratives can reveal their taken-for-granted clinical understandings. Articulating those understandings verbally and in writing can assist in making innovations and experiential learning in practice accessible to others, thereby opening the possibility of making clinical knowledge cumulative and collective, as well as generating new questions and topics for research. Innovations and new clinical understandings occur in practice, but they will remain hidden if they are not articulated and made visible so that they can be evaluated and improved. Practicing nurses develop clinical knowledge and their own moral agency as they learn from their patients and families.

Experiential learning in most work environments—particularly in high-risk settings—requires courage and supportive learning environments. Nurses' stories can reveal the particular, nuanced, and ethically driven care that nurses elaborate in the course of taking care of particular patients. Embedded in these stories is clinical wisdom that other nurses can identify with and appropriate for their own clinical practices. Local practice communities develop distinct clinical knowledge and skills.

Collecting, reflecting on, and interpreting narratives both in practice and in academic settings can uncover new knowledge and skills and identify areas of excellence as well as impediments to good practice. One way to accomplish this is through telling and writing narratives in the first person about clinical situations in which the clinician learned something new. Teaching nurses and other clinicians to think reflectively about these narratives will help clinicians not only to identify the concerns that organize the story but also to see the notions of good embedded in the story. Reflective thinking also will enhance relational, communicative, and collaborative skills and articulation of newly developing clinical knowledge.

The goal of capturing experiential learning is to articulate new clinical knowledge, which involves the forming of the story, the concerns that shape the story, and how the story ends, as revealed in the dialogue and perceptions of the storyteller. Narratives reveal contexts, processes, and content of practical moral reasoning. Thus, stories create moral imagination (i.e., the ability to perceive when ethical issues are involved and to imagine how to respond to perceived ethical demands, even as they expose knowledge gaps and paradoxes).

Narratives about experiential learning reveal moral agency and changes in the storyteller's perceptions. Moreover, they reveal shifts in styles of practice. Because all research must be evaluated and implemented by the practitioner, ways are needed to capture this process of understanding and experiential learning inherent in translating research findings into practice. Often, storytelling about experiential learning occurs in shift reports or other oral reports between clinicians. For example, "the patient transitioned into a full-blown pulmonary edema with specific changes in hemodynamic parameters." Or, first-person, experience-near narratives may be systematically gathered from clinicians who participate in interpreting the narratives. Experience-near, first-person narratives provide the storyteller's direct first-person account of an actual clinical situation. The following interview excerpt is taken from a naturalistic study of actual clinical situations in intensive care units (ICUs). In this interview, an advanced practice nurse (APN) illustrates clinical grasp and clinical forethought, as well as experiential learning:

> **APN:** A man was admitted to the ICU on a mechanical ventilator with a status post cardiac arrest. He had been intubated, on full ventilatory support for less than a day…. He did not appear to have any problems initially, at least in terms of ventilation and oxygenation, with ruling in for an MI. He was basically in a stabilization period of support. He was not instrumented with a PA catheter. He was awake, cognitively aware, at least as best as we could tell…. I remember getting a call late in the afternoon and the staff nurse thought that the patient seemed to be working a little bit harder on the ventilator, and she had approached the intern and the resident. I work in a teaching facility, and they looked at the patient, didn't really notice, particularly, that the patient was struggling with his breathing, or that there was a slight increase in the respiratory rate that seemed to be sustained. The nurse also had reported to me that the heart rate had been elevated, but the patient didn't appear to be hemodynamically compromised, so she wasn't too worried about it, but she was wondering if the ventilator settings were appropriate…. One of the first things that I noticed when I went in the room was that the patient wasn't breathing very rapidly, but he was using a lot more respiratory effort on each breath…. He was using more accessory muscles, and he was actively exhaling. The breathing appeared paradoxical, meaning he wasn't using the diaphragm; he was using accessory muscles. But there really wasn't a marked tachypnea pattern. And again, I looked at the ventilator sheets to see again how long the patient had been on the ventilator. I was wondering if it was just… maybe… an agitation situation… maybe he needed some sedation, or [to figure out] what was going on. The nurse also remarked that in the last 20 minutes, the patient's mentation had deteriorated. Where he had been a little more responsive, he was now less responsive, and so she was even more nervous. So the three us—I believe it was either the senior resident or the junior assistant resident, myself, and the staff nurse—talking in the patient's room, or looking at the ventilatory parameters, and clearly the patient's mentation had deteriorated, breathing appeared to be more labored. So, I asked them if they had taken a recent chest x-ray, or if there was anything new going on with the patient that was important, and they said, "No, the patient had a

chest x-ray in the morning as a part of a routine check, but there hadn't been any follow-up." I asked the nurse if there had been any change in breath sounds, and she said, "No." And the JR [junior resident], who was in the room, said he noticed no differences as well. So I took a listen, and the chest was really noisy, but … I thought that the breath sounds were a little more diminished on the right side as opposed to the left side. So I asked if there was any indication to repeat the chest x-ray, or if that was their finding as well. Now with breath sounds, often there isn't symmetry necessarily and… but there wasn't anything outward in terms of chest excursion… and by visual inspection it looked like it would be symmetric. But nevertheless, I went ahead and looked at the ventilator parameters. The ventilatory support settings appeared to be appropriate. Possibly the backup rate could have been a little higher, but the patient wasn't really assisting much over the control rate. The patient had a pulse oximeter. Those settings were fairly stable, in the low 90s, as I recall, and the patient was not hypotensive… was a little more tachycardic though than what the nurse had led me to believe over the phone, during our telephone conversation… somewhere around 120s, 130s… something like that. But the patient wasn't exhibiting signs of, you know, EKG changes or hypotension associated with that. He was on no vasoactive drugs at the time. There was a slight increase in the airway pressures, but it wasn't high enough that would really warn me that I felt that there was a marked change in compliance at that time. The patient appeared to be returning most of the tidal volume that was being delivered by the ventilator.

So I stayed in with the nurse, and we were talking and going over what the plan was and things we might be looking for in the evening, because it was late afternoon, and I was going to be getting ready to go home. So, right before I left—the nurse had temporarily left the room—I noticed, and at first I wasn't sure if it was just the room lighting, or, if there was a true color change. Subsequently there was a color change in the patient. But I noticed that the patient's upper torso looked a little duskier to me, especially the head and neck area. And I pulled his gown down. And I noticed there was a clear demarcation and color, and this was sort of in the midchest area, up to the neck and to the head. I listened to the breath sounds again and noticed that they appeared even more diminished on the right side, as opposed to the left side. So I was thinking that this was… maybe a pneumothorax. Again, the patient's mentation had not improved. When I brought this up to the JR, and actually the cardiology fellow was up there as well, in the latter part of the afternoon, they didn't think it was a pneumothorax because the patient was returning most of the exhaled volume. And they thought that under positive pressure, this would be a tension pneumothorax, and we should see a decrease in exhaled volumes or marked increase in airway pressures. And I know from the literature—and at least my own experience—it isn't always so clear-cut like that. So the chest x-ray was ordered, and not… probably 10 or 15 minutes from the time that I get this curbside consult with the fellow and even before Radiology came up, this patient dropped his blood pressure, his heart rate went up, and when we listened to his breath sounds, it was clear the patient's breath sounds had decreased even more.

And there happened to be an attending over on the MICU in the coronary care unit attending a postarrest who came over, and emergently inserted a chest tube and clearly it was a big pneumothorax. And I guess what sort of stood out in my mind was that people were really looking at a lot of the classic parameters that they're taught that you should see. And I don't know if it was necessarily because of what I've read, or I think a lot of it has to do with what I've seen clinically, and I try to incorporate at least what I know from knowledge and what I've seen in practice, is that it isn't always so clear-cut. I mean, it just isn't. And sometimes you really have to kind of go on physical exam findings and not necessarily—it's important to pay attention to the things you anticipate, but sometimes the things that aren't so obvious can be very clinically significant.

This narrative account of experiential learning about clinical manifestations of a tension pneumothorax contains much practical knowledge about interpreting ambiguous clinical signs and symptoms, advocating for a needed diagnostic test (i.e., chest x-ray), negotiating different interpretations by getting different opinions, and finally responding quickly to a dramatic change in the patient's rapidly changing condition. It is a good example of the kind of modus operandi (MO) thinking involved in clinical judgment. Modus operandi thinking is the kind of thinking a detective uses in solving a case. Transitions, trajectories, and evidence are studied as they are uncovered—often narratively. The patient's trajectory matters in interpreting clinical signs and symptoms, but the story also illustrates two pervasive habits of thought and action in clinical practice: **clinical grasp** and **clinical forethought**.

Clinical Grasp

Clinical grasp describes clinical inquiry in action. Clinical grasp includes problem identification and clinical judgment across time about the particular transitions of particular patient/family clinical situations. Four aspects of clinical grasp include

- Making qualitative distinctions
- Engaging in detective work
- Recognizing changing clinical relevance
- Developing clinical knowledge about specific patient populations

Making Qualitative Distinctions

Qualitative distinctions refer to those distinctions that can be made only in a particular, contextual, or historical situation. In the clinical example above, the nurse was listening for qualitative changes in the breath sounds, changes in the patient's color, and changes in the patient's mental alertness. Clinical appreciation of the context and sequence of events—the way a clinical situation changes over time—is essential for making qualitative distinctions. Therefore, it requires paying attention to transitions in the patient. Many qualitative distinctions can be made only by observing differences in the patient or patient's situation through touch, sound, or sight, as in skin turgor, color, and capillary refill (Hooper, 1995).

Engaging in Detective Work and More

Clinical situations are open-ended and underdetermined. Modus operandi thinking keeps track of the particular patient, the way the illness unfolds, and the meanings of the patient's responses as they have occurred in the particular time sequence. It requires keeping track of what has been tried and what has or has not worked with the patient. In this kind of reasoning-in-transition, gains and losses in understanding are understood by the clinician in a narrative form that culminates in the best possible clinical decisions for the patient (Benner et al., 1999; Elwyn & Gwyn, 1999). However, in the example, the clinician also thinks of the possibility of a pneumothorax. A second comparative chest x-ray is needed. Later in the interview, he states

> **APN:** I guess it could have been a pulmonary embolus. But I was really sort of focused in the differences and the fact that it was fairly similar appearance, which can happen with pulmonary emboli. The heart rhythm pattern had not changed, although it was elevated. There was some tachycardia. But it sort of was leading me to believe that this was more sort of a pulmonary problem, as opposed to a pulmonary circulation problem, you know?

The clinician is guessing that this is a problem of physically moving air in and out rather than an obstruction in pulmonary circulation. The clinical evidence from the patient's signs and symptoms is subtle, so the clinician stays open to disconfirmation but proceeds with trying to get the chest x-ray and is prepared to recognize the sudden change in the patient's respiratory status when that occurs.

Another qualitative distinction was the judgment of whether the patient's change in mental status and agitation was due primarily to anxiety or to hypoxia. With MO thinking, sequencing and context are essential to making judgments. Modus operandi thinking uses the global understanding of the situation and operates within that situated understanding. The clinician was always focusing on some respiratory problem. The overall grasp of the clinical situation determines the approach used in MO thinking.

Recognizing Changing Clinical Relevance

Recognizing changes in clinical relevance of signs and symptoms and the patient's concerns is an experientially learned skill that enables clinicians to change their interpretations of patient data and concerns based on changes in the patient's condition. The meanings of signs and symptoms are changed by sequencing and history. For example, the patient's mental status and color continued to deteriorate, and his breath sounds diminished. Once the chest tubes were in place, there was a dramatic change in the patient's color. Clinical evaluation of each of these changes in the patient's signs and symptoms was made by examining the transitions in time and sequence as they occurred.

Developing Clinical Knowledge About Specific Patient Populations

Because the clinician has had the opportunity to observe both pulmonary circulation problems and mechanical breathing problems, he can recognize a kind of "family resemblance" with other mechanical breathing problems (as opposed to pulmonary circulation problems) that he has noticed with other patients.

Refinement of clinical judgment is possible when nurses have the opportunity to work with specific patient populations. Understanding the characteristic patterns of a particular patient population well can assist with recognizing shifts in a patient's disease trajectory that do not mesh with usual patterns and that, therefore, may signal a problem.

Clinical Forethought

Clinical forethought is another pervasive habit of thought and action in nursing practice evident in the narrative example. Clinical forethought plays a role in clinical grasp because it structures the practical logic of clinicians. Clinical forethought refers to at least four habits of thought and action:

- Future think
- Clinical forethought about specific patient populations
- Anticipation of risks for particular patients
- Seeing the unexpected

Future Think

Future think is the practical logic of the practitioner situated in practice (Bourdieu, 1990). In the example, the APN states, "So I stayed in with the nurse, and we were talking and going over what the plan was and things we might be looking for in the evening." Anticipating likely immediate future events assists with making good clinical judgments and with preparing the environment so that the nurse can respond to the patient's immediate needs in a timely fashion. Without this lead time or the developing sense of salience for anticipated signs and symptoms and the subsequent preparation of the environment, essential clinical judgments and timely interventions would be impossible in rapidly changing clinical situations.

Future think influences the nurse's response to the patient. Whether in a fast-paced ICU or in a slow-paced rehabilitation setting, thinking and acting with patients' anticipated futures in mind guide clinical thinking and judgment. Future think captures the way judgment is suspended in a predictive net of thoughtful planning ahead and preparing the environment for likely eventualities.

Clinical Forethought About Specific Patient Populations

This habit of thought and action is so second nature to the experienced nurse that he or she may neglect to tell the newcomer the "obvious." Clinical forethought includes all the anticipated actions and plans relevant to a particular patient's possible trends and trajectories that a clinician prepares for in caring for the patient (Benner et al., 1999). Clinical forethought involves much local specific knowledge, such as who is a good resource and how to marshal support services and equipment for particular patients. The staff nurse used good judgment in calling the APN to assist in solving the puzzle when she was unable to convince the less clinically experienced JR. The advanced practice nurse made use of all available physicians in the area. Part of what made a timely response possible was the actual planning involved in closely monitoring the patient and marshaling other clinician resources in this situation that changed rapidly.

Examples of preparing for specific patient populations abound in all settings. For instance, anticipating the need for a pacemaker during surgery and having the equipment assembled and ready for use save essential time. Another example might be forecasting an accident victim's potential injuries when intubation or immediate surgery might be needed for the accident victim.

Anticipation of Risks for Particular Patients

The narrative example is shaped by the foreboding sense of an impending crisis for this particular patient. The staff nurse uses her sense of foreboding about the changes in the patient's breathing to initiate her problem search. This aspect of clinical forethought is central to knowing the particular patient, family, or community. Nurses situate the patient's problems almost like a map or picture of possibilities. This vital clinical knowledge that is experientially learned from particular patients needs to be communicated to other caregivers and across care borders. Clinical teaching can be improved by enriching curricula with narratives from actual practice and by helping students recognize commonly occurring clinical situations.

For example, if a patient is hemodynamically unstable, managing life-sustaining physiologic functions will be a main orienting goal. If the patient is agitated and uncomfortable, attending to comfort needs in relation to hemodynamics will be a priority. Providing comfort measures turns out to be a central background practice for making clinical judgments and contains within it much judgment and experiential learning (Benner et al., 1996).

When clinical learning is too removed from typical contingencies and strong clinical situations in practice, nurses will lack practice in active thinking-in-action in ambiguous clinical situations. With the rapid advance of knowledge and technology, nurses need to be good clinical learners and clinical knowledge developers. One way to enhance clinical inquiry is by increasing experiential learning, which requires open learning climates where transitions can be discussed and examined—including false starts or misconceptions in actual clinical situations. Focusing only on performance and on "being correct" and not on learning from breakdown or error dampens the curiosity and courage to learn experientially.

Learning from experiential learning is central to developing one's moral agency as a clinician. One's *sense* of moral agency as well as *actual* moral agency in particular situations changes with the level of skills acquired (Benner et al., 1996). Experiential learning is facilitated or hampered by learning how to relate to patients/families and engage the clinical problems at hand. Those nurses who do not go on to become expert clinicians have some learning difficulty associated with skills of involvement (i.e., communication and relationship) and consequently, difficulty making clinical judgments, particularly qualitative distinctions (Benner et al., 1996). Experienced, nonexpert nurses saw clinical problem solving as a simple weighing of facts, or rational calculation. They did not experience their own agency (i.e., their ability to influence situations). They failed to see qualitative distinctions linked to the patient's well-being.

Seeing the Unexpected

One of the keys to becoming an expert practitioner lies in how the person holds past experiential learning and background habitual skills and practices. If nothing is routinized as a habitual response pattern, practitioners cannot attend to the unexpected, particularly in emergencies. However, if expectations are held rigidly, subtle changes from the usual will be missed, and habitual, rote responses will rule.

The clinician must be flexible in shifting between what is in the background and the foreground of his or her attention. This is accomplished by staying curious and open. The clinical "certainty" associated with perceptual grasp is distinct from the kind of "certainty" achievable in scientific experiments and through measurements. It is similar to recognizing faces or family resemblances. It is subject to faulty memory and mistaken identities; therefore, such perceptual grasp is the *beginning* of curiosity and inquiry—not the end.

In rapidly moving clinical situations, perceptual grasp is the starting point for clarification, confirmation, and action. The relationship between foreground and background of attention needs to be fluid so that missed expectations allow the nurse to see the unexpected. For example, when the rhythm of a cardiac monitor changes, the nurse notices the change in the rhythm's sound, and what had been background or tacit awareness becomes the foreground of attention (i.e., focal awareness). A hallmark of expertise is the ability to notice the unexpected (Benner et al., 1996). Background expectations of usual patient trajectories form with experience. These background experiences form tacit expectations that enable the nurse to notice subtle failed expectations and to pay attention to early signs of unexpected changes in the patient's condition.

Polanyi (1958), a physician and philosopher, wrote about the distinction between focal and tacit awareness. Tacit awareness operates at a perceptual level, usually as a result of a skilled embodied takeover of experiential learning. A tacit awareness allows one to notice changes without explicitly directing attention to the potential change until it happens. Clinical expectations gained by caring for similar patient populations form a tacit clinical forethought that enables the experienced clinician to notice missed expectations. Alterations from implicit or explicit expectations from a range of scientific studies, ethical concerns, and clinical experience set the stage for experiential learning, depending on the openness of the learner.

Conclusion

Evidence-based practice must be contextualized by the nurse in particular clinical settings and particular patient–nurse relationships, concerns, and goals. Evidence-based practice can provide guidelines and intelligent dialogue with the best practice options in particular situations. It cannot be assumed that the flow of knowledge is only from science to practice; it also results from direct experiential learning in practice. Patient/family and healthcare values and concerns, as well as practice-based knowledge, must also be central to the dialogue between patient and clinician that incorporates the patients' values, concerns, and choices. In patient situations, EBP also incorporates developing expertise and using clinical judgment in conjunction with valid science to provide the best possible care.

references

Angell, M. (2000). Is academic medicine for sale? *New England Journal of Medicine, 342*, 1516–1518.

Association of Clinical Research Professionals. (2002). *White paper on future trends.* Retrieved from http://www.acrpnet.org/index_fl.html. Accessed November 24, 2002.

Benner, P. (1984; 2001). *From novice to expert: Excellence and power in clinical nursing practice.* Menlo Park, CA: Addison-Wesley.

Benner, P. (1994). The role of articulation in understanding practice and experience as sources of knowledge in clinical nursing. In J. Tully & D. M. Wenstock (Eds.). *Philosophy in an age of pluralism. The Philosophy of Charles Taylor, 9*, 136–155.

Benner, P., & Wrubel, J. (1982). Clinical knowledge development: The value of perceptual awareness. *Nurse Educator, 7*, 11–17.

Benner, P., Hooper-Kyriakidis, P., & Stannard, D. (1999). *Clinical wisdom and interventions in critical care: A thinking-in-action approach.* Philadelphia: W.B. Saunders.

Benner, P., Tanner, C. A., & Chesla, C. A. (1996). *Expertise in nursing practice: Caring, clinical judgment, and ethics.* New York: Springer.

Blum, L. (1994). *Moral perception and particularity.* Cambridge, England: Cambridge University Press.

Bodenheimer, T. (2000). Uneasy alliance: Clinical investigators and the pharmaceutical industry. *New England Journal of Medicine, 342*, 1539–1544.

Bourdieu, P. (1990). *The logic of practice.* (R. Nice, Trans.) Stanford, CA: Stanford University Press.

Brennan, T. A. (1994). Buying editorials. *New England Journal of Medicine, 331*, 673–675.

Cassel, E. J. (1991). *The nature of suffering and the goals of medicine.* New York: Oxford University Press.

Choudhry, N. K., Stelfox, H. T., & Detsky, A. S. (2002). Relationships between authors of clinical practice guidelines and the pharmaceutical industry. *JAMA, 287*, 612–617.

CenterWatch Newsletter, 9(9), September 2002.

DeAngelis, C. D. (2000). Conflict of interest and the public trust. *JAMA, 284*, 2237–2238.

Dreyfus, H. L. (1992). *What computers still can't do: A critique of artificial reason.* Cambridge, MA: MIT.

Dreyfus, H. L. (1979). *What computers can't do: The limits of artificial intelligence* (Rev. ed.). New York: Harper & Row.

Dunne, J. (1993). *Back to the rough ground, practical judgment and the lure of technique.* Notre Dame, IN: University of Notre Dame Press.

Dunne, J. (1997). *Back to the rough ground, practical judgment and the lure of technique.* Notre Dame, IN: University of Notre Dame Press.

Frankford, D. M. (1994). Scientism and economism in the regulation of health care. *Journal of Health Politics, Policy and Law, 19*, 773–799.

Gadamer, H. G. (1976). *Truth and method.* Barden G., Cumming J. (Eds. and Trans.). New York: Seabury.

Groen, G. J., & Patel, V. L. (1985). Medical problem-solving: Some questionable assumptions. *Medical Education, 19*, 95–100.

Halpern, J. (2001). *From detached concern to empathy. Humanizing medical care.* London: Oxford University Press.

Hooper, P. L. (1995). *Expert titration of multiple vasoactive drugs in post-cardiac surgical patients: An interpretive study of clinical judgment and perceptual acuity.* Unpublished doctoral dissertation, University of California at San Francisco, San Francisco.

Hunter, K. M. (1991). *Doctors' stories: The narrative structure of medical knowledge.* Princeton, NJ: Princeton University Press.

Kassirer, J. P. (1992). Clinical problem-solving–A new feature in the journal. *New England Journal of Medicine, 326*, 60–61.

Kierkegaard, S. (1962 Trans.). *The present age.* New York: Harper & Row.

Kuhn, T. S. (1970). *The structure of scientific revolutions.* (2nd ed.). Chicago: University of Chicago.

Lave, J. & Wenger, E. (1991) *Situated learning: Legitimate peripheral perspectives (Learning in doing: Social, cognitive and computational perspectives.)* Cambridge, England: Cambridge University Press.

Polanyi, M. (1958). *Personal knowledge: Towards a post-critical philosophy.* New York: Harper & Row.

Rettig, R. A. (2000). The industrialization of clinical research. *Health Affairs, 19*, 129–146.

Rubin, J. (1996). Impediments to the development of clinical knowledge and ethical judgment in critical care nursing. In P. Benner, C. A. Tanner, & C. A. Chesla (Eds.). *Expertise in nursing practice: Caring, clinical judgment, and ethics* (pp.170–192). New York: Springer.

Ruddick, S. (1989). *Maternal thinking: Toward a politic of peace.* New York: Ballantine.

Scannell, K. (2002). Interrogating the bodies of evidence: Patients and the foundations of evidence-based medicine. Kaiser Permanente: *Ethics Rounds, 11*(1), 8.

Siegel, M. (2002). When doctors say don't and the patient says do. *New York Times* (Science). Oct. 29, p. D7.

Tanenbaum, S. J. (1994). Knowing and acting in medical practice: The epistemological politics of outcomes research. *Journal of Health Politics, Policy and Law, 19*(1), 31–44.

Tanner, C. A., Benner, P., Chesla, C. A., Gordon, D. R. (1993). The phenomenology of knowing the patient. *Image, 25*, 273–280.

Taylor, C. (1993). Explanation and practical reason. In M. Nussbaum & A. Sen (Eds.). *The quality of life.* Oxford, England: Clarendon.

Taylor, C. (1994). Philosophical reflections on caring practices. In S. S. Phillips & P. Benner (Eds.). *The crisis of care: Affirming and restoring caring practices in the helping professions* (pp. 174–187.). Washington, DC: Georgetown University Press.

Vetleson, A. J. (1994). *Perception, empathy, and judgment: An inquiry into the preconditions of moral performance*. University Park, PA: Pennsylvania State University Press.

Wartofsky, M. W. (1986). Clinical judgment, expert programs, and cognitive style: A counter-essay in the logic of diagnosis. *Journal of Medicine and Philosophy, 11*, 81–92.

Wulff, H. R., Pederson, S. A., & Rosenberg, R. (1990). *Philosophy of medicine: An introduction*. Oxford, England: Blackwell Scientific.

Acknowledgment

This chapter draws heavily on two chapters in *Clinical Wisdom and Interventions in Critical Care: A Thinking-in-Action Approach*. Philadelphia: W. B. Saunders, 1999. Chapter Two, "Clinical Grasp and Clinical Inquiry: Problem Identification and Clinical Problem Solving," pp. 23–61, was developed primarily by Patricia Hooper-Kyriakidis, RN, PhD.

Advancing Optimal Care With Clinical Practice Guidelines

Doris Grinspun, Bernadette Mazurek Melnyk, and Ellen Fineout-Overholt

> *Whatever you can do or dream you can, begin it. Boldness*
>
> *has genius, power, and magic in it.*
>
> *J o h a n n   W o l f g a n g   v o n   G o e t h e*

Clinical practice variations are problematic and a well-recognized phenomenon. More than 30 years have passed since Wennberg and Gittelsohn (1973, 1982) first described the variation in treatment patterns in New England and other parts of the United States. Yet, remarkable practice differences in the diagnosis, treatment, and management of patients continue to permeate healthcare everywhere. *The Dartmouth Atlas of Health Care* (Wennberg, McAndrew, & the Dartmouth Medical School Center for Evaluative Clinical Sciences Staff, 1999) offers many queries that can assist in graphically demonstrating the variability of healthcare services in the United States. Features allow comparisons of states and resource utilization (see Table 8.1). In Canada, similar reports are available through the Institute for Clinical Evaluative Sciences (http://www.ices.on.ca). These regional variations in care and resource utilization are reflections of the many factors that influence outcomes of healthcare delivery. One critical factor that may hold the key to reducing variation in outcomes is the availability, uptake, and consistent utilization of clinical evidence at the point of care.

Practicing based on evidence includes the integration of individual clinical expertise and patient preferences with the best available evidence from systematic research (Sackett, Richardson, Rosenberg, et al., 1997) and practice-generated data (see Chapter 4). Evidence-based practice (EBP) requires clinicians to determine the clinical options that are supported by high-quality scientific evidence and corroborated with the internal evidence. Gaining access to up-to-date scientific clinical information can be very difficult, particularly where access to healthcare journals is limited, and synthesizing the information can be even more challenging. The U.S. National Library of Medicine (NLM) indicated that, in 2008, PubMed contained more than 18 million citations to articles from more than 5,200 journals published worldwide, making it impossible for the individual clinician to master the body of emerging evidence (NLM, 2008).

table 8.1 **Example of data that can be accessed from *Dartmouth health atlas***

State Name	State No.	No. of Deaths*	RNs Required Under Proposed Federal Standards per 1,000 Decedents During the Last 2 Years of Life (2001–2005)
Arizona	3	15,568	38.73
Nevada	29	6,020	48.18
New Mexico	32	6,344	35.82

*No. of Deaths are from 20% sample.

Source: http://www.dartmouthatlas.org/index.shtm

The reality of information overload is especially difficult for busy point-of-care providers who find themselves already overwhelmed by competing clinical priorities.

During a landmark workshop on clinical practice guidelines organized by the American Thoracic Society and the European Respiratory Society that drew experts from more than 40 international organizations, a vision statement was created that highlighted 10 key visions for guideline development and use (Schunemann, Woodhead, Anzueto, et al., 2009). These included

1. Globalize the evidence
2. Focus on questions that are important to patients and clinicians and include relevant stakeholders in guideline panels
3. Undertake collaborative evidence reviews relevant to healthcare questions and recommendations
4. Use a common metric to assess the quality of evidence and strength of recommendations
5. Consider comorbidities in guideline development
6. Identify ways that help guideline consumers (clinicians, patients, and others) understand and implement guidelines using the best available tools
7. Deal with conflicts of interest and guideline sponsoring transparently
8. Support development of decision aids to assist implementation of value and preference sensitive guideline recommendations
9. Maintain a collaboration of international organizations
10. Examine collaborative models for funding guideline development and implementation

Guidelines as Tools

Overwhelming evidence, competing clinical priorities, and ever-increasing accountability highlight the importance of synthesis studies and clinical practice guidelines. Meta-analyses and integrative reviews facilitate practitioners' ability to base their interventions on the strongest, most up-to-date and relevant evidence, rather than engaging with the challenging task of individually appraising and synthesizing large volumes of scientific studies. Evidence-based practice guidelines (EBPGs), which are systematically developed statements based on the best available evidence, including syntheses, make recommendations in order to assist practitioners with decisions regarding the most effective interventions for specific clinical conditions across a broad array of clinical diagnoses and situations (Tricoci, Allen, Kramer, et al., 2009). They also are designed to allow some flexibility in their application to individual patients who fall outside the scope of the guideline or who have significant comorbidities not adequately addressed in a particular guideline. These tools are increasingly being used to reduce unnecessary variations in clinical practice.

Rigorously and explicitly developed EBPGs can help bridge the gap between published scientific evidence and clinical decision making (Davies, Edwards, Ploeg, et al., 2008; Grinspun, Virani, & Bajnok, 2002; Miller & Kearney, 2004). As expected, the dramatic growth in guideline development is not without unintended consequences. The rigor of guidelines varies significantly as does the reporting on how a particular guideline is formulated. In a recent review of 53 guidelines on 22 topics by the American College of Cardiology (ACC) and the American Heart Association (AHA), Tricoci et al. (2009) found that the recommendations issued in these guidelines were largely developed from lower levels of evidence (e.g., nonrandomized trials, case studies) or expert opinion. The findings from this review indicate that the process of writing guidelines needs to improve, and the research base from which guidelines are derived needs to be expanded.

At times, one can find guidelines with conflicting recommendations, posing dilemmas for users and potentially hindering, rather than advancing, quality patient care. Finally, guidelines are often developed and written in ways that clinicians and organizations may find difficult to implement, which limits their effectiveness in influencing clinical practice and improving patient outcomes. Despite these limitations or "growing pains," the increased emphasis over the past decade on evidence-based guideline development, implementation, and evaluation is a welcome direction toward evidence-based decision making at the point of care. This chapter offers clinicians a brief overview of EBPGs and ways to access, appraise, and use these tools to improve the care and health outcomes of their patients.

How to Access Guidelines

In the past, finding EBPGs was a formidable challenge. The large number of guideline developers and topics, coupled with the various forms of guideline publication and distribution, made identification of guidelines difficult and unpredictable. Fortunately today, a two-step Google search brings forward the most commonly used EBPG sites. Use the term *practice guideline* and you will immediately access the Centre for Health Evidence (http://www.cche.net), the National Guideline Clearinghouse (NGC; http://www.guideline.gov/), the Canadian Medical Association (CMA; http://www.cma.ca), the Registered Nurses' Association of Ontario (RNAO; http://www.rnao.org), and other such reliable sources of EBPG. In addition, to make finding EBPGs easier, the term *practice guideline* can be used as a limit to define a publication type when searching NLM's PubMed database.

Access the PubMed database at
http://www.ncbi.nlm.nih.gov/pubmed

Using the search term *practice guideline* alone, without any qualifiers, yields more than 60,000 citations. Most of these citations are not actual guidelines but studies of guideline implementation, commentaries, editorials, or letters to the editor about guidelines. Thus, once a specific site (e.g., PubMed, NGC, RNAO) is accessed, it is important to refine the search by adding the clinical areas or interventions of interest. Searching citation databases for EBPGs can present challenges as not all guidelines are published in indexed journals or books, making it difficult to locate them in traditional healthcare databases.

In the last decade, individual collections that distribute international, regional, organizational, or specialty-specific guidelines have matured (see Box 8.1). The list of individual guideline developers is long, and the distribution venues for guidelines can be as plentiful as the number of developers.

---

box 8.1

Selected Guideline Databases

General

- NGC: http://www.guideline.gov
- Primary Care Clinical Practice Guidelines: http://medicine.ucsf.edu/education/resed/ebm/practice_guidelines.html
- RNAO: http://www.rnao.org
- CMA Infobase: Clinical Practice Guidelines (CPGs): http://mdm.ca/cpgsnew/cpgs/index.asp
- HSTAT: http://hstat.nlm.nih.gov
- Guidelines Advisory Committee (GAC): http://www.gacguidelines.ca
- SIGN: http://www.sign.ac.uk/guidelines/index.html
- NICE: http://www.nice.org.uk
- NZGG: http://www.nzgg.org.nz
- G-I-N: http://www.G-I-N.net

Specific

- American College of Physicians: http://www.acponline.org/clinical_information/guidelines
- American Cancer Society: http://www.cancer.org/docroot/home/index.asp
- American College of Cardiology: http://www.acc.org/qualityandscience/clinical/statements.htm
- American Association of Clinical Endocrinologists: http://www.aace.com/pub/guidelines/
- American Association of Respiratory Care: http://www.aarc.org/resources/
- American Academy of Pediatrics: http://aappolicy.aappublications.org/
- American Psychiatric Association: http://www.psych.org/psych_pract/treatg/pg/prac_guide.cfm
- Ministry of Health Services, British Columbia, Canada: http://www.gov.bc.ca/health/
- New York Academy of Medicine: http://www.ebmny.org/cpg.html
- Veterans Administration: http://www1.va.gov/health/index.asp
- National Kidney Foundation: https://www.kidney.org/professionals/doqi/guidelineindex.cfm
- American Medical Directors Association: http://www.amda.com
- Association of Women's Health, Obstetric, and Neonatal Nurses: http://awhonn.org
- National Association of Neonatal Nurses: http://www.nann.org
- Oncology Nursing Society: http://www.ons.org
- University of Iowa Gerontological Nursing Interventions Research Center: http://www.nursing.uiowa.edu/excellence/nursing_interventions/

In Canada, RNAO disseminates its production of rigorously developed clinical healthy work environment and education best practice guidelines for nurses on its website (http://www.rnao.org). The Registered Nurses' Association of Ontario's best practice guidelines are freely downloadable and widely used internationally. In addition, CMA maintains the CMA InfoBase of clinical practice guidelines for physicians (http://mdm.ca/cpgsnew/cpgs/index.asp). Guidelines are included in the CMA InfoBase only if they are produced or endorsed in Canada by a national, provincial/territorial, or regional medical or health organization, professional society, government agency, or expert panel.

In the United Kingdom, another country-specific guideline collection is the Scottish Intercollegiate Guidelines Network (SIGN) sponsored by the Royal College of Physicians (http://www.sign.ac.uk). Also, the National Institute for Health and Clinical Excellence (NICE) in England maintains a collection of guidelines to advise the National Health Service (http://www.nice.org.uk/).

In New Zealand, the New Zealand Guidelines Group (NZGG) maintains a collection of guidelines developed under its sponsorship (http://www.nzgg.org.nz/). In the United States, individual professional societies and national groups maintain collections of guidelines specific to a particular practice, professional specialty, disease screening, prevention, or management.

The ACC and the AHA have joint guideline panels and publish their guidelines in a variety of formats (http://www.acc.org/qualityandscience/clinical/statements.htm). The American Cancer Society also convenes multidisciplinary panels to develop cancer-related guidelines and to make the guidelines available on the Internet (http://www.cancer.org/). The U.S. Preventive Services Task Force (USPSTF) provides evidence-based guidelines for disease screening and prevention, including behavioral counseling (http://www.ahrq.gov/clinic/uspstfix.htm).

Globally, the Guidelines International Network (G-I-N) has the world's largest guideline library that is regularly updated with the latest information about guidelines of the G-I-N membership. The Guidelines International Network is a not-for-profit association of 93 organizational members and partners devoted to improving the quality of healthcare through the development and use of clinical practice guidelines (http://www.g-i-n.net).

In addition, there is an international collaboration of researchers, guideline developers, and guideline implementers called the ADPATE Collaboration that promotes the development and use of clinical practice guidelines through adaptation of existing guidelines. This collaboration develops and validates a generic adaptation process that fosters valid and high-quality adapted guidelines (http://www.adapte.org/rubrique/the-adapte-collaboration.php).

Although it is useful to have collections of guidelines that are specific to a disease or specialty, this can make it difficult to find guidelines in more than one clinical area. In 1998, the U.S. Agency for Health Care Policy and Research, now the Agency for Healthcare Research and Quality, released the NGC.

Access the NGC at **http://www.guideline.gov**

The National Guideline Clearinghouse was developed in partnership with the American Medical Association and the American Association of Health Plans. In developing the NGC, AHRQ intended to create a comprehensive database of up-to-date English language EBPGs (see Box 8.2). Five years later, NGC contained about 1,100 guidelines from developers all over the world. That number grew to 2,950 in 2008. The National Guideline Clearinghouse also contains an archive of guideline titles that are out of date. The archived guidelines do not get circulated on the site. The database is updated at least weekly with new content and provides guideline comparison features so that users can explore differences among guidelines, facilitating critical appraisal. A newer feature to the NGC is the guideline synthesis, which enables users to access comprehensive information with the best available evidence to support recommendations. Users can register to receive weekly e-mails listing the guideline changes on the site. The NGC receives more than 250,000 visits per week.

box 8.2

National Guideline Clearinghouse: http://www. guideline.gov

Features

- Structured abstracts (summaries) about the guideline and its development
- Links to full-text guidelines, where available, and/or ordering information for print copies
- Palm-based PDA downloads of the Complete NGC Summary for all guidelines represented in the database.
- Weekly e-mail feature
- A guideline comparison utility that gives users the ability to generate side-by-side comparisons for any combination of two or more guidelines
- Unique guideline comparisons called Guideline Syntheses, comparing guidelines covering similar topics, highlighting areas of similarity and difference
- An electronic forum, NGC-L, for exchanging information on clinical practice guidelines, their development, implementation, and use
- Annotated bibliographies on guideline development, methodology, structure, evaluation, and implementation
- Expert commentary
- Guideline archive

Inclusion Criteria

- The clinical practice guideline contains systematically developed statements that include recommendations, strategies, or information that assist healthcare practitioners and patients to make decisions about appropriate healthcare for specific clinical circumstances.
- The clinical practice guideline was produced under the auspices of medical specialty associations; relevant professional societies; public or private organizations; government agencies at the federal, state, or local levels; or healthcare organizations or plans.
- A systematic literature search and review of existing scientific evidence published in peer-reviewed journals was performed during the guideline development.
- The guideline was either developed, reviewed, or revised within the last 5 years.

Of the various guideline collections and databases, the NGC contains the most descriptive information about guidelines. It also is the most selective about the guidelines that are included in its database. Inclusion criteria are applied to each guideline to determine whether or not they will be incorporated in the database. Furthermore, guidelines in the NGC database reflect the most current version.

Another website that is very helpful is NLM Gateway. The Gateway allows users to put in a search term that is then sent out to eight different NLM databases. One of these, Health Services/Health Technology Assessment Text (HSTAT) is especially practical. Health Services/ Health Technology Assessment Text is unique because it takes large guidelines, systematic reviews, and technology assessments and enables their texts to be searchable on the Internet, making them much easier to navigate electronically.

Access the NLM Gateway at **http://gateway.nlm.nih.gov/gw/Cmd**

There is no shortage of guideline-related sites on the Internet. The challenge is finding the source of guidelines that is easiest to use and provides the best mechanisms for making sure the contents are up to date. Because so many guideline resources are now on the Internet, it is wise to consider the quality of the website when choosing a source.

Extremely useful databases of evidence-based guidelines exist. Many of these resources provide users with the guidelines and some also provide additional information on how guidelines are developed and used. Evaluation of guideline databases is necessary to ensure that the information is reliable and current.

Finding the Right Guideline

Locating and reviewing current guidelines on a particular subject are often overwhelming. Even after a guideline has been identified, it can be difficult to determine critical information of the guideline, such as who developed and funded it, who was on the panel, how the guideline was developed, what dates the literature review covered, and so on. Guidelines should provide this background and be explicit in their discussion of the evidence supporting their recommendations as well as in identifying the benefits and harms of interventions (Barratt, Irwig, Glasziou, et al., 1999; Burgers, Grol, & Eccles, 2005; DiCenso, Ciliska, Dobbins, et al., 2005). Guidelines developed using evidence of established benefit of treatments or interventions have the potential to improve healthcare and health outcomes as well as decrease morbidity and mortality (Grimshaw, Thomas, & MacLennan, 2004; Woolf, Grol, Hutchinson, et al., 1999). However, guidelines of low quality may cause harm to patients and should be carefully appraised for validity and reliability of their information and supporting evidence (Shekelle, Kravitz, & Beart, 2000).

Users of guidelines need to keep in mind that "one size *does not* fit all." Haynes describes the "three Rs" of clinical practice guideline application as their application to the *right person* at the *right time* and in the *right way* (Haynes, 1993). Davis and Taylor-Vaisey (1997) suggest that the effect of clinical guidelines on improved healthcare outcomes is dependent on taking into account their nature, the nature and beliefs of the target clinicians, and environmental factors when trying to implement them. In a landmark work, Hayward, Wilson, Tunis, et al. (1995) from the Evidence-based Medicine Working Group identified three main questions to consider when using EBPGs: (a) What are the guideline recommendations? (b) Are the guideline recommendations valid? and (c) How useful are the recommendations? Lastly, in a recent article Straus and Haynes (2009) remind us that evidence alone is never sufficient to make clinical decisions. One must weigh the evidence in context, always accounting for the values and preferences of patients, with the goal to achieve optimal shared decision making. These authors add that key to supporting clinicians is ensuring that information resources are reliable, relevant, and readable.

How to Read Recommendations?

The strength of a guideline is based upon the validity and reliability of its recommendations. In addition, guideline usefulness is highly dependent on the meaningfulness and practicality of the recommendations. Practicality relates to the ease with which a recommendation can be implemented. The recommendations should be as unambiguous as possible. They should address how often screening and other interventions should occur to achieve optimal outcomes. In addition, the recommendations should be explicit about areas where informing the patient of choices can lead to varying decisions. Furthermore, recommendations should address clinically relevant actions. The developers' assessment of the benefits against the harms of implementing the recommendation should be part of the support documentation for the recommendation.

It is important to know whether the developers focused on outcomes that are meaningful to patients and whether they were inclusive in considering all reasonable treatment options for a given condition or disease. The user should consider whether the developers assigned different values to the outcomes they evaluated, taking patient preferences into consideration. Developers need to fully describe the process used to systematically search and review the evidence on which the guideline recommendations are based. When combining the evidence, it is important to note whether the developer used a rating scheme or similar method to determine the quality and strength of the studies included, both primary studies and syntheses. Developers often use letter grades or words such as *strongly recommend* to rate their assessment of the strength of the evidence for a given recommendation. In 2002, the Research Training Institute at the University of North Carolina at Chapel Hill (RTI-UNC) Evidence-Based Practice Center completed a **systematic review** of schemes used to rate the quality of a body of evidence. While, there is no universal consensus on grading evidence or determining the strength of a body of evidence supporting a recommendation, there are well-established norms. The most notable process for grading recommendations is the one used by the USPSTF (Harris, Helfand, Woolf, et al., 2001; USPSTF, 2008; see Box 8.3).

As another example of grading recommendations in clinical practice guidelines, the ACC and the AHA use a system based on level of evidence and class or recommendation (see http://www.acc.org and http://www.aha.org). The level of evidence integrates an objective description of the existence and type of studies supporting the recommendation and expert

chapter 8

---

box 8.3

USPSTF System for Evaluating Evidence to Support Recommendations

A—The USPSTF recommends the service. There is high certainty that the net benefit is substantial. Offer or provide this service.

B—The USPSTF recommends the service. There is high certainty that the net benefit is moderate or there is moderate certainty that the net benefit is moderate to substantial. Offer or provide the service.

C—The USPSTF recommends against routinely providing the service. There may be considerations that support providing the service in an individual patient. There is at least moderate certainty that the net benefit is small. Offer or provide this service only if other considerations support the offering or providing the service in an individual patient.

D—The USPSTF recommends against the service. There is moderate or high certainty that the service has no net benefit or that the harms outweigh the benefits. Discourage the use of this service.

I—The USPSTF concludes that the current evidence is insufficient to assess the balance of benefits and harms of the service. Evidence is lacking, of poor quality, or conflicting, and the balance of benefits and harms cannot be determined. Read the clinical considerations section of the USPSTF Recommendation Statement. If the service is offered, patients should understand the uncertainty about the balance of benefits and harms.

Source: http://www.ahrq.gov/CLINIC/uspstfix.htm

consensus according to one of three categories, including: (a) Level of evidence A (i.e., the recommendation is based on evidence from multiple **randomized controlled trials** or **meta-analyses**), (b) Level of evidence B (i.e., the recommendation is based on evidence from a single randomized trial or nonrandomized studies), and (c) Level of evidence C (i.e., the recommendation is based on expert opinion, case studies, or standards of care). The class of recommendation indicates the strengths and weaknesses of the evidence as well as the relative importance of the risks and benefits identified by the evidence. The following are definitions of classes used by the ACC and AHA: (a) Class I: conditions for which there is evidence and/or general agreement that a given procedure or treatment is useful and effective, (b) Class II: conditions for which there is conflicting evidence and/or a divergence of opinion about the usefulness/efficacy of a procedure or treatment, (c) Class IIa: weight of evidence/opinion is in favor of usefulness/efficacy, (d) Class IIb: usefulness/efficacy is less well established by evidence/opinion, and (e) Class III: conditions for which there is evidence or general agreement that the procedure/treatment is not useful/effective and in some cases may be harmful (Tricoci et al., 2009).

Because guidelines reflect snapshots of the evidence at a given point in time, they require consistent updating to incorporate new evidence. Thus, it is critical that developers commit to a cyclical systematic review of their guidelines. In addition, developers can alert guideline users to ongoing research studies that may have an impact on the recommendations in the future. It is advisable that guidelines undergo peer review and pilot testing in actual practice before being released. Stakeholders' review allows a reality check to identify last-minute inconsistencies or relevant evidence that might have been overlooked. Pilot testing allows organizational or functional problems with implementing the guideline to be identified, including the cost of implementing the guideline. These can then be corrected or accommodated to enhance the chances of the guideline being implemented.

Will the Recommendations Help Patient Care?

Applying a guideline on management of heart failure in the ambulatory setting is not the same as using a guideline on management of heart failure in the hospital. Similarly, a guideline on management of heart failure in children is not comparable with a guideline on management of heart failure in adults. The guideline should: (a) fit the setting of care and the age and gender of the patients, (b) be useable by the type of clinicians providing the care, and (c) take into consideration the presence of any comorbidities. Ultimately, both the guideline user and developer must keep in mind the role evidence plays in developing recommendations. For example, most experimental studies do not take into account the characteristics of individual patients, including comorbidities and clinical settings (Berg, 1998; Burgers et al., 2005; Cook, Greengold, Ellrodt, et al., 1997). Although EBPGs do not always take into account multiple conditions and patients generally do not present with only one disease or condition, guidelines can help point clinicians in the right direction when looking for the right care for their patients. Practitioners have the responsibility to individualize guideline implementation for their particular patients' circumstances.

Tools for Evaluating Guidelines

Finding the right guideline to use is contingent on being able to critically appraise the validity and reliability of a guideline. There is ample evidence that guideline developers do not always adhere to best practices in guideline development. Two studies of guidelines developed by medical specialty societies found that a significant percentage did not adhere to accepted methodological practices in their development (Grilli, Magrini, Penna, et al., 2000; Shaneyfelt, Mayo-Smith, & Rothwangl, 1999). In a landmark work, the Institute of Medicine identified eight attributes of good guideline development, including:

- Validity
- Reliability and reproducibility
- Clinical applicability

- Clinical flexibility
- Clarity
- Documentation
- Development by a multidisciplinary process
- Plans for review (Field & Lohr, 1990, 1992)

Guidelines are complex and heterogeneous documents; therefore, evaluating them is often difficult. However, with a good guide, critical appraisal of guidelines can be accomplished (see Appendix D for rapid critical appraisal [RCA] checklists for clinical practice guidelines).

Provisional Instrument for Assessing Guidelines

Lohr and Field (1992) developed a provisional instrument for assessing clinical practice guidelines. They developed the instrument because they recognized that there was a need for an explicit mechanism to appraise the validity of individual clinical practice guidelines. The instrument was a first step in trying to identify a way to appraise critical attributes of guidelines. Nonetheless, it was long and difficult to complete. It was not intended to be used by practicing clinicians, but by groups or organizations wanting to adopt a guideline. The instrument also was appropriate for self-assessment by guideline developers.

Rapid Critical Appraisal Checklist

Rapid critical appraisal of a guideline can be accomplished by applying standardized criteria when evaluating the attributes of the guideline (see Box 8.4). The answer to each question in the

---

box 8.4

RCA Questions to Ask of Evidence-Based Guidelines

Who were the guideline developers?

Were the developers representative of key stakeholders in this specialty (interdisciplinary)?

Who funded the guideline development?

Were any of the guideline developers funded researchers of the reviewed studies?

Did the team have a valid development strategy?

Was an explicit (how decisions were made), sensible, and impartial process used to identify, select, and combine evidence?

Did its developers carry out a comprehensive, reproducible literature review within the past 12 months of its publication/revision?

Were all important options and outcomes considered?

Is each recommendation in the guideline tagged by the level/strength of evidence upon which it is based and linked with the scientific evidence?

Do the guidelines make explicit recommendations (reflecting value judgments about outcomes)?

Has the guideline been subjected to peer review and testing?

Is the intent of use provided (e.g., national, regional, local)?

Are the recommendations clinically relevant?

Will the recommendations help me in caring for my patients?

Are the recommendations practical/feasible? Are resources (people and equipment) available?

Are the recommendations a major variation from current practice? Can the outcomes be measured through standard care?

RCA checklist supplies the end user with information that, when weighed all together, enables the clinician to decide whether the given guideline is the best match for her or his setting, patient, and desired outcomes.

Agree Instrument for Assessing Guidelines

In 1992, the United Kingdom National Health Services Management Executive set in motion the development of an appraisal instrument for the National Health Services (Cluzeau, Littlejohns, Grimshaw, et al., 1999). This was the first attempt to formally evaluate the usefulness of a guideline appraisal instrument. Subsequently, the European Union provided funding for the development of the Appraisal of Guidelines for Research and Evaluation (AGREE) instrument.

> The AGREE instrument can be found at
> **http://www.agreecollaboration.org**

The AGREE instrument was developed and evaluated by an international group of guideline developers and researchers. Since its release in final form in 2001, the AGREE instrument has been translated into many languages and is gaining appeal as the standard guideline appraisal tool. The AGREE instrument contains six quality domains and 23 items (AGREE Collaboration, 2001; see Box 8.5).

The AGREE instrument recommends there be more than one appraiser for each guideline—preferably four—to increase confidence in the reliability of the instrument. The instrument is scored using a four-point Likert scale, with 1 being "strongly disagree" and 4 being "strongly agree." The domain scores are not meant to be aggregated into one overall score for the guideline. Thus, the instrument will produce individual domain scores but will not produce an overall rating for a guideline. The instrument allows the appraiser to give a subjective assessment of the guideline based on review of the individual domain scores. It is important to note that recent studies raise serious questions regarding the inter-rater reliability of the AGREE instrument and suggest that the tool could benefit from further detailed appraisal (Wimpenny & van Zelm, 2007). Alternative appraisal instruments are being developed that address more than the guidelines along other sources of evidence. A promising example is the GRADE (Grades of Recommendations, Assessment, Development and Evaluation) instrument (Atkins, Eccles, Flottorp, et al., 2004).

National Guideline Clearinghouse and Others

The National Guideline Clearinghouse produces structured summaries of each guideline in its database to aid the user in assessing the quality and appropriateness of a guideline. The summaries describe guideline attributes similar to those contained in the Lohr and Field (1992) provisional instrument, the RCA checklist, and the AGREE instrument. In addition, the Conference on Guideline Standardization (COGS) Statement recommends standardizing the development and reporting of a guideline, so developers can ensure the quality of their guidelines and make their implementation easier (Shiffman, Shekelle, Overhage, et al., 2003).

> More can be learned about the COGS appraisal guides at
> **http://gem.med.yale.edu/cogs/welcome.do**

box 8.5

AGREE Instrument

Scope and Purpose

Item 1. The overall objective(s) of the guideline is (are) specifically described.

Item 2. The clinical question(s) covered by the guideline is (are) specifically described.

Item 3. The patients to whom the guideline(s) are meant to apply are specifically described.

Stakeholder Involvement

Item 4. The guideline development group includes individuals from all relevant professional groups.

Item 5. The patients' views and preferences have been sought.

Item 6. The target users of the guideline are clearly defined.

Item 7. The guideline has been piloted among target users.

Rigor of Development

Item 8. Systematic methods were used to search for evidence.

Item 9. The criteria for selecting the evidence are clearly described.

Item 10. The methods used for formulating the recommendations are clearly described.

Item 11. The health benefits, side effects, and risks have been considered in formulating the recommendations.

Item 12. There is an explicit link between the recommendations and the supporting evidence.

Item 13. The guideline has been externally reviewed by experts prior to its publication.

Item 14. A procedure for updating the guideline is provided.

Clarity and Presentation

Item 15. The recommendations are specific and unambiguous.

Item 16. The different options for management of the condition are clearly presented.

Item 17. The key recommendations are easily identifiable.

Item 18. The guideline is supported with tools for application.

Application

Item 19. The potential organizational barriers in applying the recommendations have been discussed.

Item 20. The possible cost implications of applying the recommendations have been considered.

Item 21. The guideline presents key review criteria for monitoring and/or audit purposes.

Editorial Independence

Item 22. The guideline is editorially independent from the funding body.

Item 23. Conflicts of interest of guideline development members have been recorded.

Source: From Cluzeau, F. A., Littlejohns, P., Grimshaw, J. M., Feder, G., & Moran, S. E. (1999). Development and application of a generic methodology to assess the quality of clinical guidelines. International Journal of Quality Health Care, 11(1), 21–28.

How Guidelines are Developed

Determining when to develop guidelines should be systematically approached due to the amount of resources, skill, and time needed to accomplish these activities. In 1995, the Institute of Medicine issued guidance on setting priorities for clinical practice guidelines (Field, 1995). The report emphasized the importance of considering whether the guideline had the potential to change health outcomes or costs and the availability of scientific evidence on which to develop the recommendations (Field, 1995). Other criteria used by organizations include the following:

- The topic is clinically important, affecting large numbers of people with substantial morbidity or mortality (the burden of illness).
- The topic is complex and requires clinical practice clarity.
- There is evidence of substantive variation between actual and optimal care.
- There are no existing valid or relevant guidelines available to use.
- There is evidence available to support evidence-based guideline development.
- The topic is central to healthy public policy and serves to introduce innovation.

When it is determined that there is uncertainty about how to treat or when gaps between optimal practice and actual practice have been identified, an organization may decide to develop a clinical practice guideline. Because it is difficult and expensive to develop guidelines, many organizations would be better served by adopting or adapting existing guidelines that have already been developed. Critically appraising already developed guidelines will allow an organization to screen for the best developed and suited guidelines for their organization.

Processes and Panels

When the decision is made that a guideline will be developed, several important steps must take place. Guidelines can be developed at a central level with a good scientific basis and broad validity, or they can follow a local approach in the form of care protocols agreed upon by a department or institution. The emphasis of the latter is on practical feasibility and support of care processes (Burgers et al., 2005). These local guidelines can be developed using informal consensus, formal consensus, evidence-based methodologies, and explicit methodologies, either alone or in any combination. However, it is highly recommended that development focus on more formal and explicit processes so that another developer using similar techniques would likely come to the same conclusions.

Next, the guideline panel must be identified. The process for development of the panel should include multidisciplinary major stakeholders for the guideline, including users and patients (Field & Lohr, 1990; Shekelle, Woolf, Eccles, et al., 1999; Scottish Intercollegiate Guideline Network [SIGN], 2008). Guideline panels should be composed of members who can adequately address the relevant interventions and meaningful outcomes and can weigh benefits and harms. To increase the feasibility of implementation, it is advisable that panels be composed of subject experts who bring the different perspectives of research, clinical practice, administration, education, and policy (Grinspun et al., 2002; McQueen, Montgomery, Lappan-Gracon, et al., 2008). Variations in the composition of the guideline development panel, the developing organization, and the interpretation of the evidence are often the source of differing recommendations on the same clinical topic across guidelines (Berg, Atkins, & Tierney, 1997; Burgers et al., 2005; DiCenso & Guyatt, 2005; Lohr, 1995).

Review Questions

The next step in guideline development is the formal assessment of the clinical questions to be reviewed. This can be aided by the development of an analytic framework or causal pathway (Harris et al., 2001).

These diagrams provide a roadmap for the precise description of the target population, setting of care, interventions, and intermediate as well as final health outcomes. They also help focus the most meaningful questions that will guide the literature review and subsequent recommendations. Figure 8.1 shows an analytic framework for prevention screening used by the USPSTF (Harris et al.).

The numbers in the diagram relate to the key questions that will be considered. For example, (1) relates to whether the screening test actually reduces morbidity and/or mortality; and (5) asks the important question of whether treatment of clinically diagnosed patients results in reduced morbidity and/or mortality.

Literature Search and Review

After the key questions have been identified, a formal search and review of the literature take place. It is easiest if a systematic review has already been identified by searching databases such as the Cochrane Library, MEDLINE, CINAHL, and EMBASE. If an already completed systematic review is not found, it is necessary to develop one. The first step is to determine what types of evidence will be considered, including study design, dates of publication, and language. A search strategy of relevant citation databases should be developed, preferably with the assistance of a medical librarian familiar with electronic searches. Once the search is completed, a process for screening titles and abstracts for relevance is conducted. The remaining titles are retrieved for evaluation. These articles are then screened and data is extracted from the studies. The individual articles are reviewed for internal and external biases, and their quality is often rated based on standardized criteria. Once data are extracted from the individual studies, the results are summarized, sometimes using meta-analysis to combine results from similar studies.

Recommendations

The formal search, review, and appraisal of the literature lead to developing recommendations based on the strength of the evidence for each of the questions that were identified in the analytic

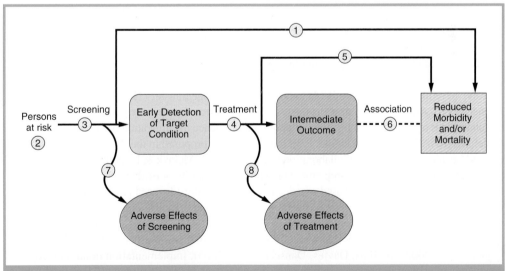

| figure 8.1 | Analytic framework for prevention screening (From Harris, R. P., Helfand, M., Woolf, S. H., Lohr, K. N., Mulrow, C. D., Teutsch, S. M., et al. [2001]. Current methods of the U.S. Preventive Services Task Force: A review of the process. *American Journal of Preventive Medicine, 20*(3 Suppl), 21–35.) |

framework. Some guideline panels choose to make recommendations based solely on evidence, whereas others will use expert opinion when the evidence is poor or lacking. When expert opinion is used, it should be identified as such and be gathered using formal, explicit methods (Grinspun et al., 2002).

Peer Review and Dissemination

After the guideline recommendations are formulated, the guideline should be subjected to peer review to uncover any omissions or misinterpretations. In some cases, pilot testing will uncover that it is not feasible to implement a certain guideline or will offer tips to facilitate contextual modifications that ease adoption. Following the peer review and pilot testing, if necessary, the guideline is revised. Then, it is published and broadly disseminated.

Implementing Evidence-Based Guidelines

Implementing guidelines into actual practice requires multifaceted and sustained interventions. Individual practitioners' commitment and organizational leadership are keys to implementation. Assessing organizational readiness for best practice guidelines implementation is a critical step and it must include all levels of administrative leadership and clinical practice staff. Studies report successful results and improvements in clinical practice and patients' outcomes following well-thought-out multilevel and multibundled interventions (Devlin, Czaus, & Santos, 2002; O'Connor, Creager, Mooney, et al., 2006). Critical elements that assist in uptake and translation of evidence into day-to-day practice include (a) facilitating staff to utilize best practice guidelines; (b) creating a positive milieu and securing structures and processes that inspire EBP (Gifford, Davies, Edwards, et al., 2006); (c) interactive education with skills building practice sessions and attention to patient education (Davies et al., 2008); (d) electronic gathering and dissemination systems offering real-time feedback and access to guidelines (Davies et al.; Doran, Carryer, Paterson, et al., 2009); (e) changing organizational policies and procedures to reflect clinical best practices and making staff aware of these changes (St-Pierre, Davies, Edwards, et al., 2007); and (f) organizational and unit-based champions, teamwork and collaboration, professional association's support, interorganizational collaboration, networks, and administrative leadership (Ploeg, Davies, Edwards, et al., 2007). Gifford et al. (2007) discuss in detail the pivotal role that managerial leadership plays in securing uptake of research evidence by point-of-care clinical staff.

Several strategies are available to facilitate knowledge transfer (Thompson, Estabrooks, & Degner, 2006). An effective example is the use of best practice champions (Santos, 2008). Best practice champions are nurses who promote, support, and influence the utilization of nursing best practice guidelines (RNAO, 2008). In addition, EBP mentors as first proposed in the Advancing Research and Clinical practice through close Collaboration (ARCC) Model (Melnyk & Fineout-Overholt, 2002) also are a promising strategy for implementation and sustainability of evidence-based guidelines and care (Melnyk, 2007). Evidence-based practice mentors, typically advanced practice nurses who have in-depth knowledge and skills in EBP as well as individual and organizational change strategies, work with direct care staff in promoting evidence-based care.

There are excellent toolkits to facilitate the implementation process (DiCenso, Virani, Bajnok, et al., 2002; Dobbins, Davies, Danseco, et al., 2005). Implementation in nursing education also is of critical importance in preparing future nurses to "think evidence." Relatively short workshops with clinical instructors have been shown to be an effective way to assist faculty in initiating integration of practice guidelines in undergraduate nursing education (Higuchi, Cragg, Diem, et al., 2006). Quality measurement and feedback mechanisms can help determine whether the guideline is actually being used in practice.

Once best practice guidelines are successfully implemented, it is vital to ensure that utilization is sustained over time. This is critical to ensure long-lasting practice changes, improved clinical outcomes for patients, as well as organizational and system effectiveness. Ongoing administrative support and staff engagement are critical elements, as is embedding the evidence in policies, procedures, and plans of clinical care. Organizational learning theory provides a complementary perspective to understanding the sustainability of practice changes. A critical aspect of this approach is that of "organizational memory," which refers to the various ways knowledge is stored within organizations for current and future use (Virani, Lemieux-Charles, Davis, et al., 2008).

Does Context Matter?

The ability of practitioners to implement a guideline's recommendations is highly dependent on **context** (i.e., the milieu or environment). A teaching hospital that has multiple clinical supports in the United States or urban Canada may differ greatly from a hospital with fewer supports in rural and remote areas in the same countries, let alone in developing nations. The level of staffing and skill mix impact guideline implementation as well as the organizational model of care delivery. A critical success factor is the continuity of the care provider within the model of care delivery.

Practice guidelines can serve to build capacity and improve clinical practice across all sectors of care. However, strategies to promote uptake may be different in public health, hospital care, nursing homes, or home healthcare agencies.

Despite the need to account for practice context, most practice guidelines focus only on clinical recommendations and overlook the critical role that work environments play, leaving it to individuals to determine the appropriate method for implementation. However, there are some guidelines that are improving on this development process. For example, RNAO's best practice guidelines contain clinical, work environment, and educational recommendations making them easier to implement into practice (Grinspun et al., 2002; Nelligan, Grinspun, Jonas-Simpson, et al., 2002).

Implications for Patient Care

Evidence-based clinical practice guidelines have the potential to dramatically improve patient care, health outcomes, and organizational/system performance. When developed rigorously and implemented consistently, they can achieve their purpose of improving healthcare quality and patient outcomes. Guidelines can be an important vehicle for translating complex research findings into recommendations that can be acted upon. Because organizations still struggle with the best mechanisms to implement research into practice, guideline developers need to continue to strive toward collaboration and avoidance of duplication. Increasing collaboration between developers and implementers will result in practice recommendations that are readily useable by point-of-care practitioners as well as more easily utilized in electronic health records and clinical decision support tools. An encouraging sign is that developers also are condensing guidelines for download onto a Personal Digital Assistant (PDA) (e.g., RNAO, NGC). Collaboration among healthcare providers and joint clinical decision making also are central to improving patients' clinical outcomes (Grinspun, 2007). Interdisciplinary EBPGs can serve as a catalyst for positive team work.

In 2002, a new international organization, the G-I-N (http://www.G-I-N.net) was formed. This organization is made up of guideline developers from throughout the world. Its mission is to improve the quality of healthcare by promoting systematic development of EBPGs and their application into practice by supporting international collaboration. The presence of G-I-N signals is a move toward globalizing evidence while still promoting localized decision making. Given the complexity and expense of developing EBPGs, this type of initiative is essential. Even more important, this collaboration signifies a universal awareness that clinical decisions can no longer be made without being informed by the best available evidence.

> *To think is easy. To act is hard. But the hardest thing in the world is to act in accordance with your thinking.*
>
> *Johann Wolfgang von Goethe*

references

AGREE Collaboration. (2001). *Appraisal of Guidelines for Research & Evaluation (AGREE) Instrument.* Available at http://www.agreecollaboration.org

Atkins, D., Eccles, M., Flottorp, S., Guyatt, G. H., Henry, D., Hill, S., et al. (2004). Systems for grading the quality of evidence and the strength of recommendations: Critical appraisal of existing approaches. The Grade Group. *BMC Health Services Research, 4*(38), 1–7.

Barratt, A., Irwig, L., Glasziou, P., Cumming, R. G., Raffle, A., Hicks, N., et al. (1999). Users' guides to the medical literature: XVII. How to use guidelines and recommendations about screening. *JAMA, 281,* 2029–2034.

Berg, A. O. (1998). Dimensions of evidence. *Journal of the American Board of Family Practice, 11,* 216–223.

Berg, A. O., Atkins, D. J., & Tierney, W. (1997). Clinical practice guidelines in practice and education. *Journal of General Internal Medicine, 12*(Suppl 2), S25–S33.

Burgers, J., Grol, R., & Eccles, E. (2005). Clinical guidelines as a tool for implementing change in patient care. In R. Grol, M. Wensign, & M. Eccles (Eds.), *Improving patient care: The implementation of change in clinical practice* (pp. 71–93). Edinburgh: Elsevier.

Cluzeau, F. A., Littlejohns, P., Grimshaw, J. M., Feder, G., & Moran, S. E. (1999). Development and application of a generic methodology to assess the quality of clinical guidelines. *International Journal of Quality Health Care, 11*(1), 21–28.

Cook, D. J., Greengold, N. L., Ellrodt, G., & Weingarten, S. R. (1997). The relation between systematic reviews and practice guidelines. *Annals of Internal Medicine, 127,* 210–216.

Davies, B., Edwards, N., Ploeg, J., & Virani, T. (2008). Insights about the process and impact of implementing nursing guidelines on delivery of care in hospitals and community settings. *BMC Health Services Research, 8*(29), 1–44.

Davis, D. A., & Taylor-Vaisey, A. (1997). Translating guidelines into practice: A systematic review of theoretic concepts, practical experience and research evidence in the adoption of clinical practice guidelines. *Canadian Medical Association Journal, 157*(4), 408–416.

Devlin, R., Czaus, M., & Santos, J. (2002). Registered Nurses Association of Ontario's Best Practice Guideline as a tool for creating partnerships. *Hospital Quarterly, Spring, 5*(3), 62–65.

DiCenso, A., & Guyatt, G. (2005). Interpreting levels of evidence and grades of health care recommendation. In A. DiCenso, G. Guyatt, & D. Ciliska, D. (Eds.), *Evidence-based nursing: A guide to clinical practice* (pp. 508–525). Philadelphia: Elsevier Mosby.

DiCenso, A., Ciliska, D., Dobbins, M., & Guyatt, G. (2005). Moving from evidence to actions using clinical practice guidelines. In A. DiCenso, G. Guyatt, & D. Ciliska (Eds.), *Evidence-based nursing: A guide to clinical practice* (pp. 154–169). Philadelphia: Elsevier Mosby.

DiCenso, A., Virani, T., Bajnok, I., Borycki, E., Davies, B., Graham, I., et al. (2002). A toolkit to facilitate the implementation of clinical practice guidelines in healthcare settings. *Hospital Quarterly, Spring, 5*(3), 55–59.

Dobbins, M., Davies, B., Danseco, E., Edwards, N., & Virani, T. (2005). Changing nursing practice: Evaluating the usefulness of a best-practice guideline implementation toolkit. *Nursing Leadership, 18*(1), 34–45.

Doran, D., Carryer, J., Paterson, J., Goering, P., Nagle, L., Kushniruk, A., et al. (2009). Integrating evidence-based interventions into client care plans. *Nursing Leadership, 143,* 9–13.

Field, M. J. (Ed.) (1995). *Setting priorities for clinical practice guidelines.* Washington, DC: National Academy Press.

Field, M. J., & Lohr, K. N. (Eds.) (1990). *Clinical practice guidelines: Directions for a new program.* Washington, DC: National Academy Press.

Field, M. J., & Lohr, K. N. (Eds.) (1992). *Guidelines for clinical practice: From development to use.* Washington, DC: National Academy Press.

Gifford, W. A., Davies, B., Edwards, N., & Graham, I. (2006). Leadership strategies to influence the use of clinical practice guidelines. *Nursing Research, 19*(4), 72–88.

Gifford, W. A., Davies, B., Edwards, N., Griffin, P., & Lybanon, V. (2007). Managerials leadership for nurses' use of research evidence: An integrative review of literature. *Worldviews on Evidence-Based Nursing, 4*(3), 126–145.

Grilli, R., Magrini, N., Penna, A., Mura, G., & Liberati, A. (2000). Practice guidelines developed by specialty societies: The need for a critical appraisal. *Lancet, 355*, 103–105.

Grimshaw, J. M., Thomas, R. E., & MacLennan, G. (2004). Effectiveness and efficiency of guidelines dissemination and implementation strategies. *Health Technology Assess, 8*(6), 1–84.

Grinspun, D. (2007). Healthy workplaces: The case for shared clinical decision making and increased full-time employment. *Healthcare Papers, 7*, 69–75.

Grinspun, D., Virani, T., & Bajnok, I. (2002). Nursing best practice guidelines: The RNAO Project. *Hospital Quarterly, Winter*, 54–58.

Harris, R. P., Helfand, M., Woolf, S. H., Lohr, K. N., Mulrow, C. D., Teutsch, S. M., et al. (2001). Current methods of the U.S. Preventive Services Task Force: A review of the process. *American Journal of Preventive Medicine, 20*(3 Suppl), 21–35.

Haynes, R. B. (1993). Where's the meat in clinical journals? *ACP Journal Club, 119*, A22–A23.

Hayward, R. S., Wilson, M. C., Tunis, S. R., Bass, E. B., & Guyatt, G. (1995). Users' guides to the medical literature. VIII. How to use clinical practice guidelines. A. Are the recommendations valid? *JAMA, 274*, 570–574.

Higuchi, K. A., Cragg, C. E., Diem, E., Molnar, J., & O'Donohue, M. S. (2006). Integrating clinical guidelines into nursing education. *International Journal of Nursing Education Scholarship 3*(1), article 12.

Lohr, K. N. (1995). Guidelines for clinical practice: What they are and why they count. *Journal of Law, Medicine and Ethics, 23*(1), 49–56.

Lohr, K. N., & Field, M. J. (1992). A provisional instrument for assessing clinical practice guidelines. In M. J. Field & K. N. Lohr (Eds.), *Guidelines for clinical practice: From development to use* (pp. 346–410). Washington, DC: National Academy Press.

McQueen, K., Montgomery, P., Lappan-Gracon, S., Evans, M., & Hunter, J. (2008). Evidence-based recommendations for depressive symptoms in postpartum women. *Journal of Obstetric, Gynecologic, & Neonatal Nursing, 37*(2), 127–135.

Melnyk, B. M. (2007). The evidence-based practice mentor: A promising strategy for implementing and sustaining EBP in healthcare systems. *Worldviews on Evidence-Based Nursing, 4*(3), 123–125.

Melnyk, B. M., & Fineout-Overholt, E. (2002). Putting research into practice. *Reflections on Nursing Leadership, 28*(2), 22–25.

Miller, M., & Kearney, N. (2004). Guidelines for clinical practice: Development, dissemination and implementation. *International Journal of Nursing Studies, 41*(1), 813–821.

National Library of Medicine. (2008). *Fact sheet: PubMed®: MEDLINE® retrieval on the world wide web*. Retrieved February 14, 2009, from http://www.nlm.nih.gov/pubs/factsheets/pubmed.html

Nelligan, P., Grinspun, D., Jonas-Simpson, C., McConnell, H., Peter, E., Pilkington, B., et al. (2002). Client-centred care: Making the ideal real. *Hospital Quarterly, Summer*, 70–76.

O'Connor, P., Creager, J., Mooney, S., Laizner, A. M., & Ritchie, J. (2006). Taking aim at falls injury adverse events: Best practices and organizational change. *Healthcare Quarterly, 9*(Special Issue), 43–49.

Ploeg, J., Davies, B., Edwards, N., Gifford, W., & Miller, P. (2007). Factors influencing best-practice guideline implementation: Lessons learned from administrators, nursing staff, and project leaders. *Worldviews on Evidence-Based Nursing, 4*(4), 210–219.

Registered Nurses' Association of Ontario. (2008). Who are best practice champions? Retrieved October 10, 2008, from http://www.rnao.org/

Research Training Institute. (2002). *RTI-UNC Evidence-Based Practice Center*. Retrieved July 29, 2009, from http://www.rti.org

Sackett, D. L., Richardson, W. S., Rosenberg, W., & Haynes, R. B. (1997). *Evidence-based medicine: How to practice and teach EBM*. New York: Churchill Livingstone.

Santos, J. (2008). Promoting best practices in long-term-care. *Perspectives, 31*(2), 5–9.

Schunemann, H. J., Woodhead, M., Anzueto, A., Buist, S., MacNee, W., Rabe, K. F., et al. (2009). A vision statement on guideline development for respiratory disease: The example of COPD. *Lancet, 373*, 774–779.

Scottish Intercollegiate Guideline Network. (2008). *SIGN 50: A guideline developers' handbook. An introduction to SIGN methodology for the development of evidence-based clinical guidelines*. Edinburgh, Scotland: Author.

Shaneyfelt, T. M., Mayo-Smith, M. F., & Rothwangl, J. (1999). Are guidelines following guidelines? The methodological quality of clinical practice guidelines in the peer-reviewed medical literature. *JAMA, 281*, 1900–1905.

Shekelle, P. G., Kravitz, R. L., & Beart, J. (2000). Are nonspecific practice guidelines potentially harmful? A randomized comparison of the effect of nonspecific versus specific guidelines on physician decision making. *Health Services Research, 34*(2), 1429–1448.

Shekelle, P. G., Woolf, S. H., Eccles, M., & Grimshaw, J. (1999). Clinical guidelines: developing guidelines. *British Medical Journal, 318*(7183), 593–596.

Shiffman, R. N., Shekelle, P., Overhage, J. M., Slutsky, J., Grimshaw, J., & Deshpande, A. M. (2003). A proposal for standardized reporting of clinical practice guidelines: The COGS statement. *Annals, 139*(6), 493–500.

St-Pierre, I., Davies, B., Edwards, N., & Griffin, P. (2007). Policies and procedures: A tool to support the implementation of clinical guidelines. *Nursing Research, 20*(4), 63–78.

Straus, S., & Haynes, B. (2009). Managing evidence-based knowledge: The need for reliable, relevant and readable resources. *Canadian Medical Association Journal, 180*(9), 942–945.

Thompson, G. N., Estabrooks, C. A., & Degner, L. F. (2006). Clarifying the concepts in knowledge transfer: A literature review. *Journal of Advanced Nursing, 53*(6), 691–701.

Tricoci, P., Allen, J. M., Kramer, J. M., Califf, R. M., & Smith, S. C. (2009). Scientific evidence underlying the ACC/AHA Clinical Practice Guidelines. *JAMA, 301*(8), 831–841.

U.S. Preventive Services Task Force. (2008). *The guide to clinical preventive services*. Rockville, MD: The Agency for Healthcare Research and Quality.

Virani, T., Lemieux-Charles, L., Davis, D., & Berta, W. (2008). Sustaining change: Once evidence-based practices are transferred, what then? *Hospital Quarterly, 12*(1), 89–96.

chapter 8

203

Wennberg, J., & Gittelsohn, A. (1973). Small area variations in health care delivery. *Science, 182*(117), 1102–1108.

Wennberg, J., & Gittelsohn, A. (1982). Variations in medical care among small areas. *Scientific American, 246*(4), 120–134.

Wennberg, J. E., McAndrew, C., & the Dartmouth Medical School Center for Evaluative Clinical Sciences Staff. (1999). *The Dartmouth atlas of health care.* Washington, DC: The American Hospital Association.

Wimpenny, P., & van Zelm, R. (2007). Appraising and comparing pressure ulcer guidelines. *Worldviews on Evidence-Based Nursing, 4*(1), 40–50.

Woolf, S. H., Grol, R., Hutchinson, A., Eccles, M., & Grimshaw, J. (1999). Clinical guidelines: Potential benefits, limitations, and harms of clinical guidelines. *British Medical Journal, 318*(7182), 527–530.

Implementing Evidence in Clinical Settings

Marilyn J. Hockenberry, Terri L. Brown, and Bernadette Mazurek Melnyk

> *I never worry about action, only inaction.*
>
> *Winston Churchill*

It is not enough to have knowledge of the best evidence to guide clinical practice; that knowledge must be translated into clinical practice to improve patient care and outcomes. Because evidence-based practice (EBP) is known to improve the quality of healthcare and patient outcomes as well as decrease healthcare costs, there is currently an increased emphasis in clinical settings on promoting EBP. However, the understanding of care based on evidence is often far removed from clinical practice (Hockenberry, Wilson, & Barrera, 2006; Rycroft-Malone, Harvey, Seers, et al., 2004). This chapter describes essential concepts for developing an **environment** that fosters a culture of EBP and key strategies for successful implementation of EBP in clinical settings. Essential mechanisms for creating an evidence-based clinical environment that will be discussed include vision, engagement, integration, and evaluation (Figure 9.1; Hockenberry, Walden, Brown, et al., 2007).

A Vision for Evidence-Based Practice

Healthcare institutions with successful EBP programs begin with a vision and an understanding of the goals to be accomplished. A clear vision gives substance to the actions needed to transform a healthcare setting into an EBP environment. The EBP vision provides a compelling and motivating image of desired changes that result in achievement of excellence in clinical practice throughout the healthcare organization. An image of the future, defined as a shared mental framework, is created to begin the transformation process (see Box 9.1).

Reasons for transforming a clinical culture into an EBP environment are numerous, depending upon the type of clinical setting and its mission. For many institutions, the vision for EBP is based on regulatory initiatives and insurance-mandated outcomes. One such regulation is the Centers for Medicare and Medicaid Services' (CMS's) decision to stop paying for

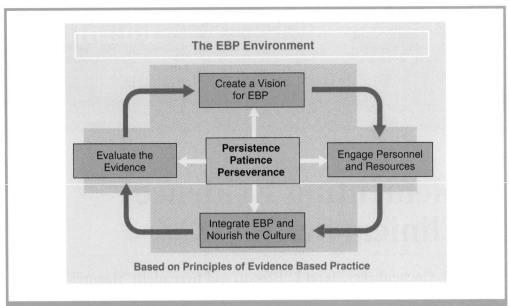

figure 9.1 — The EBP environment model (With permission from Hockenberry, M., Walden, M., Brown, T., & Barrera P. [2007]. Creating an evidence-based practice environment: One hospital's journey. *Journal of Nursing Care Quality*, 22[3]:223.)

"preventable complications" in hospitalized patients. Numerous hospital-acquired conditions that have current evidence-based guidelines for prevention were among the list that CMS ruled as nonreimbursable in late 2008. These complications that resulted from medical errors or improper care could have reasonably been avoided through the application of evidence-based guidelines (Rosenthal, 2007).

The Magnet Recognition Program also provides specific expectations for transforming a nursing culture into an environment that promotes superior performance through EBP (American Nurses Credentialing Center [ANCC], 2008). This program recognizes hospitals that demonstrate quality patient care, nursing excellence, and innovations in practice. Magnet hospitals must promote quality and disseminate best practices throughout nursing, which are attainable only through the pursuit of an EBP environment. Magnet recognition requirements include specific demonstration of expected outcomes for 2 years prior to submission of the Magnet application (ANCC). To acquire this type of evidence over time for nursing practice, an environment must promote staff use of an EBP approach to the care that is provided every day.

box 9.1

A shared mental framework exemplifies an institution's most closely held values and ideals that inspire and motivate administrators, researchers, and clinicians to participate in practice changes. It serves as the catalyst for change within the organization. With increasing emphasis on quality patient care and outcome metrics, a new image is emerging at hospitals that place tremendous value in providing excellence in care throughout the organization. A new, shared mental framework is established by administration's willingness to increase resources for quality initiatives and EBP programs.

Developing a Vision for Change

Understanding the importance of cultural change within a clinical environment frequently begins with a few passionate individuals who have a shared mental framework for the kind of quality care they want to provide their patients and families. The vision of a dedicated EBP team is critical to the success of implementation projects (Hockenberry et al., 2007). Chapter 12 elaborates further on creating a vision and motivating a change to EBP.

Early involvement of clinical experts and **EBP mentors** (i.e., clinicians who have advanced knowledge and skills in EBP as well as individual and organizational change strategies [Melnyk, 2007]) shapes the future vision for EBP at any institution. While increased knowledge and understanding are important to any EBP initiative, a key to changing actual behaviors is ownership of change. An effective method to obtain clinical support is to include experts or mentors at the beginning of an EBP project, preferably when the vision for change is first established. Administrative support for the vision is obtained as soon as those involved have organized their shared vision or mental framework. When possible, the project should be designated as an organizational priority prior to the first formal meeting. Box 9.2 provides an example of a vision for change through development of a pain prevention program within a children's hospital.

---

box 9.2

Creating a Vision for Change: Pain Prevention for Hospitalized Children

The first formal EBP initiative at the Texas Children's Hospital involved developing an EBP pain prevention protocol for use throughout the hospital. A procedural pain leadership group consisting of clinical nurse specialists from Acute Care, the Pediatric Intensive Care Unit (PICU), the Neonatal Intensive Care Unit (NICU), the Cancer Center, the chair of the Clinical Practice Council, a nurse researcher, and research assistant was established.

■ **Small steps toward change**

The pain prevention initiative began with small steps toward change. Leaders of this initiative recognized that the vision for change needed to first start within nursing. Specific nursing interventions that commonly cause pain for children were selected, and an intensive evidence review provided the strategies for improving pain management. Changes in practice began as a purposeful, selected focus rather than an attempt to transform pain management across all disciplines at once.

■ **Focusing awareness**

The evidence-based pain prevention initiative first began by increasing awareness that pain remains a major problem for hospitalized children. Many clinicians believed that pain intervention was not necessary for common nursing procedures and routinely performed painful procedures without intervention for a number of reasons because the painful period of time was limited for the child, or the clinician felt like such an expert at performing the procedure that the pain experienced was minimal. Since the procedural pain leadership group had completed an extensive review of the evidence and found that pain experiences of hospitalized children are significant and long lasting, regardless of the length of procedure or expertise of the provider, a new awareness of pain practices throughout the hospital was an essential first step for the EBP pain prevention program's vision.

table 9.1 EBP vision: transforming a clinical environment

Objective	Strategies
Develop a mental framework	• Develop a written summary of what you want to accomplish • Brainstorm with colleagues regarding the environment you want to create
Establish a motivating image for change	• Use creativity to capture attention of the clinical staff • Take advantage of real clinical scenarios to stress the need for changes in practice
Create specific goals	• Focus on short-term, attainable goals • Establish only two to three goals at a time
Gain administrative support	• Contact administrators responsible for clinical practice • Create a presentation that reflects the need for transforming the culture into an EBP environment • Seek administration support for the project to be identified as an organizational priority
Establish a leadership team	• Identify key personnel with a passion for EBP • Conduct small focus group meetings
Involve experts and EBP mentors in clinical practice	• Identify clinical experts and EBP mentors focused on the area • Engage clinical expert support

Keys to accomplishing a successful vision include preparation and planning. The old saying, "begin with the end in mind" serves vision planners well at this stage of an EBP initiative. Selecting strategies that promote small changes over time are known to be more effective than large-scale initiatives. Effective programs capture the momentum by acting quickly to disseminate the vision and by emphasizing small goals that are easily attainable (see Table 9.1). Small goals with measurable outcomes provide concrete examples of motivating the vision for change.

box 9.3

Sharing the Vision for Change

To develop a vision for needed changes in pain management, the project at the Texas Children's Hospital began by increasing awareness that hospitalized infants and children commonly experience pain. A video was used to create a dramatic image and raise nurses' emotions regarding the need for change. The video demonstrated two infants undergoing a heel stick; one infant was given a sucrose/pacifier intervention and the other infant underwent the heel stick without pain intervention. The video showed dramatic differences in infant behavior during the heel stick procedure. The infant who received standard care without pain intervention cried, moved, and thrashed his arms and legs throughout the entire procedure. The infant who received the pain intervention quietly sucked on the pacifier without movement during the entire heel stick. While a written summary of the evidence supporting sucrose as a pain intervention for young infants was given to all staff, the video was much more powerful in creating a needed change in our mental framework for managing pain. After viewing the video, numerous staff began using the sucrose/pacifier intervention prior to heel sticks as well as for other painful procedures.

Sharing the vision for excellence in practice is perhaps the most essential catalyst for promoting EBP. Initiatives that are most effective in changing the environment engage strategies that share the vision for change as early as possible. Expert clinicians may be less aware of the need for change than their nonexperienced colleagues. Emphasizing the need for change must be direct and to the point. Recognizing that one's own patient care is less than excellent is often painful for clinicians to realize (see Box 9.3). Establishing the direction for EBP in a clinical environment sets the stage for an organized approach for all future initiatives. While process toward change takes time, establishing a clear direction for change provides focus toward a common goal—improved patient outcomes.

Promote Engagement

Once a vision for EBP is created, staff at all levels must be engaged in high-priority clinical issues to develop a successful, supportive environment (see Table 9.2). Clinical staff are best positioned to identify variations in practice and ineffective processes, as they often have a vested interest in streamlining inefficiencies. Administrators, responsible for the clinical areas where changes will occur, who engage early in the planning process are likely to share ownership. A key strategy for success is involvement of staff and leaders of all disciplines who are directly impacted by the potential change, including likely early adopters as well as those who may have difficulty accepting the change.

Assess and Eliminate Barriers

Barrier assessment is an integral component throughout both the engagement and integration phases of EBP implementation (Mohide & King, 2003). Change, even when welcome, is stressful to everyone. Chapter 12 provides additional information on organizational change concepts

table 9.2 **Promoting engagement in EBP**

Objective	Strategies
Engage staff and stakeholders in assessing and eliminating barriers	• Engage stakeholders to identify educational content and strategies to learn about the practice change • Seek information about attitudes toward the affected practice directly from staff • Involve influential staff and leaders in conducting discussions with colleagues
Prioritize clinical issues	• Select clinical issues of direct interest and responsibility of clinician stakeholders • Choose issues with solid empiric evidence to begin an organizational area's EBP endeavors
Evaluate the infrastructure	• Determine the individuals and committees who have decision-making authority • Gain administrative support for adequate time and personnel for the initiative • Enlist experts to lead EBP initiatives • Ensure access to databases, search engines, and full-text articles
Develop experts in the evidence-based process	• Utilize leaders within the organization or form an academic partnership to provide expertise in research, EBP design, and evaluation • Provide formal classes and/or small-group sessions on finding and evaluating evidence • Mentor staff in critically appraising research studies and formulating practice recommendations

> **box 9.4**
>
> ## Engage Staff and Stakeholders of all Levels
>
> ■ Staff clinicians
> ■ Leadership team members (e.g., executives, administrators)
> ■ Advanced practice registered nurses
> ■ Stakeholders of all disciplines directly impacted
> ■ Physicians
> ■ Family advisory board
> ■ Allied-health professionals
> ■ Doctorally prepared nurse researchers
> ■ EBP mentors

that support processes for moving a culture toward EBP. Stakeholder resistance to change must be explored early since it frequently results from numerous factors including hesitation to break traditional practice, unfamiliarity with how evidence will improve patient outcomes, or misconceptions regarding time and effort needed to implement practice change. Box 9.4 provides examples of the types of staff and stakeholders that, when included throughout the process, can help assess and eliminate barriers. Common barriers to EBP implementation include inadequate knowledge and skills, weak beliefs about the value of EBP, poor attitudes toward EBP, lack of EBP mentors, social and organizational influences, and economic restrictions (Gale & Schaffer, 2009; Grol & Wensing, 2004; Melnyk, Fineout-Overholt, Feinstein, et al., 2004; Melnyk, Fineout-Overholt, & Mays, 2008).

Lack of knowledge can create barriers to daily evidence-based care due to inadequate understanding of EBP principles, unfamiliarity with how evidence will improve patient outcomes, and lack of specific skills and knowledge needed to implement change. The best evidence-based policies are of no value to the patients when the staff lack knowledge of how to implement them in practice; the right information must be in the right place at the right time and presented in a meaningful way (Feifer, Fifield, Ornstein, et al., 2004).

Weak beliefs about the value of EBP and attitudinal barriers can be more difficult to overcome than knowledge barriers. Focus group discussions and anonymous electronic surveys can be valuable in identifying beliefs and attitudes about current and proposed practice changes. Traditional educational techniques (e.g., lectures and web-based training), when used alone, are usually ineffective in changing attitudes. Interactive discussions with influential colleagues, seeing the positive impact of change, and removal of perceived barriers can be powerful in overcoming resistance. Box 9.5 provides an example of barrier assessment and strategies used for elimination during an EBP procedural pain initiative.

Findings from research have indicated that a lack of EBP mentors in the environment also can be a barrier to implementing EBP by point-of-care staff (Melnyk et al., 2004). Mentors who have in-depth knowledge and skills in both EBP as well as individual and organizational change strategies also are a key strategy for sustaining change once it is realized. Chapter 15 expands upon the role of the EBP mentor in advancing best practice in clinical settings.

Social and organizational barriers to change include lack of support by leaders, disagreement among clinicians, and limited resources to support change (Grol & Wensing, 2004). Effective barrier assessment includes discerning knowledge, attitudes, and beliefs of mid-level and upper-level administrators surrounding practice change and their perceived roles in communicating support for this change. Peer group discussions can be very influential, and

box 9.5

Assessing and Eliminating Barriers

In the procedural pain initiative at the Texas Children's Hospital, staff members identified several barriers to prevent pain prior to performing venipunctures. The project team members implemented multiple solutions to eliminate the barriers at the organizational level.

Assessing Barriers

- Prolonged time to obtain orders and medications and implement interventions
- Lack of knowledge about what is in the hospital formulary
- Attitude: "Even if pain medication is used, children are already stressed out/crying"; perception that meds cause vasoconstriction which leads to multiple sticks; "I'm good so it only hurts for a moment"
- Unit culture: unaccustomed to medicating prior to needlesticks

Eliminating Barriers

- Time demands were reduced through the development of a procedural pain protocol that bundled multiple medications with varying onset times: immediate (oral sucrose, vapocoolant spray), 12 minutes (buffered lidocaine injection), 10 minutes (lidocaine iontophoresis), and 30 minutes (lidocaine cream). Nurses could select floor stock medications within the protocol that were appropriate for the child's age, procedural urgency, and developmental considerations. A pharmacist reviewed and entered the protocol into the patient's medication profile upon admission to the hospital.
- Additional medications were brought into formulary to accommodate urgent needs. Bundling the medications into a protocol increased the knowledge about what was available to prevent venipuncture pain. Educational modules and skills sessions were conducted to familiarize staff nurses with new and unfamiliar medications and administration techniques.
- A multifaceted approach was used to change individual attitudes and unit cultures. Videos of infants receiving heelsticks with and without sucrose and of older children talking about their venipuncture experiences with and without lidocaine premedication were shown. Results of published research studies on the intermediate and long-term effects of unrelieved pain during procedures were disseminated through online modules. A commitment to evaluate the medication in several children was obtained from several unit IV experts. Unit administrators communicated support for the practice in staff meetings and with individual nurses. Champions for change routinely asked colleagues what medications were used when starting IVs.

chapter 9

211

informal leaders may weigh in even stronger than formal leaders on whether practice change will actually occur. Overlooked process details can impede a well-accepted practice change, including anticipated economic and workload implications. Exploring the economic and workload impact of a practice change early in a project and securing administrative support when there may be potential increase in cost or workload can prevent these barriers from impeding progress. Economic considerations must include that an increase in one type of cost may be readily offset with savings in time (i.e., workload), satisfaction, or the additional expense of patient complications when best practices are not implemented.

Prioritize Clinical Issues

In order to spark EBP, it is best to start with a clinical issue of direct interest to clinicians, since changing one's own practice can be much easier than changing the practice of another discipline or specialty. Box 9.6 provides an example of prioritizing clinical issues for EBP initiatives. Initial efforts should be focused on maximizing the likelihood of success (Graham & Harrison, 2005). Evidence-based practice changes are most likely to be successful when they are based on solid **external** as well as **internal evidence**, provide clear steps for change, and fit within the parameters of the clinician's routine practice. When an organization's readiness for change is assessed, regardless of whether the change will have a large or small impact, an easy win is more likely to occur. A practice issue that aligns with the organization/administrators' key priorities or is a focus of quality initiatives mandated by regulatory agencies, such as the Joint Commission or the Institute for Healthcare Improvement, is likely to gain administrative support more readily than an isolated initiative.

Evaluate the Infrastructure

Organizational leaders must dedicate resources, including time, to provide support for staff and their EBP mentors to ask clinical questions; search for and critically appraise evidence; analyze internal evidence; develop practice recommendations; plan changes; and develop, implement, and evaluate the EBP project. Although administrative support is crucial, it is only one of the starting points and will not lead to success on its own. Administrators should seek guidance from expert clinicians, EBP mentors, and researchers within the organization while providing authoritative as well as financial support for the EBP initiative.

---

box 9.6

Prioritize Clinical Issues

Procedures that nurses most often perform were selected as the first phase of the procedural pain initiative at the Texas Children's Hospital. Peripheral IV access, venipuncture for specimens, port access, and injections were identified as the highest priority procedures for pain prevention. Nasogastric (NG) tube and urinary catheter insertions also were considered but dropped early in the initiative. These two procedures were performed less frequently than needlesticks, and there was scant and conflicting evidence on pain prevention techniques. While important, they would have delayed protocol implementation and have a weaker evidence foundation than the other procedures.

Narrow Focus Through PICO Questions

- In children, is EMLA a better anesthetic cream than LMX in reducing pain during peripheral intravenous (PIV) access, venipuncture, and injections?
- In children, is lidocaine iontophoresis an effective anesthetic for relieving pain during PIV access?
- In infants 16 months old, is 24% sucrose more effective than 50% or 75% sucrose in decreasing crying time during and after PIV insertion?
- In children, is buffered lidocaine effective in reducing pain during PIV insertion?
- In children, is ethyl chloride effective in reducing pain without vasoconstriction during PIV access and venipuncture?
- In children, is ethyl chloride effective in reducing pain during port access?

Resources that support the ability to locate and critically evaluate relevant literature are essential for EBP implementation (Klem & Weiss, 2005). Access to an academic medical library, databases, search engines, and full-text articles needs to be available for the EBP team to be successful in securing evidence to support practice change. While PubMed and the Cochrane Library are free to search and view abstracts, to access electronic full-text articles requires a subscription to electronic journals, some of which can be accessed only through specific databases. Chapter 3 provides sources and strategies for finding relevant evidence.

Working within already-established committees and councils can be an effective strategy to gain momentum for an EBP environment. Team members should be engaged in identifying how an EBP project fits within the committee's responsibilities, priorities, and agenda. Involving multiple approval bodies within the organizational hierarchy in the engagement phase can increase the number of individuals and teams eager to ensure an EBP project's success. To allow extended time for topic exploration, focus groups may need to be formed within existing committees. Gaining consensus for a shared vision to improve patient outcomes can help break down process silos and communication barriers. Agreement that practice changes should be based on evidence, rather than individual preferences or tradition, is a critical component that EBP teams may need to revisit several times during small-group discussions (Mohide & King, 2003).

Develop Experts in the Evidence-Based Practice Process

Expertise available to lead an EBP team may exist within an organization or may require a partner from an academic or other healthcare setting. Expertise in evaluating and synthesizing the research literature is crucial. Education related to all steps of the EBP process through formal classes and/or small-group skill building sessions can expand the pool of EBP experts and mentors. Staff and clinical experts may be inexperienced at critically appraising research studies and evaluating evidence. With education and mentorship, clinicians who are novices in the EBP process can learn to analyze evidence and formulate practice recommendations within a structured environment (Benner, 1984). Gaining understanding of the *concepts* of EBP prior to the actual practice change is essential. Mentoring clinical staff eager to learn the steps of the EBP process is an important strategy that eventually develops EBP clinical experts throughout the institution (Penz & Bassendowski, 2006).

Evidence-Based Practice Integration

Ideas without action are worthless.

Helen Keller

Integrating EBP into clinical practice is one of the most challenging tasks faced by clinicians and leaders in healthcare settings (Rycroft-Malone et al., 2004; Rycroft-Malone, Kitson, Harvey, et al., 2002; Mohide & King, 2003). Evidence-based education and mentoring initiated during the engagement phase should continue during the integration phase, which is now directed toward overcoming knowledge and skill deficits along with stakeholder skepticism in order to enhance the likelihood of a positive EBP change (Melnyk, 2002; Rycroft-Malone et al., 2002, 2004). Bridging the gap between evidence and practice is essential to bring about cultural change within a clinical environment (Billings & Kowalski, 2006). Education alone will not change behavior (Melnyk, 2002). Interventions need to be tailored to target groups and settings and include individual, team, and organizational approaches (Grol & Grimshaw, 2003). Successful

table 9.3 Integrating EBP into the clinical environment

Objective	Strategies
Establish formal implementation teams	• Integrate experts in change theory at the systems level, such as advanced practice registered nurses • Include expert staff members to ensure clinical applicability, feasibility, and adoption into practice
Build excitement	• Exhibit passion for the practice change • Enlist local opinion leaders who can attest to the need for practice change • Bring in outside speakers who have the potential to connect and inspire key stakeholders • Create discomfort with the status quo
Disseminate evidence	• Utilize multifaceted strategies to overcome knowledge deficits, skill deficits, and skepticism • Promote experience sharing to emphasize the need for change and positive outcomes of change • Provide time to assimilate new practices
Develop clinical tools	• Anticipate tools and processes that the staff will need to transform practice • Revise patient care documentation records • Ensure easy access to clinical resources • Integrate alerts and reminders into workflow processes at the point of care • Repeatedly expose the staff to evidence-based information
Pilot test	• Choose pilot sites with consideration to unit leadership strength, patient population diversity, acuity, and geographic location • Address the root causes of problems • Decide to adopt, adapt, or abandon at the end of the pilot
Preserve energy sources	• Engage support personnel • Implement smaller, more manageable projects • Anticipate setbacks and have patience and persistence
Allow enough time	• Develop incremental project steps • Establish a timeline
Celebrate success	• Acknowledge the staff instrumental in process • Ensure recognition by supervisors and administration • Recognize the staff in presentations

integration occurs when evidence is robust, the physical environment is receptive to change, and the change process is appropriately facilitated (see Table 9.3).

Establish Formal Implementation Teams

Establishing a formal EBP project implementation team early in the process is an essential key to success. This leadership team should be appointed to guide EBP changes, and informal and formal coordinators must be engaged at the unit level to champion EBP (Rycroft-Malone et al., 2002, 2004). Advanced practice registered nurses are change agents adept at systems-level project design and often have the advantage of clinical experience with practice variations and outcomes evaluation (Ahrens, 2005; Melnyk, Fineout-Overholt, Williamson, et al., 2009). A leadership team that includes masters and/or doctorally prepared nurses and expert staff nurses is essential for determining the clinical applicability and feasibility of practice change recommendations and the likelihood of integrating evidence into practice and evaluating patient outcomes (Thompson, Cullum, McCaughan, et al., 2004).

Build Excitement

One of the key factors to success of any EBP change is building excitement during implementation. Team members who exhibit passion can ignite a fire in their colleagues. Recognized national experts lend stature and credibility to the idea of implementing a practice change, whereas experts within the organization can attest to the relevance of the practice in local settings and add synergy for change. It is essential to engage the staff by demonstrating the link between proposed EBP changes and desired patient outcomes (Feifer et al., 2004). Raising awareness of the need for change can be strengthened with baseline **practice-based data** (e.g., quality and performance improvement data). Creating a level of discomfort with the status quo by sharing evidence of improved outcomes at other healthcare settings can create a readiness for change. Fostering enthusiasm by unit/service-based staff and leaders can lead to a shared ownership in the success of an EBP initiative.

Disseminate Evidence

Passive educational approaches such as dissemination of clinical practice guidelines and didactic educational sessions are usually ineffective and unlikely to result in practice change (Fineout-Overholt, Melnyk, & Schultz, 2005). Education should be planned to overcome knowledge deficits, skill deficits, and skepticism. Eliminating knowledge deficits includes not only communicating what should be done (*how* to change) but also *why* a change will be beneficial (i.e., the outcome) and the *evidence* to support the change. It is important to share positive outcomes of the change including external evidence, internal evidence (e.g., quality improvement data), actual patient experiences, and stories from authentic voices (i.e., practitioners using the recommended practice). Raising the level of emotion through sharing experiences is a powerful way to increase motivation of others toward the practice change. Stories not only provide powerful images of the need for change, but also a mechanism to communicate the outcomes associated with change. The impetus for change is different for each individual; therefore, multifaceted interventions for disseminating evidence are more likely to produce change than a singularly focused endeavor (e.g., education only; Grol & Grimshaw, 2003).

Strengthening beliefs about the value of EBP and changing attitudes can be much more difficult than imparting knowledge. A shared understanding of the problem and identified gaps in outcomes can be a foundation to valuing the change in practice. Evidence summaries should be shared with practitioners, along with persons who would be involved in consensus building. Perceived barriers need to be removed, and processes may need to be streamlined to create time and support for the new practice.

Develop Clinical Tools

To enact change, the EBP implementation team must anticipate new processes and tools that the staff will need to transform practice. Development of resources that match interventions and overall strategies can greatly facilitate changes in clinical practices (Kresse, Kuklinski, & Cacchione, 2007). Clinical tools to enhance appropriateness and consistency of care may include written guidelines, EBP summaries, preprinted orders, and algorithms. Availability and ease of use are key components to the successful adoption of any of these resources. (See Box 9.7 for an example of an EBP Summary template.)

Alerts and reminders can be helpful if well integrated into workflow processes. Whether electronic or paper, optimal timing and placement of reminders in relation to decision making about the care practices are essential. Guideline prompts at the point of care can be programmed into an electronic medical record, medication administration record, or even "smart" infusion

box 9.7

Example of an EBP Critical Appraisal Template

Ask the question	**Question:**
	Background summary
Search for the evidence	**Search strategies:**
	Dates/search limits
	Key words/terms/controlled vocabulary

Rapidly critically appraise, evaluate, and synthesize the evidence

Summary of findings

Integrate the evidence

Recommendation for practice, research, or education

References

Cite all references

pumps. Clinical decision support systems that provide electronic links to EBP information within an electronic health record or organizational website can positively influence an evidence-based practitioner's use of recommended practice changes.

Pilot Test the Evidence-Based Practice Change

Implementing a new EBP change requires restructuring of the flow of daily work so that routine processes make it natural for the clinician to give care in a new way. Even educated and motivated providers can have difficulty practicing in the desired manner without daily environmental supports. Piloting changes on a small scale with a commitment to grow the practice change with staff feedback can promote positive attitudes along with engagement in the new practice. Plan to quickly respond to questions and concerns and address the root causes of problems during the pilot phase. Early evaluation results should be shared with staff at the end of each pilot cycle, and a decision should be made to adopt, adapt, or abandon the proposed practice.

Pilot testing in a select number of patient care areas before moving to widespread implementation can be useful in identifying issues of clinical applicability and feasibility that will impact future efforts at successful EBP implementation (Rosswurm & Larrabee, 1999; Titler, Kleiber, Steelman, et al., 2001). Leadership capacity, populations served, patient acuity, and geographic location are some of the initial considerations for choosing a pilot site. In addition, sites that are known to have early adopters as well as those known to be difficult or resistant implementation sites are important to consider in choosing the site to conduct a pilot project. Early adopters can serve as training sites for later adopters. Well-managed programs with a long history of successful implementation of initiatives are likely to establish practice change early in the pilot phase. However, establishing an EBP change on a struggling unit can communicate to others that change can occur even in difficult clinical settings.

Preserve Energy Sources

Change in a dynamic healthcare environment places added stress and strain on clinicians in the care setting. When implementing EBP changes, it is important to develop strategies to maintain excitement and preserve energy resources. Implementing smaller, more manageable projects in phases

box 9.8

Small Steps of Change

During the engagement phase of the procedural pain initiative at the Texas Children's Hospital, many nurses became uncomfortable with the status quo and were eager to have broader access to pain prevention medications. The protocol was anticipated to take several months to allow for critically appraising evidence, building algorithms, gaining consensus, and piloting.

Sucrose had been used for years in the hospital's NICU, but young infants admitted to other areas were not given sucrose. The first step of change was to establish an upper age limit for sucrose and permit its use anywhere in the organization. The second step was to remove a time barrier by adding sucrose and LMX (4% lidocaine cream) to floor stock in many areas. Additional medications were added to formulary and available for use by individual order as the third step of the initiative. The final step was to implement the procedural pain protocol, a group of medications for multiple procedures, and expand floor stock availability.

Protocol

Additional medications to prevent the pain caused by needlesticks brought in to hospital formulary

Sucrose and LMX as floor stock

Sucrose use outside the NICU

Sucrose use within the NICU

rather than introducing a single large EBP project may reduce fatigue and build confidence that the recommended change is achievable and sustainable given adequate time and resources (see Box 9.8). Integrating additional "champions for change" during new phases of a project can bring new energy and ownership to a project. Project leaders and teams should anticipate setbacks with patience and persistence. Periodically sharing small successes along the way can foster continued excitement for the project and reduce fatigue that is often associated with lagging outcomes (Kotter & Cohen, 2002).

Timeline for Success

Planning practice changes for an EBP project includes evaluating current practice, identifying gaps in "what is" and "what is desired," establishing incremental steps of the project, and setting timelines. Competing priorities within an area or organization can influence the timing needed to embark upon a successful EBP project. When conducting a large change, often it is easier to accomplish it when customarily busy periods are over or when leaders are as free as possible from competing responsibilities. Project timelines for EBP changes are extremely variable and can be influenced by many environmental issues, such as the size of the project, staff time commitment, EBP expertise, expediency of decision making, and the urgency of the need for practice change. (See Box 9.9 for an example of an EBP project timeline.)

Celebrate Success

Celebrate success early in the development phases of practice change recommendations. It is important to acknowledge members of the project team who are instrumental in the planning and implementation process in meetings where the practice is discussed, in hospital newsletters, or

box 9.9

Sample EBP Implementation Project Plan

Project timelines for EBP changes are highly variable. Several project components may overlap or occur simultaneously.

Project component	Timeframe
Develop a vision for change	Variable
Identify and narrow practice topic	1–3 weeks
Evaluate current practice and analyze recent quality data	4–6 weeks
Engage staff and stakeholders	4 weeks
Evaluate the infrastructure and establish formal teams	4 weeks
Develop and refine PICO questions	2–4 weeks
Develop search strategy and conduct search	4–6 weeks
Critically appraise, evaluate, and synthesize the evidence	4–8 weeks
Formulate practice recommendations	2 weeks
Celebrate success of progress to date!	Ongoing
Gain stakeholder support	2–4 weeks
Assess and eliminate barriers	Variable
Develop clinical tools	Variable
Conduct rapid cycle pilot	Variable
Celebrate success of progress to date!	Ongoing
Gain approval for change	Variable
Disseminate evidence and educate staff	4 weeks
Implement practice change	1 week
Celebrate success of progress to date!	Ongoing
Measure clinical outcomes	Ongoing
Analyze measurement data and refine practice and processes	Ongoing
Celebrate success!	Ongoing

in any venue in which materials related to the project are presented. Recognize individuals and teams who adopt and implement the new practice. Positive outcomes from preliminary measurements of success should be shared with all point-of-care providers as well as other key stakeholders. Clinicians and administrators who see the positive results of an EBP project will be more likely to engage in and support future EBP initiatives. Leaders and point-of-care providers who are responsible for promoting EBP change should be encouraged to share their findings through presentations and publications so other professionals and institutions may benefit from their EBP endeavors.

Evaluation: Linking Evidence-Based Practice to Clinical Outcomes

One of the most difficult aspects of EBP is assuring that change has occurred and, even more importantly, has resulted in positive, sustained outcomes. All too frequently, patient care outcomes in clinical settings indicate a need for changes that demand immediate action by administrators and leaders, which may place clinicians in a practice environment that is shaped by practice standards and initiatives that are not well thought out or evaluated for successful outcomes. This "crisis orientation" to clinical practice change results in less than impressive results. Well-intentioned administrators often demand changes without considering the time taken to change a culture. Policy changes that make it difficult for the clinician to provide quality care in a timely manner will never succeed. For example, EBP that requires supplies and resources that are not readily available to the clinicians will not produce positive clinical outcomes because the clinicians will not integrate changes in their practice that are difficult or impossible to perform. For sustainable change to occur, time must be taken to evaluate influence of EBP on patient care processes.

Evaluating outcomes produced by clinical practice changes is an important, yet often overlooked step in EBP (Titler et al., 2001). Outcomes reflect the impact that is being made with the change to best practice. When an effective intervention from research is translated into real-world clinical practice where confounding variables are not controlled and the patients are not the same as those involved in research, the outcomes may be different. Evaluating outcomes of an EBP change is important to determine whether the findings from research are similar when translated into the real-world clinical practice setting. It is important to measure outcomes before (i.e., baseline), shortly after (i.e., short-term follow-up), and for a reasonable length of time after (i.e., long-term follow-up) the practice change. Each of these points in time provides data on the sustainable impact of the EBP change.

The complexity of health-related outcomes associated with clinical practice presents an opportunity to evaluate the impact of EBP in the environment from multiple perspectives. Six areas of evidence, identified by the Institute of Medicine (IOM, 2000), are presented as important EBP evaluation indicators:

- Outcome measures
- Quality care improvement
- Patient-centered quality care
- Efficiency of processes
- Environmental changes
- Professional expertise

These indicators reflect evidence in the environment that demonstrates effective changes in clinical practice (see Table 9.4). Health outcome measures must be a part of the EBP environment to determine whether healthcare interventions actually make a difference.

Outcome Measures

Outcome measures have been defined as those healthcare results that can be quantified, such as health status, death, disability, iatrogenic effects of treatment, health behaviors, and the economic impact of therapy and illness management (Bethel, 2000; IOM, 2000; Titler et al., 2001). Health outcome measures are used to evaluate changes in clinical practice, support healthcare decision making, and establish new policies or practice guidelines. Outcome-based healthcare reimbursement is a growing trend that provides support for the importance of using appropriate clinical

table 9.4 **EBP evaluation in the clinical environment**

Objective	Measurement Description
Outcome measures	Outcome measures quantify medical outcomes such as health status, death, disability, iatrogenic effects of treatment, health behaviors, and the economic impact of therapy and illness management.
Quality care improvement	Managing common symptoms such as pain, fatigue, nausea and vomiting, sleep disturbances, appetite changes, and depression caused by many acute and chronic diseases.
Patient-centered quality care	Measures include effective communication with healthcare personnel; open, nonhurried interactions; presentation of all options for care; open discussion of the illness or disease; sensitivity to pain and emotional distress; consideration of the cultural and religious beliefs of the patient and family; being respectful and considerate; nonavoidance of the specific issues; empathy; patience; and a caring attitude and environment.
Efficiency of processes	Appropriate timing of interventions, effective discharge planning, and efficient utilization of hospital beds are exemplars of efficiency of processes indicators.
Environmental changes	Evaluation of policy and procedure adherence, unit resource availability, and healthcare professional access to supplies and materials essential to implement best practices.
Professional expertise	Knowledge and expertise of clinical staff.

measures. Important questions to ask regarding measurement of outcomes from an EBP implementation project include

- Are the outcomes of interest sensitive to change over time?
- How will the outcome(s) of interest be measured (e.g., subjectively through self-report and/or objectively by observation)?
- Are there existing valid and reliable instruments to measure the outcomes of interest?
- Who will measure the outcomes, and will training be necessary?
- What is the cost of measuring the outcomes?

Identifying these aspects of measurement of outcomes will assist in the quality of outcomes obtained.

Quality Care Improvement

Quality care improvement measures complement established health outcome measures by further quantifying how interventions impact the quality of patients' and families' lives (Titler et al., 2001). Quality care improvement indicators are often used to demonstrate the effectiveness of symptom management interventions. Effectively managing common symptoms caused by many acute and chronic diseases can provide specific data to demonstrate quality care improvement in clinical practice. Often, quality indicators demonstrate the existence of a clinical issue as well as provide information about successful evidence implementation and change.

Patient-Centered Quality Care

Increasing emphasis has been placed on patient-centered quality care measures (IOM, 2000). These measures are defined as the value patients and families place on the healthcare received. Patient-centered quality care requires a philosophy of care that views the patient as an equal

box 9.10

Patient-Centered Quality Care

Crucial to promoting patient-centered quality care is open, honest discussion of the illness or disease. Consideration of the cultural and religious beliefs of the patient and family, being respectful and considerate, nonavoidance of the specific issues, empathy, patience, and a caring attitude and environment are all important. Use of measures that critically evaluate key aspects of patient-centered quality care within a healthcare organization can provide crucial evidence that differentiates a good healthcare setting from an outstanding one.

Busy hospital environments often prevent family coping strategies from effectively being utilized even though evidence supports the importance of family presence. Time constraints often prevent patient-centered quality care. One family at the Texas Children's Hospital felt strongly that they needed to place a prayer rug under their child and to say a prayer over the child immediately before anesthesia. While this activity added a few more minutes to the preanesthesia preparation, it resulted in the child being relaxed and fully cooperating with the anesthesiologist once the prayer was completed. The child went to sleep without a struggle lying on the prayer rug. Parents left the anesthesia induction room feeling that their needs were met and patient/family-centered care was provided.

partner rather than a passive recipient of care, much like the EBP paradigm, in which patient preferences must be part of the decision making (see Box 9.10).

Commonly, patient-centered quality care measures have been described as "soft" indicators and received limited attention. Policy makers, healthcare organizations, and healthcare professionals now recognize the importance of organizing and managing health systems to ensure patient-centered quality care (Rosswurm & Larrabee, 1999).

Efficiency of Processes

As healthcare organizations become more sophisticated in evaluation strategies, it becomes essential to evaluate the efficiency of healthcare delivery processes. Information technology provides numerous EBP strategies to improve care delivery methods at every level in the organization. Efficiency in providing EBP care and evaluating the best possible process for implementing these practices leads to excellence in care and cost containment. Appropriate timing of interventions, effective discharge planning, and efficient utilization of hospital beds are examples of efficiency of processes indicators. These indicators are directly associated with outcomes (See Box 9.11).

Environmental Changes

Environmental change evaluation reflects the creation of a culture that promotes the use of EBP throughout the organization. Environmental outcome measures are uniquely different in comparison with efficiency of processes in that a process can change or patient outcomes change, yet there is no impact on the environment. This difference often is observed with policy and procedure changes that are carefully updated and filed into procedure manuals, yet no practice changes actually occur in the clinical setting. Examples of indicators of environmental changes include evaluation of policy and procedure adherence, unit resource availability, and healthcare professional use of supplies and materials essential to implement best practices.

---

box 9.11

Barriers that Influence Efficiency of Process Changes

Obstructive barriers to EBP implementation often impede measurable clinical outcomes. Recent implementation of an evidence-based guideline for managing bronchiolitis demonstrates the resistance to change that significantly influenced the efficiency of the EBP implementation process. An EBP review revealed that earlier discharge could occur when discharge planning was initiated earlier during hospitalization. During the implementation phase of this guideline, two different healthcare disciplines refused to compromise over who would notify the physician about early discharge orders, stating it was not their role to obtain the order. Rather than evaluate what was best for the patient and family, these professionals refused to change their practice and the administrators had to intervene to persuade a compromise.

---

box 9.12

Linking Clinical Outcomes to Professional Expertise

Placement of NG tubes in infants and children is a common and often difficult nursing procedure. Using the gold standard (radiographic documentation), Ellett, Croffie, Cohen, et al. (2005) found that more than 20% of NG tubes were incorrectly placed in 72 acutely ill children. Other studies quote misplacement as high as 43.5% in children (Ellett & Beckstrand, 1999; Ellett, Maahs, & Frosee, 1998). Displaced NG tubes can create significant morbidity and mortality.

Throughout numerous children's hospitals across the country, changes in assessing NG tube placement are being implemented because there is substantial evidence that the traditional method of auscultation is not effective in determining proper placement (Wethus, 2004). A combination of measures to ensure NG placement including pH, tube length, and physical symptoms have been shown to be more effective in the assessment of NG tube placement in children (Ellett, 2004, 2006; Ellet et al., 2005; Huffman, Piper, Jarczyk, et al., 2004; Metheny et al., 2005; Metheny & Stewart, 2002).

However, there is significant discussion throughout the country that it is difficult to change traditional nursing practice even when there is evidence to indicate that auscultation for proper NG tube placement is not safe practice. Policy changes without education and reinforcement of this new EBP approach to NG tube placement will never be effective in producing measurable change in clinical outcomes.

Professional Expertise

Excellence in providing the best possible healthcare cannot occur without expert providers. Increasing sophistication in healthcare technology places significant demands on institutions to employ healthcare professionals with appropriate expertise. Professional expertise promotes excellence by establishing expectations for adherence to accepted standards of care essential for best practice. Without healthcare providers' expertise, institutions are often unable to determine why specific outcomes are not being met (see Box 9.12).

Implementing Evidence in Clinical Settings: Examples from the Field

This section presents two examples from the field of successful EBP implementation projects. Both of these projects started with identification of the clinical problem at their hospitals as a result of a spirit of inquiry.

In the first example, Gutierrez and Smith (2008) provide a report on how an EBP implementation project reduced falls in their hospital's definitive observation unit. The problem that was identified (Step 0 in the EBP process) was that falls, which cost a hospital an average of $11,402 per fall depending upon injury and length of stay, in a high-acuity cardiac and medical surgical telemetry unit were exceeding the California Nursing Outcomes Coalition benchmark for hospitals similar in size. Therefore, the following PICOT question (Step 1 in the EBP Process) was asked: In a convenience sample of inpatients determined to be at high risk for falling (P), will identifying and modifying practices determined to be obstructive to implementation of an evidence-based fall prevention practice (I) measurably reduce the occurrence of falls (O) compared with current practice (C)? A search for the evidence to answer the PICOT question (Step 2 in the EBP Process) was conducted, which revealed 100 publications. Twenty-two of these publications underwent thorough review, and 18 were selected to guide the EBP implementation project. Critical appraisal, evaluation, and synthesis of these studies (Step 3 of the EBP process) led to the following conclusions: (a) the etiology of falls is multifactorial, and (b) interventions that reduce falls include regular hourly rounding, educational oversight of an active prevention protocol, an assessment tool, appropriate lighting, and a room clear of clutter and trip hazards.

Based on the evidence, an action plan was developed (Step 4 of the EBP process) that included a team to lead the project, which consisted of a bedside nurse (a fellow), an advanced practice nurse (the mentor), and a clinical nurse specialist (the project mentor), who worked on creating and implementing the EBP change to reduce falls. Paid time was given to work on the project (i.e., 6–8-hour paid monthly sessions over 5 months, and 48 hours paid nonclinical time). The fellow recruited the education training team that consisted of two day-shift and two night-shift registered nurses who ended up being champions for the project. Baseline data regarding current practices were collected to prevent falls, including surveys with nurses and physicians regarding what interventions they were using that helped to prevent falls. Based on the critical appraisal of external evidence found in the literature search as well as internal evidence generated from the hospital staff, a SAFE (Specialty Adult Focused Environment) area and evidence-based fall prevention protocol was embedded into a new standard of evidence-based care for fall prevention. Measurement of the baseline fall rate indicated that in the previous three quarters before the EBP protocol was implemented, fall rates rose from 3.0/1,000 patient days to 4.87/1,000 patient days. In the first phase of the EBP change, fall rates dropped to 3.59/1,000 patient days, and staff knowledge increased regarding the use of the fall prevention protocol (Step 5 of the EBP process). The authors completed the EBP process with publishing their findings (Step 6), and acknowledged that the champions on the unit were key to success of the project.

In a second example, Powers, Brower, and Tolliver (2007) report on the outcomes of an EBP project undertaken at their hospital to reduce the incidence of ventilator associated pneumonia (VAP) in neuroscience patients. As one of the most frequent complications among critically ill patients, patients with VAP have increased ICU length of stay costing an average of $57,000 per occurrence and a mortality rate of 12%–71% (Step 0 in EBP). As a result of identifying this problem, the following PICOT question was formulated: In adult neuroscience patients (P), does implementation of an evidence-based oral hygiene protocol (I) versus the current protocol being used (C) result in fewer episodes of VAP? (Step 1 in EBP). The search for evidence and critical appraisal (Steps 2 and 3 in EBP) revealed that a positive association exists between dental plaque and VAP, and findings from several studies have linked antiseptic rinses to the prevention of VAP.

Therefore, a multidisciplinary ventilator management program team was developed with a goal to decrease VAP. This team developed an evidence-based protocol for oral care that consisted of use of an antiseptic rinse with brushing the teeth every 12 hours, use of oral swabs every 4 hours, and deep oral-pharyngeal suctioning every 12 hours for ventilated neuroscience patients (Step 4 in EBP). In the first phase of implementation, the neuroscience unit went 13 weeks without any cases of VAP and 20 weeks with only one case (Step 5 in EBP). The findings were published (Step 6 in EBP), and the authors noted that 5 months into the evaluation period, several cases of VAP were identified. The cause of the cases was investigated and it was learned that the unit was out of deep oral suctioning catheters, which went undetected. The oral care kits as part of the evidence-based protocol had been introduced as a trial and the staff thought the trial was over. Therefore, the catheters are now packaged routinely as an oral care kit.

These two evidence-based implementation projects followed the seven-step EBP process (see Chapter 1). Both revealed positive outcomes as a result of EBP changes.

Summary

An EBP environment promotes excellence in clinical care resulting in improvement of patient outcomes. Transforming a healthcare institution into a setting where an EBP culture exists requires *persistence, patience*, and *perseverance* (Hockenberry et al., 2007). Persistence—to maintain steadiness on a course of action—allows time to realize how EBP can improve clinical outcomes, and is a partner with wisdom when change may create significant stress for staff. Patience—showing the capacity for endurance—provides the strength to wait for change to occur. Perseverance—adhering to a purpose—allows the team to survive the change process by resolve and dedication during a time when it is essential to stay the course and believe that EBP can transform a clinical environment (Hockenberry et al.).

references

Ahrens, T. (2005). Evidenced-based practice: Priorities and implementation strategies. *AACN Clinical Issues, 16*(1), 36–42.

American Nurses Credentialing Center. (2008). *Magnet recognition program: Application manual.* Silver Spring, MD: Author.

Benner, P. (1984). *From novice to expert: Excellence and power in clinical nursing practice.* Menlo Park, CA: Addison-Wesley.

Bethel, C. (2000). *Patient-centered care measures for the national health care quality report.* Portland, OR: Foundation for Accountability.

Billings, D. M., & Kowalski, K. (2006). Bridging the theory-practice gap with evidence-based practice. *Journal of Continuing Education in Nursing, 37*(6), 248–249.

Ellett, M. (2004). What I know about methods of correctly placing gastric tubes in adults and children. *Gastroenterology Nursing, 27*(6), 253–259.

Ellett, M. (2006). Important facts about intestinal feeding tube placement. *Gastroenterology Nursing, 29*(2), 112–124.

Ellett, M., Croffie, J. M., Cohen, M. D., & Perkins, S. M. (2005). Gastric tube placement in young children. *Clinical Nursing Research, 14*(3), 238–252.

Ellett, M. L. C., & Beckstrand, J. (1999). Examination of gavage tube placement in children. *Journal of the Society of Pediatric Nurses, 4*(2), 52–60.

Ellett, M. L. C., Maahs, J., & Forsee, S. (1998). Prevalence of feeding tube placement errors and associated risks in children. *American Journal of Maternal/Child Nursing, 23*(5), 234–239.

Feifer, C., Fifield, J., Ornstein, S., Karson, A., Bates D., Jones K., et al. (2004). From research to daily clinical practice: What are the challenges in "translation"? *Joint Commission Journal on Quality and Safety, 30*(5), 235–245.

Fineout-Overholt, E., Melnyk, B. M., & Schultz, A. (2005). Transforming health care from the inside out: Advancing evidence-based practice in the 21st century. *Journal of Professional Nursing, 21*(6), 335–344.

Gale, B. V., & Schaffer, M. A. (2009). Organizational readiness for evidence-based practice. *Journal of Nursing Administration, 39*(2), 91–97.

Graham, I. A., & Harrison, M. B. (2005). Evaluation and adaptation of clinical practice guidelines. *Evidence-Based Nursing, 8*(3), 68–72.

Grol, R., & Grimshaw J. (2003). From best evidence to best practice: Effective implementation of change in patients' care. *Lancet, 362*(9391), 1225–1230.

Grol R., & Wensing M. (2004). What drives change? Barriers to and incentives for achieving evidence-based practice. *Medical Journal of Australia, 180*(6 Suppl), S57–S60.

Gutierrez, F., & Smith, K. (2008). Reducing falls in a definitive observation unit: An evidence-based practice institute consortium project. *Critical Care Quarterly, 31*(2), 127–139.

Hockenberry, M., Walden, M., Brown, T., & Barrera, P. (2007). Creating an evidence-based practice environment: One hospital's journey. *Journal of Nursing Care Quality, 22*(3), 221–231.

Hockenberry, M., Wilson, D., & Barrera, P. (2006). Implementing evidence-based practice in a pediatric hospital. *Pediatric Nursing, 32*(4), 371–377.

Huffman S., Piper P., Jarczyk, K. S., Bayne, A., & O'Brien, E. (2004). Methods to confirm feeding tube placement: Application of research in practice. *Pediatric Nursing, 30*(1), 10–13.

Institute of Medicine. (2000). *Crossing the quality chasm.* Washington, DC: Library of Congress.

Klem, M. L., & Weiss, P. M. (2005). Evidence-based resources and the role of librarians in developing evidence-based practice curricula. *Journal of Professional Nursing, 21*(6), 380–387.

Kotter, J. P., & Cohen, D. S. (2002). *The heart of change. Real-life stories of how people change their organizations.* Boston, MA: Harvard Business School Press.

Kresse, M., Kuklinski, M., & Cacchione, J. (2007). An evidence-based template for implementation of multidisciplinary evidence-based practices in a tertiary hospital setting. *American Journal of Medical Quality, 22*(3), 148–163.

Melnyk, B. M. (2002). Strategies for overcoming barriers in implementing evidence-based practice. *Pediatric Nursing, 28*(2), 159–161.

Melnyk, B.M. (2007). The evidence-based practice mentor: A promising strategy for implementing and sustaining EBP in healthcare systems. *Worldviews on Evidence-Based Nursing, 4*(3), 123–125.

Melnyk, B. M., Fineout-Overholt, E., Feinstein, N. F., Li, H., Small, L., Wilcox, L., et al. (2004). Nurses' perceived knowledge, beliefs, skills, and needs regarding evidence-based practice: Implications for accelerating the paradigm shift. *Worldviews of Evidence-Based Nursing, 1*(3), 185–193.

Melnyk, B. M., Fineout-Overholt, E., & Mays, M. (2008). The evidence-based practice beliefs and implementation scales: Psychometric properties of two new instruments. *Worldviews on Evidence-Based Nursing, 5*(4), 208–216.

Melnyk, B. M., Fineout-Overholt, E., Williamson, K., & Stillwell, S. (2009). Transforming healthcare quality through innovations in evidence-based practice (pp. 167–191). In T. Porter-O'Grady & K. Malloch (Eds.), *Innovation Leadership: Creating the Landscape of Health Care.* Boston, MA: Jones and Bartlett.

Metheny, N. A., Schnelker, R., McGinnis, J., Zimmerman, G., Duke, C., Merritt, B., et al. (2005). Indicators of tube site during feedings. *Journal of Neuroscience Nursing, 37*(6), 320.

Metheny, N. A., & Stewart B. J. (2002). Testing feeding tube placement during continuous tube feedings. *Applied Nursing Research, 15*(4), 254–258.

Mohide, E. A., & King, B. (2003). Building a foundation for evidence-based practice: Experiences in a tertiary hospital. *Evidence Based Nursing, 6*(4), 100–103.

Penz, K., L., & Bassendowski, S. L. (2006). Evidence-based nursing in clinical practice: Implications for nurse educators. *Journal of Continuing Education in Nursing, 37*(6), 251–256, 269.

Powers, J., Brower, A., & Tolliver, S. (2007). Impact of oral hygiene on prevention of ventilator associated pneumonia in neuroscience patients. *Journal of Nursing Care Quality, 22*(4), 316–322.

Rosenthal, M. B. (2007). Nonpayment for performance: Medicare's new reimbursement rule. *New England Journal of Medicine, 357*(16), 1573–1575.

Rosswurm, M. A., & Larrabee, J. H. (1999). A model for change to evidence-based practice. *Image-The Journal of Nursing Scholarship, 31*(4), 317–322.

Rycroft-Malone, J., Harvey, G., Seers, K., Kitson, A., McCormack, B., & Titchen, A. (2004). An exploration of the factors that influence the implementation of evidence into practice. *Journal of Clinical Nursing, 13*(8), 913–924.

Rycroft-Malone, J., Kitson, A., Harvey, G., McCormack, B., Seers, K., Titchen, A., et al. (2002). Ingredients for change: Revisiting a conceptual framework. *Quality and Safety in Health Care, 11*(2), 174–180.

Thompson, C., Cullum, N., McCaughan, D., Sheldon, T., & Raynor, P. (2004). Nurses, information use, and clinical decision making: The real world potential for evidence-based decisions in nursing. *Evidence Based Nursing, 7*(3), 68–72.

Titler, M. G., Kleiber, C., Steelman, V., Rakel, B. A., Budreau, G., Everett, L. Q., et al. (2001). The Iowa model of evidence-based practice to promote quality care. *Critical Care Nursing Clinics of North America, 13*(4), 497–509.

Westhus, N. (2004). Methods to test feeding tube placement in children. *MCN: The American Journal of Maternal/Child Nursing, 29*(5), 282–291.

chapter 9

225

The Role of Outcomes in Evaluating Practice Change

Anne Wojner Alexandrov and Barbara B. Brewer

Donabedian's (1980) quality framework defines three levels of measurement: structure, process, and outcome. Healthcare providers readily accepted the charge of defining structure and measuring process, but it wasn't until the late 1990s that a focus on outcomes measurement and management began to take hold (Wojner, 2001). The focus of this chapter is the measurement of the results or outcomes of **evidence-based quality improvement** (EBQI) as well as the comparison of traditional practice with new interventions. Understanding the role of outcome evaluation is important for all healthcare providers, to both contribute to and appreciate.

Outcomes: The "End-Result Idea"

In 1917, Ernest Codman proposed an outrageous (at the time) method for aligning hospitals and physicians with the capitalist financial U.S. economic framework. Simply named the "end-result idea," Codman boldly suggested that hospitals and physicians should measure the results of their healthcare processes and make them available to the general public so that those agencies with optimal outcomes would command a leadership position within the healthcare market, while those with suboptimal performance would be challenged to improve or resign/go out of business. Sadly for Codman (1934), his suggestion was deemed as nothing short of dangerous, due to a paternalistic medical philosophy that held that patients were uneducated and cognitively unequipped to participate in both health decision making and determination of medical provider excellence. Until the emergence of Donabedian's (1980) quality framework, the prospect of outcomes measurement lay dormant.

In 1988, Paul Ellwood took up the charge for outcomes measurement when Codman left off, proposing a framework for **outcomes management** (OM). Ellwood described OM as "a technology of patient experience designed to help patients, payers, and providers make rational medical care-related choices based on better insight into the effect of these choices on patient life" (p. 1549). The principles supporting OM ascribed by Ellwood included

● Emphasizing practice standards that providers can use to select interventions
● Measuring patient functional status, well-being, and disease-specific clinical outcomes
● Pooling outcome data on a massive scale
● Analyzing and disseminating outcomes, in relation to the interventions used, to appropriate decision makers and stakeholders

Ellwood's framework for OM was published in response to a new emphasis in the mid-1980s on healthcare costs in relation to service quality and was the first to provide context for use of what were then called "best practices" (Wojner, 2001). Focusing on healthcare efficiency as key to controlling healthcare costs and improving quality, nursing case management also emerged in the late 1980s. Case management used methods that first surfaced in psychiatric social work (Wojner, 1997b). While these methods sharpened the focus on process efficiency, which continues to be a significant aspect of the case manager role today, they did little to promote the use of evidence-based interventions and failed to detail measurement of health outcomes.

In 1997, the Health Outcomes Institute's Outcomes Management Model (see Figure 10.1) was the first to take the Ellwood framework and build in actual steps to guide measurement of

chapter 10

227

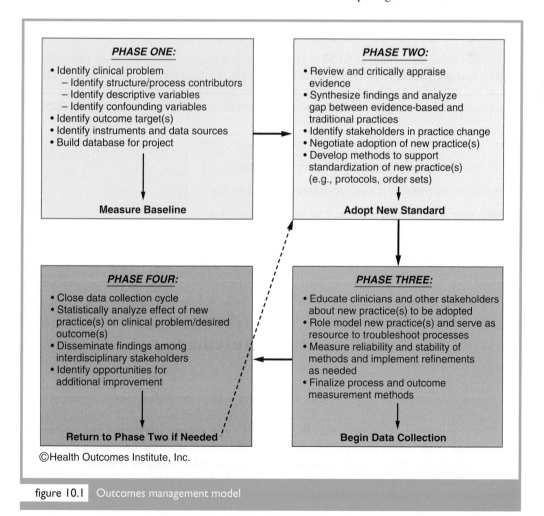

PHASE ONE:
• Identify clinical problem
 – Identify structure/process contributors
 – Identify descriptive variables
 – Identify confounding variables
• Identify outcome target(s)
• Identify instruments and data sources
• Build database for project

Measure Baseline

PHASE TWO:
• Review and critically appraise evidence
• Synthesize findings and analyze gap between evidence-based and traditional practices
• Identify stakeholders in practice change
• Negotiate adoption of new practice(s)
• Develop methods to support standardization of new practice(s) (e.g., protocols, order sets)

Adopt New Standard

PHASE FOUR:
• Close data collection cycle
• Statistically analyze effect of new practice(s) on clinical problem/desired outcome(s)
• Disseminate findings among interdisciplinary stakeholders
• Identify opportunities for additional improvement

Return to Phase Two if Needed

PHASE THREE:
• Educate clinicians and other stakeholders about new practice(s) to be adopted
• Role model new practice(s) and serve as resource to troubleshoot processes
• Measure reliability and stability of methods and implement refinements as needed
• Finalize process and outcome measurement methods

Begin Data Collection

©Health Outcomes Institute, Inc.

figure 10.1   Outcomes management model

the impact of new interventions on improving healthcare outcomes (Wojner, 1997a). The model suggested four phases to the process:

1. *Phase One*: Definition of outcome measures, along with contributing structure and process measures, and construction of a database to capture targeted variables. Measurement of baseline performance was identified as key to the process so that improvement could be clearly identified in relation to a shift in practice.

2. *Phase Two*: Contrasting and comparing traditional practice methods with those identified in the literature as best practices, interdisciplinary negotiation and adoption of new evidence-based initiatives, and construction of structured care methods (e.g., order sets, protocols) to ensure practice standardization for the purpose of improved outcomes. An emphasis was placed on interdisciplinary team engagement in the process to enhance acceptance of new practice methods.

3. *Phase Three*: Implementation of new evidence-based initiatives. This step involved role modeling and teaching new practices, making clear interdisciplinary expectations for use of newly adopted practices, determining the stability and reliability of new practices to ensure uniform use, and the subsequent measurement of outcome targets.

4. *Phase Four*: Analysis of process and outcome targets in relation to newly adopted evidence-based initiatives. A focus on interdisciplinary evaluation and dialogue about the findings achieved was emphasized, including the ability to generate new research questions or hypotheses for testing, ultimately driving refinement of standardized processes (Wojner, 1997a).

The Health Outcomes Institute's OM Model provided a road map for interdisciplinary practitioners to define outcome targets, establish measurement methods, identify practices supported by evidence, educate and train healthcare providers in the use of these methods, and subsequently measure the impact associated with implementation of new interventions on healthcare quality (Wojner, 2001).

I do believe that when we face challenges in life that are far beyond our own power, it's an opportunity to build on our faith, inner strength, and courage. I've learned that how we face challenges plays a big role in the outcome of them.

S a s h a   A z e v e d o

Quantifying the Impact of Interventions: Outcomes Measurement for Outcome Management

The process of managing health outcomes suggests that when substandard results are achieved, new practices, supported by scientific evidence, should be implemented so that outcome targets will show improvement (Ellwood, 1988; Wojner, 2001). This process is a natural fit for evidence-based practice (EBP), allowing for the establishment of clinical issues through outcomes measurement and the success or not of the implementation of an evidence-based initiative. Attitudes and beliefs that clinicians attach to traditional practices often make changing practice difficult. Acceptance of new evidence-based initiatives can be fostered among providers through measurement of failed outcomes achieved with traditional practices. Measuring outcomes of practice should be viewed as a powerful change promoter. Often these powerful outcomes are measured to demonstrate EBQI (i.e., to understand the impact of evidence-based actions on patients and organizational outcomes), often via data available through internal systems. Internal data are evidence (i.e., internal evidence) that can be used to recommend practice changes aimed at standardization of evidence-based best practices.

Healthcare organizations have a wealth of data generated by multiple individuals, often housed in multiple disparate and disconnected systems. For example, data are generated during the course of providing care to patients, as a result of tests or treatments, or by billing and financial systems. As transparency and pay-for-performance pressures have grown for providers and organizations, more and more data have been collected in response to accreditation and regulatory requirements. These types of data typically reflect evidence-based processes of care indicators that are known to produce better patient outcomes. Examples of these include (a) use of specific medications, (b) timing of antibiotics, (c) specific patient education, and (d) targeted discharge instructions. In addition, outcomes also are collected. Examples of these outcomes include (a) fall rates, (b) catheter-related infections, (c) urinary tract infections, and (d) pressure ulcer rates and stage progression. The data collection for these processes and outcomes is time consuming and expensive. Therefore, before embarking on new data collection, the usefulness of data from existing data sources for improving outcomes and demonstrating that improvement should be carefully considered.

Sources of Internal Evidence

Internal evidence sources include quality management, finance, and human resource departments; clinical systems; administration; and **electronic health records (EHRs)**. Selected sources of internal evidence are discussed in the following sections and provide examples of data typically found in each of these sources. However, this list is not intended to be exhaustive, as there may be data sources in other departments and systems within an organization.

Quality Management

In most organizations, quality management departments house data generated from incident reports, which may include falls, sentinel events (i.e., an unexpected event that culminates in death or serious injury), medication errors, and near misses (i.e., events that could have resulted in harm, but were corrected prior to it occurring). These types of data may be examined for trends related to types, locations, or other factors associated with care process errors, or they may be correlated with structural indicators such as staffing patterns (e.g., number of nurses scheduled to work). Other types of data that may be housed in quality management are patient satisfaction results and data collected through chart reviews submitted to regulatory or accreditation bodies.

Finance

Data housed in finance departments are frequently the most robust within an organization. Many of the data elements found within financial systems are generated by billing and registration systems and are used for billing purposes. Examples of these types of data are charges for tests, medications, equipment or supplies, patient days, readmission rates, and patient demographics such as name, age, ethnicity, gender, and nursing unit. Other data frequently housed in finance departments are codes for patient diagnosis, including Medicare-Severity Diagnosis Related Groups (MS-DRG) and International Statistical Classification of Diseases and Related Health Problems Version 9 (ICD-9) codes. These types of data are routinely used to measure patient volumes, to understand care processes (types of medications used or tests done), or to risk adjust for patient outcomes. They also may be used to evaluate incidence of errors within certain patient populations. For example, patients who have certain comorbid conditions, such as cancer or diabetes, may have a higher incidence of hospital-acquired infections. Evaluation of these data would assist in determining the severity of this association.

We have to have a way of dealing with this that engenders confidence [and] trust, gives us every chance of getting the right outcome, and boosts both sustainability and economic return at the same time.

John Anderson

Human Resources

Data housed in human resource departments generally include those generated from employee and payroll systems. Data generated by employee systems include turnover and staff education levels. Frequently, if available, staff education levels reflect those at time of hire and therefore may not reflect current information. Data available from payroll systems include hours by pay category or labor category and contract labor use. In some organizations, contract labor use and expense may by housed in financial systems used for expense reporting. Hours by labor category may be used to calculate provider skill mix. Hours by pay category may be used to calculate staffing.

Clinical Systems

Clinical systems are data collection and management mechanisms that can store many kinds of data. For example, these systems may house test results such as laboratory tests or point-of-care tests. They may also house pharmacy data. Pharmacy data such as numbers of doses of a medication or types of medications may be used to evaluate care process compliance or evaluate relationships among different medications and patient outcomes. In some organizations, the clinical system is the source of data for reporting outcomes in integrated reviews, such as dashboards, which is discussed in more detail later in this chapter.

Administration

Administrative departments, such as hospital administration, may provide data related to patient complaints about care and services. Such data may be in the form of a call log or table containing information about the source, type, location, and resolution of complaints.

Electronic Health Records

For those fortunate to have access to electronic health information, the numbers and types of internal data available for use in evaluating impact are vast. Data may include patient-level information such as vital signs and weights, noncharge generating clinical interventions such as indwelling urinary catheter use, or essentially any data elements captured through documentation of clinical care. One caveat related to collection of data from EHRs is that data aggregation requires standardization of language in order to collect the entire group of incidences of a particular intervention, care process, or event. Many data abstracting queries (i.e., requesting information from the EHR) use a process similar to searching for articles through an electronic database. Some searches return articles based on the precise term or terms used for the search, resulting in missing articles that were filed in the database under synonyms of the search term. Searching an EHR in some systems may work the same way. Events or care processes documented using a synonym for the search term may not be included in the query results.

Measuring Outcomes to Demonstrate Impact Begins With Asking the Right Question

One of the most frustrating situations faced by clinicians who are involved with improvement activities is getting at the data that they know exist within their organization. It is not unusual to encounter barriers to getting the data needed to answer questions about the impact of current practice. Barriers to accessing needed data usually are a result of differences in language spoken by clinicians and those who "own" the data. Differences in language typically involve the names used for the requested data elements. Other differences involve the type and form of data needed for the analysis that needs to be done, which may require patient-level data that contains data elements from multiple clinical and financial systems. For example, if a clinician wanted to evaluate glucose management over a period of time, patient-specific data such as hospital or medical record number, name, unit, point of care and/or laboratory glucose results, time and date of sample, ICD-9 codes (for diabetes), and physician name may be needed. These data elements may be generated and housed in financial, clinical, and EHR systems in an organization. Getting these data in an integrated report may require someone with specialized skills to write a query that draws data from different databases, if an organization has a query system to achieve this kind of integration.

Being clear about what data are needed from the outset will help avoid repeated requests for additional data elements needed to complete the analysis but not included in the original request. This will facilitate getting needed data in a timely fashion, which can be challenging. Generally, those individuals within an organization who have the report writing skills and access to the necessary databases are few in number and in high demand. As with any person who is in high demand, limited time is available to meet requests that are beyond normal workload requirements. Finding someone within the organization who is willing to mentor staff members who are novices at using internal evidence will minimize "forgotten" or unrecognized data needs, avoid repeated requests, and foster relationships with database owners, and may speed up the turn-around time for data requests.

Asking for data in a useable format also is important. When asking for a report, always inquire if the data are available in an electronic format. Many systems can run queries that will download data in a text file or in a format that can be opened and manipulated in spreadsheet software, such as Excel. Doing so can eliminate hours of data entry, which is necessary to convert a paper report of results into a format that can be used for analysis. Electronic formatted data also avoids potential data entry errors that can occur when entering data from a paper report to data analysis software (e.g., Excel or SPSS). It is very helpful if before requesting data analysis has been carefully considered so that data may be requested in a format that will require the least amount of manipulation (e.g., entry from paper) and cleaning (e.g., addressing missing information) to prepare for analysis. Once data have been prepared for analysis, statistical tests may be run using spreadsheet software, or the data file can be easily transferred to statistics software for further analysis.

When Existing Data Sources Are not Available

All data that are required to measure the impact of evidence-based interventions on outcome are not contained in preexisting sources, or preexisting sources of data may not be available. Therefore, it is important that collection and measurement of data that are not preexisting be discussed.

Data Collection from Nonpreexisting Sources

If data are not able to be extracted from a preexisting data source, the method of data collection may be the most important aspect of evaluating the practice change. Gathering meaningful data in an efficient manner takes forethought, ingenuity, and familiarity with how data are best collected and the importance of measurement. With evidence-based initiatives, methods and measures discovered in the evidence synthesis can be considered for use. Consideration of which patient characteristics and contextual elements might affect the outcome can increase the likelihood of collecting valid (i.e., unbiased) data. For example, if an evidence-based oral care program was initiated to reduce the incidence of ventilator-associated pneumonia (VAP), it would not be adequate to only collect data on the frequency of oral care delivery (nonpreexisting data) and the VAP rate (possibly can be obtained from preexisting data source), because there are other factors, such as patient severity, preexisting pulmonary disease, or mode of suctioning (all nonpreexisting data), that influence patients' risk for development of VAP and would need to be measured. Collecting data on a unit by care providers should be done with attention to detail and as unbiased as possible so that data precision is optimized. As described in Phase 3 of the Health Outcomes Institute's OM Model, using methods that capture the stability of processes, such as control charts, can assist in ensuring that data are collected uniformly, resulting in accurate data.

Measurement Accuracy: Establishing Validity and Reliability

Measurement instruments, whether developed in practice or through research, must be evaluated as to whether they are valid and reliable. Each instrument will have what are called **psychometric properties** that indicate its **validity** and **reliability**. These properties tend to be statistics that help the user know that these instruments will provide accurate data when used. Validity indicates that the measure or instrument actually measures what it is supposed to measure. There are actually several types of validity. For our purposes, we are going to focus on content validity, which is often reflected through an expert review of the instrument. Experts indicate whether or not they view the questions or items on the instrument as measuring the construct. For example, if a practice-developed instrument was said to measure satisfaction with the Situation-Background-Assessment-Recommendation (SBAR) communication technique, a group of experts in verbal handoffs between patients would review the instrument to indicate if the items or questions on the measure did reflect satisfaction with SBAR.

Reliability means it will measure the construct consistently every time it is used. Often this is indicated through a statistic called Cronbach alpha. A Cronbach alpha greater than 0.80 is indicative of an instrument that should perform reliably each time you use it. There are many other elements of both validity and reliability of measures that go beyond the scope of this chapter. Clinicians may be tempted to develop their own instrument; however, that is ill-advised unless they have established that valid and reliable measures do not exist. If practice-developed instruments are used, it is important to take the time to establish content validity and assess reliability. Given that whole books are dedicated to understanding measurement, including establishing validity and reliability, it would be wise for those clinicians who are developing measures to obtain one and make use of liaisons with experts in the field to facilitate accurate measurement.

Making Sense of the Data

Making sense of the data is enabled through data analysis. How data are analyzed is driven by the level of data available. In larger organizations, there may be a department or portions of a department that take on this role. However, not all organizations have such resources. Therefore, we briefly discuss this important topic, but comprehensive discussion about data analysis can be found in other resources that focus on that topic.

Levels of Data

There are two basic types of data, categorical and numerical. **Categorical variables** are those that are grouped due to a defined characteristic, such as gender, presence or absence of a disease, or possession of particular risk factors. Numbers are commonly used to label categorical data, but these numbers have no meaning and only facilitate grouping of cases into like data bundles.

Likert scales, which allow ranking of data, also are categorical in nature, in that they group data by ranks. However, data analysts often consider these types of scales numerical. Generally, the statistical methods used to analyze categorical data are **frequencies** (Giuliano & Polanowicz, 2008).

Numeric data potentially have an infinite number of possible values, for example, measures for height, weight, mean arterial pressure, and heart rate. Unlike categorical data, the mathematical intervals that separate numeric data are equal. For example, the interval between the numbers 20 and 21 is equal to the interval between 21 and 22, namely 1.

Categorical and numeric data fall within four possible levels of measurement: nominal, ordinal, interval, and ratio. The purpose of the project and the level of the data drive the selection of the statistical methods that will be used to measure the impact of the practice change. Descriptions of clinical issues that would fit within each level of measurement are discussed in the following sections.

Nominal Level Data. Data measured at the nominal level are the least sophisticated and lowest form of measurement. Nominal measurement scales assign numbers to unique categories of data, but these numbers have no meaning other than to label a group. Scales that describe the quality of a symptom by some descriptive format are nominal. For example, a nominal measure of the quality of pain may include such categories as "throbbing," "stabbing," "continuous," "intermittent," "burning," "dull," "sharp," "aching," "stinging," or "burning" (McHugh, 2003).

Ordinal Level Data. Ordinal measures use categorical data as well. Numbers assigned to categories in ordinal measures enable ranking from lowest to highest so that the magnitude of the variable can be captured. However, it is important to note that while numbers are assigned to enable sorting of findings by rank, the absolute difference in each level on an ordinal scale does not possess an equal or "true" mathematical difference in the values. Likert scales provide clinicians with ordinal level data using selections such as "very dissatisfied," "dissatisfied," "neither dissatisfied nor satisfied," "satisfied," and "very satisfied." Clearly, each progression from very dissatisfied to very satisfied describes a greater level of satisfaction, but "very satisfied" could not be described as four times more satisfied than "very dissatisfied." When developing instruments, researchers typically use four or five categories from which to rank the variable of interest on a Likert scale.

Interval and Ratio Level Data. Interval measures are the next highest level of measurement and are purely derived from numeric data with equal and consistent mathematical values separating each discreet measurement point. While ratio level data possess this same characteristic, the difference between these two levels of measurement is that interval data do not possess an absolute zero point. The best examples of interval level data are temperature measures derived from the Fahrenheit scale which assigns 32° instead of zero as the point where water freezes.

Measures derived from a ruler and temperatures measured on the Centigrade scale are both examples of ratio level data. Data measured at the interval and ratio level allow virtually all types of algebraic transformations, and therefore the greatest number of statistical options can be applied (McHugh, 2003). Given the significant amount of numeric variables used routinely in healthcare settings, many outcome targets, for example those associated with objective, quantitative physiologic data, are defined at the interval or ratio level.

When defining the outcomes to be measured, clinicians must carefully consider the instruments to measure them so that they are most accurately reflected. For example, if a project were conducted to evaluate an evidence-based weight loss strategy, the outcome of weight loss could be measured at the categorical–nominal level (e.g., "BMI <25," "BMI 25–30,"

"BMI 30–35," "BMI 35–40," and "BMI ≥41") or at the ratio level by using actual weight loss (e.g., in pounds or kilograms). Using pounds or kilograms (i.e., ratio level) would enable those evaluating the outcome to use more powerful statistical analyses. Measurement of the impact of a practice change on outcomes denotes the need to use statistical analyses that detect a difference in the outcome target that can be attributed to the evidence-based intervention. While it is beyond the scope of this chapter to provide detailed instruction on selection and use of different forms of statistical analyses, the information presented here is meant to provide some considerations for the context of outcome measurement and analysis. Collaborating with a biostatistician is a wise decision for clinicians who are analyzing more than outcome frequencies or means.

Reporting Outcomes to Key Stakeholders

Undertaking the implementation of new interventions and ultimately the measurement of their impact requires significant work on the part of the interdisciplinary healthcare team. It is paramount that all parties involved with this process (i.e., both active and passive **key stakeholder**) be afforded an opportunity to understand the results achieved, whether positive or negative. Project coordinators need to consider which reporting methods will make the outcomes easily understood by all stakeholders to enhance dissemination of results and further knowledge associated with the clinical issues in the project. Once internal data have been gathered and analyzed, reports are generated to display results. These reports can be constructed in any way the organization chooses to present the data. Scorecards and dashboards are described here as two mechanisms for communicating data to organizational stakeholders. In a study surveying 586 hospital leaders, 81% used scorecards or dashboards for tracking outcome indicators of performance and quality (Jiang, Lockee, Bass, et al., 2008).

Scorecards

Balanced scorecards are used to show how indicators from different areas may relate to each other. For example, relationships among financial performance indicators, such as hours per patient day, can be examined against clinical and safety indicators such as patient falls or infection rates. Systematically evaluating performance from a balanced perspective allows clinicians and leaders to evaluate both intended and unintended consequences of practice change. For example, if the interdisciplinary team in the emergency department (ED) implemented an evidence-based care management program that resulted in patients who normally were admitted to the hospital for observation being discharged to home with home care, it would be prudent to ensure that the new program did not negatively impact hospital readmission rates for those patients, while at the same time evaluating whether length of stay within the ED was reduced and patient satisfaction maintained or improved. Figure 10.2 provides an example of indicators that may be used in a balanced scorecard.

Scorecard indicators can include (a) identifiers of high-level strategic areas and cluster outcomes accordingly, (b) objectives that are linked to the organizational strategic plan, making the outcomes relevant across the organization, (c) the measures or metrics for each outcome, and (d) indicators of how things are going, usually in relationship to given expectations or standards, often using colors. Including these components in the scorecard integrates the performance demonstrated by internal evidence with the organization's strategic plan and mission.

Using color to enhance interpretation of indicators is extremely helpful for viewing at a glance the impact of practice on outcomes. If using the red/yellow/green color scheme, red generally indicates performance below and green indicates performance at or above goal or target. Yellow indicates performance within a certain percentage of targets, but not below or above the identified markers. Using font or background color to distinguish particular outcomes sets them apart from surrounding values. Making the scorecard easy to read and interesting to look at aids

Scorecard

Operational	Quality	Satisfaction
• Turnover • Vacancy rate • Readmission rate • Total average length of stay • Case mix index • Hours per patient day • Contract labor use • Mean wait time in ED	• Patient falls • Pressure ulcer rate • Infection rate • Compliance with evidence-based care • Mean glucose value	• Patient satisfaction • Staff satisfaction score • Medical staff satisfaction • Patient complaint rate

figure 10.2 Balanced scorecard indicators

in quick overall communication of current performance. Typically, scorecards are used to indicate performance over a single year. Months or quarters may be used as reporting intervals. The decision regarding which to use is often based on frequency of data collection and preference (see Figure 10.2).

Dashboards

Dashboards are graphic displays of information that are often used at the unit level to compare performance indicators for the population being cared for on that unit. As with scorecards, color coding enables clear displays of performance indicators of excellence and of deficiencies. The same red/yellow/green color scheme can be used for dashboards to achieve the same at-a-glance overview of performance (Modern Healthcare, 2006).

Dashboards can help healthcare providers see the direct impact on performance from the care they provided. Dematteis and Werstler (2006) indicated that the use of a unit dashboard encourages active participation of staff nurses in the continued improvement of quality because they could see the results of their contributions to patient care. Performance dashboards can help build confidence in point-of-care providers that they are indeed making a difference in the outcomes of the patients for whom they care as they implement EBPs.

Research Designs for Comparing Traditional Practice With New Interventions

When comparing a new intervention to traditional practice in a practice setting, quasi-experimental and experimental methods are typically used to generate outcomes that reflect the impact of the comparison. There are both strengths and limitations associated with these methods, but each starts with ensuring that the study is adequately powered to find a difference when a true difference does exist. The effect size of comparison of a new intervention to traditional practice, the anticipated power (usually 0.80), and the probability (i.e., alpha) (usually $p = 0.05$) are used to determine exactly how many subjects are required in each study arm to find a difference in the outcome target that is causally associated with the intervention. While it may be tempting to simply conduct a small quality study that describes the performance of an existing practice in relation to a new intervention, these studies may be less than persuasive for slow adopters to embrace new practices. Additionally, **the Health Insurance Portability and Accountability Act (HIPAA) regulations** call for ethics review boards' approval (i.e., human subject or **institutional review board [IRB]** approval of all studies involving personal health information [PHI]), and in many cases initiation of informed consent. It also is important that the knowledge learned from studies of this nature be shared, and dissemination of findings requires IRB approval prior to study conduct. Because of these factors, there can be confusion about whether implementation of evidence is considered research. Chapter 20 is more on the confusion between EBQI and research. Either approach requires IRB review to assure participant safety and to enable the demonstration of how effective a given intervention is within a particular setting. The following sections briefly address different approaches to comparing new interventions with traditional practice. Chapter 17 provides more in-depth information on generating external evidence.

The "True" Experiment

The "true" experiment is considered the most rigorous of all research designs. (See Chapter 17 for figures of different experimental designs.) While the sophistication of experiments can be built upon to encompass additional arms and methods, the basic structure is presented here. When considering measurement of the impact of a new intervention using an experimental design, the impracticality of this method must be weighed against the superior quality of the findings that will be achieved. For example, random assignment is used in which subjects are randomly assigned to treatment groups based on probability (e.g., flipping a coin). In addition, stringent controls are implemented, and a comparison or attention placebo group is used to compare outcomes against the experimental treatment group, which may make conduct of the study within a reasonable time frame challenging unless the investigators have access to a large sample of patients. Often use of a well-controlled, quasi-experimental approach provides a sound and more practical approach to the measurement of the impact of a new intervention compared to traditional practice (Wojner, 2001). See Chapter 17 for a more detailed discussion of various experimental designs.

Quasi-Experimental Designs

Many different designs support conduct of a quasi-experiment. Broadly, these designs can include the simple quasi-experiment that mirrors the true experiment, but they typically do not use random assignment or a comparison group. In addition, quasi-experiments use less stringent control methods. Examples include the repeated measures quasi-experiment, in which subjects serve as their own controls and spend time receiving both the traditional practice and the new intervention, and the pretest/posttest quasi-experiment, which typically uses different groups of patients at different times. (See Chapter 17 for figures of quasi-experimental designs.) The Health Outcomes Institute's OM Model could be used to demonstrate this design, with the pretest measurement derived from use of the traditional practice at baseline (Phase 1), and the posttest measurement reflecting adoption of the new intervention (Phase 3; Wojner, 2001).

Summary

Demonstrating that practice change has indeed brought about improved outcomes is imperative in this era of healthcare when many evidence-based initiatives have been endorsed by powerful professional healthcare organizations, as well as payers, as acceptable methods to use in the treatment of specific health conditions. With steadily emerging trends, such as pay-for-performance systems supported by use of standardized evidence-based initiatives, it is important that evaluation of outcomes be conducted in a manner that is valid and reliable. These outcomes must be accessible to healthcare leadership as well as the point-of-care providers to increase the likelihood that all those in healthcare engage in the continuous improvement of patient, provider, system, and community outcomes. Using principles of OM described in this chapter enables healthcare providers to improve healthcare practice for years to come.

references

Codman, E. A. (1917). The value of case records in hospitals. *Modern Hospitals, 9*, 426–428.

Codman, E. A. (1934). *The shoulder: Rupture of the supraspinatus tendon and other lesions in or about the subacromial bursa.* Brooklyn, NY: G. Miller.

Dematteis, J., & Werstler, J. (2006). Placing ownership for quality in the hands of the staff. *Critical Care Nurse, 26*(2), S38.

Donabedian, A. (1980). *The definition of quality and approaches to its management.* Ann Arbor, MI: Health Administration.

Ellwood, P. M. (1988). Outcomes management: A technology of patient experience. *The New England Journal of Medicine, 318*, 1549–1556.

Giuliano, K. K., & Polanowicz, M. (2008). Interpretation and use of statistics in nursing research. *AACN Advanced Critical Care, 19*, 211–222.

Jiang, H. J., Lockee, C., Bass, K., & Fraser, I. (2008). Board engagement in quality: Findings of a survey of hospital and system leaders. *Journal of Healthcare Management, 53*(2), 121–134.

McHugh, M. L. (2003). Descriptive statistics, Part I: Level of measurement. *Journal for Specialists in Pediatric Nursing, 8*(1), 35–37.

Modern Healthcare (2006). Ten best practices for measuring the effectiveness of nonprofit healthcare boards. *Bulletin of the National Center for Healthcare Leadership*, 9–20.

Wojner, A. W. (1997a). Outcomes management, from theory to practice. *Critical Care Nurse Quarterly, 19*(4), 1–15.

Wojner, A. W. (1997b). Widening the scope: From case management to outcomes management. *Case Manager, 8*(2), 77–82.

Wojner, A. W. (2001). *Outcomes management: Application to clinical practice.* St. Louis, MO: Mosby.

chapter 10

237

Creating and Sustaining a Culture for Evidence-Based Practice

Models to Guide Implementation of Evidence-Based Practice

Donna Ciliska, Alba DiCenso, Bernadette Mazurek Melnyk, Ellen Fineout-Overholt, Cheryl B. Stetler, Laura Cullen, June H. Larrabee, Alyce A. Schultz, Jo Rycroft-Malone, Robin P. Newhouse, and Deborah Dang

● Chewing gum after abdominal surgery reduces the amount of time to return of bowel function but does not decrease the length of hospital stay (Purkayastha, Tilney, & Darzi, 2008).

● Educational interventions for parents can reduce unintentional injuries in children and increase parental use of safety practices (Kendrick, Barlow, Hampshire, et al., 2007).

● Psychological interventions reduce the risk of depression after stroke (Hackett, Anderson, & House, 2008).

The clinical interventions described above are but a few of many interventions that have been evaluated and shown to have a positive impact on patient outcomes and often on cost savings for the healthcare system. However, are healthcare professionals aware of these studies? How do they learn about them? How can healthcare providers keep up to date with new knowledge that relates to their practice? Once they acquire new knowledge, how do healthcare providers change their own practices and influence others to change practice behaviors within their organizations? Are evaluations conducted to determine whether evidence-based changes in clinical practice result in beneficial outcomes? All of these questions are important to the effective implementation of evidence-based findings in clinical practice (Box 11.1).

Healthcare professionals are highly motivated to be evidence-based practitioners. However, there are many individual and organizational obstacles. At the individual level, clinicians (a) frequently have inadequate skills in searching for and evaluating research studies (Parahoo, 2000), (b) lack confidence to implement change (Parahoo), and (c) experience isolation from colleagues with whom to discuss research findings (Kajermo, Nordstrom, Krusebrant, et al., 1998). However, organizational factors often create the most significant barriers to evidence-based practice (EBP; Parahoo; Retsas, 2000). Lack of interest, motivation, leadership, vision, strategy, and direction among managers for EBP has been identified to pose a significant

---

box 11.1

Definition of Evidence-Based Practice

Evidence-based practice is the integration of best research evidence with clinical expertise and patient values to facilitate clinical decision making (Sackett, Straus, Richardson, et al., 2000). Evidence-based practice includes the following steps:

0. Cultivate a spirit of inquiry.
1. Ask the burning clinical question in PICOT format.
2. Search for and collect the most relevant best evidence.
3. Critically appraise the evidence (i.e., rapid critical appraisal, evaluation, and synthesis).
4. Integrate the best evidence with one's clinical expertise and patient preferences and values in making a practice decision or change.
5. Evaluate outcomes of the practice decision or change based on evidence.
6. Disseminate the outcomes of the EBP decision or change.

---

organizational barrier. This is especially true for the nursing profession because a change in practice, especially if it involves purchasing new equipment or changing a policy or procedure, requires administrative support (Parahoo; Retsas). For example, in the case of pressure sore prevention, nurses have the decision-making autonomy to massage weight-bearing areas and ensure frequent position changes. However, other interventions, such as the purchase of high-specification foam mattresses, require approval of the organization.

Changing clinical practice is complex and challenging. As a result, many models have been developed to systematically guide the implementation of EBP. This chapter begins by describing the components of evidence-based clinical decision making. The chapter then goes on to describe models that are designed to assist clinicians in changing practices based on evidence in their organizations.

> *Change is inevitable…adapting to change is unavoidable,*
> *it's how you do it that sets you together or apart.*
> *William Ngwako Maphoto*

The Evolution from Research Utilization to Evidence-Based Clinical Decision Making

In the past, nurses and other healthcare providers used the term *research utilization (RU)* to mean the use of research knowledge in clinical practice. Evidence-based practice is broader than RU because the clinician is encouraged to consider a number of dimensions in clinical decision making, one of which is evidence. Along with the integration of the best research evidence, evidence-based practitioners are encouraged to consider **internal evidence** (e.g., the patient's clinical status and circumstances, evidence generated internally from outcomes management or quality improvement projects), the patient's preferences and actions, healthcare resources, and clinical expertise when making clinical decisions (DiCenso, Ciliska, & Guyatt, 2004; see Figure 11.1).

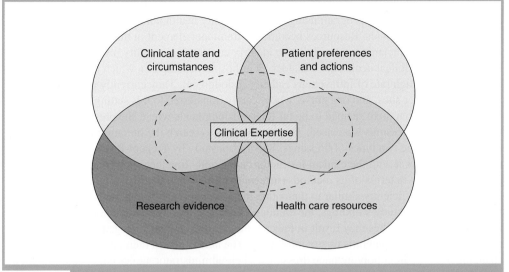

figure 11.1   Evidence-based decision making (From DiCenso, A., Ciliska, D., & Guyatt, G. [Eds.] [2004]. *Evidence-based nursing: A guide to clinical practice.* St. Louis, MO: Elsevier.)

   To illustrate how this clinical decision-making model can be implemented, consider the following examples. For many years, public health nurses have been visiting at-risk postpartum mothers in their homes to provide education and support. The nurses have the clinical expertise; the funding is available to the health department to support this nursing intervention; and the evidence shows that it has produced positive outcomes, in terms of improving the home environment for the child and reducing depression in the mothers (Shaw, Levitt, Wong, et al., 2006). However, when the community health nurse calls some clients to arrange a home visit, the clients are reluctant to agree and sometimes refuse to be visited. *Patient preferences and actions* will be the dominant element in this decision regarding a home visit. Optimally, patient values and preferences are based on careful consideration of information that provides an accurate assessment of the patient's condition and possible treatments, as well as the likely benefits, costs, and risks. In this way, clients can make informed decisions based on the best current knowledge. Patient preferences play a large role in cancer treatments where patients, having heard and understood the benefit of a chemotherapy treatment, choose not to have it because of its detrimental effects on quality of life in terms of hair loss and general malaise, for example.

   In addition to patient preferences, clinicians need to consider the *patient's clinical state, setting, and circumstances*. For example, patients who live in remote areas may not have access to the same diagnostic tests or interventions as those who live near a tertiary care medical center. Also, the effectiveness of some interventions may vary, depending on the patient's stage of illness or symptoms. Furthermore, outcomes from patients on a specific unit (i.e., internal evidence) might also be integrated into evidence-based decisions.

   Another component of clinical decision making is *healthcare resources*. Sometimes, even the best evidence cannot be utilized because the intervention is too costly. Now return to the home visiting example where the local health department would like to replace some of the community health nurses with paraprofessionals (lay home visitors) in hopes of delivering similar education and support and achieving comparable outcomes at a lower cost. The nurse manager conducts a literature search and finds an article by Olds, Robinson, O' Brien, et al. (2002), which concludes that while nurses achieved significant and important effects on numerous maternal and infant outcomes, paraprofessionals achieved small effects that were rarely statistically significant.

Though armed with this research evidence, the health department no longer has the resources to continue the home visiting program using only community health nurses, and it begins to hire and train paraprofessionals. Resources become the dominant element in this decision.

It is the clinician's responsibility to identify current, high-quality *research evidence* to inform his or her clinical decisions. Consider an in-hospital example in which nurses are concerned about the high rate of intravenous catheter dislodgment. They currently use gauze dressings on the catheter sites, and one nurse, who recently transferred to this setting from another institution, notes that there seemed to be far fewer dislodgments where she previously worked when transparent dressings were used. This nurse offers to search the literature for research studies that compare the two types of dressings. She finds a study by Trepepi-Bova, Woods, & Loach (1997) and reviews it with the clinical instructor on the unit. Together, they conclude that it is a high-quality study in terms of its methods (**internal validity**) and that the population and setting of the study are sufficiently similar to theirs that they can apply the results in their unit (**external validity**). From the study's findings, the clinicians conclude that transparent polyurethane dressings on peripheral IV sites may result in fewer catheter dislodgments than gauze dressings with no increase in rates of phlebitis or site infiltration. The nurses talk to their administrator about changing to transparent polyurethane dressings. Their administrator agrees but encourages them to evaluate whether the new type of dressing actually results in a reduction in catheter dislodgments by recording the number of dislodgments for 2 months before and after switching to transparent polyurethane dressings. Gathering internal evidence on the unit with their own patients will provide further evidence to support their change in practice.

Evidence-based decision making is influenced by the practitioner's experience and skills. Clinician skills include the expertise that develops from multiple observations of patients and how they react to certain interventions. *Clinical expertise* is essential for avoiding the mechanical application of care maps, decision rules, and guidelines. Consider an example in which healthcare professionals who work in a psychiatric outpatient facility are wondering whether they are providing the best possible care to their patients with schizophrenia. One of these providers offers to search the literature and finds a recent systematic review reporting that social skills training supported employment programs and that cognitive behavior therapy improved some outcomes in patients with schizophrenia (Wykes, Steel, Everitt, et al., 2008). In considering these interventions, the healthcare providers believed that they had the expertise to conduct social skills training, as well as access to employment programs to which they could refer their clients. However, they believed that they did not have the skills to provide cognitive behavior therapy. As a result, the healthcare providers decided to investigate avenues for learning this skill. Then, they presented a proposal to the clinic director that summarized the research evidence and outlined a plan for their continuing education and program development.

In the clinical decision-making model, clinical expertise is the mechanism that provides for the integration of the other model components. For example, the practitioner's clinical expertise will influence the

- Quality of the initial assessment of the client's clinical state and circumstances
- Problem formulation
- Decision about whether the best evidence and availability of healthcare resources substantiate a new approach
- Exploration of patient preferences
- Delivery of the clinical intervention
- Evaluation of the outcome for that particular patient

The following scenario exemplifies integrating the best available scientific evidence with clinical expertise. The local school board is concerned about the string of suicides and additional attempts at self-harm in the high schools in the last year. It asks the school nurses and counselors to implement a program for students who have attempted suicide or are otherwise engaging in self-harm. The teachers and school board are very supportive of the program, the school nurses and counselors have the skills to implement this program, and resources are sufficient to mount the program. However, the nurses and counselors search the literature and find a high-quality systematic review that shows evidence that these sorts of programs are not effective (Crawford, Thomas, Khan, et al., 2007). The school nurses and counselors recommend that the self-harm program not be offered but that instead, the school board participates in offering and evaluating a "healthy school" approach, which includes an ongoing curriculum in self-esteem enhancement, conflict resolution, and positive relationship building.

The factors in the EBP model will vary in their extent of influence in clinical decision making, depending on the decision to be made. In the past, EBP has been criticized for its "cookbook approach" to patient care. Some believe that it focuses solely on research evidence and in so doing, ignores patient preferences. Figure 11.1 shows that research evidence is only one factor in the evidence-based decision-making process and is always considered within the context of the other factors. Depending on the decision, the primary determining factor will vary. One of the advantages of this model is that healthcare providers have not traditionally considered research evidence in their decision-making process (Estabrooks, 1998), and this model serves as a reminder to them that such evidence should be one of the factors they consider in their decision making.

Models to Change Practice in an Organization

> *The mind has exactly the same power as the hands; not*
> *merely to grasp the world, but to change it.*
> *Colin Wilson*

There is increasing recognition that efforts to change practice should be guided by conceptual models or frameworks (Graham, Tetroe, & the KT Theories Research Group, 2007). Numerous models have been designed to help clinicians implement an evidence-based change in practice. Graham et al. conducted a literature review of the many models that exist and identified commonalities in terms of their steps or phases. These include the following:

- Identify a problem that needs addressing.
- Identify stakeholders or change agents who will help make the change in practice happen.
- Identify a practice change shown to be effective through high-quality research that is designed to address the problem.
- Identify, and if possible, address the potential barriers to the practice change.
- Use effective strategies to disseminate information about the practice change to those implementing it.
- Implement the practice change.
- Evaluate the impact of the practice change on structure, process, and outcome measures.
- Identify activities that will help sustain the change in practice.

In the rest of this chapter, we describe seven models that have been created to facilitate change to EBP. These seven models include

1. The Stetler model of evidence-based practice
2. The Iowa model of evidence-based practice to promote quality care

3. The model for evidence-based practice change
4. The Advancing Research and Clinical practice through close Collaboration (ARCC) model
5. The Promoting Action on Research Implementation in Health Services (PARIHS) framework
6. The clinical scholar model
7. The Johns Hopkins nursing evidence-based practice model

The Stetler Model of Evidence-Based Practice

The original Stetler/Marram model for RU was published in 1976 to fill a void regarding the realistic application of research findings to practice (Stetler & Marram, 1976). The original model has undergone three revisions in order to provide a conceptual framework and strengthen its underpinnings, integrate emerging concepts of EBP, and clarify and highlight critical concepts (Stetler, 1994a, 2001a, 2001b, in press). The core foci of all revisions were and continue to be critical thinking and a primary concern with use of research findings. However, as introduced in 1994, the model has long recognized the value of information beyond research, and in 2001, explicitly introduced additional sources of both *external* and *internal* evidence—described later in the definitions section—that could influence an ultimate "use" decision (Stetler, 1994a, 2001b). Through work on an organizational model of EBP at Baystate Medical Center, with the Stetler model as its underpinning, the 2001 version became integrally related to the concept of evidence-based nursing practice (i.e., practice that stresses "the use of research findings and, as appropriate, quality improvement data, other operational and evaluation data, the consensus of recognized experts and affirmed experience to substantiate practice" [Stetler, Brunell, Giuliano, et al., 1998, p. 49]).

Overview of the Stetler Model

The Stetler model (Figure 11.2) outlines a series of steps to assess and use research findings to facilitate safe and effective evidence-based nursing practice. Over the years of its evolution, the model has grown in complexity in order to provide more guidance around critical utilization concepts, as well as details and options involved in applying research to practice in the real world. In 2009, more modifications were made to the narrative in both pages of the model to better clarify the role of supplemental evidence and to highlight implementation tools (Stetler, in press).

The Stetler model has long been known as a practitioner-oriented model because of its focus on critical thinking and use of findings by the individual practitioner (Kim, 1999; Stetler & Marram, 1976). The 2001 version provided clarification that this guided problem-solving process also applies to groups of practitioners engaged in RU/EBP. Yet, the model maintains the bottom line assumption that even prepackaged, research-based recommendations are applied at the skilled practitioner level to individual patients, staff members, or other targets of use. Without targeted critical thinking at that level, application of research may become a task-oriented, mechanistic routine that can lead to inappropriate, ineffective, and non–evidence-based practice.

Definitions of Terms in the Stetler Model

The term *evidence* first appeared in the model in 1976 and, at that stage, referred only to research findings. However, in 1994, the concept of "substantiating evidence" was broadened to include additional sources of information because research indicates that "experiential and theoretical information are more likely to be combined with research information than they are to be ignored" (Stetler, 1994a, p. 17). By 2001, the concept of evidence had become a key element of the model (Figure 11.2; Stetler, 2001b). The following definitions underpin the multifaceted meaning of evidence within the current version (Stetler, 2001a, 2001b, in press; Stetler, et al., 1998):

● Evidence, within the context of healthcare, is defined as information or facts that are systematically obtained (i.e., obtained in a manner that is replicable, observable, credible, verifiable, or basically supportable; Stetler, 2002).

● Evidence, within the context of healthcare, can come from different sources and can vary in the degree to which it is systematically obtained and, thus, the degree to which it is perceived as basically supportable or *credible* for safe and effective use.

Different sources of evidence can be categorized as external and internal. *External* evidence comes primarily from research. Without research findings, there would be no EBP movement. However, where research findings are lacking, the consensus opinion/experience of widely recognized experts is considered supportable evidence and will often be used to supplement research-based recommendations. So, too, may credible program evaluations in the literature. *Internal* evidence comes primarily from systematically but locally obtained facts or information. It includes data from local performance, planning, quality, outcome, and evaluation activity as well as data collected through use of RU/EBP models to assess current practice and measure progress. In addition, internal evidence includes the *consensus* opinion and experience of local groups, as well as *experiential information* from individual professionals—if *affirmed*. Although an individual's isolated, unsystematic experience and related opinion are not considered to be credible evidence, those experiential observations or ways of thinking that have been reflected on, externalized, or exposed to explorations of truth and verification from various sources of data—and thus *affirmed*—are considered valid evidence in the model (Rycroft-Malone, Kitson, Harvey, et al., 2002; Rycroft-Malone & Stetler, 2004; Stetler, 2001b; Stetler et al., 1998). It is important to note, as Haynes (2002) did, the need to consider "evidence of patients' circumstances and wishes" (p. 3). Patient wishes are commonly included in EBP definitions, usually labeled as "patient preferences," and at the individual level can be considered internal evidence (Goode & Piedalue, 1999; Haynes, Sackett, Gray, et al., 1996).

Using the Stetler Model

The basic "how to" of EBP using the Stetler model is divided into the following five progressive categories or phases of activity. Figure 11.2 and related publications provide specific guidance and rationale for each of these steps (Stetler, 1994a, 2001b, in press; Stetler & Caramanica, 2007; Stetler, Morsi, Rucki, et al., 1998).

1. *Preparation*: Getting started by defining and affirming a priority need, reviewing the context in which use would occur, organizing the work if more than an individual practitioner is involved, and systematically initiating a search for relevant evidence, especially research.

2. *Validation*: Assessing a body of evidence by systematically critiquing each study and other relevant documents (e.g., a systematic review or guideline), with a *utilization* focus in mind, then choosing and summarizing the collected evidence that relates to the identified need.

3. *Comparative evaluation/decision making*: Making decisions about use after synthesizing the body of summarized evidence by applying a set of utilization criteria, then deciding whether and, if so, what to use in light of the identified need.

4. *Translation/application*: Converting findings into the type of change to be made/recommended, planning application as needed for formal use, putting the plan into action by using operational details of how to use the acceptable findings, and then enhancing adoption and actual implementation with an evidence-based change plan.

5. *Evaluation*: Evaluating the plan in terms of the degree to which it was implemented and whether the goals for using the evidence were met.

Despite the appearance that the systematic utilization of evidence is a linear, clear-cut process, it is more fluid. Figure 11.2B has serrated lines between the phases to indicate this fluidity and

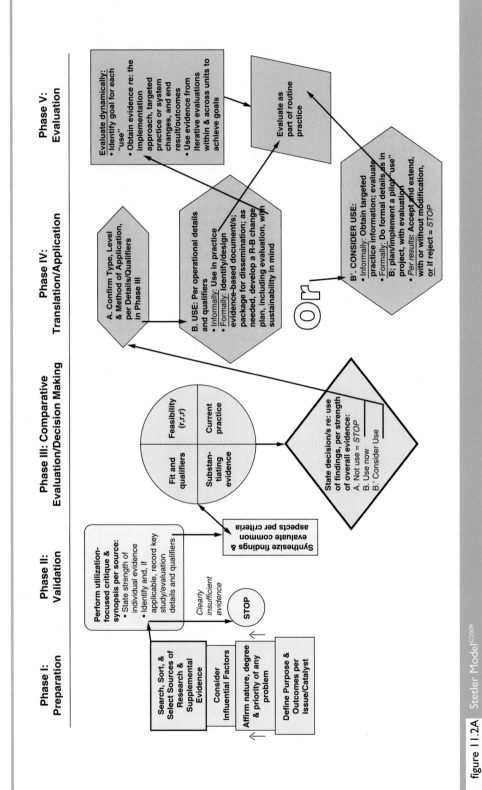

figure 11.2A Stetler Model©2009

Phase I: Preparation	Phase II: Validation	Phase III: Comparative Evaluation/Decision Making	Phase IV: Translation/Application	Phase V: Evaluation

Purpose, Context, & Sources of Evidence:
 	
• **Potential Issues/Catalysts** *= a problem, including unexplained variations; less-than-best practice; routine update of knowledge; validation/routine revision of procedures, etc; or innovative program goal*
• **Affirm/clarify perceived problem/s**, with internal evidence re: current practice *[baseline]*
• **Consider other influential internal and external factors,** e.g., timelines
• **Affirm and focus on high priority issues**
• **Decide if need to form a team, involve formal stakeholders, &/or assign project lead/facilitator**
• **Define desired, measurable outcome/s**
• **Seek out systematic reviews/guidelines first**
• **Determine need for an explicit type of research evidence, if relevant**
• **Select research sources with conceptual fit**
	Credibility of Evidence & Potential for/Detailed Qualifiers of Application:
	
	• **Critique & synopsize essential components, operational details, and other qualifying factors, per source**
	   ◦ *See instructions for use of utilization-focused review tables,* with evaluative criteria, to facilitate this task; fill in the tables for group decision making or potential future synthesis
	• **Critique** *systematic reviews and guidelines*
	• **Re-assess fit of individual sources**
	   ◦ *Rate the level & quality of each individual evidence source per a "table of evidence"*
	• **Differentiate statistical and clinical significance**
	• **Eliminate non-credible sources**
	• **End the process if there is clearly insufficient, credible external evidence that meets your need**
	
	*Stetler, Morsi, Rucki, et al. Appl Nurs Res 1998; 11(4):195-206 for noted tables, reviews, & synthesis process
		Synthesis & Decisions/Recommendations per Criteria of Applicability:
		
		• **Synthesize the cumulative findings:**
		   ◦ *Logically organize & display the similarities and differences across multiple findings, per common aspects or sub-elements of the topic under review*
		   ◦ *Evaluate degree of substantiation of each aspect/sub-element; reference any qualifying conditions for application*
		• **Evaluate degree & nature of other criteria:** *"feasibility (r,r,r = risk, resources, readiness); pragmatic fit, including potential qualifying factors to application; & nature of "current practice, including the urgency/risk of current issues/needs*
		• **Make a decision whether/what to use:**
		   ◦ *Can be a personal practitioner-level decision or a recommendation to others*
		   ◦ *"Judge strength of decision; indicate if primarily "research-based" (R-B) or, per hi use of supplemental info, "E-B"; note level of strength of recommendation/s per related" table; note any qualifying factors that may influence individualized variations*
		• **If decision = "Not use" research findings:**
		   ◦ *May conduct own research or delay use till additional research done by others*
		   ◦ *If still decide to act now, e.g., on evidence of consensus or another basis for practice, consider need for similar planned change and evaluation.*
		• **If decision = "Use/Consider Use," can mean a recommendation for or against a specific practice**
			Operational Definition of Use/Actions for Change:
			
			• **Types** *= cognitive/conceptual, symbolic &/or instrumental*
			• **Methods** *= informal or formal; direct or indirect*
			• **Levels** *= individual, group or department/organization*
			• **Direct instrumental use:** *change individual behavior (e.g., via intervention options); or change policy, procedure, protocol, algorithm, program, etc.*
			• **Cognitive use:** *validate current practice; change personal way of thinking; increase awareness; better understand or appreciate condition/s or experience/s*
			• **Symbolic use:** *develop position paper or proposal for change; or persuade others regarding a way of thinking*
			• **CAUTION: Assess whether translation/product or use goes beyond actual findings/evidence:**
			   ◦ *Research evidence may or may not provide various details for a complete policy, procedure, etc.; indicate this fact to users, and note differential levels of evidence therein*
			• **Formal dissemination & change strategies should be planned per relevant research and local barriers:**
			   ◦ *Passive education is usually not effective as an isolated strategy. Use Dx analysis* & an "implementation framework to develop a plan. Consider multiple strategies: e.g., opinion leaders, interactive education, reminders & audits.*
			   ◦ *Focus on context* to enhance sustainability of organizational-related change*
			• **Consider need for appropriate, reasoned variation**
			• **WITH B, where made a decision to use in the setting:**
			   ◦ *With formal use, may need a dynamic evaluation to effectively implement & continuously improve/refine use of best available evidence across units & time*
			• **WITH B', where made a decision to consider use & thus obtain additional, pragmatic information before a final decision**
			   ◦ *With formal consideration, do a pilot project*
			   ◦ *With a pilot project, must assess if need IRB review, per relevant institutional criteria*
				Alternative Evaluations:
				
				• **Evaluation per type, method, level:** e.g., consider conceptual use at individual level*
				• **Consider cost-benefit of change + various evaluation efforts**
				• **Use RU-as-a-process to enhance credibility of evaluation data**
				• **For both dynamic & pilot evaluations, include:**
				   ◦ *"formative, regarding actual implementation & goal progress*
				   ◦ *summative, regarding identified end goal and end-point outcomes*
				
				NOTE: Model applies to all forms of practice, i.e., educational, clinical, managerial, or other; to use effectively read 2001 & 1994 model papers.
				
				*Stetler et al, 2006 re: dx analysis
				
				**E.g.: Rogers' re: implications of attributes of a change; Rycroft-Malone et al, PARIHS (2002) & Green & Krueter's PRECEDE (1992) models re: implementation
				
				Stetler, 2003 on context &&Stetler & Caramanica, 2007 on outcomes

Part II Stetler Model©2009

figure 11.2B Stetler model of EBP has five phases (**A**, pictured and **B**, described): preparation, validation, comparative evaluation/decision making, translation/application, and evaluation. (From Stetler, C. B. [1994a]. Refinement of the Stetler/Marram model for application of research findings to practice. *Nursing Outlook, 42,* 15–25; Stetler, C. B. [2001a]. Updating the Stetler model of research utilization to facilitate evidence-based practice. *Nursing Outlook, 49,* 272–278. With permission from Elsevier Science.)

the need to occasionally revisit decisions (e.g., the relevance of specific studies and fit of various findings). Despite the model's complex appearance, its steps and concepts can be integrated into a professional's routine way of thinking about RU and EBP in general. This in turn influences how one routinely reads research and applies related findings (Stetler, 1994b; Stetler, Bautista, Vernale-Hannon, et al., 1995).

Critical Assumptions and Model Concepts

To optimize use of this model, key underlying assumptions must be understood (Stetler, 1994a, 2001b). These assumptions generate its critical thinking and practitioner orientation. For example, the model assumes that both formal and informal use of research findings—with supplemental use of other evidence—can occur in the practice setting. Formal, organization-initiated and sanctioned RU/EBP activity is most frequently discussed in the nursing literature. Often, this activity results in new policies, procedures, protocols, programs, and standards. After formal documents are disseminated, individuals are expected to use these translated and packaged findings. However, as Geyman suggests, EBP "requires the integration, patient by patient, of clinical expertise and judgment with the best available relevant external evidence" (1998, pp. 46–47). This may require reasoned variation (Stetler) in the context of a patient's circumstances, status, and preferences. Additionally, contextual and personal factors are assumed to influence an individual or group's use of research/other evidence and should be recognized up front by the user; and research and evaluative data provide probabilistic information rather than absolutes about each individual for whom the evidence is believed to generally "fit." In light of these assumptions, use of the model requires an RU/EBP competent individual.

Individual, RU/EBP competent practitioners (i.e., those who are skilled in the process of research/evidence utilization) also can informally use the model's critical thinking process in their routine practice and interactions with others (Cronenwett, 1994; Stetler, 1994a, 1994b). These practitioners may use evidence to substantiate or improve a current practice, change their way of thinking about an issue or routine, expand their repertoire of assessment or intervention strategies, or change a colleague's way of thinking about a treatment plan or issue (Stetler & Caramanica, 2007). Again, the assumption that the user possesses a certain level of knowledge and skills specifically related to the use of research and other forms of evidence is critical (Stetler, 2001b). Such knowledge and skills for the safe, appropriate, and effective use of findings include, for example, knowledge regarding research/evidence and its utilization—such as use of tables of evidence and a set of applicability criteria to determine the desirability and feasibility of using guidelines or a credible study, plus knowledge of the substantive area under consideration (Stetler).

Advanced level practitioners (e.g., clinicians with master's and doctorate degrees) are most likely to fulfill such expectations and also are more likely to routinely integrate research findings into their practices (Cronenwett, 1994; Stetler, 1994a, 1994b). Advanced-level clinicians are able to do so because of their critical thinking skills and advanced knowledge of their specialty areas—knowledge that provides them with a *body of evidence* with which to comparatively evaluate any study under consideration for application in their practice. With sufficient education and skills preparation, baccalaureate-prepared providers—in collaboration with advanced level clinicians—can and should participate in the identification of issues, development of formal evidence-based practices, and facilitation of related use.

Another of the model's underlying assumptions is that research findings and other credible evidence, such as consensus guidelines, may be used in multiple ways. Practitioners use evidence directly in observable ways to change how they behave or provide care through assessments, clinical procedures, and behavioral interventions. They also use evidence indirectly or conceptually, which is not so easy to observe but is very important to EBP. This can involve using evidence to change how one thinks about a patient or an issue. It also can involve adding evidence to one's body of knowledge, merging it with other information, and using it in the future (Stetler, 1994a). Finally, research findings and related evidence can be used symbolically (i.e., strategically) to influence the thinking and behavior of others. A key to safe use in such multiple forms, however, is that competent users will understand the strength of evidence underlying targeted uses, as well as the status of applicability criteria.

To thoroughly understand the Stetler model, it is most useful to read the 1994 paper—in particular when interested in use of research and related evidence for individual decision making—*AND* the 2001 paper, in particular when interested in the safe and effective use of research and related evidence for collective, formal decision making and related policies and practice documents.

The Iowa Model of Evidence-Based Practice to Promote Quality Care

The Iowa model of evidence-based practice to promote quality care (Titler, Kleiber, Steelman, et al., 2001) provides guidance for nurses and other clinicians in making decisions about day-to-day practices that affect patient outcomes. The Iowa model (Figure 11.3) outlines a pragmatic multiphase change process with feedback loops. The original model has been revised and updated (Titler, Kleiber, Steelman, et al., 1994; Titler et al., 2001). The model is based on the problem-solving steps in the scientific process and is widely recognized for its applicability and ease of use by multidisciplinary healthcare teams.

Using the Iowa Model

The Iowa model begins by encouraging clinicians to identify practice questions or "triggers" either through identification of a clinical problem or from new knowledge. Important triggers often come from questioning current practice. Problem-focused triggers will often have existing data that highlight an opportunity for improvement. Knowledge-focused triggers come from disseminated scientific knowledge (e.g., national guidelines, new research) leading practitioners to question current practice standards.

Staff nurses identify important and clinically relevant practice questions that can be addressed through the EBP process. A number of clinically important topics have been addressed using the Iowa model, including enteral feedings (Bowman, Greiner, Doerschug, et al., 2005), sedation management (Cullen, Greiner, Greiner, et al., 2005), verification of nasogastric tube placement (Farrington, Lang, Cullen, et al., 2009), bowel sounds assessment after abdominal surgery (Madsen, Sebolt, Cullen, et al., 2005), double gloving in the operating room (Stebral & Steelman, 2006), transfer of pediatric patients out of critical care (VanWaning, Kleiber, & Freyenberger, 2005), and drawing blood samples from umbilical artery catheters (Gordon, Bartruff, Gordon, et al., 2008). Administrative topics also have been addressed using the Iowa model (Stenger, Montgomery, & Briesemeister, 2007). Important issues have been addressed using the Iowa model well ahead of regulatory standards or changes in reimbursement (e.g., pain, falls, suicide risk, urinary catheter use) by supporting EBP projects on important clinical topics. Administrators and nurses in leadership positions can support clinicians' use of the EBP process by creating a culture of inquiry and a system supporting evidence-based care delivery (Cullen, Dawson, & Williams, 2009; Cullen et al., 2005; Davies, Edwards, Ploeg, et al., 2006; Gifford, Davies, Edwards, et al., 2006; Gifford, Davies, Edwards, et al., 2007).

Not every clinical question can be addressed through the EBP process. Identification of issues that are a priority for the organization will facilitate garnering the support needed to complete an EBP project. Higher priority may be given to topics that address high-volume, high-risk, or high-cost procedures, those that are closely aligned with the institution's strategic plan, or those that are driven by other institutional or market forces (e.g., changing reimbursement).

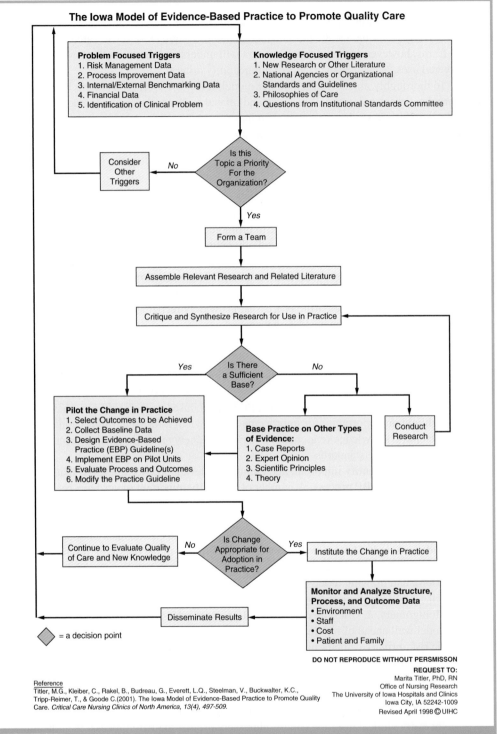

The Iowa Model of Evidence-Based Practice to Promote Quality Care

Problem Focused Triggers
1. Risk Management Data
2. Process Improvement Data
3. Internal/External Benchmarking Data
4. Financial Data
5. Identification of Clinical Problem

Knowledge Focused Triggers
1. New Research or Other Literature
2. National Agencies or Organizational Standards and Guidelines
3. Philosophies of Care
4. Questions from Institutional Standards Committee

Is this Topic a Priority For the Organization?

No → Consider Other Triggers

Yes

Form a Team

Assemble Relevant Research and Related Literature

Critique and Synthesize Research for Use in Practice

Is There a Sufficient Base?

Yes / *No*

Pilot the Change in Practice
1. Select Outcomes to be Achieved
2. Collect Baseline Data
3. Design Evidence-Based Practice (EBP) Guideline(s)
4. Implement EBP on Pilot Units
5. Evaluate Process and Outcomes
6. Modify the Practice Guideline

Base Practice on Other Types of Evidence:
1. Case Reports
2. Expert Opinion
3. Scientific Principles
4. Theory

Conduct Research

Is Change Appropriate for Adoption in Practice?

No → Continue to Evaluate Quality of Care and New Knowledge

Yes → Institute the Change in Practice

Monitor and Analyze Structure, Process, and Outcome Data
• Environment
• Staff
• Cost
• Patient and Family

Disseminate Results

◇ = a decision point

Reference
Titler, M.G., Kleiber, C., Rakel, B., Budreau, G., Everett, L.Q., Steelman, V., Buckwalter, K.C., Tripp-Reimer, T., & Goode C.(2001). The Iowa Model of Evidence-Based Practice to Promote Quality Care. *Critical Care Nursing Clinics of North America, 13(4), 497-509.*

figure 11.3 The Iowa model of evidence-based practice to promote quality care (Used with permission from Marita G. Titler, PhD, RN, FAAN, University of Iowa Hospitals and Clinics, © 1998. For permission to use or reproduce the model, please contact the University of Iowa Hospitals and Clinics at (319) 384. 9098.)

unit four

252

Considering how a topic fits within the organizational priorities can aid in obtaining support from senior leadership and other disciplines as well as in obtaining the resources necessary to carry out the practice change. If the trigger is not an organizational priority, practitioners may want to consider a different focus, different project outcomes, or other triggers for improving practice that better fit organizational needs. This and similar feedback loops within the model highlight the nonlinearity of the work and support continuing efforts for improving quality care through the EBP process.

Once there is commitment to addressing the topic, a team is formed to develop, implement, and evaluate the practice change. The team is ideally composed of stakeholders from practice, and may include the staff nurse(s), unit managers, advanced practice nurses (APNs), and interdisciplinary colleagues. Team membership requires several considerations to maximize the use of team members' skills and organizational linkages. During a recent project addressing oral mucositis using the Iowa model, team membership was designed to capture key linkages clinically and within the governance structure (Baumler, Brautigam, Bruene, et al., 2008). The team included members from pediatric and adult ambulatory and inpatient settings representing staff nurses, nurse managers, and APNs. Committee members also provided active linkages within the governance structure through their linkages with members from nursing quality management, hospital dentistry, dietary, hematology–oncology, radiation oncology, oral pathology, patient education, staff education, the products committee, the nursing policy committee, and the nursing management council. The team used these linkages to support communication, coordination, and reporting about the initiative.

Initially, the team selects, reviews, critiques, and synthesizes available research evidence. Collaboration with nursing librarians can be particularly helpful in optimizing yields from online bibliographic databases and other library resources. Librarians have expert knowledge and skills in the functionality of online resources, and when matched with clinicians' expertise, will result in yields with the best specificity to address the project trigger. If high-quality research evidence is not available or sufficient for determining practice, the team may recommend using lower levels of evidence (Gordon et al., 2008) or conduct of research to improve the evidence available for practice decisions (Kleiber, Hanrahan, Fagan, et al., 1993). When the evidence is sufficient, a practice change is piloted. The team tries the practice change to determine the feasibility and effectiveness of the EBP change in clinical care.

Piloting is an essential step in the process. Outcomes achieved in a controlled environment, when a researcher is testing a study protocol in a homogenous group of patients, may be different than those found when the evidence-based practice is used by multiple caregivers in a natural clinical setting without the tight controls of a research study. Thus, trialing the EBP change is essential for identifying issues before instituting a housewide rollout.

Piloting involves multiple steps when planning for both implementation and evaluation. The research evidence will provide direction for process and outcome indicators and measurement of baseline data, although significant modification of research measures is needed when evaluating quality improvement indicators used in EBP. Pilot evaluation is not replication research and must be narrowed to key indicators needed to provide direction for clinical decision making. Designing a draft practice guideline or protocol can take many forms including development of an evidence-based policy, procedure, care map, algorithm, or other document outlining the practice and decision points for clinician users. Implementation during the pilot requires planning and selection of effective implementation strategies (Titler, 2008; Titler & Everett, 2001; van Achterberg, Schoonhoven, & Grol, 2008). Evaluation of the process and outcome indicators is completed before and after implementation of the practice change. A comparison of prepilot and postpilot data will determine the success of the pilot, effectiveness of the evidence-based protocol, and need for modification of either the implementation process or the practice protocol.

Following the pilot, a determination is made regarding appropriateness of adoption beyond the pilot. A decision regarding adoption or modification of the practice is based upon the evaluative data from the pilot. If the practice change is not appropriate for adoption and rollout, quality or performance improvement monitoring is needed to ensure high-quality patient care. Additional steps for clinicians include watching for new knowledge, collaborating with researchers in the area, or conducting research to guide practice decisions. If the pilot results in positive outcomes, rollout and integration of the practice are facilitated through leadership support, education, and continuous monitoring of outcomes (Davies et al., 2006; Gifford et al., 2006; Gifford et al., 2007; Greenhalgh, Robert, Bate, et al., 2005; World Health Organization, 2007).

Evidence-based practice changes need ongoing evaluation with information incorporated into quality or performance improvement programs to promote integration of the practice into daily care. Monitoring and reporting trends of structure, process, and outcomes indicators with actionable feedback to clinicians can promote sustained integration of the practice change (Hysong, Best, & Pugh, 2006; Jamtvedt, Young, Kristoffersen, et al., 2006).

Dissemination of results is important for professional learning. Sharing project reports within and outside of the organization through presentations and publications supports the growth of an EBP culture in the organization, expands nursing knowledge, and encourages EBP changes in other organizations as well. Project reports can be used to learn the EBP process, to learn of practice updates, or to generate additional practice questions or triggers. Dissemination of project results is a key step in the cycle promoting adoption of EBPs within the healthcare system (Sigma Theta Tau International Research and Scholarship Advisory Committee, 2008).

The Iowa model guides clinicians through the EBP process. The model includes several feedback loops, reflecting analysis, evaluation, and modification based on the evaluative data of both process and outcome indicators. These are critical to individualizing the evidence to the practice setting and promoting adoption within the varying healthcare systems and settings within which nurses work. The feedback loops highlight the messy and nonlinear nature of EBP and support teams moving forward regardless. The Iowa model was designed to support evidence-based healthcare delivery by interdisciplinary teams (Baumler et al., 2008; Gordon et al., 2008; Stenger et al., 2007) by following a basic problem-solving approach using the scientific process, simplifying the process, and being highly application oriented. The large number of organizations using the Iowa model attests to its usefulness in practice.

The Model for Evidence-Based Practice Change

This model is a revised version of the model by Rosswurm and Larrabee (1999). The revised steps and schematic (Figure 11.4) were prompted by Larrabee's experience with teaching and leading nurses in the application of the original model since 1999 at West Virginia University hospitals and prior experience with teaching and leading nurses in RU and quality improvement (Larrabee, 2004).

The title of the revised model was changed to clarify that it was designed for guiding multiple practice change projects because the author thought the original title, "Model for Change to Evidence-Based Practice," could infer a one-time philosophical decision to pursue EBP. In its application, the actions of the original Step 3, "synthesize the best evidence," required a disproportionately longer time to conduct than the other steps. To distribute the actions in Step 3 across two steps and to retain six steps in the model, the original Step 2 was added to Step 1 and the original Step 3 was divided into two: Step 2, "locate the best evidence," and Step 3, "critically analyze the evidence" (Larrabee, 2009, p. 23). The revised model also integrates principles of quality improvement, use of team work tools, and evidence-based translation strategies to promote adoption of a new practice. The handbook (Larrabee) describing the revised model includes a number of forms and examples of their use that may be helpful to nurses applying the model.

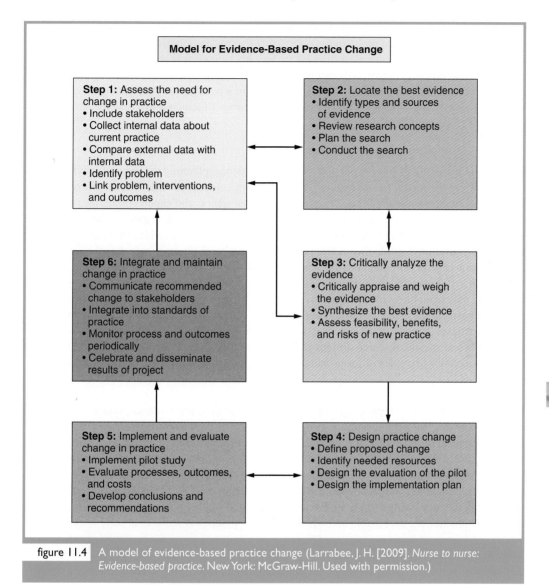

figure 11.4   A model of evidence-based practice change (Larrabee, J. H. [2009]. *Nurse to nurse: Evidence-based practice.* New York: McGraw-Hill. Used with permission.)

Progression through the six steps is illustrated by a fabricated EBP project focused on improving outcomes for patients with chronic heart failure.

Step 1: Assess the Need for Change in Practice

Key actions consist of identifying a practice problem or opportunity for improvement; creating an EBP team of stakeholders to address the practice problem; collecting internal data about that practice; collecting external data for benchmarking with the internal data; refining the practice problem statement by linking the problem with possible interventions and desired outcomes or by developing a PICOT (population-intervention-comparison-outcome-time frame) question. Often, recognition of a practice problem prompts an EBP project. Other times, an existing EBP team with the goal of conducting at least one EBP project per year will need to consider what patient outcomes most need improvement. Structured brainstorming and multivoting are team work tools that may be helpful during this process. Once the EBP team has selected a practice problem as the focus of a project, team members should collect internal and external data relevant to that practice problem to confirm that there is an opportunity for improvement. It is important to justify the focus of the EBP project because such projects are resource intensive. Statistical process control tools that may be useful during this activity include histograms and Pareto charts. The EBP team members must prepare a practice problem statement or PICO question to clarify for themselves and others what the project focus is and to use the statement or question to guide their work during Step 2.

Step 2: Locate the Best Evidence

Key actions are identifying the types and sources of evidence, planning the search for evidence, and conducting the search for the best evidence. Types of evidence include clinical practice guidelines, systematic reviews, single studies, critical appraisal topics, and expert committee reports. Sources of evidence include electronic bibliographic databases, websites, journals, and books. The search for evidence should be planned as a rigorous systematic review, which includes formulating the research question to guide the search, deciding on the search strategy, selecting the inclusion and exclusion criteria, and planning the synthesis. While planning, EBP team members can add rigor to the systematic review by selecting forms for critically appraising evidence sources, for organizing data from the evidence sources in a table of evidence, and identifying key points to use when synthesizing the evidence during Step 3. Critical appraisal forms or checklists are available in journal articles (Rosswurm & Larrabee, 1999) and online, including some that are for systematic reviews and specific research designs (Scottish Intercollegiate Guidelines Network, 2007).The handbook includes examples of forms and completed examples of their use (Larrabee, 2009).

Step 3: Critically Analyze the Evidence

Key actions are critically appraising and judging the strength of the evidence; synthesizing the evidence; and assessing the feasibility, benefits, and risks of implementing the new practice. Critical appraisal of the evidence is conducted using the forms selected during Step 2. Likewise, the forms selected during Step 2 are used to display information about the data sources in an evidence table that is then used to prepare the synthesis worksheet. After synthesizing the evidence, the EBP team members judge whether the body of evidence is of sufficient quantity and strength to support a practice change. If so, EBP team members consider whether or not benefits and risks of the new practice are acceptable and whether the new practice is feasible in their workplace.

Step 4: Design Practice Change

Key actions include defining the proposed practice change, identifying needed resources, designing the evaluation of the pilot, and designing the implementation plan. The description of the new practice may be in the form of a protocol, policy, procedure, care map, or guideline and should be supported by the body of evidence synthesized in Step 3. Needed resources will be specific for the new practice and may include personnel, materials, equipment, or forms. Even if the new practice is specific to just one unit, its use should be pilot tested to evaluate it for any necessary adaptation before making it a standard of care. Therefore, EBP team members need to design the implementation plan and the evaluation plan, considering translation strategies that promote adoption of a new practice. Some strategies include use of change champions, opinion leaders, educational sessions, educational materials, reminder systems, and audit and feedback. After designing the evaluation plan, EBP team members collect baseline data on the process and outcome indicators for which they will collect postpilot data during Step 5.

Step 5: Implement and Evaluate Change in Practice

Key actions include implementing the pilot study; evaluating process, outcomes, and costs; and developing conclusions and recommendations. The EBP team members follow the implementation plan designed during Step 4, obtaining verbal feedback from those expected to use the new practice and from the change champions who are promoting the use of the new practice. That feedback will be used to make minor adjustments in the implementation plan, if necessary. After the pilot phase concludes, the EBP team members collect and analyze the postpilot data, comparing with the baseline data. Team members use those data together with the verbal feedback to decide if they should adapt, adopt, or reject the new practice. Few teams reach this stage and decide to reject the new practice. More commonly, the new practice needs to be slightly adapted for a better fit with the organization. Once team members make this decision, they prepare conclusions and recommendations to share with administrative leaders during Step 6.

Step 6: Integrate and Maintain Change in Practice

Key actions include sharing recommendations about the new practice with stakeholders, incorporating the new practice into the standards of care, monitoring the process and outcome indicators, and celebrating and disseminating results of the project. Team members provide information about the project and their recommendations to all stakeholders, including administrative leaders who must approve making the new practice a standard of care. Once that approval is given, the EBP team members can arrange to provide inservice education to all providers expected to use the new practice. They also should make plans for ongoing monitoring of the process and outcome indicators. The frequency of this monitoring can be based on judging how well the indicators are being met. The data from ongoing monitoring can be used to identify the need for further refinements in the new practice or the need for a new EBP project. The handbook (Larrabee, 2009) provides a timeline template for preparing an annual calendar with multiple EBP projects, including ongoing monitoring of completed projects. Finally, EBP team members should consider disseminating information about their project outside the organization through presentation at professional conferences and publication.

The Advancing Research and Clinical Practice Through Close Collaboration Model: A Model for Systemwide Implementation and Sustainability of Evidence-Based Practice

The purpose of the ARCC model is to provide healthcare institutions and clinical settings with an organized conceptual framework that can guide systemwide implementation and sustainability of EBP to achieve quality outcomes. Since evidence-based clinicians are essential in cultivating an entire system culture that implements EBP as standard of care, the ARCC model encompasses key strategies for individual as well as organizational change to best practice.

The ARCC model was originally conceptualized by Bernadette Melnyk in 1999 as part of a strategic planning initiative to unify research and clinical practice in order to advance EBP within an academic medical center for the ultimate purpose of improving healthcare quality and patient outcomes (Melnyk & Fineout-Overholt, 2002). Shortly following conceptualization of the ARCC Model, advanced practice and point-of-care nurses in the medical center were surveyed about the barriers and facilitators of EBP. The results of this survey along with control theory (Carver & Sheier, 1982; Carver & Sheier, 1998) and cognitive behavioral theory (CBT; Beck, Rush, Shaw, et al. [1979]) guided the formulation of key constructs in the ARCC model. An important facilitator of EBP identified by nurses who completed the survey was a mentor, which eventually became the central mechanism for implementing and sustaining EBP in the ARCC model. Over the past decade, Melnyk & Fineout-Overholt have further developed the ARCC model through empirical testing of key relationships in the model and their extensive work with healthcare institutions to advance and sustain EBP.

The Conceptual Framework Guiding the Advancing Research and Clinical Practice Through Close Collaboration Model

Control Theory (Carver & Scheier, 1982, 1998) contends that a discrepancy between a standard or goal (e.g., systemwide implementation of EBP) and a current state (e.g., the extent to which an organization is implementing EBP) should motivate behaviors in individuals to reach the goal. However, many barriers exist in healthcare organizations that inhibit clinicians from implementing EBP, including (a) inadequate EBP knowledge and skills, (b) lack of administrative support, (c) lack of an EBP mentor, (d) lack of belief that EBP improves patient care and outcomes, and (e) perceived lack of authority to change patient care procedures (Funk, Tornquist, & Champagne, 1995; Hutchinson & Johnston, 2006; Melnyk & Fineout-Overholt, 2005). In the ARCC model, EBP mentors (i.e., typically APNs who have in-depth knowledge and skills of EBP and of individual and organizational change strategies along with mentorship skills) are developed and placed within the healthcare system as a key strategy to mitigate barriers commonly encountered by practicing clinicians when implementing EBP (see Figure 11.5). As barriers diminish, clinicians are expected to implement EBP to improve patient outcomes.

In the ARCC Model, CBT is used to guide behavioral change in individual clinicians toward EBP. CBT stresses the importance of individual, social, and environmental factors that influence cognition, learning, emotions, and behavior (Beck et al., 1979; Lam, 2005). The basic foundation of CBT is that an individual's behaviors and emotions are, in large part, determined by the way he or she thinks or his or her beliefs (i.e., the thinking-feeling-behaving triangle; Melnyk & Moldenhauer, 2006). Based on CBT, a tenet of the ARCC model contends that when clinicians' beliefs about the value of EBP and their ability to implement it are strengthened, there will be greater implementation of evidence-based care. In the ARCC model, EBP mentors work with point-of-care clinicians to strengthen their beliefs about the value of EBP and their ability to implement it.

By changing your thinking, you change your beliefs.

Author Unknown

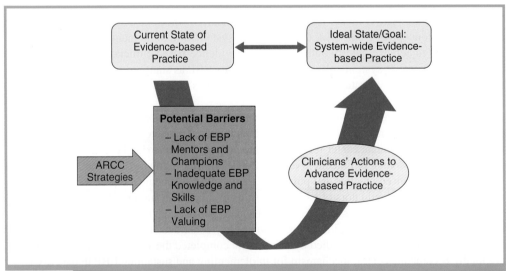

figure 11.5   Control theory as a conceptual guide for the ARCC model
(© Melnyk & Fineout-Overholt, 2005.)

Central Constructs Within and Evidence to Support the Advancing Research and Clinical Practice Through Close Collaboration Model

The first step in the ARCC model is an organizational assessment of culture and readiness for systemwide implementation of EBP (see Figure 11.6). The culture of an organization can foster EBP or stymie it. If sufficient resources are not allocated to support the work of EBP, progress in advancing EBP throughout the organization will be slow. Administrators and point-of-care providers alike must adopt the EBP paradigm for systemwide implementation to be achieved and sustained. Assessment of organizational culture can be determined with the use of the Organizational Culture and Readiness Scale for System-wide Integration of Evidence-based Practice (OCRSIEP) (Fineout-Overholt & Melnyk, 2006). With the use of this 26-item Likert scale, a description of organizational characteristics, including strengths and opportunities for fostering EBP within a healthcare system, is identified. Examples of items on the OCRSIEP include (a) To what extent is EBP clearly described as central to the mission and philosophy of your institution? (b) To what extent do you believe that EBP is practiced in your organization? and (c) To what extent is the nursing staff with whom you work committed to EBP? The scale has established face and content validity, with internal consistency reliabilities consistently greater than 0.85 (see Appendix N for a sample of the OCRSIEP scale).

Once key strengths and opportunities for fostering EBP within the organization are identified with the OCRSIEP scale, a cadre of EBP mentors is developed within the healthcare system. Evidence-based practice mentors are healthcare providers, typically APNs or baccalaureate-prepared nurses where health systems do not have APNs, who work directly with point-of-care staff to implement EBP, including (a) shifting from a traditional paradigm

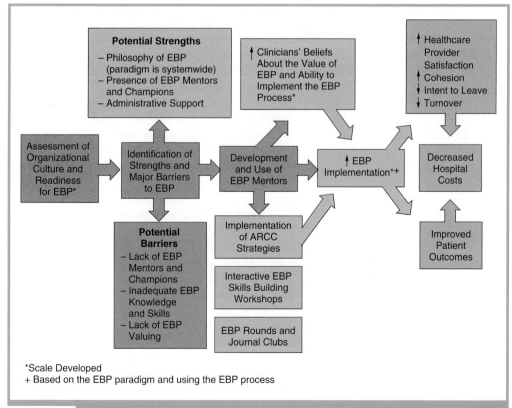

*Scale Developed
+ Based on the EBP paradigm and using the EBP process

figure 11.6   Melnyk and Fineout-Overholt's ARCC model (© Melnyk & Fineout-Overholt, 2005.)

to an EBP paradigm, (b) conducting EBP implementation (EBPI) projects, and (c) integrating practice-generated data to improve healthcare quality as well as patient and/or system outcomes. Evidence-based practice mentors also have knowledge and skills in individual behavior and organizational change strategies to facilitate changes in clinician behavior and spark sustainable changes in organizational culture, which require specific intervention strategies, time, and persistence. Some key components of the EBP mentor role as defined in the ARCC model include (a) ongoing assessment of an organization's capacity to sustain an EBP culture; (b) building EBP knowledge and skills by conducting interactive group workshops and one-on-one mentoring; (c) stimulating, facilitating, and educating nursing staff toward a culture of EBP, with a focus on overcoming barriers to best practice; (d) role modeling EBP; (e) conducting ARCC EBP enhancing strategies, such as EBP rounds, journal clubs, webpages, newsletters, and fellowship programs; (f) working with staff to generate internal evidence (i.e., practice-generated) through outcomes management and EBPI projects; (g) facilitating staff involvement in research to generate external evidence; (h) using evidence to foster best practice; and (i) collaborating with interdisciplinary professionals to advance and sustain EBP. These mentors also have excellent strategic planning, implementation, and outcomes evaluation skills so that they can monitor the impact of their role and overcome barriers in moving the system to a culture of best practice (Melnyk, 2007). Mentorship with direct care staff on clinical units by ARCC EBP mentors is important in strengthening clinicians' beliefs about the value of EBP and their ability to implement it (Melnyk & Fineout-Overholt, 2002).

In the ARCC model, beliefs about the value of EBP and a clinician's ability to implement it are measured with the EBP Beliefs Scale (EBPB; Melnyk & Fineout-Overholt, 2002). This is a 16-item Likert scale, with responses that range from 1 (strongly disagree) to 5 (strongly agree). Examples of items on the EBPB scale include (a) I am clear about the steps in EBP, (b) I am sure that I can implement EBP, and (c) I am sure that evidence-based guidelines can improve care. The EBPB scale has established face, content, and construct validity, with internal consistency reliabilities consistently greater than 0.85 (Melnyk, Fineout-Overholt, & Mays, 2008; see Appendix N for a sample copy of the scale). In the ARCC model, higher beliefs about EBP are expected to increase EBPI and, thereby, improve healthcare outcomes.

Findings from research indicate that when nurses' beliefs about the value of EBP and their ability to implement it are strong, then their implementation of EBP is greater (Melnyk, Fineout-Overholt, Feinstein, et al., 2004). Additionally, findings from a recent randomized controlled pilot study indicated that nurses who received mentoring from an ARCC EBP mentor, in comparison to those who received mentoring in physical assessment skills, had (a) stronger EBPB, (b) greater implementation of EBP, and (c) stronger group cohesion (R. Levin, personal communication, November 20, 2006), which is known to be a predictor of nurse satisfaction and turnover rates. Nurses in the ARCC EBP group also had less turnover than nurses in the physical assessment group.

Evidence-based practice implementation in the ARCC model is defined as practicing based on the EBP paradigm. This paradigm uses the EBP process to improve outcomes. The process begins with asking clinical questions and incorporates research evidence and practice-based evidence in point-of-care decision making. However, simply engaging the process is not sufficient. The results of the first three steps of the process (i.e., establishing valid and reliable research evidence) must be coupled with (a) the expertise of the clinician to gather practice-based evidence (i.e., data from practice initiatives such as Quality Improvement (QI); gather, interpret, and act on patient data; and effectively use healthcare resources and (b) what the patient and family value and prefer (see Figure 11.4). This amalgamation leads to innovative decision making at the point of care with quality outcomes as the final product. While research evidence, practice evidence, and patient/client data as interpreted through expertise and patient preferences must always be present, a context of caring allows each patient–provider encounter to be individualized (see Chapter 1, Figure 1.2). Within an organization that fosters an EBP culture, this paradigm can thrive at the patient–provider level as well as across the organization, resulting in transformed healthcare.

Evidence-based practice implementation in the ARCC model is measured with the EBPI Scale (Melnyk & Fineout-Overholt, 2002). Clinicians respond to each of the 18 Likert scale items on the EBPI by answering how often in the last 8 weeks they have performed certain EBP initiatives, such as (a) generated a PICOT question about my practice, (b) used evidence to change my clinical practice, (c) evaluated the outcomes of a practice change, and (d) shared the outcome data collected with colleagues. The EBPI has established face, content, and construct validity as well as internal consistency reliabilities greater than 0.85 (Melnyk et al., 2008; see Appendix N for a sample copy of the scale). In the ARCC model, it is contended that greater EBPI is associated with higher nurse satisfaction, which will eventually lead to less turnover rates and healthcare expenditures.

Several hospitals throughout the United States have adopted the ARCC model in their efforts to build and sustain an EBP culture in their organizations. As a part of building this culture, groups of nurses and other interdisciplinary health professionals have attended a week-long EBP mentorship immersion program, conducted by the authors of the ARCC model. These programs have prepared more than 200 nurses and interdisciplinary clinicians across the nation and globe as ARCC EBP mentors. Some of the individuals who have attended these immersion programs have negotiated roles as EBP mentors within their healthcare organizations. In addition, the authors of the ARCC model launched the nation's first 17-credit online EBP graduate certificate program that prepares expert EBP mentors through the Center for the Advancement of Evidence-Based Practice at Arizona State University. Individuals who have attended the certificate program have negotiated roles as directors of EBP, directors of quality, and vice presidents of clinical nursing practice, and have served as expert EBP mentors within their healthcare organizations. The final step in the ARCC model is for EBP mentors and other clinicians who practice according to the EBP paradigm to impact provider, patient, and system outcomes. Evidence-based practice mentors and those they influence focus on achieving the best outcomes of care, thereby making a difference in patients' lives and the success of the organization. Research is currently underway to gather additional evidence that describes the relationships in the ARCC model and establishes outcomes of the ARCC EBP mentor within healthcare systems, as the EBP mentor may very well be the key to sustainability of EBP in healthcare organizations (Melnyk, 2007).

Using the Advancing Research and Clinical Practice Through Close Collaboration Model

Because valid and reliable instruments are available to measure key constructs in the ARCC model, barriers and facilitators to EBP along with clinicians' beliefs about and actual implementation of EBP can be readily assessed and identified by organizations. There also are well-established workshops and academic offerings available that develop EBP mentors who can work closely with point-of-care staff to strengthen their beliefs about and implementation of EBP. The availability of tools to measure an organization's EBP culture as well as clinicians' EBPB and implementation also allows an organization to monitor its progress in the systemwide implementation and sustainability of EBP.

Promoting Action on Research Implementation in Health Services Framework

Getting evidence into practice is complex, multifaceted, and dynamic. The PARIHS framework was developed in an attempt to reflect these complexities, representing the interdependence and interplay of the many factors that appear to play a role in the successful implementation (SI) of evidence in practice. Previous research exploring why research evidence is not routinely used in practice has tended to focus at the level of individual practitioners and on barriers to utilization (e.g., Hunt, 1991; McSherry, Artley, & Holloran, 2006; Parahoo, 1999). While individual factors are important, getting evidence into practice requires more than a focus on addressing individual influencing factors. The PARIHS framework, which provides a conceptual map, is premised on the notion that the implementation of research-based practice depends on the ability to achieve significant and planned behavior change involving individuals, teams, and organizations. SI is represented as a function (f) of the nature and type of evidence (e), the qualities of the context (c) in which the evidence is being introduced, and the way the process is facilitated (f), whereby SI = f(E,C,F). The three elements (i.e., evidence, context, and facilitation) are each positioned on a high-to-low continuum, where in each implementation effort, the aim is to move toward "high" in order to optimize the chances of success.

Development and Refinement

The PARIHS framework has developed over time (Kitson, Harvey, & McCormack, 1998; Rycroft-Malone et al., 2002; Rycroft-Malone, Harvey, Seers, et al., 2004). It was originally conceived inductively from an analysis of practice development, quality improvement, and research project work (Kitson et al., 1998). Theoretical and retrospective analysis of four studies led to the proposal that the most SI seems to occur when evidence is scientifically robust; matches professional consensus and patients' preferences (high evidence); when the context is receptive to change with sympathetic cultures, strong leadership, and appropriate monitoring and feedback systems (high context); and when there is appropriate facilitation of change with input from skilled external and internal facilitators (high facilitation).

Since the framework's conception and publication, it has undergone research and development work. Most notably this has included a concept analysis of each of the dimensions (Harvey, Loftus-Hills, Rycroft-Malone, et al. 2002; McCormack, Kitson, Harvey, et al., 2002; Rycroft-Malone, Seers, Titchen, et al., 2004) and a research study to assess content validity (Rycroft-Malone, et al., 2004). This enabled some conceptual clarity to be gained about the framework's constituent elements and verification of its content validity. As a result of this work, the framework has been refined over time with the addition, for example, of subelements (Table 11.1). The next phase of work, currently underway, is tool development (Kitson, Rycroft-Malone, Harvey, et al., 2008).

PARIHS Elements

Evidence. Evidence is conceived in a broad sense within the framework including propositional and nonpropositional knowledge from four different types of evidence. These include research, clinical experience, patients and caregivers' experience, and local context information (see Rycroft-Malone, et al. [2004] for a detailed discussion). For evidence to be located toward high, certain criteria have to be met. These include that research evidence (qualitative and quantitative) is well conceived and conducted and that there is consensus about it, and that clinical experience has been made explicit and verified through critical reflection, critique, and debate. Patient experience is high when patients (and/or significant others) are part of the decision-making process and when patient narratives are seen as a valid source of evidence. Finally, local information/data could be considered as part of the evidence base if it has been systematically collected, evaluated, and reflected upon. Clearly, this conceptualization indicates the need for an interaction between the scientific and experiential, which requires a dialectical process.

Context. Context refers to the environment or setting in which the proposed change is to be implemented (see McCormack et al. [2002], for a detailed discussion). Within PARIHS, the contextual factors that promote SI fall under three broad subelements: culture, leadership, and

table 11.1 **PARIHS elements and subelements**

Elements	Sub-elements	
Evidence	Low	High
Research	• Poorly conceived, designed, and/or executed research • Seen as the only type of evidence • Not valued as evidence • Seen as certain	• Well-conceived, designed, and executed research, appropriate to the research question • Seen as one part of a decision • Valued as evidence • Lack of certainty acknowledged • Social construction acknowledged • Judged as relevant • Importance weighted • Conclusions drawn
Clinical experience	• Anecdote, with no critical reflection and judgment • Lack of consensus within similar groups • Not valued as evidence • Seen as the only type of evidence	• Clinical experience and expertise reflected upon, tested by individuals and groups • Consensus within similar groups • Valued as evidence • Seen as one part of the decision • Judged as relevant • Importance weighted • Conclusions drawn
Patient experience	• Not valued as evidence • Patients not involved • Seen as the only type of evidence	• Valued as evidence • Multiple biographies used • Partnerships with healthcare professionals • Seen as one part of a decision • Judged as relevant • Importance weighted • Conclusions drawn
Local data/information	• Not valued as evidence • Lack of systematic methods for collection and analysis • Not reflected upon • No conclusions drawn	• Valued as evidence • Collected and analyzed systematically and rigorously • Evaluated and reflected upon • Conclusions drawn
Context	Low	High

Culture	• Unclear values and beliefs
	• Low regard for individuals
	• Task driven organization
	• Lack of consistency
	• Resources not allocated
	• Not integrated with strategic goals
		• Able to define culture(s) in terms of prevailing values/beliefs
		• Values individual staff and clients
		• Promotes learning organization
		• Consistency of individual's role/experience to value:
		  • relationship with others
		  • teamwork
		  • power and authority
		  • rewards/recognition
		• Resources—human, financial, equipment—allocated
		• Initiative fits with strategic goals and is a key practice/patient issue

(table continues on page 264)

table 11.1 **PARIHS elements and subelements** (continued)

Elements	Sub-elements	
Evidence	Low	High
Leadership	• Traditional, command and control leadership • Lack of role clarity • Lack of teamwork • Poor organizational structures • Autocratic decision-making processes • Didactic approaches to learning/teaching/managing	• Transformational leadership • Role clarity • Effective teamwork • Effective organizational structures • Democratic inclusive decision-making processes • Enabling/empowering approach to teaching/learning/managing

Evaluation	• Absence of any form of feedback
	• Narrow use of performance information sources
	• Evaluations rely on single rather than multiple methods
		• Feedback on:
		  • individual
		  • team
		  • system
		  • performance
		• Use of multiple sources of information on performance
		• Use of multiple methods:
		  • clinical
		  • performance
		  • economic
		  • experience
		  • evaluations

Facilitation	Low inappropriate facilitation	High appropriate facilitation
Purpose Role	Task *Doing for others:* • Episodic contact • Practical/technical help • Didactic, traditional approach to teaching • External agents • Low intensity—extensive coverage	Holistic *Enabling others:* • Sustained partnership • Developmental • Adult learning approach to teaching • Internal/external agents • High intensity—limited coverage
Skills and attributes	*Task/doing for others* • Project management skills • Technical skills • Marketing skills Subject/technical/clinical credibility	*Holistic/enabling others* • Co-counseling • Critical reflection • Giving meaning • Flexibility of role • Realness/authenticity

evaluation, which operate in a dynamic, multileveled way. It is proposed that organizations that have cultures that could be described as "learning organizations" are those that are more conducive to change (high). Such cultures contain features such as decentralized decision making, a focus on relationships between managers and workers, and management styles that are facilitative. Leaders have a key role to play in creating such cultures. Transformational leaders, as opposed to those who command and control, have the ability to challenge individuals and teams in an enabling, inspiring way (high). Finally, contexts with evaluative mechanisms that collect multiple sources of evidence of performance at individual, team, and system levels comprise the third element of a high context.

Facilitation. Facilitation refers to the process of enabling or making easier the implementation of evidence into practice (see Harvey et al. [2002] for a detailed discussion). Facilitation is achieved by an individual carrying out a specific role—a facilitator—with the appropriate skills and knowledge to help individuals, teams, and/or organizations apply evidence in practice. With PARIHS, the purpose of facilitation can vary from being task-orientated, which requires technical and practical support, to enabling, which requires more of a developmental, process-orientated approach. It is argued that the skills and attributes required to fulfill the role are likely to depend on the situation, individuals, and contexts involved. Therefore, skilled facilitators are those who can adjust their role and style to the different stages of an implementation project and the needs of those with whom they are working.

Using the Framework

As each of the elements and subelements are on a continuum of high to low, it is suggested that implementation activities and processes be aimed at moving each of them toward high to increase the chances of success. As such, the framework provides a map of the elements that might require attention and a set of questions that could be asked at the outset of any implementation activity (see Kitson et al. [2008] for examples). This could provide a diagnosis of the current state or readiness to change and provide some indication of what needs to be done to move forward (e.g., Brown & McCormack, 2005). Additionally, PARIHS has the potential to be used as an evaluative tool or checklist, which could be used during or following the completion of an implementation project to assess progress or outcome (e.g., Ellis, Howard, Larson, et al., 2005; Sharp, Pineros, Hsu, et al., 2004). Furthermore, others have used the framework to model and predict the factors involved in RU (Wallin, Estabrooks, Midodzi, et al., 2006).

Future Work

There is a small but growing body of evidence from research and practice that shows that the PARIHS framework has conceptual integrity, face, and concept validity. However, there are still a number of issues that require exploration and further work. These include gaining a clearer understanding of how the elements interact during implementation and how and whether some elements are more important than others. Additionally, there are measurement challenges concerning the development of both diagnostic and evaluative tools. The next phase of work is being entered in collaboration with a wider community of researchers, practitioners, and other stakeholders.

The Clinical Scholar Model

The Clinical Scholar (CS) model was developed and implemented to promote the spirit of inquiry, educate direct care providers, and guide a mentorship program for EBP and the conduct of research at the point of care. The words of Dr. Janelle Krueger planted the seeds for the model when she encouraged the conduct and use of research as a staff nurse function and promoted the notion that clinical staff are truly in a position to be able to link research and practice. The philosophy and process used in the Conduct and Utilization of Research in Nursing project, based on Diffusion of Innovation theory, formed the early thinking for the model (Horsley, Crane, Crabtree, et al., 1983; Rogers, 2003). The concepts presented in the Clinical Scholarship resource paper published by Sigma Theta Tau International provided the overarching principles (Clinical Scholarship Task Force, 1999). The innovative ideas cultivated through the curiosity of clinical nurses and the visionary and creative leadership of a nurse researcher combined to flush out the CS model. The CS model affords a framework for building the capacity and skills for using evidence at the point of care, thus, providing a long-term solution to changing patterns of thinking and promoting evidence-based care.

Clear definitions for research and EBP are used in the model. The conduct of research is defined as the generation of new, generalizable knowledge using scientific inquiry. Research is conducted when there is no strong evidence to support a practice change. Evidence-based practice is defined as an interdisciplinary approach to healthcare practice that bases decisions and practice strategies on the best available evidence, including research findings; quality improvement data and other reliable forms of internal evidence; clinical expertise; and patient values, taking into account the feasibility of implementation and adoption, the potential risk or harm to the recipient, and the human and material costs (Schultz, Honess, Gallant, et al., 2005).

Evidence-based practice may initially be encouraged through the application of knowledge to a single intervention or project, but over time, as more nurses are educated regarding the critique, synthesis, application, and evaluation of evidence, the culture and the delivery of care will slowly change to the routine use of evidence, both formally and informally through inquisitive, reflective critical thinking. Every healthcare provider becomes responsible and accountable for providing care based on the best available evidence; not to do so is unethical. The institutionalization of evidence use in practice requires creative, critical thinkers and the support and flexibility of management to implement and evaluate change.

Clinical scholars are described as individuals with a high degree of curiosity who possess advanced critical thinking skills and continuously seek new knowledge through continuous learning opportunities. They reflect on this knowledge and seek and use a wide variety of resources in implementing new evidence in practice. They never stop asking "why?" While most CSs also are highly experienced, experience alone does not assure clinical expertise. Clinical scholarship is not the same as clinical proficiency where performing a task routinely in a highly efficient manner is

Clinical Scholar Model©
Promoting the Spirit of Inquiry

OBSERVE & REFLECT

CRITIQUE & ANALYZE

SYNTHESIZE

APPLY & EVALUATE

DISSEMINATE

(Based on the Clinical Scholarship Task Force, 1999)

figure 11.7   Clinical scholar model (Used with permission. © Alyce A. Schultz & Associates, LLC [2008].)

deemed proficient, but rather always questioning whether there is a more efficient and effective way to provide care and whether or not a particular procedure or task needs to be performed at all (Clinical Scholarship Task Force, 1999). These characteristics of CSs are very similar to the characteristics of the innovators and early adopters as described by Rogers (2003). The CS model is inductive using the innovative ideas generated in direct care and driven by the goal of building a community or cadre of CSs who will serve as mentors to other direct care providers in the critique, synthesis, implementation, and evaluation of internal evidence (e.g., quality improvement, risk management, and benchmarking data) and external evidence (i.e., empirical studies).

Clinical scholar mentors are change agents who promote clinical scholarship through the spirit of inquiry and a willingness to challenge and change traditional practice patterns and mentor other staff in fostering a culture shift. Practicing as a CS does not require that the nurses always conduct research, but it does require using an intellectual process, steeped in curiosity, that continually challenges traditional nursing practice through observation, analysis, synthesis of the evidence, application and evaluation, and dissemination (see Figure 11.7; Schultz et al. [2005]). The CS model supports the view that if research and other forms of evidence are to be used in practice, both must be understood and valued by direct care providers.

The Clinical Scholar Program

The CS program actualizes the CS model and is currently utilized in several acute care facilities across the country and as the framework for at least two nursing scholarship collaboratives (Schultz, 2008, 2009). The program is composed of equal parts of educating, processing, and mentoring in a series of six to eight all-day workshops, incorporating the components of the CS model: Observe and Reflect, Analyze and Critique, Synthesize, Apply and Evaluate, and Disseminate. The primary goals of the workshops are to (a) challenge the current nursing practices; (b) speak and understand research language; (c) critically appraise, critique, synthesize, implement, evaluate, and disseminate evidence; and (d) educate direct care providers to serve as mentors to other direct care staff. The ultimate goals are to improve the quality of care provided to patients, to measure the impact of EBP outcomes, and to base administrative and clinical decisions on the best available evidence.

An EBP environment requires both an infrastructure where change and innovation are supported and valued by management and staff and a critical mass of direct care providers (i.e., the capacity) who can conduct research and critically appraise internal and external evidence and provide leadership to practice change. The infrastructure and capacity must be embedded in a culture where interdisciplinary collaboration is fostered, policies and procedures are based on evidence, and there is a systematic approach to the evaluation of care (Stetler, 2003). Participants selected to attend the CS programs are nurses who are curious, critical thinkers who have either had a research course or are currently enrolled in a research course and are supported by their clinical supervisors to attend and carry out evidence-based projects or research studies.

The workshops begin with promoting the spirit of inquiry through **observation and reflection.** The participants learn to write clear, concise researchable questions, paying particular attention to defining the desired outcomes and the significance of the practice issue to healthcare providers, families, and patients. A librarian teaches the participants how to perform efficient and structured searches on multiple literature databases. Once scientific studies that address the clinical issues are obtained, the participants are taught how to critique the studies and identify the salient outcomes that answer their clinical questions. Evaluation of evidence is a very rigorous process, not unlike the research process; however, the emphasis is clearly on applying the evidence in practice. Using an evaluation table to delineate the **analysis and critique** of each type of research design, the principles of synthesis are taught. During these workshops, published guidelines and systematic reviews are also evaluated for their level of evidence and quality of the science. **Synthesis** is the crux of EBP. It is not a summary of the relevant articles but rather

> ### box 11.2
>
> ## Principles of Synthesis
>
> - Decide which studies to include/exclude
> - Arrange studies based on the same or very similar interventions and/or same/similar outcomes measured in the same way
> - Thoughtfully analyze inconsistencies across studies
> - Establish consensus on major conclusions for each selected outcome variable
> - Establish consensus on conclusions drawn from each study
> - Establish consensus on clinical implications of findings
> - Determine the strength of the findings for pertinent outcomes
> - Combine findings into a useful format, with recommendations for implementation in practice if applicable, based on strength of the evidence

Used with permission, Alyce A. Schultz & Associates, LLC, 2008.

a process of critical thinking built on several principles of synthesis (Box 11.2). There may be several synthesis tables, depending on how the outcomes and/or the interventions are defined. The strength of the evidence is based on levels of research designs, the quality of the studies, the consistency of the relevant findings, the number of studies measuring an independent or dependent variable, and the available internal evidence. Recommendations for practice changes are based on the strength of the evidence and utilized in the development of evidence-based guidelines, policies, procedures, or protocols. Advanced practice nurses and physicians can utilize the synthesized evidence as they develop care plans for their individual patients. Other healthcare providers often have to work through an organizational change process as the new guidelines, policies, or procedures are **applied** to a small sampling of patients and the outcomes are carefully monitored and **evaluated.** Careful adherence to the steps in the new guidelines or procedures, also known as fidelity of the intervention, is also monitored. If the outcomes for the pilot work are positive, the new guidelines, policies, or procedures are adopted for a broader patient population with outcome measurement continued until the new practices are routinized into daily patterns and positive outcomes are established for the larger group. Finally, the work is **disseminated**, not only to a local audience, but to a wider audience of direct care providers through poster or podium presentations and publications and through mass media to the general public.

"To be considered true clinical scholars, nurses must identify and describe their work, making it conscious, so that it can be shared with researchers, colleagues, other health care providers and, perhaps most important, the public" (Clinical Scholarship Task Force, 1999). The CS model for the conduct of research and EBP is based on and supports the principles of clinical scholarship. Evaluation of the model is both iterative and cumulative. The research studies and EBP projects must be continually evaluated for achieving their desired outcomes. The environment in which the work is centered must be evaluated for a sustainable change to a culture of inquiry and a breeding ground for innovation.

The Johns Hopkins Nursing Evidence-Based Practice Model

The Johns Hopkins Nursing Evidence-Based Practice (JHNEBP) model facilitates bedside nurses in translating evidence to clinical, administrative, and educational nursing practice. In 2002, the organizational leadership at The Johns Hopkins Hospital (JHH) recognized the gap in implementing research results as a standard for nursing practice. To accelerate the transfer of knowledge generated to practice, nursing leadership set a goal to build a culture of nursing practice based on evidence. The tenets of EBP support this goal because (a) nursing is both a science and profession, (b) nursing practice should be based on the best available evidence, (c) a hierarchy of evidence exists, (d) research findings should be translated to practice, and (e) nursing values efficiency and effectiveness (Newhouse, 2007). The desired outcomes were to enhance nurse autonomy, leadership, and engagement with interdisciplinary colleagues.

A team of JHH nurses formed a task force and invited faculty from Johns Hopkins University School of Nursing to participate in evaluating published EBP models and tools for application by practicing nurses within the clinical setting. A key objective was to select a model that would demystify the EBP process for bedside nurses and embed EBP into the fabric of nursing practice. For this reason, it was important that bedside nurses were involved in evaluating and piloting the model and process.

Nurses' evaluation and feedback from the pilot of a selected published model were clear—nurses wanted a mentored linear process, with accompanying tools to guide them through each step of the EBP process. Based on this feedback, the team assessed what worked in the pilot as well as the processes that participants experienced the most challenging. The JHNEBP model and process were then carefully constructed and evaluated within the organization by offering EBP educational working seminars in multiple formats. During these sessions, a question was generated; the evidence was reviewed, rated, and graded; and recommendations were made for practice. Participants were then charged to implement the recommendations and report results to the Standards of Care Committee. The details of the implementation are reported elsewhere (Dearholt, White, Newhouse, et al., 2008; Newhouse, Dearholt, Poe, et al., 2007b). The resulting JHNEBP model includes a conceptual model, a process, and tools to guide nurses through the critical steps of the process.

The model was then implemented organizationally through standardized education and integration of EBP competencies into job performance expectations. An EBP fellowship was funded by Nursing Administration, and external funding obtained to test the model in multidisciplinary teams. The EBP process was then incorporated into undergraduate research courses, and then into graduate research courses at the Johns Hopkins University School of Nursing.

Overview of the Johns Hopkins Nursing Evidence-Based Practice Model

In the JHNEBP model, EBP is

> a problem-solving approach to clinical decision-making within a health care organization that integrates the best available scientific evidence with the best available experiential (patient and practitioner) evidence, considers internal and external influences on practice, and encourages critical thinking in the judicious application of such evidence to care of the individual patient, patient population, or system (Newhouse, Dearholt, Poe, et al., 2007a, p. 3–4).

Consistent with the definition, the conceptual model (Figure 11.8) includes a core of research and nonresearch evidence within the triad of professional nursing practice (practice, education, and research). Evidence-based nursing practice is influenced by internal organizational (e.g., culture, resources) factors and external factors (e.g., accreditation, licensure). Internal and external factors can enhance or limit implementation of recommendations, conduct of the process, or the existence of EBP itself within organizations.

The Johns Hopkins Nursing Evidence-Based Practice process (Figure 11.9) contains three major components: *P*ractice question, *E*vidence, and *T*ranslation. Within these components, there are 18 prescriptive steps. Although the process appears linear, it may be iterative as the process evolves. For example, teams may discover other sources of evidence through

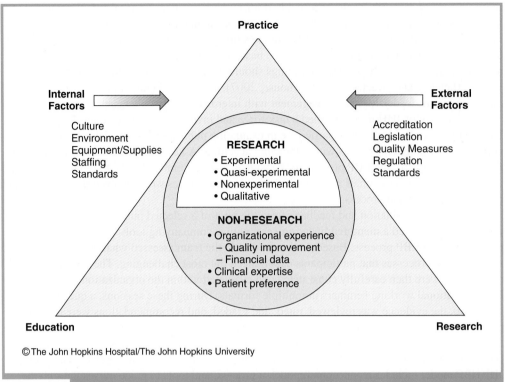

Practice

Internal Factors →

Culture
Environment
Equipment/Supplies
Staffing
Standards

← **External Factors**

Accreditation
Legislation
Quality Measures
Regulation
Standards

RESEARCH
• Experimental
• Quasi-experimental
• Nonexperimental
• Qualitative

NON-RESEARCH
• Organizational experience
 – Quality improvement
 – Financial data
• Clinical expertise
• Patient preference

Education

Research

© The John Hopkins Hospital/The John Hopkins University

| figure 11.8 | Johns Hopkins evidence-based practice conceptual model |

their review, requiring refinement of the search strategy, or evidence retrieval through footnote chasing, moving them back to the prior step(s).

During the practice question stage, a question is refined in answerable terms, a leader is designated, and a team is formed. Next, in the evidence phase, a search for evidence is conducted and evidence is screened for inclusion criteria, abstracted, appraised using a rating scale, and then summarized. Recommendations are made based on the strength, quality, and quantity of the evidence. Finally, in the translation stage, a plan is constructed for implementation of appropriate and feasible recommendations. Implementation, evaluation, and dissemination follow. The translation plan is incorporated into the organization's quality improvement framework to communicate effective (and ineffective) changes and engage the organization in adopting those changes.

Seven tools support critical steps in the process: Question Development, Evidence Rating Scale, Research Evidence Appraisal, Nonresearch Evidence Appraisal, Individual Evidence Summary, Overall Evidence Summation, and Project Management. These tools were developed with input from bedside nurses and include key questions that prompt nurses in the process. The tools were constructed to have high utility with checkbox formats, definitions, and guidelines for use on each form.

After multiple projects using different rating scales, it was clear that many publicly available scales were intended for research evidence based on randomized controlled trials (RCTs) and did not include an approach to evaluate nonresearch sources of evidence. Because the questions proposed by nurses today need an answer tomorrow, the sources of evidence are often found in nonresearch evidence such as integrated reviews, quality improvement data, or expert opinion. Nursing problems occur in natural settings, which often do not lend themselves to RCTs.

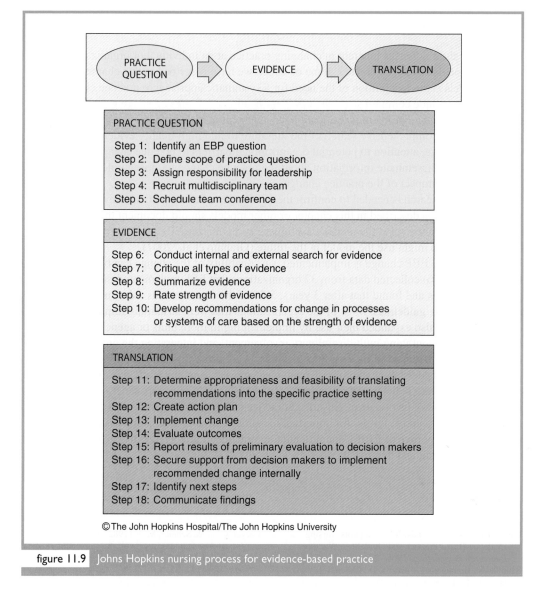

figure 11.9   Johns Hopkins nursing process for evidence-based practice

A rating scale was developed to assess the strength and quality of nonresearch evidence to enable nurses to better communicate the strength and quality of evidence on which decisions are made.

The JHNEBP model is applied to clinical, administrative, and educational nursing practice. After implementation within the hospital, the model was used in multiple settings such as community and rural hospitals; educational seminars; and academic settings at schools of nursing at the undergraduate, graduate, and doctoral level. It also has been used for state-level initiatives to review evidence (Newhouse, 2008).

A book is available with the tools to guide teams through the JHNEBP process (Newhouse et al., 2007a). A teaching guide also is available for faculty that includes strategies for learning activities to boost EBP student competencies at each level (White, Newhouse, Dearholt, et al., 2008). The model and tools have been positively evaluated by independent reviewers (Baker, 2008; Haussler, 2008; Murray, 2008) and can be used by bedside nurses to answer important practice questions using the best available evidence to inform decisions.

Conclusions

Recognizing the challenges inherent in changing practice at an individual or organizational level, numerous models have been created, some of which we have described in this chapter. Common to these models is the recognition of the need for a systematic approach to practice change. Many of the models include common steps such as identification of change agents (e.g., APNs) to lead organizational change, problem identification, engagement of stakeholders to assist with the practice change, comprehensive search of the literature to find high-quality evidence to inform the practice change, attention to potential organizational barriers to practice change, use of effective strategies to disseminate information about the practice change to those implementing it, and evaluation of the impact of the practice change.

More research is needed to confirm the advantages of using particular models. Those who use the models described in this chapter or other models should document their experiences in order to better understand the model's usefulness in facilitating EBP and to provide information to others who might use the model in the future (Graham et al., 2007).

Once the EBP change is implemented, sustainability of the change can be a challenge. Davies et al. (2006) collected data from 37 organizations that had implemented nursing best practice guidelines and found that after 3 years, 59% of the organizations were sustaining implementation of these guidelines. Most of the organizations that were sustaining implementation of the guidelines also expanded their use by implementing in more units or agencies, engaging more partners, encouraging multidisciplinary involvement, and integrating the guidelines with other quality improvement initiatives. Top facilitators for sustaining and expanding the use of guidelines were leadership champions, management support, ongoing staff education, integration of the guidelines into policies and procedures, staff buy-in and ownership, synergy with partners, and multidisciplinary involvement. Sustained practice change involves those at the front line as well as at the executive levels. An important element to ensure sustainability is an organizational culture supportive of EBP. Changing nursing practice to be more evidence-informed is a dynamic, long-term, and iterative process.

references

Baker, S. (2008). Book ends: Johns Hopkins Nursing Evidence-Based Practice and Guidelines. *Nursing Education Perspectives, 29*(4), 234.

Baumler, S., Brautigam, L., Bruene, D., Cullen, L., Dawson, C., Evans, R., et al. (2008). Assessment of oral mucositis in adult and pediatric oncology patients: An evidence-based approach. *Paper presented at the 32nd Annual Congress & Symposium of the Society of Otorhinolaryngology and Head-Neck Nurses & The Ear, Nose and Throat Nursing Foundation,* Chicago, IL.

Beck, A., Rush, A., Shaw, B., & Emery, G. (1979). *Cognitive therapy of depression.* New York: The Guilford Press.

Bowman, A., Greiner, J., Doerschug, K., Little, S., Bombei, C., & Comried, L. (2005). Implementation of an evidence-based feeding protocol and aspiration risk reduction algorithm. *Critical Care Nursing Quarterly, 28*(4), 324–333.

Brown, D., & McCormack, B. (2005). Developing post-operative pain management: Utilising the Promoting Action on Research Implementation in Health Services (PARIHS) framework. *Worldviews on Evidence-Based Nursing, 3*(2), 131–141.

Carver, C. S., & Scheier, M. F. (1982). Control theory: A useful conceptual framework for personality-social, clinical, and health psychology. *Psychological Bulletin, 92,* 111–135.

Carver C. S., & Scheier, M. F. (1998). *On the self-regulation of behavior.* Cambridge, UK: Cambridge University Press.

Clinical Scholarship Task Force. (1999). *Clinical Scholarship Resource Paper.* Retrieved June 3, 2008, from http://www.nursingsociety.org/aboutus/Documents/clinical_scholarship_paper.pdf

Crawford, M. J., Thomas, O., Khan, N., & Kulinskaya, E. (2007). Psychosocial interventions following self-harm: Systematic review of their efficacy in preventing suicide. *British Journal of Psychiatry, 190,* 11–17.

Cronenwett, C. (1994). Using research in the care of patients. In G. LoBiondo-Wood & J. Haber (Eds.), *Nursing research: Methods, critical appraisal, and utilization* (pp. 89–90). St. Louis, MO: Mosby.

Cullen, L., Dawson, C., & Williams, K. (2009). Evidence-based practice: Strategies for nursing leaders. In D. Huber (Ed.), *Leadership and Nursing Care Management* (4th ed.). Philadelphia, PA: Elsevier.

Cullen, L., Greiner, J., Greiner, J., Bombei, C., & Comried, L. (2005). Excellence in evidence-based practice: An organizational and MICU exemplar. *Critical Care Nursing Clinics of North America, 17*(2), 127–142.

Davies, B., Edwards, N., Ploeg, J., Virani, T., Skelly, J., & Dobbins, M. (2006). *Determinants of the sustained use of research evidence in nursing: Final report.* Ottawa, ON, Canada: Canadian Health Services Research Foundation & Canadian Institutes for Health Research.

Dearholt, S., White, K., Newhouse, R. P., Pugh, L., & Poe, S. (2008). Educational strategies to develop evidence-based practice mentors. *Journal for Nurses in Staff Development, 24*(2), 53–59.

DiCenso, A., Ciliska, D., & Guyatt, G. (2004). Introduction to evidence-based nursing. In A. DiCenso, D. Ciliska, & G. Guyatt (Eds.), *Evidence-based nursing: A guide to clinical practice* (pp. 3–19). St Louis, MO: Elsevier.

Ellis, I., Howard, P., Larson, A., & Robertson, J. (2005). From workshop to work practice: An exploration of context and facilitation in the development of evidence-based practice. W*orldviews on Evidence-Based Nursing, 2*(2), 84–93.

Estabrooks, C. A. (1998). Will evidence-based nursing practice make practice perfect? *Canadian Journal of Nursing Research, 30*, 15–36.

Farrington, M., Lang, S., Cullen, L., & Stewart, S. (2009). Nasogastric tube placement in pediatric and neonatal patients. *Pediatric Nursing, 35*(1), 17–24.

Fineout-Overholt, E., & Melnyk, B. M. (2006). *Organizational culture and readiness for system-wide integration of evidence-based practice.* Phoenix, AZ: Arizona State University College of Nursing & Healthcare Innovation.

Funk, S. G., Tournquist, E. M., & Champagne, M. T. (1995). Barriers and facilitators of research utilization. *Nursing Clinics of North America, 30*(3), 395–407.

Geyman, J. (1998). Evidence-based medicine in primary care: An overview. *Journal of the American Board of Family Practice, 11*, 46–56.

Gifford, W., Davies, B., Edwards, N., & Graham, I. D. (2006). Nursing research: Leadership strategies to influence the use of clinical practice guidelines. *Canadian Journal of Nursing Leadership, 19*(4), 72–88.

Gifford, W., Davies, B., Edwards, N., Griffin, P., & Lybanon, V. (2007). Managerial leadership for nurses' use of research evidence: An integrative review of the literature. *Worldviews on Evidence-Based Nursing, 4*(3), 126–145.

Goode, C., & Piedalue, F. (1999). Evidence-based clinical practice. *Journal of Nursing Administration, 29,* 15–21.

Gordon, M., Bartruff, L., Gordon, S., Lofgren, M., & Widness, J. (2008). How fast is too fast? A practice change in umbilical arterial catheter blood sampling using the Iowa model for evidence-based practice. *Advances in Neonatal Care, 8*(4), 198–207.

Graham, I. D., Tetroe, J., & the KT Theories Research Group. (2007). Some theoretical underpinnings of knowledge translation. *Academic Emergency Medicine,14*(11), 936–941.

Greenhalgh, T., Robert, G., Bate, P., Macfarlane, F., & Kyriakidou, O. (2005). *Diffusion of innovations in health service organizations.* Boston: MA: Blackwell Publishing.

Hackett, M. L., Anderson, C. S., & House, A. (2008). Interventions for preventing depression after stroke. *Cochrane Database of Systematic Reviews*, (3): CD003689.

Harvey, G., Loftus-Hills, A., Rycroft-Malone, J., Titchen, A., Kitson, A., McCormack, B., et al. (2002). Getting evidence into practice: The role and function of facilitation. *Journal of Advanced Nursing, 37*(6), 577–588.

Haussler, S. C. (2008). Resource reviews: Johns Hopkins Nursing Evidence-Based Practice Model. *Journal of Continuing Education in Nursing, 39*(9), 432.

Haynes, R. (2002). What kind of evidence is it that evidence-based medicine advocates want health care providers and consumers to pay attention to? *BMC Health Services Research, 2,* 3.

Haynes, R., Sackett, D., Gray, J., Cook, D., & Guyatt, G. (1996) EBM notebook: Transferring evidence from research into practice: 1. The role of clinical care research evidence in clinical decisions. *Evidence Based Medicine, 1,* 196–198.

Horsley, J. A., Crane, J., Crabtree, M. K., & Wood, D. J. (1983). *Using research to improve nursing practice: A guide.* Orlando, FL: Green & Stratton.

Hunt, J. (1991). Barriers to research utilisation. *Journal of Advanced Nursing, 23*(3), 423–425.

Hutchinson, A. M., & Johnston, L. (2006). Beyond the barriers scale: Commonly reported barriers to research use. *The Journal of Nursing Administration, 36*(4), 189–199.

Hysong, S. J., Best, R. G., & Pugh, J. A. (2006). Audit and feedback and clinical practice guideline adherence: Making feedback actionable. *Implementation Science, 28*(1), 1–9.

Jamtvedt, G., Young, J. M., Kristoffersen, D. T., O'Brien, M. A., & Oxman, A. D. (2006). Audit and feedback: Effects on professional practice and health care outcomes. *Cochrane Database of Systematic Reviews*, (2): CD000259.

Kajermo, K. N., Nordstrom, G., Krusebrant, A., & Bjorvell, H. (1998). Barriers and facilitators of research utilization, as perceived by a group of registered nurses in Sweden. *Journal of Advanced Nursing, 27,* 798–807.

Kendrick, D., Barlow, J., Hampshire, A., et al. (2007). Parenting interventions for the prevention of unintentional injuries in childhood. *Cochrane Database of Systematic Reviews*, (4):CD006020.

Kim, S. (1999). Models of theory-practice linkage in nursing. *Paper presented at the International Nursing Research Conference: Research to Practice*, University of Alberta, Edmonton, Canada.

Kitson, A., Harvey, G., & McCormack, B. (1998). Enabling the implementation of evidence based practice: A conceptual framework. *Quality in Health Care, 7*(3), 149–158.

Kitson, A., Rycroft-Malone, J., Harvey, G., McCormack, B., Seers, K., & Titchen, A. (2008). Evaluating the successful implementation of evidence into practice using the PARIHS framework: Theoretical and practical challenges. *Implementation Science, 3*(1), 1–12.

Kleiber, C., Hanrahan, K., Fagan, C. L., & Zittergruen, M. A. (1993). Heparin vs. saline for peripheral IV locks in children. *Pediatric Nursing, 19*(4), 376, 405–409.

Lam, D. (2005). A brief overview of CBT techniques. In S. Freeman, & A. Freeman (Eds.), *Cognitive behavior therapy in nursing practice* (pp. 29–47). New York: Springer Publishing Company.

Larrabee, J. H. (2004). Advancing quality improvement through using the best evidence to change practice. *Journal of Nursing Care Quality, 19*(1), 10–13.

Larrabee, J. H. (2009). *Nurse to nurse: Evidence-based practice.* New York: McGraw-Hill.

Madsen, D., Sebolt, T., Cullen, L., Folkedahl, B., Mueller, T., Richardson, C., et al. (2005). Listening to bowel sounds: An evidence-based practice project. *American Journal of Nursing, 105*(12), 40–50.

McCormack, B., Kitson, A., Harvey, G., Rycroft-Malone, J., Titchen, A., & Seers, K. (2002). Getting evidence into practice: The meaning of 'context.' *Journal of Advanced Nursing, 38*(1), 94–104.

McSherry, R., Artley, A., & Holloran, J. (2006). Research awareness: An important factor for evidence based practice. *Worldviews on Evidence-Based Nursing, 3*(3), 103–115.

Melnyk, B. M. (2007). The evidence-based practice mentor: A promising strategy for implementing and sustaining EBP in healthcare systems. *Worldviews on Evidence-Based Nursing, 4*(3), 123–125.

Melnyk, B. M., & Fineout-Overholt, E. (2002). Putting research into practice. *Reflections on Nursing Leadership, 28*(2), 22–25.

Melnyk, B. M., & Fineout-Overholt, E. (2005). *Evidence-based practice in nursing and healthcare: A guide to best practice.* Philadelphia, PA: Lippincott, Williams & Wilkins.

Melnyk, B. M., Fineout-Overholt, E., Feinstein, N., Li, H. S., Small, L., Wilcox, L., et al. (2004). Nurses' perceived knowledge, beliefs, skills, and needs regarding evidence-based practice: Implications for accelerating the paradigm shift. *Worldviews on Evidence-Based Nursing, 1*(3), 185–193.

Melnyk, B. M., Fineout-Overholt, E., & Mays, M. (2008). The evidence-based practice beliefs and implementation scales: Psychometric properties of two new instruments. *Worldviews on Evidence-Based Nursing, 5*(4), 208–216.

Melnyk, B. M., & Moldenhauer, Z. (2006). *The KySS guide to child and adolescent mental health screening, early intervention and health promotion.* Cherry Hill, NJ: NAPNAP.

Murray, J. S. (2008). Book review: Johns Hopkins Nursing Evidence-Based Practice and Guidelines. *Reflections on Nursing Leadership, 34*(1), 2.

Newhouse, R. P. (2007). Creating infrastructure supportive of evidence-based nursing practice: Leadership strategies. *Worldviews on Evidence-Based Nursing, 4*(1), 21–29.

Newhouse, R. P., Dearholt, S., Poe, S., Pugh, L.C., & White, K. (2007a). *Johns Hopkins Nursing Evidence-Based Practice Model and Guidelines.* Indianapolis, IN: Sigma Theta Tau International.

Newhouse, R. P., Dearholt, S., Poe, S., Pugh, L. C., & White, K. (2007b). Organizational change strategies for evidence-based practice. *Journal of Nursing Administration, 37*(12), 552–557.

Newhouse, R. P. (2008). Evidence driving quality initiatives: The Maryland Hospital Association Collaborative on Nurse Retention. *Journal of Nursing Administration, 38*(6), 268–271.

Olds, D. L., Robinson, J., O'Brien, R., Luckey, D. W., Pettitt, L. M., Henderson, C. R. Jr, et al. (2002). Home visiting by paraprofessionals and by nurses: A randomized, controlled trial. *Pediatrics, 110*(3), 486–496.

Parahoo, K. (1999). A comparison of pre-project 2000 and project 2000 nurses' perceptions of their research training, research needs and their use of research in clinical areas. *Journal of Advanced Nursing, 29*, 237–245.

Parahoo, K. (2000). Barriers to, and facilitators of, research utilization among nurses in Northern Ireland. *Journal of Advanced Nursing, 31*, 89–98.

Purkayastha, S., Tilney, H. S., & Darzi, A. W. (2008). Meta-analysis of randomized studies evaluating chewing gum to enhance postoperative recovery following colectomy. *Archives of Surgery,143*, 788–793.

Retsas, A. (2000). Barriers to using research evidence in nursing practice. *Journal of Advanced Nursing, 31*, 599–606.

Rogers, E. M. (2003). *Diffusion of innovations* (5th ed.). New York: The Free Press.

Rosswurm, M. A., & Larrabee, J. (1999). A model for change to evidence-based practice. *Image: Journal of Nursing Scholarship, 31*(4), 317–322.

Rycroft-Malone, J., Harvey, G., Seers, K., Kitson, A., McCormack, B., & Titchen, A. (2004). An exploration of the factors that influence the implementation of evidence into practice. *Journal of Clinical Nursing, 13*, 913–924.

Rycroft-Malone, J., Kitson, A., Harvey, G., McCormack, B., Seers, K., Titchen, A., et al. (2002). Ingredients for change: Revisiting a conceptual framework. *Quality & Safety in Health Care, 11*, 174–180.

Rycroft-Malone, J., Seers, K., Titchen, A., Harvey, G., Kitson, A., & McCormack, B. (2004). What counts as evidence in evidence-based practice? *Journal of Advanced Nursing, 47*(1), 81–90.

Rycroft-Malone, J., & Stetler, C. (2004). Commentary on evidence, research, knowledge: A call for conceptual clarity. *Worldviews in Evidence-Based Nursing, 1*(2), 98f.

Sackett, D. L., Straus, S. E., Richardson, W. S., Rosenberg, W. M. C., & Haynes, R. B. (2000). *Evidence-based medicine: How to practice and teach EBM.* London: Churchill Livingstone.

Schultz, A. A. (2008). The Clinical Scholar Program: Creating a culture of excellence. *RNL, Reflections on Nursing Leadership*, June, http://www.nursingsociety. org/ pub/rnl/pages/vol34_2_schultz.aspx

Schultz, A. A. (Guest Editor). (2009). Evidence-based practice. *Nursing Clinics of North America, 44*(1), xv–xvii.

Schultz, A. A. (Guest Editor), Honess, C., Gallant, P., Kent, G., Lancaster, K., Sepples, S., et al. (2005). Advancing evidence into practice: Clinical scholars at the bedside [Electronic version]. *Excellence in Nursing Knowledge.*

Scottish Intercollegiate Guidelines Network. (2007). *Critical appraisal: Notes and checklists.* Retrieved July 3, 2007, from http://www.sign.ac.uk/methodology/checklists.html

Sharp, N., Pineros, S. L., Hsu, C., Starks, H., & Sales, A. (2004). A qualitative study to identify barriers and facilitators to the implementation of pilot intervention in the Veterans Health Administration Northwest

Network. *Worldviews on Evidence-Based Nursing, 1*(4), 129–139.

Shaw, E., Levitt, C., Wong, S., & Kaczorowski, J. (2006). Systematic review of the literature on postpartum care: Effectiveness of postpartum support to improve maternal parenting, mental health, quality of life, and physical health. *Birth, 33*(3), 210–220.

Sigma Theta Tau International Research and Scholarship Advisory Committee. (2008). Sigma Theta Tau International Position Statement on Evidence-Based Practice, February 2007 Summary. *Worldviews on Evidence-Based Nursing, 5*(2), 57–59.

Stebral, L., & Steelman, V. (2006). Double-gloving for surgical procedures: An evidence-based practice project. *Perioperative Nursing Clinics, 1*(3), 251–260.

Stenger, K., Montgomery, L., & Briesemeister, E. (2007). Creating a culture of change through implementation of a safe patient handling program. *Critical Care Nursing Clinics of North America, 19*(2), 213–222.

Stetler, C. B. (1994a). Refinement of the Stetler/Marram model for application of research findings to practice. *Nursing Outlook, 42*, 15–25.

Stetler, C. B. (1994b). Using research to improve patient care. In G. LoBiondo-Wood & J. Haber (Eds.), *Nursing research: Methods, critical appraisal, and utilization* (pp. 1–2). St. Louis, MO: Mosby.

Stetler, C. B. (2001a). *Evidence-based practice and the use of research: A synopsis of basic strategies and concepts to improve care*. Washington, DC: Nova Foundation.

Stetler, C. B. (2001b). Updating the Stetler model of research utilization to facilitate evidence-based practice. *Nursing Outlook, 49*, 272–278.

Stetler, C. B. (2002). Evidence-based practice: A fad or the future of professional practice? *Paper presented at the Fourth Annual Evidence Based Practice Conference: Creating Momentum! Improving Care*! Ann Arbor, Michigan.

Stetler, C. B. (2003). Role of the organization in translating research into evidence-based practice. *Outcomes Management, 7*, 97–103.

Stetler, C. B. (in press). Stetler model. In T. Bucknall & J Rycroft-Malone, (Eds). *Models and frameworks to implementing evidence-based practice*. Oxford: Blackwell Publishing Limited.

Stetler, C. B., Bautista, C., Vernale-Hannon, C., & Foster, J. (1995). Enhancing research utilization by clinical nurse specialists. *Nursing Clinics of North America, 30*, 457–473.

Stetler, C. B., Brunell, M., Giuliano, K., Morsi, D., Prince, L., & Newell-Stokes, G. (1998). Evidence based practice and the role of nursing leadership. *Journal of Nursing Administration, 8*, 45–53.

Stetler, C. B., & Caramanica, L. (2007). Evaluation of an evidence-based practice initiative: Outcomes, strengths and limitations of a retrospective, conceptually-based approach. *Worldviews on Evidence-Based Nursing, 4*(4), 187–199.

Stetler, C. B., & Marram, G. (1976). Evaluating research findings for applicability in practice. *Nursing Outlook, 24*, 559–563.

Stetler, C., Morsi, D., Rucki, S., Broughton, S., Corrigan, B., Fitzgerald, J., et al. (1998). Utilization-focused integrative reviews in a nursing service. *Applied Nursing Research, 11*(4), 195–206.

Titler, M. G. (2008). The evidence for evidence-based practice implementation. In R. G. Hughes (Ed.), *Patient safety and quality: An evidence-based handbook for nurses* (pp. 1–49). [AHRQ Publication No. 08–0043].

Titler, M. G., & Everett, L. Q. (2001). Translating research into practice: Considerations for critical care investigators. *Critical Care Nursing Clinics of North America, 13*(4), 587–604.

Titler, M. G., Klieber, C., Steelman, V., Goode, C., Rakel, B., Barry-Walker, J., et al. (1994). Infusing research into practice to promote quality care. *Nursing Research, 43*(5), 307–313.

Titler, M. G., Kleiber, C., Steelman, V., Rakel, B. A., Budreau, G., Everett, L. Q., et al. (2001). The Iowa model of evidence-based practice to promote quality care. *Critical Care Nursing Clinics of North America, 13*(4), 497–509.

Trepepi-Bova, K. A., Woods, K. D., & Loach, M. C. (1997). A comparison of transparent polyurethane and dry gauze dressings for peripheral IV catheter sites: Rates of phlebitis, infiltration, and dislodgment by patients. *American Journal of Critical Care, 6*, 377–381.

van Achterberg, T., Schoonhoven, L., & Grol, R. (2008). Nursing implementation science: How evidence-based nursing requires evidence-based implementation. *Journal of Nursing Scholarship, 40*(4), 302–310.

Van Waning, N., Kleiber, C., & Freyenberger, B. (2005). Development and implementation of a protocol for transfers out of the pediatric intensive care unit. *Critical Care Nurse, 25*(3), 50–55.

Wallin, L., Estabrooks, C. A., Midodzi, W. K., & Cummings, G. G. (2006). Development and validation of a derived measure of research utilization by nurses. *Nursing Research, 55*(3), 149–160.

White, K. W., Newhouse, R. P., Dearholt, S. L., Poe, S. S., & Pugh, L. C. (2008). *Instructors' guide for Johns Hopkins Nursing Evidence-Based Practice Model and Guidelines*. Indianapolis, IN: Sigma Theta Tau International.

World Health Organization. (2007). *Practical guidance for scaling up health service innovations*. Geneva, Switzerland: Author.

Wykes, T., Steel, C., Everitt, B., & Tarrier, N. (2008). Cognitive behavior therapy for schizophrenia: Effect sizes, clinical models, and methodological rigor. *Schizophrenia Bulletin, 34*(3), 523–537.

chapter II

275

Creating a Vision and Motivating a Change to Evidence-Based Practice in Individuals, Teams, and Organizations

Bernadette Mazurek Melnyk and Ellen Fineout-Overholt

Shoot for the moon because even if you miss, you will land amongst the stars.

L e s   B r o w n

In today's rapidly changing healthcare environment in which health professionals are often confronted with short staffing, cost reductions, and heavy patient loads, the implementation of a change to evidence-based practice (EBP) can be a daunting process. Individual, team, and organizational changes are often a complex and lengthy process. However, there are general principles at the individual, team, and organizational levels that will expedite the process of change when thoughtfully planned and carefully implemented.

Most organizational change theories are conceptual rather than evidence-based, which limits the science base to guide decisions about implementation strategies (Prochaska, Prochaska, & Levesque, 2001). In addition, most organizational change initiatives fail because knowledge and principles of the psychology of change are not taken into consideration (Winum, Ryterband, & Stephensen, 1997).

This chapter discusses critical principles and steps for implementing change in individuals, teams, and organizations, with an emphasis on four unique non-healthcare models of organizational change that may be useful in guiding successful change efforts in healthcare institutions. Strategies to enhance team functioning as well as the cooperation of individuals with various personality styles are highlighted. A major purpose of this chapter is to stimulate innovative "out-of-the-box," or nontraditional, thinking, in motivating a change to best practice within individuals, teams, and organizations.

Although it is imperative to consider the structure, culture, and strategy for change within a system, it also is critical that the leaders and individual(s) implementing the change have a clear vision, belief in that vision, and persistence to overcome the many difficult or "character-building" experiences along the journey to bringing that project to fruition (Melnyk, 2001).

Essential Elements for Successful Organizational Change

Among the important elements that must be present for change to be accomplished successfully are vision, belief, strategic planning, action, persistence, and patience.

First Element: Vision and Goals

The first essential element for implementing change, whether it is at the **macro** (i.e., large scale) or **micro** (i.e., small scale) level, is a crystal clear vision of what is to be accomplished. A clear vision of the desired outcome is needed in order to unify stakeholders (MacPhee, 2007) and outline a plan for implementing success strategies. In numerous biographies of highly successful people, a recurrent theme is that those individuals had "big dreams" and a clear vision of the projects that they wanted to accomplish in their lives.

For example, Dr. Robert Jarvik, the man who designed the world's first artificial heart, was rejected at least three times by every medical school in the United States. However, he also had a large dream that was not going to be denied. He was finally accepted into the University of Utah School of Medicine in 1972 and, a decade later, he achieved a medical breakthrough that has gone down in history. Dr. Jarvik had none of the conventional assets (e.g., superior grades, a high score on the medical entrance exam), but he possessed important intangibles (e.g., a big dream, passion, and persistence to achieve his dream).

Dr. William DeVries, the chief surgeon who inserted the first artificial heart in a human patient, commented about how he had the vision of performing this procedure for years. Dr. DeVries repeatedly rehearsed that procedure in his mind in terms of what and how he was going to accomplish it so that when the opportunity finally presented itself, he was ready to perform.

Walt Disney visualized a dream of an amusement park where families could spend quality time together long before that dream became a reality. Walt Disney's strong visualization prompted him to take action and persist in his efforts, despite many character-building experiences. Most individuals do not realize that Walt Disney was bankrupt when he traveled across the country, showing his drawing of a mouse to bankers, investors, and friends. He faced countless rejections and tremendous mockery for his ideas for years before his dream started to become a reality. However, Disney stayed focused on his dream and thought about it on a daily basis. This intense daily focus on his dream facilitated a cognitive plan of a series of events that led him to act on that dream. Walt Disney believed that once you dream or visualize what it is that you want to accomplish, the things you need to accomplish it will be attracted to you, especially if you think about *how you can do it* instead of *why you will not be able to accomplish it*. Walt Disney died before Disney World was completed and, in the opening park ceremony, a reporter commented to his brother that it was too bad that Walt never had the opportunity to see the wonderful idea come to fruition. His brother, however, commented emphatically that the reporter was incorrect and, in fact, that Walt had seen his dream for many years.

Mark Spitz dreamed of becoming an Olympic gold medalist for many years. He prepared himself by swimming many hours a day looking at a black line on the bottom of the pool.

chapter 12

277

As he swam and looked at the black line, he kept the vision of standing on the Olympic platform and receiving an Olympic gold medal. It was that dream that kept him persisting through many character-building days of grinding practice.

If you knew it were impossible to fail, what would be the vision that you have for a change to EBP in your organization? Both within yourself and in your organization, how you think is everything. It is important to *think success* at the outset of any new individual or organizational initiative and to keep your vision larger than the fears of and obstacles associated with implementation.

Establishing an exciting shared vision with the team of individuals who will lead organizational change to EBP is important for buy-in and success of the project. When a team of leaders and individuals share a common vision for which everyone has had the opportunity for input, there is greater ownership and investment by the team members to facilitate organizational change.

Once the vision for change to EBP in your organization is established, it is imperative to create written goals with designated time frames for how that vision will be accomplished. Individuals with written goals are usually more successful in attaining them than those without written goals. For example, findings from a Harvard Business School study indicated that 83% of the population did not have clearly defined goals; 14% had goals that were not written; and 3% had written goals. The study also found that the 3% of individuals with written goals were earning 10 times that of the individuals who did not have written goals (McCormack, 1986).

Second Element: Belief

Belief in one's ability to accomplish the vision is a key element for behavior change and success (Melnyk, 2001). Too often, individuals have excellent ideas, but they lack the belief and confidence necessary to successfully spearhead and achieve their initiatives. Thus, many wonderful initiatives do not come to fruition.

Cognitive behavior theory (CBT) is a useful framework to guide individual behavioral change toward EBP, as it contends that an individual's behaviors and emotions are, in large part, determined by the way he or she thinks or his or her beliefs (i.e., the thinking-feeling-behaving triangle; Beck, Rush, Shaw, et al., 1979; Lam, 2005; Melnyk & Moldenhauer, 2006). Findings from research have supported that cognitive beliefs affect emotions as well as behaviors, including the ability to successfully function or attain goals (Carver & Scheier, 1998; Melnyk, Small, Morrison-Beedy, et al., 2006). For example, if an individual does not believe or have confidence in the ability to achieve an important goal, he or she is likely to feel emotionally discouraged and not take any action toward accomplishing that goal. Melnyk et al. (2004) also have found that when nurses' beliefs about the value of EBP and their ability to implement it are high, they have greater implementation of evidence-based care than when their beliefs are low.

Anything that the mind can conceive and believe, it can achieve.

John Heywood

Third Element: A Strategic Plan

Once an initiative is conceptualized and goals are established with deadline dates, the next essential element required for successful change is a well-defined and written strategic plan. Many initiatives fail because individuals do not carefully outline implementation strategies for each established goal. As part of the strategic planning process, it is important to accomplish a SCOT (strengths, challenges, opportunities, and threats) analysis. This analysis will

- Identify the current strengths in the system that will facilitate the success of a new project.
- Identify the challenges in the system that may hinder the initiative.
- Outline the opportunities for success.
- Delineate the threats or barriers to the project's completion, with strategies to overcome them.

Other Key Elements: Action, Persistence, and Patience

Other elements for the success of any organizational change project are action, persistence, and patience. All too often, projects are terminated early because of the lack of persistence and patience, especially when challenges are encountered or the results of action are not yet seen.

An analogy to this scenario may be seen in an Asian tree, the giant bamboo. The tree has a particularly hard seed. The seed is so difficult to grow that it must be watered and fertilized every day for 4 years before any portion of it breaks the soil. In the fifth year, the tree shows itself. Once the plant breaks the surface, it is capable of growing as fast as 4 feet a day to a height of 90 feet in less than a month. The question that is often asked is, Did the tree grow 90 feet in under a month or did it grow to its height over the 5 years? Of course, the answer is that it took 5 years to grow.

> *Nurse your dreams and protect them through the bad times and tough times to the sunshine and light which always comes.*
>
> *Woodrow Wilson*

Thomas Edison tried 9,000 different ways to invent a new type of storage battery before he found the right combination. His associate used to laugh at him, saying that he had failed 9,000 times. However, Edison kept his dream in front of him and persisted, commenting that at least he found 9,000 ways that it would not work. What would have happened if Edison had stopped his efforts to invent a storage battery on his 8,999th attempt?

The bottom line is that, no matter how outstanding a strategic plan is conceptualized and written, action, persistence, and patience are key elements for success in accomplishing any new initiative.

Four Models of Organizational Change

Chapter 11 outlined several models that have been used to stimulate EBP in the health professions. However, four organizational change models are presented because they take different elements and strategies into consideration. These models were selected because they are based either on hundreds of interviews and real-life experiences by highly qualified change experts who have worked to facilitate change in business organizations for a number of years (Duck, 2002; Kotter & Cohen, 2002; Rogers, 2003), or they are based on a behavior change model that has been empirically supported for a number of years as effective in producing behavior change in high-risk patient populations (e.g., smoking, risky sexual behavior). The principles of these models add unique perspectives and could easily be applied to healthcare organizations interested in motivating a change to EBP. Empirical testing of these models could move the field of organizational change in healthcare organizations forward.

The Change Curve Model

Duck's (2002) Change Curve model emphasizes basic assumptions for change in an organization (see Box 12.1). In addition, it emphasizes the stages of organizational change with potential areas for failure.

Stage I

The first stage of organizational change in the Change Curve model is *stagnation*. The causes of stagnation are typically a lack of effective leadership, failed initiatives, and too few resources. The emotional climate in the stage of stagnation is one in which individuals feel comfortable, there is no sense of threat, depression occurs, and/or hyperactivity exists and individuals become stressed and exhausted. Stagnation ends when action is finally taken.

Stage II

The second stage of the Change Curve model is *preparation*. In this stage, the emotional climate of the organization is one of anxiety, hopefulness, and/or reduced productivity. Buy-in from individuals is essential at this stage in which people must ask themselves what they are willing to do. The opportunity that exists at this stage is getting people excited about the vision. The danger at this stage of change is the length of preparation: The project may fail if it is too short or too long.

Stage III

The third stage of the Change Curve model is *implementation*. In this stage, it is essential to assess individuals' readiness for the change as well as to increase their confidence in their ability to help make the change happen.

In the implementation stage, Duck (2002) emphasizes that individuals must see "what is in it for them" if they are going to commit to making a change. In addition, she asserts that when emotion is attached to the reason, individuals are more likely to change.

Stage IV

The fourth stage of the Change Curve model is *determination*. If results are not being experienced by now, individuals begin to experience fatigue change. The opportunity in this stage of organizational change is to create small successes along the way to change. The danger is that this is the stage in which the initiative has the highest chance of failure.

---

box 12.1

Basic Assumptions for Change in an Organization

- ■ Changing an organization is a highly emotional process.
- ■ Group change requires individual change.
- ■ No fundamental change takes place without strong leadership.
- ■ The leader must be willing to change before others are expected to change.
- ■ The larger and more drastic the change, the more difficult the change.
- ■ The greater the number of individuals involved, the tougher the change will be to effect.

From Duck, J. D. (2002). The change monster. The human forces that fuel or foil corporate transformation and change. New York: Crown Business.

Stage V

The fifth and final stage in the Change Curve model is *fruition*. In this stage, the efforts are coming to fruition, and positive outcomes can be seen. The opportunity in this stage is to celebrate and reward individuals for their efforts as well as to seek new ways to change and grow. This stage is in danger when individuals revert back to a level of complacency and begin to stagnate again.

> *I have learned that success is to be measured not so much by the position that one has reached in life as by the obstacles which one has overcome while trying to succeed.*
>
> *Booker T. Washington*

Kotter and Cohen's Model of Change

Based on evidence gathered during interviews from more than 100 organizations in the process of large-scale change, Kotter and Cohen (2002) proposed that the key to organizational change lies in helping people to feel differently (i.e., appealing to their emotions). They assert that individuals change their behavior less when they are given facts or analyses that change their thinking than when they are shown truths that influence their feelings. In other words, there is a seeing, feeling, and changing pattern if successful behavioral change is going to occur. In their book *The Heart of Change* (2002), Kotter and Cohen outline eight steps for successful change in an organization (see Table 12.1).

Urgency

According to Kotter and Cohen, the first step in changing an organization is creating a *sense of urgency*. This is especially important when individuals in an organization have been in a rut or a period of complacency for some time.

table 12.1   Eight steps for successful change

Action	New Behavior
Step 1: Increase a sense of urgency.	"Let's go." "We need to change."
Step 2: Build the guiding team.	A group forms to guide the change and work together.
Step 3: Get the vision right.	The team develops the right vision and strategy for the change effort.
Step 4: Communicate for "buy-in."	People begin to see and accept the change as worthwhile.
Step 5: Empower action and remove barriers.	People begin to change and behave differently.
Step 6: Create short-term wins.	Momentum builds. Fewer people resist the change.
Step 7: Don't let up.	The vision is fulfilled.
Step 8: Make the change stick.	New and winning behavior continues.

Kotter, J. P., & Cohen, D. S. (2002). *The heart of change: Real-life stories of how people change their organizations.* Boston: Harvard Business School Press.

Team Selection

The second step is carefully selecting a team of individuals who can guide change. Members of the team should possess the needed knowledge, skills, respect, and trust with other individuals in the organization as well as a commitment to the project. In some prior studies that have implemented interventions to facilitate a change to EBP, **opinion leaders** (e.g., individuals who have the ability to influence others) have been a critical element in change to EBP (Oxman, Thomson, Davis, et al., 1995).

Vision and Strategy

In step three, the team guiding the project creates a clear vision with realistic implementation strategies for accomplishing that vision. In this step, it is important that the strategies are implemented in a reasonable timeframe because implementation that is too slow may lead to the initiative's failure.

Communicating the Vision

Step four of Kotter and Cohen's organizational change model emphasizes the importance of communicating the vision and strategies with "heartfelt messages" that appeal to people's emotions. For example, instead of telling individuals that EBP results in better patient outcomes, stories of real-life examples where EBP really made a difference (e.g., thousands of low-birth-weight infants were saved from dying as a result of a systematic review of randomized controlled trials, which indicated that dexamethasone injections to women in premature labor enhanced lung surfactant production in the fetus; mortality rates in ICUs dropped as a result of a change in endotracheal suctioning procedures) need to be shared with them. Repetition also is key so that everyone is clear on the strategies that need to be implemented.

Empowerment

In step five, individuals need to be empowered to change their behaviors. Barriers that inhibit successful change (e.g., inadequate resources or skills) should be removed. If not, individuals will become frustrated and change will be undermined.

Interim Successes

Step six in Kotter and Cohen's model consists of establishing short-term successes. If individuals do not experience some degree of early success in their attempts to change, they will soon become frustrated and the initiative will falter.

Ongoing Persistence

In step seven, continued persistence is essential in order to make the vision a reality. Organizational change efforts often fail because individuals try to accomplish too much in a short time or they give up too early, especially when the going gets tough.

Nourishment

In step eight, it is important to nourish the new culture to make the change last, even if the leadership team experiences transitions. This nourishment is essential if the new culture and behaviors are to be sustained.

In summary, evidence from Kotter and Cohen's work with organizations to change the behavior of professionals have indicated that change agents must communicate their vision and make their points in ways that are compelling and emotionally engaging. It is this type of communication that enables individuals to identify a problem or the solution to a problem, prompts them to experience different feelings (e.g., passion, urgency, hope), and changes behavior (i.e., they see, feel, and change).

Diffusion of Innovations

Concepts in Everett M. Rogers's (2003) theory of diffusion of innovations can be very useful when rolling out an organizational change to EBP. In this theory, a bell-shaped curve is used to describe the rate of adoption of new innovations by individuals (see Figure 12.1).

Innovators comprise 2.5% of the innovation curve in Everett's theory. They are out-of-the-box thinkers and recognize innovative opportunities readily. Next are the early adopters or opinion leaders, who comprise 13.5% of the curve. These are individuals who are highly influential in organizations and encourage others to adopt new innovations. The next group of individuals, comprising approximately 34% of the innovation curve, is the early majority. This group of individuals follows the lead of the early adopters in implementing the innovation. The late majority also comprises 34% of the innovation curve. This group of individuals spends additional time watching how the innovation is progressing and are more cautious in its adoption. Finally, the last 16% of individuals are the laggards, or the individuals who are fairly steeped in tradition and have much difficulty with change. They eventually adopt the new innovation, but not until it becomes the standard practice. According to the theory, there needs to be a critical mass of 15%–20% of innovators, early adopters, and early majority before innovative change really begins to take hold (Rogers, 2003).

If leaders who are embarking on an innovative change to EBP do not expect this pattern of diffusion, they can easily be frustrated and relinquish the initiative too prematurely. According to the theory, it is important to target the early adopters in the change effort as they are instrumental in helping to facilitate a change to EBP in the organization. Many change efforts fail because focus and energy are placed on the late majority as well as on laggards who are much slower to adopt change, instead of targeting the individuals who welcome and/or are receptive to it.

chapter 12

283

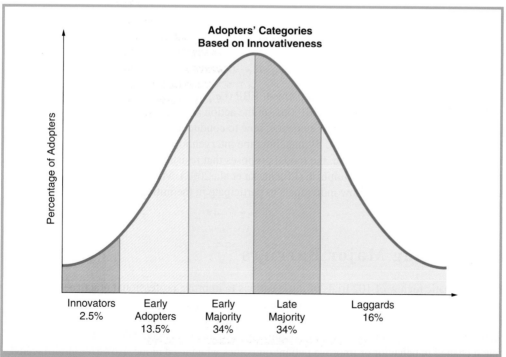

figure 12.1 Categories that describe how individuals adopt innovation (From Rogers, E. M. [2003]. *Diffusion of innovations* [5th ed.]. New York: Free Press.)

The Transtheoretical Model of Health Behavior Change

For the past two decades, the transtheoretical model of health behavior change (Prochaska & Velicer, 1997) with its five stages (i.e., precontemplation, contemplation, preparation, action, and maintenance) has been empirically supported as being useful in precipitating and explaining behavior change in patients.

In the stage of precontemplation, the individual is not intending to take action in the next 6 months. In contemplation, the individual is intending to take action in the next 6 months. In preparation, the individual plans to take action in the next 30 days. The stage of action is when overt changes were made less than 6 months ago. Finally, the stage of maintenance is when overt changes were made more than 6 months ago (Prochaska et al., 2001).

Research indicates that approximately 40% of individuals in a specific population (e.g., smokers) are in the precontemplation stage, 40% are in the contemplative stage, and 20% are in the preparation phase (e.g., Laforge, Velicer, Richmond, et al., 1999).

In applying these statistics, if only approximately 20% of the staff in an organization are preparing (preparation stage) to take action in implementing EBP, it will be challenging for the initiative to succeed because many of these individuals will likely view a change to EBP as imposed and become resistant to the idea (Prochaska et al., 2001).

The transtheoretical model is now beginning to be applied in the field of organizational change (Prochaska et al., 2001). The extension of this model to healthcare providers when a change to EBP is desired could continue to extend the theory's pragmatic efficacy. For example, when attempting to stimulate a change to EBP in individuals who are in the precontemplative and contemplative stages, the focus should be on making a connection with them and assisting them to progress to the next stage of readiness (e.g., from precontemplative to contemplative), rather than working with them on actual behavior change strategies.

Strategies to assist individuals to move from the precontemplative or contemplative stages to a stage of readiness to change might include

- Strengthening their belief that EBP results in the best patient outcomes and highest quality of care
- Supporting their self-efficacy or confidence (i.e., they can indeed make the shift to EBP)

For individuals who are planning to implement EBP (i.e., in the preparation stage) or who are actively changing their practices to EBP (i.e., in the action stage), assisting them with EBP strategies (e.g., how to search for the best evidence, how to conduct efficient critical appraisal) would be an appropriate course of action. By matching the intervention strategies to the stage in which individuals are currently engaged, the model proposes that resistance, stress, and the time needed to implement the change will diminish (Prochaska et al., 2001). Matching the intervention to the stages of change also will allow individuals to participate in the initiative, even if they are not ready to take action.

Overcoming Major Barriers

In a systematic review of 102 trials of interventions to improve professional practice, Oxman, Thomson, Davis, and Hayes (1995) concluded that there are no "magic bullets" for improving the quality of healthcare. Dissemination-only strategies (e.g., didactic conferences or the sharing of information or evidence-based guidelines among colleagues) do not tend to produce much change in behavior or improve patient outcomes when used alone. However, multifaceted interventions consisting of a variety of strategies (e.g., use of opinion leaders, outreach visits, reminders) are moderately effective in changing behavior.

Even the best written strategic plans can go awry because of a number of barriers to implementation. As a result, it is critical to conduct an organizational analysis prior to starting the change effort to identify these barriers as well as strategies for their removal (Melnyk, 2002). Some of these barriers and recommended strategies for removing are discussed in the following sections.

Overcoming Skepticism and Misperceptions About Evidence-Based Practice

Any time the suggested change is introduced in a system, there will be some degree of skepticism about it. Individuals tend to be skeptical about a change if they do not clearly understand the reason for it, if they are fearful about it, or if they have misperceptions about why the change is needed. The best strategy for overcoming this barrier is to allow individuals to express their skepticism, fears, and anxieties about the change as well as to clarify any misperceptions that they may have about EBP (e.g., that it takes too much time). Educating them about EBP in a way that appeals to their emotions and enhances their beliefs about their ability to implement it will enhance the change process.

Individual Personality Styles

Any time that change is introduced in a system, it is important to be sensitive to the personality styles of individuals. Knowing the four major personality styles will assist in the change effort by facilitating strategies to work successfully with each of them.

Rohm and Carey (1997), a seasoned psychologist who has written books on the different personality styles, uses a "DISC" model (see descriptions in the following sections) for working with individuals who possess different personality styles. Although a particular style tends to predominate, individuals often are in combinations of two or more styles.

D Personality Styles: Drivers

Individuals with "D" personality styles like to take charge of projects and are highly task oriented. They are dominant, driving, and determined. An excellent strategy for working with individuals who have this type of personality style is to create excitement by giving them opportunities to lead the way by spearheading specific tasks or initiatives.

I Personality Styles: Inspired

Individuals who possess predominantly "I" personalities are typically people who are socially oriented and like to have fun. They are inspirational, influencing, impressive, and interactive. As such, they usually get excited about a new initiative by being shown that it can be a fun and exciting process.

S Personality Styles: Supportive and Steady

Individuals with predominantly "S" personalities are typically reserved and like to be led. They tend to be supportive, steady, submissive, and shy. The best strategy for working with individuals who have this personality style is to lead the way, telling them that they will be important in helping the project to succeed but that they themselves do not need to spearhead the effort.

C Personality Styles: Contemplators

Individuals with predominantly "C" personality styles are very analytical and detail oriented. They tend to be competent, cautious, careful, and contemplative. At one extreme, they can experience "analysis by paralysis," to a point at which initiatives never get launched. These individuals, although they mean well, may prolong the planning stage of a new initiative so long that others lose enthusiasm for embarking on the change process. The best way to deal with these individuals is to show them all of the details of the specific action plan that will be used to accomplish the change to EBP.

Written Strategic Plan with Set Goals

Again, it is essential to have a written strategic plan with clearly established goals for a change to EBP to occur. Lack of a detailed plan is a major barrier to implementing a change to EBP within a system. The goals established should be SMART (i.e., specific, measurable, attainable, relevant, and time bound; Torres & Fairbanks, 1996). The established goals also should be high enough to facilitate growth in individuals and the organization but not so high that people will get easily frustrated by their inability to reach them.

Communicate the Vision and Strategic Plan

Communication is key to any successful organizational change plan. Individuals in the system need to be very clear about the vision and their role in the strategic planning efforts. Repetition and visual reminders of the vision and plan are important for the project's success. Involving individuals in creating the vision and plan will facilitate their buy-in and commitment to the project.

> *Change is stressful enough even when people are well pre-pared for its demands. Action imposed on people who are not adequately prepared can become intolerable..*
> *Prochaska et al., 2001, p. 258*

Teamwork

Team building and teamwork are essential for successful organizational change to EBP. Recent research supports that the successful implementation of new best practices is a multilevel process involving healthcare delivery teams and their effectiveness, not just individual clinicians, with the strongest link being team knowledge and skills to make the desired improvements (Lukas, Mohr, & Meterko, 2009). Furthermore, interprofessional and interdisciplinary team building is key to improving healthcare quality and patient outcomes.

Torres and Fairbanks (1996) outline six reasons for team building:

1. To establish team purpose
2. To understand the stages of team development
3. To analyze how the team works based on member role
4. To develop effective team communication
5. To examine team processes
6. To understand team leadership

It is important to understand that the team-building process is dynamic and that it requires creativity and flexibility. In addition, knowing the typical stages of team development (i.e., forming, storming, norming, and performing) will promote successful development of the team and prevent the early termination of a project due to typical team struggles, especially in the storming phase (see Table 12.2).

table 12.2 **Stages of team development with associated characteristics**

Stage	Characteristics
Forming	Anxiety, excitement, testing, dependence, exploration, and trust
Storming	Resistance to different approaches; attitude changes; competitiveness and defensiveness; tension and disunity
Norming	Satisfaction increases; trust and respect develops; feedback is provided to others; responsibilities are shared; decisions are made
Performing	Level of interaction is high; performance increases; team members are comfortable with one another; there is optimism and confidence

From Torres, C., & Fairbanks, D. (1996). Teambuilding: The ASTD trainer's sourcebook. New York: McGraw-Hill.

Organizational Context, Including Resources and Administrative Support

Organizational context (i.e., the environment or setting), including resources and administrative support, has been linked to the diffusion of EBPs throughout an organization (Rycroft-Malone, Harvey, Seers, et al., 2004). When leaders visibly express support for change or innovation, the change is more likely to occur (Lukas et al., 2009). In addition, effective leaders adopt innovation early and view change as an opportunity to learn, adapt, and improve (Rogers, 2003).

Although a large number of resources are not necessary to begin a change to EBP, there is no doubt that having ample resources as well as support and EBP role modeling from leaders and managers will expedite the process. Systems can begin to introduce small initiatives to implement a change to EBP, such as conducting journal clubs or EBP rounds. It is important to remember that small changes can have substantial impact (MacPhee, 2007).

What is the smallest change that you can make based on evidence that will have the largest impact?
Bernadette Mazurek Melnyk

Placing PICOT boxes and EBP posters visibly in clinical settings can spark a spirit of inquiry in clinicians to consistently be asking themselves what the evidence is behind the care practices that are being implemented with their patients. These have been used successfully as part of the ARCC (Advancing Research and Clinical Practice through Close Collaboration model; Melnyk & Fineout-Overholt, 2002 [see Chapter 11]). Effective teams also can be instrumental for sparking a change to EBP when there is a weak organizational context (Lukas et al., 2009).

In EBP rounds, the staff generate an important practice question. Then, they are assisted with searching for and critically appraising the evidence, followed by a presentation to other staff, where findings and implications for practice are discussed.

In systems that lack administrative support for a change to EBP, it is challenging but not impossible to ignite change. Assisting administrators to understand how a change to EBP can improve the quality and cost-effectiveness of patient care and appealing to their emotions with concrete examples of how a lack of evidence-based care resulted in adverse outcomes can help facilitate their support. Sharing of important documents that herald EBP as the standard for quality care and health professional education (e.g., Greiner & Knebel, 2003; Institute of Medicine, 2001) will support the position of implementing a change to EBP in the organization.

chapter 12

287

Overcoming Resistance

Resistance in an organization is frequently the result of poorly planned implementation and is the major reason that organizational change initiatives often fail (Prochaska et al., 2001; Winum et al., 1997). Individuals who display resistance to change are often not clear about the benefits of change and/or they have fears and anxiety about their role in implementing change or how it will impact them.

When confronted with individuals who are resisting a change to EBP, it is essential to facilitate conversations that will help them express their thoughts, hesitations, and misperceptions. Listening to these individuals' perspectives on change with respect and acceptance is essential to overcoming resistance (Corey & Corey, 2002; Prochaska et al., 2001). Once concerns are expressed, strategies to overcome them can be implemented.

Organizational Culture and Mentorship: Key Elements for Sustaining Organizational Change

It is one thing to begin implementation of EBP in a healthcare organization, but a whole other entity to sustain the momentum. Organizational culture is the attitudes, beliefs, experiences, and values of the organization. It is defined as "the specific collection of values and norms that are shared by people and groups in an organization that control the way they interact with each other and with stakeholders outside the organization" (Hill & Jones, 2001). In order to sustain EBP, adoption of the EBP paradigm by a critical mass of administrators and managers, leaders, and individual clinicians is essential. This paradigm should be reflected in the vision, mission, and goals of an organization as well as in its standards of practice, clinical ladder promotion systems, and new employee orientations.

The paradigm shift to an EBP culture does not happen overnight; it typically takes years as well as consistent and persistent effort to build and sustain. Unfortunately, many leaders give up prematurely when they are not seeing the outcomes of their efforts materialize in the time frame that they believe they should occur. Therefore, having a mechanism for support and regular recognition within the organization for individuals who are facilitating this shift to an EBP paradigm is important.

Evidence-based practice mentors are another key ingredient for the sustainability of EBP as first described in the ARCC model by Melnyk and Fineout-Overholt (2002; see Chapter 11 for a full description of ARCC). These healthcare professionals typically have (a) a master's degree; (b) in-depth knowledge and skills in EBP; and (c) knowledge and skills in individual, team, and organizational change strategies. Evidence-based practice mentors work directly with point-of-care staff on shifting from a traditional paradigm to an EBP paradigm, which includes (a) assisting clinicians in gaining EBP knowledge and skills, (b) conducting EBP implementation projects, (c) integrating practice-generated data to improve healthcare quality as well as patient and/or system outcomes, and (d) measuring outcomes of EBP implementation (Melnyk, 2007). Findings from a study in the Visiting Nurse Service indicated that nurses who received mentorship from an ARCC EBP mentor, compared to those who received instruction in physical assessment (i.e., the attention control group), had higher EBP beliefs, greater EBP implementation, and less attrition/turnover. In addition, there was no significant difference between the ARCC and attention control groups on the outcome variable of nurses' productivity, indicating that nurse involvement in learning about how to integrate EBP into their daily practice along with implementing an EBP project during work time did not affect the number of home visits made by the nurses (R. Levin, personal communication, November 20, 2006). In another study, point-of-care staff indicated that mentors were critical in assisting them with EBP (Melnyk & Fineout-Overholt, 2002). For further evidence on the outcomes of mentoring and additional information on the specific role of the EBP mentor, see Chapter 15.

Preventing Fatigue

The barrier of fatigue typically presents itself when the implementation phase of a project is exceedingly long. An excellent strategy for preventing and/or decreasing fatigue in a system is to create small successes along the course of the change project and to recognize (reward) individuals for their efforts. Recognition and appreciation are very important in demonstrating the value of individuals' efforts and sustaining enthusiasm along the course of a project.

The road to implementing a change to EBP will be challenging but extremely rewarding. Essential elements for success include a clear shared vision and a well-defined written strategic plan, as well as knowledge and skills regarding the process of organizational change, team building, and working with individuals who possess different personality styles. Lastly, an ability to persist through the multiple challenges that will be confronted along the course of an organization's change will be essential for success.

> *Never, never, never, never, never, never, never quit!*
>
> *Winston Churchill*

references

Beck, A., Rush, A., Shaw, B., & Emery, G. (1979). *Cognitive therapy of depression*. New York: The Guilford Press.

Carver, S., & Scheier, M. F. (1998). *On the selfregulation of behavior*. Cambridge, England: Cambridge University Press.

Corey, M. S., & Corey, G. (2002). *Groups: process and practice* (6th ed.). Pacific Grove, CA: Brooks/Cole.

Duck, J. D. (2002). *The change monster: The human forces that fuel or foil corporate transformation and change*. New York: Crown Business.

Greiner, A., & Knebel, E. (2003). *Health professions education: A bridge to quality*. Washington, DC: National Academy Press.

Hill, C. W. L., & Jones, G. R. (2001). *Strategic management*. New York: Houghton Mifflin.

Institute of Medicine. (2001). *Crossing the quality chasm: A new health system for the 21st century*. Washington, DC: National Academy Press.

Kotter, J. P., & Cohen, D. S. (2002). *The heart of change: Real-life stories of how people change their organizations*. Boston: Harvard Business School Press.

LaForge, R. G., Velicer, W. F., Richmond, R. L., & Owen, N. (1999). Stage distributions for five health behaviors in the USA and Australia. *Preventive Medicine, 28*, 61–74.

Lam, D. (2005). A brief overview of CBT techniques. In S. Freeman and A. Freeman (Eds., pp. 29–47), *Cognitive behavior therapy in nursing practice*. New York: Springer Publishing Company.

Lukas, C. V., Mohr, D. C., & Meterko, M. (2009). Team effectiveness and organizational context in the implementation of a clinical innovation. *Quality Management in Health Care, 18*(1), 25–39.

MacPhee, M. (2007). Strategies and tools for managing change. *Journal of Nursing Administration, 37*(9), 405–413.

McCormack, M. H. (1986). *What they don't teach you at Harvard Business School: Notes from a street smart executive*. New York: Bantam.

Melnyk, B. M. (2001). Big dreams, belief and persistence: Essential elements for achieving career success. *Advance for Nurse Practitioners, 9*(3), 85–86.

Melnyk, B. M. (2002). Strategies for overcoming barriers in implementing evidence-based practice. *Pediatric Nursing, 28*(2), 159–161.

Melnyk, B. M. (2007). The evidence-based practice mentor: A promising strategy for implementing and sustaining EBP in healthcare systems [Editorial]. *Worldviews on Evidence-Based Nursing, 4*(3), 123–125.

Melnyk, B. M., & Fineout-Overholt, E. (2002). Putting research into practice, Rochester ARCC. *Reflections on Nursing Leadership, 28*(2), 22–25.

Melnyk, B. M., Fineout-Overholt, E., Feinstein, N. F., Li, H., Small, L., Wilcox, L., et al. (2004). Nurses' perceived knowledge, beliefs, skills, and needs regarding evidence-based practice: Implications for accelerating the paradigm shift. *Worldviews on Evidence-Based Nursing, 1*(3), 185–193.

Melnyk, B. M., & Moldenhauer, Z. (2006). *The KySS guide to child and adolescent mental health screening, early intervention and health promotion*. New Jersey: National Association of Pediatric Nurse Practitioners.

Melnyk, B. M., Small, L., Morrison-Beedy, D., Strasser, A., Spath, L., Kreipe, R., et al. (2006). Mental health correlates of healthy lifestyle attitudes, beliefs, choices & behaviors in overweight teens. *Journal of Pediatric Health Care, 20*(6), 401–406.

Oxman, A., Thomson, M. A., Davis, D., & Hayes, R. B. (1995). No magic bullets: A systematic review of 102 trials of interventions to improve professional practice. *Canadian Medical Association Journal, 15*(10), 1423–1431.

Prochaska, J. M., Prochaska, J. O., & Levesque, D. A. (2001). A transtheoretical approach to changing organizations. *Administration and Policy in Mental Health, 28*(4), 247–261.

Prochaska, J. O., & Velicer, W. F. (1997). The transtheoretical model of health behavior change. *American Journal of Health Promotion, 12*(1), 38–48.

Rogers, E. M. (2003). *Diffusion of innovations* (5th ed.). New York: Free Press.

Rohm, R. A., & Carey, E. C. (1997). *Who do you think you are... anyway? How your personality style acts... reacts... and interacts with others*. Atlanta, GA: Personality Insights.

Rycroft-Malone, J., Harvey, G., Seers, K., Kitson, A., McCormack, B., & Titchen, A. (2004). An exploration of the factors that influence the implementation of evidence into practice. *Journal of Clinical Nursing, 13*, 913–924.

Torres, C., & Fairbanks, D. (1996). *Teambuilding: The ASTD trainer's sourcebook*. New York: McGraw-Hill.

Winum, P., Ryterband, E., & Stephensen, P. (1997). Helping organizations change: A model for guiding consultation. *Consulting Psychology Journal: Practice and Research, 49*, 6–16.

Teaching Evidence-Based Practice in Academic Settings

Ellen Fineout-Overholt, Susan B. Stillwell, Kathleen M. Williamson, John F. Cox III, and Brett W. Robbins

> *Without change there is no innovation, creativity, or incentive for improvement. Those who initiate change will have a better opportunity to manage the change that is inevitable.*
>
> William Pollard

Evidence-based practice (EBP) is an imperative now in healthcare and continues to rapidly replace the traditional paradigm of authority in healthcare decision making (Porter-O'Grady & Malloch, 2008). Making this transition for learners, students, or practitioners can sometimes be challenging. However, healthcare professionals, policy makers, and payers have determined that EBP is essential to providing effective patient care (American Nurses Credentialing Center, 2004; Centers for Medicare & Medicaid, 2009; Joint Commission, 2009). Almost a decade ago, the Institute of Medicine (IOM) set forth a vision that is coming to reality—that all healthcare professionals would be educated to practice patient-centered care as members of an interdisciplinary team, who, utilizing quality improvement approaches and **informatics,** based their decision making on valid, reliable evidence (Greiner & Knebel, 2003; IOM, 2001). The core competencies for healthcare education to meet the needs of the healthcare system in the 21st century were identified as

- **Provide patient-centered care**

- **Work in interdisciplinary teams**

- **Employ EBP**

- **Apply quality improvement**

- **Utilize informatics (Greiner & Knebel, p. 46)**

The Health Professions Educational Summit recommended that all education address these competencies from an oversight perspective, in essence from the top down. Professional organizations and accrediting bodies have used these competencies as standards for criteria defining successful curricula for academic programs (American Association of Colleges of Nursing [AACN], 2006; Association of American Medical Colleges, 2007). Teaching learners about how to critique and apply research using traditional methods is no longer sufficient to prepare practitioners for the level of practice expected of them (Ciliska, 2005). Practitioners are expected to bring the best and latest evidence to bear on their decision making with patients. Evidence synthesis is required to be up to date on current treatments and care modalities. To be prepared to practice based on evidence, learners will need to be challenged to incorporate valid scientific evidence; their own expertise; and their patients' choices, concerns, and values when making clinical decisions.

Getting Started: Asking the Right Questions

Teaching EBP has become an imperative in healthcare education. While much advancement has been made in integrating EBP into the classroom, the task continues to be challenging. This chapter aims to ease the potentially overwhelming nature of this imperative by providing helpful information in assessing what is needed to support teaching EBP in academic settings. The information focuses on

- Problem solving while setting up an identified infrastructure to support the integration of EBP into academic curricula
- Promoting qualities in teachers and learners of EBP to help them succeed in integrating EBP
- Choosing the best method available to teach EBP content for academic settings
- Evaluating the outcomes of the chosen teaching program

Potential curricula and programs to teach EBP are addressed. Just as EBP depends on the commitment of those healthcare providers who are dedicated to giving their patients the best care possible, successful teaching of EBP is contingent on the people teaching the concepts.

Identify Available Resources

The first step in establishing a successful program for teaching EBP, be it large or small, is to take stock of the resources available that are or could be dedicated to EBP (Fineout-Overholt & Melnyk, 2005). Asking some basic evaluation questions about the current resources that may be available to support EBP can assist you in getting started (see Box 13.1).

Institutional Support for Evidence-Based Practice

An essential question for every person who is about to undertake teaching EBP is, Does the philosophy and mission of my institution support EBP? In addition, there are some underlying questions to help determine the answer to this important first question (see Box 13.2). Asking these secondary questions can help determine whether the true philosophy and mission of the organization support EBP. If the philosophy or culture is less than supportive of EBP, primary efforts may need to focus on demonstrating to the organization the effectiveness of EBP through the success of small initiatives (e.g., student evaluations of courses taught from an EBP paradigm).

The goals and objectives of educational organization need to be congruent with a mission to produce evidence-based practitioners. Varied goals and competing agendas will need to be overcome for faculty to integrate EBP concepts into their curricula. The first step toward building an evidence-based curriculum is to obtain buy-in and support from all levels of administration. From this support will flow other necessary resources for a successful EBP program, such as qualified personnel, continuing education, databases, and computers.

> **box 13.1**
>
> ## Questions for Evaluating the Environmental Readiness for Teaching Evidence-Based Practice Successfully
>
> 1. Does the philosophy and mission of my institution support EBP?
> 2. What is the personal commitment to EBP and practice excellence among educators and administration?
> 3. Are there educators who have EBP knowledge and skills?
> 4. Do all educators have basic computer skills?
> 5. Do all students and educators have ready access to quality computers (e.g., that will support Internet access)?
> 6. Do educators have skills in using databases to find relevant evidence?
> 7. Are there librarians who have EBP knowledge and skills and who can be involved in teaching EBP?

Adapted from Fineout-Overholt, OCRSIEP Scale, 2006.

Commitment of Educators and Administrators

The next question in evaluating how ready an academic organization is to begin a program of teaching EBP is, What is the personal commitment to EBP and practice excellence among educators and administration? One way to ascertain whether educators are committed to EBP is to observe their educational practices (e.g., observe whether they teach based on evidence or on tradition [i.e., "we have always done it that way"]). Other facets of this question may involve what educators read, their database searching skills, and their receptivity to discussing

> **box 13.2**
>
> ## Secondary Questions: Does the Philosophy and Mission of My Institution Support Evidence-Based Practice?
>
> 1. How is EBP taught in my organization, throughout all mediums (e.g., inservices, formal classroom offerings, one-on-one mentoring)?
> 2. Is it a goal of the institution or practice to promote EBP?
> 3. If so, how is this mission "lived out" in the atmosphere/curriculum of the institution or practice?
> 4. Are there champions for EBP at my institution? If so, how would I describe them (having responsibility and authority)?
> 5. What kind of physical resources are available to practitioners, educators, and students to support reaching EBP goals?
> 6. What incentives are in place for practitioners and educators to incorporate EBP into practice, curriculum, and courses for which they are responsible?
> 7. What are the EBP assignments throughout the educational objectives or curriculum that evaluate the integration of EBP concepts?

Adapted from Fineout-Overholt, OCRSIEP Scale, 2006.

supporting evidence for decision making. Because commitment is not a tangible outcome, this is a more difficult question to answer. However, some ways to discern educators' commitment to EBP is to discuss EBP with them and observe their involvement in EBP initiatives. Many change theorists recommend inviting those who are the biggest resisters to assist you in advancing the change (Duck, 2002). This can also be true in teaching EBP. A strategy to encourage those who are not committed to EBP or excellence in practice is to engage them in the teaching process.

Unfortunately, lack of commitment to EBP by educators or administrators is not easily remedied. However, persistence with exposure to the benefits of EBP and how it improves outcomes with students during their education and afterward will help to build the foundation needed to move EBP forward in academic organizations.

Knowledge of Evidence-Based Practice: A Human Resource

The next question at hand is, Are there educators who have EBP knowledge and skills? Knowledge of EBP processes and its associated skills is the first human resource to evaluate. Do educators know how to construct a searchable, answerable question? Can they communicate how to search for relevant evidence? Do they know how to critically appraise all levels of evidence? Can they apply the evidence to a clinical situation? Can they efficiently guide providers in evaluating outcomes based on evidence? After it has been determined how much educators know about EBP, the challenge becomes gaining the information needed to close the gaps in knowledge. A caveat is warranted here that sometimes faculty may exhibit a high commitment to teaching EBP but may not be able to discern the gaps in their knowledge. In a survey of nurse practitioner faculty, Melnyk, Fineout-Overholt, Feinstein, et al. (2008) found that of the sample of 79 graduate educators, 97% indicated they taught EBP in their curricula; however, the top-cited teaching strategy was supporting clinical practice with a single study. The EBP paradigm focuses on what we know (i.e., a body of evidence) versus basing practices on a single study. These findings allude to faculty's commitment to teaching EBP and identify gaps in their knowledge of the EBP paradigm and what teaching EBP requires (Melnyk et al., 2008).

Gaining Knowledge

There are numerous mechanisms available to assist educators in gaining EBP knowledge and skills. There are workshops around the country that present basic and advanced EBP concepts, as well as online tutorials that can be accessed easily at one's convenience to learn about EBP (see Boxes 14.1 and 14.2 in Chapter 14 for sample listings). In addition, for those wanting a more in-depth knowledge of EBP, there are a few academic programs, such as the EBP Graduate Certificate Program at Arizona State University College of Nursing & Health Innovation that prepares faculty and advanced practice nurses to be expert EBP mentors.

Of course, there are many articles about the basic knowledge of EBP and how to teach EBP, such as the *Users' Guides to Evidence-Based Practice* (http://www.cche.net/usersguides/main.asp), the *Tips for Teaching EBP* series (e.g., Kennedy, Jaeschke, Keitz, et al., 2008; McGinn, Jervis, Wisnivesky, et al., 2008; Prasad, Jaeschke, Wyer, et al., 2008; Richardson, Wilson, Keitz, et al., 2008; Williams & Hoffman, 2008), and the *Worldviews on Evidence-Based Nursing* journal's recurring column Teaching EBP (e.g., Fineout-Overholt & Johnston, 2005; Johnston & Fineout-Overholt, 2005; Kent & Fineout-Overholt, 2007; O'Mathuna, Fineout-Overholt, & Kent, 2008). After determining the level of EBP knowledge of the key people in your institution, consider whether the workloads of those individuals can accommodate a new endeavor. Administrative involvement is essential to this preliminary evaluation step. Without administrative support of an endeavor to initiate EBP, success will be difficult to achieve (Fineout-Overholt & Melnyk, 2005).

Informatics and Computer Literacy Among Educators

Determining the basic informatics and computer literacy of educators is the next step in building the foundation for teaching EBP. Without educators that are knowledgeable in informatics, including adequate computer skills and the ability to use databases to find relevant evidence, teaching EBP will be challenging. Using technology to enhance teaching EBP will be discussed later in this chapter; however, before any technology can be considered, basic skills in informatics must be assessed.

When determining the fiscal resources for teaching EBP, funding for computers is an essential budget item. Updated, fast computers with Internet access are a must for educators and students who will be learning about EBP. Administrators will need to commit to computer access for all students, clinicians, and educators.

In addition, a commitment by administrators is essential to ensure that all learners and teachers are computer literate at a basic level. Medical librarians, who are indispensable to this process and who are excellent resources for helping both learners and teachers accomplish the goal of informatics and computer literacy, often can offer classes on computer basics and database searching techniques, among other helpful topics.

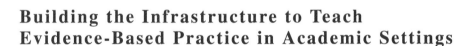

Online tutorials about basic computer function (e.g., **http://tech.tln.lib.mi.us/tutor/**) are also helpful resources

Building the Infrastructure to Teach Evidence-Based Practice in Academic Settings

Teaching EBP cannot occur without human, fiscal, and technological resources. Securing these resources prior to initiating a teaching program will help it succeed. Human resources can include EBP champions, mentors, and evidence-based librarians; knowledge of EBP; and time to accomplish the goal. Fiscal resources include committed funds for ongoing development of the teaching program, to educator the educators, and for purchasing the best technology available for enhancing the program and easing the workload of faculty. Technological resources are vast and always changing. Considering how to best use them to enhance EBP is an imperative.

Human Resources

Multilevel support for an EBP teaching program is imperative. Administrators, educators, librarians, and students are key stakeholders in this initiative. Administrators, for the purposes of this chapter, are defined as anyone who provides fiscal and managerial support to an EBP program (e.g., university presidents, academic deans, residency directors, department chairs, chief financial officers, chief executive officers). Administrators must include designated fiscal resources for EBP in their strategic plans and prospective budgets (e.g., for ongoing education, technology, evidence databases, librarian involvement, and recognition of experts' time in training and compensation). A proposal outlining the EBP teaching program and its potential benefits and costs will assist in obtaining support from administration.

Availability of Medical Librarians

An invaluable resource to assure you have on the EBP teaching team is a medical/health science librarian who is knowledgeable about EBP. It is imperative that these librarians be involved in the plan to initiate EBP. They can provide perspective and expertise in searching databases, as well as facilitate aspects of information literacy needed by students and faculty who strive to successfully teach and learn about EBP.

Early involvement of the librarian in preparing an EBP teaching program is crucial. It is an evidence-based medical/health sciences librarian's job to be proficient in knowing where to get information. Librarians' knowledge of databases, informatics resources, and information retrieval is integral to successful EBP teaching programs. Librarians can assist educators in developing database and Internet searching skills as a means of finding relevant evidence to answer clinical questions. In addition, librarians can set up direct search mechanisms in which the faculty or students pose their PICOT question electronically, and the librarian scours the databases for the answer and sends the citations and abstracts for the body of evidence to the inquirer. This approach to evidence retrieval can save enormous amounts of time and use some of the many talents of medical/health sciences librarians well.

Champions

As educators support teaching EBP, they must ensure that they are knowledgeable and skilled in EBP and able to meaningfully articulate the concepts to the students. A preliminary investment is required so that educators who are teaching EBP have the expertise required for meaningful and successful delivery and role modeling of EBP concepts. For example, assigning faculty to teach a fundamental critical appraisal methods course when their primary focus is generating evidence and they are novices at using evidence in practice is likely to be frustrating to the faculty member and students. Helping the faculty to become more proficient in understanding the EBP paradigm and how it blends with their research paradigm can facilitate their transition from frustration to champion of EBP. Educators need to be familiar with the concepts of EBP to be able to assist learners in determining whether observed practice is built on solid evidence or solely on tradition. Educators role modeling EBP concepts (e.g., addressing a student question at the time it is asked with a search of the literature and a discussion of findings and outcomes) can assist learners to integrate EBP concepts into their own practice paradigms.

Additional champions required for successful communication of EBP concepts are the learners themselves. There are always different levels of learners. Those who quickly absorb the concepts of EBP can become champions who assist other learners in integrating EBP principles into their practices. Integration of EBP concepts into one's practice is essential for learners to both see and do. Without learner champions, educating other learners will be less successful. Often in venues such as journal clubs, the learners are the ones who create an environment that encourages the less-than-enthusiastic learner to join in the process. The idea that learning EBP can be analogous to making a quilt may help learners to see the EBP process as wholly integrated. Educators, clinical preceptors, and other learners using EBP concepts are the "patches" in the quilt. When learners see EBP concepts integrated by these patches, the process takes on perspective and purpose, much as patches put together make a pattern that can be seen only in the completed quilt.

Mentors

The final champion for successfully teaching EBP is the EBP mentor, sometimes called a coach, information broker, or confidant (Melnyk, 2007). This individual's job is to provide one-on-one mentoring of educators, providing them with on-site assistance in problem solving about a how to teach EBP. Mentoring has been a long-standing tradition in academia; however, these efforts must be focused, purposeful, and supported by administration for them to be successful (Peck, Lester, Hinshaw, et al., 2009). Faculty who believe in EBP and desire to teach students to be evidence-based clinicians may find that competing priorities within an academic environment must be overcome in order for them to provide the amount of guidance they would like to their fellow educators. An EBP mentor's primary focus in the academic setting is on improving the student and faculty's understanding and integration of EBP in practice and educational paradigms. This is often accomplished through providing the right information at the right time that can assist the student to provide the best possible care to the patient and the faculty to provide the best evidence-based education to the student. These mentorships need to be formal, paid positions with time dedicated for teaching EBP. Chapter 15 has more on the concept of mentoring in EBP.

Technical Resources

Technical resources are an imperative for educators as they develop curricula using multiple instructional technologies to provide varied learning opportunities for students to improve their information literacy skills to effectively and efficiently access resources to answer their clinical questions (Pravikoff, Pierce, & Tanner, 2005; Schutt & Hightower, 2009). According to the AACN, technology affords an increased collaboration among faculties in teaching, practice, and research. In addition, technology in education may enhance the professional ability to educate clinicians for practice, prepare future healthcare educators, and advance professional science (AACN, 2002).

Information technology (IT) provides students and faculty access to evidence-based resources that are necessary for learning about evidenced-based care (Technology Informatics Guiding Education Reform [TIGER], 2007). Through IT support students can collect practice-based evidence (e.g., quality improvement data), combined with external evidence (i.e., research) and apply this evidence-based knowledge at the bedside in their clinical practicums (TIGER, 2007).

There is a call for an infusion of innovation, which includes technology, to reform nursing curricula that will prepare healthcare providers of the future (National League of Nursing [NLN], 2003). All educational programs for all levels of healthcare providers should design evidence-base curricula that are flexible, responsive to students' needs, collaborative, and technology savvy (NLN).

The Summit on Health Professions Education (Greiner & Knebel, 2003) identified the use of informatics as one of the core competencies for the 21st century health education. Through the use of informatics, medical errors can be avoided as students learn in a safe environment from experiences enhanced by technology, thereby, making mistakes without the harm to the patient (IOM, 1999; IOM 2001). In the IOM report, *Educating Health Professionals to Use Informatics* (2002), informatics is described as an enabler that may enhance patient-centered care and safety, making possible EBP, continuous improvement in quality of care, and support for interdisciplinary teams. When teaching organizations assume a leadership role in enhancing learning with technology, clinical organizations also benefit (IOM, 2001).

As technology in healthcare is increasing exponentially, educators need to integrate the use of technology into the curriculum. Students are using technologies in their everyday lives but can revert backward when in the educational milieu. There are many instructional technologies that are available to educators, including (a) simulation technology; (b) mobile devices; (c) Internet-accessed social networking sites, such as Facebook, Twitter, and Second Life; (d) course management systems, such as Blackboard™ and WebCT®, that provide distance learning through web-enhanced and online courses; (e) audio and video conferencing through Internet-based programs such as WebEx, Adobe® Acrobat® Connect™ Pro, and Skype™; and (f) clinical decision support systems (CDSSs), such as Cerner and PowerChart®. Given that most of these technologies are used in students' daily lives and/or the clinical environment, integrating technology in healthcare education is essential to prepare the student to enter such an environment and thrive. Students need to know how to use technology to access EBP resources and communicate them to others to facilitate EBP.

Simulation, mobile devices, electronic health records (EHRs), and the Internet to access social networking sites via the World Wide Web are expected to be the most used and important technologies in healthcare and healthcare education. These products have the potential of enabling students to access data and information for point-of-care decision making and support healthcare practitioners with work flow, continuing education, collaboration, and access to EBP resources. Currently, innovative technology, such as these, is being applied to enhance patient care delivery and provider productivity (Healthcare Information and Management Systems Society, 2002).

Simulation

The use of simulation technology allows healthcare educators to prepare students for the current clinical and community environments. The use of the most advanced simulator technology provides the educator with the ability to provide simulation education to challenge and test students' clinical and decision-making skills during realistic evidence-based patient care scenarios. These simulations are designed to replicate a real-life clinical situation for students so that they can experience, among other things, the integration of internal and external evidence while making decisions using the EBP paradigm. This technology affords students the opportunities to problem solve, use critical thinking skills, and perform to the best of their ability potentially without intimidation and fear.

Simulation also promotes participative learning in which students apply their knowledge and recognize the impact of a disease/disorder on a patient, family, or community situation. Simulation is enhancing student learning and is not intended to take the place of clinical sites or clinical experiences. It allows for practice of EBP knowledge and skills within a supportive and safe environment, thus allowing learners to focus on problem solving rather than on attaining a single perfect answer. In a landmark article, Morton (1997) describes how students also can receive immediate feedback from faculty, which reinforces the learning.

Advantages to providing simulation experiences include the ability to control the extraneous stimuli, keep the student directly engaged in activity, have the learner focused on instruction, and provide an opportunity to experience a specific area or event that might not occur in a clinical setting and learn to integrate the EBP process into one's clinical practice (Morgan, 2006; Morton, 1997; Rauen, 2004). Simulation allows for learners' and educators' time to be used efficiently and offers faculty an opportunity to simulate learning opportunities that might be difficult to find. In addition, learners have performed better in simulated experiences, with an increased ratio of students to faculty. Hallikainen et al. (2009) found in a randomized trial that students using simulation were 25% better in their performance of tasks than students taught traditionally. In addition, the ratio of students to faculty in the simulated group was six to one, compared to one to one in an intense clinical setting due to the extremely high risks involved.

During simulation, actions can be paused for reflection and correction. Mistakes are not only permitted, but expected as learning opportunities; multiple problems can be cleverly introduced, and, if scenarios are videotaped, replay can allow for reflection and further learning. In this way, technology prevents patient safety from being threatened. It is important that access to IT during a simulation experience mimics what students will experience in their clinical practicums, including access to EBP resources.

Creating simulation scenarios that are evidence based addresses the cognitive, affective, and psychomotor domains of learning to bridge theory and practice (Morgan, 2006; Morton, 1997; Spunt, Foster, & Adams, 2004). The evidence-based approach allows faculty to develop creative and innovative ways to teach and prepare clinicians for the demands of the workplace (Jeffries, 2005; Spunt et al., 2004). Focus on the cognitive learning domain (knowledge, comprehension, application, analysis, and synthesis) allows faculty to develop lessons that enhance learners' ability to gain knowledge and apply principles of physiology, pathophysiology, pharmacology, assessment, and management while integrating evidence from practice and research into their decision making (Morton, 1997; Starkweather & Kardong-Edgren, 2008).

table 13.1 **College of nursing simulation centers**

Arizona State University College of Nursing & Health Innovation Learning Resource Educational Simulation Program	http://nursing.asu.edu/lrc/esp.htm
Duke University Human Simulation and Patient Safety Center	http://simcenter.duke.edu/
University of Texas Arlington School of Nursing, Smart Hospital™ & Health System	http://www.uta.edu/nursing/simulation/
University of Maryland Clinical Simulation Laboratories	http://nursing.umaryland.edu/resources/simlabs/index.htm

Lessons developed using the affective domain of learning provide an opportunity for students to learn about attitudes and behaviors that are desirable, consistent, and appropriate for the professional clinician role (Kitson-Reynolds, 2009; Morton, 1997). Students learn options and formulate guidelines for expected professional behavior by choosing from alternatives: caring, empathy, sensitivity, integrity, cooperation, independence, and compassion. Students also learn how to interact with colleagues and learn to function as team players. Creative lessons that focus on the psychomotor learning domain involve scenarios that allow for hands-on skill building, such as performing clinical skills, tasks, and procedures. The focus of including all domains in simulated learning is to allow students to become comfortable with the clinical environment, technology, and processes so that evidence-based care of the patient becomes the focus rather than these environmental aspects (Morton; Skiba, Connors, & Jeffries, 2008).

Faculty teaching at all levels of the curriculum can incorporate simulation. Faculty can plan lessons and develop creative evidence-based case scenarios for students as well as integrate simulation technology into faculty development workshops. Such continuing education can encourage faculty to integrate simulation technology into the teaching and learning process, which will enhance the nursing curriculum (Skiba et al., 2008). Several schools have led the way in integrating simulation technology into their curriculum (see Table 13.1).

Mobile Devices

The use of handheld devices is being introduced with increasing frequency in many healthcare and education settings. A mobile device, such as a smart phone, BlackBerry, iPhone, and iPod touch, is characterized by its handheld size, mobility, ability to communicate with other units, and use of applications. A mobile device is a useful tool that allows one to use it as a date book, to-do list, address book, memo pad, calculator, and Internet access, and it has the ability to download health/medical software programs that can be accessed in the classroom and at the point of care.

The use of mobile devices in nursing education supports educators in the preparation of nursing students for current and future work environments. Mobile technology tests students' clinical and decision-making skills in clinical, laboratory, and classroom settings. Challenges to the use of mobile device technology include cost, faculty acceptance and education, and identification of user-friendly hardware and software (Bauldoff, Kirkpatrick, Sheets, et al., 2008; Huffstutler, Wyatt, & Wright, 2002). Technology that is accessible and usable for both faculty and students allows for the reinforcement of core knowledge for practice, strengthening of professional confidence, and access to the most up-to-date information in EBP resources (Bauldoff et al.; Kuiper, 2008; White, Allen, Goodwin, et al., 2005). Students are able to retrieve and receive information at the point of care in real time, which allows the student to have instant information when administering medications, completing a care plan,

table 13.2 Mobile device resources for medical/nursing software downloads

Product	Website
Epocrates®	http://www.epocrates.com/index.html
Pepid Medical Information Resources™	http://www.pepid.com/
Skyscape®	http://www.skyscape.com/index/home.aspx
Unbound Medicine®	http://www.unboundmedicine.com/
PDA Cortex©	http://www.rnpalm.com/index.htm

collecting disease management information, and developing patient education materials to conduct procedures and provide safe and efficient care to the patient, while simultaneously allowing learning to take place (Greenfield, 2007). By accessing healthcare information via a mobile device, the student is able to be accountable for learning, self-improvement, gathering and analyzing patient health status data, and using EBP resources (e.g., MEDLINE and PubMed), which are essential in providing quality, patient-centered, evidenced-based care (Kuiper; White et al., 2005). There are many software resources that can be downloaded to a mobile device (see Table 13.2).

Clinical Information Systems

There are many clinical information systems, such as EHRs, that have been designed to enhance productivity and that are used at the point of care or wherever the clinical staff needs to access patient information. Another example, CDSSs bring knowledge of patient data, orders, care plans, medication administration record, and nursing care together with the best evidence available to support decision at the point of care, usually within the EHR, to provide supportive evidence for why particular health treatment prescriptions are chosen. In a systematic review, Chaudhry et al. (2006) indicated that IT, including CDSSs, had a positive impact on healthcare quality, efficiency, and costs. This included CDSS features such as evidence-based prompts, alerts, and reminders. Given this positive impact, more infrastructure is necessary to make CDSSs and EHRs more common. Part of that infrastructure needs to be the academic preparation of healthcare professionals who care for patients.

The IOM (2001) supported the integration of EBP and IT infrastructure in the academic setting. As part of a national health information infrastructure to provide access to patient information for service providers, insurers, and patients, schools of nursing are forming relationships with hospitals and partnering with healthcare information organizations, such as the Cerner Corporation, to integrate clinical information systems and CDSSs into the curriculum. This integration of technology teaches students electronic information management at the same time they learn to assess patients and document clinical events through electronic media (Gassert, 2006).

The University of Kansas School of Nursing was the first to develop an academic business partnership with the Cerner Corporation to integrate a live production of a clinical information system into the nursing curriculum (http://www2.kumc.edu/son/abp.html). University of Maryland School of Nursing developed a partnership with the Cerner Corporation in 2006 to integrate clinical information software into clinical simulation laboratories (http://nursing.umaryland.edu/).

This type of partnership affords faculty the ability to integrate IT into the curriculum and develop evidence-based scenarios that can enhance the critical thinking and problem-solving abilities of students, and provides the IT infrastructure for EBP (Connors, Warren, & McNamara, 2003; Connors, Weaver, Warren, et al., 2002). Such a system allows students to access reference databases, search the Internet, and document assessments and care plans, and it teaches students necessary skills needed to be competent in the highly technical IT healthcare environment of today and tomorrow (Connors et al., 2002). Developing academic-business partnerships with clinical information system companies, such as the Cerner Corporation, provides faculty the opportunity to incorporate IT into the curriculum; develop evidence-based scenarios; demonstrate through simulated experiences how to document care; access resources; impact cost and quality of care; and promote the EBP process, dissemination and evaluation of knowledge, and research (Connors et al., 2003).

World Wide Web

The newer version of the World Wide Web provides an environment that promotes collaboration, functionality, and the ability to interact socially (Kardong-Edgren, Oermann, Ha, et al., 2009; Weberg, in press). Utilizing web-based tools, such as Wikis, blogs, podcasts, social networking sites (e.g., Facebook, Twitter, Ning), and video conferencing (e.g., Skype, Adobe® Acrobat® Connect™ Pro, WebEx, and Wimba), offers an opportunity for educators to develop interactive and creative ways to provide lessons, construct assignments, and encourage critical thinking and decision making along with a satisfactory learning experience (Murray, Belgrave, & Robinson, 2006; Skiba et al., 2008). Faculty have an immense opportunity, challenge, and responsibility to use web tools, definitions, and web resources (see Table 13.3) to teach students about healthcare so as to "reduce health care errors and improve care quality, access and cost effectiveness" (Fetter, 2009, p. 78).

table 13.3 **Web-based tools educators can use to enhance teaching and learning**

Web Tool	Definition	Resource Web Link
Wiki	Internet based pages where groups can edit the work in real time.	http://www.wiki.com/whatiswiki.htm
Blog	Places where you can write things that are of interest to you and get feedback from others.	https://www.blogger.com/start
Podcast	A video or audio recording that can be retrieved from the Internet that you can watch or listen to.	http://www.how-to-podcast-tutorial.com/
Video conferencing	Streams audio and visual in real time, bringing people in different sites together for a meeting.	http://www.skype.com/ http://www.webex.com/ http://www.adobe.com/products/acrobatconnectpro/ http://www.wimba.com/
Social networking sites	Online community on the Internet where people join and communicate and share similar interests and connect by sharing pictures, stories, and experiences.	http://www.facebook.com/ http://www.ning.com/ http://twitter.com/ http://www.linkedin.com/
Second life	A virtual world where users create an avatar (online person) and interact with others in a virtual world created by those in it.	http://secondlife.com/

Second Life, Twitter, and Facebook

Schools of nursing are reaching out and connecting with students through various social networking sites. Duke University School of Nursing has developed a virtual world in Second Life where students can access lectures and discussions in virtual classrooms (http://nursing. duke.edu/modules/son_about/index.php?id = 90). Educators need to incorporate technology courses into the curriculum and empower the future healthcare professionals with knowledge and confidence to use technology. The numbers of schools, journals, businesses, educational institutions, and hospitals are growing everyday. It is estimated that approximately 100 hospitals have some kind of Twitter account, and some 82 hospitals have a Facebook page (Snow, 2009). Social networking sites, such as Facebook, Ning, and Twitter, along with the virtual world of Second Life, allow educators to create innovative teaching and learning and promote various ways to communicate. Educators can use these methods to communicate lessons and assignments, conduct virtual office hours, promote discussions, generate new ideas, link to resources, and provide up-to-date real-time information to students (Weberg, in press).

Implementing a curriculum that integrates EBP through incorporating technology provides faculty creative avenues for innovation and offers multiple opportunities to increase students' information literacy skills (Schutt, & Hightower, 2009). Educational agencies that develop collaborative learning communities with active use of technology to move toward knowledge development, dissemination, and implementation of EBPs are on the cutting edge (TIGER, 2009). In addition, technologies need to be people centered, affordable, useable, universal, useful, and standards-based (TIGER). Healthcare educators have the opportunity to be creatively innovative as they integrate EBP and technology into curricula to give students the ability to practice in real-world settings through simulation, document care, and access to EBP resources.

With technology changing the landscape of education, there is concern over copyright and ensuring protection of intellectual property. For the purposes of this chapter, the United States copyright law indicates that a work may be used for the purpose of critique, scholarship, and for teaching, among other uses, and these purposes may be considered fair use (U.S. Copyright Law, section #107; see http://www.copyright.gov/title17/92chap1.html#107). The Teach Act (Copyright Clearance Center, 2002) addresses use of materials online.

> Additional copyright information can be found at **http://www4.law.cornell.edu/uscode/17/.** Information about the Teach Act, including a checklist for use, can be found in the Teach Act Toolkit at **http://www.lib.ncsu.edu/dspc/legislative/teachkit/overview.html**

One way of dealing with the copyright issue, which can sometimes be difficult and time consuming, is to use only links to full-text study reports as teaching tools. This places the responsibility on learners to obtain information straight from the source. The disadvantage to this practice is that there are many good teaching tools that are not full text. Despite the challenges that come with electronic information, resources such as the Internet, electronic journals, and other computer databases are essential to a successful EBP teaching program.

Characteristics of Evidence-Based Practice Teachers and Learners

Commitment to excellent patient care is central to becoming an evidence-based practitioner and the most important attribute of the learner. Practitioners who continually strive for excellence will want to understand their patients' problems thoroughly and apply the current best evidence

---

box 13.3

Qualities for Evidence-Based Practice Teachers and Learners

Commitment to:

1. Excellent patient care
2. Excellent clinical skills
3. Excellent clinical judgment
4. Diligence
5. Perspective

---

appropriately to all aspects of patient care. In other words, they will automatically gravitate toward the practice and promotion of EBP (Fineout-Overholt, Levin, & Melnyk, 2004; Melnyk, Fineout-Overholt, Feinstein, et al., 2004).

Excellence in Patient Care, Clinical Skills, and Clinical Judgment

Given the assumption that clinicians who seek after relevant information to address patient issues strive for the highest quality of care, it is imperative that those who teach EBP and those learning about EBP be committed to excellence in patient care. Box 13.3 lists the essential qualities that, when present in the learner and teacher, make for an EBP teaching/learning environment and culture.

Excellent clinical skills in patient interviewing and physical examination are needed for practitioners to accurately understand the clinical problem, the patient's unique situation and values, and the evidence-based management options related to the identified problem. In addition, excellent communication skills are essential so that practitioners and teachers of EBP can clearly explain to patients and learners the risks and benefits of the available options and evidence-based recommendations.

Excellent clinical judgment is of paramount importance because it is the skill that enables practitioners to weigh the risks and benefits targeted by the available research evidence in the light of the patient's values and preferences. Time and experience are essential elements to developing clinical judgment. Teachers will be expected to have highly developed clinical judgment, whereas early learners will grow in this quality.

Diligence

Diligence is another desirable teacher and learner quality. Teachers and learners of EBP must be consistently willing to work hard, to search the ever-expanding array of available healthcare information resources to find the best evidence for a given clinical question, and to return to the clinical scenario and apply the evidence appropriately. Diligence is needed to communicate and hone the other essential skills of interviewing, physical examination, clinical reasoning, and judgment.

Perspective

The final desirable teacher and learner quality is perspective. An ability to view newly appraised evidence appropriately in the context of the greater body of healthcare knowledge and accepted practice is the desired goal for all evidence-based practitioners. This quality is necessary for practitioners to choose, when it comes to their own practice, whether to adopt, adapt, or discard newly appraised research evidence in conjunction with their expertise and their patients' values and preferences.

Gaining perspective comes from the extensive study required to become proficient in the practice of healthcare and requires tolerance of uncertainty. If a teacher or learner has an

table 13.4 **Evidence-based practice skills inventory**

To help your preceptor improve your skills in EBP, please indicate your experience by checking the appropriate box.

	No Experience	Some Experience	Much Experience
Asking answerable questions about my patients	☐	☐	☐
Performing efficient searches for evidence that answers my clinical questions	☐	☐	☐
Selecting the best evidence from what is found in the search	☐	☐	☐
Critically appraising the evidence	☐	☐	☐
Applying the evidence to my practice	☐	☐	☐

"all-or-nothing" attitude, evidence is usually categorized as either good or bad, and this is seldom beneficial to the patient or the student. Most of the evidence that exists today is in the in-between category, neither perfectly valid nor worthy of rejection. The more mature perspective of EBP teachers will cultivate openness to uncertainty that will benefit learners.

To cultivate an environment for teaching EBP successfully, faculty need to determine how people responsible for developing an EBP initiative assess whether their EBP mentors exhibit the qualities described. In turn, EBP teachers must assess whether learners have these qualities. Working together with learners, in a clinical practicum for example, assists the teacher to assess learners' clinical skills, commitment to excellent patient care, clinical judgment, diligence, and perspective.

Often it is helpful to have a checklist to assist in the evaluation of students' skills. Table 13.4 contains an EBP skills inventory that may be used to assess teachers' and learners' self-perceived strengths and weaknesses regarding the essential skills of EBP (J. Cox, personal communication, March 30, 2009). Informal assessment has demonstrated that learners as well as teachers have gained valuable perspective from this self-assessment. Using this type of questionnaire, EBP teachers can discover learners' comfort with learning to be an evidence-based practitioner. In addition, teachers can discern the importance they attach to improving their EBP skills.

Making learning relevant is one of the most important strategies for developing learners' enthusiasm for and skill in practicing EBP. The examples, assignments, and concepts used in teaching must be based on real patients. In addition, applying the results of the process to learners' current or future practice helps to cement the concepts for them. In the academic setting, if students are given assignments that are not relevant to practice, all but the most highly motivated EBP students will perceive it as busy work and lose enthusiasm.

An effective reflection tool is the **educational prescription** (EP), originally described by Sackett et al. (1991) to teach people how to "do" critical appraisal. The educator writes an EP for an early learner when a learner does not know the answer to a question that is pertinent to the evaluation or management of his or her patient. The hope is that learners eventually start to identify their own knowledge deficits and write their own EPs. Completing the elements of an EP (see example in Box 13.4) emphasizes the qualities that are desirable in learners and teachers. Asking learners to report how the evidence they find will alter the management of their patients teaches them perspective. Fundamental to the successful use of EPs is educators' willingness

> **box 13.4**
>
> ## Example of an EP
>
> 1. To be reported (date/time): Monday, November 3, 7 AM rounds
> 2. The patient problem: 35 y/o female runner who is a new mother who has been diagnosed with type II diabetes wants to know about managing the disease with nutrition and exercise versus medication.
> 3. Educational tasks to be completed before the session:
>   a. Formulate a searchable, answerable question.
>   i. P—35-year-old women
>   ii. I—Nutrition and exercise
>   iii. C—Oral hypoglycemic agents
>   iv. O—Normal hemoglobin A1c
>   b. Look for valid, relevant evidence to answer question.
>   c. Do focused search for MeSH headings: nutrition, exercise, hypoglycemic agents, glycosylated hemoglobin
>   d. Combine various search results, limit to RCTs, limit to adult 19–44 years
>   e. Using inclusion and exclusion criteria, narrow yield to only relevant studies.
>   f. Critically appraise studies kept from the search.
>   g. Keep best studies for discussion with patient (and group).
> 4. Presentation will cover:
>   a. *How* I found what I found
>   b. *What* I found
>   c. The *validity and applicability* of what I found
>   d. How what I found would *alter my* management of the patient

chapter 13

305

to admit they do not know everything, write their own EPs, and present them to the learners, thereby modeling the desirable qualities of commitment to excellence in patient care, diligence, and perspective.

> More can be learned about EPs from the toolbox on the website for the Centre for Evidence-Based Medicine
> (**http://www.cebm.utoronto.ca/practise/formulate/eduprescript.htm**)

   Teacher efforts to cultivate desirable learner qualities must be tailored to the learner's proficiency in the steps of the EBP process. For example, learners without much experience asking questions about their patients should be encouraged to start asking questions, then coached to refine those questions into more searchable, answerable questions. In the process, learners will start to see the benefit of walking through the stages of the EBP process and that careful formulation of the question leads to a more fruitful search for information. Only after learners have developed some proficiency in asking the searchable, answerable question does it make sense to focus teaching efforts on improving searching efficiency.

   In the early stages, learners typically are excited about finding out information relevant to their patients in clinical practicums. These early learners may use textbooks to answer most of their questions. This is appropriate because many questions of early learners are background questions (i.e., those questions that ask for general information about a clinical issue). As learners gain knowledge and experience in asking pertinent questions about their patients' care, questions shift from background questions answered by a textbook to foreground questions that require more up-to-date information to answer them. Chapter 2 has an excellent discussion of foreground and background questions. Determining which type of question the learner is asking has implications for how the teacher directs the learning.

For various reasons, early learners often may neglect to report the source of their information for their clinical decision. It is necessary for teachers of EBP to prompt learners explicitly to provide their rationale for their choice of information resources used in clinical decision making. Furthermore, teachers who are at this early stage need to query their learners consistently about which resources they used to find their information and their opinion of the validity of the information they found, as well as the ease of use—or lack thereof—of the resource. Such discussion is useful for all involved because those resources that are updated regularly; are easy to search; and provide clear, evidence-based recommendations are likely to emerge as the favorites.

This discussion sets the stage for the expectation that learners will critically appraise primary articles from the literature when they progress to the point that they are using the research evidence for the purpose of answering their own questions versus performing an academic exercise. This is a shift from traditional education where learners simply received information passively. In EBP, learners must actively formulate clinical questions, search out evidence to answer them, determine the validity of the evidence, and decide how to use it in practice (Fineout-Overholt & Johnston, 2007).

Shift in Educational Paradigm: From Traditional to Evidence-Based Practice

Traditional research education focuses on preparing research generators (i.e., learning to design studies and generate hypotheses) or critiquing research for strengths and weaknesses. Evidence-based practice education focuses on preparing the learner to be an **evidence user**. The learner is taught to think of issues in the clinical area in a systematic fashion and to formulate questions around the issues in a searchable, answerable way. Teaching learners to find evidence quickly that can answer their clinical questions and critically appraise it, not only for strengths and weaknesses (validity) but also for applicability to the given patient situation, is integral to EBP education. This decision cannot be made solely on the scientific evidence itself but must include consideration of the patient's values and preferences, as well as the clinician's expertise, which incorporates internal evidence. If the scientific evidence is useful to the practitioner, the next step in learning is to understand how to apply the evidence and evaluate the outcomes of the intervention. Assisting learners to understand how the EBP process flows is essential to success in teaching EBP concepts. There are many models for implementing EBP, all of which could be discussed here (see Chapter 11 for more information). However, the EBP paradigm and the ACE Star model were selected to demonstrate the ease of learning when approached from the perspective of the EBP process.

The Evidence-Based Practice Paradigm

To understand the EBP paradigm, faculty must understand what is considered evidence. In this book, evidence has been described as internal evidence (i.e., practice-generated evidence) and external evidence (i.e., research). When using evidence (i.e., external and internal) for decision making along with patient preferences and clinician expertise, faculty and students must realize that a new responsibility comes with this broadened EBP scope: life-long problem solving that integrates (a) a systematic search for, critical appraisal, and synthesis of the most relevant and best research (i.e., external evidence) to answer a clinical question; (b) clinicians expertise, which includes abilities to interpret information generated from practice (i.e., internal evidence), from patient assessment, and from the evaluation and subsequent careful use of resources available to improved outcomes; and (c) the values and preferences of patients (see Chapter 1, Figure 1.2).

In the EBP paradigm, how the three EBP components will meld together when making a clinical decision is dependent on each patient–clinician interaction. Students practicing from this paradigm have a better sense of why they are learning about Foley catheter insertion or turning every 2 hours. The variability of the weight of each component is directly related to the characteristics of the clinician–patient clinical encounter. Clinical expertise involves how clinicians integrate knowledge of research and what they know about their work and population, as well as what they know about their patients' preferences. The best clinical decisions come when all of these are present and contributing factors in the decision-making process. Patient preferences are not uninformed preferences. When patients are not informed, clinicians have the responsibility to provide needed information in a manner that the patient can appreciate. Once informed, patients determine how they choose to proceed with the decision. For example, evidence from research might support the efficacy of one naturopathic supplement over another in treating gastrointestinal irritation. However, if the patient is likely to experience financial hardship from the preferred supplement because it is so expensive and will likely refuse to take it, and if there is another supplement with similar efficacy, the clinician has a responsibility to discuss these options with the patient. The patient can then decide which supplement works best for him or her. In this case, patient preference will outweigh the evidence from research and perhaps from clinical expertise and the healthcare provider and the patient will choose an alternative supplement with similar efficacy and tolerable financial burden that will achieve the outcome of resolving the gastrointestinal irritation. This is an important underpinning paradigm for students and faculty to understand and practice; then, the EBP process and models of EBP make sense. Otherwise, it becomes following steps. The bottom line for educators is to help students grasp why they are learning and what outcome they are striving to achieve. This clarity helps students put their energies into learning to improve outcomes versus studying to pass a test or procedural check-off.

ACE Star Model

The ACE Star model (Figure 13.1) depicts the Cycle of Knowledge Transformation. It is an EBP model that provides an inclusive framework with which to organize EBP processes and approaches. A five-point star is used to illustrate five stages of what the originators term *knowledge transformation*. These stages are

1. Knowledge discovery
2. Evidence summary
3. Translation into practice recommendations
4. Implementation into practice
5. Evaluation

As learners go from one point on the star to the next, they begin to have a context within which to place the various aspects of EBP. Evidence-based processes and methods vary from one point of the Star model to the next and depend on the "form" of knowledge at that particular stage of transformation. For example, research findings represented on the first point are transformed into a single statement by combining all research (Point 2 of the Star). The ACE Star model places previous research utilization work within the context of the more comprehensive EBP paradigm and serves as an organizer for examining and applying EBP.

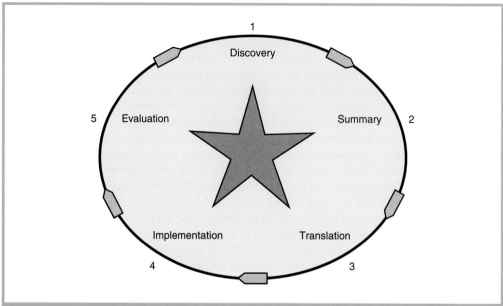

| figure 13.1 | Cycle of knowledge transformation, the ACE star model (Used with permission from the Academic Center for Evidence-Based Nursing of the University of Texas Health Science Center at San Antonio.) |

Discovery

Discovery (Point 1) on the star is the stage when new knowledge is generated by research methodologies used in traditional single, original research studies. These primary research studies may range in design from descriptive to correlational to causal and from randomized control trials to qualitative inquiries.

Evidence Summary

Evidence summary (Point 2) is unique to EBP. During this stage, evidence from all research knowledge is synthesized into a single, coherent distillation of the state of the science on the particular clinical topic. **Evidence summaries** are reviews of literature that can range from highly rigorous meta-analyses to integrative reviews of all studies that could answer a given clinical question. Systematic methods improve the certainty with which practitioners can rely on the recommendations from the evidence. Other terms used for evidence summary are *systematic review* and *evidence synthesis*. For examples see AHRQ Evidence-Based Practice Center Reports (http://www.ahrq.gov/clinic/epcix.htm).

Translation

Translation is the third point on the star. The end point of this translation stage is the evidence summary, combined with clinical expertise, to produce valid and reliable clinical recommendations. At this stage of transformation, the knowledge now reflects best practice based on best research evidence and consensus and endorsement of experts. On a local level, experts from the specific clinical agency may adapt the clinical practice guidelines to be specific to setting and population. Guidelines may also be called *care standards, clinical pathways, protocols*, or *algorithms*. Chapter 9 has more information on clinical practice guidelines.

Implementation

Implementation of EBP, the fourth stage, is perhaps the most familiar stage to healthcare providers because of prior work in nursing and other healthcare disciplines to integrate research into practice (i.e., research utilization). This step involves bringing evidence to bear on clinical decision making and changing practice. At this stage, the clinical practice guideline is activated and put into actual practice. Important considerations during planning for implementation include cost efficiency, timeliness, and usefulness for the clinician and client. For examples of resources see AHRQ Health Care Innovations Exchange (http://www.innovations.ahrq.gov/).

Evaluation

The fifth and final stage is evaluation. This last step is crucial to verifying the success of EBP. It is important to include patient, healthcare provider, and system outcomes in evaluation (Stevens, 2002). The Star Model formed the foundation for the ACE EBP Readiness Inventory (ACE-ERI). This assessment tool measures the student or nurse's self-report of confidence in the ability to apply EBP. Reliability, validity, and use of the ACE-ERI indicate that the instrument is a sound instrument and can be administered via online survey and pencil-and-paper to students and practicing nurses (Stevens, 2009b).

Application of the ACE Star Model

The Star Model was successfully used to frame a list of 93 essential competencies in EBP for nurses across all levels of education (Stevens, 2009a). These competencies are identified for each of the five stages reflected in the model for the purpose of demonstrating knowledge of the full process of EBP. These competencies and the ACE-ERI provide guidance for nursing education programs and professional development programs in preparing a nursing workforce to capably employ EBP. Educational programs use the Star Model as an organizer for integrating EBP concepts into curricula. In addition, nursing departments in hospitals have adopted the ACE Star Model as part of their plan for moving to excellence.

Strategies for Integrating Evidence-Based Practice in Academic Curricula

There are many strategies that can assist in teaching EBP in academic settings. The key to all of them is to keep it simple. Focusing on the EBP paradigm and how it is being lived/exemplified in course documents and teaching will facilitate this simplicity. A common language and the steps of the EBP process are areas of course curricula that are readily incorporated into existing courses without a tremendous upheaval.

Language

The goal of integrating EBP into the curriculum is to do so without getting overwhelmed. A good place to begin is to review course syllabi and related course documents for the opportunity to use language that reflects EBP. For example, something as simple as changing the word "rationale" to "evidence" or "improve client care" to "improve client outcomes" can facilitate learning and shifting of paradigms for learners. These small steps reflect the EBP paradigm, and students and faculty will begin to "talk" the language.

Another simple step that can be taken is to review the current learning activities and course assignments and reframe them to reflect EBP. For example, in the undergraduate nursing program at Arizona State University College of Nursing & Health Innovation, learning activities in the Professional Development course for beginning nursing students were reviewed and EBP-related criteria for the assignments were added. One assignment required students to develop aesthetic projects that represented their first nursing experience and peer review these projects. The "Critique Form" was re-titled to "Appraisal Form," which reframes the activity to look for the value or worth of the project. This parallels critical appraisal of evidence, which is step 3 of the EBP process. In addition, one question was added to this appraisal form that requested students to reflect on the EBP process: "How did this project (either yours or your peers) help you understand the evidence-based practice process?" In this almost effortless way, existing assignments became framed within the EBP paradigm, making integration of EBP into courses doable.

Consider where the best place is to introduce the theoretical underpinnings of EBP and additional courses in which it can be integrated throughout the curriculum. An imperative approach for making EBP real for students is relevance. Particularly, since these new nursing students do not have much clinical reference points, using current exemplars of how they make decisions, such as purchasing iPods, automobiles, or flight tickets, makes it much more relevant.

Steps in the Evidence-Based Practice Process

Asking the Clinical Question

First, faculty must keep in mind that step 0 of the EBP process is fostering a spirit of inquiry. Once that step is achieved, students can focus on step 1, formulating clinical questions. If handheld devices are required as part of the educational program, a number of programs can be downloaded to PDAs and iPhones. For example, a PICOmaker can be downloaded to a PDA that allows students to capture clinical issues and formulate PICOT questions (http://www.library. ualberta.ca/pdazone/pico/). Another example is searching PubMed for evidence using a PICOT format, which is available for handheld devices with wireless Internet service (http://pubmedhh. nlm.nih.gov/nlm/pico/piconew.html).

Searching for Evidence

Step 2 of the EBP process, searching for the evidence, involves competency with informatics, as has been discussed. Addressing this from an EBP perspective will help eliminate some of the reported barriers to finding answers to the clinical question (Ebell, 2009; Ely, Osheroff, Chambliss, et al., 2005; Green & Ruff, 2005).

Strategies to teach how to search for the evidence include formal classes on searching electronic databases as well as role modeling by faculty. Librarians are essential for consistency in introducing students to library resources, including access to available electronic databases. In the Internet-mediated classroom, faculty have the opportunity to role model searching techniques that may be challenging to students, such as using controlled vocabulary, Boolean connectors and limits (see Chapter 3 for more information).

Using laptops in the classroom for the immediate retrieval of evidence to answer questions generated by case studies can be learning tools to bridge the gap between practice and evidence (Rush, 2008). It is important to require search histories as part of written papers as demonstrations of the quality of search skills. This can reinforce successful skill building through feedback from the faculty/librarian as well as provide an opportunity for peer review and learner self-assessment of this critical skill (McDowell & Ma, 2007).

Planning opportunities for students to use EHRs or CDSSs can provide realistic experiences in which immediate access to data and best clinical practices offer students decision-making quandaries in which they can integrate evidence with patient preferences and their clinical expertise. An example is Nurse^2, a system available to teach nursing students how to use the EHRs (http://www.nursesquared.com/Features.html).

Critical Appraisal

Step 3 of the EBP process is critical appraisal. There are a variety of teaching strategies that have been reported in the literature to teach this concept, including journal clubs and letter writing (Edwards, White, Gray, et al., 2001). For example, a journal club was structured to have a small group of medical students present their appraisal of a preselected paper to their peers and write a letter to the journal editor based on their appraisal. In another example, a short course taken by nursing students agreed that a variety of methods (e.g., lecture, group work, interactive plenary discussion, over 11 days during a 4-week schedule) were efficient and effective ways to learn to critically appraise a scientific article (Smith-Strom & Nortvedt, 2008). In a final example, groups of five students were formed and sections of articles were used to teach the steps of EBP with the lecture component, and the remaining time was used for application and interaction. The same students remained in the same group throughout the entire course. Guided mentorship was used to teach EBP to residents in psychiatry and consisted of an EBP clinical mentoring curriculum that included evidenced-based decision-making strategies at the point of care and attendees mentoring the residents throughout the clinical rotation (Mascola, 2008).

For some educators, the challenge in teaching critical appraisal to students is delineating EBP and research (Burns & Foley, 2005). Undergraduate nursing programs have traditionally emphasized critiques of research and the development of a research proposal or even conducting research (August-Brady, 2005; McQuaid-Dvorak, Prophy, Binder, et al., 1993; Wheeler, Fasano, & Burr, 1995). More recently, however, faculty are redesigning the traditional research course to an EBP approach (Meeker, Jones, & Flanagan, 2008; Smith-Strom & Nortvedt, 2008). Research courses can be restructured to include experiential learning activities, using clinical problems as a focus and levels of evidence as the framework to approach research design and critical appraisal of the evidence.

As an example, the redesign of the undergraduate nursing research course undertaken at Arizona State University College of Nursing & Health Innovation included reframing course objectives and learning activities to specifically address EBP concepts and principles, with the goal to produce evidence users not evidence generators. This redesign was a joint effort among faculty who taught the traditional research course and an EBP working group, composed of faculty who were champions of EBP and an EBP expert who was sanctioned by the curriculum committee to lead the integration of EBP in the curriculum. Sample objectives and learning activities from the redesigned course shifted the requirements of this course from producing a research proposal to using concepts and principles of EBP in evaluating research for practice (see Box 13.5).

Clinical Decision Making: Patient Preferences

In step 4 of the EBP process, along with evidence, patient values and preferences play an integral part in clinical decision making. Learning activities focused on heightening students awareness of the importance of patient preferences can be designed around students' day-to-day experiences with patients or clients. For example, a learning activity with beginning students can include clinical experiences in which students are obtaining patient histories. This experience can provide a rich forum for discussing patients' preferences, desires, and values about their health and their expectations of healthcare.

As an additional example, students in a community/public health course learned about vulnerable populations in theory. In clinical settings, these students provided nursing care to people who were homeless, people who had mental illness and chronic disease, high-risk moms and babies, and people living in poverty, among them immigrants and refugees. Using an inductive approach, students were asked to assess the population and identify health risks and high-risk behaviors. In a written assignment, students provided the information about the population and

box 13.5

Sample Course Objectives and Learning Assignments

Course objective	Example assignment
Formulate searchable, answerable questions from clinical issues	Generate PICOT questions for written assignment
Examine clinical questions in relation to levels of evidence	Groups share and give feedback on PICOT questions
Find the best evidence to answer the clinical question through searching existing healthcare databases and other sources of evidence	Search two types of questions and post search strategies/results Groups share and give feedback to peers Paper on search for the evidence to a clinical question
Critically appraise best evidence (i.e., evaluating research methodologies for validity, reliability, and applicability) to answer selected clinical questions	Conduct a rapid critical appraisal of a quantitative study Groups share and give feedback to peers Paper on appraisal of the evidence
Discuss strategies for implementing evidence into daily practice	Paper on proposed change in practice

then were asked to gather information about common issues and solutions to identified health issues within the population. After discussion in class, students critically appraised chosen randomized controlled trials that addressed identified health concerns. At this point, students had an understanding of the population, health issues for that population, and potential solutions that were being published in the literature or lay press. Students readily engaged developing a PICOT question, as now they had some expertise with the population (K. Jarrell, personal communication, April 7, 2009)

Strategies for Teaching Evidence-Based Practice in Academic Settings

According to a systematic review conducted by Coomarasamy and Khan (2004), knowledge, skills, attitude, and behavior were improved with the clinical integration of EBP; however, stand-alone EBP courses only improved knowledge. Thus, EBP must be incorporated across all settings in healthcare education, so as to parallel learners' daily experiences (e.g., ambulatory care and inpatient experiences, direct patient care, patient rounds, change-of-shift meetings, and unit-to-unit report when a patient is being transferred).

Teaching EBP should not be restricted to one instructor or to one teaching episode (e.g., single academic course, selected clinical courses). Rather, it should be woven into the fabric of academic programs' overall curricula in such a fashion that it becomes part of the culture. The learners need to see EBP used and learned in every setting to which they are exposed. This ever-present implementation and learning of EBP concepts serve to model for the learners that EBP is not only an academic exercise but also is actively used in clinical practice.

Lectures, Group Learning, Journal Clubs, and More

Methods used to teach EBP should emphasize active participation by the learners as much as possible. Examples of potential strategies include lectures, discussion groups, small- and large-group presentations, journal clubs, elective rotations, grand rounds, unit rounds, and change-of-shift discussions for practicums. Teachers are best to act in the facilitator role while learners take front stage in working through the concepts.

Presentations Integrated with Clinical Practicum

A good way to begin any type of educational presentation on EBP is to provide a short synopsis on the definition and EBP process with examples. When teaching EBP in a classroom setting, using an interactive teaching style is preferred (e.g., Socratic questioning and group work) because the students can get lost in the content if not engaging the material. These methods facilitate student engagement.

Clinically integrated teaching-learning activities are superior to classroom teaching alone to improve knowledge, attitude, and behavior. However, classroom teaching can incorporate activities (e.g., case studies, group work, role play, hands-on learning) to be educationally effective. Clinical teaching can include didactic information by the teacher who directly applies the content to patient situations. Using interactive teaching strategies at a clinical site can make learning more effective. Didactic teaching without interactive teaching strategies is less effective and leads to rote memory (Khan & Coomarasamy, 2006). A proposed hierarchy of teaching and learning activities related to educational effectiveness has been suggested by Khan & Coomarasamy (see Box 13.6).

Small-Group Seminars

Research evidence supports that seminars targeting specific EBP skills can increase those skills to a moderate degree, at least in the short term (Amsallem, Kasparian, Cucherat, et al., 2007; Flores-Mateo & Argimon, 2007; Shuval, Berkovits, Netzer, et al., 2007; West & McDonald, 2008; Yew & Reid, 2008). If you are in doubt about what sort of topic would be of interest for small-group work, ask for suggestions from the participants. Suggestions can be offered either before the group work seminar so that predigested or preappraised examples can be used or at the time of the seminar in more of an "on-the-fly" setup. These more spontaneous sessions tend to be risky, because if the example is too difficult, the learners quickly can become lost and disheartened, potentially viewing EBP as a tedious and difficult process. A skillful teacher can build confidence in the learner by crafting or framing the issue in such a way that easily guides the learner to a clinical question that can be formulated rather easily, then to an available answer that can be found from a relatively simple search, and then to the evidence that can be easily critically appraised. This is an initial engagement step, and each group work seminar could build in difficulty and ambiguity of the EBP process. Beginning this way will enable the group to feel

---

box 13.6

Hierarchy of Teaching and Learning Activities

Level 1	Interactive and clinically integrated activities
Level 2(a)	Interactive but classroom-based activities
Level 2(b)	Didactic but clinically integrated activities
Level 3	Didactic classroom or stand-alone teaching

that the process is not only learnable but also useful and doable, because they have participated in it and accomplished many of the steps themselves.

When moving toward more focused seminars in EBP skills, remember to orient your group of learners as to where the skill you are teaching fits into the greater context of the EBP process. For example, if you are teaching a seminar on how to search the healthcare literature, it is important to stress that searching is simply a tool to be used to find the most relevant, valid research evidence and not the only—or even the most important—skill that needs to be learned in the EBP process. Whetting their appetites about the focus of the search and prompting them on to the next steps of critical appraisal and application of evidence to the clinical problem can help learners to realize the broader scope of the EBP process rather than focus on an isolated skill.

Another practical suggestion when establishing small, focused group seminars on EBP concepts is to provide time and means of hands-on practice. For example, when teaching a session on composing and formatting answerable, searchable questions, ask the participants to individually think of clinical questions from their own experience. Provide ample time for them to share their questions with the group then determine whether they are foreground or background questions (see Chapter 2 for more information on formulating clinical questions). If the question was foreground, the group would decide what type of question it was (e.g., treatment, diagnosis, harm, meaning) and construct it in the PICOT format. Then the group would access computers to search for relevant scientific evidence to answer their questions.

Alternatively, the leader could present a case to the group members, asking them to write down questions they generate during the presentation. Then the leader asks each member of the group to share the questions phrased in the PICOT format with their group. This sort of individual practice and skill building as a group is quite powerful as a teaching and learning method. All participants are working actively, not passively, to learn the concepts, and their peers in the group provide immediate feedback and "reality testing" for each individual.

Whether the learning is in a seminar or classroom, learning searching skills led by a medical librarian knowledgeable in EBP should include hands-on practice in searching for evidence to answer their own questions. This combines the principle of relevance to the learner with the evidence-based method of skill-building workshops and thereby fosters more active participation and learning.

For teaching critical appraisal skills, it is useful to work with three small groups, each group focusing on a specific appraisal criterion. (Chapters 4–7 have more information on critical appraisal of evidence.) For example, one small group would report back to the larger group on the results of the study. Another group would discuss the validity of the study results, and the third group would discuss applicability of the study findings to the given patient scenario. This process assists the learners to view the critical appraisal process as a coherent whole.

Incorporating small-group work in a classroom setting adds more opportunity for learners to discuss EBP content in a less threatening atmosphere. Small groups can be a successful forum to formulate PICOT questions from a provided clinical scenario, critically appraise studies, and report back to the class.

Journal Clubs

Another option for teaching EBP is the journal club. Consider that a journal club is not a gather of faculty or students to passively discuss topics. Rather, a journal club is an active group discussion in which all people involved participate (Fineout-Overholt, 2006). When establishing a journal club in an academic setting, it is important to begin by being explicit about the purpose, who should participate, the timing, and the format to optimize attendance. The participants can be those interested in learning and teaching EBP or students in a course. Although the leader of the group can rotate among the members, an educator-mentor who is knowledgeable in EBP is essential to validate the journal club's importance and to provide mentoring when the

> **box 13.7**
>
> ## Characteristics of a Successful Journal Club
>
> Regular and anticipated meetings
> Mandatory attendance
> Clarity of purpose
> Appropriate times to meet
> Incentives for meeting
> A leader to choose articles and lead the discussion
> Having articles circulated before the meeting
> Internet use for dissemination and storing data
> Applying established critical appraisal criteria
> Providing a summary of the club's findings

group needs her or his expertise to ask facilitating questions about each step of the EBP process (Campbell-Fleming, Catania, & Courtney, 2009).

The timing of a journal club should be amenable to participants' schedules. Scheduling journal clubs over the lunch hour may work well for some; others can attend those held in the early evening. Whatever the time, food and camaraderie are great incentives to increase attendance. Box 13.7 contains the essential elements of a journal club, which were supported in systematic review of how to run an effective journal club (Deenadayalan, Grimmer-Somers, Prior, et al., 2008).

An example of how a journal club has been used to promote EBP is by Cave and Clandinin (2007) who conducted a journal club to assist students to understand how to incorporate clinical expertise and patient preferences into decision making. In a new twist on the traditional journal club, students read books written by physicians about their practices. The facilitator focused the discussion around the role of clinical expertise and patients' preferences in clinical decision making.

Journal Club Teaching Formats: Grazing or Hunting. In journal clubs, determining which teaching format will work best for your participants is crucial. Consider first whether a "grazing" format or a "hunting" format would best meet learners' needs. Grazing formats have been the most common to this point and typically begin with a group of individuals, such as faculty wanting to learn more about EBP or students post-conference, dividing the relevant journals in their field among themselves. Each individual is then responsible for perusing—or grazing on—one to three journals for recent publications of interest to the group. At the small-group meeting, members of the group take their turns in presenting the information they have found to the rest of the group members.

Unless it is a required component during clinical experiences for students, the grazing process has its inherent inefficiencies. First, in this format, the number of journals reviewed tends to be a function of the number of individuals in the group. Thus, the group is likely to leave several journals unreviewed and, therefore, miss evidence. Second, the group effect is further complicated by members' abilities to make it to the meetings. Third, there are many citations in given journals that are of poor quality. Wading through several journals looking for quality research evidence can be quite tedious. Fourth, the time required by the group members to accomplish the given goal tends to be quite high. Due to these inefficiencies of grazing, many members may relegate the small-group meeting to just another thing on their already full to-do lists.

Despite the inherent inefficiencies, grazing is still an essential activity in keeping up with the latest information. Fortunately, there are now secondary publications that do the grazing, cutting down the time it takes to find quality research evidence. The editorial boards of these resources systematically survey the existing literature. Any relevant studies that meet certain methodologic criteria are abstracted in a quickly readable format. Examples of sources for predigested or preappraised evidence are the *Evidence-Based Nursing Journal, Worldviews on Evidence-Based Nursing, American College of Physicians Journal Club,* Clinical Evidence, InfoPoems, and American Academy of Pediatrics Grand Rounds. Thus, grazing is very helpful in keeping current, especially when grazing in these greener pastures.

An alternative to grazing is a hunting format. This format begins with a clinical issue and the question of interest to the individual or group. A question is posed from a concern about a clinical issue. The question is then converted into a PICOT question, one that is answerable and searchable. A literature search to find relevant research evidence is performed. Finally, any relevant studies are brought back to the group to critically appraise and discuss application to clinical decision making.

The hunting format has two distinct advantages. First, it is by definition relevant to the group because its own members posed the original question, rather than relying on whatever happened to be published since the last meeting. Second, it includes the question and search components of the EBP process, which are left out of the grazing format. The hunting format can easily be adapted for use in formal coursework. Simply assign group members the task of presenting the results of their question, search, and critical appraisal at the various meetings on a rotating basis.

It is important to make a distinct link between the applicable clinical scenario; the searchable, answerable search question; the search findings; and the subsequent critical appraisal and application of research evidence to allow the group to see the process as a coherent whole. Otherwise, because so much time is spent in learning critical appraisal, learners can quickly equate EBP with only critical appraisal instead of seeing it as a comprehensive process.

Case Exemplars for Teaching Evidence-Based Practice in Academic Settings

The University of Rochester Internal Medicine, Pediatrics, and Medicine-Pediatrics

A variety of teaching-learning methods in both clinical *practicum* and academic *courses* are part of residents' learning experiences (e.g., morning report, journal club, ambulatory conferences, skills blocks, and an EBP elective). During morning report, participants are required to present an EP once every month as they rotate to different patient units. The clinical questions are to be drawn from their practice experiences, with the search, critical appraisal, and application discussed among the group. This 1-hour teaching conference usually consists of two cases being presented and discussed, each for half of an hour. Once per week, an EP is presented and discussed instead of a case. The group in attendance (including a seasoned mentor) gives immediate feedback to the resident. This teaching method has been adopted with great success in a medical school residency program in Pakistan as well (Iqbal & Quadri, 2007).

Journal club meets once per week. During this noon conference, a hunting format is used, and the group is divided into smaller groups, each with the task of analyzing one aspect of a systematic review or study and presenting back to the large group. Skills blocks are specific 2-week rotations set aside for nonclinical, classroom learning of clinical concepts, with a large portion of these sessions being devoted to the teaching of EBP concepts. These skill block minicourses are quite successful in bringing beginners to a common place of facility with EBP. Table 13.5 exemplifies a workable skill block minicourse schedule.

For the more advanced learner, an EBP elective is offered. This is a 2-week course that consists of two 2-hour sessions daily. Attendance is limited to 8 to 10 participants for optimizing

table 13.5 **Example of workable skill block minicourse schedule**

Session	Topic
1. 3 h	Introduction of principles of EBP (large group) Session on asking answerable questions (large group) Break into small groups of 8–10 and select project topics
2. 2 h (large group)	Search tutorial by medical librarian
3. 1 h (small groups)	Critically appraise and discuss an article on therapy—preselected article
4. 1 h (small groups)	Critically appraise and discuss an overview (meta-analysis) This overview optimally contains the article on therapy from the previous session
5. 1 h (small groups)	Critically appraise and discuss an article on diagnostic testing—preselected article
6. 1 h (small groups)	Critically appraise and discuss an article on prognosis—preselected article
7. 2 h	Small groups—participants present their project (EP) Large group—wrap up and answer any overall questions

individual participation. In an introductory session where individual and group goals are set, learning needs are identified. A session on asking an answerable and searchable question; a search tutorial with a medical librarian; and sessions on the critical appraisal and application of articles of therapy, diagnosis, prognosis, overview, and harm using preselected articles follow the introductory session. The remainder of the elective is left open for the group to decide what to present and discuss. Individuals are required to take turns in leading these open sessions, teaching the group something they did not know beforehand. This program is designed to address the three ingredients of optimal adult learning:

1. A pretest that reveals a knowledge deficit
2. A learning phase to fill the knowledge deficit
3. A posttest where the learner presents what she or he has learned

To conclude the elective, group members individually present a project of their choosing, ranging from an appraisal of related single studies to formulating a complete EP.

Arizona State University College of Nursing & Health Innovation

Increasingly, programs are being offered online both in the United States and Europe (Coppus, et al., 2007; Davis, Chryssafidou, Zamora, et al., 2007; Durkin 2008; Gagnon, Legare, Labrecque, et al., 2007; Kulier et al., 2008; Rabensteiner, Hofer, Meier, et al., 2007). The online Doctor of Nursing program at Arizona State University College of Nursing & Health Innovation offers core courses in EBP that build knowledge and skills throughout the program. The leveling of EBP courses throughout the program focuses on building an understanding of the EBP paradigm and principles of critical appraisal and theory in the first few semesters while students are gaining expertise in clinical specialty. This sequencing enables them to apply this new paradigm to their practices. When course work for their capstone experience begins in earnest (i.e., the last four semesters of the program), the courses again are building blocks for their project. First students complete an exhaustive synthesis of a body of evidence to answer a clinical question. They begin to build the plan for implementing that evidence and determining outcomes in the outcomes management course in the second semester. The next building block is the EBP implementation and mentorship course, which enables them to conduct and evaluate their project and introduce or enhance the understanding about EBP in their work environment during the

box 13.8

Example of Outcomes Management Project Assignment Criteria

■ Background and significance of project are clear. (Support that there is insufficient evidence to answer the clinical question.)

■ Clinically meaningful question is clear. (Use PICOT to identify question components.)

■ Sources and process for identifying outcomes for project are clear. (The outcomes flow from the question. All possible outcomes are considered and addressed to answer the question.)

■ Sources and process for collecting data are clear. (How approval was obtained, collection tool, who is collecting data, and from whom or what.)

■ Data analysis approach assists in answering the clinical question. (Was the right statistical test for the level of data collected?)

■ Proposed presentation of data is clear. (Graphs are readable on slide/handout. All data are synthesized and presented to audience in written form, slide/handout.)

■ Implications for practice changes based on the data are clear. (What the data indicate that needs to be different in practice.)

■ Plan for change is clear. (Specific steps for change.)

■ Anticipated barriers, facilitators, and challenges to plan are clear.

■ Outcomes for evaluation of plan are clear and measurable.

■ Dissemination plan is clear and feasible. (What is going to be done with the information gathered in the project?)

■ PowerPoint presentation and supporting documents enhance presentation.

■ Overall argument is compelling and worthy of change in practice.

third semester. The program culminates with reflection on their project and its impact on their local organization and beyond. In each semester, a clinical component is planned with specific EBP milestones in which students plan, implement, evaluate, and disseminate the findings of their EBP capstone project. Thus, clinically integrating EBP is paramount to successful practice changes that improve patient outcomes. Some of the educational evaluation methods that help students assimilate EBP concepts can be found in Boxes 13.8 and 13.9.

Lessons Learned

Among lessons learned about the structure and content of an EBP integration curriculum, four are worth noting: set clear deadlines, carefully assess skill levels, assure education has meaning, and foster learning and growth.

First Lesson: Set Clear Deadlines

Deadlines for any product of learning are crucial. Clinicians, both teachers and learners, are very busy in a complex clinical setting. Because there are many distractions, it is important to be explicit about the goals and timeline of any assigned learning experience. Examples of this are a 2-day return on search results for a question generated by both teacher and learner, assigning an EP on a question to be presented the next day on rounds or in report, and breaking up a large project into smaller ones with shorter deadlines (e.g., divide an EBP paper assignment into

box 13.9

Example of Requirements for an Evidence Implementation Project

Purpose

This small-group project (two people per group) has been designed to assist students in searching for the best evidence and critiquing it so that scholarly, up-to-date care for patients can be provided.

Instructions

1. Identify a clinical question of interest from a patient you have cared for in your clinical experiences. Topics must be preapproved by the course faculty.
2. Briefly describe the background to the problem, its clinical significance, and how you searched for the best evidence to answer your question.
3. Present the best evidence to answer this clinical question.
4. Critique the evidence.
5. Discuss implications for practice and future research.
6. Include a glossary of all research terms used in your paper.
7. All studies critiqued must accompany paper submission (paper must be in hard and disk copy).

three stages due 1 month apart: question and search strategy, critical appraisal, and application of evidence). In short, it is important to keep the learning experience on the learner's radar screen within the context of the experience, workshop, seminar, or coursework.

Second Lesson: Carefully Assess Skill Levels

The second lesson learned is that learners begin an educational program with widely varied skills in informatics and EBP. Determining learners' skills prior to starting the teaching program is essential. Because becoming an evidence-based provider is a complex task, much like becoming a licensed practitioner, the program should be broken down into reasonable parts that learners can accomplish. It is important to meet learners where they are and to foster growth in knowledge and skills from that point. Any bar to reflect learner growth should be flexible enough to be angled upward or downward for a specific learner. This avoids the frustration that sets in when learners are overwhelmed with the material or process. Setting realistic expectations for each experience and providing formative feedback along the way in addition to summative information at the end of the experience will encourage learners' growth.

Third Lesson: Assure Education Has Meaning

The third lesson learned is to make the content, settings, formats, and methods meaningful to learners. This shows learners first hand that EBP is applicable and useful to them in their particular practice setting. Use relevant examples and scenarios. This is best accomplished by beginning the process with a question generated by the learner. It is incredibly powerful to learn the EBP process by working through a clinical issue that the learner actually cares about and that the learner can imagine herself or himself using in the future.

Fourth Lesson: Foster Learning and Growth

The fourth lesson learned is to foster learning and growth in those you teach, with the goal that they, in turn, will share their EBP knowledge with their colleagues. Focusing on getting a particular grade or checking off a required assignment will not produce life-long learners who will improve outcomes. Learners who do not readily understand PICOT questions, patient preferences, effect size, or intention-to-treat will improve their knowledge and comfort with the subject matter if they experience mentored learning.

Evaluating Success in Teaching Evidence-Based Practice

Evaluation of outcomes based on evidence is a critical step in the EBP process and in teaching EBP. Effective outcome evaluation of EBP teaching programs is as imperative as their existence. Evaluation involves an assessment of (a) learners, (b) educators/preceptors, (c) curricula, and (d) the program (Bourke & Ihrke, 2009). Most instruments used to evaluate educational programs measure EBP skills, knowledge, behaviors, and attitudes of the learners (Hart, Eato, Buckner, et al., 2008; Ireland, Martindale, Johnson, et al., 2009; Shaneyfelt, Baum, Bell, et al., 2006; Sherriff, Wallis, & Chaboyer, 2007; Varnell, Haas, Duke, et al., 2008). Shaneyfelt et al. conducted a systematic review evaluating EBP in education and found that a number of instruments were used to evaluate some dimension of EBP, and could be used to evaluate individuals as well as educational programs. Recently, job satisfaction, self-efficacy, and professional performance were measured in occupational physicians who participated in an EBP course using case method learning sessions (Hugenholtz, Schaafsma, Nieuwenhuijsen, et al., 2008). These studies did not measure the outcome of the impact EBP has on patient outcomes.

Learner Evaluation

Evaluating learners' integration of EBP concepts into their thinking, problem solving, and practice is not an easy task. However, several mechanisms are discussed that can assist in determining how well learners have integrated EBP concepts into their practices.

---

box 13.10

Description of an Evidence-Based Practice Synthesis Paper

The purpose of these assignments is to familiarize students with the independent identification and synthesis of existing evidence to answer a clinical question. Each student will select a clinically meaningful question and conduct an in-depth search for the best scientific evidence regarding that question. There will be components of this assignment due throughout the semester. Students will be provided feedback on those sections. The final paper should clearly describe the methods used to identify and retrieve the evidence and the rationale for exploring the clinical issue chosen. A discussion of these theories used to guide the research included in the review is expected. Clearly articulated recommendations for practice based on research evidence are essential to a successful paper. A summary table of included studies should be placed at the end of the paper, before references.

From Arizona State University, Core Course in EBP, 2009.

Classroom Learning

Depending upon the educational delivery program (e.g., formal classroom, online, seminars), there are many options for evaluating the specific levels of the cognitive domain related to EBP concepts. Formal testing or specific EBP assignments can assist the learners to identify areas in the process that need remedial work. However, synthesis is a higher cognitive level, and synthesis papers seem to be a common option that educators use to determine the learner's ability to comprehend, synthesize, and apply EBP concepts and principles in formal educational settings (see Box 13.10).

Student perception is another valuable evaluation strategy. Box 13.11 contains an exemplar of how these evaluations can provide important feedback on the value of a course to those taking it.

Clinical Experiences

Traditionally, clinical experiences in nursing programs used care plans, care maps, and logs to evaluate clinical knowledge and application. Application of EBP knowledge in the clinical setting can be evaluated with these tools or others, such as a case study or EBP application paper. Another evaluative method, depending upon the level of student, is to have the learner find and critically appraise the scientific evidence to support a chosen intervention, then describe how this evidence influenced decision making, taking into consideration the clinical team's expertise and the patient's preferences and values.

In addition, learners can prepare EPs as a self-assessment of learning the EBP process and journal these prescriptions, reflecting on what they need to learn, how they plan to learn the information, and on what they have learned. With any assignment, educators must carefully develop the instructions with evaluative criteria. Gaining experience in how to turn a clinical issue into a searchable, answerable question; finding relevant, valid evidence to answer the question; and coming to the point of application of evidence with confidence is not easily achieved. Evaluation of this process is equally challenging, but essential to the sustainability of clinicians' daily use of EBP in their practices.

> *What is experienced and seen in the clinical area is what will likely predict future behavior.*
>
> **Bob Berenson**

Educator and Preceptor Evaluation

Preparing educators and preceptors for teaching EBP to learners is imperative. It is known that learners emulate what they see modeled in their preceptors and educators. Berenson (2002) made that point very clear when he articulated, in a discussion about healthcare professionals' education, that even if the benefits of EBP are clearly presented in a didactic venue, what is experienced and seen in the clinical area is what will likely predict future behavior.

Whether the educational program is nursing, physical therapy, or medicine, or the level of education is baccalaureate, graduate, or postgraduate, educators/preceptors should make clear the course objectives and expectations of the learning about EBP. Knowledge of EBP should be evident in the educators'/preceptors' clinical discussions with learners and should be central to the teaching-learning process. An example of a great opportunity for demonstrating operation of the EBP process is preceptors asking advance practice nurses questions about why a particular

box 13.11

*On Change...*An Exemplar for Using Student Evaluation to Demonstrate Effective Teaching

Context: Beginning paradigm shift within the college; however, traditional focus of research course was introduction of the conduct of nursing research, including concepts, issues, processes, and methods without explicit attention to EBP.

Course: The course structure (e.g., course syllabus) remained unchanged; however, the faculty taught it with a "spirit" of inquiry. The course was launched with a simple question: "What are you curious about?" The language of research and EBP was modeled. Course content and assignments were modified. Nursing research core content was taught in the context of EBP concepts, principles, and practices. The course evaluation was simply a question: "What changes have you made?"

Invitation: A substantial body of education and nursing literature supports the importance of reflective practice; that is, taking time to "take stock" and integrate experiences from practice, peer interactions, and educational endeavors. I tapped into this powerful learning tool to assess the students' perception of their journey to a better understanding of self and their professional nursing role related to nursing research and EBP. I began the undergraduate research course (i.e., NUR362) with a reflection on change, citing the following 1872 Nightingale quote, to create an early anticipatory set for an end of course Discussion Board forum designed to capture student self-evaluation of change during their course journey and provide qualitative impact/outcome evaluation data. As the course reached its conclusion, students were invited to engage in thoughtful self-reflection and post a response to the following question: What personal and/or professional change(s)/progress have you made over the duration of NUR362?

> **"For us who Nurse, our Nursing is a thing, which, unless in it
> we are making progress every year, every month, every week,
> take my word for it, we are going back."**
>
> **~ Nightingale (1872) ~**

Captured Reflections: A PowerPoint presentation was created using selected quotes by each student, capturing the nature and power of the students' learning and change journey. This became a "surprise" presentation for the students during the last class session, and served to reinforce the student's shared perceptions, experiences, and pride related to their achievements and learning across all learning domains.

Impact/Outcomes: The student quotes speak for themselves in providing insight into the impact and outcomes of their course experience. Change in knowledge, skills, and attitudes were reflected in responses that captured:

- "I have been able to understand how important research will be in my future career."
- "I have a stronger knowledge of how research will play a part in the daily things I will be doing."
- "The idea of...actually being able to look for the answers to my questions instead of just wondering...really piqued my interest."

(box continues on page 323)

box 13.11 *(continued)*

- ■ "I feel more confident in tackling the sometimes overwhelming research journals or articles."
- ■ "When I first began this class, I was thinking to myself how boring this class was going to be....I have come to realize that research is essential for the nursing profession to further itself and to provide the best care we can."

Submitted by Karen Saewert, PhD, RN, CPHQ, CNE
Clinical Associate Professor & Director, E³: Evaluation & Educational Excellence
Arizona State University College of Nursing & Health Innovation

Ulrich, B. T. (1992). Change. In Leadership and management according to Florence Nightingale (pp. 10–13). Norwalk, CT: Appleton & Lang

treatment option was chosen or a care trajectory was decided. For instance, during the clinical experience of a student at a large southeast university, the healthcare team was discussing the appropriateness of the common practice of prescribing cytotoxicity assays for the diagnosis of *Clostridium difficile*, which take days to obtain results compared to the rapid PCR test that can be done in real time and in-house. One of the preceptors indicated that current evidence supports the use of the more efficient PCR rapid test (McFarland, 2009) and that overall, the sensitivity and specificity were superior to the traditional cytotoxitcity assay. Further discussion focused on the cost savings, timing of initiation of treatment, and patient comfort by implementing current evidence. Another clinician in the group discussed how difficult it was for clinicians to accept the new rapid test. A discussion ensued, reflecting on the use of science, expertise, and patient concerns and choices together to make the best clinical decision. The role of uncertainty in clinical practice and the benefits of clinical inquiry also were discussed. Subsequently, the student was asked to design a project that would apply EBP principles to this clinical situation and evaluate the plan, including measurement of practice outcomes. This kind of preceptor interaction to foster application of EBP principles in the clinical area is invaluable to the learner. These principles used by preceptors to teach EBP are also the ones by which they would be evaluated. Evaluation forms can be constructed that delineate these principles that students and preceptors complete to indicate the extent to which they perceive the principles were present in the learning experience.

An additional measure to evaluate educator/preceptor teaching is peer review. Course syllabi, teaching materials, lesson plans, or case studies, as well as peer observation of the educator/preceptor in the clinical or classroom setting can be one source of evaluation data to assess teaching effectiveness. Student evaluations of teaching can also assist the educator/ preceptor to reflect on aspects of teaching that are helpful or can be improved to foster student learning. Establishing a peer review rubric assists with consistency of evaluation. There are many online sources of such rubrics. For example, Google results for *peer review rubric* elicited more than 10 readily available peer review rubrics, ranging from paper rubrics to team work rubrics.

Curricula Evaluation

The design of the curriculum drives the direction for content and activities that are implemented in the program (Sauter & Applegate, 2005). Evidence-based practice in the curriculum should be sequenced logically considering the depth and breadth of the content. One way to determine this is to develop a grid or matrix that identifies EBP program outcomes and course objectives reflecting Bloom's taxonomy (http://projects.coe.uga.edu/epltt/index.php?title = Bloom%27s_ Taxonomy). The EBP content, the learning activities that relate to the objectives, and the evaluative methods that measure the learner outcomes can be entered into the matrix to determine internal consistency and vertical organization. The curricular design should mirror the institution's mission and philosophy statements, which should actively reflect EBP. Specific courses can be reviewed to determine the internal consistency of course objectives, content, learning activities, and evaluative methods, and their placement in the curriculum and how they reflect EBP knowledge, skills, and attitudes. In informal workshop or seminar formats, it is equally important to evaluate the objectives, content, learning activities, and outcomes to foster successful learning about EBP.

Program Evaluation

To evaluate the program, careful consideration of what to evaluate, when to evaluate, and who to evaluate is imperative. Evaluating learners' ongoing absorption of EBP concepts throughout an educational program is integral to knowing the success of the program. However, other outcomes of the overall program that need to be examined include program goal(s) and environmental outcomes. Some of these outcomes may be evaluated on a continual basis (e.g., graduates application of EBP in daily practice) and some may be a one-time assessment (e.g., number of attendees from different locations to measure scope of attendance).

Continual monitoring of the environment and outcomes (goals) is necessary for either teaching or implementing EBP. Periodically, the educator/preceptor champions of EBP need to determine where they are in reaching the goals of the EBP program. This first requires a commitment to setting measurable program goals that can be monitored on an ongoing basis. Evaluation of the program's foundation (environment) can be obtained by examining the questions raised in the first part of this chapter. If there are insufficient answers (e.g., educators' knowledge of up-to-date EBP concepts is lacking), the program has not been completely successful in that area. Steps then would be taken to address the areas that lack support (e.g., send the educators to an EBP conference or hold an EBP conference on the program site). The learners can provide feedback on the courses and learning experiences at the conclusion of the courses. This input can be analyzed and used to make decisions about the courses.

Program goals should address whether learners can formulate a searchable, answerable clinical question; efficiently find relevant evidence; discern what is best scientific evidence; and apply the best scientific evidence with clinical expertise and patient input to clinical decision making. Part of the Summit on Health Professions Education (Greiner & Knebel, 2003) competency regarding practicing using evidence stated that across and within disciplines, efforts must be focused on the development of a scientific evidence base. The final goal for a teaching program must be for learners to actively evaluate outcomes based on evidence.

In addition, the Summit recommended that funding sources such as the Agency for Healthcare Research and Quality (AHRQ) support ongoing clinical and education research that evaluates care based on the five specified competencies. An example of this type of research could be a study to evaluate educational outcomes for an EBP teaching program across two or more disciplines (e.g., nursing and medicine).

Final Assessment

There is usually some type of cumulative assessment for learners completing a degree program, such as comprehensive exams. However, not every discipline uses this form of outcome evaluation. National licensure and certifying exams may provide outcome evaluation for some disciplines and some levels of education. Whatever form of final assessment a teaching program in EBP employs (e.g., EBP implementation project), it must address the EBP paradigm, particularly application and evaluation. These are the most challenging steps of the EBP process to evaluate. Without evaluating the EBP process in a final evaluation, educators cannot know whether learners are prepared to apply principles they have learned in their daily practices.

Program Effectiveness

The overall EBP program is effective if the learners are successful in integrating EBP concepts into their thinking and practice. Integration of EBP concepts into daily practice can be discerned by periodic follow-up with graduates to ask them about the integration of EBP in their practices. Although self-report has its drawbacks, querying what EBP initiatives learners have been involved in during the past 12 months can assist the educator in obtaining more objective information on how they have applied EBP knowledge to practice.

At Arizona State University College of Nursing & Health Innovation, concepts and principles of EBP were integrated throughout the upper division nursing major in the undergraduate nursing program. Evaluation of the impact of EBP integration on undergraduate students' EBP beliefs and implementation of concepts and principles was planned and executed when the integration began. Foundational concepts for EBP were introduced in the first semester, with specific learning activities placed in specific courses in that semester. An introduction to the evaluation of research and its use in practice were the focus of the second semester. The specific course that focused on the underpinnings of EBP was developed and it replaced the traditional research course. At the senior level, no further didactic information was presented; however, building skills in critical appraisal and application of evidence to practice was the emphasis in the community setting, and effecting change and improving outcomes through the integration and amalgamation of evidence, clinician expertise, and patient preference were the culmination capstone project in final semester of their senior year.

Tools such as Evidence-based Practice Beliefs and Evidence-based Practice Implementation Scales (Melnyk & Fineout-Overholt, 2003a; Melnyk & Fineout-Overholt, 2003b) are being used to determine the impact of the EBP-integrated curriculum. These tools can be used to compare total scores as well as individual belief and implementation statements, which can provide information about the curriculum in terms of strengths and areas to focus EBP learning. After the implementation of the revised traditional research course to an evidence-based approach to research, EBP faculty were interested to know if this change was effective. This was part of ongoing quality improvement of the EBP integration. Students' beliefs about EBP and use of EBP principles were measured. Students who took the EBP approach to research course as compared with the students who took the traditional research course scored similarly on EBP beliefs, but significantly higher on EBP implementation. The frequency of applying principles of EBP was greater in the students who were enrolled in the EBP approach to research course. This suggested that this change in curriculum was successful. However, data collection and analysis are ongoing with plans to assess the graduates' beliefs and implementation of EBP 1 year after graduation in order to evaluate the graduates' use of principles and concepts of EBP in their practice.

Evaluating the impact of EBP programs on learners and healthcare providers' performance may involve various approaches, such as tests, papers, EPs, and self report, to evaluate various outcomes (e.g., knowledge, attitude, and behaviors). In more formal academic settings, the use of a portfolio may be a means to capture the integration of the EBP paradigm (Green, 2006).

Words can never adequately convey the incredible impact of attitude toward life. The longer I live the more convinced I become that life is 10% what happens to us and 90% how we respond to it.

I believe the single most significant decision I can make on a day-to-day basis is my choice of attitude. It is more than my past, my education, my bankroll, my successes or failures, fame or pain, what other people think of me or say about me, my circumstances, or my position. Attitude keeps me going or cripples my progress. It alone fuels my fire or assaults my hope. When my attitudes are right, there's no barrier too high, no valley too deep, no dream too extreme, no challenge too great for me.

Charles S. Swindoll

references

American Association of Colleges of Nursing. (2002). *AACN White Paper: Distance technology in nursing education: Assessing a new frontier.* Retrieved May 20, 2009, from http://www.aacn.nche.edu/Publications/positions/whitepaper.htm

American Association of Colleges of Nursing. (2006). *The essentials of doctoral education for advanced nursing practice.* Retrieved May 29, 2009, http://www.aacn.nche.edu/DNP/pdf/Essentials.pdf

American Nurses Credentialing Center. (2004). *ANCC Magnet Recognition Program.* Retrieved May 29, 2009, from http://www.nursecredentialing.org/magnet/

Amsallem, E., Kasparian, C., Cucherat, M., Chabaud, S., Haugh, M., Boissel, J. P., et al. (2007). Evaluation of two evidence-based knowledge transfer interventions for physicians: A cluster randomized controlled factorial design trial: The CardioDAS Study. *Fundamental & Clinical Pharmacology, 21*(6), 631–641.

Association of American Medical Colleges. (2007). *Advancing educators and education: Defining the components and evidence of educational scholarship.* Retrieved May 29, 2009, from http://www.aamc.org/members/facultydev/facultyvitae/winter08/feature.htm

August-Brady, M. M. (2005). Teaching undergraduate research from a process perspective. *Journal of Nursing Education, 44*(11), 519–521.

Bauldoff, G. S., Kirkpatrick, B., Sheets, D. J., Mays, B., & Curran, C. R. (2008). Implementation of handheld devices. *Nurse Educator, 33*(6), 244–248.

Berenson, B. (2002). Crossing the quality chasm: Next steps for health professions education. Major stakeholders comment on key strategies and action plans. Retrieved May 17, 2003, from http://www.kaisernetwork.org/health_cast/uploaded_files/Transcript_6.18.02_IOM_Major-Stakeholders.pdf

Bourke, M. P., & Ihrke, B. A.(2009). The evaluation process: An overview. In D. M. Billings & J. A. Halstead (Eds.), *Teaching in nursing: A guide for faculty* (pp. 391–408). St. Louis, MO: Elsevier.

Burns, H. K., & Foley, S. M. (2005) Building a foundation for an evidence-based approach to practice: Teaching basic concepts to undergraduate freshman students. *Journal of Professional Nursing, 21*(6), 351–357.

Campbell-Fleming, J., Catania, K., & Courtney, L. (2009). Promoting evidence-based practice through a traveling journal club. *Clinical Nurse Specialist, 23*(1), 16–20.

Cave, M. T., & Clandinin, D. J. (2007). Revisiting the journal club. *Medical Teacher, 29*(4), 365–370.

Centers for Medicare & Medicaid Services. (2009). *Medicaid and CHIP promising practices.* Retrieved May 28, 2009, from http://www.cms.hhs.gov/MedicaidCHIPQualPrac/MCPPDL/ItemDetail.asp?ItemID=CMS1185908

Chaudhry, B., Wang, J., Wu, S., et al. (2006). Systematic review: Impact of health information technology on quality, efficiency, and costs of medical care. *Annals of Internal Medicine, 144*, 742–752.

Ciliska, D. (2005). Educating for evidence-based practice. *Journal of Professional Nursing, 21*(6), 345–350.

Connors, H. R., Warren, J. J., & McNamara, T. J. (2003). *Academic business partnerships: KU School of*

Nursing/Cerner Partnership. Retrieved May 12, 2009, from http://www2.kumc.edu/son/abp.html

Connors, H. R., Weaver, C., Warren, J., & Miller, K. L. (2002). An academic-business partnership for advancing clinical informatics. *Nursing Education Perspectives, 23*(5), 228–233.

Coomarasamy, A., & Khan, K. (2004).What is the evidence that postgraduate teaching in evidence-based medicine changes anything? A systematic review. *British Medical Journal, 329*, 1017–1022.

Coppus, S. F. et al. (2007). A clinically integrated curriculum in evidence-based medicine for just-in-time learning through on-the-job training: The EU-EBM project. *BMC Medical Education, 7*, 46.

Copyright Clearance Center. (2002). *The TEACH Act: New roles, rules and responsibilities for academic institutions*. Retrieved May 19, 2009, from http://www.copyright.com/media/pdfs/CR-Teach-Act.pdf

Davis, J., Chryssafidou, E., Zamora, J., Davies, D., Khan, K., & Coomarasamy, A. (2007). Computer-based teaching is as good as face to face lecture-based teaching of evidence based medicine: A randomised controlled trial. *BMC Medical Education, 7*, 23.

Deenadayalan, Y., Grimmer-Somers, K., Prior, M., & Kumar, S. (2008). How to run an effective journal club: A systematic review. *Journal of Evaluating Clinical Practice, 14*(5), 898–911.

Duck, J. D. (2002). *The change monster: The human forces that fuel or foil corporate transformation and change*. New York: Crown Business.

Durkin, G. J. (2008). A comparison of the effectiveness of computer-based learning courses among nursing staff. *Journal for Nurses in Staff Development, 24*(2), 62–66.

Ebell, M. H. (2009). How to find answers to clinical questions. *American Family Physician, 79*(4), 293–296.

Edwards, R., White, M., Gray, J., & Fischbacher, C. (2001). Use of a journal club and letter writing exercise to teach critical appraisal to medical undergraduates. *Medical Education, 35*, 691–694.

Ely, J. W., Osheroff, J. A., Chambliss, M. L., Ebell, M. H., & Rosenbaum, M. E. (2005). Answering physicians' clinical questions: Obstacles and potential solutions. *Journal of the American Medical Informatics Association, 12*(2), 217–224.

Fetter, M. S. (2009). Curriculum strategies to improve baccalaureate nursing information technology outcomes. *Journal of Nursing Education, 48*(2), 78–85.

Fineout-Overholt, E. (2006). Using journal clubs to introduce EBP. In R. F. Levin & H. R. Feldman (Eds.), *Teaching evidence-based practice in nursing* (pp. 325–335). New York: Springer.

Fineout-Overholt, E., & Johnston, L. (2005). Teaching EBP: A challenge for educators in the 21st century. *Worldviews on Evidence-Based Nursing, 2*(1), 37–39.

Fineout-Overholt, E., & Johnston, L. (2007). Evaluation: An essential step to the EBP process. *Worldviews on Evidence-Based Nursing, 4*(1), 54–59.

Fineout-Overholt E., Levin R. F., & Melnyk B. M. (2004). Strategies for advancing evidence-based practice in clinical settings. *Journal of the New York State Nurses Association, 35*(2), 28–32.

Fineout-Overholt E., & Melnyk, B. (2005). Building a culture of best practice. *Nurse Leader, 3*(6), 26–30.

Fineout-Overholt, E., & Melnyk, B. M. (2006). *Organizational culture & readiness for system-wide integration of evidence-based practice*. Gilbert, AZ: ARCC Publishing.

Flores-Mateo, G., & Argimon, J. M. (2007). Evidence based practice in postgraduate healthcare education: A systematic review. *BMC Health Services Research, 7*, 119.

Gagnon, M. P., Legare, F., Labrecque, M., Fremont, P., Cauchon, M., & Desmartis, M. (2007). Perceived barriers to completing an e-learning program on evidence-based medicine. *Informatics in Primary Care, 15*(2), 83–91.

Gassert, A. (2006). Impact of technology and simulated learning on nursing shortages. *Nursing Outlook, 54*(3), 166–167.

Green, M. L. (2006). Evaluating evidence-based practice performance. *ACP Journal Club, 145*(2) Suppl A-8, A-9, A-10.

Green, M. L., & Ruff, T. R. (2005). Why do residents fail to answer their clinical questions? A qualitative study of barriers to practicing evidence-based medicine. *Academic Medicine, 80*(2), 176–182.

Greenfield, S. (2007). Medication error reduction and the use of PDA technology. *Journal of Nursing Education, 46*(3), 127–131.

Greiner, A., & Knebel, E. (Eds.) (2003). *Health professions education: A bridge to quality*. Washington, DC: National Academy Press.

Hallikainen, J., Väisänen, O., Randell, T., Tarkkila, P., Rosenberg, P., & Niemi-Murola, L. (2009). Teaching anaesthesia induction to medical students: Comparison between full scale simulation and supervised teaching in the operating theatre. *European Journal of Anaesthesiology, 26*(2), 101–104.

Hart, P., Eato, L., Buckner, M., Morrow, B., Barrett, D., Fraser, D., et al. (2008). Effectiveness of a computer-based educational program on nurses' knowledge, attitude, and skill level related to evidence-based practice. *Worldviews on Evidence-Based Nursing, 5*(2), 75–84.

Healthcare Information and Management Systems Society (2002). Using innovative technology to enhance patient care delivery. *Paper presented at the American Academy of Nursing Technology and Workforce Conference*, Chicago, IL. Retrieved May 12, 2009, from http://www.himss.org/content/files/AANNsgSummit-HIMSSFINAL_18770.pdf

Huffstutler, S., Wyatt, T. H., & Wright, C. P. (2002). The use of handheld technology in nursing education. *Nurse Educator, 27*(6), 271–275.

Hugenholtz, N., Schaafsma, F. G., Nieuwenhuijsen, K., & van Dijk, F. J. (2008). Effect of an EBM course in combination with case method learning sessions: An RCT on professional performance, job satisfaction, and self-efficacy of occupational physicians. *International Archives of Occupational and Environmental Health, 82*, 107–115.

Institute of Medicine. (1999). *To err is human: Building a safe health system*. Washington, DC: National Academy Press.

Institute of Medicine. (2001). *Crossing the quality chasm: A new health system for the 21st century*. Washington, DC: National Academy Press.

Institute of Medicine. (2002). *Educating health professionals to use informatics*. Washington, DC: National Academy Press.

Iqbal, M., & Quadri, K. H. M. (2007). Initial experience with learner-centered evidence-based format morning report. *Journal of Pakistan Medical Association, 57*, 120–122.

Ireland, J., Martindale, S., Johnson, N., Adams, D., Eboh, W., & Mowatt, E. (2009). Blended learning in education: Effects on knowledge and attitude. *British Journal of Nursing, 18*(2), 124–130.

Jeffries, P. R. (2005). A framework for designing, implementing, and evaluating simulations used as teaching strategies in nursing. *Nursing Education Perspectives, 26*(2), 96–103.

Johnston, L., & Fineout-Overholt, E. (2005). Teaching EBP: "Getting from zero to one." Moving from recognizing and admitting uncertainties to asking searchable, answerable questions. *Worldviews on Evidence-Based Nursing, 2*(2), 98–102.

The Joint Commission. (2009). *Revised 2009 accreditation requirements as of March 26, 2009: Hospital accreditation program.* Retrieved May 29, 2009, from http://www.jointcommission.org/NR/rdonlyres/C9298DD0–6726–4105-A007-FE2C65F77075/0/CMS_New_Revised_HAP_FINAL_withScoring.pdf

Kardong-Edgren, S. E., Oermann, M. H., Ha, Y., Tennant, M. N., Snelson, C., Hallmark, E., et al. (2009). Using a wiki in nursing education and research. *International Journal of Nursing Education Scholarship, 6*(1), 1–10.

Kennedy, C. C., Jaeschke, R., Keitz, S., Newman, T., Montori, V., et al. (2008). Adjusting for prognostic imbalances (confounding variables) in studies on therapy or harm. *Journal of General Internal Medicine, 23*(3), 337–343.

Kent, B., & Fineout-Overholt, E. (2007). Teaching EBP: Clinical practice guidelines: Part 1. *Worldviews on Evidence-Based Nursing, 4*(2), 106–111.

Khan, K. S., & Coomarasamy, A. (2006). A hierarchy of effective teaching and learning to acquire competence in evidence-based medicine. *BMC Medical Education, 6*(59). Retrieved April 24, 2009, from http://www.biomedcentral.com/1472–6920/6/59

Kitson-Reynolds, E. (2009). Developing decision making for students using interactive practice. *British Journal of Midwifery, 17*(4), 238, 240–243.

Kulier R., et al. (2008). Harmonising evidence-based medicine teaching: A study of the outcomes of e-learning in five European countries. *BMC Medical Education, 8*, 27.

Kuiper, R. (2008). Use of personal digital assistant to support clinical reasoning in undergraduate baccalaureate nursing students. *Computers, Informatics, Nursing, 26*(2), 90–98.

Mascola, A. J. (2008). Guided mentorship in evidenced-based medicine for psychiatry: A pilot cohort study supporting a promising method of real-time. *Academic Psychiatry, 32*, 475–483.

McDowell, D. E., & Ma, X. (2007). Computer literacy in baccalaureate nursing students during the last 8 years. *Computer Informatics Nursing, 25*(1), 30–38.

McFarland, L. (2009). Renewed interest in a difficult disease: Clostridium difficile infections – epidemiology and current treatment strategies. *Current Opinion in Gastroenterology, 25*, 24–35.

McGinn, T., Jervis, R., Wisnivesky, J., Keitz, S., Wyer, P. C., et al. (2008). Tips for teachers of evidence-based medicine: Clinical prediction rules (CPRs) and estimating pretest probability. *Journal of General Internal Medicine, 23*(8), 1261–1268.

McQuaid-Dvorak, E., Prophy, E. B., Binder, D. M., & Carlson, E. (1993). A survey of BSN curricula: Research content. *Journal of Nursing Education, 32*, 265–269.

Meeker, M. A., Jones, J. M., & Flanagan, N. (2008). Teaching undergraduate nursing research from an evidence-based practice perspective. *Journal of Nursing Education, 47*(8), 376–379.

Melnyk, B. M. (2007). The evidence-based practice mentor: A promising strategy for implementing and sustaining EBP in healthcare systems. *Worldviews on Evidence-Based Nursing, 4*(3), 23–25.

Melnyk, B., & Fineout-Overholt, E. (2003a). *Evidence-based practice beliefs scale.* Rochester, NY: ARCC Publishing.

Melnyk, B. & Fineout-Overholt, E. (2003b). *Evidence-based practice implementation scale.* Rochester, NY: ARCC Publishing.

Melnyk, B. M., Fineout-Overholt, E., Feinstein, N., Li, H. S., Small, L., Wilcox, L., et al. (2004). Nurses' perceived knowledge, beliefs, skills, and needs regarding evidence-based practice: Implications for accelerating the paradigm shift. *Worldviews on Evidence-Based Nursing, 1*(3), 185–193.

Melnyk, B. M., Fineout-Overholt, E., Feinstein, N. F., Sadler, L. S., & Green-Hernandez, C. (2008). Nurse practitioner educators' perceived knowledge, beliefs, and teaching strategies regarding evidence-based practice: Implications for accelerating the integration of evidence-based practice into graduate programs. *Journal of Professional Nursing, 24*(1), 7–13.

Morgan, R. (2006). Using clinical skills laboratories to promote theory: Practice integration during first practice placement: An Irish perspective. *Journal of Clinical Nursing, 15*(2), 155–161.

Morton, P. G. (1997). Using a critical care simulation laboratory to teach students. *Critical Care Nurse, 17*(6), 66–69.

Murray, T. L., Belgrave, L., & Robinson, V. I. (2006). Nursing faculty members competence of web-based course development systems directly influences students' satisfaction. *The ABNF Journal*, (Summer), 100–102.

National League of Nursing (2003). *Position statement: Innovation in nursing education: A call to reform.* New York: Nurse Education Perspectives, NLN.

O'Mathuna, D. P., Fineout-Overholt, E., & Kent, B. (2008). How systematic reviews can foster evidence-based clinical decisions: Part II. *Worldviews on Evidence-Based Nursing, 5*(2), 102–107.

Peck, S., Lester, J., Hinshaw, G., Stiles, A., & Dingman, S. (2009). EBP partners: Doctoral students and practicing clinicians bridging the theory-practice gap. *Critical Care Nursing Quarterly, 32*(2), 99–105.

Porter-O'Grady, T., & Malloch, K. (2008). Beyond myth and magic: The future of evidence-based leadership. *Nursing Administration Quarterly, 32*(3), 176–187.

Prasad, P., Jaeschke, R., Wyer, P., Keitz, S. Guyatt, G., et al. (2008). Tips for teachers of evidence-based medicine: Understanding odds ratios and their relationship to risk ratios. *Journal of General Internal Medicine, 23*(5), 635–640.

Pravikoff, D. S., Pierce, S. T., & Tanner, A. (2005). Evidence-based practice readiness study supported by academy nursing informatics expert panel. *Nursing Outlook, 53*(1), 49–50.

Rabensteiner, V., Hofer, B., Meier, H., & De Fiore, L. (2007). Web, workshops, e-learning for Quality improvement: An evidence-based medicine educational programme. *Recenti Progressi in Medicina, 98*(3), 169–174.

Rauen, C. A. (2004). Simulation as a teaching strategy for nursing education and orientation in cardiac surgery. *Critical Care Nurse, 24*(3), 46–51.

Richardson, W. S., Wilson, M. C., Keitz, S. A., Weyer, P. C., & EBM Teaching Scripts Working Group. (2008). Tips for teachers of evidence-based medicine: Making sense of diagnostic test results using likelihood ratios. *Journal of General Internal Medicine, 23*(1), 87–92.

Rush, K. L. (2008).Connecting practice to evidence using laptop computers in the classroom. *Computers Informatics in Nursing,* (July/August), 190–196.

Sackett, D. L., Haynes, R. B., Guyatt, G. H., & Tugwell, P. (1991). *Keeping up to date – The educational prescription in clinical epidemiology* (2nd ed.). Boston, MA: Little Brown & Co.

Sauter, M. K., & Applegate, M. H. (2005). Education program evaluation. In D. M. Billings & J. A. Halstead (Eds.), *Teaching in nursing: A guide for faculty* (pp. 543–599). St. Louis, MO: Elsevier Saunders.

Schutt, M. S., & Hightower, B. (2009). Enhancing RN-to-BSN students' information literacy skills through the use of instructional technology. *Journal of Nursing Education, 48*(2), 101–105.

Shaneyfelt, T., Baum, K. D., Bell, D., Feldstein, D., Houston, T., Kaatz, S., et al. (2006). Instruments for evaluating education in evidence-based practice: A systematic review. *American Medical Association, 296*(9), 1116–1127.

Sherriff, K. L., Wallis, M., & Chaboyer, W. (2007). Nurses' attitudes to and perceptions of knowledge and skills regarding evidence-based practice. *International Journal of Nursing Practice, 13*, 363–369.

Shuval, K., Berkovits, E., Netzer, D., Hekselman, I., Linn, S., et al. (2007). Evaluating the impact of an evidence-based medicine educational intervention on primary care doctors' attitudes, knowledge and clinical behaviour: A controlled trial and before and after study. *Journal of Evaluation in Clinical Practice, 13*(4), 581–598.

Skiba, D. J., Connors, H. R., & Jeffries, P. R. (2008). Information technologies and the transformation of nursing education. *Nursing Outlook, 56*(5), 225–230.

Smith-Strom, H., & Nortvedt, M. W. (2008). Evaluation of evidence-based methods used to teach nursing students to critically appraise evidence. *Journal of Nursing Education, 47*(8), 372–375.

Snow, K. (2009). *Hospitals embrace social networking tool for teaching.* Retrieved May 10, 2009, from http://abcnews.go.com/print?id = 7347728

Spunt, D., Foster, D., & Adams, K. (2004). Mock code: A clinical simulation module. *Nurse Educator, 29*(5), 192–194.

Starkweather, A. R., Kardong-Edgren, S. (2008). Diffusion of innovation: Embedding simulation into nursing curricula. *International Journal of Nursing Education Scholarship, 5*(1), Article 13.

Stevens, K. R. (2002). *ACE star model of EBP: The cycle of knowledge transformation.* Academic Center for Evidence-based Practice, http://www.acestar.uthscsa.edu

Stevens, K. R. (2009a). *Essential competencies for evidence-based practice in nursing* (2nd ed.). University of Texas Health Science Center at San Antonio.

Stevens, K. R., & Lowe, V. (2009b). Measuring EBP readiness. *Proceedings of the 2009 Summer Institute on EBP.* July 11, 2009. San Antonio, Texas.

Technology Informatics Guiding Education Reform (2007). *The TIGER initiative: Evidence and informatics transforming nursing: 3-year action steps toward a 10-year vision.* Retrieved May 12, 2009, from http://www.tigersummit.com/uploads/TIGER-Initiative_Report2007_Color.pdf

Technology Informatics Guiding Education Reform. (2009). *The TIGER initiative: Collaborating to integrate evidence and informatics into nursing practice and education: An executive summary.* Retrieved May 12, 2009, from http://www.tigersummit.com/uploads/TIGER_Collaborative_Exec_Summary_040509.pdf

Varnell, G., Haas, B., Duke, G., & Hudson, K. (2008). Effect of an educational intervention on attitudes toward and implementation of evidence-based practice. *Worldviews on Evidence-Based Nursing, 5*(4), 172–181.

Weberg, D. (2009). Twitter and simulation: Tweet your way to better sim. *Clinical Simulation in Nursing, 5*(2), e63–e65.

West, C. P., & McDonald, F. S. (2008). Evaluation of a longitudinal medical school evidence-based medicine curriculum: A pilot study. *Journal of General Internal Medicine, 23*(7), 1057–1059.

Wheeler, K., Fasano, N., & Burr, L. (1995). Strategies for teaching research: A survey of baccalaureate programs. *Journal of Professional Nursing, 11*, 233–238.

White, A., Allen, P., Goodwin, L., Breckinridge, D., Dowell, J., & Garvey, R. (2005). Infusing PDA technology into nursing education. *Nurse Educator, 30*(4), 150–154.

Williams, B. C. & Hoffman, R. M. (2008). Teaching tips: A new series in JGIM. *Journal of General Internal Medicine, 23*(1), 112–113.

Yew, K. S., & Reid, A. (2008). Teaching evidence-based medicine skills: An exploratory study of residency graduates' practice habits. *Family Medicine, 40*(1), 24–31.

chapter 13

329

Teaching Evidence-Based Practice in Clinical Settings

Karen Balakas and Ellen Fineout-Overholt

There have been many changes in healthcare in the last decade. Many first-time initiatives are now commonplace in acute and primary care settings (e.g., core measures, pay for performance). Other initiatives are still gaining momentum (e.g., clinical decision support systems, electronic health records). While these changes have helped to advance the use of outcomes to demonstrate what is happening in practice, often their adoption has been mandated *to* clinicians versus being generated *by* clinicians. In addition, there has been little consideration of the basic paradigm from which clinicians practice. The focus has been primarily on what clinicians are doing. For example, there are quality improvement bundles, lean strategies, and professional practice programs that have been put into place to enhance the processes of care. While these programs may be great methods for addressing clinical issues, leaders and point-of-care providers must consider that what we do in healthcare comes from what we value. Our organizational priorities indicate what we value. Consider what initiatives are targeted for elimination when the organization experiences financial limitations—often educational and, so called, enrichment positions.

What we value often is informed by what we are taught. Educators are essential for a thriving organizational culture. It is so important for all healthcare providers and leadership to consider why evidence-based practice (EBP) must be part of the culture of any organization. This paradigm must be a core value held by leadership and point-of-care providers, not just an edict from the top down. Educators in healthcare are the conduits for EBP to flow to the point of care (Penz & Bassendowski, 2006). Furthermore, many educators are EBP mentors who foster a culture of EBP within an organization (Fineout-Overholt & Melnyk, 2005).

One method that healthcare educators can employ to shift the thinking of point-of-care clinicians is to document how others have changed outcomes through the implementation of EBP. There are many examples in the literature of how clinicians have used the EBP process to improve patient outcomes. For example, Gutierrez and Smith (2008) indicated that their fall rates significantly decreased when an evidence-based protocol was put into place. In another example, Powers, Brower, and Tolliver (2007) found that an evidence-based protocol for oral care, including an accompanying care kit with all the supplies needed to provide this care, greatly reduced their incidence of ventilator-associated pneumonia. However, EBP change can be seen as temporary, unless all clinicians are aware of the process and the purpose of the initiative.

In the situation with Powers and colleagues, the kit was seen as a trial and therefore, when it was over, care changed back to care as it was before, resulting in a blip in the outcome of ventilator-associated pneumonia. Real-life examples, such as these, are very helpful to educators who are working with clinicians who experience daily the competing priorities of getting the work done and of providing evidence-based care.

Not only is EBP the right thing to do, as it improves healthcare outcomes (Balakas, Potter, Pratt, et al., 2009; Hockenberry, Brown, Walden, et al., 2008; Selig & Lewanowicz, 2008; Singleton & Levin, 2008), but regulatory and accrediting agencies have indicated that, from a safety standpoint as well as a reimbursement standpoint, organizations that are practicing based on evidence will reap rewards. Patient safety is an imperative. Organizations must know the best initiatives that reliably produce the safest environments. Educators must be able to translate for clinicians the evidence that demonstrates these expected safety outcomes. Every clinician must be aware that lives are lost every year due to preventable errors by clinicians and systems (Institute of Medicine, 2001). The National Patient Safety Goals (The Joint Commission, 2009) clearly indicate that evidence-based initiatives are to be put into place to achieve best outcomes for patients. Furthermore, the Center for Medicare & Medicaid Services (CMS) has mandated that preventable, nosocomial infections (e.g., urinary tract infections), and other complications (e.g., pressure ulcers) will no longer be reimbursed (Rosenthal, 2007). Such a mandate can foster disengagement by the point-of-care provider; however, healthcare educators have an opportunity to bring the evidence to the clinician that supports why these clinical issues are so important to address. This partnership enables innovative decision making between the patient and the provider that will bring about outcomes that will be best for the patient and, as a matter of course, comply with the mandate.

Evidence-based care makes sense from a safety perspective and from a best care perspective. Best care cannot be distilled down into safe-only care. There are issues such as cost effectiveness, quality, and satisfaction that are important to consider. Standards of excellence in care are set by such organizations and The Joint Commission (formerly known as JCAHO) and the American Nurses Credentialing Center (ANCC) Magnet program. These standards hinge on EBP underpinning healthcare, from care delivered at the bedside to decisions made in the executive boardroom. Healthcare educators have the privilege of making these standards meaningful to point-of-care clinicians as well as leadership. While this may sound simple, there are challenges to bringing EBP alive in clinical settings.

Challenges in the Clinical Setting

Evidence-based practice has become recognized as the gold standard of care, prompting many healthcare organizations to invest resources into the creation of a culture that sustains the use of evidence for direct care decision making. As nurses at the point of care are essential to the implementation of EBP, it is important to ascertain factors that may hinder its adoption. Identification of barriers to achievement of EBP has been studied extensively (Brown, Wickline, Ecoff, et al., 2009; Cadmus, Van Wynen, Chamberlain, et al., 2008; Hockenberry, Walaen, Brown, et al., 2008; Holleman, Eliens, van Vliet, et al., 2006; Pipe, Cisar, Caruso, et al., 2008; Porter-O'Grady, Alexander, Blaylock, et al., 2006; Porter-O'Grady & Malloch, 2008; Vratny & Shriver, 2007). Among the most cited barriers is the skill level of the individual nurse. Yet today's nurses are increasingly being challenged by patients and healthcare organizations to provide high-quality, measurable patient care outcomes (Holleman et al.). Since nurses most often practice nursing guided by what they learned in nursing school and through their clinical experiences, data reflecting the age and educational preparation of the registered nurse (RN) population may offer insights.

According to the 2004 National Sample Survey of Registered Nurses (NSSRN; Health Resources and Services Administration [HRSA]), the average age of a nurse was 46.8 years, reflecting a 7.9% increase from 2000, and the percent of nurses older than 54 years of age had increased to 25.2% from 20.3% in 2000. In 2008, the Michigan Center for Nursing (MCN) conducted its fifth annual survey of nurses and found the average age was 50 years with one third of the sample approaching retirement (MCN, 2008). Workforce analyst Dr. Peter Buerhaus (2008) and colleagues (2008) stated that with fewer new nurses entering the profession, the average age of the RN is climbing, and that by 2012, nurses in their 50s are expected to become the largest segment of the nursing workforce, accounting for almost one quarter of the RN population.

Educational preparation is another factor that needs to be considered when planning strategies to teach EBP. Nurses who graduated from school even 5 years ago may have not had any formal education about EBP, whether or not their program contained a research course. The 2004 NSSRN reported that while the majority of nurses obtained their primary nursing education in an associate degree program, nearly 21% eventually received a higher degree. From 2000 to 2004, the percentage of nurses whose highest initial nursing preparation was a baccalaureate degree increased from 32.7% to 34.2%, while the number of diploma prepared nurses continued to steadily decline (HRSA, 2004). Although these figures reflect a changing trend in initial nursing preparation, there is evidence to support that today's nursing population is likely to have little formal education about EBP and/or research (Albert & Siedlecki, 2008).

According to Van Patter Gale and Schaffer (2009), nurses have difficulty interpreting and applying study findings, and knowledge resulting from scientific research is seldom used in practice. Pravikoff, Tanner, and Pierce (2005) reported that the majority of nurses did not appreciate the contribution of research for practice. Their study found that the relationship between research findings and patient care outcomes had not been stressed to most practicing nurses in either educational or practice settings. They also reported that although EBP has been widely discussed in the literature over the past decade, only 46% of the nurses surveyed were familiar with the term. The limited ability of the clinical nurse to engage in any research activity is concerning, since nurses are expected to apply research and determine which findings produce better outcomes. Nurses stated that although they were aware of the existence of research to guide practice, it was often implemented through a top-down hierarchy that eliminates the staff nurse from the process. The end result is decreased commitment by staff nurses to adopt EBP or implement research findings (Reavy & Tavernier, 2008).

Nurses report that they frequently need information to support their nursing role but rarely consult with librarians or use nursing research. Nurses often lack the skills needed to locate research information and indicate that they feel much more confident asking colleagues or searching the Internet (e.g., Google Scholar) than using bibliographic databases (e.g., PubMed, CINAHL; Vratny & Shriver, 2007). Studies indicated that the majority of nurses have never searched either CINAHL or MEDLINE, even though they describe competence in using search engines to locate information (Van Patter Gale & Schaffer, 2009). This may be a reflection of the length of time since graduation from nursing school when, for many, computers, the Internet, and electronic databases did not yet exist.

Cadmus et al. (2008) found that age and educational level of nurses were significantly correlated with the frequency of seeking information and the sources used to obtain information. As the age of the nurse increased, the probability of using databases decreased. However, as the educational preparation of the nurses increased, the likelihood of using databases increased. The presence of a hospital library did not seem to increase the use of research for practice. Cadmus and colleagues also reported that 50% of the nurses had never used the library, and some did not know its location or hours of operation. The unlikely use of the hospital library was documented in other studies (e.g., Brown et al., 2009; Kajermo, Unden, Gardulf, et al., 2008; Sherriff, Wallis, & Chagoyer, 2007) and may be a reflection of the fast-paced hospital environment.

Results from the 2004 NSSRN indicated that although there have been substantial changes in the healthcare delivery system, hospitals remain the primary setting in which nurses are employed. Stressors related to shortages in the RN workforce and the demands associated with long shifts and increased patient loads have been well documented (American Health Care Association, 2008; Kane, Shamliyan, Mueller, et al., 2007). It is not surprising that a lack of time is frequently cited as one of the major barriers to the implementation of EBP (Brown et al., 2009; Van Patter Gale & Schaffer, 2009; Wells, Free, & Adams, 2007). Nurses reported that they had little time either during scheduled working hours or during their personal time to engage in activities required for EBP. For many nurses, beyond the time needed to search for evidence, there was no time to read or appraise research. Organizational skills may be a factor since nurses in practice for less than 3 years were more likely to identify time constraints as a barrier compared with more experienced nurses (Van Patter Gale & Schaffer).

Prior to the current initiative to incorporate EBP into the workplace, staff nurses and other healthcare providers have had no incentive to question current practice. Implementation of research findings into practice had been the expectation of nurses with advance degrees (Van Patter Gale & Schaffer, 2009). Adherence to institutional policies and procedures and following physician orders also were expected behaviors. Nurses incorporated safety into their practice in terms of checking medication doses and interactions, but did not seek information to support or change patient care interventions. Now they are being asked to formulate clinical questions and translate research findings for effective patient care in a changing clinical environment.

Nurses also report that managers do not always take into account the limitations of the practice setting for application of EBP (Brown et al., 2009; Kajermo, Unden, Gardulf, et al., 2008). Perhaps there is a discrepancy between a stated goal for implementation of EBP and competing organizational priorities. Hospitals are focusing on achieving and maintaining a balance that considers patient and staff safety, productivity, improved clinical outcomes, hospital financial viability, enhanced patient satisfaction, and increased staff satisfaction. Support from immediate managers and unit educators is needed to facilitate change toward evidence-based care (Brown et al., 2009; Cadmus et al., 2008; Van Patter Gale & Schaffer, 2009).

For bedside clinicians to engage in EBP, they must have the tools necessary; therefore, teaching EBP has become an imperative for healthcare organizations. Since bedside clinicians directly influence patient care outcomes, it is essential to understand their ability to implement EBP in the real practice environment. This understanding drives the design of educational initiatives to meet point-of-care providers' learning needs. The introduction of EBP education must be carefully planned and executed so that clinicians truly can incorporate EBP into their everyday practice.

According to Melnyk, Fineout-Overholt, Stillwell, et al. (2010), the crux of teaching nurses and other healthcare providers about EBP is buy-in. Perhaps buy-in is not strong enough, perhaps ownership is truly the key to successful integration of EBP into an organizational culture. When teaching point-of-care providers or healthcare administrators about EBP, the first place to start must be with what motivates daily care decisions. Often this is the traditional practice paradigm, that is, the comfort of "we've always done it that way." While most of those reading this chapter would agree that this is not the best paradigm to work from, we also would likely admit that it is reassuring to be able to predict how things are going to be done. However, the difficulty with this paradigm is that tradition does not guarantee predictable outcomes. Rather, the outcomes vary with the clinician and the interpretation of the norm.

Practicing based on the EBP paradigm (see Figure 1.2) enables variation of care processes with some standardization regarding the inclusion of the external evidence (i.e., research), patient preferences, and clinical expertise, including internal evidence. This paradigm focuses on patient outcomes. For all clinicians and administrators, the patient outcome is the unifying factor. When initiating care practices, the outcome is the driver of decisions. Consider teaching all those involved in healthcare about why they engage in care practices such as inserting an intravenous line, administering a medication, or performing a diagnostic test. Often clinicians may indicate that processes are the goal of care initiatives; however, processes lead to outcomes. The outcomes are bottom-line drivers for fiscal, resource allocation, and other decisions that establish priorities in healthcare. Some may see EBP as a burden, a challenge, or a disturbance of the status quo; however, without this kind of disruption, transformation of healthcare will not occur (Zuzelo, McGoldrick, Seminara, et al., 2006). Educators, particularly as EBP mentors, are the key to this paradigm shift at the bedside.

Organizational Readiness for Teaching Evidence-Based Practice

Teaching EBP in clinical settings is not an option, it is a necessity (Porter-O'Grady & Malloch, 2008). To make this happen, the organization must make a commitment to provide the resources and leadership necessary to transform the culture to one that demonstrates EBP daily. Transformational leadership is a requirement for an evidence-based organization. Through this leadership, the vision and value for EBP are communicated to clinicians, and an appeal for their active involvement is clearly conveyed. Leaders must be innovative and challenge assumptions. They need to partner with point-of-care providers to achieve outcomes. Transformational leaders demonstrate their commitment by setting forth the vision and providing resources necessary to establish an EBP culture (Fineout-Overholt & Melnyk, 2005).

One method for achieving mutual goals is through shared governance. Establishing a councilor structure in an EBP organization includes an EBP or Research/EBP Council to address clinical issues with evidence. This becomes part of an EBP culture. Clinicians begin to rely on this council for tackling the clinical issues that are important to bedside staff and providing guidance for applying the evidence to their organization. A Practice Council can be a partner that takes the evidence compiled and synthesized by the EBP Council and operationalizes plans for putting standards of care and other policies into place across the organization to address the given clinical issue based on evidence. Commitment to shared governance is key to providing a voice for point-of-care providers so that they are able to actively participate in evidence-based initiatives and improve outcomes (Zuzelo et al., 2006). Having an EBP Council provides an opportunity to have an impact on the spread of evidence-based decision making. When all councils begin to use evidence-based thinking, the EBP process becomes the norm for making decisions in the organization. An Education Council can make sure that programs offered are evidence based and that EBP is an essential component of orientation and continuing education for all clinical staff. A Leadership Council can ensure that essential resources are provided for clinicians to practice based on evidence and educators to facilitate a culture of EBP.

Essential Resources for Teaching Evidence-Based Practice

The first step in establishing an educational program for EBP in the clinical setting is to assess the resources that are available or could be dedicated to EBP (Schulman, 2008). Leadership in the development of educational strategies is contingent upon the human resources within the healthcare organization. A clinically focused nurse researcher who is dedicated to the vision of EBP can provide guidance and support as a program is developed. Teaching the EBP process and its associated skills requires the ability to pose searchable, answerable questions; assist in

box 14.1

A Sampling of Available Continuing Education Programs to Learn about Evidence-Based Practice

- **McMaster University** offers a 5-day course that is designed to help participants advance their critical appraisal skills, improve their skills in acknowledging and incorporating patient values and preferences in clinical decision making, and learn how to teach EBP using a variety of educational models. (http://ebm.mcmaster.ca/)
- **The University of Texas Health Science Center's Academic Center for Evidence-Based Nursing (ACE)** offers a 3-day institute on EBP that is geared toward preparing participants for an increasingly active role in EBP. Knowledge and skills gained through this interdisciplinary conference are directly pertinent to integrating EBP preparation into nursing education programs. (http://www.acestar.uthscsa.edu/)
- **The Johanna Briggs Institute** offers a 6-month workplace, evidence-based, implementation program involving two, 5-day intensive training residencies. (http://www.joannabriggs.edu.au/services/clin_fellow.php)
- **The Center for the Advancement of Evidence-Based Practice at Arizona State University's College of Nursing & Health Innovation** offers a clinical 5-day EBP immersions program that prepares staff nurses, advanced practice nurses, nurse researchers, and other healthcare providers to serve as leaders and EBP mentors in changing organizational cultures through the promotion, implementation, and sustainability of EBP from administration to the bedside. For academic educators, a 4-day EBP Mentorship Program is designed to prepare faculty to integrate EBP across their nursing curricula. In addition to these initiatives, EBP conferences, workshops, and online programs are offered throughout the year (http://nursingandhealth.asu.edu/ebp).

searching for relevant evidence; critically appraise and synthesize evidence; apply evidence in the clinical setting; and guide providers in evaluating outcomes based on evidence (Fineout-Overholt, 2006a; Fineout-Overholt & Johnston, 2005). If an individual with in-depth knowledge of EBP and research is not available within the organization, establishing a partnership with an academic institution can help to facilitate the development of a program.

The next step is to assess the knowledge level about EBP among educators within the organization to determine whether additional education may be needed. Building a team of EBP educators and mentors is a crucial component of any educational strategy and EBP culture (Fineout-Overholt & Melnyk, 2005). Interdisciplinary teams are an essential factor for building an evidence-based framework in the clinical setting (Porter-O'Grady et al., 2006). Once the gaps are identified regarding knowledge and skills needed to teach EBP, there are numerous workshops, courses, and online programs that are available throughout the country to assist team members in gaining basic and advanced EBP knowledge and skills. Some of the more established programs are listed in Box 14.1, and online tutorials that can be easily accessed are listed in Box 14.2.

Determining the basic informatics and computer literacy of educators is necessary in developing the groundwork for teaching EBP in clinical settings. Without educators who are knowledgeable in informatics, including adequate computer skills and the ability to use databases to find relevant evidence, teaching EBP will be challenging. Chapter 3 provides in-depth information for developing effective search strategies for finding relevant evidence in multiple databases to answer clinical questions.

---

box 14.2

A Sampling of Available Tutorials on Evidence-Based Practice

- *Evidence-Based Clinical Practice Tutorial* by Kathryn Nesbit, Miner Library, University of Rochester Medical Center (http://www.urmc.rochester.edu/hslt/miner/resources/evidence_based/index.cfm)
- *Evidence-Based Medicine: Finding the Best Clinical Literature* from University of Illinois at Chicago (http://www.uic.edu/depts/lib/lhsp/resources/ebm.shtml)
- *Centre for Evidence-Based Medicine* from the Mt. Sinai Hospital and University Health Network (Toronto, Ontario, Canada)—this website has supporting materials for the 3rd edition of *Evidence-Based Medicine: How to Practice and Teach EBM* by David L. Sackett et al. (http://www.cebm.utoronto.ca/teach/)
- *Users' Guides to Evidence-Based Practice* from the Canadian Centre for Health Evidence. These are similar to the series of *JAMA Users' Guides to the Medical Literature*. (http://www.cche.net/text/usersguides/therapy.asp)
- The following online slide presentations also may be helpful to assist educators increase their EBP knowledge:
  - http://www.libraries.psu.edu/instruction/ebpt-07/index.htm
  - http://www.nyam.org/fellows/ebhc/eb_teach.html

Another important issue in the preliminary evaluation of resources is to assure that you have a clinical (i.e., on the unit) or medical librarian on the teaching team who is knowledgeable about EBP. It is imperative that medical librarians be involved in the plan to initiate EBP. It is important to plan early involvement of librarians in preparing an EBP teaching program. As active partners, they can provide perspective and expertise in search strategy development as well as access to databases and other sources of evidence. In addition, medical librarians are expert in informatics and information literacy and can facilitate teaching the skills needed by nurses, physicians, and other healthcare providers who strive to be successful at EBP. Evidence-based librarians foster a culture of EBP within an organization.

An essential resource that facilitates the work of EBP mentors and educators to teach about and sustain EBP implementation is access to databases and evidence to support changes in practice (Fineout-Overholt, Hofstetter, Shell, et al., 2005; Schulman, 2008). Both PubMed and the Cochrane Library offer free access to search and read abstracts, but nurses need full-text articles to appraise and apply the evidence. Subscriptions to databases such as CINAHL or online resources such as Nurse or MD Consult and electronic journal services are usually available at academic libraries. Many hospitals have medical libraries and can include vital resources in their holdings that are necessary for clinicians to provide evidence-based care to their population of patients. If a hospital does not have a library, there are online resources that clinicians can join for a fee. DynaMed is an online reference developed for point-of-care clinicians that contains summaries for more than 3,000 topics. This resource is updated daily and monitors the content of more than 500 medical journals and systematic review databases. The literature is critically appraised, integrated into existing content, and synthesized to deliver the best available evidence.

Another online peer-reviewed resource providing evidence-based reviews is UpToDate, which contains more than 7,700 topics in 14 medical specialties and provides the user with synthesized evidence upon which to make treatment decisions. Point-of-care clinicians also can subscribe to the Nursing Reference Center to obtain relevant clinical information. All of these resources can help clinicians model and teach the critical value of EBP to provide improved patient outcomes. Chapter 3 contains more information on sources of evidence.

Information on DynaMed and a free trial can be found at
http://www.ebscohost.com/dynamed/
Information on UpToDate can be found at
http://www.uptodate.com/home/index.html
Information on the Nursing Reference Center can be found at
http://ebscohost.com/uploads/thisTopic-dbTopic-1045.pdf

A final crucial element required to teach EBP is financial support. Clinicians need protected time to participate in classes, develop clinical questions, locate evidence, read and appraise the evidence, plan for application of the evidence and implementation of practice changes, and determine evaluation strategies to assess outcomes. This means that administrators and unit-level managers must include time for EBP in their budgets. A budget that provides for dedicated time to engage in evidence-based project work demonstrates to staff nurses that the education for and implementation of EBP is valued by leadership (Schulman, 2008; Vratny & Shriver, 2007).

Educational Strategies for Teaching Evidence-Based Practice

Teaching EBP requires a tiered educational approach. It is not enough to just offer classes to bedside clinicians without first engaging direct-line managers in the process. Managers, unit educators, and advanced practice nurses serve as models of change for point-of-care staff. They can foster the implementation of EBP, if they too understand its value, their role in the process, and can see the link between the use of research and improved patient outcomes (Brown et al., 2009; Newhouse, Dearholt, Poe, et al., 2007; Pipe et al., 2008; Van Patter Gale & Schaffer, 2009). One way to accomplish this undertaking is to schedule one or several meetings to introduce the EBP model upon which the program is based, discuss the steps of EBP, and present their unique role in developing and sustaining EBP on the unit. For example, prior to launching an educational program for staff nurses, one pediatric hospital's Research/EBP committee hosted a luncheon meeting for nurse managers and administrators. This preliminary step proved to be a crucial one, since each nurse manager was needed to identify a staff nurse whose leadership skills might grow from being involved in an EBP project (Steurer, 2008). Another institution conducted monthly education classes for managers during regularly occurring Nursing Governance meetings and offered one contact hour for continuing education (Vratny & Shriver, 2007). It is vital to the success of an EBP project that it is fully supported by managers with clearly identified benefits for each unit's population. Similar presentations for supervisors, case managers, and clinical educators also are needed to sustain adoption of EBP.

Once a team of educators and EBP mentors has been developed, additional intensive efforts can begin to educate bedside caregivers. Numerous EBP educational programs for clinical staff have been documented in the literature (Balakas et al., 2009; Brewer, Brewer, & Schultz, 2009; Hockenberry, Brown, Walden, et al., 2009; Newhouse et al., 2007; Schulman, 2008; Selig & Lewandowicz, 2008; Soukup & McCleish, 2008; Steurer, 2008; Weeks, Marshall, & Burns, 2009). The length and depth of each program vary, but the basic content is consistent and includes a comprehensive overview of EBP, a presentation for each step in the process, a discussion of change theory, and often an opportunity to complete a project. Some of the programs are offered in a workshop format that may range from 2 to 7 days and are presented at one point in time or over several months (Balakas et al.; Brewer et al.). Other programs include a formal application process and are delivered in a combination of didactic classes, discussion groups, and mentored projects (Hockenberry et al.; Pipe, Timm, Harris, et al, 2009; Steurer). Classes within these programs provide the clinician with intensive guidance on the development of a PICOT question, building searching skills to locate and retrieve evidence, learning critical appraisal skills, and application of evidence for practice change. Requiring the identification of a clinical question or area of interest prior to participation in a program is very helpful, as it makes it easier for the clinicians to quickly focus on the steps of EBP. Using clinicians' PICOT questions and providing computers for interactive sessions while teaching searching skills is very effective. If a computer lab is not available, securing laptop computers and encouraging participants to work as partners can help to facilitate learning. Given that most hospitals have clinical guidelines readily available, some programs incorporate critical review and updating of the guidelines as a component of the EBP course. This exercise provides the learner with a relevant example to illustrate the application of EBP. These programs serve to not only educate clinical staff but also build a cadre of EBP mentors to lead and promote EBP initiatives within the organization. An outline of potential class topics and exercises is listed in Box 14.3.

> **box 14.3**
>
> ## Topical Outline for an Evidence-Based Practice Program
>
> 1. Introducing the principles of EBP
> 2. Incorporating the vision for EBP
> 3. Understanding the institutional EBP model
> 4. Developing focused clinical questions
>   - Defining the clinical problem
>   - Developing PICOT questions
> 5. Considering patient values and preferences for EBP
>   - Incorporating patient choices and concerns when making clinical decisions
> 6. Searching for relevant evidence
>   - Using search engines and EBP databases
>   - Finding clinical guidelines
>   - Exploring EBP websites
> 7. Defining internal and external evidence
> 8. Determining performance improvement indicators
> 9. Critically analyzing the evidence
>   - Research designs
>   - Using rapid appraisal forms
>   - Understanding the statistics
> 10. Synthesizing evidence
>   - Using an evaluation table
>   - Using a synthesis table
> 11. Translating evidence into practice
>   - Implications for practice change
>   - Defining and evaluating outcomes
> 12. Creating organizational change
> 13. Disseminating the evidence

Since not all clinicians are able to commit to a mentoring role, classes that introduce the concepts of EBP and highlight its potential for improving patient care outcomes can support continued adoption of EBP. At one institution, 3-hour sessions are routinely scheduled at convenient times for staff to learn how to (a) formulate PICOT questions that directly relate to current practice issues, (b) obtain help in finding relevant evidence, and (c) work with unit mentors to use EBP to improve clinical outcomes (Balakas et al., 2009). A seminar format was used by another hospital to guide clinical staff through the EBP process. Direct care providers, clinical nurse specialists, the medical librarian, and a nurse researcher partnered to apply EBP to a specific clinical question and then used seminars to explain and model the process (Pipe et al., 2008). Following participation in the EBP Mentorship Program at Arizona State University, two nurses at a community hospital partnered with the medical librarian and began offering 2-hour classes for bedside staff teaching how to create a PICOT question and then how to use it for searching the literature (S. Sauer, F. Mooney, and B. Mueth, personal communication, September 17, 2008). Teaching smaller classes can adapt content for relevance to the participant's clinical background and prepare a significant number of caregivers who embrace inquiry and value EBP for best practice.

Self-directed learning has been a part of healthcare education for several decades, and the benefits have been documented in the literature for more than 20 years. Self-directed learning incorporates adult learning principles and encourages participants to take an active role in the learning process (Zadvinskis, 2008; Campbell-Fleming, Catania, & Courtney, 2009). This approach may be helpful for motivated clinicians who are not able to attend face-to-face classes or conferences and wish to learn the principles of EBP. Through self-directed learning, participants have the opportunity to set their own priorities and determine their own timeframe for learning. The Department of Nursing at the University of Iowa Hospitals and Clinics offers an online continuing education course to introduce EBP and present a summary of the current state of the science of EBP. A more comprehensive program is offered through the Center for Advancement of EBP at Arizona State University's graduate certificate program for nurses and other healthcare professionals to become experts and change agents for EBP.

Self-directed learning initiatives can be created within the work environment to provide staff with the same opportunities for learning EBP as afforded by more traditional methods. One hospital developed online independent self-study modules to teach the principles of EBP in preparation for a Magnet site visit. The course was available to more than 2,000 clinical staff and required only 2 months to complete. Educators reported that independent study proved to be efficient, practical, and cost-effective while providing content relevant to the institution and reaching a large number of clinical staff (Zadvinskis, 2008). Clinical nurse specialists and a nurse researcher at another hospital created a portable journal club to provide relevant research articles and teach appraisal skills to nurses in an ambulatory care setting. Articles were posted on a tri-fold display board along with an appraisal of the research so that clinical staff could determine the usefulness of the information for clinical practice and see the actual application of EBP. These educators were careful to choose articles that were directly relevant to practice and were responsive to requests from clinical staff to leave the traveling poster in the area for several weeks to provide adequate time for reading and reflection. An unanticipated benefit of this teaching strategy was the promotion of a connection with inpatient nurses who were discussing the evidence through a traditional journal club format (Campbell-Fleming et al., 2009). The Nursing Research Council at another hospital used the strategy of traveling posters on clinical units to display the results of evidence reviews and to teach the skills for EBP. Posters were displayed on a portable cart, introduced during change of shift report, and accompanied by a self-administered short test staff could complete for continuing education credits. Over a period of several years, the posters have been successful in providing an introduction to EBP principles and generating approximately 10 requests annually for evidence reviews (Worral, 2006).

chapter 14

339

The committee structure of the organization provides another venue for teaching EBP. Hospitals traditionally support a committee dedicated to the development and review of policies and procedures that impart guidance for the care frontline staff provide to patients and families. Policies and procedures provide the direction to implement procedures, deliver patient education, and evaluate interventions. Establishing a process that supports the integration of evidence into policies, procedures, and guidelines ensures safety and rigor while embracing EBP (Balakas et al., 2009; Long, Burkett, & McGee, 2009; O'Brien-Pallas & Hayes, 2008; Oman, Duran, & Fink, 2008). To accomplish this goal, participants need to learn the skills for EBP. Evidence can be located, appraised, and then used to further develop or update documents as well as to create an evidence-based process or algorithm to guide the committee's work. Working with a nurse researcher skilled in teaching EBP, a community hospital restructured its policy and procedure committee into a Practice Council and then worked to create a process for evidence-based review of all policies and procedures. As part of their EBP initiative, the newly formed Practice Council adopted a rating system for the evidence, selected tools for critical appraisal, and created a synthesis table so that they could more easily share the basis for recommendations with staff (S. Mayberry, personal communication, November 4, 2008).

In the emergency department of another hospital, procedures and references are verified using an EBP approach to ensure best practice. An exemplar of this process involved the revision of the triage policy to include an alcohol screening by the clinical staff. Committee members found that recent guidelines supported the use of a brief alcohol consumption screen and coupling it with a short intervention. The screen and a list of resources for at-risk patients were added to the triage procedure. Following implementation, the staff found an unanticipated benefit for at-risk patients. Several individuals who screened positively for increased alcohol consumption and were later admitted as inpatients asked for additional assistance and resources. The screening intervention may have stimulated the conversation about at-risk alcohol consumption and encouraged these patients to consider assistance (Balakas et al., 2009).

Journal clubs have been used effectively for decades in the clinical setting to assist providers who want to improve the application of research into practice. Traditionally, journal clubs that have been either *topic-based* or *teaching-based* provided a forum for healthcare providers to discuss clinical issues, the current research available on the topic, and the recommended basis for clinical decisions related to treatment options. They have also been used as a teaching/learning strategy to help clinicians learn about EBP and how evidence can be used for clinical decision making. *EBP–skills-focused* journal clubs teach participants the steps needed for EBP from development of a PICOT question through application of evidence and evaluation of clinical outcomes (Fineout-Overholt, 2006b; Quinlan, 2006).

Active participation in a journal club is frequently dependent upon some knowledge of the research appraisal process. Providing classes about the critical appraisal of research, including evaluating the validity of research methods, can support bedside clinicians to become involved in unit-based journal clubs. However, participation in such classes may seem daunting for some clinical staff. Also, the additional time commitment for another meeting may compete with other hospital committees and the daily demands of patient care needs. Incorporating a modified journal club format into existing unit committee meetings is an effective teaching strategy to teach appraisal skills and engender interest in the use of research to guide practice. The EBP mentor/teacher can locate an article relevant to the unit's patient population and either post it on the unit's bulletin board or distribute it electronically prior to the meeting. The beginning of the meeting can then be used to role model appraisal of the article and brainstorm with the group potential applications for practice. This strategy has been used successfully in one hospital during unit practice committee meetings to implement bedside reporting, a new tube-feeding protocol, fall-prevention rounds, family presence during resuscitation, the effective use of capnography, and the use of noninvasive technology to assess tissue oxygenation and stroke volume. Committee members have learned the steps of EBP and can clearly articulate why they chose specific practices. As the clinical staff has become educated about EBP, they are able to communicate more effectively with other disciplines and engage more frequently in scholarly discussions (Balakas et al., 2009).

Specific disease process–focused clinical practice teams were created within one academic medical center and led by unit EBP mentors so that an EBP approach was taught and operationalized. Staff were encouraged to become members of the various committees based on their interest in the clinical topic. Some examples included an acute stroke tissue plasminogen activator reperfusion team, an acute myocardial treatment team, a pneumonia treatment team, and a sepsis treatment team. Evidence-based practice was modeled by the mentors, and staff were taught skills needed to apply the process. Through the implementation of an EBP framework, patient care delivery has been standardized and improved outcomes have been sustained over time (Balakas et al., 2009).

Modeling EBP through a committee structure was employed by another hospital as it transitioned its traditional Nursing-Quality Council into a Best Practice Council based on the institutions' EBP model. Work teams for areas of performance improvement in bloodstream infection prevention, fall prevention, pressure ulcer prevention, and hand-off communication were identified and challenged to use the steps of EBP to make recommendations for changes to policies and practices. Team leadership and teaching were provided by clinicians committed to improving patient outcomes through EBP. Clinical staff learned how to develop focused questions, search for relevant evidence, critically appraise the literature, and determine applicability and feasibility of practice changes (Anderson, Mokraceck, & Lindy, 2009).

Teaching EBP in the clinical setting also can be enhanced through partnerships with academic institutions. A nurse researcher in one community hospital collaborated with faculty from two area universities to provide a clinical site for graduate nursing students to engage in EBP. This association provided an educational opportunity for both students and clinical staff. The graduate students participated in an EBP workshop being offered for unit practice committee chairs and other clinicians. Students were then assigned policies and procedures from several clinical areas and worked with the unit staff to review and update the documents. With support from the hospital's nurse researcher and its academic faculty, students were able to locate relevant studies and lead discussions to critically appraise the evidence. Students and staff then worked together to incorporate recommendations into the policies and procedures so that they were truly evidence-based. Bedside caregivers were able to apply what they had just learned about EBP with guidance from a student in a nonthreatening environment. Students were able to experience an aspect of the advanced practice nurse role and apply what they were learning about EBP in the "real world" (A. Fish & N. Westhus, personal communication, December 5, 2008).

As clinicians become skilled in the steps of EBP and complete projects, they will need guidance in learning how to share their work through oral and poster presentations. Some staff will be required to deliver a presentation following the completion of an educational program, while others will want to communicate the results of their endeavors internally and externally (Hockenberry et al., 2009; Soukup & McCleish, 2008). In addition to individual guidance, classes in how to develop presentations can be very helpful. Promotion of attendance and presentations at local, state, and national conferences by the EBP leadership team supports previous teaching efforts and strengthens the clinician's knowledge base. Nurses from one community hospital worked for several months to address a problem with surgical site infection on their clinical unit. Using an EBP approach, they revised practices for dressing changes on the unit and created a Wound Cart to help them implement their new protocol. When a call for abstracts was received by members of the Research/EBP Committee, the staff nurses were encouraged to submit their project. Evidence-based practice mentors helped them write and submit the abstract and then develop the poster. Hospital administration financially supported the nurses' attendance at the regional EBP conference where they expanded their knowledge of EBP and returned with increased enthusiasm and commitment to EBP (J. Quinn, personal communication, March 10, 2009).

Teaching EBP in a clinical setting requires commitment, diligence, enthusiasm, creativity, and teamwork. It is not accomplished through one program, one committee, or one project. It requires an ability to set goals and then evaluate progress toward the attainment of those goals. Teaching EBP is a continuous process that will result in improved patient care outcomes, professional growth, and an empowered clinical staff. Teaching EBP can be a personally and professionally rewarding experience.

references

Albert, N., & Siedlecki, S. (2008). Developing and implementing a nursing research team in a clinical setting. *Journal of Nursing Administration, 38*(2), 90–96.

American Health Care Association. (2008). *Staffing.* Retrieved May 8, 2009, from http://www.ahcancal.org/research_data/staffing/Pages/default.aspx

Anderson, J., Mokracek, M., & Lindy, C. (2009). A nursing quality program driven by evidence-based practice. *Nursing Clinics of North America, 44*(1), 83–91.

Balakas, K., Potter, P., Pratt, E., Rea, G., & Williams, J. (2009). Evidence equals excellence: The application of an evidence-based practice model in an academic medical center. *Nursing Clinics of North America, 44*(1), 1–10.

Brewer, B., Brewer, M., & Schultz, A. (2009). A collaborative approach to building the capacity for research and evidence-based practice in community hospitals. *Nursing Clinics of North America, 44*(1), 11–25.

Brown, C., Wickline, M., Ecoff, L., & Glaser, D. (2009). Nursing practice, knowledge, attitudes and perceived barriers to evidence-based practice at an academic medical center. *Journal of Advanced Nursing, 65*(2), 371–381.

Buerhaus, P. (2008). Current and future state of the U.S. nursing workforce. *Journal of the American Medical Association, 300*(20), 2422–2424.

Buerhaus, P., Potter, V., & Staiger, D. (2008). *The future of the nursing workforce in the United States: Data, trends & implications.* Sudbury, MA: Jones & Bartlett.

Cadmus, E., Van Wynen, E., Chamberlain, B., Steingall, P., Kilgallen, M., Holly, C., et al. (2008). Nurses' skill level and access to evidence-based practice. *Journal of Nursing Administration, 38*(11), 494–503.

Campbell-Fleming, J., Catania, K., & Courtney, L. (2009). Promoting evidence-based practice through a traveling journal club. *Clinical Nurse Specialist, 23*(1), 16–20.

Fineout-Overholt, E. (2006a). Outcome evaluation for programs teaching EBP. In R. F. Levin & H. R. Feldman (Eds.), *Teaching evidence-based practice in nursing: A guide for academic & clinical settings* (pp. 143–157). New York: Springer.

Fineout-Overholt, E. (2006b). Using journal clubs to introduce EBP. In R. F. Levin & H. R. Feldman (Eds.), *Teaching evidence-based practice in nursing: A guide for academic & clinical settings* (pp. 325–335). New York: Springer.

Fineout-Overholt, E., & Johnston, L. (2005). Teaching EBP: A challenge for educators in the 21st century. *Worldviews on Evidence-Based Nursing, 2*(1), 37–39.

Fineout-Overholt, E., & Melnyk, B. (2005). Building a culture of best practice. *Nurse Leader, 3*(6), 26–30.

Fineout-Overholt, E., Hofstetter, S., Shell, L., & Johnston, L. (2005). Teaching EBP: Getting to the gold: How to search for the best evidence. *Worldviews on Evidence-Based Nursing, 2*(4), 207–211.

Gutierrez, F., & Smith, K. (2008). Reducing falls in a definitive observation unit: An evidence-based practice institute consortium project. *Critical Care Quarterly, 31*(2), 127–139.

Health Resources and Services Administration. (2004). The registered nurse population: National sample survey of registered nurses, March 2004: Preliminary findings. Retrieved May 9, 2009, from http://bhpr.hrsa.gov/healthworkforce/rnsurvey04/

Hockenberry, M., Brown, T., Walden, M., & Barrera, P. (2009). Teaching evidence-based practice skills in a hospital. *Journal of Continuing Education in Nursing, 40*(1), 28–32.

Hockenberry, M., Walaen, M., Brown, T., & Barrera, P. (2008). Creating an evidence-based practice environment: One hospital's journey. *Journal of Trauma Nursing, 15*(3), 136–142.

Holleman, G., Eliens, A., van Vliet, M., & van Achterberg, T. (2006). Promotion of evidence-based practice by professional nursing associations: Literature review. *Journal of Advanced Nursing, 53*(6), 702–709.

Institute of Medicine. (2001). *Crossing the quality chasm.* Washington, DC: National Academies Press.

The Joint Commission. (2009). *National Patient Safety Goals.* Retrieved May 12, 2009, from http://www.jointcommission.org/PatientSafety/NationalPatientSafetyGoals/09_hap_npsgs.htm

Kajermo, K., Unden, M., Gardulf, A., Eridsson, L. E., Orton, M. L., Arnetz, B. B., et al. (2008). Predictors of nurses' perceptions of barriers to research utilization. *Journal of Nursing Management, 16*(3), 305–314.

Kane, R. L., Shamliyan, T., Mueller, C., Duval, S., & Wilt, T. (2007). *Nursing staffing and quality of patient care.* Evidence Report/Technology Assessment No. 151. (Prepared by the Minnesota Evidence-Based Practice Center under Contract No. 290–02–0009.) AHRQ Publication No. 07-E005. Rockville, MD: Agency for Healthcare Research and Quality.

Long, L., Burkett, K., & McGee, S. (2009). Promotion of safe outcomes: Incorporating evidence into policies and procedures. *Nursing Clinics of North America, 44*(1), 57–70.

Melnyk, B., Fineout-Overholt, E., Stillwell, S., & Williamson, K. (2010). Transforming healthcare quality through innovations in evidence-based practice (pp. 167–194). In T. Porter-O'Grady & K. Malloch (Eds.), *The leadership of innovation: Creating the landscape for healthcare transformation.* Sudbury, MA: Jones & Bartlett.

Michigan Center for Nursing. (2008). *Survey of nurses, 2008.* Retrieved May 9, 2009, from http://www.michigancenterfornursing.org/mimages/nursesurvey08.pdf

Newhouse, R., Dearholt, S., Poe, S., Pugh, L., & White, K. (2007). Organizational change strategies for evidence-based practice. *Journal of Nursing Administration, 37*(12), 552–557.

O'Brien-Pallas, L., & Hayes, L. (2008). Challenges in getting workforce research in nursing used for decision-making in policy and practice: A Canadian perspective. *Journal of Clinical Nursing, 17*(24), 3338–3346.

Oman, K., Duran, C., & Fink, R. (2008). Evidence-based policy and procedures. *Journal of Nursing Administration, 38*(1), 47–51.

Penz, K., & Bassendowski, S. (2006). Evidence-based nursing in clinical practice: Implications for nurse educators. *The Journal of Continuing Education in Nursing, 37*(6), 250–254.

Pipe, T., Cisar, N., Caruso, E., & Wellik, K. (2008). Leadership strategies: Inspiring evidence-based practice at the individual, unit, and organizational levels. *Journal of Nursing Care Quality, 23*(3), 265–271.

Pipe, T., Timm, J., Harris, M., Frusti, D., Tucker, S., Attlesey-Pries, J., et al. (2009). Implementing a health system-wide evidence-based practice educational program to reach nurses with various levels of experience and educational preparation. *Nursing Clinics of North America, 44*(1), 43–55.

Porter-O'Grady, T., & Malloch, K. (2008). Beyond myth and magic: The future of evidence-based leadership. *Nursing Administration Quarterly, 32*(3), 176–187.

Porter-O'Grady, T., Alexander, D., Blaylock, J., Minkara, N., & Surel, D. (2006). Constructing a team model: Creating a foundation for evidence-based teams. *Nursing Administration Quarterly, 30*(3), 211–220.

Powers, J., Brower, A., & Tolliver, S. (2007). Impact of oral hygiene on prevention of ventilator-associated pneumonia in neuroscience patients. *Journal of Nursing Care Quality, 22*(4), 316–322.

Pravikoff, D., Tanner, A., & Pierce, S. (2005). Readiness of U.S. nurses for evidence-based practice. *American Journal of Nursing, 105*(9), 40–51.

Quinlan, P. (2006). Teaching evidence-based practice in a hospital setting: Bringing it to the bedside. In R. F. Levin & H. R. Feldman (Eds.). *Teaching evidence-based practice in nursing: A guide for academic & clinical settings* (pp. 279–293). New York: Springer.

Reavy, K., & Tavernier, S. (2008). Nurses reclaiming ownership of their practice: Implementation of an evidence-based practice model and process. *Journal of Continuing Education in Nursing, 39*(4), 166–172.

Rosenthal, M. (2007). Nonpayment for performance? Medicare's new reimbursement rule. *New England Journal of Medicine, 357*(16), 1573–1575.

Schulman, C. (2008). Strategies for starting a successful evidence-based practice program. *Advanced Critical Care, 19*(3), 301–311.

Selig, P., & Lewanowicz, W. (2008). Translation to practice: Developing an evidence-based practice nurse internship program. *Advanced Critical Care, 19*(3), 301–311.

Sherriff, K. L., Wallis, M., & Chaboyer, W. (2007). Nurses' attitudes to and perceptions of knowledge and skills regarding evidence-based practice. *International Journal of Nursing Practice, 13*(6), 363–369.

Singleton, J., & Levin, R. (2008). Strategies for learning evidence-based practice: Critically appraising clinical practice guidelines. *Journal of Nursing Education, 47*(8), 380–383.

Soukup, S. M., & McCleish, J. (2008). Advancing evidence-based practice: A program series. *Journal of Continuing Education in Nursing, 39*(9), 402–406.

Steurer, L. (2008, October). *An evidence-based practice scholar's program: One institution's journey toward excellence.* Podium presentation at the annual American Nurses Credentialing Center Magnet Conference, Salt Lake City, Utah.

Van Patter Gale, B., & Schaffer, M. (2009). Organizational readiness for evidence-based practice. *Journal of Nursing Administration, 39*(2), 91–97.

Vratny, A., & Shriver, D. (2007). A conceptual model for growing evidence-based practice. *Journal of Nursing Administration, 31*(2), 162–170.

Weeks, S., Marshall, J., & Burns, P. (2009). Development of an evidence-based practice and research collaborative among urban hospitals. *Nursing Clinics of North America, 44*(1), 27–31.

Wells, N., Free, M., & Adams, R. (2007). Nursing research internship: Enhancing evidence-based practice among staff nurses. *Journal of Nursing Administration, 37*(3), 135–143.

Worral, P. (2006). Traveling posters: Communicating on the front lines. In R. F. Levin & H. R. Feldman (Eds.), *Teaching evidence-based practice in nursing: A guide for academic & clinical settings* (pp. 337–346). New York: Springer.

Zadvinskis, I. (2008). Increasing knowledge level of evidence-based nursing through self-directed learning: Lessons learned for staff development. *Journal for Nurses in Staff Development, 24*(4), E13–E19.

Zuzelo, P., McGoldrick, T., Seminara, P., & Karbach, H. (2006). Shared governance and EBP: A logical partnership? *Nursing Management, 37*(6), 45–50.

chapter 14

343

ARCC Evidence-Based Practice Mentors: The Key to Sustaining Evidence-Based Practice

Ellen Fineout-Overholt and Bernadette Mazurek Melnyk

> *Mentoring is more an affair of the heart than the head—it is a 2 way relationship that is based on trust. A mentor wins and sustains the mentee's trust through constancy (staying the course), reliability (being there when it counts), integrity (honoring commitments and promises), and walking the talk.*
>
> *M.J. Tobin*

Overview of the ARCC Model and Evolution of Evidence-Based Practice Mentors

Although the implementation of evidence-based practice (EBP) is known to improve the quality of care and patient outcomes, which is a major reason why third-party payers are incentivizing organizations to deliver evidence-based care, healthcare systems are having challenges sustaining a culture of EBP. *Sustainability* has become a "buzz word" in today's world and, in its broadest sense, means an emphasis on cultivating a high quality of life for generations to come by promoting and maintaining security, clean air, and health (Melnyk, 2007). For EBP to be sustained in healthcare systems, there needs to be a key mechanism inherent in organizations to promote the continued systemwide advancement of evidence-based care once it is initiated. As first proposed in the Advancing Research and Clinical practice through close Collaboration (ARCC) Model (Melnyk & Fineout-Overholt, 2002), this key mechanism is an **EBP mentor**, typically an advanced practice clinician with in-depth knowledge and skills in EBP as well as individual behavioral and organizational change strategies. An EBP mentor, however, can be any clinician with expert knowledge of EBP and a desire to assist others in advancing excellence through evidence-based care.

The ARCC Model is a guide for systemwide implementation and sustainability of EBP in healthcare organizations that focuses on assisting clinicians with EBP knowledge, beliefs, and skills building to consistently implement evidence-based care and the building of EBP cultures to sustain best practices. The model was first conceptualized to provide a framework for advancing EBP within an academic medical center and surrounding community (see Chapter 11). Nurses identified mentorship as an important success strategy to assist point-of-care staff with the implementation of EBP (Melnyk & Fineout-Overholt, 2002). Thus, the term *EBP mentor* was coined to emphasize the key role of mentorship in promoting and sustaining the use of evidence-based care by point-of-care staff and in building cultures that support EBP (Melnyk, 2007).

A mentor is a trusted coach or teacher, whether in EBP or any other endeavor. Tobin (2004) describes the following roles of a mentor: (a) teacher, (b) sponsor, (c) advisor, (d) agent, (e) role model, (f) coach, and (g) confidante. A mentor typically provides directional guidance, fosters self-confidence, and instills values in the mentee (Wensel, 2006). Unlike having a preceptor who sets specific goals to be met in a limited period of time (Funderburk, 2008), the mentor–mentee relationship usually is enduring and dynamic, as it changes over time to meet the mentee's and mentor's needs (Bellack & Morjikian, 2005; Wensel). Characteristics of effective mentors include a minimum of beginning expert knowledge and skills, patience, enthusiasm, a sense of humor, respect, positive attitude, and good communication and listening skills (Fawcett, 2002; Kanaskie, 2006). Characteristics of good mentees include self-awareness, receptiveness to constructive feedback, and motivation/eagerness to learn.

In the ARCC Model, EBP mentors use findings from an assessment of the readiness and culture of an organization for systemwide implementation of EBP to guide them in developing a strategic plan to enhance clinicians' knowledge and skills in EBP and to foster a culture of best practice. Evidence from research has supported that EBP mentors enhance point-of-care providers' beliefs about the value of EBP and their ability to implement it, which in turn leads to greater EBP implementation (Melnyk, Fineout-Overholt, Feinstein, et al., 2004). Research further supports that when EBP implementation is enhanced, group cohesion is strengthened and turnover rates are less (R. Levin, personal communication, February 20, 2006). A key outcome of reduced staff turnover is substantial cost savings for healthcare organizations. For more specific information about the ARCC Model, please see Chapter 11.

The ARCC Evidence-Based Practice Mentor Role

Evidence-based practice mentors first ensure that those they mentor and others with whom they work have a common understanding of the definition of EBP. For these mentors, EBP is defined as a problem-solving approach to clinical practice that integrates the conscientious use of *best evidence* (internal and external) with a *clinician's expertise* and *patient preferences and values* to make decisions about the type of care that is provided and outcomes to be evaluated. In addition, these mentors ensure that the seven-step EBP process is well understood by point-of-care providers as well as managers or administrators (see Chapter 1 for more on the seven-step EBP process). The spirit of inquiry is an important focus for the EBP mentor. Without this initial element of an EBP culture, the EBP mentor role is less effective and often can be perceived as nothing more than another bureaucratic role established by administration to support their agenda.

In the ARCC Model, there are important components of the EBP mentor role, including (a) ongoing assessment of an organization's capacity to sustain an EBP culture; (b) building EBP knowledge and skills through conducting interactive group workshops and one-to-one mentoring; (c) stimulating, facilitating, and educating clinicians toward a culture of EBP, with a focus on overcoming barriers to best practice; (d) role modeling EBP; (e) conducting ARCC strategies to enhance the implementation of EBP, such as journal clubs, EBP rounds, web pages, newsletters, and fellowship programs; (f) working with staff to generate internal evidence (i.e., practice-generated) through quality improvement, outcomes management, and EBP implementation projects; (g) facilitating staff involvement in research to generate external evidence; (h) using evidence to foster best practice; and (i) collaborating with interdisciplinary professionals to advance and sustain EBP. These mentors also have excellent strategic planning, implementation, and outcomes evaluation skills so that they can monitor the impact of their role and overcome barriers in moving the system to a culture of best practice (Melnyk, 2007). Mentoring direct care staff on clinical units, primary care practice, or public health practice by ARCC EBP mentors is important in strengthening clinicians' beliefs about the value of EBP and their ability to implement it (Melnyk & Fineout-Overholt, 2002).

Each agency can individualize the role of the EBP mentor. Imperative to the role are the elements just discussed and a focus on outcomes. Often, healthcare has been focused on processes, such as measurement of time from door to discharge in the emergency department or sign-in to exit for a primary care practice. Evidence-based practice mentors are focused on both the outcomes of these processes and the processes themselves. These mentors assist with refining processes for the purpose or improving outcomes.

As systems strategists, EBP mentors (a) strategically plan, implement, and monitor/evaluate outcomes; (b) evaluate the impact of their role as EBP mentors; and (c) overcome barriers in moving to a culture of best practice. These mentors play a strategic role in sustaining an EBP culture (Ervin, 2005; Fineout-Overholt & Melnyk, 2005; Melnyk & Fineout-Overholt, 2002). Mentorship makes a difference (Sambunjak, Straus, & Marušic, 2006). Dr. Linda Olson-Keller indicated that she had been teaching public health nurses about EBP for many years, but without great success. The problem was not a knowledge deficit, and could not be resolved by teaching alone. What was missing is the mentoring component that moves EBP into the realm of the everyday, the expected norm for professional practice. (L. Olson-Keller, personal communication, June 9, 2009).

> *What is experienced and seen in the clinical area is what will likely predict future behavior.*
>
> **Bob Berenson**

Evidence to Support the Positive Impact of Mentorship on Outcomes

> *Mentoring is a brain to pick, an ear to listen, and a push in the right direction.*
>
> **John Crosby**

A body of evidence is beginning to accumulate that supports the positive impact that mentors have on individual and system outcomes. In a recent systematic review of 42 mainly cross-sectional descriptive studies that evaluated the evidence about the prevalence of mentorship and its impact on career development (Sambunjak et al., 2006), findings indicated that less than

50% of medical students and, in some fields, less than 20% of faculty had mentors. Overall, individuals with mentors had significantly higher career satisfaction scores than those without mentors. Eight studies from this systematic review reported the positive influence that mentorship had on personal development and career guidance. Furthermore, 21 studies in the review described the impact of mentoring on research development and productivity. Findings indicated that mentors increased mentees' self-confidence and provided resources and support for their activities. Mentees were more productive in the number of publications and grants than those individuals without mentors. They also were more likely to complete their theses. A lack of mentorship was reported as a barrier to completing scholarly projects and publications. Mentors were viewed as an important motivating factor in pursuing a research career. Overall, the studies from this systematic review indicated that mentorship was perceived to be important for career guidance, personal development, career choice, and productivity.

Another study by Beecroft, Santner, Lacy, et al. (2006) was conducted for the purpose of determining whether new graduate nurses in a mentoring program were (a) satisfactorily matched with mentors, (b) received guidance and support, (c) attained socialization into the nursing profession, (d) benefited from having a role model for acquisition of professional behaviors, (e) maintained contact with mentors, and (f) were satisfied with the mentorship. A survey was administered to 318 new graduate nurses who had participated in a yearlong mentoring/residency program at one healthcare institution in the United States over a 6-year period of time. Eighty-three percent of the mentees reported that they "clicked" with their mentors. Twenty-eight percent of the mentees indicated that they had a strong connection with their mentor, and approximately half met with their mentors on a regular basis. Slightly more than half of the mentees indicated that their mentors moderated stress during the residency period. Furthermore, the benefits of mentorship were more when mentors and mentees met on a regular basis.

In another outcomes evaluation study that sought to determine the impact of an 18-month mentorship program on nurse retention in five hospitals in the Southern region of the United States (Zucker, Coss, Williams, et al., 2006), findings indicated that both mentors and mentees reported that the program increased their knowledge and allowed them to become better people and colleagues. Positive comments from the mentees included that they felt a sense of importance and worth, an increased sense of loyalty, and a family atmosphere. The retention rate of new nurses in the healthcare system increased by 16%. In addition, the overall turnover rate for new graduates was reduced to 10.6% with the program. In another study (Greene & Puetzer, 2002), a substantial decrease in the number of novice staff terminations also was noted with the implementation of a mentorship program.

In a qualitative study that investigated the process through which 11 occupational therapists in Canadian healthcare institutions developed the capacity to use research evidence in their clinical practices, Craik and Rappolt (2006) found that providing mentoring to students was important for research utilization. Providing mentoring to students and colleagues was a catalyst for updating knowledge of current research and integrating research into clinical practice.

As a result of the benefits of mentoring, The Academy of Medical Surgical Nurses developed a mentoring program entitled Nurses Nurturing Nurses (N3). Some of the benefits of mentoring for mentors outlined by the Academy included (a) development of professional colleagues, self-awareness, and interpersonal relationships; (b) professional development; (c) stimulation to question practice; and (d) improved political skills. In addition, benefits for those being mentored proposed by the Academy included (a) recipient of one-to-one nurturing, (b) insight into unwritten rules and politics, (c) assistance with career development, (d) increased network of contacts, and (e) development of self-confidence and problem-solving skills (Reeves, 2004).

The process that hospitals must embark upon in seeking Magnet status from the American Nurses Credentialing Center, which is considered the gold standard for nursing practice, must include mechanisms for mentoring and professional development of nurses as well as succession planning (e.g., mentoring nurses into leadership roles). In the application process, examples must be provided that speak to mentoring for these purposes (American Nurses Credentialing Center, 2005).

Outcomes of ARCC Evidence-Based Practice Mentors

To support implementation of the ARCC Model, an EBP Mentorship Program was created as a 5-day immersion program that is held on the ASU College of Nursing & Health Innovation campus. The program prepares staff nurses, advanced practice nurses, nurse researchers, and other healthcare providers to serve as leaders and mentors in changing organizational cultures through the promotion, implementation, and sustainability of EBP from administration to the bedside. The program fosters a shift to the EBP paradigm and covers the seven-step EBP process—(0) cultivate a spirit of inquiry, (1) ask the clinically relevant question in PICOT format, (2) search for the best evidence, (3) critically appraise and synthesize the evidence, (4) plan and implement evidence, (5) evaluate the outcomes, and (6) disseminate the outcome. Additional foci are the implementation of what is known from a body of evidence and development of the EBP mentor role. The EBP mentors return to their home institutions with a strategic plan for implementing and evaluating at least one EBP project and a description of the EBP mentor role individualized for their agency.

In a recent post-program evaluation survey, almost 40% of the 38 EBP mentors from across the United States and the world (see Table 15.1) who responded were from the Southwestern United States. More than 40% were from medium-sized community hospitals, with a

unit four

table 15.1 Description of evidence-based practice mentors who completed the EBP mentorship program evaluation survey (*n* = 38)

Home Area	Percent	Description of Institution	Percent	Roles	Percent
Northeast	2.6	Academic Medical Center (affiliated with Nursing School/Division/Department)	34.2	Staff nurse	2.6
Southeast	7.8	Large Medical Center (>600 beds)	7.9	Charge nurse	0.0
Northwest	13.2	Community or Medium-sized Hospital (>150 beds and <600 beds)	42.1	Nurse manager	5.3
Southwest	39.5	Small or Rural Hospital (<150 beds)	0.0	Advanced practice nurse (clinical nurse specialist or nurse practitioner)	18.4
Midwest	31.6	Urgent Care Clinic, Primary Care or Long Term care	0.0	Clinical educator	23.7
International	5.3	Nursing Education (College of Nursing)	10.5	Academic faculty	15.8
		Other	5.3	EBP mentor	10.5
				Other	23.7

mean tenure of 6.16 years in their current role and 26.84 years as a nurse. The EBP mentors who responded to the survey were primarily Caucasian (95%) and female (97%). The majority of the respondents' exposure to EBP came from the EBP Mentorship Program (84%), with continuing education coming in as the second source of learning about EBP (52.6%). In addition, less than 20% formally learned about EBP in school.

To evaluate the EBP Mentorship Program, several scales were administered in an electronic questionnaire via Surveymonkey. To help understand the culture in which the EBP mentors worked, the 25-item Likert-scale, Organizational Culture & Readiness for System-wide Integration of EBP (OCRSIEP; Fineout-Overholt & Melnyk, 2006) was administered. Examples of scale items include (a) To what extent is EBP clearly described in the mission and philosophy of your institution? (b) To what extent do practitioners model EBP? and (c) To what extent are fiscal resources used to support EBP? The range of summed scores was between 25 and 125, with 25 representing *not much EBP organizational support for an EBP culture*; 50 representing *marginal organizational support for an EBP culture*; 75 representing *some organizational support for an EBP culture*; 100 representing *moderate organizational support for an EBP culture*; and 125 representing *full organizational support for an EBP culture*. The EBP mentors' OCRSIEP scores were compared to a similar sample of EBP workshop participants and were found to have a slightly higher mean (83 [SD = 16] and 80 [SD = 18], respectively). The EBP mentors perceived their organizations to fall between some and moderate organizational support for EBP; however, with the organization supporting the formal role of EBP mentor, it would be reasonable to expect that the organizational support for EBP would be a minimum of moderate. These findings indicate that healthcare systems in which these EBP mentors work still have room for growth to establish a sustained culture of EBP.

The EBP mentors' beliefs about EBP were measured by the 16-item EBP Beliefs (EBPB) Scale (Melnyk & Fineout-Overholt, 2003a). Participants responded from 1 (strongly disagree) to 5 (strongly agree) to each of the 5-point Likert scale items. Examples of the items on the EBPB scale include (a) "I believe that EBP results in the best clinical care for patients," (b) "I am clear about the steps of EBP," and (c) "I am sure that I can implement EBP. Scoring consists of reverse scoring two negatively phrased items (i.e., "I believe EBP takes too much time"; "I believe EBP is difficult") and then summing all 16 items, with a total score that ranges between none (16), marginal (32), some (48), moderate (64), and very strong beliefs (80) (Melnyk, Fineout-Overholt, & Mays, 2008). The Cronbach's alpha (i.e., reliability coefficient) for this sample was 0.83. The EBP mentors' mean EBPB scores increased from 61 (SD = 7.4) at baseline to 68 (SD = 6.2) after program completion. In addition, compared to a similar sample of EBP workshop participants, these mentors were found to have a slightly higher EBPB mean score (68 [SD = 6.2] and 60 [SD = 9.5], respectively). Although EBP mentors' beliefs were higher approximately 1 year after completing the EBP Mentorship Program than when they began, their beliefs in EBP remained in the moderately strong category versus moving to the high beliefs category.

The final evaluation of the effectiveness of the EBP mentorship program was actual implementation of EBP, which was measured by the 18-item EBP Implementation (EBPI) Scale (Melnyk & Fineout-Overholt, 2003b). Evidence-based practice mentors responded to each of 18 items on the 5-point frequency scale by indicating how often in the past 8 weeks they performed the item. Sample items include (a) used evidence to change my clinical practice, (b) shared an EBP guideline with a colleague, (c) promoted the use of EBP to my colleagues, and (d) shared the outcome data collected with colleagues. Scoring of the instrument consists of summing all 18 items with a range between 0 and 72, with none equal to 0 times within the past 8 weeks; 18 equal to *1–3 times* within the past 8 weeks; 36 equal to *4–5 times* within the past 8 weeks; 54 equal to *6–8 times* within the past 8 weeks; and 72 equals *greater than 8 times* within the past 8 weeks (Melnyk et al., 2008). The reliability coefficient of the EBPI with this sample was 0.95. As a group, the EBP mentors reported a mean implementation score at baseline

chapter 15

349

of 19 (SD = 13.2) (e.g., 1–3 times per week they used evidence, talked about outcomes; see Appendix N for sample scales), which is consistent with other EBP workshop samples at baseline (Mean = 20 [SD = 15.5]). About 1 year after attending the program, the mentors reported a mean implementation score of 55 (SD = 18.6) (i.e., they used evidence in their practice approximately 6–8 times within the past 8 weeks).

The EBP mentors indicated that, after attending the EBP Mentorship Program, they were (a) more influential, (b) able to speak more intelligently about evidence, (c) able to improve outcomes, and (d) able to formulate the question and find the evidence. In addition, EBP mentors indicated that they could now (a) read research, (b) lead EBP initiatives (e.g., through gaining promotions that facilitated their influence on organizational change), (c) advance their education through returning to school, (d) provide valued contributions to care, and (e) serve as sought after consultants/resources for EBP.

While EBP beliefs and implementation increased and were sustained for approximately one year after the 5-day immersion program, there remained identified barriers to the EBP mentor role that challenged the mentor to carry out the role to its fullest degree, including (a) competing clinical priorities, (b) time, (c) allocated resources, (d) existing politics in the organization, (e) lack of administrative support, and (f) no accountability for EBP. Many of these barriers have been documented in the literature (Pravikoff, Pierce, Tanner, et al., 2005). Identified facilitators to the EBP mentor role included (a) continued contact with the mentorship program faculty, (b) the ability to ask questions, (c) the availability of assistance with data analysis, (d) assistance with project development, (e) a supportive Chief Nursing Officer or Director of EBP or Nurse researcher, (f) a network of fellow EBP mentors, and (g) EBP as an expectation of the Joint Commission on the Accreditation of Healthcare Organizations (JCAHO) and Magnet.

Findings from this program evaluation with ARCC EBP mentors indicated that they were able to strengthen and sustain their EBP beliefs and increase EBP implementation for as long as one year following attendance at the workshop, despite some organizational challenges. With a strong focus on education and skills building during the 5-day immersion program, the participants were equipped to leave the program and implement into clinical practice the EBP knowledge and skills that they learned. Just as these ARCC EBP mentors are making a difference one step at a time with their clinician colleagues, so can any clinician who has a sincere desire to enhance excellence in care based on evidence. Careful documentation of outcomes will assist EBP mentors to demonstrate their impact on patient care, system outcomes, and the care practices of their colleagues.

references

American Nurses Credentialing Center. (2005). *The Magnet Recognition Program application manual.* Silver Spring, MD: Author.

Beecroft, P. C., Santner, S., Lacy, M. L., Kunzman, L., & Dorey, F. (2006). New graduate nurses' perceptions of mentoring: Six-year programme evaluation. *Journal of Advanced Nursing, 55*(6), 736–747.

Bellack, J. P., & Morjikian, R. L. (2005). The RWJ Executive Nurse Fellows Program, Part 2: Mentoring for leadership success. *Journal of Nursing Administration, 35*(12), 533–540.

Craik, J., & Rappolt, S. (2006). Enhancing research utilization capacity through multifaceted professional development. *American Journal of Occupational Therapy, 60*, 155–164.

Ervin, N. E. (2005). Clinical coaching: A strategy for enhancing evidence-based nursing practice. *CNS, 19*(6), 296–301.

Fawcett, D. (2002). Mentoring: What it is and how to make it work. *AORN Journal, 75*(2), 950–954.

Fineout-Overholt, E., Melnyk, B. M., & Schultz, A. (2005). Transforming healthcare from the inside out: Advancing evidence-based practice in the 21st century. *Journal of Professional Nursing, 21*(6), 335–344.

Fineout-Overholt, E., & Melnyk, B. (2006). *Organizational culture & readiness for system-wide integration of evidence-based practice.* Gilbert, AZ: ARCC Publishing.

Funderburk, A. E. (2008). Mentoring: The retention factor in the acute care setting. *Journal for Nurses in Staff Development, 24*(3), E1–E5.

Greene, M. T., & Puetzer, M. (2002). The value of mentoring: A strategic approach to retention and recruitment. *Journal of Nursing Care Quality, 17*(1), 63–70.

Kanaskie, M. L. (2006). Mentoring: A staff retention tool. *Critical Care Nursing Quarterly, 29*(2), 248–252.

Melnyk, B. M. (2007). The evidence-based practice mentor: A promising strategy for implementing and sustaining EBP in healthcare systems. *Worldviews on Evidence-Based Nursing, 4*(3), 123–125.

Melnyk, B. M., & Fineout-Overholt, E. (2002). Putting research into practice. *Reflections on Nursing Leadership, 28*(2), 22–25.

Melnyk, B., & Fineout-Overholt, E. (2003a). *Evidence-based practice beliefs scale*. Rochester, NY: ARCC Publishing.

Melnyk, B., & Fineout-Overholt, E. (2003b). *Evidence-based practice implementation scale*. Rochester, NY: ARCC Publishing.

Melnyk, B. M., Fineout-Overholt, E., Feinstein, N., Li, H. S., Small, L., Wilcox, L., et al. (2004). Nurses' perceived knowledge, beliefs, skills, and needs regarding evidence-based practice: Implications for accelerating the paradigm shift. *Worldviews on Evidence-Based Nursing, 1*(3), 185–193.

Melnyk, B. M., Fineout-Overholt, E., & Mays, M. (2008). The evidence-based practice beliefs and implementation scales: Psychometric properties of two new instruments. *Worldviews on Evidence-Based Nursing, 5*(4), 208–216.

Pravikoff, D. S., Pierce, S. T., Tanner, A., Bakken, S., Feetham, S. L., Foster, R. L., et al. (2005). Evidence-based practice readiness study supported by academy nursing informatics expert panel. *Nursing Outlook, 53*, 49–50.

Reeves, K. A. (2004). Nurses nurturing nurses: A mentoring program. *Nurse Leader, 2*(6), 47–54.

Sambunjak, D., Straus, S. E., & Marušic, A. (2006). Mentoring in academic medicine: A systematic review. The Journal of The American Medical Association, 296(9), 1103–1115.

Tobin, M. J. (2004). Mentoring: Seven roles and some specifics. *American Journal of Respiratory and Critical Care Medicine, 170*, 114–117.

Wensel, T. M. (2006). Mentor or preceptor: What is the difference? *American Journal Health-System Pharmacy, 63*, 1597.

Zucker, B., Coss, C., Williams, D., Bloodworth, L., Lynn, M., Denker, A., et al. (2006). Nursing retention in the era of a nursing shortage. *Journal for Nurses in Staff Development, 22*(6), 302–306.

chapter 15

351

Step Six: Disseminating Evidence and Evidence-Based Practice Implementation Outcomes

Disseminating Evidence Through Publications, Presentations, Health Policy Briefs, and the Media

Cecily L. Betz, Kathryn A. Smith, Bernadette Mazurek Melnyk, and Tom Rickey

This chapter focuses on ideas and pragmatic suggestions for disseminating evidence and evidence-based information. Whatever the venue (e.g., speaking before an audience, presenting a poster, publishing a paper, communicating with the media, writing a health policy brief), the key to being effective is sufficient preparation. Excellent preparation reduces performance anxiety, bolsters confidence, and enhances the success of any dissemination initiative. The primary goal of disseminating evidence, whatever the conduit as described in this chapter, is to facilitate the transfer and adoption of research findings into clinical practice (Oermann, Galvin, Floyd, et al., 2006). For the majority of clinicians in advanced practice and leadership roles, enrollment in some type of instructional program (e.g., a continuing education course, staff development class, or college course) to learn the knowledge and skills to successfully make presentations or publish manuscripts is rarely available (Lannon, 2007). Much of the learning for these advanced professional competencies is gained through the self-taught "trial and error approach," mentoring by knowledgeable colleagues, and modeling the observable behavior and materials developed by other professionals.

This chapter presents information on the strategies that can be used by healthcare professionals to disseminate evidence. Content covered includes podium/oral, panel, roundtable, poster, and small-group presentations, as well as podcasts/vodcasts, hospital-based and professional committees, journal clubs, and community meetings. A discussion follows on professional publishing and dissemination of evidence to influence health policy. In addition, suggestions for disseminating evidence to the media are hightlighted.

Disseminating Evidence Through Podium/Oral Presentations

An effective evidence-based presentation begins with an understanding of the characteristics and needs of the audience. In preparing for a podium or oral presentation, it is important to inquire about the audience, the context of the presentation, the desired length and format, and any special considerations (Gross, 2002; Hadfield-Law, 2001; Happell, 2008; Heinrich, 2007; McConnell, 2002; Schulmeister & Vrabel, 2002; Smith, 2000; Woodring, 2000). For presenters whose practice focus is education or research, a strategy to ensure that the presentation has relevance for clinicians is to elicit the involvement of an advanced level clinician as a copresenter. Together, the presentation can be tailored to meet the aims of imparting evidence related to clinical care in clinically meaningful language and style (Oermann et al., 2006).

> *Whether you think you can or think you can't, you're right.*
>
> *Henry Ford*

Preparing for the Presentation

As you begin preparing the presentation, specifically ask the following substantive questions:

What is the educational level and practice specialty of the audience?
What is the audience's current knowledge of the material to be presented?
Is the content for an audience with limited knowledge of the evidence-based topic?
Why is the audience interested in the presentation?
Is the audience expected to use evidence-based approaches in providing clinical care?
What other information, if any, will the audience be receiving?
What previous exposure has the audience had to the content of the presentation?
How might the members of the audience use the information from the presentation to improve their practices, teaching, or other aspects of their work?

Additional logistical questions to consider include

Number of participants expected to attend the presentation
Availability of audio-visual equipment (e.g., LCD projector for PowerPoint presentations)
Length of the presentation
Format of the presentation
Expectations regarding handouts
Specific content to be addressed (Bagott & Bagott, 2001)
Once these questions are answered, formulation of the presentation can begin. The first step in this process is creating learner objectives (e.g., at the end of the presentation, the participants will be able to describe the study's major outcomes) along with a detailed outline for the presentation. For presentations with a purpose of disseminating evidence from a study, the following topical outline is suggested.
  I. Introduction to the clinical problem (e.g., depression affects approximately 25% of adults in the United States)
 II. The purpose/primary aim of the study (e.g., to determine the short- and long-term effects of cognitive-behavior therapy [CBT] on depressive symptoms in young adults)
III. The theoretical framework used to guide the study

IV. Hypotheses (e.g., young adults who receive CBT will have less depressive symptoms than young adults who do not receive CBT) or study questions (what are the effects of CBT on depressed adults?)

V. The design (e.g., a randomized controlled trial)

    A. A description of the interventions used if an experimental study is being presented

    B. A description of the sample with inclusion and exclusion criteria (e.g., the sample included 104 depressed adults between the ages of 21 and 30 years; potential subjects were excluded if they had a mental health problem with psychotic features), as well as a concise description of the demographics of the sample

    C. The dependent variables and instruments used to measure the study's outcomes, along with validity and reliability information of each instrument (e.g., the Beck Depression Inventory was used to measure depressive symptoms; construct validity of the Beck Inventory has been supported in prior work, and internal consistency reliability is reported as consistently higher than 0.80)

VI. Findings from the study

    A. Approach to statistical analyses (e.g., types of statistical tests used [an independent *t*-test was used to test the study hypothesis])

    B. Findings (it is best to represent the findings in easy-to-read graphs or tables)

VII. Discussion of the findings, along with major strengths and limitations of the study (e.g., substantial attrition rate, difficulties in recruitment)

VIII. Implications

    A. Implications for future research (e.g., what was learned from this study that can guide future research in the area)

    B. Implications for clinical practice (e.g., how this evidence can be used to improve practice)

Once the outline is developed, major points and the content for each section of the outline can be developed along with the time allocation for each component of the presentation. Many conferences limit research/evidence-based presentations to 20 minutes or less, with it being common-place for three to four individuals to deliver their talks in the same session. For presentations with extremely limited time frames, it is critical to deliver only "nuts and bolts" information. Because many individuals, especially novices, often extend their presentation beyond the allocated time limit, it is beneficial to write out and conduct a practice presentation with colleagues before the actual conference. Having colleagues attend and critique this practice session will strengthen the final product.

Slides to Enhance the Presentation

Once the presentation is written, slides should be developed to enhance delivery and hold the attention of the audience. Many of the currently available slide programs (e.g., Microsoft PowerPoint) are easy to use. A rule of thumb is that a minimal amount of information should be contained on each slide and that there should be no more than one or two slides per minute of presentation time. Therefore, if an oral presentation is scheduled for 20 minutes, no more than 40 slides should accompany it.

    Another helpful tip in creating slides is to keep them simple in terms of the colors, graphics, and number of fonts used. A dark or medium background (e.g., navy blue or maroon) with light color lettering (e.g., yellow or white) works best. White or pale-colored backgrounds should be avoided. Individuals in the back of a room should be able to read all text. Fonts should be simple (e.g., Arial, Times New Roman). Font and background color should be consistent throughout the slide presentation. Important points should appear in boldface on slides. In addition, photographs enhance the presentation, capture the audience's interest, and assist in emphasizing important points (see Appendix F for an example of a slide presentation to accompany a 20-minute research report). Avoid the use of comics and entertaining sound effects. If acronyms are used, they should be defined by the speaker during the presentation. Moreover, there are many websites that contain helpful information for creating and delivering professional oral presentations. More recently, advances in the development of personal digital assistant (PDA) devices have resulted in their capacity to be used as projection devices for PowerPoint presentations, enabling tremendous convenience for presenters (Yam, 2005).

Excellent tutorials on creating PowerPoint slides by Epson Presenters Online, where registration is free, and templates and clip art are downloadable at

http://www.presentersonline.com/tutorials/powerpoint/slides. shtml

Other Types of Evidence-Based Oral Presentations

The following guidelines and tips for presenting evidence from a study also apply to delivering other types of evidence-based presentations (e.g., evidence-based implementation projects).

The format for presenting *systematic reviews* of evidence should include

Introduction to the clinical problem
Purpose of the systematic review or the clinical question addressed
Methods (e.g., search strategy)
Results (i.e., presentation and critical appraisal of the evidence)
Implications for future research and practice
It is important to remember that the material prepared for a conference presentation can be converted into a manuscript for publication with additional effort. The information disseminated at a conference also would be appropriate and timely for an audience targeted by print and/or electronic media (Happell, 2007).

Disseminating Evidence Through Panel Presentations

Panel presentations are effective venues for conveying divergent perspectives on evidence-based topics. This type of presentation format is especially effective in convening colleagues from various clinical settings to disseminate information on evidenced-based topics. For example, during a panel presentation, clinicians can discuss their various evidenced-based approaches to promoting spiritual support services on their hematology-oncology units. Listening to a number of different views enriches the session for the audience. The style and purpose of panel presentations vary according to the roles of the moderator and panelists. The moderator may serve as the coordinator, meaning that this individual manages the agenda of the panel by first giving background or introductory information and commentary on the subject matter to be discussed. Then, the moderator asks questions of the panel members to elicit their opinions on the topic. Questions from the audience are taken as a means of delving further into particular areas of interest or understanding the panelists' views better.

Another panel model features a more formalized approach in which members of the panel present prepared remarks, with the moderator serving as a discussion facilitator by offering commentary for panel response and eliciting audience questions. The panel format is dependent on a number of factors, including panelist expertise, public speaking experience, organizational practices, and the moderator's competence in the role.

Panelist Preparation

Serving as a panelist begins with knowing the expectations for participation (e.g., delivering a prepared presentation or sharing expert opinions with the audience). The panel format will dictate the type of preparation necessary for the presentation. Whatever the format, it is necessary to obtain contextual information.

First, the potential panelist must learn about the theme of and rationale for the panel, along with the session objectives. For example, is the panelist expected to provide a clinically based or theoretically oriented presentation? Coupled with this information, it is important to know information about the other panelists, their areas of expertise, and the topics that the other panelists will address, along with their particular biases or perspectives. It is also necessary to know the timeframe for the entire panel, including allotment of time for audience questions, each panelist's prepared remarks, and the moderator's commentary (Gross, 2002; Hadfield-Law, 2001; McConnell, 2002; Schulmeister & Vrabel, 2002; Smith, 2000; Woodring, 2000).

If a panelist is expected to prepare remarks, it is important to inquire about the availability of audiovisual equipment. In addition, the following strategies will ensure success of the panel presentation.

Limit the number of slides because having too many slides becomes distracting and deemphasizes the substance of the presentation. Slides should be used to highlight, not supplant, what is said. It is helpful to have a brief conversation with the other panelists and agree on a number of slides and timeframes so that none of the panelists dominate. Develop a time clock system (e.g., set a timepiece in front of the speaker or have the moderator invoke the time notification with signage or some other method). Use an active voice that holds the audience's attention, and illustrate content with real-life examples. Identify the major theme of the presentation, and add three to five major points to support the thrust of the theme.

If a panelist is expected to offer expert opinions in response to questions, the following preparatory steps are needed:

Gather information on the projected demographics of the audience and gear responses to the needs of the group; consulting with colleagues before the panel presentation may be useful. A representative description of the projected audience will provide insight as to appropriate direction for preparation.

Anticipate the questions that might be asked from the audience; colleagues can be asked to contribute to a potential list of questions for advance preparation.

Paraphrase questions asked from the audience before providing a response; this allows everyone in the audience to hear the questions and allows the presenter time to organize his or her thoughts.

Treat all questions with the same importance so as not to display a bias or preference for certain individuals in the audience.

During the session, panelists are expected to conduct themselves professionally, with sensitivity to the fact that they are only one of several experts sharing the stage from whom the audience wants to hear new information and practice ideas. Box 16.1 lists suggestions for panelist conduct, or what some individuals refer to as "A Panelist's Dos and Don'ts."

chapter 16

359

---

box 16.1

A Panelist's Do' s and Don'ts

DO

- Be sensitive to time limitations for both prepared and spontaneous remarks.
- Make notations of other speakers' comments for response and essential points for an organized, well-thought-out reply.

DON'T

- "Jump" on the remarks of other speakers (i.e., enable them to speak without interruption).
- Look at another panelist when responding to his or her comments; rather, speak directly to the audience.
- Insert political or partisan opinions.

Moderator Preparation

The moderator's main role during a panel presentation is to ensure that the session objectives are met, that the panelist presentations are pulled together in a cohesive fashion, and that all participants fulfill their duties without dominating the presentation. The moderator will begin the session by providing introductory remarks that include an overview of the panel's purpose, a brief biographical introduction, and the evidence-based topic of each panelist. The moderator's role is to ensure the even flow of the panel discussion and questions from the audience. At the conclusion of the panel, the moderator should provide summary statements of the major themes of each evidence-based presentation; therefore, note taking during the session will be necessary while being attentive to coordinating questions from the audience and panelist responses. Box 16.2 presents specific responsibilities of the moderator during a panel presentation.

Prior to the panel session, the moderator should contact each of the panelists to obtain sufficient information about the presentation and each panelist's area of expertise. Exchange of information about the other panel members also should occur, including contact information, so that contact by panel members can be established before the presentation. Additionally, the moderator can serve as a liaison for exchanging logistic information (e.g., audiovisual needs, room setup, projected number of individuals attending the presentation for distribution of handouts, and confirmation of

---

box 16.2

Responsibilities of the Moderator During a Panel Presentation

- Provide a brief introduction of each panelist, emphasizing his or her expertise or experience with the evidence-based topic.
- Select audience members who have questions to ask of panelists.
- Repeat questions (or have panelists do it) for the audience's benefit.
- Remind the audience members or panelists of time constraints if too much time is used.
- Redirect the panelists' comments as needed to ensure that one or two panelists do not dominate the session.

---

the meeting time and place). The moderator also needs to be responsible for ensuring that the panel adheres to time constraints and clearly conveys to panelists the methods for keeping time.

Disseminating Evidence Through Roundtable Presentations

Roundtable presentations are an informal way to share information with a small group of people—literally, the number of individuals that fit around a table. Roundtable presentations offer the opportunity not only to share specific information with a group, but also to allow the group to discuss the information, related to experiences, and how the content will be used within their own practices.

Because the group for a roundtable is generally small (e.g., 6–12 individuals), it is appropriate to start the discussion with introductions so that the group members can get acquainted, which will allow them to more easily engage in conversation about the topic. The use of audiovisual equipment is often not possible in this setting, but PowerPoint or other types of handouts can be used to identify key points or provide supplemental information (Bergren, 2000; Evans, 2000; "Teaching with Slides," 2003). As in the case of a formal lecture, it is important to understand the needs of the audience and their reasons for attending the roundtable.

Preparation for a Roundtable Discussion

In planning the presentation, it is important to allow ample time for discussion. Anticipate that one half to one third of the allotted time will be spent in discussion related to the prepared evidence-based material. Preplanned discussion questions to be used by the presenter are useful to facilitate dialogue among the participants, should spontaneous conversation not occur.

Content for a roundtable is prepared in the same way as for a lecture presentation. Delivery of the material will be different, given the small group size and intimate setting in which the roundtable takes place. After appropriate introductions, the goals of the evidenced-based presentation are stated. Any handouts are distributed and described in terms of their utility and relevance to the evidence-based practice (EBP) topic. The content of the presentation is then delivered. Because the group is small, it is important to scan the group regularly, making eye contact with each person, in order to engage all present. Questions can be answered either during the presentation or at the end. If questions are taken and discussion allowed during the delivery of the content, it is important to watch the time to assure that all content will be covered (Gross, 2002; Hadfield-Law, 2001; McConnell, 2002; Schulmeister & Vrabel, 2002; Woodring, 2000).

At the end of a roundtable session, participants should be thanked for attending, and any final questions that require additional clarification should be answered. The group may wish to exchange business cards or other identification or information so that dialogue among the members may continue. The presenter should offer his or her business card to allow future follow-up and may stay in the vicinity of the roundtable for a period of time after the session to answer individual questions.

Disseminating Evidence Through Poster Presentations

Poster presentations provide an alternative option for presenting evidence-based information to a professional audience. Poster presentations are different from those given from a podium in a number of ways. Podium presentations are more formal in both style and format. The presenter typically provides more information from the podium as contrasted with the poster, wherein only the most essential aspects of information about a study or evidence-based project are given. The podium presenter adheres to a fairly standard format for providing information, with little or no time allowed to take audience questions. The poster presenter also adheres to a defined format for displaying information; however, this type of presentation allows for more interaction between colleagues in the area of clinical interest. Typically, the presenter stands near his or her poster and answers questions or discusses key points as individuals walk by. Individuals displaying posters can explore any number of issues that are not possible with podium presentations. For example, colleagues might discuss in greater detail the clinical implications of the evidence presented, such as implementation challenges in a community-based setting compared with a tertiary care setting. Poster presentations enable the dissemination of preliminary research data or evidence reviews (Miracle, 2008).

Podium presentations are confined to limited periods of time (e.g., usually 15–20 minutes in length), whereas posters are displayed for longer periods of time (e.g., several hours), which allows the presenter more time to speak directly with colleagues about his or her work. A poster presentation is less intimidating than a podium presentation because public speaking can be uncomfortable for professionals who are not accustomed to presenting before large numbers of people (Bagott & Bagott, 2001). Displaying information also may be preferable to giving an oral presentation for individuals who process information better in visual rather than verbal format.

The key to developing an effective and eye-catching poster is to construct it in a way that captures the attention of the conference participants. It is useful to think about the attractive characteristics of poster presentations seen at various professional conferences (see the accompanying CD-ROM for two well-designed posters that were displayed at national/international conferences). Notable aspects of these posters include their design and symmetry, the contrast of colors used, use of key words or phrases to emphasize important content, and use of graphs/figures to present study findings. In contrast, posters that are poorly designed often present content in a disorganized format, contain too much or too little information, use colors that clash, and do not use figures/graphs to display content.

However, the display of graphics and organization of a poster are not enough. Knowing how to present information to colleagues in succinct, scholarly, and precise terms is just as important. Substance and design, when combined well in a poster, can serve as an effective vehicle for conveying information to colleagues. The poster becomes a magnet for attracting colleagues, not only to read about one's work but also to provide a venue for additional discussion with sharing of information that is the keystone of collegial discourse (Miller, 2007; Miracle, 2008).

Ideally, if the resources are available, it is useful to consult with a graphic design expert when constructing a poster. Consulting with an expert certainly makes it easier, but the designer has limitations as well because this individual's area of expertise is limited to graphic design, not the poster content (Taggart & Arslanian, 2000). If consulting with a graphic designer is not an option, then accessing examples of posters from print resources or the Internet or with input from colleagues is an alternative (Miller, 2007).

When a poster is accepted for presentation at a conference, authors typically receive the guidelines for construction and display of their posters (e.g., size specifications). If the guidelines are not received, it is critical to obtain them prior to beginning the poster's design so that time is not lost in preparing a product that does not meet the requirements of the poster session.

The Pragmatics of Constructing a Poster: Getting Started

The first step in developing a poster presentation is to translate ideas and images into graphic form. Sketching out or developing a mockup model of the poster with self-sticking notes or using a computer template may be useful (Hamilton, 2008). The professional meeting and/or association may specify poster requirements. Therefore, it will be important to obtain and carefully review poster guidelines, such as the poster size that is standard for the conference (e.g., the typical size is 4 feet by 6 feet). It is also important that the poster text and graphics be readable from a distance of 4 feet. Keeping the following principles in mind will enhance the readability of the poster.

Remember that English-speaking participants will read the poster from left to right and from top to bottom.

Number the order of the presentation to assist the reader in information sequencing.

Vary the font size on the poster according to the type of information being presented, for example, 72 point (pt) or larger for the poster title (readable from 20 feet), 72 pt or larger for authors' names and affiliations, 36–48 pt or larger for poster headings and subheadings, and 14–20 pt for poster text.

Use graphics or illustrations in lieu of text when appropriate, such as when reporting findings.

Keep headings and subheadings brief (fewer than five words).

Use bulleted phrases or short sentences of seven words or less.

Use high contrast with lettering and background.

Use familiar typeface (e.g., Times New Roman, Courier New, Arial) and the same font style throughout the poster.

Keep in mind that sans serif fonts (without curlicues) are the most readable.

Avoid using shadowing and underlines; use bold instead for areas of emphasis.

Use active tense (e.g., "Findings reveal…") and plain language.

Organize the poster content into four sections: background information, methodology, findings, and implications.

Limit the number of references cited on the poster by listing them on the handout or at the end of a corresponding section.

Limit text to 50 words or less.

The presentation of content should follow a logical sequence from beginning to end. This format is similar to that used for publishing research papers. The presentation of research content, although dependent on the specifications of the conference, typically includes

Introduction/Background: The focus of the introduction section is to attract the attention of colleagues about the significance of the project by emphasizing the need, prevalence of the problem, or clinical issue.

Objectives(s): This section should be brief in that it states the focus of the study.

Design/Methods: Brevity is the key unless there is something of interest about the methods or design that warrants emphasis (e.g., recruiting and training interviewers for culturally diverse populations).

Data Analysis: This section should be concise in terms of listing analyses conducted.

Study Findings: The emphasis in this section is on presenting graphs or tables with limited explanatory text to accompany them.

Conclusions: Brief statements are made regarding the most significant findings as well as the clinical implications for practice.

Acknowledgement: When applicable, it is important to recognize the names of other colleagues on the project and/or the funding source, if applicable.

Evidence-Based Poster Presentations

Similarly, the content of an evidence-based poster presentation would generally include the following sections:

Background/Significance: Provide background as to the nature or status of the clinical problem (e.g., prevalence data or other statistics demonstrating the growing importance of the problem).

Clinical Question: Specifically identify what clinical problem or question was investigated.

Search for Evidence/Accepted Practice: Identify briefly the methods and sources used to collect evidence (e.g., search strategy for the review of literature, focus groups, and surveys of institutional practices).

Presentation of and Critical Appraisal of the Evidence: Provide a succinct summary of the conclusions drawn from evaluating the scope of evidence available.

Clinical Practice Implications: Describe clinical practice implications, based on the process of collecting and evaluating the evidence.

Expectations of Poster Presenters

Poster presenters are expected to stand beside their posters in accordance with the designated time periods for display. It is disappointing for colleagues to walk among posters without the authors or investigators because one of the primary purposes for a poster presentation is to facilitate scholarly and clinical dialogue among colleagues. Having PowerPoint handouts of the poster presentation available for distribution is helpful as well (Bergren, 2000; Evans, 2000). The handouts may contain additional information that was not possible to include in the poster display (e.g., more detail on the review of pertinent literature, the theoretical framework, research instruments, and references). Contact information for later correspondence is helpful as well (Hamilton, 2008).

Helpful Resources for Constructing Posters

Many excellent resources are available via the Internet to help with constructing posters. These resources provide pragmatic details on aspects of constructing a poster (e.g., durable poster materials, display layout and format, logistics of color selection, photos and graphics). Some sites provide information on using PowerPoint and creating posters for online purposes. These sites are contained in Box 16.3. Listed below are some fail-safe suggestions for avoiding poster presentation disasters.

---

box 16.3

Helpful Websites for Creating Poster Presentations

1. *Creating Effective Poster Presentations: An Effective Poster.* This website provides succinct information on the construction of posters akin to listing of "helpful hints." Background information is presented on the rationale and benefits for considering poster sessions as an option for professional presentation.
   http://www.ncsu.edu/project/posters/NewSite/
2. *Creating Medical Poster Presentations.* This website provides information about poster sessions for medical and scientific presentations using PowerPoint software.
   http://office.microsoft.com/en-us/powerpoint/HA012265841033.aspx
3. *Designing Effective Posters.* This website provides the most comprehensive and detailed information about poster sessions of any website. Jeff Radel, Department of Occupational Therapy Education, University of Kansas Medical Center, provides detailed information on every aspect of creating a poster, from formatting the poster title to transport and storage. This website is really a must.
   http://www.kumc.edu/SAH/OTEd/jradel/Poster_Presentations/PstrStart.html
4. *The University of Medicine and Dentistry of New Jersey Center for Teaching Excellence.* This website contains numerous links to other websites to provide comprehensive information on the development of poster presentations. It is an excellent resource for obtaining information on all aspects of poster presentations.
   http://cte.umdnj.edu/career_development/career_posters.cfm

Develop a timeline that accommodates unanticipated delays in processing over which one has no
control (e.g., use of graphic designer, photo processing).

Back up files as the poster is being developed so that no data are lost through computer
malfunctioning or as a result of a virus.

Determine the best method for transporting the poster on an airplane or by train because it may
have to be carried to the passenger section and stored overhead. Sending the poster risks not
having it arrive for your presentation.

Bring a computer file of the poster, just in case it gets lost, damaged, or destroyed in transit.

Ensure the security of the poster if staying in a hotel room by properly labeling it in case it is
inadvertently misplaced.

Remember to bring materials (e.g., masking tape, double-sided tape, pins) to display the poster.

Have handouts available for colleagues who want additional information on the literature review,
methodology, and references.

Disseminating Evidence Through Small Group Presentations

Evidence-Based Grand Rounds

Grand rounds can serve as a major forum for evidence-based presentations. Very often, departments within tertiary care and academic settings will host grand rounds. Grand rounds are
forums designed for clinicians to speak directly to their colleagues on topics that are innovative (cutting edge) or that call for new approaches to care. Usually, speakers present empirically based answers to clinical practice questions, typically findings from their own or others'
studies or policy updates with clinical implications for staff. Grand rounds usually consist of
formal oral presentations accompanied by audiovisual slides or video presentations. Generally, a
question-and-answer period follows the speaker's presentation.

Just as there are journal club websites (discussed in more detail later in the chapter), grand
rounds presentations can be found on numerous Internet websites. Internet grand rounds are another
setting for experts to share evidence-based information with colleagues on a particular topic. The
Internet grand rounds topic may be presented or reviewed by numerous clinical experts, enabling
users to e-mail questions that can later be posted on the website. The advantages of Internet usage
are the widespread access that is available to users, the ability to combine the perspectives and expertise of many clinical specialists, and the convenience for the user. Additionally, users are not bound
by the time constraints of real-time meetings, enabling them to participate at their own convenience.

Evidence-Based Clinical Rounds

Evidence-based clinical rounds, smaller in scope than grand rounds, are an effective medium through
which to present evidence to guide clinical practice changes as well as intimately involve clinical
staff in the process. Evidence-based clinical rounds have been used very successfully as part of the
Advancing Research and Clinical practice through close Collaboration (ARCC) Model (Melnyk &
Fineout-Overholt, 2002). One or a few clinicians will do the following in preparation for these rounds:

Identify a clinical question (e.g., What is the most effective medication to decrease pain in postsurgical cardiac patients?).

Conduct a systematic search for the evidence to answer the clinical question.

Critically appraise the evidence found.

Recommend guidelines for practice changes based on the evidence.

These clinicians then present the information that they gathered and make recommendations for clinical practice to their colleagues, based on the evidence, in the form of an oral
presentation during a more casual session than the more formal, larger grand rounds.

Brief Consultations

Ultimately, the goal of excellence in clinical care is to integrate evidence into clinical practice as a standard of care for *all* patients under *all* circumstances. This level of practice can only be achieved by fostering the organizational environment to support it. As one expert has stated, "hallway consultations," meaning the consultation that occurs informally between colleagues in the hallways about patients, are an "on-the-ground" approach to facilitating discussion about nursing care interventions that are evidence-based. These are excellent opportunities for collegial consultation and instruction (Coralli, 2006).

Disseminating Evidence Through podcast/vodcast Presentations

More recent technological developments have enabled the use of podcasts or vodcasts for the purpose of disseminating information to targeted audiences (Savel, Goldstein, Perencevich, et al., 2007). A podcast is an instructional media that can be used "to deliver a Web-based audio broadcast via an RSS feed over the Internet to subscribers" (Dictionary.com, 2009). A vodcast (terms such as *video podcast* or *vidcast* are used as well) refers to "the online delivery of video on demand, video clip content via Atom or RSS enclosures" (Reference.com, 2009).

The advantage of podcasts/vodcasts is that the presentation, whether in audio or video format, can be archived on a designated website for later convenient use by the learner (Abe, 2007; Skiba, 2006). For example, journal clubs and presentations can be audio- and video-taped for later use for those unable to attend at the scheduled time. Podcasts and vodcasts are relatively simple to access by users and inexpensive to produce (Rowell, Corl, Johnson, et al., 2006). PowerPoint presentations can be integrated into podcasts as a means of accompanying the audiotapes (Jham, Duraes, Strassler, et al., 2008). Both podcasts and vodcasts can be downloaded to the user's own mobile device (e.g., iPods, BlackBerry, MP3 players; Abe, 2007).

Disadvantages of these web-based tools are that the user may not have the technology infrastructure for using it, and the extent to which it is known for its instructional purposes by intended audiences is limited. Additionally, unless an interactive feature is integrated into the podcast, the learning is primarily a passive instructional approach (Jham et al., 2008). Refer to Box 16.4 for a listing of websites that provide information on the development of podcasts and vodcasts.

---

box 16.4

Helpful Websites for Podcasts

The following websites provide guidance for developing podcasts:

- How to Create Your Own Podcasts-A Step by Step Tutorial
  http://radio.about.com/od/podcastin1/a/aa030805a.htm
- Learning in Hand-Create Podcasts
  http://learninginhand.com/podcasting/create.html
- Online Tools and Software for Creating Podcast Feeds and Posts
  http://radio.about.com/od/onlinepodcastcreation/Online_Tools_and_Software_For_Creating_Podcast_Feeds_and_Posts.htm
- How to Create a Podcast
  http://pharmacy.ucsf.edu/facultyandstaff/podcast/

An online clearinghouse of podcasts for higher education containing lectures, podcasts, and speeches is available at **http://ed-cast.org/default.aspx** (Skiba, 2006)

Disseminating Evidence Through Community Meetings

Individuals identified as experts in a particular area may be asked to present evidence-based information in a community setting. This type of presentation can be particularly challenging because community groups may include laypersons and the media, in addition to professionals. This requires that the speaker be able to address all members of the group in a way that is understandable to everyone. Before making the presentation, it is important to collaborate with community leaders about the nature of the content to be presented as well as to be culturally sensitive to the potential participants of the meeting. Tips for presenting to a mixed audience include the following:

Define all abbreviations and acronyms (e.g., the American College of Nurse Practitioners, rather than ACNP).

Provide definitions as you speak (e.g., ".... risk pool, that is, a group of individuals brought together to purchase insurance in order to spread the risk, or cost, among a larger group of people....").

Avoid off-hand remarks that could be misinterpreted or misquoted by any media present. Stick with the facts as you know them or offer your professional, educated opinion when asked.

Offer to answer individual questions after the session so that those who might be embarrassed to ask a question before a large group will have the opportunity to question the speaker privately.

Begin the presentation with a general overview of its purpose, followed by a review of the major points or findings.

When offering examples, consider the potentially mixed nature of the audience and offer exemplars that all members can understand.

Allow ample time for questions and answers as well as discussion of the topic.

The use of slides and corresponding handouts also is useful in keeping all participants engaged and focused on the presentation (Bergren, 2000; Evans, 2000; "Teaching with Slides," 2003). In addition, referral to relevant websites and articles is always appreciated. Make sure you check all website referrals to assure that the link is active and the content appropriate.

Disseminating Evidence Through Hospital/Organization-Based and Professional Committee Meetings

Presenting evidence-based information to a committee of fellow professionals can be a stressful and intimidating experience. Adequate preparation is again the key for ensuring success. Anticipate questions that may reflect not only the information that is being presented but also historical information, because not everyone in the group will be aware of all of the relevant history surrounding a particular issue. Consider the following:

Why is the group interested in the topic?

What is the history of the issue in the particular institution?

Has there been any controversy surrounding the issue that may interfere with the presentation? If so, should it be addressed in an open manner before the presentation begins?

Are there some members of the group who may be more resistant than others to the information presented? If it is possible to learn more about concerns ahead of time, they can be addressed more readily in the meeting.

Is there any related information that may need to be discussed during the presentation, and does the presenter have adequate knowledge in the related area?

Is this a group whose meetings are informal, or does the group maintain formal rules during its meeting process?

The most important pieces of information needed before beginning to prepare for a committee presentation are

- What is the goal of the presentation?
- Who is the audience?
- How much time will there be to share information?

Whoever invites the presenter to the meeting or is responsible for serving as chairperson should be able to describe the anticipated number of attendees, the disciplines represented, and the relevance of the information for the group. Using the questions above as a basis for exploration should result in adequate information about the audience.

Committee meetings are usually tightly scheduled with little opportunity to go beyond the allotted time. Therefore, it is important to be able to provide key information within the time-frame allowed. In addition, if the meeting is held in a hospital or other similar facility, staff members may come in and out of the meeting when they are answering pages or attending to patient care responsibilities. This movement in and out of the room can be distracting and unnerving for the speaker, so it is important to prepare mentally for this possibility and plan to focus on the topic and the members who remain at the meeting. In addition, anticipate that some latecomers will ask for information that has already been presented. The best approach is to provide the information in a brief manner and offer to discuss it more fully after the meeting.

After a brief introduction as to its relevance for the group, the presentation can generally follow the format for a journal article on an EBP topic, including

Clinical question

Search for evidence

Critical appraisal

Implications for practice

Evaluation (if the practice change had been implemented)

This should be followed by a period of discussion as to the utility of the information for the committee or the facility.

Disseminating Evidence Through Journal Clubs

The concept of journal clubs has evolved considerably over the years, especially with the use of the Internet as a vehicle for scholarly exchange. One only has to access the World Wide Web by using a search engine with the key words *journal club* to find a proliferation of online journal clubs, most of which are evidence-based in focus, and appreciate the widespread recognition of journal clubs as a conduit for the dissemination of knowledge on clinical care. Whether journal clubs are offered on website or via the Internet, they serve as another mechanism for disseminating the best evidence on which to base nursing practice. Journal clubs are a venue for use by nurses to improve their clinical practice and patient outcomes. It may be used as a strategy to foster the goals of the healthcare organization's nursing department to obtain magnet status (Rich, 2006).

On-Site Journal Clubs

Journal clubs provide an opportunity for clinicians to share and learn about evidence-based approaches at their work sites. An advanced-level clinician can serve as the leader and mentor of a journal club until other colleagues achieve the knowledge and skills necessary to lead a group. The success of the journal club will depend on several factors:

Expertise of the advanced-level clinician in selecting an appropriate review article together with other supporting articles that provide substantial sources of evidence

Organizational resources to facilitate the activities of the journal club, such as access to online bibliographic resources that include evidence-based reviews (e.g., Cochrane Controlled Trials Register)

Participation by motivated colleagues/staff

A journal club is typically led by an advanced-level clinician who understands research design, methods, and statistics. This clinician serves not only as the discussion facilitator, but also as an educator because it is likely that colleagues will ask additional contextual information (Rich, 2006). Questions from journal club participants typically focus on the type of research design used, sample selection criteria, instrumentation, and statistical analyses. Therefore, it is essential that the journal club leader have the knowledge to answer these types of questions adequately. Additionally, in order to be effective, the journal club leader needs facilitator skills to encourage members of the club to participate as well as to feel comfortable and supported in sharing input. The facilitation skills for an effective journal club leader include

Actively listening to questions asked

Using open-ended questions to facilitate discussion

Avoiding the appearance of preference or bias in responding to questions by stating that a particular question is "good" unless equivalent affirming comments are made about all questions

Clearly communicating messages about the purpose and expectations for the club

Coming to the meeting well prepared and organized to conduct the meeting smoothly (e.g., ensuring room availability and setup, as well as a sufficient number of handouts and other materials)

Monitoring the flow of discussion to ensure that it is focused on the topic

Interceding when conversation "drift" occurs, redirecting the conversation back to the topic (e.g., "getting back to our point," "as was said before," and "we were talking about …")

Reinforcing responses to questions asked by members with affirming comments in order to encourage group participation

Summarizing major points at the end of the session before concluding the meeting

The journal club leader will most likely have the responsibility for selecting the journal article to be discussed by the group participants (Rich, 2006). This article should meet the journal club criteria for an evidence-based presentation and should be appropriate to the clinical practice of the staff. Selected articles should be studies or evidence reviews that are current, use valid and reliable instrumentation, have an adequate number of subjects, and use a research design appropriate for the research question or purpose. Although there may be variations in the format for the journal club, such as including content on the "how tos" for critiquing research articles

(Dyckoff, Manela, & Valente, 2004), the standard process for the discussion of articles, focusing on the key point and not a reread of the articles, is as follows:

Study objectives/hypotheses

Design and methods, including the setting wherein the study was conducted (e.g., in the community, in the intensive care unit, in outpatient clinic, or in the home) as well as instruments used along with their validity and reliability for the sample studied

Data analyses, with rationale for the specific tests used

Findings, specifically in terms of the significance or nonsignificance of the findings, paying careful attention to whether the study had a large enough sample size with power to detect significant findings

Conclusions of the study with clinical implications, such as the clinical procedure related to aseptic management of long-term gastrostomy tubes

Efficient critical appraisal of the study, including its strengths and limitations as well as applicability to practice (e.g., clinicians might be hesitant to change their practice based on the findings from one study that had a very small number of subjects)

Journal clubs are held at regularly scheduled times and locations, enabling participants to anticipate meetings. Articles for the journal club should be distributed to members well in advance so that members can read and "digest" the material. Distribution of forthcoming meetings and identification of the topic to be discussed by e-mail via the institution's targeted mailing list is a convenient and time-efficient method (Dyckoff et al., 2004).

Online Journal Clubs

The Internet provides additional resources and opportunities for developing other types of journal clubs for healthcare professionals. There are numerous online bibliographic databases that can be accessed for obtaining evidence-based answers to questions or accessing substantive articles for a journal club.

For example, an advanced-level clinician on a pediatric unit of a major tertiary medical center wants to find a high-quality article on pediatric pain for next month's journal club. The most effective strategy for finding this article would be to access one of several online evidence-based review databases because the most current and rigorously reviewed studies can be found there. These databases include the ACP Journal Club, Evidence-Based Medicine Reviews, **Cochrane Database of Systematic Reviews**, Cochrane Controlled Trials Register, and Database of Abstracts of Reviews of Effectiveness (DARE). Searching these databases for "pediatric pain" reveals the five citations listed in Box 16.5. Based on the needs of the clinical staff, the clinician selects the article published by Jeffs (2007) because it addresses specific clinical practice issues related to pediatric pain.

There are online journal clubs that incorporate the technological advantages available with the Internet. This format enables individual users to access the journal club website at times convenient to personal work schedules, interests, and learning style. Website journal clubs, although highly individualized, are similar to the group meeting format in that an article is reviewed for its applicability for clinical practice. The difference with the online format is the process, which varies from site to site (e.g., a critical review of a clinical trial initiated by a contributing author and reviewed by website editors, individual efforts of a website editor with feedback from its users). Several online evidence-based websites are listed in Box 16.6.

Additionally, online professional journals may offer a journal club feature enabling feedback from readers. For example, the *American Journal of Critical Care* offers a supplemental section at the end of selected articles for the reader, enabling the review and critique of the study as a preliminary step in considering its application to practice. Discussion of its applicability with other journal readers is available through an online discussion using electronic letters (Kiekkas, Sakellanropoulos, Brkalaki, et al., 2008).

---

box 16.5

Results of a Search on "Pediatric Pain" in Evidence-Based Review Databases

Stanford, E. A., Chambers, C. T., & Craig, K. D. (2006, January). The role of developmental factors in predicting young children's use of a self-report scale for pain. [Journal Article. Randomized Controlled Trial. Research Support, Non-U.S. Gov't] *Pain, 120*(1–2),16–23.

Jeffs, D. A. (2007, July). A pilot study of distraction for adolescents during allergy testing. [Journal Article. Randomized Controlled Trial. Research Support, Non-U.S. Gov't] *Journal for Specialists in Pediatric Nursing: JSPN, 12*(3),170–185.

Hadden, K. L., & von Baeyer., C. L. (2005, March–April). Global and specific behavioral measures of pain in children with cerebral palsy. [Clinical Trial. Journal Article. Randomized Controlled Trial. Research Support, Non-U.S. Gov't] *The Clinical Journal of Pain, 21*(2), 140–146.

Robins, P. M., Smith, S. M., Glutting, J. J., & Bishop, C. T. (2005, July–August). A randomized controlled trial of a cognitive-behavioral family intervention for pediatric recurrent abdominal pain. [Clinical Trial. Journal Article. Randomized Controlled Trial. Research Support, Non-U.S. Gov't] *Journal of Pediatric Psychology, 30*(5):397–408.

Sinha, M., Christopher, N. C., Fenn, R., & Reeves, L. (2006, April). Evaluation of non-pharmacologic methods of pain and anxiety management for laceration repair in the pediatric emergency department. [Journal Article. Randomized Controlled Trial. Research Support, Non-U.S. Gov't] *Pediatrics, 117*(4),1162–1168.

Institutional-related journal clubs benefit from incorporating a process for evaluation. This can be done informally at the conclusion of each of the on-site meetings or at a predetermined end-point for the online sessions. Evaluation forms also can be used to evaluate the perceived benefit of journal clubs. There are numerous disadvantages and advantages in using online journal clubs. The user does not have the benefit of hearing the views of colleagues, which may limit learning regarding others' own clinical areas of expertise, critical thinking, and professional attitudes and values. Having the opportunity to participate in shared discourse on professional issues is an important activity that promotes group cohesiveness and understanding, often fostering teamwork and group morale. Some learners may benefit more from the group discussion format because it is more suitable to their learning style. Likewise, other staff members may prefer the online format because it is more convenient and accessible.

Journal club meetings enable the moderator to model professional behavior for other staff members. Professional development is an ongoing process, and the journal club is yet another opportunity for leaders to model the importance of using evidence for nursing practice, to demonstrate ways of discussing practice issues in a nonthreatening venue, and to create expectations for professional practice. Depending on a number of factors, such as website design and personnel resources, the online format may be more economical and feasible.

Disseminating Evidence Through Publishing

Many publishing options are available for individuals who are interested in sharing evidence-based information with their colleagues. Typically, writing a journal article or contributing a chapter to a book is the first idea that comes to mind when publishing is considered. Publications

---

box 16.6

Examples of Websites Containing Evidence-Based Practice Information

1. University of Minnesota, Evidenced-Based Nursing (EBN). This website provides a primer on EBN. Information is provided on what EBN is, models of evidence-based projects, barriers to EBN, evaluating the quality of nursing research, and links to nursing research journals and EBN websites.
    http://evidence.ahc.umn.edu/ebn.htm
2. Oncology Nursing Society, Evidenced-Based Practice (EBP) Research Center. This website provides a number of resources on EBP and its application to the specialty of oncology nursing practice. PowerPoint presentations on EBP can be easily accessed.
    http://onsopcontent.ons.org/toolkits/evidence/
3. New York University: Welcome to Nursing Resources: A Self-Paced Tutorial and Refresher. This online tutorial provides an overview of the online research and evidence-based resources available for nurses. As the title implies, this tutorial provides introductory information for nurses who are unfamiliar with these new approaches to professional nursing practice. Information is also provided on nursing journals.
    http://library.nyu.edu/research/health/tutorial/
4. John Hopkins Welch Medical Library. This website is a gateway to a number of nursing resources that include nursing evidence-based sites.
    http://www.welch.jhu.edu/internet/nursing.html
5. The Center for the Advancement of Evidence-Based Practice at Arizona State University College of Nursing and Health Innovation. This website contains a variety of resources on EBP.
    http://www.nursingandhealth.edu/caep/index.htm

---

of this sort may appear overwhelming in terms of time, effort, and lack of prior writing experience. However, there are many other opportunities and options available for individuals who find themselves entertaining ideas about publishing.

Publishing experience can be gained by taking on less ambitious projects, such as serving on a publishing-type of committee at work or through a professional organization. Serving on these committees enables professionals to network with and learn from each other about the logistics and mechanics of publishing. Although the specific purpose of the committee may vary slightly (e.g., a newsletter committee, a publication committee), these committees are not necessarily designed for creating or fostering collective writing efforts. Publication committees may serve as panels to review publications submitted by prospective authors to an association's newsletter or journal. Other committees may provide oversight to the production of professional materials to ensure that the association or organization's affiliation is properly represented.

Regardless of the specific type of publication committee, membership enables individuals to learn through a variety of skill-enhancing efforts on how to write and professionally publish. Ideally, seasoned committee members can serve as mentors for less experienced committee members in acquiring these skills. For example, reviewing the written work of other colleagues enables one to learn through the editing process what constitutes both a well-written manuscript and one not so well written. Writing a manuscript is not only about sharing expertise concerning evidence-based approaches, it is also about learning how to present information in a manner that enhances readability for professional audiences. Reading drafts in progress is an indirect method of learning to write. Serving on evidence-based committees provides another prospect for learning important precursor publishing skills. It is through committee participation that professionals learn the clinical framework for the organization of content and practice. Committee discussion of evidence-based issues and approaches provides an understanding of the processes involved in EBP that include

Posing the burning clinical question
Searching for the best and latest evidence
Critically appraising and synthesizing the evidence
Clinically implementing a practice change
Evaluating the change

Also, introduction to role models who have published can influence those who have not because it exposes individuals to the possibility that this new professional effort is possible.

Finding a Mentor

For individuals who have had limited publishing experience, finding a mentor is beneficial. This mentor can be found anywhere (e.g., at school or work, on the Internet, with a professional organization, and, in some instances, by contacting a nursing editor). A mentor can guide the novice writer through the process, starting with an idea for a topic and leading to the actual writing and submission process. It is important that the mentor selected be an individual who possesses sufficient prior publication experience.

There may be opportunities to collaborate on a joint writing project with a colleague with publication experience. The optimal circumstances for convening a writing team are to locate a co-writer in the same or geographically convenient community. Although the Internet has facilitated the availability of working with colleagues in distant locations, the first foray into a writing project with another colleague is best achieved with someone in close proximity. Real-time meetings involving personal contact are a prerequisite for the teaming of professionals with disparate writing experiences. This is yet another form of mentoring with extended hands-on involvement (Oermann et al., 2006).

Although experience and expertise are important, so is compatibility (e.g., writing style, temperament, and personality). A colleague who has a style of interaction that is uncomfortable for the novice is a significant detriment. Those who publish must devote extra time and effort beyond their usual workloads; therefore, engaging in an effort that is unpleasant and literally painful is likely to be short lived. Persistence with a specific publishing effort is likely to be brief if these types of negative circumstances exist. Publishing should be both a professionally rewarding and a fun experience (Farella, 2002; Fetter, 1999; Fitzgerald, 2000; Sullivan, 2002).

Generating the Idea

A component of getting started with publishing an evidence-based paper is determining the topic. Generating the topic for publication is based on an individual's area of expertise, the clinical question that arises from clinical practice, and the availability of resources to support the initial curiosity and attention to the idea. An idea for an evidence-based publication may have been germinating for some time before it is fully acknowledged as a potential publication topic. For example, a clinician may have noticed that elderly residents in assisted living facilities have extended periods of confusion following hospital admissions. This clinical interest may lead the clinician to search the literature for information on the phenomenon and to find evidence for instituting new interventions. The experience prompts the clinician to believe that other colleagues would benefit from learning about these practices. As a result, the clinician decides to write an article for a gerontology journal.

Brainstorming is another approach whereby ideas are generated through a free-association process. This process is enhanced if it can be done with other colleagues. The impetus stimulated with the rapid exchange of ideas can result in many more ideas that would otherwise not have been identified (Fitzgerald, 2000; Oermann, 1999, 2001; Pelletier, Miracle, Thom, et al., 2002).

A motivation for generating an evidence-based publication may be predicated on the conviction that current practice is inadequate to meet patient needs. For example, health outcome data may demonstrate the need for improvement in selected patient outcomes. A manuscript describing an evidence-based intervention to improve a particular set of patient outcomes is an example of a publication designed to improve both professional practice and patient outcomes (Mason & Street, 2006).

Planning the Manuscript

Once an idea or a set of ideas has been "discovered," the prospective author needs to sketch out a plan on how this initial idea or concept can be developed into a manuscript. For evidence-based papers, the formats for writing them do not vary significantly because there is a specified order for presentation of the content; the differences are based more on style rather than substance. Although publication formats vary according to the technical specifications and editorial philosophy of the journal, the standard format for an evidence-based manuscript is as follows:

- *Title page*: This is the first page of the manuscript and contains the article's title and all of the authors' names, job titles, affiliations, and contact information. If there are many authors, the corresponding author is indicated. The manuscript title should be succinct, and the key words in the title should be well known and accessible for content bibliographic searches. For example, if the author intends to write an evidenced-based manuscript about adolescents, having the term *children* in the title would be misleading for readers.
- *Abstract*: An abstract contains a brief summary or synopsis of the article. Summaries indicate to the reader whether it is a research or clinical article. The abstract also identifies the major themes or findings and clinical implications. It is important that the abstract adheres to the technical specifications of the journal (Happell, 2008).
- *Introduction*: The introduction of the manuscript should be written in a succinct manner and should not extend beyond a few paragraphs. It contains information about the purpose of the article, the importance of the topic for the professional audience, and brief supporting evidence as to why this topic is important. Supporting evidence might include prevalence data or demonstration of need.
- *Manuscript narrative*: This "middle section" of the manuscript will differ according to the type of evidence-based paper that is written, journal guidelines, and editorial philosophy. It is useful to select a couple of examples of articles published in the journal targeted for the submission to obtain a clear idea of how the narrative can be developed. Obviously, the articles published in the targeted journal represent successful submissions.
- *Conclusions and clinical implications*: The conclusions of the research evidence are presented in a summary form to emphasize the essence of the narrative discussion. For professionals who are accustomed to reading clinically oriented articles, the format of evidence-based papers may be unfamiliar and more difficult to follow. The conclusion section enables the reader to locate the information succinctly if the previous discussion has not been sequenced clearly. The clinical implications section informs the reader about how this evidence can be applied to clinical practice. As importantly, the evidence substantiates the rationale for its use in clinical practice.

Adopting a Positive Attitude

> *Your living is determined not so much by what life brings*
> *to you as by the attitude you bring to life; not so much by*
> *what happens to you as by the way your mind looks at what*
> *happens.*
>
> *John Homer Miller*

Having a positive attitude toward professional publication, especially for novice prospective authors, is an absolute must. When an individual decides to write professionally, one needs to develop a resolute attitude that the publication task will be completed, no matter what problems or challenges are encountered, because there are likely to be a number of them. Typically, authors have the unusual experience of engaging in a very solitary activity that is undertaken by literally hundreds of thousands of people. Yet, there are very few opportunities that enable authors to communicate with one another about the highs and lows of the writing experience (Heinrich, 2007). Occasionally, one will read a magazine or newspaper article about the process of writing. In 2001, Stephen King wrote a book entitled simply *On Writing* that provides insight into his life as a writer and what he has learned along the way. However, most times authors toil at their computers, writing and deleting what they have written and rewriting until the words on the page seem to make sense of the ideas they want to convey to their readers.

It is important for writers to remember that their receipt of request for revisions and rejection letters is the norm for all authors. It is essential not to take the comments personally and put aside the emotional reaction to scholarly criticism. An objective perspective of reviewing comments both negatively and positively is important to writing the revised manuscript draft (Winters, Walker, Larson, et al., 2006).

> *You measure the size of the accomplishment by the obstacles*
> *you had to overcome to reach your goals.*
>
> *Booker T. Washington*

For many authors, uncertainty and self-doubt can interfere unduly with the process of writing, resulting in an unfinished manuscript that languishes on the computer's hard drive. For others, perhaps a harsh critique is mailed to them after the review has been completed, releasing a barrage of self-doubt and shame. For some individuals, the feedback is traumatic and demoralizing. Regrettably, some individuals are unwilling to subject themselves to this harrowing experience again. However, it is important to know and appreciate that even the most successful and prominent authors have been subjected to their fair share of rejections. A major difference between those who are successful and those who are not is *persistence*. Persistence is one of the keys to getting work published.

> *Criticism, like rain, should be gentle enough to nourish a*
> *man's growth without destroying his roots.*
>
> *Frank A. Clark*

Another major factor that contributes to writing success is organization. That is, the process of getting an evidence-based publication submitted and accepted is dependent on creating the circumstances for it to occur because it does not just happen. The organizational approach to getting thoughts down on paper in an acceptable professional format will require allocation of time periods for writing and achievement of the steps described in this section on publishing. Therefore, it is useful to remember the following (Wills, 2000):

- Work on eliminating negative self-talk (e.g., "I can't do this" or "This paper will never get published").
- Remember that every author at some point in his or her career had to start at the beginning.
- Negative manuscript reviews should never be personalized, because almost everyone has received at least one.
- Some individuals should not serve as reviewers as their critical perspectives are demeaning rather than helpful.
- Manuscript reviews may reflect mixed views wherein one reviewer evaluates the paper favorably in contrast to another who is critical of the manuscript.
- There is a collective experience of feeling confident, unsure, hesitant, weary, excited, bored, and tired that all authors can relate to with writing for publication.
- Authors who are successful do not take no for an answer easily; they are able to brush aside criticism, look at it objectively, and revise the paper accordingly, resulting in a much improved document.
- Setting realistic goals for initiating and completing a writing task is essential to prevent the disappointment of unrealistic expectations and possibly abandoning the project entirely.
- Developing a plan that specifies a concrete course of action with attainable benchmarks of accomplishment enables an author to feel satisfaction associated with achieving a stated goal.

Deciding What to Publish

Professional publications on EBP can be found everywhere. The significance of its influence is demonstrated by the number of publications that can be found through bibliographic searches, the number of professional journals that regularly feature columns on EBP, and other publications that address the topic exclusively, such as this book and the journal *Evidence-Based Nursing*.

One of the first decisions an author makes in beginning the writing process is the choice of what to write and how it will be written. There are numerous opportunities for publishing that vary from something as straightforward as a letter to the editor to the complex writing project of editing a major nursing textbook. Here is a listing of the wide range of publishing options:

- Letters to the editor
- Commentaries
- Books
- Continuing education reviews
- Chapters
- NCLEX questions
- Articles
- Evidence-based clinical practice guidelines
- Newsletter inserts
- Standards of care
- Book and media reviews
- Policy Briefs

Authors with limited publishing experience may want to begin with manageable writing endeavors, such as a media review or contributing a chapter to a textbook. Students, under the tutelage of their instructors, may be encouraged to revamp their written class assignment into a manuscript for journal submission. Well-established authors, journal editors, and other professional leaders continually search for aspiring authors who have the motivation, professional expertise, and willingness to engage in the publishing process.

Selecting a Journal

The format and content of a manuscript targeted for journal submission will be dictated by the editorial guidelines and technical specifications of the journal. The author must first target a journal that corresponds to the subject matter of the manuscript. Authors intending to submit evidence-based papers will need to apprise themselves of the following journal criteria before making the decision to submit to a particular journal (Hundley, 2002):

- Is the journal peer-reviewed?
- What is the profile of the journal's readership?
- What is the turnaround period for review?
- What is the "in press" period (i.e., from time of acceptance to publication)?
- What are the technical specifications?

Manuscripts submitted to **peer-reviewed journals** are critiqued by a team of reviewers who have expertise in the subject matter of the paper. Any identification of the manuscript's author(s) is removed and, likewise, the anonymity of the reviewers is maintained during the review process. This type of review process is known as the **blind review**, meaning that neither the authors nor the reviewers know the identities of each other. It is believed that the blind review process is the most objective and fair way of judging the significance, technical competence, and contribution to the professional literature.

Peer-reviewed journals publish more rigorously reviewed manuscripts than those reviewed by other means. Generally, most authors prefer to have their manuscripts published in these journals for this reason. Manuscripts published in regularly featured columns of peer-reviewed journals may not be peer-reviewed. Authors need to ascertain this fact before submission. Another useful criterion to use in considering the choice for journal submission is the readership profile. Although the style and format of articles published by journals will be obvious to the author in terms of the type of article (e.g., data-based, clinical, or policy-oriented papers), having other editorial information is useful in terms of understanding the need to insert additional narrative on research methodology or clinical implications (Carroll-Johnson, 2001; DeBehnke, Kline, & Shih, 2001).

In most instances, information on the review process (e.g., the review period time frame and technical specifications) can be found in the "information for authors" section in each journal. Many authors are concerned about the timeliness in which manuscripts are published. Authors may worry that a research paper that has undergone a lengthy review process will not then be published in a timely manner. Concerns also exist regarding the delay in publishing an "in press" manuscript because a lengthy time frame will substantially slow the dissemination of research findings. Answers to these questions can be easily obtained from journal editors. There are currently numerous websites for nursing journals wherein technical specifications are listed, editorial philosophy is posted, and hyperlinks are available to the journal's publisher for convenient access (American Psychological Association [APA], 2002). The journal's technical specifications include the following:

- Page length
- Reference format (e.g., APA)
- Margins, font style, and size
- Use of graphics, photos, and figures
- Face page and author identifying information
- Electronic version and software

Developing the Manuscript Concept

Developing the concept for the manuscript is contingent on the author's area of clinical expertise and the need for evidence because there is a dearth of accessible information on which to base clinical practice. A clinician may want to share information with colleagues about an innovative intervention or implementation of an exemplary program, or may report the findings of testing a new approach to providing clinical services. There is an urgent need to publish articles on the search for and critical appraisal of evidence as healthcare providers increasingly desire to base their practices on empirically tested approaches.

As the author proceeds with the process of refining the concept for writing an article on EBP, the perusal of the literature will assist in distillation of the topic into an organizational outline. Reviewing the literature will enable the author to gain an understanding of how to develop this publication uniquely and in a manner that contributes to the body of evidence-based nursing literature (Betz, 2008; Farella, 2002; Siwek, Gourlay, Slawson, et al., 2002; Webb, 2002).

Review of the Literature

Throughout the discussion on methods for disseminating evidence, such as journal clubs and public presentations, the Internet was identified as a technology resource. This is also true for publishing efforts. Use of online bibliographic databases enables writers to conduct more comprehensive and better literature searches. The following bibliographic databases will be useful when proceeding with the literature search for writing evidence-based articles and reports:

- Cochrane Database of Systematic Reviews (interdisciplinary)
- Cochrane Controlled Trials Register (interdisciplinary)
- ACP Journal Club (interdisciplinary)
- Evidence-Based Medicine Reviews (interdisciplinary)
- DARE (interdisciplinary)
- Cumulative Index of Nursing and Allied Health Literature (CINAHL, a nursing and allied health literature database that contains international journals from these disciplines)
- MEDLINE (a medical literature database of international medical, nursing, and allied health journals that contains primarily medical journals and selected nursing and allied health journals that have met the criteria for inclusion)
- Google Scholar

In conducting a literature review preliminary to writing a manuscript, a few guidelines should be followed. References cited in a manuscript should be recent, meaning those published within the past 3–5 years. In some professions, it may be difficult to find current citations from the literature, thereby necessitating accessing the interdisciplinary literature representing not only health-related disciplines but also non–health-related disciplines (e.g., education, job development, and rehabilitation, to name a few). There are classic references, older than the 3–5 years time frame, from any field that should be included in a publication because these are seminal works on which subsequent publications are based and cannot be ignored.

An author will have concluded his or her search for evidence when the **saturation level** of research has been reached. The saturation level is achieved once the author no longer finds any new references, but instead, is familiar and knowledgeable with the literature. Clinicians who author evidence-based articles will rely heavily on empirically based articles as they are searching for evidence. Authors will be less likely to include clinically oriented articles other than to demonstrate the relevance to clinical practice, such as the prevalence of falls in the elderly. Textbooks should be used sparingly in evidence-based publications unless the books are written on highly specialized topics and are a compilation of perspectives from experts in the field (Heinrich, 2002).

Developing a Timeline

Healthcare professionals are well acquainted with developing and adhering to a work plan that identifies benchmarks of achievement. Having a work plan specifies in a concrete fashion the necessary tasks the author must undertake to complete the writing goal. The greater the level of specificity, the better the "roadmap" the author will have for reaching his or her goal. Together with the identified tasks, *realistic* timelines should be listed along with strategies for keeping on track with accomplishing the steps of the writing project. A writing project timeline might look like the one listed below:

- Operationalize the idea/select a topic—June 1
- Formulate the Outline—June 15
- Locate journals/author guidelines—July 15
- Survey the literature—September 15
- Develop the first draft—November 15
- Review/proofread—December 10
- Formulate revisions—January 8
- Submit—January 20

Writing Strategies

Content outlines for articles will vary according to the type of manuscript. The generic outline for an evidence-based article, as used in the ongoing evidence-based column in the journal *Pediatric Nursing*, follows this format:

- Introduction to the clinical problem
- The clinical question
- Search for the evidence (i.e., the search strategy used to find the evidence and the results)
- Presentation of the evidence
- Critical appraisal of the evidence with implications for future research
- Application to practice (i.e., based on the evidence reviewed, what should be implemented in clinical practice settings)
- Evaluation (includes outcomes of the practice change if they were measured).

Obviously, writing an article for publication involves much more than just following an outline. The writing process is a slow and tedious effort that is characterized by stops and starts, cutting and pasting, and the frequent use of the delete key. However, writers use several pragmatic tips to help them complete their writing projects. Writing begins with following the manuscript outline at whatever section that can be written, even if it means first writing the simpler portions of the manuscript (e.g., the conclusion and introduction). Placing words on paper is important to "priming the pump," meaning to write anything, even if initially the words are awkward sounding and stilted. Inspiration will not necessarily happen spontaneously.

Creativity is dependent on discipline and organizational techniques (Webb, 2002). These organizational techniques include the following:

- The manuscript outline should be followed as written. If the author discovers the narrative would be better written otherwise, the outline needs revision.
- Writing something is preferable to writing nothing. Awkward-sounding statements can always be edited and/or deleted. Initially, generating loose ideas that are difficult to couple with words can lead to more fluid thinking and word composition.
- Before completing a session of writing, leave notes within the document that can be used as prompts for the next writing activity. Leaving author notes ensures continuity with the train of thought from the last writing session and helps to facilitate recall and ease with the writing process.

- Write the paper anonymously, meaning there is no self-identification, although there may be exceptions in discussing particular programs. Use the same verb tense throughout, and avoid the use of passive voice. Note the major themes of paragraphs in the margins of the manuscript to discern the discussion sequencing, highlighting potential problems with organization.
- Avoid the use of *shoulds*, *musts*, and other words that sound opinionated and self-serving. Insert information that can be replicated and applied by others by avoiding the use of nonspecific terminology. For example, when discussing family support strategies, consider what more information can be shared with readers to enhance a clearer understanding of what is specifically meant.

Proofreading the Manuscript

If possible, the optimal proofreading strategy is to have colleagues or friends read the manuscript draft, including individuals who have expertise in the content area as well as those who possess no content expertise. Those without content expertise are specifically helpful in reading the manuscript for clarity, style, and grammatical errors. However, it is essential that whoever proofreads the draft be a good writer with the capacity to provide specific suggestions for editing purposes. Very often, faculty members whose students are writing for publication outside of their course assignments are willing to serve as proofreaders. It is important to provide colleagues with the guidelines for manuscript submission from the targeted journal so that they can review the paper with those guidelines in mind (e.g., formatting, length).

Authors can serve as their own proofreaders as well. Setting the manuscript draft aside for a week or two will create the distance needed to read it again with a set of "fresh eyes." In this manner, the author can read his or her own work more objectively and potentially single out the flaws with sentence structure, spelling, organization, and content. Once the proofreading is accomplished, the draft is revised based on collegial feedback and the author's own proofing.

Spell checking the document is an absolute must in proofing manuscripts. However, automatic spell checking is not enough in that it is not capable of detecting problems with some misspellings. The numbering of tables, graphics, and figures will need to be double-checked to ensure that they are properly matched with the sequence identified in the paper. The citation of references in the text is checked with those in the reference list for correct spelling, dates of publication, and referencing format. Other technical specifications (e.g., pagination, use of headers, margins, fonts) are reviewed to ensure conformity to those listed in the author guidelines. Permissions and transfer of copyright are included with the packet of materials that will be sent to the editorial office.

Once this process is completed, the manuscript can be submitted for review. The information for authors and/or the receipt from the editorial office will indicate the expected turnaround period for the manuscript review. If after a few weeks no feedback has been received, it is appropriate to e-mail or call the editorial office to inquire about the status of the review. As mentioned previously, it is important not to take feedback personally. An impassioned approach will serve the author well by moving beyond what might be stinging criticisms to revising the draft based on the reviewers' recommendations. It is at this juncture that the author needs to keep focused on what was and continues to be the original goal—to publish the paper and contribute to the professional literature on EBP (Ohler, 2002; Sullivan, 2002).

> *Remember that you never get a second chance to make a great first impression, so make the first submission of the manuscript as flawless as possible.*
>
> *Bernadette Melnyk*

Disseminating Evidence to Influence Health Policy

Politically, healthcare providers are in an enviable position to advocate for change because they are highly regarded and trusted by the American public. As a leading politician recently remarked to a colleague, "Political endorsements from state nursing organizations are one of the most important endorsements a politician seeks to obtain." In essence, such a testimonial is *evidence* of the potential influence that healthcare providers, individually and collectively, have to impact changes in policy and to be engaged in policy making. The key is not only recognizing this potential, but also actively taking advantage of opportunities that arise to be engaged in policy making at all levels of government and within professional organizations and service agencies.

Regrettably, opportunities to affect policy change may not be seized or recognized for their value and importance. A colleague recently witnessed the unpleasant exchange of a lawmaker's stern words directed to a nursing administrator from a local nursing education department. This nursing education administrator had been invited to provide testimony on the state's nursing shortage during a legislative hearing on this workforce crisis. Unfortunately, the nursing administrator was ill prepared and had not conducted the preparatory work necessary to offer legislative testimony. The legislator was angered with her lack of preparation and her inability to answer his questions about the state's nursing shortage and statewide nursing efforts to address this issue. Not only was this an example of inadequate professional preparation, but the circumstances also reflected negatively on the profession as a whole because the policy input on behalf of nurses was not heard.

These vignettes illustrate the continuum of possibilities for healthcare professionals to influence policy. As healthcare professionals learn to become more involved in policy making, they will be expected to integrate evidence as the basis for policy development. As policy makers, healthcare providers will be "at the table" with key stakeholders, citing evidence to improve healthcare resources and services for national and international populations. This section provides specific suggestions for integrating evidence in writing and other policy making efforts.

Writing Health Policy Issue Briefs

There is a growing recognition that current best evidence from research is needed to provide policy-related information to legislators in order to influence policy decisions that improve the quality of healthcare. Research that informs policy evaluates outcomes that are priorities for patients, healthcare providers, and payers, such as re/hospitalizations, quality of life, satisfaction, morbidities, mortality, and costs (Ross & Gross, 2009). In addition to conducting good policy research, there is an urgent need for healthcare professionals to write compelling policy briefs based on findings from sound research that legislators can readily understand. A legislator cannot bring forward legislation without having the necessary substantiation, based on various sources of evidence, as to the need or problem to be addressed (ESRC UK Centre for Evidence-Based Policy and Practice, 2001a, 2001b). However, findings from a survey with a random sample of legislators indicated that they are often overwhelmed by the huge volume of information they receive and need information provided to them to be concise and relevant to current debates (Sorian & Baugh, 2002). Unfortunately, research is often not published in readily digestible form for policy makers and their staff (Jennings, 2002).

One avenue for providing policy makers with sound evidence is by developing issue briefs (see Appendix G for a brief developed by the American Association of Colleges of Nursing to assist policy makers in drafting a bill to enhance the nursing work force). A policy brief is a powerful communication tool that provides current evidence, based on prevalence reports and research by scientists, and/or the opinion of experts that can lead to successful decision making about key policy issues (Jennings, 2002).

The key to developing issue briefs is to be succinct and direct in communicating with the intended audience. A well-written issue brief summarizes and clearly communicates to the reader the scope of the policy issue. The reader should be able to scan the document quickly and be able to comprehend the major aspects of the policy issue that is featured. Tips for organizing an issue brief include the following:

- Lead with a title on the masthead that clearly conveys the purpose.
- Identify the policy issue in the first sentence so that by the end of the opening paragraph, the reader knows the policy issue.
- Include background information that highlights the major features of the issue.
- Indicate the historical pattern of response to the problem in subsequent statements.
- Identify the inherent limitations as well as the problem and why it is still a problem.
- Include common opposing views and refute them as well.

Another format for writing policy briefs includes the following components:

- Clear statement of the issue
- Context and background of the issue/problem, most effectively captured in bullet format
- Options: Pros and cons of each recommendation listed
- Resources used to prepare the policy brief (Jennings, 2002)

An issues brief provides a systematic review and synthesis of literature based on the selected topic addressing the demonstrated clinical outcomes of interventions, cost-effectiveness, and applicability. As the supporting evidence is presented, the reader is led in a logical sequence through the presentation of information that enables a clear understanding of the need for policy change. The concluding remarks of this section provide the links between research, clinical practice, and policy making. It distills for the reader what has been done and how it can be applied to policy making, which may be difficult for the politician or stakeholders if they do not have the expertise to "point the way" (Box 16.7).

A review of the literature should be conducted differently for policy makers than for a research audience. The analysis is conducted not only with clinical knowledge in the area but also with an understanding of the practical implications for policy makers. Where the information was obtained (i.e., meaning the type of research studies reviewed and synthesized in the paper; expert opinion of researchers, clinicians, and experts) is incorporated in the brief. Once the strength of the available evidence has been analyzed, conclusions are made about where gaps in the literature exist for which further research is needed. The conclusion will be much briefer than those written for research or review of literature articles.

The healthcare provider who is involved in constructing a policy issue brief will emphasize the application for policy and practice. That is, what is being advocated for policy change? How will the policy result in a change for services, such as treatments, assessment approaches, and evaluation of intervention outcomes (e.g., What clinical outcomes for the target population are expected, such as improved health as evidenced by better cardiovascular status and a higher level of daily functioning)? Policy conclusions should delineate in detail the possible clinical implications. For example, implications would recommend

- Funding priorities in the treatment of chronic conditions
- Projected effects of funding cutbacks (e.g., a decrease in access to care and treatment)
- Longitudinal studies of various treatment approaches (e.g., hormone replacement therapy)
- Identification of actual and anticipated population outcomes

---

box 16.7

Typical Topics and Components of a Health Policy Issue Brief

Issues briefs are developed to address issues of interest to policy makers:

TYPICAL TOPICS

Healthcare financing
Risk/benefit ratio
Ways of reducing costs
Lower rates of mortality and improved morbidity
The role of technology in healthcare
Human resource needs
System change to improve services

TYPICAL COMPONENTS

Title

Background of the issue
Historical pattern of response to the problem
Inherent limitations and problems
Why it is still a problem

Review and synthesis of the literature
Clinical outcomes of interventions
Cost-effectiveness
Applicability
Policy implications

System changes
Services proposed
Population outcomes

In this way, issue briefs assist policy makers in understanding the evidence so that they can create legislation founded on the premise that policy change is based on good science and knowledge.

Design layout is a factor in conveying the message to the audience. Obvious requirements in design layout of policy briefs are to ensure that there are graphics to highlight the major propositions, problems, facts, and recommendations. Boxes that contain bulleted, succinct statements are effective. A pullout that defines terminology may be useful if the language is unfamiliar to readers. It is important to ensure the graphics are not too busy to be a distraction from the material presented. A case example to illustrate the nature of the problem or the implications of recommendations may be helpful. In a nutshell, policy makers are more likely to use information and evidence from a policy brief if

- The issue is clearly stated.
- The research evidence in the brief is focused
- The document can be skimmed quickly for salient points.
- It is synthesized, conclusion-oriented, and succinct (i.e., no more than 2–4 pages; Melnyk et al., 2003)

Use of graphics and visual pointers also enables the reader to navigate through the material easily. To add depth, briefs can be accompanied by other tools, such as slides, spreadsheets, links to articles, websites, and a list of key contacts (Melnyk et al., 2003).

Understanding the Target Audience

Daily, consumers are bombarded with new or breaking information about healthcare that includes promising new medications and treatments, hope for medical cures, and new treatment approaches. The barrage of information can be confusing for consumers. The conflicting information on hormone replacement therapy is an excellent example of the confusion women have experienced in understanding what might be the long-term effects of taking hormones. Policy experts have noted that the public seeks information that will enable them to better understand the disease pathophysiology and clinical application of that knowledge. In writing for a particular audience, the author needs to have an awareness of what type of information the audience is looking for and what would be considered most helpful.

Thoughtful and well-referenced issue briefs will be used by professional associations to assist them in the development of critical paths and practice guidelines. For example, the Agency for Healthcare Research and Quality (AHRQ) National Guidelines Clearinghouse contains more than 1,000 clinical practice guidelines that clinicians can access. The Agency for Healthcare Research and Quality (2007) is currently involved in supporting the implementation efforts of the State Child Health Insurance Program (SCHIP) by producing national performance measures through the Child Health Insurance Research Initiative for this national effort. Additionally, policy makers and other stakeholders can work with clinicians in suggesting topics for evidence review and development.

Writing in Understandable Language

The content and format of a policy brief will vary depending on the characteristics of the intended audience and whether the readers are primarily consumers, policy makers, or professionals. To illustrate, if an issue brief is written for a professional audience, the summary of the research evidence can be presented using research terminology. If issue briefs are written for consumer-oriented audiences (e.g., legislators), research terminology is altered for consumer comprehension. Generally speaking, the reading level for widespread consumer distribution should be for a sixth-grade reading level (using the Flesch Kineard Reading Level found on software tools to assess reading level is most helpful). For policy makers, the format needs to emphasize practical information that is easy to read. The content may also be adapted to the interests of individual legislators

Health literacy is now recognized as a major public health concern affecting Americans. The United States public health document entitled *Healthy People 2010* identifies the following objective to address this health literacy issue: *Improve the health literacy of persons with marginal or inadequate skills* (Objective 11.2; U.S. Department of Health and Human Services, 2000). As the national surveys and research studies demonstrate, the majority of the U.S. public have limited and inadequate understanding of the health information they receive to care for themselves and their families (Flores, Abreu, & Tomany-Korman, 2005; Kutner, Greenberg, Jin, et al., 2006; Leyva, Sharif, & Ozuah, 2005).

It is the writer's responsibility to apply or translate for the reader the synthesis of research for policy (i.e., how a particular practice can be improved and what the expected outcomes are for the targeted underserved populations). The issue brief author(s) need to keep in mind the targeted readership and the change that is being advocated. Based on these two primary criteria, the issue brief will be written in the style and format appropriate for the audience.

All knowledge must have local application in order to be used. Briefs that are effective need to be written in a matter that policy makers can see the relevance and impact for application at the local, state, and/or national levels. Lastly, the constant stream of information available today can lead to overload and be a barrier to accessing and using evidence. Having a preexisting relationship or intending to develop one with policy makers is important. It was found that seeking the advice and expertise of colleagues related to medical issues was preferable to seeking information from the literature. This model would likely apply to working with policy makers as well. Relationships and other methods of contact will strengthen the ties with policy makers, such as bulletins for decision makers that focus on a particular issue, as is done by several policy think tanks. Additionally, healthcare provider experts aware of the organizational barriers of workload, time constraints, and authority to implement change associated with projected change will be in a position to address these concerns directly through personal contacts with policy makers (Funk, Champagne, Wiese, et al., 1991). Policy briefs are designed to inform readers with analyses of research results that have policy relevance. Issue briefs are effective tools for use by nursing professionals to describe, discuss, and recommend the need for policy changes.

Disseminating Evidence to the Media

Healthcare professionals need to think critically about why a reporter would want to take time to hear about their work and to listen to what they have to say. Professionals who are serious about disseminating evidence need to be prepared to answer this question (Box 16.8).

This section provides general guidance for talking to the media about findings from research and evidence-based implementation projects. Basics are covered first, and emphasis follows with regard to the dynamic nature of news, factors influencing why reporters cover certain stories, and information about how to influence the process.

The Basics

Everyone has a story to tell. A technician witnesses a miraculous patient recovery in the middle of the night; a nurse designs a study that uncovers the ineffectiveness of a tool widely used by healthcare providers; a researcher designs a novel molecule that evolves into a drug to treat the symptoms of heart disease in millions. However, these examples all deal with healthcare. What about sports, marriage, hobbies, other professions, world politics, and travel? It is a huge world out there, full of incredible stories, amazing breakthroughs, and passionate people performing great feats. Really, it is almost too much. At any instant, people can choose from hundreds of broadcast channels beamed into living rooms, select from millions of websites, and view news from a multitude of publications. Information is coming at everyone in a flood, making it difficult for someone to listen to a healthcare provider's story or research findings.

To make a case with the media, first you must be clear about your message. What is it that you want the world to know? Have you developed an incredible new method for identifying children at risk of abuse? Might your work inspire young people to explore research or the healthcare professions? Have you developed a new method to prevent obesity and cardiovascular disease?

Second, what is your definition of "the world"? Perhaps the only person who needs to hear your message is the president of your university because your department is slated for closure and you want him or her to be aware of your colleagues' good work. The target of your message also could be a particular company to which you hope to license a new technology that you have discovered. Your target audience could be overweight individuals who should hear your message of moderation, exercise, and weight loss. Specifically, knowing or choosing your audience is just as important as shaping your message. It may be that you need to work with the media, but perhaps you simply need to make one phone call or send a letter to one individual. Not all dissemination requires the media, particularly in this era when individuals possess more tools than ever for reaching targeted audiences effectively.

Finally, it is important to conduct a reality check in terms of assessing the competition. There is a multitude of fascinating websites, libraries full of books, reports to complete, and patients to be seen, all of which compete for the public's attention. Therefore, it is important to remember that just because you want someone to listen to what you have to say about the evidence on a particular topic does not mean they will listen. This may be the most common mistake of healthcare providers (i.e., making the assumption that people will be interested in your findings because so much work has been invested in a particular project).

When attempting to make contact with the media, you will often find a very intelligent person working in a virtual frenzy because of deadlines and competitive pressures. Be prepared to state your message concisely and be ready to challenge that person into paying attention. Never presume that because you have something to say, a reporter owes you the courtesy of listening. You may be one of dozens or hundreds of people who contact the reporter on that day in the midst of a multitude of demanding tasks that need to be accomplished.

To be prepared to make your case for why the media should cover what you have to say, you should place yourself and your story through scrutiny that mirrors a review from a top journal. You should know who has done or is doing work similar to yours and how your work is different. Be prepared to justify why funding was provided for your research or project. Be ready

box 16.8

Factors that Help Determine the News Value of Research Evidence

- ■ *Interest*—Is it interesting? Does it stir the imagination?
- ■ *Relevance*—Is it relevant? Will the finding(s) make any difference in anyone's life in the next year?
- ■ *Other events*—What else is happening in the world or in the local community this day (e.g., a hospital closing, impeachment proceedings, a war)?
- ■ *Availability*—How available or reachable is the healthcare provider?
- ■ *Exceptionality*—Is the evidence out of the ordinary? (e.g., at an institution that brings in $1 million of research funding every day, a new $2 million grant is not news, at least not because of the dollar amount)
- ■ *Compatibilities*—How does the development fit into the overall strategic goals of the institution?
- ■ *Quotability*—Is the healthcare provider quotable? Does he or she speak in a relatable, nontechnical language?
- ■ *Visual appeal*—Is good artwork available?
- ■ *High-profile affiliations*—Are the study's findings being announced through a major journal or at a major meeting?
- ■ *Human interest*—Is a patient who was included in the study available so that a human face can be placed on the story?
- ■ *Clarity and applicability*—Is the take-home message clear and applicable to people's lives?
- ■ *Cost*—How much funding is involved?

to explain the significance of your work in a way that the reporter can understand, which may result in an explanation unlike one you have ever given to other colleagues. It is important to ask yourself the question, Why should my story dominate over a typical day's smattering of health news (e.g., the genetic variations of malaria, cold-weather lip care, overeating as one of life's guilty pleasures, and ski-related injuries)?

News Is Dynamic

Once you have honed your message and defined the audience that you would like to reach, as well as decided that the media might be a good way to communicate with that audience, you need to recognize the potential power of the media. When people turn to the Internet, the TV remote, or the radio, they simply hit a button, and a flurry of information comes sailing forth. There is a tendency in most of us simply to listen to what we hear, not quite unquestioningly but certainly passively. For example, people turn on the radio, hear "the day's top news," and make what they will of it. However, there is truthfully no central repository of events deemed to be "news" from which the media draws. Ordinary people decide what is news. If you remember nothing else from this chapter, remember this: *The news is up for grabs.*

As a news recipient, you are allowing your worldview to be dictated by someone else. Whether it is an announcer in a radio booth in Albuquerque, an unseen TV editor shouting across a newsroom in Los Angeles, or a webmaster spinning tales from his living room, you are subjecting yourself to someone else's choices about what you should and should not hear. People make these choices every day (i.e., which information to pass along and which to conceal or ignore). You might inform your neighbors about the interest rate you received on refinancing your house but not tell how long you spent brushing your teeth that morning. A father might tell his young child about his first experience playing baseball but not about his first experience with a girl. We are all editors.

This is also true with the media. A ferryboat sinks and 240 people die, but it is not news because it happened halfway across the globe. The same day, a single man veers off the road and escapes without a scratch, but it is a headline news story because the driver is a politician who was driving while intoxicated.

There is no single body of events that constitutes news and another set of events that constitutes non-news. Deciding the news is an incredibly dynamic process, and becoming aware of this is a huge step toward working with the media effectively. Prepare carefully first, then pursue your share of the media. It could be that the healthcare provider across town is conducting work less interesting than your own, but maybe she or he actually took the time to call a reporter. As a result, the front-page story is about the other professional's work, not yours.

In addition to the specifics of your story, there is a multitude of factors that will decide whether your news is the media's news on any given day (see Box 16.8). Being aware of these and other factors is important if your story is to make the news.

- What issues are routinely covered by the publication?
- When is the reporter's deadline, and what time of day are you contacting him or her?
- What else is going on in the world today? Has there been a big layoff locally? A major terrorism event?
- Which reporter or editor is on vacation, and who is filling in? What are his or her interests?
- What are the personal issues that the reporter is grappling with that day?
- What is the editorial approach or bias of the publication as a whole?
- From which demographics does the outlet draw the bulk of its advertising dollars?
- Who is able to provide or offer the best opportunity for artwork or a visually interesting angle?
- Which source returned the phone call most quickly?

Most of these factors cannot be controlled by you, but they mold coverage of stories. Consider, for example, a public relations (PR) specialist who prepared publicity about a research finding published in a top scientific journal (i.e., a fossil of a tropical beast known as a "champsosaur" that was found in the Arctic Circle) that included a global warming theme, a well-executed color sketch of an interesting beast, an animal whose name sounded like "chompasaurus," an accessible and engaging scientist, and a top-notch publication aligned to promise tremendous coverage. That same day, though, the U.S. House of Representatives voted to impeach President Clinton. As a result, the "chompasaurus" was redirected to the inside pages of newspapers everywhere by an event that the researcher had no hope to control. The story still received international attention but not as sweeping as would have occurred in the absence of a national high-profile event.

The point to remember is that news is a fluid medium. There are all sorts of people manipulating events to determine what you read, hear, and view. You can make the decision to sit on the sideline and receive news that is determined by others or do your best to convey your message to your audience.

You also will find that many others may attempt to manipulate your findings or story for a certain news angle. Box 16.9 provides some examples of the people who might become involved in an ordinary healthcare or research story. Your graduate student may seek to turn the findings into a job offer. The PR department may hawk the results to the media, seeking positive publicity for the institution. The fundraising office may have in mind a meeting with a donor who is ready to give millions of dollars, based on work just like yours. Your competitors will comb through the article, seeking weak spots. The company funding your pharmaceutical research may be thrilled with the results and will promote them on Wall Street. Also, politicians may rush to claim credit for supplying the funding that resulted in such important knowledge. The list goes on and on.

Much of the competition for news space and its interpretation is invisible to the typical healthcare professional, who usually spends years immersed in his or her work, compared with time spent with an actual media representative—an exposure usually measured in minutes. Thus, many healthcare professionals approach the media with a certain bravado. Although anyone who works with the media ought to be prepared for negative fallout, healthcare providers seem to be particularly vulnerable to being caught off guard when a supposedly straightforward process of communication goes awry.

The Bad, the Good, and Media Exposure in General

Media scrutiny may bring with it the realization that your quote really is not true (e.g., your project is not "the first" or "the only," as you sincerely thought it was). A collaborator's name may be unintentionally omitted from an article, causing jealousy or even a rift. Your competitors

---

box 16.9

Who Can Help Disseminate Evidence?

- Your graduate students
- Your postdoctoral fellows
- Your department chair
- Your dean
- Your colleagues
- PR office
- Fundraising office
- Technology-transfer office
- Alumni office

- Funding organization
- Journals that publish findings
- Professional organizations
- Manufacturer of the product you tested
- PR firm hired by manufacturer
- PR firm hired by journal
- Politicians
- Patient advocacy groups
- Collaborators at other institutions

(i.e., that group across the country with a huge reputation), whose work over the last 10 years will be proven completely inane if you are correct, may try and dispute your works (worse yet, they may even have better media contacts). Your colleagues down the hall may say that your work is unimportant because it was covered in the popular press when truthfully, they are jealous because prospective graduate students want to visit your team, not theirs. Or simply working with the media may consume large amounts of time that you could be spending elsewhere, and the process is no longer fun for you, but the queries keep pouring in. There are a great many pitfalls about working with the media, and the costs versus the benefits need to be weighed before deciding to pursue this avenue of dissemination.

Media attention can be extremely beneficial as well. Your student may get a great offer from an employer who was unaware of your work before it was covered in a major business magazine. You might be invited to speak at a national meeting based on an organizer's Internet search of a topic. After reading about your work, a representative from a large company may visit you, then fund your work with several hundred thousand dollars. The article may help fuel perceived momentum around an expansion of research or a healthcare topic, resulting in a spurt in donations that will fund your future initiatives. There also may be a boost in morale from the media coverage that helps your institution retain the best and brightest individuals. Publicity about the findings from a clinical trial also can speed research and fuel initiatives to better health outcomes for the public.

Publicists of research findings have witnessed all these results and more. Publicity about a nurse's study of rocking-chair therapy to treat dementia was covered by major publications around the world and is now used by dozens of nursing homes, thanks to some basic PR. Before that story was widely publicized, it was rejected by dozens of reporters. However, a single news story by a reporter at *The Boston Globe* launched the story into popularity and the research into use worldwide. Publicity about a finding on vaccines and thimerosal resulted in editorials in *The New York Times* and *The Wall Street Journal*. Also, research shows that coverage in the general press has a positive impact on the number of times a research article is cited in the scientific press. Increased citations in the scientific press, more funding, greater collaboration, jobs for students, and research making a difference in people's lives—these are all outcomes important to healthcare providers. Frequently, the first step toward disseminating these outcomes after careful preparation is conducted as outlined above is simply calling or contacting a reporter. Many healthcare professionals are hesitant to take this simple action for fear that the mere act of informing a person outside of their communities may be construed as "hyping" the results. Many individuals forget that much of the funding for their work came from taxpayers and that they have an obligation to report back to the people who paid for their work.

Some Practical Advice

Even when reluctant to call the media, chances are that you will have contact with a reporter about your study's findings eventually. When this occurs, you might want to have Box 16.10 posted nearby as a starting point or simply have handy the phone number of your PR person, who should work as your advocate. Frequently, a PR representative can clarify a reporter's questions for you or provide you with the reporter's background. It is not uncommon for a local reporter to lack total understanding about research, whereas some reporters at the largest publications will have their doctorates and will relish the opportunity to grill you in detail about the methods used in your project. A PR person also can redirect a call to someone else in the organization who is more appropriate or provide you the happenings within your organization that might influence the reporter's approach. Occasionally, a PR representative will counsel you to steer clear of a certain reporter because of that reporter's poor track record.

> ### box 16.10
>
> ## When a Reporter Calls: A Quick Guide to Action
>
> ■ Call your PR person for insight, support, and backup.
> ■ Obtain background on the reporter (e.g., What does he or she normally cover? What have the experiences of your colleagues been?).
> ■ Relax. Just because the reporter is in a frenzy does not mean that you need to be.
> ■ What messages would you like to communicate? Focus on two or three main messages that you want to convey, and be ready to work those into your answers to the reporter's questions.
> ■ Before the interview, have background materials ready, and offer to provide them to the reporter.
> ■ During the interview, think before you talk. Do not be pressured to provide immediate answers. Offer to call the reporter back, and use time to collect your thoughts. In many cases, when a person claims to have been misquoted, they are simply unhappy about what they said to the reporter.
> ■ Give the reporter your phone numbers (including home number), and say you would be happy to take calls anytime if he or she has any more questions or would like further clarification.
> ■ Do not ask to see the story in advance because you are not the reporter's boss, you do not own the publication, and you do not determine what is covered and how. Instead, offer to be a resource and encourage the reporter to contact you with further questions.

Even as you invite a PR person into your life, you must remain aware that he or she also is altering the story to some extent and placing your work in a particular context. For instance, after a PR specialist conducts a careful interview and does some reading about the topic, he or she attempts to write a summary of the healthcare professional's work in approximately 800 words (see Appendix H for an example of a press release summary). Then the summary is provided to the professional for review. Typically, a physician, nurse, or researcher will read what is written, change a couple of lowercase letters to uppercase, and perhaps strike out an erroneous word or two or insert some jargon. They typically limit their comments to the words presented to them in the summary. It never occurs to many professionals that they have left the entire interpretation of their work (e.g., the context, the emphasis) up to the PR specialist. If the words are accurate, they approve the overall theme. It is great when that happens, but healthcare professionals should be encouraged to consider whether the PR person's interpretation is accurate or one that they would choose themselves.

With the input of a PR person who specializes in covering research findings, a host of other issues will arise when disseminating evidence to the media. Briefly, here are a few of those issues:

● *Embargoes*: A news embargo (i.e., a restriction on the release of any media information about the findings from a study before they are published in a journal article) is oftentimes used by some journals or science organizations to give reporters time to develop a story on a complex or exciting topic. However, not all reporters agree to embargoes; many see them as authorized or misguided attempts to control the news—and not all embargoes are legitimate. To be safe, if you are part of an embargoed story, you need to clarify this up front with the reporter before you say anything of substance. That said, hundreds of research stories are embargoed every week, and rarely does anything go wrong. If you and the reporter agree on the embargo, it is fine to speak to the reporter, and the story will appear after the embargo lifts.

- *Off the record*: Do not go there. Anything you say is on the record, and if you talk and then say afterward, "That was off the record," the reporter has no obligation to regard those comments as off the record. You have to establish that *before* the interview. Even then, it is risky and better to avoid.

- *Peer review*: This is crucial to veteran research reporters, as crucial to them as it is to researchers. If you are making a claim, you need to have evidence that has been reviewed by someone else. Stories claiming any type of medical or scientific progress in detail usually rely on a publication in a journal or at least a presentation at a professional meeting. Even so, the rules are not always clear. A journal article almost always has much more detailed evidence and has been more rigorously reviewed than an abstract for a poster presentation, so the timing can be delicate. So, too, can the publicity be around a paper or presentation. For instance, some journals will reject manuscripts if you or your institution have actively promoted the results in the media, but they will accept them even if the media covered the previously reported results, as long as you did not initiate the coverage.

- Press conferences: Try not to be nervous when interviewed during a press conference. Visual elements should be available whenever possible. Keep comments short. Include speakers for the news value they contribute. If you are talking about research results, make sure you have presented at a meeting or published in a journal before the conference. Healthcare professionals who make claims and present study findings at a press conference without supporting evidence that has been peer-reviewed place their careers at risk.

It is also important to remember technology-transfer issues. In other words, contact your technology-transfer department and consider filing a patent on any research/program products *before* you publish or present your results.

Reporters come with a variety of interests and abilities, but all have the power to reach out to more people with your message than you will probably be able to reach without them. When dealing with a reporter on a deadline, spending 5 minutes placing an issue in perspective will save them 45 minutes of conducting research on the Web, when they really have only 5 minutes to accomplish the job. Avoiding the temptation to send them to the library, along with the other "don'ts" listed in Box 16.11, will go a long way toward building your reputation as a media source.

You will not want to be a source for all reporters because some will not be very credible and/or polite. In one instance, a reporter repeatedly demanded to see a research group's "vials containing smallpox virus," no matter how many times the group tried to clarify that it had the *vaccine*, not the *virus*.

There also are reporters who have no interest in looking objectively at news and who instead are seeking a human face to place on a story already written. Additionally, there are reporters who will try to have you tell their version of a story instead of your version. In a story about why people were volunteering to be vaccinated against smallpox, a representative from a major TV network was not satisfied with the answer provided by one participant. The answer did not match the producer's preconceived notion of why people were volunteering, so he instructed the participant to use the word *patriotism* in his answer. Because the young man had been prepared for the pressure exerted by reporters, he disregarded the advice and provided an honest answer. The story was a success, in addition to being truthful.

> ## box 16.11
>
> ## Some "Don'ts" When Working with Reporters
>
> Don't use scientific jargon.
> Don't assume you are a media expert.
> Don't wait hours to return a call; call back immediately.
> Don't expect a story to name every contributor or collaborator.
> Don't assume the reporter is familiar with the details of your project or discipline—ask.
> Don't dictate the "proper" questions or the story angle.
> Don't talk about just the positive aspects of your research findings; also discuss the limitations.
> Don't ask to see a copy of the story before it is published.

The payoff from working effectively with the press can be enormous, but the prospect also can be daunting. It is important to prepare thoroughly, seek the assistance of an experienced PR person if one is available, build up a reservoir of patience and persistence, and give it a try. Although it would be simpler if quality work attracted attention on its own, the reality is that news is a "grab bag," and you might as well capture your share of it.

unit five

392

references

Abe, D. (2007). Teacher upgrade: Podcasts uploading your childbirth class. *International Journal of Childbirth Education, 22*, 38.

Agency for Healthcare Research and Quality. (2007). *Child health insurance research initiative*. Retrieved January 20, 2009, from http://www.ahrq.gov/chiri/

American Psychological Association. (2002). *Publication manual of the American Psychological Association* (5th Ed.). Washington, DC: Author.

Bagott, I., & Bagott, J. (2001). Talk the talk: Overcome your fear of public speaking. *Nursing Spectrum (Metro Edition), 2*(7), 12–13.

Bergren, M. D. (2000). Information technology: Power up your presentation with PowerPoint. *Journal of School Nursing, 16*(4), 44–47.

Betz, C. L. (2008). Frequently asked questions.... again and again. *Journal of Pediatric Nursing, 23*, 329–330.

Carroll-Johnson, R. M. (2001). Submitting a manuscript for review. *Clinical Journal of Oncology Nursing, 5*(3 Suppl), 13–16.

Coralli, C. H. (2006). Effective case presentations: An important clinical skill for nurse practitioners. *Journal of the American Academy of Nurse Practitioners, 18*, 216–220 (Reprint from *Journal of American Academy of Nurse Practitioner, 1989*, 1).

DeBehnke, D. J., Kline, J. A., & Shih, R. D. (2001). Research fundamentals: Choosing an appropriate journal, manuscript preparation, and interactions with editors. *Academic Emergency Medicine, 8*(8), 844–850.

Dictionary.com. (2009). *Podcast*. Retrieved January 19, 2009, from http://dictionary.reference.com/browse/podcast

Dyckoff, D., Manela, J., & Valente, S. (2004). Improving practice with a journal club. *Nursing, 34*(7), 29.

ESRC UK Centre for Evidence-Based Policy and Practice. (2001a). *Working Paper 1*. London: University of London, Department of Politics.

ESRC UK Centre for Evidence-Based Policy and Practice. (2001b). *Working Paper 6*. London: University of London, Department of Politics.

Evans, M. L. (2000). Polished, professional presentation: Unlocking the design elements. *Journal of Continuing Education in Nursing, 31*(5), 213–218.

Farella, C. (2002). Read all about it! RN authors have the write stuff. *Nursing Spectrum (Greater Chicago/NE Illinois & NW Indiana Edition), 15*(1), 32–34.

Fetter, M. S. (1999). The privilege of publishing. *Medical-Surgical Nursing, 8*(3), 142–143.

Fitzgerald, T. (2000). 5 minutes with.... Carolyn Zagury, PhD, RN.... nursing and publishing. *Nurseweek (California Statewide Edition), 13*(20), 15.

Flores, G., Abreu, M., & Tomany-Korman, S. C. (2005). Limited English proficiency, primary language at home, and disparities in children's health care: How language barriers are measured matters. *Public Health Reports, 120*, 418–430.

Funk, S. G., Champagne, M. T., Wiese, R. A., & Tournquist, E. M. (1991). Barriers: The barriers to research utilization scale. *Applied Nursing Research, 4*(1), 39–45.

Gross, B. (2002). *Tools for teaching: Preparing to teach the large lecture course*. Berkeley, CA: University of California, Berkeley. Retrieved November 10, 2002, from http://teaching.berkeley.edu/bgd/largelecture.html

Hadfield-Law, L. (2001). Presentation skills. Presentation skills for nurses: How to prepare more effectively. *British Journal of Nursing, 10*(18), 1208–1211.

Hamilton, C. W. (2008). At a glance: A stepwise approach to successful poster presentations. *Chest, 134*, 457–459.

Happell, B. (2007). Conference presentations: Developing nursing knowledge by disseminating research findings. *Nurse Researcher, 15*, 70–77.

Happell, B. (2008). Conference presentations: A guide to writing the abstract. *Nurse Researcher, 15*, 79–87.

Heinrich, K. T. (2002). Manuscript development. Slant, style, and synthesis: 3 keys to a strong literature review. *Nurse Author and Editor, 12*(1), 1–3.

Heinrich, K. T. (2007). Dare to share: A unique approach to presenting and publishing. *Nurse Educator, 32*, 269–273.

Hundley, V. (2002). Research notes: How do you decide where to send an article for publication? *Nursing Standard, 16*(36), 21.

Jennings, C. P. (2002). The power of the policy brief. *Policy, Politics & Nursing Practice, 3*(3), 261–263.

Jham, B. C., Duraes, G. V., Strassler, H. E., & Sensi, L. G. (2008). Joining the podcast revolution. *Journal of Dental Education, 72*, 278–281.

Kiekkas, P., Sakellanropoulos, G. C., Brkalaki, H., Manolis, E., Samios, A., et al. (2008). Nursing workload associated with fever in the general intensive care unit. *American Journal of Critical Care, 17*, 522–533.

King, S. (2001). *On writing.* New York: Pocket Books.

Kutner, M., Greenberg, E., Jin, Y., & Paulsen, C. (2006). *The health literacy of America's adults: Results from the 2003 National Assessment of Adult Literacy* (NCES 2006–483). Washington, DC: National Center for Education Statistics.

Lannon, S. L. (2007). Leadership skills beyond the bedside: Professional development classes for the staff nurse. *The Journal of Continuing Education in Nursing, 38*, 17–21.

Leyva, M., Sharif, I., & Ozuah, O. (2005). Health literacy among Spanish-speaking Latino parents with limited English proficiency. *Ambulatory Pediatrics, 5*, 56–59.

Mason, M. A., & Street, A. (2006). Publishing outcome data: Is it an effective approach? *Journal of Evaluation in Clinical Practice, 12*, 37–48.

McConnell, E. A. (2002). Making outstandingly good presentations. *DCCN—Dimensions of Critical Care Nursing, 21*(1), 28–30.

Melnyk, B. M., Brown, H., Jones, D., Kreipe, R., & Novak, J. (2003). Improving the mental/psychosocial health of U.S. children and adolescents: Outcomes and implementation strategies from the National KySS Summit (Supplement). *Journal of Pediatric Health Care, 17*(6), S1–S28.

Melnyk, B. M., & Fineout-Overholt, E. (2002). Putting research into practice: Rochester ARCC. *Reflections on Nursing Leadership, 28*(2), 22–25.

Miller, J. E. (2007). Preparing and presenting effective research posters. *Health Services Research, 42*, 311–328.

Miracle, V. A. (2008). Effective poster presentations. *Dimensions of Critical Care Nursing, 27*, 122–124.

Oermann, M. (1999). Extensive writing projects: Tips for completing them on time. *Nurse Author and Editor, 9*(1), 8–10.

Oermann, M. H. (2001). *Writing for publication in nursing.* Philadelphia: Lippincott Williams & Wilkins.

Oermann, M. H., Galvin, E. A., Floyd, J. A., & Roop, J. C. (2006). Presenting research to clinicians: Strategies for writing about research findings. *Nursing Research, 13*(4), 66–74.

Ohler, L. (2002). Manuscript development. Manuscript revisions: The team approach. *Nurse Author and Editor, 12*(2), 1–3.

Pelletier, L. R., Miracle, V. A., Thom, C., Parse, R. R., & Hauger, J. (2002). The insider's view: Timely topics. *Nurse Author and Editor, 12*(3), 5–6,

Reference.com. (2009). Vodcast. Retrieved January 19, 2009, from http://www.reference.com/search? q = Vodcast

Rich, K. (2006). The journal club: A means to promote nursing research. *Journal of Vascular Research, 24*, 26–27.

Ross, J. S., & Gross, C. P. (2009). Policy research: Using evidence to improve healthcare delivery systems. *Circulation, 119*, 891–898.

Rowell, M. R., Corl, F. M., Johnson, P. T., & Fishman, E. K. (2006). Internet-based dissemination of educational audiocasts: A primer in podcasting-How to do it. *American Journal of Radiology, 186*, 1792–1796.

Savel, R. H., Goldstein, E. B., Perencevich, E. N., & Angood, P. B. (2007). The critical care podcast: A novel medium for critical care communication and education. *Journal of American Medical Informatics Association, 14*, 94–99.

Schulmeister, L., & Vrabel, M. (2002). Searching for information for presentations and publications. *Clinical Nurse Specialist, 16*(2), 79–84.

Siwek, J., Gourlay, M. L., Slawson, D. C., & Shaughnessy, A. F. (2002). How to write an evidence-based clinical review article. *American Family Physician, 65*(2), 251–258.

Skiba, D. J. (2006). Emerging technologies center: The 2005 word of the year: Podcast. *Nursing Education Perspectives, 27*, 54–55.

Smith, M. F. (2000). Nurse educator: Public speaking survival strategies. *Journal of Emergency Nursing, 26*(2), 166–168.

Sorian, R., & Baugh, T. (2002). Power of information: Closing the gap between research and policy. *Health Affairs, 21*(2), 264–268.

Sullivan, E. J. (2002). Top 10 reasons a manuscript is rejected. *Journal of Professional Nursing, 18*(1), 1–2.

Taggart, H. M., & Arslanian C. (2000). Creating an effective poster presentation. *Orthopaedic Nursing, 19*(3), 47–52.

Teaching with slides, PowerPoint, and Overhead Projectors. (2003). *The Journal of Continuing Education in Nursing, 34*, 245–246.

U.S. Department of Health and Human Services. (2000). *Healthy People 2010: Understanding and improving health* (2nd ed.). Washington, DC: U.S. Government Printing Office.

Webb, C. (2002). How to make your article more readable. *Journal of Advanced Nursing, 38*(1), 1–2.

Wills, C. E. (2000). Strategies for managing barriers to the writing process. *Nursing Forum, 25*(4), 5–13.

Winters, J. M., Walker, S. N., Larson, J. L., & Lanuza, D. M. (2006). True tales from publishing research. *Western Journal of Nursing Research, 28*, 751–753.

Woodring, B. C. (2000). Professional development: Preparing presentations that produce peace of mind. *Journal of Child & Family Nursing, 3*(1), 63–64.

Yam, C-S. (2005). Computers in radiology: Projecting PowerPoint presentations with a PDA. *American Journal of Radiology, 184*, 1356–1359.

chapter 16

393

Next Steps: Generating External Evidence

Start by doing what is necessary, then do what is possible, and suddenly you are doing the impossible

St. Francis of Assisi

Generating Evidence Through Quantitative Research

Bernadette Mazurek Melnyk and Robert Cole

> *Man's mind, stretched to a new idea, never goes back to its original dimensions.*
> *Oliver Wendell Holmes*

When there is a lack of research reported in the literature to guide clinical practice, it becomes necessary to design and conduct studies to generate **external evidence** (i.e., evidence generated through rigorous research that is intended to be used outside of one's own clinical practice setting). There are many areas in clinical practice that do not have an established evidence base (e.g., care for dying children, primary care interventions to improve mental health outcomes in high-risk individuals). As a result, there is an urgent need to conduct studies so that healthcare providers can base their treatment decisions on sound evidence from well-designed studies instead of continuing to make decisions that are steeped solely in tradition or opinion.

The Importance of Generating Evidence

This chapter provides a general overview and practical guide for formulating clinical research questions and designing studies to answer these questions. It also includes suggestions on when a quantitative approach would be more appropriate to answer a specific question. A variety of quantitative research designs are discussed, from **descriptive studies** to **randomized controlled trials** (RCTs), which are conducted to answer questions about the effectiveness of interventions or treatments. Techniques to enhance the rigor of quantitative research designs are highlighted, including strategies to strengthen **internal validity** (i.e., the ability to say that it was the independent variable or intervention that caused a change in the dependent variable or outcome, not other extraneous variables), as well as **external validity** (i.e., generalizability, which is the ability to generalize findings from a study's sample to the larger population). Specific principles of conducting *qualitative studies* are detailed in Chapter 18.

397

Getting Started: From Idea to Reality

> *We are told never to cross a bridge until we come to it, but*
> *the world is owned by men who have 'crossed bridges' in*
> *their imagination far ahead of the crowd.*
> *Speakers Library*

Many ideas for studies come from clinical practice situations in which questions arise regarding best practices or evolve from a search for evidence on a particular topic (e.g., Is music or relaxation therapy more effective in reducing the stress of patients after surgery? What are the major variables that predict the development of posttraumatic stress disorder in adults after motor vehicle accidents?). However, these ideas are often cast aside as competing demands for patient care or overwhelming job responsibilities prevent the transformation of ideas into study projects. Additionally, some practitioners may hesitate to conduct a study for fear they do not have adequate knowledge, skills, or resources to complete the project successfully.

Because of the nature of current clinical practice in today's healthcare environment, it is worthwhile to develop a "creative ideas" file when thoughts for studies are generated. A creative ideas file may spark practitioners to act on previous ideas at a later time. In addition, these ideas or research questions can be shared with doctorally prepared clinicians or researchers who can partner with the practitioner to launch a study. Thus, the person who had the idea or question can assume an active role on the study team but need not take on the role of the lead person, or **principal investigator (PI)**, who is responsible and accountable for overseeing all elements of the research project.

> *The greatest successful people of the world have used their*
> *imagination.... They think ahead and create their mental*
> *picture, and then go to work materializing that picture in all*
> *its details, filling in here, adding a little there, altering this*
> *a bit and that a bit, but steadily building—steadily building.*
> *Robert Collier*

Once an idea for a study is generated, it is exceedingly important to first conduct an extensive search of the literature and critically appraise all **systematic reviews** or related studies in the area. The purpose of this search and critical appraisal is to evaluate the strengths and limitations of prior work, which is critical before another study in the same area is designed.

This process prevents unknowing replication of prior work, which typically does not enhance science or clinical practice. In contrast, deliberate replication of a prior study can be a real strength of a project because it is considered good science and it creates a solid foundation of accumulating evidence on which to base practice changes.

After an idea is generated for a study and a search for and critical appraisal of the literature have been conducted, a collaborative team can be established to be part of the planning process from the outset. Because clinicians often have a host of burning clinical questions but typically need assistance with intricate details of study design, methods, and analysis, formulating a team comprising seasoned clinicians and research experts (e.g., doctorally prepared clinical researchers) will usually lead to the best outcomes. In addition, a team of interdisciplinary professionals will add value to the project, especially in the study design and interpretation of findings. Many funding agencies now expect interdisciplinary collaboration on research projects. Convening this collaborative team for a **research design meeting** at the outset of a project is exceedingly beneficial in developing the study's design and methods, as well as establishing enthusiasm and team spirit for the project.

Research design meetings are an excellent mechanism for moving an idea into the reality of a clinical study. Approximately 1 to 2 weeks before the meeting is conducted, a concise, two-page study draft should be prepared and disseminated. This draft acts as an outline or overview of the clinical problem and includes the research question and a brief description of the proposed methods (Box 17.1 for an example of a study outline, as well as Boxes 17.2 and 17.3 for completed examples of study outlines for different types of clinical studies). As the study outline develops, a list of questions related to the project should be answered:

- Is this idea feasible and clinically important?
- What is the aim of the study, along with the research question(s) or hypotheses?
- What is the best design to answer the study question(s) or test the hypotheses?
- What are the potential sources of data? Are there valid and reliable instruments to measure the desired outcomes?

(text continues on page 403)

box 17.1

Outlining Important Elements of a Clinical Study

Before developing a study protocol, it is extremely beneficial to develop a one- to two-page outline of the elements of a study.

   I. Significance of the Problem
   II. Specific Aim of the Study
      A. Research Question(s) or
      B. Hypotheses
   III. Theoretical/Conceptual Framework
   IV. Study Design
   V. Subjects
      A. Sampling Design
      B. Sampling Criteria
         1. Inclusion Criteria
         2. Exclusion Criteria
   VI. Variables
      A. Independent Variable(s) (in an experimental study, the intervention being proposed)
      B. Dependent Variable(s) (the outcomes) and Measures
      C. Mediating Variable, if applicable (e.g., the variable through which the intervention will most likely exert its effects)
      D. Confounding or Extraneous Variable(s) with potential control strategies
   VII. Statistical Issues
      A. Sample Size
      B. Approach to Analyses

box 17.2

Example of a Completed Study Outline for a Descriptive Correlational Study

A nonexperimental study entitled "Relationship Between Depressive Symptoms and Motivation to Lose Weight in Overweight Teens."

I. **Significance of the Problem**

Data from the Centers for Disease Control indicate that 18% of adolescents are overweight. The major negative consequences associated with obesity in adolescence include premature death, type 2 diabetes, hyperlipidemia, hypertension, and depression. It is known that motivation to lose weight is a key factor in weight loss, but the relationship between depressive symptoms and motivation to lose weight in adolescence has not been studied.

II. **Specific Aim of the Study with Research Question(s) or Hypotheses**

The aim of this study is to answer the following research question: What is the relationship between depressive symptoms and motivation to lose weight in overweight adolescents?

III. **Theoretical/Conceptual Framework**

Control theory contends that, when there is a discrepancy between a standard or goal (e.g., perceived ideal weight), this discrepancy should motivate individuals to initiate behaviors (e.g., exercise, healthy eating) that allow them to achieve their goal. However, there are often barriers that may inhibit an individual in being motivated to initiate these behaviors. In this study, depression is viewed as a barrier to motivation and behaviors that would allow teens to achieve their ideal weight.

IV. **Study Design**

A descriptive correlational design will be used.

V. **Subjects**

A. *Sampling Design*: A random sample of 80 overweight adolescents will be drawn from two randomly selected high schools in Phoenix, Arizona; one from the city school district and one from the suburban area.

B. *Sampling Criteria*

1. *Inclusion Criteria*: adolescents with a body mass index of 25 or greater enrolled in the two high schools.

2. *Exclusion Criteria*: adolescents with a current diagnosis of major depression and/or suicidal ideation.

VI. **Variables**

A. *Independent Variable(s)*: Not applicable.

B. *Dependent Variable(s)*: Depressive symptoms will be measured with the well-known, valid, and reliable Beck Depression Inventory (BDI-II). Motivation to lose weight will be measured with a newly constructed scale that has been reviewed for content validity with experts in the field. This new scale has been pilot tested with 15 overweight teens and found to have a Cronbach's alpha of 0.80.

box 17.2 *(continued)*

   C. *Mediating Variable, if Applicable:* Not applicable
   D. *Confounding or Extraneous Variable(s) with Potential Control Strategies:* Gender is a
      potential confounding variable, because there is a higher incidence of depression
      in adolescent females than males documented in the literature. Therefore, strati-
      fied random sampling will be used so that an equal number of males and females
      will be drawn for the sample.
VII. Statistical Issues
   A. *Sample Size:* To obtain a power of 0.8 and medium effect size at the 0.05 level of
      significance, a total of 80 adolescents will be needed.
   B. *Approach to Analyses:* A Pearson's *r* correlation coefficient will be used to deter-
      mine if a relationship exists between the number of depressive symptoms and
      motivation to lose weight in this sample.

box 17.3

Example of a Completed Study Outline for a Randomized Controlled Trial

A Randomized Clinical Trial entitled "Improving Outcomes of Hospitalized Elders and Family Caregivers" (Li, H., Melnyk, B. M., & McCann, R., funded by the National Institutes of Health/National Institute of Nursing Research, R01 #008455-01, 4/1/03–12/31/08.)

  I. Significance of the Problem
    There are more than 12 million elderly people hospitalized each year in the
    United States, many of whom experience functional decline. Family care of hospital-
    ized elders is important, given the increasing numbers of hospitalized elders, needs
    for elder care in the home after hospital discharge, and responsibilities of family
    caregivers for providing this care. Involving family caregivers in the hospital care of
    their loved ones may result in positive outcomes for both the elderly patients and
    their family caregivers. However, there is a paucity of empirical studies that have been
    conducted to evaluate the effectiveness of interventions to enhance family participa-
    tion in caring for hospitalized elders.
 II. Specific Aim with Research Question/Hypothesis
    The aim of this study is to evaluate the effects of a theoretically driven, reproducible
    intervention (CARE: Creating Avenues for Relative Empowerment) on the process
    and outcomes of hospitalized elders and their family caregivers. It is hypothesized
    that the family caregivers and elders who receive the CARE program will have better
    outcomes (e.g., less depression and functional decline) than those who receive the
    control program.

(box continues on page 402)

box 17.3 *(continued)*

III. Theoretical/Conceptual Framework

The theoretical framework for this study is derived from self-regulation theory and interactional role theory. According to self-regulation theory, it is contended that providing information to family caregivers about the potential emotions and behaviors that they can expect in their hospitalized relatives as well as signs and complications during hospitalization will facilitate the formation of a clear cognitive schema that will strengthen their beliefs about these changes as well as how to interpret them. Subsequently, stronger beliefs should lead to less worry, anxiety, and depression in the family caregivers as well as a greater participation in their loved one's care. In addition, according to role theory, it is postulated that by discussing family roles in a mutually agreed-upon family preference contract, family caregivers' beliefs about their role will be strengthened, and they will participate more in the care of their elderly relatives as well as have less role strain and more role reward and improved family-patient relationships. As a result of improved family caregivers' emotional and functional outcomes as well as role outcomes, patient outcomes also should be improved.

IV. Study Design

A RCT will be used with random assignment of subjects to either the experimental CARE group or the comparison group.

V. Subjects

A. *Sampling Criteria*: Family members who meet the following criteria will be eligible for study participation:

1. Age 21 years or older
2. Have an elderly relative (65 years or older) admitted to the three study units within the past 24–48 hours
3. Are related to the patient by blood, marriage, adoption, or affinity as a significant other (e.g., life partner and close friend)
4. Are primary caregivers
5. Can read and speak English
6. Live within a 1-hour drive of the facility (60 miles)
7. Ineligible for participation are family members who are paid care providers, whose elderly relative is hospitalized for longer than 30 days, who are unable to complete the questionnaires or provide care because of their own mental or physical impairment, or whose relative dies during the hospital stay or within 2 months after discharge.

B. *Sampling Design*: A convenience sample of family caregivers who meet the inclusion criteria will participate in the study.

VI. Variables

A. *Independent Variable(s)*: The family caregivers in the experimental group will receive the CARE program that includes both audio taped and written materials containing information on

1. Emotional responses, behavioral characteristics, and possible complications of elderly patients during hospitalization
2. How family caregivers can participate in their relative's care and prevent or care for dysfunctional syndromes. In addition, family caregivers will be assisted with the development of a specific plan for their elderly relative's hospital care,

box 17.3 *(continued)*

based on their abilities and preferences. Family caregivers in the control group will receive audio taped and written materials containing information on the hospital's services and policies.

B. *Dependent Variable(s)*: Measures of both process and outcome variables include family caregivers' outcomes (beliefs, anxiety, worry, depression, role performance, role strain, role adaptation, and role rewards); outcomes of quality of relationship between family caregiver and patient (mutuality); as well as elderly patients' outcomes (dysfunctional syndrome, length of hospital stay, readmission, depression, and cognitive status) during hospitalization and after hospital discharge.

C. *Mediating Variable, if Applicable*: It is proposed that the CARE intervention will be mediated through family beliefs about their role to improve the outcomes of family caregivers.

D. *Confounding or Extraneous Variable(s) with Potential Control Strategies*: The type of relationship between the family caregiver and the hospitalized elder (e.g., spouse, daughter/son) may confound the outcomes; therefore, a randomized block design will be used that will randomly assign equal numbers of caregivers who are spouses and children to the CARE and control groups.

VII. Statistical Issues

A. *Sample Size*: To detect a medium effect with a power of 0.8 at a 0.05 level of significance, a total of 140 family caregivers and their elders will be needed. Because this is a longitudinal study that will follow subjects for 2 months following discharge, 40 additional family caregivers and their elders will be recruited into the study in the event of attrition to assure a sample size of 140 caregivers at the end of the study.

B. *Approach to Analyses*: Cronbach's alpha will be used to determine internal consistency reliability of the study instruments. Analysis of covariance tests will be used to test the hypotheses if preliminary analysis reveals that the two groups are significantly different on certain demographic and clinical variables. With intercorrelated dependent variables, MANOVA is the first step in testing the hypotheses so that chance results will not be attributable to the experimental intervention. If the MANOVA is significant, univariate ANOVAs will be used to isolate group differences on each of the dependent variables. If differences exist between the pooled experimental and pooled comparison groups on certain demographic or clinical variables at preintervention, these differences will be controlled for statistically by the use of multivariate analysis of covariance.

● What should be the **inclusion** and **exclusion criteria** for the potential study participants?
● What are the essential elements of the intervention, if applicable, and how will **integrity of the intervention** be maintained (i.e., assurance that the intervention is being delivered exactly in the manner in which it was intended to be delivered?)

By distributing these questions along with a concise draft of the study outline that has been developed, team members will have time to reflect on these issues and be better prepared to discuss them at the research design conference.

---

box 17.4

Initial Steps in Designing a Clinical Study

- Cultivate a spirit of inquiry as you deliver care to patients in your practice setting.
- Ask questions about best practices for specific clinical problems.
- Develop a "creative ideas" file as thoughts for studies emerge.
- Pursue a clinical research question.
- Search for and critically appraise systematic reviews and prior studies in the area of interest.
- Establish a potential collaborative team for the project.
- Plan a research design meeting.
- Prepare and disseminate a concise two-page study outline.
- Conduct the research design meeting to plan specific details of the clinical study, decide on the roles of team members, and plan the writing of a grant proposal for funding if needed.

The research design planning session needs to foster an environment in which constructive critique and candid discussion will promote a finely tuned study design. It is important to discuss the roles for each of the study team members (e.g., percentage of effort on the study, specific functions, availability, and order of authorship once the study is published). In addition, potential funding sources for the study should be discussed, as well as who will assume specific responsibilities in writing a grant proposal if funding is necessary to conduct the project (see Chapter 19 for specific steps in writing a successful grant proposal and Box 17.4 for a summary of initial steps in designing a clinical study).

Designing a Clinical Quantitative Study

Box 17.5 cites several factors to consider in developing a quantitative study. The most important of these factors is a critical analysis and synthesis of prior work conducted in the clinical area.

Critical Analysis and Synthesis of Prior Data
If this critical analysis reveals numerous studies that describe a particular construct or phenomenon, such as stressors of family caregivers of hospitalized elders, as well as studies that identify the major predictors of caregiver stress during hospitalization (e.g., uncertainty regarding the

---

box 17.5

Major Factors to Consider When Designing a Quantitative Study

- Prior studies in the area
- Significance of the problem
- Innovation of the project
- Feasibility
- Setting for the study and access to potential subjects
- The study team
- Ethics of the study

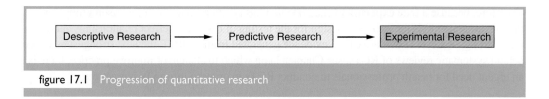

figure 17.1 Progression of quantitative research

caregiving role in the hospital, lack of knowledge regarding how best to enhance outcomes in the hospitalized elder), another descriptive study in the field may not be needed. Instead, the next logical step in this example (based on the descriptive and predictive evidence already generated from prior studies) would be to design and test an educational intervention that informs family caregivers of the functions they can perform to improve their hospitalized elder's health outcomes. In contrast, if the phenomenon of caregiver stress is not well understood or adequately measured in the literature, conducting a qualitative or descriptive study may become the beginning step in conducting research in this area. This type of study might begin with open-ended questions to allow participants to respond in their own words to such questions as, How would you describe what it is like for you to care for your partner or parent? or How have things changed for you now, while your family member is in the hospital? Thus, research in a particular area frequently begins with qualitative work in which a phenomenon or construct is explored with heavy emphasis on interview or observation data (see Chapter 18). When more is known about the nature of the phenomenon through qualitative work, quantitative research is usually undertaken in which the construct of interest is described using measurement scales, test scores, and statistical approaches (see Figure 17.1).

As Figure 17.1 shows, quantitative research designs range from descriptive and correlational descriptive/predictive studies to RCTs. **Correlational descriptive** and **correlational predictive** designs examine the relationships between two or more variables (e.g., What is the relationship between smoking and lung cancer in adults? or What maternal factors in the first month of life predict infant cognitive development at 1 year of age?). These designs are the study of choice when the **independent variable** cannot be manipulated experimentally because of some individual characteristic or ethical consideration (e.g., individuals cannot be assigned to smoke or not smoke). The goal in correlational descriptive or correlational predictive studies is to provide an indication of how likely it is that a cause-and-effect relationship might exist (Powers & Knapp, 1995).

Although RCTs, or *experiments*, are the strongest designs for testing cause-and-effect relationships (i.e., testing the effects of certain clinical practices or interventions on patient outcomes), only a small percentage of studies conducted in many of the health professions are experimental studies or clinical trials. Additionally, of those intervention studies reported in the literature, many have limitations that weaken the evidence that is generated from them, including

- Lack of random assignment to study groups
- Lack of or underdeveloped theoretical frameworks to guide the interventions
- Small sample sizes that lead to inadequate **power** to detect significant differences in outcomes between the experimental and control groups
- Omission of **manipulation checks**, assessments verifying that subjects have actually processed the experimental information that they have received or followed through with prescribed intervention activities
- Failure to limit **confounding** or **extraneous variables** (i.e., those factors that interfere with the relationship between the independent and dependent variables)
- Lack of more long-term follow-up to assess the sustainability of the treatment or intervention

Therefore, because a **true experiment** (i.e., one that has an intervention, a comparison group, and random assignment) is the strongest design for the testing of cause-and-effect relationships and provides strong, or **Level II evidence** (i.e., evidence generated from an RCT, the next strongest evidence behind systematic reviews of RCTs; see Chapter 1) on which to change or improve practice, there is an urgent need for health professionals to conduct RCTs in order to inform best practices.

Significance of the Question

A second major factor to consider when designing studies is the significance of the problem or research question. There may be research questions that are very interesting (e.g., Do pink or blue scrubs worn by intensive care unit nurses impact the mood of unit secretaries?) but answering them will not significantly improve care or patient outcomes. Therefore, a funding agency is not likely to rate the significance of the problem as important. Problems that are significant for study are usually those that affect a large percentage of the population or those that frequently affect the process or outcomes of patient care.

Feasibility

The third factor to consider when designing a study is feasibility. Before embarking on a study, important questions to ask regarding feasibility are

- Can the study be conducted in a reasonable amount of time?
- Are there adequate resources available at the institution or clinical site to conduct the study? If the answer is no, what is the potential for obtaining funding?
- Are there an adequate number of potential subjects to recruit into the study?
- Does the lead person (PI) have sufficient time and expertise to spearhead the effort?

If the answer to any of these questions is no, further consideration should be given to the feasibility of the project.

As a general rule, it typically takes more time to carry out a clinical study than is originally projected. Even when subject numbers are projected to be sufficient for the time allotted for data collection when planning a study, it is wise to incorporate a buffer period (i.e., extra time) in case subject recruitment takes longer than anticipated. Also, certain times of the year are more conducive for data collection than others (e.g., in conducting a study with elementary school students, data collection will be possible only when school is in session, not during the summer months).

Setting

The fourth major factor to consider when designing a study is the setting(s) in which it will be implemented. Certain settings are more conducive to the conduct of clinical research than others. Settings that tend to facilitate research are those in which there is administrative approval and staff "buy-in" regarding clinical studies. Settings in which staff members perceive research as burdensome to them or their patients may confound study results as well as hamper a study's progress. Obtaining administrative approval to conduct a study and getting a sense of staff support for a project is an early and critical preparatory step for a clinical research project.

Research Team

> *Alone we can do so little; together we can do so much.*
> *Helen Keller*

The fifth major factor to consider when designing a clinical study is the research team. Specifically, it is important to consider the experience, skills, interest, and commitment of each member of the team. It is typical for there to be much enthusiasm about a project at its beginning, but sustained interest and participation by each member of the study team will be important for its successful completion. Study team members should possess the skills needed to plan, implement, analyze, and interpret the research data. For a novice researcher, the addition of seasoned researchers to the project will be important for its success, especially as challenges are encountered in the course of the initiative.

> *It is literally true that you can succeed best and quickest by helping others to succeed.*
>
> *Napoleon Hill*

Ethics, Benefits, and Risks

The final major factor to consider in planning a study is whether it is ethical in terms of subject burden as well as whether the benefits of participation in the study will exceed the risks. Serious consideration also must be given to the gender, age, and racial/ethnic composition of the sample. For federal grant applications, strong rationale must be provided if women, children, and minority subjects will be excluded from the research project. In addition, study team members need to be knowledgeable regarding the ethics of conducting a study and the rights of participant subjects. Further discussion about obtaining research subjects' review approval for a clinical study appears later in this chapter and in chapter 20.

Specific Steps in Designing a Quantitative Study

When designing a quantitative clinical research study, there is a specific series of orderly steps that are typically followed (Box 17.6). This is referred to as the *scientific approach to inquiry.*

Step 1: Formulate the Study Question

The first step in the design of a study is developing an innovative, answerable study question. Cummings, Browner, and Hulley (2001) use the acronym FINER (feasible, interesting, novel, ethical, relevant) to determine the quality of the research question. Feasibility is an important issue when formulating a research question. Although a research question may be very interesting (e.g., What is the effect of a therapeutic intervention program on depression in women whose spouses have been murdered?), it could take years to collect an adequate number of subjects to conduct the statistical analysis to answer the question.

On the other hand, if a research question is not interesting to the investigator, there is a chance that the project may never reach completion, especially when challenges arise that make data collection difficult. Other feasibility issues include the amount of time and funding needed to conduct the project, as well as the scope of the study. Studies that are very broad and that contain too many goals are often not feasible or manageable.

Research questions should be novel, meaning that obtaining the answer to them should add to, confirm, or refute what is already known, or they should extend prior research findings. Replication studies are important, especially if they address major limitations of prior work.

Good research questions should be ethical in that they do not present unacceptable physical or psychological risks to the subjects in the study. The institution of strict federal

box 17.6

Specific Steps in Designing a Quantitative Clinical Study

1. Formulate the study question.
2. Establish the significance of the problem.
3. Search for and critically appraise available evidence.
4. Develop the theoretical/conceptual framework.
5. Generate hypotheses when appropriate.
6. Select the appropriate research design.
7. Identify the population/sampling plan and implement strategies to enhance external validity.
8. Determine the measures that will be used.
9. Outline the data collection plan.
10. Apply for human subjects approval.
11. Implement the study.
12. Prepare and analyze the data.
13. Interpret the results.
14. Disseminate the findings.
15. Incorporate the findings in EBP and evaluate the outcomes.

regulations surrounding research with human subjects has curtailed studies in which the risks exceed the benefits of participation in a study. As such, before a research study is conducted, review of the entire protocol by a **research subjects review board** (RSRB), sometimes referred to as an *institutional review board* (IRB), is necessary.

Many universities, such as Arizona State University, have websites that provide comprehensive information on (a) how to submit studies for review; (b) answers to frequently asked questions; and (c) information about regulations regarding research, including specific details related to HIPAA (Health Insurance Portability and Accountability Act **(see http://researchintegrity.asu.edu/humans/forms)**

In institutions where a formal RSRB is not in existence, there should be some type of ethics committee that reviews and approves research proposals.

Finally, research questions should be relevant to science and/or clinical practice. They should also have the potential to impact health policy and guide further research (Cummings et al., 2001; Box 17.7).

Step 2: Establish Significance of the Problem

The problem of interest should be one that is clinically important or that will extend the science in an area. When embarking on a study, it is imperative to ask questions about why the clinical problem is important, including

- What is the incidence of this particular problem?
- How many individuals are affected by this problem?

> **box 17.7**
>
> ## Characteristics of a Good Study Question
>
> F = Feasible
> I = Interesting
> N = Novel
> E = Ethical
> R = Relevant

Cummings, S. R., Browner, W. S., & Hulley, S. B. (2001). Conceiving the research question. In S. B. Hulley, S. R. Cummings, W. S. Browner, D. Grady, N. Hearst, & T. B. Newman (Eds.), *Designing clinical research: An epidemiologic approach* (2nd ed., pp. 17–23). Philadelphia: Lippincott, Williams & Wilkins.

- Will studying this problem potentially improve the care that is delivered to patients?
- Will studying this problem potentially influence health policy?
- Will studying this intervention lead to better health outcomes in patients?
- Will studying this problem assist clinicians in gaining a better understanding of the area so that more sensitive clinical care can be delivered?

Step 3: Search and Appraise Evidence

A thorough search for and critical appraisal of all relevant studies in the area are essential (see Chapters 3–6) before the study design is planned. It is first advantageous to begin searching for **systematic reviews** on the topic. A systematic review is a summary of evidence in a particular topic area that attempts to answer a specific clinical question using methods that reduce bias, usually conducted by an expert or expert panel on a particular topic (Melnyk, 2003). When it is conducted properly, a systematic review uses a rigorous process for identifying, critically appraising, and synthesizing studies for the purpose of answering a specific clinical question and drawing conclusions about the evidence gathered (e.g., How effective are educational interventions in reducing sexual risk-taking behaviors in teenagers? What factors predict osteoporosis in women?). In using a rigorous process to determine which types of studies will be included in a systematic review, author bias is usually eliminated, and greater credibility can be placed in the findings from the review. In systematic reviews, methodological strengths and limitations of each study included in the review are discussed, and recommendations for clinical practice as well as further research are presented (Guyatt & Rennie, 2002). As such, the availability of a systematic review in a particular topic area can provide an individual with quick access to the status of interventions or clinical studies in a particular area as well as recommendations for further study.

If a systematic review in the area of interest is not available, the search for and critical appraisal of individual studies should commence. In reading prior studies, the following information should be tabled so that a critical analysis of the body of prior work can be conducted:

- Demographics and size of the sample
- Research design employed (e.g., descriptive correlational study, RCT), including the type of intervention(s) if applicable
- Variables measured with accompanying instruments
- Major findings
- Strengths and limitations

Once a table such as this is developed, it will be easier to identify strengths as well as gaps in prior work that could possibly be addressed by the proposed study.

Step 4: Develop a Theoretical/Conceptual Framework

A **theoretical** or **conceptual framework** is made up of a number of interrelated statements that attempt to describe, explain, and/or predict a phenomenon. Developing a conceptual or theoretical framework is an important step in designing a clinical study. Its purpose is to provide a framework for selecting the study's variables, including how they relate to one another, as well as to guide the development of the intervention(s) in experimental studies. Without a well-developed theoretical framework, explanations for the findings from a study may be weak and speculative (Melnyk & Feinstein, 2001).

As an example, self-regulation theory (Johnson, Fieler, Jones, et al., 1997; Leventhal & Johnson, 1983) has provided an excellent theoretical framework for providing educational interventions to patients undergoing intrusive procedures (e.g., endoscopy) and chemotherapy/radiation. The basic premise of this theory is that the provision of concrete objective information to an individual who is confronting a stressful situation or procedure will facilitate a cognitive schema or representation of what will happen that is similar to the real-life event. As a result of an individual knowing what he or she is likely to experience, there is an increase in understanding, predictability, and confidence in dealing with the situation as it unfolds (Johnson et al., 1997), which leads to improved coping outcomes.

Through a series of experimental studies, Melnyk and colleagues extended the use of self-regulation theory to guide interventions with parents of hospitalized and critically ill children (Melnyk, 1994; Melnyk, Alpert-Gillis, Feinstein, et al., 2004; Melnyk, Alpert-Gillis, Hensel, et al., 1997), parents of low-birth-weight premature infants (Melnyk, Alpert-Gillis, Feinstein, et al., 2001; Melnyk, Feinstein, Alpert-Gillis, et al., 2006), and parents with young children experiencing marital separation and divorce (Melnyk & Alpert-Gillis, 1996). Extensive evidence in the literature from descriptive studies indicated that a major source of stress for parents of hospitalized and critically ill children is their children's emotional and behavioral responses to hospitalization. Thus, it was hypothesized that parents who receive the COPE (Creating Opportunities for Parent Empowerment) intervention program, which contains educational information about children's likely behavioral and emotional changes during and following hospitalization, would have stronger beliefs about their children's responses to the stressful event. It also was hypothesized that the COPE program would work through parental beliefs about their children and their role—the proposed **mediating variable** (i.e., the variable or mechanism through which the intervention works)—to positively impact parent and child outcomes. As a result of them knowing what to expect of their children's emotions and behaviors during and following hospitalization, it was predicted that parents who receive the COPE program would have better emotional and functional coping outcomes (i.e., less negative mood state and increased participation in their children's care) than would parents who did not receive this information. Ultimately, because the emotional contagion hypothesis (Jimmerson, 1982; VanderVeer, 1949) states that heightened parental anxiety leads to heightened child anxiety, it was expected that the children of parents who received the COPE program would have better coping outcomes than would those whose parents did not receive this educational information. Thus, through this series of clinical trials, empirical support for the effectiveness of the COPE program was generated in addition to data that explain how the intervention actually impacts patient and family outcomes (Figure 17.2).

Step 5: Generate Hypotheses When Appropriate

Hypotheses are predictions about the relationships between study variables. For example, when using self-regulation theory, a hypothesis that would logically emerge from the theory would be that parents who receive concrete objective information about their children's likely responses to hospitalization (i.e., the independent variable) would report less anxiety (i.e., the **dependent** or

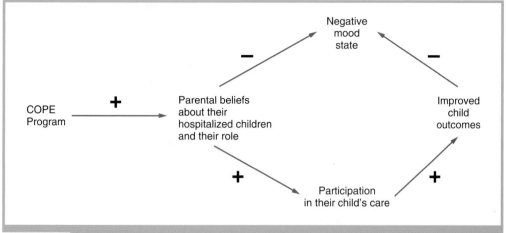

figure 17.2 Effects of the COPE program on maternal and child outcomes during and following critical care hospitalization

outcome variable) than would parents who do not receive this information. To include hypotheses in a clinical study, there should be either a theory to guide the formulation of these predictions or enough evidence from prior work to provide a sufficient foundation on which to make predictive statements. In situations where the evidence on which to base predictive statements is insufficient or where an investigator chooses not to use a theoretical or conceptual framework to guide his or her work (which is not advised), research questions should be developed instead of hypotheses (e.g., What is the effect of an educational intervention on coping outcomes of parents of critically ill children?).

Step 6: Select the Appropriate Research Design

The **design** of a clinical study is its foundation. It is the overall plan (i.e., the study protocol for testing the study hypotheses or questions) that includes the following:

- Strategies for controlling confounding or extraneous variables
- Strategies for when the intervention will be delivered (in experimental studies)
- How often and when the data will be collected

A good quantitative design is one that

- Appropriately tests the hypotheses or answers the research questions
- Lacks bias
- Controls extraneous or confounding variables
- Has sufficient **power** (i.e., the ability to detect statistically significant findings)

If the research question or hypothesis concerns itself with testing the effects of an intervention or treatment on patient outcomes, the study calls for an **experimental design**. In contrast, if the hypothesis/research question is interested in quantitatively describing a selected variable or is interested in the relationship between two or more variables (e.g., What is the relationship between the average amount of sleep and test performance in college students? What presurgery demographic variables predict successful recovery from open heart surgery?), a **nonexperimental study design** would be the most appropriate. The next section of this chapter reviews the most common designs for nonexperimental as well as experimental studies.

Nonexperimental Study Designs

Typically, nonexperimental designs are used to describe, explain, or predict a phenomenon. These types of designs also are undertaken when it is undesirable or unethical to manipulate the independent variable or, in other words, to impose a treatment. For example, it would be unethical to assign teenagers randomly to receive an illegal drug (e.g., ecstasy) in order to study its effects on sexual risk-taking behaviors. Therefore, an alternative design would be a prospective descriptive study in which sexual risk-taking behaviors are measured over time in a group of adolescents who use ecstasy, compared with a group who has never used any drugs.

Descriptive Studies. The purpose of descriptive studies is to describe, observe, or document a phenomenon that can serve as a foundation for developing hypotheses or testing theory. For example, a descriptive study design would be appropriate to answer each of the following clinical questions:

- What is the incidence of complications in women who are on bed rest with preterm labor?
- What is the average number of depressive symptoms experienced by teenagers after a critical care hospitalization?
- In adults with type 2 diabetes, what are the most common physical comorbidities?

Survey Research. Surveys are a type of descriptive study in which self-report data are typically collected to assess a certain condition or status. Most survey research is **cross-sectional** (i.e., all measurements are collected at the same point in time) versus research that is conducted over time (e.g., **cohort studies**, which follow the same sample longitudinally).

Survey data can be collected via multiple strategies (e.g., personal or telephone interviews and mailed or in-person questionnaires). For example, a group of healthcare providers might be surveyed with a questionnaire designed to measure their knowledge and attitudes about evidence-based practice (EBP). Data gained from this survey might then be used to design inservice education workshops to enhance the providers' knowledge and skills in this area.

Major advantages of survey research include rapid data collection and flexibility. Disadvantages of survey research include low response rates—especially if the surveys are mailed—and gathering information that is fairly superficial.

Correlational Studies. Correlational research designs are used when there is an interest in describing the relationship between or among two or more variables. In this type of design, even when there is a strong relationship that is discovered between the variables under consideration, it is not substantiated to say that one variable caused the other to happen. For example, if a study found a positive relationship between adolescent smoking and drug use (e.g., as smoking increases, drug use increases), it would not be appropriate to state that smoking causes drug use. The only conclusion that could be drawn from these data is that these variables **covary** (i.e., as one changes, the other variable changes as well).

Correlational Descriptive Research. When there is interest in describing the relationship between two variables, a correlational descriptive study design would be most appropriate. For example, the following two research questions would be best answered with correlational designs:

- What is the relationship between number of days that a person is on bed rest after a severe motor vehicle accident (the independent variable) and the incidence of decubiti ulcers (the dependent variable)?
- What is the relationship between watching violent television shows (the independent variable) and the number of anger outbursts in adult males (the dependent variable)?

Correlational Predictive Research. When an investigator is interested in whether one variable that occurs earlier in time predicts another variable that occurs later in time, a correlational predictive

| Level of stress in the first 3 months after starting a new job | ⟹ | Job performance 1 year later |

figure 17.3   A correlational predictive study

study should be undertaken. For example, the following research questions would best lend themselves to this type of study (Figure 17.3):

- Does maternal anxiety shortly after a child's admission to the intensive care unit (the independent variable) predict posttraumatic stress symptoms 6 months after hospitalization (the dependent variable)?
- Does the level of stress during the first 3 months after starting a new job (the independent variable) predict performance one year later?

Establishment of a strong relationship in correlational predictive studies often lends support for attempting to influence the independent variable in a future intervention study. For example, if findings from research indicated that job stress in the initial months after starting a new position as a practitioner predicted later job performance, a future study might evaluate the effects of a training program on reducing early job stress with the expectation that a successful intervention program would improve later job performance. Although it should never be definitively stated that a cause-and-effect relationship is supported with a correlational study, a predictive correlational design is stronger than a descriptive one with regard to making a causal inference because the independent variable occurs before the dependent variable in time sequence (Polit & Beck, 2008).

Case-Control Studies. Case-control studies are those in which one group of individuals (i.e., cases) with a certain condition (e.g., migraine headaches) is studied at the same time as another group of individuals who do not have the condition (i.e., controls) to determine an association between one or more predictor variables (e.g., family history of migraine headaches, consumption of red wine) and the condition (i.e., migraine headaches). Case-control studies are usually retrospective, or ex post facto (i.e., they look back in time to reveal predictor variables that might explain why the cases contracted the disease or problem and the controls did not).

Advantages of this type of research design include an ability to determine associations with a small number of subjects, which is especially useful in the study of rare types of diseases, and an ability to generate hypotheses for future studies (Newman, Browner, Cummings, et al., 2001). One of the major limitations to using this study design is **bias** (i.e., an inability to control confounding variables that may influence the outcome). For example, the two groups of individuals previously presented (i.e., those with migraines and those without migraines) may be different on certain variables (e.g., amount of sleep and stress) that also may influence the development of migraine headaches. Another limitation is that because case-control studies are usually retrospective, one is limited to data available at a prior time. Often, data on interesting variables were not thought to be important and not collected.

Cohort Studies. A cohort study follows a group of subjects longitudinally over a period of time to describe the incidence of a problem or to determine the relationship between a predictor variable and an outcome. For example, if an investigator were interested in whether daughters of mothers who had breast cancer have a higher incidence of the disease versus those whose mothers did not have breast cancer, this type of design would be appropriate. Two groups of daughters (i.e., those with and without a mother with breast cancer) would be studied over time to determine the incidence of breast cancer in each group. A major strength of prospective cohort studies includes being able to determine the incidence of a problem and its possible cause(s).

A major limitation is the lengthy nature of this type of study, the costs of which often become prohibitive.

Experimental Study Designs

A true experiment, or RCT, is the strongest design for testing cause-and-effect relationships (e.g., whether an intervention or treatment impacts patient outcomes) and provides strong evidence on which to change and improve clinical practice. For evidence to support causality (i.e., cause-and-effect relationships), three criteria must be met:

1. The independent variable (i.e., the intervention or treatment) must precede the dependent variable (i.e., the outcome) in terms of time sequence.
2. There must be a strong relationship between the independent and dependent variables.
3. The relationship between the independent and dependent variables cannot be explained as being due to the influence of other variables (i.e., all possible alternate explanations of the relationship must be eliminated).

Although true experiments are the best designs to control for the influence of confounding variables, it must be recognized that control of potential confounding or extraneous variables is very challenging when conducting studies in the real world—not in the laboratory. Other limitations of experiments include the fact that they are usually time consuming and expensive.

Intervention studies or clinical trials typically follow a five-phase development sequence:

- Phase I: Basic research that is exploratory and descriptive in nature and that establishes the variables that may be amenable to intervention or in which the content, strength, and timing of the intervention are developed, along with the outcome measures for the study
- Phase II: Pilot research (i.e., a small-scale study in which the intervention is tested with a small number of subjects so that the feasibility of a large-scale study is determined and alternative strategies are developed for potential problems)
- Phase III: Efficacy trials in which evaluation of the intervention takes place in an ideal setting and clinical efficacy is determined (in this stage, much emphasis is placed on internal validity of the study and preliminary *cost-effectiveness* of the intervention)
- Phase IV: Effectiveness of clinical trials in which analysis of the intervention effect is conducted in clinical practice and clinical effectiveness is determined, as is cost-effectiveness (in this stage, much emphasis is placed on external validity or generalizability of the study)
- Phase V: Effects on public health in which wide-scale implementation of the intervention is conducted to determine its effects on public health (Whittemore & Grey, 2002)

Many practitioners assume a leadership role in Phases I and II of this sequence and more of a participative role as a member of a research team in Phases III through V.

Randomized Controlled Trial or True Experiment. The best type of study design or "gold standard" for evaluating the effects of a treatment or intervention is an RCT, or true experiment, in that it is the strongest design for testing cause-and-effect relationships. True experiments or RCTs possess three characteristics:

1. An experimental group that receives the treatment or intervention
2. A control or comparison group that receives standard care or a comparison intervention that is different from the experimental intervention
3. **Randomization** or **random assignment**, which is the use of a strategy to randomly assign subjects to the experimental or control groups (e.g., tossing a coin)

Random assignment is the strongest method to help ensure that the study groups are similar on demographic or clinical variables at baseline (i.e., before the treatment is delivered). Similarity

R	O_1	X_1	O_2
R	O_1	X_2	O_2

figure 17.4   Two-group RCT with pretest/posttest design and structurally equivalent comparison group. R, random assignment; X, intervention/treatment, *with X_1 being the experimental intervention and X_2 being the comparison/control intervention;* O, observation/measurement, *with O_1 being the first time the variable is measured (at baseline) and O_2 being the second time that it is measured (after the intervention)*

between groups at the beginning of an experiment is very important in that if findings reveal a positive effect on the dependent variable, it can be concluded that the treatment, not other extraneous variables, is what affected the outcome. For example, results from an RCT might reveal that a cognitive behavioral intervention reduced depressive symptoms in adults. However, if the adults in the experimental and control groups were not similar on certain characteristics prior to the start of the intervention (e.g., level of social support, number of current stressful life events), it could be that differences between the groups on these variables accounted for the change in depressive symptoms at the end of the study, instead of the change being due to the positive impact of the cognitive behavioral intervention itself.

Examples of true experimental designs along with advantages and disadvantages of each are presented in Figures 17.4 through 17.9. *R* in these figures indicates random assignment, *X* represents an intervention or treatment (*X1* indicates the experimental intervention, and *X2* and *X3* indicate study groups who received an intervention different from the experimental intervention), and *O* indicates the time at which an observation or outcome measurement occurs (*O1* indicates the first time that an observation or measure is gathered, and *O2* and *O3* indicate the second and third times a measure is collected). These designations have been used for years in the literature since the publishing of a landmark book on experimental designs by Campbell and Stanley (1963). Note that time moves from left to right, and subscripts can be used to designate different groups if necessary.

The major advantage of the design illustrated in Figure 17.4 is that it is a true experiment, the strongest design for testing cause-and-effect relationships. As seen in Figure 17.4, the inclusion of a comparison group in the design that receives a different/comparison or "attention control" intervention similar in length to the experimental intervention is important, especially in psychosocial research, because it helps to support that any positive effects of the experimental intervention are not just the result of giving participants something instead of nothing but are due to experimental intervention itself. However, at the same time, it must be realized that including a comparison intervention may dilute some of the positive effects of the experimental intervention, especially if an outcome being measured in a study is tapping a psychosocial variable, such as anxiety (e.g., giving participants something instead of nothing, as would be the case with a pure control group, might reduce anxiety simply because someone spent time and provided some type of intervention). The benefits of this design (i.e., including an attention control or comparison intervention) outweigh the risk of diluting the positive effects of the experimental intervention. Although pretesting the subjects on the same measure that is being used as the outcome for the study (e.g., state anxiety) may in itself sensitize them to respond differently when answering questions on the anxiety measure the second time, this approach allows one to determine whether subjects are similar on anxiety at the beginning of the study. A disadvantage of this design, as with all experiments, is that it is typically expensive and time consuming.

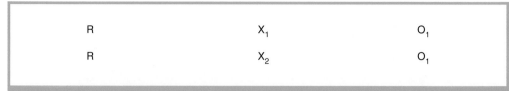

R	X_1	O_1
R	X_2	O_1

figure 17.5 Two-group RCT with posttest design only. R, random assignment; X, intervention/treatment, *with X_1 being the experimental intervention and X_2 being the comparison/control intervention;* O, observation/measurement

The advantage of conducting a two-group RCT with a posttest-only design is that there is no pretesting effect, which may confound the outcome in a study (Figure 17.5). For example, if you were interested in evaluating the effects of a fire safety educational program on school-aged children's knowledge of fire safety procedures, you may not want to pretest the experimental and attention control groups on their knowledge by asking them questions such as, What do you do if fire gets on your clothes? or What do you do if you find matches? The administration of a pretest in itself may lead the control children, who were not receiving the educational information, to ask their parents or teachers for the answers to these questions. As a result, findings may reveal no difference in knowledge between the two study groups at the end of the study—not because the intervention did not work, but due to the strong influence of pretesting effects on the outcome.

The main disadvantage of a posttest-only design is that baseline data on the study groups are unknown. Even though random assignment in the design illustrated in Figure 17.5 was used, which is the strongest strategy for controlling extraneous or confounding variables in an experimental study, there is still a chance that the two groups may be unequal or different at the start of the study. Differences in important baseline study measures between experimental groups may then negatively impact a study's outcomes or interfere with the ability to say that it was the intervention itself that caused a change in the dependent variable(s).

If an investigator is interested in whether an intervention produces both short-term and long-term effects on an outcome, it is important for a study to build into its design repeated measurements of the outcome variable of interest (Figure 17.6). The advantage of this type of design is that repeated assessments of an outcome variable over time allow an investigator to determine the sustainability of an intervention's effects. A disadvantage of this type of design is that *study attrition* (i.e., loss of subjects) may be a problem that may threaten the internal validity of the study. Another disadvantage of this design is that it is costly to follow subjects for longer periods of time. In addition, repeated follow-up on the same measures also may have the disadvantage of introducing testing effects that influence the outcome. For example, individuals may think

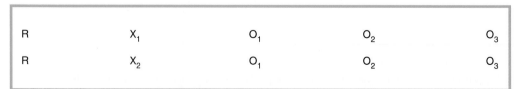

R	X_1	O_1	O_2	O_3
R	X_2	O_1	O_2	O_3

figure 17.6 Two-group RCT with long-term repeated measures follow-up. R, random assignment; X, intervention/treatment, *with X_1 being the experimental intervention and X_2 being the comparison intervention;* O, observation/measurement, *which will occur at three different time points (i.e., O_1, O_2, and O_3) after the intervention/treatment is delivered*

figure 17.7   Two-group RCT with true control group that receives no intervention. R, random assignment; X, intervention/treatment, *with X₁ being the experimental intervention*; O, observation/measurement

about their answers and change their beliefs as part of the repeated follow-up sessions, not as the result of the intervention. Also, subjects may learn how repeated follow-up sessions work and, if the study entails extensive questioning when individuals admit to certain things (e.g., being depressed or taking drugs), they may learn to respond negatively to avoid lengthy follow-up testing or interviews.

The real disadvantage to conducting an RCT with a true control group, as illustrated in Figure 17.7, is that any positive intervention effects that are found may be solely related to giving the intervention group something versus nothing or the typical standard of care. This is especially true in studies that are measuring psychosocial/mental health variables, such as depression and anxiety. For example, if a healthcare provider were studying the effects of a stress reduction program on college students with test anxiety, someone simply spending extra time with them could reduce their anxiety, regardless of whether the intervention itself was helpful.

The inclusion of a third group, as shown in Figure 17.8, allows an investigator to separate the effects of giving something (i.e., a comparison or attention control intervention) from a pure control group (i.e., a group who receives nothing or standard care)—a very strong experimental design. Disadvantages typically include the need to recruit additional subjects and costs to conduct the study.

The main advantage to conducting an experimental study that employs a **Solomon four-group design** (i.e., an experiment that uses a before-after design for the first experimental and control groups and an after-only design for the second experimental and control groups; Polit & Beck, 2008) is that it can separate the effects of pretesting the subjects (i.e., gathering baseline measures) on the outcome measure(s) (see Figure 17.9). Disadvantages include the addition of subjects as well as costs for increasing the size of the sample.

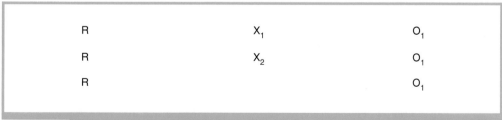

figure 17.8   Three-group RCT (i.e., one group who receives one type of experimental intervention, one group who receives a different or comparison intervention, and a pure control group who receives no intervention or standard care). R, random assignment; X, intervention/treatment, *with X₁ being the experimental intervention and X₂ being the comparison intervention*; O, observation/measurement, *which only occurs once (i.e., postintervention)*

R	O_1	X_1	O_2
R		X_1	O_2
R	O_1	X_2	O_2
R		X_2	O_2

figure 17.9 Solomon four-group design in which a pair of experimental and control groups receive pretesting as depicted by O_1 and a pair who do not receive pretesting. R, random assignment; X, intervention/treatment, with X_1 being the experimental intervention and X_2 being the comparison/control intervention; O, observation/measurement, with O_1 being the pretest (i.e., measured at baseline) and O_2 being the posttest (i.e., measured after the intervention is delivered)

A factorial design (Figure 17.10) is an experiment that has two or more interventions or treatments. A major advantage of this type of design is that it allows an investigator to study the separate and combined effects of different types of interventions. For example, if a healthcare provider were interested in the separate and combined effects of two different interventions (i.e., educational information and an exercise program) on blood pressure in adults with hypertension, this type of design would result in four groups:

1. A group of subjects who would receive educational information only
2. A group of subjects who would receive an exercise program only
3. A group of subjects who would receive both educational information and an exercise program
4. A group of subjects who would receive neither information nor exercise

A major strength of this design is that it could be determined whether education or exercise alone positively impacts blood pressure or whether a combination of the two treatments is more effective than either intervention alone. Disadvantages to this design typically include additional subjects and costs.

Quasi-Experimental Studies. Designs in which the independent variable (i.e., a treatment) is manipulated or introduced but where there is a lack of random assignment or a control group are called **quasi-experimental designs.**

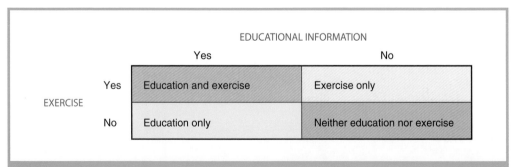

figure 17.10 2 × 2 factorial experiment that generates four study groups. **A.** A group who receives both education and exercise. **B.** A group who receives education only. **C.** A group who receives exercise only. **D.** A control group who receives neither education nor exercise

| O_1 | X_1 | O_2 |
| O_1 | X_2 | O_2 |

figure 17.11 A quasi-experiment with pretest and posttest design and a comparison/control group but lacking random assignment. X, intervention, with X_1 being the experimental intervention and X_2 being the comparison/control intervention; O, observation, with O_1 indicating measurement at baseline and O_2 indicating measurement after the intervention is delivered

Although **quasi-experiments** may be more practical and feasible, they are weaker than true experimental designs in the ability to establish cause-and-effect inferences (i.e., to say that the independent variable or treatment was responsible for a change in the dependent variable and that the change was not due to other extraneous factors).

There are times when quasi-experiments need to be conducted because random assignment is not always possible. For example, individuals cannot be assigned to smoking and non-smoking conditions. Even when it is ethically feasible to use random assignment, the study setting might preclude it. For example, school principals frequently resist assigning children to programs based on random assignment. In addition, random assignment can be disruptive in schools (e.g., taking children out of their regular classrooms for special programs). Quasi-experiments, that is, designs that compare groups created by some method other than random assignment, provide an alternative to true experiments. Despite their limitations, some of these designs can be quite powerful in their ability to eliminate alternative explanations for the relationship between an intervention and the outcomes in a study.

Two examples of quasi-experimental designs are shown in Figures 17.11 and 17.12. In Figure 17.11, there is an experimental group and an attention control group who both receive a treatment, but the subjects have not been randomly assigned to the two study groups. As a result, the probability of equal study groups cannot be assured. Therefore, a pretest is administered so that it can be determined whether the two study groups are equal at baseline before the intervention is delivered. In quasi-experiments, pretesting is especially important to assess whether the subjects are similar at baseline on the variable(s) that will be used as the outcome(s) in the study. However, even with pretesting that shows no pre-intervention differences, a quasi-experiment is still not as strong as a true experiment that uses random assignment. Because the groups are pre-existing or created by a means other than random assignment in a quasi-experiment, there could be other unexplored differences between them that might account for any differences found on the outcome variables. If only posttesting is conducted in a quasi-experimental design in which random assignment was not used, it would be very difficult to have confidence in the findings because it could not be known whether the study groups were similar on key variables at the commencement of the study. In contrast, when random assignment is used in true experimental designs, it is very likely that the study groups will be equivalent on pretest measures.

Another example of a quasi-experimental study is the interrupted time series design (Figure 17.12). In this study, there is no random assignment or comparison/attention control group. This design incorporates a long series of pretest observations, an intervention, and a long series of posttest observations.

The time series design is used most frequently in communities or agencies that maintain careful archival records. It also can be used with community survey data if the survey questions and sample remain constant over time. An intervention effect is evidenced if a stable pattern of

chapter 17

419

| O_1 | O_2 | O_3 | O_4 | X | O_5 | O_6 | O_7 | O_8 |

figure 17.12 Time series design

observations over a long period of time is found, followed by a marked change at the point of the intervention, then a stable pattern again over a long time after the intervention. For example, adolescent truancy rates might be tracked over several years, followed by an intervention with the tracking of truancy rates for several additional years. If there is a marked drop in truancy rates at the point of the intervention, there is reasonable evidence for a program's effect. Even though this is a single-group design, there is ample evidence to rule out a variety of alternative explanations.

One frequent challenge to single-group designs is the threat of **history**, which involves the occurrence of some event or program unrelated to the intervention that might account for the change observed. History remains a viable alternate explanation for a change in the dependent variable only if the event happens at the same time point as the intervention. If the event occurs earlier or later than the experimental intervention, it cannot explain a change in outcome that occurs at or around the time of the intervention.

Another possible alternate explanation for observed changes in a single-group design is the **maturation** threat. Maturation is a developmental change that occurs even in the absence of the intervention. A true maturation effect will occur gradually throughout the pretest and posttest periods and thus could not account for sharp changes that occur at the point of the intervention.

Observed changes also might occur because of repeated testing or changes in instrumentation. Repeat testing of individuals typically influences their subsequent scores. In addition, performance on skills-based tests should increase over time simply due to practice. Finally, mortality as well as attrition or movement into and out of a community also could influence the outcome data but they offer an alternate explanation only if it started at the point of treatment.

Tamburro, Shorr, Bush, et al. (2002) employed an interrupted time series design in their evaluation of the impact of the Mid-South Safe Kids Coalition on rates of serious unintentional injuries (i.e., those leading to hospitalization or death). Consistent data were available for 1990 and 1991, 2 years prior to the implementation of the coalition, and for 1993 through 1997, about 6 years following the implementation. All children in the county younger than 10 years old who were treated in a single hospital were included in the sample. Analyses showed a statistically significant drop in the rates of targeted injuries from 3.5 to 2.0 per 1,000 children, beginning precisely at the point the coalition was formed.

Pre-Experimental Studies. Pre-experiments lack both random assignment and a comparison/attention control group (Figure 17.13). As such, they are very weak in internal validity and allow too many competing explanations for a study's findings.

Other Important Experimental Design Factors. Methods to ensure quality and consistency in the delivery of the intervention (i.e., maintenance of integrity) are crucial for being able to determine whether and how well an intervention works.

Integrity and Reproducibility. Frequently, investigators spend inordinate amounts of time paying particular attention to the dependent variable(s) or measure(s) to be used in a study and do not give sufficient time and attention to how an intervention is delivered. In addition, at the outset of an intervention study, it is critical to give thought to whether the intervention will be able to be reproduced by others in different settings. Reproducibility is critical if translation of the

X O_1

figure 17.13   Pre-experiment in which there is no random assignment or no comparison/control group. X, intervention; O, observation

intervention into real-life practice settings is going to occur. As such, it is important to manualize or create standardized materials that specifically outline the content of the intervention so that others can replicate it and expect the same results in their practice settings. Use of videotapes, audio tapes, DVDs, or other types of reproducible materials to deliver an intervention is helpful in that this strategy ensures that each subject will receive all of the intervention content in exactly the same manner. However, this type of delivery is not always best suited to a particular clinical population. For example, groups may be the best strategy to deliver interventions to teens at high risk for sexually transmitted diseases because they allow for the teaching of refusal skills through role-playing.

In a study conducted by Morrison-Beedy, Carey, Aronowitz, et al. (2002a; 2002b), several healthcare providers were used to deliver an information/motivation/behavioral skills training program in four 2-hour group sessions to urban minority female adolescents. The content of the program and necessary skills to be taught for each of the sessions were detailed in a written manual. However, before the actual study commenced, intensive training of the interventionists occurred (e.g., practice groups and role-playing) to ensure that each of them would deliver the content of the program and the teaching of behavioral skills in the same manner. Once the study started, sessions were audio taped and reviewed by the investigators to ensure quality and completeness in the delivery of the educational information and behavioral skills.

If rigorous standards to ensure the integrity of an intervention do not occur in a study, it would be difficult to know whether the findings generated were the result of the intervention itself or other extraneous variables (Melnyk & Fineout-Overholt, 2005). When integrity of an intervention is maintained, greater confidence can be placed in a study's findings.

Pilot Study. Before conducting a large experimental study, it is extremely beneficial to first conduct a pilot study, which is a preliminary study that is conducted with a small number of subjects (e.g., 30–40) versus a full-scale clinical trial with large numbers of subjects. A pilot study is critical in determining the feasibility of subject enrollment, the intervention, the protocol or data collection plan for the study, and the likelihood that subjects will complete follow-up measures. With the development and implementation of new study measures, it also is essential to pilot them before use in a full-scale study to determine their validity and reliability. Pilot work enables investigators to identify weaknesses in their study design so that they can be corrected for the full-scale study. Subjects used for the pilot study should match those individuals who will be participating in the full-scale clinical trial.

Pilot studies are frequently conducted by advanced practice nurses and other master's prepared clinicians and often lead the way to full-scale clinical trials. Working through the details for a large-scale intervention trial with a pilot study saves much time, energy, and frustration, as well as provides convincing evidence that a large-scale clinical trial is feasible and well worth the effort.

Manipulation Checks. Manipulation checks are important assessments to determine whether the intervention was successfully conducted. For example, if an investigator was delivering an educational intervention intended to teach healthcare providers about a disease and its treatment in order to improve patient outcomes, a manipulation check might be a test with a number

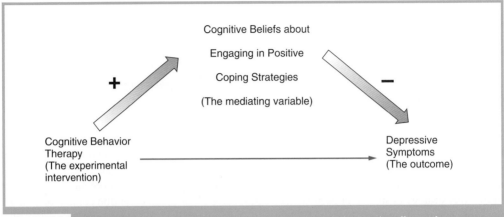

figure 17.14 The proposed mediating effect of cognitive beliefs in explaining the effects of cognitive behavioral therapy on depressive symptoms

of multiple-choice questions about the content of the intervention to which the subjects would respond. Answering a certain percentage of these questions correctly would indicate that the subjects successfully processed the educational information. As another example, an investigator may be interested in the effects of a new aerobic exercise program on weight loss in young adults. Therefore, subjects in the experimental group would be taught this program and instructed to complete the prescribed activities three times per week. A manipulation check to ensure that subjects actually complied with the prescribed exercise activities may involve keeping a log that lists the dates and number of minutes spent adhering to the program. These types of assessments are critical in order to verify that manipulation of the independent variable or completion of the treatment was achieved. If manipulation checks are not included in an experimental study and results indicate no differences between the experimental and attention control/comparison groups, it would be very difficult to explain whether it was a lack of intervention potency or the fact that subjects did not attend to or adhere to the intervention that was responsible for a lack of intervention effects.

Intervention Processes. When preparing to conduct an intervention study, it is important to think not only about the dependent variables or outcomes that the intervention might impact, but also about the process through which the intervention will exert its effects. The explanations about how an intervention works are important in facilitating its implementation into practice settings (Melnyk, 1995; Melnyk, Crean, Feinstein, et al., 2007; Melnyk & Feinstein, 2001).

For example, an investigator proposes that a cognitive behavioral intervention (the independent variable) will reduce depressive symptoms (the dependent variable) in adults with low self-esteem. At the same time, however, the investigator proposes the mechanism of action (i.e., the mediating variable) through which the intervention will work. Therefore, it is hypothesized that the experimental intervention will enhance cognitive beliefs about one's ability to engage in positive coping strategies, which in turn will result in a decrease in depressive symptoms (Figure 17.14). Conceptualization of a well-defined theoretical framework at the outset of designing an intervention study will facilitate explanations of how an intervention program may impact a study's outcomes.

Control Strategies. When conducting experimental studies, it is critical to strategize about how to control for extraneous factors that may influence the outcome(s) so that the effects of the intervention itself can be determined. These extraneous factors include those internal or intrinsic to the individuals who participate in a study (e.g., fatigue and level of maturity) and those external to the participants (e.g., the environment in which the study is conducted).

The best strategy to control for extraneous variables is randomization or random assignment. By randomly assigning subjects to study groups, there is a good probability that the subjects in the groups will be similar on important characteristics at the beginning of a study. When random assignment is not possible, other methods may be used to control extraneous or confounding variables. One of these strategies is **homogeneity**, or using subjects who are similar on the characteristics that may affect the outcome variable(s). For example, if a study were evaluating the effects of an intervention on parental stress during the critical care hospitalization of children, it may include only parents from intact marriages because divorced parents may have higher stress levels than nondivorced parents. In addition, very young mothers may have high stress levels. Therefore, this study's inclusion criteria may include only those parents who are from intact marriages as well as those who are older than 21 years. A limitation of this strategy is that at the end of the study, findings can be generalized only to married parents older than 21 years.

Another strategy to control intrinsic factors in a study is **blocking**. Blocking entails deliberately including a potential extraneous intrinsic or confounding variable in a study's design. For example, if there were a concern that level of motivation would affect the results of a study to determine the effects of aerobic exercise (i.e., the treatment) on weight loss in young adults, an investigator may choose to include motivation as another independent variable in the study, aside from the exercise program itself. In doing so, the effects of both motivation and exercise on weight loss could be studied in a 2 × 2 **randomized block design** (Figure 17.15) involving two independent variables with two levels: (a) exercise and no exercise and (b) high motivation and low motivation. The benefit of this type of design is that the interaction between motivation and exercise on weight loss also could be determined (i.e., Do individuals with high levels of motivation have greater weight loss than those with low motivation?).

Threats to Internal Validity. **Internal validity** is the extent to which it can be said that the independent variable (i.e., the intervention) causes a change in the dependent variable (i.e., outcome), and that the results are not due to other factors or alternative explanations. There are a number of major threats to the internal validity of a study that should be addressed in the planning process.

Attrition. The first threat to internal validity is **attrition**, or dropout of study participants, which may result in nonequivalent study groups (i.e., more individuals lost from the study in the attention control group than from the experimental group or more individuals with a certain characteristic withdrawing from participation). As a result of losing more subjects from the control group than from the experimental group or more subjects with a certain characteristic (e.g., high anxiety), the study findings may be different than if those individuals had remained in the study. For example, if individuals with the poorest outcomes felt that they were not gaining any benefit

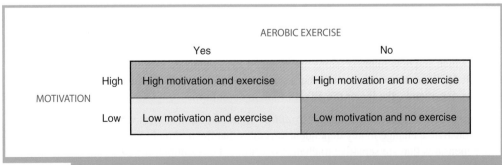

figure 17.15   A 2 × 2 randomized block design, *blocking on motivation*

from the study, which led them to drop from a study, differences between the two study groups may not surface during statistical analyses.

One strategy for preventing differential attrition is not to overly persuade potential subjects to participate in a study. There is a fine line between encouraging a potential subject to participate in a study and overly persuading him or her to participate. If someone decides to participate with much hesitation, there is an increased probability that he or she may drop from the study.

Another strategy for preventing attrition is to offer research subjects a small honorarium for participating in a study. Some studies provide an honorarium during each time point that a subject completes a specific phase of a study protocol (e.g., completing a set of questionnaires or receiving an intervention), whereas others provide an honorarium when the subjects complete the entire study protocol. Providing an honorarium sends the message that an individual's time for participating in a study is valued.

If there will be substantial time between contacts in a study, it is important to maintain communication through periodic cards or telephone calls. Lengthy lapses in communication with subjects make it easier for them not to return phone calls and questionnaires as well as to miss follow-up appointments. To prevent attrition, another helpful strategy is to maintain consistency in who provides follow-up with the participants. One consistent person on the research team who follows a subject longitudinally over time will enhance the chances of successfully obtaining repeated follow-up data.

Finally, it is important to reduce subject burden to prevent attrition from a study. Participants can become easily overwhelmed if each contact involves the completion of several questionnaires that require a lot of time. An important question to ask for each proposed dependent variable is: How key is the measurement of this outcome or is it just a nice additional piece of data to include in the study? As a general rule of thumb, the easier and less time consuming it is to participate in a study, the greater will be the probability of completion. It is also more valuable to have complete data on a few key variables than having partial data on a larger number of key and just interesting variables.

Confounding Variables/Selection. The best strategy to control for or minimize the influence of confounding variables is to randomly assign subjects to study groups. Another strategy for controlling potential confounding variables is to establish thoughtful inclusion and exclusion criteria. Finally, maintaining consistent study conditions for all participants is another strategy for controlling potential confounding variables. One way to ensure consistency is to establish clearly written study protocols so that every individual on the team understands the intricacies of when and how the interventions will be delivered, as well as the specific steps of data collection.

Nonadherence and Failure to Complete the Intervention Protocol. Designing a realistic intervention is important so that it will eventually be transportable to the real clinical practice world. There is a delicate balance in designing an intervention that will produce sustainable effects versus one that will be easy to implement in practice. As such, much thoughtful consideration must be given to the logistics of the intervention (e.g., feasibility and user-friendliness).

If there are multiple sessions with ongoing phases of the intervention, it is important to record which and how many sessions are attended and completed by study participants because this will facilitate the evaluation of whether a dose response exists (i.e., the greater the number of sessions one attends, the larger the effect of the intervention).

Measurement of Change in Outcome Variables. In intervention studies where it is important to demonstrate a change in key dependent variables that the treatment will impact, it is critical to use measures that are sensitive to change over time. For example, if a certain measure has high **test–retest reliability** (i.e., it is stable over time, such as an individual's personality), there will be little opportunity to affect a change in that measure. This is in contrast to other types of studies in which high test–retest reliabilities on certain measures are desirable (e.g., cohort studies that do not employ interventions in which you are following certain variables over time). For example, an individual's trait anxiety is the general predisposition to anxiety over time, which has been empirically shown to be a stable construct. In contrast, an individual's state anxiety fluctuates, depending on the situation. Therefore, an intervention would most likely affect state, not trait anxiety. Therefore, state anxiety would be a better outcome measure in an intervention study than would trait anxiety.

In conducting intervention studies, it is important to use the same measures longitudinally so that intervention effects over time can be determined. Carefully planning the timing of assessments is critical, especially if there is interest in both the short-term and long-term effects of an intervention. It is also important to use measures that have good variability and that have been tested in the population of interest to avoid **ceiling** and **floor** effects (i.e., participant scores that cluster toward the low end or high-end score of a measure).

In addition to measuring the outcomes of interventions with quantitative scales, it is important to administer an evaluation questionnaire at the end of a study so that subjects can provide open-ended responses to whether and how they believed the intervention was helpful. These types of responses are especially important if, by chance, the quantitative measures in the study reveal no statistically significant differences between study groups on key outcome variables.

It is also important to assess both clinical meaningfulness and statistical significance when determining whether an intervention has been successful. For example, the greater the number of subjects that are included in a study, the more statistical *power* there will be to detect statistically significant differences between groups. In contrast, the smaller the sample size, the lower the power and the more difficult it will be to detect statistically significant findings. For example, in one hypothetical study with 1,000 subjects, an investigator found that teens who were enrolled in an expensive smoking cessation program smoked two cigarettes less per day than did teens who did not receive the program. This finding was statistically significant at the 0.05 level. As a result of this significant finding, the costly smoking cessation program was widely implemented. Although the finding was statistically significant, the clinical meaningfulness of this finding is weak. In contrast, another investigator conducted the same study with 50 adolescents and found that the experimental group teens smoked 10 cigarettes less per day than did teens who did not receive the smoking cessation program. This difference, however, was not statistically significant due to a small number of subjects and low statistical power. Therefore, a decision was made not to implement the program routinely because there was not a statistically significant difference between the study groups. However, a 10-cigarette difference between groups is more clinically meaningful than a 2-cigarette difference. This is a good example of how faulty decisions can be made if only statistically significant findings are considered important and their clinical meaningfulness is ignored.

History. History is another major threat to the internal validity of a study. This condition happens when external events take place concurrently with the treatment that may influence the outcome variables. For example, if a study were being conducted to determine the effects of a violence prevention intervention on anxiety in school-aged children and a school shooting occurred that received extensive media attention during the course of the trial, children's anxiety levels at the end of the study could be high, despite any positive effects of the intervention. The best way to minimize the threat of history is random assignment because at least both groups then should be equally affected by the external event.

Maturation. The passage of time alone can impact the outcomes of a study. For example, when studying infants who are growing rapidly, an acceleration in cognitive development may occur, regardless of the effects of an intervention that is aimed at enhancing cognition. The best way to deal with the threat of maturation is to use random assignment to allocate subjects to experimental and control groups as well as to recognize it as a potential alternative explanation for a study's findings.

Testing. Completing measures repeatedly could influence an individual's responses the next time a measure is completed. For example, answering the same depression scale three or four times could program someone to respond in the same way on subsequent administrations of the scale.

On the other hand, lengthy lapses in the administration of an instrument may result in a failure to detect important changes over time. Therefore, the best way to deal with this threat to internal validity is to think very carefully about how many times subjects are being asked to complete study measures and provide a strong rationale for these decisions.

Step 7: Identify the Sample and Enhance External Validity

External validity addresses the **generalizability** of research results (i.e., our ability to apply what we learn from a study sample to the larger population from which the sample was drawn). Clearly, a great deal is learned from the samples we study. However, there is always interest in applying that knowledge to a broader population (e.g., to the next 1,000 patients, not just the 100 in a particular study).

The key to external validity is the degree to which the sample that is being studied is representative of the population from which it was drawn. Creating a representative sample is a complex and challenging task. Samples are rarely if ever perfectly representative of the populations of interest, but there can be reasonable approximations.

There are four steps to consider when building a sample (Trochim, 2001):

1. Carefully define the theoretical population. The theoretical population is the population to which you wish to generalize your results (e.g., all 3-year-old children).
2. Describe the population to which you have access (i.e., the study population). Continuing with our example, this might include all 3-year-old children in the county in which you work, or perhaps in all of the counties in which your collaborators work. At this point, it is necessary to consider how similar the study population is to the theoretical population. Typically, if the county is large and diverse, it is reasonable to assume that the study population is an acceptable substitute for the theoretical population. However, if the focus of your work is strongly influenced by regional factors, such as climate, culture, or access to services, the choice of a study population could severely limit generalizability to the theoretical population.
3. Describe the method you will use to access the population; in other words, define the sampling frame. It is highly unlikely that there will be a single comprehensive list of all 3-year-old children living in any one region at a particular time. You must find some practical method of identifying eligible children; then assess how the available methods might introduce bias or nonrepresentativeness. One strategy might be to approach the day care programs in the region. This would certainly be efficient, but not all 3-year-olds attend day care, and those who do are unlikely to be fully representative of the study population. For example, children whose mothers do not work outside the home are less likely to attend day care. Another approach might be to contact all of the pediatric offices in the region and solicit their cooperation in identifying the 3-year-olds under their care. Certainly, all young children see a pediatrician or nurse practitioner from time to time, even if they do not regularly keep their well child appointments. However, not all children in the region may receive care at the local pediatric offices. Perhaps families at one or both ends of the socioeconomic spectrum travel outside of the region for their care; perhaps others avoid care because of a lack of insurance and use only the emergency department on an as-needed basis. Finally, the records at the pediatric offices might be out of date. A child may have come in for a 2-year visit, then

moved away. Each of these possible alternatives needs to be reviewed and evaluated. The method that balances efficiency with representativeness will be the best choice. If there are more sites (day care centers and pediatric offices) than one can efficiently work with, a mechanism to choose a portion of the sites must be selected. The options will be described in the next section, along with mechanisms for selecting actual subjects from the sampling frame.

4. Typically, the sampling frame will include many more potential subjects than are required for the study. Thus, the fourth step in the process is identifying a method to select those individuals who will be invited to participate. Once again, the method chosen should balance efficiency and representativeness.

Random Sampling

Randomly selecting study sites (e.g., clinics or day care centers) and then subjects is the method most likely to avoid bias. In **random sampling**, every potential subject has an equal chance of being selected. The most straightforward way to think about random sampling is to imagine taking the list of everyone in the sampling frame, cutting it into small pieces with one name on each piece, placing all the names in a bowl, and drawing from the bowl the number of names required for the study design. This might work for selecting 6-day care programs from a list of 25, but in practice, it is an inefficient way to draw a sample of 200 children from a sampling frame of 10,000. That is quite a bit of cutting! A more efficient method is to assign everyone in the sampling frame a unique number, then, reading down the columns of a random number table or a list of random numbers generated by a computer algorithm, select those cases whose identifiers are included in the list of random numbers. If the entire sampling frame is available electronically, most computer database programs will draw random samples of cases of any specified number.

Random sampling is an efficient way in which to create a representative sample, but it does not guarantee representativeness. By definition, the process is random. However, it is possible, although quite unlikely, that a very atypical sample might emerge. In using random sampling to create a sample of 200 from 10,000 children, every possible sample of 200 has an equal chance of being drawn. It is possible, although very unlikely, that the sample drawn will contain 200 boys and no girls. More realistically, smaller (proportionately) subgroups might be underrepresented or entirely absent. If the research involves handedness or physical stature, it is possible that the selected sample will have no left-handed children or no children below or above a given height. To avoid this possibility, sampling procedures frequently incorporate **stratification**.

Stratified Sampling

Stratification involves dividing the study population into two or more subpopulations, then sampling separately from each. For example, if you would like to ensure that exactly 50% of the 200 children in the study sample are male, you would divide the study population into male and female groups and randomly sample 100 from each. This type of simple stratification works only if information about the stratification variable is included in the sampling frame data, that is, in the day care center or pediatric office records. It is unlikely that you would be able to stratify by handedness using this simple strategy. Similarly, it would be unlikely that you would be able to stratify on measures such as depression, self-esteem, or life stress because information about these variables is unlikely to be included in any accessible preexisting database.

A variation on this theme involves a second stage of information gathering and sampling. Once the initial sampling frame is identified, a brief survey is conducted with a large random sample. The survey includes questions about variables on which you would like to stratify. A second random sample can now be drawn from the sample of completed surveys. This second-stage sampling can be stratified based on this new information. Such sampling designs are somewhat more complex to analyze, but they do ensure that all of the subgroups of interest are included in adequate numbers.

Cluster (Area) Random Sampling

If the study population is spread over a wide geographical area, you can use another variation of two-stage sampling. First, you divide the large area into regions or clusters (e.g., counties or census tracts). From the full list of clusters, you can randomly sample a sufficiently manageable number of clusters. Then individual subjects from each cluster can be randomly sampled. Clearly, it is best to have the same sampling strategy and the same sampling frame within each cluster. Like the other two-stage strategies, this requires somewhat more complex approaches to data analysis, but it makes collecting data across large geographic regions economical. If, for example, your sample population is all women in a state and you randomly sample from that population (e.g., from state motor vehicle or telephone records), you then must drive all over the state to collect your data. If you divide the state into counties and randomly sample six counties, the logistics of data collection become manageable as long as you believe that these six counties fairly reflect the overall state profile.

Nonprobability or Purposive Samples

There are occasions when it is not feasible to use random sampling. Nevertheless, you should make every effort to develop a representative sample and to employ a systematic approach that can be well described. This is purposive sampling (Trochim, 2001). A good description of your sampling strategy, whether random or not, permits the readers of your work to judge for themselves the representativeness of your sample and the generalizability of your results. Simply characterizing the sampling strategy as one of "convenience" with no further discussion leaves the reader with the impression that no thought whatsoever was given to external validity and no judgment can be made about generalizability. The reader is left to believe that you are assuming that your findings are invariant across all people and all places.

Modal Instance Sampling

Unlike random sampling, you sample the most frequent or modal case. This is less useful when sampling individuals than when sampling larger units, such as counties, clinics, or schools in two-stage sampling designs or where these larger units are actually the units of analysis (i.e., where the program or treatment is applied to a region or clinic rather than to a person). For example, in a primarily rural state, when selecting counties, you would select counties with a typical profile rather than those having very few highly urban counties. With respect to schools, you might select from the comprehensive high schools rather than from magnet or other schools with specialized programming.

With respect to the sampling of individuals, if we want to sample children from predominantly middle-class schools where most children are college bound, we might want to choose students who are in fact middle class and college bound. This will not give a truly representative picture of the entire school, but it provides a reasonable reflection of the majority.

Heterogeneity Sampling

This strategy is applicable in the same situations in which modal instance sampling is applicable. However, with this approach, instead of sampling just the modal or typical case, you take care to sample heterogeneously to ensure a broad spectrum of subjects. In the example involving counties described previously, rather than sampling just the modal rural counties, you would sample rural, urban, and suburban counties. With respect to schools, you might select comprehensive, magnet, and some specialized school programs. With respect to individual children, you might sample college-bound students, those in vocational programs, and perhaps even some who have dropped out or are about to drop out of school.

Snowball Sampling

Snowball sampling is helpful when assembling a sample of infrequent or hard-to-find cases. With snowball sampling, each subject is asked to recommend other potential subjects or to inform other possible subjects about the opportunity to participate in the study. For example, if one is studying older adults with relatively rare diseases or conditions, the spouses of one case will be likely to know or at least to have met other individuals whose spouses have the same condition. In snowball sampling, the investigator is less concerned with the broad representation of a large study population and more concerned with finding the relatively few members of that population who exist.

Determination of Sample Size

The determination of sample size is an important step and should be done early in the process of designing a study. It is important to remember that the sample size estimate should be calculated on how many subjects need to be followed over the course of a study, not just enrolled (Browner, Newman, Cummings, et al., 2001), always building into the plan at least a 20% dropout rate for longitudinal designs. Too few subjects may result in low statistical power and the inability to detect significant findings in a study when they truly do exist (i.e., making a *type 2 error*, such as when an investigator accepts a false null hypothesis, which states there is no relationship between the independent and dependent variables). Many studies conducted in the health professions result in nonsignificant findings as a result of samples that are too small. On the other hand, enrolling more subjects than needed will result in greater costs to a study than necessary. When estimating sample size, it is important to obtain the statistics on the number of patients who would have met your study criteria who were available in the clinical setting during the prior year where the study will be conducted. These data will allow you to determine the feasibility of recruiting the necessary number of subjects during the course of your study.

Power analysis is a procedure used for determining the sample size needed for a study and helps to reduce type 2 errors (Polit & Beck, 2008). Readers are encouraged to refer to a good resource to assist with the process of power analysis and calculation of sample size (Cohen, 1988, 1992; Jaccard & Becker, 1990).

Refusal to Participate and Study Attrition

The actual generalizability of the results depends not on who is approached to participate in a study but on who actually completes the study. Not everyone who is approached agrees to participate, and not everyone who agrees to participate completes the study. If the number of people who refuse or who drop out is relatively small and there is no reason to believe that any subgroup of subjects was more likely to drop out than any other (i.e., the pattern of refusals and dropouts was random), the final sample will still be representative of the study population. Quite frequently, however, those who refuse to participate and those who drop out are not a random subset.

People with exhibitionist tendencies (i.e., those who like to talk about themselves), hypochondriacs (i.e., always in need of confirmation of their illness or looking for free services), people with a strong social conscience, and those generally willing to volunteer are less likely to refuse. Thus, they will be overrepresented in any sample in which there is a substantial degree of refusal or dropout (Rosenthal & Rosnow, 2008). People who volunteer also are more likely to be affluent and well educated.

The best strategy to enhance external validity is to minimize refusal and dropout rates. To assess the potential impact of these threats, it is essential to have a clear sampling frame and to keep records of who is approached, who agrees to participate, who refuses, and ultimately who completes the study. If anything is known about those who were approached and refused, the possibility of bias can be addressed by comparing those who refused with those who did not as well as those who dropped out with those who did not. Understanding the impact of refusal rates is not possible using convenience sampling in which advertisements are placed in the newspaper or signs are posted and only those who are interested are identified. Such strategies must assume that the findings of the study (e.g., the impact of the intervention or the beliefs of the participants) are invariant across people.

Strategies to Promote Participation

There are several strategies that encourage participation in a study:

- *Have direct, personal contacts with prospective subjects.* Avoid making prospective subjects take any action or demonstrate any initiative to enroll, such as requiring them to complete enrollment forms or make telephone calls. Be persistent but respectful when contacting prospective subjects. Send letters of introduction on official stationery introducing the study and stating who and when someone will call to explain the study further. Use high-powered mailings (e.g., special delivery and/or hand-addressed envelopes) because individuals are much more likely to open such mail. Have the letters come from the PI whose credentials lend credibility to the study. Finally, communicate that volunteering is normative, not unusual behavior. You do not want to start out by saying, "You are probably quite busy…." This conveys an expectation that the person will refuse and actually gives them a socially acceptable reason.
- *Make participation as easy as possible.* Do what you can to remove any barriers, such as the cost of babysitting or transportation. If possible, have babysitting available at the study site. If that is not possible, provide a sufficient honorarium to cover the cost. Cover the cost of transportation or send a cab to transport individuals to the study site. Make the study as nonthreatening, stress free, and brief as possible, given the research design. Lengthy interviews covering a number of personal topics will burden subjects. Be certain each section is essential. Train the recruiters and interviewers well. Make certain that they are comfortable with the recruitment protocol, script, and interview before working with actual subjects. Interviewers must be accepting and nonjudgmental. They must not appear shocked, awkward, or unprepared during any conversation or interview.
- *Make participation worthwhile.* Carefully and clearly explain the importance of the work and the manner in which the study results might improve care or services to patients and/or families like theirs. Make participation sound interesting. Emphasize what the subjects might learn about themselves or their families. Tell them about any activities they might actually enjoy.

Step 8: Determine Measures

Selection of measures or instruments to assess or observe a study's variables is a critical step in designing a clinical study. As a rule, it is best to choose measures that yield the highest level of data (i.e., *interval* or *ratio data*, otherwise known as *continuous variables*) because these types of measures will allow fuller assessments of the study's variables, as well as permit the use of more robust statistical tests. Examples of interval- or ratio-level data that have quantified intervals on an infinite scale of values are weight in pounds, number of glasses of beverages consumed a day, and age. **Ordinal data** are those that have ordered categories with intervals that cannot be quantified (e.g., none, a little, some, a lot, and very much so). Finally, **categorical data** have unordered categories in which one category is not considered higher or better than another (e.g., sex, gender, and race).

Measures should be both **valid** (i.e., they measure what they are intended to measure) and **reliable** (i.e., they consistently and accurately measure the construct of interest). If possible, it is best to use measures that have been used with similar samples as the study being planned, as well as those that are reported to have **reliability coefficients** of at least 0.70 or better instead of measures that have not been previously tested in prior work or have been tested with samples very different from the proposed study. It is very difficult to place confidence in a study's findings if the measures used did not have established validity or the **internal consistency reliability** of the measures was less than 0.70.

It is also important to recognize that obtaining two forms of assessment on a particular variable (e.g., self-report and observation) enhances credibility of the findings when the data from these different sources converge. For example, if a parent reports that his or her child is high on externalizing behaviors (i.e., acting-out behaviors) on an instrument that measures these behaviors, and the child's teacher also completes a teacher version of the same instrument that yields high scores, the convergence of these findings produces a convincing case for the child being high on externalizing behaviors.

If observation data are being gathered, it is important to train observers on the instrument that will be used in a study so that there is an **inter-rater reliability** or agreement on the construct that is being observed (e.g., maternal–infant interaction) at least 90% of the time. In addition, for intervention studies, it is important that observers be blind to the study group (i.e., unaware as to whether the subjects are in the experimental or control groups) to avoid bias in their ratings.

Step 9: Outline Data Collection Plan

The data collection plan typically specifies when and where each phase of the study (e.g., subject enrollment, intervention sessions, and completion of measures) will be completed and exactly when all the measures will be obtained. Careful planning of these details is essential before the study commences. A timetable is often helpful to outline the study procedures so that each member of the team is aware of the specific plan for data collection (Box 17.8).

Step 10: Apply for Human Subjects Approval

Before the commencement of research, it is essential to have the study approved by an RSRB that will evaluate the study for protection of human subjects. Federal regulations (Code of Federal Regulations, 1983) now mandate that any research conducted be reviewed to ensure the following:

- Risks to subjects are minimized.
- Selection of subjects is equitable (e.g., women, children, and individuals of a certain race/ethnicity are not excluded).
- Informed consent is obtained and documented if indicated (see Appendix J for an example of an approved consent form).
- A data and safety monitoring plan is implemented when indicated (e.g., for clinical trials; see Appendix K for an example of a data safety and monitoring plan).

---

box 17.8

Timetable for a Study's Data Collection Plan

Months 1 and 2: Hire and train research assistants. Prepare study offices, study materials, and data packets.

Months 3 to 24: Subject recruitment, completion of all hospital data collection, ongoing data collection for posthospital phases of the study, and data entry.

Months 24 to 30: Complete data collection and data entry for posthospital phases of study.

Months 31 to 36: Data analysis. Preparation of reports and manuscripts.

In addition, any individual involved in a study as an investigator, subinvestigator, study coordinator, or enroller of human subjects must pass a required test on the protection of human subjects, based on the Belmont Report. The Belmont Report was issued in 1978 by the National Commission of the Protection of Human Subjects of Biomedical and Behavioral Research and outlined three principles on which standards of ethical conduct in research are to be based:

1. Beneficence (i.e., no harm to subjects)
2. Respect for human dignity (e.g., the right for self-determination, as in providing voluntary consent to participate in a study)
3. Justice (e.g., fair treatment and nondiscriminatory selection of human subjects)

Guidelines for RSRB application and review should be obtained from the institution(s) in which the study will be conducted.

> See the Arizona State University's website at **http://researchintegrity.asu.edu/forms/** for one example of required guidelines and forms for submission of a research study for human subjects' review.

Step 11: Implement the Study

Once human subjects' approval for the study is obtained, data collection can begin. Particular detail and attention should be paid to the process of data collection for the first 5 to 10 subjects regarding the ease of enrollment and completion of study questionnaires.

These first 5 or 10 cases can be considered a pilot phase used to identify problems in the intervention, recruitment, or data gathering so that changes can be made if needed. This is a good time for the research team to work through any challenges encountered and to implement strategies to overcome them. Once the main study begins, no changes should be made. If changes are made, subjects evaluated before the changes cannot be analyzed along with subjects evaluated afterward.

During the conduct of the study, emphasis should be placed on the review of questionnaires after completion by study participants to prevent missing data that pose challenges for data analysis, as well as to determine whether subjects meet clinical criteria on sensitive measures or those that identify them as at risk for certain conditions (e.g., major depression, suicide). Weekly or biweekly team meetings are very beneficial for the research team to overcome challenges in data collection and to maintain cohesiveness during the conduct of the study.

Step 12: Prepare and Analyze Data

In the preparation phase of data analysis, it is important to assess study measures for completeness and to make determinations about what strategies will be used to handle missing data. For example, if less than 30% of the data are missing on a questionnaire, it is acceptable practice to impute the mean for missing items. If, on the other hand, more than 30% of the data are missing on a questionnaire, investigators commonly eliminate it from data analysis. There is a growing body of literature on handling missing data, although the best strategy is really avoiding it in the first place (Cole, Feinstein, & Bender, 2001).

Creating a codebook regarding how certain responses will be translated into numerical form is important before data can be entered into a statistical program, such as SPSS (Statistical Package for the Social Sciences). For example, marital status could be coded as "1" married, "2" not married, "3" divorced, or "4" married for the second or third time. Verifying all entered data also is a critical step in preparing to analyze the data.

Multiple statistical tests can be conducted to answer research questions and to test hypotheses generated in quantitative studies, and readers are encouraged to consult a statistical resource for detailed information on these specific tests. For example, Munro's text *Statistical methods for health care research* (2004) is a user-friendly book that provides excellent information and examples of common statistical analyses for quantitative studies.

Step 13: Interpret the Results

Careful interpretation of the results of a study (i.e., explaining the study results) is important and should be based on the theoretical/conceptual framework that guided the study as well as prior work in the area. Alternative explanations for the findings should always be considered in the discussion. In addition, it is important to discuss findings from prior research that relate to the current study.

Step 14: Disseminate the Findings

Once a study is completed, it is imperative to disseminate the findings to both researchers and clinicians who will use the evidence in guiding further research in the area or in making decisions about patient care. The vehicles for dissemination should include both conferences in the form of oral and/or poster presentations as well as publications (see Chapter 16 for helpful strategies on preparing oral and poster presentations, as well as writing for publication). In addition, the findings of a study also should be disseminated to the media, healthcare policy makers, and the public (see Chapter 16).

Step 15: Incorporate Findings into Evidence-Based Practice and Evaluate Outcomes

Once evidence from a study is generated, it is important to factor that evidence into a decision regarding whether it should be incorporated into patient care. Studies should be critically appraised with respect to three key questions:

1. Are the findings valid (i.e., as close to the truth as possible)?
2. Are the findings important (e.g., strength and preciseness of the intervention)?
3. Are the findings applicable to your patients? (See Unit Two.)

Once a decision is made to incorporate the findings of a study into practice, an outcomes evaluation should be conducted to determine the impact of the change on the process or outcomes of clinical care (see Chapter 10).

chapter 17

433

references

Browner, W. S., Newman, T. B., Cummings, S. R., & Hulley, S. B. (2001). Estimating sample size and power: The nitty-gritty. In S. B. Hulley, S. R. Cummings, W. S. Browner, D. Grady, N. Hearst, & T. B. Newman (Eds.), *Designing clinical research: An epidemiologic approach* (2nd ed., pp. 65–85). Philadelphia: Lippincott Williams & Wilkins.

Campbell, D. T., & Stanley, J. C. (1963). *Experimental and quasi-experimental designs for research.* Chicago: Rand McNally.

Code of Federal Regulations (1983). *Protection of human subjects*: 45CFR46 (Rev. March 8, 1983). Washington, DC: Department of Health and Human Services.

Cohen, J. (1988). *Statistical power analysis for the behavioral sciences* (2nd ed.). Mahwah, NJ: Lawrence Erlbaum.

Cohen, J. (1992). *A power primer: Psychological bulletin.* Washington, DC: American Psychological Association.

Cole, R. E., Feinstein, N. F., & Bender, N. L. (2001). What's the big deal about missing data? *Applied Nursing Research, 14,* 225–226.

Cummings, S. R., Browner, W. S., & Hulley, S. B. (2001). Conceiving the research question. In S. B. Hulley, S. R. Cummings, W. S. Browner, D. Grady, N. Hearst, & T. B. Newman (Eds.),

Designing clinical research: An epidemiologic approach (2nd ed., pp. 17–23). Philadelphia: Lippincott, Williams & Wilkins.

Guyatt, G., & Rennie, D. (2002). *Users' guides to the medical literature: Essentials of evidence-based clinical practice*. Chicago: American Medical Association.

Jaccard, J., & Becker, M. A. (1990). *Statistics for the behavioral sciences* (2nd ed.). Belmont, CA: Wadsworth.

Jimmerson, S. (1982). Anxiety. In J. Haber, A. Leach, & B. Sideleau (Eds.), *Comprehensive psychiatric nursing*. New York: McGraw-Hill.

Johnson, J. E., Fieler, V. K., Jones, L. S., Wlasowicz, G. S., & Mitchell, M. L. (1997). *Self-regulation theory: Applying theory to your practice*. Pittsburgh, PA: Oncology Nursing Press.

Leventhal, H., & Johnson, J. E. (1983). Laboratory and field experimentation: Development of a theory of self-regulation. In P. J. Woolridge, M. H. Schmitt, J. K. Skipper, Jr., & R. C. Leonard (Eds.), *Behavioral science and nursing theory* (pp. 189–262). St. Louis: Mosby.

Melnyk, B. M. (1994). Coping with unplanned childhood hospitalization: Effects of informational interventions on mothers and children. *Nursing Research, 43*, 50–55.

Melnyk, B. M. (1995). Coping with unplanned childhood hospitalization: The mediating functions of parental beliefs. *Journal of Pediatric Psychology, 20*(3), 299–312.

Melnyk, B. M. (2003). Critical appraisal of systematic reviews: A key strategy for evidence-based practice. *Pediatric Nursing, 29*(2), 125, 147–149.

Melnyk, B. M., & Alpert-Gillis, L. J. (1996). Enhancing coping outcomes of mothers and young children following marital separation: A pilot study. *Journal of Family Nursing, 2*(3), 266–285.

Melnyk, B. M., Alpert-Gillis, L., Feinstein, N. F., Crean, H., Johnson, J., Fairbanks, E., et al. (2004). Creating opportunities for parent empowerment (COPE): Program effects on the mental health/coping outcomes of critically ill young children and their mothers. *Pediatrics, 113*(6), e597–e606.

Melnyk, B. M., Alpert-Gillis, L., Feinstein, N. F., Fairbanks, E., Schultz-Czarniak, J. Hust, D., et al. (2001). Improving cognitive development of LBW premature infants with the COPE program: A pilot study of the benefit of early NICU intervention with mothers. *Research in Nursing and Health, 24*, 373–389.

Melnyk, B. M., Alpert-Gillis, L. J., Hensel, P. B., Cable-Beiling, R. C., & Rubenstein, J. S. (1997). Helping mothers cope with a critically ill child: A pilot test of the COPE intervention. *Research in Nursing & Health, 20*, 3–14.

Melnyk, B. M., Crean, H. F., Feinstein, N. F., & Alpert-Gillis, L. (2007). Testing the theoretical framework of the COPE program for mothers of critically ill children: An integrative model of young children's post-hospital adjustment behaviors. *Journal of Pediatric Psychology, 32*(4), 463–474.

Melnyk, B. M., & Feinstein, N. F. (2001). Mediating functions of maternal anxiety and participation in care on young children's posthospital adjustment. *Research in Nursing & Health, 24*, 18–26.

Melnyk, B. M., Feinstein, N. F., Alpert-Gillis, L., Fairbanks, E., Crean, H. F., Sinkin, R., et al. (2006). Reducing premature infants' length of stay and improving parents' mental health outcomes with the COPE NICU program: A randomized clinical trial. *Pediatrics, 118*(5), 1414–1427.

Melnyk, B. M., & Fineout-Overholt, E. (2005). *Evidence-based practice in nursing and healthcare: A guide to best practice*. Philadelphia: Lippincott, Williams & Wilkins.

Morrison-Beedy, D., Carey, M. P., Aronowitz, T., Mkandawire, L., & Dyne, J. (2002a). Adolescents' input on the development of a HIV-risk reduction intervention. *Journal of the Association of Nurses in AIDS Care, 13*, 21–27.

Morrison-Beedy, D., Carey, M. P., Aronowitz, T., Mkandawire, L., & Dyne, J. (2002b). An HIV risk reduction intervention in an adolescent correctional facility: Lessons learned. *Applied Nursing Research, 15*, 97–101.

Munro, B. H. (2004). *Statistical methods for health care research* (5th ed.). Philadelphia: Lippincott, Williams & Wilkins.

National Commission for the Protection of Human Subjects of Biomedical and Behavioral Research (1978). *Belmont report: Ethical principles and guidelines for research involving human subjects*. Washington, DC: U.S. Government Printing Office.

Newman, T. B., Browner, W. S., Cummings, S. R., & Hulley, S. B. (2001). Designing an observation study: Cross-sectional and case-control studies. In S. B. Hulley, S. R. Cummings, W. S. Browner, D. Grady, N. Hearst, & T. B. Newman (Eds.), *Designing clinical research: An epidemiologic approach* (2nd ed., pp. 197–123). Philadelphia: Lippincott, Williams & Wilkins.

Polit, D. F., & Beck, C.T. (2008). *Nursing research: Generating and assessing evidence for nursing practice* (8th ed.). Philadelphia: Lippincott, Williams & Wilkins.

Powers, B A., & Knapp, T. R. (1995). *A dictionary of nursing theory and research*. New York: Springer.

Rosenthal, R., & Rosnow, R. L. (2008). *Essential of behavioral research: Methods and data analysis* (3rd ed.). New York: McGraw-Hill.

Tamburro, R. F., Shorr, R. I., Bush, A. J., Kritchevsky, S. B., Stidham, G. L., & Helms, S. A. (2002). Association between the inception of s SAFE KIDS Coalition and changes in pediatric unintentional injury. *Injury Prevention, 8*, 242–245.

Trochim, W. M. (2001). *The research methods knowledge base*. Cincinnati, OH: Atomic Dog Publishing.

VanderVeer, A. H. (1949). The psychopathology of physical illness and hospital residence. *Quarterly Journal of Child Behavior, 1*, 55–79.

Whittemore, R., & Grey, M. (2002). The systematic development of nursing interventions. *Journal of Nursing Scholarship, 34*(2), 115–120.

unit six

434

Generating Evidence Through Qualitative Research

Bethel Ann Powers

> *The future depends on what we do in the present.*
> *Mahatma Gandhi*

Qualitative studies are helpful in answering particular kinds of research questions concerned with human responses in a particular situation and context and the meanings that humans bring to those situations (Grace & Powers, 2009). The choice to study human response and meaning from a qualitative perspective involves the researchers' commitment to certain philosophical assumptions within this field of research. The belief that human experience is made up of multiple realities directs researchers to designs and approaches that take these multiple realities of study participants into account. This leads to researchers' perceived need to spend time and develop close relationships with participants to observe and gain direct firsthand information from them about their experiences. Creswell (2007) provides a more detailed explication of philosophical, paradigm (i.e., worldview), and interpretive frameworks that characterize qualitative research (e.g., ontological, epistemological, theoretical, methodological).

Once the decision is made to adopt such a philosophical stance, a wide array of theoretical perspectives and technical approaches are available to qualitatively address various types of research questions about human experience. For example, when a concept or phenomenon is not well understood or is inadequately covered in the literature, conducting qualitative studies may be a good way to develop knowledge in this area. Examples of such studies include the exploration of how persons learn to eat again and resolve problems related to their sense of selfhood and social identity after an esophagectomy for cancer (Wainwright, Donovan, Kavadas, et al., 2007) and the exploration of how persons left with autobiographical memory impairments resulting from neurotrauma experience a sense of self (Medved & Brockmeier, 2008).

Qualitative studies also are helpful when much is known about a phenomenon, but what is known in certain areas is deficient in quality, depth, or detail. Thus, qualitative studies may explore specific concepts or variables, such as the inner experiences of nonphysical suffering and trust for chronically ill individuals nearing the end of life (Sacks & Nelson, 2007) or the influence of multiple chronic conditions on body image in later life (Clarke, Griffin, & The PACC Research Team, 2008).

Qualitative researchers may develop theories or offer insights that explain the processes individuals go through when dealing with an issue. Examples of such explanations include the process of parenting a child with life-threatening heart disease (Rempel & Harrison, 2007) or the interpretation of the nature of hope in the context of AIDS dementia in the era of HAART (highly active antiretroviral therapies; Kelly, 2007).

Qualitative studies may provide comprehensive views of topics from a sociocultural perspective. Some specific examples of this focus include the study of recently arrived refugees' perceptions of community-level support (Barnes & Aguilar, 2007) and discovering the disparities in healthcare for rural Hispanic immigrants in the Midwest United States (Cristancho, Garces, Peters, et al., 2008).

All qualitative studies aim to increase sensitivity to human experiences in order to enhance understanding or stimulate social action. Examples include gaining insight and increased understanding about how living with chronic non–cancer-related lymphedema affects individuals' lives (Bogan, Powell, & Dudgeon, 2007) and gaining understanding of potential issues and concerns related to the impact of childhood leukemia on survivors' career, family, and future expectations (Brown, Pikler, Lavish, et al., 2008).

Basic Understandings about Qualitative Research

Before discussing specific considerations in designing a qualitative study, it is important to address some common misunderstandings (see Box 18.1). First, the terms *qualitative* and *descriptive* are often used interchangeably and applied indistinguishably, so it is important to understand that this can create confusion. For example, referring to all nonnumerical data as descriptive or qualitative data to distinguish them from numerical or quantitative data confuses the nature of the data with the research processes that produce them. Any type of study design can produce numerical and nonnumerical data, but only qualitative studies produce qualitative data. Similarly, both quantitative and qualitative research traditions have distinct types of descriptive research designs. Therefore, it is important to distinguish between the two. Qualitative descriptive studies are not equivalent to quantitative types of descriptive research. Their purposes and underlying assumptions are very different.

Second, a single set of procedural steps for designing qualitative research studies is not possible because of the diversity and complexity of the field. Reading Chapter 6 will help readers understand the emphasis on general principles that apply to qualitative research design.

---

box 18.1

Basic Understandings About Qualitative Research

- ■ Not all descriptive research is qualitative.
- ■ Not all qualitative research is descriptive.
- ■ There is no single set of procedural steps for designing qualitative research studies.
- ■ Researchers who have been mentored in the qualitative approach their research question requires have comparative advantages over "those who try to do qualitative research by reading manuals" (Morse, 1997, p. 181).

Finally, mentored experiences are important in developing expertise in all areas of research—quantitative as well as qualitative. But well-written qualitative research reports can be captivating to the extent that some persons may mistakenly believe that reading about how to do qualitative research should be enough to enable them to conduct a qualitative research study. With that caveat in mind, the objective of this chapter is to build on the information presented in Chapter 6 on appraising qualitative research. This time, however, it is assumed that readers might be thinking about practice-based research questions that they would like to pursue in collaboration with an experienced qualitative researcher. This chapter is designed for individuals interested in such collaborative experiences.

Not All Descriptive Research is Qualitative

Descriptive studies are typically used in a preliminary way by quantitative researchers to establish the knowledge base and generate hypotheses for conducting correlational, quasi-experimental, and experimental studies (Powers & Knapp, 2006). Quantitative studies may use some of the same techniques used by qualitative researchers (e.g., observation, interviews, and descriptive statistics); however, the philosophical underpinnings, purposes, and methods of the research designs are not the same. Qualitative descriptive research reflects certain features that are common among other types of traditional qualitative research designs and differs from quantitative descriptive research in many ways.

Multiple Purposes Focus on Understanding and Meaning

Qualitative descriptive studies do not serve the unidirectional purpose of quantitative descriptive studies that are designed as preliminary steps to more controlled correlational or experimental studies. These quantitative studies are oriented toward measurement, testing, or verification of cause-and-effect relationships. Qualitative descriptive studies also are more interpretive than quantitative description [used for any purpose], which typically entails surveys or other pre-structured means to obtain a common dataset on preselected variables, and descriptive statistics to summarize them. Quantitative descriptive studies entail interpretation in that researchers set the horizon of expectations for the study … But it is a kind of interpretation that does not move beyond these preset confines, including the operational definitions of concepts and their representations as items in surveys and other measures. Quantitative description limits what can be learned about the meanings participants give to events. (Sandelowski, 2000, p. 336)

In contrast, the different purposes of qualitative studies include discovering meaning, explaining meaning in context, promoting understanding, raising awareness, and challenging misconceptions about the nature of human experiences. These purposes are different from those of research designs needed to test theory/hypotheses and answer questions related to treatment or risk.

Openness and Flexibility Accommodate the Unexpected

Qualitative researchers cast a wider net. They consider all that happens in "the field" (i.e., all that is observed or brought to their awareness in any way) as data. In addition, they expect, welcome, and accommodate the unexpected in the process of data collection. "[I]n quantitative research, there is a sharper line drawn between exploration (finding out what is there) and description (describing what has been found)" (Sandelowski, 2000, p. 336). Qualitative procedures are more flexible to allow for decision making about new directions in data gathering influenced by simultaneous collection and analysis of incoming data.

Distinctive Procedures Assure Depth, Accuracy, and Completeness

Sampling in qualitative studies is purposeful to ensure data quality and completeness (i.e., the concept of **saturation**) and to enhance theoretical generalizability (Morse, 1999). Sample size varies, and samples are often comparatively small; however, data sets are very large and dense.

Use of multiple data sources (e.g., participant observation, interview, and material artifacts) is common and ongoing. Qualitative researchers also rely on the discovery of multiple means of validation in the data collection and analysis process to ensure that findings are complete and accurate.

Presentation of Findings Involves Multiple Reporting Styles

Presentation of findings in qualitative research does not follow a uniform format. It involves multiple reporting styles. It is not structured around preselected variables and is more fully elaborated from participants' points of view and in their own words. Varied writing techniques may be used to sensitize readers to the real-life complexities and feeling tones of participants' experiences. Full narrative descriptions seek to establish "descriptive validity" through accurate portrayals of events and "interpretive validity" by accounting for the meanings that participants attribute to those events (Sandelowski, 2000, citing Maxwell, 1992).

Conclusions Are Not Based on Prior Assumptions

Qualitative researchers do not limit conclusions to those based on prior assumptions about a phenomenon (e.g., in the form of predetermined measures and items on surveys and other data collection instruments) or drawn from "the results of statistical tests, which are themselves based on sets of assumptions" (Sandelowski, 2000, p. 336). The prior assumptions of qualitative researchers are reflected upon, temporarily set aside, and ultimately treated as data to be analyzed along with study participants' accounts.

Qualitative Research is Complete and Nonhierarchical

Qualitative descriptive research may generate basic knowledge, hypotheses, and theories to be used in the design of other types of qualitative or quantitative studies. However, qualitative descriptive research, like all types of qualitative studies, is not necessarily a preliminary step to some other type of research (Morse, 1996). It is "a complete and valued end-product in itself" (Sandelowski, 2000, p. 335). This reflects the nonhierarchical nature of all qualitative research. It has no fixed counterpart to quantitative researchers' linear continuum that conceptualizes knowledge development as a progression upward from preliminary descriptive research designs to experiments and clinical trials. Therefore, more often it is assumed that "[n]o method is absolutely weak nor strong, but rather more or less useful or appropriate in relation to certain purposes" (Sandelowski, p. 335).

> *Don't let the fear of the time it will take to accomplish something stand in the way of your doing it. The time will pass anyway, we might just as well put that passing time to the best possible use.*
> *Earl Nightingale*

Not All Qualitative Research is Descriptive

Some qualitative research studies are interpretive, involving a higher degree of analytic complexity. Kearney (2001) along with Sandelowski and Barroso (2003) provide useful discussions about different features and degrees of complexity in qualitative research reports. All research involves interpretation in the natural course of describing what the findings signify and their perceived relevance. But not all research is interpretive in intent. "The defining feature of findings [characteristic of interpretive explanation] is the transformation of data to produce … science- or narrative-informed clarification or elucidation of conceptual or thematic linkages that re-present the target phenomenon in a new way" (Sandelowski & Barroso, p. 914).

Interpretive Nature of Qualitative Designs

Qualitative research designs, in varying degrees, involve the use of deliberate interpretive strategies seeking to describe a phenomenon more completely. As a result, qualitative descriptive studies are more interpretive than quantitative descriptive studies because of their purposes and the ways in which they are conceptualized, designed, and carried out. However, they are less interpretive than other qualitative approaches. Although all qualitative research studies involve description, there are certain types of studies that are not solely descriptive, such as phenomenology, ethnography, or grounded theory (Sandelowski, 2000).

      Qualitative descriptive studies differ from other qualitative studies that represent one of the interpretive traditions in several ways. First, qualitative descriptive studies do not move as far *into* the data in terms of producing "thick" descriptions. Geertz (1973) used the term **thick description** as a metaphor for the use of interpretative devices to deepen ethnographic descriptions and, specifically, to make them more eloquently revealing of taken-for-granted, hidden meanings and symbols within everyday events. Second, qualitative descriptive studies do not move as far *away from* the data in their interpretations of findings. That is, they involve "a kind of interpretation that is low-inference, or likely to result in easier consensus among … most observers" (Sandelowski, 2000, pp. 335–336) about how closely description captures the actual reality of a situation or human experience.

Description Versus Interpretation as an End Product

Finally, in qualitative descriptive studies, description is the end product. The purely descriptive study employs "a straight descriptive summary of the informational contents of data [that are] organized in a way that best fits the data" (Sandelowski, 2000, pp. 338–339). In qualitative interpretive studies, description is the means to an end. In these types of studies, researchers are expected to "put much more of their own interpretive spin on what they see and hear," representing and transforming the data by "deliberately choos[ing] to describe an event in terms of a conceptual, philosophical, or other highly abstract framework or system" (Sandelowski, p. 336).

No Single Set of Procedural Steps for Designing Qualitative Research Studies

Different types of qualitative research have unique methodological approaches that determine how researchers think about a phenomenon of interest, as well as what they do to understand it better. Creswell (2007) discusses how study designs differ across qualitative traditions, focusing on a small subset, specifically *phenomenology, narrative, grounded theory, ethnography*, and *case study*.

      In addition to having external diversity, qualitative traditions also exhibit significant internal diversity. For example, Creswell (2007) observed "a lack of orthodoxy in ethnography [due to] a number of subtypes … with different theoretical orientations and aims, [which] has resulted in pluralistic approaches" (p. 69). In like manner, grounded theory has been described as "a family of methods" in which "scholars invoke differences of approach and substance" (Bryant & Charmaz, 2007, pp. 11, 12). Differences across schools of phenomenological inquiry also have been noted, such as, the descriptive Husserlian-focused Duquesne School of phenomenological psychology, the interpretive emphasis of Heideggerian hermeneutics, van Manen's (1990/1997) humanistic pedagogical approach, and the transcendental phenomenology of Moustakas (1994). Significant differences in approaches within the same school of phenomenology have also been documented, as in Beck's (1994) comparison of methodologies of Duquesne School phenomenologists Colaizzi, Giorgi, and VanKaam.

Consequently, the diversity, complexity, and dynamic nature of the field of qualitative inquiry require that individuals be specific about the research tradition and style that they will be following. In addition, the description of procedural steps to be used needs to be consistent with standards for that particular design. Providing practical assistance in matching research question to method and within-method procedures is an important part of the mentor or qualitative coresearcher role.

Qualitative Studies Designed and Conducted by Researchers Mentored in a Specified Approach Will Have the Best Outcomes

Rising interest in conducting qualitative studies has been fueled by increased awareness of their usefulness as well as the greater availability of textbooks and articles about the various qualitative methods. Textbooks in particular, however, largely fail to communicate

- The extent of diversity within traditions
- The limitations of written descriptions that attempt to reconstruct the more creative, reflective, and cognitive processing aspects of interpretive qualitative methodologies
- Distinctions between quantitative and qualitative descriptive research
- Distinctions between descriptive and interpretive qualitative work

Sandelowski's (2000) presentation of qualitative description is especially helpful in addressing confusion and misperceptions related to choice of direction in qualitative research design. One of the confusions discussed is when a study has "overtones" of a particular qualitative approach (e.g., phenomenology, grounded theory, ethnography) but is not a pure example of that kind of study. Discussed misperceptions include mislabeling of research and "erroneous references to or misuses of methods or techniques" (p. 337).

Articles like this can do what textbooks do not do, as well—focus on select issues in closer detail. However, there is an abundance of resources on a wide range of topics. Therefore, the best approach to designing and conducting qualitative studies of any type is in partnership with a qualified researcher who can differentiate between what information will be more or less useful, who understands the clinical question and can propose possible research directions, and who has been mentored in the specific method to be used.

General Principles of Qualitative Research Design

All researchers, qualitative or quantitative, must address certain areas when designing a research study. The general principles that guide the development of qualitative research projects can be found in Box 18.2.

Identifying a Study Question

In qualitative research, the primary study question is the one that summarizes, in its most general form, what the study is about. Accompanying subquestions lend further focus, as in the following example from the literature. The primary study question is italicized for emphasis. *How do older adults with numerous chronic health issues perceive their bodies in terms of aesthetics and in*

> ## box 18.2
>
> ## General Principles of Qualitative Research Design
>
> 1. Identify a study question.
> 2. Review the literature.
> 3. Define the theoretical perspective.
> 4. Select an appropriate research design.
> 5. Formulate a purpose statement.
> 6. Establish study significance.
> 7. Describe the research procedures.
> 8. Discuss study limitations.

terms of physical functioning? (Clarke et al., 2008, p. 1086). How do gender norms, ageism, and illness experiences shape and constrain their body evaluations?

Often, identification of research questions such as these evolves from curiosity about some phenomenon in the clinical arena (e.g., what the "struggle between physical abilities and disabilities and personal goals, values, and priorities" is like for persons as they age, Clarke et al., 2008 p. 1084), hunches based on observation and experience (e.g., issues related to loss of independence and social pressures to maintain young-looking bodies), and knowledge of some literature (e.g., studies of the embodied experience of singular chronic conditions viewed from the perspective [or through the lens] of literature on body image and ageism).

Reviewing the Literature

A systematic literature review provides information about existing evidence related to study questions. It is used as a framework to explain why the study is important, to indicate what it may contribute to knowledge about the topic, and to set the stage for presentation of results in published reports. For example, Wainwright et al. (2007) described the literature framing their work as:

> The extent to which loss of appetite and body weight result from the progress of disease (cancer cachexia), the physiological changes that result from surgery (iatrogenesis), or psychosocial factors is poorly understood, and the three factors might be linked (Van Knippenberg et al., 1992) … In an important study, Kelly (1992) explored the experiences of ulcerative colitis patients who underwent radical surgery (total colectomy and ileostomy) … Esophagectomy patients have much in common with ileostomists. They, too, must adapt to profound physical change that affects a major bodily function … Clinical studies describing outcomes after esophagectomy focus on survival, mortality, morbidity, and dysphagia (difficulty swallowing). Some quantitative researchers have attempted to measure changes in quality of life after esophagectomy … but other aspects of recovery have been less well explored. Qualitative accounts of patients' experiences are particularly lacking yet provide valuable insights that might inform changes in service provision (pp. 759–760).

This example illustrates that citing an absence of literature on a topic is not enough. Exploring what about the phenomenon is poorly understood, the wider literature about recovery from illness and treatment, and the state of the science regarding studies of outcomes after esophagectomy provided evidence to support the need for further study.

Defining the Theoretical Perspective

Theoretical perspectives that guide qualitative research range from the basic philosophical assumptions that are implicit in methodological practices of all qualitative studies (Creswell, 2007) and social science theories associated with particular traditions (e.g., theories of culture in ethnographic research, symbolic interaction in grounded theory research) to particular ideological perspectives and theoretical frameworks. Implicit assumptions and embedded theories of a research tradition that guides methods may be demonstrated rather than explicitly discussed in the design of a study (i.e., through explanation of study procedures). Other theoretical or ideological perspectives that pertain to the research questions may be presented early in the design of some studies as orienting/sensitizing frameworks or at the end of others, as outcomes of the research.

In the following example, social support theories used to guide understanding in a narrative study of community social support for Cuban refugees in Texas are introduced at the beginning of the study.

> Social support has been defined … as a set of actions that assists a focal person in meeting personal goals or dealing with the demands of a particular situation … Unfortunately, this approach … places the attention and expectations on the individual … and can even lead to blame … for his or her inability to cope adequately. Historically, theorists also assumed that the immediate family was always a source of support, but that has not been supported by research with refugees … As an alternative to the focus on the individual and family, the interactional approach to social support defines support as a complex transactional process between the person and his or her social environment in which both the person and the situation must be considered (Barnes & Aguilar, 2007, p 226).

In contrast, discussion of theory occurs at the end of theory-generating studies, as in the following example:

> Mothers and fathers in this study demonstrated extraordinary parenting through a multifaceted process of safeguarding precarious survival as they pursued technologically advanced surgical treatment for their baby's lethal heart defect. Extraordinary parenting was characterized by unusual parenting activities that occurred in a taken-for-granted context of technology and family involvement. (Rempel & Harrison, 2007, p. 833)

> Consequently, defining the theoretical perspective of a qualitative study involves choices about how theory will be used. The result is less uniformity than in the case of theory-testing and theory-verification research designs that consistently begin with a theoretical framework.

Selecting an Appropriate Research Design

Qualitative description is the design of choice for many basic clinical questions that involve the desire to facilitate an understanding of a human experience as a whole through in-depth engagement with study participants, most usually in their natural environments (i.e., the field). Styles and techniques typically involve researchers in field activities that may include active participation, observation, and/or interviews.

Pursuing questions that lead to choosing another type of qualitative design should be contingent on the availability of a researcher who is a specialist in that particular methodology. Commonly used possible choices, described in broad strokes, include

- *Ethnography* when the purpose is to explain human experience in cultural context, as an interpretation or in theoretical terms
- *Grounded theory* when the purpose is to generate a theory that explains the ways in which persons move through an experience (e.g., in stages or phases)

● *Phenomenology* or *hermeneutics* when the purpose is to produce an interpretation of what an experience is like (i.e., how it feels and its meaning for individuals in the context of their everyday lives)

In selecting a design, it is important to be sensitive to two important considerations. One is that a descriptive qualitative design may involve "hues, tones, and textures … [i.e.] the look, sound, and feel of other [qualitative] approaches" (Sandelowski, 2000, p. 337). However, these studies should not be confused with or mislabeled as examples of one of these approaches. Nor should such a study be referred to as "mixed-methods" research, because these designs are explicitly constructed to maximize the use of combined qualitative and quantitative approaches (Creswell, 2008; Teddlie & Tashakkori, 2008). The second consideration is that in choosing a traditional design (e.g., ethnography, grounded theory, phenomenology, hermeneutics), one needs to consider the diversity in these fields and accurately reflect the chosen method in the study design description.

Formulating a Study Purpose

Purpose statements draw attention to the central research focus, study participants, and the nature and selected elements of the research design. The following example of a purpose statement identifies a style of counseling research (i.e., consensual qualitative research [CQR]) involving a prescribed set of interviewing and analysis techniques.

> The purpose of this qualitative study was to gain understanding of the potential career issues and concerns of childhood leukemia survivors. Firsthand accounts of the life and career development process as experienced by childhood leukemia survivors provide opportunity for helping professionals to identify the career needs of this population, as well as the challenges they encounter in their career development and life planning. Thus, our methodological framework incorporated CQR to answer two main research questions: (a) What effect does a childhood cancer diagnosis have on the survivors' education and career plans? and (b) What is the role of family in the survivors' educational and career planning? (Brown et al., 2008, p. 21)

Establishing the Significance of the Study

Although activities up to and including establishing a study's significance have been described as six separate steps, in reality these efforts at laying the groundwork for a study evolve simultaneously. Identification of researchable clinical issues and literature reviews, in particular, help establish why a study is needed and how it will contribute to improving professional practice. Often, statements of significance are combined with purpose statements, as in the following example:

> The aim of the present study is to investigate [the] question: What sort of sense of self, if any, takes shape when the strategies of memory importation, memory appropriation, and memory compensation are used in autobiographical narratives by people who have had severe anterograde memory impairments for 1 year? It is a memory deficit that reduces the ability to form memories of events occurring after neurological harm, while at the same time memories occurring before are retained … More specifically, we wanted to find out whether they experienced a sense of Nochi's (1998) "lost self," or whether they experienced themselves in a different fashion altogether. This question bears important ramifications, not least for the rehabilitation services offered to these individuals … We believe as clinical professionals we need a better understanding of how people make sense of themselves, especially under extreme circumstances, before "reaffirming" or "reconstructing" a putatively damaged "self" in people of whom the only thing we know is that they have a damaged brain (Medved & Brockmeier, 2008, p. 471).

Describing Research Procedures

There is no single set of procedural steps in qualitative research. What to do and how to do it are dictated by the topic plus background understandings and purposes of the selected study design. Typically, multiple common techniques are combined in various ways to achieve study outcomes. Areas to address include sampling and sampling strategy, ethical considerations, data collection and management, data analysis and interpretation, and standards of quality and scientific rigor.

Sample and Sampling Strategy

The sampling plan must describe the location and characteristics of the population from which a sample will be selected, the estimated sample size, inclusion/exclusion criteria, and recruitment procedures. A variety of sampling strategies may support purposeful selection of the best sources of information about an experience. Research questions, type of study, and previous studies or similar studies in the literature suggest rationales for estimating the size of the sample. Researchers also must explain how they will know when the necessary sample size has been reached, because this cannot easily be determined a priori. Commonly, this process involves monitoring the quality of databases as the research progresses. Decisions about when optimum sample size is achieved are based on judgments about (a) usefulness of the data in various informational categories, (b) types of additional data sources needed to capture an adequate view of the phenomenon, and (c) number of interviews and/or observations needed before informational categories are full and continued data collection produces no new information (concept of redundancy or saturation).

Ethical Considerations

Researchers need to keep up to date with the most current ethical guidelines for the protection of human subjects required by the federal government, funding agencies, and local institutions. Of note for qualitative researchers is the importance of addressing how use of common techniques involving close researcher–participant interaction (e.g., participant observation and in-depth interviews) over periods of time will take into account the issues of confidentiality, privacy, and concerns about nonconsenting members of a group and undue burden. Researchers need to realize that close attachments may develop between themselves and study participants, which will need to be monitored and managed kindly and professionally. They also need to be sensitive to the emotions of study participants who may experience distress at the baring of painful memories and be prepared to describe the steps the researcher will take if such distress occurs.

Data Collection and Data Management

Qualitative researchers may use multiple data collection strategies in a single study. Most important is matching and explaining how particular strategies will meet stated study aims. Examples of what will be observed, sample interview questions, and descriptions of other kinds of data sources (e.g., documents, artifacts, audiovisual materials) serve as indicators of the kinds of data that will be collected. Who will be collecting the data and how information will be recorded need to be described in detail. If there are multiple data collectors, how they are trained and supervised, as well as checks for interrater reliability also require explanation.

Data management systems for record keeping, storage, organization, and retrieval of information are an important consideration in research that typically generates large volumes of data. It is wise to lay out a plan prior to data collection. The plan may be a combination of a physical filing system for raw field notes, audiotapes, documents, and hard copy transcriptions and a computer software program, of which there are many varieties. The researcher needs to keep in mind that although some software programs support data analysis through features beyond storage and retrieval that enable manipulation and various displays of data, they do not actually perform analyses. Analysis of qualitative data is an intellectual process.

Data Analysis and Interpretation

Data analysis is an ongoing activity that occurs simultaneously with data collection. Therefore, description of procedures involves outlining approaches that will be used throughout the course of the research. For instance, it might be useful to describe the process for deciding about the need to modify the direction of questions and observation in response to new insights and informational needs. This will include how decisions and analytic thoughts and questioning of the data will be recorded and used. Specific analytic steps vary with different types of qualitative designs. Some of the more generic steps of data analysis involve

- Reading through all the data to get a general sense of what is there and reflecting on possible meanings
- Coding/labeling, categorizing, and writing reflective notes about the data to examine it from all angles
- Generating detailed written descriptions
- Searching for recurring themes and patterns

Interpretive strategies move beyond description of what is there to reflection on the possible meaning of data (e.g., what it may suggest or symbolize, what there is to be learned as a result of new insights). An explanation of procedures might project how the interpretation will appear in the final written report. For example, meaning may be expressed by re-presenting participants' perspectives within a new explanatory or sensitizing framework that reflects what the researcher has come to understand of the participants' reality. A researcher also may use reflection, intuition, and imaginative play (i.e., mentally stretching/varying different aspects of the data via the imagination) to arrive at a creative synthesis that produces a richly textured picture of the experience. Continuous writing and rewriting are a natural part of developing strong, oriented portrayals of all the experiential aspects of a phenomenon.

Whether the end product tends more toward description or interpretation, it is important to explain how data integration and conclusions will be reached, particularly in designs where more than one data source will be used. The importance and potential usefulness of findings need to be part of this discussion.

Standards of Quality and Scientific Rigor

How quality will be monitored and scientific rigor will be maintained needs to be directly addressed. Because general criteria for evaluating qualitative studies are discussed extensively in Chapter 6, comments here are limited to identifying broad areas to consider in designing a qualitative study. Greatest emphasis usually is placed on validity relating to concerns about accuracy, credibility, and confirmability (i.e., evidence in the data to support findings and interpretations). Researchers may choose the most appropriate steps for ensuring quality and rigor from among a variety of strategies.

Similarly, strategies for documenting how decisions were made throughout the course of the study (the concept of an audit trail) may be described. This is thought by some to be similar to quantitative researchers' notions of reliability. Most important is that selected criteria are consistent with study aims and chosen design because although there are common strategies, there are no hard and fast rules about what procedures must be followed in every research approach. And some quality measures that are effective for one approach may not serve well for another.

Discussing Study Limitations

All types of research are delimited/bounded and limited by their scope and degree of generalizability. Qualitative researchers engaged in theory generation most often refer to the need for further research to determine generalizability, for example:

> Although there is some agreement between the theory developed in this study [the dynamic nature of trust in the individual's nonphysical suffering experience] and existing literature (Kahn & Steeves, 1995; Morse, 2001), there are fundamental differences between what non-physical suffering is and what the experience encompasses ... but nursing has not developed any effective interventions to "move" the individual through the suffering experience across settings. Findings in this study suggest that establishing and supporting trust and developing relationships might be a future area of research or intervention when caring for a suffering individual (Sacks & Nelson, 2007, p. 689).

In this instance, theory testing in intervention studies might lead to an estimate of statistical generalizability (i.e., the extent to which inferences based on this and/or other extant theoretical models may apply to a larger population). Verification, extension, or development of new theory, in turn, would need to be based on accumulated evidence of many studies.

Transferability, or **theoretical generalizability**, of qualitative research refers to the extent to which the evidence, knowledge, understandings, or insights gained may be thought to be meaningful and applicable to similar cases or other situations. For example, health professionals involved in caring for persons with AIDS dementia, on the basis of their own experience, will be able to judge the extent to which Kelly's (2007) interpretive ethnography of the lived experiences of hope and loss in the HAART era of treatments is theoretically generalizable. Clinicians can do this by asking such questions as:

- Does the description of ways in which treatments influence the experience of personal hope and "living loss" fit/make sense/ring true/resonate with my own observations?
- Does it provide insights or make me think differently or reflect more deeply on my own experiences?
- Would the understandings generated about what the experience is like be helpful to new practitioners or individuals/families undergoing this experience?
- Does it add new understandings to existing knowledge in this field?
- Can insights from this study also be valuable when applied to situations of persons with other types of life-threatening illnesses whose hopes are structured in accordance with evolutionary advances in treatments and new technologies?

In other words, "[t]he knowledge gained is not limited to demographic variables; it is the fit of the topic or the comparability of the problem that is of concern. Recall, it is the knowledge that is generalized" (Morse, 1999, p. 6).

Validation of study findings might come in the form of application of the knowledge in practice. Researchers often will describe their interpretation of findings based on sample selection as a natural limitation of the research. For example, Cristancho et al. (2008) stated, "Our use of purposive sampling is a limiting factor in our ability to generalize our findings beyond small rural Midwestern communities that have experienced a rapid increase in their Hispanic immigrant populations" (p. 644). Bogan et al. (2007) indicated that they used purposive sampling of these extreme cases [individuals who had completed a lymphedema rehabilitation program in an inpatient setting for 2–3 weeks] to provide information-rich experiences to illuminate both the unusual and the typical (Patton, 2002) ... [However], the high rates of compliance described by participants might be related to the relatively short period since their inpatient treatment within the previous 5 years. [And] the role of their histories of living with severe and debilitating lymphedema over many years as a motivation for compliance with self-management is unlikely to represent what would inspire individuals with less complicated and less advanced presentations of the condition. (pp. 215, 223)

Other research limitations include potential pitfalls in chosen methods and issues related to the nature of the study topic. For example, researchers investigating the so-called sensitive topics (e.g., drug cultures, deviance, crime, and abuse) or working with vulnerable populations (e.g., children or persons who are mentally ill, cognitively impaired, institutionalized, or incarcerated) must address limitations in terms of anticipated ethical, practical, and methodological issues associated with their research plans.

In summary, this chapter offers broad considerations for generating qualitative evidence within the context of a research world that comprises both qualitative and quantitative approaches to evidence-based practice. Because neither approach exists in a vacuum, some necessary distinctions have been drawn in the interests of promoting clearer communication. However, the primary focus has been on general principles that guide the development of qualitative research projects. This discussion does not take the place of more specific guidance that researchers planning an actual study would need to obtain through training and consultation, as appropriate.

> *Use what talent you possess: The woods would be very*
>
> *silent if no birds sang except those that sang best.*
>
> *Henry Van Dyke*

chapter 18

447

references

Barnes, D. M., & Aguilar, R. (2007). Community social support for Cuban refugees in Texas. *Qualitative Health Research, 17,* 225–237.

Beck, C. T. (1994). Reliability and validity issues in phenomenological research. *Western Journal of Nursing Research, 16,* 254–267.

Bogan, L. K., Powell, J. M., & Dudgeon, B. J. (2007). Experiences of living with non-cancer-related lymphedema: Implications for clinical practice. *Qualitative Health Research, 17,* 213–224.

Brown, C., Pikler, V. I., Lavish, L. A., Keune, K. M., & Hutto, C. J. (2008). Surviving childhood leukemia: Career, family, and future expectations. *Qualitative Health Research, 18,* 19–30.

Bryant, A., & Charmaz, K. (2007). *The SAGE handbook of grounded theory.* London: Sage.

Clarke, L. H., Griffin, M., & The PACC Research Team. (2008). Failing bodies: Body image and multiple chronic conditions in later life. *Qualitative Health Research, 18,* 1084–1095.

Creswell, J. W. (2007). *Qualitative inquiry and research design: Choosing among five approaches* (3rd ed.). Thousand Oaks, CA: Sage.

Creswell, J. W. (2008). *Research design: Qualitative, quantitative, and mixed methods approaches* (3rd ed.). Thousand Oaks, CA: Sage.

Cristancho, S., Garces, D. M., Peters, K. E., & Mueller, B. C. (2008). Listening to rural Hispanic immigrants in the Midwest: A community-based participatory assessment of major barriers to health care access and use. *Qualitative Health Research, 18,* 633–646.

Geertz, C. (1973). Thick description: Toward an interpretive theory of culture. In C. Geertz (Ed.), *The interpretation of cultures* (pp. 3–30). New York: Basic Books.

Grace, J. T., & Powers, B. A. (2009). Claiming our core: Appraising qualitative evidence for nursing questions about human response and meaning. *Nursing Outlook, 57*(1), 27–34.

Kahn, D. L., & Steeves, R. H. (1995). The significance of suffering in cancer care. *Seminars in Oncology Nursing, 11,* 9–16.

Kearney, M. H. (2001). Levels and applications of qualitative research evidence. *Research in Nursing & Health, 24,* 145–153.

Kelly, M. (1992). Self, identity, and radical surgery. *Sociology of Health & Illness, 14,* 390–415.

Kelly, A. (2007). Hope is forked: Hope, loss, treatments, and AIDS dementia. *Qualitative Health Research, 17,* 866–872.

Maxwell, J. A. (1992). Understanding and validity in qualitative research. *Harvard Educational Review, 62,* 279–299.

Medved, M. I., & Brockmeier, J. (2008). Continuity amid chaos: Neurotrauma, loss of memory, and sense of self. *Qualitative Health Research, 18,* 469–479.

Morse, J. M. (1996). Is qualitative research complete? *Qualitative Health Research, 6,* 3–5.

Morse, J. M. (1997). Learning to drive from a manual? *Qualitative Health Research, 7,* 181–183.

Morse, J. M. (1999). Qualitative generalizability. *Qualitative Health Research, 9,* 5–6.

Morse, J. M. (2001). Toward a praxis theory of suffering. *Advances in Nursing Science, 24,* 47–59.

Moustakas, C. (1994). *Phenomenological research methods.* Thousand Oaks, CA: Sage.

Nochi, M. (1998). "Loss of self" in the narratives of people with traumatic brain injuries: A qualitative analysis. *Social Science and Medicine, 46,* 869–878.

Patton, M. Q. (2002). *Qualitative research and evaluation methods* (3rd ed.). Thousand Oaks, CA: Sage.

Powers, B. A., & Knapp, T. R. (2006). *Dictionary of nursing theory and research* (3rd ed.). New York: Springer.

Rempel, G. R., & Harrison, M. J. (2007). Safeguarding precarious survival: Parenting children who have life-threatening heart disease. *Qualitative Health Research, 17,* 824–837.

Sacks, J. L., & Nelson, J. P. (2007). A theory of nonphysical suffering and trust in hospice patients. *Qualitative Health Research, 17,* 675–689.

Sandelowski, M. (2000). Whatever happened to qualitative description? *Research in Nursing & Health, 23,* 334–340.

Sandelowski, M., & Barroso, J. (2003). Classifying the findings in qualitative studies. *Qualitative Health Research, 13,* 905–923.

Teddlie, C., & Tashakkori, A. (2008). *Foundations of mixed methods research: Integrating quantitative and qualitative techniques in the social and behavioral sciences.* Thousand Oaks, CA: Sage.

Van Knippenberg, F. C. E., Out, J. J., Tilanus, H. W., Mud, H. J., Hop, W. C. J., & Verhage, F. (1992). Quality of life in patients with resected esophageal cancer. *Social Science & Medicine, 35,* 139–145.

van Manen, M. (1990/1997). *Researching lived experience: Human science for an action sensitive pedagogy.* London, Ontario: University of Western Ontario & State University of New York Press.

Wainwright, D., Donovan, J. L., Kavadas, V., Cramer, H., & Blazeby, J. M. (2007). Remapping the body: Learning to eat again after surgery for esophageal cancer. *Qualitative Health Research, 17,* 759–771.

Acknowledgments

The author wishes to thank Jeanne T. Grace, PhD, RN, WHNP, and *anonymous* reviewers for reading and commenting on earlier drafts of this chapter.

Writing a Successful Grant Proposal to Fund Research and Evidence-Based Practice Implementation Projects

Bernadette Mazurek Melnyk and Ellen Fineout-Overholt

There's always a way if you are willing to pay the price of time, energy, or effort.

Robert Schuller

Once a decision has been made to conduct a study to generate evidence that will guide clinical practice or to implement and evaluate a practice change as part of an evidence-based practice (EBP) implementation or outcomes management project, the feasibility of conducting such an initiative must be assessed. Although certain studies or outcome management projects can be conducted with few resources, most projects (e.g., randomized controlled trials) typically require funding to cover items such as research assistants, staff time, instruments to measure outcomes of interest, intervention materials, and data management and analyses. This chapter focuses on strategies for developing a successful grant proposal to fund research as well as EBP implementation or outcome management projects. Many of these grant-writing strategies are similar, whether applying for large-scale grants from federal agencies, such as the National Institutes of Health (NIH) or the Agency for Healthcare Research and Quality (AHRQ), or more small-scale funding from professional organizations or foundations. Potential funding sources and key components of a project budget also will be highlighted.

449

Preliminary Strategies for Writing a Grant Proposal

A grant proposal is a written plan outlining the specific aims, background, significance, methods, and budget for a project that is requesting funding from sources such as professional organizations, federal agencies, or foundations. It is not uncommon for the process of planning, writing, and revising a rigorous detailed grant proposal for certain funding sources (e.g., NIH, AHRQ, the Centers for Disease Control and Prevention [CDC]) to take several months. In contrast, other sources (e.g., foundations and professional organizations) may require only the submission of a concise abstract or two- to three-page summary of the project for funding consideration. When embarking on the road to writing a successful grant proposal, whether for a large or small project, there are five critical qualities that the writer must possess—the five "Ps": passion, planning, persuasion, persistence, and patience.

The Five Ps

The first quality is *passion* for the proposed initiative. Passion for the project is essential, especially because many "character-building" experiences (e.g., writing multiple drafts, resubmissions) will surface along the road to successful completion.

Second, detailed *planning* must begin. Every element of the project needs to be carefully considered, along with strategies for overcoming potential obstacles. Developing a strong team to carry out the project as well as plan and write the grant facilitates success.

The third element for successful grant writing is *persuasion*. The grant application needs to be written in a manner that excites the reviewers and creates a compelling case for why the project should be funded.

Finally, *persistence* and *patience* are indispensable qualities, especially because the grant application process is very competitive across federal agencies, professional organizations, and foundations. In many cases, repeated submissions are required to secure funding. Therefore, resubmitting applications and being patient and receptive to grant reviewers' feedback are crucial ingredients for success. One tip for success is to surround yourself with uplifting motivational quotes to inspire and encourage you through the writing process (Box 19.1).

---

box 19.1

Motivational Quotes for Success with Grant Writing

Failures are only temporary setbacks and "character-building" experiences.
  —Les Brown

Most people give up just when they're about to achieve success. They quit on the one-yard line. They give up at the last minute of the game, one foot from a winning touchdown.
  —H. Ross Perot

I do not think there is any other quality so essential to success of any kind as the quality of perseverance. It overcomes almost everything, even nature.
  —John D. Rockefeller

First Impressions

Remember that you never get a second chance to make a great first impression. Paying attention to details and being as meticulous as possible for the first grant submission will be well worth the effort when your grant is reviewed.

Once the idea for a study project is generated, the literature searched and critically appraised, and a planning meeting conducted to determine the design and methods (see Chapters 17 and 18), a search for potential funding sources should commence.

Credentials

To obtain grants from most national federal funding agencies (e.g., NIH and AHRQ), a doctoral degree is usually the minimum qualification necessary for the principal or lead investigator on the project. However, many clinicians with master's degrees make substantial contributions to federally funded studies as members of research teams that are spearheaded by clinicians with doctorates. For many professional organization and foundation funding sources, a master's degree is usually sufficient to obtain grant funding, although it typically fares well in the peer review of the grant proposal to have a researcher with a doctorate as part of the team.

Potential Funding Sources

Academic medical centers, schools within university settings, and healthcare organizations frequently have internal mechanisms available to fund small research projects (e.g., pilot and feasibility studies), often through a competitive grants program. External funding agencies, such as NIH and AHRQ; foundations, such as the W.T. Grant Foundation; for-profit corporations, such as pharmaceutical companies; and professional organizations, such as the Society of Critical Care Medicine and the American Heart Association, often list priorities or areas that they are interested in supporting (e.g., palliative care, pain management for critically ill patients, symptom management, and HIV risk reduction).

Establishing a list of potential funding agencies whose priorities are matched with the type of study or project that you are interested in conducting will enhance chances for success. Internet links to various potential funding agencies/organizations are listed in Table 19.1.

Additional helpful resources are databases that match a clinician's interests with federal and foundation research grant opportunities. Two databases that most universities have available to provide this type of matching include the Sponsored Programs Information Network (SPIN) and Genius Smarts. With information from thousands of different sponsoring agencies, SPIN facilitates the identification of potential grants in an individual's area of interest, once specified in the database. Genius Smarts sends e-mail messages to people who are registered in the SPIN database whenever there is a match between the identified areas of interest and potential funding opportunities.

Another continuously updated database that is accessible on the Internet is GrantsNet, a resource of funding opportunities in biomedical research. GrantsNet is free of charge and provides excellent grant-writing tools and tips.

GrantsNet can be found at **http://sciencecareers.sciencemag.org/ funding**

table 19.1 Internet links to various potential funding agencies

Type	Organization	Internet Link
M	National Institute of Mental Health	http://gopher.nimh.nih.gov/
V	National Institutes of Health	http://www.nih.gov/
M	National Alliance on Mental Illness	http://www.nami.org/research/policy.html
V	National Institute of Nursing Research	http://www.ninr.nih.gov/
N	American Nurses Foundation (American Nurses Association)	http://www.anfonline.org/
V	Sigma Theta Tau International	http://www.nursingsociety.org/research/smallgrants/pages/grants_small.aspx
N	American Academy of Nursing	http://www.aannet.org/
V	Agency for Healthcare Research and Quality	http://www.ahrq.gov/fund/
V	Centers for Disease Control and Prevention	http://www.cdc.gov/
M	Substance Abuse and Mental Health Services Administration	http://www.samhsa.gov/
G	National Institute on Aging	http://www.nia.nih.gov/
M	National Institute on Drug Abuse	http://www.drugabuse.gov/funding
V	National Center for Complementary and Alternative Medicine	http://nccam.nih.gov/research/
M	Alzheimer's Association	http://www.alz.org/
M	American Academy of Child & Adolescent Psychiatry	http://www.aacap.org/
N	National League for Nursing	http://www.nln.org/research/grants.htm
M	American Psychiatric Association	http://www.psych.org/
V	Foundation Center	http://www.foundationcenter.org
V	GrantsNet	http://www.grantsnet.org/
V	Robert Wood Johnson Foundation	http://www.rwjf.org/
P	The Annie E. Casey Foundation	http://www.aecf.org/
O	Oncology Nursing Society	http://www.ons.org/
O	American Cancer Society	http://www.cancer.org/

N, nursing issues (e.g., recruitment/retention, competencies, etc.); G, geriatric; M, mental health; O, oncology; P, pediatric; V, multi-type (nonspecific, general categories).

Foundation Center is an Internet site that assists individuals in learning about and locating foundations that match with their individual interests. The Center's mission is to support and improve institutional philanthropic efforts by promoting public understanding of the field and assisting grant applicants to succeed. Helpful online education and tutorials on grant writing are also available at this website. Registration is free for Foundation Center.

The Foundation Center can be found at **http://foundationcenter.org**

Application Criteria

Before proceeding with an application to a specific funding agency or organization, the criteria required to apply for a grant need to be identified. For example, to be eligible for a research grant from some professional organizations, membership in the organization is required. In addition, some foundations require that the grant applicant live in a particular geographical area to apply for funding. Obtaining this type of information as well as conducting a background investigation on a particular organization or foundation will save precious time and energy in that grant applications will be submitted only to sources that match your interest area and qualifications.

Some grant writers find it helpful to contact an individual from the agency or to write a letter of inquiry that contains an abstract of the proposed project before actually writing and submitting the full proposal for funding. The names and contact information for program officers (i.e., the program development/administration contact personnel for grant applicants) are typically listed on an agency's home page. Although some individuals prefer to write the grant abstract after the entire proposal is completed, others find it worthwhile to develop the abstract first and seek up-front consultation about the project's compatibility with a potential funding agency's interests.

Importance of the Abstract

The proposal's abstract is key to the success of the proposal and should create a compelling case for why the project needs to be funded. Important components of the abstract should include

- Clinical significance of the project
- The study's aims or hypotheses/study questions
- Conceptual or **theoretical framework**
- Design and methods, including sample and outcome variables to be measured, as well as the intervention if the study is a clinical trial
- Approach to analyses

Finding a Match

If the preconsultation indicates that the proposed work is not a good match for the potential funding agency, fight off discouragement. Much time and energy will be saved in developing a grant proposal for an agency that is interested in the project as opposed to one that is not. Because grant funding is very competitive, consider targeting several potential funding sources to which your proposal can be submitted simultaneously. However, first determine whether multiple submissions of essentially the same proposal to different funding agencies are allowable by carefully reading the guidelines for submission or asking the program officer from the funding source. Also, keep in mind that various agencies may be willing to fund specific parts of the overall project budget.

Once potential funding agencies are identified, it is extremely beneficial to obtain copies of successfully funded proposals if available. Review of these proposals for substantive quality as well as layout and formatting often strengthens the proposal, especially for first-time grant applicants. Federal agencies (e.g., NIH, AHRQ) will provide copies of successfully funded proposals upon request.

A copy of a well-written NIH grant can be accessed at
http://www.niaid.nih.gov/ncn/grants/app/default.htm. In addition,
abstracts of past and currently funded federal proposals are available at
http://projectreporter.nih.gov/reporter.cfm

For copies of grants funded by professional organizations and foundations, requests should be made directly to the investigator(s). Abstracts of currently funded projects from professional organizations and foundations are often available on their websites or publicized in their newsletters.

Guidelines for Submission

Before writing the proposal, guidelines for grant submission should be obtained from each potential funding source (e.g., length of the proposal, desired font, specifications on margins), reviewed carefully, and followed meticulously. Some funding agencies will return grants if all directions are not followed, which may delay evaluation of the grant proposal until the next review cycle. Also, be sure that the grant proposal looks pleasing aesthetically and does not contain grammatical and typographical errors. A well-organized proposal that is clear and free of errors indicates to reviewers that the actual project will be carried out with the same meticulous detail (Cummings, Holly, & Hulley, 2001).

454

Tips and answers to frequently asked questions for new applicants who
are applying to the NIH for grant funding can be obtained at
http://www.nigms.nih.gov/Research/Application/Tips.htm

Criteria for Rating and Reviewing

In addition to obtaining the guidelines for grant submission, ask whether the funding agency provides grant applicants with the criteria on which grants are rated and reviewed.

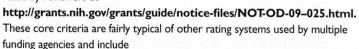

The NIH publishes the review criteria on which grant applications are
rated by reviewers at
http://grants.nih.gov/grants/guide/notice-files/NOT-OD-09–025.html.
These core criteria are fairly typical of other rating systems used by multiple
funding agencies and include

- Significance of the study: Is the problem important? If the aims are
  accomplished, how will knowledge be extended or clinical practice be
  improved?
- Investigator(s): Are the investigators well qualified or suited for the
  project?
- Innovation: Is the project novel or cutting edge?
- Approach: Are the design and methods proposed appropriate to the
  aims of the study?
- Environment: Are there adequate resources available to support the
  project's success?
- Additional review criteria include (a) protection for human subjects and
  (b) inclusion of women, minorities, and children

Develop the Outline

Before writing the proposal, it is helpful to develop an outline that includes each component of the grant application with a timeline and deadline for completion. If working within a team, the lead investigator can then assign specific sections of the grant proposal to various team members. Team members should be informed that before the final product is ready for submission, the document may require several revisions.

As a rule of thumb, it is important to avoid the "old and predictable." Grant reviewers look favorably on projects that are innovative. In addition, never assume that the reviewers will know what you mean when you are writing the grant. Writing with clarity and providing rationales for the decisions that you have made about your design and methods are instrumental in receiving a positive grant review.

At the same time, avoid promising too much or too little within the context of the grant. Thinking that it is advantageous to accomplish a multitude of goals within one study is a commonly held belief, but projects that are so ambitious in scope that feasibility is in question tend to fare poorly in review.

Any time your team lacks a particular expertise related to your project, it is important to obtain expert consultants who can provide guidance in needed areas. These individuals can critique the proposal to strengthen the application before it is submitted. Of additional benefit is a mock review in which successful grant writers and others with expertise in the project area are convened to critique the grant's strengths and limitations. With this type of feedback, you can strengthen the grant application before it is ever submitted for funding consideration. Another strategy is to ask individuals with no expertise in the project area to read the grant proposal and provide feedback on its clarity.

Some individuals find it helpful to place a draft of the grant aside for a few days, then read it again. A fresh perspective a few days later is often invaluable in making final revisions. Additionally, obtaining an editorial review of the grant proposal before submitting it is important in achieving the strongest possible product. See Box 19.2 for a summary of general strategies for successful grant writing.

---

box 19.2

General Strategies for Writing and Funding Grant Proposals

- Possess the five Ps: passion, planning, persuasion, persistence, patience.
- Remember, you never get a second chance to make a first great impression. Submit a high-quality proposal the first time.
- Formulate a great team.
- Write a concise, compelling abstract of the project.
- Identify potential funding sources that are a match with your project.
- Obtain presubmission consultation from staff at the potential funding agency to determine whether the project is a good match with the agency's priorities.
- Obtain and meticulously follow the guidelines for grant submission from the potential funding agency.
- Review successfully funded proposals from the same funding agency.
- Obtain the criteria on which grants are rated if available from the funding agency.
- Develop a topical outline of the proposal with a timeline for when specific components will be completed.

(box continues on page 456)

box 19.2 *(continued)*

- Be innovative; avoid the "old and predictable."
- Write with clarity and provide rationales for your decisions; always justify!
- Do not promise too much or too little.
- Conduct a mock review of the proposal in which both experts and nonexperts in the area provide critique.
- Make the document look aesthetically pleasing.
- Spell check and also personally review the document for grammatical and typographical errors.
- Obtain editorial review before the proposal is submitted.
- Celebrate successful completion of the grant!

Specific Steps in Writing a Successful Grant Proposal

The typical components of a grant proposal are listed in Box 19.3. Although not all of these components may be required for every grant, it is helpful to consider each one when planning the project.

The Abstract

A large amount of time should be invested in developing a clear, compelling, comprehensive, and concise abstract of the project. Because it is a preview of what is to come, the abstract needs to pique the interest and excitement of the reviewers so that they will be compelled to read the rest of the grant application. A poorly written abstract will immediately set the tone for the review and may bias the reviewers to judge the full proposal negatively or dissuade them from reading the rest of the proposal, given that reviewers typically review multiple grant applications simultaneously. Please see Box 19.4 for two examples of grant abstracts from funded grants that are clear and comprehensive but concise and compelling.

Table of Contents

The table of contents containing the components of the grant and corresponding page numbers must be completed accurately so that a reviewer who wants to refer back to a section of the grant can easily identify and access it.

Budget

Many hospitals and universities have research centers or offices with an administrator specifically skilled in developing budgets for grant proposals. It is helpful to seek the assistance of this person, if available, when developing the budget for your project to avoid overestimating or underestimating costs. Knowing which expenses the funding organization will and will not cover is important before developing the budget. This information is often included in the potential funder's guidelines for grant submission.

Most budgets are delineated into two categories: personnel and nonpersonnel (e.g., travel, costs associated with purchasing instruments, honoraria for the subjects). Many professional organizations pay only for **direct costs** (i.e., those costs directly required to conduct

> ### box 19.3
>
> ## Typical Components of a Grant Application
>
> - Abstract
> - Table of contents
> - Budget
> - Biosketches of investigators (usually a condensed two-page to three-page curriculum vitae or resume)
> - Specific aims
> - Introduction to the problem
> - Goals or objectives of the study
> - Research hypotheses or research questions
> - Background for the study, including background and innovation of the project
> - Critical review and synthesis of the literature (consider the inclusion of a table that summarizes findings from prior studies)
> - Discussion on how the proposed work will fill a gap in prior work or extend what is known
> - Theoretical/conceptual framework
> - Prior research experience of the investigators
> - Inclusion of prior studies by the principal investigator and research team as well as professional experience
> - Research methods
> - Design (e.g., experimental, nonexperimental)
> - Methods
> - Sample and setting (selection criteria, sampling design, plans for recruitment of subjects)
> - Intervention if applicable (detailed descriptions of experimental and control or comparison interventions)
> - Variables with measures (validity and reliability information for each measure)
> - Procedure for data collection
> - Approach to data analysis
> - Potential limitations with alternative strategies
> - Timetable for the proposed work
> - Human subjects and ethical considerations
> - Consultants
> - References
> - Appendix
> - Letters of support
> - Instruments
> - Resources available and environment
> - Prior publications

the study, such as personnel, travel, photocopying, instruments, and subject fees) and not for **indirect costs** (i.e., those costs that are not directly related to the actual conduct of the study but are associated with the "overhead" in an organization, such as lights, telephones, office space). Reviewers will critically analyze whether there are appropriate and adequate personnel to carry out the study and whether the costs requested are allowable and reasonable. In applying for

box 19.4

Examples of Grant Abstracts from Two Funded Studies

FUNCTIONAL OUTCOMES AFTER INTENSIVE CARE AMONG ELDERS

Funded by the American Nurses Foundation (Principal investigator: Diane Mick, PhD, RN, CCNS, GNP; Total costs = $2,700).

Objective: Both age and probability of benefit have been suggested as criteria for allocation of healthcare resources. This study will evaluate elders' functional outcomes after intensive care in an effort to discern benefit or futility of interventions.

Methods: A descriptive correlational design will be used. Subjects who are 65 years of age will be identified as "elderly" or "frail elderly" on admission to the Intensive Care Unit (ICU), using Katz's Index of Activities of Daily Living scale. Illness severity will be quantified using the Acute Physiology and Chronic Health Evaluation II Scale. Functional status at admission and at discharge from the ICU, and at 1-month and 3-month post-ICU discharge intervals will be quantified with the Medical Outcomes Study 36-Item Short-Form Health Survey (SF-36). Significance of relationships among age, frailty, gender, illness severity, and functional outcomes will be determined, as well as which patient characteristics and clinical factors are predictive of high levels of physical functioning after ICU discharge.

Significance: Findings may be useful as an adjunct to clinical decision making. As the clinicians who are closest to critically ill elderly patients, nurses are positioned to facilitate dialogue about elderly patients' wishes and expectations.

IMPROVING OUTCOMES OF LOW-BIRTH-WEIGHT (LBW) PREMATURE INFANTS AND PARENTS

Funded by the NIH/National Institute of Nursing Research (Principal investigator: Bernadette Melnyk, PhD, CPNP, PMHNP, FAAN; Co-investigators: Linda Alpert-Gillis, PhD, and Nancy Feinstein, PhD, RN-C [R01#05077]; Total costs = $2.44 million).

Although the mortality rate of LBW premature infants has declined dramatically over the past several years, morbidity remains high as the result of negative cognitive, neurodevelopmental, and behavioral sequelae. Studies indicate that parents of LBW premature infants experience multiple ongoing stressors that result in short-term and long-term negative coping outcomes, such as anxiety and depression, as well as dysfunctional parenting patterns. In the proposed study, we will build upon our prior work and previous studies that have supported the positive benefits of educational-behavioral interventions with mothers of hospitalized young children and LBW premature infants. Among the unique contributions of this study include the following: (a) development of a theoretically driven, reproducible intervention that can be easily translated into clinical practice and widely disseminated; (b) evaluation of our intervention with fathers/significant others as well as mothers; (c) a prospective cost-effectiveness analysis; and (d) an intervention that begins early in the NICU stay, prior to parents developing negative perceptions of their infants and the establishment of ineffective parent-infant interactions.

The primary aim of this multisite study is to evaluate the effects of a theoretically driven, reproducible intervention (COPE = Creating Opportunities for Parent Empowerment) on the process and outcomes of mothers and fathers/significant others' coping with an LBW premature infant and infant developmental outcomes. The secondary

box 19.4 *(continued)*

aims are to (a) explore how the coping process and outcomes of mothers and fathers together contribute to the outcomes of LBW premature infants, (b) determine the cost-effectiveness of the COPE program, and (c) explore what factors moderate the effects of the intervention program (e.g., temperament, family structure, socioeconomic status). A two-group experiment will be used with 240 mothers and 240 fathers/significant others of LBW premature infants in the NICU. Measures of both process and outcome variables, including parental beliefs, anxiety, depression, parent-infant interaction, and infant developmental outcomes, will be assessed during hospitalization and up to the infants' 2-year corrected ages. Findings from a recent pilot study with 42 mother-infant dyads support undertaking this full-scale clinical trial in that mothers who received the COPE program versus those who received a comparison program had more positive coping outcomes, and their infants scored significantly higher (14 points) on the Mental Development Index of the Bayley Scales of Infant Development at 6 months corrected age.

small grants from professional organizations and foundations, which may not provide enough funds to cover a portion of the salaries for the investigators/clinicians who will implement the project, it is important to negotiate release time with administrators during the preparation of the grant so that there will be ample time to successfully complete the project if funded. Typically, subscriptions to journals, professional organization memberships, and entertainment are examples of nonallowable costs. See Table 19.2 for an example of a grant application's proposed budget.

Biosketches of the Principal Investigator and Research Team Members

For the review panel to assess the qualifications of the research team so that it can make a judgment about the team's ability to conduct the proposed project, **biosketches** are typically required as part of the grant application. A biosketch is a condensed two-page to three-page document, similar to a resume or brief curriculum vita, which captures the individual's educational and professional work experience, honors, prior research grants, and publications.

Introduction and Specific Aims

The significance of the problem should be immediately introduced in the grant proposal so that the reviewers can make the judgment that the project is worth funding right from the beginning of the proposal. For example, the following introduction is quickly convincing of the need for more intervention studies with teenagers who use tobacco:

> Approximately 3,000 adolescents become regular tobacco users every day. Evidence from prior studies indicates that teens who smoke are more likely to abuse other substances, such as alcohol and drugs, than teens who do not smoke. There is also accumulating evidence that morbidities associated with cigarette smoking include hypertension, hypercholesteremia, and lung and heart disease.

In the introduction to the grant, it also is important to be clear about what it is that the study will accomplish (i.e., the goals or objectives). For example, "This proposal will evaluate the effects of a conceptually driven, reproducible intervention program on smoking cessation in 15-to 18-year-old adolescents."

table 19.2 **Example of a grant application's proposed budget**

Principal Investigator Funding Agency Submission Date Earliest Start Date		First Year						
Personnel	Role of project	Type of Appointment	% of Effort	$ Base Salary	$ Salary	Benefit Rate%	$ Benefits	$ Total Salary & Benefits
Mary Smith	Principal investigator	12	5	68,000	3,400	28.50	969	4,369
Roberta Picarazzi	Co-investigator	12	5	68,000	3,400	28.50	969	4,369
TBA (24 hours @ $38/hr)	Research associate	12			912	28.50	260	1,172
TBA (49 hours @ $18/hr)	Research assistant	12			882	31.00	273	1,155
					0		0	0
					8,594		2,471	11,065
Consultant costs								0
NA								
Equipment								0
NA								
Supplies								50
General office supplies			50					
Travel								0
Local								
Domestic								
Other expenses								4,350
Lab supplies								
Pharmacy setup fee			500					
Drug/material costs and labor	$15/day × 3 days	3,600		Sample size = 80				
Photocopying			50					
Instrument for data collection								
Patient satisfaction tool								
Human subjects consent form								
Presentation materials (poster & slides)			200					
Subtotal direct costs for initial budget period								15,465
Consortium/ Contractual costs								
Direct costs								
Indirect costs								
Total direct costs for initial budget period								15,465
Less equipment costs								*15,465*
Indirect costs								–

NA, not applicable; TBA, to be announced.

Background and Significance

In this section of the grant proposal, it is important to convince the reviewers that the problem being presented is worthy of study in that the findings are likely to improve the clinical practice and/or health outcomes of a specific population. How the proposal will extend the science in the area or positively impact clinical practice should be explicitly stated. In addition, a comprehensive but concise review of prior studies in the area should be presented, along with a critical analysis of their major strengths and limitations, including the gaps of prior work. It is beneficial to use a table to summarize the sample, design, measures, outcomes, and major limitations of prior studies. The literature review must clearly provide justification for the proposed study's aims, hypotheses, and/or research questions.

The inclusion of a well-defined conceptual or theoretical framework is important in guiding the study and explaining findings of study. If a separate section devoted to the conceptual or theoretical framework is not specified in the guidelines for grant submission, it is typically included in the background section of the proposal. When crafted appropriately, it is clear how the theoretical/conceptual framework is driving the study hypotheses, the intervention if applicable, and/or the relationship between the proposed study variables. This section of the grant also should include definitions of the constructs being measured, along with a description of how the constructs to be studied relate to one another.

For example, if an individual is using a coping framework to study the effects of a stress-reduction intervention program with working women, it would be important in the theoretical framework to state that coping comprises two functions: emotional coping, which regulates emotional responses (e.g., anxiety and depression), and functional coping, which is the solving of problems (e.g., the ability to demonstrate high-quality work performance). Therefore, a study of working women that uses this coping framework should evaluate the effects of the stress-reduction program on the outcome measures of anxiety, depression, and work performance.

The background section should conclude with the study's **hypotheses,** which are statements about the predicted relationships between the **independent** and **dependent** or outcome variables. Hypotheses should be clear, testable, and plausible. The following is an example of a well-written hypothesis:

> Family caregivers who receive the CARE program (i.e., the independent variable) will report less depressive symptoms (i.e., the dependent variable) than family caregivers who receive the comparison program at 2 months following their relative's discharge from the hospital.

When there is not enough prior literature on which to formulate a hypothesis, the investigator may instead present a research question to be answered by the project. For example, if no prior intervention studies have been conducted with family caregivers of hospitalized elders, instead of proposing a hypothesis, it may be more appropriate to ask the following research question: "What is the effect of an educational intervention on anxiety and depressive symptoms in family caregivers of hospitalized elders?"

Prior Research Experience

A summary of professional experience and/or prior work conducted by the principal investigator or project coordinator as well as the research team members should be included in the grant application. Inclusion of this type of information demonstrates that a solid foundation has been laid on which to conduct the proposed study and leaves the reviewers feeling confident that the research team will be able to complete the work that it is proposing.

Study Design and Methods

The design of the study should be clearly described. For example, "This is a randomized clinical trial with repeated measures at 3 and 6 months following discharge from the neonatal intensive care unit." Another example might be, "The purpose of this 6-month project is to determine the effect of implementing interdisciplinary rounds on care delivery and patient outcomes in the burn/trauma unit of a large tertiary hospital."

In discussing the study's methods, it is important to provide rationales for the selected methods so that the reviewers will know that you have critically thought about potential options and made the best decision, based on your critical analysis. Nothing should be left to the reviewers' imagination, and all decisions should be justified.

If the proposed study is an intervention trial, it is very important to discuss the strategies that will be undertaken to strengthen the **internal validity** of the study (i.e., the ability to say that it was the independent variable or the treatment that caused a change in the dependent variable, not other extraneous factors). Please see Chapter 17 for a discussion of strategies to minimize threats to internal validity in quantitative studies.

The sample should be described in this section of the proposal, including its inclusion criteria (i.e., who will be included in the study) and exclusion criteria (i.e., who will be excluded from participation), as well as exactly how the subjects will be recruited into the study. The feasibility of recruiting the targeted number of subjects should also be discussed, and support letters confirming access to the sample should be included in the grant application's appendix. In addition, a description of how subjects from both genders as well as diverse cultural groups will be included is essential. If people younger than 21 years will not be included in the research sample, it is imperative to provide a strong rationale for their exclusion because Public Law 103–43 requires that women and children be included in studies funded by the federal government. In quantitative studies, a **power analysis** (i.e., a procedure for estimating sample size) should always be included (Cohen, 1992). This calculation is critical so that the reviewers will know that there is an adequate sample size for the statistical analysis. Remember, **power** (i.e., the ability of a study to detect existing relationships among variables and thereby reject the null hypothesis that there is no relationship [Polit & Beck, 2007]) in a study increases when sample size increases. Many clinical research studies do not obtain significant findings solely because the sample size is not large enough and the study does not have adequate power to detect significant relationships between variables.

Next, the sampling design (e.g., **random** or **convenience sampling**) should be described. When it is not possible to randomly sample subjects when conducting a study, strategies to increase representativeness of the sample and enhance **external validity** (i.e., **generalizability**) should be discussed. For example, the investigators might choose to recruit subjects from a second study site.

For intervention studies/clinical trials, the intervention must be clearly described. Discussion about how the theoretical/conceptual framework guided the development of the intervention is beneficial in assisting the reviewers to see a clear connection between them. Issues of reproducibility and feasibility of the proposed intervention should also be discussed. In addition, it is important to include information about what the comparison or control group will receive throughout the study.

For intervention studies, it is important to provide details regarding how the integrity of the intervention will be maintained (i.e., the intervention will be delivered in the same manner to all subjects), as well as assurance that the intervention will be culturally sensitive. Additionally, it is important to include a discussion about what type of **manipulation checks** (i.e., assessments to determine whether subjects actually processed the content of the intervention or followed through with the activities prescribed in the intervention program) will be used in the study. **"Booster" interventions** (i.e., additional interventions at timed intervals after the initial intervention) are a good idea to include in the study's design if long-term benefits of an intervention are desired.

It is important to include how outcomes of the study will be measured. If using formal instruments, description of each measure must be included in the grant proposal, including

face, content, and **construct validity** (i.e., does the instrument measure what it is intended to measure?) and **reliability** (i.e., does the instrument measure the construct consistently?). In addition, a description of the scoring of each of the instruments should be included, along with their cultural sensitivity. Justification for why a certain measure was selected is important, especially if there are multiple valid and reliable instruments available that tap the same construct. If collecting patient outcomes, descriptions of how, when, and by whom the data will be collected should be included in the proposal.

     Internal consistency reliability (i.e., the degree to which all the subparts of an instrument are measuring the same attribute [Polit & Beck, 2007] of an instrument) should be at least 70%, whereas **interrater reliability** (i.e., the degree to which two different observers assign the same ratings to an attribute being measured or observed [Polit & Beck, 2007]) should be at least 90% and assessed routinely to correct for any **observer drift** (i.e., a decrease in interrater reliability). For intervention studies, it is important to include measures that are sensitive to change over time (i.e., those with low test–retest reliabilities) so that the intervention can demonstrate its ability to affect the study's outcome variables.

     When conducting research, both self-report as well as nonbiased observation measures should be included whenever possible because convergence on both of these types of measures will increase the credibility of the study's findings. In addition, the use of valid and reliable instruments is preferred whenever possible over the use of instruments that are newly developed and lacking established validity and reliability.

     The procedure or protocol for the study should be clearly described. Specific information about the timing of data collection for all measures should be discussed. Using a table helps to summarize the study protocol in a concise snapshot so that reviewers can quickly grasp when the study's measures will be collected (see Table 19.3).

     The description of data analysis must include specific and clear explanations about how the data to answer each of the study hypotheses or research questions will be analyzed. Adding a statistical consultant to your study team who can assist with the writing of the statistical section and the analysis of the study's data will fare favorably in the review process.

     Even if the guidelines for the proposal do not call for it, it is very advantageous to include a section in the grant that discusses potential limitations of the proposal with alternative approaches. By doing so, it demonstrates to the reviewers that potential limitations of the study have been recognized, along with plans for alternative strategies that will be employed to overcome them. For example, inclusion of strategies to guard against study attrition (i.e., loss of subjects from your study) would be important to discuss in this section.

     A timetable that indicates when specific components of the study will be started and completed should be included in the grant application (see Figure 19.1). This projected timeline should be realistic and feasible.

Human Subjects

When writing a research proposal, it is essential to discuss the risks and benefits of study participation, protection against risks, and the importance of the knowledge to be gained from the study. The demographics of the sample that you intend to recruit into your study are also very important to describe in the proposal. In addition, the process through which informed consent will be obtained needs to be discussed, along with how confidentiality of the data will be maintained. Some funding agencies require the proposal to be reviewed and approved by an appropriate research subjects review board, and others require proof of approval if funding is awarded before commencement of the project.

     In addition, if a study is a clinical trial, federal agencies (e.g., NIH) require a **data and safety monitoring plan,** which outlines how adverse effects will be assessed and managed.

table 19.3 **A summary table of a study's protocol**

Example of a study protocol for a randomized controlled trial to determine the effects of an intervention program on the coping outcomes of young critically ill children and their mothers											
			Time								
Variables	Measures	Cronbach's Alphas	1	2	3	4	5	6	7	8	9
Maternal Emotional Outcomes											
State anxiety	State anxiety inventory (A-State)	0.94–0.96	•	•	•	•		•	•	•	•
Negative mood state	Profile of mood states (POMS, short form)	0.92–0.96	•	•	•	•		•	•	•	•
Depression	Depression subscale, POMS	0.92–0.96	•	•	•	•	•	•	•	•	
Stress related to PICU	Parental stressor scale: PICU (PSS:PICU)	0.90–0.91	•	•							
Posthospitalization stress	Posthospitalization stress index for parents	0.83–0.85	•	•	•	•					
Maternal Functional Outcomes											
Parent participation in care	Index of parent participation	0.85	•	•							
Other Key Maternal Variables											
Parental beliefs	Parental beliefs scale	0.91	•								
Manipulation checks evaluation	Manipulation checks Self-report questionnaire	NA	•	•	•	•					
		NA	•	•	•	•					
Child Adjustment Outcomes											
Posthospitalization stress	Posthospitalization stress index for children	0.78–0.85	•	•	•	•					
Child behavior	Behavioral assessment scale for children	0.92–0.95	•	•	•	•					

Time 1, Phase I intervention (6–16 hours after PICU admission); Time 2, Phase II intervention (16–30 hours after PICU admission); Time 3, Phase III intervention (2–6 hours after transfer to pediatric unit); Time 4, Observation contact (24–36 hours after transfer to pediatric unit); Time 5, Phase III intervention (2–3 days following hospital discharge); Time 6, 1 Month postdischarge follow-up (1 month following hospital discharge); Time 7, 3 Months postdischarge follow-up (3 months following hospital discharge); Time 8, 6 Months postdischarge follow-up (6 months following hospital discharge); Time 9, 12 Months postdischarge follow-up (12 months following hospital discharge).

If applying to the NIH for funding, Public Law 103–43 requires that women and minorities be included in all studies unless there is acceptable scientific justification provided as to why their inclusion is not feasible or appropriate with regard to the health of the subjects or the purpose of the research. NIH also requires that children younger than 21 years be included in research unless there are ethical or scientific reasons for their exclusion.

> More specific information on the protection and inclusion of human subjects can be found in Chapter 20 and at
> **http://grants.nih.gov/grants/frequent_questions.htm**

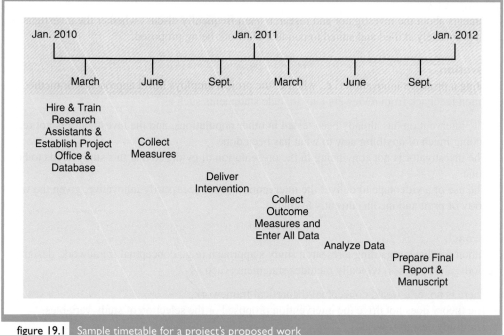

Consultants, References, and Appendices

A section for consultants is often included in grant applications. The expertise and role of each consultant on the project should be described.

Each citation referenced in the grant proposal should be included in the reference list. All references should be accurate, complete, and formatted according to the guidelines for submission (e.g., American Psychological Association [APA] or American Medical Association [AMA] formatting).

Grant applications typically require or allow the investigator to include letters of support from consultants or study sites, copies of instruments that will be used in the study, lists of resources available, and publications of the research team that support the application. Support letters from consultants indicate to the reviewers that they are enthusiastic about the proposed study or project and that they are committed to their role on the project. Letters of support from study sites are helpful to indicate enthusiasm for the study and permission for subjects to be recruited from those sites.

Common Feedback from Grant Reviews

This section of the chapter describes feedback that is commonly provided by reviewers of federal grants and some professional organizations. It is organized according to typical categories used for rating grant applications. Feedback from a grant review should help to strengthen the proposed study and facilitate the professional growth of the investigator.

Significance

Reviewers typically judge the significance of a project by whether the study addresses an important problem or extends what is known in the area. Common feedback in this category may include statements such as

- The literature does not capture the entire body of information on the selected concepts.
- The argument for why an intervention in this particular population is needed is not strong.
- It is not clear how this study or project builds on prior work in the area.

Investigators

Comments about the investigator and research team frequently discuss whether the investigators are appropriately skilled and suited to conduct the work being proposed.

Innovation

In rating a project's innovation (i.e., whether the project employs novel approaches or methods), common feedback from reviewers may include statements such as

- The intervention has already been tested in other populations, and the investigator is not really adding much of anything new to what has been done.
- The investigator is not convincing in the presentation of evidence that this study needs to be done.
- The use of a videotape to deliver the intervention is not necessarily innovative, given the wide array of print and media currently available.

Approach

Common feedback regarding a research study's approach (e.g., conceptual framework, design, methods, and analyses) typically includes statements such as

- There is no, or a weak, conceptual/theoretical framework.
- The theory does not drive the intervention proposed or the selection of study variables.
- The study design is weak.
- Some of the details for the methods are unclear.
- The sample size is not adequate to test the hypotheses.
- The measures are not adequately described.
- The data analysis section needs a fuller discussion.
- The number of measures being used creates too much burden for the subjects.
- The project is too ambitious for the timetable proposed.

In addition, comments from reviewers about intervention studies typically focus on concerns about cross-contamination between the experimental and control groups (e.g., sharing of experimental information), reproducibility and feasibility of the intervention, and cultural sensitivity.

Environment

Reviewers typically comment on whether the environment is conducive to support the work being proposed (e.g., whether there is evidence of enough resources and institutional support for the project).

Major Pitfalls of Grant Proposals

There are numerous weaknesses in grant proposals that limit their ability to fare well during the review process. Box 19.5 outlines these common pitfalls.

Major Characteristics of Funded Grant Proposals

Unlike proposals that are weak, strong proposals have characteristics that enhance their fundability. These characteristics include

- Creativity and innovation
- High scientific quality
- Clarity

---

box 19.5

Major Pitfalls of Grant Proposals

- Lack of new or original ideas
- Failure to acknowledge published relevant work
- Fatal flaws in the study design or methods
- Applications that are incomplete or do not contain enough detail about the methods
- Unrealistic amount of work
- Uncritical approach
- Human subjects concerns
- Absence of a theory or conceptual framework
- Absence of links to current literature
- Lack of significance
- Inappropriate or weak data analysis plan
- Promising too much or too little

- Excellent technical quality (e.g., organized, easy to read, and free of grammatical and spelling errors)
- Potential to impact the clinical field
- Greater depth in thinking about conceptual issues

Successful grant proposals also include a thoughtful discussion about the limitations of the proposed work, as well as strategies for dealing with potential problems without overemphasizing these issues (Cummings et al., 2001). Copies of successful grant applications funded by NIH as well as various professional organizations can be obtained on request.

A Nonfunded Grant: Strategies for Resubmission

Many individuals feel dejected when their proposals are not successful in securing funding. However, openness to constructive feedback, continued belief in one's ability to be successful, and persistence are often necessary to turn a nonfunded proposal into a funded one.

> *The only limit to our realization of tomorrow will be our doubts of today.*
> *Franklin Delano Roosevelt*

> *If you believe you can, you probably can. If you believe you won't, you most assuredly won't. Belief is the ignition switch that gets you off the launching pad.*
> *Dr. Dennis Waitley*

Even the most successful grant writers face rejection at times during their careers. When confronted with a rejected proposal, being able to seek the advice of a seasoned mentor who has faced and overcome grant rejections is invaluable in addressing how you will handle the revisions and further pursuit of funding.

Once a grant proposal is rejected, it is important to determine whether a resubmission will be allowed by the funding agency. If permitted, it is important to ask whether there are specific guidelines for resubmission and, if so, to obtain them. For example, the NIH allows one resubmission of a grant proposal. Individuals who are resubmitting are allowed a certain number of pages as an introduction to the revised proposal in which they specifically respond to how they have addressed the reviewers' concerns and suggestions.

If a resubmission is allowed, it is helpful to discuss the plans for addressing the reviewers' comments with the appropriate program officer or contact person at the funding agency. Individuals from the funding agency can often provide insights into the critique and make suggestions for revision.

After reading the reviewers' feedback, recognize that it is normal to feel sad, frustrated, and/or angry about the critique. It is also common to believe that the reviewers did not read your grant thoroughly or to feel that they did not understand your work and were overly critical of it. After reading the review comments, it is helpful to file them away for a week or two until you can come back to them with an open mind to begin the process of revising the proposal.

In the introduction to the revised application, first inform the review committee that its critique has assisted you in clarifying and strengthening your proposed work. It is critical to respond point by point to the major issues raised by the review panel, without a defensive posture. If you disagree with a recommendation from the review panel, do so gently and astutely. Be sure to include a good rationale, as in the following example:

> We agree that cross-contamination is always a concern in clinical intervention studies and have given it thoughtful consideration. However, we believe that this potential problem can be minimized by taking several precautions. For example, we will administer the interventions to the subjects in a private room adjacent to the intensive care unit so that the staff nurses will not overhear the content of the interventions and begin to share it with the families.

Finally, revise the text enough so that reviewers will note that you took their suggestions seriously, but do not completely rewrite the application as though it were new. Guidelines for resubmission will often inform applicants to use a boldface or italic font to identify the content that has been changed within the context of the grant proposal.

Unhelpful responses in the resubmission process include not taking the reviewers' critique seriously by ignoring their suggestions, as well as denigrating the review panel's criticisms. In addition, changing the research design in an attempt to please the review panel without critical thought and analysis will not fare well in the re-review of the grant proposal.

Specific Considerations in Seeking Funds for Outcomes Management or Quality Improvement Projects

Evidence-based practice implementation and outcomes management projects as well as quality improvement initiatives that focus on improving practice performance, including changes in care delivery modalities (e.g., primary nursing versus team nursing), system supports for the health-care team (e.g., electronic health record with clinical decision support system), and evaluation of the effect of a practice change on patient outcomes within a particular environment (e.g., how substance abusers respond to education about drug rehabilitation and the subsequent effect on the recurrence of abuse in a small county rehabilitation program), are usually not funded by federal agencies. Internal funding sources and foundations are typically the most viable places to obtain funding for these types of endeavors. The application process for a foundation can range in rigor from a one-page to two-page abstract to a full-scale NIH-style grant proposal.

For internal sources of funding within one's institution (e.g., schools of nursing, academic health centers, hospitals), guidelines are usually available upon request from the research office, if one exists, or from the department that handles professional, educational, or research affairs. As with other types of grant applications, obtaining and explicitly following the guidelines for submission are essential for success. In both cases, one of the primary tenets of securing funding is that the project reflects the mission and stated goals of the organization or foundation. Specifically, the grant application needs to be an excellent match, often between what the funding source desires and what can be provided. Generally, foundations are very clear about the specific areas in which they are willing to provide fiscal support. For example, a major funding area for the Kellogg Foundation is vulnerable children.

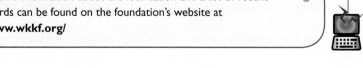

More specific information about the foundation and a list of recent grant awards can be found on the foundation's website at **http://www.wkkf.org/**

Many universities and medical centers have a foundation relations office that can assist individuals in locating a good foundation match and pursuing funding for their proposals. In fact, some universities and medical centers require that all requests for foundation funds be streamlined through their foundation relations office so that multiple applications from various departments are not submitted simultaneously to the same foundation.

One way to determine whether the foundation that you wish to query about funding is a good match with your project is to peruse projects that were recently funded, which can typically be found on the foundation's website. Scanning the list of these funded projects can provide a sense of the types of projects that are currently being funded. If few to no healthcare projects are funded, realize that this may not be a good match and that more inquiry is necessary before soliciting funding from that organization. If you determine that a foundation is a good match for your project, carefully study the requirements for proposal submission. Some foundations require that the first step in the application process include only an abstract of the proposed project. If the abstract matches the organization's goals and is reviewed favorably, the applicant may be asked to provide a more detailed proposal. However, some foundations or organizations may provide funding based on the abstract alone, especially if the budget request is small (e.g., less than $10,000). Other foundations require a full-scale proposal, including detailed budgets and biographical sketches for the project director and team members. By carefully following the guidelines provided by the organization, the chance of funding will increase.

Keep in mind that most foundations require that the sponsoring organization meet the regulations of the United States Internal Revenue Service as a 501c3 organization (i.e., tax exempt). When preparing to seek foundation funding, be aware that many foundations seldom provide large funding relative in size to federal grants. In perusing foundation websites, you may note that, on average, most foundation grants range between $500 and $50,000.

An example of an organization that funds initiatives such as outcomes management or quality improvement projects is the American Association of Critical-Care Nurses (AACN).

Information about AACN's small grant opportunities along with specific requirements for submission can be found at **http://www.aacn.org**

Funding for Evidence-Based Practice Implementation Projects

Evidence-based practice implementation projects are typically clinical projects that use research findings to improve clinical practice. They are usually conceived in response to an identified clinical problem. Unlike research studies that have a goal to generate new knowledge, EBP implementation projects are usually meant to solve clinical problems through the application of existing research-based knowledge (e.g., evidence-based clinical practice guidelines).

The application of the pain management guidelines developed by AHRQ to healthcare settings nationwide is a good example of an EBP implementation project in action. These guidelines were based on sound scientific evidence and developed by nationally known clinical experts. Managers, clinical specialists, and educators then implemented the published guidelines in their clinical settings, measuring clinical outcomes pre-implementation and post-implementation.

Sources that fund EBP implementation projects, such as AACN's Small Project Grants, do not generally require the scientific rigor of a typical research proposal. Because the nature of this type of funding is small (i.e., usually $500–$1,500), the timeline from funding to project implementation is short (usually less than 12 months), and the project usually involves the application of well-established research evidence (e.g., guidelines, procedures, and protocols). Thus, the application process is modified accordingly and typically includes

- Cover letter
- Grant application form
- Timetable for the project
- Budget: Funding requested and justification for funding requested
- Evidence of ethical review: If an institutional review board is not available in the institution, a letter of approval from facility administration should be requested, indicating that they are aware of the project and its implications for their patients.
- Participant consent: All subjects in the project must give written consent, especially if the eventual publication of project results is anticipated (exception: data abstraction from medical records with elimination of all patient-specific identifying data).
- Program questions: Specific to each grant, these questions should be answered in detail. When describing the project, use the information outlined in the methods section of this chapter as a general guide.

Remember that many organizations require membership or registration on their websites to be eligible to apply for funding or to gain access to funding guidelines.

Foundations typically restrict their focus to certain populations or service areas (e.g., rural nursing homes). For example, the Washington Square Health Foundation focuses on increasing access to healthcare among at-risk populations and expanding the community's capacity to address important healthcare needs. Its mission is to grant funds in order to promote and maintain access to adequate healthcare for all people in the greater Chicago area. This foundation awards funding to medical and nursing educational programs, medical research institutions, and direct healthcare services (e.g., outcomes management initiatives).

General guidelines for submitting a grant proposal to the Washington Square Health Foundation include

- Collected assessment data about the healthcare needs of high-risk, underserved, and/or disadvantaged populations in the service area
- Implemented targeted activities to increase the accessibility of healthcare services to one or more high-risk, underserved, and/or disadvantaged populations
- Designed and implemented with community involvement, new or expanded services to address the healthcare needs of one or more high-risk, underserved, and/or disadvantaged populations
- Identified opportunities to increase assets of high-risk, underserved, and/or disadvantaged communities, such as by employing community members as staff in health programs, locating health service delivery sites in the community, and negotiating purchasing contracts with local businesses for health service–related products

> The Washington Square Health Foundation can be found at
> **http://www.wshf.org**

Some foundations fund demonstration and quality improvement projects as well as community initiatives versus research because of the desire to influence practice or healthcare improvements quickly. For example, the Fan Fox & Leslie R. Samuels Foundation has shifted the focus of its healthcare program from applied research to patient-based and social service activities that assist older adults in New York City. The refocused program is designed to improve the mechanism for health and social services to be delivered through support to organizations that reflect inventive, useful, competent, and thoughtful care to their patients. Requirements for a grant application to the Fan Fox & Leslie R. Samuels Foundation include the following:

- The program will improve the overall quality of life or healthcare service delivery to New York City's elderly.
- The program has a realistic, achievable work plan and a rational, well-justified budget.
- The program staff members who will perform the work are experienced and highly qualified.
- The sponsoring organization is stable, competent, and committed.

To submit an abstract for funding to the Fan Fox & Leslie R. Samuels Foundation, applicants must compile a cover sheet with the following information: legal name, address, phone, fax, and e-mail and website addresses (if available) of the institution or organization; the program director's name, address, phone, fax, and e-mail (if available); the name and exact title of the organization's CEO; the program title and its duration; the total dollar amount requested; and a one paragraph summary of the proposed program. In addition, a three-page letter (1-inch margins, 12-point font) that clearly states the following must be submitted:

- The general problems and issues being addressed and their importance
- A brief description of the nature of the program and its significance, with clear goals and objectives
- The recommended approach to care or services that represents an improvement over how services are delivered now; how the proposed program makes care or service provision better
- A description of the anticipated benefit of the program to older adults, including the number of individuals who will be impacted

- The program's overall significance
- A summary of the critical activities to be performed, the timeframe for the proposed program, and a brief breakdown of the projected budget
- If successful, the likelihood that the program will be continued by the institution
- The commitment of the sponsoring institution (e.g., contribution of salaries, space, overhead) during and after the grant term

The Fan Fox & Leslie R. Samuels Foundation can be found at **http://www.samuels.org/**

The pursuit of foundation funding is a good option to follow for EBP implementation or quality improvement projects and outcomes management initiatives. Most requirements for foundation applications are readily available on the Internet, which enhances the timeliness of application submission. As with any other funding endeavor, assuring that the foundation or organization's goals are a good match for your project, carefully following the supplied guidelines, and providing the clearest and most informative presentation of the project, whether that be only an abstract or a full proposal, will increase chances for successful funding.

Conclusion

The process of writing a grant proposal is a challenging but rewarding experience. Formulating a great team, judicious planning, careful attention to the detailed requirements of the grant application, and background homework on potential funding sources as well as prior work in the area will facilitate the writing of an innovative, compelling, clear proposal that is matched appropriately for the potential funding agency.

It is helpful to remember that the process of writing a grant proposal resembles the eating of a 2-ton chocolate elephant. If you sit on a stool in front of the elephant and look up, the whole elephant appears too large to consume. However, if you sit on the stool looking straight ahead and consume the part of the elephant that is directly in front of you, then move the stool to the next parts in sequential order and consume them one at a time, soon the whole chocolate elephant will be eaten! In addition, when writing a grant proposal, it is helpful to remember the following individuals who succeeded in their endeavors as the result of not being afraid to take risks in combination with strong belief in themselves and sheer persistence:

- *Babe Ruth struck out 1,330 times. In between his strikeouts, he hit 714 home runs.*
- R.H. Macy failed in retailing seven times before his store in New York became a success.
- Abraham Lincoln failed twice in business and was defeated in six state and national elections before being elected President of the United States.
- Theodor S. Geisel wrote a children's book that was rejected by 23 publishers. The 24th publisher sold six million copies of it—the first "Dr. Seuss" book—and that book and its successors are still staples of every children's library (Kouzes & Posner, 2002, p. 214).

Remember, people often fail their way to success. This also applies to the process of grant writing. Therefore, prepare well, believe in yourself and your team's ability to write a great grant proposal, seek mentorship and critique, and stay persistent to resubmit until your project is funded!

chapter 19

references

Cohen, J. (1992). A power primer. *Psychological Bulletin, 112*(1), 155–159.

Cummings, S. R., Holly, E. A., & Hulley, S. (2001). Writing and funding a research proposal. In S. B. Hulley, S. R. Cummings, W. S. Browner, (Eds.), *Designing clinical research. An epidemiologic approach* (2nd ed., pp 285–299). Philadelphia, PA: Lippincott Williams & Wilkins.

Kouzes, J. M., & Posner, B. Z. (2002). *The leadership challenge* (3rd ed.). San Francisco, CA: Jossey-Bass.

Polit, D. F., & Beck, C. T. (2007). *Nursing research: Generating and assessing evidence for nursing practice* (8th ed.). Philadelphia, PA: Lippincott, Williams & Wilkins.

Ethical Considerations for Evidence Implementation and Evidence Generation

Dónal P. O'Mathúna

> *In great affairs men show themselves as they wish to be seen; in small things they show themselves as they are.*
>
> Nicholas Chamfort

Evidence-based practice (EBP) should lead to improved outcomes through applying evidence to practice, which requires careful evaluation of these outcomes. Without such evaluation, our confidence in applying the evidence can be weak. Though the impetus for evaluating the implementation of evidence may arise from a commitment to EBP itself, it should arise from a commitment to ethical practice and improving outcomes. Ethical principles influence both the importance of evaluating the impact of evidence on patients and the way those evaluations are conducted.

Some of the motivations underlying the advancement of EBP are, at their core, ethical issues. Individual studies and reports by organizations in the United States such as the Institute of Medicine (IOM) and the Agency for Healthcare Research and Quality (AHRQ) have found "detailed, compelling evidence of serious problems with the quality of American healthcare" (Baily, Bottrell, Lynn, et al., 2006, p. S7). In the United States and other countries, medication errors are one example of serious and widespread problems in healthcare practice. Every year, 1.5 million people are harmed in the United States through medication errors at a cost of $3.5 billion in hospital costs alone (IOM, 2006).

Other countries also report serious problems with their healthcare systems. In a survey of seven developed countries (i.e., Australia, Canada, Germany, the Netherlands, New Zealand, the United Kingdom, and the United States), each scored low on some quality criteria (Schoen, Osborn, Doty, et al., 2007). In every country, more than half of the respondents stated that fundamental changes were needed in their healthcare systems. Patients with chronic illnesses continue to report system-wide problems with the quality of their healthcare (Schoen, Osborn, How, et al., 2009). In addition, problems in developing countries raise a host of other ethical issues that will not be addressed in this chapter (O'Mathúna, 2007).

The IOM has developed a conceptual framework to help understand healthcare quality and how it can be improved practically. It defines quality as "the degree to which health services for individuals and populations increase the likelihood of desired health outcomes and are consistent with current professional knowledge" (IOM, 2009). The core dimensions of quality, as articulated in several IOM reports, are safety, effectiveness, patient-centeredness, timeliness, equity, and efficiency (Baily et al., 2006).

Each of these dimensions is underpinned by ethical principles (see Box 20.1). For example, the ethical principle of balancing benefit and harm promotes safety. The ethical principle of equality, justice, and equity promotes the use of resources according to effectiveness in a timely, equitable fashion. The ethical principle of human dignity (i.e., respect for persons) promotes patient-centeredness and equity. Thus, promotion of healthcare quality can be seen as an ethical enterprise. Evidence-based practice, as the backbone of all quality initiatives, also is underpinned by the same ethical principles. However, that does not mean that every approach to improving quality is necessarily ethical or evidence-based.

Situations where evidence-based quality improvement (EBQI) initiatives could conflict with ethical principles include (a) attempts to improve quality for some patients that may inadvertently cause harm for others, if people or resources are diverted away from them; (b) strategies intended to improve quality that may turn out to be ineffective and waste scarce resources; and (c) activities declared to be quality improvement that may be more accurately described as clinical research or visa versa. The term *clinical research* will be used here, although *human subjects research* also is used, especially in regulatory contexts. Clinical research is defined as research where investigators directly interact with human subjects or material of human origin (National Institutes of Health, 2005). If research activities are carried out without patient informed consent,

> ### box 20.1
>
> ## Fifteen Ethical Principles of the *Universal Declaration on Bioethics and Human Rights* (United Nations Educational, Scientific and Cultural Organization, 2008)
>
> 1. Human dignity and human rights
> 2. Benefit and harm
> 3. Autonomy and individual responsibility
> 4. Consent
> 5. Persons without the capacity to consent
> 6. Respect for human vulnerability and personal integrity
> 7. Privacy and confidentiality
> 8. Equality, justice, and equity
> 9. Nondiscrimination and nonstigmatization
> 10. Respect for cultural diversity and pluralism
> 11. Solidarity and cooperation
> 12. Social responsibility and health
> 13. Sharing of benefits
> 14. Protecting future generations
> 15. Protection of the environment, the biosphere, and biodiversity

they may be seen as an unethical use of patients as research subjects (Baily et al., 2006). In contrast, it may be seen as unethical to require patients to provide their consent for care that is known to provide them with better outcomes compared to their acceptance of mediocre care that does not have that guarantee. Despite these issues, if efforts are not made to improve quality, healthcare professionals may violate their ethical responsibility to provide patients with the most safe and effective clinical care possible. When this violation happens, patients will continue to be put at risk from lower quality healthcare.

One approach to improving the quality of healthcare is referred to as performance improvement (PI) or quality improvement (QI). Such projects can be defined as "systematic, data-guided activities designed to bring about immediate improvements in healthcare delivery in particular settings" (Lynn, Baily, Bottrell, et al., 2007, p. 667). These activities include an array of methods designed to solve practical clinical problems and to bring about and evaluate change, sometimes based on evidence. Some similarity between QI and EBP can be seen in the description of QI as an approach that "means encouraging people in the clinical care setting to use their daily experience to identify promising ways to improve care, implement changes on a small scale, collect data on the effects of those changes, and assess the results" (Baily et al., 2006, p. S5). This is much like the EBP paradigm that requires clinicians to bring their expertise as well as empiric knowledge into innovative clinical decision making. However, the QI approach does not explicitly require the participation of the patient as does EBP.

The EBP implementation approach can be centered on an issue arising in a unit, an institution, or a system. Evidence can be applied to bring about change for one patient, or it may be intended to effect change across a system or profession. Documenting the change is the imperative. Here is where the EBP implementation approach is often confused with clinical research. These two enterprises involve human participants and sometimes use similar methods to evaluate outcomes. For some, EBP implementation activities are seen as a form of clinical research that should come under the same ethical and regulatory requirements. Others claim that some EBP implementation activities are sufficiently different that they should not be considered clinical research; however, specific ethical principles still apply. One issue that often distinguishes these two approaches is the generalizability of their findings. Clinical research should be conducted with samples that are representative of the population of interest so that the findings can be applied to that population. Implementation of evidence in practice is the application of interventions, practices, or approaches that are known to produce outcomes with some degree of confidence; however, the people to whom the care is provided are not usually representative of a population. Rather they are the patients under that provider's care, no matter what the setting (e.g., hospital, community, primary care practice, or long-term care facility). This type of process occurs often in improving the quality of care; however, to generalize the process or the findings (i.e., outcomes) from EBP implementation is not the goal. Rather the goal is to initiate and sustain meaningful change within the clinicians' practice and for those patients or clients.

Nevertheless, confusion still exists around the ethical issues surrounding EBP implementation and how it compares to clinical research. The formal processes often seem to be a confusing factor for institutional review boards (IRBs; otherwise known as research ethics committees in Europe). Some IRBs and regulators view the EBP implementation process as research based on descriptions of the deliberate application of an evidence-based practice across all patients and the evaluation of outcomes. However, if clinicians withheld known beneficial treatment from patients, they could be considered unethical. In addition, collection of data, in and of itself, cannot be misconstrued as clinical research. To follow that logic would require that daily intake and output values that are totaled and described would be considered research that produced generalizable knowledge. Research is knowledge that is generated in such a way that it can be applied to a broader population than those from whence it came. Evidence-based practice implementation is applying research, with internal evidence, to improve care. To guard against this issue hindering best practice for patients, clinicians and IRBs must use caution to ensure that unique ethical requirements for research are applied to research and that the ethical requirements fitting to EBP implementation are appropriately applied.

This ethical debate has raged in the literature for a number of years. Given that the answers accepted will significantly impact efforts to improve the quality of healthcare, it is important to understand these ethical issues. While much of the debate has been triggered by how these issues have been dealt with in the United States, the ethical issues have relevance for other jurisdictions. Two cases are presented in the following section to highlight the issues involved.

> *It is not fair to ask of others what you are unwilling to do yourself.*
>
> *Eleanor Roosevelt*

Two Ethical Exemplars

Bloodstream infections related to catheters lead to about 28,000 deaths in intensive care units (ICUs) in the United States each year (Pronovost, Needham, Berenholtz, et al., 2006). About three times as many catheter-related infections occur each year, with resulting care costing more than $2 billion annually. Researchers at Johns Hopkins University coordinated a prospective cohort study to examine the impact of introducing evidence-based strategies to reduce infection rates in all ICUs in Michigan (to be referred to in this chapter as the Michigan ICU study). Just more than 100 ICUs participated in the 18-month study during 2004 and 2005. A large and sustained reduction in rates of catheter-related infections occurred (up to 66% reduction). The median number of infections per 1,000 catheter-days decreased from 2.7 at baseline to 0 during the final study period ($p < 0.002$).

The study involved a number of educational interventions targeted at ICU personnel to improve patient safety. This included designating one physician and one nurse as team leaders in each ICU. The researchers developed a checklist to promote clinicians' use of five evidence-based procedures recommended by the Centers for Disease Control and Prevention. These were (a) hand washing; (b) using full-barrier precautions during insertion of central venous catheters; (c) cleansing the skin with chlorhexidine prior to catheter insertion; (d) avoiding, where possible, the femoral site for catheter insertion; and (e) removing unnecessary catheters. Neither expensive technology nor additional ICU staff was required, though each hospital provided adequate staff to implement the educational intervention.

The study had limitations and, as with any study, required critical appraisal (Daley, 2007; Jenny-Avital, 2007). Nonetheless, the results were praised in *The New York Times* as "stunning" because of how the study saved more than 1,500 lives during its 18 months (Gawande, 2007). However, a few weeks after the study results were published, the Office for Human Research Protections (OHRP), the federal agency charged with protecting people involved in research in the United States, ordered an investigation into possible ethical violations in the study (Miller & Emanuel, 2008). In November 2007, the OHRP ruled that the project had violated ethics regulations and was to be shut down, including planned expansions in other states (Gawande, 2007).

The OHRP held that the Michigan ICU study had violated two ethics regulations. The study was submitted to the Johns Hopkins University Institutional Review Board, which deemed it exempt from review. The IRB viewed the project as an EBP implementation and QI initiative, not clinical research. The OHRP disagreed and held that it was research. Informed consent was not obtained in the project because it was considered exempt from IRB review (Pronovost et al., 2006). OHRP held that informed consent should not have been waived for this reason because it viewed the project as clinical research.

Wide application of OHRP's approach could mean that "whole swaths of critical work to ensure safe and effective care would either halt or shrink" (Gawande, 2007). In the resolution to the situation, both parties agreed that the study was clinical research because an educational intervention of unknown efficacy was being tested on clinicians (OHRP, 2008). At the same time, the study most likely would have satisfied the regulations for expedited IRB review since it involved no more than minimal risks (Miller & Emanuel, 2008). The IRB review could also have determined that informed consent was not ethically required since the five infection-control guidelines were evidence-based (i.e., their expected outcomes had been demonstrated previously through research) and patients were not being put at additional risks (OHRP). The protocol could have been introduced as part of standard clinical practice and covered by patients' consent to treatment. The OHRP also concluded that since the Michigan ICU study demonstrated the effectiveness of its interventions, future implementation and monitoring of the checklists would not be research but improving clinical care.

The importance of establishing whether a project is research or evidence implementation is revealed by another exemplar, this time in Spain. An educational program on compliance with evidence-based guidelines in patients with severe sepsis was prospectively evaluated for its impact on mortality (Ferrer, Artigas, Levy, et al., 2008). About 20% of Spain's ICUs participated. Based on the results, the authors concluded that if the educational program was implemented in all Spanish hospitals, 490 lives might be saved each year. As with any project or study, there were limitations to this project, and it must be critically appraised, especially as the project design falls at a lower level of evidence in the intervention hierarchy, making it difficult to establish causation (Kahn & Bates, 2008). However, it is a good example of an educational program introduced to promote evidence-based guidelines on a national level, along with an objective evaluation of its impact.

The project was subsequently criticized for ethical reasons based on the belief that it represented clinical research (Lemaire, 2008). The project coordinators did not obtain informed consent from the patients involved, which would have been required if it had been viewed as a research study. The authors defended their decision because they viewed the project as EBQI and part of good clinical care (Ferrer, Artigas, & Levy, 2008). They gave several reasons why they did not view their project as clinical research. Foremost amongst these was that the educational program taught previously established evidence-based guidelines and did not expose patients to test interventions. In particular, they noted that the project was reviewed by the research ethics committee at every participating hospital and in that way ensured that appropriate ethical standards were maintained.

> *If the people who make the decisions are the people who will also bear the consequences of those decisions, perhaps better decisions will result.*
>
> *John Abrams*

Practical Consequences

Much of the controversy has revolved around establishing whether evidence implementation activities fall within the definition of clinical research. The focus of this chapter is on the ethical aspects of this distinction, which have important practical and regulatory implications.

The OHRP can impose severe penalties on organizations found to be violating U.S. regulations. The OHRP has regularly viewed research as very broadly defined and thereby often included QI activities (Lynn et al., 2007). Similar regulatory uncertainty and confusion can exist in the United Kingdom (Hill & Small, 2006) and elsewhere in Europe (Lemaire, Ravoire, & Golinelli, 2008).

Another practical consequence of "getting it wrong" can arise if clinicians decide to pursue publication of their findings. Many journals will not publish articles they deem to be clinical research if they have not already had IRB review (Lynn et al., 2007). Sometimes clinicians conducting evidence implementation activities decide to pursue publication only after the project is completed and the findings are viewed as having broader interest (Hill & Small, 2006). Some journals evaluate the ethics of a study or project themselves regardless of whether or not an ethics committee reviewed the original proposal, but not all take the time and effort this requires (Abbasi & Heath, 2005).

The more significant consequences relate to patients. Since responsibility for classifying a project or study as research currently rests with the investigators, inappropriate classification could avoid ethical review, which could have highlighted ethical problems or concerns if this approach were taken (Abbasi & Heath, 2005). If, however, EBP project coordinators view an ethics application as an onerous, lengthy, and perhaps nonrelevant process, they may decide to forego conducting important practice evaluations. Given that current practice has quality problems, this may leave practitioners unwilling to make evidence-based changes, putting patients at risk for continued lower quality care, or to promote the introduction of practice changes without monitoring their effects (Lynn et al., 2007). It is important that the ethical considerations that apply to EBP initiatives, such as protection of privacy, be addressed by project coordinators; however, other ethical safeguards designed for clinical research, such as informed consent, may not be appropriate for EBP implementation projects.

Distinguishing Research from Quality Improvement

Much has been written on ways to distinguish research from QI; therefore, this section of the chapter discusses the differences. Before reviewing some of the key distinctions, two other terms must be mentioned: ***quality assurance*** and ***audit***. Both terms are designed to assess how well current practice compares with best practice (Casarett, Karlawish, & Sugarman, 2000). Research can be viewed as generating the evidence upon which practice should be based. Quality assurance involves planned, systematic processes, which should be evidence-based, designed to assure patients and providers that quality of care is addressed in a systematic and reliable manner. An audit evaluates whether or not current (or past) practice is based on the best available evidence. Different approaches are also taken within QI projects. Evidence-based quality improvement includes a set of activities designed to change practice so that it is more closely implemented according to the best available evidence. Current practice must be assessed before and after change is introduced within EBQI, and therefore in this chapter, audit and quality assurance will be subsumed under the term EBQI (Casarett et al.).

Evidence-based quality improvement has much in common with clinical research, which is why distinctions are difficult. Rather than making a clear-cut distinction, a spectrum of activities are involved. At one end of the spectrum, randomized controlled trials are clearly clinical research that requires specific protection of study participants from harm due to unknown outcomes. At the other end of the spectrum, individual practitioners may introduce something new to their practice. Let's say they read a well-done systematic review about the benefits of exercise for patients like those for whom they care. Before making the change, they gather data on relevant outcomes to establish what the current outcomes are that may be affected by the exercise intervention. They introduce the evidence-based intervention and collect more data to evaluate whether the intervention achieved the same outcomes in their patients that the evidence indicated. They look back over all the data and notice some important changes. As a result, the practitioners talk about the evidence-based exercise intervention as part of their routine clinical discussions with patients. Through an EBQI activity like this, the quality of care provided to patients would be improved because evidence was implemented in practice.

Along this spectrum of EBQI and research are a range of activities. A practitioner might tell colleagues about an evidence-based change that improved care. They decide to introduce this change across the unit. Others hear about it and decide to evaluate the outcomes from units that applied the evidence and compare them to outcomes from other units without the change. Some suggest the activities should be written up and submitted for publication. When considered from an ethical viewpoint, the question arises if at some point the project has become one that needs to be submitted for ethical approval. This would clearly be the case if the project was deemed clinical research. However, even if it was not a research project, it could benefit from ethical review to ensure, for example, that all appropriate steps were being taken to protect patient privacy. This raises a question about who could provide such ethical review, which is a matter we will consider later in the chapter.

Evidence-based quality improvement overlaps in many ways with the U.S. regulatory definition of research as "a systematic investigation, including research development, testing and evaluation, designed to develop or contribute to generalizable knowledge" (Baily et al., 2006, p. S28). The methods of research and EBQI can be similar, which is why much of the ethical debate has been triggered.

Quality Improvement "uses the kind of reasoning that is inherent in the scientific method, it involves systematic investigations of working hypotheses about how a process might be improved, and it frequently employs qualitative and quantitative methods and analytic tools that are also used in research projects" (Baily et al., 2006, p. S11).

Hence, people can look at the same project and come to different conclusions as to whether or not it should be classified as research and fall under the ethical requirements of research studies. Two articles by research ethicists came to the opposite conclusions regarding whether the Michigan ICU study should have been regulated as clinical research, thus requiring informed consent. Miller and Emanuel (2008) held that the study was research because it prospectively implemented a protocol, tested hypotheses, and had a goal of contributing to generalizable knowledge as inferred from its publication. However, Baily (2008) concluded that it was not clinical research because it was designed to promote clinicians' use of evidence-based procedures and placed patients at no additional risk.

Clear distinctions between research and EBQI are sometimes difficult to determine. However, there are differences and some of them are ethically significant. When examining a study, these factors must be taken into account in determining what ethical issues may arise and how they should be addressed. From an ethical perspective, classifying a project as research or QI is not the most important factor. Such an approach can lead to an overly simplistic approach to ethics. The OHPR criticized Johns Hopkins University for its general conclusion that EBQI studies were not clinical research (OHRP, 2007). Several ethical issues must be addressed, no matter how a study is classified. Overall, protecting and promoting the well-being of everyone involved in a study should be paramount. This suggests that some ethical evaluation of EBQI projects is important. Whether or not an IRB is the best place for that review is a question that we will return to toward the end of the chapter.

Research is focused on questions for which answers are not known. When we don't know whether this intervention is better than that intervention, research in the form of a randomized controlled trial may be conducted. We don't know how diet impacts the risk of cancer, so epidemiological research is conducted. We don't know how patients experience and cope with a disability, so qualitative research is carried out. Research is focused on *generating* evidence *for* practice, whereas EBQI is focused on *implementing* evidence *in* practice. Activities should be regarded as EBQI when they seek to change practice to improve outcomes so that they are more evidence-based. Evidence-based quality improvement starts with answers to what works best, and seeks to promote use of the best available evidence so that practice outcomes are improved.

Research is not an integral part of routine clinical practice. Clinical practice relies on knowledge generated by research, but patients do not need to be involved in research projects in order to receive quality clinical care. Research may occur in clinical settings, but if so, patients should only be enrolled if they volunteer for research. "In contrast, QI is *an integral part of the ongoing management of the system for delivering clinical care*, not an independent, knowledge-seeking enterprise" (Baily et al., 2006, p. S12). This distinction is crucial, and will be discussed in more detail later in the chapter.

Research often carries risks for patients, which is one of the reasons for informed consent. Research on interventions involving risk is justified when researchers do not know which alternative is best. The risks may be side effects, known or unknown. The risks may be that a patient receives an intervention that turns out to be less effective. Because research is pursuing knowledge that is not known, risks are inherent. The risks with EBQI activities are usually very low, such as revealing personal information in questionnaires or interviews. Some activities may carry risk of harm, and must be evaluated when designing the project. However, sometimes the risks may be greater if the EBQI activities are *not* implemented and the old way of doing things remains in place.

Those conducting research studies are often not part of the clinical team caring for patients, whereas EBQI is almost always carried out by those caring for the patients involved. This supports the notion that EBQI is part of routine clinical practice and can foster a culture of continual improvement. Evidence-based quality improvement often uses data that practitioners have regular access to in their clinical roles. Research is usually distinct from clinical care and often generates data that would not otherwise be available.

Funding for research often is generated externally, while EBQI projects are usually conducted using the resources available to the clinical team. External funding can generate conflicts of interest for researchers. The research study itself may put researchers' interests at odds with those of the subjects, which is one reason for IRB review. In contrast, EBQI projects, by their nature, are intended to improve the quality of care patients receive.

Research and EBQI have been distinguished on the basis of generalizability, but this is not clear-cut. Some have taken the goal of publication as an indicator of generalizability, but that also is not necessarily the case. A comparison with case reports may be helpful here. As discussed in Chapter 5, case reports should not be considered generalizable information, but they remain valuable to practitioners. Case reports, and case series, describe clinical practice in a systematic way, yet they are reports of clinical practice, not research. They reflect on what has happened in clinical practice and help others to learn from those experiences.

In the same way, publication of EBQI activities provides opportunities for others to learn from those experiences. A desire to share the findings of EBQI activities should be seen as part of the ethical commitment to help others improve patient outcomes, either by introducing the same evidence-based changes or avoiding them if they turn out to be unhelpful. However, the extent to which the original activities were context dependant must be taken into account if others implement the results elsewhere. Publication of the results should not change the nature of the original activities.

In research, publication is usually envisioned as one of the outcomes expected, if not required, for the project to be successful. In EBQI, this is not always the case, and publication is unlikely to be a strong motivation for the project. However, the final step in the EBP process is the dissemination of results. In some cases publication may be preplanned, but in others, "it is more

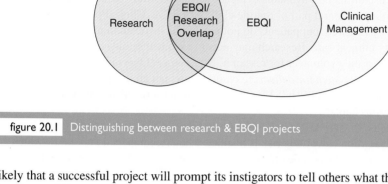

figure 20.1 Distinguishing between research & EBQI projects

likely that a successful project will prompt its instigators to tell others what they have done, [and] that there will be a retrospective decision to seek publication" (Hill & Small, 2006, p. 103).

Overall, discussions will be needed to determine whether a project is better defined as clinical research or EBQI. Figure 20.1 is an adaptation of a diagram used to represent the distinctions (Baily et al., 2006). This also points out that some studies should be classified as overlapping research and EBQI. For example, a systematic investigation might be designed to bring about local clinical improvements but also develop generalizable knowledge at the same time (Baily et al.). The Michigan ICU study and the Spanish sepsis study could both be placed in this overlapping region. This serves to highlight that the important factor is not how a study is classified, but whether the activity is ethically appropriate.

Ethical Principles as Applied to Research and Evidence-Based Quality Improvement

Much has been written on research ethics (Emanuel, Grady, Crouch, et al., 2008). A set of seven ethical requirements have been proposed as the ethical foundations upon which clinical research should be based (Emanuel, Wendler, & Grady, 2000). They are summarized in the following sections as originally proposed for clinical research, and their relevance for EBQI activities is also described, where appropriate (Baily et al., 2006). All seven principles are ethically important and are not listed in any order of priority.

Social or Scientific Value

For research to be ethical, it should be worth doing. Appropriate use of resources is an ethical issue because of the principle of justice. Further research on questions that have been adequately answered by prior studies is ethically questionable. Exposing human subjects to any level of risk is unethical if the research does not have value to society or healthcare. This also places an ethical obligation on researchers to share their results and findings with others so that they can benefit from the new knowledge.

Similarly, EBQI activities are only ethical if they are worth doing. The value of the activity may initially be very local. Practitioners should identify significant clinical outcomes that could benefit from improvements. The value of different proposed activities may need to be compared to determine which have the potential to improve care the most. After conducting a local EBQI activity, its wider value may be noted. For example, the results of the Michigan ICU study were extremely valuable worldwide, and it would have been unethical not to disseminate them broadly.

Scientific Validity

To be ethical, a research project must be methodologically rigorous to ensure a well-done study that can produce generalizable, valid findings. In addition, poorly designed or implemented projects waste the resources and time of those involved. Exposing people to any risk in a flawed project is unethical.

The requirement for rigorous methods also applies to EBQI; however, the focus of the rigor is to carefully evaluate the outcomes and avoid wasting resources and exposing people to unnecessary risk. The goal of EBQI is usually local improvement, not generalizable knowledge, so different methods may be used. Context and local factors are embedded in EBQI, while they are usually minimized in research by the methodological rigor.

Fair Subject Selection

The selection of subjects for research studies should be fair so that risks and benefits are shared equally. Inclusion and exclusion criteria for recruiting study participants should be based on good scientific reasons, not convenience or vulnerability. People should not be selected *because* they are marginalized, powerless, or poor. Such groups may become human subjects, but only if the research is relevant to people in those groups. Those groups that bear the risks and burdens of research should have the potential to benefit from the results.

The same criteria should apply in EBQI activities. Who is involved in an EBQI project may be determined more by where EBQI is carried out within an organization rather than recruiting techniques aimed at representative sampling. If resources prevent improving care in all areas that would be appropriate, decisions should be made fairly, not based on the status of people with various conditions. Clinics or services that serve the underprivileged are as entitled to improvement as any other service. Services for the underprivileged should not be left without EBQI while resources are continually committed to fee-paying or profitable services only.

Favorable Risk–Benefit Ratio

Both research and EBQI should be committed to minimizing the risks and maximizing the gains of all studies and projects. Risks in research can range from very high to none, while risks in EBQI are usually low. Risks may be physical, but can also include risks to privacy and respect. Wherever possible, the risk–benefit ratio should be improved as much as possible.

Independent Review

Independent review of research is ethically required because of the potential conflicts of interest. Research subjects are inherently used as means to a goal of securing new knowledge. They may be placed at risk of harm for the good of others. In clinical contexts, the potential exists to exploit patients as research subjects because what is best for the research project may not be what is best for patients.

Different views exist on the nature of the review that EBQI activities ethically require. The view argued here in more detail below is that this can vary with different types of activities.

Respect for Potential and Enrolled Subjects

Research has scientific goals, but respect for the participants involved in the research must remain paramount. As the Declaration of Helsinki states, "In medical research involving human subjects, the well-being of the individual research subject must take precedence over all other interests" (World Medical Association, 2008). This respect applies to those who are asked to become research subjects and decide not to do so. It includes protecting privacy and confidentiality, maintaining participants' welfare during the project, keeping them informed of significant changes during the research, and allowing them to withdraw from research.

In EBQI activities, respect for patients also must take precedence. Improving their outcomes is the goal of EBQI and inherent to the nature of the activities. As with research, it includes protecting privacy and confidentiality, maintaining welfare, and keeping patients informed. However, the issue of withdrawing from EBQI (i.e., initiatives designed to produce known improvement in outcomes) is tied up with informed consent and its appropriateness to EBQI is discussed later in this chapter.

Informed Consent

Informed consent is one of the bedrocks of research ethics. Participating in research is viewed as voluntary, and this places an ethical obligation on researchers to provide information so that subjects make informed decisions to enroll or not. This requirement is based on the importance of respecting an individual's autonomy over his or her body and health. Researchers must provide information regarding the risks and benefits of participation and help people understand this information. Informed consent is a process that often must be revisited as subjects engage in the research and understand its expectations and implications more fully. The issue of informed consent and EBQI is one of the more widely debated ethical issues and will be examined in depth in the following section.

> *The bravest thing you can do when you are not brave is to profess courage and act accordingly.*
> *Corra Harris*

Informed Consent and Evidence-Based Quality Improvement

One of the important issues debated within implementation of evidence is whether informed consent is necessary. Part of the reason for informed consent is to protect patients, both physically but also in terms of respecting them as people. People who come to health services do not usually expect to become subjects of research. Therefore, to respect them as individuals, they are offered the opportunity to participate. If they agree, a *process* of informed consent will be initiated. From an ethical perspective, this process is not simply one of getting an informed consent form signed, but an ongoing dialogue between researcher and participant about the research study.

Many activities happen when patients are within the health services. These activities are designed to restore or maintain optimal health for those patients. Patients enter the healthcare system trusting that clinicians are there to assist them toward health and minimize their risks while in their care. Therefore, obtaining informed consent for each individual action or intervention would not be practical. Collecting multiple informed consents likely would be unethical if this took away from the care patients received because so much time would be spent garnering informed consents. Consequently, separate informed consent is usually not expected when patients engage in what they might normally anticipate to be part of usual care.

Debate over informed consent can be seen as a question of whether patients should expect EBQI to be seen as part of standard healthcare practice. Some argue that "much of QI is simply good clinical care combined with systematic, experiential learning. Individual practitioners are constantly learning by doing and taking steps to improve their own practice" (Baily et al., 2006, p. S8). The ethical commitment to care for and do good for patients, coupled with an avoidance of harm, implies a commitment to improve clinical practice wherever possible. Taking steps to improve one's own practice includes evaluating whether or not improvement has occurred. This can be done through formal examinations, peer feedback, and other methods. A commitment to improving care more generally should similarly include steps to evaluate the quality of care (i.e., outcomes) in formal and informal ways. Evidence-based quality improvement activities play a role in this, and as such, professionals and organizations have an ethical responsibility to conduct EBQI projects to demonstrate whether or not change improves outcomes.

This understanding of EBQI also places a responsibility on patients to participate in such activities. In that case, informed consent would not be necessary. This can be seen as similar to the responsibilities of teachers and students. If teachers have a responsibility to evaluate and improve their teaching, feedback from students is vital. This could be viewed as a mutual ethical responsibility, so students must provide feedback in response to the teaching. Certainly, protections need to be put in place, such as ensuring that the feedback is anonymous so that students who point out problems will do so without fear of repercussion. Since students benefit from improved teaching, students have a responsibility to provide information that will contribute to improved learning and therefore signed informed consent is not necessary. In fact, it may be counterproductive, as such forms may be the only items that identify which students provided feedback and which did not.

This understanding of healthcare (and education) may not sit well with the current emphasis on autonomy and individualism. Individual rights should be valued in healthcare, but sometimes individual autonomy is prioritized over all other ethical principles. A culture can exist in which patients see themselves primarily as customers, purchasing the services they desire. This can foster an environment in which patients feel little or no obligation to the service or system that provides their care. They may feel they are paying for a service and can go elsewhere if they are not satisfied.

An individualistic paradigm brings a significant loss of the sense of a social commitment to improve the healthcare services that will be available to everyone. Viewing healthcare as primarily a business can have this same effect. Customers rightly feel little sense of responsibility to improve the quality of a local hardware store or the goods they buy from the store. The market is supposed to take care of that. But healthcare is not the same type of commodity as hardware.

In addition, such individualism is not realistic in healthcare and does not produce quality care. Patients are part of a social network and benefit from the experiences of others who have participated in prior clinical research and EBQI. What is needed is an appropriate balance between individual autonomy and group responsibility (Kearns, O'Mathúna, & Scott, 2010). Patients should be able to see with gratitude how others have contributed to the service they receive and be willing to become involved in helping improve healthcare outcomes. We can all do this by accepting responsibility to participate in EBQI activities and managing our own health to maximize limited resources. Such a sense of moral obligation to the quality of our healthcare services is vital if the outcomes are to improve. Paradoxically, a commitment by everyone to improve the healthcare available for everyone should mean that we will each individually receive higher quality healthcare when we need to avail of those services and resources.

Such a view of healthcare places ethical responsibilities on healthcare organizations, professionals, and patients to participate in improving the quality of healthcare processes as well as outcomes. Patients may be unaware of this responsibility. For a long time, patients were afforded little opportunity to give feedback to healthcare professionals. In some cases, such feedback was overlooked, and in some, the feedback was actively rejected. The necessity of improving healthcare means that the voices of patients must be heard. This also places an ethical responsibility on patients to engage with improvement processes. And it will require strategies to inform the general public that healthcare organizations are committed to improving outcomes through implementing evidence, and that their help is needed to do so.

"This means that someone seeking care from a healthcare organization cannot insist on the freedom to opt out completely from efforts to improve the quality of care in that organization without jeopardizing the very benefits he or she seeks. In fact, it is in the best interest of patients to cooperate with QI activities and even to seek out the healthcare organizations that are the most committed to QI. As an ethical matter, the responsibility of patients to cooperate in QI activities is justified by the benefits that each patient receives because of the cooperation of the others in the collective enterprise" (Baily et al., 2006, p. S28).

Conclusion: Reviewing Evidence-Based Quality Improvement Projects

Review of research studies by an IRB is important. This safeguards those people participating in research. Some ethical review activities involve an overlap between research and EBQI. These situations could continue to be sent to IRBs for review, but the IRB has an obligation to examine them with the distinctions between EBQI and research in mind.

The majority of EBQI is low risk and could be reviewed within clinical management and supervision structures. This is based on the view that EBQI is part of normal clinical activities and is thus "a systematic, data-guided form of the clinical and managerial innovation and adaptation that has always been an integral part of clinical and managerial practice. The fact that QI is a normal healthcare operation focused on improving local care has been critical to our argument that ethical review of QI should be incorporated into the system of accountability for clinical care" (Baily et al., 2006, p. S28).

Various practical structures could be put in place to facilitate this type of review. In some cases, external review may be necessary, for example, when projects involve more risk or seem to become more like research. Clinicians and ethical review boards need flexibility and knowledge of the purpose of the project or study. One benefit of keeping the review in the clinical setting would be that it could contribute to fostering a culture of evidence implementation in practice.

"There is a danger that scrutiny is seen as a burden, a problem to be circumvented. It may, rather, help clarify why we are doing what we are proposing; how we came to assume benefits would accrue; and how we justify in terms of the likelihood and extent of these benefits the extra burden and risk patient participants undergo, extra demands on professionals, and extra costs to participating organizations. But we have to have a scrutiny process that can recognize when a light hand is needed. We have to be able to deconstruct projects, be they research audit or QI, such that appropriate scrutiny is imposed—to improve the proposed activities and to defend the interests of those subjected to them" (Hill & Small, 2006, p. 105).

Bringing EBQI review into the normal routine of clinical management offers an opportunity to enhance ethical and EBP. It gives everyone the opportunity to become more familiar with the review of EBQI activities and how their ethical standards can be upheld. It requires adequate knowledge and skills in critical appraisal and ethical reflection. And it is a chance to remind everyone of the importance of continual improvement, monitoring or change, and ethical practice. The idea of a one-size-fits-all ethical review does not apply to the current complex culture that incorporates both EBQI and generation of research.

references

Abbasi, K., & Heath, I. (2005). Ethics review of research and audit. *BMJ, 330*, 431–432.

Baily, M. A. (2008). Harming through protection? *New England Journal of Medicine, 358*(8), 768–769.

Baily, M. A., Bottrell, M., Lynn, J., & Jennings, B. (2006). The ethics of using QI methods to improve health care quality and safety. *Hastings Center Report, 36*(4), S1–S408.

Casarett, D., Karlawish, J. H. T., & Sugarman, J. (2000). Determining when quality improvement initiatives should be considered research: proposed criteria and potential implications. *Journal of the American Medical Association, 283*(17), 2275–2280.

Daley, M. R. (2007). Catheter-related bloodstream infections [letter]. *New England Journal of Medicine, 356*(12), 1267–1268.

Emanuel, E. J., Grady, C., Crouch, R. A., Lie, R., Miller, F., & Wendler, D. (Eds.). (2008). *The Oxford textbook of clinical research ethics*. New York: Oxford University Press.

Emanuel, E. J., Wendler, D., & Grady, C. (2000). What makes clinical research ethical? *Journal of the American Medical Association, 283*(20), 2701–2711.

Ferrer, R., Artigas, A., & Levy, M. (2008). Informed consent and studies of a quality improvement program [letter]. *Journal of the American Medical Association, 300*(15), 1762–1763.

Ferrer, R., Artigas, A., Levy, M. M., Blanco, J., González-Díaz, G., Garnacho-Montero, et al. (2008). Improvement in process of care and outcome after a multicenter severe sepsis educational program in Spain. *Journal of the American Medical Association, 299*(19), 2294–2303.

Gawande, A. (2007). A lifesaving checklist. *The New York Times*. Retrieved March 10, 2009, from http://www.nytimes.com/2007/12/30/opinion/30gawande.html

Hill, S. L., & Small, N. (2006). Differentiating between research, audit and quality improvement: governance implications. *Clinical Governance: An International Journal, 11*(2), 98–107.

Institute of Medicine. (2006). *Preventing medication errors*. Washington, DC: National Academy Press.

Institute of Medicine. (2009). *Crossing the quality chasm: the IOM health care quality initiative*. Retrieved March 10, 2009, from http://www.iom.edu/CMS/8089.aspx

Jenny-Avital, E. R. (2007). Catheter-related bloodstream infections [letter]. *New England Journal of Medicine, 356*(12), 1267.

Kahn, J. M., & Bates, D. W. (2008). Improving sepsis care: the road ahead. *Journal of the American Medical Association, 299*(19), 2322–2323.

Kearns, A. J., O'Mathúna, D. P., & Scott, P. A. (2010). Diagnostic self-testing: Autonomous choices and relational responsibilities. *Bioethics, 24*(4), 199–207.

Lemaire, F. (2008). Informed consent and studies of a quality improvement program [letter]. *Journal of the American Medical Association, 300*(15), 1762.

Lemaire, F., Ravoire, S., & Golinelli, D. (2008). Non-interventional research and usual care: definition, regulatory aspects, difficulties and recommendations. *Thérapie, 63*(2), 103–106.

Lynn, J., Baily, M. A., Bottrell, M., Jennings, B., Levine, R. J., Davidoff, F., et al. (2007). The ethics of using quality improvement methods in health care. *Annals of Internal Medicine, 146*(9), 666–673.

Miller, F. G., & Emanuel, E. J. (2008). Quality-improvement research and informed consent. *New England Journal of Medicine, 358*(8), 765–767.

National Institutes of Health. (2005). *Glossary: clinical research*. Retrieved May 8, 2009, from http://grants.nih.gov/grants/policy/hs/glossary.htm

Office for Human Research Protections. (2007). RE: human subject research protections under federalwide assurances FWA-5752, FWA-287, and FWA-3834. Retrieved March 9, 2009, from http://www.hhs.gov/ohrp/detrm_letrs/YR07/nov07c.pdf

Office for Human Research Protections. (2008). RE: human subject research protections under federalwide assurances FWA-5752, FWA-287, and FWA-3834. Retrieved March 2, 2009, from http://www.hhs.gov/ohrp/detrm_letrs/YR08/feb08b.pdf

O'Mathúna, D. P. (2007). Decision-making and health research: ethics and the 10/90 gap. *Research Practitioner, 8*(5), 164–172.

Pronovost, P., Needham, D., Berenholtz, S., Sinopoli, D., Chu, H., Cosgrove, S., et al. (2006). An intervention to decrease catheter-related bloodstream infections in the ICU. *New England Journal of Medicine, 355*(26), 2725–2732.

Schoen, C., Osborn, R., Doty, M. M., Bishop, M., Peugh, J., & Murukutla, N. (2007). Toward higher-performance health systems: adults' health care experiences in seven countries, 2007. *Health Affairs, 26*(6), w717–w734.

Schoen, C., Osborn, R., How, S. K. H., Doty, M. M., & Peugh, J. (2009). In chronic condition: experiences of patients with complex health care needs, in eight countries, 2008. *Health Affairs, 28*(1), w1–w16.

United Nations Educational, Scientific and Cultural Organization. (2008). *Bioethics core curriculum*. Paris: United Nations Educational, Scientific and Cultural Organization. Retrieved May 8, 2009, from http://unesdoc.unesco.org/images/0016/001636/163613E.pdf

World Medical Association. (2008). *Declaration of Helsinki*. Retrieved March 14, 2009, from http://www.wma.net/e/policy/b3.htm

chapter 20

487

Case Examples: Evidence-Based Care and Outcomes in Depressed Adults and in Critically Ill Children

Case Example A-1: Evidence-Based Care and Outcomes in Adult Depression

An evidence-based approach to changing treatment modality for depressed adults in an in-patient psychiatric unit

As a new psychiatric/mental healthcare provider on an adult in-patient unit, you observe that various therapists are using different treatment modalities (e.g., group cognitive-behavior therapy, individual cognitive-behavior therapy, relaxation therapy, interpersonal therapy) with depressed patients. When asked about the different treatment modalities, the unit director tells you that therapists should employ the treatments they have found to work the best from their own clinical experiences. However, the director is open to further discussion and learning about the empirical effectiveness of different treatment modalities for adults with depressive disorders. Therefore, you volunteer to search the literature to answer the following PICOT clinical questions: (1) In adults hospitalized in psychiatric units, how does group cognitive-behavioral therapy (CBT) versus individual CBT reduce depression? and (2) In adults hospitalized in psychiatric units, how does CBT in comparison to relaxation therapy and interpersonal therapy reduce depression?

A search for systematic reviews of randomized controlled trials, the strongest level of evidence upon which to base practice changes, is first undertaken in the Cochrane Database of Systematic Reviews. The key words searched include adults, psychiatric units, group therapy, depression, and cognitive-behavior therapy. Results of this search reveal that there are no systematic reviews in the Cochrane Library published specifically to answer the clinical questions. A search for evidence-based clinical guidelines is then performed at the National Guidelines Clearinghouse at www.guideline.gov. A total of 42 guidelines are uncovered when "depression in hospitalized adults" is searched; however, there are no guidelines that contain data regarding effectiveness of group versus individual CBT.

The search continues with MEDLINE and CINAHL using the same key words. The results include one meta-analysis of 13 clinical trials comparing CBT, mainly in group form, with other treatment modalities (e.g., relaxation therapy, interpersonal treatment therapy) and indicate an overall positive effect for CBT with 63% of patients showing clinically significant improvement at the end of treatment compared to approximately a 20% lesser improvement in patients receiving other types of treatments. Critical appraisal of this meta-analysis and five randomized controlled trials lead to the conclusion that CBT is the most effective treatment for depression. Not enough evidence is available to support a definitive conclusion that individual CBT is more effective than group CBT.

This evidence is shared with the unit director. As a result, the unit director decides to implement a practice change on the unit. Therapists are now required to conduct group CBT with the depressed patients instead of using other modes of therapy, unless individual or family factors or preferences warrant another type of treatment. As a result of this practice change, positive outcomes measured and achieved include

- A shorter length of stay, resulting in reduced costs
- More positive interactions and communication between the patients and the staff
- Higher job satisfaction among the therapists
- More time available for therapists to spend with the most complicated mental health patients

Case Example A-2: Evidence-Based Care and Outcomes in Critically Ill Children

An evidence-based approach to identifying critically ill children at highest risk for negative mental health outcomes.

As a nurse working in a pediatric intensive care unit (PICU) for the past two decades, you note that the characteristics of pediatric hospitalization have been drastically changing in recent years. For example, the number of general pediatric beds has been decreasing, but the numbers of pediatric intensive care unit beds are increasing. From reviewing the literature, you also note that critical care hospitalization has the potential for long-lasting negative outcomes on children and their parents, such as posttraumatic stress disorder syndrome as well as negative behavioral, emotional, and academic outcomes as many as 10 years after hospitalization.

Because of higher nursing caseloads in the intensive care unit along with short staffing and less time available to deliver intensive psychosocial interventions to patients and their families, you believe it is critical for you to answer the following clinical question, "What demographic variables and factors during a child's critical care hospitalization predict poor outcomes 6 months after the hospital experience?" You believe that the answer to this question is critical in order to assist healthcare professionals in identifying high-risk children before their discharge from the hospital so that targeted interventions to reduce negative outcomes can be implemented.

Your search for evidence begins with the Cochrane database of systematic reviews and National Guidelines Clearinghouse™, which reveals no systematic reviews or EBP guidelines published on predictors of outcomes following childhood critical care hospitalization. As a result, you continue your search for individual studies from the past 20 years using MEDLINE, CINAHL, and PsycINFO databases, which reveal nine predictive studies that can assist you in answering your question (Small, 2002; Small & Melnyk, 2006). Through your critical appraisal of these studies, you conclude that the following factors have accumulated enough evidence to support them as predictors of negative outcomes in critically ill children:

- Increased parental anxiety and depressive symptoms
- A high number of family life stressors

- Marital stress and divorce
- A less cohesive family environment
- Younger age
- Male gender
- First-time hospital admissions

After presenting the results of your search and critical appraisal to your nurse manager and medical director as well as to your colleagues, a working group was formed on your unit to develop a risk scale that could be completed by each child's primary nurse within 24–48 hours of admission to the PICU. With the assistance of clinical researchers from the affiliated schools of nursing and psychology, the scale was then refined and tested on a full-scale level to determine the range of scores that would predict the poorest posthospital discharge outcomes.

As a result of this EBP initiative, each child in the PICU now receives a risk assessment using a valid and reliable tool. All critically ill children who score in the highest risk category and their families are now provided with an evidence-based educational/behavioral intervention program (*COPE* = *C*reating *O*pportunities for *P*arent *E*mpowerment), which has been shown to result in less externalizing behavior problems (e.g., aggression, acting out) and less attention problems for children and less posttraumatic stress symptoms for parents, up to 1 year following discharge from the hospital (Melnyk, Alpert-Gillis, Feinstein et al., 2004). As a result, the number of children and their parents who suffer long-term negative outcomes as a result of critical care hospitalization at your medical center is substantially lower than when there was no risk assessment and intervention program being implemented in your PICU.

appendix A

491

references

Melnyk, B.M., Alpert-Gillis, L., Feinstein, N.F., Crean, H., Johnson, J., Fairbanks, E., Small, L., Rubenstein, J., Slota, M., & Corbo-Richert, B. (2004). Creating opportunities for parent empowerment (COPE): Program effects on the mental health/coping outcomes of critically ill young children and their mothers. *Pediatrics* (Electronic Pages), *113*(6), e597–e607.

Small, L. (2002). Early predictors of poor coping outcomes in children following intensive care hospitalization and stressful medical encounters. *Pediatric Nursing, 28*(4), 393–398, 401.

Small, L., & Melnyk, B.M. (2006). Early predictors of post-hospital adjustment problems in critically ill young children. *Research in Nursing & Health, 29*(6), 622–635.

Template for Asking PICOT Questions

An electronic copy of the question templates appears on the CD-ROM that accompanies the text.

Intervention

In _____ (P), how does _____ (I) compared to _____
(C) affect _____ (O) within _____ (T)?

Etiology

Are _____ (P), who have _____ (I) compared with those without
_____ (C) at _____ risk for/of _____ (O) over
_____ (T)?

Diagnosis or Diagnostic Test

In _____ (P) are/is _____ (I) compared with _____ (C)
more accurate in diagnosing _____ (O)?

Prognosis/Prediction

In _____ (P), how does _____ (I) compared to _____
(C) influence _____ (O) over _____ (T)?

Meaning

How do _____ (P) with _____ (I) perceive _____ (O)
during _____ (T)?

Short Definitions of Different Types of Questions

Intervention: Questions addressing how a clinical issue, illness, or disability is treated.

Etiology: Questions that address the causes or origin of disease, the factors which produce or predispose toward a certain disease or disorder.

Diagnosis: Questions addressing the act or process of identifying or determining the nature and cause of a disease or injury through evaluation.

Prognosis/Prediction: Questions addressing the prediction of the course of a disease.

Meaning: Questions addressing how one experiences a phenomenon—or why we need to approach practice differently.

Sample Questions

Intervention: In African American female adolescents with hepatitis B (P), how does acetaminophen (I) compared to ibuprofen (C) affect liver function (O)?

Etiology: Are 30- to 50-year-old women (P) who have high blood pressure (I) compared with those without high blood pressure (C) at increased risk for an acute myocardial infarction (O) during the first year after hysterectomy (T)?

Diagnosis: In middle-aged males with suspected myocardial infarction (P), are serial 12-lead ECGs (I) compared to one initial 12-lead ECG (C) more accurate in diagnosing an acute myocardial infarction (O)?

Prognosis/Prediction: **(1)** For patients 65 years and older (P), how does the use of an influenza vaccine (I) compared to not receiving the vaccine (C) influence the risk of developing pneumonia (O) during flu season (T)?

(2) In patients who have experienced an acute myocardial infarction (P), how does being a smoker (I) compared to being a nonsmoker (C) influence death and infarction rates (O) during the first 5 years after the myocardial infarction (T)?

Meaning: How do 20-something males (P) with a diagnosis of below the waist paralysis (I) perceive their interactions with their romantic significant others (O) during the first year after their diagnosis (T)?

Walking the Walk and Talking the Talk: An Appraisal Guide for Qualitative Evidence

Qualitative Description

#1 **Sword, W., Busser, D., Ganann, R., McMillan, T., & Swinton, M. (2008). Women's care-seeking experiences after referral for postpartum depression.** *Qualitative Health Research, 18,* **1161–1173.**

Question: What were women's experiences of seeking care after referral from public health nurse for probable postpartum depression, including responses to being referred, specific factors that hindered or facilitated care seeking, experiences seeking care, and responses to interventions offered?

Design: **Qualitative description**…"the method of choice when straight descriptions of phenomena are desired…The description in qualitative descriptive studies entails the presentation of the facts of the case in everyday language…[It] is less interpretive than phenomenological, theoretical, ethnographic, or narrative descriptions…[but] more interpretive than quantitative description, which typically entails surveys or other prestructured means to obtain a common dataset on preselected variables…" (Sandelowski, 2000, pp. 336, 339).

Sample: New mothers ($N = 18$) recruited from an early prevention and intervention initiative (Healthy Babies, Healthy Children) who accepted, as part of the program, the offer of a home visit by a public health nurse

Procedures: In-depth, semistructured telephone interviews conducted approximately 4 weeks after screening for postpartum depression were thought to be less burdensome on new mothers than asking for face-to-face interviews in their homes or another location. Two trained research assistants used an interview guide containing broad, open-ended questions about women's feelings about being referred for probable postpartum depression and their subsequent care-seeking experiences. The conversational interview style included probes and reflective statements to obtain clarification and to encourage more detailed description. The interviews, averaging 40–50 minutes in length, were audiotaped and transcribed verbatim. In addition, participants' demographic data were obtained from the women's completion of a structured questionnaire.

Data entry and management in NVivo qualitative data software supported conventional content analysis as described by Hsieh and Shannon (2005). Preliminary codes were assigned to meaningful units of data (sentences or phrases). Further data reduction occurred over the course of the analysis, as related codes were subsumed under broader emergent categories. Focusing on the research questions led to development of a rich description of women's care seeking after referral for postpartum depression.

Appraisal:

● *Are the results valid/trustworthy and credible?* Yes. **[Sample selection]:** English-speaking women in the public health program, Healthy Babies, Healthy Children, with an Edinburgh Postnatal Depression Scale (EPDS) score of 12 or higher, indicative of probable depression (Cox & Holden, 2003), were eligible to participate in the study. "The EPDS is a well-validated and widely used instrument to assess the presence of depressive symptoms (p.1163)." **[Accuracy and Completeness]:** Accuracy (credibility) was assured through analysis of each interview by multiple independent coders followed by research team review and the arrival at initial and final coding schemes through a process of discussion and consensus. Transcripts were reviewed to ensure that the final coding scheme had been consistently applied to all the data. Completeness of data (credibility) was assured by a search for negative cases (outliers/exceptions to identified informational categories and concepts). Goodness of fit between analysis and data from which it was generated (confirmability) was demonstrated by the use of quotes and examples. Reliability (dependability) was assured by careful documentation of the research process (the audit trail), including a record of evolving and finalized coding decisions and data analysis procedures. **[Plausibility/Believability]:** Quotes that give voice to study participants and illustrate different aspects of the phenomenon are well chosen and appropriately introduced. These representations of the women's thoughts and feelings illuminate and draw the reader into their experience.

● *What were the results of the study?* *[Approach/Purpose/Phenomenon]:* Qualitative description accomplishes the intended purpose to produce a detailed and straightforward report of women's experiences related to seeking care following referral for probable postpartum depression. "A socioecological framework of health services utilization was used as an orienting framework for data collection (p.1163)." *[Reported Results]:* Specific barriers and facilitators of care seeking were identified at individual, social network, and health system levels of influence. At the *individual level*, women's normalizing of symptoms, limited understanding, waiting for symptoms to improve, discomfort discussing mental health concerns, and fears deterred care seeking. Symptom awareness and not feeling like oneself prompted women to seek care. At the *social network level*, normalizing of symptoms and limited understanding of postpartum depression on the part of family and friends posed barriers; while expressions of worry or concern and encouragement to seek care facilitated women's care seeking. *Health system level* barriers included normalizing of symptoms, offering unacceptable interventions, and disconnected care pathways (communication and timing disruptions). Care seeking was facilitated by having established and supportive relationships, legitimization of postpartum depression, outreach and follow-up, and timeliness of care.

● *Will the results help me in caring for my patients?* **[Relevance]:** Promotion of knowledge and awareness of postpartum depression is needed among both the general public and health care professionals, since normalizing symptoms and limited understanding were found to be barriers to care seeking at all three levels of influence. The research reflects patient values (preferences, concerns, and expectations) and circumstances (clinical state). **[Application]:** All care providers coming in contact with new mothers should be alert for symptoms; and consistent use of screening instruments should be considered. Findings also highlight the importance of interpersonal skills in establishing trust and supportive relationships that include acknowledgement of women's fears about discussing mental health concerns, assistance to making informed decisions, and efforts to learn about various treatment modalities that may be used to more effectively match interventions with women's individual needs and preferences. Analysis further suggests that improved coordination of care would broaden opportunities for appropriate assessment and treatment of women with postpartum depression.

Ethnography

#2   Scott, S. D., Estabrooks, C. A., Allen, M., & Pollock, C. (2008). A context of uncertainty: How context shapes nurses' research utilization behaviors. *Qualitative Health Research, 18,* **347–357.**

Question: How do characteristics of the work environment context and culture influence nurses' research utilization behaviors?

Design: **An ethnographic study**...Cultural understanding obtained through ethnographic fieldwork requires researcher presence in study participants' environments. Participant observation is the central fieldwork technique combined with in-depth interviewing and also collection of artifacts as appropriate to the purposes of the research.

Sample: A maximum variation sampling strategy (i.e., selection of persons, events, and/or settings that offer or represent a wide variety of perspectives related to the phenomenon of interest) was used to purposefully sample events where research use occurred (e.g., patient care rounds and reports) and providers ($N = 29$ nurses, nurse leaders, physicians, and allied health care professionals) on a pediatric critical care unit. The majority of patients, aged from 1 month to 16 years, had recently undergone cardiac surgery, were sedated and ventilated, and required one-on-one care.

Procedures: Systematic observations of approximately 2 hours in length were recorded in fieldnotes and completed over a 7-month period. Observation on all nursing shifts and on all days of the week focused on everyday communication patterns associated with unit routines, patient care rounds, nursing report times, and breaks. Interviews of purposefully selected unit members were 1–4 hours in length (average length – 75 minutes). Interviews were tape-recorded and transcribed verbatim. Analysis, guided by Fetterman's (1998) description of ordering (coding and grouping) and interpreting (identifying patterns in) the data, led to identification of uncertainty ("a cognitive state of being unable to anticipate the meaning and/or outcome of an experience" p. 350) as the unit's primary characteristic that shaped nurses' work and the nature of valued knowledge (i.e., a higher value and reliance placed on immediately available knowledge gained through clinical experience and advanced practice than the value placed on research knowledge).

Appraisal:

● *Are the results valid/trustworthy and credible?* Yes. **[Sample Selection]:** Events and ICU personnel were selected purposefully to ensure comprehensive observations of organizational patterns and a broad representation of views, as described above. **[Accuracy and Completeness]:** Credibility was assured by prolonged engagement in the field, documentation of researcher biases and preconceptions, broad sampling for diverse variations and common patterns, and triangulation of data sources. Dependability and confirmability were addressed by documentation of research materials, research process, and decisions (an audit trail). And rich descriptions of the nursing unit were provided in sufficient detail to allow readers to make judgments about transferability. **[Plausibility/Believability]:** A table of data excerpts supporting each source of uncertainty and well-staged examples provide a realistic/authentic cultural portrait of study participants' work world (see authenticity criteria—Guba & Lincoln, 1989).

● *What were the results of the study?* [**Approach/Purpose/Phenomenon**]: An ethnographic research design is well suited to research purposes such as this one that sought to understand how context and organizational culture shape the phenomenon of interest—nurses' research utilization behaviors. [**Reported Results**]: In this high intensity technology-driven work environment, uncertainty was reported to shape nurse study participants' behaviors to an extent that research use was seen as irrelevant. Four major sources of uncertainty were described and illustrated by excerpts from the data. Sources of uncertainty included (a) the precarious status of seriously ill patients, (b) the inherent unpredictability of nurses' work, (c) the complexity of teamwork in a highly sophisticated environment, and (d) a changing management. "In response to the context of uncertainty on this unit, these nurses chose to retreat to a zone of safety, doing what they were told, focusing on routine, and deferring to the authority of others... [They] did not perceive that managers expected them to use research... [and although] they believed research was important... they did not believe that accessing and assessing research was part of their role (p.355)."

● *Will the results help me in caring for my patients?* [**Relevance**]: The influence of context and organizational culture on research utilization in complex organizational structures is an important and understudied phenomenon. "Clearly, the concepts of culture and context overlap. In this article [the authors] use the term context to signify those aspects of the work setting that extend beyond the unit examined. [They] use the term culture to refer to aspects that are particular, but not unique, to the unit examined (p. 348)." [**Application**]: In this research, the perceived arbitrariness and unpredictability of physicians' and/or administrators' responses to nurses' actions produced a lack of confidence in their own decision making, thus affecting their willingness to use research in their practice. The authors suggest that "particular organizational qualities or features (i.e., certainty) must be present to create and sustain clinical environments that are ideal for research utilization. [Consequently,] uncertainty must be controlled or reduced [before attempting to introduce] research utilization interventions..." Efforts to do so may be facilitated by an appreciation for how organizational context influences research utilization behaviors and an understanding of possible sources of uncertainty that could be]..."prevent[ing] nurses from going outside of the 'safe zone' (p. 356)."

appendix C

497

Video-Assisted Ethnography

#3 **Carroll, K., Iedema, R., & Kerridge, R. (2008). Reshaping ICU ward round practices using video-reflexive ethnography.** *Qualitative Health Research, 18,* **380–390.**

Question: What are the ways in which clinicians can enhance their communication processes through the use of video-ethnographic and reflexive research methodology?

Design: **Video-reflexive ethnography**…a combination of an ethnographic focus on observation and interviewing with video filming and analysis of video-reflexive sessions (involving study participants' responses to viewings of the video recordings).

Sample: Medical ICU ward rounds and planning meetings in a metropolitan 800-bed tertiary referral and teaching hospital ($N = 1$) was the field site for this study.

Procedures: The medical communication reflexive session held with staff was preceded by 12 days (approximately 193 hours) of participant observation and interviewing to establish trust relationships and orient to the culture of the unit. Observations captured medical ward rounds, planning meetings, nursing handovers, and organizational aspects such as staffing allocation and assignments, allied health practice, and work-related informal hallway conversations. Observations and opportunistic interviews with medical, nursing, allied health, and clerical staff were recorded in handwritten fieldnotes and stored in computerized files. Eight hours of video data capturing formal medical communication were coded by the primary researcher, and analysis was guided by two key questions: Who is or is not speaking? What information is being communicated? Selected footage, representative of three themes emerging from the analysis, was used to produce a 10-minute DVD for the feedback component of the study. In the video reflective session, which lasted 90 minutes and was attended by 10 intensivists, clinicians engaged in problem-solving their own communication difficulties.

Appraisal:

● *Are the results valid/trustworthy and credible?* Yes. **[Sample Selection]:** The selection of ICU ward rounds and daily planning meetings was based on the agreed upon importance of these communication mechanisms to patient care and clinician-identified tensions surrounding their purposes, length, and complexities. **[Accuracy and Completeness]:** Credibility was assured by prolonged engagement and persistent observation in the field, triangulation of data sources and methods, and validation of study outcomes in partnership with study participants. **[Plausibility/Believability]:** Detailing of significant participant responses before and after the video-reflexive session demonstrates how the method may both empower individuals to act (tactical authenticity) and stimulate action (catalytic authenticity) (Guba & Lincoln, 1989).

● *What were the results of the study?* **[Approach/Purpose/Phenomenon]:** Use of video data for reflexive feedback narrows and strengthens the ethnographic focus on details of the research phenomenon (communication processes in cultural context) while offering "interventionist possibilities…[b]y creating a space for inquiry that goes beyond epidemiological and descriptive approaches to health service provision…(Shojania & Grimshaw, 2006) (p. 381)." **[Reported Results]:** The first theme ("the big picture"), including talk of patient trajectory and medical diagnosis, was generally communicated by senior intensivists with little input from junior and other staff. The second theme ("small detail"), involving current physiological knowledge of each patient, was communicated by junior doctors. The third theme was the lack of multidisciplinary voice, evidenced by the absence of talk time for other health professionals in the recorded video data. The article focuses on one feedback meeting that catalyzed changes in morning rounds and planning meetings. Changes included greater time efficiency, a greater presence of intensivists in the ICU, increased nursing staff satisfaction, and a handover sheet to improve the structure of clinical information exchanges.

● *Will the results help me in caring for my patients?* **[Relevance]:** This type of video-assisted research, by emphasizing the role of participants as partners, is directly responsive to their immediate interests and concerns. **[Application]:** The authors suggest that taking an interventionist rather than a descriptive approach, by using video-ethnographic and reflexive research methodology, enhances clinicians' and researchers' understanding of the complexity of contemporary hospital-based work, thus enabling clinicians to appraise and reshape existing practices as in this example of enhancing communication processes.

Grounded Theory

#4   Marcellus, L. (2008). (Ad)ministering love: Providing family foster care to infants with prenatal substance exposure. *Qualitative Health Research, 18,* 1220–1230.

Question: What is the process of becoming and providing family foster care giving in the context of caring for infants with prenatal drug and alcohol exposure?

Design: **A constructivist approach to grounded theory (Charmaz, 2006)**. "A number of the disputes among grounded theorists and critiques by other colleagues result from where various authors stand between interpretive and positivist traditions…Constructivist grounded theory is part of the interpretive tradition…Constructivists study *how*—and sometimes *why*—participants construct meanings and actions in specific situations…to show the complexities of particular worlds, views, and actions (pp. 129, 130, 132)."

Sample: Foster families ($N = 11$) in five different communities; all but one with at least one foster child in the home; and 10 of whom had their own children participating in the study, with ages ranging from 5 to 31.

Procedures: The primary data collection strategy was open-ended, semistructured family interviews lasting between 1 and 2 hours. Interviews were recorded, transcribed, and mailed back to family participants for editing and elaboration on further thoughts they may have had while reading the transcript. Researcher observations and reactions were recorded after each interview. Additional data collection strategies included follow-up telephone calls and e-mails, attendance at foster parent events and child welfare conferences, examination of relevant government documents related to child-in-care policies and guidelines, and review of professional and lay literature and media. Three social workers, all with at least 10 years of experience supporting foster families, also were interviewed. Data analysis involved grounded theory techniques of constant comparison, increasingly abstract consideration of the data, and identification of a basic social process.

Appraisal:

- *Are the results valid/trustworthy and credible?* Yes. **[Sample Selection]:** Families were recruited through the Guardianship Branch of the British Columbia Ministry for Child and Family Development, a Canadian government agency responsible for administering foster care services. The initial goal of locating families at different time points (to represent families waiting their first placement, novice and experienced families) was limited by the gatekeeper role of resource workers, reluctance of all family members to participate, and the effect of overall low morale of families in the child welfare system. Within these constraints, "following identification of the initial group of participants, recruitment decisions were then based on the emerging theory and the principles of theoretical sampling (p. 1221)." **[Accuracy and Completeness]:** Validation strategies included periodic review of and discussion about the emerging analysis with an interdisciplinary grounded theory seminar group (peer debriefing), study participants (member checking), and other foster parents and social workers (triangulation of sources of information). **[Plausibility/Believability]:** Depiction of a model/diagram of the theory and selective use of quotes enhance plausibility and direct reader attention to the phases of this experiential process (starting out, living as a foster family, and moving on).

- *What were the results of the study?* **[Approach/Purpose/Phenomenon]:** Use of a grounded theory approach suits the theory generating purpose of this research on the phenomenon of family foster care of infants with prenatal substance exposure. **[Reported Results]:** The basic social process—*(Ad)ministering Love*—is described as having several phases that represent the tension families experience between providing love and guidance for a special needs infant within the restrictions and scrutiny of a child protective system. *Phase 1* (starting out) involves determining family readiness to foster, meeting the requirements of the system, immersing (plunging into the experience) for the first time, and finding their niche (discovering age and gender preferences for foster children that were good fits with the strengths and demands of the family). *Phase 2* (living as a foster family), the middle phase of this process, is depicted as circular and ongoing. Key elements of this phase include rebalancing family life with each placement (being expected to suddenly care for and integrate the infant into family life in addition to being ready to let go with little notice), honoring limits (such as family need for respite), experiencing an emotional double bind (developing attachments and experiencing grief and loss when having to let go), working (i.e., navigating rules of) the child welfare system, feeling a powerless responsibility (responsibility over day-to-day decisions with no control over the long-term decisions affecting the child's future), and public parenting (living with pressure to meet a high level of parenting expertise and effectiveness under supervision by the state). *Phase 3* (moving on) involves relinquishing the role of foster family (no longer actively accepting new placements for various reasons, e.g., to commit to long-term foster placements or adoption of the foster children), losing fit (because of changes in family focus, needs or composition), and transferring child focus (moving away from full-time active fostering while continuing to be connected to caring for children in some way, e.g., volunteering with child-related activities).

● *Will the results help me in caring for my patients?* [**Relevance**]: The varied aspects of the described process of fostering an infant with special needs bring families into contact with many persons, including, nurses, physicians, and infant development specialists. However, in spite of ongoing oversight by the system, families' work within their homes along with its demands and rewards "remain generally unseen, unknown, and unacknowledged by others (p. 1230)." [**Application**]: Understanding the nature and consequences of this type of care giving is an important factor in being able to effectively support foster families and the infants and children in their care.

Grounded Theory

#5   Denz-Penhey, H., & Murdoch, J. C. (2008). Personal resiliency: Serious diagnosis and prognosis with unexpected quality outcomes. *Qualitative Health Research, 18,* **391–404.**

Question: What is common in stories of persons with serious disease who have less than a 10% chance of survival and have a good quality of life at the time of first interview?

Design: **A Glaserian grounded theory approach (Glaser 1978, 1992)** in which attention is focused on emergence of theory from data without the use of a preestablished formula. Theoretical sensitivity (Glaser, 1978) is emphasized in Glaserian grounded theory. This acquired or enhanced natural personal quality of the researcher is exemplified by the ability to grasp subtleties of meaning in empirical data, to interact or dialog with the data, to reflect on interactions between data with the help of theoretical terms and concepts, and to consider boundaries of emerging interpretations (i.e., the possibilities for alternative interpretations) in developing theoretical understanding of a phenomenon. Glaser argues that the acquisition and use of theoretical sensitivity is what makes the development of a grounded, well-integrated and conceptually dense theory possible. The authors of this article comment on an initial attempt to use Strauss and Corbin's (1990) paradigm model approach to grounded theory without success before deciding on a Glaserian approach.

Sample: Participants ($N = 11$) varied in age from 20 to 77 at first diagnosis and from 23 to 89 at first interview, which was conducted between 2 and 40 years after the first illness. Each had a life-threatening disease: seven had metastatic cancer, one had acute myeloid leukemia, one had Eisenmenger's syndrome (congenital heart disease), one had multiorgan failure, and one had congestive heart failure with multiple chronic conditions.

Procedures: A total of 26 open-ended semistructured interviews were conducted, with each participant interviewed between two and four times. First interviews averaged 2.5 hours in length and 1 hour for follow-up interviews (with one lasting 5 hours at the first interview and 3.5 hours at the second). Participants determined the length of time they wished to speak. A constant comparative method of data analysis was used, with participants' reported information compared for similarities, variations, and differences; creation of categories; and reflection on the bigger picture and the core category that links categories together.

Appraisal:

- *Are the results valid/trustworthy and credible?* Yes. **[Sample Selection]:** Selection criteria included (a) participants who, in their own and their doctors' opinions, were exhibiting a good quality of life at first contact with the interviewer; (b) participants who had recovered, were in remission, or whose medical condition had stabilized when this was not expected given the diagnosis, prognosis, and treatment; (c) participants with less than 10% chance of survival with their conditions, according to their attending physicians, at the time of the first interview; and (d) participants whose less than 10% chance of survival, in each case, was confirmed, on the basis of documented evidence, by a medical practitioner with specialty expertise in their condition but no prior knowledge of them. "The first six participants accepted were the first to be referred to the study by their doctors. The final five participants were [purposefully] chosen in an attempt to find disconfirming data [negative case analysis] to modify the developing theory (p. 392)." **[Accuracy and Completeness]:** Sampling was purposeful with theoretical sampling proceeding after analysis of data from the first six participants to seek excellent examples for the evolving theory and to check for disconfirming data. Member checks were performed to assure accuracy of information and plausibility of information categories and interpretations. Participants were provided with verbatim transcripts for confirmation and correction. Confirmation of fit among data, categories, and conceptual development of the theoretical framework was achieved by the primary analyst working with a second analyst, frequent and extensive memoing, creation of an audit trail, and peer debriefing (consensus building with two project supervisors). **[Plausibility/Believability]:** A table illustrating the various dimensions and dimensional aspects of the theory draws together the variables of interest whose relationships are logically laid down in the reporting and discussion of study results. There are some well-selected quotes that illustrate points that the authors wish to make. But these are limited because "there is no mandate in grounded theory write-ups [as in some other studies] to foreground the perspectives and voices of individual participants… Data are used only to show how a theory was constructed, and that it was indeed constructed from these data (Sandelowski, 1998, p. 377).

- *What were the results of the study?* **[Approach/Purpose/Phenomenon]:** The selection of a grounded theory approach was used to sort out the variables, relationships, and content relevant to the phenomenon of personal resiliency. The authors explain that "…in the field of patient care in serious illness we do not yet know the full range of variables that need to be explored…the basic exploratory study of allowing the data to define the variables common to the stories of people who have had unexpectedly good outcomes in terminal disease has not yet been done, and this study attempts to do so (p. 392)." **[Reported Results]:** The core category in stories of persons who had survived unexpectedly was *Personal resiliency: The illness as secondary to a quality-connected life.* The five dimensions of this "way of being and acting in the world" (p. 394) were *social connectedness* (friendships; community and group participation), *connectedness to family* (giving, receiving, participating, belonging), *connectedness to the physical environment* (enjoying/appreciating multiple aspects of place, i.e., home, landscape, nature, animals, and/or plants), *connectedness to experiential inner wisdom* (wisdom of bodily needs and tolerances, life-changing insights, intuitive inner wisdom), and *connectedness to a strong psychological self—"This is Me"* (values providing a sense of meaning and purpose in their lives and positive mindsets that supported a way of being that included a strong sense of acceptance, mental flexibility, ability to change activities and lifestyles in response to new information, mental stamina, and active participation in decisions related to their disease treatment and management).

● *Will the results help me in caring for my patients?* [**Relevance**]: Healthcare professionals need to be as attentive to advising patients on life activities and relationships as they are to prescribing biomedical interventions. Knowledge of how resiliency has helped other persons faced with similar circumstances may be useful to patients and their families. [**Application**]: The authors say: "Patient-directed quality of life is an ethical way to practice and medical carers can use this information to support patient autonomy. Improved quality of life is a beneficial outcome in itself, and if increased longevity should occur as well, that can be regarded as an additional bonus (pp. 402–203)."

Descriptive Phenomenology

#6   Wongvatunyu, S., & Porter, E. (2008). Helping young adult children with traumatic brain injury: The life-world of mothers. *Qualitative Health Research, 18,* **1062–1074.**

Question: What is the personal–social context of the experience of mothers who are helping young adult survivors of moderate or severe traumatic brain injury (TBI)?

Design: **Porter's (1995) descriptive phenomenological method based on Husserlian phenomenology and the phenomenological sociology of Schutz and Luckman (1973).** This involved bracketing (avoiding ideas and use of language that suggest preconceptions of the experience) and asking mothers, in an open neutrally worded way, simply to talk about their experiences as caregivers and to describe what their lives were like before and after the TBI. Probes were employed to encourage clarification and elaboration. Example: "When the mothers related an intention basic to the helping experience, the first author asked them to explain their reason(s) for having that intention (p. 1064)." Thus, the authors explain (p. 1064), in differentiating data pertaining to lifeworld from data pertaining to intentions (Porter, 1995), reasons (rationales) for intentions (particular things mothers did to help their children) were identified as reflections of the mothers' lifeworld to be described in "objectivated categories" (Schutz & Luckman, 1973, p. 180).

Sample: Participants ($N = 7$) were recruited by posting notices in local clinics for TBI survivors and in meeting rooms of family support groups at the local rehabilitation center. Mothers' ages ranged from 46 to 64 years ($M = 53$) and their young adult TBI survivors (five males and two females) ranged in age from 20 to 36 years. The young adults had been injured at least 6 months earlier and lived with their mothers, with the exception of one man who recently had left his mother's home to live with his wife and children.

Procedures: Three in-depth, tape-recorded interviews were conducted with each mother over a 2-month period. Most of the 1-hour interviews took place at the mothers' homes, with some done in private meeting rooms at the university for the mothers' convenience. Each interview was transcribed immediately so that discussion of ideas generated by them could be used to guide exploratory questions in subsequent interviews. In the analysis, a 3-level classification scheme was used to document consistencies among the mothers' lifeworlds. "From specific to general, the levels of the lifeworld were (a) "element" (Porter, 1995, p. 35), (b) "descriptor" (Porter, 1995, p. 35), and (c) feature (Spiegelberg, 1994) (Wongvatunyu & Porter, 2008, p. 1064)." An element was common to some or all the women. Descriptors were coined to capture the similarities that pertained to particular lifeworld features. Feedback from each mother was obtained in the third interview to determine if labels for phenomena and lifeworld features were descriptive of her experience.

Appraisal:

● *Are the results valid/trustworthy and credible?* Yes. [**Sample Selection**]: The focus on mothers of young adults allows for examination of what happens when young adults return to the parental home as TBI survivors. "Mothers…engage in supportive and emotional activities

(Francis-Connolly, 2000) rather than basic caregiving such as youngsters need…[but] factors relevant to developmental tasks can resurface, such as functional status, history of the mother–child relationship (Verhaeghe, Defloor, & Grypdonck, 2005), and reintegration into the community (Winstanley, Simpson, Tate, et al., 2006) (p. 1063). **[Accuracy and Completeness]:** Accuracy of data and plausibility of interpretations were assured by member checking (repeating several key questions at second and third interviews to check reliability and soliciting feedback on labels and features used in the interpretation of findings) and prompt discussion of each interview. **[Plausibility/Believability]:** A table of lifeworld features and their component descriptors is accompanied by quotes that faithfully capture study participants' values (preferences, concerns, and expectations) and unique circumstances. These lend authenticity (Guba & Lincoln, 1989) to and provide validation of the reported research findings

- *What were the results of the study?* **[Approach/Purpose/Phenomenon]:** A descriptive (Husserlian) phenomenological study is the method of choice when exploration is directed toward uncovering and illuminating the empirical essence of the lifeworld…in this case, the lifeworld of mothers helping young adult children with TBI. **[Reported Results]:** Five lifeworld features basic to the maternal experience of helping young adult TBI survivors and their accompanying descriptors were identified. *Having a child who survived a TBI as a young adult* was characterized as "particularly complex" (p. 1065), involving nine descriptors of mothers' common experience which included *feeling unprepared to take it all in, looking for answers that no one has, thinking positively about my child's situation, holding on to the child who has been mine all this time, getting to know my child now, knowing all about my child, starting over with my baby, continuing to mother my child,* and *hoping for the best for my child.* Six months or more after the injury, mothers were aware of *perceiving that life has really changed,* involving *living with changes in my relationship with my child, living with changes in my own life, putting my life on hold,* and *perceiving the changes as part of my life and as life-long. Having sufficient support/feeling bereft of any help* pertained to situations of either *receiving that kind of support/lacking that kind of support from health professionals* where the support was that which was consistent with what was needed at various times during the postinjury period. Descriptors of the lifeworld feature—*believing that my child is still able*—reflected mothers' common experience of *perceiving that my child can work on that issue, perceiving that my child is trying hard to progress,* and *perceiving that my child is able to do more in life.* Mothers' faith in their own helping abilities—*believing that I can help my child*—were "basic facets of the lifeworld" (p. 1070). Mothers mentioned *having personality traits* and *having previous experience that are relevant to helping my child now.* Most mothers talked about the importance of having patience or trying to become more patient.

- *Will the results help me in caring for my patients?* **[Relevance]:** TBI is noted to be a leading cause of death and disability among young persons in the United States. Thus, caregivers need to understand the personal–social factors affecting involved family members. The authors claim to report what they believe is "the first study to illuminate the lifeworld of …mothers" of young adult TBI survivors (p. 1063), the rationale for which is described above under "sample selection." **[Application]:** The authors suggest that during conversations with mothers of TBI survivors, healthcare professionals could adopt some of the phrases used to characterize these findings to offer support (e.g., "mothers of TBI survivors can feel as though they are looking for nonexistent answers") and recognize mothers' unique expertise (e.g., "What are special things about your child that you feel I should know?"… "To broach discussion of changed relationships, practitioners can ask mothers about ways in which their children seem like different people (p. 1071)." Sensitivity to the different types of support needed at different times postinjury should involve making sure that mothers are aware of opportunities for help that they might not be aware of needing in the aftermath of the injury as they focus their concentration on the injured child. Finally, findings about the importance of patience and the never-ending nature of the experience should encourage healthcare professionals to provide opportunities at each encounter for mothers to talk about the impact of the injury on their lives rather than asking only about the progress of the young adult.

Hermeneutic Phenomenology

#7   Woodgate, R. L., Ateah, C., & Secco, L. (2008). Living in a world of our own: The experience of parents who have a child with autism. *Qualitative Health Research, 18,* 1075–1083.

Question: What is the lived experience of parents who have a child with autism?

Design: **Hermeneutic phenomenology as described by van Manen.** According to van Manen (1990): "Hermeneutic phenomenology tries to be attentive to both terms of its methodology: it is a *descriptive* (phenomenological) methodology because it wants to be attentive to how things appear, it wants to let things speak for themselves; it is an *interpretive* (hermeneutic) methodology because it claims that there are no such things as uninterpreted phenomena (p. 180)." Phenomenologists using this approach are especially interested in how the phenomenon of interest is related to the everyday world of human experience. That is, they adhere to a theory of interpretation that assumes the need to explain meaning in relation to context. An understanding of the meaning of the phenomenon is revealed though analysis and interpretation of the texts created from conversations with persons who know what it is like to be living the experience as well as other informational sources that support reflection on essential themes that characterize it.

Sample: Participants ($N = 21$) were parents from 16 families of children with autism (16 mothers and 5 fathers) all but 2 of whom had at least one other child. The children with autism (all boys except for 2 girls) ranged in age from 3 to 9 years, with age at initial diagnosis ranging from 2.5 to 3.5 years.

Procedures: Data collection involved tape-recorded open-ended interviews during which participants were asked to tell what life was like for them before, during, and after their child was diagnosed with autism. Probes were used as needed to facilitate the telling of stories in a conversational manner. Interviews were between 1.5 to 3 hours in length. Observations of the contexts of interviews were recorded in fieldnotes. Tapes were transcribed and the interview and fieldnote texts were analyzed, using van Manen's selective highlighting approach. This involved selecting and highlighting sentences or sentence clusters suggestive of thematic content, writing notes (analytic memos) about themes related to the experience, and reducing all textual data (through processes of writing and rewriting) until "essential themes" emerged which were defined as "unique to the phenomenon of parents who have a child with autism and…fundamental to the overall shared description of living the experience (pp. 1077–1078)."

Appraisal:

● *Are the results valid/trustworthy and credible?* Yes. **[Sample Selection]:** "The only legitimate informants in phenomenological research are those who have lived the reality… (p. 1077)." Participants were recruited through a support group. Children's conditions, as described by their parents, varied in terms of difficulties with communication, social relations, and repetitive, stereotypical behavior. "The extent of treatment the children received was dependent both on what services were available to them and what parents could afford (p. 1077)." **[Accuracy and Completeness]:** Accuracy was addressed by rigorous writing and rewriting to include all meaningful themes and ensure that they were presented as disclosed. In van Manen's (1990) approach to phenomenology, writing and rewriting are a vital part of the analytic process that helps produce a heightened awareness of the phenomenon and deepen the interpretation. "Writing is a reflexive activity that involves the totality of our physical and mental being…To be able to do justice to the fullness and ambiguity of the experience of the lifeworld, writing may turn into a complex process of rewriting (rethinking, reflecting, recognizing) …Writing and rewriting are the thing. (van Manen, 1990, p. 131, 132)." Other measures to ensure rigor were prolonged engagement with participants and the data, careful line-by-line analysis of transcripts, and detailed memo writing. Accuracy and credibility also were enhanced by discussion of preliminary interpretations with participants during and following each interview. **[Plausibility/Believability]:** Themes were fully explained and supported by examples and well-selected quotes. Quotes were used strategically to validate findings and establish a mood (Sandelowski, 1994) reflective of parents' values/concerns and actions/reactions.

- *What were the results of the study?* **[Approach/Purpose/Phenomenon]:** The human science approach of this phenomenological method is a good fit with the study interest in stimulating reflection on lived experiences in the everyday lives of parents of children with autism, with the intent to increase thoughtfulness (pedagogic understanding) about how best to respond and offer support to such families. **[Reported Results]:** *The essence (essential nature) of the parents' experiences (i.e. what the experiences were like) was "living in a world of our own"* that left them feeling isolated. Their sense of isolation was attributed to four main sources: society's lack of understanding, missing a "normal" way of life, being disconnected from their families, and dealing with an unsupportive "system" (bureaucracies of child-related agencies, healthcare facilities, and educational settings). "Parents expressed feeling completely defeated and on their own when they felt that family members, friends, professionals within the system, and others in their lives were not there to support their sense of hope that things would get better for their child (p. 1079)." *Three themes support the essence* in terms of demonstrating how parents struggled to remove the isolation that they felt enveloped themselves and their children. *Theme 1: vigilant parenting,* incorporated strategies of (a) *acting sooner rather than later*/keeping abreast of care needs, (b) *doing all you can,* and (c) *staying close to your gut feelings. Theme 2: sustaining the self and family,* involved sustaining family integrity while enhancing protective measures for the child with autism through (a) *working toward a healthy balance* of self-needs and the child's needs, (b) *cherishing different milestones* in the child's development, and (c) *learning to let go*/accepting and allowing situations that cannot be changed play out. *Theme 3: fighting all the way,* referred to making "the system" work for parents and their children by (a) *learning all you can,* and (b) *educating others.*

- *Will the results help me in caring for my patients?* **[Relevance]:** What was found to be unique about these research findings was that, from parents' perspectives, their sense of isolation mainly resulted from lack of understanding and support from external sources (society, family, and the conglomerate structure of child health/assistance systems). **[Application]:** Thus, the study reinforces the need to educate persons who lack understanding of the impact of autism on children and parents and to address gaps in helping services in order to create "a seamless system that will help foster more enduring relationships between parents and all professionals involved in the care of children with autism (p. 1082)." Additionally, "given [their] expertise, …parents [themselves] could become invaluable assets in helping professionals understand human relationships and responses (p. 1083)."

Narrative/Life Story Methods

#8   Thomas, S. P., & Hall, J. M. (2008) Life trajectories of female child abuse survivors thriving in adulthood. *Qualitative Health Research, 18,* 149–166.

Question: How have thriving female adult survivors of child abuse been able to achieve success in their lives?

Design: **Narrative/life story methods.** Life story/life history approaches represent a form of biographical research that involves the recording of a person's life story as told to the researcher by the person him/herself. The researcher then may use different investigative strategies to explore this recorded record of the individual's life. Narrative methods (the study of stories or narratives of human experiences) involve "an analysis of meaning in context through interpretation of persons' life experiences…for the purpose of evoking a response from readers and promoting dialog (Powers & Knapp, 2006, p. 110)."

Sample: Participants were women ($N = 27$) ranging in age from 29 to 79 who had experienced childhood abuse, beginning as early as infancy and continuing, in most cases, until they left home. A majority (74%) experienced sexual abuse, combined with other forms (physical/emotional abuse and neglect), with adult males commonly the sexual/physical aggressors and mothers tending to be nonprotective and/or verbally abusive. Nearly all had experienced depression, anxiety-related symptoms, and other signs of posttraumatic stress disorder. However, the study's exclusion criteria prohibited women who were currently in crisis—those experiencing severe depression, psychotic symptoms, suicidality, interpersonal violence, drug or alcohol abuse, or acute physical illness—from participation in the study. "Provision for psychiatric care was made and a referral list was given to each participant, in the event that an interview caused distress (p. 151)."

Procedures: Three open-ended interviews were conducted by the same interviewer (a graduate-level psychiatric nurse) across a time span of 6–12 months in settings of the women's choice (home, workplace, university office). Free flowing storytelling was encouraged, with little use of interviewer probes, in order to allow women to share details of their lives in their own words and in their own ways. Analysis of interview transcripts occurred in three phases. *Phase I* involved content mapping, through development and use of a concept list, to reduce and summarize the texts in accordance with the aims of the study. Summary Narrative Assessment (SNA) forms also were developed to enable the research team to shift analytic focus between the SNAs and the original transcripts in a dialectical (conversational style of reasoning) process. "Women were classified into four groups: "thrivers" who made upward progress since their 20s ($n = 8$), 30s ($n = 8$), or 40s ($n = 6$) and "strugglers" ($n = 5$) who had made some progress but were hindered by frequent thinking about abusive dynamics and were less successful in work and relationships (p. 152)." Graphs of healing trajectories showed no predominant pattern. Identified turning points also were diverse with aftermaths that were often negative (brought about by crises such as divorce, death in the family, and others related to women's personal thoughts or epiphanies). *Phase II* involved a systematic examination of the direction and nature of the aftermath of turning points, using a coding scheme to identify the redemption (a painful event made better) and contamination (a good experience ruined/undermined) sequences that followed. The full transcripts (rather than the SNAs) were read and analyzed line-by-line to enhance understanding. *Phase III* involved creation of "detailed trajectories of exemplar cases, to highlight turning points and the most significant redemptive sequences in [the women's] lives; they often explicitly identified those as lifesaving. A new concept, *setbacks*, was incorporated in Phase III, to differentiate adverse events that had lesser impact and duration than turning points, not necessarily changing the direction of a life trajectory (p. 152)."

Appraisal:

● *Are the results valid/trustworthy and credible?* Yes. **[Sample Selection]:** The majority of participants responded to a feature article in a local newspaper about the study and its focus on success stories rather than problems associated with the abuse. Flyers and network sampling were other means of recruitment. Telephone screening was used to determine that potential participants were not currently in crisis. **[Accuracy and Completeness]:** "Throughout the analysis, the larger multidisciplinary team was used as a sounding board for…emergent discoveries. In addition to weekly or biweekly evening meetings over a 4-year period, the team held half-day retreats; notes taken at these meetings constitute an audit trail for the project. Critique and consensual validation by team members from varied disciplines (psychology, psychiatry, nursing) and by several experiential consultants (CM survivor not in the study) enhanced the rigor and credibility of the analysis (p. 153)." **[Plausibility/Believability]:** Verisimilitude (a criterion of good literary style—evocative, creative writing) was established through multiple figures illustrating the report's storied turning points, redemption and contamination sequences, setbacks, and life trajectories (steady upward progression, roller-coaster, and struggler patterns).

- *What were the results of the study?* **[Approach/Purpose/Phenomenon]:** Narrative/life story methods are a good fit with research aims to examine surviving and thriving after childhood maltreatment (CM). The authors explain that this methodology was chosen "because it permits us to learn how people interpret their own traumatic experiences. 'Telling narratives is a major way that individuals make sense of disruptive events in their lives' (Riessman, 1990, p. 1199)(p. 149)." **[Reported Results]:** *Diverse patterns of healing* included a roller-coaster pattern, patterns of steady upward progress, and patterns of continued struggle. *Four types of redemption narratives* were found: redemption by counseling or psychotherapy, redemption by a loving relationship, redemption by God, and self-redemption. *Three common threads* interwoven throughout all of the women's narratives were issues related to: telling/not telling, remembering/not remembering, and forgiving/ not forgiving.

- *Will the results help me in caring for my patients?* **[Relevance]:** The article foregrounds participants' voices that "command attention of clinicians and policy makers because earlier and more efficacious interventions could have fostered earlier thriving and mitigated years of suffering (p. 164)." **[Application]:** The authors advise "patience, gentleness, and sensitivity… in working with CM survivors, not pressuring women to remember abuse, not urging them to confront (or forgive) abusers if they do not wish to do so (p. 163)." To foster thriving, earlier and longer, rather than short-term, therapies are needed as well as tolerance for some distortion of the early experience that may be a healthy self-protective mechanism commonly observed among trauma survivors.

Focus Group Analysis

#9 Morgan, D. G. et al. (2008). Taking the hit: Focusing on caregiver "error" masks organizational-level risk factors for nursing aide assault. *Qualitative Health Research,* **18, 334–346.**

Question: What are nursing aide (NA) perceptions of the characteristics of incidents of physical aggression against themselves by nursing home residents?

Design: **Focus group analysis.** Focus groups generate data on a particular topic through discussion and interaction. Sessions are moderated by a group leader and are conducted as informal semistructured interviews. In this research, as in many studies, the group interview technique was used in conjunction with other forms of data collecting. The study plan involved use of structured prospective event-reporting logs (diaries) in which NAs were to document consecutive incidents of resident aggression (time, place, type of activity taking place, views on what caused it, and their emotions and behavior) followed by focus groups to further explore the NAs' perceptions of these events. This article is limited solely to reporting outcomes of the focus group analysis.

Sample: Participating nursing homes included eight with special care units (SCUs) for persons with dementia and three non-SCU facilities, since comparison of perceptions of employees in nursing homes with and without SCUs was of interest. All NAs were eligible to participate. A total of 19 focus groups were conducted with 138 NAs. The focus groups were of two types. Those necessitated by a need to understand barriers to participation in the study ($N = 9$) were conducted in five facilities with a total of 74 NAs. Those aimed at exploring physical aggression, as originally planned ($N = 10$), were conducted in the remaining six facilities with a total of 63 NAs. An individual interview also was conducted in one facility where staffing levels limited formation of a second group.

Procedures: A semistructured interview guide was designed as a follow-up to questions in the diary. Due to NAs' discomfort with sessions being tape-recorded, a flip chart was used to document discussion points. Researchers also wrote detailed notes, including verbatim quotes, which were entered into a word processing program. Concurrent data collection and analysis enabled subsequent interviews to be guided by the analysis of those that had gone before. The narrative text data were analyzed using grounded theory techniques to identify themes.

Appraisal:

- *Are the results valid/trustworthy and credible?* Yes. **[Sample Selection]:** The research design called for follow-up in-depth interviews (focus groups) in approximately half of the participating facilities to deepen understanding of the larger study findings. This plan was modified to include focus group follow-up in all nursing homes in order to address low response rates to the structured event-reporting log/diary approach. Posters, brochures, and unit communication books were used to publicize the focus groups, groups were scheduled for ease of attendance by workers on different shifts, and funding was offered for staff relief during meeting times. **[Accuracy and Completeness]:** Explanation of sampling strategies and facilitation of the group process are thorough and the purpose of focus groups in the overall study, to enhance accuracy and credibility through triangulation of data sources, is established. **[Plausibility/Believability]:** Sets of quotes are sequenced and contextualized around NA responses to reports of physical aggression (feeling blamed, lack of acknowledgement and action, desire for respect and involvement, and factors influencing risk of exposure). The effect intensifies the feeling and mood of study participants' contributions at the same time that the quotes support plausible arguments about organizational conditions that underlie NAs' reactions.

- *What were the results of the study?* **[Approach/Purpose/Phenomenon]:** This study was part of a larger study on rural dementia care in the midwestern Canadian province of Saskatchewan. A focus group format fit the researchers' need to further explore and follow up on NA perceptions of barriers to study participation and views on the phenomenon of physical aggression they experienced at the hands of nursing home residents. **[Reported Results]:** Although each of the two sets of focus groups was conducted for a different purpose, the analysis converged around consistent themes. Specifically, NAs' reluctance to participate in the diary component of the study was directly linked to perceptions of their experiences in caring for residents demonstrating physically aggressive behavior. *Consistent themes that were the cause of frustration* were (a) NAs' perceptions of being blamed when they reported resident aggression, (b) lack of acknowledgment and action in response to reports of aggression, and (c) NAs' desire for respect and involvement in decision and policy making within the organization. The third theme derived from a perception of themselves "at the bottom of the organizational hierarchy" even though they were the caregivers who had "extensive knowledge of individual residents and their needs" (p. 340). *Factors influencing risk of exposure to physical aggression* included workload, inflexible routines, limited access to specialized programs and personnel for behavior management assessment, and inadequate education for NAs, RNs, and physicians. "Rushing care" for residents, particularly those with dementia who need a slower pace, was the most frequently cited problem. Rigid institutional routines (care according to predetermined schedules) contributed to rushing of care that led to resident agitation and aggression. NAs also reported that poorly controlled pain led to resident aggression as well as difficulty to get aggressive residents assessed for a behavioral medication management solution "because the nurses were concerned about medication cost and side effects (p. 342)." There was little difference between reports of NAs who worked on SCUs and those who did not.

- *Will the results help me in caring for my patients?* **[Relevance]:** Resident aggression in nursing homes is a serious problem. NAs, because they provide the majority of care, are most at risk for both verbal aggression and physical assault. Small rural nursing homes, in particular, may have fewer resources, including specialized dementia care programs, which places even higher job-related strain on personnel, especially NAs. **[Application]:** The authors suggest that "to fully address the issue of NA assault there must be a shift in focus away from the behavior of individual NAs to the broader system level…The analysis points to the need for multiple changes at the organizational level…the difficulties of finding effective strategies should not prevent organizations from acknowledging and responding more actively to the plight of NAs who are 'taking the hit,' both literally and figuratively, for the current situation in long-term care (pp. 342, 343, 344)."

Metasynthesis/Meta-ethnography

#10 Yick, A. G. (2008). A metasynthesis of qualitative findings on the role of spirituality and religiosity among culturally diverse domestic violence survivors. *Qualitative health Research, 18,* 1289–1306.

Question: What can a synthesis of existing qualitative findings tell us about the role of culture, spirituality, and religion on domestic violence? Specifically: (a) How do domestic violence victims and survivors use religious and spiritual resources to cope and find meaning? (b) How do religion and spirituality overtly and covertly promote abuse? (c) How does culture affect the intersection of religion or spirituality and domestic violence?

Design: **Metasynthesis as outlined by Noblit and Hare.** Noblit and Hare (1988) provide a step-by-step approach to performing meta-ethnography, a metasynthesis approach in the anthropological/ethnographic tradition. It involves a systematic comparison of qualitative research reports on a designated topic to obtain a full understanding of the phenomenon and a determination of how the key metaphors of each study relate to one another (i.e., translating the studies into one another). Synthesis of these multiple translations refers to the researcher's formulation of overarching metaphors that remains faithful to the interpretations found in the original research sources and accurately portrays their shared and unique findings.

Sample: The sample consisted of *six qualitative research studies* (i.e., eight articles, taking into account three studies that were published from the same dataset). Table 1 summarizes the characteristics of each study. All studies met the following criteria: (a) use of a qualitative design, (b) use of direct quotes from participants from the original study, (c) use of English language, and (d) examination of women who were (or were at the time of the original study) affected by domestic violence. "This study focused solely on male perpetrators and female spouses or intimate partners. A decision was made to focus on heterosexual relationships because the dynamics are different in gay and lesbian domestic violence and domestic violence perpetrated by females (p. 1293)." *Women who were participants in the original studies (N = 62)* were from diverse racial/ethnic and religious backgrounds: more than half (*n* = 34) African American, nine Asian women, nine White women, and several from other ethnic groups with Catholic, Protestant, Muslim, and Buddhist backgrounds. (The demographics of this population are displayed in Table 4.)

Procedures: Each study was read in its entirety to obtain a sense of it as a whole. In subsequent readings, words and terms were highlighted to capture concepts. Table 2 illustrates how meanings from units of text were condensed and then summarized into an interpretation with an underlying meaning and subthemes. Table 3 shows how nine identified overarching themes were linked back to the concepts in the original studies.

Appraisal:

● *Are the results valid/trustworthy and credible?* Yes. **[Sample Selection]:** Diverse databases were used in the library search, including Ebscohost, PsyArticles, CINAHL, ProQuest, Medline, SocIndex, and Sage Sociology and Psychology Collections. **[Accuracy and Completeness]:**

The researcher identified and used a recognized approach (Noblit & Hare, 1988). Search strategies and sample selection are described. Strengths and limitations of the study are discussed. Tables reflect the approach that was used. They also support the rigor and credibility of the analysis by reducing explanation of procedures and outcomes to easy-to-understand visual displays. This helps readers to focus on the key ideas contained in the report. **[Plausibility/ Believability]:** Tables tracking and organizing the characteristics of the studies and the stages of the analytic process illustrate and increase confidence in the plausibility of the reported results.

● *What were the results of the study?* **[Approach/Purpose/Phenomenon]:** In this research, metasynthesis addresses what the researchers describe as "the problem with findings from individual studies…that end up as 'little islands of knowledge' (Glaser & Strauss, 1971, p. 181) or what Paterson, Thorne, & Canam, et al. (2001) coined 'many individual pieces of the jigsaw puzzle'(p. 4). Because of minimal efforts to examine, synthesize, and draw inferences from a line of similar studies, advancement of the knowledge base is often precluded (Finfgeld, 2003; Walsh & Downe, 2005) (p. 1290)." **[Reported Results]:** The main themes and concepts from the six studies were reduced to nine themes. (a) *Strength and resilience stemming from a spiritual or religious base* was expressed as an intangible form (invoking God or a higher being) and also as tangible forms of support from organizational and nonorganizational spiritual or religious resources. (b) *Tension stemming from the definitions or standards of an ideal family* by their church/religion/culture "might [have been] deeply woven into these women's makeup, making it difficult for them to leave abusive relationships (p. 1299)." (c) *Tension stemming from religious or cultural definitions of gender role expectations* may also "trigger confusion and guilt (p. 1300)." (d) *The experience of a spiritual vacuum* described in four of the six studies "[did] not seem to revolve around religion but rather that transcendent dimension that guides an individual's life…[a loss of] personhood (p. 1300). (e) *Reconstruction as part of the spiritual journey* involved spiritual growth and changing views on life's meaning with religious connotations. (f) *Recouping (or recovering) the spirit and self* "included learning interpersonal skills and self-awareness capacities and establishing personal boundaries…an integration process [for the women's previously fragmented identities] (p. 1301)." (g) *New interpretations of definitions of "submission"* involved decision making about what practices and beliefs were disempowering to women and noting features within religious guidelines (e.g., the context of scriptures) that might make deviation from particular tenets appropriate. (h) *Forgiveness as healing* was a theme in four studies that included not only forgiving abusive husbands or partners but also satisfying a need to feel forgiven. "Because of gender role expectations and the church community's disapproval of divorce, self-blame was prevalent, which made the need to feel forgiven that much stronger… [The need for God's forgiveness helped women] move on and heal (p. 1302)." (i) *Giving back—social activism* "was a product of these women's spiritual awakening and their recouping their sense of self and spirit…Sharing their stories [to reach out to other women and girls and instill values in their children was] at the heart of their social activism (p. 1302)."

● *Will the results help me in caring for my patients?* **[Relevance]:** The premise underlying the importance of developing knowledge in this area is that the effect of culture, spirituality, and religion on domestic violence may be one that enables victims to cope and find meaning or one that overtly and covertly promotes the abuse. Thus, it is important to develop a better understanding of how differences among these orientations may be harnessed or reframed by pulling together women's reported views on the topic.

[Application]: The author observes a need for collaboration on the part of practitioners, churches, and faith communities "to develop culturally competent best practices in working with domestic violence victims and survivors (p. 1303)." Healthcare providers could work with survivors and victims on rebuilding a "sense of self"; explore how race, culture, and ethnicity influence definitions of forgiveness; and find ways to connect individuals with their communities "so they can give back and recoup their sense of self (pp. 1303–1304)."

references

Carroll, K., Iedema, R., & Kerridge, R. (2008). Reshaping ICU ward round practices using video-reflexive ethnography. *Qualitative Health Research, 18,* 380–390.

Charmaz, K. (2006). *Constructing grounded theory: A practical guide through qualitative analysis.* Thousand Oaks, CA: Sage.

Cox, J., & Holden, J. (2003). *Perinatal mental health: A guide to the Edinburgh Postnatal Depression Scale (EPDS).* London: Gaskell.

Denz-Penhey, H., & Murdoch, J. C. (2008). Personal resiliency: Serious diagnosis and prognosis with unexpected quality outcomes. *Qualitative Health Research, 18,* 391–404.

Fetterman, D. (1998). *Ethnography: Step-by-step* (2nd ed.). Thousand Oaks, CA: Sage.

Finfgeld, D. L. (2003). Metasynthesis: The state of the art – So far. *Qualitative Health Research, 13,* 893–904.

Francis-Connolly, E. (2000). Toward an understanding of mothering: A comparison of two motherhood stages. *American Journal of Occupational Therapy, 54,* 281–289.

Glaser, B. (1978). *Theoretical sensitivity: Advances in the methodology of grounded theory.* Mill Valley, CA: Sociology Press.

Glaser, B. (1992). *Basics of grounded theory analysis: Emergence vs. forcing.* Mill Valley, CA: Sociology Press.

Glaser, B., & Strauss, A. (1971). *Status passage: A formal theory.* Chicago: Aldine.

Guba, E. G., & Lincoln, Y. S. (1989). *Fourth generation evaluation.* Newbury Park, CA: Sage.

Hsieh, H. F., & Shannon, S. E. (2005). Three approaches to qualitative content analysis. *Qualitative Health Research, 15,* 1277–1288.

Marcellus, L. (2008). (Ad)ministering love: Providing family foster care to infants with prenatal substance exposure. *Qualitative Health Research, 18,* 1220–1230.

Morgan, D. G., Crossley, M. F., Stewart, N. J., D'Arcy, C., Forbes, D. A., Normand, S. A., & Cammer, A. L. (2008). Taking the hit: Focusing on caregiver "error" masks organizational-level risk factors for nursing aide assault. *Qualitative Health Research, 18,* 334–346.

Noblit, G. W., & Hare, R. D. (1988). *Meta-ethnography: Synthesizing qualitative studies.* Newbury Park, CA: Sage.

Paterson, B. L., Thorne, S. E., Canam, C., & Jillings, C. (2001). *Meta-study of qualitative health research: A practical guide to meta-analysis and meta-synthesis.* Thousand Oaks, CA: Sage.

Porter, E. J. (1995). The life-world of older widows: The context of lived experience. *Journal of Women & Aging, 7*(4), 31–46.

Powers, B. A., & Knapp, T. R. (2006). *Dictionary of nursing theory and research* (3rd ed). New York: Springer.

Riessman, C. K. (1990). Strategic uses of narrative in the presentation of self and illness. *Social Science and Medicine, 30,* 1195–1200.

Sandelowski, M. (1994). The use of quotes in qualitative research. *Research in Nursing & Health, 17,* 479–482.

Sandelowski. M. (1998). Writing a good read: Strategies for re-presenting qualitative data. *Research in Nursing & Health, 21,* 375–382.

Sandelowski, M. (2000). Whatever happened to qualitative description? *Research in Nursing & Health, 23,* 334–340.

Schutz, A., & Luckman, T. (1973). *The structures of the life-world* (R.M. Zaner & H.T. Engelhardt, Jr., Trans.). Evanston, IL: Northwestern University Press.

Scott, S. D., Estabrooks, C. A., Allen, M., & Pollock, C. (2008). A context of uncertainty: How context shapes nurses' research utilization behaviors. *Qualitative Health Research, 18,* 347–357.

Shojania, K. G., & Grimshaw, J. M. (2005). Evidence-based quality improvement: The state of the science. *Health Affairs, 24,* 138–151.

Spiegelberg, H. (1994). *The phenomenological movement: A historical introduction* (3rd revised and enlarged ed.). Dordrecht, the Netherlands: Kluwer Academic Press. Strauss, A., & Corbin, J. (1990). *Basics of qualitative research: Grounded theory procedures and techniques.* Newbury Park, CA: Sage.

Sword, W., Busser, D., Ganann, R., McMillan, T., & Swinton, M. (2008). Women's care- seeking experiences after referral for postpartum depression. *Qualitative Health Research, 18,* 1161–1173.

Thomas, S. P., & Hall, J. M. (2008). Life trajectories of female child abuse survivors thriving in adulthood. *Qualitative Health Research, 18,* 149–166.

van Manen, M. (1990). *Researching lived experience: Human science for an action sensitive pedagogy.* London, Canada: Althouse.

Verhaeghe, S., Defloor, T., & Grypdonck, M. (2005). Stress and coping among families of patients with traumatic brain injury: A review of the literature. *Journal of Clinical Nursing, 14,* 1004–1012.

Walsh, D., & Downe, S. (2005). Meta-synthesis method for qualitative research: A literature review. *Journal of Advanced Nursing, 50*(2), 204–211.

Winstanley, J., Simpson, G., Tate, R., & Myles, B. (2006). Early indicators and contributors to psychological distress in relatives during rehabilitation following severe traumatic brain injury: Findings from the brain injury outcomes study. *Journal of Head Trauma Rehabilitation, 21,* 453–466.

Wongvatunyu, S., & Porter, E. J. (2008). Helping young adult children with traumatic brain injury: The life-world of mothers. *Qualitative Health Research, 18,* 1062–1074.

Woodgate, R. L., Ateah, C., & Secco, L. (2008). Living in a world of our own: The experience of parents who have a child with autism. *Qualitative Health Research, 18,* 1075–1083.

Yick, A. G. (2008). A metasynthesis of qualitative findings on the role of spirituality and religiosity among culturally diverse domestic violence survivors. *Qualitative Health Research, 18,* 1289–1306.

Rapid Critical Appraisal Checklists

Electronic copies of rapid critical appraisal (RCA) checklists can be found on the accompanying CD-ROM.

Rapid Critical Appraisal Checklist for Case–Control Studies

1. Are the Results of the Study Valid?

a. How were the cases obtained?	Yes	No	Unknown
b. Were appropriate controls selected?	Yes	No	Unknown
c. Were data collection methods the same for the cases and controls?	Yes	No	Unknown

2. What Are the Results?

a. Is an estimate of effect given (do the numbers add up)?	Yes	No	Unknown
b. Are there multiple comparisons of data?	Yes	No	Unknown
d. Is there any possibility of bias or confounding?	Yes	No	Unknown

3. Will the Results Help Me in Caring for My Patients?

a. Were the study patients similar to my own?	Yes	No	Unknown
b. How do the results compare with previous studies?	_____		
c. What are my patients/family's values and expectations for the outcome?	_____		

appendix D

513

Rapid Critical Appraisal Checklist for Cohort Studies

1. Are the Results of the Study Valid?

a. Was there a representative and well-defined sample of patients at a similar point in the course of the disease?	Yes	No	Unknown
b. Was follow-up sufficiently long and complete?	Yes	No	Unknown
c. Were objective and unbiased outcome criteria used?	Yes	No	Unknown
d. Did the analysis adjust for important prognostic risk factors and confounding variables?	Yes	No	Unknown

2. What Are the Results?

a. What is the magnitude of the relationship between predictors (i.e., prognostic indicators) and targeted outcome? _____

b. How likely is the outcome event(s) in a specified period of time? _____

c. How precise are the study estimates? _____

3. Will the Results Help Me in Caring for My Patients?

a. Were the study patients similar to my own?	Yes	No	Unknown
b. Will the results lead directly to selecting or avoiding therapy?	Yes	No	Unknown
c. Are the results useful for reassuring or counseling patients?	Yes	No	Unknown

Rapid Critical Appraisal Checklist for Randomized Clinical Trials

1. Are the Results of the Study Valid?

A. Were the subjects randomly assigned to the experimental and control groups?	Yes	No	Unknown
B. Was random assignment concealed from the individuals who were first enrolling subjects into the study?	Yes	No	Unknown
C. Were the subjects and providers blind to the study group?	Yes	No	Unknown
D. Were reasons given to explain why subjects did not complete the study?	Yes	No	Unknown
E. Were the follow-up assessments conducted long enough to fully study the effects of the intervention?	Yes	No	Unknown
F. Were the subjects analyzed in the group to which they were randomly assigned?	Yes	No	Unknown
G. Was the control group appropriate?	Yes	No	Unknown
H. Were the instruments used to measure the outcomes valid and reliable?	Yes	No	Unknown
I. Were the subjects in each of the groups similar on demographic and baseline clinical variables?	Yes	No	Unknown

2. What Are the Results?

A. How large is the intervention or treatment effect (NNT, NNH, effect size, level of significance)? _____

B. How precise is the intervention or treatment (CI)? _____

3. Will the Results Help Me in Caring for My Patients?

A. Were all clinically important outcomes measured?	Yes	No	Unknown
B. What are the risks and benefits of the treatment? _____			
C. Is the treatment feasible in my clinical setting?	Yes	No	Unknown
D. What are my patients/family's values and expectations for the outcome that is trying to be prevented and the treatment itself? _____			

Modified from Melnyk, B. (2004). Rapid Critical Appraisal of Randomized Controlled Trials (RCTs): An Essential Skill for Evidence-Based Practice, Melnyk, Pediatric Nursing Journal.

Rapid Critical Appraisal Checklist for Systematic Reviews of Clinical Intervention Studies

I. Are the Results of the Review Valid?

A.	Are the studies contained in the review randomized controlled trials?	Yes	No
B.	Does the review include a detailed description of the search strategy to find all relevant studies?	Yes	No
C.	Does the review describe how validity of the individual studies was assessed (e.g., methodological quality, including the use of random assignment to study groups and complete follow-up of the subjects)?	Yes	No
D.	Were the results consistent across studies?	Yes	No
E.	Were individual patient data or aggregate data used in the analysis?	Yes	No

2. What Were the Results?

A.	How large is the intervention or treatment effect (OR, RR, effect size, level of significance)?	_____
B.	How precise is the intervention or treatment (CI)?	_____

3. Will the Results Assist Me in Caring for My Patients?

A.	Are my patients similar to the ones included in the review?	Yes	No
B.	Is it feasible to implement the findings in my practice setting?	Yes	No
C.	Were all clinically important outcomes considered, including risks and benefits of the treatment?	Yes	No
D.	What is my clinical assessment of the patient and are there any contraindications or circumstances that would inhibit me from implementing the treatment?	Yes	No
E.	What are my patient's and his or her family's preferences and values about the treatment that is under consideration?	Yes	No

© *Fineout-Overholt & Melnyk, 2005. This form may be used for educational and research purposes without permission.*

Rapid Critical Appraisal Checklist for Qualitative Evidence

1) Are the Results of the Study Valid (i.e., Trustworthy and Credible)?

(a) How were study participants chosen? _____

(b) How were accuracy and completeness of data assured? _____

(c) How plausible/believable are the results?

    (i) Are implications of the research stated?   Yes   No   Unknown

        (1) May new insights increase sensitivity to others' needs?

        (2) May understandings enhance situational competence?

(d) What is the effect on the reader?

        (1) Are results plausible and believable?   Yes   No   Unknown

        (2) Is the reader imaginatively drawn into the experience?   Yes   No   Unknown

2) What Were the Results?

(a) Does the research approach fit the purpose of the study?   Yes   No   Unknown

    (i) How does the researcher identify the study approach?   Yes   No   Unknown

        (1) Are language and concepts consistent with the approach?   Yes   No   Unknown

        (2) Are data collection and analysis techniques appropriate?   Yes   No   Unknown

    (ii) Is the significance/importance of the study explicit?   Yes   No   Unknown

        (1) Does review of the literature support a need for the study?   Yes   No   Unknown

        (2) What is the study's potential contribution? _____

    (iii) Is the sampling strategy clear and guided by study needs?   Yes   No   Unknown

        (1) Does the researcher control selection of the sample?   Yes   No   Unknown

        (2) Do sample composition and size reflect study needs?   Yes   No   Unknown

(b) Is the phenomenon (human experience) clearly identified?

    (i) Are data collection procedures clear?   Yes   No   Unknown

        (1) Are sources and means of verifying data explicit?   Yes   No   Unknown

        (2) Are researcher roles and activities explained?   Yes   No   Unknown

    (ii) Are data analysis procedures described?   Yes   No   Unknown

        (1) Does analysis guide direction of sampling and when it ends?   Yes   No   Unknown

        (2) Are data management processes described?   Yes   No   Unknown

(c) What are the reported results (description or interpretation)?

    (i) How are specific findings presented? _____

        (1) Is presentation logical, consistent, and easy to follow?   Yes   No   Unknown

        (2) Do quotes fit the findings they are intended to illustrate?   Yes   No   Unknown

    (ii) How are overall results presented? _____

        (1) Are meanings derived from data described in context?   Yes   No   Unknown

        (2) Does the writing effectively promote understanding?   Yes   No   Unknown

3) Will the Results Help Me in Caring for My Patients?

(a) Are the results relevant to persons in similar situations?   Yes   No   Unknown

(b) Are the results relevant to patient values and/or circumstances?   Yes   No   Unknown

(c) How may the results be applied in clinical practice? _____

Rapid Critical Appraisal Checklist for Evidence-Based Clinical Practice Guidelines

Credibility

(1)	Who were the guideline developers?			_____
(2)	Were the developers representative of key stakeholders in this specialty (interdisciplinary)?	Yes	No	Unknown
(3)	Who funded the guideline development?			_____
(4)	Were any of the guidelines developers funded researchers of the reviewed studies?	Yes	No	Unknown
(5)	Did the team have a valid development strategy?	Yes	No	Unknown
(6)	Was an explicit (how decisions were made), sensible and impartial process used to identify, select, and combine evidence?	Yes	No	Unknown
(7)	Did its developers carry out a comprehensive, reproducible literature review within the past 12 months of its publication/revision?	Yes	No	Unknown
(8)	Were all important options and outcomes considered?	Yes	No	Unknown
(9)	Is each recommendation in the guideline tagged by the level/strength of evidence upon which it is based and linked with the scientific evidence?	Yes	No	Unknown
(10)	Do the guidelines make explicit recommendations (reflecting value judgments about outcomes)	Yes	No	Unknown
(11)	Has the guideline been subjected to peer review and testing?	Yes	No	Unknown

Applicability/Generalizability

(12)	Is the intent of use provided (e.g., national, regional, local)?	Yes	No	Unknown
(13)	Are the recommendations clinically relevant?	Yes	No	Unknown
(14)	Will the recommendations help me in caring for my patients?	Yes	No	Unknown
(15)	Are the recommendations practical/feasible (e.g., resources–people and equipment—available)?	Yes	No	Unknown
(16)	Are the recommendations a major variation from current practice?	Yes	No	Unknown
(17)	Can the outcomes be measured through standard care?	Yes	No	Unknown

Modified from Slutsky, J. (2005). Using evidence-based guidelines: Tools for improving practice, In B.M. Melnyk & E. Fineout-Overholt (Eds.), Evidence-based practice in nursing & healthcare. A guide to best practice (pp. 221–236). Philadelphia, PA: Lippincott, Williams & Wilkins.

Templates for Evaluation and Synthesis Tables for Conducting an Evidence Review

Evaluation Table Template

Caveats

(1) The **only studies** you should put in these tables are the ones that you know answer your question after you have done rapid critical appraisal.
(2) This evaluation is **for the purpose** of synthesis.
(3) Simplicity is key to a successful evaluation table.

Citation	Conceptual Framework	Design/ Method	Sample/ Setting	Major Variables Studied and Their Definitions	Measurement	Data Analysis	Findings	Appraisal: Worth to Practice

The topics below are prompts for each column. Please do not repeat the topics, just provide the appropriate data extracted from the studies.

| Author, Year, Title | Theoretical basis for study | Indicate design & briefly describe what was done in the study | Number, Characteristics, Attrition rate & why? | Independent variables (e.g., IV1 = IV2 =) Dependent variables (e.g., DV =) | What scales were used to measure the outcome variables (e.g., name of scale, author, reliability info [e.g., Cronbach alphas]) | What stats were used to answer the clinical question (i.e., all stats do not need to be put into the table) | Statistical findings or qualitative findings (i.e., for every statistical test you have in the data analysis column, you should have a finding) | • strengths and limitations of the study
 • Risk or harm if study intervention or findings implemented
 • Feasibility of use in your practice
 • Remember: level of evidence + quality of evidence = strength of evidence & confidence to act |

Evidence Synthesis Tables

Comparisons of Variable of Interest: Outcome, Intervention, Measurement, Definition of variable, Levels of evidence [design] Across Studies

The table below is one template for constructing a sythesis table that focuses on comparing interventions across studies.

Studies	A	B	C	D	E	F
Interventions						
1	X	X			X	X
2			X	X		X
3			X	X		X

A, B, C, etc = study author & year, X = presence of the intervention in that study.

The table below is another example of a template for a synthesis table that compares *design*, *sample*, and *outcome* across studies. You can choose any of the studies' characteristics to focus on in the synthesis, as the purpose is to tell the story of how studies are different and how they are alike; however, do not choose all of them. If you use all of the characteristics then the table becomes an evaluation table, not a synthesis table.

	Design	Sample	Outcome
Studies			

Example of a Slide Show for a 20-Minute Paper Presentation

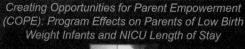

Creating Opportunities for Parent Empowerment (COPE): Program Effects on Parents of Low Birth Weight Infants and NICU Length of Stay

Bernadette Mazurek Melnyk, PhD, CPNP/PMHNP, FAAN
Dean and Distinguished Foundation Professor in Nursing
ASU College of Nursing and Health Innovation
Nancy F. Feinstein, PhD, RNC; Linda Alpert-Gillis, PhD
Hugh Crean, PhD; Eileen Fairbanks. MS, RN, PNP
University of Rochester

Center for Improving Health Outcomes in Children, Teens & Families

Funding for this Study by:
The National Institutes of Health/
National Institute of Nursing Research R01#05077

Background/Significance

- Over 500,000 premature infants are born every year in the U.S.

- Evidence has accumulated to support that LBW premature infants experience a host of adverse physical and mental health/ behavioral outcomes which persist well into the school-age and adolescent years

Background/Significance

- Adverse outcomes for preterm children include delays in cognitive and neurological development, behavior problems and attention deficit disorder

- The costs associated with a NICU stay (i.e., approximately $1,250 to $2,000 per day) and increased medical utilization by these children are exorbitant

Background/Significance

- Parents of preterms experience high stress levels and often lack adequate knowledge of how to parent and interact with them in a developmentally sensitive manner

- Adverse outcomes for parents of preterms include:
  -anxiety and depressive disorders
  -dysfunctional parenting interactions and the vulnerable child syndrome

Background/Significance

- Interventions to enhance coping and mental health outcomes in parents of LBW premature infants to improve both parent and child outcomes have not kept pace with the rapid technological advances to sustain survival

Background/Significance

- Most programs for parents of preterm infants have commenced the interventions at or shortly after NICU discharge, after parental perceptions of their infants and altered parenting interaction trajectories have been established

(This is way too late!)

The COPE NICU Program

An educational-behavioral skills building program for parents of premature infants that prepares parents for the characteristics to expect in their ill and premature children and how to parent them in developmentally sensitive ways to enhance their health outcomes

The COPE NICU Program

- 4 part series of audio tapes that provides parents with infant behavior information and parent role information
  - 2-4 days after admission to NICU
  - 2-4 days after the first intervention
  - 1-4 days prior to discharge
  - 1 week after discharge

- Parent skills building activities that help parents implement the COPE information

ASU College of Nursing & Healthcare Innovation
ARIZONA STATE UNIVERSITY

The First Component of COPE:
Audio taped and written information that teaches parents about the behaviors, physical characteristics and alert states of premature infants

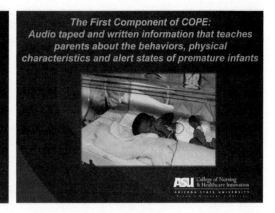

ASU College of Nursing & Healthcare Innovation
ARIZONA STATE UNIVERSITY

COPE information also teaches parents how best to parent and interact with their infants

ASU College of Nursing & Healthcare Innovation
ARIZONA STATE UNIVERSITY

The Second Component of COPE

- Skills building activities that assist parents with:
  - Identifying the special characteristics of their infants
  - Describing their infants' stress cues
  - Identifying strategies to assist their infants when stressed
  - Implementing behaviors that will help their infants to grow and develop

ASU College of Nursing & Healthcare Innovation
ARIZONA STATE UNIVERSITY

The Theoretical Framework

- Self-Regulation Theory (Leventhal & Johnson)

- Control Theory (Carver & Scheier)

- The Emotional Contagion Hypotheses (VanderVeer)

Hypothesized Effects of the COPE Program on the Process and Outcomes of Parental and Infant Development/Adjustment

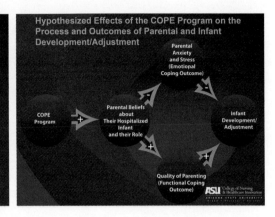

COPE Program

Parental Beliefs about Their Hospitalized Infant and their Role

Parental Anxiety and Stress (Emotional Coping Outcome)

Infant Development/ Adjustment

Quality of Parenting (Functional Coping Outcome)

THE DESIGN
A randomized controlled trial at 2 study sites involving 260 LBW Premature Infants and their mothers and fathers with follow-up through 3 years corrected age

---

Study Inclusion Criteria

- Gestational age of 26 to 34 weeks inclusive
- Birth-weight of less than 2500 grams and appropriate for gestational age
- Anticipated survival
- Singleton birth
- No severe handicapping conditions, including Grade III or IV IVH
- Born at the study sites

The Sample

- 260 families, including 258 mothers (147 in the COPE group; 113 in the comparison group) and 154 fathers (81 in the COPE group and 73 in the comparison group)

- 13 families were eliminated from the study because of infant death (n=3), transfer of child custody (n=2), completion of only baseline measures (n=7), and a significant congenital anomaly (n=1)

The Sample of Mothers

- Mean age = 27.8 years
- Completion of high school = (n=212; 82.2%)
- On public assistance = 86 (33.3%)
- Married = 138 (53.4%)
- Never married = 98 (38.0%)
- Race/Ethnicity
  - White, not Hispanic Origin (n=174; 67.4%)
  - African-American (n=58; 22.5%)
  - Other (n= 26; 10.1%)

The Sample of Fathers

- Mean age = 30.6 years
- Completion of high school = (n=126;83.4%)
- Married = 96 (63.6%)
- Never married = 39 (25.8%)
- Race/Ethnicity
  - White, not Hispanic Origin (n=115; 76.2%)
  - African-American (n=23; 15.2%)
  - Other (n= 13; 8.6%)

The Sample of Infants

- Mean gestational age = 31.3 weeks (range = 26 to 35 weeks).
- Mean birth-weight = 1650 grams, with 102 infants weighing less than 1500 grams
- Males = 126 (48.5%)
- Females = 134 (51.5%)
- Mean CRIB score = 1.7; range = 0 to 12

The Sample of Infants

- Mean discharge weight = 2150.3 grams
- Mean total length of NICU stay = 35.2 days
- Transferred to another hospital before discharge (n=61; 24.3%)

ASU College of Nursing & Healthcare Innovation
ARIZONA STATE UNIVERSITY

Dependent Variables & Measures

Variable	Measure	Cronbach's Alpha
State Anxiety	*State Trait Anxiety Inventory*	.83-.92
Depressive Symptoms	*Beck Depression Inventory*	.83-.90

ASU College of Nursing & Healthcare Innovation
ARIZONA STATE UNIVERSITY

Dependent Variables & Measures

Variable	Measure	Cronbach's Alpha
Stress related to the NICU	*Parental Stressor Scale (PSS: NICU)*	.94-.96
Quality of Parent-infant Interaction in the NICU	*Index of Parent Behavior-NICU (IPBN)*	.83-.86

ASU College of Nursing & Healthcare Innovation
ARIZONA STATE UNIVERSITY

Process Variable & Measure

Variable	Measure	Cronbach's Alpha
Parental beliefs	*Parental Beliefs Scale*	.90-.93

ASU College of Nursing & Healthcare Innovation
ARIZONA STATE UNIVERSITY

Infant Outcomes

Variable	Measure	Cronbach's Alpha
Length of Stay in NICU	*Length of Stay in Days*	N/A
Total Length of Stay (NICU, plus Transfer Hospital)	*Length of Stay in Days*	N/A

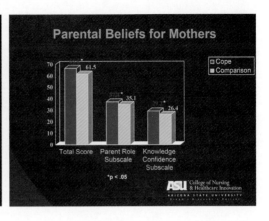

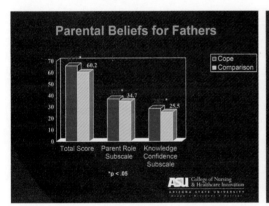

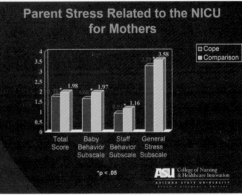

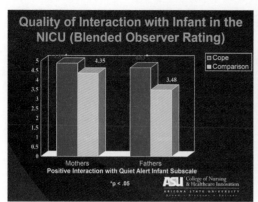

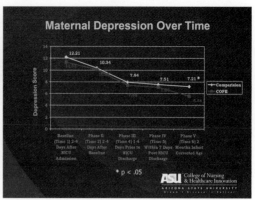

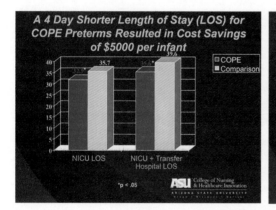

Cost Savings for the Healthcare System to Implement COPE

- At $5,000 per infant x 500,000 premature infants born every year, routine implementation of the COPE program could save the U.S. healthcare system 2.5 billion dollars per year

Other Key Findings

- Parental beliefs about their parental role and what to expect from their infants were significantly correlated with a shorter NICU length of stay

- Mothers and fathers' positive parenting behavior ratings on the IPBN were significantly correlated with NICU LOS and Total Length of Stay

Parents' Evaluation Comments about the COPE Program Information

"It helped me to pay attention to my baby instead of my fears."

"It made me feel like everything was going to be alright."

"It gave you other things to concentrate on besides your baby's illness. It helped you to see the positive milestones your baby met."

Mothers' Evaluation Comments about the COPE Activities

"The activities gave me a chance to interact with my baby."

"They helped me to form an emotional bond to my baby."

"I did not know how important reading was to a tiny baby. Those things we were told changed a lot of the way we were thinking."

Conclusions

- This is the first full-scale RCT to demonstrate that a reproducible theory-based intervention with parents of preterm infants that commences early in the NICU stay results in less parental stress, more positive parent-infant interactions in the NICU, less parental anxiety and depressive symptoms following hospitalization, and a reduced LOS for preterms

Conclusions

- Findings support the theoretical framework

- Launching this positive parent-infant interactional trajectory shortly after admission in the NICU is critical in that prior studies have indicated that early interaction patterns between parents and infants in the NICU are likely to remain consistent over time

Our Vision

- To improve the clinical care and outcomes for all premature infants and their parents

- Standard implementation of COPE in every NICU in the country and coverage by insurers

Contact Information

Bernadette.Melnyk@asu.edu

602-496-2200

Example of a Health Policy Brief

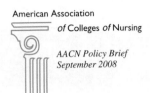

American Association

of Colleges *of* Nursing

AACN Policy Brief
September 2008

Ensuring Access to Safe, Quality, and Affordable Healthcare through a Robust Nursing Workforce

Making the Case for Healthcare Reform

America's healthcare delivery system is in desperate need of reform. Since the early 1990s, healthcare appeared to shift from a system based on providing quality care to one driven by market-based economic models. Demands by the customers (business and government) to lower costs and adhere to a structured business plan overrode the public's ideal of health care as a humanitarian service.[1] The shift received significant attention. In 1995 the American Hospital Association referred to the changes as the "worst disaster to hit US hospitals" explaining that patient errors, malpractice suits, and union activities all increased under this flawed model.[1] Within the next six years, institutions such as the Health Research and Services Administration (HRSA) and the Institute of Medicine (IOM) looked critically at the failing system. Landmark IOM studies such as *"To Err is Human"* and *"Crossing the Quality Chasm"* showed that the healthcare system was in crisis.[2,3] Adverse outcomes were on the rise with as many as 98,000 Americans dying each year from avoidable medical errors.[2] These numbers sent shockwaves throughout the healthcare community and on Capitol Hill. The basic premises of healthcare-quality, and safety- were being compromised.

The national healthcare system is at a crossroads. It can no longer continue to function under the current circumstances, but there are positive aspects that must be retained. It is the role of the new Administration, Congress, and vested stakeholders to differentiate what must be kept, from what must be reformed. The nursing workforce fits squarely in both of these categories. Registered Nurses (RNs) are the backbone of the healthcare system representing the largest group of healthcare professionals with 2.4 million practicing nurses in the United States. Yet, the ongoing shortage of nurses is contributing to the breakdown of the nation's ability to ensure access to safe, quality, and affordable healthcare. Unfortunately, the demand for RNs continues to outpace the supply of new nurses entering the healthcare system each year.

As a stakeholder in healthcare reform, the American Association of Colleges of Nursing (AACN) offers its expertise by recommending that a significant investment be made to increase the capacity of nursing schools to educate more nurses. Without

ADVANCING HIGHER EDUCATION IN NURSING

One Dupont Circle NW, Suite 530 · Washington, DC 20036 · 202-463-6930 *tel* · 202-785-8320 *fax* ·
www.aacn.nche.edu

a robust nursing workforce, the healthcare system will not be able to offer safe, affordable, and quality health care. Outlined below is an overview of the nursing shortage crisis and AACN's specific recommendations of healthcare reform from the nursing education perspective.

Nursing Shortage

- According to the latest projections from the U.S. Bureau of Labor Statistics, more than one million new and replacement nurses will be needed by 2016.[4] This estimate takes into consideration the overburdened healthcare system, the growing complexity of nursing care, and the basic demand for nurses as the baby boomer population ages. However, the perception that "just more nurses" are needed is flawed. The greatest need is for nurses prepared at the baccalaureate and graduate levels.

Demand for a Highly Educated Nursing Workforce

- RNs provide services along the entire spectrum, including lifesaving interventions and preventative care. Patients who enter the nation's hospitals and healthcare facilities typically suffer from multiple co-morbidities such as obesity, diabetes, and hypertension. More acute patients have fundamentally changed the intensity of nursing care. The changes in how health care is delivered have created demand for nursing personnel who can function with more independence in clinical decision-making and case management, perform the traditional role of clinical caregiver, and teach patients how to comply with treatment regimens and maintain good health. Knowing that patients today are more complex and require an advanced level of specialized care, the need for nurses who are highly educated is critical. Therefore, the nursing shortage and its impact on patient care cannot be solved by simply increasing the pipeline. The workforce must be fortified with more highly-educated and well-qualified nurses, specifically nurses with a baccalaureate degree or higher.

- Unlike graduates of diploma or associate-degree nursing programs, the nurse with a baccalaureate degree is prepared to practice in all health care settings - critical care, outpatient care, public health, and mental health. In addition to the liberal learning and global perspective gained from a four-year baccalaureate education, the curriculum includes clinical, scientific, decision-making, and humanistic skills, including preparation in community health, patient education, as well as nursing management and leadership. Such skills are essential for today's professional nurse who must make quick, sometimes life-and-death decisions; design and manage a comprehensive plan of nursing care; understand a patient's treatment, symptoms, and danger signs; supervise other nursing personnel and support staff; master advanced technology; guide patients through the maze of healthcare resources in a community; and educate patients on healthcare options and how to adopt healthy lifestyles.

- The National Advisory Council on Nurse Education and Practice, policy advisors to Congress and the U.S. Secretary for Health and Human Services on nursing issues, has urged that at least two-thirds of the nurse workforce hold baccalaureate or higher degrees in nursing by 2010. Currently, only 47.2% of nurses hold degrees at the baccalaureate level and above.[5] Organizations such as AACN, the American Nurses Association, and the American Organization of Nurse Executives are calling for all professional registered nurses to be educated at the baccalaureate level in an effort to adequately prepare nurses for their challenging and complex roles. However, this task is not easily achieved.

The Nurse Faculty Shortage

- The nursing educational system in the United States is significantly strained. Despite marked increases in nursing school enrollment and graduations, capacity barriers have prohibited schools from accepting more students. Last year AACN reported that 40,285 qualified applicants were turned away from baccalaureate and graduate nursing programs. The top reason cited by schools of nursing for not increasing enrollment was a lack of faculty. According to a *Special Survey on Vacant Faculty Positions* released by AACN in July 2008, data show a national nurse faculty vacancy rate of 7.6%.[6] Most of the vacancies (88.1%) were faculty positions requiring or preferring a doctoral degree.[6] Yet, enrollment in research-focused doctoral nursing programs was up by only 0.9% from the 2006–2007 academic year.[6] More concerning, only one in ten of our nation's registered nurses hold master's or doctoral degrees, which are required to teach. If action is not taken to educate the next generation of nurses and nurse faculty, health care in America will continue to suffer.

The Solution

As Congress looks towards healthcare reform, AACN strongly suggests that the nursing workforce be increased. A robust nursing workforce is needed before quality, access, and affordability of health care can be addressed. AACN is committed to working with Congress to address the nursing and nurse faculty shortage through legislative efforts that not only increase the number of nurses, but ensure that they are qualified to practice in a demanding healthcare environment. Provided below are AACN's top recommendations to Congress as they address the nursing shortage as a component of healthcare reform:

- **Reauthorize the Title VIII Nursing Workforce Development Programs, which are authorized under the Public Health Service Act, (42 U.S.C. 296 et seq.)**

  - Over the last 44 years, Nursing Workforce Development programs have addressed all aspects of nursing shortages – education, practice, retention, and recruitment. As the largest source of federal funding for nursing education, these programs bolster RN education from entry-level preparation through graduate study. The Title VIII programs award grants to schools of nursing, as well as direct support to nurses and nursing students through loans, scholarships, traineeships, and programmatic grants. By supporting the supply and distribution of qualified nurses, these programs help to ensure that nurses are available to provide care to individuals in all healthcare settings. Additionally, the Title VIII programs also favor institutions that educate nurses for practice in rural and medically underserved communities. However, authorization of all Title VIII programs has expired.

Increase funding for the Title VIII Nursing Workforce Development Programs.

During the nursing shortage of the 1970s, Congress addressed the problem by providing increased levels of funding for Title VIII programs. Specifically, in 1973 Congress appropriated $160.61 million to the authorities; the largest appropriation of funds Title VIII has ever received. In today's dollars this would be a commitment of over $763 million. Currently, Title VIII receives $156.05 million to focus on a similar, critical national nursing shortage. Compounding the impact of this low appropriation level is the stagnant nature of Title VIII funding in the face of escalating education costs. In FY 2006 and 2007, $149.68 million was appropriated to Title VIII. This allocation supported 75,946 nursing students and nurses in 2006 while only 71,729 in 2007, due in part to increased tuition costs and inflation.

---

[1] Curtin, L.L. (2007). The perfect storm: Managed care, aging adults, and a nursing shortage. *Nursing Administration Quarterly*, 31(2), 105–110.

[2] Institute of Medicine (2002). *To err is human: Building a safer health system*. Washington, DC: The National Academies Press.

[3] Institute of Medicine. (2001). *Crossing the quality chasm: A new health system for the 21st century*. Washington, DC: The National Academies Press.

[4] Bureau of Labor and Statistics, (2007). *Occupational projections to 2016*. Accessed July 29, 2008 from www.bls.gov/opub/mlr/2007/11/art5full.pdf

[5] Health Resources and Services Administration (2004). *National Sample Survey of Registered Nurses*. Accessed February 19, 2008 from http://bhpr.hrsa.gov/healthworkforce/reports/rnpopulation/preliminaryfindings.htm

[6] American Association of Colleges of Nursing. (2008). *Special Survey on Vacant Faculty Positions*. Washington, DC.

Example of a Press Release

U.S. Department of Health and Human Services

NIH News

National Institutes of Health

<u>National Institute of Nursing Research (NINR)</u>

EMBARGOED FOR RELEASE
Wednesday, November 1, 2006
12:00 a.m. ET

CONTACT:
<u>NINR Communications Office</u>
301-496-0207

E-mail this page
☑ Subscribe

Neonatal Intensive Care Unit Program Reduces Premature Infants' Length of Stay and Improves Parents' Mental Health Outcomes

An educational intervention program for parents of infants born prematurely that is implemented early in the Neonatal Intensive Care Unit (NICU) can reduce parental stress, depression and anxiety, enhance parent-infant interactions, and reduce hospital length of stay, according to a study led by Dr. Bernadette Melnyk, Dean and Distinguished Foundation Professor in Nursing at Arizona State University College of Nursing & Healthcare Innovation, Phoenix.

The study, which was funded by the National Institute of Nursing Research (NINR), a component of the National Institutes of Health, set out to evaluate the efficacy of an intervention program [Creating Opportunities for Parent Empowerment (COPE)] that was designed to make parent-infant interactions a more positive experience and enhance parent mental health outcomes for the ultimate purpose of improving child development and behavior outcomes.

Two hundred and sixty families with preterm infants participated in a randomized, controlled trial conducted from 2001 to 2004 in two NICUs, in Rochester and Syracuse, New York. Subjects at each of the two study sites were randomly assigned to receive the COPE program or a comparison intervention program.

The researchers describe COPE as a four-phase educational-behavioral intervention program, with each phase providing parents with information on:

- The appearance and behavioral characteristics of premature infants and how parents can participate in their infant's care, meet their infant's needs, make interactions with their infant a more positive experience, and aid in their infant's development;
- Activities that assist parents in implementing the experimental information, such as recognizing their infants' alert states and stress cues, and identifying special characteristics of their infants.

Phase I of the COPE program occurred 2 to 4 days after the infants' admission to the NICU; Phase II occurred 2 to 4 days after completion of Phase I; Phase III occurred 1 to 4 days before discharge; Phase IV was delivered in the parents' home 1 week after infant discharge.

The investigators packaged the intervention as audiotaped and written information along with prescribed activities so that it could be easily reproduced and administered to all parents of preterm infants in NICUs at low cost. Their goal was for the COPE program to achieve widespread use without requiring intensive staff training and time.

The study, which appears in the November issue of Pediatrics, found that mothers in the COPE program reported significantly less stress in the NICU and less depression and anxiety than mothers in the comparison group when evaluated 2 months following the intervention. Trained observers in the study rated mothers and fathers in the COPE program as more positive in interactions with their infants. Mothers and fathers also reported stronger beliefs about their parental role and what behaviors and characteristics to expect of their infants during hospitalization. Also, infants in the COPE program had a 3.8-day shorter NICU length of stay and a 3.9-day shorter total hospital length of stay than did comparison infants. In addition, for very low birth weight infants in the study (those less than 1500 grams), the COPE infants had an eight-day shorter length of stay than comparison infants.

The researchers also report that the COPE group's shortened hospital stay resulted in decreased hospital costs of $5000 per infant (4 days x $1,250/day). They further note that with 480,000 low birth weight premature infants born every year in the U.S., approximately $2.4 billion could be saved annually within our national health care system if the COPE program were to be adopted by NICUs across the country.

According to the investigators, this is believed to be the first randomized controlled trial to demonstrate that a reproducible theory-based intervention with parents of premature infants that commences early in the NICU produces less parental stress in the NICU, more positive parent-interactions in the NICU, less parental anxiety and depressive symptoms following hospitalization, and reduced length of stay for preterms.

"This study demonstrates the important role that nurse scientists can play not only in helping families cope during a highly stressful period in their lives, but also in contributing to a family's long-term quality of life and well being," said Dr. Patricia A. Grady, Director, National Institute of Nursing Research.

The research team is continuing to follow these children and their parents to determine if these lower patterns of depressive and anxiety symptoms will continue over time through 3 years of age or escalate as developmental changes occur and lags in infant development are discovered.

Dr. Melnyk and her team point out that "interventions such as the COPE program, targeted to lessen depressive symptoms, are especially important in that depressed mothers have been found to be less responsive, affectionate, and positive during interactions with their infants, which leads to later adverse child outcomes. Specifically, maternal depression has been empirically linked with family violence, marital discord, impaired cognitive development, child abuse and neglect, and childhood mental health and behavior disorders." "Despite the high incidence of maternal depression in women with premature infants, these women rarely seek professional assistance for their condition, often unaware of their symptoms or minimizing them," they conclude.

Dr. Melnyk's key research collaborators include Dr. Nancy Feinstein, Dr. Linda Alpert-Gillis, Eileen Fairbanks, Dr. Hugh Crean, and Dr. Xin Tu, University of Rochester, New York; Dr. Leigh Small, Arizona State University College of Nursing and Healthcare Innovation; Dr. Robert Sinkin, The University of Virginia Medical Center; Dr. Steve Gross, Crouse Hospital in Syracuse, New York; and Dr. Pat Stone, Columbia University, New York.

The primary mission of the NINR, one of 27 Institutes and Centers at the National Institutes of Health, is to support clinical and basic research and establish a scientific basis for the care of individuals across the life span. For additional information, visit the NINR web site at http://ninr.nih.gov/.

The National Institutes of Health (NIH) — *The Nation's Medical Research Agency* — includes 27 Institutes and Centers and is a component of the U.S. Department of Health and Human Services. It is the primary federal agency for conducting and supporting basic, clinical and translational medical research, and it investigates the causes, treatments, and cures for both common and rare diseases. For more information about NIH and its programs, visit *www.nih.gov*.

Home > News & Events   E-mail this page   ☑ Subscribe to receive future NIH news releases

Example of a Successful Media Dissemination Effort: When Rocking Chairs in Nursing Homes Make the News[1]

Nancy Watson

I am the case study of what happens when the media strikes! I am going to tell you what it was like to have your research or your story picked up by the public press. It all began when I was sitting in my office and the phone rang. It was a person from the public relations (PR) office at the university where I worked. He had heard I was presenting my research about our rocking chair study at a conference, and he wanted to know about it. He had a research abstract but wanted me to explain it to him in laymen's terms.

The rocking chair study was directly aimed at improving the clinical problem that we examined in prior studies, the well-being of people with dementia in nursing homes. Our research team, led by the original principal investigator Dr. Thelma Wells, tried a simple intervention of using rocking to improve psychological well-being and improve balance.

What we found was that it worked. We were able to reduce anxiety/depression when the residents rocked long enough and also improve balance in those who seemed to like it. This study spoke directly to a clinical need that came straight from practice and has gone back to practice. We have received hundreds of requests for intervention teaching materials. It is exciting when an intervention actually changes practice in a variety of settings.

The PR representative asked really hard and very specific questions (e.g., "how many did people improve?" "how much did they improve in numerical terms?" and "what does that mean for a patient?"). These questions required rethinking and reframing, even recalculating numbers to recast the findings in a form that would be most easily understood by the average reader. The PR representative also asked why we thought rocking might be beneficial (i.e., what was the idea [theory] behind it, and what was the clinical hunch that led to it?). All of this was a preparation for the actual interviews that followed.

The press release came next. This document translated our research into a form that would hopefully catch the public's imagination. But, before the press release went out, I had to

[1] 2001 Sigma Theta Tau International Research Dissemination Award.

check it very carefully to make sure it was accurate. It was a bit of a culture shock to see our technical research reframed in terms that the public would care about. But that reframing was *key* to why our story was so far-reaching.

The first interview was with the Boston Globe's science reporter. I was scared to death. It was on the Thursday before the Saturday conference at which we were to present our research. The interview lasted about 40 minutes, I think, though it seemed like forever. Though the interview was intense, our PR representative had primed me well. I had a sheet of paper in front of me with all the bits and pieces of things I might need to have at my fingertips (e.g., sample size, significant findings with the statistics). I also had the citations for key supportive studies and the references for the theoretical basis of the study right in front of me…and I was glad I had them. The reporter actually wanted to know the *exact* citations that this work was based upon and wrote them down. I am certain the reporter must have looked them up as a way of being sure that we were "for real" and knew what we were talking about.

The reporter wanted to release the story before the "embargo" (i.e., an agreed upon time before which information about a study cannot be released) that was Saturday 12 noon when the study would be presented at the conference. The reporter really pushed, as he wanted to release the story for the Saturday morning paper, promising that he was sure he could get it on the front page of the Saturday edition. Our PR representative had told me to stand firm, so I did.

Low and behold, the story showed up on the front page of the Sunday edition. The Boston Globe headline was "Rock of Aged: Chairs' Sway May Soothe Ailing Elders." One important point is that they attributed the study to a nurse researcher. And this is no small point and not by accident. It was because I went to great pains to convince this reporter that this was important *to me*. I made it clear every time I talked to a reporter that I wanted him or her to be sure to mention that I was a nurse. I did not care about being a PhD, but the nurse part was very important to me.

Even on Saturday, the press release started the phone ringing. On the day of the conference, in between sessions, I was on a pay phone calling reporters back who were interested in the story. In addition, on that same day, two of the local networks picked up the story, and it quickly went national. San Francisco, New York City, Seattle, Los Angeles, Philadelphia, Boston, Richmond, Columbus, and Tulsa, to name a few, aired the story.

I think part of the reason the story got so much television coverage was because we had the pictures of people using the rocking chairs, and this made the story visually interesting. To use the pictures, we had to alert families, who had already given permission for the training video, that their loved one might be on television. This preparation was done ahead of time, when we first learned that this story might hit the press.

When the Boston Globe article hit on Sunday, things really heated up…and the phone was ringing off the hook. Our PR representative and I were tied at the hip! He could reach me anywhere; I had all his numbers and he had all my numbers, and he needed them.

The biggest thing that happened was that USA Today called on Sunday to do a story for the next morning. The reporter stated at 5 PM on Sunday evening that she had to talk to me *immediately*. I called her right back and we did the interview over the phone. The next morning the story was on the front page of the Life Style section of USA Today. I bought 10 copies (almost cleaned out the Seven-Eleven Store) and delivered copies to the nursing home that had been the study site. I left one for the Administrator and one for the Director of Nursing. I made sure to put one on the unit where we did the study.

The lesson to be learned here is that you have to act fast and be available to respond to the many reporters wanting to get the story out. USA Today was just ready to go to press when I called them back on Sunday. They were eager to get the story that the Boston Globe had scooped in their next day's edition. So being *reachable* and *ready* made the difference.

The next week was wild. Most notable were the radio reports and interviews on most of the major networks, including a long interview with the BBC that aired worldwide. These interviews included such questions as "how could people living the jungle fashion somewhat to rock—like a swing in a tree?" So I had to translate the principles of the rocking experience into terms that could be applied in a very foreign culture. This was a wonderful opportunity to reach a worldwide audience. I again told the reporter that it was really important to me that he mention that I was a nurse.

The next onslaught came from the wire services, wanting to pick up the story, including Reuters, Associated Press, and UPI. As a result of the wire services running the story, newspaper articles popped up everywhere. We had alumni sending us articles from their local papers from across the country. This spin-off effect was very exciting. But there was also a feeling that the story was taking on a life of its own; and it *was*!

Next, Time Magazine wanted to pick up the story and included a piece in their "GOOD NEWS" Health Report about 3 weeks later. It was attributed to the Eastern Nursing Research Society, thus, keeping the nursing connection. Websites were also picking up the story, including ABC, CBS, Associated Press, and NewsDay. These stories also involved interviews with freelance writers who would call and need to talk to us directly to get their *own* spin on the story. To be prepared, I needed to keep my notes out and ready for these calls too.

One of the most meaningful articles was the one in the Alzheimer's Association's Advances for families and caregivers. It was significant because it directly reached the people who needed it most, the people who love and care for persons with dementia, and that really meant a lot. This story lent real credibility to our work. Families and caregivers saw that nurses were important contributors to the effort to care for those persons with dementia.

That is how my story unfolded and some of what it is like to be caught up in the maelstrom of the public press. It was harrowing; it was very exciting; and it was rewarding. It was an opportunity to get the research to the people who could truly use it, and that made it worth it. My experience may not be typical, but I learned a lot from it. I hope that some of my experience may help you prepare for a similar experience with your work.

A science reporter for the university PR department calling on that April day enabled this to happen. He really walked me through it, and as a novice to this process, I really appreciated his sage advice. You may wonder how everything turned out and what happened as a result of our media attention. Our experience with the rocking chair study served to get the word out that nurses do research that matters. Nursing, having waited long and hard, had an opportunity to have the work nurses do be recognized!

But more than that, the initial coverage has continued to have a ripple effect. Recently, I did a live interview, via phone, with a news radio in London about the use of rocking chairs to relieve stress. For the last 5 years, I have had reporters call periodically wanting to know about whether or not rocking might be good for older people in general or if rockers in airports are a good idea. These questions stretch beyond our research, but that is fine. What I say is that our research was on people with dementia, but it is possible that it *could* have application for older persons, *BUT WE DO NOT KNOW THAT FROM OUR* RESEARCH. Nevertheless, it is good to be asked and to be willing to help the reporter to be able to reference for their his or her piece in a different context.

In addition to the continuing ripple effect with the media, we have gotten numerous phone calls from families, clinicians, and entrepreneurs. First, you would be surprised how many people (i.e., the entrepreneurs) have created rocking devices and contacted us wanting an endorsement. Our stand has always been that we cannot endorse specific products, only the idea that there *may* be value in rocking that is *self-propelled*. Our experience is somewhat typical in this respect, as press coverage may result in this type of response quite often, and you need to be ready for it. One variation on the calls from entrepreneurs has been the calls from the sales representatives from the company that manufactured the chair we used in the study. They have been interested in using our research to recommend that particular chair. However, we have taken the position that there are many chairs that meet the basic requirements that could be used safely for rocking *not* just one brand. We have tried not to let our research be used for promotional purposes.

The families we have heard from have been our real joy. We have had phone calls from families with loved ones at home and in nursing homes, all wanting to know "what rocking chair we used" and if they should get one for their family member. These calls are our reward. They are our opportunity to make our research really matter. We have an opportunity to talk one to one with caregivers and to explain to them how to go about it and what to look for in a chair. As a part of our funding, we already had created a video to teach people how to select a chair, orient a person to the chair and teach them to rock. So, when families called, we were ready with the video and clear written instructions to help them.

We also have had calls from nurses and other professionals, asking questions about using rocking chairs in their facilities. We have heard from nurses working in nursing homes, in psychiatric facilities, and in Veterans Administration (VA) hospitals. They have reported wonderful success with the rocking therapy, especially in calming people down when they are acutely upset. That is something that we observed anecdotally but did not study directly.

Here is one testimonial that we just received this past August. It is from an Occupational Therapist (OT) working at the VA system in California. She wrote, "Thank you very much for sending the video. Yesterday, I gave an inservice on Rocking Chair Therapy. It was such a huge success that three units — dementia, nursing home and hospice — would like to implement rocking chairs *ASAP*. I was able to get one [of the manufacture's chairs] for a trial use for one month. The manufacture's representative drove up from Southern California to deliver the chair to me the day before the inservice. I did a [slide] presentation, the chair was on display and I showed a two-minute clip of your video. Tomorrow, I am giving an inservice to the dementia nurses to implement the one rocking chair.

Today, my OT supervisor and I spent one hour with one of [our] more difficult dementia patient[s] and had him rock in the chair. At first, it wasn't working, but we gave him a teddy bear. Oh it was, incredible! He didn't want to leave the chair. He just kept on rocking. The patient has three children and maybe he thought he was rocking one of them. We're planning another rocking session with him tomorrow. I just want to thank you for all your great work on the rocking chair study and I want you to know that I know it is going to benefit the west coast VA sites in many positive ways. Again, thank you and I will keep you informed of our progress."

This is just one example of what we are still hearing. This truly is our reward. The media coverage has helped us get a clinical innovation out to the world in much shorter time than the usual 17 years that it takes to change clinical practice. It has communicated the "evidence" to those who can use it. The research article (Watson, Wells & Cox, 1998) is important to communicate the science to the professionals, but the public media is how this simple idea of rocking has been so widely disseminated, to all those it affects, professional and lay persons.

Based on our experience, the media is an important tool for nurses to use in communicating their research and in making our practice more evidence-based. I hope you will have the opportunity to use it to get your story out too.

reference

Watson, N.W., Wells, T.J. & Cox, C. (1998). Rocking chair therapy for dementia patients: Its effect on psychosocial well-being and balance, *American Journal of Alzheimer's Disease 13*(6), 296–308.

Example of an Approved Consent Form for a Study

Freshman Five to Thrive: COPE (Creating Opportunities for Personal Empowerment)/ Healthy Lifestyles

ID#_____

Freshman Five to Thrive: COPE (Creating Opportunities for Personal Empowerment)/ Healthy Lifestyles

College Student Consent Form
Arizona State University

Introduction
The purposes of this form are to provide you (as a prospective research study partici-pant) information that may affect your decision as to whether or not to participate in this research and to record the consent of those who agree to be involved in the study. We are asking you to take part in a research study because we are trying to learn more about choices that college students make and how these choices affect their health.

Researchers
Dr. Bernadette Melnyk PhD, RN, CPNP/NPP, FAAN, College of Nursing & Healthcare Innovation and her research staff have invited you to participate in this research study.

Study Purpose
The purpose of this intervention study is to evaluate the effects of a healthy life-styles program on the physical and mental health outcomes of college freshman.

Description of Research Study
The information from this study will be given to you in the Freshman Five to Thrive course you have enrolled in. Course content in the course you have enrolled in will remain as described in the course syllabus and the university's schedule of classes. The class will include different information about making your college experience a happy, successful and fulfilling one.

If you agree to participate in the study, you will be asked to complete questionnaires (a written set of questions), which will take approximately one to two hours. You will be asked questions that may be sensitive to answer. If you are uncomfortable answering a question, then it will be ok to leave the answer blank. You will be asked to complete questionnaires at the beginning of the semester, at the end of the semester (Class #14), 6 months after the end of the semester and yearly thereafter for 4 years or until you receive your undergraduate degree or withdraw from the university for a total of no more than 6 years. Your participation will take approximately the 14 weeks

ASU IRB
Approved
Sign_____
Date_____

Initials _____

Freshman Five to Thrive: COPE (Creating Opportunities for Personal Empowerment)/ Healthy Lifestyles

ID#_____

(42 hours classroom time) of the class semester, one to two hours 6 months after the end of the semester and one to two hours yearly (maximum 6 years) thereafter until graduation or withdrawal from the university. You will be requested to wear a pedometer as a requirement for this course. As a study participant, you will be asked to record the number of steps you take each day. Approximately 75 subjects will be participating in this study on the Tempe campus of Arizona State University.

You may not participate in this study if you have any physical medical condition(s) that prevents you from performing regular physical exercise. This includes, for example, any pre-existing cardiac conditions or pregnancy. Withdrawal from the course during the semester will also exclude you from further participation in the study.

Your height and weight will be measured at the beginning of the study and at the end of the semester (prior to Class #14), 6 months after the end of the semester and yearly (maximum 6 years) thereafter until undergraduate graduation or withdrawal from the university. We will check your weight and height in a private area in the LivWELL Assessment Center in the Student Recreation Center at ASU.

Risks

You may feel uncomfortable completing study questionnaires that ask personal or sensitive information. You may leave any question unanswered if you so choose without affecting your participation in the study. Physical activities are planned in this course which will increase your heart and respiratory rate but will not reach the intensity as to prevent you from carrying on a comfortable conversation with research staff and faculty. You will be educated as to the signs and symptoms of exceeding comfortable exertion levels and research personnel will monitor class physical activity.

Benefits

Scores on one of the questionnaires may indicate moderate or extremely elevated anxiety and depression. You will be immediately notified if this occurs and we will support you in seeking mental health evaluation and treatment at the student health center, by Dr. Bernadette Melnyk or, if not in immediate danger of self-harm, by a mental health provider of your own choosing or from a list of providers that will be given to you.

Acquisition of knowledge will be provided in each of the classes concerning lifestyle choices and life management will increase coping, promote self-efficacy and build beliefs/confidence in your ability to adapt to the stresses of your environment. As a result, you should be able to persist in your education, graduate from college, and become a healthy member of society.

Confidentiality

Confidentiality of student responses will be maintained at all times. All physical measurements will be kept private. All study materials collected by the research staff will be identified with a coded number in order to separate your name from study materials. Any personal information that can be linked with your study materials will be locked in the research office and only project coordinators will have access to this information.

Initials _____

Freshman Five to Thrive: COPE (Creating Opportunities for Personal Empowerment)/ Healthy Lifestyles

ID#_____

All information obtained in this study is strictly confidential. The results of this study may be used in reports, presentations, and publications but the researchers will not identify you and the results will be reported in aggregate (together with other subjects).

Withdrawal Privilege

You do not have to be in this study. If you do not participate in the study, you will still receive the usual classroom course content as described in the course catalog and syllabus. No one will be angry at you if you decide not to participate in this study. Even if you start the study, you can stop later if you want. Your grade in your class will not be affected if you decide not to participate in the study. You may ask questions about the study at any time.

Costs and Payments

In order to recognize your contribution to this research study, you can receive up to $80 in gift cards for participating for the entire length of the study. $10 in a gift card will be given after the completion of the first set of questionnaires at the beginning of the semester and at the completion of the semester (Class #14) (Total $20). Six months after the end of the semester and at yearly follow up data collection points (maximum 6 years) or until undergraduate graduation or withdrawal from the university, you will earn $10 in a gift card for completing questionnaires and reporting your height and weight (Maximum Total of $60). It will not cost you anything to participate in this study.

Compensation for Illness and Injury

If you agree to participate in the study, then your consent does not waive any of your legal rights. However, in the event of harm or injury arising from this study, neither Arizona State University nor the researchers are able to give you any money, insurance coverage, free medical care, or any compensation for such injury.

Voluntary Consent

Any questions you have concerning the research study or your participation in the study, before or after your consent, will be answered by Dr. Bernadette Melnyk, 500 N. 3rd Street, Phoenix, AZ 85004, 602-496-2200. You may also contact the project coordinator, Diana Jacobson MS, RN, CPNP, 500 N. 3rd Street, Phoenix, AZ 85004, 602-496-0863 with any questions.

If you have questions about your rights as a subject/participant in this research or if you feel you have been placed at risk, you can contact the Chair of the Human Subject Institutional Review Board, through the ASU Research Compliance Office, at 480-965-6788.

Your signature below indicates that you have read this form and consent to be in this study.

Subject's Signature _____

Printed first and last name _____

Date_____

Initials _____

Freshman Five to Thrive: COPE (Creating Opportunities for Personal Empowerment)/ Healthy Lifestyles

ID#_____

Investigator's Statement

"I certify that I have explained to the above individual the nature and purpose, the potential benefits and possible risks associated with participation in this research study, have answered any questions that have been raised, and have witnessed the above signature. These elements of Informed Consent conform to the Assurance given by Arizona State University to the Office for Human Research Protections to protect the rights of human subjects. I have provided the subject/participant with a copy of this signed consent document".

Signature of Investigator _____

Printed first and last name _____

Date_____

appendix J

Initials _____

A Data and Safety Monitoring Plan for an Intervention Study

Study: Improving Outcomes of LBW Premature Infants and Parents

Funded by the National Institutes of Health/National Institute of Nursing Research (R01#NR05077)
Principal Investigator (PI): Melnyk, Bernadette; Coinvestigators: Alpert-Gillis, Linda and Feinstein, Nancy Fischbeck

Data and Safety Monitoring Plan

The potential risk of this clinical trial is considered to be minimal because of the nature of the intervention. The study has no adverse events expected for participants based upon the pilot study. Since this grant application fits in the category of Clinical Trial (Phase II) study, we developed a plan for appropriate oversight and monitoring of the conduct of the clinical trial to ensure the safety of the participants and the validity and integrity of the data.

(a) The PI had already obtained the policies of the University of Rochester internal review board (IRB) specifically regarding the adverse events associated with clinical trials. The PIs will adhere to those policies and maintain a copy of the policies in the study file.

(b) The PI will meet with the research assistants and the coinvestigators on a biweekly basis during the data collection phase and identify any risks of adverse effects resulting from the data collection process and data review.

(c) The PI, coinvestigators, and consultants will make decisions about necessary protocol and operational changes based on discussion and review of data and the data collection process. Any proposed changes in the consent form or research procedures resulting from the report will be prepared/identified by the PI and submitted with the report to the IRB for approval.

(d) The following policies required by our IRB and National Institutes of Health (NIH) will be adhered to: (1) any adverse events that are serious and unexpected and are related (possibly or probably) to the study will be reported to the IRB and NIH within 15 calendar days; (2) adverse events that are both unexpected and related that either are life threatening or result in death will be reported to IRB and NIH immediately; and (3) adverse events that do not meet the criteria above will be documented in the summary report submitted to the IRB and NIH annually at the time of the study's continuing review. Because the proposed study has a low risk intervention, we do not anticipate any serious adverse effects described in the first two categories from a result of participating in this study.

(e) The PI will ensure that the NIH (funding Institute and Center) is informed of actions, if any, taken by the IRB as a result of its continuing review, and recommendations that emanate from the monitoring activities.

(f) The Rochester site will be responsible for reporting adverse events or unanticipated problems involving risks to subjects or others to the local IRB. If problems are considered related to the trial, the IRB at the Syracuse site will also be notified.

(g) The PI will be responsible for the monitoring of this plan throughout the life of the study.

System-Wide ARCC Evidence-Based Practice Mentor Role Description

ORGANIZATIONAL CULTURE	1. <u>Role Responsibilities</u>: Assesses organization for readiness & sustainability of an EBP culture with valid & reliable instruments Activities include, but are not limited to: ▪ Evaluates decision making pattern across disciplines ▪ Reviews and leads revision of philosophy to reflect EBP ▪ Establishes a critical mass of healthcare providers with knowledge & skills in EBP ▪ Conducts other ARCC interventions (e.g., journal club, EBP rounds) to foster an EBP culture
	Feedback:
PROFESSIONAL PRACTICE	2. <u>Role responsibilities</u>: Stimulates, facilitates, and educates nursing staff toward a culture of evidence-based practice. Activities include, but are not limited to: • Leads regularly scheduled classes with varying levels of complexity to educate point-of-care staff about using evidence in practice • Provides in-house projects to foster point-of-care staff's use of external & internal evidence in making clinical decisions
	Feedback:
INTERNAL & EXTERNAL EVIDENCE	3. <u>Role responsibilities</u>: Mentors point-of-care staff in generating evidence through participating in studies and outcome management, evidence-based QI, and EBP implementation projects. Activities include, but are not limited to: • Assists with study or project design and proposal development • Facilitates data analysis for research and evidence-based implementation & QI projects • Develops and sustains processes that facilitate corroboration of internal & external evidence
	Feedback:
TEAMWORK	4. <u>Role Responsibilities</u>: Acts as Chair or Co-chair for House-wide Evidence-based Practice Committee Activities include, but are not limited to: • Collaborates with co-chair in planning agenda that is focused on house-wide clinical issues • Reviews ongoing research and QI projects at each meeting • Facilitates teamwork on house-wide evidence-implementation projects • Discusses implications of project outcome data for future practice & policy change
	Feedback:
INTER-DISCIPLINARY TEAM COLLABORATION	5. <u>Role Responsibilities</u>: Collaborates & fosters collaboration among healthcare providers in the use of evidence in clinical decision-making. Activities include, but are not limited to: • Discusses practice concerns with various clinician groups to foster best practices • Participates in interdisciplinary groups in relation to use of research in decision-making activities.
	Feedback:
ACADEMIC & SERVICE PARTNERSHIP	6. <u>Role Responsibilities</u>: Serves as a liaison between hospital and university professors. Activities include, but are not limited to: • Solicits and facilitates collaborative research opportunities with university professors • Partners with university professors in development of nursing research proposals
	Feedback:
KNOWLEDGE TRANSLATION	7. <u>Role Responsibilities</u>: Uses external & internal evidence to foster best practice . Activities include, but are not limited to: • Translates external & internal evidence for point-of-care staff in clinical decision-making • Uses external & internal evidence to stimulate change in standards of practice.
	Feedback:
RETURN ON INVESTMENT (ROI) FOR EBP	8. <u>Role Responsibilities</u>: Fosters & assists with measurement of outcomes based on evidence. Activities include, but are not limited to: ▪ Administers budget for EBP implementation (QI) & research generation ▪ Generates income through contributions/grants/ participation in research generation with various academic and other partners
	Feedback:

Timeline for an ARCC EBP Implementation Project

An electronic copy of the ARCC EBP Implementation Plan can be found on the accompanying CD-ROM.

ARCC EBP Implementation Plan

PICOT Question:		
Team Members		
EBP Mentor & Contact Info		
Preliminary Checkpoint	○ Who are the stakeholders for your project ○ Active (on the implementation team) & Supportive (not on the team, but essential to success) ○ identify project team roles & leadership ○ Begin acquisition of any necessary approvals for project implementation and dissemination (e.g., system leadership, unit leadership, ethics board [IRB]) ○ ***Begin relationship with EBP Mentor***	Notes:
Checkpoint One	○ Hone PICOT question & assure team is prepared ○ Build EBP knowledge & skills ○ ***Begin relationship with EBP Mentor***	Notes:
Checkpoint Two	○ Conduct literature search & retain studies that meet criteria for inclusion ○ Connect with librarian ○ Meet with implementation group - TEAM BUILD ○ ***Begin relationship with EBP Mentor***	Notes:
Checkpoint Three	○ Critically appraise literature ○ Meet with group to discuss how completely evidence answers question; pose follow-up questions and re-review the literature as necessary ○ ***Begin relationship with EBP Mentor***	Notes:
Checkpoint Four	○ Meet with group ○ Summarize evidence with focus on implications for practice & conduct interviews with content experts as necessary to benchmark ○ Begin formulating detailed plan for implementation of evidence ○ Include who must know about the project, when they will know, how they will know ○ ***Begin relationship with EBP Mentor***	Notes:

appendices

Checkpoint Five	o Define project purpose- connect the evidence & the project o Define baseline data collection source(s) (e.g., existing dataset, electronic health record), methods, & measures o Define post project outcome indicators of a successful project o Gather outcome measures o Write data collection protocol o Write the project protocol (data collection fits in this document) o Finalize any necessary approvals for project implementation & dissemination (e.g., system leadership, unit leadership, IRB) o ***Begin relationship with EBP Mentor***	Notes:
Checkpoint Six (about mid-way)	o Meet with implementation group o Discuss known barriers & facilitators of project o Discuss strategies for minimizing barriers & maximizing facilitators o Finalize protocol for implementation of evidence o Identify resources (human, fiscal, & other) necessary to complete project o Supply EBP Mentor with written IRB approval & managerial support o Begin work on poster for dissemination of initiation of project & progress to date to educate stakeholders about project - get help from support staff o Include specific plan for how evaluation will take place: who, what, when, where & how and communication mechanisms to stakeholders o ***Begin relationship with EBP Mentor***	Notes:
Checkpoint Seven	o Meet with implementation group to review proposed poster o Make final adjustment to poster with support staff o Inform stakeholders of start date of implementation & poster presentation o Address nay concerns or questions of stakeholders (active & supportive) o ***Begin relationship with EBP Mentor***	Notes:

Checkpoint Eight	○ Poster presentation (preferred event is a system-wide recognition of quality, research or innovation) ○ LAUNCH EBP implementation project ○ *Begin relationship with EBP Mentor*	Notes:
Checkpoint Nine	○ Mid-project meet with all key stake-holders to review progress & provide outcomes to date. ○ Review issues, successes, aha's, & triumphs of project to date. ○ *Begin relationship with EBP Mentor*	Notes:
Checkpoint Ten	○ Complete final data collection for project evaluation ○ Present project results via poster presentation - locally & nationally ○ *Celebrate with EBP Mentor & Agency Leadership*	Notes:
Checkpoint Eleven	○ Review project progress, lessons learned, new questions generated from process ○ *Consult with EBP Mentor about new questions*	Notes:

©*Fineout-Overholt, 2009 This form may be used for educational purposes without permission. If you use it for your practice change, please let us know by emailing ellen@transforminghealthcarewitharcc.com*

Instruments to Evaluate Organizational Culture and Readiness for System-Wide Integration of EBP, EBP Beliefs, and EBP Implementation with Psychometrics

Organizational Culture & Readiness for System-Wide Integration of Evidence-based Practice Survey

Below are 18 questions about evidence-based practice (EBP). Please consider the culture of your organization and its readiness for system wide implementation of EBP and indicate which answer best describes your response to each question. There are no right or wrong answers.

Item	None at All	A Little	Somewhat	Moderately	Very Much
1. To what extent is EBP clearly described as central to the mission and philosophy of your institution?	1	2	3	4	5
2. To what extent do you believe that EBP is practiced in your organization?	1	2	3	4	5
3. To what extent is the nursing staff with whom you work committed to EBP?	1	2	3	4	5
4. To what extent is the physician team with whom you work committed to EBP?	1	2	3	4	5
5. To what extent are there administrators within your organization committed to EBP (i.e., have planned for resources and support [e.g., time] to initiate EBP)?	1	2	3	4	5
6. In your organization, to what extent is there a critical mass of nurses who have strong EBP knowledge and skills?	1	2	3	4	5
7. To what extent are there nurse scientists (doctorally prepared researchers) in your organization to assist in generation of evidence when it does not exist?	1	2	3	4	5
8. In your organization, to what extent are there Advanced Practiced Nurses who are EBP mentors for staff nurses as well as other APNs?	1	2	3	4	5
9. To what extent do practitioners model EBP in their clinical settings?	1	2	3	4	5
10. To what extent do staff nurses have access to quality computers and access to electronic databases for searching for best evidence?	1	2	3	4	5
11. To what extent do staff nurses have proficient computer skills?	1	2	3	4	5
12. To what extent do librarians within your organization have EBP knowledge and skills?	1	2	3	4	5
13. To what extent are librarians used to search for evidence?	1	2	3	4	5
14. To what extent are fiscal resources used to support EBP (e.g., education-attending EBP conferences/workshops, computers, paid time for the EBP process, mentors)	1	2	3	4	5
15. To what extent are there EBP champions (i.e., those who will go the extra mile to advance EBP) in the environment among:					
a. Administrators?	1	2	3	4	5
b. Physicians?	1	2	3	4	5
c. Nurse Educators?	1	2	3	4	5
d. Advance Nurse Practitioners?	1	2	3	4	5
e. Staff Nurses?	1	2	3	4	5
16. To what extent is the measurement and sharing of outcomes part of the culture of the organization in which you work?	1	2	3	4	5

Item	None	25%	50%	75%	100%
17. To what extent are decisions generated from:					
a. direct care providers?	1	2	3	4	5
b. upper administration?	1	2	3	4	5
c. physician or other healthcare provider groups?	1	2	3	4	5

Item	Not ready	Getting Ready	Been Ready but Not Acting	Ready to Go	Past Ready & onto Action
18. Overall, how would you rate your institution in readiness for EBP	1	2	3	4	5
19. Compared to 6 months ago, how much movement in your organization has there been toward an EBP culture. (place a hatch mark on the line to the right that indicates your response)	None ———————————————— A Great Deal				

EBP Beliefs Scale

Below are 16 statements about evidence-based practice (EBP). Please circle the number that best describes your agreement or disagreement with each statement. There are no right or wrong answers.

	Strongly Disagree	Disagree	Neither Agree nor Disagree	Agree	Strongly Agree
1. I believe that EBP results in the best clinical care for patients.	1	2	3	4	5
2. I am clear about the steps of EBP.	1	2	3	4	5
3. I am sure that I can implement EBP.	1	2	3	4	5
4. I believe that critically appraising evidence is an important step in the EBP process.	1	2	3	4	5
5. I am sure that evidence-based guidelines can improve clinical care	1	2	3	4	5
6. I believe that I can search for the best evidence to answer clinical questions in a time efficient way.	1	2	3	4	5
7. I believe that I can overcome barriers in implementing EBP.	1	2	3	4	5
8. I am sure that I can implement EBP in a time efficient way.	1	2	3	4	5
9. I am sure that implementing EBP will improve the care that I deliver to my patients.	1	2	3	4	5
10. I am sure about how to measure the outcomes of clinical care.	1	2	3	4	5
11. I believe that EBP takes too much time.	1	2	3	4	5
12. I am sure that I can access the best resources in order to implement EBP.	1	2	3	4	5
13. I believe EBP is difficult.	1	2	3	4	5
14. I know how to implement EBP sufficiently enough to make practice changes.	1	2	3	4	5
15. I am confident about my ability to implement EBP where I work.	1	2	3	4	5
16. I believe the care that I deliver is evidence-based.	1	2	3	4	5

EBP Implementation Scale

Below are 18 questions about evidence-based practice (EBP). Some healthcare providers do some of these things more often than other healthcare providers. There is no certain frequency in which you should be performing these tasks. Please answer each question by circling the number that best describes **how often each item has applied to you in the past 8 weeks**.

In the **past 8 weeks**, I have:

	0 times	1-3 times	4-5 times	6-7 times	8 or more times
1. Used evidence to change my clinical practice…	0	1	2	3	4
2. Critically appraised evidence from a research study…	0	1	2	3	4
3. Generated a PICO question about my clinical practice…	0	1	2	3	4
4. Informally discussed evidence from a research study with a colleague...	0	1	2	3	4
5. Collected data on a patient problem...	0	1	2	3	4
6. Shared evidence from a study or studies in the form of a report or presentation to more than 2 colleagues…	0	1	2	3	4
7. Evaluated the outcomes of a practice change…	0	1	2	3	4
8. Shared an EBP guideline with a colleague…	0	1	2	3	4
9. Shared evidence from a research study with a patient/family member…	0	1	2	3	4
10. Shared evidenced from a research study with a multi-disciplinary team member…	0	1	2	3	4
11. Read and critically appraised a clinical research study…	0	1	2	3	4
12. Accessed the Cochrane database of systematic reviews…	0	1	2	3	4
13. Accessed the National Guidelines Clearinghouse…	0	1	2	3	4
14. Used an EBP guideline or systematic review to change clinical practice where I work…	0	1	2	3	4
15. Evaluated a care initiative by collecting patient outcome data…	0	1	2	3	4
16 Shared the outcome data collected with colleagues…	0	1	2	3	4
17. Changed practice based on patient outcome data…	0	1	2	3	4
18. Promoted the use of EBP to my colleagues…	0	1	2	3	4

The Evidence-Based Practice Beliefs and Implementation Scales: Psychometric Properties of Two New Instruments

Bernadette Mazurek Melnyk, RN, PhD, CPNP/NPP, FAAN, FNAP, Ellen Fineout-Overholt, RN, PhD, FNAP, Mary Z. Mays, PhD

ABSTRACT

Background: Implementation of evidence-based practice (EBP) by health professionals is a key strategy for improving health care quality and patient outcomes as well as increasing professional role satisfaction. However, it is estimated that only a small percentage of nurses and other health care providers are consistently using this approach to clinical practice.

Aim: The aim of this study was to report on the development and psychometric properties of two new scales: (1) the 16-item EBP Beliefs Scale that allows measurement of a person's beliefs about the value of EBP and the ability to implement it, and (2) the 18-item EBP Implementation Scale that allows measurement of the extent to which EBP is implemented.

Methods: Nurses (N = 394) attending continuing education workshops volunteered to complete the scales. Data were analysed to evaluate reliability and validity of both instruments.

Results: Cronbach's alpha was > .90 for each scale. Principal components analysis indicated that each scale allowed measurement of a unidimensional construct. Strength of EBP beliefs and the extent of EBP implementation increased as educational level increased ($p < .001$) and as responsibility in the workplace increased ($p < .001$).

Conclusion: In this study, initial evidence was provided to support the reliability and validity of the EBP Beliefs and Implementation Scales in a heterogeneous sample of practicing nurses.

Evidence to Action: Use of the scales in future research could generate evidence to guide EBP implementation strategies in practice and education. Results could establish the extent to which EBP is being implemented and its effect on clinician satisfaction and patient outcomes.

KEYWORDS evidence-based practice, measurement, reliability, validity, nursing, beliefs

Worldviews on Evidence-Based Nursing 2008; 5(4):208–216. Copyright ©2008 Sigma Theta Tau International

Evidence-based practice (EBP) is a problem-solving approach to the delivery of care that incorporates the best evidence from well-designed studies in combination with a clinician's expertise and patients' preferences within a context of caring (Sackett et al. 2000; Melnyk & Fineout-Overholt 2005b). Because there has been support for better outcomes as a result of evidence-based versus tradition-based care (Heater et al. 1988; Grimshaw et al. 2006), national and federal organisations as well as recent summit meetings held by the Institute of Medicine and leaders of health care professions have recommended its teaching and implementation (Greiner & Knebel 2003; Melnyk et al. 2005). However, the uptake by health care professionals of research findings into practice and implementation of EBP has been slow and inconsistent because of multiple intra-personal and environmental barriers (Eccles et al. 2005; Fineout-Overholt et al. 2005; Parahoo 2000).

Findings from a recent survey to assess nurses' readiness to engage in EBP conducted by the Nursing Informatics Expert Panel of the American Academy of Nursing with a United States' (U.S.) sample of 1,097 randomly selected registered nurses indicated that: (1) almost half were not familiar with the term "EBP," (2) more than half reported that they did not believe their colleagues use research

Bernadette Mazurek Melnyk, Dean and Distinguished Foundation Professor in Nursing, **Ellen Fineout-Overholt**, Clinical Associate Professor and Director, Center for the Advancement of Evidence-Based Practice, **Mary Z. Mays**, Associate Professor, Arizona State University College of Nursing & Healthcare Innovation, Phoenix, Arizona. Address correspondence to Bernadette Mazurek Melnyk, Arizona State University College of Nursing & Healthcare Innovation, 500 North 3rd Street, Phoenix, AZ 85004; Bernadette.Melnyk@asu.edu

Accepted 4 October 2007
Copyright ©2008 Sigma Theta Tau International
1545-102X/08

findings in practice, (3) only 27% of the respondents had been taught how to use electronic databases, (4) most do not search information databases (e.g., Medline and CINAHL) to gather practice information, and (5) those who search these resources do not believe they have adequate searching skills (Pravikoff et al. 2005). As a result of these findings, along with other major barriers to EBP (e.g., lack of EBP mentors, negative attitudes toward research, inadequate resources at the point of care, competing priorities, perceived lack of time to implement EBP) (Kajermo et al. 2000; Fineout-Overholt et al. 2005; Hutchinson & Johnson 2006), it is estimated that it takes approximately 17 years to translate research findings into clinical practice to improve patients' outcomes (Balas & Boren 2000).

Furthermore, there is a crisis in nursing workforce shortages in several countries throughout the world. The crux of this shortage is largely two-fold: (1) too few nurses, and (2) dissatisfaction with work environments that do not support professional nursing practice.

The demands placed upon nurses as a result of the shortage have led to increasing reports of job dissatisfaction and intent to leave the profession. Research has shown that while most nurses are committed to their profession, they are highly dissatisfied with their work environments (U.S. General Accounting Office 2001). In one study, 23% of nurses reported intending to leave the profession with another 37% uncertain of their future (Larrabee et al. 2003). High turnover rates are very costly to the health care system and negatively affect patient outcomes (Vahey et al. 2004). The Nurse Reinvestment Act (NRA, PL 107–205[h1]) indicates that nurse dissatisfaction contributes to the nursing shortage, and that retention might be increased and patient outcomes improved by nurse involvement in evidence-based clinical decision making.

Although only a few studies have provided direct evidence, clinicians who use research evidence in their practices are more satisfied with their role and their patients have better clinical outcomes (Ciliska et al. 1996; Retsas 2000; Maljanian et al. 2002). In addition, anecdotal reports from nurses support that providing evidence-based care (EBC) renews the professional spirit of the nurse, a key variable in professional satisfaction. EBP also supports nurses to become "strong patient advocates, focused on improving the quality of the care given to patients" (Strout 2005, p. 39).

Future investigations of the effect of EBP on clinical care and job satisfaction could be facilitated by instruments to measure: (1) the strength of beliefs in EBP, and (2) the extent to which EBP is implemented. Therefore, the purpose of this study was to begin validation of two new instruments: (1) a 16-item EBP Beliefs Scale that allows measurement of an individual's beliefs about the value of EBP

and the ability to implement it; and (2) an 18-item EBP Implementation Scale that allows measurement of the extent of actual EBP implementation.

The Theoretical Model that Guided Development of the Two EBP Scales

The transtheoretical model of health behaviour change (Prochaska & Velicer 1997), which is now being extended to the field of organisational change, and the ARCC (Advancing Research and Clinical practice through close Collaboration) model (Melnyk & Fineout-Overholt 2002) guided development of the two EBP scales. The transtheoretical model has five stages that show the process through which an individual makes a change in behaviour (i.e., pre-contemplation, contemplation, preparation, action, and maintenance; Prochaska & Velicer 1997). Within this model are 10 processes that might produce a change in actual behaviour, including three that show the following cognitive beliefs: (1) appreciating that the change is important to one's success (i.e., self-re-evaluation), (2) believing that a change can succeed and making a firm commitment to the change (i.e., self-liberation), and (3) appreciating that the change will have a positive effect on the work environment (i.e., environmental re-evaluation; Prochaska et al. 2001). From this theory, the literature and the ARCC model, a 52-item descriptive survey was developed by the first two authors and used in a previous study with 160 nurses who were attending EBP workshops in the Northeast region of the U.S. (Melnyk et al. 2004a). The 52-item survey tapped nurses' demographic variables as well as their knowledge and beliefs about EBP, the extent to which they implemented EBP, and barriers and facilitators to EBP implementation. Seven items on the 52-item survey specifically assessed nurses' knowledge, beliefs, and ability to implement EBP. Findings from this survey indicated that nurses who held stronger beliefs about the value of EBP and their ability to implement it reported a higher level of implementation than did nurses with weaker EBP beliefs. Therefore, in an attempt to more fully study EBP beliefs and their relationship to EBP implementation, three items from the 52-item descriptive survey that tapped beliefs about EBP served as the foundation for an expanded 16-item EBP Beliefs instrument.

The EBP Beliefs Scale also was adapted from previous beliefs scales developed by Melnyk (1994) and Melnyk et al. (2001, 2006) and was specifically designed to measure a clinicians' beliefs about the value of EBP and their beliefs/confidence in implementing it in practice. The constructs of self-re-evaluation, self-liberation, and environmental re-evaluation from the transtheoretical model of change also were incorporated into the scale. The relationship between an individual's beliefs/confidence about his

appendix N

563

or her ability to implement certain behaviours and actual implementation of those behaviours has been empirically supported in many studies (Melnyk 1995; Melnyk et al. 2001; Arora et al. 2005; Reynolds & Magnan 2005; Melnyk et al. 2006; Rhodes & Plotnikoff 2006).

The ARCC model was first conceptualised in 1999 as a system-wide implementation model of EBP. ARCC is guided by control theory (Carver & Scheier 1982, 1998), which contends that a discrepancy between a standard or goal (e.g., system-wide implementation of EBP) and a current state (e.g., the extent to which an organisation is implementing EBP) will motivate behaviours to reach the standard or goal. However, in health care organisations, many barriers exist that inhibit nurses and other health care professionals from implementing EBP. In the ARCC Model, strategies are implemented (e.g., EBP mentors who assist clinicians with implementation of EBP and providing EBP skills building workshops) to remove barriers so that nurses and other health care providers can implement EBC in order to achieve system-wide implementation.

The first step to system-wide implementation of EBC in ARCC is an organisational assessment of readiness and the context for EBP so that the strengths and barriers in a system can be identified. Inherent to successful advancement of EBP in the system is the key role of an EBP mentor, an advanced practice nurse who has in-depth skills in EBP as well as working knowledge of how to remove barriers to organisational change. Mentorship with direct-care nurses on clinical units by the EBP mentors throughout the system is important in strengthening nurses' beliefs about the value of EBC and their ability to implement it. Evidence from previous research has supported the premise that when nurses have stronger beliefs about their ability to implement EBP, implementation of EBC is higher than when they have weaker beliefs (Melnyk et al. 2005). Continued research on these issues will be facilitated by instruments that allow systematic measurement of EBP beliefs and implementation.

Congruent with the theoretical model, beliefs in EBP were defined as "endorsement of the premise that EBP improves clinical outcomes and confidence in one's EBP knowledge/skills." Implementation of EBP was defined as "engaging in relevant behaviours," including: (1) seeks and appraises scientific evidence, (2) shares evidence or data with colleagues or patients, (3) collects and evaluates outcome data, and (4) uses evidence to change practice. The two new instruments were created to measure these constructs on a continuum from strong disagreement to strong agreement in the case of EBP beliefs and from never to daily for EBP implementation.

Validation of an instrument is a long-term process of accumulating a persuasive body of evidence (Nunnally &

Bernstein 1994; Goodwin 2002; Worthington & Whitaker 2006). This study is the first in a series of planned studies designed to refine and validate two new instruments (i.e., the EBP Beliefs and EBP Implementation Scales) that are used to measure EBP beliefs and implementation, and provide initial evidence of their reliability, construct validity, and criterion validity.

METHODS

Participants

The sample comprised 394 nurses from five states in the U.S. who attended continuing education workshops on EBP provided by the first two authors during 2005 and 2006. Age of the nurses ranged from 21 to 69 years ($M = 45$, $SD = 10$). The sample was composed predominantly of women (96%). Participants' self-identified race/ethnicity as White (89%), African American (5%), Asian/Pacific Islander (2%), Native American (2%), Hispanic (2%), or Other (< 1%). They were residents of Arizona, Colorado, New Jersey, Ohio, and Texas in the U.S. The majority of participants were employed full-time (82%) and the majority worked the day shift (78%). Educational achievement of the participants ranged from diploma nurses with less than 5 years of experience since attaining the diploma to doctorally prepared nurses with more than 20 years experience since attaining the doctorate. The majority of participants had a bachelor's degree or higher: 5% doctorate, 33% master's, 41% bachelor, 16% associate, and 4% diploma.

Procedure

Each group of participants was asked to complete the paper and pencil scales prior to commencement of the EBP workshops they were attending. Participants received an explanation about how their data would be used to establish the psychometric properties of the EBP Beliefs and Implementation scales. Completion of the scales by the participants served as their consent to participate in the study. All scales were completed anonymously and participants completed the two scales in less than 15 minutes. The institutional review board of Arizona State University approved the study.

Item development. The EBP Beliefs Scale (Melnyk & Fineout-Overholt 2002), was an outgrowth of earlier work (Melnyk 1994, 1995, Melnyk et al. 1997, 2004a, 2006). On the scale, clinicians are asked to respond to each of 16 items (Table 1) on a 5-point Likert-scale that ranges from 1 (strongly disagree) to 5 (strongly agree). Scoring of the instrument consists of reverse scoring two negatively phrased items (Table 1) and then summing responses to the 16 items for a total score that ranges between 16 and 80.

TABLE 1

Percentage endorsement ($N = 333$) and factor loadings on items of the EBP beliefs scale

ITEM	STRONGLY AGREE OR AGREE	LOADING
8. I am sure that I can implement EBP in a time efficient way.	48%	0.77
3. I am sure that I can implement EBP.	66%	0.76
6. I believe that I can search for the best evidence to answer clinical questions in a time efficient way.	62%	0.73
15. I am confident about my ability to implement EBP where I work.	46%	0.72
7. I believe that I can overcome barriers in implementing EBP.	61%	0.71
10. I am sure about how to measure the outcomes of clinical care.	44%	0.67
14. I know how to implement EBP sufficiently enough to make practice changes.	35%	0.67
12. I am sure that I can access the best resources in order to implement EBP.	57%	0.67
9. I am sure that implementing EBP will improve the care that I deliver to my patients.	94%	0.65
4. I believe that critically appraising evidence is an important step in the EBP process.	91%	0.63
2. I am clear about the steps of EBP.	53%	0.61
5. I am sure that evidence-based guidelines can improve clinical care.	96%	0.56
1. I believe that EBP results in the best clinical care for patients.	94%	0.53
16. I believe the care that I deliver is evidence-based.	47%	0.52
13. I believe EBP is difficult. (reverse scored)	47%	0.43
11. I believe that EBP takes too much time. (reverse scored)	56%	0.38

The EBP Implementation Scale was developed from a review of literature on the essential components and steps of EBP. Participants were asked to respond to each of the 18 items on a 5-point frequency scale (Table 2) by indicating how often in the past 8 weeks they performed the item. The scale ranges from 0 meaning "0 times" to 4, meaning ">8 times." Scoring consisted of summing responses to the 18 items for a total score that could range from 0 to 72.

TABLE 2

Percentage implementation ($N = 319$) and factor loadings on items of the EBP implementation scale

ITEM	5 OR MORE TIMES IN THE LAST 8 WEEKS	LOADING
16. Shared the outcome data collected with colleagues.	17%	0.83
6. Shared evidence from a study/ies in the form of a report or presentation to > 2 colleagues.	25%	0.83
8. Shared an EBP guideline with a colleague.	16%	0.83
10. Shared evidence from a research study with a multidisciplinary team member.	18%	0.81
14. Used an EBP guideline or systematic review to change clinical practice where I work.	11%	0.79
17. Changed practice based on patient outcome data.	16%	0.79
15. Evaluated a care initiative by collecting patient outcome data.	17%	0.78
7. Evaluated the outcomes of a practice change.	20%	0.78
18. Promoted the use of EBP to my colleagues.	23%	0.78
1. Used evidence to change my clinical practice.	24%	0.77
9. Shared evidence from a research study with a patient/family member.	17%	0.76
11. Read and critically appraised a clinical research study.	31%	0.76
4. Informally discussed evidence from a research study with a colleague.	37%	0.75
2. Critically appraised evidence from a research study.	33%	0.74
3. Generated a PICO question about my clinical practice.	13%	0.73
5. Collected data on a patient problem.	34%	0.70
13. Accessed the National Guidelines Clearinghouse.	12%	0.68
12. Accessed the Cochrane database of systematic reviews.	15%	0.60

Evidence-Based Practice Beliefs and Implementation Scales

During item development, the face and content validity of early drafts of the instruments were assessed in convenience samples of practicing staff nurses ($N = 15$) and EBP subject-matter experts ($N = 8$) who reviewed the two questionnaires for content and clarity. Final versions of the instruments were scored for readability: Flesch-Kincaid reading grade level was 8.0 for the EBP Beliefs Scale and 9.6 for the EBP Implementation Scale.

Statistical procedures. Reliability was assessed using: (1) the Cronbach procedure for measuring internal consistency, and (2) the equal-length, split-half Spearman-Brown procedure for measuring intra-scale correlation. Reliability statistics were calculated after reverse coding of items was completed.

The goal of the instrument development process was to develop two brief scales, each measuring a single global factor. Attainment of this goal was evaluated with a principal components analysis (PCA) of each scale. The validity of the two scales was analysed separately because, congruent with their different purposes, they used response-rating scales that were semantically and numerically distinct, precluding their combination into a single PCA.

The PCA method was chosen over other factor-analysis methods such as "principal axis factoring" or "common factor analysis" for three reasons. First, this initial analysis was largely exploratory, rather than confirmatory, designed to identify essential items for measuring the construct, rather then the latent structure of the instrument (Worthington & Whitaker 2006). Second, PCA allows users to take into account all of the variance in items, not simply the shared variance, and to identify factors in order of the percentage of variance accounted for; that is, the first factor in PCA accounts for the maximum amount of total variability. Third, PCA identifies only orthogonal factors, when multiple factors are identified. Thus, PCA can quickly highlight items not contributing to the construct, which can then be considered for deletion from the scale. The inter-item correlation matrix was used as the basis for the PCA, because the sample was a broad cross-section of the target audience. List-wise deletion of cases was used in each procedure.

Differences in attitudes and behaviours among subgroups were evaluated to determine whether the scales could distinguish between the subgroups, an indication of criterion validity. An independent samples t test was used to compare two subgroups formed by degree of prior exposure to EBP. One-way analysis of variance (ANOVA) was used to compare five subgroups defined by educational level, four defined by nursing roles, and five defined by age. Results were considered statistically significant when $p < .05$.

TABLE 3
Reliability coefficients of the EBP beliefs and implementation scales

Survey	N	Cronbach α	Spearman-Brown r
EBP Beliefs Scale	330	.90	0.87
EBP Implementation Scale	319	.96	0.95

RESULTS

Response Patterns

The percentage of participants who responded strongly agree or agree is shown in Table 1 for each item on the EBP Beliefs scale. Items with high levels of endorsement were focused on beliefs about the positive effect of EBP. Items with low levels of endorsement were focused on confidence in implementing EBP.

The percentage of participants who responded five or more times in the last 8 weeks is shown in Table 2 for each item of the EBP Implementation scale. The most common implementation item was critical appraisal of scientific evidence. The least common implementation item was accessing or using a published EBP guideline.

Reliability

Cronbach α and Spearman-Brown r reliability coefficients exceeded 0.85 for each of the scales (Table 3).

Construct Validity: Exploratory PCA

List-wise deletion resulted in a sample of 333 participants for PCA of the EBP Beliefs scale. The scree plot of eigenvalues indicated that the major discontinuity occurred between the first and second factors. The first factor had an eigenvalue of 6.44 and accounted for 40% of the variance in the scale. Three other factors had eigenvalues > 1.0 (1.8, 1.3, and 1.1, respectively). They accounted for 11%, 8%, and 7% of the variance in the scale, respectively, not meaningfully more than the 6.3% variance that could be accounted for by any single item (Steger 2006). Thus, a single-factor solution was the most parsimonious interpretation of the results. Factor loadings for each item in the single-factor solution are shown in Table 1. The unidimensional nature of the scale is supported by the high factor loadings. Every item on the scale has a factor loading > 0.35; it is noteworthy that the only items with factor loadings < 0.50 are the two reverse-scored items. These high loadings combined with the high Cronbach α (.90) indicate that a single construct is being measured (Linn 1968; Hakstian et al. 1982; Nunnally & Bernstein 1994; Steger 2006;

TABLE 4

Comparison of prior exposure subgroups

	N	*M (SD)*	*p*
EBP beliefs scale			
No exposure to EBP	133	54.68 (12.45)	=.67
Prior exposure to EBP	197	55.46 (18.60)	
EBP implementation scale			
No exposure to EBP	133	8.60 (10.74)	<.001
Prior exposure to EBP	183	18.27 (16.60)	

Worthington & Whitaker 2006). However, given that this orthogonal factor accounts for <50% of the variance in total scores, it is possible that a shorter version of the scale could be developed.

List-wise deletion resulted in a sample of 319 participants for PCA of the EBP Implementation scale. The scree plot indicated a single factor that the major discontinuity occurred between the first and second factors. The first factor had an eigenvalue of 10.53 and accounted for 59% of the variance in the scale. One other factor had an eigenvalue > 1.0; at 1.5, it accounted for only 8% of the variance in the scale, not meaningfully more than the 5.5% variance that could be accounted for by any single item (Steger 2006). Again, the single-factor solution appeared to be the best fit to the data. Factor loadings for each item in the single factor solution are shown in Table 2; all items have loadings >0.60. These high loadings combined with the high Cronbach α (.96) indicate that a single unidimensional construct is being measured (Linn 1968; Hakstian et al. 1982; Nunnally & Bernstein 1994; Steger 2006; Worthington & Whitaker 2006).

Criterion Validity: Known Groups Comparisons

Prior exposure. Participants who indicated that they had been exposed to the principles of EBP in school, during continuing education coursework, or by reading professional literature were compared to those who indicated that they had little or no prior exposure to EBP. Average scores on the scales are shown for each subgroup in Table 4. Individuals who had prior exposure to EBP had beliefs about EBP that were similar to those who had no prior exposure. However, those with prior exposure scored twice as high on average on the Implementation scale.

The nature of this relationship is further indicated by the different correlations between scores on the Beliefs and Implementation scales for the two groups. Although both correlations were significantly different from 0 ($p < .001$), the correlation was significantly higher ($p = .05$) for participants who had prior exposure to EBP

($r = 0.51$) than for participants with little or no experience with EBP ($r = 0.35$). That is, when participants had prior exposure to EBP through formal training, their beliefs in EBP were more strongly related to the frequency with which they implemented EBP.

This pattern of relationships shows that, in a sample of individuals seeking new or additional training in EBP, individuals might have strong beliefs in EBP that are not based on formal training in EBP (the two groups were similar in beliefs), but lack of training in EBP might be a barrier to actual implementation of EBP (the two groups were dissimilar in implementation and implementation was more strongly correlated with beliefs among those with prior training).

Education level. Participants were divided into five subgroups on the basis of the highest level of education achieved. The strength of beliefs in EBP significantly increased with the level of education, $F(4, 344) = 7.03$, $p < .001$: Participants with associate degrees scored lowest ($M = 49.70$, $SD = 19.95$), while those with doctoral degrees scored highest ($M = 64.06$, $SD = 9.14$). Similarly, scores on the Implementation scale significantly increased with level of education, $F(4, 331) = 7.46$, $p < .001$: Participants with associate degrees scored lowest ($M = 8.37$, $SD = 12.96$), while those with doctoral degrees scored highest ($M = 25.50$, $SD = 21.08$).

Nursing roles. Four subgroups of participants had roles that should systematically vary in the number of opportunities for implementing EBP: staff nurse ($N = 111$), nurse manager ($N = 33$), clinical nurse specialist ($N = 27$), and educator/faculty ($N = 59$). The strength of beliefs in EBP significantly increased from staff nurse to educator/faculty, $F(3, 233) = 9.34$, $p < .001$: Staff nurses scored lowest ($M = 48.72$, $SD = 21.63$) and educator/faculty scored highest ($M = 61.50$, $SD = 8.51$). The frequency of implementing EBP significantly increased from staff nurse to educator/faculty, $F(3, 226) = 6.97$, $p < .001$: Staff nurses scored lowest ($M = 10.36$, $SD = 13.54$) and educator/faculty scored highest ($M = 20.85$, $SD = 18.71$).

Age. Participants were divided into five subgroups on the basis of age decades. The strength of beliefs in EBP significantly increased with age, $F(4, 337) = 5.60$, $p < .001$: The youngest participants, age 21 to 30 years, scored lowest ($M = 48.35$, $SD = 23.87$), while the oldest, age 61 to 70 years scored highest ($M = 59.75$, $SD = 4.74$). Scores on the Implementation scale did not vary significantly with age. Age was not meaningfully associated with role, time in current position, employment status, shift worked, hours worked per week, or educational level. Thus, it appears that unidentified chronological or secular trends operate to increase endorsement of EBP, but not implementation of EBP across the life span.

DISCUSSION

Both the EBP beliefs and implementation scales had good psychometric properties. Response patterns on individual items and total scores indicated that the scales were sensitive to a wide range of attitudes and behaviours. High Cronbach coefficients indicated that the internal consistency of the scales was excellent. Although the choice of factor analysis procedure in exploratory factor analysis and the best method of extracting factors have been widely debated (Linn 1968; Hakstian et al. 1982; Steger 2006; Worthington & Whitaker 2006), the pattern of results seen in this study clearly support the premise that the scales are measuring unidimensional constructs. The criterion validity of the scales was supported by the differences seen between subgroups. The strength of beliefs in EBP was strongly associated with the frequency of implementing EBP and this relationship was strongest among participants who had prior training in EBP, suggesting that while formal training in EBP was not a prerequisite to beliefs about EBP, training facilitated implementation of EBP. Similarly, level of education was strongly associated with beliefs about EBP and implementation of EBP, suggesting that graduate education increases appreciation of the positive impact of EBP and instills a desire to use EBP to improve patient outcomes. Like educational level, role was significantly associated with EBP beliefs and implementation with nurse educators and faculty having significantly stronger beliefs in EBP and implementing EBP significantly more frequently than did staff nurses.

IMPLICATIONS FOR RESEARCH, EDUCATION, AND PRACTICE

This initial validation study had some limitations. Test-retest reliability was not measured, so the instruments' stability is unknown. Cross-validation studies are needed to confirm the factor structure of the scales, to derive the optimal scale length, and to establish the reliability and validity of the scales in other populations. A longitudinal study should be conducted to determine the predictive validity of the EBP Beliefs scale (i.e., whether the strength of EBP beliefs allows predictions of EBP implementation rates). Such a study could also allow reassessment of the relationship of age to EBP beliefs and implementation rates and defining how the relationship of beliefs to implementation is affected by chronological and secular trends. Finally, a controlled intervention study should be conducted to assess the instruments' sensitivity to changes in beliefs and implementation as a function of educational intervention.

The results of this study were consistent with prior work suggesting that beliefs are amenable to change with educational interventions (Melnyk 1995; Melnyk et al.

1997; Melnyk & Feinstein 2001; Melnyk et al. 2004a; Melnyk et al. 2006). Therefore, strategies such as educational and skills-building sessions on EBP with nurses should strengthen their beliefs about the value of EBP and their ability to implement it, which should, in turn, increase its implementation rate. Concepts of EBP can be introduced into educational curricula at all levels. In associate degree education, nursing students can be exposed to the EBP paradigm, helped to develop a spirit of inquiry, and taught the importance of data-driven decision making. In addition to these EBP foundations, baccalaureate curricula should emphasise how to use valid research to inform EBP (American Association of Critical Care Nurses 2004; Ciliska 2005). Furthermore, baccalaureate programs should teach students the steps of EBP so they can use this problem-solving approach to deliver the highest quality of care. Graduate education programs should emphasise the need to expand the science of EBP principles and measure the effect of EBP on clinical outcomes.

In order for EBP to be consistently implemented in health care organisations, a culture of best practice needs to be established, in which all nursing professionals, regardless of educational preparation, have an important role in advancing EBC. The development of EBP mentors may be key to implementing and sustaining an EBP culture (Fineout-Overholt et al. 2005; Melnyk 2007). In a recent randomised controlled pilot study with staff nurses in a Visiting Nurse Service in the Northeastern U.S., presence of an ARCC EBP mentor led to higher EBP beliefs in nurses, which in turn, led to greater EBP implementation (Levin et al. 2007). Subsequently, greater EBP implementation by the nurses who had an ARCC mentor versus an advanced practice nurse who taught physical assessment skills led to higher group cohesion, which is a predictor of nurse job satisfaction and retention (Levin et al. 2007). Therefore, ARCC advanced practice mentors might be central to not only advancing EBC, but also to enhancing nurse satisfaction and retention at a time in which several countries are facing serious nursing shortages.

CONCLUSION

The EBP Beliefs and EBP Implementation scales are psychometrically sound instruments that can be used to systematically study the effect of EBP educational and mentorship programs on EBP skills, clinical care, job satisfaction, and retention.

References

American Association of Critical Care Nurses. (2004). *Position statement on nursing research*. Retrieved May 28, 2008, from http://www.aacn.nche.edu/Publications/positions/NsgRes.htm.

Arora N.K., Avanian J.Z. & Guadagnoli E. (2005). Examining the relationship of patients' attitudes and beliefs with their self-reported level of participation in medical decision-making. *Medical Care, 43*(9), 865–872.

Balas E.A. & Boren S.A. (2000). Managing clinical knowledge for healthcare improvements. In V. Schattauer (Ed.), *Yearbook of medical informatics* (pp. 65–70). New York: Stuttgart.

Carver C.S. & Scheier M.F. (1982). Control theory: A useful conceptual framework for personality-social, clinical, and health psychology. *Psychological Bulletin, 92,* 111–135.

Carver C.S. & Scheier M.F. (1998). *On the self-regulation of behavior.* Cambridge, UK: Cambridge University Press.

Ciliska D. (2005). Educating for evidence-based practice. *Journal of Professional Nursing, 21*(6), 345–350.

Ciliska D., Chambers L., Hayward S., James M. & Underwood J. (1996). Increasing evidence-based decisions about public health interventions. *Canadian Journal of Public Health, 87*(6), 376, 410.

Eccles M., Grimshaw J., Walker A., Johnston M. & Pitts N. (2005). Changing the behavior of healthcare professionals: The use of theory in promoting the uptake of research findings. *Journal of Clinical Epidemiology, 58*(2), 113–116.

Fineout-Overholt E., Melnyk B.M. & Schultz A. (2005). Transforming health care from the inside out: Advancing evidence-based practice in the 21st century. *Journal of Professional Nursing, 21*(6), 335–344.

Goodwin L.D. (2002). Changing conceptions of measurement validity: An update on the new standards. *Journal of Nursing Education, 41,* 100–106.

Greiner A. & Knebel E. (2003). *Health professions education: A bridge to quality.* Washington, DC: National Academic Press.

Grimshaw J., Eccles M., Thomas R., MacLennan G., Ramsay C., Fraser C. & Vale L. (2006). Toward evidence-based quality improvement. Evidence (and its limitations) of the effectiveness of guideline dissemination and implementation strategies 1966–1998. *Journal of General Internal Medicine, 21*(Suppl. 2), S14–S20.

Hakstian A.R., Rogers W.D. & Cattell R.B. (1982). The behavior of numbers of factors rules with simulated data. *Multivariate Behavioral Research, 17,* 193–219.

Heater B., Becker A. & Olsen R. (1988). Nursing interventions and patient outcomes: A meta-analysis of studies. *Nursing Research, 37,* 303–307.

Hutchinson A.M. & Johnston L. (2006). Beyond the barriers scale: Commonly reported barriers to research use. *Journal of Nursing Administration, 36*(4), 189–199.

Kajermo K.N., Nordstrom G., Krusebrant A. & Bjorvell H. (2000). Perceptions of research utilization: Comparisons between health care professionals, nursing students and a reference group of nurse clinicians. *Journal of Advanced Nursing, 31*(1), 99–109.

Larrabee J.H., Janney M.A., Ostrow C.L., Withrow M.L., Hobbs G.R. Jr. & Burant C. (2003). Predicting registered nurse job satisfaction and intent to leave. *Journal of Nursing Administration, 33,* 271–283.

Levin R., Vetter M.J., Fineout-Overholt E., Melnyk B.M. & Barnes M. (2007). Advancing research and clinical practice through close collaboration (ARCC): A pilot test of an intervention to improve evidence-based care and patient outcomes in a community health setting. Paper presented at the 8th Annual National/International Evidence-Based Practice Conference, Translating Research into Best Practice with Vulnerable Populations. Phoenix, Arizona, February 23.

Linn R.L. (1968). A Monte Carlo approach to the number of factors problem. *Psychometrika, 33,* 37–71.

Maljanian R., Caramanica L., Taylor S.K., MacRae J.B. & Beland D.K. (2002). Evidence-based nursing practice, Part 2: Building skills through research roundtables. *Journal of Nursing Administration, 32*(2), 85–90.

Melnyk B.M. (1994). Coping with unplanned childhood hospitalization: Effects of interventions on mothers and children. *Nursing Research, 43*(1), 50–55.

Melnyk B.M. (1995). Coping with unplanned childhood hospitalization: The mediating functions of parental beliefs. *Journal of Pediatric Psychology, 20*(3), 299–312.

Melnyk B.M. (2007). The evidence-based practice mentor. A promising strategy for implementing and sustaining EBP in healthcare systems. *Worldviews on Evidence-Based Nursing, 4*(3), 123–125.

Melnyk B.M. & Feinstein N.F. (2001). Mediating functions of maternal anxiety and participation in care on young children's posthospital adjustment. *Research in Nursing & Health, 24,* 18–26.

Melnyk B. & Fineout-Overholt E. (2002). Putting research into practice. *Reflections on Nursing Leadership, 28,* 22–25.

Melnyk B.M. & Fineout-Overholt E. (2005a). *Evidence-based practice in nursing & healthcare. A guide to best practice.* Philadelphia: Lippincott, Williams & Wilkins.

Melnyk B.M. & Fineout-Overholt E. (2005b). Outcomes and implementation strategies from the first U.S. Evidence-Based Practice Leadership Summit. *Worldviews on Evidence-based Nursing, 2,* 185–193.

Melnyk B.M., Alpert-Gillis L.J., Hensel P.B., Cable-Billing R.C. & Rubenstein J. (1997). Helping mothers cope with a critically ill child: A pilot test of the COPE Intervention. *Research in Nursing and Health, 20,* 3–14.

Melnyk B.M., Alpert-Gillis L., Feinstein N.F., Fairbanks E., Schultz-Czarniak J., Hust D., Sherman L., LeMoine

C., Moldenhauer Z., Small L., Bender N. & Sinkin R.A. (2001). Improving cognitive development of LBW premature infants with the COPE program: A pilot study of the benefit of early NICU intervention with mothers. *Research in Nursing and Health*, 24, 373–389.

Melnyk B.M., Alpert-Gillis L., Feinstein N.F., Crean H., Johnson J., Fairbanks E., Small L., Rubenstein J., Slota M. & Corbo-Richert B. (2004a). Creating opportunities for parent empowerment (COPE): Program effects on the mental health/coping outcomes of critically ill young children and their mothers. *Pediatrics*, 113(6). Accessed December 17, 2004, from http://www.pediatrics.org/cgi/content/full/113/6/e597-e607.

Melnyk B.M., Fineout-Overholt E., Feinstein N., Li H., Small L., Wilcox L. & Kraus R. (2004b). Nurses' perceived knowledge, beliefs, skills, and needs regarding evidence-based practice: Implications for accelerating the paradigm shift. *Worldviews on Evidence-based Nursing*, 1, 185–193.

Melnyk B.M., Fineout-Overholt E., Stetler C. & Allan J. (2005). Outcomes and Implementation Strategies from the First U.S. EBP Leadership Summit. *Worldviews on Evidence-Based Nursing* 2(3), 113–121.

Melnyk B.M., Feinstein N.F., Alpert-Gillis L., Fairbanks E., Crean H.F., Sinkin R., Stone P.W., Small L., Tu X. & Gross S.J. (2006). Reducing premature infants length of stay and improving parents' mental health outcomes with the COPE NICU program: A randomized clinical trial. *Pediatrics*, 118(5), 1414–1427.

Nunnally J.C. & Bernstein I.H. (1994). *Psychometric theory* (3rd Ed.). New York: McGraw-Hill.

Parahoo K. (2000). Barriers to, and facilitators of, research utilization among nurses in Northern Ireland. *Journal of Advanced Nursing*, 31(1), 89–98.

Pravikoff D.S., Pierce S.T. & Tanner A. (2005). Evidence-based practice readiness study supported by academy nursing informatics expert panel. *Nursing Outlook*, 53, 49–50.

Prochaska J.O. & Velicer W.F. (1997). The transtheoretical model of health behavior change. *American Journal of Health Promotion*, 12(1), 38–48.

Prochaska J.M., Prochaska J.O. & Levesque D.A. (2001). A transtheoretical approach to changing organizations. *Administration and Policy in Mental Health*, 28(4), 247–261.

Retsas A. (2000). Barriers to using research evidence in nursing practice. *Journal of Advanced Nursing*, 31(3), 599–606.

Reynolds K.E. & Magnan M.A. (2005). Nursing attitudes and beliefs toward human sexuality: Collaborative research promoting evidence-based practice. *Clinical Nurse Specialist*, 19(5), 255–259.

Rhodes R.E. & Plotnikoff R.C. (2006). Understanding action control: Predicting physical activity intention-behavior profiles across 6 months in a Canadian sample. *Health Psychology*, 25(6), 292–299.

Sackett D.L., Straus S.E., Richardson W.S., Rosenberg W. & Hayes R.B. (2000). *Evidence-based medicine: How to practice and teach EBM*. London: Churchill Livingstone.

Steger M.F. (2006). An illustration of issues in factor extraction and identification of dimensionality in psychological assessment data. *Journal of Personality Assessment*, 86(3), 263–272.

Strout T.D. (2005). Curiosity and reflective thinking: Renewal of the spirit. *Excellence in Nursing Knowledge*. Indianapolis, IN: Sigma Theta Tau International.

U.S. General Accounting Office. (2001). *Nursing workforce: Emerging nurse shortages due to multiple factors. Report to the Chairman, Subcommittee on Health, Committee on Way and Means, House of Representatives* [GAO-01–944]. Washington, DC: Author.

Vahey D.C., Aiken L.H., Sloane D.M., Clarke S.P. & Vargas D. (2004), Medical Care, 42(2 Suppl): II 57–66.

Worthington R.L. & Whitaker T.A. (2006). Scale development research a content analysis and recommendations for best practices. *The Counseling Psychologist*, 34(6), 806–838.

appendices

570

glossary

A

Absolute risk increase (ARI): The absolute risk increase for an undesirable outcome is when the risk is more for the experimental/ condition group than the control/comparison group.

Absolute risk reduction (ARR): The absolute risk reduction for an undesirable outcome is when the risk is less for the experimental/condition group than the control/comparison group.

Accountability (HIPAA) Act: The Health Insurance Portability and Accountability Act (HIPAA) was approved by the United States Congress in 1996 to protect the privacy of individuals. It enforces protections for works that improve portability and continuity of health insurance coverage.

Action research: A general term for a variety of approaches that aim to resolve social problems by improving existing conditions for oppressed groups or communities.

Adoption of research evidence: A process that occurs across five stages of innovation (i.e., knowledge, persuasion, decision, implementation, and confirmation).

Analysis: The process used to determine the findings in a study or project.

Analytic notes: Notes researchers write to themselves to record their thoughts, questions, and ideas as a process of simultaneous data collection and data analysis unfolds.

Applicability of study findings: Whether or not the effects of the study are appropriate for a particular patient situation.

Article synopsis: A summary of the content of an article.

Attrition: When subjects are lost from or drop their participation in a study (see loss of subjects to follow-up).

Audit: To examine carefully and verify the findings from a study or project.

Author name: The name of the person who wrote a paper.

Axial coding: A process used in grounded theory to relate categories of information by using a coding paradigm with predetermined subcategories (Strauss & Corbin, 1990).

B

Background questions: Questions that need to be answered as a foundation for asking the searchable, answerable foreground question. They are questions that ask for general information about a clinical issue.

Basic social process (BSP): The basis for theory generation—recurs frequently, links all the data together, and describes the pattern followed regardless of the variety of conditions under which the experience takes place and different ways in which persons go through it. There are two types of BSP, a basic social psychological process (BSPP) and a basic social structural process (BSSP).

Benchmarking: The process of looking outward to identify, understand, and adapt outstanding [best] practices and [high performance] to help improve performance.

Bias: Divergence of results from the true values or the process that leads to such divergence.

Biography: An approach that produces an in-depth report of a person's life. Life histories and oral histories also involve gathering of biographical information and recording of personal recollections of one or more individuals.

Biosketch: A 2 to 3 page document, similar to a resume or brief curriculum vitae, that captures an individual's educational and professional work experience, honors, prior research grants, and publications.

Blind review: A review process in which identification of the author/creator/researcher is removed and, likewise, the identity of the reviewers so that anonymity of both parties is assured.

Blocking: A strategy introduced into a study that entails deliberately including a potential extraneous intrinsic or confounding variable in a study's design in order to control its effects on the dependent or outcome variable.

Booster interventions: Interventions that are delivered after the initial intervention or treatment in a study for the purpose of enhancing the effects of the intervention.

Bracketing: Identifying and suspending previously acquired knowledge, beliefs, and opinions about a phenomenon.

C

Care delivery outcomes: The outcomes that are influenced by the delivery of clinical care.

Case–control study: A type of research that retrospectively compares characteristics of an individual who has a certain condition (e.g., hypertension) with one who does not (i.e., a matched control or similar person without hypertension); often conducted for the purpose of identifying variables that might predict the condition (e.g., stressful lifestyle, sodium intake).

Case reports: Reports that describe the history of a single patient, or a small group of patients, usually in the form of a story.

Case study: An intensive investigation of a case involving a person or small group of persons, an issue, or an event.

Categorical data/variables: Data that is classified into categories (e.g., gender, hair color) instead of being numerically ordered.

Ceiling effects: Participant scores that cluster toward the high end of a measure.

Clinical forethought: All the anticipated actions and plans relevant to a particular patient's possible trends and trajectories that a clinician prepares for in caring for the patient.

Clinical decision support system: Interactive computer programs designed to assist healthcare providers in making clinical decisions.

Clinical grasp: Clinical inquiry in action. Includes problem identification and clinical judgment across time about the particular transitions of particular patient/family clinical situations. Four aspects of clinical grasp include making qualitative distinctions, engaging in detective work, recognizing changing relevance, and developing clinical knowledge about specific patient populations.

Clinical inquiry: A process in which clinicians gather data together using narrowly defined clinical parameters; it allows for an appraisal of the available choices of treatment for the purpose of finding the most appropriate choice of action.

Clinical practice guidelines: Systematically developed statements to assist clinicians and patients in making decisions about care; ideally, the guidelines consist of a systematic review of the literature, in conjunction with consensus of a group of expert decision makers, including administrators, policy makers, clinicians, and consumers who consider the evidence and make recommendations.

Clinical significance: Study findings that will directly influence clinical practice, whether they are statistically significant or not.

Cochrane Central Register of Controlled trials: A bibliography of controlled trials identified by contributors to the Cochrane Collaboration and others.

Cochrane Database of Methodology Reviews: Contains full text of systematic reviews of empirical methodological studies prepared by The Cochrane Empirical Methodological Studies Methods Group.

Cochrane Database of Systematic Reviews: Contains reviews that are highly structured and systematic with evidence included or excluded on the basis of explicit quality criteria, to minimize bias.

Cochrane Methodology Register: A bibliography of articles and books on the science of research synthesis.

Cohort study: A longitudinal study that begins with the gathering of two groups of patients (the cohorts), one that received the exposure (e.g., to a disease) and one that does not, and then following these groups over time (prospective) to measure the development of different outcomes (diseases).

Computer-assisted qualitative data analysis: An area of technological innovation that, in qualitative research, has resulted in uses of word processing and software packages to support data management.

Conceptual framework: A group of interrelated statements that provide a guide or direction for a study or project; sometimes referred to as a theoretical framework.

Confidence interval (CI): A measure of the precision of the estimate. The 95% confidence interval (CI) is the range of values within which we can be 95% sure that the true value lies for the whole population of patients from whom the study patients were selected.

Confirmability: Demonstrated by providing substantiation that findings and interpretations are grounded in the data (i.e., links between researcher assertions and the data are clear and credible).

Confounding: Occurs when two factors are closely associated and the effects of one confuses or distorts the effects of the other factor on an outcome. The distorting factor is a confounding variable.

Confounding variables: Those factors that interfere with the relationship between the independent and dependent variables.

Constant comparison: A systematic approach to analysis that is a search for patterns in data as they are coded, sorted into categories, and examined in different contexts.

Construct validity: The degree to which an instrument measures the construct it is supposed to be measuring.

Contamination: The inadvertent and undesirable influence of an experimental intervention on another intervention.

Content analysis: In qualitative analysis, a term that refers to processes of breaking down narrative data (coding, comparing, contrasting and categorizing bits of information) and reconstituting them in some new form (e.g., description, interpretation, theory).

Content validity: The degree to which the items in an instrument are tapping the content they are supposed to measure.

Context: The conditions in which something exists.

Control group: A group of subjects who do not receive the experimental intervention or treatment.

Controlled vocabulary or thesaurus: A hierarchical arrangement of descriptive terms that serve as mapping agents for searches; often unique to each database.

Convenience sampling: Drawing readily available subjects to participate in a study.

Correlational descriptive study: A study that is conducted for the purpose of describing the relationship between two or more variables.

Correlational predictive study: A study that is conducted for the purpose of describing what variables predict a certain outcome.

Covariate: A variable that is controlled for in statistical analyses (e.g., analysis of covariance); the variable controlled is typically a confounding or extraneous variable that may influence the outcome.

Critical appraisal: The process of evaluating a study for its worth (i.e., validity, reliability, and applicability to clinical practice).

Critical inquiry: Theoretical perspectives that are ideologically oriented toward critique of and emancipation from oppressive social arrangements or false ideas.

Critical theory: A blend of ideology (based on a critical theory of society) and a form of social analysis and critique that aims to liberate people from unrecognized myths and oppression, in order to bring about enlightenment and radical social change.

Critique: An in-depth analysis and critical evaluation of a study that identifies its strengths and limitations.

Cronbach alpha: An estimate of internal consistency or homogeneity of an instrument that is comprised of several subparts or scales.

Cross-contamination: Diffusion of the treatment or intervention across study groups.

Cross-sectional study: A study designed to observe an outcome or variable at a single point in time, usually for the purpose of inferring trends over time.

Culture: Shared knowledge and behavior of people who interact within distinct social settings and subsystems.

D

Database of Abstracts of Reviews of Effects (DARE): Database that includes abstracts of systematic reviews that have been critically appraised by reviewers at the NHS Centre for Reviews and Dissemination at the University of York, England.

Data and safety monitoring plan: A detailed plan for how adverse effects will be assessed and managed.

Dependent or outcome variable: The variable or outcome that is influenced or caused by the independent variable.

Descriptive studies: Those studies that are conducted for the purpose of describing the characteristics of certain phenomena or selected variables.

Design: The overall plan for a study that includes strategies for controlling confounding variables, strategies for when the intervention will be delivered (in experimental studies) and how often and when the data will be collected.

Dialogical engagement: Thinking that is like a thoughtful dialog or conversation.

Dimensional analysis: A method for generating grounded theory using an explanatory matrix (Schatzman, 1991).

Direct costs: Actual costs required to conduct a study (e.g., personnel, subject honoraria, instruments).

Discourse analysis: A general term for approaches to analyzing recorded talk and patterns of communication.

Dissemination: The process of distributing or circulating information widely.

E

EBP mentor: Typically, an advanced practice clinician with in-depth knowledge and skills in EBP as well as in individual behavior and organizational change.

Educational prescription (EP): A written plan (usually self-initiated) for identifying and addressing EBP learning needs. The EP contains each step of the EBP process, but may have a primary focus on one or two steps, such as searching or critical appraisal.

Effect measures: Measures used to compare the differences in occurrences of outcomes between groups.

Effect size: The strength of the effect of an intervention.

Electronic health record: An individual's health record in a digital format.

Emergence: Glaser's (1992) term for conceptually driven ("discovery") versus procedurally driven ("forcing") theory development in his critique of Strauss and Corbin (1990).

Emic and etic: Contrasting "insider" views of informants (emic) and the researcher's "outsider" (etic) views.

Environment: Surroundings.

Epistemologies: Ways of knowing and reasoning.

Essences: Internal meaning structures of a phenomenon grasped through the study of human lived experience.

Ethnographic studies: Studies of a social group's culture through time spent combining participant observation and in-depth interviews in the informants' natural setting.

Evaluation: An evaluation of worth.

Event rate: The rate at which a specific event occurs.

Evidence-based clinical practice guidelines: Specific practice recommendations that are based on a methodologically rigorous review of the best evidence on a specific topic.

Evidence-based decision making: The integration of best research evidence in making decisions about patient care, which should also include the clinician's expertise as well as patient preferences and values.

Evidence-based practice (EBP): A paradigm and life-long problem solving approach to clinical decision-making that involves the conscientious use of the best available evidence (including a systematic search for and critical appraisal of the most relevant evidence to answer a clinical question) with one's own clinical expertise and patient values and preferences to improve outcomes for individuals, groups, communities, and systems.

Evidence-based quality improvement (EBQI): Quality improvement initiatives based on evidence.

Evidence-based theories: A theory that has been tested and supported through the accumulation of evidence from several studies.

Evidence summaries: Syntheses of studies (see systematic reviews).

Evidence-user: Anyone who uses valid evidence to support or change practice; demonstrating skills in interpreting evidence, not generating evidence.

Excerpta Medica Online: A major biomedical and pharmaceutical database.

Exclusion criteria: Investigator-identified characteristics that are (a) possessed by individuals who would exclude them from participating in a study; (b) specified to exclude studies from a body of evidence.

Experiential learning: Experience requiring a turning around of preconceptions, expectations, sets, and routines or adding some new insights to a particular practical situation; a way of knowing that contributes to knowledge production; should influence the development of science.

Experimental design/experiment: A study whose purpose is to test the effects of an intervention or treatment on selected outcomes. This is the strongest design for testing cause-and-effect relationships.

External evidence: Evidence that is generated from rigorous research.

External validity: Generalizability; the ability to generalize the findings from a study to the larger population from which the sample was drawn.

Extraneous variables: Those factors that interfere with the relationship between the independent and dependent variables.

F

Face validity: The degree to which an instrument appears to be measuring (i.e., tapping) the construct it is intended to measure.

Factorial design: An experimental design that has two or more interventions or treatments.

False positive: A condition where the test indicates that the person has the outcome of interest when, in fact, the person does not.

False negative: A condition where the test indicates that the person does not have the outcome of interest when, in fact, the person does.

Feminist epistemologies: A variety of views and practices inviting critical dialogue about women's experiences in historical, cultural, and socioeconomic perspectives.

Field notes: Self-designed observational protocols for recording notes about field observations.

Field studies: Studies involving direct, firsthand observation and interviews in informants' natural settings.

Fieldwork: All research activities carried out in and in relation to the field (informants' natural settings).

Fixed effect model: Traditional assumption that the event rates are fixed in each of the control and treatment groups.

Floor effects: Participant scores that cluster toward the low end of a measure.

Focus groups: This type of group interview generates data on designated topics through discussion and interaction. Focus group research is a distinct type of study when used as the sole research strategy.

Foreground questions: Those questions that can be answered from scientific evidence about diagnosing, treating, or assisting patients with understanding their prognosis, focusing on specific knowledge.

Forest plot: Diagrammatic representation of the results (i.e., the effects or point estimates) of trials (i.e., squares) along with their confidence intervals (i.e., straight lines through the squares).

Frequency: The number of occurrences in a given time period.

Full text: An article published electronically in its entirety.

Funnel plot: The plotting of sample size against the effect size of studies included in a systematic review. The funnel should be inverted and symmetrical if a representative sample has been obtained.

G

Generalizability: The extent to which the findings from a study can be generalized or applied to the larger population (i.e., external validity).

Gold standard: An accepted and established reference standard or diagnostic test for a particular illness.

Grey literature: Refers to publications such as brochures and conference proceedings.

(Grounded) formal theory: A systematic explanation of an area of human/social experience derived through meta-analysis of substantive theory.

(Grounded) substantive theory: A systematic explanation of a situation-specific human experience/social phenomenon.

Grounded theory: Studies to generate theory about how people deal with life situations that is "grounded" in empirical data and describes the processes by which they move through experiences over time.

H

Harm: When risks outweigh benefits.

Health Technology Assessment Database: Database containing information on health-care technology assessments.

Health topic summaries: Concise overviews of a health topic.

Hermeneutics: Philosophy, theories, and practices of interpretation.

Hierarchy of evidence: A mechanism for determining which study designs have the most power to predict cause-and-effect. The highest level of evidence is systematic reviews of RCTs, and the lowest level of evidence is expert opinion and consensus statements.

History: The occurrence of some event or program unrelated to the intervention that might account for the change observed in the dependent variable.

Hits: Studies obtained from a search that contain the searched word.

Homogeneous study population/Homogeneity: When subjects in a study are similar on the characteristics that may affect the outcome variable(s).

HSR Queries: Health and safety regulation questions.

Hyperlink: A connection to organized information that is housed in cyberspace and usually relevant to the site on which it was found.

Hypotheses: Predictions about the relationships between variables (e.g., adults who receive cognitive behavioral therapy will report less depression than those who receive relaxation therapy).

I

Incidence: New occurrences of the outcome or disorder within the at-risk population in a specified time frame.

Inclusion criteria: Essential characteristics specified by investigator that (a) potential participants must possess in order to be considered for a study; (b) studies must meet to be included in a body of evidence.

Independent variable: The variable that is influencing the dependent variable or outcome; in experimental studies, it is the intervention or treatment.

Indirect costs: Costs that are not directly related to the actual conduct of a study, but are associated with the "overhead" in an organization, such as lights, telephones, and office space.

Informatics: How data, information, knowledge, and wisdom are collected, stored, processed, communicated, and used to support the process of healthcare delivery to clients, providers, administrators, and organizations involved in healthcare delivery.

Institutional Review Board (IRB): A committee that approves, monitors, and reviews research involving human subjects for the purpose of protecting the rights and welfare of research subjects.

Integrative reviews: Systematic summaries of the accumulated state of knowledge about a concept, including highlights of important issues left unresolved.

Integrity of the intervention: The extent to which an intervention is delivered as intended.

Internal consistency reliability: The extent to which an instrument's subparts are measuring the same construct.

Internal evidence: Evidence generated within a clinical practice setting from initiatives such as quality improvement, outcomes management, or EBP implementation projects.

Internal validity: The extent to which it can be said that the independent variable (i.e., the intervention) causes a change in the dependent variable (i.e., outcome), and the results are not due to other factors or alternative explanations.

Interpretive ethnography: Loosely characterized, a movement within anthropology that generates many hybrid forms of ethnographic work as a result of crossing a variety of theoretical boundaries within social science.

Interrater reliability: The degree to which two individuals agree on what they observe.

Interval data: Data that has quantified intervals and equal distances between points, but without a meaningful zero point (e.g., temperature in degrees Fahrenheit); often referred to as continuous data.

Introspection: A process of recognizing and examining one's own inner state or feelings.

J

Journal title: The title of a journal.

K

Key informant: A select informant/assistant with extensive or specialized knowledge of his/her own culture.

Key stakeholder: An individual or institution that has an investment in a project.

L

Level of evidence: A ranking of evidence by the type of design or research methodology that would answer the question with the least amount of error and provide the most reliable findings. Leveling of evidence, also called hierarchies, vary by type of question asked. An example is provided for intervention questions.

Level I evidence: Evidence that is generated from systematic reviews or meta-analyses of all relevant randomized controlled trials or evidence-based clinical practice guidelines based on systematic reviews of randomized controlled trials; the strongest level of evidence to guide clinical practice.

Level II evidence: Evidence generated from at least one well-designed randomized clinical trial (i.e., a true experiment).

Level III evidence: Evidence obtained from well-designed controlled trials without randomization.

Level IV evidence: Evidence from well-designed case–control and cohort studies.

Level V evidence: Evidence from systematic reviews of descriptive and qualitative studies.

Level VI evidence: Evidence from a single descriptive or qualitative study.

Level VII evidence: Evidence from the opinion of authorities and/or reports of expert committees.

Likelihood ratio: The likelihood that a given test result would be expected in patients with a disease compared to the likelihood that the same result would be expected in patients without that disease.

Lived experience: Everyday experience, not as it is conceptualized, but as it is lived (i.e., how it feels).

Loss of subjects to follow-up: The proportion of people who started the study but do not complete the study, for whatever reason.

M

Macrolevel change: Change at a large-scale level (e.g., nationwide systems or large institutions).

Magnitude of effect: Expressing the size of the relationship between two variables or difference between two groups on a given variable/outcome (i.e., the effect size).

Manipulation checks: Assessments verifying that subjects have actually processed the experimental information that they have received or followed through with prescribed intervention activities.

Maturation: Developmental change that occurs, even in the absence of the intervention.

Mean: A measure of central tendency, derived by summing all scores and dividing by the number of participants.

Mediating processes: The mechanisms through which an intervention produces the desired outcome(s).

Mediating variable: The variable or mechanism through which an intervention works to impact the outcome in a study.

Meta-analysis: A process of using quantitative methods to summarize the results from the multiple studies, obtained and critically reviewed using a rigorous process (to minimize bias) for identifying, appraising, and synthesizing studies to answer a specific question and draw conclusions about the data gathered. The purpose of this process is to gain a summary statistic (i.e., a measure of a single effect) that represents the effect of the intervention across multiple studies.

Method: The theory of how a certain type of research should be carried out (i.e., strategy, approach, process/overall design, and logic of design). Researchers often subsume description of techniques under a discussion of method.

MeSH: MEDLINE®'s controlled vocabulary: **Me**dical **S**ubject **H**eadings.

Micro level Change: Change at a small-scale level (e.g., units within a local healthcare organization or small groups of individuals).

N

Narrative analysis: A term that refers to distinct styles of generating, interpreting, and representing data as stories that provide insights into life experiences.

Narrative review: A summary of primary studies from which conclusions are drawn by the reviewer based on his or her own interpretations.

National Guidelines Clearinghouse: A comprehensive database of up-to-date English language evidence-based clinical practice guidelines, developed in partnership with the American Medical Association, the American Association of Health Plans, and the Association for Healthcare Research and Quality.

Naturalistic research: Commitment to the study of phenomena in their naturally occurring settings (contexts).

News embargo: A restriction on the release of any media information about the findings from a study before they are published in a journal article.

NHS Economic Evaluation Database: A register of published economic evaluations of healthcare interventions.

Nominated/snowball sample: A sample obtained with the help of informants already enrolled in the study.

Nonexperimental study design: A study design in which data are collected but whose purpose is not to test the effects of an intervention or treatment on selected outcomes.

Nonhomogeneous sample: A sample comprised of individuals with dissimilar characteristics.

Null hypothesis: There is no relationship between or among study variables.

Number needed to harm (NNH): The number of clients, who, if they received an intervention, would result in one additional person being harmed (i.e., having a bad outcome) compared to the clients in the control arm of a study.

Number needed to treat (NNT): The number of people who would need to receive the experimental therapy to prevent one bad outcome or cause one additional good outcome.

O

Observation: Facts learned from observing.

Observation continuum: A range of social roles encompassed by participant-observation and ranging from complete observer to complete participant at the extremes.

Observer drift: A decrease in interrater reliability.

Occurrence rate: The rate at which an event occurs.

Odds ratio (OR): The odds of a case patient (i.e., someone in the intervention group) being exposed (a/b) divided by the odds of a control patient being exposed (c/d).

Opinion leaders: Individuals who are typically highly knowledgeable and well respected in a system; as such, they are often able to influence change.

Ordinal data: Variables that have ordered categories with intervals that cannot be quantified (e.g., mild, moderate, or severe anxiety).

Outcomes management: The use of process and outcomes data to coordinate and influence actions and processes of care that contribute to patient achievement of targeted behaviors or desired effects.

Outcomes measurement: A generic term used to describe the collection and reporting of information about an observed effect in relation to some care delivery process or health promotion action.

Outcomes research: The use of rigorous scientific methods to measure the effect of some intervention on some outcome(s).

P

Paradigm: A worldview or set of beliefs, assumptions, and values that guide clinicians' and researchers' thinking. For example, where the researcher stands on issues related to the nature of reality (ontology), relationship of the researcher to the researched (epistemology), role of values (axiology), use of language (rhetoric), and process (methodology) (Creswell, 1998).

Participant-observation: Observation and participation in everyday activities in study of informants' natural settings.

Participatory action research (PAR): A form of action research that is participatory in nature (i.e., researchers and participants collaborate in problem definition, choice of methods, data analysis, and use of findings); democratic in principle; and reformatory in impulse (i.e., has as its objective the empowerment of persons through the process of constructing and using their own knowledge as a form of consciousness raising with the potential for promoting social action).

Patient preferences: Values the patient holds, concerns the patient has regarding the clinical decision/treatment/situation, and choices the patient has/prefers regarding the clinical decision/treatment/situation.

Peer reviewed: A project, paper, study, etc. is reviewed by a person(s) who is a peer to the author and has expertise in the subject.

Phenomenologic: Pertaining to the study of essences (i.e., meaning structures) intuited or grasped through descriptions of lived experience.

Phenomenological reduction: An intellectual process involving reflection, imagination, and intuition.

PICOT format: A process in which clinical questions are phrased in a manner that yields the most relevant information from a search; P = patient population; I = Intervention or issue of interest; C = Comparison intervention or status; O = Outcome; T = Time frame for (I) to achieve the (O).

Placebo: A sham medical intervention or inert pill; typically given to subjects in experimental research studies to control for time and attention spent with subjects getting the experimental intervention.

Plan-Do-Study-Act cycle: Rapid cycle improvement in healthcare settings in which changes are quickly made and studied.

Power: The ability of a study design to detect existing relationships between or among variables.

Power analysis: Procedure used for determining the sample size needed for a study.

Practice-based data/evidence: Data that is generated from clinical practice or a healthcare system.

Pragmatism: A practical approach to solutions.

Prevalence: Refers to the persons in the at-risk population who have the outcome or disorder in a given "snapshot in time."

Principal investigator (PI): The lead person who is responsible and accountable for the scientific integrity of a study as well as the oversight of all elements in the conduct of that study.

Prognosis: The likelihood of a certain outcome.

Psychometric properties: The validity and reliability information on a scale or instrument.

Purposeful/theoretical sample: A sample intentionally selected in accordance with the needs of the study.

p value: The statistical test of the assumption that there is no difference between an experimental intervention and a control. p value indicates the probability of an event, given the assumption that there is no true difference. By convention, a p value of 0.05 is considered a statistically significant result.

Q

Qualitative data analysis: A variety of techniques that are used to move back and forth between data and ideas throughout the course of the research.

Qualitative data management: The act of designing systems to organize, catalogue, code, store, and retrieve data. System design influences, in turn, how the researcher approaches the task of analysis.

Qualitative description: Description that "entails a kind of interpretation that is low-inference (close to the 'facts'), or likely to result in easier consensus (about the 'facts') among researchers" (Sandelowski, 2000b, p. 335).

Qualitative evaluation: A general term covering a variety of approaches to evaluating programs, projects, policies, and so on using qualitative research techniques.

Qualitative studies: Research that involves the collection of data in nonnumeric form, such as personal interviews, usually with the intention of describing a phenomenon.

Quality assurance: The process of ensuring that initiatives or the care being delivered in an institution is of high quality.

Quality improvement data: Data that is collected for the purpose of improving the quality of healthcare or patient outcomes.

Quality improvement projects: Initiatives with a goal to improve the processes or outcomes of the care being delivered.

Quantitative research: The investigation of phenomena using manipulation of numeric data with statistical analysis. Can be descriptive, predictive, or causal.

Quantitative studies: Research that collects data in numeric form and emphasizes precise measurement of variables; often conducted in the form of rigorously controlled studies.

Quasi-experiments: A type of experimental design that tests the effects of an intervention or treatment but lacks one or more characteristics of a true experiment (e.g., random assignment; a control or comparison group).

R

Random assignment (also called randomization): The use of a strategy to randomly assign subjects to the experimental or control groups (e.g., tossing a coin).

Random error: Measurement error that occurs without a pattern, purpose, or intent.

Random sampling: Selecting subjects to participate in a study by using a random strategy (e.g., tossing a coin); in this method of selecting subjects, every subject has an equal chance of being selected.

Randomized block design: A type of control strategy used in an experimental design that places subjects in equally distributed study groups based on certain characteristics (e.g., age) so that each study group will be similar prior to introduction of the intervention or treatment.

Randomized controlled trial (RCT): A true experiment (i.e., one that delivers an intervention or treatment in which subjects are randomly assigned to control and experimental groups); the strongest design to support cause-and-effect relationships.

Ratio level data: The highest level of data; data that has quantified intervals on an infinite scale in which there are equal distances between points and a meaningful zero point (e.g., ounces of water; height); often referred to as continuous data.

Reference population: Those individuals in the past, present, and future to whom the study results can be generalized.

Reflection: The act of contemplating.

Relative risk (RR): Measures the strength of association and is the risk of the outcome in the exposed group (Re) divided by the risk of the outcome in the unexposed group (Ru). RR is used in prospective studies such as RCTs and cohort studies.

Relative risk reduction (RRR): Proportion of risk for bad outcomes in the intervention group compared to the unexposed control group.

Reliability: The consistency of an instrument in measuring the underlying construct.

Reliability coefficients: A measure of an instrument's reliability (e.g., often computed with a Cronbach alpha).

Reliability of study findings: Whether or not the effects of a study have sufficient influence on practice, clinically and statistically; that is, the results can be counted on to make a difference when clinicians apply them to their practice.

Reliable measures: Those that consistently and accurately measure the construct of interest.

Representation: Part of the analytic process that raises the issue of providing a truthful portrayal of what the data represent (e.g., essence of an experience; cultural portrait) that will be meaningful to its intended audience.

Research design meeting: A planning meeting held for the purpose of designing a study and strategizing about potential funding as well as the roles of all investigators.

Research subjects review board (RSRB): Often referred to as an institutional review board (IRB); a group of individuals who review a study before it can be conducted to determine the benefits and risks of conducting the research to study participants.

Research utilization: The use of research knowledge, often based on a single study, in clinical practice.

Risk: The probability that a person (currently free from a disease) will develop a disease at some point.

Risk ratio: See relative risk.

Rules of evidence: Standard criteria for the evaluation of domains of evidence; these are applied to research evidence to assess its validity, the study findings, and its applicability to a patient/system situation.

S

Saturation: The point at which categories of data are full and data collection ceases to provide new information.

Saturation level: The level at which a searcher no longer finds any new references, but instead, is familiar and knowledgeable with the literature.

Semiotics: The theory and study of signs and symbols applied to the analysis of systems of patterned communication.

Semistructured interviews: Formal interviews that provide more interviewer control and question format structure but retain a conversational tone and allow informants to answer in their own ways.

Sensitivity: The probability of a diagnostic test finding disease among those who have the disease or the proportion of people with disease who have a positive test result (true positive).

SnNout: When a test has a high Sensitivity, a Negative result rules out the diagnosis.

Sociolinguistics: The study of the use of speech in social life.

Solomon four group design: A type of experimental study design that uses a before–after design for the first two experimental groups and an after-only design for the second experimental and control groups so that it can separate the effects of pretesting the subjects on the outcome measure(s).

glossary

581

Specificity: The probability of a diagnostic test finding NO disease among those who do NOT have the disease or the proportion of people free of a disease who have a negative test (true negatives).

Spirit of inquiry: A persistent questioning about how to improve current practices; a sense of curiosity.

SpPin: When a test has a high Specificity, a Positive result rules in the diagnosis.

Standard error: An estimate due to sampling error of the deviation of the sample mean from the true population mean.

Statistical significance: The results of statistical analysis of data are unlikely to have been caused by chance, at a predetermined level of probability.

Stratification: A strategy that divides the study population into two or more subpopulations and then samples separately from each.

Structured, open-ended interviews: Formal interviews with little flexibility in the way that questions are asked, but with question formats that allow informants to respond on their own terms (e.g., "What does…. mean to you?" "How do you feel/think about…?").

Symbolic interaction: Theoretical perspective on how social reality is created by human interaction through ongoing, taken-for-granted processes of symbolic communication.

Synthesis: The process of putting together parts to make a whole (e.g., integrating the results of several studies to tell a story about an entire body of evidence).

Systematic review: A summary of evidence, typically conducted by an expert or expert panel on a particular topic, that uses a rigorous process (to minimize bias) for identifying, appraising, and synthesizing studies to answer a specific clinical question and draw conclusions about the data gathered.

T

Techniques: Tools or procedures used to generate or analyze data (e.g., interviewing, observation, standardized tests and measures, constant comparison, document analysis, content analysis, statistical analysis). Techniques are method-neutral and may be used, as appropriate, in any research design—either qualitative or quantitative.

Test–retest reliability: A test of an instrument's stability over time assessed by repeated measurements over time.

Textword: A word that is not a part of the database's controlled vocabulary/thesaurus. Textwords are searched only in titles and abstracts. Sometimes called keywords.

Thematic analysis: Systematic description of recurring ideas or topics (themes) that represent different, yet related, aspects of a phenomenon.

Theoretic interest: A desire to know or understand better.

Theoretical framework: The basis upon which a study is guided; its purpose is to provide a context for selecting the study's variables, including how they relate to one another as well as to guide the development of an intervention in experimental studies.

Theoretical generalizability: See transferability.

Theoretical sampling: Decision making, while concurrently collecting and analyzing data, about what further data and data sources are needed to develop the emerging theory.

Theoretical sensitivity: A conceptual process to accompany techniques for generating grounded theory (Glaser, 1978).

Thick description: Description that does more than describe human experiences by beginning to interpret what they mean, involving detailed reports of what people say and do, incorporating the textures and feelings of the physical and social worlds in which people move, with reference to that context (i.e., an interpretation of what their words and actions mean).

Transferability: Demonstrated by information that is sufficient for a research consumer to determine whether the findings are meaningful to other people in similar situations (analytic or theoretical *vs.* statistical generalizability).

True experiment: The strongest type of experimental design for testing cause-and-effect relationships: true experiments possess three characteristics: (a) a treatment or intervention; (b) a control or comparison group; and (c) random assignment.

Type 1 error: Mistakenly rejecting the null hypothesis when it is actually true.

Type 2 error: Mistakenly accepting (not rejecting) the null hypothesis when it is false.

U

Unstructured, open-ended interviews: Informal conversations that allow informants the fullest range of possibilities to describe their experiences, thoughts, and feelings.

V

Valid measures: Those that measure the construct that they are intended to measure (e.g., an anxiety measure truly measures anxiety, not depression).

Validity of study findings: Whether or not the results of the study were obtained via sound scientific methods.

Volunteer/convenience sample: A sample obtained by solicitation or advertising for participants who meet study criteria.

Y

Yield: The number of hits obtained by a literature search; this can be per database and/or total yield; there can be several levels of yield (e.g., first yield and final yield, that is, only those studies that were kept for review).

All Cochrane definitions came from
http://www.update-software.com/cochrane/content.htm

index

Note: Page numbers followed by "b" denote boxes; those followed by "f" denote figures; those followed by "t" denote tables.